# CRIMINAL LAW:
# TEXT AND MATERIALS

AUSTRALIA
Law Book Co.
Sydney

CANADA and USA
Carswell
Toronto

HONG KONG
Sweet and Maxwell
Asia

NEW ZEALAND
Brookers
Auckland

SINGAPORE and MALAYSIA
Sweet and Maxwell Asia
Singapore and Kuala Lumpur

# CRIMINAL LAW:
# TEXT AND MATERIALS

*Fifth Edition*

by

## C. M. V. CLARKSON, B.A., LL.B., LL.M.
*Professor of Law, University of Leicester*

## H. M. KEATING, LL.M.
*Senior Lecturer in Law, University of Sussex*

LONDON
SWEET & MAXWELL
2003

Published in 2003 by
Sweet & Maxwell Limited of
100 Avenue Road,
London NW3 3PF
(*http://www.sweetandmaxwell.co.uk*)
Typeset by
Mendip Communications Ltd,
Frome, Somerset
Printed and bound in Great Britain by
TJ International Ltd, Padstow, Cornwall

First Edition ............................................ 1984
Reprinted ............................................... 1986
Reprinted ............................................... 1988
Second Edition......................................... 1990
Reprinted ............................................... 1991
Reprinted ............................................... 1993
Third Edition .......................................... 1994
Reprinted ............................................... 1994
Reprinted ............................................... 1995
Fourth Edition ........................................ 1998
Reprinted ............................................... 1999
Reprinted ............................................... 2000
Reprinted................................... 2001 (twice)
Reprinted ............................................... 2002
Fifth Edition............................................ 2003

A CIP catalogue record for this book
is available from The British Library

ISBN 0 421 78420 2

No natural forests were destroyed to make this product,
only farmed timber was used and re-planted

# PREFACE

---

The aim of this book is to examine the main principles and rules of the criminal law and to expose the theoretical bases upon which they are founded.

The criminal law is the backdrop to the operation of the whole criminal justice system. It informs the way in which victims, the public, the police and other law enforcement agencies, the C.P.S. and judges and other court personnel react and operate. It is, therefore, inextricably linked to issues of criminal procedure, criminology, moral philosophy and penology. Fletcher has stated that "the criminal law should express the way we live". It is a reflection of community values aimed at isolating the blameworthy who are deserving of punishment. Equally, it is a means of social control; it attempts to uphold, as well as reflect, these community values; it sets a standard, albeit at times a minimal one, of necessary compliance. In short, it is a set of moral commandments that are backed up by the legal threat of punishment. It thus follows that whether sanctions are imposed on the basis of desert or on utilitarian grounds, the rules of the criminal law and the punishment of offenders are the two sides of the same coin. A whole range of substantive issues—such as, whether "recklessness" should include "inadvertence", whether one can justify the existence of offences of "strict liability", how the boundaries of the law of "attempt" and "accessorial" crime should be drawn, and so on—are, in reality, issues relating to the justification of punishment in such cases. A true appreciation of the substantive criminal law must thus involve some understanding of the rationale of punishment and why conduct is criminalised—and it is in this context that we have sought to present the main rules of the law.

Like many other works in this field, this is a book on the actual rules of the criminal law. We have attempted to provide a full analysis of these main rules on the topics covered. But, in doing this, we have attempted the more ambitious task of using the law to extract, and develop, some fundamental ideas underlying the law. We have tried to explore, in the context of punishment, such issues as: the relationship between blame and harm, the criteria for identifying the blameworthy, the structure of offences in relation to each other and whether such structure fairly represents the differing wrongdoing involved, and the role of the general defences. In short, we have attempted to subject the criminal law to the beginnings of a philosophical analysis that can throw some light on the substantive rules.

The criminal law changes with great rapidity and therefore this book has been substantially rewritten and updated for the fifth edition. This is particularly the case for those sections of the book dealing with punishment, the meaning of "intention", mistake, strict liability, homicide, theft, fraud, the partial defences of provocation and diminished responsibility and the general defences such as self-defence and the emerging defence of necessity. Since the publication of the last edition the Human Rights Act 1998, incorporating the European Convention on Human Rights, has come into force. The implications of this are considered in the new text.

v

We have been anxious to ensure that this book be accessible to, and easily digestible by, undergraduate and other students concerned with criminal law. We have approached our task, and included appropriate materials, with this concern very much in mind. We have tried to cover the range of competing views and present them in a discursive manner allowing the reader to make choices—while not being afraid to state our own preferences.

A brief word about the format of this book is necessary. It is neither a straight "textbook", nor a "cases and materials" book. Instead, we have tried to combine what we regard as the best features of both such styles—a book with the flow and coherence of a textbook thus providing the reader with guidance and direction, but one that also enables a substantial amount of original material from a diversity of sources to be absorbed.

We are very grateful to our publishers for their help and patience during the preparation of this book.

Chris Clarkson would like to thank Sue Smith, of the University of Leicester library, for her invaluable help in tracing references and materials. He is indebted, yet again, to his wife, Barbara, for her support during the writing of this book.

Heather Keating would like to express her gratitude to her family, co-author and other friends for their support and understanding during the writing of this edition.

This book has been written with reference to the law as it stood on March 31, 2003 although it has been possible to incorporate some subsequent changes to the law.

April 2003

C. M. V. CLARKSON
H. M. KEATING

# ACKNOWLEDGMENTS

Grateful acknowledgment is made to the following authors and publishers for permission to quote from their works:

Adler, Zsuzanna: "Rape—the Intention of Parliament and the practice of the Courts" (1982) 45 MLR 664, Blackwell Publishers

Alexander, F and Staub, H: *The Criminal, The Judge and the Public* (1956) pp. 212, 213. Free Press, a Division of Macmillan, Inc. Copyright © 1957 by the Free Press, copyright renewed 1985 by Anita Alexander

Allen, F: *the Decline of the Rehabilitive Ideal: Penal Policy and Social Purpose* (1981). Published by Yale University Press. © Yale University Press London

Andenaes, J: "General Prevention" (1952) 43 J Crim L, C & PS 176. © J. Andenaes. Reprinted by special permission of Northwestern University School of Law, *Journal of Criminal Law and Criminology*

——: "The General Preventive Effects of Punishment" (1966) 114 UpaLRev 949, 960–970. © University of Pennsylvania Law Review and Fred B. Rothman and Company

Ashworth, Andrew: "Belief, Inent and Criminal Liability" in Eekelaar, J and Bell, J, Oxford Essays in Jurisprudence (1987). Reprinted by permission of Oxford University Press

——: "Intoxication and General Defences" [1980] Crim L Rev 556

——: *Principles of Criminal Law* (1999, 3rd ed.) Clarendon Press. Published by Oxford University Press

——: "Robbery Re-assessed" [2002] Crim L Rev 851

——: "The Scope of Liability of Omissions" (1989) 105 LQR 424

——: *Sentencing and Criminal Justice* (2000, 3rd ed.), Butterworths a division of LexisNexis Butterworths Tolley

——: *Sentencing and Penal Policy* (1983), Butterworths a division of LexisNexis Butterworths Tolley

——: "Testing Fidelity to Legal Values: Official Involvement and Criminal Justice" (2000) 63 MLR 633, Blackwell Publishers

——: "Transferred Malice and Punishment for Unforeseen Consequences" in PR Glazebrook (ed.) *Reshaping the Criminal Law* (1978). Oxford University Press. Reprinted by permission of Oxford University Press

"Attorney-General's Reference (No. 1 of 1985) [1986] 83 Criminal Appeal Review 70

Austin, J: *Lecturers on Jurisprudence* (5th ed) XVIII-XIX Vol 1. Thoemmes Press

Beale, JH: "Retreat from a Murderous Assault" (1903) 16 Harv L Rev 567

Bentham, J: "An Introduction to the Principles of Morals and Legislation" in Bentham and Mill, *The Utilitarians* (1961) © Anchor Publishing

Bergman, D: *Deaths at Work: Accidents or Corporate Crime*, 1991. Reprinted by permission of Workers Educational Association

Blom-Cooper, L: "Criminal Law that leaves Children at Risk" *The Independent*, August 7, 1989

Bottoms, AE: "An Introduction to 'The Coming Crisis'" in Bottoms, AE and Preston, RH, *The Coming Penal Crisis* (1980). Reprinted by permission of Scottish Academic Press Ltd

Box, S: *Power, Crime and Mystification* (1983) Routledge

Brady, J: "Punishing Attempts" (1980) 63 *THE MONIST* 246. © 1980, *THE MONIST: An International Quarterly Journal of General Philosophical Inquiry*, Peru, Illinois, USA 61354. Reprinted by permission

Brady, JB: "Recklessness, Negligence, Indifference and Awareness" (1980) 43 MLR 381, Blackwell Publishers

——: "Strict Liability Offenses: A Justification". From the Criminal Law Bulletin, Volume 8, Number 3, April 1972

Braithwaite, J: *Crime, Shame and Reintegration* (1989). Cambridge University Press

—— and Pettit, P: *Not Just Deserts: A Republican Theory of Criminal Justice* (1990). By permission of Oxford University Press

Brett, Peter: *Inquiry into Criminal Guilt* (1963). Reproduced with the expressed permission of the © Lawbook Co, part of Thomson Legal & Regulatory Limited, *http://thomson.com.au*

Brownlee, Ian D: "Superior Orders – Time for a New Realism?" [1989] Crim L Rev 296

Buchanan and Virgo: "Duress and Mental Abnormality" [1999] Crim L Rev 517

Butterworth Law Publishers Ltd: All England Law Reports; extracts from various other publications

Buxton, Richard: "The Human Rights Act and the Substantive Criminal Law" [2000] Crim L Rev 331

Card, Richard: "The Criminal Revision Committees Working Paper on Sexual Offences" [1981] Crim L R 361

——: "Reform of the Law of Conspiracy" [1973] Crim L Rev 674

Cardozo, BN: "What Medicine Can do For Law" (from *Law and Literature*) © 1947 F.B. Rothman, Littleton, Colorado

Clarkson, CMV: "Context and Culpability in Involuntary Manslaughter: Principle or Instinct?" in Ashworth and Mitchell (eds) *Rethinking English Homicide Law* (2000). Oxford University Press

——: "Corporate Culpability" (1997) Web Journal of Current Legal Issues". Reprinted by kind permission of Blackstone Press Limited

——: *Understanding Criminal Law* (2001). Reprinted by permission of Collins

—— and Keating, HM: "Codification: Offences against the Person under the Draft Criminal Code" (1986) 50 J Crim L 405. Reprinted by permission of Vathek Publishing

Cohen, Morris R: "Moral Aspects of the Criminal Law" (1940) 49 Yale Law Journal 987–1026. Reprinted by permission of the Yale Law Journal Company and William S. Hein Company from *The Yale Law Journal*

Colvin, E: "Corporate Personality and Criminal Liability", Criminal Law Forum 6 (1995), p.8. Reprinted by permission of Kluwer Academic Publishers B.V

Conklin, JE: *Criminology*. © Allyn & Bacon Publishing, Boston, MA

"The Conspiracy Dilemma: Prosecution of Group Crimes or Protection of Individual Defendants" (1948) 62 Harv L Rev 276

Cowley, D: "The Retreat from Morgan" [1982] Crim L Rev 198

Cross, R: "Relfections on *Bratty*'s Case" (1962) 78 LQR 236

——, Sir Rupert and Ashworth, Andrew: *The English Sentencing System* (1981, 3rd ed.), Butterworths a division of LexisNexis Butterworths Tolley

"*Davidge v Bunnett*" [1984] Crim L Rev 297

Devlin Patrick: "Morals and the Criminal Law", in *Enforcement of Morals* (1965) published by Oxford University Press with permission from the British Academy

Davis, M: "Why Attempts Deserve Less Punishment than Complete Crimes", Law & Philosophy 5 (1986), p.28–29. Reprinted by permission of Kluwer Academic Publishers B.V

Dennis, Ian: "Duress, Murder and Criminal Responsibility" (1980) 96 LQR 208

Dessian, GH: "Justice After Conviction" (1951) 25 Connecticut Bar Journal, Copyright © Connecticut Bar Association

Devlin, P: "Morals and the Criminal Law", reprinted in the *Enforcement of Morals* (1965) Oxford University Press

Dressler, J: *Understanding Criminal Law* (1987). M. Bender

Duff, RA: *Criminal Attempts* (1986) Oxford University Press

——: "Intentions Legal and Philosophical" (1989) 9 Oxford Journal of Legal Studies 76. By permission of Oxford University Press

——: *Intention Agency and Criminal Liability: Philosophy of Action and the Criminal Law* (1990). Basil Blackwell

——: "Recklessness" [1980] Crim L Rev 282

——: *Trials and Punishments* (1986). Cambridge University Press

Duff, A and von Hirsch, A: "Responsibility, Retribution and the 'Voluntary': A Response to Williams" [1997] CLJ 103. © A Duff and A von Hirsch

Editorial "The Criminology of Attempts" [1986] Crim L Rev 769

Farrier, MD: "The Distinction between Murder and Manslaughter in its Procedural Context" (1976) 39 MLR 414, Blackwell Publishers

Feinberg, J: "The Expressive Function of Punishment" (1965) *THE MONIST*, Vol. 49, No. 3, 397–423. © 1965, *THE MONIST: An International Quarterly Journal of General Philosophical Inquiry*, Peru, Illinois, USA 61354. Reprinted by permission

——: *Harmless Wrongdoing (The Moral Limits of the Criminal Law* Vol 4) (1988). Oxford University Press

——: *Harm to Others* by Joel Feinberg, © 1984 by Oxford University Press, Inc. Used by permission of Oxford University Press, Inc

Feldman, D: *Civil Liberties and Human Rights in England and Wales* (2002, 2nd ed.). By permission of Oxford University Press

Fine, RP and Cohen, GM: "Is Criminal Negligence a Defensible Basis for Penal Liability" (1967) 16 Buffalo L Rev 749. Reprinted by permission of Buffalo Law Review

Finnis, J: "Intention and Side-effects" in Frey, RG, and Morris, CW (eds) *Liability and Responsibility* (1991). Cambridge University Press

——: "The Restoration of Retribution" (1971) 32 Analysis 131. Basil Blackwell

Fisse, B: "Recent Developments in Corporate Criminal Law and Corporate Liability to Monetary Penalties" (1990) 13 UNSWLV 1. Reprinted by permission of the University of New South Wales Law Journal

—— and Braithwaite, J: "The Allocation of Responsibility for Corporate Crime: Individualism, Collectivism and Accountability" (1988) 11 Sydney Law Review 468

Fletcher, GP: *Rethinking Criminal Law* (1978). Reprinted by permission of Little, Brown & Co., Boston

——: "The Theory of Criminal Negligence: A Comparative Analysis" (1971) 119 Upal Rev 401. Reprinted by permission of University of Pennsylvania Law Review

Frankel, Marvin: *Criminal Sentences: Law Without Order*. Copyright © 1973 by
  Marvin E. Frankel. Reprinted by permission of Hill and Wang, a division of
  Farrar, Strauss and Giroux, LLC
Franklin, RL: *Freewill and Determinism* (1968, Routledge & Kegan Paul Ltd.
  Published by Humanities Press Inc. in the USA)
Freeman, S: "Criminal Liability and the Duty to Aid the Distressed" (1994) C142
  Upal Rev 1455. Reprinted by permission of University of Pennsylvania Law
  Review

Gardiner, G: "The Purposes of Criminal Punishment" (1958) 21 MLR 117,
  Blackwell Publishers.
Gardner, J: "The Gist of Excuses" (1998) 1 Buffalo Criminal Law Review 575
——, John: "Justifications and Reasons" in Simester and Smith (eds) *Harm and
  Culpability* (1996) Clarendon Press. Published by Oxford University Press
—— and Jung, H: "Making Sense of *Mens Rea*: Anthony Duff's Account" (1991)
  11 OJLS 559. By permission of Oxford University Press
—— and Macklem, Timothy: "Compassion without Respect? Nine Fallacies in *R v
  Smith*" [2001] Crim L Rev 623
——, Simon: "Appreciating *Olugboja*" (1996) 16 Legal Studies 275, Butterworths
  a division of LexisNexis Butterworths Tolley
Gerber, R and McAnnay, PD: "Punishment: Current Survey of Philosophy and
  Law" (1967) 11 St Louis ULJ 491. Reprinted with permission of the Saint Louis
  University *Law Journal* © 1967 St. Louis University School of Law, St. Louis,
  Missouri
Glazebrook, PR: "Thief or Swindler: Who Cares?" [1991] CLJ 389. © PR
  Glazebrook
Goff, Lord: "The Mental Element in the Crime of Murder" (1988) 104 LQR 30
Goldstein, A: *The Insanity Defense* (1967). Published by Yale University Press. ©
  Yale University Press London
Goldstein, Abraham S: "Conspiracy to Defraud the United States" (1959) 68 Yale
  Law Journal 405–463. Reprinted by permission of The Yale Law Journal
  Company and William S. Hein Company from *The Yale Law Journal*
——, Joseph and Katz, Jay: "Abolish the "Insanity Defense": Why Not?" (1963)
  72 Yale Law Journal 853–876. Reprinted by permission of The Yale Law
  Journal Company and William S. Hein Company from *The Yale Law Journal*
Griew, Edward: "Dishonesty: The Objections to *Feely* and *Ghosh*" [1985] Crim L
  Rev 341
Gross, Hyman: *A Theory of Criminal Justice* (1979) Routledge

Hart, HLA: "Immorality and Treason", 62 *Listener* 162–163 (July 30, 1959)
——: *Punishment and Responsibility, Essays in the Philosophy of Law* (1968, ©
  Reprinted by permission of Oxford University Press)
—— and Honoré, AM: *Causation in the Law* (2nd ed, 1985) © Oxford University
  Press 1959. Reprinted by permission of Oxford University Press
Hart, HLA: "Prolegomenon to the Principles of Punishment" in *Punishment and
  Responsibility, Essays in the Philosophy of Law* (1968) published by Oxford
  University Press with permission from the Aristotelian Society
Hart, HLA: "Punishment and Elimination of Responsibility" in *Punishment and
  Responsibility, Essays in the Philosophy of Law* (1968) published by Oxford
  University Press with permission from Athlone Press and the London School of
  Economics

Henderson, D and Gillespie, RD: *Textbook of Psychiatry for Students and Practitioners* revised by Ivor RC Batchelor (17th ed, 1950), pp 125, 191. Reprinted by permission of Oxford University Press

Hepburn, J.: "Occasional Property Crime", Meier, R (ed.) *Major Forms of Crime* (1984), pp 88–89, © 1984 by Sage Publications. Reprinted by Permission of Sage Publications, Inc

Her Majesty's Stationery Office: Various extracts

von Hirsch, A: *Doing Justice—The Choice of Punishments (Report of the Committee for the Study of Incarceration)* Copyright © 1976 by Andrew von Hirsch. Reprinted by permission of Hill and Wang, a division of Farrar, Strauss and Giroux, LLC

——: *Past or Future Crimes: Deservedness and Dangerousness in the Sentencing of Criminals* (Crime, Law and Deviance Series) © 1985, Rutgers, The State University, Rutgers University Press

——: "Prediction of Criminal Conduct and Preventative Confinement of Convicted Persons" (1972) 21 Buffalo L Rev 717. Reprinted by permission of Buffalo Law Review

——: *Censure and Criminal Sanctions* (1993). By permission of Oxford University Press

—— and Ashworth, A (eds): *Principled Sentencing* (1992)

—— and Jareborg, N: "Gauging Criminal Harm: A Living-Standard Analysis" (1991) 11 Oxford Journal of Legal Studies 1. By permission of Oxford University Press

Hodge, J: *Alcohol and Violence* (1993). Reprinted by permission of Royal College of Physicians, London

Honoré, AM: "Responsibility and Luck" (1988) 104 LQR 530

Honoré, T: "The Dependence of Morality on Law" (1993) 13 Oxford Journal of Legal Studies 1. By permission of Oxford University Press

——: *Responsibility and Fault* (1999) Hart Publishing. Reprinted with permission of Hart Publishing Ltd

Horder, J: *Provocation and Responsibility* (1992). By permission of Oxford University Press

——: "Sobering Up? The Law Commission on Criminal Intoxication" (1995) 58 MLR 534, Blackwell Publishers

——: "Intention in the Criminal Law – a Rejoinder" (1995) 958 MLR 678, Blackwell Publishers.

——: "Criminal Law: Between Determinism, Liberalism, and Criminal Justice" (1996) 49 Criminal Legal Problems 159, Oxford University Press

Horder, Jeremy: "How Culpability Can, and Cannot, be denied in Under-age Sex Crimes" [2001] Crim L Rev 15

Howard, Colin: "Strict Responsibility in the High Court of Australia" (1960) 76 LQR 547

Hughes, Graham: "Criminal Omissions" (1958) 67 Yale Law Journal 590–637. Reprinted by permission of The Yale Law Journal Company and William S. Hein Company from *The Yale Law Journal*

——: "Morals and the Criminal Law" (1962) 71 Yale Law Journal 662–682. Reprinted by permission of The Yale Law Journal Company and William S. Hein Company from *The Yale Law Journal*.

Husak, Douglas: "Does Criminal Liability Require An Act" in Duff, A (ed) *Philosophy and the Criminal Law* (1998). Cambridge University Press

The Incorporated Council of Law Reporting for England and Wales: Weekly Law Reports, Queen's Bench Division, Appeal Cases and King's Bench Law Reports

Johnson, Philip: *The Unnecessary Crime of Conspiracy* (1973) 61 California Law Review 1137. © 1973 by the California Law Review. Reprinted from the California Law Review Vol. 61, No. 5, Pp: 1157–1158 by permission of the Regents of the University of California

Kadish, SH: *Excusing Crime* (1987) 75 California Law Review 257. © 1987 by the California Law Review. Reprinted from the California Law Review Vol. 75, No. 1, Pp: 261, 264 by permission of the Regents of the University of California
——: "The Crises of Over-criminalization" (1967) Vol. 374 of The Annals. © 1967 The American Academy of Political and Social Science
—— and Paulsen, MG: *Criminal Law and Its Process* (1969, Little, Brown & Co, Boston)
Kaplan, J: "The Role of Law in Drug Control" [1971] *Duke Law Journal* 1065. © (1971) J Kaplan. Published by Duke University School of Law
Katz, L: *Bad Acts and Guilty Minds* (1987). Reprinted by permission of The University of Chicago Press
Kenny, A: *Freewill and Responsibility* (1978) Routledge
Koh, KL, Clarkson, C and Morgan, N: Criminal Law in Singapore and Malaysia: Text and Materials (1989). Malayan Law Journal

Lacey, Nicola: *State Punishment: Political Principles and Community Values* (1988) Routledge
——, Well, C and Meure, D: *Reconstructing Criminal Law: Text and Materials* (1998, 2nd ed.) Weidenfeld & Nicolson
La Fave, WR and Scott, AW: *Criminal Law* (2nd ed, 1986). Reprinted by permission of the West Group
Lanham, David: "Accomplices and Transferred Malice" (1980) 96 LQR 110
——: "Accomplices, Principles and Causation" (1980) 12 *Melbourne University Law Review* 490, 510–11
——: "Larsonneur Revisited" [1976] Crim L Rev 276
Lawson, FH and Rudden, B: *The Law of Property* (1982) Oxford University Press
Leavens, Arthur: *A Causation Approach to Criminal Omissions* (1988) 76 California Law Review 547. © 1988 by the California Law Review. Reprinted from the California Law Review Vol. 76, No. 3, Pp: 572–575 by permission of the University of California, Berkeley
Leigh, LH: (With assistance of Susannah Brown) "Crimes in Bankruptcy" in Leigh, LH, ed. *Economic Crime in Europe* (1980) Macmillan Press Ltd. Reprinted with permission of Palgrave Macmillan
——: *Strict and Vicarious Liability* (1983), Sweet & Maxwell
Lewis, CS: "The Humanitarian Theory of Punishment" (1953) VI *Res Judicatae* 224. Reprinted by permission of the *Melbourne University Law Review*
Lloyd-Bostock, S: "The Ordinary Man, and the Psychology of Attributing Causes and Responsibility" (1979) 45 MLR 143, Blackwell Publishers

McGregor, J: "Why When She Says No She Doesn't Mean Maybe and She Doesn't Mean Yes: A Critical Reconstruction of Consent, Sex and the Law (1996) 2 Legal Theory 175, Cambridge University Press
MacKenna, Sir Brian: "Causing Death by Reckless or Dangerous Driving: A Suggestion" [1970] Crim L Rev 67

Magistrates Association: *Magistrates' Court Sentencing Guidelines* (September 2000). Reproduced with the permission of the Magistrates' Association, 28 Fitzroy Square, London W1T 6DD

Mandil, DM: "Chance, Freedom and Criminal Liability". This article originally appeared at 87 Colum.L.Rev. 125 (1987). Reprinted by permission

Mead, G: "Contracting into Crime: A Theory of Criminal Omissions" (1991) 11 Oxford Journal of Legal Studies 147. By permission of Oxford University Press

Model Penal Code: Extracts from Tentative Drafts No. 4 (1955), 8 (1958) and Model Penal Code Proposed Official Draft (1962). © American Law Institute. Reprinted with permission. All rights reserved

Morawetz, TH: *The Philosophy of Law: An Introduction* (1980, Macmillan US). Copyright © 1980 by Thomas H. Morawetz

Morris, Allison: *Women, Crime and Criminal Justice* (1987) © Reprinted by permission of Basil Blackwell

Morris, H: "Persons and Punishment" (1968) *THE MONIST*, Vol. 52, 397–423. © 1968, *THE MONIST: An International Quarterly Journal of General Philosophical Inquiry*, Peru, Illinois, USA 61354. Reprinted by permission

Morris, N: *Madness and the Criminal Law* © 1982 by The University of Chicago Press, pp. 31–32, 61–64. All rights reserved

—— and Howard, C: *Studies in Criminal Law* © Oxford University Press 1964, pp 175–176, 199. Reprinted with permission by Oxford University Press

Morris, T and Blom-Cooper, L: *A Calendar of Murder: Criminal Homicide in England since 1957* (1964) Michael Joseph Publishers Ltd. © Dr Terence Morris and Louis Blom-Cooper 1964. Reproduced by permission of Penguin Books Ltd.

Mueller: "*Mens Rea* and the Law Without It" (1955) 58 W. Va. L. Rev. 34, 37–38. © G Mueller

Murphy, DJ: *Customers and Thieves—An Ethnography of Shoplifting* (1986, Ashgate Publishing Ltd). © DJ Murphy

Nicolson, Donald and Sanghvi, Rohit: "Battered Women and Provocation: The Implications of *R v Ahluwalia*" [1993] Crim L Rev 728

Norrie, A: "A Critique of Criminal Causation" (1991) 54 MLR 685, Blackwell Publishers

——: "After *Woollin*" [1999] Crim L Rev 532

——: *Crime, Reason and History: A Critical Introduction to Criminal Law* (2001, 2nd ed.), Butterworths a division of LexisNexis Butterworths Tolley

——: "From Criminal Law to Legal Theory: The Mysterious Case of the Reasonable Glue Sniffer" (2002) 65 MLR 538, Blackwell Publishers

——: "Subjectivism, Objectivism and the Limits of Criminal Recklessness" (1992) 12 Oxford Journal of Legal Studies 45. By permission of Oxford University Press

O'Donovan, K: "Defences for Battered Women Who Kill" (1991) 18 JL & S 219, Blackwell Publishers

Packer, HL: *The Limits of The Criminal Sanction.* Copyright © 1968 by Herbert L. Packer. Used with the permission of Stanford University Press, *www.sup.org*

——: "Mens Reas and the Supreme Court" (1962) Sup. Ct. Rev. 107 at 109. Reprinted by permission of The University of Chicago Press

Parry, Deborah L: "Judicial Approaches to Due Diligence" [1995] Crim L Rev 675

Pickard, T: "Culpable Mistakes and Rape: Relating Mens Rea to the Crime", (1980) 30 *University of Toronto Law Journal* 75

Richardson, Genevra: "Strict Liability for Regulatory Crime: The Empirical Research" [1987] Crim L Rev 295

Robinson, P: "Criminal Law Defences: A Systematic Analysis" (1982) 82 Columbia Law Review 199

——: *Criminal Law Defences*, Vol 2, 1984. Reprinted by permission of the West Group

Robinson, P: "Hybrid Principles for the Distribution of Criminal Sanctions" (1988) 82 *Northwestern University Law Review* 19. © P. Robinson. Reprinted by special permission of Northwestern University School of Law, *Northwestern University Law Review*

Rosenham, DL: "On Being Sane in Insane Place". *Science* (1973) Vol 199, pp 250–258. Reprinted (abstracted/excerpted) with permission. Copyright (1973) by the American Association for the Advancement of Science

Rumney, Philip and Morgan-Taylor, Martin: "Recognizing the Male Victim: Gender Neutrality and the Law of Rape" (1997) 26 Anglo-American Law Review 198. Tolley Publishing a division of LexisNexis Butterworths Tolley

Rychlak, RJ: "Society's Moral Right to Punish: A Further Exploration of the Denunciation Theory of Punishment" (1990) 65 Tul. L. Rev. 299–338. Reprinted with the permission of the Tulane Law Review Association, which holds the copyright

Schulhofer, S: "Harm and Punishment: A Critique of emphasis on the results conduct in the Criminal Law" (1974) 122 UpaLRev 1497. Reprinted by permission of University of Pennsylvania Law Review

——: *Unwanted Sex: The Culture of Intimidation and the Failure of the Law* (1998) Harvard University Press. Reprinted with permission of Harvard University Press

Shute, S and Horder, J: "Thieving and Deceiving: What is the Difference?" (1993) 56 MLR 548, Blackwell Publishers

Silber, JR: "Being and Doing" 35 Univ. of Chicago L.R. 47 at 61, 62, 90. Reprinted by permission.

Simpson, AWB: "The Butler Committee's Report: The Legal Aspects" (1976) 16 British Journal of Criminology. By permission of Oxford University Press

Smith, ATH: "Error and Mistake in Law in Anglo-American Criminal Law" (1985) 14 Anglo-American Law Review 3. Tolley Publishing a division of LexisNexis Butterworths Tolley

——: "The Idea of Criminal Deception" [1982] Crim L Rev 721

——: "Stealing the Body and its Parts" [1976] Crim L Rev 622

Smith, JC: "Commentary on *Broome v Perkins*" [1987] Crim L Rev 272

——: "Commentary on *DPP v Huskinson*" [1988 Crim L Rev 621

——: "Commentary on *DPP v Morgan*" [1975] Crim L Rev 717

——: "Commentary on *Lambie*" [1981] Crim L Rev 716–717

——: "Commentary on *R v Walker*" [1984] Crim L Rev 113

——: "The Element of Chance in Criminal Liability" [1971] Crim L Rev 63

Smith, KJM: *A Modern Treatise on the Law of Complicity* (1991), Oxford University Press

——: "Duress and Steadfastness: In Pursuit of the Unintelligible" [1999] Crim L Rev 363

Spencer, JR: "The Theft Act 1978" [1979] Crim L Rev 24

Stuart, Donald: "*Mens Rea* Negligence and Attempts" [1968] Crim L Rev 647

Szasz, TS: "The Myth of Mental Illness" (1960) 15 American Psychologist 113. American Psychological Association

Tadros, V: "The Characters of Excuse" (2001) 21 Oxford Journal of Legal Studies 495. By permission of Oxford University Press

Taylor, R: "Complicity and Excuses" [1983] Crim L Rev 656

Tempkin, J: "Do we need the Crime of Incest?" (1991) 44 Current Legal Problems 185

The Times: Extract from *Winzar v Chief Constable of Kent*, March 28, 1983 and *R v Emmett*, October 15, 1999. © Copyright by Times Newspapers Ltd

Tolmie, Julia: "Alcoholism and Criminal Liability" (2001) 64 MLR 688, Blackwell Publishers

Tonry, M: *Sentencing Matters* by Michael Tonry, © 1996 by Michael Tonry. Used by permission of Oxford University Press, Inc

Veltford, H and Lee, G: "The Coconut Grove Fire: A Study in Scapegoating" Journal of Abnormal and Social Psychology XXXVIII (No. 2 Clinical Supp 1943) 138. American Psychological Association

Walker, N: *Punishment, Danger and Stigma* (1980). Reproduced by permission of Basil Blackwell

Wasik, Martin: "Abandoning Criminal Intent" [1980] Crim L Rev 785

——: "Partial Excuses in the Criminal Law" (1982) 45 MLR 516, Blackwell Publishers

Welchsler, H: "The Challenge of a Model Penal Code" (1952) 65 Harv L Rev 1097

Wells, Celia: "Swatting the Subjectivist Bug" [1982] Crim L Rev 209

White, RW: The Abnormal Personality, pp 203–205, 288. Copyright © 1948 Ronald Press Co. This material is used by permission of John Wiley and Sons, Inc

Williams, Glanville: "Divergent Interpretation of Recklessness" (1982) 132 New LJ 289 © Glanville Williams. Butterworths a division of LexisNexis Butterworths Tolley

——: *The Mental Element in Crime* (1965) Magnes Press

——: "Recklessness Redefined" [1982] CLJ 252. © Glanville Williams

——: "Temporary Appropriation should be Theft" [1981] Crim L Rev 129

——: *Textbook of Criminal Law* (1st ed, 1978, 2nd ed, 1983, Sweet & Maxwell)

Wilson, W: "Doctrinal Rationality after *Woollin*" (1999) 62 MLR 448, Blackwell Publishers

——: "Is Hurting People Wrong" 1992 Journal of Social Welfare and Family Law 388, Routledge. Reprinted with permission of Taylor & Francis Ltd, *www.tandf.co.uk/journals*

——: "Murder and the Structure of Homicide" in Ashworth and Mitchell (eds) *Rethinking English Homicide Law* (2000). Oxford University Press

Wolfgang, ME: "Victim—Precipitated Homicide" (1957) 48 J Crim L, C & PS 2–3. Reprinted by special permission of Northwestern University School of Law, *Journal of Criminal Law and Criminology*

Wooton, Lady B: *Crime and Penal Policy, Reflections on Fifty Years Experience* (2nd ed., 1981, George Allen & Unwin (Publishers) Ltd)

——: *Crime and The Criminal Law* (2nd ed, 1981, Sweet & Maxwell)

Zeitlin, L: "A Little Larceny can do a lot for Employee Morale". Psychology Today Magazine. Copyright © 1971 (PT Partners, LP)

While every care has been taken to establish and acknowledge copyright, and contact the copyright owners, the publishers tender their apologies for any accidental infringement. They would be pleased to come to a suitable arrangement with the rightful owners in each case.

# CONTENTS

# 4.   CAUSATION                                                     438

# 5.   INCHOATE OFFENCES                                             463

# TABLE OF CASES

# TABLE OF STATUTES

# TABLE OF STATUTORY INSTRUMENTS

# 1

# CRIME AND PUNISHMENT

---

## I. INTRODUCTION

An attempt to comprehend the rules of criminal law must involve some understanding of the function of those rules. It would of course be possible simply to list the rules relating to various offences, *e.g.* murder, rape, and attempt, but such a stark analysis would not be particularly helpful or illuminating. The student of criminal law must be in a position to evaluate such rules and answer important questions. Why do we regard murder as more serious than manslaughter, when in both cases the victim has been killed? In rape does or should it make any difference whether the "rapist" believed his victim was consenting? Why do we hold someone liable for attempted murder if no harm has been caused to the victim, because, say, the gun was defective and could never have injured anyone? Should such a person be held liable? These and numerous other fundamental questions that will be posed in the course of this book cannot be answered, and the present rules and reform proposals cannot be evaluated, without understanding the objective of these rules.

The function of the criminal law is to lay down a set of standards of what is permissible or not. It is a method of social control, a framework specifying the parameters of acceptable behaviour. The same is, of course, true of all law and indeed of ethical systems such as morality and religion. Family law, for example, is a set of rules stating whom one may marry, when a divorce may be obtained and so on. If one breaches these rules, for example, by trying to marry a close relative, the law provides a sanction, namely, the marriage is void. Similarly, the law of contract details how and when a contract comes into existence and stipulates the sanction for failing to comply with these rules (the contract may be void) or for failing to perform one's obligations under the contract (one may be liable for damages). All these rules are designed to ensure compliance therewith and the sanctions are those deemed most appropriate to ensure such compliance.

Similarly, the criminal law is a series of rules, with its own set of sanctions, aimed at controlling behaviour. For example, the rules provide that if you drive a motor car, you must drive carefully; if you operate a business, you must ensure that the work environment is not dangerous; you must not steal or kill or injure other people and so on. What distinguishes the criminal law from other mechanisms of social control, and from other branches of law, is the sanction that is employed to back up the rules, namely, stigmatic punishment. If you steal property, the law of property (concerned with regulating property rights) might say that the "transaction" is void and you do not become the owner of the property. The criminal law, on the other hand, provides its own special sanction: if you steal property you are liable to be sent to prison for a maximum of seven years. The convicted thief is subjected to the shame and censure of public punishment.

Of course, one must not assume from this that the criminal law (or any other mechanism of social control) will operate perfectly. At all stages of the process from criminalisation to punishment there is scope for the mechanism to falter. It may well be that there are groups in society powerful enough to prevent the criminalisation of behaviour that otherwise appears to be a prime candidate for such treatment. An enormous number of crimes are never reported to the police, many persons who offend go undetected or are not prosecuted or not punished. The entire criminal justice system is riddled with discretion which tends to give the system the appearance of incoherence, but it is our view that, as a backdrop against which all these decisions must be made, there is a system of criminal law that is capable of internal consistency and it is that system that will be explored in this book.

In order to make sense of the criminal law and of the substantive rules that make up the whole, it is important to establish a framework. First, what conduct should be prohibited by the criminal law? If one accepts that one of the objects of the criminal law is to prevent people unjustifiably being deprived of their property, why should it be theft (a criminal offence) if you take property away from someone, but only breach of contract (generally, not a criminal offence) if you take their property pursuant to a contract without performing your obligations under that contract? If one understands why theft is criminalised, but breach of contract is not, one can begin to understand how theft should be defined so as to distinguish it from breach of contract. The substantive rules can start making sense (or be seen to be in need of reform to the extent they do not make sense).

Secondly, why do we *punish* those who break the rules of the criminal law? In the above theft example, why is the property law sanction not sufficient? Who do we punish and how much punishment should be imposed? Do we punish people simply because they deserve punishment or because we wish to make an example of them in order to deter others and so on? Again, the answer to these questions will often provide the key to an understanding of the rules themselves. For example, should duress be a defence in the criminal law, and if so, to what crimes? If punishing largely for desert reasons, such a defence should be available as a person subjected to duress is blameless and does not deserve punishment. On the other hand, if deterrence is seen as the main rationale of punishment, perhaps there ought to be no defence of duress, or it should not be available for the most serious crimes. A person subjected to duress might need the threat of punishment as a deterrent against giving in to the threat. In short, the structure of the substantive rules of the criminal law will depend on the view taken as to the purposes of punishment; the issue is of more fundamental importance than whether an individual judge happens to stress deterrence or reform when sentencing. Understanding the rationale of punishment will enable us to understand, evaluate, criticise and suggest reforms of those substantive rules.

It is these two crucial questions that are the subject of this first chapter.

## II. WHAT CONDUCT OUGHT TO BE CRIMINAL?

### A. *Introduction*

What conduct should be criminalised? We seem content to leave some "wrongful" conduct to morality or religion: for example, telling lies as to why an essay has not been completed on time. Other such conduct is left to the law of tort, for example, telling lies about other people so as to damage their reputation, or to the law of contract, for example, deliberately not performing one's obligations under a contract. On the other hand, if we tell a lie as a result of which another person gives us property, we commit the crime of obtaining property by deception, contrary to section 15 of the Theft Act 1968. Is there any *principle* explaining why the last form of conduct is criminalised but not the others? Why, in a competitive capitalist society, is insider dealing (using privileged information to buy and sell shares on the stock exchange) a criminal offence?[1] On what basis was the decision made to make possession of indecent photographs of children a criminal offence as well as the taking of them?[2] Why should incest be a criminal offence? Similar questions can be addressed to many areas of human conduct, but, in an attempt to sharpen the focus of this section, we shall lay particular emphasis on the laws relating to incest and sado-masochism between consenting adults.

It must be conceded at the outset that many, if not most, decisions to criminalise conduct are simply a response either to pressure groups or to perceived public opinion. This is well illustrated by the campaign to criminalise the possession of most handguns—even those held in sports clubs—in the wake of the Dunblane massacre where one man, armed with a handgun, shot and killed 16 children. A combination of factors—an organised campaign by a pressure group comprising parents of the children, a well-orchestrated press crusade and a Government and an opposition party preparing for a general election and both determined to demonstrate a toughness against crime—conspired to ensure the speedy passage of the Firearms (Amendment) Act 1997 through Parliament. The creation of numerous other offences in recent years can be accounted for in the same way. For example, the alleged rise in football hooliganism led to the Football (Offences) Act 1991 which creates the offences of throwing missiles, indecent or racialist chanting and going on to the playing area at designated football matches. As a result of several highly-publicised cases of fighting dogs severely injuring people, the Dangerous Dogs Act 1991 creates various offences relating to breeding, selling or allowing such dogs to be in public places without a muzzle and lead. In short, over the past two decades there has been an alarming tendency on the part of the Government, in particular, to adopt the view that if there is a problem, an instant panacea is to found by criminalising the conduct in question. This has led some commentators to assert that it is not possible to find any unifying thread explaining the content of the criminal law.[3] However, occasionally a more principled debate

---

[1] Criminal Justice Act 1993, s.52.

[2] Possession of indecent photos of children was made a criminal offence by s.160 of the Criminal Justice Act 1988; the taking of such photos was made a criminal offence under the Protection of Children Act 1978, s.1(1)(a).

[3] Lacey, "Contingency and Criminalisation" in Loveland (ed.), *Frontiers of Criminality* (1995).

emerges. For instance, in the 1950s the Wolfenden Committee[4] which investigated offences of homosexuality and prostitution sought to provide a theoretical framework against which the decision to criminalise conduct should be made. More recently, the Law Commission undertook a similar task in examining the extent to which consent should be a defence to various activities such as sado-masochism and various types of fighting. The aim of this section is to explore whether there are any principles that *ought* to inform a debate on whether conduct should be criminalised or decriminalised.

## B. *Criteria for Criminalisation*

It is common to assert that there are two conditions that need to be satisfied before criminalisation of conduct is justified:

(i)   The conduct must be *wrongful*.

(ii)  It must be *necessary* to employ the *criminal law* to condemn or prevent such conduct.[5]

(iii) It must be *permissible* to criminalise the activity. Criminalisation of the conduct must not contravene the European Convention on Human Rights brought into force in the United Kingdom by the Human Rights Act 1998.

### 1. Wrongful conduct

Conduct should not be prohibited unless it can be regarded as wrongful. There is, however, no agreement as to the criteria for establishing wrongfulness. Three main strands of thinking can be discerned. First, there is the view that conduct is wrongful if it is immoral (legal moralism). Secondly, many assert that conduct is only wrongful if it causes harm or serious offence to others (the harm principle or liberalism). Thirdly, there are those who assert that conduct is wrongful if it causes harm to others or to the actor (paternalism). Each of these competing views will be discussed in turn.

#### (i) *Legal Moralism*

Few would deny that the criminal law has a moral content[6]; many actions prohibited by the criminal law, such as theft and violence to the person, are undoubted moral wrongs. Even in the absence of a prohibitory law, a large majority would still feel that the actions were deeply wrong. Immoral conduct is something that offends against the community spirit. In a secular age, it need have no special religious connotations at all; immorality is not necessarily the same thing as sin, which has a religious connotation.[7] It is, however, no simple matter to define what it means for something to be "morally wrong".

---

[4] Report of the Committee on Homosexual Offences and Prostitution (1957).

[5] Packer, *The Limits of the Criminal Sanction* (1969).

[6] Some theorists, adopting a conflict view of society, would argue that the criminal law represents nothing more than the vested interests of the powerful, *e.g.* Quinney, *The Social Reality of Crime* (1970).

[7] Hughes, "Morals and the Criminal Law" (1962) 71 Yale L.J. 662 at 666–669.

### Tony Honoré, "The Dependence of Morality on Law" (1993) 13 O.J.L.S. 1 at 2:

"How are we to understand morality, a term with rather uncertain limits? It is concerned with conduct that has a significant impact on other people, and perhaps also animals, individually or collectively, and with the restraints on behaviour that we should accept because of this. Moral criticism assesses behaviour in the light of its impact on others. It excludes purely self-regarding behaviour. Moreover, since we live in groups and communities, and belong to states and other political entities, the central core of morality is concerned with how to co-exist and co-operate with others. The core of morality is, in a broad sense, political."

Moreover, one needs to be alert to the difficulties inherent in ascertaining moral opinion. Not only does moral opinion change over time but,

"[t]o assume a common culture or a normative consensus in American society (for example) as in most modern societies, is to ignore the deep and divisive role of class, ethnic, religious, status, and regional culture conflicts which often produce widely opposing definitions of goodness, truth, and moral virtue."[8]

Leaving aside the problem of defining morality, one must still question the nature of the relationship between immorality and the criminal law. Is it just historical coincidence that both should operate so often in the same fields of activity or is it possible to state some more definite relationship?

### Hyman Gross, A Theory of Criminal Justice (1979), pp. 13–15:

"It seems obvious that those crimes of violence, theft and destruction that stand as paradigms of crime and comprise the core of any penal code are also moral wrongs. Everyone has a right to be free of such harm inflicted by others, and when murder, rape, arson, assault or larceny is committed there is also a moral wrong since a moral duty to refrain from doing harm to others has been breached. The right to be free of such harm does not have its origin in law but in a general consensus on the rights enjoyed by any member of society, or even by any person, no matter how he lives. This consensus is a more fundamental element of society even than the law, and for that reason the violation of such a right is a moral wrong and not simply a legal wrong.

But beyond the most obvious crimes, legions of others are on the books for the reason that doing what is prohibited (or failing to do what is required) makes life hazardous or unpleasant. Members of the public are entitled to live and to work in safety and to enjoy life in public places without fear, disquiet or embarrassment ... these rights are also moral rights and not simply legal rights, since entitlement to the security and freedom that they represent is a matter of fundamental social consensus and not a matter simply of legal enactment.

Other crimes that are not common crimes are morally wrong for a different reason. Income tax fraud or draft evasion seem to place an unfair burden on others or deprive others of what is due to them."[9]

---

[8] Gusfield, "On Legislating Morals: The Symbolic Process of Designating Deviance" (1968) 56 Cal.L.Rev. 54 at 55–56.

[9] Gross argues further that committing a crime is necessarily a moral wrong because it involves violating a "solemn promise to live according to the rules" of society. However, we are here concerned with the *content* of these rules and their relationship to morality.

### Herbert L. Packer, The Limits of the Criminal Sanction (1969), pp. 262–264:

"Can we ... assert that there is any kind of connection between the immorality of a category of conduct and the appropriate use of the criminal sanction? I think we can, but only on a prudential basis. Leaving aside for the moment what we mean by immoral, we may discern an analogy between the requirement of culpability in the individual case and a limiting criterion for the legislative invocation of the criminal sanction: only conduct generally considered 'immoral' should be treated as criminal. Several reasons support this prudential limitation. To begin with, the principles of selection we use in determining what kinds of undesirable conduct to treat as criminal should surely include at least one that is responsible to the basic character of the criminal sanction, *i.e.* its quality of moral condemnation. To put it another way, we should use the strengths of the sanction rather than ignore or undermine them. If the conduct with which the original sanction deals is already regarded as being morally wrong, the processes of the criminal law have, so to speak, a 'leg up' on the job. This is a matter partly of public attitude and partly of the morale maintained by those who operate the criminal process. The way to keep those processes running at peak efficiency is to ensure that those who operate them are convinced that what they are doing is right. The surest way to persuade them that what they are doing is right is to have them act only against what they think is wrong. If the criminal sanction is widely used to deal with morally neutral behaviour, law enforcement officials are likely to be at least subconsciously defensive about their work, and the public will find the criminal law a confusing guide to moral, or even acceptable, behaviour. [Packer then dismisses the argument that the criminal law can be used to shape people's views on immorality, and continues]: ... The question remains: whose morality are we talking about? It is easy to slide into the assumption that somewhere in society there is an authoritative body of moral sentiment to which the law should look. That assumption becomes particularly dangerous ... when it is used to buttress the assertion that the immorality of a given form of conduct is a *sufficient* condition for declaring the conduct to be criminal. But when one is talking about immorality as a *necessary* condition for invocation of the criminal sanction, the inquiry should simply be whether there exists any significant body of dissent from the proposition that the conduct in question is immoral. Is there a social group that will be alienated or offended by making (or keeping) the conduct in question criminal? If there is, then prudence dictates caution in employing the criminal sanction.

We can sum up this prudential limitation as follows: the criminal sanction should ordinarily be limited to conduct that is viewed, without significant social dissent, as immoral. The calendar of crimes should not be enlarged beyond that point and, as views about morality shift, should be contracted."

Is incest immoral?

### Jennifer Temkin, "Do We Need the Crime of Incest?" (1991) 44 Current Legal Problems 185 at 188–189:

"There must be some doubts about the strengths of this social taboo. Indeed, the very fact that many scholars argue that incest between consenting adults should be legalised, or that incest is not to be regarded as universally aberrant, or harmful, tends somewhat to suggest that its hold is rather weaker than might be supposed. A variety of studies provide some support for this view. In her study of incest in County Antrim, Northern Ireland, Lukianowicz reports one daughter as saying of her father with whom she had sexual relations, 'I think it was quite natural for him to do so after his wife had left him.' Her husband added, 'many fathers have intercourse with their daughters. You just have to accept it.' Her findings as a whole led her to hypothesize that the incestuous behaviour between fathers and daughters revealed in her study should be regarded 'as the expression of a type of sexual behaviour accepted by the particular subculture of their social group'. David Finkelhor goes further to suggest that in America as a whole the taboo is weaker than might be thought. He states:

'Incest is often called the "ultimate taboo". ... In fact, however, incest is regarded ambivalently. On the one hand, it is treated as a serious threat to the social order. ... On the other hand, unlike sexual abuse, incest is often the subject of ribald humour, innuendo and the like. ... Such an undercurrent of humour about a supposed taboo can be an indicator of a counterculture, a covert belief among people—often held simultaneously with the taboo—that "it's really not so bad" or that "under some circumstances at least, it would be OK." The humour reflects a kind of challenge to the taboo. ... In contrast, truly serious taboos ... are not the subject of any humour to speak of ... For a crime of allegedly universal revulsion, sex within the family seems to be remarkably widespread.'"

What of sado-masochistic encounters between consenting adults? In *Brown*[10] the House of Lords was called upon to decide whether consent to sado-masochistic acts could be a defence to charges of assault occasioning actual bodily harm contrary to section 47 of the Offences Against the Person Act 1861. By a majority of three to two it was decided that consent was no defence to such charges. Lord Templeman (in the majority) stated: "Society is entitled and bound to protect itself against a cult of violence. Pleasure derived from the infliction of pain is an evil thing. Cruelty is uncivilised."[11] Lord Lowry (also in the majority) argued that "[w]hat the appellants are obliged to propose is that the deliberate and painful infliction of physical injury should be exempted from the operation of statutory provisions the object of which is to prevent or punish that very thing, the reason for the proposed exemption being that both those who will inflict and those who will suffer the injury wish to satisfy a perverted and depraved sexual desire. Sado-masochistic homosexual activity cannot be regarded as conducive to the enhancement or enjoyment of family life or conducive to the welfare of society."[12] Finally, Lord Mustill (in the minority) was of the view "that whatever the outsider might feel about the subject matter of the prosecutions—perhaps horror, amazement or incomprehension, perhaps sadness—very few could read even a summary of the other activities without disgust".[13]

Even if one accepts that the House of Lords is in tune with current morality, does this mean that one is *bound* to criminalise sado-masochistic conduct?

Some commentators have argued that it is possible to pinpoint more precisely the relationship between the criminal law and morality: they believe that not only is immorality a necessary condition for invocation of the criminal sanction, but that it is a sufficient one. It is not necessary to search for further justification (harm, enforceability, etc.) before the criminal law can be brought into action; the fact that the conduct is morally wrong is enough. This view is epitomised by such statements by James Fitzjames Stephen as "How can the State or the public be competent to determine any question whatever if it is not competent to decide that gross vice is a bad thing? I do not think the State ought to stand bandying compliments with pimps."[14]

Graphic though this picture is, the view that immorality is a sufficient condition is now likely to be couched in more qualified terms.

[10] [1994] 1 A.C. 212. The facts and an extract from the case are given at pp. 289–292.
[11] *ibid.* at 237.
[12] *ibid.* at 255.
[13] *ibid.* at 256–257.
[14] *Liberty, Equality, Fraternity* (1874) at 138.

## Patrick Devlin, Morals and the Criminal Law (reprinted in The Enforcement of Morals) (1965), pp. 7–8, 14–17:

"I think it is clear that the criminal law as we know it is based upon moral principle. In a number of crimes its function is simply to enforce a moral principle and nothing else. The law, both criminal and civil, claims to be able to speak about morality and immorality generally. Where does it get its authority to do this and how does it settle the moral principles which it enforces? Undoubtedly, as a matter of history, it derived from Christian teaching. But I think that the strict logician is right when he says that the law can no longer rely on doctrines in which citizens are entitled to disbelieve. It is necessary therefore to look for some other source ... I have framed three interrogatories addressed to myself to answer.

(1) Has society the right to pass judgment at all on the matters of morals? Ought there, in other words, to be a public morality, or are morals always a matter for private judgment?

(2) If society has the right to pass judgment, has it also the right to use the weapon of the law to enforce it?

(3) If so, ought it to use that weapon in all cases or only in some: and if only in some on what principles should it distinguish? ...

[Lord Devlin then explained that a public morality is one of the vital ingredients of a society, and that the State has the right to safeguard anything that is essential to its existence. In other words, he answered the first two questions affirmatively.]

In what circumstances the State should exercise its power is the third of the interrogatories I have framed. But before I get to it I must raise a point which might have been brought up in any one of the three. How are the moral judgments of society to be ascertained ... It is surely not enough that they should be reached by the opinion of the majority; it would be too much to require the individual assent of every citizen. English law has evolved and regularly uses a standard which does not depend on the counting of heads. It is that of the reasonable man. He is not to be confused with the rational man. He is not expected to reason about anything and his judgment may be largely a matter of feeling ... for my purpose I should like to call him the man in the jury box ...

Immorality then, for the purpose of the law, is what every right-minded person is presumed to consider immoral. Any immorality is capable of affecting society injuriously and in effect to a greater or lesser extent it usually does: this is what gives the law *locus standi*. It cannot be shut out. But—and this brings me to the third question—the individual has a *locus standi* too; he cannot be expected to surrender to the judgment of society the whole conduct of his life. It is the old familiar question of striking a balance between the rights and interests of society and those of the individual ... there must be toleration of the maximum individual freedom that is consistent with the integrity of society. Nothing should be punished by the law that does not lie beyond the limit of tolerance. It is not nearly enough to say that a majority dislike a practice: there must be a real feeling of reprobation ... I do not think one can ignore disgust if it is deeply felt and not manufactured. Its presence is a good indication that the bounds of toleration are being reached ...

[B]efore a society can put a practice beyond the limits of tolerance there must be a deliberate judgment that the practice is injurious to society ... We should ask ourselves in the first instance whether, looking at it calmly and dispassionately, we regard it as a vice so abominable that its mere presence is an offence. If that is the genuine feeling of the society in which we live, I do not see how society can be denied the right to eradicate it."

Criminal sanctions, according to Devlin, should be determined by the deep disgust (dispassionately felt) of the right-minded person, or, more accurately, they should depend upon the law-maker's interpretation of the likelihood of the right-minded person being deeply disgusted.

Devlin's criteria are easily applied to many crimes, such as murder and rape. Other crimes such as theft would also undoubtedly be regarded as immoral and generally attract "the real feeling of reprobation", even if not "disgust".

This thesis becomes more difficult when applied to Devlin's own example of homosexuality (he was responding to the Wolfenden Report, which had recommended decriminalising homosexual acts between consenting adult males in private). According to Devlin, although "some people sincerely believe that homosexuality is neither immoral nor unnatural",[15] there is nevertheless a collective judgment against it, and a deep feeling of disgust towards it.[16] But as Hughes states:

"One cannot help suspecting that the morality of an established caste is being too uninquiringly preferred here as the morality of the right-thinking majority. For is it not a strange society that is disgusted at private, consensual, homosexual behaviour, but can look with equanimity upon fox and stag hunting?

... It is not beyond the bounds of possibility that proper inquiry might reveal that, while the ordinary man contemplates homosexual behaviour with aversion and distaste, the knowledge of this practice by others does not disgust him so deeply as Lord Devlin suspects ...

There is no suggestion of an inquiry into the harm such homosexual behaviour does to society, into the effectiveness of criminal prohibition as a check, or into the evils which may attend criminal prohibition. The only yardstick is the depth of disgust."[17]

Was is it just a coincidence that the activities in *Brown* took place during homosexual encounters? It has been pointed out that prostitutes regularly receive beatings as part of their sexual encounters, even if the degrees of sado-masochism described in *Brown* are probably rarer. The implication for some commentators is that, despite all the window-dressing that talk of "harm" provides, this is really a case about the immorality of certain types of homosexual encounters.[18]

Whether one accepts such an argument or not, the result of the wide ruling in *Brown* is that most such violent encounters must be regarded as illegal if actual bodily harm results. It is irrelevant whether sexual pleasure is involved as consent is no defence. Some have applauded this conclusion:

### William Wilson, "Is Hurting People Wrong?" [1992] Journal of Social Welfare and Family Law 388 at 393, 395:

"[*Brown*] should be treated, not as a test case for sexual freedom but for the idea that even a tolerant, pluralistic society must enforce one fundamental residual moral value. Quite simply, it may be argued, hurting people is wrong, and this is so whether the victim consents or not, and whether the purpose is to fulfil a sexual need, to induce a state of euphoric narcosis, punish an errant child. ...

How is the balance between freedom and coercion to be drawn? Is the public interest to be secured, in other words, by allowing citizens absolute licence to pursue their own conceptions of the good life, which we take to be the basic moral premise upon which coercion is to be ordered? Or is it to be restricted in order to achieve some more valuable

---

[15] At p. 8.
[16] In 1987 it was estimated that 74 per cent of the population regarded homosexual relations as "always" or "mostly" wrong (Harding, "Trends in Permissiveness" in Jowell, Witherspoon and Brook (eds), *British Social Attitudes, the 5th Report* (1988), p. 36. However, by 2001 that figure had fallen to 47 per cent (*British Social Attitudes*, 19th Report, 2002).
[17] Hughes, "Morals and the Criminal Law" (1962) 71 Yale L.J. 662 at 676–678.
[18] Bibbings and Alldridge accuse their Lordships of being homophobic: "Sexual Expression, Body Alteration, and the Defence of Consent" (1993) J. Law & Soc. 356 at 358.

public good, namely societal cohesion and public order? ... [A] fundamental building block in our moral society is the social taboo against the infliction of injury on another. Remove this building block and not only do sensibilities stand to be damaged but, over time, perhaps our very commitment to the sanctity of life. To reduce this fundamental moral issue to an issue about the presence or absence of consent may be to miss what is really at stake, namely our humanity, as presently conceived. If sadism is allowable, if consented to, then it is consent rather than moral conviction which polices the barrier between a society of would-be sadists and the kind of society most of us would like to inhabit."

A line has to be drawn between that which society will allow, or turn a blind eye to, or condemn informally and that which it will condemn by means of the criminal law. One yardstick offered by Devlin is the depth of disgust. Another, offered by Wilson, is that of autonomy being "trumped" where the activity is against the "public interest". In the case of *Brown*, Lord Mustill dissented on the issue of where this line should be drawn:

### R. v Brown [1994] 1 A.C. 212 (House of Lords)

Lord Mustill:
"When proposing that the conduct is not rightly so charged I do not invite your Lordships' House to endorse it as morally acceptable. Nor do I pronounce in favour of a libertarian doctrine specifically related to sexual matters. ... What I do say is that these are questions of private morality; that the standards by which they fall to be judged are not those of the criminal law; and that if these standards are to be upheld the individual must enforce them upon himself according to his own moral standards, or have them enforced against him by moral pressures exerted by whatever religious or other community to whose ethical ideals he responds. The point from which I invite your Lordships to depart is simply this, that the state should interfere with the rights of an individual to live his or her life as he or she may choose no more than is necessary to ensure a proper balance between the special interests of the individual and the general interests of the individuals who together comprise the population at large. Thus, whilst acknowledging that very many people, if asked whether the appellants' conduct was wrong, would reply, 'Yes, repulsively wrong', I would at the same time assert that this does not in itself mean that the prosecution of the appellants ... is well-founded."

However, according to the law as it now stands, boxing, for example, stands one side of the line, while sado-masochism falls on the other.

A similar debate exists in relation to incest. Incest (which was not criminalised until 1908 by a private member's bill[19]) probably figures as an example where a large number of people would feel exactly the sort of emotions described by Lord Devlin.

### Jennifer Temkin, "Do We Need the Crime of Incest?" (1991) 44 Current Legal Problems 185 at 187–188:

"For those who are dedicated to the institution of the family and the maintenance of family life, incest must remain an anathema. It is destructive both to those who participate in it and to those who are directly involved. ... It is vital to the actual security and sense of security of all members of that unit that within it certain boundaries are set and preserved. Of these boundaries the sexual one is the most fundamental. Women living or in contact with fathers and brothers need to know that sex between them is not and never will be on the agenda ... it is fitting therefore for the criminal law to place its weight behind that boundary

[19] Punishment of Incest Act 1908. The offence is now governed by ss.10 and 11 of the Sexual Offences Act 1956.

and endeavour thereby to protect the individual's safety in the family situation. An incest law must seek both to protect the family and protect the individual from the family."

Clearly, therefore, incest is against the "public interest". The difficulty lies, however, in dissecting this creature "public interest" or "public policy". Perhaps this can only be done by assessing its relationship to "harm". However, what can be concluded at this stage is that Lord Devlin's yardstick is not a sound basis upon which to take decisions to criminalise, especially if cloaked behind a mask of public interest. Not only may it be a thin disguise for the criminalisation of immorality *simpliciter*[20] (as advocated by Stephen more than a century ago) but the criteria employed are too limited. One cannot, as Lord Devlin has done, throw rationality completely to the winds in order to replace it with the reasonable man's disgust—which, as Hart points out, may be based on "ignorance, superstition or misunderstanding".[21] Instead,

> "the examination of existing law and the debate about proposed laws should be conducted by making as explicit a statement as is possible of the values that the law is designed to protect, by a careful investigation of the harm done to those values by the conduct prohibited or which it is sought to prohibit, and by a careful consideration of the probable efficacy of legal prohibition. In this debate the prevalence of feelings of disgust or revulsion in the community is one factor to be considered and no more than that."[22]

In other words, whilst immorality (with all its attendant difficulties of identification) may be a necessary condition for the imposition of the criminal law, it ought not to be a sufficient one.

### (ii) *The Harm and Offence Principle*

A basic tenet of liberalism is that respect must be shown to the principle of individual autonomy—the notion that people possess free will and must be allowed, to the maximum extent possible, to make free choices. The state should only intervene to restrict autonomy when it is necessary to prevent harm or serious offence to others.

**The Law Commission, Consent in the Criminal Law (Consultation Paper No. 139, 1995) Appendix C, para. C.85:**

> "The liberal and the moralist disagree fundamentally about the value of autonomy. The liberal can agree with the moralist that the world would be a better place with less of this evil in it, and the liberal might even set about trying to reduce the evil by argument, persuasion, exhortation and/or education of the young. But she will not use the criminal law to this end because she accords primacy to the value of autonomy and the mutually reinforcing ideals of value pluralism and toleration. Given the diversity of human needs, tastes and talents there must be a diversity of eligible life-styles, careers and options to give everybody a fair chance of living a fulfilling, stimulating and enjoyable life. Some of these life-styles will be

---

[20] For a defence of Lord Devlin, see Rostow, "The Enforcement of Morals" [1960] C.L.J. 174 where he suggests that Lord Devlin so qualifies his central conditions with cries for tolerance, etc., that the gap between him and his critics is very small.

[21] Hart, "Immorality and Treason" 62 Listener 163 (July 30, 1959).

[22] Hughes (*above*, n.7, at p. 682). He points out that this approach will still contain elements of irrationality but that it is better than the "throwing the baby out with the bath water" (Hart, "Immorality and Treason", *ibid.* p. 163) approach of Devlin.

incompatible or even mutually contradictory, but the liberal will demand that each should extend to the others a degree of tolerance and respect, within the limits set by the harm and offence principles. The liberal asserts that her political theory is the most appropriate for a multicultural and pluralistic society."

## H. L. A. Hart, "Immorality and Treason" 62 Listener 162–163 (July 30, 1959):

"The Wolfenden Committee on Homosexual Offences and Prostitution recommended by a majority of 12 to 1 that homosexual behaviour between consenting adults in private should no longer be a criminal offence. One of the Committee's principal grounds for this recommendation was expressed in its report in this way: 'There must remain a realm of private morality and immorality which in brief and crude terms is not the law's business.' I shall call this the liberal point of view: for it is a special application of those wider principles of liberal thought which John Stuart Mill formulated in his essay on Liberty. Mill's most famous words, less cautious perhaps than the Wolfenden Committee's were:

'The only purpose for which power can be rightfully exercised over any member of a civilized community against his will is to prevent harm to others. His own good, either physical or moral, is not a sufficient warrant. He cannot rightfully be compelled to do or forbear ... because in the opinion of others to do so would be wise or even right.'

The liberal point of view has often been attacked, both before and after Mill. I shall discuss here the repudiation of it made by Sir Patrick Devlin ...

Mill's formulation of the liberal point of view may well be too simple. The grounds for interfering with human liberty are more various than the single criterion of 'harm to others' suggests: cruelty to animals or organizing prostitution for gain do not, as Mill himself saw, fall easily under the description of harm to others. Conversely, even where there is harm to others in the most literal sense, there may well be other principles limiting the extent to which harmful activities should be repressed by law. So there are multiple criteria, not a single criterion, determining when human liberty may be restricted. Perhaps this is what Sir Patrick means by a curious distinction which he often stresses between theoretical and practical limits. But with all its simplicities the liberal point of view is a better guide than Sir Patrick to clear thought in the proper relation of morality to the criminal law: for it stresses what he obscures—namely, the points at which thought is needed before we turn popular morality into criminal law.

No doubt we would all agree that consensus of moral opinion on certain matters is essential if society is to be worth living in. Laws against murder, theft, and much else would be of little use if they were not supported by a widely diffused conviction that what these laws forbid is also immoral. So much is obvious. But it does not follow that everything to which the moral vetoes of accepted morality attach is of equal importance to society; nor is there the slightest reason for thinking of morality as a seamless web: one which will fall to pieces carrying society with it, unless all its emphatic vetoes are enforced by law. Surely even in the face of the moral feeling that is up to concert pitch—the trio of intolerance, indignation, and disgust—we must pause to think. We must ask a question at two different levels which Sir Patrick never clearly enough identifies or separates. First, we must ask whether a practice which offends moral feeling is harmful, independently of its repercussion on the general moral code. Secondly, what about repercussion on the moral code? Is it really true that failure to translate this item of general morality into criminal law will jeopardize the whole fabric of morality and so society?

We cannot escape thinking about these two different questions merely by repeating to ourselves the vague nostrum: 'This is part of public morality and public morality must be preserved if society is to exist.' Sometimes Sir Patrick seems to admit this, for he says in words which both Mill and the Wolfenden Report might have used, that there must be the maximum respect for individual liberty consistent with the integrity of society. Yet this, as his contrasting examples of fornication and homosexuality show, turns out to mean only that the immorality which the law may punish must be generally felt to be intolerable. This plainly is no adequate substitute for a reasoned estimate of the damage to the fabric of society likely to ensue if it is not suppressed.

Nothing perhaps shows more clearly the inadequacy of Sir Patrick's approach to this problem than his comparison between the suppression of sexual immorality and the suppression of treason or subversive activity. Private subversive activity is, of course, a contradiction in terms because 'subversion' means overthrowing government, which is a public thing. But it is grotesque, even where moral feeling against homosexuality is up to concert pitch, to think of the homosexual behaviour of two adults in private as in any way like treason or sedition either in intention or effect. We can make it *seem* like treason only if we assume that deviation from a general moral code is bound to affect that code, and to lead not merely to its modification but to its destruction. The analogy could begin to be plausible only if it was clear that offending against this item of morality was likely to jeopardize the whole structure. But we have ample evidence for believing that people will not abandon morality, will not think any better of murder, cruelty, and dishonesty, merely because some private sexual practice which they abominate is not punished by the law."

An immediate problem with the harm and offence principle is that one needs a careful definition of these terms. A trader who sets up a legitimate business in competition with another can severely harm that other person by taking away all her business but, in a capitalist society where business competition is encouraged, this can hardly constitute the sort of harm that ought to be criminalised. Similarly, picking one's nose in public might cause deep offence to observers but, again, it would be unthinkable to assert that such conduct should be criminal.

With regard to the concept of harm, a distinction is often drawn between primary and secondary harms.

### J. Kaplan, "The Role of the Law in Drug Control" [1971] Duke L.J. 1065 at 1065–1068:

"Typically the use of the law to prevent conduct which harms only the actor himself is distinguished from the use of the law as a means of preventing the individual from harming others, including society at large. In practice, however, this is not an easy distinction to draw, for there are few actions in which one can engage that threaten harm only to himself.

The purest example of laws aimed at such conduct are the statutes which require the driver of a motorcycle to wear a protective helmet. It is true that one can argue that the helmet really protects others, since it shields the motorcyclist from thrown pebbles which might make him lose control and injure innocent pedestrians or automobile drivers. Though this approach makes the problem easier, it is disingenuous. As a result, many courts and commentators have refused to take it and have assumed that the helmet protects only the cyclist himself.

Though the helmetless cyclist does not expose others to any appreciable physical danger, he does drive in a society that is committed to preventing people from dying of their injuries. Thus, rather than allowing the cyclist to die unnecessarily, society is prepared to undertake the enormous expense of treating him until he either expires or recovers. In Professor Robert Bartel's apt phrase, the helmetless cyclist exposes others to 'public ward' harm—the danger of having to treat him should he not be killed outright. It is on this theory that society feels it has the right to demand that he do his share to protect himself.

The expense and inconvenience that the helmetless driver may cause does not, however, stop at public ward harm. Insofar as his failure to wear a helmet results in his own injury, he may force society to assume the cost of his neglected responsibilities to others. Here the issue cannot be avoided by saying that it is all society's fault for not letting him die in the street at minimal cost, because his responsibilities must still be fulfilled. As an emotional matter, moreover, non-support justifications for laws which attempt to prevent self-harming conduct often command considerably more power than do public ward justifications. Thus, despite the enormous public ward justifications for halting alcohol abuse, one of the most powerful Prohibitionist posters contained a drawing of a saloon with a father drinking at the bar while his clean, but poorly dressed little daughter stood in the doorway saying, 'Father, Father, please come home. Mother needs you.' The same public interest which underlies non-support laws, then, can also justify helmetless cyclist laws—at least in the case of those who owe someone a support obligation.

In addition to the public ward and non-support justifications for forbidding conduct which on first glance would appear to harm only the actor, a further justification exists which might be called the 'modelling' justification. Modelling is the psychological term for the process by which one repeats a type of behaviour one sees in others. Modelling of behaviour may thus occur where the watcher first learns that the behaviour which he had thought impossible can indeed be performed; where the watcher, by observing, learns how to do it; where he simply gets the idea from watching; or where he, for any one of many reasons, imitates the action. It is true, of course, that the same values which underlie the freedom of communication may interfere with preventing the harm caused by modelling. The individual who models the helmetless cyclist does so without coercion, and, apart from the indirect harms discussed, he harms only himself. Nevertheless, where those persons society tries to protect from modelling are children, the fact that the helmetless cyclist in a causal sense may have caused the modelling, which in turn might lead to injury, may be very significant. Children are regarded as much more likely than adults to model dangerous conduct, and we certainly acknowledge a greater responsibility to protect them from harm.

The final justification by which some may find social harm in conduct which appears to harm only the actor might be called the 'categorical imperative' justification. This relies on the fact that although an act might harm only the actor if performed by relatively few people, it could cause harm to everyone if it were performed by almost all. This justification is not heard in the helmetless cyclist case, but it is heard with respect to some sexual and drug laws."

If one were to apply the distinction made by Kaplan between harms which may be referred to as primary (involving direct harm to others) and secondary (involving indirect harm to others) to the examples we have employed before, theft would clearly belong to the former category; it causes harm to others and can be criminalised on that basis. Clearly also, incest involving a non-consenting child can be criminalised on this basis (although that still leaves unresolved the issue of whether one needs a law of *incest* rather than utilising provisions designed to deal with child abuse more generally[23]). But what of consensual incest between a brother and sister who have both attained their majority? In the face of a recommendation that it should cease to be unlawful if both parties are over 21,[24] it has been argued that continued protection is required since the chances are that the incest will have commenced when the "victim" was under age and that the reality of the relationship is more likely to have been founded upon coercion and exploitation than upon consent.[25] In addition to this harm to the victim one might wish to make reference to the eugenic risks involved and one could also employ Kaplan's "modelling" and "categorical imperative" justifications.

Similar arguments were raised in the case of *Brown*[26] as was an incident of corruption of a young man into the sado-masochistic ring. In other words, the

[23] See Temkin, "Do We Need the Crime of Incest?" (1991) 44 C.L.P. 185 at 193–194 who argues that there is a strong case for retention of the specific crime of incest.
[24] Criminal Law Revision Committee, Fifteenth Report, Sexual Offences (Cmnd.9213), paras 8.15–8.36.
[25] Temkin, "Do We Need the Crime of Incest?" (1991) 44 C.L.P. 185 at 201.
[26] [1994] 1 A.C. 212.

potential, if not the reality, for harm to others existed. In addition, the majority stressed other relevant harms. Lord Jauncey stated that "it would appear to be good luck rather than good judgment which has prevented serious injury from occurring. Wounds can easily become septic if not properly treated, the free flow of blood from a person who is HIV positive or who has AIDS can infect another and an inflicter who is carried away by sexual excitement or by drink or drugs could very easily inflict pain and injury beyond the level to which the receiver had consented. ... When considering the public interest potential for harm is just as relevant as actual harm."[27] Furthermore, arguments based again upon the "modelling" and "categorical imperative" justifications could be made.

What this discussion suggests is that the distinction between primary and secondary harms does not provide us with a basis for making decisions as to whether to criminalise conduct. Not only may it be a front for the criminalisation of immorality *simpliciter* but also it does not enable us to answer which (if any) secondary harms should be prohibited by the criminal law. Just as no-one today argues that all immoral acts ought to be criminal, so no-one argues that all secondary harms ought to be criminal. "The obvious secondary harm resulting from such almost universally performed acts as over-eating or poor nutrition is the *reductio ad absurdum* of such arguments."[28]

One of the most sophisticated efforts at defining the harm and offence principle is that provided by Joel Feinberg in a series of books, spanning four volumes, entitled *The Moral Limits of the Criminal Law*.

## Joel Feinberg, The Moral Limits of the Criminal Law: Harm to Others (1984), pp. 33, 34, 36, 215–216:

"Harm ... [means] the thwarting, setting back, or defeating of an interest ... One's interests ... consist of all those things in which one has a stake ... Only setbacks of interests that are wrongs, and wrongs that are setbacks to interest, are to count as harms in the appropriate sense ...

This interpretation thus excludes set-back interests produced by justified or excused conduct ('harms' that are not wrongs) ... A harm in the appropriate sense then will be produced by morally indefensible conduct that not ony sets back the victim's interest, but also violates his right ...

Minor or trivial harms *are* harms despite their minor magnitude and triviality, but below a certain threshold they are not to count as harms for the purposes of the harm principle, for legal interference with trivia is likely to cause more harm than it prevents ...

Where the kind of conduct in question ... does create a danger to some degree, legislators employing the harm principle must use various rules of thumb as best they can:

   a. the greater the *gravity* of a possible harm, the less probable its occurrence need be to justify prohibition of the conduct that threatens to produce it;
   b. the greater the *probability* of harm, the less grave the harm need be to justify coercion;
   c. the greater the *magnitude of the risk* of harm, itself compounded out of gravity and probability, the less reasonable it is to accept the risk;
   d. the more *valuable* (useful) the dangerous conduct, both to the actor and others, the more reasonable it is to take the risk of harmful consequences ...
   e. the more reasonable the risk of harm (the danger), the weaker is the case for prohibiting the conduct that creates it."

---

[27] At 245–246.
[28] Kaplan, p. 1068.

## Joel Feinberg, The Moral Limits of the Criminal Law: Offense to Others (1985), pp. 1–2, 26:

"It is always a good reason in support of a proposed criminal prohibition that it would probably be an effective way of preventing serious offense (as opposed to injury or harm) to persons other than the actor, and that it is probably a necessary means to that end ...

The offense principle requires that the disliked state of mind ... be produced wrongfully by another party ...

[It is necessary] to weigh, in each main category and context of offensiveness, the seriousness of the offense caused to unwilling witnesses against the reasonableness of the offender's conduct. The seriousness of the offensiveness would be determined by (1) the intensity and durability of the repugnance produced, and the extent to which repugnance could be anticipated to be the general reaction of strangers to the conduct displayed or represented (conduct offensive only to persons with an abnormal susceptibility to offense would not count as *very* offensive); (2) the ease with which unwilling witnesses can avoid the offensive displays; and (3) whether or not the witnesses have willingly assumed the risk of being offended either through curiosity or the anticipation of pleasure ...

These factors would be weighed as a group against the reasonableness of the offending party's conduct as determined by (1) its personal importance to the actors themselves and its social utility generally, remembering always the enormous social utility of unhampered expression (in those cases where expression is involved); (2) the availability of alternative times and places where the conduct in question would cause less offense; (3) the extent, if any, to which the offense is caused with spiteful motives. In addition, the legislature would examine the prior established character of various neighbourhoods, and consider establishing licensed zones in areas where the conduct in question is known to be already prevalent, so that people inclined to be offended are not likely to stumble on it to their surprise ...

[Feinberg argues that the law should not treat offence as if it was as serious as harm and, where possible, should use other modes of regulation such as injunctions or licensing procedures (p.3).]"

## The Law Commission, Consent in the Criminal Law (Consultation Paper No. 139, 1995), Appendix C, para. C.41:

"Liberals support the offence principle because some forms of offence can be so extreme and protracted that they unacceptably infringe the autonomy of unwilling observers and are therefore, on liberal principles, legitimate candidates for criminalisation. The liberal is, however, extremely cautious in using the criminal law to this end and will only endorse an offence principle that is properly qualified and carefully circumscribed. The reason is clear; since just about every conceivable activity might give offence to *somebody, everybody's* autonomy would be severely and unacceptably curtailed if the criminal law routinely targeted offensive conduct ... The liberal, at any rate, will only countenance criminalising offence which is extreme and unavoidable, and this can never be said of activity which takes place in private."

It follows that while picking one's nose in public might be an offence to sensibility,[29] it could never, using Feinberg's criteria, amount to *serious* offence. On the other hand, if one were travelling on a bus and the passengers in the seat directly opposite perform mutual fellatio or cunnilingus to climax accompanied by sound effects,[30] it could be argued that the test of serious offence is made out.

[29] Gross, *A Theory of Criminal Justice* (1979), p. 120.
[30] Feinberg, *The Moral Limits of the Criminal Law: Offense to Others* (1985), p. 12.

The critical definition of harm and offence is that it involves a *wrongful* set-back to another's interests. Whether conduct is wrongful is ultimately to be based on moral judgments. Accordingly, if a victim consents to injury or the risk of injury, as is the case with sado-masochistic beatings, that person has not been wronged and so has not been harmed. Similarly, the legitimate businessperson has not wronged the competitor and so no harm has been caused.

### (iii) *Legal Paternalism*

Legal paternalism involves allowing the criminal law to be used to protect a person from harm to himself. The law is entitled to interfere with a person's autonomy for his own good and to enhance his welfare. If it were established that consuming certain drugs was harmful to the person concerned, the paternalist would criminalise the sale and possession of such drugs. The legal paternalist is, however, only interested in enhancing the interests that a person actually has and not in protecting interests that he ought to have. As Roberts puts it: "So a paternalist in my sense may interfere with another person's self-regarding actions in order to protect those interests which the other would recognise as authentically his (*e.g.* his interests in continued life and bodily security) but not for the sake of interests the other disowns (*e.g.* his (moral) interest in not having gay sex)."[31] There are, however, problems with a paternalistic approach.

**The Law Commission, Consent in the Criminal Law (Consultation Paper No. 139, 1995), Appendix C, para. C.63:**

"[T]he paternalist argues from a philosophical slippery slope and is at constant risk of taking a tumble. The fact is that many of us make life-style choices which do not promote our immediate or long-term interests. Smoking certainly falls into this category of choices: for the paternalist it should be a clear target for criminalisation. But the point goes much further. If (as seems plausible) a balanced, healthy diet and regular exercise would be in every person's interests, the paternalist has a reason for criminalising fatty foods and sedentary life-styles. Risk-taking without good reason would also be ruled out. Sky-diving, mountaineering and most contact sports would have to be criminalised. In principle, the paternalist seems to be committed to using the criminal law to turn us all into super-fit, clean-living 'spartans' whether we like it or not."

Despite this,[32] the Law Commission has proposed, in relation to sado-masochistic activities, that the law be based on an approach "redolent of a paternalism that is softened at the edges".[33] Accordingly, while people should be generally entitled to make choices for themselves and consent to injury, even fairly serious injury, they should not be permitted to consent to seriously disabling injury. Because people have interests in their physical health, the normal functioning of their bodies and in avoiding intense pain or grotesque disfigurement, the Law Commission takes the view that anybody who consents to seriously disabling injury "has made a mistake and that to be really disabled is against his or her interests".[34] An exception is,

---

[31] "The Philosophical Foundations of *Consent in the Criminal Law*" (1997) 17 O.J.L.S. 389 at 394.
[32] "Appendix C: Consent and the Criminal Law: Philosophical Foundations" was specially commissioned by the Law Commission and written by Paul Roberts. While reproducing his advice, the Law Commission felt itself unable to adopt the approach he favours (para. 2.1).
[33] Para. 2.15.
[34] Para. 2.18.

however, proposed in relation to activities that are "very widely regarded as beneficial"[35] such as surgery and risky sports. By allowing people to consent to a range of injuries in sado-masochism, the Law Commission clearly regards its paternalistic view as being softened in favour of liberalism. However, by not allowing people to consent to seriously disabling injuries in the course of sado-masochism while not criminalising the same injuries in the course of, say, boxing, it is possible to assert that in reality the Law Commission has adopted a stance of paternalism hardened at the edges by legal moralism.

### 2. Is it necessary to employ the criminal law?

Whichever of the above views is adopted as the correct basis upon which to justify the determination that conduct is wrongful, most commentators accept that this is merely a minimal or necessary, but not a sufficient, condition. Assuming the conduct in question is adjudged to be wrongful, there is a further condition to be established. It must be *necessary* to use the *criminal law* to condemn and try to prevent the wrongful conduct.

### Herbert L. Packer, The Limits of the Criminal Sanction (1969), pp. 266–272:

"The question is not one of whether or not there will be harm done; it is one of the remoteness and probability of the harm. Some things are more harmful than others. Homicide is more harmful than muttering voodoo incantations; rape is more harmful than reading dirty books. And in a world of limited resources, we need to draw discriminations about the gravity and remoteness of harms. Seen in this light, 'harm to others' is a prudential criterion rather than a hard and fast distinction of principle.

'Harm to others' does not, of course, mean identifiable others. It has become fashionable to talk about 'victimless crimes,' meaning those in which there is no immediately identifiable victim to lodge a complaint. The absence of an identifiable victim can make enforcement difficult, and can encourage undesirable enforcement practices. But the prospect of these difficulties should not end the inquiry into the wisdom of any given use of the criminal sanction. Many offenses against the administration of government are 'victimless crimes' in the sense that there is nobody to complain. Consensual transactions like bribery and espionage are admittedly difficult to detect because of the absence of an identifiable victim; yet they do not necessarily cause so little 'harm to others' that we can forget about subjecting them to the criminal sanction.

The 'harm to others' formula seems to me to have two uses that justify its inclusion in a list of limiting criteria for invocation of the criminal sanction. First, it is a way to make sure that a given form of conduct is not being subjected to the criminal sanction purely or even primarily because it is thought to be immoral. It forces an inquiry into precisely what bad effects are feared if the conduct in question is not suppressed by the criminal law. Second, it immediately brings into play a host of secular inquiries about the effects of subjecting the conduct in question to the criminal sanction. One cannot meaningfully deal with the question of 'harm to others' without weighing benefits against detriments. In that sense, it is a kind of threshold question, important not so much in itself as in focusing attention on further considerations relevant to the ultimate decision. It is for these two instrumental reasons rather than for either its intrinsic rightness or its ease of application that it deserves inclusion ... [Packer then considers the further conditions.]

---

[35] *ibid.*

Goals of Punishment:

To begin with, there is the obvious point that unless at least *one* utilitarian mode of prevention is likely to be served by employing the criminal sanction against a particular form of conduct, we had better forget about it. Sneezing in church is a relatively uncontroversial example ...

[A] utilitarian case for defining conduct as criminal can best be made in situations where both deterrence and incapacitation are effective: where people are relatively likely to be deflected by the possibility of being caught *and* where punishment is likely to prevent the commission of further crimes. There are many situations in which the two are not correlated and ... very few in which they are ...

Remoteness and Triviality:

The conduct proscribed by any criminal code can be ranked in a hierarchy of remoteness from the ultimate harm that the law seeks to prevent. We prohibit the sale of liquor to an intoxicated person to lessen the likelihood that he will drive while drunk (an offense), crash into another car (an offense), injure an occupant of the other car (an offense), or cause the death of someone in the other car (an offense). There we have a spectrum of remoteness ranging from the illegal sale of liquor to manslaughter. Similarly, we make it an offense to possess tools specially adapted for burglary so that we may reduce the incidence of burglary (an offense), and thereby reduce the incidence of further offences, such as larceny, robbery, rape, and even murder, that can ensue from burglary. Mayhem or murder might not be intended by most burglars, but they are nonetheless possible results of the confrontation between burglar and victim.

One of the most delicate problems in framing criminal proscriptions is to locate the point farthest removed from the ultimate harm apprehended at which meaningful preventive intervention can take place. If dangerous conduct can be deterred and dangerous persons identified well short of the point at which the danger becomes acute, so much the better. Or so it seems. Actually, increasing the radius of the criminal law in the interest of early intervention is a very risky business. The first question in every case is, or should be: how high is the probability that the preparatory conduct, if not inhibited by the threat of criminal punishment, will result in an ultimate harm of the sort that the law should try to prevent? A related consideration is whether the preparatory conduct is itself socially useful, or at least neutral, so that its proscription or curtailment might unduly inhibit people from doing what they should otherwise be free to do. To put the issue in terms that are familiar in the law, is the risk substantial and is it justifiable? ...

Still another consideration relates to the problem of enforcement. By and large, the further removed the conduct in question is from the ultimate harm apprehended, the more difficult it is going to be to detect the occurrence of the conduct and to apprehend people who engage in it. Considerations of maximizing personal freedom and of minimizing the strain on law enforcement combine, then, to suggest considerable caution in the progression towards the remote end of the spectrum.

An example that is amusing because it is so extreme is a recent action of the New York City Council. At the urgent request of the Fire Commissioner, the Council voted to make it a criminal offense, punishable by a hundred-dollar fine, a thirty-day jail term or both, to smoke in bed in a hotel, motel, or other place of public abode. A subsidiary provision required that a notice to that effect be displayed by the proprietor of every place covered by the ban. Now, nobody doubts that a great many serious and sometimes fatal accidents are caused by people's smoking in bed and that it would be a far better thing if people did not smoke in bed. But consider the impossibility of enforcing such a prohibition without the most detailed kind of surveillance. Consider the invasions of privacy that such surveillance would entail. And, enforcement problems aside, consider the effect of announcing that such commonly engaged in conduct has now become criminal. One wonders what was accomplished by the criminal prohibition that would not equally well be accomplished by requiring hotels to display in each room a notice warning about the danger. Alternatively, the solution might have been to make it criminal to cause a fire by smoking in bed, regardless of the amount of harm done. That kind of prohibition would at least have been enforceable, whether or not it was enforced. As it is, given the well-known relationship between intoxication and fires resulting from smoking in bed, I suppose travellers should be grateful that the City Council did not go one step further and make it a crime to go to bed drunk in a New York hotel.

The idea of a criminal conviction no longer inspires the awe that it once did, because of the tendency of legislative bodies (like the New York City Council in this example) to prescribe criminal penalties simply as a means of expressing their disapproval of conduct. This tendency results in two kinds of triviality: triviality of object and triviality of intention. By triviality of object I mean the selection of behaviour for which the regular imposition of criminal punishment is disproportionate. By triviality of intention I mean an attitude of indifference or cynicism on the part of legislators toward the actual enforcement of the proscriptions they vote for. Both forms of triviality should be carefully avoided. A rational legislator should not vote to subject previously legal conduct to criminal proscription unless he is prepared to say, first, that the conduct being proscribed is so threatening to important social interests that he is willing to see people who engage in it subjected to criminal punishment and, second, that he expects law enforcement to devote adequate resources to detecting, apprehending, and convicting violators. The two will tend in most cases to be complementary ... [Such trivial offences should be decriminalised and made 'civil offences' or 'infractions.']"

Packer then identifies further conditions that need to be taken into account when making the "ultimate decision" about criminalisation. In addition to what has been said so far, we need to avoid the possibility of creating a "crime tariff"[36]; by this he means that the demand for the illegalised activity or product may be so inelastic that rather than reducing the incidence of the activity, it merely drives it underground and forces the price up. The provision of illegal abortions and the sale of narcotics are cases in point. The same may well be true of sado-masochistic activities.

We may finally consider dangers pointed to by both Packer[37] and Kadish (in the context of a discussion of sexual crimes) which are all too likely to materialise if conduct is criminalised (or not decriminalised) without careful investigation:

### Sanford Kadish, "The Crisis of Overcriminalisation" (1967) 374 Annals 157 at 159–162:

"But law enforcement pays a price for using the criminal law ... [to enforce morality]. First, the moral message communicated by the law is contradicted by the total absence of enforcement; for while the public sees the conduct condemned in words, it also sees in the dramatic absence of prosecutions that it is not condemned in deed. Moral adjurations vulnerable to a charge of hypocrisy are self-defeating no less in law than elsewhere. Second, the spectacle of nullification of the legislature's solemn commands is an unhealthy influence on law enforcement generally. It tends to breed a cynicism and an indifference to the criminal-law processes which augment tendencies towards disrespect for those who make and enforce the law, a disrespect which is already widely in evidence. In addition: 'Dead letter laws, far from promoting a sense of security, which is the main function of the penal law, actually impair that security by holding the threat of prosecution over the heads of people whom we have no intention to punish.'[38]

[36] Packer, pp. 277–282.
[37] pp. 282–295.
[38] Since the enactment of the Prohibition of Female Circumcision Act 1985 there has been no prosecution in England; the practice nevertheless continues (Atoki, "Should Female Circumcision Continue to be Banned?" (1995) 3 *Feminist Legal Studies* 223 at 235.

Finally, these laws invite discriminatory enforcement against persons selected for prosecution on grounds unrelated to the evil against which these laws are purportedly addressed, whether those grounds be 'the prodding of some reform group, a newspaper-generated hysteria over some local sex crime, a vice drive which is put on by the local authorities to distract attention from defects in their administration of the city government.'
...

Despite the fact that homosexual practices are condemned as criminal in virtually all states, usually as a felony with substantial punishment, and despite sporadic efforts at enforcement in certain situations, there is little evidence that the criminal law has discouraged the practice to any substantial degree. The Kinsey Report as well as other studies suggest a wide incidence of homosexuality throughout the country. One major reason for the ineffectiveness of these laws is that the private and consensual nature of the conduct precludes the attainment of any substantial deterrent efficacy through law enforcement. There are no complainants, and only the indiscreet have reasons for fear.

... [T]he use of the criminal law has been attended by grave consequences. A commonly noted consequence is the enhanced opportunities created for extortionary threats of exposure and prosecution ... But, of more significance for the administration of justice, enforcement efforts by police have created problems both for them and for the community. Opportunities for enforcement are limited by the private and consensual character of the behaviour ... To obtain evidence, police are obliged to resort to behaviour which tends to degrade and demean both themselves personally and law enforcement as an institution. However one may deplore homosexual conduct, no one can lightly accept a criminal law which requires for its enforcement that officers of the law sit concealed in ceilings, their eyes fixed to 'peepholes,' searching for criminal sexuality in the lavatories below; or that they loiter suggestively around public toilets or in corridors hopefully awaiting a sexual advance. Such conduct corrupts both citizenry and police and reduces the moral authority of the criminal law, especially among those portions of the citizenry—the poor and subcultural—who are particularly liable to be treated in an arbitrary fashion. The complaint of the critical [is] that the police have more important things to do with their time."

In returning to the examples of incest and sado-masochism it may be useful at this point to summarise Packer's criteria:

### Herbert L. Packer, The Limits of the Criminal Sanction (1969), p. 296:

"(1) The conduct is prominent in most people's view of socially threatening behaviour, and is not condoned by any significant segment of society.

(2) Subjecting it to the criminal sanction is not inconsistent with the goals of punishment.

(3) Suppressing it will not inhibit socially desirable conduct.

(4) It may be dealt with through even-handed and nondiscriminatory enforcement.

(5) Controlling it through the criminal process will not expose that process to severe qualitative or quantitative strains.

(6) There are no reasonable alternatives to the criminal sanction for dealing with it.

These criteria can be used in making up a kind of priority list of conduct for which the legislature might consider invoking the criminal sanction."

What conclusions are to be drawn about the examples used throughout this section?

The crime of incest covers a wide variety of situations—from consensual adult relationships between siblings to forced sexual intercourse by a father with his young daughter. Given the stance taken by the law to homosexual relationships between consenting adults, should the law continue to prohibit incest between consenting adults? Whilst the answer for some is clearly affirmative because of the special position of the family, the dangers of exploitation and the difficulty of proving other charges,[39] others have questioned the need for an *incest* law at all.

### Louis Blom-Cooper, "Criminal Law That Leaves Children at Risk," The Independent, August 7, 1989:

"The real question is how to deal with incestuous relationships. Is there any need for a criminal offence of incest? It is axiomatic that children need to be protected against incestuous adults. But how? Protection, so far as it is possible for it to be provided through legal measures, is already provided by statutes dealing with child cruelty and neglect. Incest is only one manifestation of child abuse, and by no means the worst. . . .

The 1908 legislation could be justified as an attempt to protect children at a time when legal protection was minimal . . . the essence of any prohibition on incest must be the protection of dependants unable to protect themselves.

The experience of 80 years of law enforcement against incestuous adults does not encourage one to believe that the criminal process has done much to control incestuous conduct. The Lord Chief Justice himself confessed that incestuous relationships might well be 'a situation which arose more often than was generally realised.' There are about 100 prosecutions each year. Incest surfaces to public knowledge only when there has been a rupture in the family. . . . The gross inequity in the application of the law cannot command public respect. And the infliction of imprisonment on the few who are caught does little to help society with the problem of child abuse. . . .

Something more subtle than the heavy hand of the criminal law needs to be deployed in order to provide optimum protection for abused children."[40]

Finally, we return to the problem of sado-masochism and the decision of *Brown*. The activities all took place with the consent of the passive partners. Was it appropriate to invoke the criminal law? The majority felt that the public interest took over at the point of actual bodily harm. Consent can thus only operate as a defence to a narrow range of activities involving minimal harm. They largely dealt with the matter as one of violence. But, surely, "violence" presupposes something that is against the will of the recipient. The whole approach of the majority amounts to little more than pure moralism. Piercing of genitals is unlawful. Ear-piercing is lawful. As has been commented: "Eroticism makes a difference."[41] The minority, on the other hand, dealt with the matter as one of private sexual morality and felt that it was only when grievous bodily harm had been caused that consent should be no defence. There are two possible, and radically different, responses to this. First, one could argue, as Susan Edwards has done, that there are dangers in such an approach: "In our desire to preserve privacy, individual liberty, and freedom from state intervention we are in danger of missing what lies at the heart of sado-masochism—its potential for violence. Why is it that for some the prefix 'sex' functions as a protective shield? We need to recognise, as we move increasingly into a world of sexual violence, the dangers of placing this so-called 'sex' beyond the rule of law."[42]

---

[39] Temkin, *above*, n.23 at 193.
[40] See also Morton, "The Incest Act 1908—Was it Ever Relevant?" (1988) 138 New L.J. 59; Card, "Sexual Relations with Minors" [1975] Crim.L.R.370; Bailey and McCabe, "Reforming the Law of Incest" [1979] Crim.L.R.749.
[41] Bibbings and Alldridge, "Sexual Expression, Body Alteration, and the Defence of Consent" (1993) 20 J. Law & Soc. 356 at 362.
[42] "No Defence For a Sado-masochistic Libido" (1993) 143 New L.J. 406 at 407.

The alternative response is that Edwards misses the point as in *Brown* all parties were sexually motivated. This was not a case of one person using "sex" as a shield or mask for the assertion of power and infliction of violence upon hapless victims. What could be more fundamental to individual autonomy than being able to express one's sexuality with other like-minded persons?

### 3. Is it permissible to criminalise the conduct?

Even assuming the above criteria have been met, namely that the conduct is regarded as "wrongful" and it is thought "necessary" to invoke the powers of the criminal law to condemn the activity, there is a final hurdle to be overcome before the conduct should be declared (or remain) criminal. Such criminalisation must not contravene the European Convention on Human Rights which was made directly applicable in English law by the Human Rights Act 1998.

These provisions operate in two ways. First, any new Bill proposing to criminalise conduct must be accompanied by a statement by the Minister responsible that the provisions of the Bill are compatible with the Convention.[43]

Secondly, it is possible that existing criminal offences are structured in such a way as to offend the provisions of the ECHR. For example, the European Commission has found that it was a contravention of Article 8 (respect for private life) and Article 14 (non-discrimination) to have different ages of consent for heterosexuals and homosexuals.[44] This led to a change of English law, rendering the age of consent the same for all persons.[45] Under the Human Rights Act 1998, courts are obliged to interpret all legislation "so far as it is possible to do so" in a manner that is compatible with Convention rights.[46] Courts are thus mandated to *interpret* legislation to achieve this result if possible, but they are not permitted to *legislate* (in the sense of rewriting statutory provisions): "if it is necessary in order to obtain compliance to radically alter the effect of the legislation this will be an indication that more than interpretation is involved."[47] While every effort must be made to interpret provisions to ensure compatibility, if this is not possible then, as "a measure of last resort",[48] the High Court and appellate courts may make a declaration of incompatibility. While this does not affect the actual validity of the incompatible legislation, there is an obligation to bring the law into conformity with the Convention since otherwise the United Kingdom will not meet its obligations under Article 1 of the Convention "to secure to everyone within their jurisdiction the rights and freedoms" set out in the Convention.

Similarly, courts are obliged to ensure compatibility between the common law and the Convention even if this involves courts having to override previous authority. While English courts have displayed some reluctance to go down this route, increasingly challenges to established authorities are being mounted. For example, in *Gemmel and Richards*[49] the Court of Appeal was faced with the

---

[43] Human Rights Act 1988, s.19: this applies to all Bills and not only those creating criminal offences.
[44] *Sutherland and Morris v UK* [1998] E.H.R.L.R. 117.
[45] Sexual Offences (Amendment) Act 2000, s.1.
[46] Human Rights Act 1998, s.3(1).
[47] *Poplar Housing and Regeneration Community Association Ltd v Donoghue* [2002] Q.B. 48.
[48] *R. v A (No. 2)* [2002] A.C. 45.
[49] [2003] 1 Cr.App.R. 23.

argument that certain aspects of a leading House of Lords decision, *Caldwell*,[50] were incompatible with the Convention. While rejecting this argument on its merits, the Court of Appeal clearly regarded itself as having such a power. A court in Jersey has actually exercised this power in holding that the common law defence of insanity is incompatible with the ECHR.[51]

While the importance of the ECHR cannot be over-estimated, it must be conceded that its impact on the substantive criminal law (as opposed to criminal procedure, evidence and sentencing) has, to date, been somewhat limited. For example, Article 8 provides a right to respect for private life. *Prima facie*, one might think that the decision in *Brown* would be incompatible with this: all the sado-masochistic activities in this case were consensual and in private. If a right to private life is to mean anything, it ought to encompass persons expressing their sexuality in the privacy of their own homes. Indeed, the decision in *Brown* was challenged on this basis in the European Court of Human Rights in *Laskey, Jaggard and Brown v UK*.[52] However, the European Court, while conceding that there was a violation of the right to respect for private life in Article 8(1), nevertheless ruled that criminalisation in cases involving "violence" was justifiable under Article 8(2) which permits invasions of privacy if it is "necessary in a democratic society ... for the protection of health or morals".

It remains to be seen, now that the Convention applies directly in English law, whether English judges will adopt a less moralistic/paternalistic stance.[53] The Convention could, potentially, affect many aspects of substantive criminal law such as self-defence, abortion and euthanasia (Article 2: right to life); defence of parental chastisement (Article 3: right not to be subjected to torture or inhuman or degrading treatment); defence of insanity (Article 5: right to liberty and security); strict liability and reverse burdens of proof (Article 6: presumption of innocence); sexual offences and child abduction (Article 8: right to respect for private life); blasphemy (Article 9: freedom of religion); obscenity, contempt of court, criminal libel, racial hatred offences, incitement to disaffection (Article 10: right to freedom of expression); breach of the peace and public order offences (Article 11: right to freedom of assembly and association).[54]

However, the early indications are not propitious with the English courts holding, for example, that Article 6 is "not concerned with the fairness of provisions of substantive law" and that Contracting States are free "to choose how to define the essential elements of an offence".[55] The precise effect of the

---

[50] [1982] A.C. 341.

[51] *Attorney-General v Jason Prior*. See Mackay and Gearty [2001] Crim.L.R.560. This conclusion was rejected on appeal. See Mackay [2002] Crim.L.R.728.

[52] (1997) 24 E.H.R.R. 39.

[53] Recourse to the European Court of Human Rights is still retained if all domestic remedies have been exhausted (ECHR, Art.34).

[54] Ashworth, *Principles of Criminal Law* (3rd ed., 1999), pp. 63–64; Simester and Sullivan, *Criminal Law: Theory and Doctrine* (2000), pp. 39–40. See generally, Emmerson and Ashworth, *Human Rights and Criminal Proceedings* (1999).

[55] *Gemmel and Richards* [2003] 1 Cr.App.R. 23. See also *Concannon* [2002] Crim.L.R.211. Arkinstall and O'Brien, "Table of Cases under the Human Rights Act" [2002] E.H.R.L.R. 364 provide a comprehensive list of English cases under the Human Rights Act 1998: in only one case was there a successful challenge under the Act (*Percy* [2001] EWHC Admin 1125 concerned with the Public Order Act 1985, s.5).

Convention and the nature of the various challenges to the substantive criminal law will be explored in the relevant sections of this book, particularly in relation to the structure of the defences to criminal liability which is the area that seems most likely to be affected. For present purposes, it is sufficient to conclude that while the test of permissibility of criminalisation under the ECHR could provide some check on unbridled moralism, the ultimate decision whether any particular criminalisation is justifiable will remain to be determined by the other criteria considered above.

### C. *Conclusion*

The question which we have attempted to answer in this chapter is startling in its apparent simplicity: what sort of conduct ought to be prohibited by the criminal law? That the answer is by no means clear-cut should by now be obvious, but it is submitted that in assessing the relationship between immorality and the criminal law, and the concept of harm and the criminal law, a framework, now supported by the ECHR, has been provided by which specific activities can be adjudged. It is not enough that a practice is widely regarded as immoral. Nor is it enough that it should cause harm. And the mere fact that an offence, or proposed offence, is not incompatible with the ECHR should not be conclusive. All these are minimal conditions for action by means of the criminal law but they are not sufficient. Whenever, throughout this book, we refer to the necessity for "harm done", it is envisaged that the harm will have been subjected to rigorous scrutiny such as that suggested by Feinberg and Packer. The fact that this is not always true of the present criminal law will become clear as the book progresses. Having passed through a phase of reducing the net of criminal liability, the opposite now appears to be true. All too often the criminal law is invoked without a clear analysis of whether it is appropriate to do so or what is hoped to be achieved thereby. A cry of "something has to be done" is set up and the criminal law is proposed as an instant panacea instead of being reserved as the tool of last resort.

### III. PUNISHMENT

There are four main "theories" of punishment:

1. retribution
2. deterrence
3. incapacitation
4. rehabilitation

In the interests of clarity of exposition we shall first examine these competing theories. Most of them are usually addressing the question: why do we punish? However, we shall see that there are other questions that also need answering, namely: who do we punish?; how much do we punish?; what type of punishment should be imposed? These questions will be addressed after the theories have been explored.

The retributive theory looks back to the crime, and punishes *because* of the crime. The remaining three theories all look forward to the consequences of punishment and hope to achieve something thereby, namely, crime reduction. They are thus often termed consequentialist or *utilitarian* theories. (A consequentialist seeks to achieve a consequence at any price; a utilitarian sets a price on the achievement of that goal—in this context, only the minimum amount of punishment thought necessary to achieve the consequence can be justified.) The boundaries between these theories are far from clear with several of them containing sub-categories, many of which are perceived quite differently by different writers.[56]

## A. *Retribution*

The word "retribution" is used in several senses. Sometimes it is employed to indicate either vengeance or expiation, but more commonly today it refers to giving the offender his or her just deserts and/or using punishment as a system of censure or denunciation.

## 1. Vengeance

### James Fitzjames Stephen, A History of the Criminal Law of England Vol. II (1883), pp. 81–82:

"[T]he infliction of punishment by law gives definite expression and a solemn ratification and justification to the hatred which is excited by the commission of the offence, and which constitutes the moral or popular as distinguished from the conscientious sanction of that part of morality which is also sanctioned by the criminal law. The criminal law thus proceeds upon the principle that it is morally right to hate criminals, and it confirms and justifies that sentiment by inflicting upon criminals, punishments which express it ... I am also of opinion that this close alliance between criminal law and moral sentiment is in all ways healthy and advantageous to the community. I think it highly desirable that criminals should be hated, that the punishments inflicted upon them should be so contrived as to give expression to that hatred, and to justify it so far as the public provision of means for expressing and gratifying a healthy natural sentiment can justify and encourage it."

This desire for vengeance supposedly operates at two levels. First, it is asserted that punishment satisfies the victim's (or relatives' and friends') desire for vengeance and the state is merely exacting vengeance on their behalf to prevent private retaliation.

Secondly, it is asserted that there is a public need for vengeance. It is argued that there is an instinctive demand which is active in every human being to retaliate—just as an animal strikes back with hate at those who attack it. This reaction is not only understandable but desirable as a socially acceptable outlet for our aggressions. If there were no punishment our aggressions would become repressed to the point when they might break out in an anti-social manner.[57] Such views find little serious support today and have been alleged to "represent the

---

[56] The role of restorative or reparative justice which concentrates on compensating the victim (and possibly the community) for the effects of crime is not discussed here since such a "restorative theory is not a rationale for punishment but a justification for rather different responses to lawbreaking" (Ashworth, *Sentencing and Criminal Justice* (3rd ed., 2000), p. 76).

[57] See Puttkammer, *Administration of Criminal Justice* 9 (1953) for a discussion and criticism of such a view.

breakdown of human intelligence, as well as good will. It shows perhaps the ugliest phase of our human nature".[58]

## 2. Expiation

According to this view the offender must be made to work off his guilt; he must be purified through suffering. This is regarded as a species of retribution in that the offender is "paying his debt" owed to society, and, in so doing, becomes reconciled with that society. The focus is on the past crime; the attempt is to wipe the slate clean.

These ideas stem largely from the religious influences on our culture, but some would argue that there is a deeper psychological explanation underlying an offender's need for expiation. From the time we are children we are conditioned to expect punishment when we have done wrong. Guilt is a state of tension which gives rise to a need for the removal of this tension. We are conditioned to expect this relief through punishment. The most famous illustration of this form of punishment comes from Dostoyevsky's *Crime and Punishment* in which Raskolnikov, after committing a brutal murder, becomes obsessed with feelings of guilt and eventually gives himself up as the only means of coming to terms with himself and achieving peace of mind. Some of these ideas are illustrated by the following case. The defendant was to be punished so that he could expiate his sins, and thereafter become an accepted member of society again.

### R. v Williams [1974] Crim.L.R.558 (Court of Appeal, Criminal Division)

"*Facts*: Pleaded guilty to attempting to bugger a sheep and aiding and abetting another to do so. The offence was committed about midnight after the defendants had been drinking heavily. They were seen by a man taking his dog for a walk. Sentenced to twelve months' imprisonment. *Previous convictions*: eight for dishonesty and road traffic offences: probation, fined, six months' imprisonment. *Special considerations*: they lived in a small community and the judge said: 'I fully appreciate that it is going to be a matter of comment about you for years to come and I think the kindest thing I can do is to visit upon you the outrage which I think anybody with any decent feelings would feel about it so that nobody can say, in your village, that you haven't paid for it.' *Decision*: it had been submitted that, the remarks indicated that the judge included a deterrent factor in the sentence. The court did not so regard them. The judge was giving the defendants an opportunity to expiate their offences and there was nothing wrong in his approach. However, having regard to the circumstances, and the remorse they had shown and the fact that they had been in custody for six weeks, and in the hope that they had learned their lesson, the sentence would be suspended for two years."[59]

While society might offer an offender the opportunity of expiation, it clearly cannot insist or demand it as the will or desire for *true* expiation must proceed from the defendant himself. But, of course, as *Williams* makes clear, one is not necessarily dealing with true expiation of sin. Society simply deems the offender to have purged his guilt by punishment.

---

[58] Cohen, "Moral Aspects of the Criminal Law" (1940) 49 Yale L.J. 987 at 1025.
[59] See also, *Morgan* [1991] Crim.L.R.214.

## 3. Desert

Over the last two decades "theories" of punishment such as deterrence and rehabilitation have come under increasing attack both by academics and lawmakers.[60] The view that has fast gained ascendency is that we punish criminals primarily because they deserve it.[61] The Criminal Justice Act 1991 is largely based on this philosophy. The Act followed a government White Paper which proclaimed that the aim was "better justice through a more consistent approach to sentencing, so that convicted criminals get their 'just deserts' ".[62] A majority of states in the United States have undertaken major sentencing reforms based primarily on just deserts thinking.

Just desert theorists have tended to follow the ideas of Kant that people deserve to be punished if they have broken the law. In this way we are according them respect as autonomous and responsible human beings who have chosen to commit a crime whereas "to be punished for reform reasons is to be treated like a dog".[63] Under a general theory of political obligation all persons owe duties to others not to infringe their rights. Justice and fairness insist that all persons must bear the sacrifice of obeying the law equally. By committing a crime, offenders have gained an unfair advantage over all others who have "toed the line" and restrained themselves from committing crime. They are "free riders" who have failed to observe the moral constraints that others have accepted.[64] Punishment is necessary to take away the benefits gained. Social equilibrium must be restored. Offenders deserve punishment in order to destroy their unfair advantage.

Jean Hampton, in a variation on this theme, argues that crime involves the infliction of a moral injury; the victim is diminished in value. Punishment is necessary "to vindicate the value of the victim".[65] The defendant by committing the crime is asserting an unjustified superiority over the victim which must be nullified through punishment.

### Andrew von Hirsch, Doing Justice—The Choice of Punishments (Report of the Committee for the Study of Incarceration) (1976), pp. 45–49:

"In everyday thinking about punishment, the idea of desert figures prominently. Ask the person on the street why a wrongdoer should be punished, and he is likely to say that he 'deserves' it . . .

To say someone 'deserves' to be rewarded or punished is to refer to his *past* conduct, and assert that its merit or demerit is reason for according him pleasant or unpleasant treatment. The focus on the past is critical. That a student has written an outstanding paper is grounds for asserting that he deserves an award; but that the award will yield him or others future benefits (however desirable those might be) cannot be grounds for claiming he deserves it. The same holds for punishment: to assert that someone deserves to be punished is to look at his past wrongdoing as reason for having him penalized. This orientation to the past

---

[60] For a good bibliography, see von Hirsch and Ashworth, *Principled Sentencing* (2nd ed., 1998), pp. 209–211.

[61] This is (and probably always has been) the view of the public: Walker and Hough, *Public Attitudes to Sentencing* (1988), pp. 185–186.

[62] Home Office White Paper, *Crime, Justice and Protecting the Public* (1990) Cm.965, para. 1.6.

[63] Mabbott, "Freewill and Punishment" in *Contemporary British Philosophy* (1956), pp. 289, 303.

[64] Morris, "Persons and Punishment" (1968) 52 *Monist* 475.

[65] Hampton, "Correcting Harms versus Righting Wrongs: The Goal of Retribution" (1992) 39 U.C.L.A. Law Review 1659 at 1686.

distinguishes desert from the other purported aims of punishment—deterrence, incapacitation, rehabilitation—which seek to justify the criminal sanction by its prospective usefulness in preventing crime ...

A useful place to begin is with Kant's explanation of deserved punishment, which he based on the idea of fair dealing among free individuals. To realise their own freedom, he contended, members of society have the reciprocal obligation to limit their behaviour so as not to interfere with the freedom of others. When someone infringes another's rights, he gains an unfair advantage over all others in the society—since he has failed to constrain his own behaviour while benefitting from other persons' forbearance from interfering with his rights. The punishment—by imposing a counterbalancing disadvantage on the violator—restores the equilibrium: after having undergone the punishment, the violator ceases to be at advantage over his non-violating fellows. (This righting-of-the-balance is not a matter of preventing future crimes. Aside from any concern with prospective criminality, it is the violator's *past* crime that placed him in a position of advantage over others, and it is that advantage which the punishment would eliminate.) As Herbert Morris puts it in a recent restatement of the Kantian argument:

> 'A person who violates the rules has something others have—the benefits of the system [of mutual non-interference with others' rights]—but by renouncing what others have assumed, the burdens of self-restraint, he has acquired an unfair advantage. Matters are not even until this advantage is in some way erased ... Justice—that is punishing such individuals—restores the equilibrium of benefits and burdens ...' ("Persons and Punishment", 52 *The Monist* 475, 478 (1968).)

Kant's theory, however, accounts only for the imposition of *some* kind of deprivation on the offender to offset the 'advantage' he obtained in violating others' rights. It does not explain why that deprivation should take the peculiar form of punishment. Punishment differs from other purposefully inflicted deprivations in the moral disapproval it expresses: punishing someone conveys in dramatic fashion that his conduct was wrong and that he is blameworthy for having committed it. Why, then, does the violator deserve to be *punished*, instead of being made to suffer another kind of deprivation that connotes no special moral stigma?

To answer this question it becomes necessary, we think, to focus specifically on the reprobation implicit in punishment and argue that *it* is deserved. Someone who infringes the rights of others, the argument runs, does wrong and deserves blame for his conduct. It is because he deserves blame that the sanctioning authority is entitled to choose a response that expresses moral disapproval; namely, punishment. In other words, the sanction ought not only to deprive the offender of the 'advantage' obtained by his disregard of the rules (the Kantian explanation); but do so in a manner that ascribes blame (the reprobative explanation).

This raises the question of what purpose the reprobation itself serves. Blaming persons who commit wrongful acts is, arguably, a way of reaffirming the moral values that were infringed. But to speak of reaffirming such values prompts the further question: Why should the violator be singled out for blame to achieve that end? The answer must ultimately be that the censure is itself deserved: that someone who is responsible for wrongdoing is blame*worthy* and hence may justly be blamed."

## John Finnis, "The Restoration of Retribution" (1971) 32 Analysis 131:

"These obscurities about the nature and occasion of the criminal's profiting can be cleared up if we ... say that

(1) what the criminal gains in the act of committing crime (whatever the size and nature of the loot, if any, and indeed quite apart from the success or failure of his overall purpose) is the advantage of indulging a (wrongful) self-preference, of permitting himself an excessive freedom in choosing—this advantage (of exercising a wider freedom and of acting according to one's tastes ...) being something that his law-abiding fellow citizens have denied themselves insofar as they have chosen to

conform their will (habits and choices) to the law even when they would 'prefer' not to;

(2) this advantage is gained at the time of the crime, because and insofar as the crime is ... a free and 'responsible' exercise of self-will; the wrongfulness of gaining this advantage is the specifically relevant moral turpitude adverted to in the retributivist's talk of criminal 'guilt'; and the advantage is one that cannot be lost, unless and until ...

(3) the criminal has the disadvantage of having his wayward will restricted in its freedom by being subjected to the representative 'will of society' (the 'will' which he disregarded in disregarding the law) through the process of punishment; a punishment is thus to be defined not, formally speaking, in terms of the infliction of pain (nor as incarceration), but rather in terms of the subjection of will (normally, but not necessarily, effected through the denial of benefits and advantages of social living: compulsory employment on some useful work which the criminal would not of himself have chosen to do would satisfy the definition) ...

It is not just the victim and the wrongdoer who should be put back on a footing of equality: the 'satisfaction' which the wrongdoer gains is an advantage not only as against the victim but also as against all those who might have been wrongdoers but restrained themselves ...

Aquinas ... [said,] 'anyone who has indulged his will more than he ought [*plus voluntati suae indulsit quam debuit*], by transgressing the law, should either of his own accord or without his consent undergo something opposed to what he wills—so that the quality of justice may thus be restored [*reintegretur*].'

On this view ... we can say ... that the restoration of a fair distribution of advantages and disadvantages as between citizens is *an aim* of punishment ...

At the end of a period one should be able to look back over the *whole* period and say that, because of the adjustments that were made in response to criminal disruption of that order, no one has (overall and taking the period as a whole) been disadvantaged unfairly by attempting to live in strict accordance with that basic order of fairness."

## C. S. Lewis, "The Humanitarian Theory of Punishment" (1953) VI Res Judicatae 224:

"My subject is ... that theory of punishment ... [that] ... may be called the Humanitarian theory. Those who hold it think that it is mild and merciful. In this I believe that they are seriously mistaken. I believe that the 'Humanity' which it claims is a dangerous illusion and disguises the possibility of cruelty and injustice without end. I urge a return to the traditional or Retributive theory not solely, not even primarily, in the interests of society, but in the interests of the criminal.

According to the Humanitarian theory, to punish a man because he deserves it, and as much as he deserves, is mere revenge, and therefore barbarous and immoral. It is maintained that the only legitimate motives for punishing are the desire to deter others by example or to mend the criminal. When this theory is combined, as frequently happens, with the belief that all crime is more or less pathological, the idea of mending tails off into that of healing or curing and punishment becomes therapeutic. Thus it appears at first sight that we have passed from the harsh and self-righteous notion of giving the wicked their deserts to the charitable and enlightened one of tending the psychologically sick. What could be more amiable? One little point which is taken for granted in this theory needs, however, to be made explicit. The things done to the criminal, even if they are called cures, will be just as compulsory as they were in the old days when we called them punishments. If a tendency to steal can be cured by psychotherapy, the thief will no doubt be forced to undergo the treatment. Otherwise, society cannot continue.

My contention is that this doctrine, merciful though it appears, really means that each one of us, from the moment he breaks the law, is deprived of the rights of a human being.

The reason is this. The Humanitarian theory removes from Punishment the concept of Desert. But the concept of Desert is the only connecting link between punishment and justice. It is only as deserved or undeserved that a sentence can be just or unjust. I do not here contend that the question 'Is it deserved?' is the only one we can reasonably ask about a punishment. We may very properly ask whether it is likely to deter others and to reform the criminal. But neither of these two last questions is a question about justice. There is no sense in talking about a 'just deterrent' or a 'just cure.' We demand of a deterrent not whether it is just but whether it will deter. We demand of a cure not whether it is just but whether it succeeds. Thus when we cease to consider what the criminal deserves and consider only what will cure him or deter others, we have tacitly removed him from the sphere of justice altogether: instead of a person, a subject of rights, we now have a mere object, a patient, a 'case.'

The distinction will become clearer if we ask who will be qualified to determine sentences when sentences are no longer held to derive their propriety from the criminal's deservings. On the old view the problem of fixing the right sentence was a moral problem. Accordingly, the judge who did it was a person trained in jurisprudence: trained, that is, in a science which deals with rights and duties ... And when (say, in eighteenth century England) actual punishments conflicted too violently with the moral sense of the community, juries refused to convict and reform was finally brought about. This was possible because, so long as we are thinking in terms of Desert, the propriety of the penal code, being a moral question, is a question on which every man has the right to an opinion, not because he follows this or that profession, but because he is simply a man, a rational animal enjoying the Natural Light. But all this is changed when we drop the concept of Desert. The only two questions we may now ask about a punishment are whether it deters and whether it cures. But these are not questions on which anyone is entitled to have an opinion simply because he is a man. He is not entitled to an opinion even if, in addition to being a man, he should happen also to be a jurist, a Christian and a moral theologian. For they are not questions about principle but about matter of fact ... Only the expert 'penologist' (let barbarous things have barbarous names), in the light of previous experiment can tell us what is likely to deter: only the psychotherapist can tell us what is likely to cure. It will be in vain for the rest of us, speaking simply as men, to say, 'but this punishment is hideously unjust, hideously disproportionate to the criminal's deserts.' The experts with perfect logic will reply 'but nobody was talking about deserts. No one was talking about *punishment* in your archaic vindictive sense of the word. Here are the statistics proving that this treatment deters. Here are the statistics proving that this other treatment cures. What is your trouble?'

The Humanitarian theory, then, removes sentences from the hands of jurists whom the public conscience is entitled to criticize and places them in the hands of technical experts whose special sciences do not even employ such categories as rights or justice ...

If we turn from the curative to the deterrent justification of punishment we shall find the new theory even more alarming. When you punish a man *in terrorem*, make of him an 'example' to others, you are admittedly using him as a means to an end: someone else's end. This, in itself, would be a very wicked thing to do. On the classical theory of Punishment it was of course justified on the ground that the man deserved it. That was assumed to be established before any question of 'making him an example' arose. You then, as the saying is, killed two birds with one stone; in the process of giving him what he deserved you set an example to others. But take away desert and the whole morality of the punishment disappears. Why, in Heaven's name, am I to be sacrificed to the good of society in this way?—unless, of course, I deserve it ...

To be 'cured' against one's will and cured of states which we may not regard as a disease is to be put on a level with those who have not yet reached the age of reason or those who never will: to be classed with infants, imbeciles, and domestic animals. But to be punished however severely, because we have deserved it, because we 'ought to have known better,' is to be treated as a human person ...

[T]he Humanitarian theory wants simply to abolish Justice and substitute Mercy for it. This means that you start being 'kind' to people before you have considered their rights, and then force upon them supposed kindnesses which they in fact had a right to refuse, and finally kindnesses which no one but you will recognise as kindnesses and which the recipient will feel as abominable cruelties. You have overshot the mark. Mercy detached from Justice, grows unmerciful. That is the important paradox. As there are plants which will flourish only in mountain soil, so it appears that Mercy will flower only when it grows in the crannies of the rock of Justice: transplated to the marshlands of mere Humanitarianism, it becomes a man-eating weed, all the more dangerous because it is still called by the same name as the mountain variety. But we ought long ago to have learned our lesson. We should be too old now to be deceived by those humane pretensions which have served to usher in every cruelty of the revolutionary period in which we live. These are the 'precious balms' which will 'break our heads.' "

The concept of just deserts has, however, attracted criticism.

### John Braithwaite and Philip Pettit, Not Just Deserts: A Republican Theory of Criminal Justice (1990), pp. 158–159:

"A first objection to this justification for punishment is that law-abiding conduct is not always burdensome and crime is not always advantageous. The rapist might contract syphilis or the burglar break a leg. The conspiracy or the attempted murder might fail. Is the crime to be punished even though no benefits accrued?

The benefits and burdens theorist has a reply to this. He can say that it is self-restraint which is the burden, and unrestricted liberty the benefit that criminals gain by eschewing self-restraint. But is the self-restraint of not committing murder really a burden to our law-abiding readers? ... Even under conditions of unrestricted liberty most of us have no interest in or attraction to committing murder, and so the burden is no actual inconvenience. On the contrary, one influential view is that educating ourselves to adopt a moral character which abhors evil makes us 'better off' ...

[It has been argued that] the burden of self-restraint still does limit options ... and to have choice is better than not having it ... Is it a burden in this sense that you are unable to fly to Mars tomorrow? The point we would stress is that some burdens have practical significance for people and some do not. It seems a weak basis for locking people up that they renounced burdens which are not felt to be burdens by most law-abiding citizens."

### Nicola Lacey, State Punishment: Political Principles and Community Values (1988), pp. 24–26:

"[Desert theories do not give] very clear practical guidance about the fair measure of punishment in particular cases. What actual punishment would forfeit a set of rights equivalent to those violated by a rapist, a petty thief, a reckless driver? ... As in the case of the law of the talion and the culpability principle, resort to arguments from conventionally agreed, customary or consequence-based penalty scales seem hard to avoid. Secondly, real difficulties have been raised about the social contract tradition itself; in what sense can a *fictitious* agreement generate obligations for real people? ... Furthermore, these views are dependent for their force, as we have already noted, on the existence of a fair set of rules. This is not fatal in itself, but the criteria which dictate that there is indeed a just equilibrium which can be restored are not generated by the forfeiture of rights or unfair advantage principles alone. The views do pre-suppose an independent account of what counts as an unfair advantage and a just equilibrium.

Finally, it seems legitimate to ask whether the metaphorical ideas of restoring relationships of justice or moral equilibria outweigh the obvious disvalues attached to the suffering and other costs of punishment. Do these theories really ignore such costs completely? If not, what weight do they accord to them? In what real sense does punishment 'restore the right'? Do these theories really remove the mystery attaching to the original, simple desert principle, or are they, too, a form of moral alchemy? Or, in trying to avoid the mystery, do they not collapse into versions of utilitarian or other consequentialist justification? ... Even the more sophisticated versions barely rise above the level of metaphor, and leave us with the suspicion that the idea of desert cannot be distinguished from a principle of vengeance or the unappealing assertion that two wrongs somehow make a right."

There are two main advantages to punishment based on just deserts. First, it means that limits are placed on state power in that excessive exemplary or incapacitative sentences become unacceptable. Second, it helps reduce unjustifiable sentencing disparity in that two offenders committing the same crime will receive similar punishments, irrespective of race, culture or background. These are matters to which we shall return in due course.[66]

## 4. Censure or denunciation

While some just deserts theorists claim that desert is in itself the only purpose of punishment in that "punishing the guilty achieves something good—namely, justice",[67] others argue that punishment based on desert is necessary to express disapproval and censure of the conduct and the offender.[68]

In 1934, a German court in Leipzig found one Marinus van der Lubbe guilty of arson and high treason. He was sentenced to death and duly decapitated. After years of legal wrangling, a ruling in 1967 cleared van der Lubbe of high treason, but upheld his conviction of arson. His sentence was reduced from death to eight years' imprisonment.[69] Why did the German court sentence a dead man to eight years' imprisonment?

In *Sutcliffe* the defendant, the notorious "Yorkshire Ripper" who raped and murdered many women, pleaded guilty to manslaughter and the prosecution were content to accept this plea. However, the judge refused to accept it and insisted on a trial with the result that he was convicted of murder and sentenced to life imprisonment.[70] Why did the judge insist upon a costly public trial when he could have accepted the original plea and would almost certainly have sentenced the defendant to the same sentence, namely, life imprisonment?

**Joel Feinberg, "The Expressive Function of Punishment" (1965) Vol. 49, No. 3, The Monist, 397–423:**

"[P]unishment is a conventional device for the expression of attitudes of resentment and indignation, and of judgments of disapproval and reprobation, on the part either of the punishing authority himself or of those 'in whose name' the punishment is inflicted. Punishment, in short, has a *symbolic significance* largely missing from other kinds of penalties.

[66] See further, *below*, pp. 68–81.
[67] Moore, "The Moral Worth of Retribution" in Schoeman (ed.), *Responsibility, Character, and the Emotions: New Essays in Moral Philosophy* (1987).
[68] von Hirsch, *Past or Future Crimes* (1985), p. 52.
[69] "Raking the Reichstag Ashes," *The Sunday Times*, January 4, 1981, 13.
[70] *The Times*, April 30, 1981; *The Times*, May 23, 1981.

That the expression of the community's condemnation is an essential ingredient in legal punishment is widely acknowledged by legal writers. Henry M. Hart, for example, gives eloquent emphasis to the point:

> 'What distinguishes a criminal from a civil sanction and all that distinguishes it, it is ventured, is the judgment of community condemnation which accompanies ... its imposition. As Professor Gardner wrote not long ago, in a distinct but cognate connection:
> "The essence of punishment for moral delinquency lies in the criminal conviction itself. One may lose more money on the stock market than in a court-room; a prisoner of war camp may well provide a harsher environment that a state prison; death on the field of battle has the same physical characteristics as death by sentence of law. It is the expression of the community's hatred, fear, or contempt for the convict which alone characterises physical hardship as punishment."
> If this is what a 'criminal' penalty is, then we can say readily enough what a 'crime' is ... It is conduct which, if duly shown to have taken place, will incur a formal and solemn pronouncement of the moral condemnation of the community ... Indeed the condemnation plus the added [unpleasant physical] consequences may well be considered, compendiously, as constituting the punishment.' ("The Aims of the Criminal Law," *Law and Contemporary Problems*, 23 (1958), II, A, 4.) ...

Consider the standard international practice of demanding that a nation whose agent has unlawfully violated the complaining nation's rights should punish the offending agent. For example, suppose that an airplane of nation A fires on an airplane of nation B while the latter is flying over international waters. Very likely high authorities in nation B will send a note of protest to their counterparts in nation A demanding, among other things, that the transgressive pilot be punished. Punishing the pilot is an emphatic, dramatic, and well-understood way of *condemning* and thereby *disavowing* his act. It tells the world that the pilot had no right to do what he did, that he was on his own in doing it, that his government does not condone that sort of thing. It testifies thereby to government A's recognition of the violated rights of government B in the affected area and, therefore, to the wrongfulness of the pilot's act. Failure to punish the pilot tells the world that government A does not consider him to have been personally at fault. That in turn is to claim responsibility for the act, which in effect labels that act as an 'instrument of deliberate national policy' and hence an act of war. In that case either formal hostilities or humiliating loss of face by one side or the other almost certainly will follow. None of this scenario makes any sense without the clearly understood reprobative symbolism of punishment. In quite parallel ways punishment enables employers to disavow the acts of their employees (though not civil liability for those acts), and fathers the destructive acts of their sons ...

This symbolic function of punishment was given great emphasis by Kant, who, characteristically, proceeded to exaggerate its importance. Even if a desert island community were to disband, Kant argued, its members should first execute the last murderer left in its jails, 'for otherwise they might all be regarded as participators in the [unpunished] murder ...' (*The Philosophy of Law*, tr. W. Hastie, 198). This Kantian idea that in failing to punish wicked acts society endorses them and thus becomes *particeps criminis* does seem to reflect, however dimly, something embedded in common sense."

### Royal Commission on Capital Punishment, Minutes of Evidence, Ninth Day, December 1, 1949, Memorandum Submitted by the Rt. Hon. Lord Justice Denning, 207:

"Punishment is the way in which society expresses its denunciation of wrong doing: and, in order to maintain respect for law, it is essential that the punishment inflicted for grave crimes should adequately reflect the revulsion felt by the great majority of citizens for them. It is a mistake to consider the objects of punishment as being deterrent or reformative or preventive and nothing else. If that were so, we should not send to prison a man who was guilty of motor manslaughter, but only disqualify him from driving; but would public opinion be content with this? The truth is that some crimes are so outrageous that society insists on adequate punishment, because the wrong-doer deserves it, irrespective of whether it is a deterrent or not ... In my view the ultimate justification of any punishment is, not that it is a deterrent, but that it is the emphatic denunciation by the community of a crime."

### Antony Duff and Andrew von Hirsch, "Responsibility, Retribution and the 'Voluntary': A Response to Williams" [1997] C.L.J. 103 at 111–112:

"To see criminal punishment as a communicative, censuring institution is to see it as, at least to a significant extent, a formal or institutional analogue to our extra-legal practice of moral blame or criticism. In our ordinary moral lives we criticise, condemn or censure others for the wrongs that they do (and should be ready to accept or respond to their criticisms of our conduct). If we ask why such responses are appropriate, the answer is that we owe it to each other and to the values to which we are committed) to respond in such a fashion to wrongdoing—that this is what is involved in treating or respecting each other as moral agents ...

... [W]e should ... have a communicative censuring institution of criminal punishment not because this is the most efficient way of preventing crime (though it might help prevent crime) but also (at least, in part) because this is how a state should respond to its citizens as moral agents."

### Ronald J. Rychlak, "Society's Moral Right to Punish: A Further Exploration of the Denunciation Theory of Punishment" (1990–1991) 65 Tulane Law Review 299 at 331–332:

"This theory holds that society must register its disapproval of wrongful acts and reaffirm the values violated by these acts. Punishment declares that this society will not tolerate this conduct, regardless of any future deterrent effect ...

One of the most visible aims of denunciation is the maintenance of social cohesion ... The most important aim of the denunciatory theory ... is to reassure the majority of society that the system does work.

Denunciation serves to satisfy the majority's need to know that its rules (reflecting its values and goals) are being enforced. In other words, denunciation shows law-abiding society not only that the criminal system works, but that the society itself works."

Denunciation theory can also serve to educate the public by reaffirming social values and reinforcing inhibitions against crime. The utilitarian benefits of this theory, termed educative deterrence, will be discussed later.[71]

## B. *Deterrence*

Unlike retributive theories, deterrent theories are forward looking in that they are concerned with the consequences of punishment; their aim is to reduce further crime by the threat or example of punishment. Deterrence supposedly operates at three levels:

### 1. Individual deterrence

The deterrent theories seek to discourage crime. In the case of individual or specific deterrence it is hoped that the experience of punishment will be so unpleasant that the offender will not reoffend. The task of the sentencer is, therefore, to look to the future and select the sentence which is likely to have most

---

[71] See *below*, pp. 41–45.

impact on the individual. In the case of some offenders, no punishment at all may be necessary as the risk of the convicted person reoffending may be minimal. In other cases the required sentence may be so severe as to be inhumane.

It is often said that every time a crime is committed the theory of deterrence is weakened; it is an argument that has some force when applied to the reoffender. One can argue that a reconviction reveals the failure of the previous sentence. However, it is notoriously difficult to measure and assess this.[72] The overall reconviction rate in 1994 was 56 per cent and increased with each further conviction to the point that the rate was 74 per cent for persons with eleven or more previous convictions.[73] However, such figures tell us nothing about those who are not reconvicted; it could simply be that they were not caught.

Nevertheless, the figures could be construed to suggest that what is needed is a more severe sentence than that merited by the present offence at an early stage in the defendant's criminal career to have a strong deterrent effect. Indeed, this kind of approach was encapsulated in the much discussed "short, sharp shock" that imposed detention centre orders on young offenders under the Criminal Justice Act 1982.[74] Even if research established (and all indications are to the contrary[75]) that such measures were more effective in preventing recidivism, there is the problem of whether it is just to impose a more severe punishment than that merited by the offence.

## 2. General deterrence

Under this theory it is the threat of punishment that deters people from committing crimes. At the legislative level, Parliament lays down penalties to threaten those who might contemplate crime. At the sentencing level, offenders are punished in order that others will be discouraged from committing crimes; this punishment is held up as an example of what will happen if others engage in similar activities.

There are two aspects to this theory. First, punishment "at the normal rate" must be imposed in most cases to keep the threat of punishment alive. Secondly, when a specific type of crime is on the increase or has attracted much publicity, then excessively severe penalties (known as "exemplary sentences") may be imposed to try to prevent that particular crime. For example, exemplary sentences were imposed to suppress attacks on ethnic minority groups in Notting Hill in 1958,[76] to prevent the sudden increase of muggings on elderly people in the early 1970s[77] and to contain football hooliganism in the late 1970s.[78] In 1985 concern over the rise of football hooliganism led to an exemplary sentence of life imprisonment for riotous assembly outside a football ground.[79]

---

[72] Walker and Padfield, *Sentencing: Theory, Practice and Law* (2nd ed., 1996), pp. 79–95.

[73] Kershaw, *Reconvictions of Offenders Sentenced or Discharged from Prison in 1994, England and Wales* (H.O.R.S., 1999).

[74] Abolished by the Criminal Justice Act 1988, s.123.

[75] This was the main reason for the abolition of detention centre orders (Emmins and Scanlan, *Criminal Justice Act 1988* (1988), p. 101).

[76] *e.g. Hurst, The Times*, November 26, 1958; see [1958] Crim.L.R.709.

[77] *e.g. Storey* (1973) 57 Cr.App.R.840.

[78] *e.g. Motley* (1978) 66 Cr.App.R.274; *Bruce* (1977) 65 Cr.App.R.148.

[79] *Whitton, The Times*, November 9, 1985. This sentence was reduced to three years' imprisonment on appeal (*Whitton, The Times*, May 20, 1986).

The theory of general deterrence rests upon one crucial assumption—that people are deterred from committing crime by the threat of punishment. Is this assumption justifiable?

## J. Andenaes, "The General Preventive Effects of Punishment" (1966) 114 U.Pa.L.Rev. 949 at 960–970:

"Reports on conditions of disorganisation following wars, revolution or mutinies provide ample documentation as to how lawlessness may flourish when the probability of detection, apprehension and conviction is low. In these situations, however, many factors work together. The most clear cut examples of the importance of the risk of detection itself are provided by cases in which society functions normally but all policing activity is paralyzed by a police strike or a similar condition. For example, the following official report was made on lawlessness during a 1919 police strike, starting at midnight on July 31st, during which nearly half of the Liverpool policemen were out of service: 'In this district the strike was accompanied by threats, violence and intimidation on the part of lawless persons. Many assaults on the constables who remained on duty were committed. Owing to the sudden nature of the strike the authorities were afforded no opportunity to make adequate provision to cope with the position. Looting of shops commenced about 10pm on August 1st, and continued for some days. In all about 400 shops were looted. Military were requisitioned, special constables sworn in, and police brought from other centers.' (Mannheim, *Social Aspects of Crime in England Between the Wars*, 156–157 (1940).)

A somewhat similar situation occurred in Denmark when the German occupation forces arrested the entire police force in September, 1944. During the remainder of the occupation period all policing was performed by an improvised unarmed watch corps, who were ineffective except in those instances when they were able to capture the criminal red handed. The general crime rate rose immediately, but there was a great discrepancy between the various types of crime. The number of cases of robbery increased generally in Copenhagen during the war, rising from ten per year in 1939 to ten per month in 1943. But after the Germans arrested the police in 1944, the figure rose to over a hundred per month and continued to rise. Larcenies reported to the insurance companies quickly increased tenfold or more. The fact that penalties were greatly increased for criminals who were caught and brought before the courts did not offset the fact that most crimes were going undetected. On the other hand, crimes like embezzlement and fraud, where the criminal is usually known if the crime itself is discovered, do not seem to have increased notably . . .

The involuntary experiments in Liverpool and Copenhagen showed a reduction in law obedience following a reduction of risks. Examples of the opposite are also reported—the number of crimes decreases as the hazards rise. Tarde mentions that the number of cases of poisoning decreased when research in chemistry and toxicology made it possible to discover with greater certainty the causes as well as the perpetrator of this type of crime. (Tarde, Penal Philosophy 476 (1912)). A decline in bank robberies and kidnappings in the United States is reported to have followed the enactment of federal legislation which increased the likelihood of punishment (Taft, *Criminology* 322, 361 (rev. ed. 1950)) . . .

The decisive factor in creating the deterrent effect is, of course, not the objective risk of detection but the risk as it is calculated by the potential criminal. We know little about how realistic these calculations are. It is often said that criminals tend to be overly optimistic— they are confident that all will work out well. It is possible that the reverse occurs among many law abiding people; they are deterred because of an over-estimation of the risks. A faulty estimate in one direction or the other may consequently play an important part in determining whether an individual is to become a criminal. If fluctuations in the risks of detection do not reach the potential offender, they can be of no consequence to deterrence. If on the other hand, it were possible to convince people that crime does not pay, this assumption might act as a deterrent even if the risks, viewed objectively, remained unchanged . . .

It seems reasonable to conclude that as a general rule, though not without exceptions, the general preventive effect of the criminal law increases with the growing severity of penalties. Contemporary dictatorships display with almost frightening clarity the conformity that can be produced by a ruthlessly severe justice."

### T. Sellin, "The Law and Some Aspects of Criminal Conduct" in Aims and Methods of Legal Research (1955), 113 at 119–120:

"Our statistics suggest the imperative need for paying more legislative attention to law enforcement, since it is law enforcement in the broad sense, which gives the law any intimidating effect it may be assumed to possess. In this connection reference might be made to the extremely interesting experiment performed in New York City last year. It was prompted by the felt need for increasing the personnel of the police department of the city. The 25th precinct . . . was chosen, an area with high crime rates. . . . The experiment began on September 1, 1954, and lasted four months. Essentially, it consisted of increasing the number of police in the area. The foot and motor patrol was increased from 25 to 99 men, plus a special squad of sixteen patrolmen for the evening and early morning hours. The detective squad was increased from 33 to 54, thirteen of whom were formed into a special narcotics squad. A special unit of the Juvenile Aid Bureau was set up, consisting of seventeen officers.

The effect of the experiment was interesting indeed, when the data covering the period are compared with those of the last four months of the year before. Eight persons were murdered in the area compared with six in 1953, adding further proof of the absence of any specially deterrent effect in the law so far as this crime is concerned. The number of rapes declined from 12 to 9, of which five were statutory, and felonious assaults fell from 185 to 132. Robberies declined from 166 to 50, burglary from 425 to 148, grand larceny from 153 to 46, and auto thefts from 78 to 24. On the other hand, cases of possessing dangerous weapons rose from 13 to 27, cases of sale or possession of narcotics from 78 to 186, and disorderly conduct cases from 77 to 177. Prostitution cases dropped slightly, while gambling cases rose from 125 to 170, mostly in connection with the policy racket and card playing, while arrests for dice games declined sharply. The number of juvenile delinquency referrals rose from 135 to 372. Summonses, mostly in connection with parking violations, increased 140%."

With regard to those crimes, such as robbery and burglary, that declined in the 25th precinct, it would be interesting to know if there was any increase in surrounding precincts. If extra policing causes a burglar to transfer his plans to a house in another street or area, this can hardly be described as true deterrence.[80]

### Gerald Gardiner, "The Purposes of Criminal Punishment" (1958) 21 M.L.R. 117 at 122–125:

"The belief in the value of deterrence rests on the assumption that we are rational beings who always think before we act, and then base our actions on a careful calculation of the gains and losses involved. These assumptions, dear to many lawyers, have long since been abandoned in the social sciences. No economist would seriously maintain them today, and even to the uninformed the movements of shares on the stock exchange—where one might expect to see Bentham's principle of 'enlightened self-interest' vindicated most clearly—demonstrate that men's actions are governed quite as much by fear or greed as by reason; and that the ability to ignore hard facts and to see only what you want to see, is shared by a surprisingly large and influential section of the community.

[80] Walker, *Why Punish?* (1991), p. 13. It is interesting to compare this with research in England into neighbourhood watch schemes which seem to have had little effect in reducing crime. See Bennett, *Evaluating Neighbourhood Watch* (1990). There is some evidence that the introduction of CCTV into town centres has had the effect of moving crime into other areas.

Amongst criminals, foresight and prudent calculation is even more conspicuous by its absence. . . . Even though there is no consensus amongst doctors about the exact description of the so-called 'psychopaths,' experienced Prison Medical Officers, and for that matter, Prison Governors, are agreed that there is a type of prisoner who is quite incapable of foresight, who cannot learn even from the experience of punishment, much less from the threat of it. Yet other offenders, notably some sex-offenders (but also others subject to compulsive behaviour) are sometimes at the mercy of their impulses, and unable, without proper help and treatment, to control themselves adequately. Such persons are frequently in conflict, not only with society, but also with themselves.

Another factor on which the effectiveness of deterrence depends is the certainty of conviction. But according to the latest official Criminal Statistics, only 48 per cent. of the offences known to the police are 'cleared up.' Offences cleared up include those for which a person is arrested or summoned, or for which he is cautioned, those taken into consideration by a court when the offender is found guilty on another charge, and even some which are strongly suspected but which cannot be definitely cleared up; for instance, where the suspect dies or commits suicide before the case has been tried. Even so, this still leaves an unknown quantity of offences which remain undetected altogether, so that the chances of your *not* being caught are distinctly better than those of your being apprehended and brought to trial. Add to this the fact that by no means all those who come before the courts are found guilty, and it is clear that the threat of punishment loses something of its persuasive force."

### George H. Dessian, "Justice after Conviction" (1951) 25 Connecticut Bar Journal 215:

"I suppose that it is evident that the deterrent effect of any particular sentence imposed must depend on two things: the way in which the convict sentenced is capable and has been conditioned to respond to such a prescription; and the way in which others of comparable personality and similar inclination in the general population are capable and have been conditioned to respond to the example of the sentence inflicted on the convict. If deterrence is to work the latter must presumably identify with the convict, must be averse to suffering a similar sentence themselves, and must be made aware that there is a high probability of the latter eventuality.

For these reasons it seems to me that we must rule out as promising subjects for the deterrence approach those who will consider any expected sentence a martyrdom preferable to conformity with the law (the political fanatic who identifies with an alien hostile culture, the religious fanatic, the patriot who engages in espionage on behalf of his own country abroad), those in whom the conscious awarenesses involved in the process of being deterred will not be controlling (the mental defective in a complicated situation, the psychotic in many situations, the intoxicated or drug-influenced, the extremely neurotic offender who 'does not know why he did it' in the sense that he was driven by subconscious or not altogether conscious impulses, and the 'temporarily insane' offender who happened to be confronted by a situation with which he could not otherwise emotionally cope), and those who will not identify with the convict and hence not take him as an example (members of elite groups in the community who may consider themselves, rightly or wrongly, as exempt from the law or regulation in question, persons who feel that in any event they have adequate protection, and persons who feel that they are sufficiently smarter than the convict to avoid getting caught)."

Research into the behaviour of criminals supports many of the points made in the preceding extracts. For example, Gill's research, based on interviews with commercial robbers, concluded that few of them thought there was a high chance of being caught. The less organised and amateurish robbers did not plan their crimes, acted impulsively and gave no thought to being caught or to the consequences of their actions. On the other hand, the more organised and professional robbers planned to minimise the risks and concluded there was a low chance of apprehension.[81] Wright and Decker's American research into burglary found that most burglars in their sample perceived themselves, when committing the offence, to be "in a situation of immediate need" and "consciously refused to dwell on the possibility of getting caught".[82] Similar English research confirms that most burglars are not rational calculators but act on the spur-of-the-moment.[83]

Research into the effectiveness of punishment as a deterrent tends to distinguish between absolute deterrence (whether the existence of punishment in general affects criminal conduct) and marginal deterrence (whether increasing the severity of a punishment affects the prevalence of an offence). A major Cambridge analysis of recent research found that there was not much evidence that increased severity of punishment had any substantial marginal deterrent effect. The Report concluded that increasing sentence severity could have "possible counterproductive effects relating to reduced differential disincentives against the most serious crimes of violence" and could cause "destigmatisation of punishment ... if severe sanctions are very widely employed".[84]

Following earlier research findings, the White Paper preceding the Criminal Justice Act 1991 concluded that "it is unrealistic to construct sentencing arrangements on the assumption that most offenders will weigh up the possibilities in advance and base their conduct on rational calculation".[85] The 1991 Act followed this by outlawing exemplary sentences and, subject to exceptions, endorsing the concept of desert.[86] However, despite overwhelming evidence of ineffectiveness, the Conservative Government in the lead-up to the 1997 General Election reaffirmed its belief in general deterrence[87] and enacted the Crimes (Sentences) Act 1997 containing mandatory and minimum sentences for certain offences when committed a second or third time.[88] Most of these provisions were then brought into force by the newly-elected Labour Government. While a desire to incapacitate dangerous offenders was a major force behind these new sentences (and so they will be discussed more fully in the next section), much of the rhetoric[89] surrounding them was based on deterrence. Whatever the "evidence", successive governments believe (or think the electorate believe) in the effectiveness of punishment as a deterrent. It is unfortunate that such thinking is not informed by the distinction, referred to above, between absolute deterrence (few doubt that

[81] Gill, *Commercial Robbery* (2000), p. 106.

[82] Wright and Decker, *Burglars on the Job: Streetlife and Residential Break-ins* (1994), pp. 61, 137.

[83] Bennett and Wright, *Burglars on Burglary* (1984).

[84] Von Hirsch *et al*, *Criminal Deterrence and Sentence Severity* (1999), pp. 41, 48.

[85] *Crime, Justice and Protecting the Public* (1990) Cm.965, para. 2.8.

[86] This is now Powers of Criminal Courts (Sentencing) Act 2000, s.80(2)(a). Despite this, exemplary sentences are occasionally given. See, for example, *Attorney-General's Reference (Nos 62 and 63 of 1997) (McMaster)* [1998] 2 C.App.R.(S.) 300.

[87] Home Office, *Protecting the Public: The Government's Strategy on Crime in England and Wales* (1996), paras 1.12, 1.14.

[88] This is now consolidated in the Powers of Criminal Courts (Sentencing) Act 2000.

[89] Kahan, "The Secret Ambition of Deterrence" (1999) 113 Harv.L.Rev.413 argues that in general "the real value of deterrence—its secret ambition—is to quiet illiberal conflict between contending cultural styles and moral outlooks"; the rhetoric of deterrence is a liberal ploy to defuse or suppress contentious moral issues; it is a cover-up: "the real significance of liberal theory [relating to deterrence] lies not in what it says but in what it stops us from saying".

punishment in general does have a broad deterrent effect for at least some crimes) and marginal deterrence where evidence that increasing the severity of punishments has an increased deterrent effect is noticeably lacking.

### 3. Educative deterrence

Under the theory of general deterrence a person who is contemplating committing a crime is deterred by the positive threat that he or she will suffer the same punishment as others have suffered. But punishment can have a more profound subconscious effect on society. Punishment of criminals builds up in the community over a period of time the habit of not breaking the law. It creates unconscious inhibitions against committing crimes and thus serves to educate the public as to the proper distinction between good and bad conduct. Every time someone is punished for theft the public morality that theft is wrong is strengthened and our habit of not stealing is reinforced. If suddenly nobody were to be punished for theft and this state of affairs were to endure for a considerable period of time, our inhibitions against stealing and our moral view that theft was wrong would start breaking down. The habit would be broken; we might start stealing. This theory goes a long way towards explaining the prevalence of petty white-collar crime in offices and factories. Take, for example, the use of the office telephone for private phone calls beyond those permitted by the employer. This is a criminal offence carrying a maximum penalty of five years' imprisonment.[90] The fact that prosecutions in this context are so rare has resulted in a lack of public morality on the subject; the public has not been educated to accept the gravity of the conduct. There is no subconscious inhibition against committing the crime. For most people the only inhibition is that the employer "might disapprove". This does not have the same powerful impact on the subconscious that punishment for this offence would have. If we were to cease punishing for other offences, *e.g.* theft, they could, in time, come to be regarded as no more serious than using the office telephone for unauthorised private calls.

### Hyman Gross, A Theory of Criminal Justice (1979), pp. 400–401:

"There is a third version of deterrence, one that places no stock in considerations of intimidation and makes no claim that the law has a general tendency to scare off would-be wrongdoers by its threat. In this version stress is still placed on the threats made by the law, and for that reason it can be called a deterrence theory . . .

According to this theory, punishment for violating the rules of conduct laid down by the law is necessary if the law is to remain a sufficiently strong influence to keep the community on the whole law-abiding and so to make possible a peaceable society. Without punishment for violating these rules the law becomes merely a guide and an exhortation to right conduct. No doubt even without liability to punishment an appreciation of the consequences of crime would itself encourage many to forbear in the face of temptation. But most of us would sometimes succumb on occasions when the urge was particularly strong if getting away with it was a certainty because liability for crime was something unknown in the community. Only saints and martyrs could be constantly law-abiding in a community that had no system of criminal liability, for at the very least in acts of retaliation and of self-preservation everyone else would occasionally do what the law prohibited. The threats of the criminal law are necessary, then, only as part of a system of liability ensuring that those who commit

---

[90] Theft Act 1968, s.13.

crimes do not get away with them. The threats are not laid down to deter those tempted to break the rules, but rather to maintain the rules as a set of standards that compel allegiance in spite of violations by those who commit crimes. In short, the rules of conduct laid down in the criminal law are a powerful social force upon which society is dependent for its very existence, and there is punishment for violation of these rules in order to prevent the dissipation of their power that would result if they were violated with impunity."

## J. Andenaes, "The General Preventive Effects of Punishment" (1966) 114 U.Pa.L.Rev. 949:

"Interesting lessons may be drawn from an experiment launched in some of the Scandinavian countries to fight drunken driving. In Norway, for example, the motor vehicle code prohibits the driving of motor vehicles when the alcohol percentage in the driver's blood exceeds 0·05 ... [T]he consistent policy of the courts has been to give prison sentences for violations, except in cases involving very exceptional circumstances. The prison terms are short, usually not more than the minimum jail period of twenty-one days, but the penalty is exacted on anyone who is detected, whether or not the driving was dangerous or caused damage.

A person moving between Norway and the United States can hardly avoid noticing the radical difference in the attitudes towards automobile driving and alcohol. There is no reason to doubt that the difference in legal provisions plays a substantial role in this difference in attitudes. The awareness of hazards of imprisonment for intoxicated driving is in our country a living reality to every driver, and for most people the risk seems too great. When a man goes to a party where alcoholic drinks are likely to be served, and he is not fortunate enough to have a wife who drives but does not drink, he will leave his car at home or he will limit his consumption to a minimum. It is also my feeling—although I am here on uncertain grounds—that the legislation has been instrumental in forming or sustaining the widespread conviction that is wrong, or irresponsible, to place oneself behind the wheel when intoxicated. 'Alcohol and motorcar driving do not belong together' is a slogan commonly accepted. Statistics on traffic accidents show a very small number of accidents due to intoxication."

## J. Andenaes, "General Prevention" (1952) 43 J.Crim.L., C. & P.S. 176 at 179–181:

"Later theory puts much stress on the ability of penal law to arouse or strengthen inhibitions of another sort. In Swedish discussion the *moralising*—in other words the *educational*—function has been greatly stressed. The idea is that punishment as a concrete expression of society's disapproval of an act helps to form and to strengthen the public's moral code and thereby creates conscious and unconscious inhibitions against committing crime. Unconscious inhibitions against committing forbidden acts can also be aroused without appealing to the individual's concepts of morality. Purely as a matter of habit, with fear, respect for authority or social imitation as connecting links, it is possible to induce favourable attitudes toward this or that action and unfavourable attitudes toward another action. We find the clearest example of this in the military, where extended inculcation of discipline and stern reaction against breach thereof can induce a purely automatic, habitual response—not only where obeying specific orders is concerned, but also with regard to general orders and regulations. We have another example in the relationship between an occupying power and an occupied population. The regulations set down by the occupier are not regarded by the people as morally binding; but by a combination of terror and habit formation a great measure of obedience can be elicited—at any rate in response to commands which do not conflict too greatly with national feelings ...

... To the lawmaker, the achievement of inhibition and habit is of greater value than mere deterrence. For these apply in cases, where a person need not fear detection and punishment, and they can apply without the person even having knowledge of the legal prohibition."

## Franz Alexander and Hugo Staub, The Criminal, the Judge and the Public (1956), p. 123:

"We can state now that the power of the Superego over our instinctive life is undermined, not only when some one is punished unjustly and too severely, but also when the offender escapes punishment and thus fails to pay for his offence. Unwarranted acquittal means simply that the court permits the defendant to do things which we prohibit to ourselves. Under such circumstances, the righteous member of the community finds himself facing the following dilemma: he must either give up his own inhibitions and give in to his own anti-social tendencies, or he must demand that the offender be punished without fail. 'What I do not allow myself must not be allowed others; if others are not called upon to pay for their violations of the law, then I shall not abide by my self-imposed restrictions.'

We may say, then, that what creates the public demand for atonement is one's anxiety lest his own Superego be overturned and that one's own impulses, which have been curbed with so much difficulty, might break through to expression. This anxiety is quite justified, because before our Superego was set up, our unbridled impulses kept us always in a state of painful conflict with the outside world. Was not the Superego set up for the purpose of ridding ourselves of or escaping from such painful situations? Moreover, the original pressure of our instinctual drives remains so strong that man's Superego, if it is to preserve its power of repression, always needs the support of outside authorities. Hence, in the case of every violation of the law, our Ego makes an appeal for the atonement of the transgression; it does this in order to enforce the opposition of the Superego against the pressure of its instincts. The example of a criminal has a stimulating effect on our own repressed impulses, and increases the pressure coming from them. That is why our Ego needs the constant reinforcement of our Superego; it can obtain this reinforcement only from those in authority, who are the prototype of our Superego. If the Ego can show that the secular authorities agree with the Superego, then it is able to keep the instinctual impulses in check: if, however, these secular authorities happen to disavow the Superego by setting a guilty man free, then the individual feels that no support is given him to counteract a pending breaking through of his own anti-social tendencies. The demand that every crime should be expiated represents, then, a defence reaction on the part of the Ego against one's own instinctual drives; the Ego puts itself at the service of the inner repressing forces, in order to retain the state of equilibrium, which must always exist between the repressed and the repressing forces of the personality. The demand that the lawbreaker be punished is thus a demonstration against one's own inner drives, a demonstration which tends to keep these drives amenable to control: 'I forbid the lawbreaker what I forbid myself.'

[T]he greater the pressure coming from repressed impulses, the more aware becomes the Ego that it needs the institution of punishment as an intimidating example, acting against one's own primitive world of repressed instinctual drives. In other words, the louder man calls for the punishment of the lawbreaker, the less he has to fight against his own repressed impulses. ... If and when, however, the criminal is duly punished, our demand for atonement is thoroughly satisfied and we feel that we have proved to ourselves that we are good and loyal to society; under such circumstances, we can afford, as we do, to express sympathy with and kindliness towards the very same criminal. What happened is this: through the gratification of our demand for expiation of the crime, we won a victory over the evil within ourselves: we may well be grateful to the criminal, for *he* paid for what *we* unconsciously wished to do. That is why our forefathers preferred a penitent sinner to a hundred righteous men, for the repenting sinner is much more helpful to us in our struggle against our own repressed impulses."

## John Braithwaite, Crime, Shame and Reintegration (1989), pp. 77–79:

"Community-wide shaming is necessary because most crimes are not experienced within the average household. Children need to learn about the evil of murder, rape, car theft, and environmental pollution offenses through condemnation of the local butcher or the far away image on the television screen. But the shaming of the local offender known personally to children in the neighborhood is especially important, because the wrongdoing and the shaming are so vivid as to leave a lasting impression.

Much shaming in the socialization of children is of course vicarious, through stories. Because they are not so vivid as real-life incidents of shaming, they are not so powerful. Yet they are necessary because so many types of misbehavior will not occur in the family or the neighborhood. A culture without stories for children in which morals are clearly drawn and evil deeds clearly identified would be a culture which failed the moral development of its children. . . .

Essentially, societal processes of shaming do three things:

1. They give content to a day-to-day socialization of children which occurs mainly through induction. As we have just seen, shaming supplies the morals which build consciences. The evil of acts beyond the immediate experience of children is more effectively communicated by shaming than by pure reasoning.

2. Societal incidents of shaming remind parents of the wide range of evils about which they must moralize with their children. Parents do not have to keep a checklist of crimes, a curriculum of sins, to discuss with their offspring. In a society where shaming is important, societal incidents of shaming will trigger vicarious shaming within the family so that the criminal code is eventually more or less automatically covered. . . . Of course societies which shame only half-heartedly run a risk that the full curriculum of crimes will not be covered. Both this point and the last one could be summarized in another way by saying that public shaming puts pressure on parents, teachers and neighbours to ensure that they engage in private shaming which is sufficiently systematic.

3. Societal shaming in considerable measure takes over from parental socialization once children move away from the influence of the family and the school. Put another way, shaming generalizes beyond childhood principles learnt during the early years of life.

This third principle is about the 'criminal law as a moral eye-opener' as Andenaes calls it. As a child, I may have learnt the principle that killing is wrong, but when I leave the familiar surroundings of the family to work in the unfamilar environment of a nuclear power plant, I am taught by a nuclear safety regulatory system that to breach certain safety laws can cost lives, and so persons who breach them are treated with a comparable level of shame. The principle that illegal killing is shameful is generalized. To the extent that genuine shame is not directed against those who defy the safety rules, however, I am liable to take them much less seriously. Unfortunately, societal shaming processes often do fail too generalize to organizational crime.

Recent years in some Western societies have seen more effective shaming directed at certain kinds of offenses—drunk driving, occupational health and safety and environmental offenses, and political corruption, for example. This shaming has for many adults integrated new categories of wrongdoing (for which they had not been socialized as children) into the moral frameworks pre-existing from their childhood.

While most citizens are aware of the content of most criminal laws, knowledge of what the law requires of citizens in detail can be enhanced by cases of public shaming. Through shaming directed at new legal frontiers, feminists in many countries have clarified for citizens just what sexual harassment, rape within marriage, and employment discrimination mean. Social change is increasingly rapid, particularly in the face of burgeoning technologies which require new moralities of nuclear, environmental and consumer safety, responsible use of new technologies of information exchange and electronic funds transfer, ethical exploitation of new institutions such as futures exchanges, and so on. Shaming is thus particularly vital in sustaining a contemporarily relevant legal and moral order."

In the United States these ideas have been pushed to the limit by the introduction of "shaming penalties". For example, persons convicted of drunken driving have been required to put special bumper stickers on their cars,[91] or wear a pink fluorescent bracelet,[92] publicising their conviction. A woman has been made to

---

[91] *Goldschmitt v State*, 490 So.2d 123 (Fla. 1986).
[92] *Ballenger v State*, 210 Ga.App.627, 436 S.E. 2d 793 (1993).

place an advertisement in her local paper stating that she bought drugs in front of her children.[93] There are, however, limits to the degree of public humiliation to which an offender can be exposed. In *State v Meyer*[94] an offender was required, as a condition of his probation sentence, to place bold signs at all entrances to his family farm stating: "Warning! A Violent Felon Lives Here. Enter at Your Own Risk." On appeal this was held to be an unreasonable condition of probation and the order was vacated.[95]

This theory should be contrasted with the retributive theory of denunciation. The theories are similar in that punishment, under both theories, is performing a symbolic, expressive function—but there is an important difference between them. The idea of denunciation, as with all retributive theories, is not concerned with the effects of punishment. It is not a forward looking theory aimed at preventing crime. Rather, it is concerned with the relation of the punishment to the past event, the crime. It is concerned that there be a relationship between the gravity of the offence and the degree of censure or denunciation. The educative theory, on the other hand, is exclusively forward-looking, as are all deterrent theories. Punishment is used as a means of preventing crime and maintaining obedience to the law.

The educative theory rests upon an important premise, namely, that public morality and inhibitions against committing crimes are created and/or preserved by the regular punishment of others. This is a difficult premise to test although some research suggests a clear link between criminality and moral assessments of behaviour. For instance, Kaufmann asked a group of subjects to evaluate the morality of certain behaviour (failing to rescue a drowning man). Some subjects were told that this behaviour was criminal; others were told that there was no duty to rescue. The former group judged the inaction more harshly than the latter group.[96] Similarly, Walker and Marsh discovered that subjects stated that their disapproval of not wearing a seat-belt would increase when this became an offence.[97] Clearly most laws are designed to have some symbolic or expressive function. The point asserted here (and so difficult to validate—although one's intuitions do indicate some plausibility to the claim) is that *punishment* (or at least the real possibility thereof) pursuant to criminal liability is what gives the law its sting.[98] For instance, we have civil laws against race and sex discrimination whose function is not merely to provide a remedy but to underline the important message that such discrimination is *wrong*. The argument here is that if such discrimination had been made *criminal* and offenders *punished*, the message would have been stronger. This of course raises many questions, including the critical one of determining when conduct is sufficiently "wrong" for criminalisation to be justifiable—an issue addressed at the beginning of this chapter.

---

[93] *The Guardian*, February 4, 1997.
[94] 176 Ill. 2d 372; 680 N.E. 2d 315 (Ill., 1997).
[95] See, generally, Kahan, "What Do Alternative Sanctions Mean?" (1996) 63 U.Chi.L.Rev. 591.
[96] Kaufmann, "Legality and Harmfulness of a Bystander's Failure to Intervene as Determinants of Moral Judgment" in Macaulay and Berkowitz (eds), *Altruism and Helping Behaviour: Social Psychological Studies of Some Antecedents and Consequences* (1970).
[97] Walker and Marsh, "Do Sentences Affect Public Disapproval?" (1984) 24 Brit. J. Criminol. 27.
[98] *Contra* Walker and Marsh (*ibid.*) who concluded that public disapproval of conduct was not influenced by *severity* of punishment.

## C. *Incapacitation*

In the case of *Sargent*,[99] Lawton L.J. acknowledged "that there are some offenders for whom neither deterrence nor rehabilitation works. They will go on committing crimes as long as they are able to do so. In those cases the only protection which the public has is that such persons should be locked up for a long period." Such protective sentencing aims to render the criminal incapable of committing more crimes; it thus "incapacitates" the offender. The particular punishment chosen at one stage in our penal history might have been the death penalty, severance of limbs or deportation to a colony. Today it is likely to be imprisonment, although other sentences such as a curfew order or disqualification from driving can also be viewed as incapacitative sentences. The real hallmark of an incapacitative sentence, however, is that it is likely to be longer or more severe than that which would normally be imposed for the offence.

### R. v Hatch [1997] 1 Cr.App.R.(S.) 22 (Court of Appeal, Criminal Division)

The appellant, aged 46, pleaded guilty to four counts of buggery of boys aged 10 or 11, two counts of gross indecency and two counts of indecent assault on a male. He was sentenced to life imprisonment and appealed against his sentence.

Bennett J.:
"[T]he Crown accepted that the appellant used no violence or threats upon the boys, and that the boys were 'willing' partners in the acts of buggery ...

His record gives very serious cause for concern. The appellant first came before the courts as a juvenile in 1965 (when he was aged 16). He was put on probation for an offence of indecent assault with a five year old boy. In August 1970, when the appellant was 21 years old, he was convicted of indecently assaulting a boy aged seven and was put on probation. In November 1972, when the appellant was 23 years old, he was convicted of nine counts of indecent assault on boys aged between six and 10, and was sentenced to a total of 18 months' imprisonment. In April 1976, when he was 26 years old, the appellant was convicted of indecent assault on a boy and was sentenced to a term of imprisonment of two years. In January 1979, when the appellant was 29 years old, he was convicted of two counts of buggery on a boy, two counts of indecent assault on a boy and a count of indecent assault on a girl. For those offences he was sentenced to a total term of imprisonment of six years. In September 1983, when the appellant was 34 years old, he was convicted of indecently assaulting a boy aged 14 and sentenced to three years' imprisonment. In June 1987, when he was 38 years old, he was convicted on two counts of indecently assaulting a male and was sentenced to a term of imprisonment of five years in all. In February 1991, when the appellant was 41 years old, he was convicted on four counts of indecently assaulting a male and a further count of gross indecency with a boy aged 14. For those offences he was sentenced to a total term of imprisonment of five years.
[During his last term of imprisonment the appellant had received psychotherapeutic treatment but felt it had not helped.] ...
He described his behaviour in terms of indecent assaults as being 'cold and calculating'. He told Dr Naismith [a consultant forensic psychiatrist] that he was addicted to the danger and to his own fear. He likened it to a chess game where he was controlling the situation. He also said he needed to know the parents and for the parents to know him ... [H]e knew that he

[99] (1975) 60 Cr.App.R.74.

was in potential threat of his life from the parents, but ..5 . he liked the fear and also the control ... [H]e stated that he needed to make sure that the child was an accomplice ...

Dr Naismith was of the opinion: ...
'2. He (the appellant) does not suffer from mental illness, mental impairment, severe mental impairment or psychopathic disorder ...
4. It is generally accepted that the best predictor of future behaviour is past behaviour ...
8. ... [T]he likelihood is that Mr Hatch will continue to exhibit the potential for the forseeable future for the behaviour which appears to have characterised him in the past. I regret that I cannot put before the Court any prospect for medical treatment which would effectively and reliably result in the cessation of such proclivities.'

Dr McClelland [a consultant psychiastrist reported that the appellant] 'is aware of the immorality of his thoughts, actions and offences but preserves his self esteem by insisting that he would never harm a child and that any resistance by a child would immediately "kill the sex" ... On his own account therefore he has not been violent with children ... He is kindly in principle but in practice a child is a sexual object ... Mr Hatch does not suffer from any mental illness. I cannot recommend any psychiatric treatment ...'

Mr Reeds [counsel for the appellant] ... submitted the offences of buggery in the circumstances of this particular case were not grave offences ...

In our judgment although the appellant is not suffering from a mental illness or disorder ... he is strongly attracted sexually to young boys and positively enjoys controlling the situation. Not only are these very serious offences, but also his record shows that he has manifested perverted sexual tendencies at least for the whole of his adult life. There is no treatment for his disorder. He is, and will continue to be, a real danger to young boys, and thus is likely to continue to commit sexual offences against them in the future."

**Appeal dismissed**

There is much public support for the view that there are cases where society needs protection[1] and that it is permissible to incarcerate dangerous offenders who pose a threat to society for longer than non-dangerous offenders committing the same offence. The Floud Report on Dangerous Offenders[2] took it "as axiomatic that the public is entitled to the protection of a special sentence"[3] against grave harm and recommended a special sentencing framework of sentencing for dangerous offenders. This was done by a utilitarian balancing of risks argument: the harm done to the convicted offender in being punished longer than is deserved is outweighed by the prospect of harm done to the public should the offender be released at an earlier time. In short, where there is a risk of grave harm to potential victims, the rights of such victims should prevail over the rights of a convicted offender.

Further, research has revealed that a significant amount of crime is being committed by relatively few persons, for example, those on bail, and so "a policy of selective incapacitation aimed at such 'career criminals' promises a high yield of crime prevention for a low investment of resources".[4]

There are, however, significant objections to incapacitative sentencing. First, such a practice can only be justified (if at all) if predictions of dangerousness are accurate.

[1] Walker and Hough, *Public Attitudes to Sentencing* (1988), pp. 178–179.
[2] Floud and Young, *Dangerousness and Criminal Justice* (1981).
[3] Floud, "Dangerousness and Criminal Justice" (1982) 22 Brit. J. Criminol. 213 at 220.
[4] Duff and Garland, *A Reader on Punishment* (1994), p. 239.

### Andrew von Hirsch, "Prediction of Criminal Conduct and Preventive Confinement of Convicted Persons" (1972) 21 Buffalo Law Review 717 at 735–736:

"What makes violence so particularly difficult to predict is not merely its rarity, but its situational quality. Deterministic models to the contrary notwithstanding, violence generally is not a quality which inheres in certain 'dangerous' individuals: it is an occurrence which may erupt—or may not—in certain crisis situations. Whether it does erupt, whether it is reported, whether the perpetrator is apprehended and punished depends upon a wide variety of fortuitous circumstances, largely beyond the actor's control. Not only the actor's proclivities, but the decisions of other individuals—the victim, the bystanders, the police, the magistrate—may determine whether an act of violence occurs and whether it comes to be included in the criminal statistics."

The substantial literature that has developed on the subject of prediction is in broad agreement that for every three persons predicted to commit violent offences, only one will do so. It has become common to refer to those who do not reoffend as "false positives" and for most commentators this is taken to mean that a false prediction of dangerousness was made. However, that view has been challenged by Norval Morris. He argues that if an unexploded bomb were found in the early post-war days in London and then safely defused no-one would talk about it subsequently as if it had not been dangerous simply because it had not caused any damage. He thinks there is no difference in principle between the analogy of the bomb and dangerous people: "In sum, that the person predicted as dangerous does no future injury does not mean that the classification was erroneous."[5]

### Nigel Walker, Punishment, Danger and Stigma (1980), pp. 98–99:

"[In challenging the anti-protectionist's view] ... let us accept that in our present state of partial ignorance any labelling of the individual as a future perpetrator of violence is going to be mistaken in the majority of cases. Does it follow that it is wrong to apply this label? Only if we swallow two assumptions. One is that it is *morally wrong* to make mistakes of this kind. Everyone would agree that it is *regrettable*; but if the decision is taken with good intentions, and one has done one's best, with the available information, to minimise the percentage of mistaken detentions, is it *morally wrong*? Only if we swallow the second assumption—namely the anti-protectionist's insistence that our overriding objective must be to minimise the total number of mistaken decisions, treating a mistaken decision to detain as exactly equal to a mistaken decision to release. The anti-protectionist is using two neat rhetorical tricks at once. By referring to mistaken detentions and mistaken releases simply as 'mistakes,' he is implying that they all count the same; and by glossing over the difference between 'regrettable' and 'morally wrong,' he is implying that it is our moral duty to go for the smallest number of mistakes irrespective of their nature.

To put this point in concrete terms, suppose that you have in custody three men who have done serious violence to more or less innocent victims. Suppose too that the best actuarial information you can get tells you that one of them—but not *which* one—will do more violence if released. The anti-protectionist is saying that it is your moral duty to release all three instead of continuing to detain all three because release will involve only one mistaken decision instead of two mistaken decisions. Yet the one mistaken release would mean injury or death to someone, while the two mistaken detentions would mean something quite

---

[5] Morris, "On 'Dangerousness' in the Judicial Process" (1982) Record of Association of the Bar of the City of New York 102 at 115.

different: the continued deprivation of freedom for three men of whom an unidentifiable two would not do anybody injury if released."[6]

Most other commentators, however, have greater difficulty justifying the continued incarceration of offenders when predictions are so inaccurate and when many of the most useful predictors are controversial. Beyond the obvious factors of number and type of previous convictions, other considerations might be indicative of future offending. However, to include predictors such as sex, race, age, intelligence, educational attainments, etc. would be unacceptable as "factors which are beyond the offender's control and not logically related to culpability".[7]

The second central objection to incapacitative sentences is that, even if predictions were accurate, it is wrong in principle to punish someone for what he might do in the future. Such a practice amounts to a radical departure from the constraints of just desert under which punishment should be proportionate to the seriousness of the current offence committed.

### Andrew von Hirsch, Past or Future Crimes (1985), p. 11:

"Advocates of the desert model opposed the use of individual prediction in sentencing as a matter of principle, not merely because of such forecasts' tendency to error. Their objection to predictive sentencing was simply that it led to undeserved punishments and would do so even if the false-positive rate could be reduced. The use of predictions, accurate or not, meant that those identified as future recidivists would be treated more severely than those not so identified, not because of differences in the blameworthiness of their past conduct, but because of crimes they supposedly would commit in future. It was felt that punishment, as a blaming institution, was warranted only for past culpable choices and could not justly be levied for future conduct. Unless the person actually made the wrongful choice he was predicted to make, he ought not to be condemned for that choice—and hence should not suffer punishment for it."

Most commonly, predictions of dangerousness are based on previous convictions (along, sometimes, with psychiatric reports). The objection to this is that the offender has already been punished for the past crimes and so this amounts to punishing him or her again for these offences.

It is, however, possible to justify attaching weight to previous convictions within a retributive framework. There are two views here that are employed by just deserts theorists. First, under the principle of "cumulative sentencing", persistent offenders can be regarded as more blameworthy because they have failed to learn lessons from previous convictions and ensuing punishments. They have persisted in criminal behaviour after being specifically warned and punished. Under this view, there should be no ceiling to the possible punishment. With each repeated defiance of the law, the offender is more blameworthy and deserving of greater punishment.

An alternative way of justifying, in terms of desert, extra weight attaching to previous convictions is the theory of "progressive loss of mitigation".

---

[6] For a critique of Walker's views, see Wood, "Dangerous Offenders and the Morality of Protective Sentencing" [1988] Crim.L.R.424 at 425–429.

[7] Tonry, "Prediction and Classification: Legal and Ethical Issues" in Gottfredson and Tonry (eds), *Prediction and Classification: Criminal Justice Decision Making* (1987), p. 397.

### Andrew Ashworth, Sentencing and Criminal Justice (3rd ed., 2000), p. 166:

"The argument ... is based on the idea of a lapse ... [and] the idea of giving someone a 'second chance'. So the justification for the discount for first offenders rests partly on recognition of human fallibility, and partly on respect for people's ability to respond to the censure expressed in the sentence. The justification for the gradual losing of that mitigation on second and subsequent convictions is that the 'second chance' has been given and not taken: the offender has forfeited the tolerance, and its associated sentence discount, because through his subsequent criminal choices he has not responded to the public censure."

According to this theory, with each successive conviction the argument that this was a "lapse" loses plausibility and so the degree of mitigation should progressively diminish until after a certain number of convictions it is lost entirely.[8] It has been suggested that this progressive loss of mitigation could be represented on a graph with an upward slope followed by a plateau.[9]

While this theory has its attractions, it is unlikely to be politically acceptable as it would involve treating an offender with 30 previous convictions the same as one with three or four convictions. The danger is that these theories can be seized upon as providing an intellectual justification for increasing sentencing severity within a desert framework when in reality the previous convictions are simply being used as predictors of future re-offending or dangerousness. For example, the Halliday Report endorses the notion that persons with previous convictions deserve, in retributive terms, greater punishment but then adds that this "coincidentally" enables the risk of re-offending to be taken into account. The Report then goes on to suggest that levels of punishment can be adjusted up or down by "plus or minus 100 per cent". An example is given of an "entry point", based on offence seriousness of 18 months' imprisonment: a first offender might be accorded mitigation and receive a non-custodial sentence while an offender with a large number of previous convictions could receive a sentence of three years' imprisonment.[10] An effective increase of 200 per cent for a repeat, as opposed to a first, offender is not compatible with any desert-based theory permitting weight to be attached to previous convictions. This is simply rampant incapacitative sentencing.

These tensions between the constraints of just deserts and the desire to incapacitate the dangerous led to a policy of bifurcation being adopted by the Criminal Justice Act 1991. Non-threatening offenders are sentenced on the just deserts principle of proportionality, while dangerous violent and sexual offenders are not subject to such contraints. They may receive custodial sentences even though such a sentence would not be justified on the basis of offence-seriousness[11] and they may receive longer custodial sentences than would be justified on the basis of proportionality in order to protect the public from serious harm.[12] In interpreting what is meant by a "longer than normal" sentence, the courts have

---

[8] It has been suggested that this could occur as soon as after a third conviction (von Hirsch, "Desert and Previous Convictions" in von Hirsch and Ashworth, *Principled Sentencing* (2nd ed., 1998) at p. 192).

[9] Wasik and von Hirsch, "Section 29 Revisited: Previous Convictions in Sentencing" [1994] Crim.L.R.409.

[10] Home Office, *Making Punishments Work: Report of a Review of the Sentencing Framework for England and Wales* (Halliday Report) (2001).

[11] Now consolidated in Powers of the Criminal Courts (Sentencing) Act 2000, s.79(2)(b).

[12] *ibid.*, s.80(2)(b).

paid lip-service to the requirement of proportionality by stating that the sentence must bear a "reasonable relationship" to the seriousness of the offence.[13] However, this appears to be little more than empty rhetoric with one research finding revealing that these provisions were resulting in sentences for violent and sexual offenders being increased on average by some 73 per cent.[14] In another study it was found that the average sentence in section 80(2)(b) cases for violent offences was 7.2 years' imprisonment compared to 2.3 years' imprisonment for commensurate sentences.[15]

Other forms of incapacitative sentence are also available. First, an "extended sentence" may be imposed under what is now section 85 of the Powers of Criminal Courts (Sentencing) Act 2000. Where the offender has committed a violent or sexual offence and the court considers that the normal period of licence would not be adequate to prevent the commission of further offences, a longer licence period may be specified by the court. This extension period must not exceed five years in the case of a violent offence or ten years in the case of a sexual offence. Secondly, a discretionary sentence of life imprisonment may be passed in respect of certain serious offences, such as rape or manslaughter, carrying that maximum penalty. The criteria for the imposition of such a sentence are not only that the offence should be grave enough to require "a very long sentence" but also that the offender is "likely to commit such offences in future".[16] In such cases, the "more likely it is that an offender will offend again, and the more grave such offending is likely to be if it does occur, the less emphasis the court might lay on the gravity of the original offence".[17]

A final, and most significant, step, in relation to the sentencing of persistent and dangerous offenders was taken by the Crime (Sentences) Act 1977, whose provisions have now been consolidated in sections 109–111 of the Powers of the Criminal Courts (Sentencing) Act 2000. These provisions draw inspiration from the "Three Strikes and You're Out" laws introduced in numerous states in the United States following a 1993 Washington state referendum mandating life sentences for third-time felons.[18] For example, in California courts are obliged to sentence offenders to at least 25 years' imprisonment without parole on their third felony conviction.[19] In one notorious case, a man with prior convictions was

---

[13] *Crow and Pennington* (1995) 16 Cr.App.R.(S.) 409.

[14] Clarkson, "Beyond Just Deserts: Sentencing Violent and Sexual Offenders" (1997) 36 Howard JCJ 284.

[15] Flood-Page and Mackie, *Sentencing Practice: An Examination of Decisions in Magistrates' Courts and the Crown Court in the mid–1990s* (H.O.R.S. No.180, 1998), p. 92.

[16] *Hodgson* (1968) 52 Cr.App.R.113.

[17] *Chapman* [2000] 1 Cr.App.R.(S.) 377 at 385.

[18] Tonry, *Sentencing Matters* (1996), pp. 3–4. Parole is abolished in such cases meaning that the offender will spend the remainder of his or her life in prison (Prison Reform Trust, *Lessons from America: Washington: The State that Invented 'Three Strikes'* (1997).

[19] Cal. Penal Code, s.667. The previous convictions must be for "violent" or "serious" offences, but the third conviction need not be for such an offence. This is known as a "petty with a prior" law: for example, petty theft can be charged as a felony if there are prior felony convictions (Prison Reform Trust, *Lessons from America: Automatic Life Sentences: The Californian Experience* (1996). See, generally, Shichor and Sechrest, *Three Strikes and You're Out: Vengeance as Public Policy* (1996).

sentenced to 25 years' imprisonment for stealing a slice of pizza.[20] Under the English provisions three types of offenders are liable to mandatory or minimum sentences if they have previous convictions. First, dealing with violent and sexual offenders, where a person, who already has a conviction for a "serious offence", is convicted of another "serious offence"[21] a life sentence must be imposed unless there are "exceptional circumstances" which justify the imposition of a different sentence.[22] In *Offen*[23] it was held that the rationale of this provision was the protection of the public and so if the offender posed no significant risk this would constitute "exceptional circumstances". It was further held that under this more flexible interpretation section 109 did not infringe the provisions of the ECHR.[24]

Secondly, where a person who has two convictions for trafficking class A drugs is convicted for a third time for such an offence, the court is obliged to impose a sentence of at least seven years' imprisonment unless there are specific circumstances rendering such a sentence unjust. Thirdly, where a person is convicted for a third time of domestic burglary the court must impose a sentence of at least three years' imprisonment unless there are specific circumstances rendering such a sentence unjust.

These provisions, aimed at being both a general deterrent and a means of incapacitating the persistent and dangerous offender, could result in an enormous increase in the prison population.[25] The Home Office estimated that bringing section 111 (the burglary provisions) into force would increase the prison population by about 5,000 by 2010.[26] Defendants with previous convictions would be under great pressure to plead guilty to lesser charges to avoid the possibility of a life or minimum sentence.[27] Such provisions are difficult to reconcile with any known version of just deserts. As the Prison Reform Trust, commenting on the Californian experience, puts it: "Offences do differ markedly in their gravity and circumstances; offenders have greater or lesser culpability and show greater or lesser remorse. Mandatory sentences do not allow for such distinctions. They are a denial of justice, reducing sentencing to a rubber stamp exercise."[28] As one English sentencing judge, in feeling obliged to impose a mandatory life sentence, put it: "This may give cause to the public ... to wonder if this kind of statute is the kind of statute that they really want in a civilised society".[29]

[20] *Williams, The Independent*, March 4, 1995. See, further, Prison Reform Trust, *ibid.*, who report that 85 per cent of all offenders who have been sentenced under this law have been sentenced for non-violent offences (p. 3).
[21] The definition of serious offence in s.109(5) is not the same as that of a "violent or sexual" offence under s.80(2)(b) (as interpreted) of the PCCS Act 2000.
[22] PCCS Act 2000, s.109.
[23] [2001] 1 W.L.R. 253.
[24] Art. 7: retrospective penalties; art. 3: inhuman or degrading treatment or punishment; art. 5: right to liberty and security.
[25] Baker, "From 'Making Bad People Worse' to 'Prison Works': Sentencing Policy in England and Wales in the 1990s" (1996) 7 *Criminal Law Forum* 639 at 641.
[26] Howard League Magazine, vol. 18, no. 1, Feb. 2000, p. 3.
[27] Tonry, *Sentencing Matters* (1996), ch. 5.
[28] Prison Reform Trust, *above*, n.19 at 6.
[29] Swanson H.H.J. in *Turner* (Sheffield Crown Court) cited by Henham, "Sentencing Dangerous Offenders: Policy and Practice in the Crown Court" [2001] Crim.L.R.693 at 704.

## D. *Rehabilitation*

Punishment with the aim of reforming or rehabilitating the offender has constituted one of the most ambitious developments in penal theory. The aim is to secure conformity, not through fear (which is the more limited object of deterrence) but through some inner positive motivation on the part of the individual. The process has been described as "improving [the offender's] ... character so that he is less often inclined to commit offences again even when he can do so without fear of the penalty."[30] The source of the change in motivation or improvement in behaviour has been variously described but remains one of the ambiguities of the concept of reform.

The origins of the rehabilitative ideal are inextricably linked with the humanitarian movement for prison reform and many who defend the ideal stress the welfare aspect. Adopting this more humane response can help soften strict "law and order" attitudes.[31] The great penal reformers of the eighteenth century, Beccaria, Bentham, Eden and Romilly, all advocated a system of punishment which combined deterrent with reformative features. It was their belief, however, that reform could come from punishment itself—by, for example, a period of solitude which would induce remorse, repentance and reform. Indeed, the first penitentiary in the United States was created by the Quakers in Philadelphia in 1793 in order that prisoners could pay "penance" for their sins and thereby become "cleansed".[32] The object was to make offenders "better persons" capable of being reintegrated into society (rather than simply purging their sins and thereby repaying their debt to society, which is the more limited object of expiation). When, towards the end of the nineteenth century the aim of rehabilitation became (with deterrence) part of official penal policy in this country, there was more than an element of this thinking present in the measures taken.

Whilst it soon became clear that, far from making "better individuals", solitude had a severely damaging impact upon offenders, the belief that reform should be a concomitant of punishment continued to hold sway for the first half of the twentieth century at least. The moral or religious exhortations to improve were gradually replaced by the behavioural sciences and medicine. As more was learned about the antecedents of human behaviour it was hoped that therapeutic measures could be designed which would improve the offender's behaviour. Put simply, crime was seen as a symptom of an "illness" that could, with the appropriate remedy, be cured.

### H. Weihofen, "Retribution is Obsolete," National Probation and Parole Association News, XXXIX (1960) 1, 4:

"Crime and criminal responsibility are not mere interesting abstractions for the amusement of philosophers dreaming up metaphysical constructs. Crime is a reality, an ever present danger which in some cases is literally a matter of life and death.

---

[30] Walker "Punishing, Denouncing or Reducing Crime" in Glazebrook (ed.), *Reshaping the Criminal Law* (1978), p. 393.

[31] See, *e.g.* Cullen and Gilbert, *Reaffirming Rehabilitation* (1982).

[32] See Walker, *Crime and Punishment in Great Britain* (1968), pp. 134–138, and Morris, *The Future of Imprisonment* (1974).

The voices of ignorance and hate are loud enough now to shout down almost every effort to improve criminal administration by substituting rational for irrational solutions, a rehabilitative for a punitive approach. The rationale of these programs calls for understanding the sociological, economic and cultural sources of criminality, the psychology of criminals and our reactions to criminality. This is too sophisticated for the single-minded devotees of punishment...

I resent the apostles of punishment-for-its-own-sake arrogating to themselves words like 'moral' and 'justice' and implying in consequence that those who scorn their metaphysics are amoral or at least unconcerned with moral values. Surely the feeling of concern for the offender as a human being; the desire to save him from a criminal career and to help him redeem himself as a member of the human family; the even wider concern to prevent others from falling into criminality by searching out the influences and conditions that produce those frustrating and embittering defeats, degradations and humiliations of the human spirit that turn a man against his fellow men; the effort, therefore, to give men those advantages that will help them to keep their feet on the right path—better education, more healthful dwellings, readier aid for casualties of sickness, accident and failures of employment—surely all of this is not a less moral ideal than that which knows only one measure of morality, an eye for an eye and a tooth for a tooth.

Half a century ago, Winston Churchill said, in the House of Commons:

'The mood and temper of the public with regard to the treatment of crime and criminals is one of the most unfailing tests of the civilisation of any country. A calm, dispassionate recognition of the rights of the accused, and even of the convicted criminal against the State—a constant heart searching by all charged with the duty of punishment—a desire and eagerness to rehabilitate in the world of industry those who have paid their due in the hard coinage of punishment: tireless efforts towards the discovery of curative and regenerative processes: unfailing faith that there is a treasure, if you can only find it, in the heart of every man. These are the symbols which, in the treatment of crime and criminals mark and measure the stored-up strength of a nation.'

Yes; and I would add, these are the sign and proof of its morality."

Rehabilitative sentencing involves a focus on the individual offender's needs ensuring that the sentence, or programme within a sentence, will help change the offender's behaviour, attitude and responses. A number of non-custodial measures were introduced in the 1960s and 1970s, such as probation and community service orders, about which rehabilitative claims were made – although the introduction of such measures was perhaps more influenced by a desire to reduce the prison population.

However, despite the attractiveness of the idea of rehabilitating offenders so that they would not wish to re-offend, the 1970s saw a major decline in the rehabilitative ideal. As can be seen from the following extracts, criticism has taken many forms. The gist of the case against the rehabilitative ideal is as follows. First, it is highly interventionist and ultimately gives the State the power to try to alter the character and personality of the offender. Apart from raising images of a "Clockwork Orange" society and presenting grave human rights concerns, it also means that judges, who are trained in law and not psychiatry, are not the most appropriate persons to carry out the task of sentencing. This would be best left to "experts" (psychiatrists etc.). Such ideas were condemned as removing the requirement of justice from sentencing.

The second casualty of the rehabilitative ideal is proportionality. Instead of looking to the past—to the offence committed—the sentencer is only concerned with the future needs of the offender. The sentence should then be chosen which has the best chance of bringing about the desired change; thus the principle of treating like cases in a like manner has no part to play. Proportionality links punishment to the seriousness of the offence whereas under the rehabilitative ideal there are no like cases. Each case has to be determined on its own merits. There ought, in theory at least, to be complete individualisation of sentences—the sentences should depend, not on the offence, but on the offender. This, of course, inevitably leads to widespread sentencing disparity which breaches a fundamental principle of justice that people be accorded equal treatment before the law. It also leads in some cases to excessively long sentences being passed to allow time for rehabilitation.[33]

Finally, research began to question whether rehabilitative programmes actually work. In an important article in 1974 Martinson concluded that "with few and isolated exceptions, the rehabilitative efforts that have been reported so far have had no appreciable effect on recidivism.[34] Initially such attacks were deflected by the argument that the criminal justice system was not truly committed to rehabilitation; often it was sacrificed completely to other competing ideals (such as deterrence), or that appropriate means had yet to be found to have the desired impact upon the defendant.

Whether a rehabilitation has been successful is normally measured by studies of recidivism, few of which lent much support to the idea that rehabilitation works for the majority of offenders. However, there were some studies concentrating on treatment strategies for specific categories of offenders which revealed some success and, indeed, Martinson wrote an article in 1979 in which he partially recanted on his earlier views.[35] Nevertheless, the notion that "nothing works" had entered the currency of penology and that, coupled with ethical concerns about the treatment model, led to a demand that punishment be more firmly linked to just deserts.

### Francis Allen, The Decline of the Rehabilitative Idea: Penal Policy and Social Purpose (1981), p. 47:

"One immediate consequence of a rehabilitative regime is a drastic enlargement of state concerns. The state's interests now embrace not only the offender's conduct but, as Michael Foucault has put it [*Discipline and Punish*], his 'soul': his motives, his history, his social environment. A traditional restraint on governmental authority is the notion of relevance: the state is limited in its inquiries and actions to that which is pertinent to its legitimate purposes. But when there are no clear limits on what may be relevant to the treatment process and when the goals of treatment have not been clearly defined, the idea of relevance as a regulatory of public authority is destroyed or impaired."

### A. E. Bottoms, "An Introduction to 'The Coming Crisis' " in A. E. Bottoms and R. H. Preston, The Coming Penal Crisis (1980), pp. 1–3:

"First, and the dominant factor in much current penal consideration, comes *the collapse of the rehabilitative ideal*. ... A succession of negative research reports has—with a few exceptions which do not seriously disturb the conclusion—suggested that different types of

---

[33] Cross, *Punishment, Prison and the Public* (1971).

[34] "What Works?" (1974) Public Interest 35. Martinson's article has been misquoted as stating that nothing works and has proved to be highly influential. See also, Lipton, Martinson and Wilks, *Effectiveness of Correctional Treatment* (1975).

[35] Martinson, "New Findings, New Views: A Note of Caution Regarding Sentencing Reform" (1979) 7 Hofstra L.Rev.243.

treatment make little or no difference to the subsequent reconviction rates of offenders. ...
As the Serota Report (ACPS 1977) succinctly put it:

> 'A steadily accumulating volume of research has shown that, if reconviction rates are used
> to measure the success or failure of sentencing policy, there is virtually nothing to choose
> between different lengths of custodial sentence, different types of institutional regime, and
> even between custodial and non-custodial treatment; (para. 8).'

Very recently, the Home Office's *Review* has endorsed this view. ...
But the objections to the treatment (or rehabilitation) ethic have not been solely based on
empirical demonstrations of lack of efficacy. Strong theoretical objections have also been
raised, perhaps most influentially in the American Friends Service Committee's (1971)
*Struggle for Justice*, which argued that there was:

> 'compelling evidence that the individualised-treatment model, the ideal towards which
> reformers have been urging us for at least a century, is theoretically faulty, systematically
> discriminatory in application, and inconsistent with some of our most basic concepts of
> justice (p. 12).'

What lies behind these claims?
(i) *'Theoretically faulty'*—because, it can be claimed, the treatment model implies that
criminal behaviour has its roots in the deficiencies of the individual and his upbringing, and
that if these are remedied, the crime rate will be cut; but this medical analogy is
inappropriate, and crime is far more a result of the overall organization of society than of the
deficiencies of the individual.
(ii) *'Systematically discriminatory'*—because the treatment model typically takes more
severe coercive action in cases of 'unsatisfactory' home circumstances or 'dubious' moral
background; but these judgments are made by middle-class workers who unwittingly but
systematically discriminate against the poor and the disadvantaged, and in favour of the
'good' homes of the privileged.
(iii) *'Inconsistent with justice'*—because judgments involving the liberty of the individual are
made (in the name of 'casework' or whatever) on the basis of extremely impressionistic
evidence which is usually not revealed to the offender, and which he cannot therefore
challenge; and the result may be, for example, that some will serve long sentences for trivial
crimes because their 'attitudes have not improved,' while others convicted of serious crime
but who have allegedly 'responded' are let out.
Underneath criticisms like these, it will be noted, lies a fundamental conviction by the critics
as to the essentially *coercive* nature of the rehabilitative ideal.... Many adherents of the
ideal blinded themselves as to this coerciveness, in the false belief that benevolent intentions
preclude a coercive result."

## M. Cohen, "Moral Aspects of the Criminal Law" (1940) 49 Yale L.J. 987 at 1012–1014:

"The growing belief in education and in the healing powers of medicine encourages
people to suppose that the delinquent may be re-educated to become a useful member of
society. Even from the strictest economic point of view, individual men and women are the
most valuable assets of any society. Is it not better to save them for a life of usefulness rather
than punish them by imprisonment which generally makes them worse after they leave than
before they entered?
There are, however, a number of highly questionable assumptions back of this theory
which need to be critically examined.
We have already had occasion to question the assumption that crime is a physical or
mental disease. We may now raise the question whether it is curable and if so at what cost to
society? Benevolent social reformers are apt to ignore the amount of cold calculating
business shrewdness among criminals. Some hot-blooded ones may respond to emotional
appeal; but they are also likely to back-slide when opportunity or temptation comes along.
Human beings are not putty that can be remolded at will by benevolent intentions. ... The

analogy of the criminal law to medicine breaks down. The surgeon can determine with a fair degree of accuracy when there is an inflamed appendix or cancerous growth, so that by cutting it out he can remove a definite cause of distress. Is there in the complex of our social system any one cause of crime which any social physician can as readily remove on the basis of similarly verifiable knowledge?

Let us abandon the light-hearted pretension that any of us know how all cases of criminality can be readily cured, and ask the more modest and serious question: to what can criminals be re-educated or re-conditioned so that they can live useful lives? It would indeed be illiberal dogmatism to deny all possibility and desirability of effort along this line. Yet we must keep in mind our human limitations.

If the causes of crime are determined by the life of certain groups, it is foolish to deal with the individual as if he were a self-sufficient and self-determining system. We must deal with the whole group to which he naturally belongs or gravitates and which determines his morale. Otherwise we have to adapt him completely to some other group or social condition, which is indeed a very difficult problem in social engineering.

And here we must not neglect the question of cost. When we refer to any measure as impracticable, we generally mean that the cost is too great. There is doubtless a tremendous expense in maintaining our present system of punishment. But this expense is not unlimited. Suppose that fiendish perpetrators of horrible crimes on children could be reformed by being sent first for several years to a special hospital. Will people vote large funds for such purposes when honest law-abiding citizens so often cannot get adequate hospital facilities?"

### R. J. Gerber and P. D. McAnany, "Punishment: Current Survey of Philosophy and Law" (1967) 11 Saint Louis University L.J. 491 at 502–535:

"To begin with rehabilitation, it is clear that its image has been tarnished by a series of exposés. The initial discovery has shown that rehabilitation has frequently been a cover for neglect. Persons put into penal incarceration in the name of social reform have been left there interminably because they are being 'cured.' The ugly truth is that few states have facilities to implement a rehabilitation program at the level at which their policy insists on treatment under terms of confinement. The result is far worse than an entirely punitive system whose sanctions are carefully measured by law.

A second serious charge made against the treatment-minded is that their approach is an invitation to personal tyranny and denial of human rights. Once a prisoner is placed in the hands of the doctor to be cured before he is released, there is no one who can predict how long the cure will take, nor control the autonomy of the doctor's judgment. The real impact of [the] C. S. Lewis ... article[36] comes in the fact that all of 'treatment' is done in the name of a benevolent, but uncontrolled, humanitarianism. It is not Lewis' point, nor any other of its critics, that rehabilitation is not a valid goal of society, but they all insist that some other more fundamental justification must be present to provide support for what must be conceived as only ancillary to the essential nature of punishment. Not only must we seek justification for punishment elsewhere, but a clear limit must be placed on what criminals can be forced to undergo for their own benefit ....

Finally, an argument is made that all the science in the world cannot really rehabilitate a person whose attitudes are anti-social. The only way to change a man is from the inside out, beginning with the heart. While this may sound a bit revivalistic, behind it is couched a theory as to the real nature of the 'cure'. Do criminals need psychotherapy, job-training, education, or do they have a more basic need to draw them from criminal ways, a need for 'repentance' and forgiveness? To put the issue at a practical level, what possible motivations can a social scientist give a prisoner when he is not interested in the prisoner as a person? Can

[36] *Above*, p. 30.

we really expect to have a good program without a proper understanding of motivations in the personal sense? Further, can a rehabilitation expert give proper motivation when he himself has no commitment to the motives he insists on, or can he insist on the goals of 'normal' society when these are at best morally ambiguous?... Society at large has not been overly successful in offering a pattern for living except to the already successful."

### Andrew von Hirsch, Doing Justice—The Choice of Punishments (Report of the Committee for the Study of Incarceration) (1976), pp. 16–18:

"Some advocates of rehabilitation attribute the current failures to inadequate screening. Programs are applied indiscriminately to heterogenous groups of offenders, some of whom may be responsive while others are not... It is, they say, like using insulin to treat all diseases:... Arguably, outcomes could begin to improve were one able in rehabilitation as in medicine, to identify with greater precision the particular subgroups of offenders who are amenable to different types of treatment. However, ignorance of the causes of crime remains a serious barrier to successful screening...

It would be an exaggeration to say that no treatment methods work, for some positive results have been reported, which further follow-up may confirm. But, certainly, few programs seem to succeed; and it is still uncertain to what extent the claimed success would survive replication or close analysis.

In those special instances where it might be possible to find treatment that works, the more difficult question has to be confronted: aside from effectiveness, what other limitations should there be on the rehabilitative disposition? Is it just, for example, to impose dissimilar sentences for treatment purposes upon offenders convicted of similar crimes? We shall argue later that there are limitations of justice on the rehabilitative disposition, even if the treatment were known to be effective.

But in the more commonplace instances where no successful treatments are known, the rehabilitative disposition is plainly untenable. It cannot be rational or fair to sentence for treatment, without a reasonable expectation that the treatment works."

Von Hirsch later suggested that much of the true appeal of rehabilitative ideology lies in the fact that its advocates were able both to have their cake and eat it:

"(I)t offered both therapy and restraint. One did not have to assume that all criminals were redeemable but could merely hope that some might be. Thereapy could be tried on apparently amenable defendants, but always with a faile-safe: the offender who seemed unsuitable for, or unresponsive to, treatment could be separated from the community."[37]

Despite these concerns, the rehabilitative ideal underwent something of a revival in the 1990s with the catch-phrase "what works" replacing the gloom of "nothing works" that had dominated the previous decade. Various programmes have been introduced for offenders who have received both custodial and non-custodial sentences. Apart from drug and alcohol programmes, there has been a growing implementation of cognitive-behavioural programmes: these focus on training offenders in decision-making and problem-solving, management of emotions (such as anger-management), negotiation skills and critical reasoning with offenders being encouraged to reflect on the consequences of their actions. Programmes also include various educational and life-skills courses, such as ones aimed at improving literacy and numeracy, designed to improve offenders' chances of employment.

---

[37] *Past or Future Crimes* (1985), p. 5.

New statistical techniques of meta-analysis (aggregating findings from a number of smaller studies) have been employed and are revealing some success for these programmes particularly in relation to certain types of offenders.[38] For example, it has been suggested that corporate offenders may be more amenable to rehabilitation than other groups.[39]

Since the 1997 election there has been a greater commitment to evidence-based initiatives and research. The important Halliday Report,[40] proposing a radical overhaul of sentencing, strongly endorses the "What Works" strategies and programmes and estimates that they could lead to a reduction in the overall reconviction rate of 5 to 15 per cent[41] on the basis that "some things can work for some people, provided the right programmes are selected and implemented properly."[42]

However, while there is now emerging evidence that some rehabilitative measures can be effective, the other central concerns over the rehabilitative ideal still remain.

## Norval Morris and Colin Howard, Studies in Criminal Law (1964), pp. 175–176:

"Principles will now be suggested by which we may keep the advantages of these utilitarian, reformative, socially protective approaches to punishment and yet avoid the dangers to human rights implicit in them. . . .

First, *power over a criminal's life should not be taken in excess of that which would be taken were his reform not considered as one of our purposes.* Let the maximum of his punishment be never greater than that which would be justified by the other aims of our system of criminal justice. Within the term of that sentence, let us utilise our reformative skills to assist him towards social readjustment, but never put forward the possibility of reforming him to justify an extension of power over him. The jailer in a white coat with a degree in a behavioural science remains a jailer."

The Criminal Justice Act 1991 (now consolidated in the Powers of the Criminal Courts (Sentencing) Act 2000), to some extent, endorsed this submission. For instance, one of the criteria for the imposition of a probation order (now a "community rehabilitation order") is that supervision must be desirable in the interest of the rehabilitation of the offender[43] but such a sentence can only be imposed within the confines of a system based primarily on proportionality. Similarly, the Halliday Report, while strongly endorsing rehabilitative sentencing, stresses that any such sentence must be imposed within the limits of a "punitive envelope" whose limits are shaped by the principle of desert. This notion of combining the various theories is the subject of the next section.

[38] McGuire (ed.), *What Works: Reducing Reoffending*, 1995; Raynor, "Community Penalties: Probation, Punishment and 'What Works'" in Maguire, Morgan and Reiner (eds), *The Oxford Handbook of Criminology* (3rd ed, 2002); Parliamentary All-Party Penal Affairs Group, *Changing Offending Behaviour—Some Things Work* (1999).
[39] Gobert, "Controlling Corporate Criminality: Penal Sanctions and Beyond" [1998] 2 Web J.C.L.I.
[40] *Above*, n.10.
[41] Para.1.49.
[42] Para.1.50.
[43] Powers of the Criminal Courts (Sentencing) Act 2000, s.41(1).

### E. *Combining the Theories*

It is difficult to make any sense of the above competing "theories" until one knows precisely what question they are trying to answer. Building on the work of Hart[44] one can distinguish four separate questions:

1. What is the purpose of punishment?
2. Who may be punished?
3. How much punishment should be imposed?
4. What type of punishment should be imposed?

Many commentators have attempted to combine both retributive and utilitarian considerations in answering these questions. One approach, exemplified by Hart, is that a distinction needs to be drawn between two issues. First, one needs to ascertain what the purpose of the whole institution of punishment is; Hart called this "the general justifying aim" and the justification for this was to be found in utilitarian considerations. In short, the reason why we have an institution of punishment is because we want to reduce crime. However, there is a second separate issue of "distribution": this relates to the second two questions above, namely, who to punish and how much punishment? According to Hart the question of distribution should be answered in retributive terms. Only persons who have committed criminal offences deserve punishment and the amount of punishment should be proportionate to the seriousness of the crime. According to this approach, one could say that the aim of the institution of punishment was, for example, deterrence but one would not be justified in punishing innocent people (say, the children of the offender) purely because this might be an effective deterrent. Punishment can only be justified in a particular case on the retributive basis that it is deserved.

### George Fletcher, Rethinking Criminal Law (1978), p. 419

"The analogy that comes to mind is the distinction between justifying the income tax as a whole and justifying the imposition of burdens on particular taxpayers. The justification of the system as a whole is raising revenue for the government; the justification of burdens on particular taxpayers is (roughly) the taxpayer's relative ability to pay. It would obviously be improper to interweave these two levels of justification and justify the denial of claim for a charitable deduction on the ground of the claimant's relative ability to pay. Similarly, if the justification for the criminal law as a whole is the isolation of dangerous offenders, it is improper to decide particular cases by appealing to the alleged offender's relative dangerousness."

One could advocate such a "dualist"[45] approach but, instead of accepting Hart's views, one could argue, for instance, that the aim of the institution of punishment is desert but that one needs utilitarian justifications to punish in individual cases.[46] Much of this chapter has been devoted to answering the first question: what is the

[44] "Prolegomenon to the Principles of Punishment" in *Punishment and Responsibility* (1969), p. 1.
[45] Wood, "Retribution, Crime Reduction and the Justification of Punishment" (2002) 22 O.J.L.S. 301.
[46] Goldman, "The Paradox of Punishment" (1979) 9 Philosophy and Public Affairs 42.

purpose of punishment? Nothing further need be added here. The focus of the remainder of this section is on whether a dualist approach is justifiable and, if so, how matters of distribution of punishment should be determined. In assessing this it is helpful to examine the above three distributive questions separately.

## 1. Who may be punished?

### H. L. A. Hart, "Prolegomenon to the Principles of Punishment" in Punishment and Responsibility (1968), pp. 11–13, 21–24:

"First, though we may be clear as to what value the practice of punishment is to promote, we have still to answer as a question of Distribution 'Who may be punished?'. Secondly, if in answer to this question we say 'only an offender for an offence' this admission of retribution in Distribution is not a principle from which anything follows as to the severity or amount of punishment: in particular it neither licenses nor requires, as Retribution in General Aim does, more severe punishments than deterrence or other utilitarian criteria would require.

The root question to be considered is, however, why we attach the moral importance which we do to retribution in Distribution. ...

The standard example used by philosophers to bring out the importance of retribution in Distribution is that of a wholly innocent person who has not even unintentionally done anything which the law punishes if done intentionally. It is supposed that in order to avert some social catastrophe officials of the system fabricate evidence on which he is charged, tried, convicted and sent to prison or death. Or it is supposed that without resort to any fraud more persons may be deterred from crime if wives and children of offenders were punished vicariously for their crimes. In some forms, this kind of thing may be ruled out by a consistent sufficiently comprehensive utilitarianism. Certainly expedients involving fraud or faked charges might be very difficult to justify on utilitarian grounds. We can of course imagine that a negro might be sent to prison or executed on a false charge of rape in order to avoid widespread lynching of many others; but a *system* which openly empowered authorities to do this kind of thing, even if it succeeded in averting specific evils like lynching would awaken such apprehension and insecurity that any gain from the exercise of these powers would by any utilitarian calculation be offset by the misery caused by their existence. But official resort to this kind of fraud on a particular occasion in breach of the rules and the subsequent indemnification of the officials responsible might save many lives and so be thought to yield a clear surplus of value. Certainly vicarious punishment of an offender's family might do so and legal systems have occasionally resorted to this. An example of it is the Roman *Lex Quisquis* providing for the punishment of the children of those guilty of *majestas*. In extreme cases many might still think it right to resort to these expedients but we should do so with the sense of sacrificing an important principle. We should be conscious of choosing the lesser of two evils, and this would be inexplicable if the principle sacrificed to utility were itself only a requirement of utility. ...

It is clear that like all principles of Justice it (punishment) is concerned with the adjustment of claims between a multiplicity of persons. It incorporates the idea that each individual person is to be protected against the claim of the rest for the highest possible measure of security, happiness or welfare which could be got at his expense by condemning him for a breach of the rules and punishing him. For this a moral licence is required in the form of proof that the person punished broke the law by an action which was the outcome of his free choice, and the recognition of excuses is the most we can do to ensure that the terms of the licence are observed. Here perhaps, the elucidation of this restrictive principle should stop. Perhaps we (or I) ought simply to say that it is a requirement of Justice, and Justice simply consists of principles to be observed in adjusting the competing claims of human beings which (i) treat all alike as persons by attaching special significance to human voluntary action and (ii) forbid the use of one human being for the benefit of others except in return for his voluntary actions against them. ...

We may look upon the principle that punishment must be reserved for voluntary offences from two different points of view. The first is that of the rest of society considered as *harmed* by the offence (either because one of its members has been injured or because the authority of the law essential to its existence has been challenged or both). The principle then appears as one securing that the suffering involved in punishment falls upon those whose who have voluntarily harmed others: this is valued, not as the Aim of punishment, but as the only fair terms on which the General Aim (protection of society, maintenance of respect for law, etc.) may be pursued.

The second point of view is that of society concerned not as harmed by the crime but as *offering* individuals including the criminal the protection of the laws on terms which are fair, because they not only consist of a framework of reciprocal rights and duties, but because within this framework each individual is given a *fair* opportunity to choose between keeping the law required for society's protection or paying the penalty. From the first point of view the actual punishment of a criminal appears not merely as something useful to society (General Aim) but as justly extracted from the criminal who has voluntarily done harm; from the second it appears as a price justly extracted because the criminal had a fair opportunity beforehand to avoid liability to pay."

This dualist approach has been criticised on the basis that confining retribution to the issue of distribution of punishment amounts to a down-grading of its importance.[47] It has been further suggested that the whole dualist enterprise is flawed.

### Nicola Lacey, State Punishment: Political Principles and Community Values (1988), pp. 51–52:

"All these hybrid theories proceed on the assumption that there are genuinely separate questions to be answered: ... It seems to be true ... that rules themselves contain their own conditions of application. No sensible system has rules and then fails to apply them: prima facie, the reasons for having the rules generate the reasons for applying them in individual cases. This seems to indicate that the principle of distribution, if one is (as it seems to be) needed, must come in at the first stage: *a* principle of distribution is inevitably contained within or at least envisaged by the general justifying aim of the rules. And if the general justifying aim is straightforwardly utilitarian, the project of grafting on a separate distributive principle, begins to look deeply problematic, for utilitarianism does *not*, as its critics sometimes claim, lack such a principle. It rather embodies criteria of distribution which are vulnerable to serious objection. It is necessary, then, to identify an alternative general justifying aim which incorporates or is consistent with an acceptable distributive principle, rather than to separate different questions and give different answers to them. Conversely, I think it can be argued that a justification for institutions of punishment must include a justification for their actual use in individual cases, and that the individual question is in some ways primary: can any single infliction of punishment ever be justified? The mere fact that such an infliction is according to rules does not seem to generate any additional justification in itself. In justifying a system of rules, we generally assume that those rules will be applied: therefore the justification which we seek must also justify the application of the rules. For these reasons it is my belief that the ... Hartian distinction does not really withstand close analysis."[48]

Lacey's approach is, however, dependent on the "general justifying aim" itself embodying *effective* criteria of "distribution". To assess this let us briefly consider

---

[47] Wood, *above* n.45 at 307.
[48] For a similar argument, see Braithwaite and Pettit, *Not Just Deserts* (1990), p. 167.

the utilitarian response to the problem of punishing the innocent. Why not punish an innocent person if, say, it would be an effective deterrent? The answer here is that such punishment could never in fact be an effective deterrent as punishment would become a lottery and there would be no special disincentive to would-be offenders. Punishing the innocent would cause suffering to the victim, general insecurity, disrespect for the law and could encourage the guilty person to reoffend. In short, such punishment would cause more evil than it prevented and thus could not be justifiable.

There are problems with this approach. Suppose that a judge, concerned about people speeding through his town, sentenced his clerk to a long sentence of imprisonment for a speeding offence. In fact the clerk was innocent and had agreed to the exercise and never actually served the sentence. Apart from a few court and prison officials, no-one else ever discovered the truth although the punishment imposed received much publicity. In such a case the victim does not suffer at all, there is no real offender escaping liability and no insecurity or disrespect for the law is caused. However, even if this sentence were proved to have an effective deterrent effect, it is still manifestly unjust. It represents a distortion and a mockery of the criminal justice system which is why there would be an outcry if the truth were discovered.

Further, even if the "general justifying aim" did embody criteria of distribution, *why would they be any better* than those yielded by the concept of just desert, which, as demonstrated in the Hart extract above, provides fair, consistent and just results?

## 2. How severely do we punish?

The amount of punishment imposed again depends on the rationale for the imposition of that punishment.

Let us start with the utilitarian view of punishment. How would a utilitarian determine the amount of punishment to be imposed for a particular offence? If it were thought necessary, for example, for reasons of deterrence, could extreme sentences be imposed that bore no relationship to the seriousness of the crime? Could one give life sentences for parking on double yellow lines if this were thought to be an effective deterrent? Could one give life sentences to persons who repeatedly stole milk bottles from doorsteps if this would prevent the recurrence of the crime?

The classic answer to this question is still that provided by Jeremy Bentham, that all punishment is evil and ought only to be imposed to achieve some greater good—and, accordingly, one should only impose the minimum punishment necessary to achieve that objective.

### Jeremy Bentham, An Introduction to the Principles of Morals and Legislation, Chap. 13, in Bentham and Mill, The Utilitarians (1961), pp. 162, 166:

"The general object which all laws have, or ought to have, in common, is to augment the total happiness of the community; and therefore, in the first place, to exclude, as far as may be, every thing that tends to subtract from that happiness: in other words, to exclude mischief.

But all punishment is mischief: all punishment in itself is evil. Upon the principle of utility, if it ought at all to be admitted, it ought only to be admitted in as far as it promises to exclude some greater evil.

It is plain, therefore, that in the following cases punishment ought not to be inflicted.

1. Where it is *groundless:* where there is no mischief for it to prevent, the act not being mischievous upon the whole.
2. Where it must be *inefficacious:* where it cannot act so as to prevent the mischief.
3. Where it is *unprofitable;* or too *expensive:* where the mischief it would produce would be greater than what it prevented.
4. Where it is *needless:* where the mischief may be prevented, or cease of itself, without it: that is, at a cheaper rate ....

Now the evil of the punishment divides itself into four branches, by which so many different sets of persons are affected. 1. The evil of *coercion* or *restraint:* or the pain which it gives a man not to be able to do the act, whatever it be, which by the apprehension of the punishment he is deterred from doing. This is felt by those by whom the law is *observed.* 2. The evil of *apprehension:* or the pain which a man, who has exposed himself to punishment, feels at the thought of undergoing it. This is felt by those by whom the law has been *broken,* and so feel themselves in *danger* of its being executed upon them. 3. The evil of *sufferance:* or the pain which a man feels, in virtue of the punishment itself, from the time when he begins to undergo it. This is felt by those by whom the law is broken, and upon whom it comes actually to be executed. 4. The pain of sympathy, and the other *derivative* evils resulting to the persons who are in *connection* with the several classes of original sufferers just mentioned."

Accordingly, the utilitarian reason why we do not punish parking on a double yellow line with life imprisonment is that it is thought that the aim of deterrence can be effectively achieved at a lower cost—and crime must be prevented as economically in terms of the suffering of the offender as possible. Further, such an extreme sentence would undoubtedly attract public sympathy for the offender and thus "instead of reaffirming the law and intensifying men's consciousness that the kind of act punished is wrong, will have the opposite effect of casting discredit on the law and making the action of the law-breaker appear excusable or even almost heroic".[49]

The problem with this approach is that while it might explain why preposterous sentences cannot be imposed for minor crimes, it does not necessarily prohibit exemplary sentences (discussed earlier) whereby one person is given *a longer sentence than is deserved.* Desert theory is emphatic here: the crime itself provides the necessary guidance as to the amount of punishment necessary. The punishment must be proportionate to the crime; it must "fit" the crime. Modern desert theorists, such as von Hirsch, argue that punishment must be proportionate to the seriousness of the crime in order to reflect an *appropriate degree of censure.*

### Andrew von Hirsch, Past or Future Crimes: Deservedness and Dangerousness in the Sentencing of Criminals (1985), pp. 35–36:

"The requirement of proportionate punishment is derived directly from the censuring implications of the criminal sanction. Once one has created an institution with the condemnatory connotations that punishment has, then it is a requirement of justice, not merely of efficient law enforcement, to punish offenders according to the degree of reprehensibleness of their conduct. Disproportionate punishments are unjust not because they are ineffectual or possibly counterproductive, but because the state purports to condemn the actor for his conduct and yet visits more or less censure on him than the gravity of that conduct warrants.

[49] Ewing, "A Study of Punishment II: Punishment as viewed by the Philosopher" (1943) 21 Can.B.Rev. 102 at 116.

... As long as the state continues to respond to violence, theft, or fraud, or similarly noxious conduct through the institution of the criminal sanction, it is necessarily treating those whom it punishes as wrongdoers and condemning them for their conduct. If it thus condemns, then the severity of the state's response ought to reflect the degree of blameworthiness, that is, the gravity, of actors' conduct.

This argument uses a commonly understood concept, employed in everyday life: the notion of censure. The idea is that once one has established a condemnatory institution to respond to criminal acts, one ought then to allocate its sanctions in a manner that comports with the reprehensibleness of those acts."

How does one determine what level of punishment is proportionate to the seriousness of the crime?

### Andrew von Hirsch, "Ordinal and Cardinal Desert" in Andrew von Hirsch and Andrew Ashworth (eds.), Principled Sentencing (1992), pp. 209–210[50]:

"One must distinguish between *ordinal* and *cardinal* magnitudes of punishment: That is, between (1) the question of how defendants should be punished relative to each other, and (2) the question of what absolute severity levels should be chosen to anchor the penalty scale ...

For modern desert theory, this distinction is critical. Advocates of desert-oriented sentencing such as myself do not assert that desert is determinative for all purposes. Rather, our claim is a more restricted one, to wit: desert is a determinative principle in deciding ordinal magnitudes, but only a limiting principle in deciding cardinal magnitudes. To see what this means in practice, consider the crime of burglary. The issues of ordinal magnitude deal with how a particular burglary should be penalized compared to other burglaries and to other more or less serious crimes. When desert theorists assert that desert is a determining principle here, they mean that the ordering of penalties must meet the following two requirements. The first is the requirement of *parity*: criminal conduct of equal seriousness should be punished equally, with deviations from such equality permitted only where special circumstances alter the harm or culpability—that is, the degree of blameworthiness—of the defendant's conduct. The other is that of *rank ordering*: penalties should be ranked and spaced to reflect the ranking and spacing in degree of seriousness among crimes. What desert theorists object to is deciding these questions of *comparative* punishments on grounds other than the blameworthiness of the defendant's conduct: for example, to punish a particular burglar more severely than other burglars not because his particular crime is any worse but because he is a worse risk or because giving him a higher-than-usual punishment would make him an example to others.

To espouse this view does not, however, require one to hold that desert is determinative in deciding cardinal magnitudes. Here, rather, most modern desert theorists—certainly I—would admit that desert is a limiting principle only. I do not claim to know precisely how tough or lenient a sentencing scale should be, but only that punishments beyond certain levels of harshness or leniency are *undeserved*."

A final, but critical, issue remains. *Must* one punish to the exact extent dictated by the seriousness of the crime, or does the concept of just desert merely provide a ceiling beyond which punishment is undeserved?

The strict Kantian response is that the offender must be punished to that extent, *no more and no less*, which is necessary to destroy the unfair advantage gained from committing the crime. A failure to punish the offender, either at all, or to the extent necessary to eliminate the advantage gained, would not restore social

---

[50] This is an amended version of von Hirsch, "Equality, 'Anisonomy,' and Justice: A Review of *Madness and the Criminal Law*" (1984) 82 Michigan Law Review 1093.

equilibrium and would amount to society endorsing the criminal's acts and thus becoming participants in it. It would further involve failing to treat the criminal as a responsible human being who deserves the consequences of his actions.

On the other hand, it could be that the concept of just desert should only specify the maximum possible penalty beyond which punishment is undeserved.[51] Within a permissible range, punishment is deserved—one is justified in punishing—but one has a choice as to the severity of the punishment, that choice being informed by all the circumstances of the offence and perhaps even by utilitarian considerations. In short, within a range set by desert principles, the precise allocation of punishment could be determined on a utilitarian basis. This approach, sometimes called limited or negative retributivism, has recently been endorsed in England and Wales by the Halliday Report[52] and forms the main plank of the Government's proposals for a radical restructuring of the approach to sentencing.[53]

The Halliday Report proposes that desert should provide a "punitive envelope"[54] indicating a permissible range of sentence. No sentence outside that range is permissible. However, once the "envelope is opened", the actual sentence imposed, within the defined limits, will depend on utilitarian considerations. Within the range the sentencer will select the punishment that would most closely serve the purpose of crime reduction (and reparation) in the individual case. This will involve an assessment of the likelihood of re-offending and the measures most likely to reduce that risk.[55]

### Nicola Lacey, State Punishment: Political Principles and Community Values (1988), pp. 54–55:

"The idea that desert furnishes the state with a non-conclusive reason to punish raises the question of what types of extra reasons must be adduced in order to produce a justification of particular acts of punishment. On some accounts, apparently no-utilitarian factors are appealed to—factors such as fairness and justice. But it is clear that the most obvious candidates are utilitarian reasons such as prevention, deterrence, avoidance of private vengeance and so on. It is important to note that on most weak retributivist views desert operates not only as the central justification but also as a limit on the amount of punishment: the only function of the consequentialist considerations is to add an element which provides the sufficient reason for some punitive action. On this view, consequentialism cannot tell us whom to punish or how much to punish; it merely defeats the argument from the pointlessness of purely retributive punishment. The difficulty here is that these utilitarian arguments do purport to provide not just an explanation of when we may exercise our right or power of punishment, but actually to make it right for us to punish. According to utilitarianism, it is right to punish wherever such an action maximises the aggregate of pleasure over pain. It is thus hard to see how it is that the weak retributive principle fails to become redundant. In addition, it is not clear whether the desert argument is intended to apply to the design of institutions and the utilitarian one to individual acts of punishment . . . If this were so, we would be invited to endorse the unattractive vision of a legal system based on a principle of desert, in which individual acts of punishment were left to judicial

---

[51] Morris, *Punishment, Desert and Rehabilitation* (1976).
[52] Home Office, *Making Punishments Work: Report of the Sentencing Framework for England and Wales* (2001).
[53] *Justice for All* Cm.5563 (2002); Criminal Justice Bill, 2003.
[54] Para. 2.39.
[55] Para. 2.31. See Baker and Clarkson, "Making Punishments Work? An Evaluation of the Halliday Report on Sentencing in England and Wales" [2002] Crim.L.R.81.

discretion which should be exercised on the basis of consequentialist reasoning, or else of a system in which the legislator made utilitarian generalisations in framing the rules which were nevertheless primarily based on considerations of desert."

The Halliday Report demonstrates that the central tension here is how best to combine desert and utilitarian considerations in sentencing. As Lacey makes clear, sentencing cannot be left to unfettered judicial discretion. Justice demands that like cases be treated alike. There needs to be an organising principle to structure and control such discretion. The Halliday Report makes some effort in this direction—but is ultimately flawed for two reasons. First, the limits of permissible punishment based on desert are overly influenced by the existence of previous convictions.[56] This leaves too broad a band within which punishment is "deserved". Secondly, once the envelope has been opened, utilitarianism takes complete control and there is insufficient guidance as to the relationship between the various utilitarian considerations.

## 3. What type of punishment?

### Paul H. Robinson, "Hybrid Principles for the Distribution of Criminal Sanctions" (1988) 82 Northwestern University Law Review 19 at 34–36:

"The [next] issue, concerning the method of sanction, is distinguishable from the distribution of amount. Two offenders may merit the same *amount* of sanction yet different *methods* of sanctioning may be suitable for imposing that amount. These two issues—how much for whom and what method—are not only functionally distinguishable but also may properly be subject to different distributive principles.

Each of the distributive purposes may treat the different issues differently. Effective crime control can be furthered through a variety of mechanisms—by setting the amount or the method of sanction, as well as by setting enforcement and prosecution patterns and expenditures. Satisfaction of desert concerns, by contrast, depends almost exclusively on the amount issue—who receives how much; the method issue (as well as the resource allocation issues) is generally not relevant.

The desert requirement of a proper ordinal ranking of offenders by overall blameworthiness, for example, concerns the ranking of *amounts* of sanction. As long as the ordinal ranking is correct, the *method* by which each amount is imposed is not relevant to desert. If one month in the state prison is the punitive equivalent to five months of weekends in the local jail, then desert is satisfied even if the more blameworthy offender gets probation, with a condition of seven months of weekends in jail, while the less blameworthy offender goes to prison for one month. It is critical, of course, that the sanction equivalencies be properly set. Some empirical research has been done on perceptions of relative seriousness of sanctions, but the work is still in its infancy.

With an estimate of equivalencies, one can construct a sentencing system that allows independent determination of the amount and method issues. The principles governing the 'amount' issue can generate total 'sanction units' for each offender, which can then be allocated to a particular sanctioning method or combination of methods according to a different set of 'method' principles. As long as the issues can be effectively segregated in

[56] See p. 50.

practice, one can develop a hybrid distributive principle for governing the amount of sanction that is different from the principle used to determine the method of sanction. One could, for example, emphasize desert in determining the amount of sanction, but ignore it in determining the method. The selection of method could be made to maximize pure utilitarian concerns without infringing desert interests—a precious no-loss, all-win opportunity.

The separation of amount and method issues has other important collateral advantages. For example, unwarranted disparity in sentencing primarily concerns disparity in amount, rather than disparity in method. Thus, one might significantly reduce judicial sentencing discretion on the amount issue, in order to reduce disparity among judges, yet maintain broad judicial discretion on the method issue. As long as the total 'sanction units' for an offender are satisfied and the sanction equivalencies are properly set, it does not matter what method or methods an individual judge selects; the punitive 'bite' will be the same."

According to this analysis, within a desert framework, decisions as to the type of punishment can be based on utilitarian considerations. For example, the decision whether to impose a community rehabilitative order (formerly, a probation order) or a community punishment order (formerly, a community service order) could be determined by rehabilitative considerations. This approach has been endorsed by the Halliday Report but, as seen above, where the Halliday Report is flawed is that it would permit utilitarian considerations to determine not only the *type* of punishment, but also the *amount* of punishment.

## F. *Sentencing Guidelines*

Until the rise of the just deserts movement, sentencers were generally free to impose whatever sentence they deemed appropriate—up to the maximum permitted. In England there were constraints: a "tariff" was developed by the judges which broadly indicated a range of sentences for "normal cases" and defendants had a right of appeal where an excessive penalty beyond the tariff was imposed. It is interesting to contrast this with the position in the United States where the just deserts movement began its revival. Judicial sentencing discretion there was virtually unlimited and in a majority of states no appeal against sentence was permitted.

Such broad discretionary powers meant several things in both jurisdictions. Different judges could impose different sentences for different reasons without having to give any explanation in open court. For example, some judges could impose a sentence for deterrent reasons but other judges in similar cases could sentence offenders in order to rehabilitate them. Even the same judge was not always consistent in sentencing. There was no agreement among judges as to what criteria ought to be taken into account in the sentencing decision and what weight ought to be given to factors such as previous convictions, age, good family, perceived future dangerousness, whether the accused pleaded guilty and other such matters. Criticism of this lack of consistency was speedily met with the response that sentences were individualised; they were tailored to meet the needs of the defendant and therefore consistency in punishments for similar crimes was not to be expected. The result was widespread sentencing disparity with similar cases being treated differently.

In England a 1979 study on sentencing practice in the Magistrates' Court revealed sometimes wide disparities in the use of fines and imprisonment: "Almost all clerks and chairmen emphasised the necessity for the establishment and maintenance of a consistent policy in their own individual courts but this concern did not extend to maintaining consistency with their neighbours. It was more important, they believed, that the decision taken by the courts should be determined by the particular characteristics of the offenders coming before it and of the district it served than that wider consistency be achieved at the expense of sensitivity."[57]

Even more startling evidence of sentencing disparity began to emerge from the United States.

## Marvin E. Frankel, Criminal Sentences—Law Without Order (1973), pp. 21–22:

"Take, for instance, the case of two men we received last spring. The first man had been convicted of cashing a cheque for $58.40. He was out of work at the time of his offence, and when his wife became ill and he needed money for rent, food and doctor's bills, he became the victim of temptation. He had no prior criminal record. The other man cashed a cheque for $35.20. He was also out of work and his wife had left him for another man. His prior record consisted of a drunk charge and a non-support charge. Our examination of these two cases indicated no significant differences for sentencing purposes but they appeared before different judges and the first man received 15 years in prison and the second man 30 days...

In one of our institutions a middle-aged credit union treasurer is serving 117 days for embezzling $24,000 in order to cover his gambling debts. On the other hand, another middle-aged embezzler with a fine past record and a fine family is serving 20 years, with 5 years probation to follow."

Another consequence of judges sentencing for a mixture of reasons, many of them utilitarian, was that excessively long sentences were being imposed in some cases. In particular, the rationale of exemplary sentencing resulted in some persons receiving sentences in excess of those imposed on others committing similar crimes.

One final point about the pre-just desert era ought to be borne in mind. Offenders sent to prison were entitled to remission of their sentence (for good behaviour in prison) and to release on parole after a specified period. The decision whether to release someone on parole was highly discretionary and effectively amounted to a prisoner being sentenced a second time—but this time behind closed doors. This meant that when two offenders received the same sentence for the same crime, one could be released far sooner than the other. This, of course, could lead to even greater real disparity.

It was a combination of all these factors that provided fertile soil for the growth of the just deserts movement. The agenda was set: judicial discretion had to be controlled; sentencing disparity had to be eliminated: this would necessarily involve eliminating disproportionately long sentences; there needed to be "truth in sentencing": equal sentences imposed in open court had to mean the same thing for different offenders. The concept of just desert with its liberal emphasis on justice involving like cases being treated alike was the obvious facilitator. However, it was clearly not enough simply to embrace the concept of just desert and reduce the

---

[57] Tarling and Weatheritt, *Sentencing Practice in Magistrates' Courts*, (H.O.R.S. No. 56, 1979) p. 45. See also N.A.C.R.O., *The Real Alternative* (1989), pp. 10–17; Corbett, "Magistrates' Courts Clerks' Sentencing Behaviour: An Experimental Study" in Lloyd-Bostock and Pennington (eds), *The Psychology of Sentencing* (1987), pp. 205 *et seq.*; and Liberty, *Unequal before the Law; Sentencing in Magistrates' Courts in England and Wales 1981–1990* (1992).

importance of utilitarian considerations. Different judges could have different conceptions of what sentence was deserved in any particular case. What was needed was a mechanism for ensuring that judicial discretion was controlled by forcing judges to sentence in accordance with agreed and objective standards of desert. The response in many states in the United States was sharp and dramatic. In England it has been slower and somewhat different. Let us consider the developments in each country in turn.

## 1. United States

In the United States most states have developed sentencing guidelines under which judicial discretion is retained, but specific criteria or guidelines are developed to structure and control the exercise of that discretion. The legislature continues to set maximum terms. A specialised body, usually referred to as a Sentencing Commission, is created to establish sentencing guidelines within these broad statutory boundaries. These guidelines are generally based on two factors: the severity of the offence and the offender's prior criminal history. Offences are ranked in order of their seriousness and the Commission specifies a limited number of aggravating and mitigating circumstances which increase or decrease the severity of the offence. Factors relating to the offender's prior criminal history include previous convictions, prior incarcerations and whether the person was on parole or probation at the time the offence was committed. For each combination of offence and offender, including a consideration of aggravating or mitigating circumstances, the guidelines provide a narrow sentencing range. The sentencing judge is expected to impose a sentence within this range, but if there are special circumstances not adequately taken into account by the guidelines, there may be a departure from the guidelines; reasons for the departure must be given and the sentence then becomes automatically subject to appellate review.

Under such schemes the sentence imposed on an offender is the sentence that will actually be served (except for "good time" reductions). Accordingly, there is no necessity for a Parole Board.

The role of the Sentencing Commission is viewed as crucial. Unlike the legislature, such a body would have the time and expertise to establish guidelines on the basis of careful study of existing sentencing practices; it could periodically alter these guidelines on the basis of on-going experience; theoretically, it would be removed from partisan politics; it would be a publicly accountable body; its rule-making would be on the record and open to public scrutiny.

The best known example of such guidelines is to be found in Minnesota (Figure 1). The italicised numbers within each grid denote the presumptive sentencing range in months within which a sentence may be imposed without it being deemed a departure. All felony offences are assigned an appropriate level of severity. The offences listed on the grid are examples of frequently occurring offences within each severity level. The offender's criminal history score is computed by assigning points to previous convictions (one-half point for each previous conviction at levels 1–2; one point for each previous conviction at levels 3–5; one and a half points for convictions at levels 6–8; and 2 points for convictions at levels 9–11), custody status at the time of the offence (for example, if the offender was on probation), prior misdemeanour record and prior juvenile record. Cumulative points may accrue on a single occasion when offenders are sentenced concurrently for more than one offence.[58]

---

[58] *State v Hernandez*, 311 N.W. 2d 478 (Minn. 1981).

*Figure 1 Minnesota Sentencing Guidelines Grid, Effective August 1, 2002*

## Presumptive Sentence Lengths in Months

Italicized numbers within the grid denote the range within which a judge may sentence without the sentence being deemed a departure. Offenders with nonimprisonment felony sentences are subject to jail time according to law.

| SEVERITY LEVEL OF CONVICTION OFFENSE (Common offenses listed in italics) | | CRIMINAL HISTORY SCORE | | | | | | |
|---|---|---|---|---|---|---|---|---|
| | | 0 | 1 | 2 | 3 | 4 | 5 | 6 or more |
| Murder, 2nd Degree (intentional murder; drive-by-shootings) | XI | 306 *299–313* | 326 *319–333* | 346 *339–353* | 366 *359–373* | 386 *379–393* | 406 *399–413* | 426 *419–433* |
| Murder, 3rd Degree Murder, 2nd Degree (unintentional murder) | X | 150 *144–156* | 165 *159–171* | 180 *174–186* | 195 *189–201* | 210 *204–216* | 225 *219–231* | 240 *234–246* |
| Criminal Sexual Conduct, 1st Degree[2] Assault, 1st Degree | IX | 86 *81–91* | 98 *93–103* | 110 *105–115* | 122 *117–127* | 134 *129–139* | 146 *141–151* | 158 *153–163* |
| Aggravated Robbery 1st Degree | VIII | 48 *44–52* | 58 *54–62* | 68 *64–72* | 78 *74–82* | 88 *84–92* | 98 *94–102* | 108 *104–112* |
| Felony DWI | VII | 36 | 42 | 48 | 54 *51–57* | 60 *57–63* | 66 *63–69* | 72 *69–75* |
| Criminal Sexual Conduct, 2nd Degree (a) & (b) | VI | 21 | 27 | 33 | 39 *37–41* | 45 *43–47* | 51 *49–53* | 57 *55–59* |
| Residential Burglary Simple Robbery | V | 18 | 23 | 28 | 33 *31–35* | 38 *36–40* | 43 *41–45* | 48 *46–50* |
| Nonresidential Burglary | IV | 12[1] | 15 | 18 | 21 | 24 *23–25* | 27 *26–28* | 30 *29–31* |
| Theft Crimes (Over $2,500) | III | 12[1] | 13 | 15 | 17 | 19 *18–20* | 21 *20–22* | 23 *22–24* |
| Theft Crimes ($2,500 or less) Check Forgery ($200–$2,500) | II | 12[1] | 12[1] | 13 | 15 | 17 | 19 | 21 *20–22* |
| Sale of Simulated Controlled Substance | I | 12[1] | 12[1] | 12[1] | 13 | 15 | 17 | 19 *18–20* |

☐ Presumptive commitment to state imprisonment. First Degree Murder is excluded from the guidelines by law and continues to have a mandatory life sentence.

▨ Presumptive stayed sentence; at the discretion of the judge, up to a year in jail and/or other non-jail sanctions can be imposed as conditions of probation. However, certain offenses in this section of the grid always carry a presumptive commitment to state prison. These offenses include Third Degree Controlled Substance Crimes when the offender has a prior felony drug conviction, Burglary of an Occupied Dwelling when the offender has a prior felony burglary conviction, ...

[1] One year and one day

[2] Pursuant to M.S. section 609.342, subd. 2, the presumptive sentence for Criminal Sexual Conduct in the First Degree is a minimum of 144 months.

The presumptive sentence for cases contained in cells below and to the left of the solid line should be "stayed" (delayed until some future date; if the offender complies with imposed conditions until that date, the case is discharged). The presumptive sentence for cases contained in cells above and to the right of the solid line should be "executed" (served immediately).

The presumptive penalty may be departed from in cases involving "substantial and compelling circumstances". The Sentencing Guidelines provide a non-exclusive list of mitigating factors (for example, that the victim was the aggressor in the incident) and aggravating factors (for example, that the victim was particularly vulnerable due to age or infirmity) that may be used as reasons for departure. They are also explicit that race, sex, employment and social factors may *not* be used as reasons for departure. Parole is abolished and replaced by a specified reduction (up to one-third off) for good behaviour in prison.

These guidelines appear to have been tolerably successful in reducing disparity. In 1991 the overall departure rate was 16 per cent, three-quarters of which were mitigated and one-quarter aggravated departures.[59] This can, of course, be justified. Justice not only demands that like cases be treated alike, but that different cases be treated differently. It is inevitable that in reducing all serious crimes to only eleven categories over-generalised solutions are imposed and fine-tuning has to be achieved on a case-by-case basis which involves departing from the presumptive penalty.

Further, it must be recalled that the guidelines only deal with the control of discretion at the sentencing stage of the criminal justice process. Inevitably, since the introduction of the guidelines much discretion has been shifted to the prosecutor who, in agreeing a reduced charge, is effectively determining the sentence in most cases. This means that offenders are not being sentenced for the crime they committed, but rather for the crime to which they have pleaded guilty.[60] This, coupled with an apparent tendency on the part of prosecutors to insist that offenders plead guilty to a number of charges so that their offender score is raised,[61] can lead to disparity and injustice being removed to an earlier and less visible stage of the process.

Finally, a very real danger of implementing such a guideline system must be emphasised. In Minnesota the original guidelines were introduced in 1980 with the avowed and laudable aim of reducing prison populations. Such guidelines are, however, amenable to hijack by the law-and-order brigade intent on increasing penalties. This has occurred in Minnesota where the presumptive penalties have been increased twice since their inception. In 1989, after several highly-publicised homicides and considerable legislative pressure, the Sentencing Commission

---

[59] Frase, "Sentencing Guidelines in Minnesota and Other American States: A Progress Report" in Clarkson and Morgan, *The Politics of Sentencing Reform* (1995).

[60] The United States Sentencing Commission initially sought to introduce guidelines allowing offenders to be sentenced according to the real crime they committed rather than the one for which they admitted guilt. The Commission was, however, ultimately forced to abandon such a scheme because of difficulties of establishing the "real" crime (United States Sentencing Commission, *2001 Federal Sentencing Guideline Manual*, A.4(a)).

[61] Tonry, "Sentencing Guidelines and Sentencing Commissions—the Second Generation" in Pease and Wasik (eds), *Sentencing Reform* (1987), p. 39.

*doubled* several initial penalties: for example, the presumptive penalty for aggravated robbery was increased from 24 to 48 months. At the same time it doubled the number of points accorded to prior convictions thereby again increasing the potential for, and duration of, imprisonment. The result was an increase in the incarceration rate.[62]

## Michael Tonry, Sentencing Matters (1996), pp. 13–24:

"The irony of 'just deserts' is that it backfired. The overriding aim was to make sentencing principled and fair ... If indeterminate sentencing sometimes produced racial and class disparities, other unwanted disparities, and sentences grossly out of proportion to the crimes of which offenders were convicted, there was much to be said for proposals to scale the severity of punishments to the seriousness of crimes and thereby to satisfy the first tenet of equal treatment to: 'treat like cases alike.' In practice the effect was to focus attention solely on offenders' crimes and criminal records, to the exclusion of ethically important differences in their circumstances, and thereby to fail the second tenet of equal treatment to 'treat different cases differently.'

Reduced to their core elements, just desert theories are based on the intuitively powerful idea that punishment should be *deserved*, the empirical premise that most people agree about the comparative seriousness of crimes, and the proposal that crimes be ranked in order of their seriousness and punishments proportioned to those rankings. ... In practice, however, while most academic proponents of desert theories favor overall *reduction* in the severity of punishments, the result has been both to make punishment more severe and to create disparities as extreme as any that existed under indeterminate sentencing.

... [B]ecause desert theories place primary emphasis on linking deserved punishments to the severity of crimes, in the interest of treating like cases alike, they lead to disregard of other ethically relevant differences between offenders—like their personal backgrounds and the effects of punishment on them and their families—and thereby often treat unlike cases alike ...

Just deserts, sometimes characterized as expressing a 'principle of proportionality', is sound in theory but defective in practice. In an ideal world in which all citizens have equal opportunities for self-realization and material advancement, the idea that deserved punishments can be calibrated precisely to the offender's culpability, and that punishments should be apportioned accordingly, has much to commend it. Somewhat awkwardly for desert theories, however, ours is a world that in a number of respects falls short of the ideal.

... In just deserts principle, two offenders who commit the same offense and have similar criminal records deserve the same penalty. If applicable guidelines specify a two-year prison sentence, both should receive it. If one, however, is unemployed and has no permanent residence, and the other works and supports a family, many people will want to treat them differently. Partly, this is because the second seems more stable, more integrated into society, and somehow more worthy. Partly also, and equally important, it is because the second offender's spouse and children—who have committed no crime—will also suffer ...

Judges, prosecutors, and other officials make decisions about whole people, and not about generic offenders who have committed offence X and have criminal history Y. Not surprisingly, they often feel moved to take the individual offender's circumstances into account in deciding what to do.

Another defect ... [is that in] objective terms, punishments that technically are the same may be very different. A 'generic' two-year prison sentence ... may range from time spent in a crowded, fear-ridden maximum security prison under lockup twenty-three hours per day to confinement under electronic monitoring in the offender's home, with medium and minimum security prisons, forestry camps, and halfway houses in between. All count as two years' deprivation of liberty, but all offenders and most observers see them as vastly different.

---

[62] Frase, *above*, n.59.

In subjective terms as well, two years' imprisonment in a single setting will have very different meanings to different offenders who have committed the same crime. Two years' imprisonment in a maximum security prison may be a rite of passage for a Los Angeles gang member. For an attractive, effeminate twenty-year-old, it may mean the terror of repeated sexual victimization. For a forty-year-old head of household, it may mean the loss of a job and a home and a family. For the unhealthy seventy-year-old, it may be a death sentence.

... By offering policy makers a rationale for sentencing that reduced relevant considerations to two that can be scaled on the axes of grids, [just desert theories] reified three-dimensional defendants into two-dimensional abstractions. When policy makers think of abstractions rather than people, it is easy to respond to an electoral opponent's possible 'soft on crime' accusations by voting to increase sentences or to establish mandatory penalties ... If a two-dimensional grid is chalked on to a legislative committee's blackboard, it takes little effort to erase numbers and replace them with higher ones."

## 2. England and Wales

There have been significant responses in England and Wales. First, since 1989 the Attorney-General has been able to refer an unduly lenient sentence, imposed by the Crown Court, to the Court of Appeal which has the power to increase that sentence.[63] A disparate sentence can be an unduly light one as well as an unduly heavy one and so this right of appeal does go some way towards the elimination of unwarranted disparity. However, it is only Crown Court sentences (and not ones from magistrates' courts), and only ones imposed for "indictable only" offences, that are referable. These account for fewer than 20 per cent of sentences imposed in the Crown Court.[64] Nevertheless, betwen 60 and 80 sentences are reviewed by the Court of Appeal for undue lenience each year and 88 per cent of these are found to be unduly lenient.[65]

Secondly, as we have seen, the Criminal Justice Act 1991 endorsed the concept of just desert in declaring that the sentence of imprisonment must be proportionate to the seriousness of the offence.

Thirdly, the early release rules were thoroughly revised by the Criminal Justice Act 1991 to try to reduce discretion and introduce more "truth in sentencing". These rules are now consolidated in section 116 of the Powers of the Criminal Courts (Sentencing) Act 2000. Very broadly speaking, all persons sentenced to less than four years' imprisonment are *entitled* to release after serving one-half of their sentence. For those serving sentences of more than one year, there is supervision on licence until the three-quarter point of the sentence. Persons serving four years or longer are *entitled* to release after serving two-thirds of their sentence but the Parole Board has the power to recommend release on licence after one-half of the sentence has been served. Thus while the Parole Board retains some discretion in these latter cases, the overall effect of these provisions has been to reduce significantly their powers.

Fourthly, the Magistrates' Association has drawn up and issued guidelines for magistrates' courts in an attempt to establish consistency in sentencing. Guidelines for a variety of offences have been drawn up and a few offences have been subdivided. For example, there are separate guidelines for general theft and theft in breach of trust. An example of these guidelines is set out in Figure 2.

[63] Criminal Justice Act 1988, s.36.
[64] Shute, "Who Passes Unduly Lenient Sentences? How Were They Listed?: A Survey of Attorney-General's Reference Cases, 1989–1997" [1999] Crim.L.R.603.
[65] *ibid.*

| Theft Act 1968 s.1<br>Triable either way – see Mode of Trial Guidelines<br>Penalty: Level 5 and/or 6 months<br>May disqualify where committed with reference<br>to the theft or taking of the vehicle | **Theft** |
| --- | --- |

---

## CONSIDER THE SERIOUSNESS OF THE OFFENCE
### *(INCLUDING THE IMPACT ON THE VICTIM)*

*IS DISCHARGE OR FINE APPROPRIATE?*

**GUIDELINE: →**    *IS IT SERIOUS ENOUGH FOR A COMMUNITY PENALTY?*

*IS IT SO SERIOUS THAT ONLY CUSTODY IS APPROPRIATE?*

*ARE MAGISTRATES' SENTENCING POWERS APPROPRIATE?*

---

 ## CONSIDER AGGRAVATING AND MITIGATING FACTORS

**for example**
- High value
- Planned
- Sophisticated
- Adult involving children
- Organised team
- Related damage
- Vulnerable victim
- *This list is not exhaustive*

**for example**
- Impulsive action
- Low value
- *This list is not exhaustive*

---

*If racially aggravated, or offender is on bail, this offence is more serious*

*If offender has previous convictions, their relevance and any failure to respond to previous sentences must be considered – they may increase the seriousness*

---

## TAKE A PRELIMINARY VIEW OF SERIOUSNESS, THEN
## CONSIDER OFFENDER MITIGATION

**for example**
- Age, health (physical or mental)
- Co-operation with police
- Voluntary compensation
- Evidence of genuine remorse

---

## CONSIDER YOUR SENTENCE

*Compare it with the suggested guideline level of sentence and reconsider your reasons carefully if you have chosen a sentence at a different level. Consider a discount for a timely guilty plea.*

---

## DECIDE YOUR SENTENCE
### *NB. COMPENSATION – Give reasons if not awarding compensation*

---

**Remember: These are GUIDELINES only**

While such guidelines are to be welcomed, caution is necessary. In cases involving a mixture of positive and negative factors no indication is given as to the relative weight to be attached to the factors.[66] It must also be remembered that these guidelines are entirely voluntary although a survey has suggested that 75 per cent of magistrates were using a predecessor of the present guidelines.[67] However, it must be stressed that the guidelines are sufficiently broad and general that two magistrates using the same guidelines in the same case could come up with very different results. It has been suggested that there is still "postcode justice" with sentences of differing severity being imposed in different areas of the country. For instance, only 3.5 per cent of offenders convicted of handing stolen goods in Reading received a custodial sentence compared with 48 per cent in Greenwich and Woolwich in south-east London compared with 62 per cent in Bradford.[68] Nevertheless, encouraging uniformity of approach must be an improvement on allowing magistrates complete freedom to sentence purely on the basis of their intuitions.

Finally, in an attempt to structure sentencing discretion in the Crown Court, the Court of Appeal in the 1970s started handing down *guideline judgments*. These usually occur when a number of appeals are heard at the same time and the Court of Appeal takes the opportunity to make generalised statements about sentencing for that type of offence.

There are now guideline judgments dealing with a wide-range of offences. There is evidence that many of these decisions have resulted in sharp increases in sentencing levels. For example, in 1986 the Court of Appeal delivered a landmark guideline judgment on rape in *Billam*.[69] In 1984, 30 per cent of those convicted of rape received sentences of at least five years' imprisonment. By 1987, the year following *Billam*, the figure had risen to 80 per cent.[70] However, it is uncertain to what extent these guideline judgments have helped control sentencing disparity. Research on cases after *Billam* concluded that both sentencing judges and the Court of Appeal tend "to nod in the direction of *Billam* criteria but to scale ... sentences apparently unconstrained by the *Billam* scaling implications".[71] The problem was that these guideline judgments, while helpful in indicating starting points for the severity of sentences, and in listing aggravating and mitigating circumstances, were insufficiently precise, in mathematical terms, as to how much sentences could be increased or decreased.[72] Further, such guideline judgments tended to concentrate on the more serious crimes with the result that there was insufficient guidance for cases dealing with less serious crimes where non-custodial sentences were likely.[73]

[66] Wasik and Turner, "Sentencing Guidelines for the Magistrates' Courts" [1993] Crim.L.R.345 at 351, 353.
[67] Turner, "Sentencing in the Magistrates' Court" in Munro and Wasik, *Sentencing, Judicial Discretion and Training* (1992), p. 193. There are similar guidelines for traffic offences. This same survey revealed that 89 per cent of magistrates were utilising these guidelines.
[68] *Criminal Statistics England and Wales 2000* (2001), cited in *Justice for All*, Cm.5563 (2002).
[69] (1986) 82 Cr.App.R.347.
[70] Home Office White Paper, *Crime, Justice and Protecting the Public* (1990) Cm.965, para.2.14.
[71] Ranyard, Hebenton and Pease, "An Analysis of a Guideline Case as Applied to the Offence of Rape" (1994) 33 Howard JCJ 203 at 215.
[72] Ranyard, Hebenton and Pease, "An Analysis of a Guideline Case as Applied to the Offence of Rape" (1994) 33 Howard JCJ 203 at 208–209.
[73] Ashworth, *Sentencing and Criminal Justice* (3rd ed., 2000), p. 32.

In response to such criticisms a Sentencing Advisory Panel was established in 1999.[74] Where a court is seised of an appeal it must consider whether guidelines need to be framed or revised for offences of that category and, if so, the Panel must be notified. After formulating its views, the Panel must communicate them to the court. The court shall "have regard to these views" (section 80(3)(e)) and, if practicable or at the next appropriate opportunity, include guidelines in its judgement. Under section 81(3) the Panel may at any time propose to the court that guidelines be framed or revised for a particular category of offence. The following is an example of a more recent guideline judgment where the Court of Appeal has been strongly influenced by the Sentencing Advisory Panel.

## R. v McInerney and Keating [2002] EWCA Crim 3003

The Lord Chief Justice:

"1. These appeals have been listed before us so that we can give a guideline judgment as to the appropriate sentencing levels in the case of offences of domestic burglary. The guidance that we have decided to give is the result of the advice of the Sentencing Advisory Panel ('the Panel') dated 9 April 2002. It only applies directly to sentences in connection with domestic burglaries where the trespass is accompanied by theft or an intention to steal.

2. Guidance was previously given by this court, presided over by Lord Bingham Chief Justice, as to sentencing in cases of domestic burglary in *R. v Brewster & Others* [1998] 1 Cr.App.R(S.) 181:

### 'The offence

... Generally speaking domestic burglaries are the more serious if they are of occupied houses at night; if they are the result of professional planning, organisation or execution; if they are targeted at the elderly, the disabled and the sick; if there are repeated visits to the same premises; if they are committed by persistent offenders; if they are accompanied by vandalism or any wanton injury to the victim; if they are shown to have a seriously traumatic effect on the victim; if the offender operates as one of a group; if goods of high value (whether actual or sentimental) are targeted or taken; if force is used or threatened; if there is a pattern of repeat offending. It mitigates the seriousness of an offence if the offender pleads guilty, particularly if the plea is indicated at an early stage and there is hard evidence of genuine regret and remorse.'

### The Panel's Proposals:

#### A Standard Burglary
17.  ... A standard domestic burglary is a burglary, which has the following features:

 (i)  it is committed by a repeat offender;

 (ii)  it involves the theft of electrical goods such as a television or video;

(iii)  the theft of personal items such as jewellery;

(iv)  damage is caused by the break-in itself;

 (v)  some turmoil in the house, such as drawers upturned or damage to some items occurs;

(vi)  no injury or violence, but some trauma is caused to the victim ...

## Aggravating and Mitigating Features
20. Having established what they regarded and what we also treat as a standard burglary the Panel went on in the conventional way to identify what they regarded as being aggravating and mitigating factors. ...

---

[74] Crime and Disorder Act 1988, ss.80–81.

21. The Panel divided the aggravating factors into two categories. We consider this is helpful as long as it appreciated there is no clear line between the categories and they can overlap. The high-level aggravating factors are:

- force used or threatened against the victim;

- a victim injured (as a result of force used or threatened);

- the especially traumatic effect on the victim, in excess of the trauma generally associated with a standard burglary;

- professional planning, organisation or execution;

- vandalism of the premises, in excess of the damage generally associated with a standard burglary;

- the offence was racially aggravated;

- a vulnerable victim deliberately targeted (including cases of 'deception' or 'distraction' of the elderly).

22. The medium-level aggravating features are:

- a vulnerable victim, although not targeted as such;

- the victim was at home (whether daytime or night-time burglary);

- goods of high value were taken (economic or sentimental);

- the burglars worked in a group. . . .

24. The Panel, rightly in our view, did not seek to indicate what percentage uplift should result from the presence of either the high-level or medium-level factors. They did, however, indicate, and again we would agree, that it is appropriate for the sentencer 'to reflect the degree of harm done, including the impact of the burglary upon the victim whether or not the offender foresaw that result or the extent of that impact'. If, of course the offender foresees a result of the offending behaviour then that increases the seriousness of the offence.

25. The Panel also identified features (again they should not be regarded as an exhaustive list), which obviously are appropriate to take into account in mitigating the seriousness of the offence. They are:

- a first offence;

- nothing, or only property of very low value, is stolen;

- the offender played only a minor part in the burglary;

- there is no damage or disturbance to property.

The fact that the crime is committed on impulse may also be a mitigating factor. . . .

28. In addition, the offender's age or state of health, both physical and mental can be a mitigating fact, so can evidence of genuine remorse, response to previous sentences and ready co-operation with the police.

29. We have already agreed that the fact that it is a first offence should be regarded as a mitigating factor. . . .

### The Starting Points Suggested by the Panel After a Trial

32. In relation to adult offenders, not taking into account any aggravating or personal mitigating factors or the discount for a guilty plea, in relation to a completed, as opposed to an attempted, burglary of domestic premises, the Panel divided their recommendations into four categories: . . .

'(a) For a low-level burglary committed by a first-time domestic burglar (and for some second-time domestic burglars), where there is no damage to property and no property (or only property of very low value) is stolen, the starting point should be a *community sentence* ... Other types of cases at this level would include thefts (provided they are of items of low value) from attached garages or from vacant property ...

(b) For a domestic burglary displaying most of the features of the standard domestic burglary [see paragraph 17] above ... the starting point should be *a custodial sentence of nine months*. A case at this level would, on a guilty plea, be suitable for disposal in a magistrates' court ... The starting point for a second-time domestic burglar committing such an offence should be *a custodial sentence of 18 months*. When the offence is committed by an offender with two or more previous qualifying convictions for domestic burglary, the starting point is *a custodial sentence of three years*—i.e. the presumptive minimum now prescribed by law in these circumstances.

(c) In the case of a standard domestic burglary which additionally displays any one of the 'medium relevance' factors referred to in paragraph [22 above], but committed by a first-time domestic burglar, the starting point should be *a custodial sentence of 12 months*. The starting point for a second-time domestic burglar committing such an offence should be *a custodial sentence of two years*. When the offence is committed by an offender with two or more previous convictions for domestic burglary the starting point is *a custodial sentence of three and a half years (42 months)*.

(d) In the case of a standard domestic burglary which additionally displays any one of the 'high relevance' factors mentioned in [paragraph 21], but committed by a first-time domestic burglar, the starting point should be *a custodial sentence of 18 months*. The starting point for a second-time domestic burglar committing such an offence should be *a custodial sentence of three years*. When the offence is committed by an offender with two or more previous convictions for domestic burglary the starting point is *a custodial sentence of four and a half years (54 months)*. The presence of more than one "high relevance" factor could bring the sentence for an offence at this level significantly above the suggested starting points.' ...

### Our starting points

34. As to the starting points contained in (d), we would endorse the recommendation of the Panel. We also endorse the non-custodial approach recommended in (a).

35. In relation to (b) and (c) we adopt a different approach. ...

### Guidance

44. We therefore propose that instead of adopting a stepped approach as suggested by the Panel in sub-paragraphs (b) and (c) in cases in which courts would otherwise be looking to starting point of up to 18 months imprisonment, the initial approach of the courts should be to impose a community sentence subject to conditions that ensure that the sentence is (a) an effective punishment and (b) one which offers action on the part of the Probation Service to tackle the offender's criminal behaviour and (c) when appropriate, will tackle the offender's underlying problems such as drug addiction. If, and only if the court is satisfied the offender has demonstrated by his or her behaviour that punishment in the community is not practicable, should the court resort to a custodial sentence. ...

48. Where a custodial sentence is necessary, then it should be no longer than necessary. In the case of repeat offenders and aggravated offences long sentences will still be necessary as indicated by the Panel in sub-paragraphs (b) (c) and (d) above. As to the incremental increases, we agree with the Panel, that the increase in sentencing levels should slow significantly after the third qualifying conviction. It is necessary to retain a degree of proportionality between the level of sentence for burglary and other serious offences."

Initially, the Court of Appeal showed some reluctance to accept the advice of the Sentencing Advisory Panel, but, more recently, there has been a tendency to adopt the Panel's recommendations. For example, the Court of Appeal has adopted the

Panel's advice on offences relating to opium,[75] on racially aggravated offences,[76] on handling stolen goods[77] and on extended sentences.[78]

While this constitutes a major step towards ensuring consistency in sentencing, a major problem remains that each guideline judgment only focuses on a particular offence without considering the relationship of that offence to other offences in terms of seriousness and without any overall strategy or view of the aims of punishment.[79] What is needed is an attempt to structure sentencing discretion within a coherent scheme having a clear overall view of the purposes of punishment. Perhaps the English system is more suited to the setting up of a sentencing commission that lays down statements of principle such as those favoured in parts of Scandinavia.[80] Following such thinking, the Halliday Report has proposed major reforms to the legal framework within which sentencing decisions are taken. A Penal Code would articulate the main principles of sentencing and codified guidelines for all main offences would be drawn up by a special body.

### Home Office, Making Punishments Work, Report of a Review of the Sentencing Framework for England and Wales (Halliday Report) (2001), para. 0.23:

"For a new framework, an Act of Parliament should set out the general principles, specify the newly designed sentences, provide for review hearings, prescribe enforcement procedures and require guidelines to be drawn up. The Act should take the form of a Penal Code, which would be kept continuously available in up to date form. New guidelines for the use of judicial discretion will be an essential part of the new framework, in order to avoid unpredictable consequences, for example, in the sentencing of persistent offenders. Such guidelines would be set out in a separate, published Code, that would apply to all criminal courts. The guidelines would specify graded levels of seriousness of offence, presumptive 'entry points' of sentence severity in relation to each level of seriousness, how severity of sentence should increase in relation to numbers and types of previous conviction, and other possible grounds for mitigation and aggravation. Responsibility for producing, monitoring, revising and accounting for the guidelines should be placed on an independent body ... The Sentencing Advisory Panel should have a new remit to enable it to advise on all aspects of the guidelines, and produce drafts."

The Criminal Justice Bill 2003 seeks to implement these proposals.

### Justice For All, Cm.5563 (2002)

"5.8 For the first time, we will set out in legislation the purposes of sentencing. Sentences should:

---

[75] *Mashaollahi* [2001] 1 Cr.App.R.(S.) 96.
[76] *Kelly and Donnelly* [2001] 2 Cr.App.R.(S.) 341.
[77] *Webbe* [2002] 1 Cr.App.R.(S.) 82.
[78] *Nelson* [2002] 1 Cr.App.R.(S.) 565.
[79] Ashworth, "Four Techniques for Reducing Sentence Disparity" in von Hirsch and Ashworth (eds), *Principled Sentencing* (2nd ed., 1998), pp. 228–229.
[80] Jareborg, "The Swedish Sentencing Reform" in Clarkson and Morgan, *The Politics of Sentencing Reform* (1995); von Hirsch and Jareborg, "Sweden's Sentencing Statute Enacted" [1989] Crim.L.R.275. See also the Report of the Canadian Sentencing Commission, *Sentencing Reform—A Canadian Approach* (1987).

- first and foremost protect the public. This is paramount;

- act as a punishment and ensure the punishment fits the crime;

- reduce crime. Sentencing must be an effective tool, which leads to fewer crimes;

- deter (this includes both the general effect on the population at large and the specific effect on the offender);

- incapacitate, where offenders are physically prevented from committing crimes by removing them partly or entirely from society;

- reform and rehabilitate, so that the offender can learn new skills and attitudes which make him or her less likely to reoffend; and

- promote reparation. We must actively encourage offenders to make amends for the crimes they have committed. ....

5.14 We need to have a consistent set of guidelines that cover all offences and should be applied whenever a sentence is passed. We must work to eradicate the wide sentencing disparity in sentencing for the same types of offences and the public's mistrust of the system that comes partly from this inconsistent sentencing.

5.15 In consultation with the judiciary, we will legislate for and establish a Sentencing Guidelines Council, chaired by the Lord Chief Justice, which will be responsible for setting guidelines for the full range of criminal offences ...

5.17 We will ask Parliament to have a role in considering and scrutinising the draft guidelines drawn up by the Council. This will ensure democratic engagement ...

5.18 The Sentencing Advisory Panel provides only the Court of Appeal with advice. It will now offer advice to the Sentencing Guidelines Council. The guidelines produced by the new Council will apply to all courts. In every individual case, the judge or magistrate will continue to make his or her own decision as to sentence, but will be required to operate within the Council's guidelines or explain why they do not apply to the case in question. The task of the Council is a complex one, but subject to legislation the Sentencing Guidelines Council will be established and begin work immediately."

Structurally, such a framework has much to commend it as a system for controlling judicial discretion and reducing sentencing disparity. However, as always, "the devil is in the detail". As already seen, the Halliday Report proposes that for each offence there should be a sentencing range, shaped by desert considerations but heavily influenced by the existence of previous convictions. Within that range the actual sentence will be determined by crime reduction considerations, in particular, risk-assessments and the availability of suitable rehabilitative programmes. Making final decisions that depend on such predictive and individualised assessments is, of course, a recipe for sentencing disparity.

## 2

# THE GENERAL PRINCIPLES OF CRIMINAL LIABILITY

## I. Introduction

The criminal law is an institution of blame and punishment. Blame is attached to the defendant's conduct and if that conduct violates the law she is punished for it (whether for retributive or deterrent, etc., reasons). But in what circumstances are we to blame someone for their conduct, and blame them to a degree sufficient to justify the imposition of punishment? And in what circumstances can someone's actions be said to have violated the law?

Generally, the law is concerned with punishing harmful actions that are committed in circumstances or in conditions in which we can fairly blame the perpetrator of the actions. This is, of course, only a general proposition. Not all acts that are criminal cause an obvious harm. With the crime of attempt, for instance, no actual harm has been caused.[1] Similarly, criminal liability is often imposed in circumstances where many feel that no blame can be attached to the actor. Thus, in crimes of strict liability a person who has acted to the best of his ability can be punished if, albeit inadvertently, he violates a statute making certain conduct criminal. The question whether such conduct, which either involves no obvious harm, or is generally perceived to involve no blameworthiness, should be punishable will be considered later in this book.

Let us return to the general proposition which can be broken down into two limbs.

**1. Harmful conduct:** Sometimes "conduct" can in itself be forbidden on the basis that it constitutes or threatens a harm. Alternatively, it is conduct that causes a harmful result that is forbidden by the criminal law. The word "conduct" is here used in its broadest sense to encompass an omission to act or even a state of affairs. The law has developed a short-hand term, *actus reus*, to describe this.

**2. Committed in conditions in which we can fairly blame the actor:** The problem here is to determine the indicators of blame. It is widely accepted that two such indicators exist:

---

[1] No injury has been sustained, no property lost etc. It is of course possible to define "harm" expansively, enabling one to conclude that there is indeed a "harm" (a "secondary harm") in all such cases. See p. 465.

(a) *Mental element.* Some would only blame those who acted with a subjective mental element. Others would blame those whose actions objectively failed to conform to a set standard. Either way, the law has developed a short-hand term, *mens rea*, to describe this.

(b) *Absence of defence.* A defendant might have committed an *actus reus* and have *mens rea* but, because of the circumstances, we might not wish to hold him liable and punish him. He might have a valid defence in that he acted, say, in self-defence or under duress. (There might be further indicators of blame. For the sake of simplicity, a discussion of these will be reserved until later in the book.)

One way of interpreting this is that the constituent ingredients of a crime are three-fold, *actus reus, mens rea* and the absence of a valid defence.[2]

There are, however, other modes of analysing the constituent elements of a crime. Glanville Williams, for instance, argued that all elements of a crime are divisible into either *actus reus* or *mens rea* and that the *actus reus* requirement includes absence of defence.[3] Others argue that *mens rea* means blameworthiness in the sense of mental element plus absence of defence.[4]

This divergence of views can be illustrated simply. The crime of murder is defined as the "unlawful killing of a human being with malice aforethought". The constituent elements of this crime can be analysed in three ways:

(1) There are three elements—the *actus reus* of killing a human being, the *mens rea* of malice aforethought, and the requirement of unlawfulness indicating the absence of any defence.

(2) The *actus reus* is unlawfully killing a human being; the requirement of unlawfulness (absence of defence) is part of the *actus reus*.[5] The *mens rea* requirement is malice aforethought.

(3) The *actus reus* is killing a human being. The *mens rea* is the element of blameworthiness which encompasses both the malice aforethought and the unlawfulness (absence of defence) requirement.

The possible importance of these different modes of analysis will be discussed later but, for the moment, the fact that there are these very different modes of analysis serves to emphasise an important point. The terms *actus reus* and *mens rea* are no more than tools that are useful in the exposition of the criminal law. Dividing crime into its constituent elements in this way should be no more than a matter of analytical convenience.[6] Whether defendants are to be convicted should depend on important principles aimed at deciding whether their conduct deserves condemnation as criminal; such questions should not be answered by reference

---

[2] Lanham, "Larsonneur Revisited" [1976] Crim.L.R.276.
[3] *Criminal Law: The General Part* (1961), p. 20; Williams, "Statutory Exceptions to Liability and the Burden of Proof" (1976) 126 New L.J. 1032 at 1034; see also *Williams (Gladstone)* (1984) 78 Cr.App.R.276.
[4] Kadish, "The Decline of Innocence" (1968) 26 C.L.J. 273 at 273–275.
[5] This claim is only plausible with regard to justificatory defences. The distinction between justificatory and excusatory defences is discussed at pp. 270–283.
[6] See, however, pp. 188–204 where judicial decisions have lost sight of this simple point and made criminal liability dependent upon a particular mode of analysing the constituent elements of a crime.

only to definitions of *actus reus* and *mens rea*. Questions of policy should not be determined by reference to definition and terminology.[7]

In *Miller*, Lord Diplock disapproved of such terminology:

> "My Lords, it would I think be conducive to clarity of analysis of the ingredients of a crime that is created by statute, as are the greater majority of criminal offences today, if we were to avoid bad Latin and instead to think and speak ... about the conduct of the accused and his state of mind at the time of that conduct, instead of speaking of *actus reus* and *mens rea*."[8]

In this chapter we have chosen to disregard Lord Diplock's command. We shall analyse crimes in terms of *actus reus*, *mens rea* and absence of defence. We do this for the simple reason that as long as one appreciates that these terms are no more than tools, they are tools that *can* usefully aid the clear exposition of the rules of criminal law. Further, they have been so much part of the criminal law vocabulary for hundreds of years, and still are, that many of the cases to be discussed in this book would be highly confusing, if not totally meaningless, without some understanding of the orthodox meaning of these terms. In later chapters, however, we shall be suggesting that it is the concept of "blame" that ought to provide one of the fundamental bases upon which criminal liability is imposed. *Mens rea* is always an important indicator of blame, but by no means the only one. But such proposals and ideas can make no sense until the concept *mens rea* (as commonly understood) has been closely examined.

In this chapter we shall consider the primary basis of criminal liability in terms of *actus reus* and *mens rea*. For the sake of clarity the discussion of the general defences has been reserved for a separate chapter.

## II. Actus Reus

### A. *Introduction*

To many people, evil thoughts, desires and intentions are as reprehensible as evil deeds and, if we had the means to detect such criminal propensities, we would be justified in punishing such persons. The law, however, is not concerned with punishing people for thinking evil thoughts or having evil intentions.[9] The law will not interfere unless there has been some conduct, some physical manifestation of the evil intention. Some crimes only require the slightest manifestation: in conspiracy, for example, all that is needed is an agreement. However, minimal as it might be, this agreement is nevertheless a physical manifestation of the evil intention; it is conduct and can form the basis of an *actus reus*.

Why does the law insist upon an *actus reus* as a prerequisite of criminal liability?

---

[7] Smith, "On *Actus Reus* and *Mens Rea*" in Glazebrook (ed.), *Reshaping the Criminal Law* (1978), pp. 95, 96, 102.

[8] [1983] A.C. 161, 175. See also Robinson, "Should the Criminal Law Abandon the *Actus Reus* and *Mens Rea* Distinction?" in Shute, Gardner and Horder (eds), *Action and Value in Criminal Law* (1993) who argues that these phrases are misleading and obscure understanding.

[9] For a view that it could be justifiable to punish evil intentions alone, see Husak, "Does Criminal Liability Require an Act?" in Duff (ed.), *Philosophy and the Criminal Law* (1998).

### Powell v State of Texas 392 US 514 (1968) (Supreme Court of the United States)

Black J.:

"The reasons for this refusal to permit conviction without proof of an act are difficult to spell out, but they are nonetheless perceived and universally expressed in our criminal law. Evidence of propensity can be considered relatively unreliable and more difficult for a defendant to rebut: the requirement of a specific act thus provides some protection against false charges. Perhaps more fundamental is the difficulty of distinguishing, in the absence of any conduct, between desires of the day-dream variety and fixed intentions that may pose a real threat to society; extending the criminal law to cover both types of desire would be unthinkable, since '[t]here can hardly be anyone who has never thought evil. When a desire is inhibited it may find expression in fantasy; but it would be absurd to condemn this natural psychological mechanism as illegal.' (Glanville Williams (1961), p. 2.)"

Further, in addition to it being morally inappropriate to punish mere intentions, there is doubt as to whether people have sufficient control over their thoughts to be held responsible for them.[10]

### A. Goldstein, "Conspiracy to Defraud the United States" (1959) 68 Yale L.J. 405 at 405–406:

"[The notion of not punishing evil intentions alone] expresses today, as it did three centuries ago, the feeling that the individual thinking evil thoughts must be protected from a state which may class him as a threat to its security. Rooted in scepticism about the ability either to know what passes through the minds of men or to predict whether antisocial behaviour will follow from antisocial thoughts, the act requirement serves a number of closely-related objectives: it seeks to assure that the evil intent of the man branded a criminal has been *expressed in a manner signifying harm to society*; that there is no longer any substantial likelihood that he will be deterred by the threat of sanction; and that there has been an identifiable occurrence so that multiple prosecution and punishment may be minimized."

As seen above, a mere agreement to commit a crime is regarded as a sufficient manifestation of evil intentions to constitute the *actus reus* of conspiracy; similarly, mere words of instruction or encouragement are sufficient to render one liable for aiding and abetting a crime. Whether these *ought* to be regarded as a sufficient manifestation of evil intentions to justify the imposition of criminal liability is a question to be considered later.

### B. *Constituent Elements of Actus Reus*

The *actus reus* of every crime is different. The *actus reus* of theft is "the appropriation of property belonging to another"[11] and the *actus reus* of rape is "sexual intercourse with a person (whether vaginal or anal) who at the time of the intercourse does not consent to it".[12] With all crimes the *actus reus* is the external element of the crime—the objective requirement necessary to constitute the offence. Crimes can be divided into two categories and the essential elements of an *actus reus* depend on which of these two species of crime one is dealing with. First, there are crimes, known as conduct crimes, where the only external element

---

[10] Robinson, *above*, n.8 at 191.
[11] Theft Act 1968, s.1.
[12] Sexual Offences Act 1956, s.1(1), as amended.

required is the prohibited conduct itself. Thus the *actus reus* of the offence of dangerous driving is simply "driving a mechanically propelled vehicle dangerously on a road or other public place".[13] No harm, no consequence of that dangerous driving need be established. Secondly, there are other crimes, known as result crimes, where the external elements of the offence require proof that the conduct caused a prohibited result or consequence. Thus the *actus reus* of the offence of causing death by dangerous driving is "causing the death of another person by driving a mechanically propelled vehicle dangerously on a road or other public place".[14] Here it is necessary to establish that the same dangerous driving caused the forbidden consequence specified in the *actus reus*, namely, the death of another person.

Conduct crimes provide a good illustration of the criminal law punishing offenders who have caused no obvious harm. However, it can be argued that in the above example there is a harm, namely causing danger to other road users. If this is indeed a harm, it is clearly a lesser harm than actually killing another road-user. Should this difference be reflected by differing penalties for the two offences? Or should one proceed on the basis that as the forbidden conduct is the same in both offences the result (death) could be entirely fortuitous, thus not reflecting upon the driver's responsibility and consequently the two offences should carry the same penalty? This is an issue to which we shall return later in the book.

From the above it can be seen that both conduct crimes and result crimes have two elements in common: (1) Both require an "act" or conduct, *i.e.* dangerous driving; (2) Both require that the act be carried out in defined *legally relevant circumstances*, *i.e.* on a road or other public place. If the same act of driving the car occurred in a private field, the *actus reus* of the offence would not be made out. It is only dangerous driving *on a road or other public place* that is prohibited. Similarly, the *actus reus* of theft requires that the property "belong to another". In the absence of this circumstance, for example, if the property is owned by the would-be thief, the *actus reus* of the crime is not made out. Just as *mens rea* may or may not be required for the act and for the consequences in result crimes, liability may similarly depend upon whether the accused has the required mental state in relation to the legally defined relevant circumstances. The *actus reus* of rape, for example, requires the act of intercourse to be committed in the circumstance of the victim not consenting. In *Morgan*[15] the House of Lords ruled that if the defendant honestly believes that the victim is consenting to the act of intercourse, he cannot be liable. In such a case there would be no *mens rea* in relation to a vital element of the *actus reus*.

With result crimes it is necessary to establish an additional third element, namely, that the act *caused* the prohibited consequence, for example, *caused* the death of another person. If poison is put into the drink of another person with intent to kill that person who subsequently dies with the drink found beside them, liability for murder cannot exist unless it was the poison that caused the death. If the deceased had died of a heart attack, the only possible charge would be attempted murder.[16]

[13] Road Traffic Act 1988, s.2, as amended.
[14] *ibid.*, s.1.
[15] [1976] A.C. 182.
[16] *White* [1910] 2 K.B. 124; See also *Hensler* (1870) 11 Cox C.C. 570. Causation is discussed in Chap. 4.

Putting these elements together it is common to find an *actus reus* described as:

(1) an "act";
(2) committed in legally relevant circumstances; and
(3) (for result crimes) causing the prohibited result.

The issue of causation is thus treated as part of the *actus reus* requirement.

One final point needs to be made by way of introduction. Whilst many crimes are so defined that the defendant may be convicted on the basis of the *actus reus* alone without need for proof of *mens rea* (crimes of so-called strict liability), the converse is not true. There must always be an *actus reus* for liability to be at issue at all. If, for example, in an alleged case of theft, the property already belongs to the person taking it, then despite any intention to steal, the actions cannot amount to the crime of theft. Similarly, where a defendant persuades another to purchase his car by representing that it is free from encumbrances, believing he is lying, he cannot be found guilty of obtaining property by deception if it turns out that it was in fact free from encumbrances.[17] The defendant has unwittingly told the truth; the car was his to sell and his dishonest state of mind counts for nothing. The fact that a defendant believes he has committed an *actus reus* is not enough. The *actus reus* must be proved objectively to exist.

We are now in a position to examine in greater detail the requirement of an act.

## C. *The Act must be Voluntary*

The distinction between an act and any accompanying mental element required by the law for the imposition of liability has already been drawn. Thus, if we define murder as killing when there is an intention to kill or cause serious harm we can readily accept the acquittal of someone whose claim that it was all a dreadful accident is accepted by the courts. But the circumstances of the accident might lead us to very different conclusions about the basis of the acquittal. If the defendant claims that the accident lay in thinking the weapon was an imitation one rather than a real one then this translates into a denial of *mens rea*; the defendant did not have the necessary intention to kill or cause serious harm. But if the defendant claims to have shot the victim as a result of stumbling down some icy steps—the "accident" here appears to be of a more fundamental kind. The act itself seems defective. Even had we been describing situations where no accompanying mental state was required for liability (so-called crimes of strict liability), we would question a decision to punish such a defendant. The difficulty lies in trying to pin-point the defect. The law has generally shied away from identifying why it is inappropriate to punish in such circumstances beyond affirming that acts must be "voluntary". Instead, it has been left to academic lawyers and philosophers to explore what this means.

### John Austin, Lectures on Jurisprudence (5th ed.) (XVIII–XIX) Vol. I, 411–415:

"Certain movements of our bodies follow invariably and immediately our wishes and desires for those same movements. Provided, that is, that the bodily organ be sane, and the

---

[17] *Deller* (1952) 36 Cr.App.R.184. This case is commonly discussed in relation to *Dadson* (1850) 2 Den. 35.

desired movement be not prevented by any outward obstacle. ... These antecedent wishes and these consequent movements, are human volitions and acts (strictly and properly so-called). ... And as these are the only volitions, so are the bodily movements by which they are immediately followed the only acts or actions (properly so-called). It will be admitted on the mere statement, that the only objects which can be called acts are consequences of volitions. A voluntary movement of my body, or a movement which follows a volition, is an act. The *involuntary* movements which (for example) are the consequences of certain diseases, are *not* acts."

We are asked, therefore, to divide the human act into two elements: the desire for the muscular movement and the movement itself. In the case of the defendant who kills another as a result of falling down some steps, there would be no accountability for the harm done because of the absence of a willed or desired muscular movement. However, this breakdown of human behaviour has been fiercely criticised. Hart points out that described in these terms it cannot apply to omissions (where to speak of the necessity for a willed failure to move one's muscles is not only clumsy but an inaccurate reflection of the law).[18] Furthermore, such an analysis does not reflect the reality of our movements.

### H. L. A. Hart, Punishment and Responsibility (1968), pp. 101–102:

"[A] desire to contract our muscles is a very rare occurrence: there are no doubt *some* special occasions when it would be quite right to say that what we are doing is contracting our muscles, and that we have a desire to do this. An example of this is what we may do under instruction in a gymnasium. The instructor says 'lift your right hand and contract the muscles of the upper arm.' If we succeed in doing this (and it is not so easy) it would be quite appropriate to say we desired to and did contract our muscles. ... [But] when we shut a door, or when we hit someone, or when we fire a gun at a bird, these things are done without any previous thought of the muscular movements involved and without any desire to contract the muscles. ... The simple but important truth is that when we deliberate and think about actions, we do so not in terms of muscular movements but in the ordinary terminology of actions."

### Glanville Williams, The Mental Element in Crime (1965), pp. 17–18:

"[O]ne cannot by introspection, identify a conscious exercise of will previous to movement. Indeed, one cannot always find an exercise of will at all. Many acts are performed unthinkingly; not only a reflex like dropping a hot poker but much of the routine of life, such as shaving, eating, walking. We seem to switch on an 'automatic pilot' for many of the familiar tasks we perform; yet we are undoubtedly acting. Even when we make a conscious decision and act to carry it out, the act is something different from the preceding deliberation."

In this statement Williams, in accordance with other English commentators, tacitly upholds the distinction drawn in English law between *mens rea* and *actus reus*. But other critics of the willed movement principle do not. Welzel,[19] a German

---

[18] Hart, *Punishment and Responsibility* (1968), p. 100: "It is surely absurd even to attempt to fit omissions into such a picture of voluntary or involuntary conduct ... [because] in the case of omissions no muscular movement or contraction need occur ... [Such a theory] would have very unwelcome consequences for legal responsibility: for the only omissions which would then be culpable would be deliberate omissions. We could then only punish those who failed to stop at traffic lights if they deliberately shot the lights."

[19] For a discussion of Welzel's view, see Fletcher, *Rethinking Criminal Law* (1978), pp. 434–439. See also the discussion of dualism, pp. 213–216.

philosopher, is convinced that the causal theory upon which this principle, and much of the criminal law rests, is misconceived. He does not accept that there are a set of desires which *cause* the movements to occur. Instead, he favours a view of acting that looks to the actor's goal. The distinction between a bodily movement and an "act" lies not in any preceding will but in the purpose of the actor—what he was seeking to achieve. According to this philosophical stance, not only is it wrong to divide up the act, as Austin and supporters do, but to divide any mental state from its act would be equally invalid. The two, he would claim, are inextricably linked and are incapable of separate analysis. We shall return to this view later in our discussion of *mens rea*.

More representative of the standard approach is the view of Williams that:

"Notwithstanding these difficulties of definition everyone understands the proposition that an act is something more than bodily movement—for bodily movement might occur in tripping and falling, which would not be described as an act." [20]

And, we could add, ought not to render the "actor" answerable for the movements. Broad consensus does seem to exist that it would be unjust to punish in these situations, despite the harm done. Those who feel that the willed movement analysis is unhelpful argue that what is missing is an ability to control one's actions. [21] In no real sense are the actions "his". [22] For most commentators, this absence of "the ordinary link between mind and behaviour", [23] is more fundamental than that involved when, for example, duress is pleaded. The defendant who shoots another because there is a gun pointed at his partner's head accepts that he has done it, but pleads that he lacked any real opportunity to do otherwise. The defendant who shoots another as a result of falling down steps denies authorship. The law describes this latter case as one involving "automatism" and the defendant escapes criminal liability.

However, it has been argued that "physical or literal involuntariness, rather than being regarded as a distinct exculpatory factor, is best analysed as representing a spectrum or continuum of potentially excusing conditions running from total incapacitation or involuntariness, as in sleep-walking or muscular spasm, to cases say of (concussion-induced) confusion. These conditions are all reducible to an absence of fault and therefore, ... share the same underlying rationale of other excusing conditions such as duress, provocation and diminished responsibility." [24]

---

[20] *The Mental Element in Crime* (1965), p. 18.

[21] The lack of control may arise through classical automatism, such as unconsciousness or in other ways. In *Burns v Bidder* [1966] 3 All E.R. 29, the defendant was acquitted of failing to accord precedence to a pedestrian when his brakes failed. In *Neal v Reynolds* [1966] Crim.L.R.393, the defendant was convicted of the same crime which had occurred as a result of a pedestrian unforeseeably stepping out into the road. Can the control test reconcile these two different results?

[22] This is not, as Packer says, to "be read as plunging into the deep waters of free will vs determinism ... The law is not affirming that some conduct is the product of the free exercise of conscious volition; it is excluding, in a crude kind of way, conduct that in any view is not." (*The Limits of the Criminal Sanction* (1969), p. 76).

[23] Ashworth, *Principles of Criminal Law* (3rd ed., 1999), p. 101.

[24] Smith and Wilson, "Impaired Voluntariness and Criminal Responsiblity: Reworking Hart's Theory of Excuses—The English Judicial Response" (1993) 13 O.J.L.S. 69 at 74.

In short, a person whose actions are classified as involuntary can be afforded a type of defence called an *excuse* and can be exempted from criminal liability. The essence of an excuse is that the actor is blameless. If it were the actor's own fault that the involuntary conduct occurred, the law will not excuse that conduct. If the reason the person fell down the stairs was that he was extremely drunk we are entitled to say that carrying a loaded gun in that state of intoxication is culpable conduct and, accordingly, the resultant death or injury ought not to be excused.

It follows that the precise nature and effect of a defence of involuntariness or automatism depends on a variety of circumstances surrounding the involuntary conduct and, accordingly, detailed consideration of the various excuses relating to involuntariness is best left to Chapter 3 where excuses and other defences are considered.

### D. *Status Offences*

The requirement that there must be an act and that this involves voluntary human conduct has caused particular problems in the context of what are known as "status offences" or "situational liability".

A crime can be defined in such a manner that no conduct is required, but the crime is committed when a certain state of affairs exists or the defendant is in a certain condition or is of a particular status. The following notorious case is a classic example of this.

### R. v Larsonneur (1933) 24 Cr.App.R.74 (Court of Criminal Appeal)

A French subject was permitted to land in the United Kingdom subject to certain conditions endorsed on her passport. These conditions were subsequently varied by a condition requiring her to depart from the United Kingdom not later than a certain date. On that date she went to the Irish Free State. An order for her deportation from the Irish Free State was made by the executive authorities of that country, and she was subsequently brought back to Holyhead in the custody of the Irish Free State police, who there handed her over to the police of the United Kingdom, by whom she was detained. She was convicted on a charge that she "being an alien to whom leave to land in the United Kingdom has been refused was found in the United Kingdom," contrary to Articles 1(3)(g) and 18(1)(b) of the Aliens Order, 1920, as amended. She appealed against her conviction.

Marston Garsia, for the appellant:
"For an alien to whom leave to land has been refused to commit an offence under Art. 18(1)(b) of the Order three elements are necessary:
  i. the alien must land in the United Kingdom;
  ii. such landing must be contrary to Art. 1 of the Order;
  iii. the alien, having so landed in the United Kingdom, must be found therein.
Therefore the mere fact of being found in the United Kingdom after the time limited for her departure therefrom had expired was not in itself an offence, unless it could be proved in addition that she landed in the United Kingdom in contravention of Art. 1. Here the evidence showed that she had not landed at all, but that she had been landed by a superior force over which she had no control. Having thus come to be found in the United Kingdom, she was not guilty of any offence under Art. 18(1)(b)."

J. F. Eastwood, for the Crown:
"The whole point is whether the appellant was found within the United Kingdom; how she got here makes no difference at all. The word 'found' was used deliberately in the section so that if any alien who had no right to be here is here an offence is committed. By reason of

Art. 1(4) of the Order she falls within the same category as one who had originally been prohibited from landing."

Hewart, L.C.J.:

"The fact is, as the evidence shows, that the appellant is an alien. She has a French passport, which bears this statement under the date March 14, 1933, 'Leave to land granted at Folkstone this day on condition that the holder does not enter any employment, paid or unpaid, while in the United Kingdom,' but on March 22 that condition was varied and one finds these words: 'The condition attached to the grant of leave to land is hereby varied so as to require departure from the United Kingdom not later than March 22, 1933.' Then follows the signature of an Under-Secretary of State. In fact, the appellant went to the Irish Free State and afterwards, in circumstances which are perfectly immaterial, so far as this appeal is concerned, came back to Holyhead. She was at Holyhead on April 21, 1933, a date after the day limited by the condition on her passport.

In these circumstances, it seems to be quite clear that Art. 1(4) of the Aliens Order, 1920 ... applies. The article is in the following terms: 'An immigration officer, in accordance with general or special directions of the Secretary of State, may, by general order or notice or otherwise, attach such conditions as he may think fit to the grant of leave to land, and the Secretary of State may at any time vary such conditions in such manner as he thinks fit, and the alien shall comply with the conditions so attached or varied. An alien who fails to comply with any conditions so attached or varied, and an alien who is found in the United Kingdom at any time after the expiration of the period limited by any such conditions, shall for the purposes of this Order be deemed to be an alien to whom leave to land has been refused.'

The appellant was, therefore, on April 21, 1933, in the position in which she would have been if she had been prohibited from landing by the Secretary of State and, that being so, there is no reason to interfere with the finding of the jury. She was found here and was, therefore, deemed to be in the class of persons whose landing had been prohibited by the Secretary of State, by reason of the fact that she had violated the condition on her passport. The appeal, therefore, is dismissed and the recommendation for deportation remains."

**Appeal dismissed**

What is objectionable about convictions for status offences such as that in *Larsonneur* is that the defendant's actions are involuntary. There is nothing objectionable about the offence *per se* in *Larsonneur* and had Larsonneur brought herself voluntarily into the UK her conviction would have aroused no comment. It was the involuntary nature of her forced entry that provoked the controversy. In short, status offences are not objectionable if the defendant has control over the status. It would be wrong to have an offence of having a common cold but, as Husak argues, it could be justifiable to have an offence of having a beard, as this is a process over which one has control.[25] Under section 11(1) of the Terrorism Act 2000 it is a criminal offence to belong to a proscribed organisation such as the I.R.A. This provision is not aimed merely at prohibiting the "act" of joining the I.R.A.; it applies equally to those who joined before the date of commencement of the Act. This looks as though it is punishing persons for the mere status of being members of the I.R.A. However, section 11(2) provides a defence if one became a member before the organisation was proscribed and if one has not taken part in any of its activities while the organisation is proscribed. Thus, what is being punished in reality is a status over which there is control—evidenced by action (*i.e.* either

[25] Husak, *Philosophy of Criminal Law* (1987), p. 102. Similarly, while it would be contrary to principle to make it an offence to be H.I.V. positive, it could be permissible to make it an offence to have sexual intercourse while H.I.V. positive.

joining the I.R.A. after the date of commencement of the Act or, if one joined before then, taking part in its activities).

### Douglas Husak, "Does Criminal Liability Require An Act" in Antony Duff (ed.), Philosophy and the Criminal Law (1998), pp.75, 77–79:

"[P]ersons typically have *control* over their choices, and persons are responsible and deserve punishment only for those states of affairs over which they exercise control. I submit that the absence of control, and not the absence of action, establishes the outer boundary of deserved punishment and responsibility. I claim, in other words, that what I will call the *control requirement* should be substituted for the act requirement as a necessary condition of criminal liability and deserved punishment. ... The core idea behind the control requirement is that a person lacks responsibility for those states of affairs he or she is unable to prevent from taking place or obtaining. If the state of affairs for which he is responsible is an action, he must have been able not to perform that action. If the state of affairs is a status, he must have been able not to have that status. .... I propose to explicate control in terms of what it is reasonable to expect of persons. A person lacks control over a state of affairs and neither is nor ought to be criminally liable for it if it is unreasonable to expect him or her to have prevented that state of affairs from obtaining. ...

[T]he issue of whether an agent has control over a state of affairs admits of degrees ... and one person may have more control over the same kind of state of affairs than another person. ... [L]ess control is needed before responsibility is imposed for an especially bad state of affairs than for a not-so-bad state of affairs."

Following this reasoning, status offences are only unjustifiable if the person had no control over their status. However, as seen earlier when examining involuntary conduct, the general requirement of voluntariness can be dispensed with if it was the defendant's own fault that her actions were involuntary, for example, if she chose to get very drunk. So, too, liability for a status offence becomes justifiable if it was the defendant's own fault she got into that status or was in that situation. It has even been argued that the decision in *Larsonneur* was justifiable because it was her own fault that she was in the situation of being an illegal immigrant.

### David Lanham, "Larsonneur Revisited" [1976] Crim.L.R.276 at 278–280:

"[The defence of physical compulsion is] not an absolute defence. It may, at least with regard to certain types of crime, be defeated if the defendant has been at fault in bringing about the situation which has exposed him to compulsion. .... It is the thesis of this paper that Miss Larsonneur was probably the author of her own misfortune and that the fact that at the last moment she was acting under compulsion was properly regarded as affording her no defence. .... Miss Larsonneur's recorded confession is worth quoting: ...

'A short time ago my sister Mrs McCorry came to see me in France and invited me to visit her in London. On my arrival my sister introduced me to a Frenchman named René, who was living with her, and also introduced me to an Englishman named Harold Brown. René and Brown said they would arrange a marriage for me with an Englishman and they later introduced me to a man named George Drayton. We tried to get married at Guildford but the police stopped the marriage. They took my French passport from me but returned it the same day, telling me that the Home Office had ordered me to leave the country at once. Brown and René told me not to worry as they were going to get legal advice.

Next day I went to Ireland with Brown. We travelled as Mr & Mrs Wiggins. Brown said he had seen a solicitor, and that if I went to Ireland I would be in order. I naturally believed him. René and Drayton also travelled to Ireland, but not with us. There were difficulties in Ireland about marrying and eventually the police told me to leave Ireland by April 17. I wanted to leave Ireland at once, but René and Brown told me that everything would be alright (*sic.*), and that they were trying to find an Irish priest willing to marry us. I think it terrible that I should be the only one to suffer.' "

It is difficult to see that this justifies the decision in *Larsonneur*. What is meant by the defendant being "at fault"? Surely the fault must be related in some way to the offence charged. In our earlier example of the drunken person carrying a gun and falling down the stairs, it is legitimate to assert that the ensuing results were the fault of the defendant. The fault of getting drunk while in possession of a gun and any offence committed with that gun are clearly connected. Trying to go through a marriage of convenience (not an unlawful act) is not connected in the same way to the offence committed by Larsonneur.

### Alan Norrie, Crime, Reason and History: A Critical Introduction to Criminal Law (2nd ed., 2001), p. 119:

"The fault to be discovered in [*Larsonneur*] is only tangentially related to the offence with which the accused is charged, but if a broader moral fault is to be admitted in the intoxication cases, there is no reason why it should not be employed in other cases too. The problem with this line of argument is that once the game of opening up the time frame to past culpable acts is started, there is in principle no end. One can continue going back into the accused's history to find the original voluntary act that set the rest of his conduct in motion and blame him for that, but then the technical concept of actus reus becomes a fraud, a mere bagatelle, too obviously introduced or excluded to suit the perceptions of right and wrong of the judiciary."

### Winzar v Chief Constable of Kent, *The Times*, March 28, 1983, Co/1111/82 (Lexis) (Queen's Bench Divisional Court)

The defendant was brought on a stretcher to hospital. The doctor discovered that he was merely drunk and asked him to leave. He was later seen slumped on a seat in the corridor and so the police were called. They removed him to the roadway, "formed the opinion he was drunk", and placed him in their car parked nearby. He was charged with being found drunk in a highway and convicted.

Robert Goff L.J.:
"Does the fact that the Appellant was only momentarily on the highway and not there of his own volition, prevent his conviction of the offence of being found drunk in a highway? ...
In my judgment, looking at the purpose of this particular offence, it is designed ... to deal with the nuisance which can be caused by persons who are drunk in a public place. This kind of offence is caused quite simply when a person is found drunk in a public place or in a highway. .... [A]n example ... illustrates how sensible that conclusion is. Suppose a person was found as being drunk in a restaurant or a place of that kind and was asked to leave. If he was asked to leave, he would walk out of the door of the restaurant and would be in a public place or in a highway of his own volition. He would be there of his own volition because he had responded to a request. However, if a man in a restaurant made a thorough nuisance of himself, was asked to leave, objected and was ejected, in those circumstances, he would not be in a public place of his own volition because he would have been put there either by a gentleman on the door of the restaurant, or by a police officer, who might have been called to deal with the man in question. It would be nonsense if one were to say that the man who responded to the plea to leave could be said to be found drunk in a public place or in a highway, whereas the man who had been compelled to leave could not.
This leads me to the conclusion that a person is 'found to be drunk in a public place or in a highway,' within the meaning of those words as used in the section, when he is perceived to

be drunk in a public place. It is enough for the commission of the offence if (1) a person is in a public place or a highway, (2) he is drunk, and (3) in those circumstances he is perceived to be there and to be drunk. Once those criteria have been fulfilled, he is liable to be convicted of the offence of being found drunk in a highway. Finally, I turn to the question: Does it matter if the Appellant was only momentarily in the highway? In my judgment, it makes no difference. A man may be perceived to be drunk in the highway for five minutes, for one minute or for ten seconds. However short the period of time, if a man is perceived to be drunk in a highway, he is guilty of the offence under the section. Of course, if the period of time is very short, the penalty imposed may be minimal; indeed in such circumstances a police officer, using his discretion, may think it unnecessary to charge the man. The point is simply that the offence is committed if a person is perceived to be drunk in a public place or in the highway. Once that criterion is fulfilled, then the offence is committed."

**Conviction affirmed**

Again it could be argued that it was Winzar's "fault" he was in that situation. The report does not make it clear how he got to be taken to the hospital. Presumably he must have been found in some public place, or have summoned medical assistance when he was only drunk and not in need of such attention.

A different approach to a similar problem was adopted by the Supreme Court of Alabama.

### Martin v State, 31 Ala. App. 334, 17 So. 2d 427 (1944) (Alabama Court of Appeals)

Simpson J.:
"Appellant was convicted of being drunk on a public highway, and appeals. Officers of the law arrested him at his home and took him onto the highway where he allegedly committed the proscribed acts, viz. manifested a drunken condition by using loud and profane language. The pertinent provisions of our statute are:
'Any person who, while intoxicated or drunk, appears in any public place where one or more persons are present, . . . and manifests a drunken condition by boisterous or indecent conduct, or loud and profane discourse, shall, on conviction be fined.' (Code 1940, Title 14, Section 120.)
Under the plain terms of this statute a voluntary appearance is presupposed. The rule has been declared, and we think it sound, that an accusation of drunkenness in a designated public place cannot be established by proof that the accused, while in an intoxicated condition, was involuntarily and forcibly carried to that place by the arresting officer.
Conviction of appellant was contrary to this announced principle and in our view, erroneous. It appears that no legal conviction can be sustained under the evidence, so, consonant with the prevailing rule, the judgment of the trial court is reversed and one here rendered discharging appellant."[26]

Can this case be reconciled with *Larsonneur* and *Winzar* on the basis that Martin was arrested in his own home and therefore could not in any way be blamed for his resultant situation?

### Herbert L. Packer, The Limits of the Criminal Sanction (1969), pp. 78–79:

"There is a strong tradition in Anglo-American law of treating certain kinds of status, such as vagrancy, as criminal. To be a person 'without visible means of living who has the physical ability to work, and who does not seek employment, nor labor when employment is

---

[26] See also *O'Sullivan v Fisher* [1954] S.A.S.R. 33 (S. Aust.); *Achterdam* (1911) E.D.L. 336 (S.A.).

offered him' (in the words of a now-repealed California statute) may perhaps be characterized as engaging in a kind of omissive conduct: but common sense rebels at the use of the word 'conduct' to describe a condition that does not 'take place' but rather exists without reference to discrete points of time. It must be acknowledged that when the law makes the status of vagrancy or the status of 'being a common drunkard' (that phrase redolent of Elizabethan England) a criminal offense, it is departing from the restriction to conduct. Laws of this sort are in fact very much on the way out. Courts are giving them a helpful push on the road to oblivion. . . .

Offenses of status can best be understood as embodiments of the preventive ideal at a time when the criminal law offered no alternatives. Their demise is the result, whatever the rubric under which it is accomplished, of the development of alternatives that have permitted us the previously unavailable luxury of recognizing that such offenses are anomalies in the criminal law. There has always been pressure to rid the community of people who are perceived as dangerous, threatening, or merely odd. That pressure, until fairly recently, has had to find its outlet almost entirely in the criminal law. But the extraordinary expansion of the concept of illness, and especially of mental illness, that has taken place during the last century has furnished us another set of outlets. Now we can afford to insist on the doctrinal purity from which crimes of status represent so marked a lapse."

The European Convention on Human Rights, Article 3, provides a right not to be subjected to "inhuman or degrading treatment". This is similar to the Eighth Amendment to the United States Constitution which prohibits cruel and unusual punishment.

### Powell v State of Texas 392 US 514 (1968) (Supreme Court of the United States)

Marshall J.:

"[The appellant was convicted in a Texas court of 'being found in a state of intoxication in any public place' and fined \$20. His defence was that he was a chronic alcoholic, and that his public drunkenness was therefore involuntary. The trial court ruled that chronic alcoholism was no defence.]

Appellant, however, seeks to come within the application of the Cruel and Unusual Punishment Clause announced in *Robinson v State of California*, 370 US 660, which involved a state statute making it a crime to 'be addicted to the use of narcotics.' This Court held there that 'a state law which imprisons a person thus afflicted [with narcotic addiction] as a criminal, even though he has never touched any narcotic drug within the State or been guilty of any irregular behaviour there, inflicts a cruel and unusual punishment . . .' *ibid.* at 667, and 82 S. Ct., at 1420–1421.

On its face the present case does not fall within that holding, since appellant was convicted, not for being a chronic alcoholic but for being in public while drunk on a particular occasion. The State of Texas thus has not sought to punish a mere status as California did in *Robinson*; nor has it attempted to regulate appellant's behaviour in the privacy of his own home. Rather, it has imposed upon appellant a criminal sanction for public behaviour which may create substantial health and safety hazards, both for appellant and for members of the general public, and which offends the moral and esthetic sensibilities of a large segment of the community. This seems a far cry from convicting one for being an addict, being a chronic alcoholic, being 'mentally ill, or a leper. . . .' *ibid.* at 666, and 82 S.Ct., at 1420."

Fortas J. dissenting:

"*Robinson* stands upon a principle which, despite its sublety, must be simply stated and respectfully applied because it is the foundation of individual liberty and the cornerstone of the relations between a civilized state and its citizens: Criminal penalties may not be inflicted upon a person for being in a condition he is powerless to change. In all probability, Robinson at some time before his conviction elected to take narcotics. But the crime as defined did not punish this conduct. The statute imposed a penalty for the offense of 'addiction'—a condition which Robinson could not control. Once Robinson had become an addict, he was utterly powerless to avoid criminal guilt. He was powerless to choose not to violate the law.

In the present case, appellant is charged with a crime composed of two elements—being intoxicated and being found in a public place while in that condition. The crime, so defined, differs from that in *Robinson*. The statute covers more than a mere status. But the essential constitutional defect here is the same as in *Robinson*, for in both cases the particular defendant was accused of being in a condition which he had no capacity to change or avoid. The trial judge sitting as trier of fact found upon the medical and other relevant testimony, that Powell is a 'chronic alcoholic.' He defined appellant's 'chronic alcoholism' as 'a disease which destroys the afflicted person's will power to resist the constant, excessive consumption of alcohol.' He also found that 'a chronic alcoholic does not appear in public by his own volition but under a compulsion symptomatic of the disease of chronic alcoholism.' I read these findings to mean that appellant was powerless to avoid drinking; that having taken his first drink, he had 'an uncontrollable compulsion to drink' to the point of intoxication; and that, once intoxicated, he could not prevent himself from appearing in public places."

**Affirmed**

The majority in *Powell* are drawing a distinction between punishment for a status and punishment for the manifestations of that status. Presumably they would hold it to be wrong to punish someone for having a common cold, but permissible to punish him for sneezing. Is this a valid distinction? This seems extraordinary and quite inconsistent with the view that it is the question of control and voluntariness that ought to be decisive in these cases. The dissenting judgment, on the other hand, does recognise this and focuses on the voluntariness of the defendant's actions. On this basis the question is simply whether Larsonneur, Winzar, Martin and Powell had control over their status or, even if they did not, whether it was their own fault that they allowed themselves to get into that status. It is only this latter approach that is likely to be regarded as compatible with the ECHR.

## E. *Omissions*

Most crimes are committed by positive action and thus the requirement of an "act" will usually be met by a positive act. But in certain circumstances a passive failure to act may be deemed to constitute the requisite "act". A failure to act may result in the imposition of criminal liability in two situations.

1. In conduct crimes the failure to act may itself, without more, constitute the crime. This usually occurs in statutory crimes which are specifically defined in terms of an omission to act, for example, failing to provide for a child in one's care[27] or failing to provide a specimen of breath under the breathaliser legislation.[28]

2. In result crimes the failure to act may contribute towards the harm specified in the offence and may thus, in certain circumstances, be deemed the requisite "act" for the purposes of the offence. This will only be so if the actor is under a duty to act. For example, a father would be under a duty to rescue his child drowning in a shallow pool; his failure to act would constitute the requisite "act" of the crime of

[27] Children and Young Persons Act 1933, s.1(2)(a).
[28] Road Traffic Act 1988, s.6(4).

homicide. However, a stranger could with impunity watch the same child drowning; there is no general duty to act in English law. As Lord Diplock stated in *Miller*:

> "The conduct of the parabolical priest and Levite on the road to Jericho may have been indeed deplorable, but English law has not so far developed to the stage of treating it as criminal."[29]

Thus criminal liability in these cases is completely dependent upon the existence of a duty to act. It is to this, and other related problems, that we now turn.

## 1. Duty to Act

It is not entirely certain when a duty to act will arise[30] but it is generally thought that the following situations cover the present English law:

### (i) *Where there is a special relationship*

The most commonly cited example of a duty to act is where there is a close personal relationship. Parents are under a duty to aid their small children; husbands and wives are under a duty to aid each other.[31]

In *Downes*[32] a parent, being a member of a religious sect called the Peculiar People, who believed in prayer rather than in medicine, failed to call a doctor for his sick child who died. Downes was convicted of manslaughter.[33]

It used to be asserted that the reason for the imposition of a duty of care in such cases was that the blood or marriage relationship was so strong as to generate a legal duty to preserve life. In the United States decision of *People v Beardsley*,[34] for instance, it was held that a man owes no duty to act to aid his "week-end mistress", as distinguished from his wife. However, such a rationale can no longer be accepted. The true reason for the existence of a duty in such cases must be the interdependence that springs from shared family life or close communal living.[35] In such a situation one comes to rely on the other members of the family and it is this reliance and expectation of assistance, if necessary, that generates the duty to act, rather than any blood tie. Thus in *Shepherd*[36] it was held that no duty to act is owed

---

[29] [1983] 2 A.C. 161, 175.

[30] The first draft of the Criminal Code Bill specified the circumstances in which one would be under a duty to act (cl. 20(2)). These detailed proposals were dropped from the revised Draft Criminal Code; they are matters that must remain for the development of the common law (Law Com. No. 77, Vol. 2, para. 7.12). The Draft Criminal Law Bill 1993, cl. 19, follows this latter approach (Law Com. No. 218, *Legislating the Criminal Code: Offences against the Person and General Principles*, Cm.2370 (1993)).

[31] *Smith* [1979] Crim.L.R.251.

[32] (1875) 13 Cox C.C. 111.

[33] In this case and in *Shepherd* (*below*, n.36) it was indicated that the duty was imposed by statute (Poor Law Amendment Act 1868, s.37—making it an offence if any parent wilfully neglected to provide (*inter alia*) medical aid for his child, being in his custody under the age of 14 years, whereby the health of such child had been or was likely to be seriously injured). In *Downes*, Coleridge C.J. deliberately left open the question whether there would be a duty to act in the absence of such a statutory duty. While many of the earlier cases were decided on this basis, it is now generally accepted that there is a *common law* duty to act in such cases but there is little express authority on this point.

[34] 150 Mich. 206; 113 N.W. 1128; 13 L.R.A.(N.S.) 1020; 121 Am.St.Rep. 617; 13 Ann.Cas. 39 (1907). This case was cited with approval in England in *Sinclair*, unreported, 1998 WL 1044437.

[35] Fletcher, *Rethinking Criminal Law* (1978), p. 613.

[36] (1862) 9 Cox C.C. 123.

by a parent to her 18 year old "entirely emancipated" daughter. In such a case there would not be the same expectation of assistance as with a dependent child. Thus it is suggested that separated spouses owe no duty to each other, and with other relatives it is not a question of blood relationship but the assumption of responsibility that generates the reliance and expectation of assistance and hence the legal duty to act. In *Stone and Dobinson* Lane L.J. did allude to the fact that the victim "was a blood relation of the appellant" but it is clear from his ensuing comments that the true basis of the duty to act was the fact that the appellant had taken the victim into his home and assumed responsibility for her.[37]

(ii) *Where responsibility has been assumed*

If the defendant assumes responsibility towards another or voluntarily assumes a duty towards another, then he or she becomes under a legal duty to act.

### R. v Instan [1893] 1 Q.B. 450 (Court for Crown Cases Reserved)

The defendant lived with her 73-year-old aunt. The aunt, who had been healthy until shortly before her death, developed gangrene in her leg. During the last twelve days of her life she could not fend for herself, move about or summon help. Only the defendant knew of her state and gave her aunt no food and did not seek medical assistance. The defendant was charged with manslaughter and convicted.

Lord Coleridge C.J.:

"We are all of the opinion that this conviction must be affirmed. It would not be correct to say that every moral obligation involves a legal duty; but every legal duty is founded on a moral obligation. A legal common law duty is nothing else than the enforcing by law of that which is a moral obligation without legal enforcement. There can be no question in this case that it was the clear duty of the prisoner to impart to the deceased so much as was necessary to sustain life of the food which she from time to time took in, and which was paid for by the deceased's own money for the purpose of the maintenance of herself and the prisoner; it was only through the instrumentality of the prisoner that the deceased could get the food. There was, therefore, a common law duty imposed upon the prisoner which she did not discharge.

Nor can there be any question that the failure of the prisoner to discharge her legal duty at least accelerated the death of the deceased, if it did not actually cause it. There is no case directly in point; but it would be a slur upon and a discredit to the administration of justice in this country if there were any doubt as to the legal principle, or as to the present case being within it. The prisoner was under a moral obligation to the deceased from which arose a legal duty towards her; that legal duty the prisoner has wilfully and deliberately left unperformed, with the consequence that there has been an acceleration of the death of the deceased owing to the non-performance of that legal duty. It is unnecessary to say more than that upon the evidence this conviction was most properly arrived at."

**Conviction affirmed**

In *Stone and Dobinson*[38] the defendants took the anorexic and infirm sister of

---

[37] [1977] 1 Q.B. 354.
[38] [1977] 1 Q.B. 354. An extract from this case can be found at pp. 112–114.

one of them into their home. She failed to look after herself or feed herself properly and eventually died. The defendants were held to have assumed a responsibility by taking her into their home and so were under a legal duty either to summon help or to care for her.

## R. v Sinclair, unreported, WL 1044437 (Court of Appeal, Criminal Division)

Sinclair and his friend, the deceased, visited a flat owned by Johnson in order to buy methadone from another man there. Needles and syringes were available in the flat. Sinclair and the deceased each injected themselves with the methadone at 2.30pm. The deceased became unconscious. Sinclair remained with him for much the afternoon and night. Both he and Johnson took limited and ineffectual remedial action such as pouring water over the deceased (and Johnson administered a saline solution) but an ambulance was only called at 6.30am the following morning. The deceased was certified dead on arrival at hospital. Sinclair and Johnson were convicted of manslaughter and appealed.

Rose L.J.:
"[Counsel for the defendant] referred to a decision of the New South Wales Supreme Court in *Tak Tak* 1988 NSWLR 226 which emphasised, as a pre-condition for a legal duty of care to arise, the need for the disabled person to be secluded by the defendant to prevent others from affording aid ...
[T]he trial judge ... [should have] focused his attention on the need, before the matter was considered by the jury, for him to consider what facts were capable of giving rise to the existence of a duty of care. So far as Johnson is concerned, there is no English authority in which a duty of care has been held to arise, over a period of hours, on the part of a medically unqualified stranger. *Beardsley* and *Tak Tak* are both persuasive authorities pointing away from the existence of any such duty, although we do not accept in the light of *Stone and Dobinson*, that the concept of seclusion is, in English law, a necessary prerequisite to the existence of a legal duty of care. But Johnson did not know the deceased. His only connection with him was that he had come to his house and there taken methadone and remained until he died. Others were coming and going in the meantime. The fact that Johnson had prepared and administered to the deceased saline solutions does not, as it seems to us, demonstrate on his part a voluntary assumption of a legal duty of care rather than a desultory attempt to be of assistance. In our judgment, the facts in relation to Johnson were not capable of giving rise to a legal duty of care ...
Sinclair is in a different position. The evidence was that he was a close friend of the deceased for many years and the two had lived together almost as brothers. It was Sinclair who paid for and supplied the deceased with the first dose of methadone and helped him to obtain the second dose. He knew that the deceased was not an addict. He remained with the deceased throughout the period of his unconsciousness and, for a substantial period, was the only person with him. In the light of this evidence, there was in our judgment material on which the jury properly directed, could have found that Sinclair owed the deceased a legal duty of care.
[The appeal was, however, allowed on the ground that a fuller direction on causation should have been given: as to whether acceleration of the moment of death was other than minimal.]"

**Appeal allowed**

## Geoffrey Mead, "Contracting into Crime: A Theory of Criminal Omissions" (1991) 11 O.J.L.S. 147 at 168:

"The presence of an undertaking often gives rise to other reasons for the presence of a duty ... If D has given an undertaking he may be in the best position to avert the harm. I shall refer to this as the 'Best Position' argument. This may be for one or more of the following reasons.

First, he is more likely to be aware that a person may be in a position of peril and in need of assistance. He will know of the vulnerability of the victim in a way that others may not. Second, he may be more capable of carrying out the required task than will a third party. We might assume that, in most cases where D undertakes to do a particular thing, he feels he has the ability to do it, whereas a third party, who has not given such an undertaking will not necessarily possess the required skills to do what is needed in order to avert danger to V. The third point is that if other people are aware of the undertaking they might feel it unproductive for them to get involved as well. They might reasonably think that they would simply get in the way and hinder the proper completion of the task in question."

The real problem in these cases is one of determining the circumstances in which a person can be said to have undertaken a duty towards another. A ship captain would be liable for failing to pick up a seaman, or a passenger, who had fallen overboard.[39] Depending on the circumstances of employment, an employer could be liable for failing to aid his endangered employee. And as LaFave and Scott assert:

"If two mountain climbers, climbing together, are off by themselves on a mountainside, and one falls into a crevass, it would seem that the nature of their joint enterprise, involving a relationship of mutual reliance, ought to impose a duty upon the one mountaineer to extricate his imperilled colleague. So also if two people, though not closely related, live together under one roof, one may have a duty to act to aid the other who becomes helpless."[40]

Following this, in *Beardsley* if the parties had lived together or embarked on a dangerous joint enterprise together, as opposed to an adulterous weekend, the defendant would probably have been held to have assumed a duty to act. Again, as suggested before, it ought to be a question of whether, because of the relationship or the circumstances or both together, the parties rely on assistance from each other. *Sinclair* is explicable on this basis. While Johnson was effectively in as good a position as Sinclair to render aid (following Mead's Best Position argument), it was the closeness of the relationship between Sinclair and the deceased and their embarking on the enterprise of procuring drugs together that would have led the deceased to rely on assistance from Sinclair. Although at his house, Johnson was a stranger. There would not have been the same reliance on, and expectation of, assistance from him.

### (iii) *Where a duty has been assumed by contract*

A duty to assist others may arise out of a contract. A lifeguard employed at a swimming pool to ensure the safety of swimmers cannot sit idly by while a swimmer is drowning.

In *Pittwood*[41] a railway gate-keeper, who was employed to keep a gate shut whenever a train was passing, was held liable for manslaughter when he forgot to shut the gate with the result that a train hit a hay-cart crossing the railway line and killed a man.

Again, the basis of the duty in these cases is not so much the contract itself, but rather the fact that the contract is evidence of an assumption of responsibility creating an expectation in the mind of others that the defendant will act. The public

---

[39] *US v Knowles*, 26 Fed.Cas. 800 (N.D. Cal. 1864).
[40] *Criminal Law* (2nd ed., 1986), p. 204.
[41] (1902) 19 T.L.R. 37.

expect railway gate-keepers to act and close the gates of railway crossings when trains are approaching. It is their reliance on this fact that creates the duty to act. The fact that the railway gate-keeper has contracted to perform these duties is merely strong evidence that he has assumed these responsibilities. It is submitted that the position would be no different if, during a strike, a volunteer offered (without any contract) to perform these duties. The fact that he had undertaken this responsibility would cause the public to rely upon his performing these tasks. On this basis, this whole category (along with the first category above) simply becomes a species of the second category, namely the assumption of responsibility.

### (iv) *Where a duty is imposed by statute*

A failure to act may in itself, without more, constitute a criminal offence. Failing to provide for a child in one's care is a criminal offence contrary to section 1(1) of the Children and Young Persons Act 1933, even if this failure to act causes no ulterior harm. This same statutory duty to act may, if breached, constitute the necessary "act" for the purpose of an ulterior offence if further harm results from the breach of duty.

In *Lowe*[42] a man neglected his nine-week-old daughter by failing to call for a doctor when she became ill. He was charged with neglecting the child contrary to section 1(1) of the Children and Young Persons Act 1933 and with manslaughter. One way in which manslaughter can be committed is by committing an unlawful act that is dangerous and causes death (constructive manslaughter). It was held that the requirement of an unlawful act was not satisfied by an omission. Phillimore L.J stated:

> "We think there is a clear distinction between an act of omission and an act of commission likely to cause harm. Whatever may be the position in regard to the latter it does not follow that the same is true of the former. In other words if I strike a child in a manner likely to cause harm it is right that if the child dies I may be charged with manslaughter. If, however, I omit to do something with the result that it suffers injury to health which results in its death, we think that a charge of manslaughter should not be an inevitable consequence, even if the omission is deliberate."

This case provides an interesting illustration of the reluctance of the English courts to impose criminal liability for omissions to act. Phillimore L.J. is suggesting that there needs to be a higher degree of blameworthiness for crimes committed through omission than for crimes where there has been a positive act of commission and so an omission will not suffice for constructive manslaughter because this only requires a relatively low degree of culpability. This approach is only justifiable if positive acts are regarded as "worse" than omissions.[43]

However, if the crime requires a higher degree of blameworthiness, an omission where there is a duty imposed by statute will suffice. For example, manslaughter can also be committed by gross negligence. This route to conviction could have been employed in *Lowe* if this higher level of culpability could have been

---

[42] [1973] 1 Q.B. 702. An extract from this case can be found at p. 659.
[43] See pp. 110–111.

established on the facts. In such a case, liability would have been based on the common law duty and not on an unlawful act.

Sections 2–7 of the Health and Safety at Work Act 1974 impose duties on employers to operate a safe working environment. A specific penalty is provided for breach of this duty. If a worker were to die as a result of a breach of this duty, it is doubtful whether the employer would be liable for constructive manslaughter because, as the Law Commission has noted, Parliament, in creating this duty, has provided a specific and limited punishment for its breach.[44] However, if a higher degree of blameworthiness (gross negligence) can be attributed to the employer, this breach of a statutory duty would not be treated any differently to breach of a common law duty. On this basis individual employers, and even a few companies, have been held liable for manslaughter by gross negligence.

### (v) *Where the defendant has created a dangerous situation*

### R. v Miller [1983] 2 A.C. 161 (House of Lords)

One night while squatting in someone else's house, the appellant lit a cigarette and then lay down on a mattress in one of the rooms. He fell asleep before he had finished smoking the cigarette and it dropped onto the mattress. Later he woke up and saw that the mattress was smouldering. He did nothing about it; he merely moved to another room and went to sleep again. The house caught fire. The appellant was rescued and subsequently charged with arson, contrary to s.1(1) and (3) of the Criminal Damage Act 1971. At this trial he submitted that there was no case to go to the jury because his omission to put out the fire, which he had started accidentally, could not in the circumstances amount to a sufficient *actus reus*. The judge ruled that once he had discovered the mattress was smouldering the appellant had been under a duty to act. The appellant was convicted. The Court of Appeal upheld his conviction on the ground that his whole course of conduct constituted a continuous *actus reus*. On appeal, to the House of Lords:

Lord Diplock:
"The first question is a pure question of causation.... If ... the question ... to: 'Did a physical act of the accused start the fire which spread and damaged property belonging to another?,' is answered 'Yes,' as it was by the jury in the instant case, then for the purpose of the further questions the answers to which are determinative of his guilt of the offence of arson, the conduct of the accused, throughout the period from immediately before the moment of ignition to the completion of the damage to the property by the fire, is relevant; so is his state of mind throughout the period.

Since arson is a result-crime the period may be considerable, and during it the conduct of the accused that is causative of the result may consist not only of his doing physical acts which cause the fire to start or spread but also of his failing to take measures that lie within his power to counteract the danger that he has himself created. And if his conduct, active or passive, varies in the course of the period, so may his state of mind at the time of each piece of conduct. If at the time of any particular piece of conduct by the accused that is causative of the result, the state of mind that actuates his conduct falls within the description of one or other of the states of mind that are made a necessary ingredient of the offence of arson by s.1(1) of the Criminal Damage Act 1971 (*i.e.* intending to damage property belonging to another or being reckless whether such property would be damaged) I know of no principle of English criminal law that would prevent his being guilty of the offence created by that subsection. Likewise I see no rational ground for excluding from conduct capable of giving rise to criminal liability, conduct which consists of failing to take measures that lie within

---

[44] Law Commission Consultation Paper No. 122, *Legislating the Criminal Code: Offences against the Person and General Principles* (1992), para. 6.19.

one's power to counteract a danger that one has oneself created, if at the time of such conduct one's state of mind is such as constitutes a necessary ingredient of the offence....

I cannot see any good reason why, so far as liability under criminal law is concerned, it should matter at what point of time before the resultant damage is complete a person becomes aware that he has done a physical act which, whether or not he appreciated that it would at the time when he did it, does in fact create a risk that property of another will be damaged; provided that, at the moment of awareness, it lies within his power to take steps, either himself or by calling for the assistance of the fire brigade if this be necessary, to prevent or minimise the damage to the property at risk.

Let me take first the case of the person who has thrown away a lighted cigarette expecting it to go out harmlessly, but later becomes aware that, although he did not intend it to do so, it has, in the event, caused some inflammable material to smoulder and that unless the smouldering is extinguished promptly, an act that the person who dropped the cigarette could perform without danger to himself or difficulty, the inflammable material will be likely to burst into flames and damage some other person's property. The person who dropped the cigarette deliberately refrains from doing anything to extinguish the smouldering. His reason for so refraining is that he intends that the risk which his own act had originally created, though it was only subsequently that he became aware of this, should fructify in actual damage to that other person's property; and what he so intends, in fact occurs. There can be no sensible reason why he should not be guilty of arson. If he would be guilty of arson, having appreciated the risk of damage at the very moment of dropping the lighted cigarette, it would be quite irrational that he should *not* be guilty if he first appreciated the risk at some later point in time but when it was still possible for him to take steps to prevent or minimise the damage....

The recorder, in his lucid summing up to the jury ... told them that the accused having by his own act started a fire in the mattress which, when he became aware of its existence, presented an obvious risk of damaging the house, became under a duty to take some action to put it out. The Court of Appeal upheld the conviction, but its ratio decidendi appears to be somewhat different from that of the recorder. As I understand the judgment, in effect it treats the whole course of conduct of the accused, from the moment at which he fell asleep and dropped the cigarette on to the mattress until the time the damage to the house by fire was complete, as a continuous act of the accused, and holds that it is sufficient to constitute the statutory offence of arson if at any stage in that course of conduct the state of mind of the accused, when he fails to try to prevent or minimise the damage which will result from his initial act, although it lies within his power to do so, is that of being reckless whether property belonging to another would be damaged.

My Lords, these alternative ways of analysing the legal theory that justifies [the] decision ... provoked academic controversy. Each theory has distinguished support. Professor J. C. Smith espouses the 'duty theory' (see [1982] Crim.L.R.526 at 528); Professor Glanville Williams ... now prefers that of the continuous act (see [1982] Crim.L.R.773). When applied to cases where a person has unknowingly done an act which sets in train events that, when he becomes aware of them, present an obvious risk that property belonging to another will be damaged, both theories lead to an identical result; and since what your Lordships are concerned with is to give guidance to trial judges in their task of summing up to juries, I would for this purpose adopt the duty theory as being the easier to explain to a jury; though I would commend the use of the word 'responsibility,' rather than 'duty' which is more appropriate to civil than to criminal law, since it suggests an obligation owed to another person, *i.e.* the person to whom the endangered property belongs, whereas a criminal statute defines combinations of conduct and state of mind which render a person liable to punishment by the state itself....

[A] suitable direction to the jury would be: that the accused is guilty of the offence under s.1(1) of the Criminal Damage Act 1971 if, when he does become aware that the events in question have happened as a result of his own act, he does not try to prevent or reduce the risk of damage by his own efforts or if necessary by sending for help from the fire brigade, and the reason why he does not is either because he has not given any thought to the possibility of there being any such risk or because, having recognised that there was some risk involved, he has decided not to try to prevent or reduce it."

Appeal dismissed

Lord Diplock's reasoning is to be welcomed. We all bear a responsibility for our actions, even if those actions are unintentional. They are *our* actions. Where others are placed in danger from these actions, they expect us to "do something". They would rely on us to provide reasonable assistance, even if that only amounts to summoning help. Further, "the person who creates a danger may be more aware than others of the existence of the danger, and ought not feel a reluctance to intervene that may be felt by others".[45] Accordingly, we should be under a duty to act when we become aware of the danger. On this basis it is irrelevant whether the defendant's initial actions involved any fault. Thus if, as in *Fagan v M.P.C.*,[46] the defendant accidentally parks his car with a wheel resting on a policeman's foot, we would surely be justified in saying that the defendant had assumed a responsibility (to get off the foot); his initial action would raise an expectation on the part of the police officer that he would act. He is under a duty to act.

It is, however, difficult to determine the precise circumstances in which a duty can be said to arise because of the creation of a "dangerous situation".

### R. v Khan and Khan [1998] Crim.L.R.830; Lawtel No. 9705543X3 (Court of Appeal, Criminal Division)

The defendants, who were drug dealers, sold and supplied a quantity of heroin to a 15–year-old girl who was inexperienced as a heroin user and who snorted an excessive quantity through her nose and swallowed it. She became obviously very ill and in need of medical attention. The appellants left her alone in a flat where she died. They were convicted of murder and appealed.

Swinton Thomas L.J.:
"[The trial judge] did not make any ruling as to whether the facts were capable of giving rise to the relevant duty and he did not direct the jury in relation to that issue. To extend the duty to summon medical assistance to a drug dealer who supplies heroin to a person who subsequently dies on the facts of this case would undoubtedly enlarge the class of person to whom, on previous authority, such a duty may be owed. It may be correct to hold that such a duty does arise. However, before that situation can occur, the Judge must first make a ruling as to whether the facts as proved are capable of giving rise to such a duty and, if he answers that question in the affirmative, then to give the jury an appropriate direction which would enable them to answer the question whether on the facts as found by them there was such a duty in the case being tried by them."

Appeal allowed

This decision is not helpful. In *Miller*, Lord Diplock is clear in his model direction that if the defendant started the events in question he *is* (as a matter of law) under a duty to act. The suggestion in *Khan and Khan* is that it is ultimately for the jury to determine (as a matter of fact) whether there was such a duty. This cannot be

---

[45] Meade, "Contracting into Crime: A Theory of Criminal Omissions" (1991) 11 O.J.L.S. 147 at 171.
[46] [1969] 1 Q.B. 439. The actual reasoning adopted in this case was somewhat different to the proposal here: see p. 182.

correct. Whether a duty exists is a matter of law. It is simply not open for a jury to hold, for example, that a stranger is under a duty to rescue an imperilled child; it is clear that she is not. Accordingly, it should be for the courts to lay down legal principles as to whether, on facts such as those in *Khan and Khan*, the defendant is under a duty or not.

## 2. Performance of Duty

Assuming the defendant is under a duty to act, how much danger, inconvenience or expense must he or she undergo in order to fulfil that duty and avoid criminal liability?

### United States v Knowles, 26 Fed.Cas. 801 (No. 15, 540) (N.D. Cal. 1864) (District Court, Northern District California)

The defendant was captain of the American ship *Charger* when a seaman, Swainson, accidentally fell into the sea and drowned. The defendant was charged with manslaughter on the ground that death had been caused by his wilful omission to rescue Swainson when it was his duty to do so.

Field, Circuit Justice (charging jury):
"Now, in the case of a person falling overboard from a ship at sea, whether a passenger or seaman, when he is not killed by the fall, there is no question as to the duty of the commander. He is bound, both by law and by contract, to do everything consistent with the safety of the ship and of the passengers and crew, necessary to rescue the person overboard, and for that purpose to stop the vessel, lower the boats, and throw to him such buoys or other articles which can be readily obtained, that may serve to support him in the water until he is reached by the boats and saved. No matter what delay in the voyage may be occasioned, or what expense to the owners may be incurred, nothing will excuse the commander for any omission to take these steps to save the person overboard, provided they can be taken with a due regard to the safety of the ship and others remaining on board. Subject to this condition, every person at sea, whether passenger or seaman, has a right to all reasonable efforts of the commander of the vessel for his rescue, in case he should by accident fall or be thrown overboard. Any neglect to make such efforts would be criminal, and if followed by the loss of the person overboard, when by them he might have been saved, the commander would be guilty of manslaughter, and might be indicted and punished for that offense.

In the present case it is not pretended that any efforts were made by the defendant to save Swainson. . . . The positions taken in the defense of the accused are: (1) That Swainson was killed by his fall from the yard; (2) that if not killed, it would have been impossible to save him in the existing condition of the sea and weather; (3) that to have attempted to save him would have endangered the safety of the ship and the lives of the crew. If in your judgment either of these positions is sustained by the evidence the defendant is entitled to an acquittal. . . .

If you are satisfied that the fall was not immediately fatal, the next inquiry will be whether Swainson could have been saved by any reasonable efforts of the captain, in the then condition of the sea and weather. That the wind was high there can be no doubt. The vessel was going at the time, at the rate of twelve knots an hour; it had averaged, for several hours, ten knots an hour. A wind capable of propelling a vessel at that speed would, in a few hours, create a strong sea. To stop the ship, change its course, go back to the position where the seaman fell overboard, and lower the boats, would have required a good deal of time, according to the testimony of several witnesses. In the meanwhile, the man overboard must have drifted a good way from the spot where he fell. To these considerations, you will add the probable shock and consequent exhaustion which Swainson must have experienced from the fall, even supposing that he was not immediately killed.

It is not sufficient for you to believe that possibly he might have been saved. To find the defendant guilty, you must come to the conclusion that he would, beyond a reasonable doubt, have been saved if proper efforts to save him had been reasonably made, and that his death was the consequence of the defendant's negligence in this respect. Beside the condition of the weather and sea, you must also take into consideration the character of the boats attached to the ship. According to testimony of the mate, they were small and unfit for a rough sea.

During the trial, much evidence was offered as to the character of the defendant as a skilful and able officer and as a humane man. The act charged is one of gross inhumanity; it is that of allowing a sailor falling overboard, whilst at work upon the ship, to perish, without an effort to save him, when by proper efforts, promptly made, he could have been saved. If there be any doubt as to the conduct of the defendant, his past life and character should have some consideration with you.

With these views, I leave the case with you. It is one of much interest, but I do not think that, under the instruction given, you will have any difficulty in arriving at a just conclusion."

**The jury returned a verdict of acquittal**

## Vehicle Inspectorate v Nuttall [1999] 1 W.L.R. 629 (House of Lords)

The defendant, an owner of a coach business, did not examine charts produced by tachographs installed in his vehicles and was convicted of permitting his drivers to contravene various requirements of section 96(11A) of the Transport Act 1968.

Lord Hobhouse of Woodborough:
"This offence of permitting is a crime of omission which arises from the duty to act and involves the failure to perform that duty. What actual conduct will amount to the offence of permitting will be a question of fact depending on the circumstances of the particular case. For example, an employer whose employees are always, to his knowledge, back in the yard within the required time need not carry out the same checks as one whose employees are sent out on longer journeys which will necessitate the taking of breaks if the Regulations are not to be infringed. Such an employer must certainly carry out some checks. ... The test of reasonableness must be applied objectively having regard to the relevant circumstances which will vary from case to case. But it is not a question of the employer doing what he thinks is reasonable. He must do whatever is involved in taking the reasonable steps to prevent breaches. It is an objective not a subjective criterion. If he does not perform his duty, he has committed the *actus reus* of the offence ...

The employer is under a positive duty to take the steps which an employer can reasonably take to detect and prevent breaches. He is not required to do the impossible; but he is not at liberty to omit to take those reasonable steps."

## 3. Distinguishing Positive Acts from Omissions

The distinction between positive acts and omissions is crucial as criminal liability will only be imposed for the latter if a duty to act can be established. But it is not always clear whether one is dealing with a positive act or an omission. For example, if a road worker digs a deep hole in the road and then forgets to place a cover over it with the result that a child falls in the hole and is killed, has the death been caused by the positive act of digging the hole or the omission to cover the hole?

Katz has suggested that the test for distinguishing an act from an omission should be as follows: "if the defendant did not exist, would the harmful outcome in question still have occurred in the way it did?"[47] On this test the road worker is clearly acting as his existence is critical to the causing of death. On the other hand, there is an omission where the stranger fails to rescue the drowning child because

---

[47] Katz, *Bad Acts and Guilty Minds* (1987), p. 143.

the child would still have died even if the stranger had not existed. In *Environmental Agency v Empress Car Co. (Abertillery) Ltd*[48] a company maintained a diesel oil tank on its premises. An outlet from the tank, governed by a tap, had no lock. A vandal opened the tap causing pollution to a river. The House of Lords held that "maintaining a tank of diesel is doing something" and therefore amounted to a positive act. This is consistent with Katz's theory. If the company had not existed, the pollution would never have occurred.

### 4. Omissions and Causation

Where a mother fails to rescue her drowning child, how can her inactivity be said to cause the death of the child? Hogan has written:

"[T]here is no way you can *cause* an event by doing nothing ... to prevent it. If grandma's skirts are ignited by her careless proximity to the gas oven, the delinquent grandson cannot be said to have killed her by his failure to dowse her ... To say to the child, 'You have killed your grandmother' would simply be untrue."[49]

This view cannot be tenable. When we examine causation we shall see that many actions could potentially be classed as "causes" of consequences. When the child drowns in the pool with the mother watching and doing nothing, we could say that the causes of the child's death were the following: that the child was in the park and was taken near the pool, that the child fell in the pool, that there was sufficient water in the pool for him to drown, that he could not swim, that his lungs filled with water, or that his mother did not rescue him when she could easily have done so. Hart and Honoré, in the leading work on causation, argue that in selecting a cause from a list such as this, one will count as causes those things or events that are a deviation from normal or required behaviour: "when man made normal conditions are established, deviation from them will be regarded as exceptional and so rank as the cause of harm."[50] In our list there are two exceptional occurrences: the child fell in the pool and the mother failed to rescue him. Both are deviations from what might be expected and can thus be held to be causes of the death of the child.

### Arthur Leavens, "A Causation Approach to Criminal Omissions" (1988) 76 Cal. L.Rev. 547, 572–575:

"[I]t seems at first inappropriate to apply commonsense causation analysis to an individual's failure to engage in particular conduct. If one focuses solely on the circumstances of an omission at the time directly preceding the harm, the omission often appears not to have affected the at rest state of affairs. For example, a person sitting in the park while a nearby flower dies from lack of water is usually not considered to have caused the plant's demise, even if a full watercan sits nearby ...

The difficulty in conceptualizing an omission as a causal force is that omissions do not seem to fit within the parameters of the physical cause and effect model. In the physical paradigm, there is a direct and identifiable chain of events through which the actor can readily be seen as intervening and changing what existed before. In cases of omission,

---

[48] [1999] 2 A.C. 22.
[49] "Omissions and the Duty Myth" in Smith (ed.), *Criminal Law: Essays in Honour of J. C. Smith* (1986), pp. 85–86.
[50] Hart and Honoré, *Causation in the Law* (2nd ed., 1985), p. 37.

however, the actor does not physically alter the status quo, but rather appears simply to permit the preexisting state of affairs to continue. Without direct physical involvement in the causal process leading to a particular result, an omitter seems no more causally responsible for the result than anyone else . . .

Such a view of causation is flawed because its inquiry is too limited. It depends on a definition of the status quo as the existing physical state of affairs at the precise time of the omission, much as if we took a picture of the scene at the moment before the omission and then compared it to a similar picture taken immediately thereafter, searching for a change in circumstances physically attributable to the omissive conduct. Our everyday notions of causation, however, are not so limited because we understand that the status quo encompasses more than the physical state of affairs at a given time. Indeed, in everyday usage the status quo is taken to include expected patterns of conduct, including actions designed to avert certain unwanted results. When, for example, a driver parks a car on a steep hill, it is normal to set the parking brake and put the car in gear. If the driver forgets to do so and the car subsequently rolls down the hill, smashing into another car, we would say that the failure to park properly was a departure from the status quo. This failure, not the visibly steep hill or the predicate act of pulling the car to the curb, was the cause of the collision.

Once we realize that a particular undesirable state of affairs can be avoided by taking certain precautions, we usually incorporate these precautions into what we see as the normal or at rest state of affairs. A failure to engage in the preventive conduct in these cases can thus be seen as an intervention that disturbs the status quo. When such a failure to act is a necessary condition (a 'but for' cause) of a particular harm, then that failure fairly can be said to cause that harm. In the above example, the driver's failure to park the car in a proper manner caused the accident as surely as if he had actually driven his car into the other . . .

[W]e do expect certain persons to engage in particular types of preventive conduct as a matter of routine. Because of this expectation, we perceive any failure of those persons to take prescribed actions as a departure from normality. While we do not see the bystander's failure to water the flower as the cause of its withering away, we take a different view of such a failure by the park's gardener. We expect that the gardener will take reasonable steps to prevent the flower's demise, that is, his preventive conduct represents normality. A departure from that status quo—his failure to water—is thus more than a necessary condition of the flower's death: it causes that result every bit as much as the act of an intruder pulling the plant from its soil.

Of course, society's expectation of particular preventive conduct could be described as merely another formulation of 'duty.'

A 'duty' sufficient to support criminal sanctions must be founded on both an empirically valid expectation that persons in similar circuumstances will act to prevent a harm—the probability aspect of normality—and also a deeply ingrained common understanding that society relies on that individual to prevent the harm—the normative aspect of normality. Thus parents have a 'duty' to prevent harm to their children because empirically, almost all parents act this way, and normatively, our society would consider it reprehensible if they did not. It is this combination of deviance—departing from a pattern of regular performance— and reprehensibility—being blameworthy—that makes us conclude that failure to act caused the harm."

Following this reasoning, it is only those who are under a duty to act, according to the rules examined above, that can be said to cause a result through their failure to act. This conclusion has important implications in the next section where we consider there should be a general duty to act.

### 5. A General Duty to Act?

It is often asserted that liability for omissions ought not to be restricted to those cases where there is a legal duty to act, as currently defined. The person who sees a strange child drowning in a shallow pool of water and neglects to rescue him when she could have easily done so with no danger to herself, has killed that child as surely as if she had held the child's head under the water and ought to be punished to the same extent. If one of the objects of the criminal law and punishment is to stimulate socially approved conduct then the imposition of criminal liability in such cases would encourage people to act in situations such as these.

## Andrew Ashworth, "The Scope of Liability for Omissions" (1989) 105 L.Q.R. 424 at 430–432:

"Individuals tend to place a high value on interpersonal contacts, relationships, mutual support and the fulfilment of obligations, and a society which values collective goals and collective goods may therefore provide a wider range of worthwhile opportunities for individual development ... The counter-argument to the conventional view is thus that a duty to co-operate with or to assist others should not be ruled out *ab initio* by an asocial and falsely restricted view of individual autonomy ...

Individuals need others, or the actions of others, for a wide variety of tasks which assist each one of us to maximise the pursuit of our personal goals. A community or society may be regarded as a network of relationships which support one another by direct and indirect means ...

It follows that there is a good case for encouraging co-operation at the minimal level of the duty to assist persons in peril, so long as the assistance does not endanger the person rendering it ...

The foundation of the argument is that a level of social co-operation and social responsibility is both good and necessary for the realisation of individual autonomy. Each member of society is valued intrinsically, and the value of one citizen's life is generally greater than the value of another citizen's temporary freedom. Thus it is the element of emergency which heightens the social responsibility in 'rescue' cases, and which focuses other peoples vital interests into a 'deliberative priority,' and it is immediacy to me that generates my obligation. The concepts of immediacy and the opportunity of help (usually because of physical nearness) can thus be used to generate, and to limit the scope of, the duty of assistance to those in peril."

## Samuel Freeman, "Criminal Liability and the Duty to Aid the Distressed" (1994) 142 University of Pennsylvania Law Review 1455 at 1489:

"Given ... the significant fact that each of us is about as likely to benefit from this duty as to be inconvenienced by it, the political argument for the legalization of a duty to aid the distressed is that it promotes a common good, namely the safety and security of all persons in society. Since each person is sufficiently likely to benefit from this legal duty at some crucial point in their lifetime, it is a collectively rational legal constraint."

Feinberg argues that any person in peril becomes one's neighbour for the purposes of the moral exhortation "love thy neighbour" and is therefore owed a duty:

"[I]n certain basic respects the 'special relationship duties' of neighbors in the strict sense find parallels in the moral relationships that exist between any pair of human beings whose life paths happen to cross in a time of crisis for one. When it comes to *aiding the imperiled*, all people who happen to find themselves in a position to help—all who have by chance wandered into the vicinity, or 'portable neighborhood,' of the imperiled party—are his 'neighbors,' with reciprocal dependencies, expectations, duties, and claims."[51]

---

[51] *Harm to Others* (1984), p. 133.

## Graham Hughes, "Criminal Omissions" (1958) 67 Yale L.J. 590 at 626, 634:

"But a view of moral responsibility is surely outmoded which imposes liability on the father who does not warn his child of the precipice before him, but not on a stranger who neglects to warn the child.... The law often lags a half century or so behind public mores, but the spectacle cannot be lightly entertained in a field of this importance. The duty to take active steps to save others, and a liability for homicide in the absence of such action, could well be based on the defendant's clear recognition of the victim's peril plus his failure to take steps which might reasonably be taken without risk to himself to warn or protect the victim....

Conventional criticisms of the imposition of a duty to rescue are usually based on objections to compelling one man to serve another, to creating a fear of prosecution which might cause citizens to interfere officiously in the affairs of others, and to the feasibility of imposing liability on a crowd of spectators all of whom had knowledge of the peril but were too selfish to intervene. These objections, however, do not seem to have much merit. To the first, the reply may be made that the evil of interfering with individual liberty by compelling assistance is much outweighed by the good of preserving human life. The second is a speculation which would be difficult to support. The third point appears to pose a real difficulty, but it is no different from a situation which commonly occurs in offenses of commission. In a riot, for example, it is difficult if not impossible to bring all the participants to book, but this has never been considered an obstacle to trial and punishment of those who can be reached. If a crowd of spectators stands by and watches a child drown in shallow water, nothing seems objectionable in trying and punishing all who can be tracked down and cannot show a reasonable excuse. To think that such an example of selfish group inertia could exist in our society is distressing, but, if it did, there would be every reason for invoking the criminal law against it.

The time is ripe for Anglo-American systems to translate into legislative fact the modern consciousness of interdependence. Surely, it is not in socialist countries alone that the duty of a citizen to help his fellows in these situations of extreme peril can be recognized."

There are many arguments as to why English law should not introduce a general duty to act. The central argument relates to individual liberty and autonomy. Our freedom should only be restricted insofar as it is necessary to prevent persons causing harm to others. Further, "the criminal law should recognise an individual's choices rather than allowing liability to be governed by chance, and the obligation to assist someone in peril may be thrust upon a chance passer-by, who may well prefer not to become involved at all".[52] It is further argued that the imperilled stranger has no *right* to be rescued and therefore the defendant is under no *duty* to rescue.[53]

These arguments are fortified by the claim that it is basic to our morality that it is worse to, say, shoot or drown a victim than merely to look the other way when he is drowning. As Fletcher puts it: "The difference between killing and letting die, between creating a risk, and tolerating a risk, is one of the principles that sets the framework for assessing moral responsibility."[54] This point is underlined by

[52] Ashworth, "The Scope of Criminal Liability for Omissions" (1989) 105 L.Q.R. 424 at 425–426.
[53] Murphy, "Blackmail: A Preliminary Inquiry" The Monist 63, No. 2 (1980) n.6; Stell, "Dueling and the Right to Life" 90 (1979) Ethics 7 at 12 cites John Stuart Mill's distinction between perfect and imperfect obligations: "Duties of perfect obligation are those duties in virtue of which a correlative right resides in some person or persons; duties of imperfect obligation are those moral obligations which do not give birth to any right." (*Utilitarianism* (1957), p. 61).
[54] *Rethinking Criminal Law* (1978), p. 601.

Moore: "Drowning [a child] makes the world a worse place, whereas not preventing its drowning only fails to improve the world."[55]

### Leo Katz, Bad Acts and Guilty Minds (1987), p. 145:

"[T]he consequences of an omission are generally less certain than those of an act. Holding somebody's head under water is more likely to kill him than not throwing him a life vest.

But there is a deeper, moral, reason why killing-by-omission offends us less than killing-by-commission. Compare these two situations. (1) Bert will die unless Berta gives him one of her kidneys. Berta is ailing and doesn't want to risk an operation. So she lets Bert die. (2) Berta will die unless Bert gives her his only kidney. She kills Bert and takes his kidney. In both 1 and 2 Berta brings about Bert's death to assure her own survival; in 1 she does it by an omission, in 2 by an act. Why are we less offended by her conduct in 1 than 2? Because in 1 she simply holds on to her own kidney, whereas in 2 she appropriates somebody else's kidney. We value personal autonomy and Berta's conduct in 2 offends against that value, while her conduct in 1 doesn't. Our sentiments about every other case of omission can be understood by analogizing it to these two cases. The person who fails to prevent harm that would occur even if he didn't exist simply fails to give away something he owns. The person who brings about harm that wouldn't occur if he didn't exist takes away something owned by someone else. Both persons may be callous, but only the latter offends our sense of personal autonomy."

Husak suggests the reason why it is worse to kill than to let die is because the defendant has more control in the former than in the latter situation: "persons generally exercise far less control over what happens as a result of their omission than as a result of their positive actions. Control over a consequence is typically exercised by positive action."[56]

English law has endorsed this view that it is worse to kill than to "let die." In *Airedale NHS Trust v Bland* the House of Lords ruled that in certain circumstances it was lawful for doctors to let a patient die but it was illegal actively to bring a patient's life to an end: "So to act is to cross the Rubicon which runs between on the one hand the care of the living patient and on the other hand euthanasia—actively causing his death to avoid or to end his suffering. Euthanasia is not lawful at common law."[57]

### Earl Winkler, "Is the Killing/Letting-Die Distinction Normatively Neutral?" Dialogue XXX (1991) 309 at 313:

"There may still be general, extrinsic reasons that condemn active killing while permitting letting die ... Consider the wholly germane claim that to permit any practice of active killing within medical contexts would be extremely unwise because of the risk of social disutility in the long run, through inevitable abuse, misapplication, further decline in general respect for human life and so forth ... On general consequentialist grounds it is reasonable to think that society will be benefitted by absolutely minimizing legitimate exceptions to a prohibition against killing. Therefore, concerning the issue of euthanasia, whenever appropriate humanitarian goals could be achieved equally by passive rather than active means a rule-utilitarian perspective will favour the passive measures. This reasoning alone will preserve the moral relevance of the killing/letting die distinction."

---

[55] *Act and Crime: The Philosophy of Action and Its Implications for Criminal Law* (1993), p. 59.
[56] *Philosophy of Criminal Law* (1987), p. 100. Husak advocates replacing the *actus reus* requirement in criminal law generally with a "control principle".
[57] [1993] A.C. 789 at 865.

Additionally, there are many objections of a more practical nature to any idea of introducing a general duty to act. If a large crowd watches someone drown, would they all be liable? How much help would need be given? After dragging a drowning person from the sea, would one be under a duty to provide mouth-to-mouth resuscitation (irrespective of risk of disease) and then drive the rescued person to the nearest hospital if necessary? How much danger would the rescuer be expected to risk? What if the rescuer's efforts exacerbated the situation and worsened the plight of the imperilled person? Might not such a law be counterproductive in that fear of being forced to intervene might keep people away from places where they might be called upon to help?

A final objection to any attempt to introduce a general duty to act is that it will not usually be possible to establish causation in situations other than those where at present there is a duty to act.

### R. v Stone and Dobinson [1977] 1 Q.B. 354 (Court of Appeal, Criminal Division)

The facts appear from the judgment of Geoffrey Lane L.J.

Geoffrey Lane L.J.:
"[The two appellants were convicted of manslaughter and now appeal against conviction. Stone and his housekeeper/mistress, Dobinson, admitted Stone's younger sister, Fanny, aged 61, to their household].

[Fanny] was eccentric in many ways. She was morbidly and unnecessarily anxious about putting on weight and so denied herself proper meals. She would take to her room for days. She would often stay in her room all day until the two appellants went to the public house in the evening when she would creep down and make herself a meal.

In early Spring 1975 the police called at the house. Fanny had been found wandering about in the street by herself without apparently knowing where she was. This caused the appellants to try to find Fanny's doctor. They tried to trace him through Rosy, [a sister of Fanny's with whom she had previously lived] but having walked a very considerable distance in their search they failed. It transpired that they had walked to the wrong village. Fanny herself refused to tell them the doctor's name. She thought she would be 'put away' if she did. Nothing more was done to enlist outside professional aid.

In the light of what happened subsequently there can be no doubt that Fanny's condition over the succeeding weeks and months must have deteriorated rapidly. By July 1975 she was, it seems, unable or unwilling to leave her bed and, on July 19, the next-door neighbour, Mrs Wilson, gallantly volunteered to help the female appellant to wash Fanny. She states:
'On July 19 Mrs Dobinson and I went to Fanny's room in order to clean her up. When I went into the room there was not a strong smell until I moved her. Her nightdress was wet and messed with her own excreta and the dress had to be cut off. I saw her back was sore; I hadn't seen anything like that before. I took the bedclothes off the bed. They were all wet through and messed. And so was the mattress. I was there for about two hours and Mrs Dobinson helped. She was raw, her back, shoulders, bottom and down below between her legs. Mrs Dobinson appeared to me to be upset because Fanny had never let her attend to her before. I advised Mrs Dobinson to go the social services.'

Emily West, the licensee of the local public house, the Crossed Daggers, gave evidence to the effect that during the whole of the period, from July 19 onwards, the appellants came to the public house every night at about 7 p.m. The appellant Dobinson was worried and told Emily West that Fanny would not wash, go to the toilet or eat or drink. As a result Emily West immediately advised Dobinson to get a doctor and when told that Fanny's doctor lived at Doncaster, Emily West suggested getting a local one. It seems that some efforts were made to get a local doctor, but the neighbour who volunteered to do the telephoning (the appellants being incapable of managing the instrument themselves) was unsuccessful.

On August 2, 1975 Fanny was found by Dobinson to be dead in her bed. The police were called. On arrival they found there was no ventilation in the bedroom, the window had to be hammered open and the bed was so sited that it was impossible to get the door fully open. At one side of the bed on a chair was an empty mineral bottle and on the other chair a cup. Under the bed was an empty polythene bucket. Otherwise there was no food, washing or toilet facilities in the room. There was excrement on the bed and floor. It was a scene of dreadful degradation.

The pathologist, Dr Usher, gave evidence that the deceased was naked, emaciated, weighing five stone and five pounds, her body ingrained with dirt, lying in a pool of excrement. On the bed on which she was lying were various filthy and crumpled bed-clothes, some of which were soaked in urine. There was excrement on the floor and wrapped in newspapers alongside the bed. There was a tidemark of excreta corresponding with the position in which her body was lying. At the mortuary, Dr Usher found the deceased's body to be ulcerated over the right hip joint and on the underside of the left knee; in each case the ulceration went down to the bone. There were maggots in the ulcers. ... Such ulcers could not have been produced in less than two or three weeks. The ulcers were due to the general poor condition of the skin and protruding bones which would have had a greater effect upon her than a normal person. She was soaked in urine and excreta. Her stomach contained no food products but a lot of bile stained fluid. She had not eaten recently. He found no natural disease. The disinclination to eat was a condition of anorexia nervosa which was not a physical condition but a condition of the brain or mind. She had been requiring urgent medical attention for some days or even weeks. He said:

'If two weeks prior to my seeing the body she had gone into hospital there is a distinct possibility that they may have saved her; and three weeks earlier the chances would have been good. If her condition on July 19 was no worse than that described by Mrs Wilson, then her survival would have been probable.' ...

The prosecution alleged that in the circumstances the appellants had undertaken the duty of caring for Fanny who was incapable of looking after herself, that they had, with gross negligence, failed in that duty, that such failure caused her death and they they were guilty of manslaughter. ...

[Counsel for the appellant] suggests that the situation here is unlike any reported case. Fanny came to this house as a lodger. Largely, if not entirely due to her own eccentricity and failure to look after herself or feed herself properly, she became increasingly infirm and immobile and eventually unable to look after herself. Is it to be said, asks [counsel for the appellant] rhetorically, that by the mere fact of becoming infirm and helpless in these circumstances she casts a duty on her brother and the appellant Dobinson to take steps to have her looked after or taken into hospital? The suggestion is that, heartless though it may seem, this is one of those situations where the appellants were entitled to do nothing; where no duty was cast upon them to help, any more than it is cast upon a man to rescue a stranger from drowning, however easy such a rescue might be.

This court rejects that proposition. Whether Fanny was a lodger or not she was a blood relation of the appellant Stone; she was occupying a room in his house; the appellant Dobinson had undertaken the duty of trying to wash her, of taking such food to her as she required. There was ample evidence that each appellant was aware of the poor condition she was in by mid-July. It was not disputed that no effort was made to summon an ambulance or the social services or the police despite the entreaties of Mrs Wilson and Mrs West. A social worker used to visit Cyril. No word was spoken to him. All these were matters which the jury were entitled to take into account when considering whether the necessary assumption of a duty to care for Fanny had been proved.

This was not a situation analogous to the drowning stranger. They did make efforts to care. They tried to get a doctor; they tried to discover the previous doctor. The appellant Dobinson helped with the washing and the provision of food. All these matters were put before the jury in terms which we find it impossible to fault. The jury were entitled to find that the duty had been assumed. They were entitled to conclude that once Fanny became helplessly infirm, as she had by July 19, the appellants were, in the circumstances, obliged either to summon help or else to care for Fanny themselves."

**Appeal dismissed**

If there were a general duty to act in English law, would Mrs Wilson (whose daughter was a nurse) and even Emily West be charged with manslaughter? If either of them had summoned medical assistance Fanny's life might have been saved.

The answer here must be in the negative. It is possible to hold that Stone and Dobinson caused Fanny's death because it was their deviation from an expected norm that stands out as exceptional among the candidates for causation. The inactions of Mrs Wilson and Emily West do not stand out as wholly exceptional. Fanny was dependent and reasonably relied upon Stone and Dobinson. It is this reliance that generates a duty on their part to take care of her. It is the breach of this duty that stands out as a "deviation" and thus a cause. On the other hand, Fanny did not rely on Mrs Wilson or Emily West any more than she would have relied on a passing milkman who happened to become aware of her situation. This lack of reliance means that Mrs Wilson and Emily West will not be held to have assumed a responsibility towards Fanny under the present law. Their failure to act will not stand out as exceptional or a deviation from the norm. They did not cause her death.

Does this thesis, which would be fatal to any argument in favour of a general duty to act, apply in all cases? It will be recalled that Leavens, in an earlier extract,[58] used the example of a person sitting on a park bench watching a flower die from lack of water even though a full watercan was nearby. We would not say that that person caused the death of the flower. Because she was under no duty to water the flower, her failure to act was unexceptional. But we would say that the park's gardener caused the death of the flower if he failed to water it. Because of his duty (by contract), his failure becomes significant; it represents a marked alteration of the status quo and can count as a cause.

What of the mother and the stranger who fail to rescue the child from the shallow pool of water? It has been argued that there is no difficulty in establishing a causal link in both these cases.[59] In one sense, the actions of both did cause the death of the child: but for their failures to act, the child would have survived. But, again, it is the mother's failure that stands out as the more significant cause of death. Like the appellants in *Stone and Dobinson* the mother has a special responsibility to the child. It is the failure to exercise this responsibility that is "exceptional" or a significant "deviation" from the expected and thus the substantial cause of the death. It is the existence of this duty that converts a mere cause into a legally sufficient cause. The stranger has no special responsibility towards the child and therefore, while his omission might be morally deplorable, it is not "exceptional" in the same sense as when the mother fails to save her own child.

Another way of expressing this is that a cause alters the status quo. The status quo is something that exists, "including expected patterns of conduct",[60] whether

---

[58] See pp. 107–108.
[59] Hughes, "Criminal Omissions" (1958) 67 Yale L. J. 590 at 627; Hall, *General Principles of Criminal Law* (1947), pp. 256–266.
[60] Leavens, see, p. 108.

we are there or not. A mother has a special relationship towards her drowning child. *That relationship becomes part of the status quo.* Her failure to act alters the status quo and is thus a cause of the result. The stranger's failure to act has no impact on the status quo. Events simply take their normal (but tragic) course; the stranger's acts do not count as a legal cause of the consequence.

Thus, to summarise, it would be pointless to impose a general duty to act as the only people who could be held responsible in terms of causation would be those who owed duties to their victims under one of the recognised heads. It is only *because of* the special relationship, the assumption of duty etc. that causation is established. Without this pre-existing duty the causative link between the inactivity and the ensuring consequence would be too remote.[61]

In discussing whether there ought to be a general duty to act we have, until now, assumed that the purpose of such a general duty is that a breach thereof constitutes the requisite "act" for the purposes of some ulterior offence—for example, a failure to rescue becomes the requisite act for the purposes of the crime of homicide. It is, however, not necessary to go as far as this. The law could still issue its moral directive that people must render assistance to others, but avoid all problems of causation and *mens rea*, by the creation of separate offences imposing limited and complete liability for a failure to act. A failure to act would render one liable for this separate offence. In the United States the state of Vermont has such a provision.

### 12 Vt. Stat. Ann., s.519. (Emergency Medical Care):

"(a) A person who knows that another is exposed to grave physical harm shall, to the extent that the same can be rendered without danger or peril to himself or without interference with important duties owed to others, give reasonable assistance to the exposed person unless that assistance or care is being provided by others.

(b) A person who provides reasonable assistance in compliance with subsection (a) of this section shall not be liable in civil damages unless his acts constitute gross negligence or unless he will receive or expects to receive remuneration. Nothing contained in this subsection shall alter existing law with respect to tort liability of a practitioner of the healing arts for acts committed in the ordinary course of his practice.

(c) A person who wilfully violates subsection (a) of this section shall be fined not more than $100.00."[62]

If such a provision were part of English law then defendants such as Stone and Dobinson could have been charged with this offence instead of manslaughter. Some might argue that this would have been preferable: in moral terms one can condemn Stone and Dobinson for neglecting Fanny; but can we really condemn them morally for *killing* Fanny? Of course, if such a provision were introduced in England, without more, Stone and Dobinson would have been guilty of both this offence *and* manslaughter, their duty to act being now statutory in addition to the other grounds giving rise to their duty. Thus in England, section 1(1) of the Children and Young Persons Act 1933 creates a separate criminal offence of

---

[61] This point was recognised in *Miller* [1983] A.C. 161, when Lord Diplock indicated that a "passive bystander" could not be said to have caused a fire, or presumably any injuries sustained in the fire.

[62] Many continental Criminal Codes contain similar and even broader provisions. See Ashworth and Steiner, "Criminal omissions and public duties: the French experience" (1990) 10 L.S. 153; Hughes, *above*, n.59, at 631–634.

neglecting a child for whom one is responsible. As the case of *Lowe*[63] demonstrates, the existence of such an offence does not preclude the possibility of liability for (gross negligence) manslaughter if the child dies. If the new provision were to *replace* the possibility of any criminal liability for an ulterior offence, this would need to be made explicit. On the other hand, where there is a duty under one of the already established heads, we would generally want to continue imposing criminal liability for the ulterior offence. Thus the mother who watches her young child drown in the shallow pool *ought* arguably to be liable for manslaughter (at least) and not merely liable for a lesser offence of failing to act. Such a result could easily be achieved by maintaining the present law and introducing the new provision with a proviso that it, by itself, will not give rise to a statutory duty to act for the purposes of any ulterior offence. This would still leave the problem of defendants like Stone and Dobinson unresolved. Should they simply be charged with the new statutory offence? Or should they be charged with manslaughter on the basis that they have breached one of the existing categories of duty? Should such a decision be left to prosecutorial discretion?

### 6. Punishment of Omissions

Under English law, once liability for an offence has been established, one is liable to any punishment up to the maximum, regardless of whether one's "act" consisted of positive action or an omission to act. This approach can be defended: the harm is the same in both cases and sometimes it is difficult to distinguish between acts of commission and omissions to act.

On the other hand, it can be argued that omissions ought on principle to be punished less severely than positive acts and that this lesser level of punishment should be clearly articulated. One of the views considered earlier was that it was worse to "kill" than to "let die". If this were accepted, it should be reflected at the punishment level. In *Morgan* a sentence for reckless manslaughter was reduced on the ground, *inter alia*, that the offence was "arguably a crime of omission".[64] Lesser punishment should be imposed when the harm has occurred through a failure to act when action is required. Such an approach might also have the advantage of encouraging the courts to be less inflexible in their attitude towards the imposition of criminal liability based on omissions.

### III. MENS REA

### A. *Blame and Responsibility*

The normal consequence of a criminal conviction is punishment. The offender is subjected to censure and blame. Blame and censure is only appropriate if the offender was morally responsible for his or her behaviour. We do not blame animals, small children and the insane who have caused a harm because we do not hold them responsible. In a liberal society where political freedom is valued people

---

[63] [1973] 1 Q.B. 702. See p. 101.
[64] [1991] Crim.L.R.214.

must be free from criminal liability and punishment unless they "voluntarily" break the law[65] in the sense of doing something that they can properly acknowledge as wrongdoing.[66] A morally responsible agent is one who understands the social norms to which he is subject[67] and can understand and accept responsibility for wrongdoing (whether or not this is associated with feelings of guilt). Such an agent can understand the "communicative enterprise of punishment"[68] in a way that young children and the insane cannot. The state may use its coercive powers against citizens who lack responsibility (for example, imposing tax on the purchase of goods[69]), but the use of its censuring powers of punishment in such cases would not be consistent with the demands of political freedom. There would be no freedom in a state that chose to punish persons with green eyes. In short, the link between responsibility and criminal liability is one of the hallmarks of a free society.

How is responsibility assessed? There are two main theories: the capacity theory and the character theory.[70] Under the former, the necessary attributes are knowledge, reason, and control (which includes the capacity to make choices).[71]

## United States v Currens, 290 F.2d 751 (3rd Cir. 1961), (United States Court of Appeals)

Biggs, Chief Judge:
"The concept of *mens rea*, guilty mind, is based on the assumption that a person has the capacity to control his behaviour and to choose between alternative courses of conduct. This assumption, though not unquestioned by theologians, philosophers, and scientists, is necessary to maintenance and administration of social controls. It is only through this assumption that society has found it possible to impose duties and create liabilities designed to safeguard persons and property ... Essentially these duties and liabilities are intended to operate upon the human capacity for choice and control of conduct so as to inhibit and deter socially harmful conduct. When a person possessing capacity for choice and control, nevertheless breaches a duty of this type he is subjected to the sanctions of the criminal law."

## Nicola Lacey, State Punishment: Political Principles and Community Values (1988), p. 63:

"This conception of responsibility [from H. L. A. Hart's *Punishment and Responsibility* (1968)] consists in both a cognitive and a volitional element: a person must both understand

---

[65] Williams, "Moral Responsibility and Political Freedom" [1997] C.L.J. 96.
[66] Duff and von Hirsch, "Responsibility, Retribution and the 'Voluntary': A Response to Williams" [1997] C.L.J. 103 at 109.
[67] Jacobs, *Criminal Responsibility* (1971), p. 13.
[68] Duff and von Hirsch (*above*, n.66) at 109.
[69] *ibid.* at 104.
[70] Lacey, *State Punishment: Political Principles and Community Values* (1988), pp. 62–68. For a general discussion of these and other theories, see Horder, "Criminal Culpability: The Possibility of a General Theory" (1993) 12 *Law and Philosophy* 193. See also Lacey, "In Search of the Responsible Subject: History, Philosophy and Social Sciences in Criminal Law Theory" (2001) 64 M.L.R. 350.
[71] Arenella would insist that an actor also be capable of some form of moral evaluation and be able to incorporate these moral beliefs and values into practical judgments about how to act. ("Convicting the Morally Blameless: Reassessing the Relationship between Legal and Moral Accountability" (1992) 39 U.C.L.A. Law Rev. 1511.) This approach is not accepted by present English law.

the nature of her actions, knowing the relevant circumstances and being aware of possible consequences, and have a genuine opportunity to do otherwise than she does—to exercise control over her actions, by means of choice. If she has not a real opportunity to do otherwise, if she has not genuinely chosen to act as she does, she cannot be said to be truly responsible, and it would be unfair to blame, yet alone to punish her for her actions."

According to this traditional view, because the defendant could choose to do otherwise we are entitled to hold her morally blameworthy and to punish her. Because it is difficult to say that the mentally disordered defendant could have done otherwise she is exonerated from blame and punishment.[72]

This capacity theory can be applied to crimes of recklessness and negligence.

### Antony Duff and Andrew von Hirsch, "Responsibility, Retribution and the 'Voluntary': A Response to Williams" [1997] C.L.J. 103 at 109–110:

"We might do better to focus on the notion of rational agency. By this, we mean not action that is in fact guided by good reasons; but action which is in principle susceptible to being guided by reasons, done by an agent who would be capable of recognising whether such reasons are good ones . . . [I]t seems to us to be the best way to try to capture the idea of moral responsibility which is appropriate to ascriptions of criminal liability: what we condemn the agent for is a failure to recognise, to accept, or to be adequately motivated by, reasons for action (those offered by the law) which were within his grasp."

There have been many challenges to this notion that people are free or autonomous agents capable of rational action and free choice. The argument here is that this conception of individuals as autonomous, self-determined beings ignores the social context within which people operate. As Norrie puts it: "while we feel in control of what we say or do, we sometimes appear only to speak the parts bequeathed to us by history and context".[73] Further discussion of such claims, which would have a profound impact upon the construction of criminal liability, is delayed until the more orthodox approach employed by the law has been canvassed.

An alternative conception of responsibility has been developed based upon the character of the defendant. "(A)ctions for which we hold a person fully responsible are those in which her usual character is centrally expressed. . . . The finding of a mental element such as intention or recklessness on the character model provides an important piece of evidence from which the existence of character responsibility may be inferred, given that single acts do not always indicate settled dispositions."[74] Thus we would hold responsible a person who makes unreasonable mistakes because such behaviour manifests an undesirable character trait of practical indifference to others. On the other hand, a person who acts under duress is not expressing his usual character. Because he has been forced to act in a particular way we are unable to draw an inference to a flawed character. This approach does have certain attractions; not least it accords with our tendency to regard as significant the fact that someone acts "out of character" and may be more

---

[72] Because of the danger of repetition of harm in such circumstances, it might be necessary to retain control over the defendant. See *below*, p. 399.

[73] "The Limits of Justice: Finding Fault in the Criminal Law" (1996) 59 M.L.R. 540 at 552.

[74] Lacey, *State Punishment: Political Principles and Community Values* (1988), p. 66.

in keeping with the function of the criminal law as a form of social control. However, it is this intuitive appeal that reveals a central weakness of this character theory. The infliction of a serious harm could be regarded as non-culpable if the agent acted "out of character".[75] But how would we know if any action were uncharacteristic of the agent? This theory is unlikely to replace the capacity conception of responsibility because it looks too much like punishing people for what they are rather than what they do. Such a person "remains a moral cripple, a flawed person in his own eyes, a person who understands that he committed a crime because of 'the kind of person he is' ... [This amounts to an] enormous and sadistic cruelty."[76]

## B. *Blame and Mens Rea*

We only blame those who are responsible for their actions. This means that the indicators of blame are largely fashioned according to which of the above competing conceptions of responsibility we adopt. For example, if we adopted the "character conception" of responsibility, we might need to evaluate an actor's motivations because a laudable motive would not reveal a flawed character. The law, however, has been fearful of adopting such a course as it might necessitate exempting from blame those who rob the rich to give to the poor or who, as in *Chandler v D.P.P.*,[77] commit offences to express their opposition to nuclear weapons. Accordingly, the law adopts the stance that motive is generally irrelevant to the assessment and has instead preferred the "capacity conception" of responsibility. We blame those who have control over their actions and have chosen to commit a crime. The process of choosing to commit a crime is a mental process involving *cognition* (knowing or realising that a consequence could occur or that a circumstance could exist). This mental state became known as *mens rea*.

## J. F. Stephen, History of the Criminal Law of England, Vol. II (1883), pp. 94–95:

"The maxim, '*Actus non facit reum nisi mens sit rea*', is sometimes said to be the fundamental maxim of the whole criminal law; but I think that, like many other Latin sentences supposed to form part of the Roman law, the maxim not only looks more instructive than it really is, but suggests fallacies which it does not precisely state.

It is frequently though ignorantly supposed to mean that there cannot be such a thing as legal guilt where there is no moral guilt, which is obviously untrue, as there is always a possibility of a conflict between law and morals.

It also suggests the notion that there is some state of mind called a '*mens rea*,' the absence of which, on any particular occasion, deprives what would otherwise be a crime of its criminal character. This also is untrue. There is no one such state of mind, as any one may convince himself by considering the definitions of dissimilar crimes. A pointsman falls

---

[75] Moore, "Choice, Character and Excuse" (1990) 7 *Social Philosophy and Policy* 29; Horder, "Criminal Culpability: The Possibility of a General Theory" (1993) *Law and Philosophy* 193 at 207.
[76] Lindgren, "Criminal Responsibility Reconsidered" (1987) 6 *Law and Philosophy* 89 at 94.
[77] [1964] A.C. 763.

asleep, and thereby causes a railway accident and the death of a passenger; he is guilty of manslaughter. He deliberately and by elaborate devices produces the same result: he is guilty of murder. If in each case there is a *mens rea*, as the maxim seems to imply, *mens rea* must be a name for two states of mind, not merely differing from but opposed to each other, for what two states of mind can resemble each other less than indolence and an active desire to kill?

The truth is that the maxim about *mens rea* means no more than that the definition of all or nearly all crimes contains not only an outward and visible element, but a mental element, varying according to the different nature of different crimes. Thus, in reference to murder, the *mens rea* is any state of mind which comes within the description of malice aforethought. In reference to theft the *mens rea* is an intention to deprive the owner of his property permanently, fraudulently ... Hence the only means of arriving at a full comprehension of the expression *mens rea* is by a detailed examination of the definitions of particular crimes, and therefore the expression itself is unmeaning."

*Mens rea* is the term used to indicate the mental element required by the definition of the crime. Older law and statutes used evaluative terms such as "malice aforethought" and "maliciously". For the past century, and particularly the last half-century, more cognitive terms such as knowledge and belief in relation to circumstances, and intention and recklessness in relation to consequences, have become prevalent. The courts have embraced these new concepts and have reinterpreted the older terms in the light of them. For example, "maliciously" in section 20 of the Offences against the Person Act 1861 has been construed as meaning "recklessly". Other forms of affective (as opposed to cognitive) *mens rea* also exist. For example, theft requires "dishonesty": this is a state of mind relating to the wrongfulness of actions.

Further, the term *mens rea* has been used to describe other forms of culpability that do not necessarily involve a "state of mind" in its cognitive sense of intending or being subjectively aware that a consequence could occur. Most important here has been the development of an "objective" test of recklessness that involves a failure to foresee an obvious risk. Also, certain crimes can be committed negligently. While many would dispute that this is a species of *mens rea*, it is often classed as such, particularly when used as a positive culpability requirement.[78]

Whether these latter concepts are classified as species of *mens rea* is perhaps unimportant. What does matter is that they do suffice to establish the requisite culpability for the offences to which they apply. Indeed, it might be more helpful to avoid terms such as *mens rea* and recognise that for the core, more serious, offences[79] the issue is whether the defendant is blameworthy or culpable. Having *mens rea* is a prime indicator of blameworthiness but an assessment of blame can be based on other non-cognitive factors. For example, a defendant can be blamed for causing a harm when, even though there was no awareness of the possibility of the harm occurring at the time of acting, it was the defendant's own fault for getting herself into a situation (for example, intoxicated) whereby she was deprived of the capacity for awareness. Also, the fact that a defendant has *mens rea* does not conclusively establish that she is blameworthy. She might intentionally bring about a prohibited harm but be exempt from blame because of a recognised excuse or justification (for example, duress or self-defence).

---

[78] As opposed to being a basis for determining whether there is a defence to certain crimes of strict liability.

[79] A majority of crimes are, in fact, ones of strict liability where *mens rea* does not have to be proved. About half of all indictable offences have a strict liability element (Ashworth and Blake, "The Presumption of Innocence in English Criminal Law" [1996] Crim.L.R.306).

The problem with this approach is that the concept of "blameworthiness" can be vague and uncertain. It is reminiscent of the older law that employed evaluative concepts such as "malice". Indeed, English courts have been wary of adopting this broader approach[80] and have preferred to stick to the orthodoxy of "*mens rea*".

Accordingly, this chapter will be largely confined to an analysis of the traditional concept of *mens rea*. However, it must be borne in mind that the term "*mens rea*" is no more than a tool in the identification of culpability. And, further, it must be emphasised that the shape of construction of the various *mens rea* terms, such as recklessness, should be governed by the central quest of identifying blameworthiness. For example, in assessing whether "recklessness" should be interpreted as including a failure to consider obvious risks, the central issue is whether such a failure can be regarded as sufficiently culpable to justify the imposition of criminal liability.

We are now in a position to examine some of the core *mens rea* concepts, in particular, intention, recklessness and negligence. Other *mens rea* concepts, such as dishonesty and knowledge, are discussed later in the book in relation to the offences to which they apply.

For many crimes it is unnecessary to distinguish intention from recklessness because proof of either will suffice. For example, section 1(1) of the Criminal Damage Act 1971 provides that it is an offence to destroy or damage any property belonging to another "intending to destroy or damage any such property or being reckless as to whether any such property would be destroyed or damaged". But there are some crimes that can only be committed intentionally: for example, section 18 of the Offences Against the Person Act 1861 makes it an offence to wound or cause grievous bodily harm "with intent to cause grievous bodily harm". For these crimes it is essential to define intention with some precision in order to distinguish it from recklessness.

## 1. Intention

### (i) *The Law*

There is no statutory definition of intention in English law. Section 8 of the Criminal Justice Act 1967 lays down an evidential rule as to *how* intention is to be proved:

> "A court or jury, in determining whether a person has committed an offence—(a) shall not be bound in law to infer that he intended or foresaw a result of his actions by reasons only of its being a natural and probable consequence of those actions; but (b) shall decide whether he did intend or foresee that result by reference to all the evidence, drawing such inferences from the evidence as appear proper in the circumstances."

This makes it clear that intention is a subjective state of mind. What matters is whether the defendant intended the result, not whether the reasonable man would have intended it. In trying to ascertain what the defendant did intend the court or jury must draw inferences from all the relevant evidence.

However, while this is clear as to the process for ascertaining intention, there is no agreement in English law as to the actual meaning of the word "intention". There are two views.

---

[80] See generally, Clarkson, *Understanding Criminal Law* (3rd ed., 2001), pp.17–20.

(1) A consequence is intended when it is the aim or the objective of the actor. This is often called "direct" intent.

(2) A consequence is intended when it is the aim or objective of the actor, or is foreseen as a *virtual, practical* or *moral certainty*. If this state of mind is classed as intention, it is usually called "oblique intention".

The courts used to adopt an even broader view in holding that a consequence was intended when it was foreseen as a probable or likely result of the defendant's actions.[81] In *Hyam*,[82] for instance, Mrs Hyam poured petrol through the letterbox of the house of her lover's new mistress and then ignited it knowing people were asleep in the house. She claimed that she had not meant to kill but had foreseen death or grievous bodily harm as a highly probable result of her actions. Her conviction was upheld with the House of Lords arguably ruling that her state of mind amounted to an *intention* to kill or cause grievous bodily harm.

However, over the past two decades there has been a retreat from this position and it is now clear that foresight of a consequence as probable, likely or even highly probable does *not* amount to intention. However, the precise status and meaning of "oblique intention" has greatly troubled the courts.

### R. v Moloney [1985] A.C. 905 (House of Lords)

The appellant and his stepfather, both of whom had been drinking heavily, engaged in a contest to ascertain who was quicker on the draw with a shotgun. The appellant shot and killed his stepfather but claimed he had not realised the gun was pointing at him. He was convicted of murder and his appeal was dismissed by the Court of Appeal. He appealed to the House of Lords.

Lord Bridge of Harwich:
"[L]ooking on their facts at the decided cases where a crime of specific intent was under consideration, they suggest to me that the probability of the consequence taken to have been foreseen must be little short of overwhelming before it will suffice to establish the necessary intent. ...

The golden rule should be that, when directing a jury on the mental element necessary in a crime of specific intent, the judge should avoid any elaboration or paraphrase of what is meant by intent, and leave it to the jury's good sense to decide whether the accused acted with the necessary intent, unless the judge is convinced that, on the facts and having regard to the way the case has been presented to the jury in evidence and argument, some further explanation or elaboration is strictly necessary to avoid misunderstanding. In trials for murder or wounding with intent, I find it very difficult to visualise a case where any such explanation or elaboration could be required, if the offence consisted of a direct attack on the victim with a weapon ... Even where the death results indirectly from the act of the accused, I believe the cases that will call for a direction by reference to foresight of consequences will be of extremely rare occurrence. ...

I do not, of course, by what I have said in the foregoing paragraph, mean to question the necessity, which frequently arises, to explain to a jury that intention is something quite distinct from motive or desire. But this can normally be quite simply explained by reference to the case before the court or, if necessary, by some homely example. A man who, at

---

[81] This was the view (*obiter*) of the House of Lords in *Lemon* [1979] A.C. 617 and was *arguably* the view adopted in *Hyam* [1975] A.C. 55. The alternative interpretation of *Hyam* is that the House of Lords was there defining "malice aforethought", the *mens rea* of murder—and not defining "intention". See generally, Buzzard, " 'Intent' " [1978] Crim.L.R.5 and Smith, " 'Intent': A Reply" [1978] Crim.L.R.14.

[82] [1975] A.C. 55.

London Airport, boards a plane which he knows to be bound for Manchester, clearly intends to travel to Manchester, even though Manchester is the last place he wants to be and his motive for boarding the plane is simply to escape pursuit. The possibility that the plane may have engine trouble and be diverted to Luton does not affect the matter. By boarding the Manchester plane, the man conclusively demonstrates his intention to go there, because it is a moral certainty that that is where he will arrive ...

Starting from the proposition ... that the mental element in murder requires proof of an intention to kill or cause really serious injury, the first fundamental question to be answered is whether there is any rule of substantive law that foresight by the accused of one of those eventualities as a probable consequence of his voluntary act, where the probability can be defined as exceeding a certain degree, is equivalent or alternative to the necessary intention. I would answer this question in the negative ...

The irrationality of any such rule of substantive law stems from the fact that it is impossible to define degrees of probability, in any of the infinite variety of situations arising in human affairs, in precise or scientific terms. ...

I am firmly of opinion that foresight of consequences, as an element bearing on the issue of intention in murder, or indeed any other crime of specific intent, belongs, not to the substantive law, but to the law of evidence. ...

In the rare cases in which it is necessary to direct a jury by reference to foresight of consequences, I do not believe it is necessary for the judge to do more than invite the jury to consider two questions. First, was death or really serious injury in a murder case (or whatever relevant consequence must be proved to have been intended in any other case) a natural consequence of the defendant's voluntary act? Secondly, did the defendant foresee that consequence as being a natural consequence of his act? The jury should then be told that if they answer yes to both questions it is a proper inference for them to draw that he intended that consequence."

**Appeal allowed**

## R. v Hancock and Shankland [1986] A.C. 455 (House of Lords)

The defendants, two striking miners, pushed a large lump of concrete from a bridge on to a convoy of cars below carrying a miner to work. The concrete struck a taxi's windscreen and killed the driver. The defendants claimed they had not meant to kill or cause serious injury. Their plan was to drop the concrete in the middle lane of the carriageway while the convoy was in the nearside lane. Their aim was to frighten the miner or block the road in order to prevent him from getting to work. The defendants were convicted of murder. The Court of Appeal allowed their appeals and substituted verdicts of manslaughter. The Crown appealed to the House of Lords.

Lord Scarman:

"[T]he cases to which the guidance was expressly limited by the House in *Moloney, i.e.* the 'rare cases' in which it is necessary to direct a jury by reference to foresight of consequences, are unlikely to be so rare or so exceptional as the House believed. As the House then recognised, the guidelines as formulated are applicable to cases of any crime of specific intent, and not merely murder. But further and disturbingly crimes of violence where the purpose is by open violence to protest, demonstrate, obstruct, or frighten are on the increase. Violence is used by some as a means of public communication. Inevitably there will be casualties: and inevitably death will on occasions result. If death results, is the perpetrator of the violent act guilty of murder? It will depend on his intent. ...

The question for the House is, therefore, whether the *Moloney* guidelines are sound. ...

[Lord Bridge of Harwich in *Moloney*] omitted any reference in his guidelines to probability. ... I agree with the Court of Appeal that the probability of a consequence is a factor of sufficient importance to be drawn specifically to the attention of the jury and to be explained. In a murder case where it is necessary to direct a jury on the issue of intent by reference to foresight of consequences the probability of death or serious injury resulting from the act done may be critically important. Its importance will depend on the degree of probability: if the likelihood that death or serious injury will result is high, the probability of that result may be seen as overwhelming evidence of the existence of the intent to kill or injure. Failure to explain the relevance of probability may, therefore, mislead a jury into thinking that it is of little or no importance ... In my judgment, therefore, the *Moloney* guidelines as they stand are unsafe and misleading. They require a reference to probability. They also require an explanation that the greater the probability of a consequence the more likely it is that the consequence was foreseen and that if that consequence was foreseen the greater the probability is that that consequence was also intended. But juries also require to be reminded that the decision is theirs to be reached upon a consideration of all the evidence. ...

In a case where foresight of a consequence is part of the evidence supporting a prosecution submission that the accused intended the consequence, the judge, if he thinks some general observations would help the jury, could well, having in mind section 8 of the Criminal Justice Act 1967, emphasise that the probability, however high, of a consequence is only a factor, though it may in some cases be a very significant factor, to be considered with all the other evidence in determining whether the accused intended to bring it about. The distinction between the offence and the evidence relied on to prove it is vital. ...

For these reasons I would hold that the *Moloney* guidelines are defective and should not be used as they stand without further explanation."

**Appeal dismissed**

## R. v Nedrick [1986] 1 W.L.R. 1025 (Court of Appeal, Criminal Division)

The appellant poured paraffin through the letterbox of a house and set light to it. The house caught fire and a child died. The appellant claimed that he did not want anyone to die. He was convicted of murder and appealed.

Lord Lane C.J.:
"What then does a jury have to decide so far as the mental element in murder is concerned? It simply has to decide whether the defendant intended to kill or do serious bodily harm. In order to reach that decision the jury must pay regard to all the relevant circumstances, including what the defendant himself said and did.

In the great majority of cases a direction to that effect will be enough, particularly where the defendant's actions amounted to a direct attack upon his victim, because in such cases the evidence relating to the defendant's desire or motive will be clear and his intent will have been the same as his desire or motive. But in some cases, of which this is one, the defendant does an act which is manifestly dangerous and as a result someone dies. The primary desire or motive of the defendant may not have been to harm that person, or indeed anyone. In that situation what further directions should a jury be given as to the mental state which they must find to exist in the defendant if murder is to be proved?

We have endeavoured to crystallise the effect of their Lordships' speeches in *R. v Moloney* and *R. v Hancock* in a way which we hope may be helpful to judges who have to handle this type of case.

It may be advisable first of all to explain to the jury that a man may intend to achieve a certain result whilst at the same time not desiring it to come about ...

When determining whether the defendant had the necessary intent, it may therefore be helpful for a jury to ask themselves two questions. (1) How probable was the consequence which resulted from the defendant's voluntary act? (2) Did he foresee that consequence?

If he did not appreciate that death or serious harm was likely to result from his act, he cannot have intended to bring it about. If he did, but thought that the risk to which he was exposing the person killed was only slight, then it may be easy for the jury to conclude that he did not intend to bring about that result. On the other hand, if the jury are satisfied that at the material time the defendant recognised that death or serious harm would be virtually certain (barring some unforeseen intervention) to result from his voluntary act, then that is a fact from which they may find it easy to infer that he intended to kill or do serious bodily harm, even though he may not have had any desire to achieve that result.

As Lord Bridge of Harwich said in *R. v Moloney* [1985] A.C. 905, 925: 'the probability of the consequences taken to have been foreseen must be little short of overwhelming before it will suffice to establish the necessary intent.' At p. 926 he uses the expression 'moral certainty'; he said, at p. 929 'will lead to a certain consequence unless something unexpected supervenes to prevent it.'

*Where the charge is murder and in the rare cases where the simple direction is not enough, the jury should be directed that they are not entitled to infer the necessary intention, unless they feel sure that death or serious bodily harm was a virtual certainty (barring some unforeseen intervention) as a result of the defendant's actions and that the defendant appreciated that such was the case.*[83]

Where a man realises that it is for all practical purposes inevitable that his actions will result in death or serious harm, the inference may be irresistible that he intended that result, however little he may have desired or wished it to happen. The decision is one for the jury to be reached upon a consideration of all the evidence."

**Appeal allowed**
**Conviction of manslaughter substituted**

## R. v Woollin [1999] 1 A.C. 82 (House of Lords)

The appellant lost his temper with his three-month-old son and threw him with great force causing the child to hit his head on something hard and die. In an interview the appellant admitted that he had realised there was a risk of serious injury. The trial judge directed the jury that they might infer intention if they were satisfied that the appellant appreciated that there was a substantial risk that he would cause serious harm. The appellant was convicted of murder and appealed on the ground that the judge should not have used the phrase "substantial risk", which is a test of recklessness, but should have used the phrase "virtual certainty".

Lord Steyn:
"The Crown did not contend that the appellant desired to kill his son or to cause him serious injury. The issue was whether the appellant nevertheless had the intention to cause serious harm. ...

I approach the issues arising on this appeal on the basis that it does not follow that 'intent' necessarily has precisely the same meaning in every context in the criminal law. The focus of the present appeal is the crime of murder.

Lord Bridge observed in *Moloney* [that] ...

'But looking on their facts at the decided cases where a crime of specific intent was under consideration, including *Reg v Hyam* [1975] A.C. 55 itself, they suggest to me that the probability of the consequence taken to have been foreseen must be little short of overwhelming before it will suffice *to establish* the necessary intent.' (My emphasis added.)

Lord Bridge paraphrased this idea in terms of 'moral certainty.' In the result the House adopted a narrower test of what may constitute intention which is similar to the 'virtual certainty' test in *Nedrick.* ...

In *Hancock*, Lord Scarman did not express disagreement with the test of foresight of a probability which is 'little short of overwhelming' as enunciated in *Moloney* ... Moreover, Lord Scarman thought that where explanation is required the jury should be directed as to the relevance of probability without expressly stating the matter in terms of any particular level of probability. The manner in which trial judges were to direct juries was left unclear. ...

[His Lordship then cited from *Nedrick*, including the italicised passage on p. 125]

While I have thought it right to give the full text of Lord Lane's observations, it is obvious that the italicised passage contains the critical direction. The effect of the critical direction is that a result foreseen as virtually certain is an intended result.

It is now possible to consider the Crown's direct challenge to the correctness of *Nedrick*. First, the Crown argued that *Nedrick* prevents the jury from considering all the evidence in

---

[83] This section was italicised by Lord Steyn in *Woollin* when he cited this passage with approval.

the case relevant to intention. The argument is that this is contrary to the provisions of section 8 of the Act of 1967. This provision reads:

'A court or jury, in determining whether a person has committed an offence—(a) shall not be bound in law to infer that he intended or foresaw a result of his actions by reasons only of its being a natural and probable consequence of those actions; but (b) shall decide whether he did intend or foresee that result by reference to all the evidence, drawing such inferences from the evidence as appear proper in the circumstances.'

... The Crown's argument relied on paragraph (b) which is concerned with the function of the jury. It is no more than a legislative instruction that in considering their findings on intention or foresight the jury must take into account all relevant evidence: *Nedrick* is undoubtedly concerned with the mental element which is sufficient for murder ... But, as Lord Lane C.J. emphasised in the last sentence of *Nedrick*, at p. 1028: 'The decision is one for the jury to be reached upon a consideration of all the evidence.' *Nedrick* does not prevent a jury from considering all the evidence: it merely stated what state of mind (in the absence of a purpose to kill or to cause serious harm) is sufficient for murder. I would therefore reject the Crown's first argument.

In the second place the Crown submitted that *Nedrick* is in conflict with the decision of the House in *Hancock*. Counsel argued that in order to bring some coherence to the process of determining intention Lord Lane C.J. specified a minimum level of foresight, namely virtual certainty. But that is not in conflict with the decision in *Hancock* which, apart from disapproving Lord Bridge's 'natural consequence' model direction, approved *Moloney* in all other respects. And in *Moloney* Lord Bridge said, that if a person foresees the probability of a consequence as little short of overwhelming, this 'will suffice *to establish* the necessary intent' (my emphasis) ...

The Crown did not argue that as a matter of policy foresight of a virtual certainty is too narrow a test in murder. ... Moreover, over a period of 12 years since *Nedrick* the test of foresight of virtual certainty has apparently caused no practical difficulties. It is simple and clear. It is true that it may exclude a conviction of murder in the often cited terrorist example where a member of the bomb disposal team is killed. In such a case it may realistically be said that the terrorist did not foresee the killing of a member of the bomb disposal team as a virtual certainty. That may be a consequence of not framing the principle in terms of risk-taking. Such cases ought to cause no substantial difficulty since immediately below murder there is available a verdict of manslaughter which may attract in the discretion of the court a life sentence ... I am satisfied that the *Nedrick* test, which was squarely based on the decision of the House in *Moloney*, is pitched at the right level of foresight ...

It may be appropriate to give a direction in accordance with *Nedrick* in any case in which the defendant may not have desired the result of his act. But I accept the trial judge is best placed to decide what direction is required by the circumstances of the case.

It follows that the judge should not have departed from the *Nedrick* direction. By using the phrase 'substantial *risk*' the judge blurred the line between intention and recklessness, and hence between murder and manslaughter. The misdirection enlarged the scope of the mental element required for murder. It was a material misdirection ... The conviction of murder must be quashed.

*The status of Nedrick*

In my view Lord Lane C.J.'s judgment in *Nedrick* provided valuable assistance to trial judges ... [His Lordship then repeated part of Lord Lane's judgment]:

'... (B) Where the charge is murder and in the rare cases where the simple direction is not enough, the jury should be directed that they are not entitled to infer the necessary intention, unless they feel sure that death or serious bodily harm was a virtual certainty (barring some unforeseen intervention) as a result of the defendant's actions and that the defendant appreciated that such was the case. (C) Where a man realises that it is for all practical purposes inevitable that his actions will result in death or serious harm, the inference may be irresistible that he intended that result, however little he may have desired or wished it to happen. The decision is one for the jury to be reached upon a consideration of all the evidence.' (Lettering added.)

... [It has been observed] that the use of the words 'to infer' in (B) may detract from the clarity of the model direction. I agree. I would substitute the words 'to find'. Thirdly, the first sentence of (C) does not form part of the model direction. But it would always be right for the judge to say, as Lord Lane C.J. put it, that the decision is for the jury upon a consideration of all the evidence in the case."

**Appeal allowed**

The following propositions would seem to appear from these cases:

### 1. Wanting result

A defendant who wants a result to happen—when it is the aim or objective ("direct" intention in the first view above)—clearly intends that result.

### R. A. Duff, Intention, Agency and Criminal Liability: Philosophy of Action and the Criminal Law (1990), pp. 47–48:

"To say that she intended to bring about a particular result is to say that that result formed at least part of her reason for acting as she did ... What Mrs Hyam did fitted both the description 'setting fire to the house' and the description 'making work for the fire brigade': what makes the former description, but not the latter, appropriate as a description of her intended action is its relation to her reasons for action."

Duff goes on to suggest that direct intention can be measured by employing a "test of failure": would the defendant count her actions as a failure if the result did not ensue?[84] Employing this test Mrs Hyam did not directly intend to kill or cause injury because she would not have regarded her actions as a failure had no one been killed or injured.

Such wanted results are intended even if the chances of the result occurring are slim: if the defendant shoots at his victim half a mile away knowing he could easily miss, he still intends to kill because that is what he is trying to do. Lord Reid has expressed this point in terms of a golfing analogy:

"If I say I intend to reach the green, people will believe me although we all know that the odds are ten to one against my succeeding."[85]

However, no matter how much one may want to achieve a result, one can only be said to intend it if one recognises that there is a chance of achieving it. If one does not believe that the consequence is a possible result of one's actions one can hardly be said to be trying to achieve it.[86]

### 2. Question of fact for jury

In the normal case the term "intention" should not be given a legal definition. Judges should refrain from giving juries guidance as to what it means. This is particularly true in common cases where there has been a direct attack upon the victim.[87] Whether a defendant intended a result is a question of fact which only the jury, applying their common sense to an ordinary English word, can answer. It is

---

[84] At p. 61. See also Duff, "Intention, Mens Rea and the Law Commission Report" [1980] Crim.L.R.147 at 150–151.
[85] *Gollins v Gollins* [1964] A.C. 644 at 664.
[86] Duff, "The Obscure Intentions of the House of Lords" [1986] Crim.L.R.771 at 779; Duff, *Intention, Agency and Criminal Liability* (1990), p. 58.
[87] *Gregory and Mott* [1995] Crim.L.R.507; *Fallon* [1994] Crim.L.R.519.

thus impossible to define intention or to know precisely what it means. It could well mean different things to different juries. Presumably, although one is only guessing, most juries will opt for the ordinary, common-sense meaning, namely, "as 'a decision to bring about a certain consequence' or as the aim."[88]

### 3. "Exceptional" cases: oblique intention

However, there may be other cases where a defendant has a purpose other than causing the prohibited harm—but where that result is an inevitable or likely consequence. For example, the defendant's main aim in *Nedrick* was to burn down the house in order to frighten its occupant but, in so doing, causing death was a likely result. In *Woollin*, it was again emphasised that a direction was only necessary in cases where the defendant does not desire the consequence that has occurred. In *Maloney*, Lord Bridge thought such guidance would only be necessary in "rare" and "exceptional" cases.[89] However, Lord Scarman in *Hancock* recognised that such cases would not be at all rare or exceptional—and, accordingly, guidance to the jury will be necessary in most cases where the defendant has a primary aim in acting other than causing the prohibited harm.[90]

In these cases it is permissible to give juries some guidance. However, it is far from clear precisely what form this guidance should take and what exactly intention does mean in such cases. The central problem is that there are two possible interpretations of *Woollin*:

[i] *Definitional interpretation*: a new extended *definition* of intention has been laid down. If a consequence is foreseen as virtually certain the jury may be told that this *amounts* to intention. This view is supported by two passages in *Woollin*. First, Lord Steyn cited with approval from *Maloney* that "if a person foresees the probability of a consequence as little short of overwhelming, this will suffice *to establish* the necessary intent" (Lord Steyn's emphasis). Secondly, after citing the italicised passage from *Nedrick* (p. 125), Lord Steyn added: "The effect of the critical direction is that a result foreseen as virtually certain *is* an intended result" (our emphasis). This interpretation is strengthened by the fact that in *Woollin* the Crown did not contend that the appellant desired to kill or seriously injure his son. The case proceeded on the basis that there could be another species of intention apart from direct intention.

[ii] *Evidential interpretation*: there is still no definition of intention. Where a consequence is foreseen as virtually certain this is *evidence* entitling a court or jury to find intention. Lord Steyn emphasised his approval of the critical direction in *Nedrick* (the italicised passage on p. 125). While he substituted "infer" with "find",[91] he endorsed the *Nedrick* view that the jury was "not

---

[88] *Mohan* [1976] 1 Q.B. 1.
[89] See also *Gilmour* [2000] Cr.App.R.407.
[90] In *Walker and Hayles* (1990) 90 Cr.App.R.226, it was held that a mere request from a jury for a further direction did not make the case a rare and exceptional one requiring a direction on foresight.
[91] Some commentators have suggested that the substitution of "find" for "infer" "seems a clear indication that the connection between virtual certainty and intention is not merely evidential" (Simester, (1999) 115 L.Q.R. 17). However, the jury is only *entitled* to find intention suggesting that this is still an evidential proposition.

entitled to [find] the necessary intention unless they feel sure that death or serious bodily harm was a virtual certainty … and the defendant appreciated that such was the case". While endorsing the virtual certainty test as evidence from which the jury is entitled to find intention, Lord Steyn immediately went on to rule that the *Nedrick* proposition (first sentence of (C) cited in *Woollin* on p. 126) that the inference may be irresistible, does not form part of the model direction. This seems to confirm that there is no test of intention. While foresight of a virtual certainty is a prerequisite to a finding of intention, the jury *may* (is "entitled to") find intention in such cases, but equally they *may not*. Under this view, if intention (A) *may* be found from foresight of a virtual certainty (B), (A) and (B) must logically mean different things. But what does intention (A) mean? It is not foresight of a virtual certainty (B) because that is merely an evidential pre-condition.[92] Possibly it should bear its ordinary meaning of aim, purpose (direct intent). The problem with this is that the jury are only permitted to receive a *Nedrick/Woollin* direction in cases where the defendant does *not* aim at achieving the consequence. It is a logical nonsense to tell the jury that because the defendant does not want the result they are going to be given the special direction but that if they are satisfied he foresaw the consequence as a virtual certainty, they may conclude that he did want it after all.

Which of these interpretations is preferable? The definitional interpretation has the advantage of being simpler and more workable. There are two separate species of intent: direct intent (aim/purpose) and oblique intent (foresight of virtual certainty). Each is clearly defined and proof of either will suffice (for murder, at any rate: see below). It avoids the absurdity of having to infer one state of mind (intention) from another state of mind (foresight of virtual certainty).

### William Wilson, "Doctrinal Rationality after Woollin" (1999) 62 Modern Law Review 448 at 451–452:

"What a person foresees is not necessarily even probative of what he means to achieve. Direct intention and foresight are different states of mind, in the same way that love is different from acquisitiveness. Proving that a person foresees a consequence as probable/highly probable is no more conclusive of an intention to produce that consequence than counting an art dealer's acquisitions can establish his love of art."

This approach also avoids the problem with the evidential interpretation that if one is inferring (or finding) intention from foresight of a virtual certainty, one must know what intention means. So, under the evidential interpretation, what does

---

[92] Wilson, "Doctrinal Rationality after Woollin" (1999) 62 M.L.R. 448 at 155.

intention mean? It should not mean direct intention[93] because, as seen, juries should not be given a *Nedrick/Woollin* direction in such cases so it can only mean something mysterious: "some ineffable, indefinable notion of intent, locked in the breasts of the jurors".[94] Where there is such a "logical gap"[95] between foresight of a virtual certainty and this mysterious, undefined concept of intention, it becomes difficult to predict when and in what circumstances the finding will or will not be made. Such an approach allows the jury maximum flexibility to make moral assessments of the defendant's actions and to do justice as they perceive it.[96]

On the other hand, the definitional interpretation places the jury in a moral straight-jacket. If the defendant foresees a consequence as virtually certain the jury is bound (in theory) to conclude that the test of oblique intention is satisfied.

### Alan Norrie, "After Woollin" [1999] Criminal Law Review 532 at 538:

"[There] are cases where there is a 'moral threshold' such that even though the accused could foresee a result as virtually certain, it is so at odds with his moral conception of what he was doing that it could not be conceived as a result that he intended. ... [T]here is a good argument for saying that a person does not intend indirectly those results which may be foreseen as virtually certain where they are at serious moral odds with what he intended to do. ... [Judges] and juries would be 'entitled' to find, in terms of *principle* and without strain, that the moral threshold between what the accused intended and what she foresaw as virtually certain was sufficiently large to avoid attribution of fault."

In most cases (certainly murder cases) what the defendant foresees is not going to be "at serious moral odds with what he intended to do". Such defendants are usually engaged in reprehensible conduct and it will be almost inevitable that juries will infer intention. In *Matthews and Alleyne*[97] the defendants were engaged in appalling conduct in deliberately throwing a non-swimmer into a deep, wide river. It was stated in the Court of Appeal that *Woollin* had *not* laid down a *definition* of murder but it was added that there was "very little to choose between a rule of evidence and one of substantive law" and that *on the facts* the inference was "irresistible" and that if the defendants appreciated the virtual certainty of death, it would be "impossible" for the jury not to find the requisite intention to kill.

However, as argued by Norrie, the advantage of the evidential interpretation is that in other cases where their sympathy is aroused the jury is given a "get out clause"[98] in that while they entitled to find intention, equally they are entitled not to find intention. This approach gives juries "moral elbow-room",[99] without having

---

[93] Norrie has argued that one can only infer intention from foresight where intention connotes direct intention plus foresight of a moral certainty (oblique intention) because one cannot infer a mental state (A) from the facts (b) where A and b are qualitatively different (Norrie, "Oblique Intention and Legal Politics" [1989] Crim.L.R.793 at 803). However, as Duff has effectively responded: "intention is inferable from foresight only if they *are* distinct"; if they are the same thing, no further inference is needed ("The Politics of Intention: A Response to Norrie" [1990] Crim.L.R.637 at 639).

[94] Smith [1998] Crim.L.R.891.

[95] Duff, "The Obscure Intentions of the House of Lords" [1986] Crim.L.R.771.

[96] This approach is criticised in Clarkson, *Understanding Criminal Law* (3rd ed., 2001), p. 204. Norrie says it "permits the law to have its principled cake of subjectivism, and to eat it" ("Oblique Intention and Legal Politics" [1989] Crim.L.R.793 at 806).

[97] [2003] EWCA Crim 192.

[98] Wilson, "Doctrinal Rationality after *Woollin*" (1999) 62 M.L.R. 448 at 456.

[99] Horder, "Intention in the Criminal Law – A Rejoinder" (1995) 58 M.L.R. 678 at 687.

to resort to perverse verdicts, to acquit in such cases without having to resort to perverse verdicts. As Wilson puts it: by not having a strict definition of intention the judge or jury have a "flexible friend, which, in appropriate circumstances can allow good intentions to take doctrinal precedence over knowledge".[1]

## R. v Steane [1947] K.B. 997 (Court of Criminal Appeal)

The appellant, a British film actor was resident and working in Germany before World War II. When war broke out he was arrested. As a result of threats to place his wife and children in a concentration camp and physical threats to himself, the appellant reluctantly agreed to broadcast on the radio for the Germans. For Four months he read the news three times a day. After the war he was convicted of doing acts likely to assist the enemy, with intent to assist the enemy, contrary to Regulation 2A of the Defence (General) Regulations 1939 and was sentenced to three years' imprisonment. He appealed against the conviction.

Goddard L.C.J.:
"The appellant also asserted ... that he never had the slightest idea or intention of assisting the enemy and what he did was done to save his wife and children. ...

The ... difficult question that arises, however, is in connection with the direction to the jury with regard to whether these acts were done with the attention of assisting the enemy. ... While no doubt the motive of a man's act and his intention of doing the act are in law different things, it is nonetheless true that in many offences a specific intention is a necessary ingredient, and the jury have to be satisfied that a particular act was done with that specific intent. ...

An illustration ... would be if a person deliberately took down his blackout curtains or shutters with the result that light appeared on the outside of his house, perhaps during an air raid; it might well be that no evidence or explanation were given and if all that was proved was that during that raid the prisoner exposed lights by a deliberate act, a jury could infer that he intended to signal or assist the enemy. But if the evidence in the case showed, for instance, that he or someone was overcome by heat and that he tore down the blackout to ventilate the room, the jury would certainly have to consider whether his act was done with the intent to assist the enemy or with some other intent, so that while he would be guilty of an offence of against the Blackout Regulations, he would not be guilty of the offence of attempting to assist the enemy. ...

British soldiers who were set to work on the Burma Road, or if invasion had unhappily taken place, British subjects who might have been set to work by the enemy digging trenches would undoubtedly be doing acts likely to assist the enemy. It would be unnecessary surely in their cases to consider any of the niceties of the law relating to duress because no jury would find that merely doing this work they were intending to assist the enemy. ... The proper direction to the jury in this case would have been that it was for the prosecution to prove the criminal intent, and that while the jury would be entitled to presume that intent if they thought that the act was done as the result of the free uncontrolled action of the accused, they would not be entitled to presume it if the circumstances showed that the act was done in subjection to the power of the enemy or was as equally consistent with an innocent intent as with a criminal intent, for example, a desire to save his wife and children from a concentration camp. They should only convict if satisfied by the evidence that the act complained of was in fact done to assist the enemy and if there was doubt about the matter the prisoner was entitled to be acquitted."

**Conviction quashed**

If this case were decided today under the definitional interpretation of *Woollin*,

---

[1] "Murder and the Structure of Homicide" in Ashworth and Mitchell (eds), *Rethinking English Homicide Law* (2000) at 48.

the jury would be forced (short of a perverse verdict) to conclude that Steane intended to assist the enemy: he would certainly have foreseen that consequence as a virtual certainty. However, under the evidential interpretation the jury would have the moral elbow-room to conclude that, despite such foresight, the result was not intended.

This approach also provides flexibility in medical cases where doctors administer drugs or other treatment with lawful motives (for example, to relieve pain) but knowing the treatment will kill the patient.

### Re A (conjoined twins: surgical separation) [2000] 4 All E.R. 961 (Court of Appeal, Civil Division)

The issue in this case was whether a declaration should be made that it would be lawful for doctors to separate conjoined twins even though such a procedure would certainly result in the death of the weaker twin. One of the matters canvassed was whether the doctors would have the *mens rea* of murder, namely, an intention to kill or cause grievous bodily harm.

Ward LJ:
"I have to ask myself whether I am satisfied that the doctors recognize that death or serious harm will be virtually certain (barring some unforeseen intervention) to result from carrying out this operation. If so, the doctors intend to kill or do that serious harm even though they may not have any desire to achieve that result. It is common ground that they appreciate that death to Mary would result from the severance of the common aorta. Unpalatable though it may be ... to stigmatise the doctors with 'murderous intent', that is what in law they will have if they perform the operation and Mary dies as a result.

The doctrine of double effect ... teaches that an act which produces a bad effect is nevertheless morally permissible if the action is good in itself, the intention is solely to produce the good effect, the good effect is not produced through the bad effect and there is sufficient reason to permit the bad effect. It may be difficult to reconcile with *R. v Woollin* ... I can readily see how the doctrine works when doctors are treating one patient administering pain-killing drugs for the sole good purpose of relieving pain, yet appreciating the bad side effect that it will hasten the patient's death. I simply fail to see how it can apply here where the side-effect to the good cure for Jodie is another patient's, Mary's, death, and when the treatment cannot have been undertaken to effect any benefit for Mary."

Brooke LJ:
"[A]n English court would inevitably find that the surgeons intended to kill Mary, however little they desired that end, because her death would be the virtual certain consequence of their acts, and they would realize that for all practical purposes her death would inevitably follow ..."

Robert Walker LJ:
"However the stark facts of *R. v Woollin* and the speeches in the House of Lords in that case say nothing at all about the situation in which an individual acts for a good purpose which cannot be achieved without also having bad consequences (which may be merely possible, or very probable, or virtually certain). This is the doctrine (or dilemma) of double effect. In one class of case the good purpose and the foreseen but undesired consequence (what Bentham called 'oblique intention') are both directed at the same individual. This can be illustrated by a doctor's duty to his patient. ... [H]e may in order to palliate severe pain, administer large doses of analgesics even though he knows that the likely consequence will be to shorten the patient's life. ... In these cases the doctrine of double effect prevents the doctor's foresight of accelerated death from counting as a guilty intention. This type of double effect cannot be relevant to conduct directed towards Mary. ...

There is another class of case in which a person may be faced with the dilemma of whether to save himself or others at the cost of harm or even death to a third person. The dilemma generally arises as the result of an emergency ... [such as] disasters at sea. ... If a person, faced with such a dilemma, acts with the intention of saving his own life (or the lives of others) it may be said that that leaves no room for a guilty intention to harm or even kill the third person. Equally, it may be said that although he must (on *R. v Woollin* principles) be taken to have intended the death which he foresaw as virtually certain, he has a defence of necessity. That is the way the submission was put by Miss Davies. ...

In *Gillick v West Norfolk and Wisbech Area Health Authority* [1986] 1 A.C. 112 at 190, Lord Scarman ... said ...

'The bona fide exercise by a doctor of his clinical judgment must be a complete negation of the guilty mind which is an essential ingredient of the criminal offence ...'

Here the court is concerned with the possibility of the commission of a much more serious criminal offence, that is murder. But in the wholly exceptional case of these conjoined twins I consider that the same principles apply. ... Mary's death would be foreseen as an inevitable consequence of an operation which is intended, and is necessary, to save Jodie's life. But Mary's death would not be the purpose or intention of the surgery."

This case is significant in two respects. First, it demonstrates the difference between the two interpretations of intention. Ward LJ and Brooke LJ, in effect, followed the definitional interpretation. The doctors would foresee death as a virtual certainty and therefore they *would* intend death. However, Robert Walker LJ (implicitly) allowed himself moral elbow-room in holding that the doctors would not intend to kill the weaker twin because that was not "the purpose or intention of the surgery."

Secondly, this divergence of approach brings to the fore a central dilemma here. Is intention a psychological state of mind or a moral conclusion?[2] While Robert Walker LJ clearly adopted the latter view that there was no intention because the doctors would not be morally responsible for the death, the other two members of the Court of Appeal proceeded on the basis that intention is a psychological state. The issue was quite simply whether the doctors would, as a matter of fact, foresee death as a virtual certainty.

A conclusion that a defendant is criminally liable must, of course, involve a judgment of moral responsibility but the issue is ascertaining where such moral assessments should be located: ought they to be part of the question whether the defendant intended a result or should they affect the issue of whether a defence is available? For example, Ward LJ and Brooke LJ were clear that the doctors would not be guilty of murder but they achieved this result by holding that, while they would intend death, they would be afforded a defence of medical necessity. Similarly, *Steane* could have been decided on the basis that he did intend to assist the enemy but had a defence of duress because he was forced to broadcast.

The argument in favour of the view that intention should be a moral conclusion is that actions must pass a "threshold of responsibility" before there can be intention. For example, the teacher who gives a student a (deserved) bad mark knowing it will upset the pupil does not intend such upset because of a moral assessment by the teacher that he is only performing his duty to grade properly.[3] On this basis Norrie argues that "there is a *moral* objection in common sense to saying [that Steane obliquely intended to assist the enemy], which stems from the duress under which Steane operated. The threats to his family represented the basis of a

---

[2] Simester and Shute [2000] Crim.L.R.204.
[3] Duff, "Intention, *Mens Rea* and the Law Commission Report" [1980] Crim.L.R.147 at 152–154.

*moral* excuse for saying that he did not possess the oblique intention to assist the enemy, but only intended to save his family."[4] This approach is, however, problematic when there is uncertainty as to whether the defendant does have a moral excuse or not.

## Chandler v D.P.P. [1964] A.C. 763 (House of Lords)

The appellants were deeply opposed to nuclear weapons. In order to demonstrate their opposition they planned non-violent action to immobilise an aircraft at an RAF station for a period of six hours. They were convicted of conspiracy to commit a breach of section 1 of the Official Secrets Act 1911, namely to enter a prohibited place for "a purpose prejudicial to the safety or interests of the state". The trial judge ruled that they were not entitled to call evidence to show that it would be for the benefit of the country to give up nuclear armaments. He directed the jury to convict if they were satisfied that the immediate purpose of the appellants was the obstruction of an aircraft. Their appeal was dismissed by the Court of Criminal Appeals. They appealed to the House of Lords.

Radcliffe L.J.:
"The trial judge ... directed the jury that they should not be influenced by what, he said, was the undisputed fact that the views as to the wrongness and, indeed, unwisdom of nuclear weapons held by the appellants were deeply and passionately held and that they were honest and sincere views. In effect he put it to the jury that they should look on the appellants as having made their entry for two separate purposes, an immediate purpose of obstructing the airfield, and a further or long-term purpose of inducing or compelling the Government to abandon nuclear weapons in the true interests of the state. His ruling was that, if they found the immediate purpose proved, that of obstruction, they ought to find the appellants guilty of offences under section 1 of the Act, regardless of whether they might think the long-term purpose in itself beneficial or, at any rate, non-prejudicial to the interests and safety of the state. In my opinion there was nothing defective in law in this ruling."

**Appeal dismissed**

Following the definitional interpretation of *Woollin* the defendants in *Chandler* would clearly be liable—a view consistent with the notion that intention is a psychological state of mind. The moral judgment as to liability would be left to the determination of whether they should be afforded a defence—which they would not.[5] On the other hand, under the evidential interpretation of *Woollin*, the jury would be able to evaluate the motives of the defendants in deciding whether to find intention or not. There are, however, problems with this latter approach. First, whether intention would be "found" or not in a case such as *Chandler* would depend largely on the "political" persuasions of the jury, thus generating uncertainty and inconsistency. Secondly, it results in a blurring of the distinction between the elements of an offence and exculpatory defences.[6] Would it mean that Steane could have done *anything* (for example, blow up an aeroplane killing hundreds of people) to save his family?"[7]

[4] "Oblique Intention and Legal Politics" [1989] Crim.L.R.793 at 797.
[5] See p. 330–332.
[6] Wilson, "A plea for Rationality in the Law of Murder' (1990) 10 L.S. 307 at 310.
[7] Duff, "The Politics of Intention: A Response to Norrie" [1990] Crim.L.R.637 at 638.

Such an important question as whether duress should be a defence to murder should not be left to the vagaries of a jury decision. It raises fundamental moral questions, which should be determined as a matter of law within the parameters of the defence of duress.

## 4. A variable meaning?

In *Moloney* and *Hancock* it was stressed that the court was not only dealing with murder, but with all crimes of "intention". In short, according to these cases intention bears the same meaning throughout the criminal law.

However, Lord Steyn in *Woollin* was careful to limit the scope of his judgment: "I approach the issues arising on this appeal on the basis that it does not follow that 'intent' necessarily has the same meaning in every context in the criminal law." The impact of this limitation is, of course, dependent on which of the two interpretations of *Woollin*, discussed above, is adopted. If *Woollin* is interpreted as not defining intention, but simply confirming *Nedrick* that the jury is "entitled to find" intention where there is foresight of a virtual certainty, then this limitation is unimportant as the *Nedrick* test was broadly accepted as applying to all crimes that required intention.[8] But, if *Woollin* is interpreted as laying down a definition of intention, this would mean that there is a definition of intention for the crime of murder, but for all other crimes resort would still have to be had to *Nedrick*.

It is, of course, possible to argue that the concept "intention" should have a chameleon-like character and change its meaning according to its context. For example, Glanville Williams has argued that "intent" should generally include foresight of a virtual certainty, but that there are three exceptions where it should bear its narrowest, purposive meaning of "direct" intent: namely, offences of causing mental stress or annoyance; certain instances of complicity; and treason.[9] Duff, on the other hand, also argues for a concept of "oblique" intention but with three different exceptions where only "direct" intention should suffice. His exceptions are attempted crimes, other "with intent" crimes where there has to be an intention to cause a result not specified in the *actus reus* of the crime and, finally, the doctrine of implied malice.[10]

It is submitted that such an approach is unacceptable. As can be seen from the divergent views of the above writers, agreement as to which crimes should require which type of intention would be impossible to secure and would only increase the uncertainty in this area of law. Further, it is difficult to see that there is any justifiable legal policy underpinning a variable meaning for "intention". Also, such an approach would simply lead to complication and complexity. If the *Woollin* limitation were accepted it would mean that intention to cause grievous bodily harm for murder would be governed by *Woollin* but for section 18 of the Offences against the Person Act 1861 it would be governed by *Nedrick*.

Both in terms of principle and pragmatism, the concept "intention" should bear

---

[8] This view was adopted in *Purcell* (1986) 83 Cr.App.R.45; A.M.K. *Property Management Ltd* [1985] Crim.L.R.600; *Bryson* [1985] Crim.L.R.669; *Burke* [1988] Crim.L.R.839.

[9] "Oblique Intention" [1987] C.L.J. 417 at 435–437.

[10] Duff, "Intention, Mens Rea and the Law Commission Report" [1980] Crim.L.R.147; Duff, "Intentions Legal and Philosophical" (1989) 9 O.J.L.S. 76. A similar argument for a variable meaning has been put forward by Judge Buzzard ("Intent" [1978] Crim.L.R.5).

the same meaning throughout the criminal law. If it were felt that for certain crimes this fixed meaning was inappropriate, then an additional or alternative species of *mens rea* should be stipulated—without the concept of "intention" having to shrink or expand to meet the exigencies of all situations.

(ii) *Evaluation*

From the above discussion, it should be clear that in the wake of *Woollin* foresight of a virtual certainty is an alternative species of intention or, at least, an evidential precondition to a finding of intention. The implications of these two interpretations have been assessed. But, a final question remains. *Should* foresight of a virtual certainty suffice for intention? Is such an approach too narrow in that intention should perhaps be found to exist in a wider range of cases, where a consequence is foreseen as probable or likely? Or, is the foresight of a virtual certainty approach too broad in that intention should be restricted to its core meaning of direct intention (aim/purpose)? It is suggested that an appropriate meaning can only be ascribed to "intention" after the following three matters have been considered.

1. There ought to be some semantic precision about the law's use of the word "intention" so that it correlates with the layman's perceptions of the word.

Intention is an ordinary word in everyday usage. The criminal law ought to reflect the values of society and thus, if the word "intention" is to have any useful function, it ought to bear this ordinary meaning. As Duff states:

> "[T]he 'appeal to ordinary language' should not be despised: not just because it may cause confusion if the law uses terms whose legal and extra-legal meanings differ radically; but because the term's ordinary usage reflects our moral understanding of its relevance to ascriptions of responsibility, and of those distinctions which we regard as morally significant. Thus if it is any part of the law's purpose to assign legal liability in accordance with moral responsibility, there must be a presumption in favour of preserving the ordinary meanings of the concepts through which responsibility is assigned."[11]

Further, the task of the jury is made easier when legal terms are given their ordinary meanings. It was this desire to avoid confusing juries that led the Court of Appeal in *Belfon* to reject broader interpretations of intention:

> "There has never been any need to explain what 'intent' means since the specific intent is defined in the section. Juries do not seem to have experienced any difficulty in understanding the word 'intent' without further explanation."[12]

It was this reasoning that led Lord Bridge in *Moloney* to his view that generally juries needed no guidance as to the meaning of "intention". It was a matter of fact to be decided by them according to the ordinary usage of the word.

On the other hand, as Lacey has suggested, "if ordinary usage is as consistent and reliable as [the House of Lords] presumably think it is given the importance they accord to it, guidelines would be irrelevant."[13] In short, it is not always easy to ascertain the "ordinary, everyday" meaning of words. This difficulty in assigning

---

[11] Duff, "Intention, *Mens Rea* and the Law Commission Report" [1980] Crim.L.R.147 at 148.
[12] (1976) 63 Cr.App.R.59 at 60.
[13] Lacey, "A Clear Concept of Intention: Elusive or Illusory?" (1993) M.L.R. 621 at 634.

an "ordinary" meaning to intention is illustrated by the fact that while most commentators agree with the Oxford English Dictionary definition of "intend" as aim or design, Lord Cross in the now discredited House of Lords decision of *Hyam* considered that the "ordinary man" would equate foresight of injury with intentionally causing injury. It may well be that Lord Cross was falling into the common trap of confusing the issue of how ordinary people would describe the concept of intention with the issue of whom ordinary people would want to hold responsible for their actions. However, despite this potential problem, it seems tolerably clear that to most people the term "intend" means "aiming at" or "meaning to achieve". The consequence must be one's purpose, objective or goal. Even the Law Commission in an earlier draft Bill accept that they are attributing an artificial meaning to the word intention when they defined their "standard test of intention" as being "**either** [to] intend ... **or** have no substantial doubt".[14] Having no substantial doubt is clearly accepted as being something different from intention. As has been stated: "Oblique intention is not really any kind of intention at all. It is a label for a different sort of mental state altogether, namely foresight or, in Model Penal Code terminology, knowledge. Calling it a species of intention is pure obfuscation."[15]

Should intention be defined or simply left to the jury? It is becoming increasingly common in criminal law to leave crucial issues such as this to the jury. For instance, one of the critical concepts in theft, "dishonesty", is largely left to jury determination. However, a concept such as "dishonesty" involves the application of standards; ethical stances have to be taken. In short, a judgment has to be made as to the morality of the defendant's actions. The jury, as the mouthpiece of community values, is probably the most appropriate body to express such judgments. It has been argued that this is no less true of the concept "intention" and that judicial reliance on "the haven of 'ordinary language' "[16] allows judges to let in through the back door ethical questions concerning the appropriateness of criminal liability "under the guise of supplementing conceptual analysis in a value-neutral way".[17] As already seen, however, many commentators argue that the meaning to be attributed to "intention" should involve moral judgments but these are less various, and perhaps more capable of reduction to a single formula, than the never-ending range of factors affecting ethical judgments as to the meaning of a concept such as dishonesty.[18] Accordingly, it would be preferable for "intention" to be given a legal definition, and that definition should largely reflect the ordinary meaning of the word.

2. The law ought to define intention in such a manner that it can be clearly distinguished from recklessness. One of the main problems with the old *Hyam*

---

[14] Law Com. No. 89, *Report on the Mental Element of Crime* (1978), p. 56.

[15] Finkelstein, "No Harm No Foul? Objectivism and the Law of Attempts" (1999) 18 Law and Philosophy 69 at 75.

[16] Lacey, *above*, n.13 at 633. Lacey has argued that the appeal to "ordinary usage" implies that the criminal law "operates on the basis of widely shared meanings and widely endorsed judgments. It hence suppresses the idea that criminal law is hierarchical, an exercise of power, based on meanings which are imposed" (p. 636).

[17] Horder, "Intention in the Criminal Law—a Rejoinder" (1995) 58 M.L.R. 678 at 679, summarising Lacey's views.

[18] Clarkson and Keating, "Codification: Offences against the Person under the Draft Criminal Code" (1986) 50 J.Crim.L. 405 at 410.

formulation that foresight of a probable or highly probable consequence amounted to intention was that no principle could be discerned to establish the cut-off point between recklessness and intention. Foreseeing a consequence as probable or likely was intention but foreseeing it as less than probable was recklessness. Such a test involved having to define "probable" and "likely".[19] While these problems are perhaps reduced after *Woollin*, they have not been eradicated. The boundary between intention and recklessness has simply shifted. If a consequence is foreseen as extremely likely this will presumably still amount to recklessness whereas if it is foreseen as virtually certain it can count as intention (or intention can be found). No principled basis for distinguishing between these two states of mind exists because, in both situations, the consequence is not the objective of the action. In both, it is simply a by-product of the actor's actions that is foreseen as having varying chances of occurring. The only clear basis for drawing the distinction would be to limit intention to direct intention.

3. The final factor to be taken into account in ascribing a meaning to the concept intention is the most important, but also the most elusive. Is there a moral difference between foreseeing a consequence as likely, foreseeing it as virtually certain and aiming at it? If so, where should this "moral line" be drawn?

First, should intention be given a broad meaning so as to include foresight of a consequence as merely probable or likely? If there is no significant moral difference between the person who aims to achieve a consequence and the person who merely foresees that a consequence is probable, then one *might* be justified in describing both as intention; but if there is a moral distinction between the two, this distinction will need to be reflected by the law in order that different levels of liability and punishment can be imposed.

### H. L. A. Hart, "Intention and Punishment" in Punishment and Responsibility (1968), pp. 119–122:

"[Hart cites the case of *R. v Desmond, Barrett and Others* (*The Times*, April 28, 1868) where the defendant, Barrett, dynamited a prison wall in order to effect the escape of two Irish Fenians imprisoned therein. Though the plot failed, the explosion killed some persons living nearby].

[F]or the law, a foreseen outcome is enough, even if it was unwanted by the agent, even if he thought of it as an undesirable by-product of his activities, and in Desmond's case this is what the death of those killed by the explosion was. It was no part of Barrett's purpose or aim to kill or injure anyone; the victims' deaths were not a means to his end; to bring them about was not his reason or part of his reason for igniting the fuse, but he was convicted on the ground that he foresaw their death or serious injury. . . .

The reason [that the law should neglect the difference between direct intention and foreseeing the consequence] is, I suggest, that both the case of direct intention and that of oblique intention share one feature which any system of assigning responsibility for conduct must always regard as of crucial importance. This can be seen if we compare the actual facts of the Desmond case with a case of direct intention. Suppose Barrett shot the prison guard in order to obtain from them the keys to release the prisoners. Both in the actual Desmond case and in this imaginary variant, so far as Barrett had control over the alternative between the victims' dying or living, his choice tipped the balance; in both these cases he had control over and may be considered to have chosen the outcome, since he consciously opted for the course

[19] For a discussion of these issues, see the previous edition of this book at p. 147.

leading to the victims' deaths. Whether he sought to achieve this as an end or a means to his end, or merely foresaw it as an unwelcome consequence of his intervention, is irrelevant at the stage of conviction where the question of control is crucial. However, when it comes to the question of sentence and the determination of the severity of punishment it may be (though I am not at all sure that this is in fact the case) that on both a retributive and a utilitarian theory of punishment the distinction between direct and oblique intention is relevant."

This "control" test of intention is similar to the views of Lord Diplock in *Hyam* when he equated desiring a consequence with foreseeing that consequence as likely because "what is common to both these states of mind is willingness to produce the particular evil consequence".

Even if one accepts Hart's premise that the actor has "control" in both situations, does this necessarily mean that both states of mind must be defined as "intention", and that both deserve the same level of criminal liability? The actor who acts recklessly in merely foreseeing a remote possibility of a consequence occurring, is also "in control", but if one were to designate such actions as being intentional, one would have eliminated much of the concept of recklessness.

This view that intention should include foresight of probable consequences has been firmly rejected by English law (in *Maloney* and *Hancock*) and no longer commands serious support from commentators and so will not be considered further.

The prevailing view, both judicial and extra-judicial, is that intention should extend beyond its core meaning to include foresight of a consequence as a virtual, practical or moral certainty ("oblique intent").

### Glanville Williams, Textbook of Criminal Law (2nd ed., 1983), pp. 84–85:

"Clearly, a person can be taken to intend a consequence that follows under his nose from what he continues to do, and the law should be the same where he is aware that a consequence in the future is the certain or practically certain result of what he does. As Lord Hailsham said in *Hyam*, 'intention' includes 'the means as well as the end and the inseparable consequences of the end as well as the means.' (What he evidently meant was the consequences known to the defendant to be inseparable.) ...

To take a hypothetical case: suppose that a villain of the deepest dye sends an insured parcel on an aircraft, and includes in it a time-bomb by which he intends to bring down the plane and consequently to destroy the parcel. His immediate intention is merely to collect on the insurance. He does not care whether the people on board live or die, but he knows that success in his scheme will inevitably involve their deaths as a side-effect. On the theoretical point, common sense suggests that the notion of intention should be extended to this situation; it should not merely be regarded as a case of recklessness. A consequence should normally be taken as intended although it was not desired, if it was foreseen by the actor as the *virtually certain* accompaniment of what he intended. This is not the same as saying that any consequence foreseen as *probable* is intended. ...

Clearly, one cannot confine the notion of foresight of certainty to certainty in the most absolute sense. It is a question of human certainty, or virtual certainty, or practical certainty. This is still not the same as speaking in terms of probability."

The view that foresight of a virtual certainty amounts to intention was embraced by the Criminal Law Revision Committee[20] and was essentially the test adopted by the

---

[20] 14th Report, *Offences against the Person*, Cmnd.7844 (1980), para. 10.

Law Commission in their Draft Criminal Code.[21] In 1998 the Government published a Consultation Document and Draft Bill which, if enacted, would result in legislative acceptance of this test for all non-fatal offences against the person. Such a statutory provision would not, of course, directly apply to other offences such as murder.

### Draft Offences against the Person Bill 1998, clause 14(1):

"A person acts intentionally with respect to a result if—
  (a) it is his purpose to cause it, or
  (b) although it is not his purpose to cause it, he knows that it would occur in the ordinary course of events if he were to succeed in his purpose of causing some other result."

### The Law Commission (Law Com. No. 177), A Criminal Code for England and Wales, Commentary on Draft Criminal Code Bill (1989), paras 8.14–8.16:

"Acting in order to bring about a result is, as it were, the standard case of 'intending' to cause a result. But we are satisfied that a definition of 'intention' for criminal law purposes must refer, as Lord Hailsham of St Marylebone L.C. expressed it in *Hyam* to 'the means as well as the end and the inseparable consequences of the end as well as the means.' Where a person acts in order to achieve a particular purpose, knowing that this cannot be done without causing another result, he must be held to intend to cause that other result. The other result may be a pre-condition—as where D, in order to injure P, throws a brick through the window behind which he knows P to be standing; or it may be a necessary concomitant of the first result—as (to use a much quoted example) where D blows up an aeroplane in flight in order to recover on the insurance covering its cargo, knowing that the crew will inevitably be killed. D intends to break the window and he intends to kill the crew. But there is no absolute certainty in human affairs. P *might* fling up the window while the brick is in flight. The crew *might* make a miraculous escape by parachute. D's purpose *might* be achieved without causing the second result—but these are only remote possibilities and D, if he contemplates them at all (which may be unlikely), must know that they are only remote possibilities. The result will occur, and D knows that it will occur, 'in the ordinary course of events ... unless something supervenes to prevent it.' It is, and he knows it is, 'a virtual certainty.' We have adopted the phrase, 'in the ordinary course of events' to ensure that 'intention' covers the case of a person who knows that the achievement of his purpose will necessarily cause the result in question, in the absence of some wholly improbable supervening event.

A person's awareness of any degree of probability (short of virtual certainty) that a particular result will follow from his acts ought not, we believe, to be classed as an 'intention' to cause that result for criminal law purposes. This accords with the general tendency of modern decisions on offences defined in terms of intention. Liability based on the awareness of a probable result can be provided for by casting the offence in terms of recklessness."

There are, however, contrary views that intention should not be expanded so as to include oblique intention. The argument here is that there are strong moral

---

[21] Law Com. No. 177 (1989), clause 18. It also represents the common law position in the United States where Burger C.J. in *United States v United States Gypsum* (438 US 422) held that a person intended a result "when he knows that the result is practically certain to follow from his conduct, whatever his desire may be as to that result". The Canadian Law Reform Commission produced an even stricter definition that the defendant must act "in order to effect: (a) that consequence; or (b) another consequence which he knows involves that consequence" (Report 31, *Recodifying Criminal Law* (1987); see Smith, "A Note on 'Intention' " [1990] Crim.L.R.85).

justifications for distinguishing between an actor who foresees a result as virtually certain and one who tries to achieve that result. A person's objectives or aims influence our perceptions of their character as a moral agent. Actions become more reprehensible if they are deliberate and purposeful. A boy, throwing a ball dangerously near a window and realizing that there is a better than even chance that in the course of his game he could break the window, will instinctively cry out: "I didn't mean to break it", when the window is duly shattered. Our characterisation of the boy as amoral agent would be different if he had deliberately taken aim and thrown the ball, trying to break the window. As Duff says:

"To do what I believe will help the enemy, or cause injury, may be counted criminal even when I do it for reasons which have nothing to do with helping the enemy or causing injury: but to act with the *intention of helping* the enemy, or causing injury, gives a quite different moral character to the action, which we may wish to mark by making only that an offence, or by making it a more serious offence."[22]

### John Finnis, "Intention and Side-effects" in R. G. Frey and Christopher W. Morris, Liability and Responsibility (1991), p. 46:

"[I]t is well to recall how foreign to the commonsense concept of intention is the academics' notion that what is foreseen as certain is intended.

One who hangs curtains knowing that the sunlight will make them fade does not thereby intend that they shall fade. Those who wear shoes don't intend them to wear out. Those who fly the Atlantic foreseeing certain jetlag don't do so with the intention to get jetlag; those who drink too heavily rarely intend the hangover they know is certain ... Indeed, we might call the academics' extended notion of intent the Pseudo-Masochist Theory of Intention—for it holds that those who foresee that their actions will have painful effects upon themselves *intend* those effects."

### R. A. Duff, Intention, Agency and Criminal Liability: Philosophy of Action and the Criminal Law (1990), pp. 111–113:

"[A] non-consequentialist view ... finds an intrinsic moral difference in intended action; a significance which depends not on its expected consequences, but on the intentions which structure it. ... One who tries to kill me ... *attacks* my life and my most basic rights; and the harm which I suffer in being murdered (or in being the victim of an attempted murder) essentially involves this wrongful attack on me. The point is not that a murder victim suffers the same (consequential) harm of death as a victim of natural causes, and also suffers the *separate* harm of being attacked: it is that she suffers the distinctive harm of being killed by one who attacks her life. The 'harm' at which the law of murder is aimed is thus not just the *consequential* harm of death, but the harm which is *intrinsic* to an attack on another's life ... [A]n attack is an action which is *intended* to do harm ... It is through the intentions with which I act that I engage in the world as an agent, and relate myself most closely to the actual and potential effects of my actions; and the central or fundamental kind of wrong-doing is to *direct* my actions towards evil—to *intend* and to *try* to do what is evil."[23]

This is the approach recommended in the United States by the American Law Institute's Model Penal Code and which has been widely adopted in state code

---

[22] "Intention, *Mens Rea* and The Law Commission Report" [1980] Crim.L.R.147 at 159.

[23] Duff does, however, go on to argue that such direct intention should only be required in exceptional cases (see, *above*, p. 135).

revisions throughout the United States. The Code does not adopt the view of intention favoured by the Law Commission and leading commentators in England. It adopts the narrower view that a person acts intentionally "when ... it is his conscious object to engage in conduct of that nature or to cause such a result".[24] What of foresight of a virtual certainty? The Model Penal Code does not assimilate this with intention, nor does it relegate it to the realms of recklessness. Instead, it has created a special category of *mens rea* between intention and recklessness, namely, knowledge. Section 202(2)(b) defines "knowingly" in the following terms:

> "A person acts knowingly with respect to a material element of an offense when: ... (ii) if the element involves a result of his conduct, he is aware that it is practically certain that his conduct will cause such a result."

The commentary to this sub-section recognises that the distinction drawn is a narrow one and is "no doubt inconsequential for most purposes of liability". But apart from being conceptually necessary and helping to promote clarity of definition, the distinction does have some practical utility as

> "there are areas where the discrimination is required.... This is true in treason, for example, in so far as a purpose to aid the enemy is an ingredient of the offense ... and in attempts and conspiracy, where a true purpose to effect the criminal result is requisite for liability.... The distinction also has utility in differentiating among grades of an offense for purposes of sentence, *e.g.* in the case of homicide."[25]

Thus, according to this view, there is a moral, as well as a linguistic, justification for drawing this fine distinction. Indeed there are some states in the United States that have employed this Model Penal Code terminology and have felt the distinction to be sufficiently material to warrant using it as the basis for a grading of homicide offences. Alaska provides that it is murder in the first degree to kill "with intent to cause the death of another person", but only murder in the second degree to kill "knowing that the conduct is substantially certain to cause death".[26] New Hampshire provides that it is first degree murder to kill "purposely" and second degree murder to kill "knowingly"[27] and Louisiana, while not following the Model Penal Code formulation, has adopted a similar distinction under which "specific intent" requires that the offender "actively desired the prescribed criminal consequences to follow his act" but a "general intent" includes "advert[ing] to the prescribed criminal consequences as reasonably certain to result from his act".[28]

One final question remains. How should one classify cases where a consequence is foreseen as *certain*, as opposed to virtually certain? In these situations the consequence is foreseen as something that *must* happen; it is a condition precedent to the occurrence of the actor's primary aim.[29] To take the classic example where I

---

[24] American Law Institute, Model Penal Code, s.202(2)(a) prefers the term "purposely". However, most code revisions have used this same definition for the term "intention".

[25] American Law Institute, Model Penal Code, Tent. Draft No. 4 (1955) Art. 2, pp. 124, 125.

[26] Alaska Stat. tit. 11, ss.11.41.100, 110.

[27] N.H. Rev.Stat.Ann. ss.630: 1–a, b.

[28] La.Rev.Stat. s.14–10 (1997).

[29] This need not be scientific certainty, but the consequence must be inseparable in terms of the agent's conception of the world as he understands it (Simester, "Moral Certainty and the Boundaries of Intention" (1996) 16 O.J.L.S. 445 at 459).

intend to shoot you; you are standing behind a glass window that cannot open. Do I intend to break the window? In this case I foresee it as certain that I will break the glass; I cannot shoot you without doing so. This means that breaking the glass *is* my aim or objective, albeit only a secondary aim or objective to my main one of killing you. It is a necessary and "wanted" means to my end. I intend to break the window. Lord Hailsham in *Hyam* endorsed this when he spoke of "intention, which embraces, in addition to the end, all the necessary consequences of an action including the means to the end and any consequences intended along with the end".[30]

But where an undesired consequence is only foreseen as "virtually certain" or "morally certain" it ceases to be an inescapable consequence or a necessary means to an end. It thus ceases to be a secondary aim and should no longer be described as intention. In the celebrated example where I blow up an aircraft in flight in order to obtain the insurance money and the passengers are killed, I would foresee the death of these passengers as virtually certain. But, if it is not my object to kill them, the fact that there is a chance (albeit one in a million) that they could parachute to safety, means that their death is not a necessary means to an end and cannot be described as intention. Using Duff's "test of failure",[31] blowing up the aeroplane without killing the occupants would not mark the failure of the enterprise, but would represent the ultimate in success. Similarly, flying across the Atlantic and not suffering jetlag would be a cause for celebration. On the other hand, failing to break the window represents a failure of the agent's action because this necessarily involves not killing the person behind it. The line of demarcation is a thin one and would only apply in the most exceptional cases.[32] Nevertheless, it is a conceptually clear distinction and provides a principled basis for distinguishing intention from recklessness. There is no intention to kill the passengers on the aeroplane, but there is an intention to break the glass.

If there are indeed linguistic, practical and moral justifications for distinguishing between intention (including the condition precedent cases) and foresight of the virtually certain, English law would surely not be justified in following the Law Commission's proposal to treat both as "intention".

## 2. Recklessness

### (i) *The background*

Some crimes, such as attempt, can only be committed intentionally and it is thus crucial to be able to distinguish intention from recklessness. This line of demarcation depends, as we have just seen, on how broadly one chooses to define

---

[30] [1975] A.C. 55 at 73.

[31] See p. 127.

[32] Ashworth, *Principles of Criminal Law* (3rd ed., 1999), pp. 178–179. Norrie, *above*, n.4 at 801 and the Law Commission, *above*, n.21 all deny the possibility of drawing such a distinction on the basis that virtual certainty "denote[s] the only kind of certainty that it is ever possible to have in any practical intervention in the natural or social world." (Norrie) This ignores the fact that one is dealing with a subjective concept. It is the defendant's aims and foresight that matter. To most defendants firing at the person standing behind the window, it is only possible to shoot the victim *by* breaking the glass. The fact that it might actually be possible to achieve the result without breaking the window (an earthquake might break the glass at the critical moment) does not alter the fact that the defendant is trying to break the window.

"intention". Any degree of foresight less than that specified in the definition of intention will constitute recklessness. But a vast number of crimes can be committed "intentionally or recklessly". Indeed, the Draft Criminal Code 1989 proposes that recklessness should be the basic fault element for *all* offences (unless otherwise stated).[33] For all these crimes the distinction between intention and recklessness is unimportant; what matters, instead, is the distinction between recklessness and negligence or other forms of conduct not regarded as equally blameworthy. This demarcation is vital as it has been the general policy of English law to punish reckless wrongdoing, but, with exceptions, to exempt negligent wrongdoing from criminal liability.

### (ii) *Two species of recklessness*

The concept "recklessness" has had a chequered and uncertain history with judges vacillating as to whether it meant "gross negligence"[34] (an objective *major* deviation from the standards of the reasonable person) or whether it should be limited to cases where the defendant subjectively realised that there was a possibility of the consequence occurring (or the circumstance existing) but carried on regardless.

### (a) Cunningham recklessness

By the late 1970s, following the leading decision of *Cunningham*,[35] the subjective meaning of recklessness had clearly been approved. Recklessness entailed the conscious running of an unjustifiable risk. The following case was illustrative of this approach.

### R. v Stephenson [1979] 1 Q.B. 695 (Court of Appeal, Criminal Division)

The appellant, who had crept into a hollow in the side of a large straw stack to sleep, felt cold and lit a fire of twigs and straw inside the hollow. The stack caught fire and was damaged. The appellant admitted that he had lit the fire but said the damage was an accident. He was charged with arson contrary to section 1(1) of the Criminal Damage Act 1971. Evidence on his behalf was given by a consultant psychiatrist that the appellant suffered from schizophrenia, and that the schizophrenia could have the effect of depriving him of the ability of a normal person to foresee or appreciate the risk of damage from the act of lighting the fire. The judge directed the jury that a person who without lawful excuse destroyed or damaged another's property was "reckless as to whether any such property would be destroyed or damaged," within section 1(1) of the 1971 Act, if he closed his mind to the obvious fact of risk from his act, and that schizophrenia might be a reason which made a person close his mind to the obvious fact of risk. The jury returned a verdict of guilty and the appellant was convicted. He appealed against the conviction on the ground, *inter alia*, of a misdirection by the judge on what constituted recklessness.

---

[33] Law Com. No. 177 (1989), cl. 20(1).
[34] *Andrews v D.P.P.* [1937] A.C. 576.
[35] [1957] 2 Q.B. 396. See also *Briggs* [1977] 1 W.L.R. 605; *Parker* [1977] 1 W.L.R. 600; Law Commission, *Report on the Mental Element in Crime* (Law Com. No. 89), 1978, paras 20–21.

Geoffrey Lane L.J.:

"The problem is not difficult to state. Does the word 'reckless' require that the defendant must be proved actually to have foreseen the risk of some damage resulting from his actions and nevertheless to have run the risk (the subjective test), or is it sufficient to prove that the risk of damage resulting would have been obvious to any reasonable person in the defendant's position (the objective test)? In our view it is the subjective test which is correct.

What then must the prosecution prove in order to bring home the charge of arson in circumstances such as the present? They must prove that ... the defendant either (a) intended to cause the damage to the property, or (b) was reckless as to whether the property was damaged or not. A man is reckless when he carries out the deliberate act appreciating that there is a risk that damage to property may result from his act. It is however not the taking of every risk which could properly be classed as reckless. The risk must be one which it is in all the circumstances unreasonable for him to take.

Proof of the requisite knowledge in the mind of the defendant will in most cases present little difficulty. The fact that the risk of some damage would have been obvious to anyone in his right mind in the position of the defendant is not conclusive proof of the defendant's knowledge, but it may well be and in many cases doubtless will be a matter which will drive the jury to the conclusion that the defendant himself must have appreciated the risk. The fact that he may have been in a temper at the time would not normally deprive him of knowledge or foresight of the risk. If he had the necessary knowledge or foresight and his bad temper merely caused him to disregard it or put it to the back of his mind not caring whether the risk materialised, or if it merely deprived him of the self-control necessary to prevent him from taking the risk of which he was aware, then his bad temper will not avail him. This was the concept which the court in *R. v Parker (Daryl)* [1977] 1 W.L.R. 600, 604 was trying to express when it used the words 'or closing his mind to the obvious fact that there is some risk of damage resulting from that act....' We wish to make it clear that the test remains subjective, that the knowledge or appreciation of risk of some damage must have entered the defendant's mind even though he may have suppressed it or driven it out....

How do these pronouncements affect the present appeal? The appellant, through no fault of his own, was in a mental condition which might have prevented him from appreciating the risk which would have been obvious to any normal person. When the judge said to the jury 'there may be ... all kinds of reasons which make a man close his mind to the obvious fact—among them may be schizophrenia'—we think he was guilty of a misapprehension, albeit possibly an understandable misapprehension. The schizophrenia was on the evidence something which might have prevented the idea of danger entering the appellant's mind at all. If that was the truth of the matter, then the appellant was entitled to be acquitted. That was something which was never left clearly to the jury to decide."

**Appeal allowed**

Under this "subjective" approach the definition of recklessness, both as to consequences and circumstances,[36] imposes a double test:

(1) whether the defendant foresaw the possibility of the consequence occurring; and

(2) whether it was unjustifiable or unreasonable to take the risk.

Whether a risk is justifiable or not depends on the social importance of the acts and on the chances of the forbidden consequence occurring. As the Law Commission has stated:

"The operation of public transport, for example, is inevitably accompanied by risks of accident beyond the control of the operator, yet it is socially necessary

---

[36] For the sake of simplicity the remainder of this section will refer only to consequences, but this should be taken to include circumstances.

that these risks be taken. Dangerous surgical operations must be carried out in the interests of the life and health of the patient, yet the taking of these risks is socially justifiable."[37]

Thus if there is perceived to be a one in a thousand chance of high speed trains being involved in an accident, the social value of high-speed public transport is such as to render the taking of such a remote risk justifiable, but if it is realised that there is a one in twenty chance of these trains being involved in an accident, then the chances of an accident occurring outweighs the social importance of the activity and it becomes unjustifiable to take such a risk. On the other hand, if there is the same (subjectively perceived) one in a thousand chance of killing a friend while playing Russian roulette, the complete absence of any social value attached to the activity renders the taking of the risk unjustifiable. Thus the test involves a subtle balancing operation between the following questions: how socially useful is the activity? What are the perceived chances of the harm occurring? How serious is the harm that could occur? For example, in *Vehicle Inspectorate v Nuttall*[38] it was stated that if one was dealing with conduct that could imperil the safety of the public, foresight of the slightest possibility (of a breach of contraventions) would suffice.

Whether a risk is justifiable or unreasonable is an objective issue and does not depend on the defendant's view of the matter. For example, in *Dodman*[39] it was stated that it was irrelevant that the defendant did not know his conduct was wrongful. Of course, the question whether there is any social utility in an activity is a highly evaluative one which has led some writers to argue that the concept of recklessness is an inherently political one.[40] This is true inasmuch as a value judgment is involved, a point that can always be made when employing a value-ridden concept such as "reasonableness".[41] The advantage, however, of employing such a concept and leaving it to the jury is that they can reflect the ever-shifting notions of social utility.

The Law Commission in the Draft Criminal Law Bill 1993[42] has endorsed this "subjective" approach, as has the Draft Offences Against the Person Bill 1998, clause 14(2) of which provides:

"A person acts recklessly with respect to a result if he is aware of a risk that it will occur and it is unreasonable to take that risk having regard to the circumstances as he knows or believes them to be."

### (b) Caldwell/Lawrence recklessness

In 1981 there was a radical change of direction when the House of Lords handed down two judgments on the same day, both concerned with the meaning of recklessness. It should be stressed that this change only affects the first limb of the

---

[37] Law Com. No. 31, *Working Paper on the Mental Element in Crime*, p. 53.
[38] [1999] 1 W.L.R. 629.
[39] [1998] 2 Cr.App.R.338
[40] Norrie, "Subjectivism, Objectivism and the Limits of Criminal Recklessness" (1992) 12 O.J.L.S. 45.
[41] Griffiths, *The Politics of the Judiciary* (4th ed., 1991).
[42] Law Com. No. 218, *Legislating the Criminal Code: Offences against the Person and General Principles* (1993).

test cited above, namely, whether the defendant must foresee the possibility of harm occurring. It does not affect the second requirement that it be unjustifiable to take the risk.

## R. v Caldwell [1982] A.C. 341 (House of Lords)

The respondent had done some work for the owner of a hotel as the result of which he had a quarrel with the owner, got drunk and set fire to the hotel in revenge. The fire was discovered and put out before any serious damage was caused and none of the ten guests in the hotel at the time was injured. The respondent was indicted on two counts of arson under section 1(1) and (2) of the Criminal Damage Act 1971. At his trial he pleaded guilty to the lesser charge of intentionally or recklessly destroying or damaging the property of another, contrary to section 1(1) but pleaded not guilty to the more serious charge under section 1(2) of damaging property with intent to endanger life or being reckless whether life would be endangered. He claimed that he was so drunk at the time that the thought that he might be endangering the lives of the people in the hotel had never crossed his mind. The trial judge directed the jury that drunkenness was not a defence to a charge under section 1(2) and he was convicted.

The Court of Appeal allowed his appeal. The Crown appealed to the House of Lords, where in order to decide whether drunkenness was a defence to a charge under section 1(2), the House ruled that it was necessary to decide upon the precise meaning of the term recklessness as employed in section 1(2).

Lord Diplock (with whom Lord Keith and Lord Roskill concurred):

"My Lords, the Criminal Damage Act 1971 replaced almost in their entirety the many and detailed provisions of the Malicious Damage Act 1861. . . .

In the Act of 1861, the word consistently used to describe the mens rea that was a necessary element in the multifarious offences that the Act created was 'maliciously' . . . *R. v Cunningham* . . . approved, as an accurate statement of the law, what had been said by Professor Kenny in the first edition of his *Outlines of Criminal Law* published in 1902:

'In any statutory definition of a crime, malice must be taken . . . as requiring either (1) an actual intention to do the particular kind of harm that in fact was done; or (2) recklessness as to whether such harm should occur or not (*i.e.* the accused has foreseen that the particular kind of harm might be done and yet has gone on to take the risk of it).'

My Lords, in this passage Professor Kenny was engaged in defining for the benefit of students the meaning of 'malice' as a term of art in criminal law. To do so he used ordinary English words in their popular meaning. Among the words he used was 'recklessness,' the noun derived from the adjective 'reckless,' of which the popular or dictionary meaning is careless, regardless, or heedless, of the possible harmful consequences of one's acts. It presupposes that if thought were given to the matter by the doer before the act was done, it would have been apparent to him that there was a real risk of its having the relevant harmful consequences; but, granted this, recklessness covers a whole range of states of mind from failing to give any thought at all to whether or not there is any risk of those harmful consequences, to recognising the existence of the risk and nevertheless deciding to ignore it. Conscious of this imprecision in the popular meaning of recklessness as descriptive of a state of mind, Professor Kenny, in the passage quoted, was, as it seems to me, at pains to indicate by the words in brackets the particular species within the genus reckless states of mind that constituted 'malice' in criminal law. This parenthetical restriction on the natural meaning of recklessness was necessary to an explanation of the meaning of the adverb 'maliciously' . . . but it was not directed to and consequently has no bearing on the meaning of the adjective 'reckless' in section 1 of the Criminal Damage Act 1971. To use it for that purpose can, in my view, only be misleading.

My Lords, the restricted meaning that the Court of Appeal in *R. v Cunningham* had placed upon the adverb 'maliciously' in the Malicious Damage Act 1861 in cases where the prosecution did not rely upon an actual intention of the accused to cause the damage that was in fact done, called for a meticulous analysis by the jury of the thoughts that passed through the mind of the accused at or before the time he did the act that caused the damage, in order to see on which side of a narrow dividing line they fell. If it had crossed his mind that there was a risk that someone's property might be damaged but, because his mind was affected by rage or excitement or confused by drink, he did not appreciate the seriousness of the risk or trusted that good luck would prevent its happening, this state of mind would amount to malice in the restricted meaning placed upon that term by the Court of Appeal; whereas if, for any of these reasons, he did not even trouble to give his mind to the question whether there was any risk of damaging the property, this state of mind would not suffice to make him guilty of an offence under the Malicious Damage Act 1861.

Neither state of mind seems to me to be less blameworthy than the other; but if the difference between the two constituted the distinction between what does and what does not in legal theory amount to a guilty state of mind for the purposes of a statutory offence of damage to property, it would not be a practicable distinction for use in a trial by jury. The only person who knows what the accused's mental processes were is the accused himself—and probably not even he can recall them accurately when the rage or excitement under which he acted has passed, or he has sobered up if he were under the influence of drink at the relevant time. If the accused gives evidence that because of his rage, excitement or drunkenness the risk of particular harmful consequences of his acts simply did not occur to him, a jury would find it hard to be satisfied beyond reasonable doubt that his true mental process was not that, but was the slightly different mental process required if one applies the restricted meaning of 'being reckless as to whether' something would happen, adopted by the Court of Appeal in *R. v Cunningham.*

My Lords, I can see no reason why Parliament when it decided to revise the law as to offences of damage to property should go out of its way to perpetuate fine and impracticable distinctions such as these, between one mental state and another. One would think that the sooner they were got rid of, the better.

When cases under section 1(1) of the new Act ... first came before the Court of Appeal, the question as to the meaning of the expression 'reckless' in the context of that subsection appears to have been treated as soluble simply by posing and answering what had by then, unfortunately, become an obsessive question among English lawyers: Is the test of recklessness 'subjective' or 'objective'? The first two reported cases, in both of which judgments were given off the cuff, are first *R. v Briggs (Note)* [1977] 1 W.L.R. 605 which is reported in a footnote to the second, *R. v Daryl Parker* [1977] 1 W.L.R. 600. Both classified the test of recklessness as 'subjective.' This led the court in *R. v Briggs (Note)* to say: 'A man is reckless in the sense required when he carries out a deliberate act knowing that there is some risk of damage resulting from that act but nevertheless continues in the performance of that act.' This leaves over the question whether the risk of damage may not be so slight that even the most prudent of men would feel justified in taking it, but it excludes that kind of recklessness that consists of acting without giving any thought at all to whether or not there is any risk of harmful consequences of one's act; even though the risk is great and would be obvious if any thought were given to the matter by the doer of the act. *R. v Daryl Parker*, however, opened the door a chink by adding as an alternative to the actual knowledge of the accused that there is some risk of damage resulting from his act and his going on to take it, a mental state described as 'closing his mind to the obvious fact' that there is such a risk.

*R. v Stephenson* ... slammed the door again upon any less restricted interpretation of 'reckless' as to whether particular consequences will occur than that originally approved in *Briggs* ... It made the assumption that ... [Parliament] intended the words [being reckless] to be interpreted in precisely the same sense as that in which the single adverb 'maliciously' had been construed by Professor Kenny in the passage that received the subsequent approval of the Court of Appeal in *R. v Cunningham.*

My Lords, I see no warrant for making any such assumption in an Act whose declared purpose is to revise the then existing law as to offences of damage to property, not to perpetuate it. 'Reckless' as used in the new statutory definition of the mens rea of these offences is an ordinary English word. It had not by 1971 become a term of legal art with some more limited esoteric meaning than that which it bore in ordinary speech—a meaning which surely includes not only deciding to ignore a risk of harmful consequences resulting from one's acts that one has recognised as existing, but also failing to give any thought to whether or not there is any such risk in circumstances where, if any thought were given to the matter it would be obvious that there was.

If one is attaching labels, the latter state of mind is neither more nor less 'subjective' than the first. But the label solves nothing. It is a statement of the obvious; mens rea is by definition, a state of mind of the accused himself at the time he did the physical act that constitutes the actus reus of the offence; it cannot be the mental state of some non-existent, hypothetical person.

Nevertheless, to decide whether someone has been 'reckless' as to whether harmful consequences of a particular kind will result from his act, as distinguished from his actually intending such harmful consequences to follow, does call for some consideration of how the mind of the ordinary prudent individual would have reacted to a similar situation. If there were nothing in the circumstances that ought to have drawn the attention of an ordinary prudent individual to the possibility of that kind of harmful consequence, the accused would not be described as 'reckless' in the natural meaning of that word for failing to address his mind to the possibility; nor, if the risk of the harmful consequences was so slight that the ordinary prudent individual upon due consideration of the risk would not be deterred from treating it as negligible, could the accused be described as 'reckless' in its ordinary sense if, having considered the risk, he decided to ignore it. (In this connection the gravity of the possible harmful consequences would be an important factor. To endanger life must be one of the most grave.) So to this extent, even if one ascribes to 'reckless' only the restricted meaning, adopted by the Court of Appeal in *R. v Stephenson* and *R. v Briggs (Note)*, of foreseeing that a particular kind of harm might happen and yet going on to take the risk of it, it involves a test that would be described in part as 'objective' in current legal jargon. Questions of criminal liability are seldom solved by simply asking whether the test is subjective or objective.

In my opinion, a person charged with an offence under section 1(1) of the Criminal Damage Act 1971 is 'reckless as to whether any such property would be destroyed or damaged' if (1) he does an act which in fact creates an obvious risk that property will be destroyed or damaged and (2) when he does the act he either has not given any thought to the possibility of there being any such risk or has recognised that there was some risk involved and has nonetheless gone on to do it. That would be a proper direction to the jury; cases in the Court of Appeal which held otherwise should be regarded as overruled. [His Lordship then went on to consider the defence of drunkenness.]"

Lord Edmund-Davies (with whom Lord Wilberforce concurred) dissenting:
"I have to say that I am in respectful, but profound, disagreement. The law in action compiles its own dictionary. In time, what was originally the common coinage of speech acquires a different value in the pocket of the lawyer than when in the layman's purse. Professor Kenny used lawyers' words in a lawyer's sense to express his distillation of an important part of the established law relating to mens rea, ... And it is well known that the Criminal Damage Act 1971 was in the main the work of the Law Commission, who, in their Working Paper No. 31, Codification of the Criminal Law, General Principles, The Mental Element in Crime (issued in June, 1970) defined recklessness by saying, at p. 52:

'A person is reckless if, (a) knowing that there is a risk that an event may result from his conduct or that a circumstance may exist, he takes that risk, and (b) it is unreasonable for him to take it, having regard to the degree and nature of the risk which he knows to be present.'

It was surely with this contemporaneous definition and the much respected decision of *R. v Cunningham* in mind that the draftsman proceeded to his task of drafting the Criminal Damage Act 1971.

It has therefore to be said that, unlike negligence, which has to be judged objectively, recklessness involves foresight of consequences, combined with an objective judgment of the reasonableness of the risk taken. And recklessness in vacuo is an incomprehensible notion. It *must* relate to foresight of risk of the particular kind relevant to the charge preferred, which, for the purpose of section 1(2), is the risk of endangering life and nothing other than that.

So if a defendant says of a particular risk, 'it never crossed my mind,' a jury could not on those words alone properly convict him of recklessness simply because they considered that the risk ought to have crossed his mind, though his words might well lead to a finding of negligence. But a defendant's admission that he 'closed his mind' to a particular risk could prove fatal, for: 'A person cannot, in any intelligible meaning of the words, close his mind to a risk unless he first realises that there is a risk; and if he realises that there is a risk, that is the end of the matter.' See Glanville Williams, *Textbook of Criminal Law* (1978), p. 79.

In the absence of exculpatory factors, the defendant's state of mind is therefore all-important where recklessness is an element in the offence charged and section 8 of the Criminal Justice Act 1967 has laid down that:

'A court or jury, in determining whether a person has committed an offence—(a) shall not be bound by law to infer that he intended or foresaw a result of his actions by reason only of its being a natural and probable consequence of those actions; but (b) shall decide whether he did intend or foresee that result by reference to all the evidence, drawing such inferences from the evidence as appear proper in the circumstances.'

My Lords, it is unnecessary to examine at length the proposition that ascertainment of the state of mind known as 'recklessness' is a *subjective* exercise for the task was expansively performed by Geoffrey Lane L.J. in *R. v Stephenson* ... [His Lordship then went on to consider the defence of drunkenness]."

**Appeal dismissed**

## R. v Lawrence [1982] A.C. 510 (House of Lords)

The appellant was riding his motorcycle at an excessive speed along an urban road and ran into and killed a pedestrian who was crossing the road. The appellant was convicted of causing death by reckless driving, contrary to section 1 of the Road Traffic Act 1972 and appealed against his conviction.

Lord Diplock (with whom Lord Fraser, Lord Roskill and Lord Bridge agreed):

"[His Lordship cited sections 1 and 2 of the Road Traffic Act 1972, as amended by section 50(1) of the Criminal Law Act 1977:

'1. A person who causes the death of another person by driving a motor vehicle on a road recklessly shall be guilty of an offence.

2. A person who drives a motor vehicle on a road recklessly shall be guilty of an offence.'[43]

He then contrasted these with the 'lesser offence' of section 3 of the Road Traffic Act 1972:

'If a person drives a motor vehicle on a road without due care and attention, or without reasonable consideration for other persons using the road, he shall be guilty of an offence.']

So section 3 takes care of the kind of inattention or misjudgment to which the ordinarily careful motorist is occasionally subject without its necessarily involving any moral turpitude, although it causes inconvenience and annoyance to other users of the road. ...

The conclusion reached by the majority [in *Caldwell*] was that the adjective 'reckless' when used in a criminal statute, *i.e.* the Criminal Damage Act 1971, had not acquired a special meaning as a term of legal art, but bore its popular or dictionary meaning of careless, regardless, or heedless of the possible harmful consequences of one's acts. The same must be true of the adverbial derivative 'recklessly.'

The context in which the word 'reckless' appears in section 1 of the Criminal Damage Act 1971 differs in two respects from the context in which the word 'recklessly' appears in sections 1 and 2 of the Road Traffic Act 1972, as now amended. In the Criminal Damage Act 1971 the actus reus, the physical act of destroying or damaging property belonging to another, is in itself a tort. It is not something that one does regularly as part of the ordinary routine of daily life, such as driving a car or a motor cycle. So there is something out of the

---

[43] The Road Traffic Act 1988, as amended by the Road Traffic Act 1991, has replaced these offences with those of causing death by dangerous driving (s.1) and dangerous driving (s.2).

ordinary to call the doer's attention to what he is doing and its possible consequences, which is absent in road traffic offences. The other difference in context is that in section 1 of the Criminal Damage Act 1971 the mens rea of the offences is defined as being reckless as to whether particular harmful consequences would occur, whereas in sections 1 and 2 of the Road Traffic Act 1972, as now amended, the possible harmful consequences of which the driver must be shown to have been heedless are left to be implied from the use of the word 'recklessly' itself. In ordinary usage 'recklessly' as descriptive of a physical act such as driving a motor vehicle which can be performed in a variety of different ways, some of them entailing danger and some of them not, refers not only to the state of mind of the doer of the act when he decides to do it but also qualifies the manner in which the act itself is performed. One does not speak of a person acting 'recklessly,' even though he has given no thought at all to the consequences of his act, unless the act is one that presents a real risk of harmful consequences which anyone acting with reasonable prudence would recognise and give heed to. So the actus reus of the offence under sections 1 and 2 is not simply driving a motor vehicle on a road, but driving it in a manner which in fact creates a real risk of harmful consequences resulting from it. Since driving in such a manner as to do no worse than create a risk of causing inconvenience or annoyance to other road users constitutes the lesser offence under section 3, the manner of driving that constitutes the actus reus of an offence under sections 1 and 2 must be worse than that; it must be such as to create a real risk of causing physical injury to someone else who happens to be using the road or damage to property more substantial than the kind of minor damage that may be caused by an error of judgment in the course of parking one's car. . . .

I turn now to the mens rea. My task is greatly simplified by what has already been said about the concept of recklessness in criminal law in *R. v Caldwell*. Warning was there given against adopting the simplistic approach of treating all problems of criminal liability as soluble by classifying the test of liability as being either 'subjective' or 'objective.' Recklessness on the part of the doer of an act does pre-suppose that there is something in the circumstances that would have drawn the attention of an ordinary prudent individual to the possibility that his act was capable of causing the kind of serious harmful consequences that the section which creates the offence was intended to prevent, and that the risk of those harmful consequences occurring was not so slight that an ordinary prudent individual would feel justified in treating them as negligible. It is only when this is so that the doer of the act is acting 'recklessly' if before doing the act, he either fails to give any thought to the possibility of there being any such risk or, having recognised that there was such risk, he nevertheless goes on to do it.

In my view, an appropriate instruction to the jury on what is meant by driving recklessly would be that they must be satisfied of two things:

*First*, that the defendant was in fact driving the vehicle in such a manner as to create an obvious and serious risk of causing physical injury to some other person who might happen to be using the road or of doing substantial damage to property; and

*Second*, that in driving in that manner the defendant did so without having given any thought to the possibility of there being any such risk or, having recognised that there was some risk involved, had nonetheless gone on to take it.

It is for the jury to decide whether the risk created by the manner in which the vehicle was being driven was both obvious and serious and, in deciding this, they may apply the standard of the ordinary prudent motorist as represented by themselves.

If satisfied that an obvious and serious risk was created by the manner of the defendant's driving, the jury are entitled to infer that he was in one or other of the states of mind required to constitute the offence and will probably do so; but regard must be given to any explanation he gives as to his state of mind which may displace the inference."

**Appeal dismissed**

## R. v Reid (1992) 95 Cr.App.R.393 (House of Lords)

The appellant was driving in the inside lane of a dual carriageway. He was trying to overtake another car on its nearside. Further down the road in the nearside lane there was an obstruction: a taxi-drivers' rest hut protruded some 6ft into the road. Lines were painted on the road to show that it was necessary to move towards the middle of the road to avoid the obstruction. The appellant's car struck the hut killing his front seat passenger. He was convicted of causing death by reckless driving. The Court of Appeal dismissed his appeal against conviction and certified the following point of law for consideration by the House of Lords: "In a case of reckless driving, should the jury be directed in the terms of the *ipsissima verba* of Lord Diplock's suggested instruction to the jury ... [in] *Lawrence* without modifications?"

Lord Keith of Kinkel:
"The precise state of mind of a person who drives in the manner indicated must in the vast majority of cases be quite incapable of ascertainment. Absence of something from a person's mind is as much part of his state of mind as its presence. Inadvertence to risk is no less a subjective state of mind than is disregard of a recognised risk. If there is nothing to go upon apart from what actually happened, the natural inference is that the driver's state of mind was one or other of those described by Lord Diplock ..."

Lord Goff of Chieveley:
"I think it is wise to bear in mind the possibility that words such as reckless or recklessly, which can be used in a number of different contexts, may not necessarily be expected to bear the same meaning in all statutory provisions in which they are found ...
[Recklessness includes] cases where the defendant's perception is impaired by drink or by blind rage or by some other excitement, with the result that he fails to give any thought to the possibility of such risk. But there may be other cases. For example, the defendant's state of mind may be such that he does not care whether any such risk exists or not, which has been described as an attitude of indifference, or of not caring less ... In other cases, the defendant's state of mind may be one of wilful blindness, where he simply closes his mind to the possibility of risk. In yet other cases, perhaps the most common, the defendant simply does not think about the matter at all, perhaps because he is acting impetuously on the spur of the moment without addressing his mind to the possibility of risk ...
Then there are the young joy-riders who take other people's cars, often fast cars such as GTIs, and drive them at high speed around housing estates. They, too, may well give no thought to the possibility of risk to other people or other vehicles in the vicinity ... I cannot help thinking that in ordinary speech all these people would be described as driving recklessly. Certainly, I do not think that ordinary people would regard it as a relevant inquiry to ascertain whether these drivers had in fact addressed their minds to the possibility of risk before they could be said to have acted recklessly. Indeed, I would go further and say that this category of recklessness on the roads may well be as prevalent as the category in which the driver actually foresees the risk and decides to disregard it ... Indeed, it can be argued with force that, in many cases of failing to think, the degree of blameworthiness to be attached to the driver can be greater than that to be attached in some cases to the driver who recognised the risk and decided to disregard it. This is because the unspoken premise which seems to me to underlie Lord Diplock's statement of the law in *Lawrence* (and perhaps also in *Caldwell*) is that the defendant is engaged in an activity which he knows to be potentially dangerous.
[Their Lordships held that it was not necessary that Lord Diplock's *ipsissima verba* in *Lawrence* should be followed.]"

**Appeal dismissed**

The effect of these decisions upon English criminal law will be assessed at appropriate points throughout this book. At this stage, however, several important issues need to be addressed.

**1. Ruling out the risk.** This *Caldwell/Lawrence* test of recklessness, particularly as articulated in Lord Diplock's model direction, appears to exclude from its ambit the defendant who stops to think whether there is a risk, concludes there is no risk and consequently acts. Such a person does not come within the test which requires that the actor must have either "not given any thought to the possibility of there being any such risk" (because thought has been given to such a possibility) or must have "recognised that there was some risk involved" (because the possibility of there being a risk has been dismissed). Accordingly, there can be no recklessness. This has been described as a "lacuna" (a gap) in the law of recklessness.[44] Thus if Stephenson could have established that he had contemplated the possibility of the straw stack catching fire but had dismissed the possibility (say, because of his schizophrenia) then he could not be held reckless under Lord Diplock's test. Such an actor would of course be negligent. The existence of the lacuna is an important feature distinguishing negligence from *Caldwell/Lawrence* recklessness.

### Chief Constable of Avon v Shimmen (1987) 84 Cr.App.R.7 (Queen's Bench Division)

The defendant who held a green belt and yellow belt in the Korean art of self-defence was showing off his skills to some friends. He aimed a kick at a plate-glass window contending that he believed he had the necessary muscular control and skill to avoid breaking the window. He did however break it and was charged with criminal damage contrary to section 1(1) of the Criminal Damage Act 1971. The justices concluded that the defendant "after considering such risk concluded that no damage would result" and so dismissed the charge. The prosecutor appealed by way of case stated.

Taylor J.:

"[A] number of the writers have expressed the view that between the two possible states of mind constituting recklessness as defined in *R. v Caldwell*, there exists or could exist a lacuna, that is a state of mind which fell into neither of the two alternative categories posed by Lord Diplock ... Professor Griew ('Reckless Damage and Reckless Driving: Living with Caldwell and Lawrence' [1981] Crim.L.R.743, 748) cited two hypothetical cases....

'The following cases are outside the terms of the model direction in *Caldwell*. (a) M. does give thought to whether there is a risk of damage to another's property attending his proposed act. He mistakenly concludes that there is no risk; or he perceives only a risk such as would in the circumstances be treated as negligible by the ordinary prudent individual. He missed the obvious and substantial risk. (b) N.'s case is a more likely one. He is indeed aware of the kind of risk that will attend his act if he does not take adequate precautions. He takes precautions that are intended and expected to eliminate the risk (or to reduce it to negligible proportions). But the precautions are plainly, though not plainly to him, inadequate for this purpose. These appear not to be cases of recklessness. Evidence of conscientiousness displaces what would otherwise be an available inference of recklessness, (to use the language of Lord Diplock in *Lawrence*, ... )' ...

Those two examples which were given by Professor Griew seem to me not to be 'on all fours.' In the first example, it may well be arguable that the lacuna exists because it is not a case where M. failed to give any consideration to the possibility of a risk. It is a case where he did give consideration to the possibility of the risk and concluded, albeit mistakenly, that there was no risk. In terms, therefore, of Lord Diplock's definition, he has not recognised that there was some risk involved. He therefore is outside the second possible state of mind referred to in *R. v Caldwell*.

A different situation, however, seems to me to apply in the case of N. posed by Professor Griew. He was aware of the kind of risk which would attend his act if he did not take

---

[44] Williams, "Recklessness Redefined" [1981] C.L.J. 252 at 278–281; Williams, "Divergent Interpretations of Recklessness" (1982) 132 N.L.J. 289, 313, 336 at 313–314, 336; Smith [1981] Crim.L.R.393, 394.

adequate precautions. He seeks to rely upon the fact that he did take precautions which were intended, and by him expected, to eliminate the risk. He was wrong, but the fact that he was conscientious to the degree of trying to minimise the risk does not mean that he falls outside the second limb of Lord Diplock's test. Lord Diplock's second limb is simply whether or not he has recognised that there was some risk. It seems clear to me that in the case of N., as posed by Professor Griew, N. certainly did recognise that there was some risk and went on to do the act.

In my judgment, therefore, the second example given by Professor Griew does not constitute any lacuna in the definition given by Lord Diplock. Applying those examples to the present case, it seems to me that ... this defendant did recognise the risk. It was not a case of his considering the possibility and coming to the conclusion that there was no risk. What he said to the justices in cross-examination should be quoted. He said: 'I thought I might break the window but then I thought I will not break the window ... I thought to myself, the window is not going to break.' A little later on he said: 'I weighed up the odds and thought I had eliminated as much risk as possible by missing by two inches instead of two millimetres.'

The specific finding of the justices was as follows: '... the defendant perceived there could be a risk of damage but after considering such risk concluded that no damage would result.' It seems to me that what this case amounts to is as follows; that this defendant did perceive, which is the same as Lord Diplock's word 'recognise,' that there could be a risk, but by aiming off rather more than he normally would in this sort of display, he thought he had minimised it and therefore no damage would result. In my judgment, that is far from saying that he falls outside the state of mind described by Lord Diplock in these terms, '... has recognised that there was some risk involved, and has nonetheless gone on to do it.'

In my judgment, therefore, whatever may be the situation in a hypothetical case such as that of M. as detailed by Professor Griew, which may need to be considered on another occasion, so far as this case is concerned, the justices were wrong in coming to the conclusion that this was not recklessness."

**Appeal allowed**
**Case remitted with direction to convict**

There can be no doubt that the defendant in this case had not truly ruled out the risk. Glanville Williams commented on this case that:

"This was a case where the defendant needed to be cross-examined. 'Would you have kicked with such force towards your girl friend's or wife's or your baby's head, relying on your ability to stop within an inch of it? No? Then you knew that there was some risk of your boot travelling further than you intended.' A person may be convinced of his own skill, and yet know that on rare (perhaps very rare) occasions it may fail him."[45]

This judgment is unsatisfactory in many respects. The Divisional Court is drawing an impossibly fine distinction. A defendant who rules out a risk by mistakenly concluding that there is no risk is not reckless. On the other hand, the defendant who thinks there is no risk because he is taking all steps to eliminate the risk, is reckless. Such hair-splitting distinctions, apart from lacking any solid moral foundation, can only give rise to numerous interpretive problems. A better approach was suggested, *obiter*, in *Merrick*.[46] In this case the defendant, in

---

[45] "The Unresolved Problem of Recklessness" (1988) 8 L.S. 74 at 75.
[46] [1996] 1 Cr.App.R.130.

removing electrical equipment from the ground, exposed a live electrical cable for six minutes before taking reasonable precautions to eliminate the danger. It was held (rightly) that he did not fall within the lacuna as the risk that life would be endangered had already been created before he attempted to eliminate it. However, it was stated, contrary to *Shimmen*, that a person who takes steps to prevent a risk arising at all (rather than remedying it once it has arisen) could escape liability.[47] There seems little distinction in moral terms between a defendant who thinks there is no risk because he has made a mistake and one who thinks there is no risk because he has done everything necessary in his estimation to eliminate the risk.

A further objection that can be levelled at *Shimmen* relates to the apparent acceptance that there is no recklessness where the defendant "perceives only a risk such as would in the circumstances be treated as negligible by the ordinary prudent individual". This cannot be correct. If a defendant perceives *any* risk of the harmful consequence occurring he has not "ruled out the risk" and will be reckless provided the remaining components of the *Caldwell* test have been satisfied—and provided the risk is an unjustifiable one in the circumstances.

## R. v Reid (1992) 95 Cr.App.R.393 (House of Lords)

The facts are given above at pp. 151–152.

Lord Ackner:
"[In assessing recklessness the jury] must have regard to any explanation which accounts for [the defendant's] conduct. In short, they must have regard to all the available evidence. Mr Alun Jones provided your Lordships with a cogent example. The driver of a left-hand drive car was driving up a hill with a car in front of him and before overtaking asks his passenger, sitting on his right, if the road is clear ahead. He is given an affirmative answer but the passenger has misunderstood the question as an inquiry as to whether there is any car approaching. Relying on this answer the driver pulls out to overtake. In that example the driver recognised that there might be some risk involved, reasonably sought and thought he had obtained an assurance that it did not in fact exist. He had not therefore proceeded on the basis that, appreciating there was a significant risk, he decided to run that risk. I suggested in the course of the argument as another possible example, a driver of a powerful car who decided to overtake when there was plenty of time for him to do so. However, when he was in the process of accelerating there was a wholly unexpected failure of the performance by the car, due to a failure in the fuel injection system, which caused a collision with an approaching car. Another, but different example, would be the taking of a high-risk avoiding action in order not to collide with a child, who suddenly ran across the road."

Lord Goff of Chieveley:
"I accept that, if the defendant is addressing his mind to the possibility of risk and suffers from a bona fide mistake as to a specific fact which if true would have excluded the risk, he cannot be described as reckless though he may be guilty of careless driving. ...

[Dangerous driving is not necessarily reckless driving.] This may occur where the defendant considers the possibility of risk but nevertheless concludes that there is none. But we have to remember that, *ex hypothesi*, the defendant is driving dangerously in the sense I have described; and in practice his evidence that in such circumstances he thought that there was no risk is only likely to carry weight if he can point to some specific fact as to which he was mistaken and which, if true, would have excluded the possibility of risk—which might

---

[47] At 137.

occur if, for example, as my noble and learned friend Lord Ackner has pointed out, he misunderstood in good faith some direction or instruction, or if he drove the wrong way down a one-way street at a normal speed in the mistaken belief that it was a two-way street. If that was indeed the case, his driving might well not be described as reckless, though such cases are likely to be rare. It has been suggested that there is therefore a 'loophole' or 'lacuna' in Lord Diplock's definition of recklessness. I feel bound to say that I myself regard these expressions as misleading. The simple fact is that Lord Diplock was concerned to define driving recklessly, not dangerous driving; and it is not in every case where the defendant is in fact driving dangerously that he should be held to be driving recklessly, although in most cases the two will coincide."

Such an approach has much to commend it. It seems odd to assert that one who positively believes that something will not happen is reckless as to that thing happening. There would appear to be a clear moral difference between a person who is *convinced* that no harm will occur and who does not bother to think of the risks involved in his conduct. If there is a moral difference the law ought to provide the vocabulary (negligence and recklessness respectively) to make the necessary discriminations.

On the other hand, there are problems with such an approach. Surely we do not want to acquit appalling drivers "whose unshakeable faith in their ability to avoid danger displays an arrogance bordering on lunacy".[48] Further, it is possible to argue that *everyone* who does not subjectively foresee a risk must believe the act is safe, which is another way of saying that the risk has been ruled out.[49] Acceptance of such a view would destroy the rule in *Caldwell* and is unlikely to be accepted. Indeed, it is going to be difficult in any case to convince a jury that the defendant actually did contemplate an obvious risk but ruled it out. Such a contention may simply not be believed in many cases. Further, such an argument would necessitate "a meticulous analysis by the jury of the thoughts that passed through the mind of the accused".[50] It was such fine distinctions that Lord Diplock was rejecting, yet he appears, albeit by omission, to have perpetuated them in this one sphere. It is interesting to note that despite judicial acceptance of the "lacuna",[51] there has been no case to date in which a defendant has actually escaped liability on the basis of having ruled out the risk.

**2. Creating an obvious risk.** Lord Diplock defined recklessness as (i) doing an act "which in fact creates an obvious risk" of the relevant harm occurring and (ii) "when he does the act he either has not given any thought to the possibility of there being any such risk or has recognised that there was some risk involved and has nonetheless gone on to do it".

A major problem is to ascertain what is meant by the phrase "creates an obvious risk". Obvious to whom? To the reasonable person? Or, to the defendant? A strong argument has been put forward that the risk must have been obvious to the defendant himself had he bothered to think about the matter.[52] Indeed, there are

---

[48] Birch, "The Foresight Saga: The Biggest Mistake of All?" [1988] Crim.L.R.4 at 5.
[49] Williams, *above*, n.44.
[50] *Caldwell, above*, p. 147.
[51] *Coles* [1995] 1 Cr.App.R.157; *Merrick* [1996] 1 Cr.App.R.130.
[52] Williams, "Recklessness Redefined" [1981] C.L.J. 252; Syrota, "A Radical Change in the Law of Recklessness" [1982] Crim.L.R.97.

dicta in *Caldwell* that recklessness "presupposes that, if thought were given to the matter *by the doer* before the act was done, it would have been apparent *to him*"[53] that there were risks involved.

### Glanville Williams, "Divergent Interpretations of Recklessness" (1982) 132 N.L.J. 289, 313, 336 at 289–290:

"The main problem in the theory of subjective recklessness concerns the person who knew of a particular risk in a general way but did not think of it at the moment when he was acting ... Just as we may be said 'to know' a thing because we can instantly recall it, even though it is not at the moment present in our minds, so it is not unreasonable to say that a person knows of a risk for the purpose of the law of recklessness if he would be aware of it the moment he attended to it, even though, being intent upon something else, he does not consciously attend to it. What is required is not present awareness but general knowledge, given the will and ability to recall the knowledge. It does not matter whether we say the defendant 'really' knew of the risk but paid no attention to it, or that he would have known of it if he had paid attention; the difference between these two modes of statement is only verbal ....

This is how Mr George Syrota explains the decision ...:

'Their Lordships were merely seeking to ensure that juries would not in future become "bogged down" in a particular intractable and fruitless inquiry: was D's knowledge of the risk at the forefront or the back of his mind at the moment he committed the *actus reus*.' ([1982] Crim.L.R.102).

If this is what the rule in *Caldwell* means it can be fully accepted."

On this view the schizophrenic Stephenson would presumably still have to be acquitted as even if he had stopped and thought, he still might not have appreciated the risks involved in his activities as knowledge of the risks would not even be at the back of his mind. If this view is correct, why then did Lord Diplock expressly overrule *Stephenson*?

Indeed, this whole interpretation seems somewhat tenuous[54] and has been rejected by the courts. There are numerous passages in both *Caldwell* and *Lawrence*, fortified by the model direction in *Caldwell*, that the risk must have been obvious to the "ordinary prudent individual".

### Elliott v C. (A Minor) (1983) 77 Cr.App.R.103 (Queen's Bench Divisional Court)

The defendant was a 14-year-old schoolgirl, with learning difficulties. After staying out all night without sleep she poured white spirit on the carpet of a garden shed and then threw two lighted matches on the spirit. The shed was destroyed by fire. She was charged with criminal damage contrary to section 1(1) of the Criminal Damage Act 1971, it being alleged that she had been reckless as to whether the shed be destroyed. The justices concluded that because of her age, lack of understanding, lack of experience and exhaustion, the risk of destroying the shed would not have been obvious to her if she had given any thought to the

---

[53] *Above*, p. 147 (emphasis added).
[54] See Smith [1981] Crim.L.R.660; Griew, "Reckless Damage and Reckless Driving: Living with Caldwell and Lawrence" [1981] Crim.L.R.743 at 748. The problems associated with this approach are well exposed in Duff, "Professor Williams and Conditional Subjectivism" [1982] C.L.J. 273.

matter. Accordingly they found she was not reckless and dismissed the information. The prosecutor appealed by way of case stated.

Glidewell J.:

"Mr Moses [counsel for the prosecution] ... submits that the phrase 'creates an obvious risk' means that the risk is one which must have been obvious to a reasonably prudent man, not necessarily to the particular defendant if he or she had given thought to it. It follows, says Mr Moses, that if the risk is one which would have been obvious to a reasonably prudent person, once it has also been proved that the particular defendant gave no thought to the possibility of there being such a risk, it is not a defence that because of limited intelligence or exhaustion she would not have appreciated the risk even if she had thought about it.

It is right to say, as Mr Moses pointed out to us, that there are passages in the speech of Lord Diplock in *R. v Caldwell* which suggest that his Lordship was indeed using the phrase 'creates an obvious risk' as meaning, 'creates a risk which was obvious to the particular defendant.' ...

In the light of [the authorities, *viz. Caldwell, Lawrence and Miller*] ... , we are in my judgment bound to hold that the word 'reckless' in section 1 of the Criminal Damage Act 1971 has the meaning ascribed to it by Mr Moses. ... The questions posed by the case were: '1. Whether properly directing themselves and upon a true construction of section 1(1) of the Criminal Damage Act 1971, the justices were correct in their interpretation of the meaning of reckless, namely, that a defendant should only be held to have acted recklessly by virtue of his failure to give any thought to an obvious risk that property would be destroyed or damaged, where such risk would have been obvious to him if he had given any thought to the matter? 2. Whether properly directing themselves on the evidence the justices could properly have come to their decision that the defendant had acted neither intentionally nor recklessly in destroying by fire the shed and its contents?'

I would answer 'No' to both questions, and allow the appeal."

Robert Goff L.J.

"I agree with the conclusion reached by Glidewell J. but I do so simply because I believe myself constrained to do so by authority. I feel moreover that I would be lacking in candour if I were to conceal my unhappiness about the conclusion which I feel compelled to reach ...

This is not a case where there was a deliberate disregard of a known risk of damage or injury of a certain type or degree; nor is it a case where there was mindless indifference to a risk of such damage or injury, as is expressed in common speech in the context of motoring offences (though not, I think, of arson) as 'blazing on regardless'; nor is it even a case where failure to give thought to the possibility of the risk was due to some blameworthy cause, such as intoxication. This is a case where it appears that the only basis upon which the accused might be held to have been reckless would be if the appropriate test to be applied was purely objective—a test which might in some circumstances be thought justifiable in relation to certain conduct, (*e.g* reckless driving), particularly where the word 'reckless' is used simply to characterise the relevant conduct. But such a test does not appear at first sight to be appropriate to a crime such as that under consideration in the present case, especially as recklessness in that crime has to be related to a particular consequence.

[His Lordship, however, felt himself bound to follow *Caldwell*.]"

**Appeal allowed**

This approach has been followed. In *R. (Stephen Malcolm)*,[55] it was held that the risk had to be obvious to an ordinary prudent person and it was *not* appropriate to endow such an ordinary prudent person with the characteristics of the defendant— say, age and sex.[56] In *Bell*,[57] the defendant, who had a history of mental illness,

---

[55] (1984) 79 Cr.App.R.334.

[56] This approach of endowing the reasonable person with such characteristics has been employed with regard to the partial defence of provocation and the defence of duress. See, *below*, pp. 694–716 and 336–337.

[57] [1984] 3 All E.R. 842.

suffered a schizophrenic attack and feeling he was being driven on by an outside force which he thought was God, used his car as a "weapon to attack various targets which he regarded as evil", namely, a Butlins holiday camp. He was held to be acting recklessly in that he had failed to foresee obvious risks. The fact that he might have been unable to foresee those risks was irrelevant—they were obvious to ordinary prudent people.[58] Under this purely objective test the schizophrenic Stephenson would clearly be regarded as having acted recklessly.

It follows that not only does the ordinary prudent person have no inadequacies, but also he possesses no particular expertise.

### R. v Sangha [1988] 2 All E.R. 385 (Court of Appeal, Criminal Division)

The defendant set fire to a mattress and two armchairs in a flat with the result that the premises were burnt out. The defendant was charged with causing criminal damage by fire, being reckless whether the life of another would be thereby endangered, contrary to section 1(2)(b) of the Criminal Damage Act 1971. In fact, but unknown to the defendant, because of the construction of the flat there was no danger of the fire spreading to adjoining properties. As there was no-one in the flat in which he started the fire he claimed he had not created a risk of danger to the lives of others. He was convicted and appealed to the Court of Appeal.

Tucker J:
"In our judgment, when consideration is given whether an act of setting fire to something creates an obvious and serious risk of damaging property and thereby endangering the life of another, the test to be applied is this: is it proved that an ordinary prudent bystander would have perceived an obvious risk that property would be damaged and that life would thereby be endangered? The ordinary prudent bystander is not deemed to be invested with expert knowledge relating to the construction of the property, nor to have the benefit of hindsight. The time at which his perception is material is the time when the fire is started.

Section 1(2) of the 1971 Act uses the word 'would' in the context of recklessness whether property would be destroyed or damaged, and whether the life of another would be thereby endangered. We interpret this word 'would' as going to the expectations of the normal prudent bystander.

Applying this test to the facts of the case before us, it is clear that in setting fire to these armchairs as the jury found the appellant did, he created a risk which was obvious and serious that property would be damaged and that the life of another would thereby be endangered. The fact that there were special features here which prevented that risk from materialising is irrelevant."

**Appeal dismissed**

While for some time this purely objective approach seemed beyond doubt,[59] later dicta from the House of Lords suggested a possible change of direction.

### R. v Reid (1992) 95 Cr.App.R.393 (House of Lords)

Lord Keith of Kinkel:
"[T]here may be special circumstances which require [Lord Diplock's formulation] to be

---

[58] The mental illness was only relevant in so far as a verdict of not guilty by reason of insanity was possible.

[59] For an interesting counter-argument, see Field and Lynn, "The Capacity for Recklessness" (1992) 12 L.S. 74.

modified or added to, for example, where the driver acted under some understandable and excusable mistake or where his capacity to appreciate risks was adversely affected by some condition not involving fault on his part."

Lord Goff of Chieveley:
"Another example where [there is no recklessness] [is] where a driver who, while driving, is afflicted by illness or shock which impairs his capacity to address his mind to the possibility of risk; it may well not be right to describe him as driving recklessly in such circumstances."

Lord Ackner:
"Mr Hill [counsel for the appellant] ... [submitted] that the requisite mens rea would be lacking, if the ignorance of the risk was attributable to incapacity due, for example, to age or mental deficiency of the defendant. He submitted that this was so even though the manner of his driving created a serious risk of injury or damage to property which would have been apparent to an ordinary prudent individual. It is true that in *R. v Caldwell*, where the recklessness was related essentially to the consequences of the action, Lord Diplock postulated as the basis of recklessness, that the risk of the relevant harm would have been apparent 'to the doer' of the act, if he had given thought to the matter ... But as Lord Diplock pointed out in *Lawrence* ... , the actus reus, the physical act of destroying someone else's property is a civil wrong. It is not part of the ordinary everyday routine of daily life such as driving a motor vehicle. The element of recklessness is thus tied to the proscribed conduct, the driving, and more loosely to the required state of mind than in the context of offences under the Criminal Damage Act, where recklessness characterises the consequences. I cannot therefore accept Mr Hill's modified proposition."

Lord Keith's dictum is wide enough to embrace and exempt from liability the girl in *Elliot v C*. Lord Goff only talks of sudden incapacities (illness or shock) exempting from liability. While a sudden and temporary incapacity can be distinguished from a permanent one on the basis that the former is unforeseeable while the latter is already in existence, there is nevertheless a strong case for having the same rule in all such situations. Lord Ackner does not go as far as this but does seem to suggest that with some result crimes such as causing criminal damage (where the *mens rea* element needs to be related to the consequence) the risk must have been apparent to the defendant if he had thought about the matter. It is extraordinary that he could have expressed this view without even citing *Elliott v C*. On the other hand, he stated that with other crimes that do not require the *mens rea* to be related to the consequence, such as reckless driving, the risk need only be obvious to the ordinary, prudent individual. The *mens rea* in criminal damage relates to cognition: the link between the mental element and the prohibited consequence. However, the *mens rea* in reckless driving (and causing death by reckless driving) relates more to a general attitude of indifference; it describes the quality of the actions rather than the defendant's foresight or otherwise of the consequence. This approach has little to commend it. It is far from clear why incapacity should be relevant only in result crimes. Even with conduct crimes such as reckless driving, a driver, say one suffering from senile dementia,[60] might simply not be capable of appreciating the risks involved.

Despite this move towards a more flexible approach in *Reid*, the orthodox position was confirmed in *Coles*[61] where it was held that psychological evidence of a 15–year-old's low mental capacity was not admissible. However, the court,

---

[60] Leigh, "Recklessness After Reid" (1993) 56 M.L.R. 214.
[61] [1995] 1 Cr.App.R.157.

somewhat bafflingly, added that: "adolescents of varying stages of maturity and brightness are all within the common experience of jurors."[62] This seems to suggest that a jury might be permitted to consider whether the risks would be obvious to an ordinary adolescent. However, this dictum was not even alluded to in the following case.

## R. v Gemmel and Richards [2003] 1 Cr.App.R.23 (Court of Appeal, Criminal Division)

Two boys, aged 11 and 12 respectively, set fire to newspapers and threw them under a wheelie-bin. The bin was set alight and adjoining buildings caught fire causing some £1 million damage. They claimed they thought the lit newspapers would burn themselves out on the concrete floor and that it never crossed their minds that there was a risk of the fire spreading. They were convicted of arson with the trial judge ruling that whether there was an obvious risk of the property being damaged was to be assessed by reference to the reasonable man and not a person endowed with the characteristics of the defendants: "the ordinary bystander is an adult". The defendants were convicted and appealed on the grounds that (1) the *Caldwell* test does not apply to children; and/or if it does, it is incompatible with Article 6 of the European Convention on Human Rights which requires, *inter alia*, that "everyone is entitled to a fair ... hearing".

Dyson L.J.:

"[I]n *Caldwell*, Lord Diplock was propounding a test at a high level of generalisation, which he intended to apply at least to all cases under section 1 of the 1971 Act. ... Although Lord Diplock criticised the use of the labels "subjective" and "objective", it is clear that he opted for what it is convenient to call the "objective" test. There is nothing in his speech to indicate that he considered that any qualities or characteristics were relevant other than that the person should be ordinarily prudent. A number of characteristics may affect a person's ability to see a risk for what it is: he may be too young, or too old; he may be of poor intelligence or suffer from some relevant psychological condition; or from physical disabilities which impair his ability to appreciate the existence of a risk. If Lord Diplock had considered that any of these factors was relevant to the obviousness of the risk, he would have said so. He would not have repeatedly referred to the ordinary prudent individual. ...

In our judgment, it is for the House of Lords to decide whether the time has come to revisit the *Caldwell* test. Although we see great force in the criticisms of the first leg of the *Caldwell* test that have been made, it is not open to this court to depart from it. ...

Mr Newman advances the following propositions: (a) to judge the moral and legal culpability of a child by reference to the understanding and life experience of an adult is irrational and, therefore, unfair; (b) the *Caldwell* test is disproportionately harsh given the serious consequences that can potentially flow from a conviction of an offence under section 1(1) of the 1971 Act (detention for life); and (c) the *Caldwell* test effectively renders an offence under section 1(1) an offence of strict liability in the case of a child, because a child is incapable of advancing a defence based on his or her immaturity and lack of understanding. ...

In our judgment, Mr Newman's submissions are misconceived. We fully accept that Article 6 should be given a broad and purposive interpretation. But it seems to us that it is clear, even without the assistance of Strasbourg jurisprudence, that on any natural reading of it, Article 6 is not concerned with the fairness of provisions of *substantive* law. It contains

---

[62] At 168.

three distinct elements: access to a court; provisions regarding the organisation and constitution of the court; and minimum standards of fairness concerning the conduct of proceedings. Mr Newman argues that the phrase 'a fair hearing', which appears in the body of the article, is sufficient to include the fairness of substantive law. But if the article is read as a whole, we have no doubt that this phrase does not bear the weight for which Mr Newman contends.

The distinction between procedural and substantive law is clear and important. It is not a matter of mere 'labelling'. A provision which defines the mental element or mens rea that is a necessary element of an offence is plainly not a matter of procedure. It is a matter of substantive law since it is part of the very definition of what constitutes the offence. ...

It is a matter for the Contracting State to choose how to define the essential elements of an offence. Thus, it has been established that an offence of strict liability, as opposed to one requiring a mental element, does not violate Article 6(2). ...

The position is quite clear. So far as Article 6 is concerned, the fairness of the provisions of the substantive law of the Contracting States is not a matter for investigation. The content and interpretation of domestic substantive law is not engaged by Article 6. It may, however, be engaged by other articles of the ECHR. ... We are in no doubt that the fairness of the *Caldwell* test, in so far as it is applied to children, is not justiciable under Article 6."

**Appeals dismissed**

This decision is important in two respects. First, it confirms that the ECHR is not likely to have a major impact on English substantive criminal law. But, secondly, there are strong indications that even if *Caldwell* recklessness is not incompatible with the ECHR, that does not necessarily mean it is a justifiable test and it can be anticipated that the House of Lords will soon revisit the issue. When that occurs it is to be hoped that the House of Lords will recognise that it is only possible to defend the *Caldwell/Lawrence* test of recklessness if one is dealing with an actor who is *capable* of improving his behaviour. We have seen that the notion of responsibility, upon which the doctrine of *mens rea* is premised, is based on choice. We can blame a defendant for making the wrong choice. But how can we realistically blame the schizophrenics in *Stephenson* or *Bell* or the young girl in *Elliott v C.*? They were not able to assume the responsibility we expect most people to shoulder. They "chose" to act as they did only in the most meaningless sense of the word "choice". And, crucially, their actions did not demonstrate lack of concern; they were simply the inevitable product of their inadequacy. No civilised society should blame people for inadequacies or immaturity over which they have no control (as opposed to self-induced inadequacies such as the drunkenness in *Caldwell*).

**3. Distinguishing recklessness from negligence.** Negligence is a failure to exercise such care, skill or foresight as a reasonable person would exercise in the circumstances. The test is a purely objective one. The conduct of the defendant is measured against that of an ordinary, reasonably careful person. Negligence is not widely employed as a basis of criminal liability in English law although it is increasingly being utilised in modern statutes.[63]

The *Caldwell/Lawrence* recklessness test is widely regarded as laying down an objective standard in that the defendant need not subjectively realise that there are

---

[63] Many hybrid offences (prima facie strict liability but allowing due diligence defences) can be described as crimes of negligence. See *below*, p. 232–235.

risks involved. Following *Elliott v C.*, it is only necessary that those risks be obvious to the ordinary prudent individual. This looks at first glance like a definition of negligence. However, closer inspection reveals that there is still a distinction between such recklessness and negligence for the following reasons.

First, it is now tolerably clear that a defendant who considers a risk, but rules it out, is not acting recklessly. Such a defendant may, however, be acting negligently if the reasonable person in that situation would not have so dismissed the risk.

Secondly, Lord Diplock's judgment in *Lawrence* indicates that something more than negligence *simpliciter* is required for a finding of recklessness. He insisted that an "obvious and serious risk" be established. "Serious" risk here seems to refer to the degree of likelihood of the risk materialising.[64] There is a distinction between a risk being merely "obvious" (negligence) and being "obvious and serious" (recklessness). Lord Goff in *Reid* endorsed this: for reckless driving (as opposed to careless driving) the driving must be of "a certain dangerous character ... driving in such a manner as to create a serious risk of harm". However, he also added that "the harm must be more substantial than the kind of minor damage associated with an error of judgment (careless driving),"[65] thus endorsing the view that there must be a risk of serious harm, as opposed to a serious risk of harm.

Lord Diplock encapsulated this distinction in *Lawrence* by indicating that there must be "moral turpitude" for a finding of recklessness, while no such "moral turpitude" was necessary for the "lesser offence" of careless driving which is a crime of negligence.[66] Crimes of recklessness are "worse" than crimes of negligence. In the former, the defendant, by failing to consider the consequences of actions (or considering them and acting regardless), manifests an attitude of indifference which is culpable. A negligent actor simply makes an "error of judgment".

This distinction is difficult to draw. Lord Ackner in *Reid* felt it was self-evident that a swimmer who dived from a high diving board into a busy swimming pool was reckless if he overlooked the risk of collision with someone under the diving board. But if one alters the example slightly to a swimmer jumping from the side of the pool, it is not immediately obvious whether such action displays the necessary "moral turpitude" to amount to recklessness. In these two examples it is only the extent of harm that varies. In short, it would appear that the *Caldwell/Lawrence* test has taken us back to the pre-subjective days earlier this century when recklessness was equated with gross negligence, typified by Lord Atkin's famous comment in *Andrews v D.P.P.*:

> "Simple lack of care such as will constitute civil liability is not enough. For the purposes of the criminal law there are degrees of negligence, and a very high degree of negligence is required to be proved before the felony is established. Probably of all the epithets that can be applied 'reckless' most nearly covers the case."[67]

---

[64] Williams, "Recklessness Redefined" [1981] C.L.J. 252 at 276. In *Lamb* [1990] Crim.L.R.522 it was held that juries *must* be directed that the risk must be serious in reckless driving cases.

[65] (1992) 95 Cr.App.R.393 at 410.

[66] *Simpson v Peat* [1952] 2 Q.B. 24.

[67] [1937] A.C. 576 at 583.

Leaving aside the fact that there is a "lacuna", this could be a statement of *Caldwell/Lawrence* recklessness today. Support for the view that recklessness and gross negligence are virtually synonymous can be found in tracing the history of manslaughter cases. There had long been a species of manslaughter known as "gross negligence manslaughter". After *Caldwell/Lawrence* it was assumed that this new test applied to such crimes.[68] A decade later the courts reverted back to a test of gross negligence as though the two tests were almost interchangeable—the only real difference between the two (apart from the lacuna) relating to the degree of harm risked.

**4. A variable meaning.** The concept recklessness is employed in both statutory and common law offences. Sometimes it is given a particular meaning. For example, the Sexual Offences (Amendment) Act 1976, section 1(2) expressly endorses a "subjective" test in relation to defendants who believe the other person is consenting. Most statutes, however, do not provide any such definition and the question arises whether in such offences—and in common law crimes— recklessness is to be given its *Cunningham* or its *Caldwell/Lawrence* meaning.

In *Seymour* the House of Lords indicated that recklessness should bear its *Caldwell/Lawrence* meaning throughout the criminal law, whether the offence was a statutory or a common law one. However, in *Reid* it was made clear that recklessness could be interpreted differently for different offences. Lord Goff said of recklessness that "as used in our law, it has more than one meaning". Lord Browne-Wilkinson said that he did "not accept that the constituent elements of recklessness must be the same in all statutes. In particular [various] factors may lead to the word being given different meanings in different statutes."[69]

We are thus left in the unfortunate situation that for some offences recklessness bears its *Caldwell/Lawrence* meaning but for other offences it bears its *Cunningham* meaning. For example, the *Caldwell/Lawrence* test of recklessness applies to criminal damage while the subjective *Cunningham* test applies to aiding and abetting offences.[70]

One of the most important and controversial questions is which test applies to non-fatal offences against the person. Section 20 of the Offences against the Person Act 1861 employs the concept "maliciously" which had in the past been interpreted as meaning "intentionally or recklessly".[71] While Lord Diplock's dislike of *Cunningham*, and its subjective interpretation of recklessness for statutory offences employing the term "maliciously" was plain, he was nevertheless careful to distinguish such offences: "maliciously" was a "term of art" whereas "recklessness" was not and should bear its ordinary meaning. This approach has now been confirmed by the House of Lords in *Savage; Parmenter*.[72] "Maliciously" is a quite different concept from recklessness and bears a subjective meaning that the defendant must recognise the risk of some harm.

---

[68] *Seymour* [1983] 1 A.C. 493.
[69] At 412. Lord Ackner endorsed this view (at 402).
[70] *Blakely, Sutton* [1991] Crim.L.R.763. See also *James, The Times*, October 2, 1997 where it was held that *Cunningham* recklessness applied to the crime of false imprisonment.
[71] *Cunningham* [1957] 2 Q.B. 396; *Flack v Hunt* (1979) 70 Cr.App.R.51.
[72] [1992] 1 A.C. 699.

But what of common assault and assault occasioning actual bodily harm contrary to section 47 of the Offences against the Person Act 1861? Both these offences can be committed recklessly.[73] Which definition of recklessness applies? In *D.P.P. v K (a Minor)*[74] it was held that "in the light of the authorities" the *Caldwell* test of recklessness applied to the common law offence of assault. Since then, however, it has been held in *Spratt*[75] and several other Court of Appeal decisions[76] that subjective foresight under the *Cunningham* test is required. The leading House of Lords decision in the area, *Savage; Parmenter*,[77] however, remained silent on this point. In the light of the Court of Appeal decisions, particularly in the very cases on appeal, it can be argued that by not dealing with this issue the House of Lords "may be taken to leave it as settled law that it is intention or *Cunningham* recklessness that is required."[78] The alternative view is that their Lordships would not have bothered to devote a very substantial part of the judgment to explaining why "maliciously" is a separate concept from recklessness and thus can bear a subjective meaning if they were content to accept that recklessness itself bears its *Cunningham* meaning.

While this point will doubtless be resolved in time, the real problem is that there are countless statutes creating criminal offences which can be committed recklessly and it is impossible to predict with confidence which test will be employed. For example, in *Large v Mainprize*[79] the Divisional Court adopted the subjective meaning of recklessness when interpreting an E.C. Regulation prohibiting persons recklessly furnishing false information as to a fishing catch, contrary to reg.3(2) of the Sea Fishing (Enforcement of Community Control Measures) Regulations 1985. Similarly, in *Mir*[80] it was held that *Cunningham* recklessness applied to conspiracy to damage property being reckless as to whether life was endangered and in *Okosi*[81] it was assumed that subjective recklessness was the appropriate test for the antiquated offence of causing bodily harm by wanton and furious driving contrary to section 35 of the Offences against the Person Act 1861. On the other hand, in *Warburton-Pitt*[82] it was held that the *Caldwell/Lawrence* test applied to Art. 45 of the Air Navigation Order 1980, made under sections 60 and 61 of the Civil Aviation Act 1982 prohibiting reckless acts likely to endanger aircraft or persons therein. In *Data Protection Registrar v Amnesty International*[83] the *Caldwell/Lawrence* test was again endorsed for an offence under section 5 of the Data Protection Act 1984.

---

[73] *Venna* [1976] Q.B. 421.
[74] [1990] 1 All E.R. 331.
[75] (1990) 91 Cr.App.R.362.
[76] *Savage* (1990) 91 Cr.App.R.317; *Parmenter* (1991) 92 Cr.App.R.68; *Nash* [1991] Crim.L.R.768.
[77] [1992] 1 A.C. 699.
[78] Smith, Commentary on *Savage;Parmenter* [1992] Crim.L.R.288. At one stage of the judgment Lord Ackner makes oblique reference to a defendant who "neither intends nor adverts to the possibility" of harm and concludes that there would be no assault. This supports *Cunningham* recklessness. See Stone, "Reckless Assaults after Savage and Parmenter" (1992) 12 O.J.L.S. 578 at 582.
[79] [1989] Crim.L.R.213.
[80] *The Independent*, May 23, 1994.
[81] [1996] Crim.L.R.666.
[82] (1991) 92 Cr.App.R.136.
[83] [1995] Crim.L.R.633.

The result is needless confusion and unpredictability. What is required is that one or the other test (or some alternative) be applied consistently throughout the law, or, alternatively, if both tests are to co-exist, there be some *principled* basis for determining which is to apply in any given situation.


### (iii) *Evaluation*

The argument over the merits or otherwise of *Caldwell/Lawrence* is a dispute as to whether blameworthiness is dependent on *cognition*. Are we justified in blaming only those who realise that their actions could cause the prohibited harm? The phrase "advertence-based culpability"[84] sums this up neatly.

Lord Diplock's reasoning in *Caldwell* and *Lawrence* has been described as "pathetically inadequate",[85] "slap-happy", and "profoundly regrettable".[86] The case for "advertence-based culpability" is that recklessness is a species of *mens rea* and *mens rea* is based on the notion of responsibility which involves ideas of *choice*. The defendant has chosen to act in a certain way and that choice only becomes blameworthy if there was knowledge that the actions could cause the prohibited harm. For example, in the infamous case of *Lamb*[87] the defendant pointed a revolver at his best friend in jest and pulled the trigger. His friend was similarly treating the incident as a joke. The revolver had a five-chambered cylinder which, unknown to the defendant, rotated clockwise each time the trigger was pulled. There were two bullets in the chambers but, before firing, neither was in the chamber opposite the barrel. The pulling of the trigger caused the cylinder to rotate, placing a bullet opposite the barrel so that it was struck by the striking pin or hammer. The bullet was discharged killing his friend. Lamb's defence was that he was unaware that the pulling of the trigger would bring one bullet into the firing position opposite the barrel and thus the killing was an accident. Lamb was convicted of manslaughter and sentenced to three years' imprisonment. On appeal this conviction was quashed because of a misdirection on the law of manslaughter. However, the Court of Appeal stated that with a proper direction, Lamb would have been convicted and no criticism was made of the sentence originally imposed. Glanville Williams has written of this:

> "I do not hesitate to say that I regard the sentence as outrageous, a wholly mistaken exercise of judicial discretion. Lamb was a fool, but there is no need to punish fools to that degree. There is no need to punish Lamb at all. He had killed his friend, and that was punishment enough."[88]

Because there was no advertence to the possibility of the consequence occurring, blame becomes inappropriate. The following extract not only supports the view that actors such as Lamb have simply made an "error in judgment", but also suggests utilitarian reasons why liability should be linked to cognition. While this

---

[84] Gardner and Jung, "Making Sense of *Mens Rea*: Anthony Duff's Account" (1991) 11 O.J.L.S. 559.
[85] Smith [1981] Crim.L.R.393 at 394.
[86] Williams, "Recklessness Redefined" [1981] C.L.J. 252.
[87] [1967] 2 Q.B. 981.
[88] *Above*, n.86 at 281–282.

extract, and the one following it, are assessing whether negligence is a justifiable basis for criminal liability, the arguments apply with equal force to the non-advertent recklessness test adopted in *Caldwell/Lawrence*.

### Robert P. Fine and Gary M. Cohen, "Is Criminal Negligence a Defensible Basis for Penal Liability" (1967) 16 Buffalo L.Rev. 749 at 750–752:

"Since negligence involves no *mens rea*, the question is raised as to the advisability of punishing negligent conduct with criminal sanctions. Professor Edwin Keedy responded to this question as follows: 'If the defendant, being mistaken as to the material facts, is to be punished because his mistake is one an average man would not make, punishment will sometimes be inflicted *when the criminal mind does not exist*. Such a result is contrary to fundamental principles, and is plainly unjust, for a man should not be held criminal because of lack of intelligence.' (Keedy, "Ignorance and Mistake in the Criminal Law" 22 Harv.L.Rev. 75, 84 (1908) (Emphasis added)). This argument is persuasive, especially when considered in conjunction with the traditional concepts and goals of criminal punishment.

The concept of criminal punishment is based on one, or a combination, of four theories: deterrence, retribution, rehabilitation and incapacitation.

The deterrence theory of criminal law is based on the hypothesis that the prospective offender knows that he will be punished for any criminal activity, and, therefore, will adjust his behaviour to avoid committing a criminal act. This theory rests on the idea of 'rational utility,' *i.e.* prospective offenders will weigh the evil of the sanction against the gain of the contemplated crime. However, punishment of a negligent offender in no way implements this theory, since the negligent harm-doer is, by definition, unaware of the risk he imposes on society. It is questionable whether holding an individual criminally liable for acts the risks of which he has failed to perceive will deter him from failing to perceive in the future.

The often-criticised retributive theory of criminal law presupposes a 'moral guilt,' which justifies society in seeking its revenge against the offender. This 'moral guilt' is ascribed to those forms of conduct which society deems threatening to its very existence, such as murder and larceny. However, the negligent harm-doer has not actually committed this type of morally reprehensible act, but has merely made an error in judgment. This type of error is an everyday occurrence, although it may deviate from a normal standard of care. Nevertheless, such conduct does not approach the moral turpitude against which the criminal law should seek revenge. It is difficult to comprehend how retribution requires such mistakes to be criminally punished.

It is also doubtful whether the negligent offender can be rehabilitated in any way by criminal punishment. Rehabilitation presupposes a 'warped sense of values' which can be corrected. Since inadvertence, and not a deficient sense of values, has caused the 'crime', there appears to be nothing to rehabilitate.

The underlying goal of the incapacitation theory is to protect society by isolating an individual so as to prevent him from perpetrating a similar crime in the future. However, this approach is only justifiable if less stringent methods will not further the same goal of protecting society. For example, an insane individual would not be criminally incarcerated, if the less stringent means of medical treatment would afford the same societal protection. Likewise, with a criminally negligent individual, the appropriate remedy is not incarceration, but 'to exclude him from the activity in which he is a danger'.

The conclusion drawn from this analysis is that there appears to be no reasonable justification for punishing negligence as a criminal act under any of these four theories. It does not further the purposes of deterrence, retribution, rehabilitation or incapacitation; hence, there is no rational basis for the imposition of criminal liability on negligent conduct
. . .

In addition, Hall ("Negligent Behaviour Should be Excluded from Penal Liability" 36 Colum.L.Rev. (1963)), suggests scientific arguments for the exclusion of negligence from penal liability. One contention is that the incorporation of negligence into the penal law imposes an impossible function on judges, namely, to determine whether a person, about whom very little is known, had the competence and sensitivity to appreciate certain dangers in a particular situation when the facts plainly indicate that he did not exhibit that competence."

The alternative view has not concentrated on such utilitarian considerations although it can be asserted that "punishment supplies men with an additional motive to take care before acting, to use their faculties and to draw upon their experience".[89] Further, perhaps those who fail to consider the obvious consequences of their actions reveal their dangerousness and need incapacitation (say, having their driving licence removed) and rehabilitation.

Rather, the other view has stressed that judgments of blameworthiness should not be limited to cases where the defendant realises that harm could occur. Even accepting the premise of responsibility involving the notion of choice, we can blame those who make choices of which we disapprove. We can blame Lamb for acting as he did in total disregard of an obvious and serious risk. Lord Diplock in *Caldwell* regarded non-advertence as no less blameworthy than advertence. Lord Goff in *Reid* went further and said that "it can be argued with force that, in many cases of failing to think, the degree of blameworthiness to be attached to the driver can be greater than that to be attached in some cases to the driver who recognised the risk and decided to disregard it".[90]

### George P. Fletcher, "The Theory of Criminal Negligence: A Comparative Analysis" (1971) 119 U.Pa.L.Rev. 401 at 415–418:

"At first blush it seems odd that anyone would argue that negligence is not an appropriate ground for censuring the conduct of another … In daily conduct, we all confidently blame others who fail to advert to significant risks. If we confront a motorist driving without his lights on and thereby endangering the lives of many others, we would hardly condition our condemnation of his conduct on whether he knew his lights were off. His failure to find out whether his lights were on or off would itself be a basis for condemning him.[91] Yet theorists have repeatedly argued that this judicial practice is primitive and that, as a matter of principle, an actor must *choose* to do harm in order to be culpable and fairly subject to penal sanctions. Jerome Hall has vigorously advanced this view … [T]he proponents of punishing negligence have relied upon the same reply: the culpability of negligence is not the culpability of choice, but rather of failing to bring to bear one's faculties to perceive the risks that one is taking … The battleground of one segment of the literature is the role of culpability in justifying criminal sanctions. Jerome Hall argues, for example, that 'in the long history of ethics … *voluntary* harm-doing is the essence of (culpability).' From this premise he reasons that negligence is involuntary, and that therefore it is unjust to punish negligent risk-taking. The question Hall raises is the right one. We do wish to know whether it is just to punish the negligent actor. It is not enough to show that punishing negligence has a deterrent impact on other potential risk-creators, for the goal of deterrence, however sound, does not speak to the fairness of forcing the specific defendant to be the object of exemplary sanctioning. Yet the issue of fairness to the defendant is not resolved by positing that negligence is not

---

[89] A.L.I., Model Penal Code, Tentative Draft No. 4, pp. 126–127.

[90] (1992) 95 Cr.App.R.393 at 406.

[91] Compare Williams, *above*, n.86 at 261: "can it possibly be said, with justice, that a driver who opens his door being momentarily forgetful of risk is 'no less blameworthy' than the driver who realises the possibility of causing injury to a cyclist whom he sees approaching but flings open his door regardless?".

voluntary and therefore not culpable. Surely, the negligent actor, like the intentional actor, has the capacity of doing otherwise; he could have brought to bear his faculties to perceive and to avoid the risk he created. That is all we typically require to label conduct as voluntary ...

With the idea of forfeiture in the foreground, culpability functions as the touchstone of the question whether by virtue of his illegal conduct, the violator has lost his moral standing to complain of being subjected to sanctions. If his illegal conduct is unexcused, if he had a fair chance of avoiding the violation and did not, we are inclined to regard the state's imposing a sanction as justified. The defendant's failure to exercise a responsibility shared by all, be it a responsibility to avoid intentional violations or to avoid creating substantial and unjustified risks, provides a warrant for the state's intrusion upon his autonomy as an individual. From the viewpoint of culpability as a standard of moral forfeiture, it seems fair and consistent to regard negligence as culpable and to subject the negligent offender to criminal sanctions."

This non-advertence-based culpability is often described as "objective" as opposed to "subjective" culpability which involves advertence or cognition. As the House of Lords in *Reid* emphasised, such labels can be misleading because recklessness based on non-advertence does still involve looking at *the defendant's* attitude, motive, emotional state and capacities.[92] As we have seen, there is a distinction between recklessness and negligence. Not all cases of inadvertence are regarded as involving blameworthiness. In *Reid* it was stated that where the inadvertence arose from drink, rage, an attitude of indifference or wilful blindness the defendant can be adjudged blameworthy and therefore reckless. But where the lack of foresight arose from some other factor over which the defendant had no control such as "some condition not involving fault on his part" (Lord Keith in *Reid*) there is no blame and no recklessness:

"So the principle is that the actor is to be blamed for his inadvertence, and so reckless, if he could have avoided the accident by making an effort to exercise discipline over his mind."[93]

### John Gardner and Heike Jung, "Making Sense of Mens Rea: Anthony Duff's Account" (1991) 11 O.J.L.S. 559 at 574–575:

"Recklessness is a vice or personal fault, like dishonesty, cowardice and self-indulgence ... Vices are identified in part by reference to the *ends* or *motives* of those whose actions exhibit them. A reckless person, in morality, is one who takes large risks for the sake of relatively unimportant ends. Recklessness, as a moral phenomenon cannot be identified except in terms of the agent's flimsy motives ...

It is true that the presence or absence of advertence to a risk on the part of an agent can sometimes make a difference, like so many other factors, to the scale of that agent's moral culpability. 'Objectivists' are wrong if they deny this. But inadvertence only mitigates a reckless agent's moral culpability, as a rule, if she has attenuated cognitive capacities, and even then it does not normally entail that her fault is converted from recklessness to something else, like carelessness, but only that her recklessness is diminished in scale. The

---

[92] Stannard, "Subjectivism, Objectivism, and the Draft Criminal Code" (1985) 101 L.Q.R. 540 at 543.
[93] Gardner, "Recklessness Redefined" (1993) 109 L.Q.R. 21 at 23.

quality of the motive is an essential part of what distinguishes a reckless person from a careless person in moral evaluations, and that distinction cannot be replicated by relying on any other factor instead, such as advertence to the risk."

## R. A. Duff, "Recklessness" [1980] Crim.L.R.282 at 289–292:

"[There is a] view that inadvertence, however negligent, cannot constitute *mens rea* since we cannot blame a man for what he does not know. That view has been convincingly demolished: whether I notice some aspect of my action or its context may depend on the attention I pay to what I am doing, and be thus within my control; failures of attention may be as 'voluntary' and culpable as other omissions ...

Some failures of attention or realisation may manifest, not mere stupidity or 'thoughtlessness,' but the same indifference or disregard which characterises the conscious risk-taker as reckless. If I intend to injure someone seriously, I may not realise that this might kill them: not because I am *mistaken* about the likely effect of my assault, but because it 'just doesn't occur to me'—I am blind to that aspect of my action. But such blindness to such an essential and integral aspect of a serious assault, though possible, itself manifests a 'reckless disregard' for my victim's life no different from that of an assailant who knows he is endangering life ...

[M]y failure to realise this aspect of my action expresses a certain attitude to it. I do not realise it because I regard it as unimportant; my failure expresses my complete lack of concern about it. In general, the extent to which I notice or realise the various aspects of my action, its context, and its results, is a function as much of my attitudes and values as of my powers of observation and attention: to say that I forgot or did not realise something is to admit that I thought it unimportant, and thus to convict myself of a serious lack of concern for it (which is why a bridegroom would hardly mitigate his offence of missing his wedding by the plea that he forgot it). If, as I have suggested, an agent is reckless to the extent that his actions manifest a serious kind of 'practical indifference,' a 'willingness' to bring about some harm, then such recklessness, indifference, and willingness can be exhibited as much in his failure to notice obvious and important aspects of his action as in his conscious risk-taking. A man may be reckless even though, and even partly *because*, he does not realise the risk which is in fact an essential and significant aspect of his action."

## R. A. Duff, Intention, Agency and Criminal Liability: Philosophy of Action and the Criminal Law (1990), p. 172:

"[A]n appropriate general test of recklessness would be—did the agent's conduct (including any conscious risk-taking, any failure to notice an obvious risk created by her action, and any unreasonable belief on which she acted) display a seriously culpable practical indifference to the interests which her action in fact threatened?"

Duff stresses that this is still a subjective test. What matters is *the defendant's* "practical indifference"; it is subjective to him or her. Recklessness is not just failing to conform to an objective standard: "for what matters is not just *that*, but why, the agent fails to notice an obvious risk; she is reckless only if she fails to notice it because she does not care about it."[94] On this basis he rejects the conclusion in *Caldwell*: it cannot be established that because Caldwell failed to notice the risk to life from his actions that he was displaying reckless indifference thereto. On the other hand, the defendant in *Lawrence* was driving recklessly: no-one could drive

---

[94] Duff, *Intention, Agency and Criminal Liability* (1990), pp. 165–166. Similarly, Horder argues that rather than basing culpability on cognition, we should adopt "a moral theory whose focus is the evaluation of actions stemming from the desires associated with emotions." ("Cognition, Emotion, and Criminal Culpability" (1990) 106 L.Q.R. 469 at 476.)

in the manner in which he did unless they were utterly indifferent to the safety of others.

This approach, endorsed to some extent in *Reid*, presents an immediate problem. On what basis are we to decide that Lawrence displayed this practical indifference but that Caldwell did not?

### Alan Norrie, "Subjectivism, Objectivism and the Limits of Criminal Recklessness" (1992) 12 O.J.L.S. 45 at 50–52:

"This then raises the broader question of how one could tell the callous from the stupid, the negligent or the thoughtless. Is it not likely that one person's callousness will be another person's stupidity, negligence or thoughtlessness? [What matters] on Duff's analysis is the attitude of the interpretive audience to the conduct on display. It is the inference which 'we,' the observers of the events, or the jury, draw from the facts of the case which is relevant ...

[Norrie then gives the rape example of a man who makes an unreasonable mistake as to the woman's consent to sexual intercourse. While Duff would describe this as utter practical indifference to the woman's interests and therefore recklessness, there might be others in our 'society characterised by male chauvinism' who might have different views 'about how willing women are to be forcibly seduced.']

This is not a matter of social consensus in a sexist society. The world ought to be as Duff wants it to be but it is not. So the 'we' who judge callous indifference to consent to be unreasonable cannot claim that our judgment is apolitical because universal. And the attribution of responsibility on the basis of a conception of practical indifference therefore relies here upon an interpretation of behaviour and attitude that may have nothing to do with the way in which the defendant himself would explain them. It requires the reading onto, the imposition of an interpretation of, an attitude on behaviour from 'outside.' It is practical indifference as interpreted objectively by an audience, and having no necessary subjective link with the accused. The accused does not necessarily share Duff's worldview, and hence interpretation of attitudes, yet may be adjudged subjectively guilty on Duff's account. It may be right to argue politically that the law ought to promote Duff's enlightened values through the requirement of a particular moral attitude, but it should not be presented as a form of subjectivism."

There is much to be said for Norrie's criticisms. Why is Duff so confident that Lawrence did not care about the risks of his driving? Presumably, driving as he did posed severe risks to his own life and safety as well. Was he indifferent to that as well? Lord Diplock in *Lawrence* was clearly imposing (his own) objective standard "to ensure that young tearaways and others who drive cars or motor cycles disgracefully will not get off a charge of reckless driving by saying that they were perfectly convinced that their manner of driving presented no danger, because they were so clever that they could always avoid a mishap ... The object of the offence of reckless driving is to catch the driver who flagrantly disregards rules of prudence, whatever he may think about the safety of his behaviour."[95]

Nevertheless, Duff's test of "practical indifference" does offer the distinct advantage that it enables one to escape from some of the rigours of the more formally objective test as laid down in *Caldwell* and then subsequently applied in *Elliott v C (a Minor)* without having to return to a full-blooded test based on cognition. Indeed, one might not *really* ascertain what the defendant's true attitude was, but equally under the cognitive tests one never *really* establishes what the

---

[95] Williams, "Recklessness Redefined" [1981] C.L.J. 252 at 272.

defendant foresaw. One simply draws inferences from facts and then tries to deduce what that state of mind must have been. The *Caldwell/Lawrence* test of recklessness (assuming the dicta in *Reid*, qualifying it, are built upon) is at least asking the right questions: who can we adjudge to be reckless in the sense that they are blameworthy and deserving of punishment? Those who advert to the risks involved in their actions might[96] well be blameworthy but there is no reason why the inquiry should stop there.

The case being made here is that the *Caldwell/Lawrence* concept of recklessness has been rightly freed from the shackles of cognition and that provided the dicta in *Reid*, which are not dissimilar to the ideas of Duff, are accepted, this recklessness test is to be welcomed. Whether we might *ever* want to distinguish advertence from inadvertence in assessing appropriate levels of criminal liability or punishment is a matter to which we shall return shortly.[97]

## 3. Negligence

### (i) *Introduction*

"A person is negligent if he fails to exercise such care, skill or foresight as a reasonable man in his situation would exercise."[98]

"A person acts negligently with respect to a material element of an offence when he should be aware of a substantial and unjustifiable risk that the material element exists or will result from his conduct. The risk must be of such a nature and degree that the actor's failure to perceive it, considering the nature and purpose of his conduct and the circumstances known to him, involves a gross deviation from the standard of care that a reasonable person would observe in the actor's situation."[99]

When people cause harm accidentally, in circumstances where they were acting impeccably, they will not be blamed; indeed, they will probably get our sympathy. However, the "accident" may have been one which, with some simple care and precautions, could have been avoided. In this latter situation our tendency is now to blame the actor: "You should have known what could happen." The question is whether this moral blame should be translated into criminal liability.

The legal concept of negligence has developed to reflect this responsibility that is attributed in everyday life. However, traditionally, criminal liability for negligent conduct has been more limited than might have been expected given society's attitude.[1] Nevertheless, in more recent years there has been an increasing trend towards the creation of offences based on negligence (for example, driving without due care and attention[2] and harassment[3], particularly those that refer to the

---

[96] It is interesting that Duff concludes that advertent risk-taking necessarily exhibits practical indifference whereas inadvertent risk-taking has to pass the "lack of concern" test thereby demonstrating indifference. This is criticised by Gardner and Jung, *above*, pp. 169–170.

[97] See *below*, p. 177.

[98] Law Commission, Working Paper No. 31, p. 57.

[99] American Law Institute, Model Penal Code, Proposed Official Draft, 1962, s.202(2)(d).

[1] The reluctance to punish negligent conduct has arguably left the way open for the more stringent concept of strict liability to develop.

[2] Road Traffic Act 1988, s.3.

[3] Protection from Harassment Act 1997, ss.1(1), 2(1).

requirement of reasonableness in relation to the surrounding circumstances. For example, section 25 of the Firearms Act 1968 makes it an offence to sell firearms or ammunition to "another person whom he knows or has reasonable cause for believing to be drunk or of unsound mind". Further, as we shall see, many prima facie strict liability offences allow "due diligence" defences. If the defendant can establish that he was not negligent he will escape liability. For example, section 21 of the Food Safety Act 1990 provides a defence to any person who "took all due diligence to avoid the commission of the offence".

At common law, however, there has been resistance to the development of crimes of negligence, although there has long been a trend that mistakes in relation to certain defences must be reasonable. But with regard to the definitional elements of the offence, particularly with the more serious offences, the view has always been held that punishment of ordinary carelessness or negligence would be unjust and wrong. However, in extreme cases where death resulted the law has been prepared to depart from its traditional strict insistence on advertence and allow liability for negligence, provided the defendant had shown such lack of care that the conduct could be regarded as extremely negligent. The law thus developed the idea that there can be degrees of negligence and that a person can be liable for manslaughter if there is gross negligence.

### (ii) *Is negligence a state of mind or an objective failure to comply with a set standard of behaviour?*

One view of negligence is that it is a *blank* state of mind; it is inadvertence. The argument is usually expressed in the form: if negligence is a failure to think about the possible consequences of one's actions, it is, therefore, not thinking. Not thinking equals a blank state of mind. This approach has important implications for the commonly accepted view that there can be degrees of negligence. If the mind is empty how can one possibly talk about degrees of negligence or emptiness? How, for example, can negligence be "gross" for the purposes of manslaughter? One cannot have degrees of nothing. However, as the following extract demonstrates, it is possible to assert that negligence is a state of mind and that there can be degrees of such negligence.

### Peter Brett, An Inquiry into Criminal Guilt (1963), pp. 98–100:

"[T]here are two brute facts which cannot be ignored. The first is that people who cause harm by their carelessness feel guilt. The second is that the threat of punishment can deter people from acting carelessly. It is common knowledge that as soon as traffic police appear on the roads drivers begin to pay great attention to what they are doing, and the standard of driving care rises sharply. If the theory that a careless person has a 'blank mind' on the matter is correct, it is difficult to understand why this should happen. ...

Faced with these problems, let us see whether the philosophers can help us. The account given by Ryle (*The Concept of Mind* (1949)) of recklessness and negligence, or carelessness, is useful. He points out that both these concepts are what he terms heed concepts. When we say that a person has been careless, we are stating that he was not minding what he was doing. And 'minding, in all its sorts, can vary in degree. A driver can drive a car with great care, reasonable care, or slight care, and a student can concentrate hard or not very hard' (at p. 136). ... [Ryle] continues:

'To describe someone as now doing something with some degree of some sort of heed is to say ... [h]e is in a "ready" frame of mind, for he both does what he does with readiness to do just that in just this situation and is ready to do some of whatever else he may be called on to do. To describe a driver as taking care does not entail that it has occurred to him that a donkey may bolt out of that side street. He can be ready for such contingencies without having anticipated them. Indeed, he might have anticipated them without being ready for them' (p. 147).

This is surely in accord with the ordinary usage of the terms under discussion, and also with our own personal experience of how we behave when we are either being careful or being careless. And just as there can be varying degrees of readiness, so there can be varying degrees of unreadiness. It thus makes sense to talk of gross negligence, or of recklessness as a very high degree of carelessnes, and to distinguish such forms of carelessness for legal purposes from 'mere inadvertence.' In all these cases we are stating that the person concerned was not minding what he was doing; and that although he possessed the capacity to react in a proper way to the situation, he failed to react properly because he was not at the time ready to react."

Brett accepts that negligence is being in an unready "frame" of mind and has no difficulty in distinguishing between degrees of unreadiness. The criminal law can make the same distinctions and decide at which level negligence becomes blameworthy.

However, the more common approach is to assert that negligence is not merely inadvertence to the consequence of one's actions; it is not a blank state of mind. It is the failure to comply with a standard of behaviour objectively assessed.

### Glanville Williams, "Recklessness Redefined" [1982] C.L.J. 252 at 256:

"But failing to think can be called a state of mind only in the sense that unconsciousness is a state of mind; that is to say, it is an absence of a relevant state of mind. To say that absence of a state of mind is a state of mind is an abuse of language. Not to think about risks is, of course, legal fault if a reasonable man would have thought about them; but that does not make not-thinking a state of mind ... [it] is negligence, and properly punishable as such (in order to impress upon people that this is a dangerous situation in which they are required to stop and think)."

It is this view of negligence that has been accepted by law reform bodies in both England and the United States.[4]

### (iii) *Negligence and Capacity*

Hart, although accepting that negligence is an objective standard of liability (as opposed to a state of mind), has suggested a test of negligence that does allow the characteristics and capacities of the defendant to be taken into account.

---

[4] Law Com. Working Paper No. 31, p. 51 (the final Report however did not think it necessary to define negligence; *The Mental Element in Crime* (Law Com. No. 89), para. 68); Model Penal Code, Proposed Official Draft, 1962, s.3.02(2)(d). The Draft Criminal Code Bill 1989 (Law Com. No. 177) also does not utilise the concept of negligence at all.

## H. L. A. Hart, "Negligence, Mens Rea and the Elimination of Responsibility" in Punishment and Responsibility (Essays in the Philosophy of Law) (1968), pp. 152–157:

"What is crucial is that those whom we punish should have had, when they acted, the normal capacities, physical and mental, for doing what the law requires and abstaining from what it forbids, and a fair opportunity to exercise these capacities. Where these capacities and opportunities are absent, as they are in different ways in the varied cases of accident, mistake, paralysis, reflex action, coercion, insanity, etc., the moral protest is that it is morally wrong to punish because 'he could not have helped it' or 'he could not have done otherwise' or 'he had no real choice'. But ... there is no reason (unless we are to reject the whole business of responsibility and punishment) *always* to make this protest when someone who 'just didn't think' is punished for carelessness. For in some cases at least we may say 'he could have thought about what he was doing' with just as much rational confidence as one can say of any intentional wrong-doing 'he could have done otherwise'.

Of course, the law compromises with competing values over this matter of the subjective element in responsibility ...

The most important compromise which legal systems make over the subjective element consists in its adoption of what has been unhappily termed the 'objective standard'. This may lead to an individual being treated for the purposes of conviction and punishment as if he possessed capacities for control of his conduct which he did not possess, but which an ordinary or reasonable man possesses and would have exercised. The expression 'objective' and its partner 'subjective' are unhappy because, as far as negligence is concerned, they obscure the real issue. We may be tempted to say with Dr Turner that just because the negligent man does not have 'the thought of harm in his mind,' to hold him responsible for negligence is *necessarily* to adopt an objective standard and to abandon the 'subjective' element in responsibility. It then becomes vital to distinguish this (mistaken) thesis from the position brought about by the use of objective standards in the application of laws which make negligence criminally punishable. For, when negligence is made criminally punishable, this itself leaves open the question: whether, before we punish, both or only the first of the following two questions must be answered affirmatively.

(i) Did the accused fail to take those precautions which any reasonable man with normal capacities would in the circumstances have taken?

(ii) Could the accused, given his mental and physical capacities, have taken those precautions?

... If our conditions of liability are invariant and not flexible, *i.e.* if they are not adjusted to the capacities of the accused, then some individuals will be held liable for negligence though they could not have helped their failure to comply with the standard. In *such* cases, indeed, criminal responsibility will be made independent of any 'subjective element', since the accused could not have conformed to the required standard. But this result is nothing to do with negligence being taken as a basis for criminal liability; precisely the same result will be reached if, in considering whether a person acted intentionally, we were to attribute to him foresight of consequences which a reasonable man would have foreseen but which he did not. 'Absolute liability' results, not from the admission of the principle that one who has been grossly negligent is criminally responsible for the consequent harm even if 'he had no idea in his mind of harm to anyone,' but from the refusal in the application of this principle to consider the capacities of an individual who has fallen below the standard of care.

It is of course quite arguable that no legal system could afford to individualise the conditions of liability so far as to discover and excuse all those who could not attain the average or reasonable man's standard. It may, in practice, be impossible to do more than excuse those who suffer from gross forms of incapacity, *viz.* infants, or the insane, or those afflicted with recognisably inadequate powers of control over their movements, or who are clearly unable to detect, or extricate themselves, from situations in which their disability may work harm. Some confusion is, however, engendered by certain inappropriate ways of describing these excusable cases, which we are tempted to use in a system which, like our own, defines negligence in terms of what the reasonable man would do. We may find ourselves asking whether the infant, the insane, or those suffering from paralysis did all that a reasonable man would *in the circumstances* do, taking 'circumstances' (most queerly) to include personal qualities like being an infant, insane or paralysed. This paradoxical approach leads to many difficulties. To avoid them we need to hold apart the primary question (1) What *would* the reasonable man with ordinary capacities have done in these circumstances? from the second question (2), *Could* the accused with *his* capacities have done that? Reference to such factors as lunacy or disease should be made in answering only the second of these questions. This simple, and surely realistic, approach avoids difficulties which the notion of individualising the standard of care has presented for certain writers; for these difficulties are usually created by the mistaken assumption that the only way of allowing for individual incapacities is to treat them as part of the 'circumstances' in which the reasonable man is supposed to be acting. Thus Dr Glanville Williams said that if 'regard must be had to the make-up and circumstances of the particular offender, one would seem on a determinist view of conduct to be pushed to the conclusion that there is no standard of conduct at all. For if every characteristic of the individual is taken into account, including his heredity the conclusion is that he could not help doing as he did.' (The General Part (1st Ed.) p. 82.)

But 'determinism' presents no special difficulty here. The question is whether that individual had the capacity (inherited or not) to act otherwise than he did, and 'determinism' has no relevance to the case of one who is accused of negligence which it does not have to one accused of intentionally killing."

Punishment for negligent conduct can, therefore, be justified if a combination of objective (the reasonable person) and subjective (the capacity of the particular person) factors are taken into account.

Some support for Hart's approach is to be found in the case of *Hudson*[5] where the appellant was convicted of having sexual intercourse with a defective, contrary to section 7 of the Sexual Offences Act 1956 and sentenced to eighteen months' imprisonment. He raised a defence under section 7(2) of the Sexual Offences Act 1956 which then read: "A man is not guilty of an offence under this section because he has unlawful sexual intercourse with a woman if he does not know and has no reason to suspect her to be a defective." In considering whether the appellant had "reason to suspect her to be a defective", Ashworth J. stated:

"Equally, in considering his state of mind, in the view of this court a jury is entitled and indeed bound to take into account the accused himself. There may be cases, of which this is not one, where there is evidence before the jury to show that the accused himself is a person of limited intelligence, or possibly suffering from some handicap which would prevent him from appreciating the state of affairs which an ordinary man might realise. That is a matter again which in the appropriate case would no doubt receive consideration in the summing-up."[6]

We have seen that in assessing recklessness the courts (for example, in *Elliott v C (a Minor)*) have not taken any account of personal weaknesses or idiosyncracies of the defendant. If capacity to appreciate the consequences of one's actions is to be ignored for the purposes of recklessness, it is most unlikely to be considered relevant in assessing negligence. This is extremely unfortunate and perhaps goes some way to explaining the hostility towards the concept of negligence by law reform bodies. The Draft Criminal Code Bill 1989 makes no mention of negligence, stating that "every offence requires a fault element of recklessness with respect to

[5] [1966] 1 Q.B. 448.
[6] At 455.

each of its elements other than fault elements, unless otherwise provided".[7] And, as we have seen, recklessness under the Code Bill is only given its *Cunningham* advertence-based meaning. We have argued that this approach in relation to recklessness is not justifiable. Similarly, following the arguments of Brett and Hart above, it seems that liability for negligence in lesser offences could perhaps be justified, provided, of course, that the defendant possessed the necessary capacity to have acted otherwise.

## 4. Levels of culpability

An important final point needs consideration. Assuming defendants who act with non-advertent recklessness or negligence are to be blamed for the harms they cause, are they *as* blameworthy as those who might have caused the same harms intentionally or with subjective foresight of the risks they were running? If not, should the law reflect the differences in culpability by imposing different levels of liability and/or punishment? Should the law reflect the view that "to break your Ming china, deliberately or intentionally, is worse than to knock it over while waltzing wildly round the room and not thinking of what might get knocked over"?[8] Further, is it worse to break your Ming china while waltzing round the room realising that you might knock it over than when you have no such realisation?

### A. Kenny, Freewill and Responsibility (1978), pp. 85–92:

"In the same way as the justification of the general requirement of *mens rea* flows from the nature of punishment and the nature of practical reasoning, so the justification of distinguishing between different degrees of *mens rea* arises from the different degrees of proximity to the actuality or possibility of practical reasoning in particular criminal behaviour. The same act, when performed negligently, may be punished less severely than when performed knowingly, and the same act when performed recklessly may be punished less severely than when performed intentionally. We must ask why this is so, and whether it should be so ...

No doubt almost everyone would regard a reckless killer as more wicked than an inadvertent killer; but the law's principal concern is the prevention of harm, and the harm done by either killer is identical. Should not the penalty too be identical? No: for the point at which the threat of punishment is intended to be brought to bear upon practical reasoning is different in the two cases. The threat of punishment for negligence is meant to enforce at all times a standard of care to ensure that one's actions do not endanger life: the threat of punishment for recklessness is meant to operate at the specific points at which one is contemplating a course of action known to be life-endangering. The actions, therefore, on which the threat of punishment for negligence is brought to bear are less dangerous than those on which the threat of punishment for recklessness is brought to bear: for in general actions which, for all one knows, may be dangerous are less dangerous than actions which one positively knows to be a risk to life. Hence the more severe threat of punishment is held out to the citizen contemplating the more dangerous action.

Just as actions known to be likely to cause death are in general more dangerous than those not known to be so likely, so actions done with the intention of causing death are in general more dangerous than those merely foreseen as likely to cause death. (The latter, for instance, unlike the former, are compatible with the taking of precautions against the causing of death.) This perhaps offers a reason for punishing intentional homicide more severely than

[7] Law Com. No. 177, clause 20(1).
[8] Hart, *above*, p. 175, at 136.

reckless homicide, just as reckless homicide is punished more severely than negligent homicide . . .

Thus we have seen the rationale, on the deterrent theory of punishment, for the discriminations made in law between the different forms of *mens rea* from negligence, recklessness and basic intent up to specific intent. It may well be thought that the theory behind such discriminations presupposes a coolness in calculation and a competence in the theory of games which it is unrealistic to impute to the average citizen tempted to commit a crime. On the other hand, it is surely not a mere accident that the gradations of severity in punishment which a comparatively recondite application of the theory of deterrence suggests should correspond in such large measure with the intuitions of moral common sense about the comparative wickedness of frames of mind.

In practice, of course, the deterrent effect of the law operates unevenly and erratically. The elaborate efforts of lawyers and academics to sort offences into precise categories and to fit crimes to punishment on impeccable theoretical grounds may well strike a layman as resembling an attempt to make a town clock accurate to a millisecond in a community most of whom are too short-sighted to see the clock-face, too deaf to hear the hours ring, and many of whom set no great store on punctuality in any case."

Do such utilitarian arguments adequately explain why we distinguish between different levels of culpability and reflect this by different punishments for each?

### James B. Brady, "Recklessness, Negligence, Indifference and Awareness" (1980) 43 M.L.R. 381 at 396–399:

"What is the justification for the decreasing culpability attaching to intentional, reckless and negligent conduct? . . . First of all, I do not believe that an utilitarian rationale concerning the purpose of punishment will suffice. For example, it has been argued that the culpability distinction between intentional action and recklessness may be justified since there is a greater likelihood that an intentional action will result in harm. If the purpose of punishment is the prevention of harm, the argument goes, the degree of seriousness of the offence should be proportionate to the degree of dangerousness. On this theory we punish the intentional offender more because (a) a more severe penalty may be necessary to deter a person from accomplishing a result that is his aim or purpose than to deter one who acts knowing that there is a risk but whose purpose is not to bring about that result, and (b) the intentional offender may require a longer sentence, for purpose of reform or special deterrence, than the reckless or negligent offender. . . . [T]hese arguments from an utilitarian rationale are not persuasive in general. For example, considering the class of negligent or reckless offenders as contrasted with the class of intentional offenders there seems to be no reason to believe that the former pose less of a continuing threat of harm than the latter. If the degree of seriousness of the offence were only dictated by utilitarian reasons, negligence might well be viewed as more serious, in light of the greater number of negligent harms in comparison to intentional harms, and might in special cases require more punishment for purposes of general or special deterrence than intentional offences require.

These distinctions between different modes are to be viewed as distinctions of culpability in the strict sense. If they are justified at all, they are justified because they mark moral distinctions. The strongest argument is that unless the law is to treat morally disparate cases alike the law should reflect these distinctions . . .

There does not seem to be any single criterion which fully captures our intuitions concerning degrees of culpability. One might argue, for example, that the distinctions could be maintained on the basis of the degree of voluntariness of the action. The reason that negligence, where the agent is unaware of the risk, is less blameworthy than recklessness is that negligent conduct is less voluntary than reckless conduct. But this will not explain the distinction between intentional and reckless conduct. Since in reckless conduct the agent is aware of the risk, it would seem that in both reckless and intentional action the agent has the choice of forbearing from his action. From a consideration of control of conduct, therefore, reckless conduct seems to be as voluntary as intentional conduct.

Suppose that we consider another theory, that it is the factor of likeliness to cause harm which is the criterion of blame. This is a different theory than the one discussed earlier which attempts to explain these distinctions on utilitarian grounds relating to a greater degree of likelihood of harm. The argument here is that the greater likelihood of harm marks a moral distinction and that one who engages in conduct which is more likely to cause harm is more *culpable* than one who engages in conduct with a lesser chance of harm. Under this theory the reason that intentional conduct is more culpable than recklessness causing the same harm is that harm is judged more likely to occur if that is the purpose of one's action than if it is the merely foreseen consequence of one's action.

To a certain extent this factor might explain some of the distinctions in culpability. It seems to be part of the reason, for example, for one who hopes that the harm will not occur, is more blameworthy than one who 'doesn't care one way or the other' in regard to a less likely risk. In this case 'hoping not' is not a mitigating factor because of the greater likelihood of the harm occurring.

But while the likelihood of harm is an important factor, it cannot explain other distinctions. For example, a person who causes harm with the desire of bringing about that harm is thought more culpable, even where the chance of his succeeding was slight, than a person who causes harm by recklessly taking a substantial risk. This cannot, of course, be explained on the grounds of likelihood of harm since the likelihood where the person intentionally takes a 'long shot' is less than where the person acts recklessly in regard to a likely risk. And in cases regarding the same risk, the person's hopes that the harm will not occur does reduce culpability in comparison with one who does not care at all. Again, the difference in degree cannot be explained on the basis of greater likelihood of harm since the risk is the same. Similarly, this theory evidently cannot explain the distinctions between negligent and reckless conduct involving the same risk of harm since, of course, the likelihood of harm is the same. Why then do we blame the reckless agent more? Here the answer seems to be that recklessness manifests a trait of the person that is not present to the same degree in negligence. The person who realises the risk would not have acted unless he was indifferent, in the broad sense, to the interests of others. We properly blame him more, since he is more indifferent. And the person who hopes that harm will not occur is less indifferent, in regard to the same risk, than one who does not care at all. Though again in some cases involving different degrees of risk 'hoping not' does not show a lesser degree of indifference."

Assuming that we wish to maintain these distinctions between intention, advertent recklessness, non-advertent recklessness and negligence, there are further problems to be considered. In particular, we would need to decide whether these distinctions should be reflected at the substantive level (*i.e.* different criminal offences for the different states of mind) or at the sentencing stage (*i.e.* same crime, but differing punishments depending on state of mind). If the latter, should this be left to judicial discretion or be prescribed by law in some way (say, in a guideline model of sentencing)?

## IV. RELATIONSHIP OF MENS REA TO ACTUS REUS

### A. *Introduction*

A general rule of the criminal law is that *mens rea* must exist in relation to the *actus reus*. Bearing in mind that an *actus reus* can consist of:

(1) an act;
(2) committed in certain specified circumstances; and

(3) leading to the prohibited consequence,

*mens rea* should exist in relation to each of these separate elements. But it does not necessarily follow that the same degree of *mens rea* is required in relation to each. Thus the crime of attempt, for example, could require (1) an intentional act, (2) recklessness as to surrounding circumstances, and (3) an intention to bring about the forbidden consequences. But whatever the level of *mens rea*, it must exist "in relation to" the *actus reus*, or, to put it another way, the *actus reus* must be attributable to the *mens rea*. In order to understand this rule it is necessary to investigate two "principles" that are well established in criminal law, and to consider the problem of mistake.

### B. *Coincidence of Actus Reus and Mens Rea*

In the Rhodesian case of *Shorty*[9] the defendant violently assaulted the deceased with intent to kill him. The defendant, genuinely believing the victim to be dead, attempted to dispose of the "body" by putting it down a sewer. The deceased was in fact still alive at the time but died of drowning in the sewer. The court ruled that these actions must be divided into:

(1) the assault which did not cause death—this was accompanied by an intent to kill, and
(2) the *actus reus* of murder (placing the "body" in a sewer with resultant drowning)—but this was not accompanied by *mens rea* at this stage.

Because the *actus reus* of murder did not coincide with the *mens rea* thereof, the defendant could not be convicted of murder. He was convicted only of attempted murder (stage 1), the *actus reus* of which did coincide with the requisite *mens rea*.

Is such a result realistic? The defendant intended to kill his victim; he did kill him. Should his mistake as to the method and time of death affect his liability?

### Thabo Meli v R. [1954] 1 All E.R. 373 (Privy Council)

The appellants, in accordance with a pre-arranged plan, took a man to a hut, gave him beer so that he was partially intoxicated and then struck him over the head. Believing him to be dead, they took his body and rolled it over a low cliff, making the scene look like an accident. In fact the man was not dead, but died of exposure when unconscious at the foot of the cliff.

Lord Reid:
"The point of law which was raised in this case can be simply stated. It is said that two acts were done:—first, the attack in the hut; and, secondly, the placing of the body outside afterwards—and that they were separate acts. It is said that, while the first act was accompanied by *mens rea*, it was not the cause of death; but that the second act, while it was the cause of death, was not accompanied by *mens rea*; and on that ground, it is said that the accused are not guilty of murder, though they may have been guilty of culpable homicide. It is said that the *mens rea* necessary to establish murder is an intention to kill, and that there could be no intention to kill when the accused thought that the man was already dead, so their original intention to kill had ceased before they did the act which caused the man's death. It appears to their Lordships impossible to divide up what was really one series of acts

---

[9] (1950) S.R. 280.

in this way. There is no doubt that the accused set out to do all these acts in order to achieve their plan, and as parts of their plan; and it is much too refined a ground of judgment to say that, because they were under a misapprehension at one stage and thought that their guilty purpose had been achieved before, in fact, it was achieved, therefore they are to escape the penalties of the law. ... Their crime is not reduced from murder to a lesser crime merely because the accused were under some misapprehension for a time during the completion of their criminal plot."

**Appeal dismissed**

Dealing with a similar situation (except there was no preconceived plan) in *Church*,[10] it was stated that the jury should have been told they could convict of murder "if they regarded the appellant's behaviour from the moment he first struck her to the moment when he threw her into the river as a series of acts designed to cause death or grievous bodily harm".[11]

## R v Le Brun (1992) 94 Cr.App.R.101 (Court of Appeal, Criminal Division)

The defendant hit his wife on the chin knocking her unconscious. While trying to drag her body away (probably to avoid detection) he dropped her causing her to fracture her skull and die. He was convicted of manslaughter and appealed.

Lord Lane C.J.:
"[After citing *Church* with approval his Lordship continued]
It seems to us that where the unlawful application of force and the eventual act causing death are parts of the same sequence of events, the same transaction, the fact that there is an appreciable interval of time between the two does not serve to exonerate the defendant from liability. That is certainly so where the appellant's subsequent actions which caused death, after the initial unlawful blow, are designed to conceal his commission of the original unlawful assault.
It would be possible to express the problem as one of causation. The original unlawful blow to the chin was a *causa sine qua* of the later *actus reus*. It was the opening event in a series which was to culminate in death: the first link in the chain of causation, to use another metaphor. It cannot be said that the actions of the appellant in dragging the victim away with the intention of evading liability broke the chain which linked the initial blow with the death.
In short, in circumstances such as the present ... the act which causes death and the necessary mental state to constitute manslaughter need not coincide in point of time ...
[The trial judge had drawn a correct distinction] between actions by the appellant which were designed to help his wife and actions which were not so designed: on the one hand that would be a way in which the prosecution could establish the connection if he was not trying to assist his wife; on the other hand if he was trying to assist his wife, the chain of causation would have been broken and the *nexus* between the two halves of the prosecution case would not exist."

**Appeal dismissed**

Ashworth argues that these decisions "take a rather elastic view of the contemporaneity principle, and seem to be motivated by considerations akin to constructive liability".[12] However, in all the above cases the so-called problem of a "coincidence of *actus reus* and *mens rea*" is illusory. In each case the defendant's

---

[10] (1965) 49 Cr.App.R.206.
[11] See also *Moore* and *Dorn* [1975] Crim.L.R.229. In *Att-Gen's Reference (No. 4 of 1980)* [1981] 1 W.L.R. 705 the Court of Appeal left open the question whether this "series of acts" test was a correct extension of the *Thabo Meli* principle.
[12] *Principles of Criminal Law* (3rd ed., 1999), p. 165.

actions caused the ultimate death (that is, the chain of causation was not broken); the defendant was held liable for either murder or manslaughter[13] depending on the *mens rea* present at the time of the original assault.

This approach was confirmed by the House of Lords in *Attorney-General's Reference No. 3 of 1994* where Lord Mustill stated: "The existence of an interval of time between the doing of an act by the defendant with the necessary wrongful intent and its impact on the victim in a manner which leads to death does not in itself prevent the intent, the act and the death from together amounting to murder, so long as there is an unbroken causal connection between the act and the death".[14] Lord Hope added that "the act which caused the death and the mental state which is needed to constitute manslaughter need not coincide in point of time ... [as long as] the original unlawful and dangerous act, to which the required mental state is related, and the eventual death of the victim are both part of the same sequence of events".[15]

Where, however, there are two separate incidents which cannot be conflated into a continuous act or the "same sequence of events", the jury must be unanimous as to which of the acts forms the basis of the defendant's liability.[16] In *Boreman*[17] the defendant seriously assaulted the victim (with the *mens rea* of murder) and later (perhaps accidentally) started a fire at the victim's flat. The victim died but the medical evidence was divided as to the cause of death. It was held that "where the two possible means by which the killing is effected comprise completely different acts, happening at different times, it can properly be said that the jury ought to be unanimous on which acts leads them to the decision to convict". However, the appeal was dismissed on the ground that the jury must have been satisfied that the injuries were an operating cause of death.

There are other "coincidence cases" where the initial act is not accompanied by *mens rea* but the defendant forms *mens rea* at a later stage in the sequence of events.

## Fagan v Metropolitan Police Commissioner [1969] 1 Q.B. 439 (Queen's Bench Divisional Court)

The appellant was told by a police officer to park his car in an exact position against the kerb. He drove the vehicle forward and stopped with its front off-side wheel on the constable's left foot. When told to reverse off, the appellant replied, "Fuck you, you can wait," and turned off the ignition. After several further requests, the appellant reversed the vehicle off the constable's foot. He was convicted of assaulting a police officer in the execution of his duty. On appeal he claimed that the initial driving on to the foot was unintentional and therefore not an assault, and that his refusal to drive off was not an "act" capable of amounting to an assault.

---

[13] This solution was not adopted in *Shorty* (*above*, n.9). It is submitted that under English causation principles, *Shorty* would be regarded as wrong.

[14] [1997] 3 All E.R. 936 at 942.

[15] *ibid.* at 956–957.

[16] *Brown* (1983) 79 Cr.App.R.115.

[17] [2000] 1 All E.R.307.

James J.:

"We think that the crucial question is whether, in this case, the act of the appellant can be said to be complete and spent at the moment of time when the car wheel came to rest on the foot, or whether his act is to be regarded as a continuing act operating until the wheel was removed. In our judgment, a distinction is to be drawn between acts which are complete—though results may continue to flow—and those acts which are continuing. ... For an assault to be committed, both the elements of *actus reus* and *mens rea* must be present at the same time. ... It is not necessary that *mens rea* should be present at the inception of the *actus reus*, it can be superimposed on an existing act. On the other hand, the subsequent inception of *mens rea* cannot convert an act which has been completed without *mens rea* into an assault. ...

There was an act constituting a battery which at its inception was not criminal because there was no element of intention, but which became criminal from the moment the intention was formed to produce the apprehension which was flowing from the continuing act. The fallacy of the appellant's argument is that it seeks to equate the facts of this case with such a case as where a motorist has accidentally run over a person and, that action having been completed, fails to assist the victim with the intent that the victim should suffer."

**Appeal dismissed**

In *Miller*[18] the defendant fell asleep holding a lit cigarette which started a fire. When he awoke he failed to do anything about the fire but simply moved to another room. The House of Lords adopted the "duty theory" that by creating the dangerous situation (starting the fire) the defendant became under a duty to act and so could be held responsible for the omission to act. Lord Diplock, however, conceded that the "continuous act" theory would provide an alternative route to liability.

## R. v Miller [1983] A.C. 161 (House of Lords)

Lord Diplock:

"[T]he conduct of the accused, throughout the period from immediately before the moment of ignition to the completion of the damage to the property by the fire, is relevant; so is his state of mind throughout that period. ...

[The ratio decidendi of the Court of Appeal] treats the whole course of conduct of the accused, from the moment at which he fell asleep and dropped the cigarette on to the mattress until the time the damage to the house by fire was complete, as a continuous act of the accused, and holds that it is sufficient to constitute the statutory offence of arson if at any stage in that course of conduct the state of mind of the accused, when he fails to try to prevent or minimise the damage which will result from his initial act, although it lies within his power to do so, is that of being reckless as to whether property belonging to another would be damaged."

*Fagan* presents no problem. A battery involves the application of force to another. At the time the defendant was applying force by keeping the car on the constable's foot, he was doing so deliberately. There was thus the necessary coincidence of *actus reus* and *mens rea*. *Miller* is less easily resolved in that the original action of starting the fire was unaccompanied by *mens rea* as he was asleep. The Government has published a Consultation Document containing a Draft Bill which would deal with the problem in *Miller* in the following manner.

[18] [1983] A.C. 161. A fuller extract from this case is provided at pp. 102–104.

### Home Office, Violence: Reforming the Offences Against the Person Act 1861, Draft Offences Against the Person Bill 1998, clause 16:

"(1) Where it is an offence under this Act to be at fault in causing a result by an act and a person lacks the fault required when he does an act that may cause or does cause the result, he nevertheless commits the offence if—

(a) being aware that he has done the act and that the result may occur or (as the case may be) has occurred and may continue, and

(b) with the fault required,

he fails to take reasonable steps to prevent the result occurring or continuing and it does occur or continue."

This is, as indicated in *Miller*, a better way of resolving the problem. Rather than resorting to fictions concerning a "continuing *actus reus*", the defendant is effectively treated as having created a dangerous situation. This generates a duty to take reasonable steps to prevent harm resulting from that danger.

### Nicola Lacey and Celia Wells, Reconstructing Criminal Law: Text and Materials (2nd ed., 1998), pp. 48–49:

"If in cases such as these [*Miller* and *Thabo Meli*], doctrinal analysis can be manipulated to extend the timeframe on which the law focuses, why should that timeframe not be extended in other cases too? Why, for example, should legal analysis not concern itself with *how* a defendant came to be in the situation in which she has apparently acted negligently, recklessly or intentionally? This would, of course, lead to significant extensions and reductions of liability according to the circumstances of different cases. ... [E]xactly these kinds of factors *do* in fact enter in to legal judgments as well as into quasi-legal judgments such as the decision to prosecute for a 'strict' liability offence? Can doctrine give any coherent account of which timeframe is settled upon in which instances? Once again, the coherence and determinacy of doctrine appears to be in doubt."

### C. *Transferred Malice*

There are two well-established and accepted rules of criminal law:

(a) If a defendant causes the *actus reus* by a different method than he intended he is nevertheless liable. Thus if the defendant intended to kill his victim by stabbing him but after the first stab the victim fell and struck his head on a kerb, the blow killing him, the defendant is clearly guilty of murder and cannot claim the death is accidental. He intended to kill his victim; by his actions he has killed the victim; he has *mens rea* in relation to the *actus reus*; he is liable.

(b) If the defendant is mistaken as to the identity of her victim, she is nevertheless liable. Thus if the defendant shoots at her victim thinking he is Smith but in fact it is Jones and Jones dies, the defendant is clearly guilty of murder. Again she committed the *actus reus* of murder; she had the requisite *mens rea*; she is liable.

However, what of the following scenarios?

(a) What if the defendant fires his gun at Smith, but misses and hits a passing stranger, Jones, and kills him? If the defendant was unaware of the existence of Jones, can he nevertheless be liable for murder?

(b) What if the defendant throws a brick at Smith, but misses and breaks a window near Smith? If the defendant was unaware of the existence of the window, can she be liable for criminal damage?

The response of English law to these two situations is clear:

(a) The defendant will be liable for murder. He intended to cause the *actus reus* of murder; he did cause the *actus reus* of murder. His malice against Smith is transferred to Jones. The *actus reus* of murder is killing *a* human being. This he has done, intentionally; the identity of his victim is irrelevant. The leading illustration of this principle is *Latimer*[19] where the defendant swung his belt at a man with whom he was quarrelling but the belt hit the face of a woman to whom he was talking. Lord Coleridge C.J. held:

> "if a person has a malicious intent towards one person, and in carrying into effect that malicious intent he injures another man, he is guilty of what the law considers malice against the person so injured."

(b) The defendant will *not* be liable for criminal damage because the doctrine of transferred malice does not apply where the *actus reus* (criminal damage) is different from the *mens rea* (of an offence against the person). Only if the *actus reus* intended and the *actus reus* caused are the same can the malice be transferred from the one to the other. In *Pembliton*,[20] where the facts were similar to the hypothetical example, the defendant was acquitted (on appeal) of malicious damage to a window.

The rationale of, and limits to, the doctrine of transferred malice were explored in the following case. In order to understand the decision it is necessary to appreciate two rules to be explored in Chapter 8. First, a foetus cannot be the victim of a crime of violence. If the foetus dies *in utero*, it cannot be murder or manslaughter. If, however, the child is born alive but later dies from violence aimed at it while *in utero*, the assailant may be liable for murder or manslaughter. Secondly, the *mens rea* of murder is satisfied by either an intention to kill or an intention to cause grievous bodily harm.

**Attorney-General's Reference (No. 3 of 1994) [1998] A.C. 245 (House of Lords)**

The appellant stabbed a pregnant woman intending to cause her grievous bodily harm. As a result her child was born prematurely and 121 days later died because of the prematurity of the birth. The trial judge directed the jury to acquit the appellant of both murder and manslaughter because the foetus, at the time of the attack, was not a live person. The doctrine of transferred malice was not applicable because "the intent to stab the mother (a

---

[19] (1886) 17 Q.B.D. 369. For a more recent illustration of transferred malice (and where the doctrine was expressly approved), see *Mitchell* (1983) 75 Cr.App.R.293. In *Jones (Peter)* [1987] Crim.L.R.701 the doctrine was applied in a provocation case.

[20] (1874) 12 Cox 607.

live person) could not be transferred to the foetus (not a live person)". On a reference by the Attorney-General, the Court of Appeal allowed the appeal on the ground that the foetus is part of the mother so that an intention to cause grievous bodily harm to the mother is equivalent to the same intent directed towards the foetus. The appellant appealed to the House of Lords.

Lord Mustill:
"[His Lordship rejected the Court of Appeal's views on the ground that] the mother and the foetus were two distinct organisms living symbiotically, not a single organism with two aspects. The mother's leg was part of the mother; the foetus was not. . . .
I turn to . . . 'transferred malice' . . . One explanation [of this rule is that it is] founded on the notion of risk. The person who committed a crime took the chance that the outcome would be worse than he expected . . . but as a foundation of a modern doctrine of transferred malice broad enough to encompass the present case it seems to me quite unsupportable . . .
[T]here was [also] the idea of 'general malice', of an evil disposition existing in the general and manifesting itself in the particular, uniting the aim of the offender and the result which his deeds actually produced. According to this theory, there was no need to 'transfer' the wrongful intent from the intended to the actual victim; for since the offender was . . . 'an enemy to all mankind in general', the actual victim was the direct object of the offender's enmity. Plainly, this will no longer do, for the last vestiges of the idea disappeared with the abolition of the murder/felony doctrine.
What explanation is left: for explanation there must be, since the 'transferred malice' concept is agreed on both sides to be sound law today? . . . [His Lordship then discussed *Pembliton* and *Latimer*.] I find it hard to base a modern law of murder on these two cases . . . [although the answers they gave] would be the same today. But the harking back to a concept of general malice, which amounts to no more than this, that a wrongful act displays a malevolence which can be attached to any adverse consequence, has long been out of date. And to speak of a particular malice which is 'transferred' simply disguises the problem by idiomatic language. The defendant's malice is directed at one objective, and when after the event the court treats it as directed at another object it is not recognising a 'transfer' but creating a new malice which never existed before. As Dr Glanville Williams pointed out . . . the doctrine is 'rather an arbitrary exception to general principles'. Like many of its kind this is useful enough to yield rough justice . . .
My Lords, the purpose of this enquiry has been to see whether the existing rules are based on principles sound enough to justify their extension to a case where the defendant acts without an intent to injure either the foetus or the child which it will become. In my opinion they are not. To give an affirmative answer requires a double 'transfer' of intent: first from the mother to the foetus and then from the foetus to the child as yet unborn . . . For me, this is too much . . . I am willing to follow old laws until they are overturned, but not to make a new law on a basis for which there is no principle.
Moreover, even on a narrower approach the argument breaks down. The effect of transferred malice, as I understand it, is that the intended victim and the actual victim are treated as if they were one, so that what was intended to happen to the first person (but did not happen) is added to what actually did happen to the second person (but was not intended to happen), with the result that what was intended and what happened are married to make a notionally intended and actually consummated crime. The cases are treated as if the actual victim had been the intended victim from the start. To make any sense of this process there must, as it seems to me, be some compatibility between the original intention and the actual occurrence, and this is, indeed, what one finds in the cases. There is no such compatibility here. The defendant intended to commit and did commit an immediate crime of violence to the mother. He committed no relevant violence to the foetus, which was not a person, either at the time or in the future, and intended no harm to the foetus or to the human person which it would become . . . I would not overstrain the idea of transferred malice by trying to make it fit the present case.
Accordingly, . . . the judge was right to direct an acquittal on the count of murder.

[His Lordship then went on to hold that the appellant could have been guilty of manslaughter for which recourse to transferred malice was not necessary.]"

**Appeal allowed**

Lord Mustill's clear dislike of the doctrine of transferred malice echoes the earlier views of Ashworth.

### A. J. Ashworth, "Transferred Malice and Punishment for Unforeseen Consequences" in P. R. Glazebrook (ed.), Reshaping the Criminal Law (1978), pp. 77, 84–89:

"The principle that a person should not be convicted of an offence unless he brought about the proscribed harm either intentionally or recklessly is frequently urged. ... The doctrine known as transferred malice seems to stand out as an exception to this principle, for it results in criminal liability for consequences which would in ordinary language be described as accidental. The doctrine applies 'when an injury intended for one falls on another by accident.' ...

But if the indictment charges D with wounding P with intent to do grievous bodily harm to P, contrary to section 18 of the Offences Against the Person Act 1861, is it not an affront to common sense to convict him in the knowledge that his intent was to harm O and not P?[21] ... The apparent illogicality can of course be ignored in the belief that transferred malice represents a higher principle of criminal liability which must be applied even where the particular words of a statute do not sit happily with it. ...

What, if anything, would be lost if the doctrine were abolished here? Does our criminal law offer any acceptable alternative methods of dealing with these cases? There are two obvious possibilities—liability for the crime attempted (thus ignoring the accidental result), and liability for the actual result based on recklessness—and these will be examined in turn. ...

A conviction for attempt is possible in virtually all cases which fall within the doctrine of transferred liability ... In *Latimer*, for example, D could quite simply have been convicted of the attempted unlawful wounding of O; and likewise in *Pembliton* there were strong grounds for convicting D of attempted unlawful wounding of persons in the crowd ...

In many of the cases to which transferred malice applies, the harm to P was quite unforeseen. But in some of them D could be held liable for harm to P without invoking transferred malice—on the basis that, in attempting to harm O, he was reckless as to harming P. ... It is often said that in *Pembliton* the jury should have found D reckless as to damaging the window, and that this would have spared counsel and the courts much fruitless argument ...

The doctrine could, then, be abolished without material loss to criminal justice; and it is desirable that it should be. For, quite apart from any problems over the consistency of the doctrine with general principles of criminal liability, it attributes significance to matters of chance and results in a mischaracterisation of D's criminality which could simply and effectively be avoided by charging an attempt. What, then, are the objections to using the law of attempts?

The first is that it would be wrong for a person who intended to cause harm of a certain kind and did cause such a harm to escape with a lighter sentence merely because he was charged with an attempt ...

A second objection ... is that even if the punishment were the same, it is more appropriate to convict of the completed crime in the 'transferred malice' situation. Where D set out to cause harm of a certain kind and did cause harm of that kind, it seems empty and insufficient

---

[21] This point was accepted in *Slimmings* [1999] Crim.L.R.69. The indictment would need to specify that D caused grievous bodily harm to P with intent to cause grievous bodily harm to O.

to convict him of a mere attempt. He has actually caused a loss to the community of the kind he intended to cause, and that fact should be recorded. Once again, however, this reasoning leans too heavily on results which may be entirely a matter of chance. In a system based on subjective liability, the legal label attached to D's offence should generally reflect his intentional act and not the chance result."

While one can agree that the doctrine of transferred malice was inapplicable in *Attorney-General's Reference (No. 3 of 1994)* because what was intended (grievous bodily harm to the mother) was qualitatively different to what occurred (death of the child who, at the time of the attack, was not legally a person), the hostility of Lord Mustill and Ashworth seems misplaced. Where the defendant intends to kill another human being and does kill another human being, albeit a different one from the one intended, is it fair to describe that result as a "matter of chance," exempting the defendant from liability for murder? Is this mistake as to the identity of his victim relevant in any *material* way?[22] Murder involves the intentional killing of a human being. If the defendant tries to kill Smith and instead kills Jones, the difference in result can hardly be sufficient to avoid the conclusion that the defendant intentionally killed a human being and deserves the label "murderer". The Law Commission and the Draft Offences Against the Person Bill 1998 have accepted the doctrine of transferred malice in its present form and have proposed a statutory provision to that effect.[23]

For those crimes that can be committed by *Caldwell* recklessness, such as criminal damage in the earlier window hypothetical, the doctrine of transferred malice will be of limited utility in the future. Using the *Cunningham* subjective test of recklessness, it might be difficult to establish that the defendant was reckless as to the precise harm caused. But under *Caldwell* recklessness this would be easily established. In most cases the reasonable person would have been aware that there was an obvious risk of the actual harm ensuing—or the defendant himself would have been so aware if he had stopped to think.

### D. *Mistake*

A defendant may make many different types of mistake. Sometimes she will think she is committing no crime at all. At other times she will think she is committing a different crime from the one that transpires. What is the law's response to such pleas?

In order for a mistake to be considered as a possible exculpatory factor, it must relate in a *relevant* way to the elements of the crime. If a driver makes a mistake and puts his foot on the accelerator thinking he is putting it on the brake and so kills a pedestrian, this is not a relevant mistake as to an element of the crime of causing death by dangerous driving.[24] Indeed, instead of being an exculpatory factor, such a mistake is important evidence in establishing the critical element required for the crime, namely that the driving was "dangerous".

---

[22] See Stroud, *Mens Rea* (1914), p. 184; Williams, "Convictions and Fair Labelling" [1983] C.L.J. 85 at 86–88.

[23] Draft Criminal Law Bill 1993, cl. 32 (Law Com. No. 218, 1993); Draft Offences Against the Person Bill 1998, cl. 17.

[24] *Attorney-General's Reference No. 4 of 2000* [2001] Crim.L.R.578.

A mistake might have relevance to an exemption from liability in the following three situations:

1. mistake as to one of the elements of the *actus reus*; or
2. mistake as to a defence element; or
3. mistake as to law.

As we shall see, it is difficult to distinguish rigidly between these three, but such a classification is useful for purposes of exposition.

### 1. Mistake as to element of actus reus

For most crimes the defendant must have *mens rea* in relation to the *actus reus*. This means she must have *mens rea* in relation to every element of the *actus reus*—often referred to as the "definitional elements". However, the mistake must not simply be one as to *some quality* of the definitional element. It must be as to the *existence* of the definitional element. For example, the *actus reus* of criminal damage is *destroying or damaging any property belonging to another*.[25] If the defendant thinks the property belongs to Smith when in fact it belongs to Jones, his mistake is irrelevant because he knows that the property *belongs to another*. On the other hand, if the defendant thinks the property belongs to *himself* this mistake now negates his *mens rea*. He does not have *mens rea* in relation to a definitional element and would thus escape liability.[26]

Section 170(2) of the Customs and Excise Management Act 1979 makes it an offence to be knowingly concerned in the fraudulent evasion of the prohibition on the importation of prohibited goods. In *Ellis*[27] the defendants believed they were importing prohibited pornographic goods but in fact it was prohibited drugs. Their convictions were upheld. They had *mens rea* in relation to the definitional element "prohibited goods". The precise nature and quality of such prohibited goods was of no more relevance than whether the property belonged to Smith or Jones in the earlier example.[28]

This principle is illustrated in the following case.

### R. v Forbes [2002] 1 Cr.App.R.1 (House of Lords)

The appellant was stopped at Heathrow Airport on arrival from Amsterdam in possession of two video films, labelled respectively "Spartacus" and "The Godfather 2". The videos in fact contained footage which included indecent photographs of teenage boys under the age of 16. He claimed he thought the videos contained "The Exorcist" and "Kidz" which he believed were prohibited films but, in fact, were not. The appellant was convicted under section 170(2) of the Customs and Excise Management Act 1979 in that he was "knowingly concerned in any fraudulent evasion . . . of any prohibition" on the importation of goods. The issue on appeal was whether the defendant must be proved to have known that he was

[25] Criminal Damage Act 1971, s.1(1).
[26] *Smith (David)* [1974] Q.B. 354.
[27] [1987] Crim.L.R.44.
[28] Smith has pointed out that this decision might have been unexceptional when the importation of prohibited drugs and pornographic material were both punishable with two years imprisonment—but it becomes questionable now that the penalties in relation to drugs have been increased ([1987] Crim.L.R.46). In *Leeson* [2001] 1 Cr.App.R.233 the defendant was in possession of cocaine (a class A drug) but believed it was an amphetamine (a class B drug). The court concluded that the relevance of the different classes of drugs related only to sentencing.

importing an indecent photograph of a child (as opposed to an indecent photograph of an adult which is not unlawful under Community law if the photograph comes from another Member State).

Lord Hope of Craighead:
"[T]he certified questions are misconceived. This is because it is not necessary, for the purposes of a prosecution under section 170(2)(b) of the Customs and Excise Management Act 1979, for the prosecutor to prove that the defendant knew the identity of the goods which were the subject of the prohibition which he was evading or attempting to evade. It is sufficient for him to prove that the defendant knew that the goods, whatever they happened to be, were the subject of a prohibition and that he also knew that the operation on which he was engaged was an evasion of that prohibition. If that is right, the question whether the defendant knew that the photographs which were the subject of the operation were indecent photographs of children does not arise. The prosecutor does not even need to go so far as to prove that the defendant knew that the goods were photographs. . . .

There are only two positions that can logically be adopted. One is to say that the Crown must prove that the defendant knew that the operation on which he was engaged involved prohibited goods because he knew what the *goods* were and that they were prohibited goods. The other is to say that the Crown must prove that the defendant knew that the operation on which he was engaged involved goods which were prohibited because he knew that the *operation* was designed to avoid a prohibition against the importation of those goods.

The justification for the adoption of the latter position by the Court of Appeal was that to adopt the former position would rob the provision of its effect in those cases . . . where the defendant did not know and could not have known what the goods were, because he was merely a courier. . . .

In *R. v Taaffe* [1984] AC 539 the defendant was charged with having been knowingly concerned in the fraudulent evasion of the prohibition on the importation of cannabis resin. His defence was that . . . he believed the substance to be currency which, contrary to his belief, was not subject to any prohibition on importation. . . . In the House of Lords, Lord Scarman said that . . . the principle that a man must be judged upon the facts as he believed them to be was an accepted principle of the criminal law when the state of a man's mind and his knowledge are ingredients of the offence with which he is charged.

In the present case the appellant's defence was based on the decision in *R. v Taaffe*. He said that he did not know that the video cassettes contained indecent photographs of children. . . . The trial judge left it to the jury to decide whether they believed the appellant's explanation. He made it clear that they should judge the appellant's knowledge of the facts as he believed them to be, and that unless they were sure that his defence was untrue they should find him not guilty. Plainly they did not believe his explanation, because they convicted him.

The appellant nevertheless says that he was wrongly convicted because the trial judge ought not to have directed the jury that what the prosecution had to establish was simply that he knew that he was importing prohibited material. He maintains that he should have directed them that the prosecution had to prove not only that he knew that the videos contained indecent photographs but also that they were indecent photographs of children. I would reject that argument. . . .

It was, of course, open to the appellant to say, if this was the fact, that he believed the videos to contain indecent photographs of adults and that he acted as he did because he believed, contrary to the fact, that they were prohibited. The line of defence which was approved in *R. v Taaffe* [1984] A.C. 539 ensures the acquittal of people who genuinely believe that they are importing indecent photographs of adults which are not obscene, when they are in fact photographs of children. But it is for the defendant to put forward that defence. The prosecution does not have to prove what the accused knew the goods were which he was seeking to import knowing that they were prohibited goods."

**Appeal dismissed**

Where the mistake is as to the existence of a definitional element the position used to be that the defendant would only escape liability if the mistake was a reasonable one. In *Tolson*[29] the defendant's husband deserted her and sailed for America. Inquiries revealed that the ship had been sunk and so, believing herself to be a widow, five years later she went through a marriage ceremony with another man. Later that year her husband returned from America and the defendant was charged with bigamy. Her conviction was quashed, on the basis that she had believed "in good faith and on reasonable grounds" that her husband was dead.

However, the House of Lords in the following case effected a radical change of direction by holding that in certain circumstances an honest mistake would exempt a defendant from criminal liability. It was no longer necessary that the mistake be reasonable.

### D.P.P. v Morgan [1976] A.C. 182 (House of Lords)

A husband invited a number of companions to have sexual intercourse with his wife, apparently in order to be avenged for her real or imagined infidelity. He suggested that she might put up a struggle but that they were not to take it seriously; it was her way of increasing her sexual satisfaction. The men, so urged, had intercourse in turn without her consent. They were tried and convicted of rape; the husband was convicted of aiding and abetting rape. The judge directed the jury that the men were guilty of rape even if they in fact believed that Mrs Morgan consented if such belief was not based on reasonable grounds.

The question certified to the House of Lords was whether the defendants' belief in her consent had to be based on reasonable grounds.

Lord Cross:

"In fact, however, I can see no objection to the inclusion of the element of reasonableness in what I may call a 'Tolson' case. If the words defining an offence provide either expressly or impliedly that a man is not to be guilty of it if he believes something to be true, then he cannot be found guilty if the jury think that he may have believed it to be true, however inadequate were his reasons for doing so. But, if the definition of the offence is on the face of it 'absolute' and the defendant is seeking to escape his prima facie liability by a defence of mistaken belief, I can see no hardship to him in requiring the mistake—if it is to afford him a defence—to be based on reasonable grounds. As Lord Diplock said in *Sweet v Parsley* [1970] A.C. 132, there is nothing unreasonable in the law requiring a citizen to take reasonable care to ascertain the facts relevant to his avoiding doing a prohibited act. To have intercourse with a woman who is not your wife is, even today, not generally considered to be a course of conduct which the law ought positively to encourage and it can be argued with force that it is only fair to the woman and not in the least unfair to the man that he should be under a duty to take reasonable care to ascertain that she is consenting to the intercourse and be at the risk of prosecution if he fails to take such care. So if the Sexual Offences Act 1956 had made it an offence to have intercourse with a woman who was not consenting to it, so that the defendant could only escape liability by the application of the 'Tolson' principle, I would not have thought the law unjust.

But, as I have said, section 1 of the Act of 1956, does not say that a man who has sexual intercourse with a woman who does not consent to it commits an offence; it says that a man who rapes a woman commits an offence. Rape is not a word in the use of which lawyers have a monopoly and the question to be answered in this case, as I see it, is whether according to the ordinary use of the English language a man can be said to have committed rape if he believed that the woman was consenting to the intercourse and would not have attempted to have it but for his belief, whatever his grounds for so believing. I do not think that he can. Rape, to my mind imports at least indifference as to the woman's consent. I think, moreover, that in this connection the ordinary man would distinguish between rape and bigamy. To the question whether a man who goes through a ceremony of marriage with a woman believing his wife to be dead, though she is not, commits bigamy, I think that he would reply 'Yes,—but I suppose that the law contains an escape clause for bigamists who are not really to blame.' On the other hand, to the question whether a man, who has intercourse with a woman believing on inadequate grounds that she is consenting to it, though she is not, commits rape, I think that he would reply 'No. If he was grossly careless then he may deserve to be punished but not for rape.' That being my view as to the meaning of the word 'rape' in ordinary parlance, I next ask myself whether the law gives it a different meaning. There is very little English authority on the point but what there is—namely, the reported directions of several common law judges in the early and the middle years of the last century—accords with what I take to be the proper meaning of the word ... For these reasons, I think that the summing up contained a misdirection.

The question which then arises as to the application of the proviso [to section 2(1) of the Criminal Appeal Act 1968] is far easier of solution ... The jury obviously considered that the appellant's evidence as to the part played by Mrs Morgan was a pack of lies and one must assume that any other jury would take the same view as to the relative culpability of the parties. ... So I would apply the proviso and dismiss the appeal."

Lord Hailsham:
"If it be true, as the learned judge says [in his summing up at the trial] 'in the first place', that the prosecution have to prove that 'each defendant intended to have sexual intercourse without her consent, not merely that he intended to have intercourse with her but that he intended to have intercourse without her consent', the defendant must be entitled to an acquittal if the prosecution fail to prove just that. The necessary mental ingredient will be lacking and the only possible verdict is 'not guilty'. If, on the other hand, as is asserted in the passage beginning 'secondly', it is necessary for any belief in the woman's consent to be 'a reasonable belief' before the defendant is entitled to an acquittal, it must either be because the mental ingredient in rape is not 'to have intercourse and to have it without her consent' but simply 'to have intercourse' subject to a special defence of 'honest and reasonable belief', or alternatively to have intercourse without a reasonable belief in her consent. Counsel for the Crown argued for each of these alternatives, but in my view each is open to insuperable objections of principle. No doubt it would be possible, by statute, to devise a law by which intercourse, voluntarily entered into, was an absolute offence subject to a 'defence' of belief whether honest or honest and reasonable, of which the 'evidential' burden is primarily on the defence and the 'probative' burden on the prosecution. But in my opinion such is not the crime of rape as it has hitherto been understood. The prohibited act in rape is to have intercourse without the victim's consent. The minimum *mens rea* or guilty mind in most common law offences, including rape, is the intention to do the prohibited act, and that is correctly stated in the proposition stated 'in the first place' of the judge's direction. ...

The only qualification I would make to the direction of the learned judge's 'in the first place' is the refinement for which, ... there is both Australian and English authority, that if the intention of the accused is to have intercourse nolens volens, that is recklessly and not caring whether the victim be a consenting party or not, that is equivalent on ordinary principles to an intent to do the prohibited act without the consent of the victim. ...

Once one has accepted, what seems to me abundantly clear, that the prohibited act in rape is non-consensual sexual intercourse, and that the guilty state of mind is an intention to commit it, it seems to me to follow as a matter of inexorable logic that there is no room either for a 'defence' of honest belief or mistake, or of a defence of honest and reasonable belief or mistake. Either the prosecution proves that the accused had the requisite intent, or it does not. In the former case it succeeds, and in the latter if fails. Since honest belief clearly negatives intent, the reasonableness or otherwise of that belief can only be evidence for or against the view that the belief and therefore the intent was actually held, and it matters not whether, to quote Bridge J. ... 'the definition of a crime includes no specific element beyond the prohibited act'. ... Any other view, as for insertion of the word 'reasonable' can only have the effect of saying that a man intends something which he does not. ...

I am content to rest my view of the instant case on the crime of rape by saying that it is my opinion that the prohibited act is and always has been intercourse without consent of the victim and the mental element is and always has been the intention to commit that act, or the equivalent intention of having intercourse willy-nilly not caring whether the victim consents or no [*sic*]. A failure to prove this involves an acquittal because the intent, an essential ingredient, is lacking. It matters not why it is lacking if only it is not there, and in particular it matters not that the intention is lacking only because of a belief not based on reasonable grounds. . . .

For the above reasons I would answer the question certified in the negative, but would apply the proviso to the Criminal Appeal Act on the ground that no miscarriage of justice has or conceivably could have occurred. In my view, therefore, these appeals should be dismissed."

Lord Simon:
"Does an honest but unreasonable belief that the woman is consenting to sexual intercourse suffice to negative the charge of rape? . . .

It remains to consider why the law requires, in such circumstances, that the belief in a state of affairs whereby the *actus* would not be *reus* must be held on reasonable grounds. One reason was given by Bridge J. in the Court of Appeal . . . :

'The rationale of requiring reasonable grounds for the mistaken belief must lie in the law's consideration that a bald assertion of belief for which the accused can indicate no reasonable ground is evidence of insufficient substance to raise any issue requiring the jury's consideration.'

I agree; but I think there is also another reason. The policy of the law in this regard could well derive from its concern to hold a fair balance between victim and accused. It would hardly seem just to fob off a victim of a savage assault with such comfort as he could derive from knowing that his injury was caused by a belief, however absurd, that he was about to attack the accused. A respectable woman who has been ravished would hardly feel that she was vindicated by being told that her assailant must go unpunished because he believed, quite unreasonably, that she was consenting to sexual intercourse with him. The policy behind s.6 of the Sexual Offences Act is presumably that Parliament considered that a girl under 16 is generally unlikely to be sufficiently mature to realise the full implications of sexual intercourse; so that her protection demands that a belief by a man under the age of 24 that she herself was over the age of 16 should not be only an honest but also a reasonable belief . . .

I would therefore answer the question certified for your Lordships' consideration, Yes. But, even did I consider that it should be answered No, I would, for the reasons given by my noble and learned friends, think this a suitable case to apply the proviso.

I would therefore dismiss the appeal.

[Lord Fraser held that the defendant's belief in the woman's consent did not have to be based on reasonable grounds; Lord Edmund-Davies, however, felt that only the legislature could effect such a reform in the law.]"

**Appeal dismissed**

Despite initial suggestions that *Morgan* should be confined to the crime of rape,[30] it is now clear that it applies throughout English law—at least to all those offences requiring proof of intention or recklessness as to each of the definitional elements.

### R. v Kimber [1983] 1 W.L.R. 1118 (Court of Appeal, Criminal Division)

The appellant was charged with indecent assault, contrary to section 14(1) of the Sexual Offences Act 1956. He had sexual contact with a mentally disordered female patient in a mental hospital but claimed he thought she was consenting.

[30] *Phekoo* [1981] 1 W.L.R. 1117. See also *Brown* [1984] 1 W.L.R. 1211.

Lawton L.J.:

"[D]id the jury have to consider merely whether his belief was honestly held or, if it was, did they have to go on to consider whether it was based on reasonable grounds? Another way of putting these points is to ask whether the principles upon which the House of Lords decided *R. v Morgan* should be applied to a charge of indecent assault on a woman ...

The burden of proving lack of consent rests upon the prosecution ... The consequence is that the prosecution has to prove that the defendant intended to lay hands on his victim without her consent. If he did not intend to do this, he is entitled to be found not guilty; and if he did not so intend because he believed she was consenting, the prosecution will have failed to prove the charge. It is the defendant's belief, not the grounds on which it was based, which goes to negative the intent.

In analysing the issue in this way we have followed what was said by the majority in *R. v Morgan* ... If, as we adjudge, the prohibited act in indecent assault is the use of personal violence to a woman without her consent, then the guilty state of mind is the intent to do it without her consent. Then, as in rape at common law, the inexorable logic, to which Lord Hailsham referred in *R. v Morgan*, takes over and there is no room either for a 'defence' of honest belief or mistake, or of a 'defence' of honest and reasonable belief or mistake ...

In our judgment the recorder should have directed the jury that the prosecution had to make them sure that the appellant never had believed that [the woman] was consenting. [Lawton L.J., however, concluded that no reasonable jury would have accepted the appellant's version of the facts. He was, at least, reckless as to whether she was consenting. Accordingly, there had been no miscarriage of justice.]"

**Appeal dismissed**

## B (A Minor) v D.P.P. [2000] A.C. 428 (House of Lords)

The defendant, a 15–year-old boy, invited a 13–year-old girl to perform oral sex with him on a bus. He was charged with the offence of inciting a girl under the age of 14 to commit an act of gross indecency, contrary to section 1(1) of the Indecency with Children Act 1960. He honestly believed that she was over 14 years of age.

Lord Nicholls of Birkenhead:

"The 'reasonable belief' school of thought held unchallenged sway for many years. But over the last quarter of a century there have been several important cases where a defence of honest but mistaken belief was raised. In deciding these cases the courts have placed new, or renewed, emphasis on the subjective nature of the mental element in criminal offences. The courts have rejected the reasonable belief approach and preferred the honest belief approach. When mens rea is ousted by a mistaken belief, it is as well ousted by an unreasonable belief as by a reasonable belief. In the pithy phrase of Lawton L.J. in *Regina v Kimber*, it is the defendant's belief, not the grounds on which it is based, which goes to negative the intent. ...

Considered as a matter of principle, the honest belief approach must be preferable. By definition the mental element in a crime is concerned with a subjective state of mind, such as intent or belief. To the extent that an overriding objective limit ('on reasonable grounds') is introduced, the subjective element is displaced. To that extent a person who lacks the necessary intent or belief may nevertheless commit the offence. When that occurs the defendant's 'fault' lies exclusively in falling short of an objective standard. His crime lies in his negligence. A statute may so provide expressly or by necessary implication. But this can have no place in a common law principle, of general application, which is concerned with the need for a mental element as an essential ingredient of a criminal offence. ...

There has been a general shift from objectivism to subjectivism in this branch of the law. It is now settled as a matter of general principle that mistake, whether reasonable or not, is a defence where it prevents the defendant from having the mens rea which the law requires for the crime with which he is charged. It would be in disharmony with this development now to rule that in respect of a defence under subsection 1(1) of the Act of 1960 the belief must be based on reasonable grounds."

**Appeal allowed**

One year later the House of Lords reaffirmed this approach in *R. v K*,[31] an appeal involving indecent assault on a girl under the age of 16 contrary to section 14(1) of the Sexual Offences Act 1956. A 26–year-old man committed sexual acts with a consenting 14–year-old girl believing she was aged 16 or over. Under section 14(2) a girl under the age of 16 cannot give valid consent for the purposes of this offence. It was held that the *actus reus* of this offence involved "an indecent act done ... with or without the consent of the other person being a person under the age of 16 years" and that, as regards *mens rea*, the prosecution "must be prepared to prove that the defendant did not have an honest belief that the other person was in fact consenting and not under 16 years of age." Lord Bingham did, however, stress that while the defendant's belief need only be honest and genuine and need not be reasonable, "the more unreasonable the belief, the less likely it is to be accepted as genuine."

Several points need to be made in relation to the above decisions. First, it is incorrect to talk of a "defence of mistake". It is not a defence: the defendant does not have to prove anything. The prosecution has to prove *mens rea*. If there is a mistake as to an *actus reus* element, the prosecution will have failed to prove its case. The principle is clear. A mistake as to a definitional element can negate *mens rea*; it is irrelevant whether the mistake is reasonable or not.

Secondly, given this clear principle, what is the status today of *Tolson* which required a mistake, for the crime of bigamy, to be reasonable? This case was approved in *Morgan* with Lord Cross stating that *Tolson* was dealing with a *prima facie* strict liability offence and in such cases any "defence of mistaken belief" needed to be reasonable. This view was disapproved in *B(A Minor) v D.P.P.* Lord Nicholls, in addition to the passages extracted above, cited *Sweet v Parsley* on this point and concluded that this view was "out of step with this recent line of authority" and that the dicta from those cases "must in future be read as though the reference to reasonable grounds were omitted". It thus appears that *Tolson* is no longer good authority.

Thirdly, while we are currently witnessing a decline in the importance of *Caldwell/Lawrence* in offences other than criminal damage, it ought to be pointed out that the *Caldwell* principle is not inconsistent with the highly subjectivist approach adopted in the above cases. A defendant who makes a genuine mistake is not one who has failed to consider the possible risks. He has addressed his mind to the matter in question and has "ruled out any risks"; he has reached a clear view (albeit a mistaken one) as to the relevant facts. Even under *Caldwell/Lawrence*, and especially after *Reid*, such a defendant is not reckless. This view was endorsed in several common law cases on reckless rape.[32] These cases indicate that if a defendant genuinely believes that the woman is consenting to intercourse he cannot be liable. He is only reckless if he "could not care less" or was "indifferent" as to whether she was consenting; such a defendant has clearly *not* made a genuine mistake.

---

[31] [2002] 1 A.C. 462.
[32] *Satnam and Kewal* (1984) 78 Cr.App.R.149; *Breckenridge* (1984) 79 Cr.App.R.244.

Horder[33] rejects the highly subjectivist analysis adopted in *B (A Minor) v D.P.P.* He argues that the age of 14 chosen for the offence in section 1(1) of the Indecency with Children Act 1960 is arbitrary and of no moral significance—unlike the age of 16 which, in the context of consent to sexual offences, has, despite originally being arbitrary, acquired a moral resonance and "structured people's moral thinking in [a] significant way". Accordingly, the defendant's mistake in *B (A Minor) v D.P.P.* was irrelevant; it was not a "guiding reason" for his actions. The real wrong committed by the defendant – "the guiding reason against which D acted"—was sexually propositioning a child under the age of 16. However, he continues, a defendant ought not to be adjudged blameworthy if humane and decent people would regard the behaviour as "tolerable" (even if wrong) in modern society and if the defendant believed this would be people's belief. This belief becomes plausible when dealing with teenagers of roughly the same age engaged in "sexual banter" and no actual sexual contact is involved.[34]

### Jeremy Horder, "How Culpability Can, and Cannot, be Denied in Under-age Sex Crimes" [2001] Crim.L.R.15:

"[A] mistaken belief that V is aged 14 is a mistake about a matter of moral indifference, unlike a mistaken belief that V is aged 16.

So, where the consenting V is mistakenly but reasonably believed by D to have just turned 16, then (other things being equal) this belief provides D with a morally justifiable ground for acting as does, because the question of whether V is aged 16 is a question with moral significance. ... The criteria relevant to culpability ought only to be those which relate to guiding moral reasons for the actions in question; and D's belief that V is aged 14 is not such a guiding reason. It is not in itself a moral reason for doing as he does. ...

[W]hat age D believed V to be (if he had any belief about V's age) can have practical moral significance, but of a kind quite different from that emphasised in *B (A Minor) v DPP*. The significance of B's belief about V's age was that he believed her to be *about the same age as him*. Such a belief to some extent furbishes his case for saying that he believed the contact he had with V might be regarded by decent, humane people as tolerable, even if far from admirable. ... D's belief about V's age did not, in and of itself, have practical moral significance. Its significance comes into play only as part of a broader claim focused on the 'tolerable conduct' exception."

There is much to be said, in principle, for such a nuanced, context-sensitive approach to the ascertainment of culpability. Given that, on average, teenagers have their first sexual experience at 15.3 years,[35] it hardly seems justifiable to criminalise a mere sexual proposition by a 15–year-old to a 13–year-old. However, there are practical problems in making culpability depend on a defendant's belief about what other people regard as tolerable.[36] And who are these other people? It is possible (perhaps, likely) that even "decent, humane" adults would regard requests for oral sex on a bus as intolerable—even between similarly aged teenagers. However, it could be that "decent, humane" teenagers, used to the rough-and-tumble of the school bus, could regard it as tolerable. But if the test was focused on

---

[33] "How Culpability Can, and Cannot, be Denied in Under-age Sex Crimes" [2001] Crim.L.R.15.

[34] Horder is "agnostic" whether the actual defendant in *B v D.P.P.* would qualify here because of the *repeated* requests for oral sex.

[35] Cited by Horder.

[36] See pp. 794–796 for the problems associated with such a test when applied to offences of "dishonesty".

the attitude of teenagers, how could juries, as adults, determine the views of teenagers? Perhaps, what is really at issue here is whether section 1(1) of the Indecency with Children Act 1960, as currently drafted, is itself justifiable. Given the desire to protect children against paedophiles, if one accepts the view that teenage banter should not be criminalised, perhaps the way forward is to follow the approach of other countries where, for example, it is a defence to some consensual sexual offences to show that the defendant was no more than two years older than the other person.[37]

For Horder the age of 16 is of moral significance and he would exempt from liability those who honestly *and reasonably* believed the other was 16 or over. However, as seen, the House of Lords in *R. v K* has reaffirmed its purely subjectivist approach in relation to an offence where 16 was the relevant age. This raises a final point for consideration in relation to all the above cases. Is it justifiable that defendants should escape liability on the basis that they have made an honest but unreasonable mistake? Responses to this point will be delayed until mistakes as to defence elements have been considered.

### 2. Mistake as to a defence element

There is another type of mistake a defendant can make. He might have made a mistake in thinking he was entitled to a defence. For example, a defendant might admit that he intentionally killed another but claim that he thought he was being attacked and was therefore defending himself, when, in reality, he had made a mistake and was not under attack.[38]

Originally, and even for a few years after *Morgan*, the courts insisted that only *reasonable* mistakes as to defence elements would suffice to exempt a person from liability.[39] However, in relation to mistakes affecting self-defence the courts have now abandoned the requirement that the mistake be reasonable. Whether this subjectivist approach is compatible with Article 2 of the European Convention on Human Rights will be considered later.[40]

### R. v Williams (Gladstone) (1984) 78 Cr.App.R.276 (Court of Appeal, Criminal Division)

The appellant saw a man, Mason, dragging a youth along a street and striking him; the youth was calling for help. Mason claimed he was a police officer and was arresting the youth for mugging a lady. When he was unable to produce a warrant card, a struggle ensued during which the appellant punched Mason, who sustained injuries to his face. The appellant, who was charged with assault occasioning actual bodily harm, claimed that he honestly believed Mason was unlawfully assaulting the youth and that he was trying to rescue the youth. (One is entitled to use reasonable force to prevent an unlawful assault on another.) However, the appellant had made a mistake. While Mason was not a police officer, he had nevertheless seen the youth seize the woman's handbag and was acting lawfully in restraining the youth with a view to taking him to a police station. At his trial, the jury were

---

[37] See the examples such as Victoria and the Australian Capital Territory cited by Horder. See also Home Office, *Setting the Boundaries: Reforming the Law on Sexual Offences* (2000), which proposes that the defence of mistake of age should only be available to persons under the age of 21 (para. 3.6.16).

[38] There is a further type of mistake that a defendant can make with regard to self-defence. He might mistakenly believe that it is necessary to use more force than is actually necessary. See pp. 309–311.

[39] *Albert v Lavin* [1982] A.C. 546.

[40] At p. 306.

directed that the appellant's mistake would only be relevant if it were a reasonable one. He was convicted and appealed on the ground of a misdirection.

Lane L.C.J.:

"'Assault' ... is an act by which the defendant, intentionally or recklessly, applies unlawful force to the complainant. There are circumstances in which force may be applied to another lawfully. Taking a few examples: first, where the victim consents, as in lawful sports, the application of force to another will, generally speaking, not be unlawful. Secondly, where the defendant is acting in self-defence: the exercise of any necessary and reasonable force to protect himself from unlawful violence is not unlawful. Thirdly, by virtue of section 3 of the Criminal Law Act 1967, a person may use such force as is reasonable in the circumstances in the prevention of crime or in effecting or assisting in the lawful arrest of an offender or suspected offender or persons unlawfully at large. In each of those cases the defendant will be guilty if the jury are sure that first of all he applied force to the person of another, and secondly that he had the necessary mental element to constitute guilt.

The mental element necessary to constitute guilt is the intent to apply unlawful force to the victim. We do not believe that the mental element can be substantiated by simply showing an intent to apply force and no more.

What then is the situation if the defendant is labouring under a mistake of fact as to the circumstances? What if he believes, but believes mistakenly, that the victim is consenting, or that it is necessary to defend himself, or that a crime is being committed which he intends to prevent? He must then be judged against the mistaken facts as he believes them to be. If judged against those facts or circumstances the prosecution fail to establish his guilt, then he is entitled to be acquitted.

The next question is, does it make any difference if the mistake of the defendant was one which, viewed objectively by a reasonable onlooker, was an unreasonable mistake? ...

[I]n our judgment the answer is provided by the judgment of this Court in *Kimber* ... by which ... we are bound ...

... The reasonableness or unreasonableness of the defendant's belief is material to the question of whether the belief was held by the defendant at all. If the belief was in fact held, its unreasonableness, so far as guilt or innocence is concerned, is neither here nor there. It is irrelevant. Were it otherwise, the defendant would be convicted because he was negligent in failing to recognise that the victim was not consenting or that a crime was not being committed and so on. In other words the jury should be directed first of all that the prosecution have the burden or duty of proving the unlawfulness of the defendant's actions; secondly, if the defendant may have been labouring under a mistake as to the facts, he must be judged according to his mistaken views of the facts; thirdly, that is so whether the mistake was, on an objective view, a reasonable mistake or not. ...

We have read the recommendations of the Criminal Law Revision Committee, Part IX, paragraph 72(a), in which the following passage appears: 'The common law defence of self-defence should be replaced by a statutory defence providing that a person may use such force as is reasonable in the circumstances as he believes them to be in the defence of himself or any other person.' In the view of this Court that represents the law as expressed in *Morgan* and in *Kimber*."

**Appeal allowed**

## Beckford v R. [1988] A.C. 130 (Privy Council)

The appellant was a police officer who was a member of an armed posse which chased, shot and killed a fleeing man. The appellant claimed he had killed in self defence. The trial judge directed the jury that the belief that life was in danger had to be a reasonable belief. The Court of Appeal of Jamaica confirmed this. The appellant appealed to the Privy Council.

Lord Griffiths:

"There can be no doubt that prior to the decision of the House of Lords in *R. v Morgan* the whole weight of authority supported the view that it was an essential element of self-defence not only that the accused believed that he was being attacked or in imminent danger of being attacked but also that such belief was based on reasonable grounds ...

The question then is whether the present Lord Chief Justice, Lord Lane, in *R. v Williams (Gladstone)*, was right to depart from the law as declared by his predecessors in the light of the decision of the House of Lords in *R. v Morgan*. ...

It is because it is an essential element of all crimes of violence that the violence or the threat of violence should be unlawful that self-defence, if raised as an issue in a criminal trial, must be disproved by the prosecution. If the prosecution fail to do so the accused is entitled to be acquitted because the prosecution will have failed to prove an essential element of the crime namely that the violence used by the accused was unlawful.

If then a genuine belief, albeit without reasonable grounds, is a defence to rape because it negatives the necessary intention, so also must a genuine belief in facts which if true would justify self-defence be a defence to a crime of personal violence because the belief negatives the intent to act unlawfully. ...

There may be a fear that the abandonment of the objective standard demanded by the existence of reasonable grounds for belief will result in the success of too many spurious claims of self-defence. The English experience has not shown this to be the case. The Judicial Studies Board with the approval of the Lord Chief Justice has produced a model direction on self-defence which is now widely used by judges when summing up to juries. The direction contains the following guidance:

'Whether the plea is self-defence or defence of another, if the defendant may have been labouring under a mistake as to the facts, he must be judged according to his mistaken belief of the facts: that is so whether the mistake was, on an objective view, a reasonable mistake or not.'"

**Appeal allowed**

Does this approach apply to mistakes made when claiming other defences? Take duress, for example: what is the position if a defendant honestly, but unreasonably, believes he is being subjected to duress when in fact he is not?

In *Graham*[41] and *Howe*[42] it was held that the defence of duress would only be available to one who *reasonably* believed that he was being subjected to the requisite threats for a defence of duress. The same test was applied in *Martin*[43] to "duress of circumstances".[44] In *O'Grady*[45] it was held that a person who made a drunken mistake in thinking he was being attacked was not entitled to a defence. In *Fotheringham*[46] the defendant made a drunken mistake when having non-consensual intercourse with his 14 year-old baby-sitter: he thought it was his wife. It was held that such a drunken mistake was no defence. While it was held in both these cases that a drunken mistake was no defence, there can be little doubt that if, in fact, despite the defendant's drunkenness, the mistake made was a perfectly reasonable mistake that an ordinary sober person would have made, it would be a defence. In this latter situation the drunken defendant would not in any way be

[41] [1982] 1 W.L.R. 294.
[42] [1987] A.C. 417.
[43] [1989] 1 All E.R. 652.
[44] However, in *Martin (D.P.)* [2000] 2 Cr.App.R.42 it was held that the *Williams (Gladstone)* principle did apply to duress. It will be argued (at p. 335) that this decision is wrong and ought not to be followed.
[45] [1987] Q.B. 995.
[46] (1989) 88 Cr.App.R.206 at 416.

profiting from his drunkenness. The drunkenness would be irrelevant as the same mistake would probably have been made if he had been sober.

How can this divergence of approach, between mistakes as to consent and self-defence on the one hand, and duress, duress of circumstances and drunkenness on the other hand, be explained?

In *Williams (Gladstone)* and *Beckford* the court drew a distinction between mistakes which affect definitional elements (where the mistake need only be genuine) and mistakes as to a defence element (where the mistake must be reasonable). According to these cases it is part of the definitional elements that the defendant be acting "unlawfully"; self-defensive action renders conduct lawful and so if a defendant has made a mistake as to the need for self-defensive action, there is no *mens rea* in relation to that definitional element of "unlawfulness".

### Glanville Williams, Textbook of Criminal Law (2nd ed., 1983), p. 138:

"No other rule of the substantive criminal law distinguishes between the definitional and defence elements of a crime, and it is a distinction that is impossible to draw satisfactorily. (Our notion of what issue is a 'defence,' in so far as we have any clear notion, seems to depend largely on whether we think that the defendant should be required to take the initiative in introducing it, *i.e.* on whether he should bear an evidential burden in respect of it. But there is no reason why the distribution of evidential burdens should affect the rules of liability. See 2 Leg. Stud. 255). A rule creating a *defence* merely supplies additional details of the scope of the *offence*. To regard the offence as subsisting independently of its limitations and qualifications is unrealistic. The defence is a negative condition of the offence, and is therefore an integral part of it. What we regard as part of the offence and what as part of a defence depends only on traditional habits of thought or accidents of legal drafting; it should have no bearing on the important question of criminal liability. For example, it is purely a matter of convenient drafting whether a statute says, on the one hand, that damaging the property of another without his consent is a crime, or, on the other hand, that damaging the property of another is a crime but that his consent is a defence. In fact we regard the non-consent of the owner as a definitional element, but there is no particular reason why this should be so, and the question of guilt or innocence should not depend on it."

It is difficult to determine on what basis an offence or a defence requirement should be classified as either a definitional or a defence element.[47] For example, if a defendant honestly believes he is being subjected to duress, could one not say that he lacks *mens rea* in relation to the definitional element of "unlawfulness"? If so, why did *Graham, Howe* and *Martin* insist that such mistakes be reasonable?

It is interesting to note that the main group of cases where the requirement of reasonableness has been dispensed with are cases concerning consent and self-defence. These are both "justificatory" defences. On the other hand, the areas where a mistake will only exculpate if it is reasonable, namely duress and intoxication, raise "excusatory" defences.[48] The distinction between justifications

---

[47] See Tur, "Subjectivism and Objectivism: Towards Synthesis" in Shute, Gardner and Horder, *Action and Value in Criminal Law* (1993) 213 at 217–222 for a view that this process of reclassifying defence elements as definitional elements has been largely a matter of "dry legal technique" flowing from a commitment to subjectivism with the consequence that pressing moral and public concerns have been overlooked.

[48] It is uncertain how "duress of circumstances" is to be classified. The approach in *Martin (above,* n.43) suggests it is an excuse while in *Martin (D.P.)* [2000] 2 Cr.App.R.42 it was held that the defence was analogous to self-defence, which is a justificatory defence.

and excuses is an important one to be considered later[49] but, at its very simplest, boils down to this:

[i] when conduct is "justified" it is in effect "approved of"—or, at least, tolerated as acceptable conduct. Thus a person acting in self-defence is effectively doing "right"; he is doing what we expect him to do; he is restricting unprovoked aggression; in effect, he is acting lawfully. A person who honestly thinks he is acting in a justified and thus lawful manner is not blameworthy and there is no point punishing him. Accordingly, an honest mistaken belief will suffice to exempt from criminal liability.

[ii] when conduct is excused, it remains wrong and unacceptable (*i.e.* unlawful) but because the defendant has an excuse, we punish him less or not at all. If, thinking he is being subjected to duress a defendant robs a bank, this is "wrong and disapproved of" conduct—but we might wish to exempt the defendant from liability if he had been subjected to terrible threats. But because the conduct remains wrong we will only excuse those who have a plausible excuse—and a plausible excuse is a reasonable one.

The same analysis is true of drunken mistakes. The defendant has acted unlawfully and will only be afforded an excuse if the mistake was one that a sober, reasonable person would have made.

To summarise, the position at the moment would seem to be that with regard to mistakes as to definitional elements (which include mistakes as to justificatory defences) an honest mistake will exempt a defendant from criminal liability. However, with regard to mistakes as to excusatory defences, only a reasonable mistake will entitle a defendant to such exemption.

This whole approach had been condemned by the Law Commission who in the Draft Criminal Code Bill 1989 proposed that "a person who acts in the belief that a circumstance exists has any defence that he would have if the circumstance existed".[50]

This leads us to the final question. How are we to evaluate the law's response to the problem of mistake? Are we to approve of *Morgan* and its progeny? Are the present distinctions drawn by the law based upon sound policy considerations or should we adopt the Law Commission's proposal of allowing an honest mistake to exculpate in all cases?

### D. Cowley, "The Retreat from Morgan" [1982] Crim.L.R.198 at 206–208:

"What is particularly remarkable about the apparent eagerness to retreat from *Morgan* is the lack of any really convincing justification for requiring reasonableness in mistake cases.

...

One theory suggests that whether the objective test of mistake applies depends upon where in respect of the relevant issue the evidential burden lies, and that where an evidential burden lies on the accused to show that he believed in facts inconsistent with the offence, 'a bald assertion of belief for which the accused can indicate no reasonable ground is evidence of insufficient substance to raise any issue requiring the jury's consideration.' (*per* Lord Simon in *Morgan* at 367). It is respectfully submitted that this theory is unsound and that

---

[49] Below, p.270.
[50] Law Commission, No. 177, cl. 41(1).

there is no connection between the incidence of the evidential burden and the question whether the mistake must be reasonable, the main reason being that an evidential burden on the defendant merely requires him to give some *reasonable evidence of belief* as opposed to *evidence of reasonable belief*. It may well be the case that his assertion of belief is not 'bald' but is fully corroborated by independent evidence leading the jury to accept that the unreasonable belief was in fact held and, in such circumstances, the defendant will have discharged the burden cast upon him.

An alternative reason for requiring the belief to be reasonable put forward by Lord Simon is the fact that the victim must be 'vindicated' by punishing *e.g.* an assailant who has made an unreasonable mistake: 'the policy of the law in this regard could well derive from its concern to hold a fair balance between the victim and the accused. It would hardly seem just to fob off a victim of a savage assault with such comfort as he could derive from knowing that his inquiry was caused by a belief, however absurd, that he was about to attack the accused.' One cannot but agree with Professor Williams' opinion ((1975) New L.J. p. 968) that this is not only a somewhat old-fashioned view of the criminal law but also fails to explain who is vindicated when a bigamist is punished. The lawful spouse, in particular, may not care a jot about the bigamy.

Perhaps the current judicial insistence on there being reasonable grounds for mistaken belief can, rather, be put down to a simple lack of confidence in the jury as the final arbiter of fact. If so, such judicial mistrust is very reminiscent of the somewhat misconceived and blinkered popular reaction to the decision in *Morgan*. What was apparently overlooked by those whose passions were aroused by *Morgan's* effect on the law of rape, and those whose railing against the case implied a serious lack of faith in the tribunal of fact in criminal cases, was not only the total lack of gullibility of that particular jury who decided that the defendants' tale as to Mrs Morgan's consent to their intercourse with her was a 'pack of lies', but also the ultimate result of the case—the dismissal of the defendants' appeals against conviction. There is little evidence there to support the often heard claim that a requirement of mere honest belief facilitates bogus defences, and before seeking to impose any kind of restriction upon the freedom of the jury to determine issues of fact the judiciary might reflect upon the oft-quoted words of Dixon J. that a 'lack of confidence in the ability of a tribunal correctly to estimate evidence of states of mind and the like can never be sufficient ground for excluding from inquiry the most fundamental element in a rational and humane criminal code.' *Thomas v R.* (1937) 59 C.L.R. 278 at 309."

## Celia Wells, "Swatting the Subjectivist Bug" [1982] Crim.L.R.209 at 212–213:

"If there is sufficient evidence to satisfy a jury that consent was absent, can it not be argued that this is sufficient to distinguish in terms of culpability, the mistaken defendant from those men who have never had sexual intercourse with a woman who was not consenting? If the defendant is so out of touch with the reality of the situation, is there not a suggestion that he should take more care to ensure that his sexual partner is willing? Social protection might be better served by the punishment of a defendant who failed to acquaint himself with this (seemingly) elementary fact. But would the pillar of personal guilt be demolished in the process? Is a system of criminal law only 'just' if it confines itself to punishing those who 'feel' culpable? 'The state of the actor's mind or conscience is a factual claim. Guilt, fault and culpability are normative judgments, based on an evaluation of the actor's conduct and state of mind.' (Fletcher: at p. 509.) Fletcher goes on to suggest that an alternative method of answering culpability would combine both objective and subjective elements.

'The assessment of attribution and accountability obviously requires the application of standards to the particular situation of the actor ... the standard has a variety of forms, but it always recurs to the same normative question. Could the actor have been fairly expected to avoid the act of wrongdoing? Did he or she have a fair opportunity to perceive the risk, to avoid the mistake, to resist the external pressure ...' (at 510)

It could be argued, that although the mistaken rapist is culpable, he is not as culpable as the deliberate rapist and that his crime should not be rape but some lesser offence such as 'negligent sexual invasion.' "

## George P. Fletcher, Rethinking Criminal Law (1978), pp. 696–697, 707, 709–710:

"[W]e would be naive to think we had a definitive, unassailable solution to the enduring problem of determining when mistakes must be reasonable in order to have an exculpatory effect. The thesis is tentative, and to aid those who might wish to carry the effort further, we should restate the critical premises for recognising that some mistakes have a categorical exculpatory effect.

1. The definition of an offence is the violation of a prohibitory norm.
2. The prohibitory norm identifies the minimal set of objective circumstances necessary, in the given cultural context, to state a coherent moral or social imperative.
3. There is no violation of a prohibitory norm unless the actor acts intentionally or knowingly with respect to the elements of the definition (the prohibitory norm). ...

A mistake as to one of these elements ... has the same effect in barring liability for an intentional offence as the absence of one of the objective elements. ... Of course, if the offense is one that can be committed negligently, then the mistake only bars conviction for the intentional offence. The premises supporting the alternative track requiring mistakes to be reasonable are the following:

4. Relevant mistakes about elements extrinsic to the definition are excuses.
5. Elements of justification are extrinsic to the definition.
6. Excuses are not valid unless they negate the actor's culpability.
7. A mistake does not negate culpability unless the making of the mistake was blameless.
...

[Fletcher admits that this distinction is as yet fragile. For example, he finds the issue of consent in *Morgan* to be justificatory, rather than definitional.] ... [I]n the field of putative self-defense and other imagined circumstances of justified conduct, it is generally assumed that the mistake must be reasonable. We could interpret this requirement as a concern about whether the actor's mistake is free from fault. But the doctrine could also be read as a theory about the justifying effect of appearances. If the circumstances warrant a reasonable belief, the actor is entitled to rely upon appearances, whatever the facts may actually be. ... [C]ommon-law courts are reluctant to reveal to the jury the extent to which a conviction rests on a moral assessment of the actor's wrongful conduct. ... As a step toward overcoming these inhibitions about moral discourse, we should try to state precisely how individuals can be fairly blamed for making mistakes or for remaining inadvertent to the risks implicit in their conduct. The inquiry encompasses not only mistakes in the narrow sense, but the culpability of inadvertent negligence."

## Andrew Ashworth, Principles of Criminal law (3rd ed., 1999), p. 242:

"[T]he belief principle ... focuses on D's attitude of mind at the time, but includes no reference to the circumstances of the act, to D's responsibilities, or to social expectations of conduct in that situation. ... [T]he law on mistake should be more context-sensitive. Thus in rape cases those considerations militate in favour of a requirement of reasonable grounds for any mistake; and a similar argument might be developed in relation to the responsibilities of a police officer with firearms training, as in *Beckford v R*. Of course, any such infusion of objective principles must recognize the exigencies of the moment, and must not expect more of D than society ought to expect in that particular situation. That is a necessary safeguard of individual autonomy. The general point, however, is that there may be good reasons for society to require a certain standard of conduct if the conditions were not to preclude it, particularly where the potential harm involved is serious."

This "context-sensitive" approach can be welcomed. Because of their training we can legitimately expect a higher standard of responsibility from police officers or members of the armed forces who inflict force on others believing they are acting in self-defence: we can insist that their mistakes be reasonable if they are to escape liability. So too with rape: because of the necessary proximity between the parties and thus the ease of ascertaining whether there is consent, only reasonable mistakes should exculpate. Similarly, the basis of the decision in *R. v K* is flawed. The effect of this case is that a middle-aged paedophile can escape liability for an indecent assault on a girl under the age of 16 on the basis that he genuinely believed, albeit unreasonably, that she was 16. Surely, if older men want to have sex with "children" they should be under a duty to ensure that the person is at least 16 and ought only to be able to "rely on appearances" (Fletcher) if other reasonable people would also have thought the girl was over 16.

However, as these examples show, looking at the problem another way, the question becomes: in what contexts will a mere honest, but unreasonable, mistake serve to exculpate? Given the sorts of interests the criminal law seeks to protect (bodily integrity, property rights etc.), can we not demand of all defendants that only reasonable mistakes will suffice for exemption of liability? Most people would accept that Williams (Gladstone) be allowed to "rely on appearances"—but, again, this means only relying on reasonable mistakes. Ashworth argues that we should not expect more of a defendant "than society ought to expect in that particular situation". Following the above argument, we ought always to expect ordinary persons to avoid making unreasonable mistakes. However, we can have no such expectations when dealing with defendants whose mental capacities are such that they are unable to achieve this standard, for example, mentally vulnerable defendants with severe learning difficulties. This argument then reduces itself to a proposition similar to that encountered earlier when we examined Hart's favoured test of negligence: we are entitled to blame persons for their unreasonable conduct (and unreasonable mistakes) provided they had the capacity to act according to that standard.

### 3. Mistake as to law

Traditionally, mistakes of law have been regarded as generally irrelevant. The citizen is presumed to know the law of the land—her ignorance or mistake cannot avail her.[51]

However, this proposition that mistakes of law are irrelevant is somewhat misleading. Some mistakes of law can be highly relevant. In this context it is necessary to distinguish between:

(i) mistake as to civil law, and
(ii) mistake as to criminal law.

#### (i) *Mistake as to civil law*

Some mistakes of civil law may negate the *mens rea* required for a crime. So if a defendant takes a bicycle thinking that the bicycle is her own because, say, she

---

[51] The reason often given is that the law sets an objective standard; a citizen should not be able to make it subjective by his mistaken view of it (Hall, *General Principles of Criminal Law* (2nd ed., 1960)), or that it might encourage ignorance (Holmes, *The Common Law* (1881), p. 45).

mistakenly thinks that a legal sale had taken place, she has made a mistake of the civil law relating to sale of goods; as a result of this mistake she would lack the intention to appropriate property *belonging to another*[52]; she would escape all liability.

In essence, a mistake of civil law is (or results in) a mistake of *fact*—e.g. thinking one is appropriating a bicycle belonging to oneself. Accordingly, such mistakes will be governed by the principles discussed above. So, where a defendant mistakenly believes her first marriage has been dissolved by a foreign divorce entitled to recognition in England, she will, following the demise of *Tolson,* escape liability if her mistake as to the civil law on recognition of foreign divorces was honest and genuine.

(ii) *Mistake as to criminal law*

Here the maxim "ignorance of the law is no defence" comes into operation. A mistake as to whether one's actions are criminal will generally be irrelevant. So if a defendant thinks it is legal to have more than one wife, the *actus reus* and *mens rea* of the crime of bigamy are present; he is merely alleging that he did not know bigamy was a crime and such a mistaken belief is irrelevant.[53]

This same principle extends to persons who know that a particular activity is criminal but mistakenly think they have not committed the crime. In *Lee*[54] the defendant honestly believed he had not failed a roadside breathalyser test and so, believing his arrest to be unlawful, punched the police officers. It was held that his belief in his innocence did not negate his liability for the offence of assault with intent to resist lawful arrest contrary to section 38 of the Offences against the Person Act 1861. This decision is uncontroversial. Any other solution would have given carte blanche to all arrested persons to resist that arrest on the ground that they believed they were innocent and so the arrest was unlawful.[55]

In many cases, however, there are problems in distinguishing between mistakes of civil law and criminal law, and much turns on the wording of particular statutory provisions. Three cases demonstrate this. In *Grant v Borg*[56] the offence charged was under section 24(1)(b)(i) of the Immigration Act 1971, which makes it an offence if a non-patrial "having only limited leave to ... remain ... knowingly ... remains beyond the time limited by the leave".

The House of Lords held that a mistake as to whether "leave" had expired was a mistake of law and thus irrelevant. Lord Bridge went so far as to state that:

"The principle that ignorance of the law is no defence in crime is so fundamental that to construe the word 'knowingly' in a criminal statute as requiring not merely knowledge of the facts material to the offender's guilt, but also

---

[52] The Theft Act 1968, s.2(1) specifically provides that there is no dishonesty for the purposes of the Theft Act if the defendant has a "belief that he has in law the right to deprive the other of (the property)."

[53] The Draft Criminal Code Bill 1989 (Law Com. No. 177, 1989) endorses this approach: "Ignorance or mistake as to a matter of law does not affect liability to conviction of an offence except—(a) where it is so provided; or (b) where it negatives a fault element of the offence." (clause 21).

[54] [2001] 1 Cr.App.R.293.

[55] See also *Doring* [2002] Crim.L.R.817 where a defendant claimed she did not believe what she was doing amounted to "management" of companies for the purpose of bankruptcy offences. This belief was dismissed as irrelevant.

[56] [1982] 1 W.L.R. 638.

knowledge of the relevant law, would be revolutionary and, to my mind, wholly unacceptable."[57]

But in this case there was no dispute that the defendant knew it was a crime to overstay his leave. The question was whether he might have been mistaken as to when his leave had expired—surely a question of civil law.

In *Secretary of State for Trade and Industry v Hart*[58] a somewhat different approach was adopted. In this case the defendant acted as the auditor of two companies while being disqualified from so acting because he was a director of the companies. He was charged with an offence under section 13(5) of the Companies Act 1976 which prohibits a person acting as auditor of a company "at a time when he knows that he is disqualified for appointment to that office". The defendant admitted he knew all the facts or circumstances disqualifying him, but did not know that he was disqualified in law—in other words, he was unaware of the disqualification and its criminal sanctions—surely a mistake as to whether he had committed a crime which, in principle, is not dissimilar to the mistake made in *Lee*. Yet the Divisional Court held the defendant must know he was disqualified; an awareness of the statutory restrictions was a prerequisite of liability. As Ormrod L.J. said:

> "If that means that he is entitled to rely on ignorance of the law as a defence, in contrast to the usual rule, the answer is that the section gives him that right."[59]

In *Attorney-General's Reference (No. 1 of 1995)*[60] the defendant was charged with an offence, contrary to section 3(1) of the Banking Act 1987, of accepting deposits in the course of acting as a deposit-taking business without being authorised to do so by the Bank of England. The defendants knew they were accepting deposits but had "no idea" they needed to be licensed by the Bank of England. It was held that as long as the defendants knew the facts which constituted the offence (which they did), they would be liable. The fact that they did not know it was an offence to act as they did without a licence was mere ignorance of the law and no defence. This decision seems correct. If they had mistakenly believed they had acquired a licence, this would be a mistake of fact or civil law (depending on the circumstances). Not knowing it was a crime to fail to acquire a licence was a mistake of criminal law.

A final question remains for consideration. Is it right that mistake or ignorance of the law should have no bearing on the imposition of criminal liability?

### Paul Robinson, Criminal Law Defences (Vol. 2) (1984), pp. 375–376:

"Austin argues that to permit mistakes as to criminality as an excuse for criminal conduct would be to present insoluble problems of proof (Austin on Jurisprudence: 13th ed. 1920). Everyone could claim such ignorance and it could be disproved only with considerable difficulty.

An examination of the structure of a general mistake excuse gives this concern considerable support. It is the one excuse that has no disability, no observance and verifiable abnormality, to lend support to the actor's claim of an excusing condition. The mistaken

---

[57] At 646. See to similar effect, *Millward* [1985] Q.B. 519.
[58] [1982] 1 W.L.R. 481.
[59] At 487.
[60] [1996] 4 All E.R. 21.

actor, except for his mistake, is indistinguishable from all other 'normal' persons. Evidence of the defendant's excusing condition, of his ignorance of criminality, must come solely from circumstantial evidence of his state of mind.

The absence of a distinguishing abnormality not only makes it difficult to distinguish the defendant and to establish his excusing condition, but also makes it more difficult to maintain the integrity of the prohibition violated while excusing the actor for his violation. '[O]nce the conduct has been so defined [as criminal], one cannot usurp the lawmaking function by pleading that his ignorance must mean that the conduct is not criminal as to him.' (Packer, "The Model Penal Code and Beyond" 63 Colum. L. Rev. 594, 596–97, 1963). In light of the heightened need for clear proof and the simultaneous increased difficulty in reliably determining mistake of law claims, one may reasonably concur with Holmes that 'to admit [such an] excuse at all would be to encourage ignorance where the lawmaker has determined to make men know and obey . . .' (Holmes, The Common Law 48, 1881). It is on the basis of these arguments that 'ignorance of the law is no excuse' is a maxim of long standing."

### A. T. H. Smith, "Error and Mistake of Law in Anglo-American Criminal Law" (1985) 14 Anglo-Am. L.R. 3 at 16–18:

"1. Problems of proof.

. . . [I]t may be argued that mistakes of fact and law and mistakes of law are not essentially different in kind, and since the inquiry is manifestly not impossible in the case of the former, it is equally not impossible in the latter. This response does not directly confront the brutal utilitarianism that lies behind the objection; it is not so much that proof is impossible but that the pursuit of absolute justice must be curtailed by considerations of social utility and the distribution of resources . . .

2. To admit the defence would be to encourage ignorance. . . .

Even the utilitarian should allow that where a particular individual can show that he has taken all the steps that he conceivably can to conform his conduct to what he reasonably believes to be the dictates of the law, he has done all that can be asked of him.

3. The argument from legality. According to Jerome Hall, (1976) 24 Am. Jo. Comp. Law 680) if the law were to assess a defendant's culpability on the footing of the law as he believed it to be, then for those purposes the law would be thus and so. This could undercut the rule of law, which relies on an objective law impartially administered by officials who declare what the law is. But this, as has been most persuasively argued, is to fail to distinguish between wrong-doing and attribution, justification and excuse. The mere fact that an individual is not held to be legally accountable for a wrong act does not mean that the act is not condemned; it means only that the actor is not to be blamed for what he did."

The present approach of English law is perhaps justifiable in relation to the major offences where there is a close correlation between law and morality, for instance, crimes of murder and rape and so on. It can also be defended in relation to specialist activities in which the actor may be engaged.[61] However, when turning to the plethora of legislation surrounding modern life, one is forced to question whether this approach is either just or efficacious.

Ashworth argues that (at least) in cases where the defendant has relied upon incorrect official assurances there should be a defence of mistake of law or any prosecution should be stayed as an abuse of the process of court. He cites two cases. In the first, *Cambridgeshire and Isle of Ely County Council v Rust*[62] the defendant,

---

[61] Some countries provide a defence of mistake of law but exclude it in such situations, *e.g.* Norway, (Penal Code of 1902, §57, added 1939). See also A.L.I. Model Penal Code, Proposed Official Draft 1962, s.2.04(3), Fletcher, *Rethinking Criminal Law* (1978), pp. 713–736.
[62] [1972] 1 Q.B. 426.

having made enquiries of local and national authorities, set up a stall beside a highway. After operating and paying rates on the stall for three years, the defendant was prosecuted and convicted of an offence with the Divisional Court holding that his mistake of law was irrelevant. However, in *Postermobile v Brent London Borough Council*[63] a prosecution was stayed for abuse of process in a case where the defendant had been told by officials from the Brent planning department that it would be lawful to erect advertising hoardings. It was held that persons should be able to rely on the statements of public officials: "it was not as though they had requested planning advice from one of the council's gardeners."

### Andrew Ashworth, "Testing Fidelity to Legal Values: Official Involvement and Criminal Justice" (2000) 63 M.L.R. 633 at 637–641:

"[W]e now pass to consideration of the principal rationales for recognising the claim of officially-induced error of law...

The *first* possible rationale is that it should be regarded as reasonable, in the light of what the State may fairly expect of individual citizens, to place reliance on official advice. This rationale may be related to John Gardner's illuminating distinction between excuses as denials of responsibility and excuses as assertions of reasonable response to the circumstances prevailing. The claim of reliance on official advice is not a denial of responsibility. Its essence lies in an assertion of responsible and reasonable conduct. It is surely reasonable for a citizen to rely on an interpretation of the law proffered by an official. ... The citizen has behaved as a good citizen, and done what it was reasonable to do – approaching all the relevant authorities. ... [I]t is important to consider what factors might make the reliance more or less reasonable, where an official has offered an assurance. One question is when it is reasonable to assume that the official has the authority to offer the guidance: it is possible to rule out extreme cases, as where the official does not work in the relevant department or where the official is manifestly too junior, but the only general test is whether a reasonable citizen would regard the particular official to have responsibility for the enforcement of administration of the relevant law. ...

The *second* possible rationale connects the claim of reasonable reliance on official legal advice with the principle of legality. ... [as] declared (for example) in Article 7 of the European Convention on Human Rights ... [which] make[s] it unfair to convict someone for contravening a law about which he did not know (and could not reasonably have been expected to know) and to which he could therefore not adjust his conduct. The principle of legality sustains ... the principle of fair warning. ... In cases where a person is advised by an official that the law is such-and-such, and adjusts her conduct to that advice, it seems plainly unfair to convict her of an offence if the court decides that the legal advice was erroneous. All the reasons supporting the principle of legality apply, by way of strong analogy, to reasonable reliance on official legal advice. ... [F]rom the point of view of the mistaken citizen, it is as if the conduct did not constitute an offence, because of the official source of the assurance on which she reasonably relied. The connection with ... the principle of fair warning is therefore clear. ...

The *third* rationale is of a different kind: that if the State through its officials implants or confirms a particular view of the law, it is hardly proper for it then to bring a prosecution founded on a different view of the law. This has sometimes been cast as an estoppel-based rationale, arguing that the State should be estopped from prosecuting someone to whom it has given advice that turns out to be mistaken. ...

Similar in some respects is the *fourth* rationale, grounded in the integrity principle: that for the criminal justice system to produce a conviction of a person who has been advised by an official that the conduct would be lawful would involve the system in a disreputable self-contradiction, and would compromise its integrity. ...

[63] *The Times*, 8 December, 1997.

The ... implication of the estoppel and integrity principles is that they do not point necessarily towards the creation of a *defence* of reasonable reliance on an official assurance. Rather, they point towards the stronger remedy that no prosecution should be allowed where there was reasonable reliance on official legal advice."

While Ashworth's last two rationales only apply to cases of reliance on official statements of law, his first two rationales open up the possibility of reliance on the advice of lawyers and other experts. Of course, as Ashworth concedes, there could be problems in some of these cases if defendants sought to buy immunity by hiring lawyers to give them the advice they want to hear. However, such cases could be brought within his first rationale: in the circumstances, was it reasonable to rely on the advice? Indeed, this principle could be broadened out beyond reliance situations to apply to all cases of reasonable mistake of law. Whether a mistake is one of fact or law, the central issue is one of moral blame: can the defendant be fairly blamed for having made such a mistake? With the vast array of regulatory offences, with constantly changing and varying standards of permissible conduct, for example, in relation to obscenity, with the law often being unclear and uncertain even to lawyers, do we necessarily blame all defendants who have made mistakes as to the criminal law? The paradigmatic blameworthy defendant is one who has culpably brought about the prohibited result or state of affairs and has acted in open defiance of the law. With mistake of law there is no such flouting of the rules. Bearing in mind that one is not justifying the wrong done, but merely excusing the actor—and, therefore, an excuse should only be available if the mistake was a *reasonable* one—there must surely be a strong case for exempting such an actor from criminal liability.

## V. Dispensing with Mens Rea

Whether we should dispense with *mens rea* depends, of course, on what is meant by the phrase "*mens rea*". For present purposes this phrase will be given its traditional meaning of a blameworthy state of mind in the sense of intention or subjective recklessness. If one were to conclude that *mens rea* in this sense should be dispensed with, one would then need to decide on what basis liability should be imposed. Should liability be generally imposed on the ground of gross negligence, negligence, or should liability be generally strict?

The case for dispensing with *mens rea* in its purely subjective sense falls broadly into four categories:

(1) There is no difference in moral terms between intention, recklessness and negligence; the law ought not to reflect distinctions devoid of moral content. These arguments were canvassed in the earlier sections on recklessness and negligence and will not be repeated here. Some go further and advocate that, at least for many if not all offences, what matters is the causing of the

prohibited harm. Liability should be strict. These arguments will be addressed in the later section on strict liability.

(2) It is impossible to prove what a person's state of mind was when she committed a crime. It is an illusion, and perhaps even a deception, for the law to pretend that this is what it is doing.

(3) The idea of subjective *mens rea* embraces outmoded philosophical and psychological ideas based on "dualism". If modern philosophy and psychology have rejected such a concept, the law ought to follow suit.

(4) *Mens rea* is based on notions of responsibility and free will. However, these notions have been strongly challenged by the proponents of "determinism"; the law ought not to ignore this challenge.

## 1. The Problem of Proof

The subjective theory of criminal liability assumes that a person's state of mind is ascertainable. But is it possible to inquire into a person's mind to ascertain what her intentions were when she committed the crime (maybe many months or even years previously)? As Ackner J. said in his summing-up to the jury in *Hyam*:

"There is no scientific measurement or yardstick for gauging a person's intention. Unfortunately, there is no form of meter which one can fix to an accused person, like an amp meter or something of that kind, in order to ascertain what the intention is, no X-ray machine which will produce a useful picture."[64]

This immense difficulty in proving a person's state of mind was an important reason behind Lord Diplock's conclusion in *Caldwell* that recklessness should be given a more objective meaning. He described the distinction between consciously running a risk and failing to appreciate a risk as "not being a practicable distinction for use in a trial by jury". He stated that "[t]he only person who knows what the accused's mental processes were is the accused himself, and probably not even he can recall them accurately when the rage or excitement under which he acted has passed". He was not prepared to perpetuate such "fine and impracticable distinctions".

This, taken to its logical conclusion, is the argument that because it is unrealistic to believe that one can reliably determine the state of a person's mind, the criminal law should not attempt to make criminal liability turn on states of mind.

In order to assess the strength of this claim, it is first necessary to inquire how courts try to establish intention or other subjective states of mind.

Without direct evidence of a person's state of mind, such as a confession (but even this might not be reliable), *mens rea* has to be established by drawing inferences from facts; the jury must consider all the circumstantial evidence—the conduct of the defendant before, during and after the crime, motive, statements by the defendant, type of weapon used etc.,—and from that infer what the defendant must have intended. The jury can only perform this task by trying to ascertain what

[64] No. 6530, C. 72, Warwick Crown Court; tried November 22 to 24, 1972.

any normal or reasonable person would have intended or foreseen in those circumstances. From this developed the important maxim that a man must be taken to intend the natural and probable consequences of his actions. This maxim, which of course went a long way towards destroying any subjective notion of *mens rea*, was interpreted rigidly by the House of Lords in the following decision.

## Director of Public Prosecutions v Smith [1961] A.C. 290 (House of Lords)

The respondent was driving a car in which there was stolen property. He was stopped by a police officer who told him to draw into the near side. The respondent began to do so and the constable walked beside the car. Then the respondent suddenly accelerated down an adjoining road. The constable succeeded in hanging on to the car which pursued an erratic course until the constable was thrown off in the path of a vehicle which ran over him, killing him.

At his trial for capital murder, the respondent maintained that he had no intention of killing or causing serious injury to the constable. Donovan J. directed the jury: "if you are satisfied that ... he must, as a reasonable man, have contemplated that grievous bodily harm was likely to result to that officer ... and that such harm did happen and the officer died in consequence, then the accused is guilty of capital murder."

The jury returned a verdict of guilty. The Court of Criminal Appeal quashed his conviction on the ground of misdirection. The Crown appealed to the House of Lords.

Viscount Kilmuir:
"The unlawful and voluntary act must clearly be aimed at someone in order to eliminate cases of negligence or of careless or dangerous driving. Once, however, the jury are satisfied as to that, it matters not what the accused in fact contemplated as the probable result or whether he ever contemplated at all, provided he was in law responsible and accountable for his actions, that is, was a man capable of forming an intent, not insane within the M'Naghten Rules and not suffering from diminished responsibility. On the assumption that he is so accountable for his actions, the sole question is whether the unlawful and voluntary act was of such a kind that grievous bodily harm was the natural and probable result. The only test available for this is what the ordinary responsible man would, in all the circumstances of the case, have contemplated as the natural and probable result. That, indeed, has always been the law....

[T]here seems to be no ground upon which the approach by the trial judge in the present case can be criticised. Having excluded the suggestion of accident, he asked the jury to consider what were the exact circumstances at the time as known to the respondent and what were the unlawful and voluntary acts which he did towards the police officer. The learned judge then prefaced the passages of which complaint is made by saying, in effect, that if in doing what he did he must as a reasonable man have contemplated that serious harm was likely to occur then he was guilty of murder.

My only doubt concerns the use of the expression 'a reasonable man', since this to lawyers connotes the man on the Clapham omnibus by reference to whom a standard of care in civil cases is ascertained. In judging of intent, however, it really denotes an ordinary man capable of reasoning who is responsible and accountable for his actions, and this would be the sense in which it would be understood by a jury.

Another criticism of the summing-up and one which found favour in the Court of Criminal Appeal concerned the manner in which the trial judge dealt with the presumption that a man intends the natural and probable consequences of his acts. ... The real question is whether the jury should have been told that it was rebuttable. In truth, however, as I see it, this is merely another way of applying the test of the reasonable man. Provided that the presumption is applied, once the accused's knowledge of the circumstances and the nature of his acts have been ascertained, the only thing that could rebut the presumption would be proof of incapacity to form an intent, insanity or diminished responsibility. In the present case, therefore, there was no need to explain to the jury that the presumption was rebuttable."

**Appeal allowed**

This decision was greeted with howls of derision by most English commentators.[65] The exact effect of the decision was never settled: did it lay down an irrebuttable evidential presumption that intention was to be ascertained objectively for all crimes? Or did it lay down a new *mens rea* for murder—a completely objective test where it was only necessary to establish that death or grievous bodily harm was objectively foreseeable? Either way, its effect was profound. Murder (and possibly all crimes) had been transformed into a crime of negligence: if the reasonable man would have foreseen the harm, the defendant was liable. It is interesting to note that Viscount Kilmuir emphasised that the defendant must be capable of forming the intent; this is, in essence, Hart's test of negligence.[66]

Intense criticism of this decision[67] led to the passing of the Criminal Justice Act 1967, section 8:

"A court or jury, in determining whether a person has committed an offence—
   (a) shall not be bound in law to infer that he intended or foresaw a result of his actions by reason only of its being a natural and probable consequence of these actions; but
   (b) shall decide whether he did intend or foresee that result by reference to all the evidence, drawing such inferences from the evidence as appear proper in the circumstances."

The legislature has thus clearly endorsed the idea that intention is to be subjectively ascertained—as must foresight.[68] But what is foresight? At the time it was generally assumed that foresight was synonymous with recklessness,[69] but the correctness of this view was affected by *Caldwell* and subsequent cases. Foresight is a component of recklessness. For those crimes where recklessness in the sense of foresight is required the jury must pursue the task identified in section 8(b). But for those crimes which may be satisfied by a failure on the defendant's part to foresee an obvious risk, section 8 is irrelevant.

One further, highly unfortunate (and unforeseen) consequence of section 8 has been that in laying particular emphasis upon *mens rea*, the police have had to exert more pressure to get confessions from defendants to strengthen the case for the prosecution.[70] The results have been seen in a number of successful appeals against convictions.

Section 8 does not actually solve the practical problem of proving *mens rea* at all; it merely states what *ought* to be done in theory. It is true that if there is clear

---

[65] Fletcher regards the reaction to this case as "even more unfortunate" than the decision itself in that English judges and commentators have "gone to the opposite extreme" in eschewing "any reliance on the projected behaviour of a reasonable person" (*Rethinking Criminal Law*, 1978, p. 704).

[66] *Above*, p. 175.

[67] *e.g.*, Law Commission, *Imputed Criminal Intent (Director of Public Prosecutions v Smith)*, 1965.

[68] See, also, *Frankland* [1987] A.C. 576 where the Privy Council reiterated the point that the test is a subjective one.

[69] Williams, *Textbook of Criminal Law* (1st ed., 1978), p. 63; Lord Edmund-Davies' dissenting judgment in *Caldwell*.

[70] Sanders, "Some Dangers of Policy Oriented Research—The Case of Prosecutions" in Dennis (ed.), *Criminal Law and Justice* (1987), p. 208.

evidence that the defendant did not intend a result, the jury can so find. But in what circumstances would a jury conclude that while a reasonable man would have foreseen a result, the defendant did not? Surely this would generally only occur where there was clear evidence that the defendant's state of mind was in some material way different from that of the reasonable man—say, because he was a schizophrenic. But Viscount Kilmuir in *D.P.P. v Smith* was careful to exclude those persons not capable of conforming to the standards of the reasonable man—just as Hart excluded such persons from his test of negligence.

In other cases, however, it is doubtful if juries can do otherwise than draw inferences from conduct and apply their own standards, the standards of ordinary people: "If I had been in that situation, what would I have foreseen?" Perhaps this is what was meant by the startling extract from a training manual for magistrates: "It is sometimes said on the defendant's behalf that he did not intend to inflict the particular injury which the victim suffered. This is always a weak point because any sane person who commits an act of violence must expect injury to result. The fact that it happens to be greater than anticipated provides no excuse whatsoever."[71] The Court of Appeal can sometimes pay lip-service to section 8 and quash convictions because the jury were not clearly directed that the test of intention is subjective.[72] Critics of *Caldwell* can maintain that "no evidence is quoted to show that the distinction (between subjective foresight and failing to foresee) has not worked perfectly well in practice",[73] and can claim "the truth is that arguments based upon the jury system are worthless".[74] But if the reality is that section 8 is impracticable and juries in fact have to apply objective tests in most cases, then surely the time has come for a drastic rethinking of the concept *mens rea* in its subjective form. The law of the books should correlate with the law in action. If the whole system of criminal law is based upon an impracticable premise, might not the time have come to rethink the premise?

## 2. Dualism

At the start of this chapter the view was expressed that the criminal law sees man as generally responsible for his actions; one can attribute blame and praise to him for his actions. He could, if he had wished to, have done otherwise and we, therefore, punish the "deliberate" actor who has made the wrong choice and caused harm.

Such thinking is based on the premise that there is a distinction between what a person does and what she thinks about her actions: she *decides* to act. The twin concepts *actus reus* and *mens rea* explored in this chapter could be said to accept this "dualist" viewpoint. The implications of dualism may, however, not be as supportive to the legal theory of *mens rea* as might at first sight appear.

The modern concept of dualism draws a distinction between mind and body and owes its formulation to the work of René Descartes.[75] Its roots, however, are much

---

[71] Bartle, *Crime and the New Magistrate* (1985), quoted from Nelken, "Criminal Law and Criminal Justice" in Dennis (ed.), *Criminal Law and Justice* (1987), p. 149.
[72] *Ingram* [1975] Crim.L.R.457.
[73] Smith [1981] Crim.L.R.393 at 394.
[74] Williams, "Divergent Interpretation of Recklessness" (1982) 132 N.L.J. 313 at 314.
[75] Hence the term "Cartesian" dualism.

deeper and can be traced back (through the concept of the Christian immortal soul) to the ideas of Plato. It was he who postulated the existence of two elements in man: the soul (which entered the body at birth and left at death) and the body.[76] This view was modified and defended by Descartes as a result of the onslaught of scientific investigation.

### Peter Brett, An Inquiry into Criminal Guilt (1963), p. 46:

"Descartes was both scientifically inclined and religiously devout. He perceived strong implications of the broadening scientific research, and in response to the change developed the doctrine of the dual existence of mind and body in its modern form.... In Descartes' view, every human being possesses a mind and a body. The mind corresponds to what had been termed by older writers the soul; it was responsible for directing the actions of the body. Taken by itself, the body could be seen to work on more or less well-defined mechanical principles. But if human action is merely the result of a series of causes and effects operating in accordance with mechanical laws, there is no longer any place for a belief in the freedom of human choice, or for the attribution of praise or blame to human conduct. Such a view was quite incompatible with Descartes' religious views, and he accordingly sharply distinguished from the material body the non-material mind, which directed and governed the actions of the body. The body was like a clock, which goes when wound up; the winder was the mind."

Using this analogy we could refer simplistically to the *actus reus* of a crime as a clock, and the *mens rea* as the result of the winder operating. We find from dualism, therefore, support for these concepts. However, the ground is not as safe as might appear. It is all very well to refer to the analogy of the clock and the winder; we know precisely how the one operates the other through a mechanical process. But is the same true of the workings of the body and the mind? According to dualism the mind is inevitably a separate private realm. We can only draw inferences about the hidden mental state from the behaviour which we observe.

### R. A. Duff, Intention, Agency and Criminal Liability (1990), pp. 120–121:

"Now inferences from the observed to the unobserved are usually based on and justified by an observed and regular correlation between them. My doctor's inference from the rash on my body to the diagnosis that I have measles is justified by the previously discovered regular correlation between rashes like this and the relevant virus: she can infer the presence of that regularly unobserved virus only because it has been observed to be regularly correlated with the kind of rash which she now observes. But our inferences from another's behaviour to his mental states cannot be based on correlations which we have observed between the behaviour of others and their mental states: for we can never directly observe the mental states of others. The only case in which we can observe correlations between external behaviour and inner mental states is our own. I am directly aware of my own mental states, and can observe correlations between them and my external behaviour and situation; these observed correlations must provide the basis of my inferences from the behaviour of others to their mental states.

---

[76] Plato considered the soul to be tripartite. The immortal soul resided in the mind and governed the activities of the two elements of the mortal soul. They in turn were responsible for emotions and feelings of the body. One was responsible for emotions of courage and love, the other for feelings like hunger and thirst. It was Plato's view of the soul, of an entity separable from the body (rather than Aristotle's concept of inseparable aspects of the body) that became an integral part of western religious doctrine.

This is the Argument from Analogy. I see bodies around me, which resemble mine and behave in ways similar to mine. I know that my body is connected to a mind. So I infer, by analogy with my own case, that these other bodies are also connected to minds.... [and have similar responses to mine to stimuli].

But can such inferences be reliable? Inferences from the observed to the unobserved are usually thought reliable only if they are based on a large number of cases in which the relevant correlation has been observed: we should reject inferences based on what has been observed in just one case ('I know that this man will attack me because he is red-haired and the only other red-haired man I met attacked me'). How then can I properly base my claim to know what another is thinking or feeling on the correlations between behaviour and mental state which I have observed in just one case—my own?"

Because, according to dualists, the mind is necessarily private and because, as we have seen, the inferences which we draw are suspect,[77] one might feel tempted to abandon the entire concept of *mens rea* and concentrate instead upon the behaviour which we can observe. Perhaps liability ought to be strict. However, the alternative conclusion may be thought preferable: not to jettison *mens rea*, but to jettison dualism. "Despite its apparent plausibility ... Dualism is a deeply mistaken doctrine: it distorts what it seeks to explain and has vitiated attempts to provide an adequate account of intention in the law."[78] For Duff, for example, the key to understanding the relationship between mind and behaviour is not to separate them into two distinct realms.

### R. A. Duff, Intention, Agency and Criminal Liability (1990), pp. 129, 132:

"We must claim instead that we begin with people and their actions: that these are what we can directly observe and directly know; that these are not reducible by philosophical analysis to such supposedly simpler or more basic constituents as bodies and their colourless movements ... When I read a philosophical book, what I see are not mere marks on paper, but words and sentences. In working out the book's meaning, I am not trying to make inferences from what I read to some separate realm of meaning: I am trying to identify the pattern and direction of thought which can be discerned in the book, given the wider context of thought in which it is set; and my account of its meaning will show how its parts are related to each other and to that wider context. So too, in trying to understand a person's actions (what he is doing and why), I am trying to see what they mean; to discern the pattern of which they are part, their relation to their context, and the direction in which they are moving."

A different criticism arises from the way in which the law has confined its inquiries to the reasoning processes of the mind only. Modern psychology has presented a strong case for many other mental processes being involved as well. Feelings, desires and subconscious motivations also need to be included if we are to understand the relationship between action and mind.

### John R. Silber, "Being and Doing" (1967) 35 Univ. of Chicago L.R. 47 at 61, 62, 90:

"I urge ... that there are relevant facts about human action which are denied when one insists that a person has to be conscious of what he intends in order to have an intention....

---

[77] We seek to explain the action by reference to a state of mind which is in itself evidenced by the action: a circular investigation. See also the discussion on difficulties of proof (*above*, pp. 210–213).

[78] Duff, *Intention, Agency and Criminal Liability* (1990), p. 119.

[C]onsider the Christmas dinner at which the spinster aunt ... delivers a temperance lecture while the father is opening a bottle of wine saved for the occasion. Are we to deny that the aunt's dislike of the father for having destroyed her only immediate family by marrying her sister, and the aunt's envy of her sister for being the mother in another family, are expressed in her action? Are we to believe that she does not desire and intend to hurt this family, to dampen the pleasures of its Christmas feast? Yet who would call the aunt a liar when later, in tears, she apologises for having spoiled the celebration while she continues to insist that her only concern was for the welfare of the father and mother and children who are going to destroy their health by drinking.... [S]ince her actions are *hers*, it is not surprising that they should reveal much more of herself than she consciously intends to express: what she *does* is a function of *all* that she *is*, all her loves, hates, and wants, and not merely the expression of what she consciously intends when she acts. In this case all of her action, including its disruptive consequences and its good and bad will, was intended and was done intentionally, despite the fact that her conscious intention was merely to save the family she loved from alcoholism. The most accurate account of this situation is one which simply accepts *as fact* the presence of unconscious and often ambivalent intentions. ...

We have neither understanding of man nor a basis for moral and legal judgment of him, unless we recognise the human person as a unity of being and doing."

Acceptance of such reasoning would mean that sharp distinctions presently drawn between mental states such as intention and recklessness would almost certainly have to be abandoned. Indeed, the whole concept of *mens rea*, as presently understood, is incompatible with such reasoning. Yet most lawyers do not even pause to consider such ideas. Has the time not come when such issues ought to be faced?

### 3. Determinism

Notions of responsibility and *mens rea* presuppose that there is freedom of will. This feature distinguishes people from inanimate plants and animal life. It is the ability to choose that provides the "humanness" of people. This concept of freedom of will rests on a dualist framework. The freely choosing will or mind decides between one course of action and another. Descartes was thus able to have his cake and eat it. The will chooses freely (satisfying religious feelings) but governs the operations of the body (dealing with scientific objections). The difficulty he experienced in identifying the nature of the relationship between mind and body has already been introduced. We may now examine an alternative version of the relationship: that the operations of the mind are themselves *caused*. This means that people's actions are governed by preceding events and conditions. They are "determined" and freedom of will is a myth. We thus encounter the philosophical confrontation between those who accept freedom of will and those who assert determinism in a variety of forms.[79] The confrontation rests on the acceptance or rejection of choice in man's make-up.

---

[79] Whilst the most influential work on determinism has come from dualists, another branch of determinism—"monism"—does exist. "Monists" believe that the mind is merely one of the many functions of the body, in the same way that the heartbeat is merely one function of the body. The mind is nothing more than a series of electrochemical impulses inside the brain just as, for instance, a computer programme is nothing more than a series of electronic blips inside a computer. We would not (or should not) praise or blame a computer, so we cannot praise or blame man. *Cf.* Brett *An Inquiry into Criminal Guilt* (1963), pp. 63–65.

## Thomas Morawetz, The Philosophy of Law (1980), p. 183:

"The debate over free will and determinism is one of the oldest in philosophy. It begins with the observation that the habit of thinking of oneself as having free will is deeply ingrained in human nature. All thoughts about choice, decision, and responsibility are based on the assumption of free will. At the same time (it is said), the more we find out about human nature through science, the more the assumption that there is such a thing as free will conflicts with other closely held and well-based beliefs.

This incompatibility is explained in the following way. The progress of scientific knowledge is progress in being able to give causal explanations; we come to understand events better as we come to know their causes. In the world of everyday experience all events are caused and the idea of an uncaused or free event is an absurdity. (Philosophers have made this point in various ways. Hume said that persons inevitably form the habit of thinking in causal terms. Kant said that causation was one of the categories through which the understanding operates.)

As we learn to explain events causally, we learn to predict and control them. To know that certain conditions are sufficient to cause an event is to be able to predict with certainty that the event will occur. If one can manipulate the antecedent conditions, one can bring about the event. Prediction and control will obviously be easier in some fields than others, easier in chemistry than in history because chemical events can be isolated and duplicated by experiment. But in all fields the principle of explanation is the same: to understand events is to understand them as parts of determinate causal chains.

It is clear why someone who holds this general view of causal explanation and of the explainability of all events would reject the notion of free will. He sees the doctrine of free will as the doctrine that when persons choose or decide to act, and do so freely, their actions are not in turn caused by anything else. Persons are uncaused causers. The determinist points out, in opposing this conclusion, that there is no reason to think that human action is exempt from causal explanation. In fact, it is explainable from several different perspectives; biochemistry, physiology, psychology, and sociology are only some of the sciences that involve the prediction and/or the control of human behaviour.

... [T]o say that an action is free is to say that the actor could have done otherwise; to say it is caused is to say that the actor could not have done otherwise."

## R. L. Franklin, Freewill and Determinism (1968), pp. 4–5:

"The central issue may be put in terms of a contrast between two notions, which may be called self-determinism and indeterminism. No one other than an absurd fatalist would suggest that a man is in normal circumstances at the mercy of his environment, as a rudderless boat is driven by the waves. It is we who decide how to act, and act as we decide. We respond to situations with more or less intelligence and integrity. Another person, or we in a different mood, might respond to the same situation quite differently. No account of a man's environment and external stimuli would usually enable us to know what he will do; the answer will depend on his own deliberation and choice. We might express this manifest ability of human beings to transcend a mere immediate reaction to stimuli by saying that they are *self-determined*. But this is quite compatible with saying that there are causal or scientific laws (for example, psychological ones about thought-processes, or physiological ones about brain-processes) which govern an agent's decision. The fact that a full causal account would have to be enormously complicated, that it would have to include statements about the agent as well as about his environment, and that it cannot in practice be achieved, does not show that it is in principle unobtainable. So self-determinism is compatible with determinism; indeed it is the only intelligent form of determinism. The determinist says that this self-determinism is the only sense (if any) in which a man is free, and ... that it is in fact all we mean when we speak of human freedom. The libertarian, however, denies this. He insists that such laws, if they existed, would be incompatible with our most basic conception of freedom. His view may be put by saying that man's freedom is *undetermined*."[80]

Three propositions are thus identifiable:

(1) That man is an uncaused causer; he possesses the freedom to do otherwise— "libertarianism".

(2) That man possesses the freedom to do otherwise but is influenced in his choice by a variety of factors—"self-determinism".[81]

(3) That man could not have done otherwise; his actions are the net sum of antecedent conditions and events—"determinism".

The concept of responsibility is based on one of the first two propositions. One must accept that man could have done otherwise, that he could choose to obey, in order to find him morally blameworthy. *Mens rea*, the means by which the blameworthy are traditionally and primarily identified, is dependent upon this philosophical stance.

If, on the other hand, one accepts that all actions are the result of complex mental processes and antecedent environmental, biological, or even chemical, conditions of the body, one loses the basis for blame and praise. How can a person be brought to account and held responsible for something that he was inevitably going to do? As the following case demonstrates, *mens rea* would be redundant and some other basis would have to be found for dealing with those whose actions constitute a menace to the community.[82]

### State v Sikora 44 N.J. 453, 210 A. 2d. 193 (1965) (Supreme Court of New Jersey)

The defendant, Sikora, was charged with murder (in the first degree). In a detailed statement Sikora had given a large number of details about the events leading up to the shooting, but claimed to have "lost his head" when he shot a man who had beaten him up earlier in the same evening. All the psychiatrists agreed that he was sane; the defence of insanity was not in issue.

Francis J.:
"[The evidence of Dr Galen who] ... had three years training as a psychoanalyst ... taught him that people are a product of their own life history, their own genetic patterns, and that they all feel differently under the stresses of their daily lives. As a result of his study and experience, he believes that mental disturbance and disorder, as distinguished from objective disease, are merely gradients, that people range from being essentially normal, perceiving the world substantially in its normal appearance, all the way to marked distortion of the thinking mechanism, and between the two extremes is a rather jagged line which is prone to and open to many variations. In short, all human behaviour is distributed upon an infinite spectrum of fine gradations, there being no all or none in human dynamics. It is his view that mental disorder is one degree of an indeterminate line between gross disorganization and normal functioning, and it is often impossible to say at what point on the line a particular

---

[80] Both extracts (and many other commentators do the same) speak of determinism in terms of a (complicated) cause and effect relationship. This has been criticised as adopting a view long since abandoned by the physical sciences which look instead for invariable relationships. Night always follows day, but it does not mean that day causes night. Even if human behaviour is invariably predictable it may be unwise to transform this into a causal relationship.

[81] Much difficulty has been experienced with this "compatibility" approach. *Cf.* Kenny, *Freewill and Responsibility* (1978), pp. 22–34.

[82] Baroness Wootton, *Crime and the Criminal Law* (1981).

person is functioning at a given time. Mental illness or disorder in this context is a relative term as he sees it; it is a disorganization of the personality which causes a person to react in a specific way to a specific kind of stress, in a way characteristic for him.

Psychodynamics is the study of what makes a man 'tick.' In effect the doctor said its purpose is to seek an explanation of an individual's mental condition at a given time in terms of his lifelong emotional development; to relate his questioned conduct and its accompanying emotional symptoms to their long antecedent, predetermining factors. In appearing as a witness, Dr Galen indicated his function was to help the court understand 'the dynamics of what happened to this man with his particular history at this particular time in his life.' It was not his place as a psychiatrist to consider the premeditation aspect of murder in terms of right or wrong or good or evil. Evil is a philosophical concept. In his view the psychodynamic psychiatrist cannot consider the aspect of first degree murder which in law requires the conceiving of a design to kill in terms of evil, or evil intent. These moral judgments are best left to the courts to decide. Such a physician deals with the problem in a scientific way by applying his knowledge of the 'way people operate,' his knowledge of stress and 'the way people react to particular kinds of stress, based on their personality disorganization'. He feels 'somewhat medieval in talking about evil'. Basically Dr Galen's thesis is that man is a helpless victim of his genes and his lifelong environment; that unconscious forces from within dictate the individual's behaviour without his being able to alter it....

[W]hen Dr Galen made his examination about four months after the homicide for about one and three-quarter hours, he obtained substantially the history detailed above. Sikora had a clear recollection of his previous life and of the events of the fatal night, and he was able to give the doctor a step-by-step account of the circumstances of the shooting. On the basis of the history, it was his opinion that at the time of the crime (and perhaps all his adult life) Sikora was suffering from a personality disorder of a passive-dependent type, with aggressive features. This kind of disorder is a function of his personality 'which is his way of dealing with himself and with life and with people and with stress'. He found no evidence of any overt hallucinations, delusions or ideas of reference; nor any evidence of organic mental disease. The accused's insight and judgment were consonant with his education, emotional status and intellect; he was 'estimated' to have a normal to dull-normal level of intelligence....

According to Dr Galen, tensions had been building up in Sikora, particularly since his female friend rejected him. When he was humiliated in the tavern by the remarks about her availability for other men because she had broken with him, and then physically beaten by Hooey and his companions, the tensions mounted to the point where they represented a situation in life with which he felt unable to cope. So he began to act in an automatic way; the manner in which a person with his personality inadequacy would characteristically act. He responded to the stress in the way which inevitably would be his way of dealing with that kind of stress....

The beating administered by Hooey in the tavern precipitated the disorganisation of his personality to the extent that from then on he probably 'acted in at least a semi-automatic way, and probably an automatic way.'...

In short the doctor opined that the circumstances to which Sikora had been subjected imposed on his personality disorder a stress that impaired or removed his ability consciously to premeditate or weigh a design to kill. The tension was so great that he could handle it only by an automatic reaction motivated by the predetermined influence of his unconscious. Plainly the doctor meant that Sikora's response was not a voluntary exercise of his free will. The stress was such as to distort his mechanisms. During the various actions Sikora took leading up to the killing, which so clearly indicate conception, deliberation and execution of a plan to kill, he was thinking but the thinking was automatic; it was simply subconscious thinking or reaction; it was not conscious thinking. The doctor said Sikora's anxieties at the time were of such a nature that conceivably, his reaction in that automatic way and the commission of the homicide, actually prevented a further disorganisation of his personality. The killing, said the doctor, was 'a rational murder' but 'everything this man did was irrational,' and engaged in when he could not conceive the design to kill....

The question now presented is whether psychiatric evidence of the nature described is admissible in first degree murder cases on the issue of premeditation. Defendant argues that it should have been received at the trial on that issue. . . .

For protection of society the law accepts the thesis that all men are invested with free will and capable of choosing between right and wrong. In the present state of scientific knowledge that thesis cannot be put aside in the administration of the criminal law. Criminal blameworthiness cannot be judged on a basis that negates free will and excuses the offence, wholly or partially, on opinion evidence that the offender's psychological processes or mechanisms were such that even though he knew right from wrong he was predetermined to act the way he did at that time because of unconscious influences set in motion by the emotional stresses then confronting him. In a world of reality such persons must be held responsible for their behaviour. . . .

Criminal responsibility must be judged at the level of the conscious. If a person thinks, plans and executes the plan at that level, the criminality of his act cannot be denied, wholly or partially, because although he did not realise it, his conscious was influenced to think, to plan and to execute the plan by unconscious influences which were the product of his genes and his lifelong environment. So in the present case criminal guilt cannot be denied or confined to second degree murder (when the killing was a 'rational murder' and the product of thought and action), because Sikora was unaware that his decisions and conduct were mechanistically directed by unconscious influences bound to result from the tensions to which he was subjected at the time. If the law were to accept such a medical doctrine as a basis for a finding of second rather than first degree murder, the legal doctrine of *mens rea* would all but disappear from the law. Applying Dr Galen's theory to crimes requiring specific intent to commit, such as robbery, larceny, rape, etc., it is difficult to imagine an individual who perpetrated the deed as having the mental capacity in the criminal law sense to conceive the intent to commit it. Criminal responsibility, as society now knows it, would vanish from the scene, and some other basis for dealing with the offender would have to be found. At bottom, this would appear to be the ultimate aim of the psychodynamic psychiatrist. . . .

[F]or purposes of administration of the criminal law in this State, we cannot accept a thesis that responsibility in law for a criminal act perpetrated by a legally sane defendant, can be considered non-existent or measured by the punishment established for a crime of lower degree, because his act was motivated by subconscious influences of which he was not aware, and which stemmed inevitably from his individual personality structure. A criminal act of that nature is nothing more than the consequence of an impulse that was not resisted.

In first degree murder cases psychiatric testimony of the type adduced here should be admitted but its probative function limited to the area of sentence or punishment."

                                                                        Conviction affirmed

### George P. Fletcher, Rethinking Criminal Law (1978), pp. 801–802:

"It is difficult to resolve [the issue of determinism and responsibility] except by noting that we all blame and criticise others, and in turn subject ourselves to blame and criticism, on the assumption of responsibility for our conduct. In order to defend the criminal law against the determinist critique, we need not introduce freighted terms like 'freedom of the will.' Nor need we 'posit' freedom as though we were developing a geometric system on the basis of axioms. The point is simply that the criminal law should express the way we live. Our culture is built on the assumption that, absent valid claims of excuse, we are accountable for what we do. If that cultural presupposition should someday prove to be empirically false, there will be far more radical changes in our way of life than those expressed in the criminal law."

### Jeremy Horder, "Criminal Law: Between Determinism, Liberalism, and Criminal Justice" (1996) 49 Current Legal Problems 159 at 164–165:

"In duress cases, the person threatened may regard herself as faced by an appalling dilemma, or may believe instead that she has no choice but to take the course of action that she does. Her claim to excuse, however, will be based on whether she dealt with the threat in an acceptable way, showing an appropriate degree of courage, and so on. Questions about whether she 'really' had a choice are irrelevant, or subordinated to this ethical evaluation of the conduct in which she engaged. What is true of ... duress is true generally. Individual criminal responsibility is about whether someone has done the wrong thing, without having an exemption, excuse or justification. Ethically speaking, if there was no exemption, excuse, or justification, whether this wrongdoing involved or was experienced as a choice to do wrong (from amongst alternatives) does not matter at all ...

The important point ... is to accept that determinism cannot challenge the existence of and need for evaluation of beliefs and of conduct, in the light (*inter alia*) of reasons as well as causes. Judgments of responsibility and blame in law are clearly focused on such evaluations."

### Tony Honoré, Responsibility and Fault (1999), pp. 135–137:

"It is sometimes said that determinism, if true, is irrelevant to the moral and legal responsibility of human agents. But can this be the case, given that intelligent people have been and are concerned to show that the things that go wrong in our society are better tackled by eliminating the causes of wrongdoing than by punishing, censuring or isolating the wrongdoers?

To avoid a superficial discussion of a complex issue, I assume that it makes sense to treat people as the authors of and hence responsible for their actions ...

The worry remains that, though it may make sense to treat people as responsible for their conduct, if human actions are caused by circumstances, people are not *really* responsible for what they do. However beneficial it may be to treat them as if they were, to do so is to resort to a salutary lie. And salutary lies stop being salutary when the deception is revealed. Are people's actions in fact caused by their hereditary make-up and external circumstances? No one can be sure. Though valuable work has been done by psychologists, neurologists and sociologists the precise regularities involved, if they exist, await discovery ... Even so, we tend to assume that *something* determines people's decisions. That nothing determined them would imply that they were not merely unpredictable but inexplicable: a belief that would be truly alarming.

Should this disturb us? It seems that even 'strong psychophysical explanations' bordering on psychological laws are compatible with the notions of choice, decision, action and intention to which we are committed when we treat people as responsible. To suppose, as a working hypothesis, that our decisions are determined does not make it implausible or illogical to treat ourselves as the authors of our actions when we judge ourselves and others as social beings. How far back is it rational to go in tracing causes must depend on the purpose for which we want to get at the cause of something that has gone wrong. This must also apply to the causes of human conduct. It is rational to treat people as the authors of their actions in the context of a system of responsibility that we regard as valuable both for individuals and for society as a whole. To treat human action as a stopping point beyond which causal inquiries are not ordinarily pursued is sensible and indeed indispensable."

### VI. STRICT LIABILITY

### 1. Introduction

Under the general principles considered above, a finding of culpability or blameworthiness is necessary for the imposition of criminal liability. While this proposition is true for most serious criminal offences, there are nevertheless many offences for which no culpability need be established.[83] These are called crimes of strict liability. Liability is "strict" because the prosecution is relieved of the necessity of proving *mens rea* in relation to one or more of the of the elements of the *actus reus*[84] In the first "modern" case of strict liability,[85] for example, the defendant was accused of selling adulterated milk. It was sufficient to prove that the milk was adulterated and that he was selling it; his mistake that he had thought the milk was pure was irrelevant. Similarly, in the much later case of *Alphacell v Woodward*[86] liability was established under section 2(1)(a) of the Rivers (Prevention of Pollution) Act 1951 by the defendants causing polluted water to enter a river. The fact that they had not known that the pollution was taking place and that they had mistakenly thought that their filtering system was operating efficiently did not exonerate them.[87]

## 2. The Law

How are the courts to determine whether an offence is one of strict liability? At first sight the issue resolves itself into a problem of statutory interpretation. Where the legislature has done its job efficiently, there is no difficulty. It may indicate, by the inclusion of terms such as "knowingly" or "recklessly" that the offence being created is one requiring *mens rea*. It may, alternatively, make it clear that an offence of strict liability is being created.

All too often, however, legislation is enacted with no indication as to whether the offence is one requiring proof of *mens rea*. In such cases it is for the courts to determine whether the offence is one of strict liability. The mere absence of *mens rea* terms is by no means indicative that no culpability is required. On the contrary, there is an "established common law presumption that a mental element, traditionally labelled *mens rea*, is an essential ingredient unless Parliament has indicated a contrary intention either expressly or by necessary implication".[88]

### (i) *The presumption of mens rea*

#### Sweet v Parsley [1970] A.C. 132 (House of Lords)

The defendant, a teacher, let rooms to students in a farmhouse in which she did not reside although she occasionally stayed overnight in the one room retained for her use. She exercised no control over the students beyond collecting rent from them and occasionally shouting at them to be quiet if on her visits there was excessive noise late at night.

She was convicted of being concerned in the management of premises which were used for the purpose of smoking cannabis contrary to section 5(b) of the Dangerous Drugs Act 1965, when such substances were found during a police search. The Divisional Court upheld her

---

[83] It has been estimated that more than half the roughly 8,000 crimes in English law are ones involving strict liability (Ashworth, "Is the Criminal Law a Lost Cause?" (2000) 116 L.Q.R. 225).

[84] Most of these offences are statutory in origin.

[85] *Woodrow* (1846) 153 E.R. 907 (Exch.).

[86] [1972] A.C. 824.

[87] Most discussions of strict liability centre around some mistake of fact being made by the defendant which means that he lacked *mens rea*. For example, in the case of *F.J.H. Wrothwell Ltd v Yorkshire Water Authority* [1984] Crim.L.R.43 the defendant, in a prosecution under the same Act as in *Alphacell*, mistakenly thought that the drains from his factory led into the public sewer system (and on that basis poured concentrated herbicide down them). In fact the drains led to a nearby stream. This lack of *mens rea* was not seen as fatal to the prosecution; liability was "strict".

[88] *B (A Minor) v D.P.P.*[2000] 2 A.C. 428 at 460, per Lord Nicholls.

conviction on the basis that she was not only in a position of being able to choose her tenants but could have made it a term of the letting that the smoking of cannabis was prohibited.[89] She appealed to the House of Lords.

Lord Reid:
"How has it come about that the Divisional Court has felt bound to reach such an obviously unjust result? It has in effect held that it was carrying out the will of Parliament because Parliament has chosen to make this an absolute offence. And, of course, if Parliament has so chosen the courts must carry out its will, and they cannot be blamed for any unjust consequences. But has Parliament so chosen? ... Our first duty is to consider the words of the Act: if they show a clear intention to create an absolute offence that is an end of the matter. But such cases are very rare. Sometimes the words of the section which creates a particular offence make it clear that *mens rea* is required in one form or another. Such cases are quite frequent. But in a very large number of cases there is no clear indication either way. In such cases there has for centuries been a presumption that Parliament did not intend to make criminals of persons who were in no way blameworthy in what they did. That means that whenever a section is silent as to *mens rea* there is a presumption that, in order to give effect to the will of Parliament, we must read in words appropriate to require *mens rea*. ...

In the absence of a clear indication in the Act that an offence is intended to be an absolute offence, it is necessary to go outside the Act and examine all relevant circumstances in order to establish that this must have been the intention of Parliament. I say 'must have been' because it is a universal principle that if a penal provision is reasonably capable of two interpretations, that interpretation which is most favourable to the accused must be adopted."

Lord Pearce:
"My Lords, the prosecution contend that any person who is concerned in the management of premises where cannabis is in fact smoked even once, is liable, though he had no knowledge and no guilty mind. This is, they argue, a practical act intended to prevent a practical evil. Only by convicting some innocents along with the guilty can sufficient pressure be put upon those who make their living by being concerned in the management of premises. Only thus can they be made alert to prevent cannabis being smoked there. And if the prosecution have to prove knowledge or *mens rea*, many prosecutions will fail and many of the guilty will escape. I find that argument wholly unacceptable.

The notion that some guilty mind is a constituent part of crime and punishment goes back far beyond our common law. And at common law *mens rea* is a necessary element in a crime. Since the Industrial Revolution the increasing complexity of life called into being new duties and crimes which took no account of intent. Those who undertake various industrial and other activities, especially where these affect the life and health of the citizen, may find themselves liable to statutory punishment regardless of knowledge or intent, both in respect of their own acts or neglect and those of their servants. But one must remember that normally *mens rea* is still an ingredient of any offence. Before the court will dispense with the necessity for *mens rea* it has to be satisfied that Parliament so intended. The mere absence of the word 'knowingly' is not enough. But the nature of the crime, the punishment, the absence of social obloquy, the particular mischief and the field of activity in which it occurs, and the wording of the particular section and its context, may show that Parliament intended that the act should be prevented by punishment regardless of intent or knowledge."

**Appeal allowed**
The strength of this presumption of *mens rea* has recently been strongly affirmed.

---

[89] *cf.* Smith [1968] Crim.L.R.328 who identifies the emptiness of such reasoning. Even had such a term appeared in the letting agreement it would not have absolved the defendant from liability if the crime were, as was stated by the court, one of strict liability. She could, therefore, have done everything reasonable—and more—and still have been found guilty. Her crime was, in effect, "being concerned in the management of premises".

## B (A Minor) v D.P.P. [2000] 2 A.C. 428 (House of Lords)

The defendant, a 15–year-old boy, invited a 13–year-old girl to perform oral sex on him on a bus. He was charged with the offence of inciting a girl under the age of 14 to commit an act of gross indecency, contrary to section 1(1) of the Indecency with Children Act 1960. He honestly believed she was over 14 years of age.

Lord Nicholls of Birkenhead:
"[T]he starting point for a court is the established common law presumption that a mental element, traditionally labelled mens rea, is an essential ingredient unless Parliament has indicated a contrary intention either expressly or by necessary implication. . . .

In section 1(1) of the Indecency with Children Act 1960 Parliament has not expressly negatived the need for a mental element in respect of the age element of the offence. The question, therefore, is whether, although not expressly negatived, the need for a mental element is negatived by necessary implication. 'Necessary implication' connotes an implication which is compellingly clear. Such an implication may be found in the language used, the nature of the offence, the mischief sought to be prevented and any other circumstances which may assist in determining what intention is properly to be attributed to Parliament when creating the offence.

I venture to think that, leaving aside the statutory context of section 1, there is no great difficulty in this case. The section created an entirely new criminal offence, in simple unadorned language. The offence so created is a serious offence. The more serious the offence, the greater is the weight to be attached to the presumption, because the more severe is the punishment and the graver the stigma which accompany a conviction. Under section 1 conviction originally attracted a punishment of up to two years' imprisonment. This has since been increased to a maximum of ten years' imprisonment. The notification requirements under Part I of the Sex Offenders Act 1997 now apply, no matter what the age of the offender: see Schedule 1, paragraph 1(1)(b). Further, in addition to being a serious offence, the offence is drawn broadly ('an act of gross indecency'). It can embrace conduct ranging from predatory approaches by a much older paedophile to consensual sexual experimentation between precocious teenagers of whom the offender may be the younger of the two. The conduct may be depraved by any acceptable standard, or it may be relatively innocuous behaviour in private between two young people. These factors reinforce, rather than negative, the application of the presumption in this case. . . .

Similarly, it is far from clear that strict liability regarding the age ingredient of the offence would further the purpose of section 1 more effectively than would be the case if a mental element were read into this ingredient. There is no general agreement that strict liability is necessary to the enforcement of the law protecting children in sexual matters."

Lord Hutton:
"[I]t would be reasonable to infer that it was the intention of Parliament that liability under section 1(1) of the Act of 1960 should be strict so that an honest belief as to the age of the child would not be a defence. But the test is not whether it is a reasonable implication that the statute rules out mens rea as a constituent part of the crime – the test is whether it is a necessary implication. Applying this test, I am of the opinion that there are considerations which point to the conclusion that it is not a necessary implication."

**Appeal allowed**

This approach was reaffirmed by the House of Lords in *R. v K*[90] where it was held that the offence of indecent assault on a girl under the age of 16, contrary to section 14(1) of the Sexual Offences Act 1956 was an offence requiring *mens rea* and so the defendant, believing the girl to be aged 16 or over, could not be liable. Lord Steyn

[90] [2002] 1 A.C. 462.

emphasised the point made by Lord Nicholls in *B (A Minor) v D.P.P.* that the presumption of *mens rea* can only be displaced by "necessary implication ... which is compellingly clear".

In these cases where the presumption is applied, it is necessary for the courts to specify the precise form of *mens rea* that is being implied. This is generally taken to mean intention or subjective recklessness or knowledge or belief.[91] Negligence has not been regarded as sufficiently blameworthy for this purpose. Perhaps, despite the strength of the presumption emphasised in the above cases, it is this "all or nothing" approach (full subjective *mens rea* or strict liability) that has resulted in the presumption being displaced so often. If the courts had been prepared to utilise negligence as an appropriate fault requirement here, the presumption might have been applied in a wider range of situations.

## (ii) *Displacing the presumption*

### Gammon Ltd v Attorney-General of Hong Kong [1985] 1 A.C. 1 (Privy Council)

Lord Scarman:
"In their Lordships' opinion, the law ... may be stated in the following propositions...: (1) there is a presumption of law that *mens rea* is required before a person can be held guilty of a criminal offence; (2) the presumption is particularly strong where the offence is 'truly criminal' in character; (3) the presumption applies to statutory offences, and can be displaced only if this is clearly or by necessary implication the effect of the statute; (4) the only situation in which the presumption can be displaced is where the statute is concerned with an issue of social concern, and public safety is such an issue; (5) even where a statute is concerned with such an issue, the presumption of *mens rea* stands unless it can also be shown that the creation of strict liability will be effective to promote the objects of the statute by encouraging greater vigilance to prevent the commission of the prohibited act."

The presumption in favour of *mens rea* can be overridden. Guiding criteria have gradually emerged as to when this is appropriate. These criteria, encapsulated in the "*Gammon* principles" are now regularly applied as the appropriate test to determine whether an offence is one of strict liability.[92]

### (1) *Type of offence*
Strict liability is more likely to be imposed in relation to offences that:

- pertain to matters of social regulation and public welfare such as health and safety or road traffic;
- are regarded generally as only "quasi-criminal"; that is, there is little or no stigma attached to their violation; and
- carry a light punishment, typically a fine.

Such offences are often termed "regulatory" offences—although this term is only strictly accurate for those offences that exist within a scheme of regulation such as that which applies to health and safety at work. As shall be seen, strict liability offences can exist quite independently of any such regulatory framework.

---

[91] This was the approach adopted in both *B (A Minor) v D.P.P.* and *R. v K.*
[92] *Bezzina* (1994) 99 Cr.App.R.356; *Brockley* (1994) 99 Cr.App.R.385; *Blake* [1997] 1 All E.R. 963; *Paine* [1998] 1 Cr.App.R.36.

### Staples v United States 511 US 600 (1994) (Supreme Court of the United States)

Stevens J.:

" 'Public welfare' offenses share certain characteristics: (1) they regulate 'dangerous or deleterious devices or products or obnoxious waste materials'; (2) they 'heighten the duties of those in control of particular industries, trades, properties or activities that affect public health, safety or welfare'; . . . Public welfare statutes render criminal 'a type of conduct that a reasonable person should know is subject to stringent public regulation and may seriously threaten the community's health or safety.' . . . 'The purposes of this legislation thus touch phases of the lives and health of people which, in the circumstances of modern industrialism, are largely beyond self-protection' . . . [A]n overriding public interest in health or safety may outweigh that risk [of injustice] when a person is dealing with products that are sufficiently dangerous or deleterious to make it reasonable to presume that he either knows, or should know, whether those products conform to special regulatory requirements."[93] (citations omitted)

### Lim Chin Aik v The Queen [1963] A.C. 160 (Privy Council)

(For facts see *below*, p. 230.)

Lord Evershed:

"Where the subject matter of the statute is the regulation for the public welfare of a particular activity—statutes regulating the sale of food and drink are to be found among the earliest examples—it can be and frequently has been inferred that the legislature intended that such activities could be carried out under conditions of strict liability. The presumption is that the statute or statutory instrument can be effectively enforced only if those in charge of the relevant activities are made responsible for seeing that they are complied with. When such a presumption is to be inferred, it displaces the ordinary presumption of *mens rea*. Thus sellers of meat may be made responsible for seeing that meat is fit for human consumption and it is no answer for them to say that they were not aware that it was polluted. If that were a satisfactory answer, then . . . the distribution of bad meat (and its far-reaching consequences) would not be effectively prevented."

It is, however, not always clear what a "public welfare" offence is. "The connection between 'public welfare'/'quasi' crime and strict liability is self-fulfilling at both a legislative and an interpretive level."[94] An offence can be held to be one of strict liability because it is only "quasi-criminal" and then because it is an offence of strict liability it can be labelled a "public welfare offence".

### Muhamad v R. [2003] 2 W.L.R. 1050 (Court of Appeal, Criminal Division)

The appellant was convicted of materially contributing to the extent of his insolvency by gambling contrary to section 362(1)(a) of the Insolvency Act 1986 and appealed.

Dyson L.J.:

"It is not clear to us whether an offence under section 362(1)(a) would have been classified by Lord Reid as 'quasi-criminal', or 'truly criminal'. A maximum penalty of two years' imprisonment is by no means insignificant, although it is towards the lower end of the scale of maximum custodial sentences. On the other hand, it is open to doubt whether, at any rate in 2002, such an offence would be regarded as 'truly criminal'. . . .

The question whether the presumption of law that mens rea is required applies, and, if so, whether it has been displaced can be approached in two ways. One approach is to ask

---

[93] It has been stressed in the United States that even with public welfare offences *mens rea* is "generally" required (*Posters 'N' Things Ltd v United States*, 511 US 513 (1994).

[94] Wells, *Corporations and Criminal Responsibility* (1993), p. 8.

whether the act is truly criminal, on the basis that, if it is not, then the presumption does not apply at all. The other approach is to recognise that any offence in respect of which a person may be punished in a criminal court is, *prima facie*, sufficiently 'criminal' for the presumption to apply. But the more serious the offence, the greater the weight to be attached to the presumption, and conversely, the less serious the offence, the less weight to be attached. It is now clear that it is this latter approach which, according to our domestic law, must be applied.

The starting point, therefore, is to determine how serious an offence is created by section 362(1)(a), and accordingly how much weight, if any, should be attached to the presumption. Some weight must undoubtedly be given to the presumption, but in our judgment it can be readily displaced. As we have said, the maximum sentence indicates that Parliament considered this to be an offence of some significance, but not one of the utmost seriousness. This is not surprising. We do not believe that great stigma attaches to a conviction of this offence... In our view, this is not, and never has been, a particularly serious offence....

First, the 1986 Act created a clear and coherent regime. The majority of the offences include an express requirement of a mental element. This is achieved either in the section which creates the offence (for example, section 356(2)); or by reference to section 352 (which contains a reverse onus of proof provision). Only a few, of which section 362(1)(a) is one, do not specify a mental element. In our judgment, this is a clear pointer to Parliament's intention in relation to section 362(1)(a)....

Further support for the displacement of the presumption in relation to section 362(1)(a) emerges when a comparison is made of the maximum sentences provided for by the various offences created in Chapter VI of the 1986 Act. The offences where no mental element is specified, for the most part, attract considerably lower maximum sentences than those where a mental element is specified....

The next point relied on by [the prosecution] is the fact that gambling which harms a gambler's creditors is a matter of social concern. That is obviously right. It follows that this is a case where the fourth and fifth of Lord Scarman's propositions are engaged. So too they were in *Harrow London Borough Council v Shah* [1999] 2.Cr.App.R.457. In that case, the Divisional Court had to decide whether the offence of selling National Lottery tickets to a person under the age of 16 was an offence of strict liability. The court decided that it was. In giving the leading judgment, Mitchell J said that the legislation dealt with an issue of social concern, and that it was an excellent example of the sort of legislation contemplated by Lord Scarman's fifth proposition. He said: 'That strict liability attaches to this offence will unquestionably encourage greater vigilance in preventing the commission of the prohibited act' ...

It is self-evident that section 362(1)(a) is aimed at an issue of social concern. ... [A]n offence of strict liability may have a more chilling effect on gambling that may materially contribute to insolvency than an offence which requires a mental element. We are satisfied that strict liability will encourage greater vigilance to prevent gambling which will or may materially contribute to insolvency....

We conclude, therefore, that ... the offence created by section 362(1)(a) of the 1986 Act is one of strict liability."

**Appeal dismissed**

The approach towards offence seriousness expressed in the above cases is by no means universally applied. There are glaring examples of cases where strict liability has been imposed where the crime has the stamp of traditional criminality. For example, in *Warner*[95] it was held that the serious crime of possession of dangerous drugs contrary to section 1 of the Drugs (Prevention of Misuse) Act 1964 involved strict liability. Similarly, in *Land*[96] it was held that the offence of possessing an

---

[95] [1969] A.C. 256.
[96] [1998] 1 All E.R. 403. See also *Lemon*, [1979] A.C. 617.

indecent photograph of a child contrary to section 1(1)(c) of the Protection of Children Act 1978 was one of strict liability.

### R. v Blake [1997] 1 All E.R. 963 (Court of Appeal, Criminal Division)

The defendant, a disc jockey, was convicted of using a station for wireless telegraphy without a licence contrary to section 1(1) of the Wireless Telegraphy Act 1949. He claimed he had believed he was making a demonstration tape and was not aware he was in fact transmitting. He appealed on the ground that the offence was not one of strict liability.

Hirst L.J.:
"[S]ince throughout the history of s.1(1), an offender has been potentially subject to a term of imprisonment, the offence is 'truly criminal' in character, and [thus] ... the presumption in favour of mens rea is particularly strong. However, it seems to us manifest that the purpose behind making unlicensed transmissions a serious criminal offence must have been one of social concern in the interests of public safety ... since undoubtedly the emergency services and air traffic controllers were using radio communications in 1949, albeit in a much more rudimentary form than nowadays. No doubt the much greater sophistication of these modes of communication, and the wider prevalence of pirate radio stations 40 years on, led to the substantial increase in the penalty in 1990.
Clearly, interference with transmissions by these vital public services poses a grave risk to wide sections of the public ...
... [T]he imposition of an absolute offence must surely encourage greater vigilance on the part of those establishing or using a station, or installing or using the apparatus, to avoid committing the offence, *e.g.* in the case of users by carefully checking whether they are on air; it must also operate as a deterrent ...
In these circumstances, we are satisfied that s.1(1) does create an absolute offence."

**Appeal dismissed**

As seen in *Muhamad*, it is often stated that the level of punishment attached to a crime is important in assessing whether the offence is one of strict liability. In the United States, the Model Penal Code advocates that the possibility of imprisonment should conclusively indicate that the offence is not one of strict liability.[97]

### Staples v United States 511 US 600 (1994) (Supreme Court of the United States)

The point on appeal was whether the defendant had to know that a gun he possessed was capable of automatic firing so as to make it a machine gun as defined by the National Firearms Act.

Thomas J.:
"The potentially harsh penalty attached to [the offence] ... —up to 10 years' imprisonment—confirms our reading of the Act. Historically, the penalty imposed under a statute has been a significant consideration in determining whether the statute should be

[97] Art. 6.02(4).

construed as dispensing with *mens rea*. Certainly, the cases that first defined the concept of public welfare offence almost uniformly involved statutes that provided for only light penalties such as fines or short jail sentences, not imprisonment in the state penitentiary ...

In rehearsing the characteristics of the public welfare offense, we, too, have included in our consideration the punishments imposed and have noted that 'penalties commonly are relatively small and conviction does no grave damage to an offender's reputation' (*Morissette*, 342 US 15 at 256)."

However, this is again only a guiding principle. In many cases offences carrying reasonably severe penalties have been held to be crimes of strict liability. In *Hussain*,[98] the defendant was convicted of unlawful possession of a firearm contrary to section 1 of the Firearms Act 1968 even though he believed it was a toy used by his son. Despite the fact that this offence carried a maximum penalty of three years' imprisonment, it was held to be one of strict liability.

### Gammon Ltd v Attorney-General of Hong Kong [1985] 1 A.C. 1 (Privy Council)

The appellants were charged under Hong Kong Building Ordinances with deviating in a material way from work shown on an approved plan. It had to be determined whether they had to know that their deviation was *material* or whether liability was strict in relation to that element of the offence, the maximum penalty for which was a fine of $250,000 and imprisonment for three years.

Lord Scarman:
"The severity of the penalties is a more formidable point. But it has to be considered in the light of the Ordinance read as a whole. ... [T]here is nothing inconsistent with the purpose of the Ordinance in imposing severe penalties for offences of strict liability. The legislature could reasonably have intended severity to be a significant deterrent, bearing in mind the risks to public safety arising from some contraventions of the Ordinance. ... It must be crucially important that those who participate in or bear responsibility for the carrying out of works in a manner which complies with the requirements of the Ordinance should know that severe penalties await them in the event of any contravention or non-compliance with the Ordinance."

**Appeal dismissed**

### (2) *Statutory context*

It has been repeatedly stated by the House of Lords that the presumption of *mens rea* can only be displaced if this is clearly or by necessary implication the effect of the statute. As the wording of the statute usually leaves the matter open, what is important is the statutory context of the provision in question.

### Pharmaceutical Society of Great Britain v Storkwain Ltd (1986) 83 Cr.App.R359 (House of Lords)

The appellants, retail chemists, supplied prescription-only drugs in accordance with a forged prescription. They were charged with an offence contrary to section 58(2)(a) of the Medicines Act 1968 which provides that "no person shall sell by retail, or supply in circumstances corresponding to retail sale, a medical product of a description, or falling within a class, specified in an order under this section except in accordance with a prescription by an appropriate practitioner. ..." It had to be determined whether this was an offence of strict liability.

---

[98] (1981) 47 Cr.App.R.143.

Lord Goff of Chieveley:

"It is, in my opinion, clear from the Act of 1968 that Parliament must have intended that thr presumption of *mens rea* should be inapplicable to s.58(2)(a). First of all, it appears from the Act of 1968 that, where Parliament wished to recognize that *mens rea* should be an ingredient of an offence created by the Act, it has expressly so provided. Thus, taking first of all offences created under provisions of Part II of the Act of 1968, express requirements of *mens rea* are to be found in both s.45(2) and in s.46(1), (2) and (3) of the Act. More particularly, in relation to offences created in Part III and Parts V and VI of the Act of 1968, section 121 makes detailed provision for a requirement of *mens rea* in respect of certain specified sections of the Act, including ss.63 to 65 (which are contained in Part III), but significantly not s.58. ... It is very difficult to avoid the conclusion that, by omitting s.58 from those sections to which s.121 is expressly made applicable, Parliament intended that there should be no implication of a requirement of mens rea in s.58(2)(a)."[99]

## (3) *Effectiveness in promoting the objectives of the statute*

## Lim Chin Aik v The Queen [1963] A.C. 160 (Privy Council)

The defendant was convicted of contravening an immigration ordinance by remaining in Singapore after he had been declared a prohibited immigrant. There was no evidence that the prohibition order had been brought to his attention or that any effort had been made to do so. He appealed.

Lord Evershed:

"But it is not enough in their Lordships' opinion merely to label the statute as one dealing with a grave social evil and from that to infer that strict liability was intended. It is pertinent also to inquire whether putting the defendant under strict liability will assist in the enforcement of the regulations. That means there must be something he can do, directly or indirectly, by supervision or inspection, by improvement of his business methods or by exhorting those whom he may be expected to influence or control, which will promote the observance of the regulations. Unless this is so, there is no reason in penalising him, and it cannot be inferred that the legislature imposed strict liability merely in order to find a luckless victim. ... Their Lordships prefer ... [this] to the alternative view that strict liability follows simply from the nature of the subject matter and that persons whose conduct is beyond any sort of criticism can be dealt with by the imposition of a nominal penalty. ...[1]

Where it can be shown that the imposition of strict liability would result in the prosecution and conviction of a class of persons whose conduct could not in any way affect the observance of the law, their Lordships consider that, even where the statute is dealing with a grave social evil, strict liability is not likely to be intended. ... The subject-matter, the control of immigration, is not one in which the presumption of strict liability has generally been made. Nevertheless, if the courts of Singapore were of the view that unrestricted immigration is a social evil which it is the object of the Ordinance to control most rigorously, their Lordships would hesitate to disagree. That is a matter peculiarly within the cognisance of the local courts. But [counsel for the respondent] was unable to point to anything that the appellant could possibly have done so as to ensure that he complied with the regulations. It was not, for example, suggested that it would be practicable for him to make continuous inquiry to see whether an order had been made against him. Clearly one of the objects of the

---

[99] See also *Sherras v De Rutzen* [1895] 1 Q.B. 918, *Neville v Mavroghenis* [1984] Crim.L.R.42 and *Bradish* [1990] Crim.L.R.723.

[1] As happened in the case of *Hussain* (*above*, n.98) where the defendant was only fined £100.

Ordinance is the expulsion of prohibited persons from Singapore, but there is nothing that a man can do about it if, before the commission of the offence, there is no practical or sensible way in which he can ascertain whether he is a prohibited person or not."

**Appeal allowed**

## 3. Defences to strict liability

### (1) *General defences*

A crime of strict liability is one where *mens rea* is not required in relation to one or more elements of the *actus reus*. Liability is thus strict and not absolute, although courts often misleadingly use this latter term. The importance of this point is only fully realised when one comes to consider what, if any, defences are available to a defendant charged with a strict liability offence. If the offence were "absolute" then no defences would save the defendant from the consequences of his actions. But, given that this is not the case, one has to consider whether the defendant may plead, for example, duress or self-defence or even automatism in answer to a charge. What would be the position if a dangerous dog was properly secured inside premises but let loose by a burglar? *Prima facie* the owner of the dog would be liable under section 3(1) of the Dangerous Dogs Act 1991 as this is a strict liability offence.[2] But in such circumstances there is surely a strong case that the defendant should be afforded a defence of involuntariness.

One approach would be to make the availability of a defence depend upon the nature of the defence being raised. As we shall see, it is possible to distinguish between defences that are justificatory in nature (resulting in a determination that there was no wrongful act at all) and those that are excusatory (relieving the defendant from blame whilst acknowledging the wrongfulness of the conduct). In relation to strict liability offences, it would be logical to allow the defendant to plead defences that are justifications for conduct (such as self-defence) but to deny defences that are excuses (because the defendant is really claiming absence of blame, which is not in any event required). If this argument were adopted, the excusatory defences of insanity, infancy, intoxication, duress and automatism would be denied to the defendant. An approach consistent with this view was adopted in *D.P.P. v H*[3] where it was held that insanity could only be a defence to crimes requiring *mens rea* and, accordingly, was not a defence to the strict liability offence of driving with excess alcohol.

The above argument, however, presupposes that the distinction between justificatory and excusatory defences is clear which, as will be seen, is not always the case. Further, if the underlying rationale of strict liability is the promotion of higher standards of care, this seems unlikely to be served by the punishment of, say, infants, the insane or others whose actions were involuntary. In *Hill v Baxter*[4] automatism was successfully pleaded to a charge of dangerous driving. If

---

[2] *Bezzina* (1994) 99 Cr.App.R.356. In this case the court was invited to consider this problem but declined to do so as the issue was not raised on the facts before it.
[3] *The Times*, May 2, 1997.
[4] [1958] 1 Q.B. 277.

non-insane automatism can be a defence here, so too should insane automatism. After all, the essence of an automatism defence is a denial of the "voluntary act" requirement, which is an essential element of the *actus reus*, and not merely a denial of *mens rea*. Going even further, in *Martin*[5] it was held that duress of circumstances (classically regarded as an excuse) was a defence to the strict liability offence of driving while disqualified. As we shall see, whether strict liability offences are *ever* justifiable is a controversial matter. Recognising that *all* established defences are available to such offences would go a long way towards "sweetening the bitter pill" of their (perhaps necessary) existence.

### (2) *Due diligence defences*

In addition to any general defences that may be available, there is the growing possibility that the offence may contain within it a specific defence. This will be based upon showing an absence of fault; these are often called "due diligence" defences. An example of such a defence is to be found in the Food Safety Act 1990. This Act creates a number of offences relating to the preparation and sale of food. Section 14, for example, creates an offence of selling food which is not of the nature or substance or quality demanded. Section 21 creates a due diligence defence.

### Food Safety Act 1990, section 21

"(1) In any proceedings for an offence under any of the preceding provisions of this Part (in this section referred to as 'the relevant provision'), it shall ... be a defence for the person charged to prove that he took all reasonable precautions and exercised all due diligence to avoid the commission of the offence by himself or by a person under his control.
　(2) Without prejudice to the generality of subsection (1) above, a person charged with an offence under section 8, 14 or 15 above who neither—
　(a) prepared the food in respect of which the offence is alleged to have been committed; nor
　(b) imported it into Great Britain,
　　　shall be taken to have established the defence provided by that subsection if he satisfies the requirements of subsection (3) or (4) below.
　(3) A person satisfies the requirements of this subsection if he proves—
　(a) that the commission of the offence was due to an act or default of another person who was not under his control, or to reliance on information supplied by such a person;
　(b) that he carried out all such checks of the food in question as were reasonable in all the circumstances, or that it was reasonable in all the circumstances for him to rely on checks carried out by the person who supplied the food to him; and
　(c) that he did not know and had no reason to suspect at the time of the commission of the alleged offence that his act or omission would amount to an offence under the relevant provision.
　(4) A person satisfies the requirements of this subsection if he proves—
　(a) that the commission of the offence was due to an act or default of another person who was not under his control, or to reliance on information supplied by such a person;
　(b) that the sale or intended sale of which the alleged offence consisted was not a sale or intended sale under his name or mark; and

[5] [1989] 1 All E.R. 652.

(c) that he did not know, and could not reasonably have been expected to know, at the time of the commission of the alleged offence that his act or omission would amount to an offence under the relevant provision."

## Colin Howard, "Strict Responsibility in the High Court of Australia" (1960) 76 L.Q.R. 547 at 547–548:

"A court faced with the task of deciding into which class a new minor statutory offence falls, may find itself in a difficulty. If it decides that the offence requires full *mens rea*, it may put an impossible burden upon P and thereby virtually nullify the legislation. But if it decides that P need prove no mental element at all, it runs the risk of penalising innocent and guilty alike, to the detriment of justice and respect for the law. Yet this difficulty is often illusory. 'There is a half-way house between *mens rea* and strict responsibility which has not yet been properly utilised and that is responsibility for negligence.' (Williams, *Criminal Law: The General Part* (1953), p. 21). The object of most of those offences for which one is now strictly responsible is to impose a high standard of care. Nothing is to be gained by convicting D if he proves that he took reasonable care, or, if this be desired, all possible care. To impose strict responsibility in such circumstances is to punish a useful member of society for a consequence which he has done his utmost to avoid, which is a pointless exercise. If the danger to society from any error at all is so great, then the activity itself should be prohibited; yet no one seriously suggests that the sale of milk should be abolished. If in the cases where strict responsibility is now the rule, responsibility for negligence had been imposed instead, there would have been nothing to prevent the standard of care being set very high, if the court thought this desirable in the public interest; and if the burden upon P were still too great, D could have been required to prove any ground of exculpation on the balance of probability."

## L. H. Leigh, Strict and Vicarious Liability (1983), pp. 79, 115:

"In respect of many activities, particularly in relation to public health and consumer safety and standards such [due-diligence] defences do exist. They tend to follow roughly standardised forms, are particular in their address, and enable persons and companies who show that they have complied with their exacting requirements to avoid conviction. Generally speaking, the courts have applied them strictly but sensibly, certain exceptions apart. Much, therefore, of the debate concerning the supposed rigour of the law and the absence of any recognition of a fault principle is beside the point. To a marked extent Parliament has supplied the omission of the courts.... [Such defences] coupled with a wide measure of discretion on the part of enforcement authorities, do much to minimise injustice in the operation of the law. Plainly, they do not cover the whole ground. If we have not as yet avoided subjecting the 'blameless harmdoer' to the risk of criminal conviction, we have at least gone a long way towards reconciling his interest in individual justice with the need to protect the public against a variety of evils associated primarily with carrying on particular trades and industries."

## Deborah L. Parry, "Judicial Approaches to Due Diligence" [1995] Crim.L.R.695 at 701–702:

"[The author examined a series of cases dealing with the due diligence defence provided by section 39 of the Consumer Protection Act 1987 and concluded that while a flexible attitude was apparent in pricing cases, a very demanding standard was required for safety-related offences.]

[W]hilst at the trial a due diligence defence may succeed in a safety-related matter, in none of the appeal cases has it been established ... [This causes] concern as strict liability offences may be appearing more like absolute offences ...

If ... it is felt by businesses that no one can ever 'win', there is a risk of the offences being viewed as unavoidable and of removing any stigma from convictions if it is known that even 'careful' defendants are convicted. It could certainly encourage many to opt for a plea of guilty plus mitigation, rather than expend time and money on establishing a defence."

Placing the burden on the defendant to establish due diligence does, however, present problems. In *Woolmington v D.P.P.*[6] the House of Lords declared that it was for the prosecution to establish the guilt of the defendant. It was not the responsibility of the defendant to establish his or her innocence. Article 6(2) of the European Convention Human on Rights provides that "everyone charged with a criminal offence shall be presumed innocent until proven guilty according to law". In *Kebilene*[7] a majority of the House of Lords indicated that a reverse burden of proof would not contravene article 6(2) as it merely placed an evidential burden on the defendant as opposed to a probative or legal burden. A legal or probative burden on the defendant requires him or her to prove on a balance of probabilities that, in this context, he or she has exercised due diligence or reasonable care. An evidential burden merely requires the defendant to raise sufficient evidence to show that the defence could apply but the burden remains on the prosecution to establish beyond reasonable doubt that the defence does not apply.

This approach was followed in *Lambert*.[8] The defendant was charged with possession of a controlled drug with intent to supply, contrary to section 5(3) of the Misuse of Drugs Act 1971 but raised the due diligence defence available in sections 28(2) and (3) that he did not know or suspect that he was possessing controlled drugs. The House of Lords declared, *obiter*, that placing a legal burden on the defendant would be incompatible with Article 6(2) as being a disproportionate measure for such a serious offence. However, the majority stated that sections 28(2) and (3) should be "read down" so that only an evidential burden was placed on the defendant and this would not be incompatible with the presumption of innocence established in Article 6(2).[9]

This "reading down" approach was not adopted in *L v D.P.P.*[10] where the defendant was charged with possession of a lock-knife contrary to section 139 of the Criminal Justice Act 1988 and claimed a due diligence defence under section 139(4) that he had good reason or lawful authority for having the article with him in a public place. It was held that this reverse burden of legal proof was not incompatible with Article 6(2) because it was a justifiable and proportionate response for a "democratically elected legislature" to seek "to deter the carrying of bladed or sharply pointed articles in public to the extent of placing the burden of proving a good reason on the carrier". Similarly, in *Drummond*[11] it was held that

---

[6] [1935] A.C. 462.
[7] [1999] 3 W.L.R. 972.
[8] [2001] 2 Cr.App.R.511.
[9] A similar approach was adopted in *Carass* [2002] 2 Cr.App.R.4 and in *Sheldrake* [2003] 2 All E.R. 497.
[10] [2002] 1 Cr.App.R.420.
[11] [2002] Crim.L.R.666.

not all persuasive burdens of proof need be "read down". It was necessary to determine whether Parliament intended to impose a persuasive burden and whether such a burden was justifiable and whether the interference with the presumption of innocence was no greater than necessary. In *Carass*[12] it was held that the onus on those seeking to establish that a legal or persuasive burden is necessary is "a high one".

The result of this approach is inevitable uncertainty. It is difficult to see why "a strong public interest in bladed articles not being carried in public" makes a due diligence defence a proportionate response while a similar defence to possession of drugs is a disproportionate response. Since the coming into force of the Human Rights Act 1998 the English courts have considered the status of a few strict liability offences and have held that they are not, *per se*, incompatible with the European Convention.[13] If such (admittedly lesser) offences without due diligence defences represent a proportionate response to a problem, it would be odd to hold that affording a due diligence defence with a reverse burden of legal proof (admittedly for more serious offences) could be incompatible with the ECHR. We shall shortly examine the many objections to offences of strict liability. As a response to these problems, courts in some Commonwealth countries, such as Canada, have declared that all strict liability offences should presumptively be construed as incorporating due diligence defences. It would be a sad irony if human rights concerns, as expressed in *Lambert*, were to lead to a foreclosure of this option.

## 4. Are strict liability offences justifiable?

In considering possible justifications for the imposition of strict liability, the general purposes of punishment need to be re-examined.

### Herbert L. Packer, "Mens Rea and the Supreme Court" (1962) Sup.Ct.Rev. 107 at 109:

"To punish conduct without reference to the actor's state of mind is both inefficacious and unjust. It is inefficacious because conduct unaccompanied by an awareness of the factors making it criminal does not mark the actor as one who needs to be subjected to punishment in order to deter him or others from behaving similarily in the future, nor does it single him out as a socially dangerous individual who needs to be incapacitated or reformed. It is unjust because the actor is subjected to the stigma of a criminal conviction without being morally blameworthy."

This attack by Packer requires careful consideration; two major questions are involved:
   (i)  can strict liability be justified on deterrent or other utilitarian grounds?
   (ii)  is it a morally justifiable doctrine?

---

[12] [2002] 2 Cr.App.R.4.
[13] *Muhamad* [2003] 2 W.L.R. 1050. See also *Kearns* [2003] 1 Cr.App.R.7.

(i) *The utilitarian arguments*

(a) In favour of strict liability, it is claimed that the interests of the public require that the highest possible standards of care be exercised by people engaged in certain forms of conduct.[14] This, in utilitarian terms, is the greater good to be achieved by occasionally convicting someone who may have taken all reasonable care to abide by the law; this greater good could not be achieved to the same extent, if, for example, the defence of reasonable mistake were available.

### United States v Dotterweich, 320 US (1943) 277 at 284–285 (Supreme Court of the United States)

Dotterweich, the president of a pharmaceutical company, was convicted of introducing into interstate commerce drugs that were misbranded. Despite his lack of knowledge of this, his conviction was upheld on appeal.

Frankfurter J.:

"The Food and Drugs Act of 1906 was an exertion by Congress of its power to keep impure and adulterated food and drugs out of the channels of commerce. By the Act of 1938, Congress extended the range of its control over illicit and noxious articles and stiffened the penalties for disobedience. The purposes of this legislation thus touch phases of the lives and health of people which, in the circumstances of modern industrialism, are largely beyond self-protection. Regard for these purposes should infuse construction of the legislation if it is to be treated as a working instrument of government and not merely as a collection of English words. The prosecution to which Dotterweich was subjected is based on a now familiar type of legislation whereby penalties serve as effective means of regulation. Such legislation dispenses with the conventional requirement for criminal conduct—awareness of some wrongdoing. In the interest of the larger good it puts the burden of acting at hazard upon a person otherwise innocent but standing in responsible relation to a public danger.... And so it is clear that shipments like those now in issue are 'punished by the statute if the article is misbranded (or adulterated), and that the article may be misbranded (or adulterated), without any conscious fraud at all. It was natural enough to throw this risk on shippers with regard to identity of their wares. ...' (*United States v Johnson*, 221 US 488, 497–98.)

Hardship there doubtless may be under a statute which thus penalizes the transaction though consciousness of wrongdoing be totally wanting. Balancing relative hardships, Congress has preferred to place it upon those who have at least the opportunity of informing themselves of the existence of conditions imposed for the protection of consumers before sharing in illicit commerce, rather than to throw the hazard on the innocent public who are wholly helpless."

### A. Kenny, Freewill and Responsibility (1978), p. 93:

"The application of strict liability can be justified in special cases: particularly with regard to the conduct of a business. In such a case, even a strict liability statute makes an appeal to

---

[14] Commentators vary in the range of activities they would be prepared to include; some limit it to ultra-hazardous activities, others to "trader offences". See, for example, Nemerson, "Criminal Liability without Fault: A Philosophical Perspective" (1975) 75 Col. L.R. 1517; Brady, "Strict Liability Offences: A Justification" (1972) 8 Crim.L.Bull. 217.

the practical reasoning of the citizens: in this case, when the decision is taken whether to enter the business the strictness of the liability is a cost to be weighed. Strict liability is most in place when it is brought to bear on corporations. In such cases there may not be, in advance, any individual on whom an obligation of care rests which would ground a charge of negligence for the causing of the harm which the statute wishes to prevent: the effect of the legislation may be to lead corporations to take the decision to appoint a person with the task of finding out how to prevent the harm in question."

However, opponents of strict liability have argued that there is no evidence that a higher standard of care results from the imposition of strict liability. Those engaged in activities will only do what is reasonable to prevent harm. Indeed, some have argued that strict liability may operate as a disincentive to do even this. If operators know that prosecution could flow whatever precautions they take, they may be tempted to take none whatsoever. In other words, the defendant may as well be "hanged for a sheep as for a lamb".[15] Such an attitude scarcely increases respect for the law. There may be further disutile effects: the innocent may be made to feel insecure not only in general psychological terms but to the extent that they may be deterred from entering into socially beneficial enterprises governed by strict liability.[16]

### James B. Brady, "Strict Liability Offences: A Justification" (1972) 8 Crim.L. Bulletin 217 at 224:

"There are two replies to this argument. First, there is little evidence to show that the effect of strict liability offences has been to make these socially beneficial enterprises less attractive. The second, and more important point is that a person who does not have the capacity to run (for example) a dairy in such a manner as to prevent the adulteration of milk is not to be protected on the sole ground that he is engaged in a 'socially beneficial' enterprise. An incompetent carrying on an enterprise in which there is the danger of widespread harm actually is *not* engaged in a 'socially beneficial' enterprise. There can be no objection, therefore, to his choosing not to enter the business."

(b) In addition to the arguments above, one more broadly utilitarian (in the sense that the greater good sought is based on expediency) argument may be adduced. Because of the sheer volume of criminal offences, particularly those of a regulatory nature, it is argued that it would be too time-consuming to require the prosecution to prove a mental element. There is, instead, a presumption of culpability on the part of "responsible" members of a concern that need not be proved.

### Norval Morris and Colin Howard, Studies in Criminal Law (1964), p. 199:

"[It is often alleged that there is] an administrative problem. Prosecutions are numerous: if P were required to prove a wrongful intention, in itself impossible in most regulatory offence

---

[15] Brett, *An Inquiry into Criminal Guilt* (1963), p. 8.
[16] Brandt, *Ethical Theory* (1959), p. 493. *Contra* Nemerson, *above*, n.14.

cases, the speed at which these charges can at present be dealt with would be much diminished and overwhelming arrears of work would accumulate. . . . There is no evidence of an administrative problem. Proof of absence of fault is admissible in mitigation of punishment. If such proof is admissible for one purpose, no loss of time is involved in admitting it for another. Prosecutions for regulatory offences may be numerous but so are prosecutions for many other offences, particularly the various forms of larceny. No one suggests that the pressure of work should be relieved by removing the requirement of *mens rea* from larceny. Indeed, it is arguable that, far from saving time, strict liability often wastes time by necessitating legal argument as to whether it applies to the case in hand."

### Mueller, "Mens Rea and the Law Without It" (1955) 58 W.Va.L.Rev. 34 at 37–38:

"[With regard to the claim that] the courts would be overburdened . . . It is certainly true that there is hardly any aspect of human activity which has escaped control by the law. When we eat, the (pure food and drug) law eats with us; when we walk, the (traffic) law walks with us; and even the health and soundness of our sleep is regulated by law. To litigate every one of the regulated problems of daily life would surely hamper the administration of justice. But what good will it to do punish indiscriminately, regardless of guilt or innocence, merely to save the time it would take to determine the validity of a defense? And what of the deterrent effect of such a frustrating law? Would it not ease the burden on the court and reduce the length of the court calendar much more if, for instance, in January we would prosecute only blond culprits, in February only bald ones, in March brunettes, etc.? That would at least deter some of the culprits some of the time, whereas absolute criminal liability is totally without deterrent effect."

Supporters of the expediency argument sometimes temper their support by claiming that prosecutorial discretion will prevent the obviously blameless being charged. There are, however, great difficulties with this approach. Prosecutorial discretion is notoriously unreliable; there is no guidance as to how extreme the case must be to justify a prosecution. And, most importantly, it amounts to a negation of strict liability. To some extent at least, liability is being made to depend upon fault. We shall return to this point later.[17]

### (ii) *Is strict liability morally justifiable?*

It has already been noted that the concept of *mens rea* is deeply embedded in the development of the criminal law. For some commentators its importance is so great that it cannot be trumped by utilitarian considerations. According to this view, the criminal law should only be invoked when there is blameworthy conduct—when the defendant has done something deserving of blame. Somebody who has taken all reasonable precautions is not blameworthy and does not deserve to be punished.

This argument has been answered at two levels, both of which have been subjected to much criticism:

(a) crimes of strict liability are not crimes at all in the real sense, and
(b) the question of moral blameworthiness is a misconceived one. We ought instead to concentrate on the harm done.

---

[17] *Below*, p. 244.

## (a) Strict liability offences are not "real" crimes

In *Wings Ltd v Ellis* Lord Scarman referred to the Trade Descriptions Act 1968, which creates consumer protection offences, as being "not a truly criminal statute. Its purpose is not the enforcement of the criminal law but the maintenance of trading standards."[18]

### Peter Brett, An Inquiry into Criminal Guilt (1963), pp. 114–116:

"Let us now consider what ought to be the future of the doctrine of strict liability. There are those who believe that there is no great objection to it, and even that it serves a useful and proper social purpose. Sayre's general conclusion ('Public Welfare Offences', 33 Col. L. Rev. 55 (1933)) was that the doctrine was applicable only to the minor public welfare offences, despite his recognition of its applicability in some other fields, which he attempted to distinguish on special grounds. In his view there is no objection to applying strict liability so long as only a light penalty is involved; but it ought not to be applied to 'true crimes'. This seems rather like saying that it is all right to be unjust so long as you are not too unjust. My own position is that any doctrine which permits the infliction of punishment on a morally innocent man is reprehensible.

If my view is accepted, we are then faced with the question whether it can be implemented without imperilling the social fabric. There seems to be a strong belief that it cannot. The argument is that the regulation of public welfare has been successfully accomplished under a regime of strict liability, and that it is thus proved that 'strict liability regulation works'. This is doubtless true, but it does not take us one step further to the proposition that effective public welfare regulation will not work without strict liability. That proposition must for most countries remain empirically unverified, for the simple reason that it has never been tried out in practice.

A school of thought has sprung up in recent years which attempts to resolve the question by attaching new labels to strict liability offences. Thus it has been argued that the strict liability offences should be termed 'civil offences', and that to such offences mistake of fact should not be a defence. They would be punishable only by a fine, and not by any form of imprisonment.[19] The *Model Penal Code* appears to accept this basic position save that it proposes to treat the strict liability offences as still being criminal in nature, but classes them as violations: as such the punishment which may be imposed when they are committed without fault is strictly limited, and the determination whether to class an offence as a violation is left to the legislature.

The difficulty which I have with proposals of this kind is that their proponents seem to regard the injustice of punishing innocent conduct as a matter which may be disregarded if it takes place under a different label. My own view is that the injustice remains unaffected despite the semantic change. A fine continues to be a punishment whether it is labelled civil or criminal. I do not deny that the change of label may accomplish a removal of part, if not the whole, of the stigma which results from the mere fact of conviction for a crime; nor would I wish to diminish the importance of such a step. But when this step has been taken, there still remains the brute fact that a man is being *punished* for innocent behaviour. I cannot reconcile this with any theory of justice with which I am acquainted."

The distinction drawn between "real" and "regulatory" crimes (sometimes known as crimes *mala in se* and *mala prohibita*), although one employed by many

---

[18] [1984] 3 All E.R. 577 at 587.
[19] This view is, of course, relevant also to the deterrent argument. Some commentators have argued (*e.g.* Brady and Nemerson, *above*, n.14) that higher penalties might increase the deterrent effect.

judges, is open to further criticism. Leigh has pointed out that regulatory crimes may cause as much, if not more, harm than real crimes. "Murder can, no doubt, be contrasted with illegal parking, but is it clear that theft necessarily poses a graver violation of a basic rule than does the pollution of a beach in a resort which depends upon its summer trade for prosperity? ... Is assault necessarily worse than reckless driving?"[20] Baroness Wootton also entered into the debate by asserting that the distinction being drawn between crimes *mala in se* and *mala prohobita* does not rest on any inherent characteristics of the former category other than the antiquity of such crimes.[21] The complexities of this debate are increased by the argument that imposing strict liability for regulatory offences "marginalises" such offences; nobody, least of all the perpetrator, has to take them seriously because, after all, they are not *really* criminal.

### (b) The justifiability of strict liability on the basis of harm done

### R. v Lemon [1979] A.C. 617 (House of Lords)

A magazine aimed at homosexual readers, Gay News, published a poem and accompanying drawings describing and depicting in detail various acts of sodomy and fellatio upon the crucified body of Christ. A prosecution for blasphemous libel was brought. The editor, Lemon, claimed *inter alia*, that while he had knowingly published the poem and drawings, he had no *mens rea* as to its blasphemous nature.

Lord Russell:
"Why then should this House, faced with a deliberate publication of that which a jury with every justification has held to be a blasphemous libel, consider that it should be for the prosecution to prove, presumably beyond reasonable doubt, that the accused recognised and intended it to be such or regarded it as immaterial whether it was? I see no ground for that. It does not to my mind make sense: and I consider that sense should retain a function in our criminal law. The reason why the law considers that the publication of a blasphemous libel is an offence is that the law considers that such publications should not take place. And if it takes place, and the publication is deliberate, I see no justification for holding that there is no offence when the publisher is incapable for some reason particular to himself of agreeing with a jury on the true nature of the publication."[22]

**Appeal dismissed**

Some commentators have gone further than this and have argued for an increase in strict liability crimes. Baroness Wootton believed that punishment should be based on harm done rather than on some perceived wickedness involved in certain states of mind.[23]

### Baroness Wootton, Crime and the Criminal Law (2nd ed., 1981), pp. 43, 46–48:

"[The] alternative theory [is] that the wickedness of an action is inherent not in the action itself, but in the state of mind of the person who performs it. To punish people merely for

---

[20] Leigh, *Strict and Vicarious Liability* (1982), p. 104.

[21] *Crime and the Criminal Law* (2nd ed., 1981), pp. 42–44.

[22] See also *Gibson* [1991] 1 All E.R. 439 where the Court of Appeal held it was no defence to a charge of outraging public decency to claim that the defendant did not consider the act of exhibiting freeze-dried human foetuses as earrings would cause such outrage.

[23] This would avoid what Baroness Wootton believed to be an impossible search; a person's responsibility (in the sense of capacity to conform to the law's requirements) cannot be ascertained by any rational means.

what they have done, it is argued, would be unjust, for the forbidden act might have been an accident, for which the person who did it cannot be held to blame. Hence the requirement to which traditionally the law attaches so much importance, that a crime is not, so to speak, a crime in the absence of *mens rea*. ...

[Baroness Wootton continues by claiming that the attack on strict liability by most commentators is based upon this premise: that those with *mens rea* are the wicked who deserve punishment. The function of the criminal law is, therefore, punitive.]

If, however, the primary function of the courts is conceived as the prevention of forbidden acts, there is little cause to be disturbed by the multiplication of offences of strict liability. If the law says that certain things are not to be done, it is illogical to confine this prohibition to occasions on which they are done from malice aforethought; for at least the material consequences of an action, and the reasons for prohibiting it, are the same whether it is the result of sinister malicious plotting, of negligence or of sheer accident. A man is equally dead and his relatives equally bereaved whether he was stabbed or run over by a drunken motorist or by an incompetent one; and the inconvenience caused by the loss of your bicycle is unaffected by the question whether or not the youth who removed it had the intention of putting it back, if in fact he had not done so at the time of his arrest. It is true, of course, as Professor Hart has argued, that the material consequences of an action by no means exhaust its effects. 'If one person hits another, the person struck does not think of the other as *just* a cause of pain to him. ... If the blow was light but deliberate, it has a significance for the person struck quite different from an accidental much heavier blow.' To ignore this difference, he argues, is to outrage 'distinctions which not only underlie morality but pervade the whole of our social life.' That these distinctions are widely appreciated and keenly felt no one would deny. Often perhaps they derive their force from a purely punitive or retributive attitude; but alternatively they may be held to be relevant to an assessment of the social damage that results from a criminal act. Just as a heavy blow does more damage than a light one, so also perhaps does a blow which involves psychological injury do more damage than one in which the hurt is purely physical.

The conclusion to which this argument leads is, I think, not that the presence or absence of the guilty mind is unimportant, but that *mens rea* has, so to speak—and this is the crux of the matter—*got into the wrong place*. Traditionally, the requirement of the guilty mind is written into the actual definition of a crime. No guilty intention, no crime, is the rule. Obviously this makes sense if the law's concern is with wickedness: where there is no guilty intention, there can be no wickedness. But it is equally obvious, on the other hand, that an action does not become innocuous merely because whoever performed it meant no harm. If the object of the criminal law is to prevent the occurrence of socially damaging actions, it would be absurd to turn a blind eye to those which were due to carelessness, negligence or even accident. The question of motivation is *in the first instance* irrelevant.

But only in the first instance. At a later stage, that is to say, after what is now known as a conviction, the presence or absence of guilty intention is all-important for its effect on the appropriate measures to be taken to prevent a recurrence of the forbidden act. The prevention of accidental deaths presents different problems from those involved in the prevention of wilful murders. The result of the actions of the careless, the mistaken, the wicked and the merely unfortunate may be indistinguishable from one another, but each case calls for a different treatment. Tradition, however, is very strong, and the notion that these differences are relevant only after the fact has been established that the accused committed the forbidden act seems still to be deeply abhorrent to the legal mind."

Hart has taken issue with these claims by putting forward what has become the classic justification of the doctrine of *mens rea*.[24] He clearly believed in man's ability to determine his own actions and rested his defence of *mens rea* upon that belief. His view was that even if one accepts man as "responsible", it does not mean that the notion of "wickedness" need automatically be accepted as well, nor that one,

[24] *Punishment and Responsibility* (1968), Chapter 3.

therefore, punishes retributively on the basis of it. Instead, as we have seen, the value of punishment rests on the "simple idea that unless a man has the capacity and a fair opportunity or chance to adjust his behaviour to the law its penalties ought not to be applied to him".[25] By punishing when there is some mental element one acknowledges a person's capacity and has given him the chance not to overstep the legal boundaries of action. It gives man the maximum power to determine his own future. The person who has exercised self-restraint and who has made the right choices is not made to suffer for mistakes or accidents.

Hart then adds a more general justification:

### H. L. A. Hart, Punishment and Responsibility (1968), p. 183:

"If you strike me, the judgment that the blow was deliberate will elicit fear, indignation, anger, resentment: these are not voluntary responses; but the same judgment will enter into deliberations about my future voluntary conduct towards you and will colour all my social relations with you. Shall I be your friend or enemy? Offer soothing words? Or return the blow? All this will be different if the blow is not voluntary. This is how human nature in society actually is and as yet we have no power to alter it. The bearing of this fundamental fact on the law is this. If as our legal moralists maintain it is important for the law to reflect common judgments of morality, it is surely even more important that it should in general reflect in its judgments on human conduct distinctions which not only underlie morality, but pervade the whole of our social life. This it would fail to do if it treated men merely as alterable, predictable, curable or manipulative things."

### 5. Strict liability and the European Convention on Human Rights

It has already been seen that in certain circumstances strict liability offences with reverse burdens of proof could be incompatible with Article 6(2) of the European Convention. There is, however, a further argument that some strict liability offences could, in dispensing with any fault element, contravene not only Article 6 but also Article 7 of the Convention. This approach has not been adopted by the English courts.

### Muhamad v R. [2003] 2 W.L.R. 1050 (Court of Appeal, Criminal Division)

The appellant was convicted of materially contributing to the extent of his insolvency by gambling, contrary to section 362(1)(a) of the Insolvency Act 1986.

Dyson L.J.:
"[It is argued that Article 7] requires the criminal law to be sufficiently accessible and precise to enable an individual to know in advance whether his conduct is criminal ... No gambler can necessarily know, when he places his bet, whether he runs a real risk of prosecution if he loses. The only way to avoid running this risk is not to gamble at all, or to gamble for low stakes. Without *mens rea* the offence is objectionably uncertain. Furthermore, a construction of strict liability is neither necessary in a democratic society, nor proportional to any legitimate aim ...

[T]he narrow question that arises is whether the fact that the offence is one of strict liability is disproportionate so as to render it in breach of Article 7. We accept that a strict liability offence is easier to prove than one requiring a mental element, and that, if section 362(1)(a) is interpreted as creating an offence of strict liability, it may deter persons from gambling who, if the offence required a mental element, might not be so deterred. We do not consider that either of these consequences indicates that it is disproportionate to hold that

---

[25] *ibid.*, p. 181.

the section creates an offence of strict liability ... [I]f strict liability does have a chilling effect on gambling, we are not convinced that the imposition of strict liability is a disproportionate response to the need, in the public interest, to deter persons from gambling in such a way as to cause loss to their creditors.

We should add that, so far as concerns the ECHR, there is nothing objectionable in principle with strict liability offences. In *Salabiaku v France* 13 EHRR 379, at paragraph 27 the EctHR said:

'27. As the Government and the Commission have pointed out, in principle the Contracting States remain free to apply the criminal law to an act where it is not carried out in the normal exercise of one of the rights protected under the Convention and, accordingly, to define the constituent elements of the resulting offence. In particular, and again in principle, the Contracting States may, under certain conditions, penalise a simple or objective fact as such, irrespective of whether it results from criminal intent or from negligence. Examples of such offences may be found in the laws of the Contracting States.'

In our judgment, therefore, there is nothing in the ECHR and in particular in Article 7 which requires us to reach a different conclusion from that which we expressed earlier on the basis of an application of domestic law principles. Upon its true construction, section 362(1)(a) creates an offence of strict liability."

So, strict liability offences are "under certain conditions" not incompatible with the European Convention.[26] It remains to be seen under what conditions, if any, they could be held incompatible.

### 6. Enforcement

One of the classic arguments against strict liability is that it results in the prosecution and conviction of people who were not at fault and who might even have done everything they possibly could to avoid bringing about the harm. However, empirical studies of the enforcement of many strict liability offences do not always support this conclusion.

The case of *Storwain*[27] provides an intersting case study. In this case the defendants were found guilty of the strict liability offence of supplying prescription-only drugs without a valid prescription; it had been forged. At first sight it seems that the defendants could not be blamed for what had happened. How, in a busy chemist, could checks be made as to the validity of every prescription? Yet closer examination of the case reveals that the Pharmaceutical Society (the regulatory body) which wanted to confirm the principle of strict liability, actually believed the pharmacist's conduct fell short of normal good practice. The prescription was a blatant forgery and another was also questionable. Moreover, because the prescription was for controlled drugs it was expected that the pharmacist would telephone for confirmation. He did so, but, rather than checking in the directory, rang the number given on the prescription. Not surprisingly, the forgery was confirmed by an accomplice at the end of the phone. In conclusion then, the pharmacist was prosecuted because he was at fault; even a due diligence defence, had one existed, would not have saved him.[28]

Empirical studies of many strict liability offences also point to highly selective enforcement practices amongst different enforcement agencies. In an annual report the Health and Safety Executive has stated:

---

[26] See also *Kearns* [2003] 1 Cr.App.R.7.
[27] (1986) 83 Cr.App.R.359.
[28] See Jackson, "Storkwein: A Case Study in Strict Liability and Self-Regulation" [1991] Crim.L.R.892.

"It is not our policy to prosecute for every breach of health and safety legislation which comes to our knowledge. This would be neither practicable nor productive. The policy of the Executive is to prosecute where employers or others concerned appear deliberately to have flouted the provisions of the legislation; where they have been reckless in exposing people to hazards, or where there is a record of repeated infringements of the legislation. Each case must be looked at on its merits but we are naturally concerned where death or serious injury has resulted from failure to comply."[29]

Fault appears to play a leading role, therefore, in the decision to prosecute (although the magnitude of the harm is also significant) as far as this regulatory body is concerned. Compliance is more normally secured by means of co-operation rather than coercion and the self-image of the inspectors is that of educators and advisers rather than as police. Advice, repeat visits, warnings, improvement notices and the like are all much more likely to be used to secure compliance. For example, in 2001/02 the Health and Safety Executive commenced 1,930 prosecutions yet, in contrast, issued 11,162 enforcement notices (improvement notices, immediate prohibition notices and deferred prohibition notices).[30] The emphasis is on administrative procedures with the criminal law being a remedy of last resort. A similar picture emerges from Carson's study of the Factory inspectorate.[31]

Other regulatory bodies may have a rather different self-image which will play a significant part in shaping prosecution policies. The Inland Revenue, Customs and Excise and the DSS (as far as national insurance contributions are concerned) see their role as revenue collectors[32] and will try to secure a negotiated settlement in preference to prosecution. This does not mean, however, that such regulatory bodies would be happy to see *mens rea* incorporated into the substantive offences.

### Genevra Richardson, "Strict Liability for Regulatory Crime: The Empirical Research" [1987] Crim.L.R.295 at 303:

"[T]he existing research also indicates that despite their effective rejection of strict liability in practice the majority of enforcement officers regard it with favour and urge its retention. Although prosecution and its direct threat are seldom used, routine enforcement is conducted against a background of the criminal law and the implicit threat of its invocation. The fewer the uncertainties which attach to the law, therefore, the stronger is the agencies' bargaining position."[33]

Not all agencies operate in the same way, however. As far as supplementary benefit payments are concerned, the DSS appears to be much more willing to prosecute.[34]

---

[29] *Annual Report of the Health and Safety Executive 1976*, cited in Rowan-Robinson, Watchman and Barker, *Crime and Regulation* (1990), p. 212. See also Paulus, *The Search for Pure Food: A Sociology of Legislation in Britain* (1974).

[30] Health and Safety Commission, *Annual Report 2001/02* (2002), p. 75.

[31] Carson, "White-Collar Crime and the Enforcement of Factory Legislation" (1970) 10 Brit. J. Criminol. 383.

[32] *Above*, n.29, pp. 207–210.

[33] See also Nelken's study of landlords and harrassment: *The Limits of the Legal Process* (1983).

[34] Cook, *Rich Law, Poor Law: Different Responses To Tax and Supplementary Benefit Fraud* (1989). There appears also to be some disparity in levels of punishment.

This policy, which appears to have been initiated by senior staff within the DSS, has resulted in a number of initiatives against such fraudsters. It is rather more common, however, for enforcement policies to emerge from "the bottom up".

Such selective enforcement practices are disturbing in a number of respects. Most importantly, those policies which result in only flagrant breaches being prosecuted help to perpetuate in the mind of offenders and society the view that such activities are not really criminal despite the undoubted (and sometimes very substantial) harm caused.

The discrepancy in enforcement practices between the Inland Revenue and the DSS has prompted one writer to go further: "At the heart of the contradictions in policy and practice ... is the ideological representation of the taxpayer as a 'giver' to the state and the supplementary benefit claimant as a 'taker' from the state."[35]

One final point must be made here. There are a large number of strict liability offences that fall outside the schemes discussed above and where liability tends, indeed, to be strict. Many of the summary motoring offences, such as exceeding a speed limit, driving whilst disqualified, etc., would be cases in point. In this particular context, with prosecuting policies varying considerably from one area to another, it is much harder to ascertain what role, if any, is played by fault.

## 7. Sentencing

Sentences for strict liability offences (particularly white collar crimes) are generally light. This may be because a defendant is regarded as blameless. On the other hand, there may be a number of other factors having little to do with blame or the amount of harm caused that influence such sentencing practices. The fact that the defendant has lost his job or business may be seen as punishment enough. The level of fine may be affected by the sentencer's perception of the defendant's ability to pay.[36] The defendant's previous good character may be persuasive but likely to figure is, once again, the judgment that such offences are not really criminal. The result is that the fines imposed may be no more than "pin-pricks" to an organisation which may be able to write them off as a minor business expense.[37]

A further concern is the lack of uniformity in sentencing practice. Within an area of activity (for example, pollution) sentences can be erratic.[38] This problem is exacerbated when sentences from different areas of activity are compared. Research has suggested, for example, that those engaged in supplementary benefits fraud are likely to be regarded less sympathetically than those engaged in tax evasion.[39]

## 8. Conclusion

Despite the weight of the arguments against strict liability offences it would be naïve to imagine that they can all be transformed into offences requiring full *mens*

---

[35] *ibid.*, p. 160.
[36] Padfield, "Clean Water and Muddy Causation: Is Causation a Question of Law or Fact, or Just a Way of Allocating Blame?" [1995] Crim.L.R.683 at 693.
[37] Croall, *White Collar Crime* (1992), pp. 112–125.
[38] Padfield, *above* n.36.
[39] Cook, *Rich Law, Poor Law, above.*, n.34.

*rea* or that they could all be decriminalised. It seems clear that strict liability for the most minor of offences is a necessity. However, for the rest a number of possibilities exist.

First, it is open to the courts to extend the presumption in favour of *mens rea*.[40] One important enhancement, copied from Canada, would be to state that if the penalty for the offence involves imprisonment, then strict liability is precluded.[41]

Secondly, again following the lead set elsewhere,[42] existing offences of strict liability could be converted into what would amount to offences of negligence by the general, rather than selective, use of due diligence defences.

This would not have the effect of making the prosecutor's task too difficult because the onus would be on the defendant to show that he was not negligent. However, as seen, it is possible that such a general shifting of the burden of proof could be incompatible with the ECHR.

Thirdly, increased use could be made of administrative procedures to secure compliance. Whether actual decriminalisation is the appropriate way forward, is, however, a moot point. As we have seen, those enforcement agencies already involved in such procedures rely upon the stick of the criminal sanction as their last resort. It might be, however, that the threat of, for example, closure of a business, might be as potent a weapon. In any event, using the criteria discussed in chapter one it would have to be decided that these offences were better dealt with outside the criminal law and that the loss of procedural safeguards thereby occasioned was not likely to lead to administrative malpractice.

Finally, given the widely disparate enforcement and sentencing practices, the time might be ripe to consider differentiating between individual and corporate responsibility in this context. Many, if not most, strict liability offences govern the operations not of individuals but of businesses. Those who argue against strict liability on the basis of individual responsibility might be prepared to support its use for corporations, especially if due diligence defences were also available.

In any event, this is an area of the law where growth has been rapid, unstructured and almost unchecked. What is needed is a reappraisal of strict liability offences and their future role at the legislative level. It has been left to the courts to make what best they can out of the mass of modern legislation for far too long.

## VII. Corporate Criminal Liability

### A. *Introduction*

The criminal law has developed as a mechanism for responding to individual wrongdoing. Individuals are regarded as autonomous. They are free to control

---

[40] Under the Draft Criminal Code, clause 20, there is a presumption in favour of *mens rea* "unless otherwise provided".

[41] See [1987] Crim.L.R.721 at 721–723.

[42] *e.g.*, see the American Law Institute, Model Penal Code, Tent. Draft No. 4, 1985, s.2.05 and comment at p. 140. In Australia, statutes that in other jurisdictions have been held to impose strict liability are held by the High Court to impose liability for negligence instead. See, for example, *Master Butchers v Laughton* [1915] S.A. L.R. 3; *Maher v Musson* (1954) 52 C.L.R. 100. To impose strict liability the legislature must expressly exclude the defence of reasonable mistake.

their actions, to think and make decisions, including the choice to do wrong. Accordingly, such persons can be held responsible for those choices and can be praised or blamed and punished for them. This individualistic notion of responsibility does not naturally encompass artificial organisations such as companies.

Much of our lives today is affected by companies: we work for them (in conditions that might be dangerous); we purchase their products (that might explode or poison us); we travel in their ferries and trains (that might be unsafe); we drink the water they provide (which might be unclean) and we breathe the air (into which they might have emitted their fumes). In short, companies can kill or injure us. But can they be held criminally responsible?

Interest in this subject has been heightened by two sets of developments. First, there has been a series of highly publicised "disasters" in which large numbers of persons have been killed. In 1988 there was the Piper Alpha oil rig explosion in which 167 people were killed. The inquiry which followed identified "unsafe practices", "grave shortcomings" and "significant flaws" in the management's approach to safety as causes of the explosion and subsequent deaths.[43] In 1987 there was the King's Cross fire in which 31 people died, the cause being the failure of the various groups and individuals within the overall corporate structure to identify their respective areas of responsibility.[44] And, most infamously, in 1987 there was the Zeebrugge "disaster" in which the ferry, *Herald of Free Enterprise*, capsized killing 192 people. The official inquiry found that "from top to bottom the body corporate was infected with the disease of sloppiness ... The failure on the part of the shore management to give proper and clear directions was a contributory cause of the disaster."[45] More recently, there have been a series of high-profile train crashes (Southall: 7 killed; Paddington: 31 killed; Hatfield: 4 killed) accompanied by mounting accusations of incompetence and complacency and poor safety management by the rail companies concerned.[46]

Secondly, there has been an increased awareness of the numbers of persons annually being killed and seriously injured in their places of work. In 2000/01, 295 people were killed at work. Over the same year, 27,303 workers sustained serious injuries and 133,112 workers suffered injuries at their workplace.[47] These deaths and injuries were the result of violent incidents: people being "crushed, electrocuted, asphyxiated, burnt, drowned, impaled and so forth".[48] These figures

---

[43] Dept. of Energy, *The Public Inquiry into the Piper Alpha Disaster* (The Cullen Report) (1990) Cm.1310, paras 11.4, 11.14, 14.52.

[44] *Investigation into the King's Cross Underground Fire* (1988) (Fennell Report).

[45] Dept. of Transport, *The Merchant Shipping Act 1894, M.V. Herald of Free Enterprise*, Report of Court No. 8074 (Sheen Report) at para. 14.1.

[46] For example, the Cullen Report on the Paddington (Ladbroke Grove) train crash accused Railtrack of complacency and "underlying deficiencies in the management of safety" (*Ladbroke Grove Rail Enquiry* (Cullen Report), 2001). Other "disasters" that have contributed to the growing clamour for corporate accountability have included the Clapham Junction rail disaster in 1988 where faulty signalling caused the death of 35 people, the Purley train crash in 1989 where 5 people were killed and there were strong claims that B.R. management shortcomings had contributed to the crash.

[47] Health and Safety Commission, *Health and Safety Statistics 2000/01* (2001).

[48] Slapper, "Corporate Manslaughter: An Examination of the Determinants of Prosecutorial Policy" [1993] SLS 423 at 427.

merely represent reported cases. It has been estimated that only 44 per cent of reportable injuries at work are in fact reported to the authorities.[49]

The vast majority of these incidents were the result of corporate fault. The Health and Safety Executive itself has publicly stated that 90 per cent of the deaths could have been prevented and that "in 70 per cent of cases positive action by management could have saved lives".[50]

## B. *The Law*

There are two ways in which a company can be criminally liable:

### 1. Vicarious liability

With many offences of strict liability and negligence a company can be vicariously liable for the acts of its employees in the course of their duties.

### National Rivers Authority v Alfred McAlpine Homes East Ltd
#### [1994] 4 All E.R. 286 (Queen's Bench Divisional Court)

The defendant company was charged with causing pollution, namely, wet cement, to enter controlled waters contrary to section 85(1) of the Water Resources Act 1991. Two employees of the company, the site agent and the site manager, accepted responsibility for the pollution. At their trial in the magistrates' court the company was acquitted on the ground that a company can only be criminally liable if the criminal acts are committed by senior persons within the company. The prosecution appealed by way of case stated.

Simon Brown L.J.:
"I for my part see *Alphacell* as an illustration of vicarious liability ... [A]n employer is liable for pollution resulting from its own operations carried out under its essential control, save only where some third party acts in such a way as to interrupt the chain of causation ... It is sufficient that those immediately responsible on site (those who in the event acknowledged what had occurred) were employees of the company and acting apparently within the course and scope of that employment."

Morland L.J.:
"The object of the relevant words of s.85(1) and the crime created thereby is the keeping of streams free from pollution for the benefit of mankind generally and the world's flora and fauna. Most significantly deleterious acts of pollution will arise out of industrial, agricultural or commercial activities ... In almost all cases the act or omission will be that of a person such as a workman, fitter or plant operative in a fairly low position in the hierarchy of the industrial, agricultural or commercial concern.

In my judgment, to make the offence an effective weapon in the defence of environmental protection, a company must by necessary implication be criminally liable for the acts or omissions of its servants or agents during activities being done for the company."

**Appeal allowed**
**Case remitted for rehearing**

The doctrine of vicarious liability is well established in English law in relation to strict liability offences dealing with matters such as pollution, food and drugs and health and safety at work.[51] It has also been applied to hybrid offences which are

---

[49] Health and Safety Commission, *Health and Safety Statistics 2000/01* (2001).
[50] Health and Safety Executive, *Blackspot Construction* (1988), p. 4.
[51] *British Steel plc* [1995] I.C.R. 586.

prima facie strict liability offences but allow a due diligence defence. However, it is clear that vicarious liability will not necessarily apply to all offences of strict liability. In *Seaboard Offshore Ltd v Secretary of State for Transport*[52] the House of Lords held that the doctrine of vicarious liability did not apply to the offence before it[53] irrespective of whether the offence was one of strict liability or not. Whether vicarious liability applies or not is a matter of statutory interpretation, taking into account the policy of the law and whether vicarious liability will assist enforcement.[54] For example, in *McAlpine* the law could only be made effective by holding the company vicariously liable. In *Seaboard* it was concluded that the statute was aimed at the safety policies of the company itself rather than the actions of menial employees. The result is that at present it is rather difficult to predict whether an offence will be held to be one to which the doctrine of vicarious liability will be applicable.

Is the doctrine of vicarious liability justifiable? The doctrine can be defended on pragmatic grounds. It is easy to apply. As long as someone (anyone) acting in the course of their employment has committed a crime the company can be held liable. It prevents companies shielding themselves from criminal liability by delegating potentially illegal operations to employees. Companies delegate powers to act, in their respective spheres, to all their employees and accordingly should be held responsible for their criminal acts. It is also argued that optimum deterrence is achieved through the imposition of vicarious liability in that companies will "know where they stand".[55] These arguments are, of course, particularly powerful when applied to strict liability offences. If no fault is required on the part of the individual committing the crime, there seems little point in requiring fault on the part of the company to be established. There are, however, strong arguments against the doctrine.

### Eric Colvin, "Corporate Personality and Criminal Liability" (1995) 6 Criminal Law Forum 1 at 8:

"Vicarious corporate liability has been criticized for being both underinclusive and overinclusive. It is underinclusive because it is activated only through the criminal liability of some individual. Where offenses require some form of fault, that fault must be present at the individual level. If it is not present at this level, there is no corporate liability regardless of the measure of corporate fault. Yet vicarious liability is also overinclusive because, if there is individual liability, corporate liability follows even in the absence of corporate fault. The general objection to vicarious liability in criminal law—that it divorces the determination of liability from an inquiry into culpability—applies to corporations as it does to other defendants. The special characteristics of corporations do not insulate them from the stigmatizing and penal consequences of a criminal conviction."

An example of the overinclusiveness of the doctrine is that a company could be liable for an offence despite having adopted clear policies and having issued express instructions to avert the wrongdoing. It hardly seems justifiable to hold a company

---

[52] [1994] 2 All E.R. 99.
[53] Merchant Shipping Act 1988, s.31: failing to take reasonable steps to ensure that a vessel is operated in a safe manner.
[54] See, for example, *Gateway Foodmarkets Ltd* [1997] 2 Cr.App.R. 40.
[55] Sullivan, "The Attribution of Culpability to Limited Companies" [1996] C.L.J. 515 at 541.

liable for the actions of a lowly employee who decides to breach company rules and commit a crime.

A possible compromise would be to make companies prima facie vicariously liable for all offences committed by employees in the course of their employment (whether a particular individual could be identified or not), but to afford a due diligence defence.

### Council of Europe, Liability of Enterprises for Offences, Recommendation No. R (88) 18 (1990), 6–7:

"1(2) The enterprise should be [criminally] liable, whether a natural person who committed the acts or omissions constituting the offence can be identified or not.
(4) The enterprise should be exonerated from liability where its management is not implicated in the offence and has taken all the necessary steps to prevent its commission."

A similar proposal would allow vicarious liability to apply to all offences, but only afford a due diligence defence to "non-regulatory offences that carry a stigma".[56]

### 2. Direct liability: the identification doctrine

When it comes to crimes involving blameworthiness the commitment to individualistic notions of responsibility meant that English criminal law was reluctant to hold companies criminally liable. However, as company law developed the fiction of corporate personality—the idea that a company was a legal 'person' that could sue and be sued in its own name—the criminal law did not take long to lift this fiction and superimpose it on its individualist conception of criminal liability. The courts started "lifting the veil" of companies to see if there was an individual who had committed the *actus reus* of a crime with the appropriate *mens rea*. This individual had to be sufficiently important in the corporate structure for his or her acts to be identified with the company itself; in such circumstances the company could be criminally liable (as well as the individual). This is known as the identification doctrine.

### Tesco Supermarkets Ltd v Nattrass [1972] A.C. 153 (House of Lords)

Tesco were prosecuted under section 11(2) of the Trade Descriptions Act 1968 for advertising outside their shop that they were selling goods for less than they were being offered for sale inside the shop. The fault for the incorrect advertisement lay with the local manager whose system of daily checks had broken down. Tesco claimed a defence under section 24 of the same Act that the "failure was due to the default of another person." The question then arose whether the local manager was "another person" or whether he was to be identified with the company.

Lord Reid:
"I must start by considering the nature of the personality which by a fiction the law attributes to a corporation. A living person has a mind which can have knowledge or intention or be negligent and he has hands to carry out his intentions. A corporation has none of these: it must act through living persons, though not always one or the same person. Then the person who acts is not speaking or acting for the company. He is acting as the

[56] Sullivan, *ibid.* at 544.

company and his mind which directs his acts is the mind of the company. There is no question of the company being vicariously liable. He is not acting as a servant, representative, agent or delegate. He is an embodiment of the company or, one could say, he hears and speaks through the persona of the company, within his appropriate sphere, and his mind is the mind of the company. If it is a guilty mind then that guilt is the guilt of the company. It must be a question of law whether … a person … is to be regarded as the company or merely as the company's servant or agent …

Reference is frequently made to the judgment of Denning L.J. in *H.L. Bolton (Engineering) Co. Ltd v T.J. Graham & Sons Ltd* [1957] 1 Q.B. 159. He said, at p. 172: 'A company may in many ways be likened to a human body. It has a brain and nerve centre which controls what it does. It also has hands which hold the tools and act in accordance with directions from the centre. Some of the people in the company are mere servants and agents who are nothing more than hands to do the work and cannot be said to represent the mind or will. Others are directors and managers who represent the directing mind and will of the company, and control what it does. The state of mind of these managers is the state of mind of the company and is treated by the law as such.' In that case the directors of the company only met once a year: they left the management of the business to others, and it was the intention of those managers which was imputed to the company. I think that was right. There have been attempts to apply Lord Denning's words to all servants of a company whose work is brain work, or who exercise some managerial discretion under the direction of superior officers of the company. I do not think that Lord Denning intended to refer to them. He only referred to those who 'represent the directing mind and will of the company, and control what it does.'

[The local manager was not to be identified with the company. He was, therefore, 'another person'.]"

**Appeal allowed**

There were significant objections to this strict interpretation of the identification doctrine particularly with larger companies where it is most unlikely that a senior manager will actually commit the *actus reus* of an offence with the accompanying *mens rea*. Accordingly, a more flexible approach was adopted by the Privy Council in the following case.

## Meridian Global Funds Management Asia Ltd v Securities Commission [1995] 2 A.C. 500 (Privy Council)

The chief investment officer and senior portfolio manager of Meridian, unknown to the board of directors and managing director, invested in another company without making disclosures to the stock exchange as required by section 20(3) of the New Zealand Securities Amendment Act 1988. The company was convicted of failing to comply with section 20. The New Zealand Court of Appeal upheld the conviction on the basis that the investment manager was the directing mind and will of the company and so his knowledge was attributable to the company. The company appealed to the Judicial Committee of the Privy Council.

Lord Hoffmann:

"Any proposition about a company necessarily involves a reference to a set of rules. A company exists because there is a rule (usually in a statute) which says that a *persona ficta* shall be deemed to exist and to have certain of the powers, rights and duties of a natural person … It is … a necessary part of corporate personality that there should be rules by which acts are attributed to the company. These may be called 'the rules of attribution'. …

… Judges sometimes say that a company 'as such' cannot do anything; it must act by servants or agents. … [A] reference to a company 'as such' might suggest that there is something out there called the company of which one can meaningfully say that it can or cannot do something. There is in fact no such thing as the company as such, no *ding an sich*, only the applicable rules. To say that a company cannot do something means only that there is no one whose doing of that act would, under the applicable rules of attribution, count as the act of the company.

... [T]he criminal law ... ordinarily impose[s] liability only for the *actus reus* and *mens rea* of the defendant himself. How is such a rule to be applied to a company?

... In such a case, the court must fashion a special rule of attribution for the particular substantive rule. This is always a matter of interpretation: given that it was intended to apply to a company, how was it intended to apply? Whose act (or knowledge, or state of mind) was *for this purpose* intended to count as the act etc. of the company? One finds the answer to this question by applying the usual canons of interpretation, taking into account the language of the rule (if it is a statute) and its content and policy.

... The policy of section 20 of the Securities Amendment Act 1988 is to compel, in fast-moving markets, the immediate disclosure of the identity of persons who become substantial security holders in public issuers. Notice must be given as soon as that person knows that he has become a substantial security holder. In the case of a corporate security holder, what rule should be implied as to the person whose knowledge for this purpose is to count as the knowledge of the company? Surely the person who, with the authority of the company, acquired the relevant interest. Otherwise the policy of the Act would be defeated. Companies would be able to allow employees to acquire interests on their behalf which made them substantial security holders but would not have to report them until the board or someone else in senior management got to know about it. This would put a premium on the board paying as little attention as possible to what its investment managers were doing. Their Lordships would therefore hold that upon the true construction of section 20(4)(e), the company knows that it has become a substantial security holder when that is known to the person who had authority to do the deal. ...

It was therefore not necessary in this case to inquire whether [the investment officer] could have been described in some more general sense as the 'directing mind and will' of the company. But their Lordships would wish to guard themselves against being understood to mean that whenever a servant of a company has authority to do an act on its behalf, knowledge of that act will for all purposes be attributed to the company. It is a question of construction in each case as to whether the particular rule requires that the knowledge that an act has been done, or the state of mind with which it was done, should be attributed to the company. ... [T]he fact that a company's employee is authorised to drive a lorry does not in itself lead to the conclusion that if he kills someone by reckless driving, the company will be guilty of manslaughter. There is no inconsistency. Each is an example of an attribution rule for a particular purpose, tailored as it always must be to the terms and policies of the substantive rule."

**Appeal dismissed**

This more flexible approach is to be welcomed. However, the decision is ambiguous and could lead to uncertainty. Lord Hoffmann states that "the court must fashion a special rule of attribution for the particular substantive rule". On the facts of *Meridian* this was easy. The issue was whether the company knew it had invested in another company without making the required disclosures. The person who had "authority to do the deal" was the investment manager; his knowledge was attributed to the company. But what was the "special rule of attribution" that enabled this sensible result to be achieved? Is Lord Hoffmann saying that, depending on the statute, one has a choice between utilising the identification doctrine and imposing vicarious liability—and that the company here was vicariously liable for the acts of its investment manager? Or, does it mean that, again depending on the statute, one can broaden the identification doctrine so that a company can be directly liable for the acts of someone not traditionally associated with the "controlling mind" of the company, which in this case was the investment manager? Perhaps the answer to these questions is not important. After all, the identification doctrine can be viewed as a very narrow form of vicarious liability[57]: companies can only be held "vicariously" liable for the acts of persons representing the controlling mind of the company. Whichever route is adopted, the effect of *Meridian* is the same. Companies can be liable for *mens rea* offences on the basis of acts by persons not traditionally regarded as senior enough under the *Tesco Supermarkets Ltd v Nattrass* formulation of the identification doctrine.

But how is this approach to be applied where there is no statute to be construed as is the case with manslaughter? If the acts and knowledge of an investment manager can be attributed to a company for investment offences, logic would dictate that the acts and knowledge of a health and safety manager should be attributed to a company for all health and safety purposes which would include manslaughter. In *Odyssey v OIC Run-Off Ltd.*[58] it was stated that the *Meridian* principle was of general application and could be applied to "a substantive rule of judge made law" (whether the finality of a judgment could be displaced by the perjury of a party). In this case a company was identified through the acts of a former director because at the trial where the perjury took place, he was "part of a team which was helping to row [the company] to victory". However, Brooke L.J. was careful to emphasise that this was a civil case where the approach to corporate liability was "fundamentally different". In a strong dissent, Buxton L.J. stated that the same rules of attribution should be applied in both criminal and civil cases. His view was that *Meridian* is "at best an imperfect guide to the correct approach to the rule for attribution of a crime" and that he was "bound by *Tesco v Nattrass* to apply the 'directing mind and will' formulation, or something very near to it".

Indeed, the following criminal decision has confirmed that any flexibility introduced by *Meridian* in relation to statutory offences has no application to the common law offence of manslaughter.

### Attorney-General's Reference (No. 2 of 1999) [2000] 2 Cr.App.R.207 (Court of Appeal, Criminal Division)

Following a train collision at Southall, seven passengers died and 151 were injured. Great Western Trains was prosecuted for manslaughter but was acquitted, as there was no human being with whom the company could be identified. On reference by the Attorney General:

Rose L.J.:
"There is, as it seems to us, no sound basis for suggesting that, by their recent decisions, the courts have started a process of moving from identification to personal liability as a basis for corporate liability for manslaughter. . . . [T]he identification principle is in our judgment just as relevant to the *actus reus* as to *mens rea*. . . .

In our judgment, unless an identified individual's conduct, characterisable as gross criminal negligence, can be attributed to the company the company is not, in the present state of the common law, liable for manslaughter. Civil negligence rules . . . are not apt to confer criminal liability on a company.

None of the authorities relied on by [counsel] as pointing to personal liability for manslaughter by a company supports that contention. In each, the decision was dependent on the purposive construction that the particular statute imposed. . . . In each case there was

---

[57] Simester and Sullivan, *Criminal Law: Theory and Doctrine* (2000), p. 248.
[58] 2000 W.L. 19127 (CA).

an identified employee whose conduct was held to be that of the company. In each case it was held that the concept of directing mind and will had no application when construing the statute. But it was not suggested or implied that the concept of identification is dead or moribund in relation to common law offences. ... Indeed, Lord Hoffmann's speech in the *Meridian* case, in fashioning an additional special rule of attribution geared to the purpose of the statute, proceeded on the basis that the primary 'directing mind and will' rule still applies although it is not determinative in all cases. In other words, he was not departing from the identification theory but re-affirming its existence.

 ... [T]he identification principle remains the only basis in common law for corporate liability for gross negligence manslaughter."

**Opinion accordingly**

From this, it follows that, for manslaughter at least, a company can only be liable if a person representing the controlling mind of the company actually commits the offence. This is intolerably narrow. Managing Directors do not drive trains and it would be extraordinarily difficult, if not impossible, to establish that their gross negligence in the boardroom *caused* the death of workers or members of the public.

Even if the more flexible *Meridian* approach were adopted, there would still be immense problems with the identification doctrine. It still requires an individual to be identified within the company whose acts and knowledge can be attributed to the company. In many cases the wrong might have occurred for the very reason that there was no person within the company responsible for, say, health and safety. Alternatively, the company's structures may be so complex and impenetrable, with decision-making buried at many different departmental levels, that it becomes impossible to pin-point any individual with responsibility for a particular area of activity. It is for these, and other, reasons, explored below, that there has been a call for the complete abandonment of the identification doctrine in English law.

## C. The Law in Action

The only criminal penalty that can be imposed on a company in English law is a fine. Accordingly, a company cannot be convicted of murder as this carries a mandatory sentence of life imprisonment. It is also unlikely that a company could commit crimes of a "very personal nature" such as sexual offences and bigamy.[59] However, there seems no reason in principle why a company should not be capable of committing any other criminal offence provided the identification doctrine has been satisfied.

However, while liability is possible in many such cases, the reality is that there have only ever been four successful prosecutions for manslaughter in England and Wales[60] and prosecutions for other serious offences against the person are virtually unknown. The reasons for this are two-fold.

---

[59] *P&O European Ferries (Dover) Ltd* (1991) 93 Cr.App.R.72 at 73. In *Richmond upon Thames L.B.C. v Pinn & Wheeler Ltd*, *The Times*, February 14, 1989, it was held that a company could not be convicted of an offence of driving a lorry without a permit. The act of driving was a physical act which could only be performed by a natural person. In *Robert Millars (Construction) Ltd* [1970] 1 All E.R. 577 a company was convicted of causing death by dangerous driving. This was, however, on the basis that the company had counselled and procured the offence.

[60] *Kite and Others*, *The Independent*, December 9, 1994; *Jackson Transport (Ossett) Ltd*, Health and Safety at Work, November 1996, p. 4. *English Bros Ltd*, August 2001; *Dennis Clothier and Sons*, October 2002 (www.corporateaccountability.org/manslaughter.htm).

The first explanation relates to enforcement procedures and public attitudes moulded by the media, the state and companies themselves. When persons are killed or seriously injured at work (even when they are members of the public) the typical response is to describe this as an "accident"—which in turn structures the official response.[61] Crime in the streets is still regarded as worse than crime in the suites.[62] In an attempt to increase safety at work and prevent such "accidents" the Health and Safety at Work Act 1974 makes it an offence for an employer to breach a duty "to ensure, so far as is reasonably practicable, the health, safety and welfare at work of all his employees".[63] This and other similar offences under the Act are drafted without any reference to whether a worker is killed or injured or not. The crime is simply the failure to maintain proper safety standards. This stands in strong contrast to the offences available when persons are killed or injured outside their workplaces which are structured in terms of the seriousness of the harm caused. This is true not only in cases of personal violence but also under the Road Traffic Act 1988. The different structure of the health and safety offences contributes to the overall sense that death and injury at work is not "real crime". The main body set up to enforce this legislation is the Health and Safety Executive (HSE) which has the power to notify companies that certain safety matters require attention or to bring a criminal prosecution. The result is that when someone is seriously injured at work it is extremely rare for the police to conduct an investigation into the incident.[64] For example, in 1996/97, even the HSE only investigated 4 per cent of the 50,000 major injuries at work[65] and it is only since 1998, as a result of a protocol agreed between the HSE, the CPS and the Association of Chief Police Officers (ACPO), that the police now attend the scene of every sudden workplace death.[66]

After a death or serious injury at work an investigation may be conducted by the HSE. While this is the usual practice following a death at work, less than 12 per cent of non-fatal serious injuries are investigated by the HSE.[67] Further, in those cases where an investigation is undertaken, the HSE does not regard its primary function as being one of initiating prosecutions, but rather as one of "assisting and advising the generality of well-conducted companies, and of determining good practice". The HSE, under-manned and under-resourced, with its policy of advising rather than prosecuting companies, will only press charges in cases that they believe represent a flagrant breach of the Health and Safety at Work Act 1974 with the result that only 20 per cent of workplace deaths lead to companies being prosecuted by the HSE.[68] A majority of these prosecutions are brought in the magistrates' court (72 per cent) as this is quicker and cheaper for the HSE.[69] Until

---

[61] Wells, *Corporations and Criminal Responsibility* (2nd ed., 2001), p. 11.
[62] For some evidence that corporate crime is being taken more seriously, see Croall, *White Collar Crime* (1992), pp. 109–125 and references cited therein.
[63] Section 2(1).
[64] Bergman, *Deaths at Work: Accidents or Corporate Crime* (1991), p. 17.
[65] Trotter, "The Paddington Rail Crash" (1999) N.L.J. 1505.
[66] HSE, *Work-Related Deaths: A Protocol for Liaison* (1998).
[67] Bergman, *The Case for Corporate Responsibility* (2000), p. 83.
[68] Bergman, *ibid.* at 11–12.
[69] Hutter and Lloyd-Bostock, "The Power of Accidents" (1990) 30 Brit.J.Criminol. 409: "an inspector working on a prosecution or on a public inquiry is not out making visits to other premises" (p. 421).

1992 the maximum fine there was £2000, now generally raised to £5000 for all offences[70] but to £20,000 for breaches of sections 2–6 of the Health and Safety at Work Act 1974.[71] As the Director General of the HSE has said: "the law was specifying higher penalties for the death of bluebells than people".[72] This displacement of police powers by the primarily regulatory HSE simply marginalises corporate crime and contributes, even in those cases where there is a prosecution, to the general feeling that such deaths and injuries are not really "crime" or the products of corporate violence.

This marginalisation of corporate crime is reinforced by the procedures adopted at inquests into workplace deaths where a verdict of "accidental death" is virtually automatic.

### David Bergman, Deaths at Work: Accidents or Corporate Crime (1991), pp. 43–64:

"Bereaved families have no right to legal aid at an inquest. This is a particular problem when the deceased worker was not a member of a trade union ... The decreasing levels of Trade Union membership over recent years and the relative youth of many of the workers who are killed at work means that [lack of legal representation] is not a rare occurrence ...

There are two major reasons why inquests are so cursory and why juries habitually return verdicts of accidental death. The first is the absence of company managers and directors who had responsibility for the safety of the worker. The second is the failure to thoroughly examine the witnesses present ... [T]he only company officers who are likely to be summoned are low level managers who do not have overall responsibility for the area of safety in question, and who work within constraints and frameworks decided upon by senior company officials. They are often only implementing procedures and practices which, if inadequate, would be the responsibility of more senior company officers ... The failure to call managers and directors as witnesses can sometimes make it appear as though responsibility for the accident lies with the deceased worker and their colleagues ...

The traditional emphasis of trade unions upon civil liability and compensation rather than on criminal accountability and deterrence—despite the wishes of the families themselves—has meant that their solicitors are automatically instructed to attend the inquest only to 'ascertain the facts necessary for a civil claim' ... Lawyers may also be concerned about antagonising companies with whom they may have to negotiate out of court financial settlements on behalf of the bereaved families."

Again, such procedures legitimate the current role of the police and the HSE and reinforce public conceptions that most of these deaths are "accidents". Recent proposals that the holding of an inquest should become discretionary in case of "accidents at work"[73] could well result in even fewer cases being prosecuted.

The second reason for the lack of criminalisation of corporate violence is that the identification doctrine makes a conviction extremely difficult.

---

[70] Magistrates' Courts Act 1980, s.32(9), as amended by the Criminal Justice Act 1991, s.17(2)(c).

[71] Health and Safety at Work Act 1974, s.33(1A), as amended by the Offshore Safety Act 1992, s.4(2).

[72] (1991) 187 Health and Safety Information Bulletin 21 in (1991) 491 Industrial Relations Review and Report. The average fine imposed in all courts in 2000/01 was £6,250 Health and Safety Commission, *Health and Safety Statistics 2000/01* (2001).

[73] Fundamental Review of Death Certification and the Coroner Service in England, Wales and Northern Ireland, *Certifying and Investigating Deaths in England, Wales and Northern Ireland: An Invitation for Views: A Consultation Paper* (2002).

## R. v H.M. Coroner for East Kent, ex parte Spooner and others (1989) 88 Cr.App.R. 10 (Queen's Bench Divisional Court)

The applicants sought judicial review of the coroner's decision that a company could not be indicted for manslaughter and that the acts or omissions of the company personnel could not be aggregated so as to render the company liable.

Bingham L.J.:

The inquest arises from the capsize of the vehicle ferry 'Herald of Free Enterprise' off Zeebrugge on March 6, 1987 and the huge loss of life, both of passengers and crew, to which that tragic disaster gave rise. Nearly 200 lives were lost, causing widespread grief, and the facts of the disaster are etched not only on the recollections of all who were involved, directly or indirectly, but on the consciousness of the nation as a whole.

Very shortly after the Secretary of State for Trade ordered a formal investigation under section 55 of the Merchant Shipping Act 1970. Sheen J. sitting with Assessors, was appointed to conduct it. . . .

The investigation found that the immediate cause of the vessel's loss was that she sailed with her bow doors opened trimmed by the head, *i.e.* with her nose down. The manoeuvre in which she engaged led to the entry of water into the vehicle deck, the heavy listing of the vessel and her speedy capsize.

Sheen J. criticised a number of individuals who had failed to perform their duty, in particular those responsible for failing to close the bow doors, failing to see that the doors were closed and sailing without knowing that the doors were closed. He expressed his criticisms in strong terms. The vessel was owned and operated by Townsend Car Ferries Ltd, and that company also was the subject of severe criticism.

It is right that I should refer to the terms in which Sheen J. expressed those criticisms. In paragraph 14.1 of his report he said this:

'At first sight the faults which led to this disaster were the aforesaid errors of omission on the part of the Master, the Chief Officer and the assistant bosun, and also the failure by Captain Kirby to issue and enforce clear orders. But a full investigation into the circumstances of the disaster leads inexorably to the conclusion that the underlying or cardinal faults lay higher up in the Company. The Board of Directors did not appreciate their responsibility for the safe management of their ships. They did not apply their minds to the question: What orders should be given for the safety of our ships? The Directors did not have any proper comprehension of what their duties were. There appears to have been a lack of thought about the way in which the HERALD ought to have been organised for the Dover/Zeebrugge run. All concerned in management, from the members of the Board of Directors down to the junior superintendents, were guilty of fault in that all must be regarded as sharing responsibility for the failure of management. From top to bottom the body corporate was infected with the disease of sloppiness. . . . The failure on the part of the shore management to give proper and clear directions was a contributory cause of the disaster. This is a serious finding which must be explained in some detail.'

The report then goes into very considerable detail and in the course of the present hearing three points are relied on as being particularly relevant. First, it is pointed out that the company and its representatives failed to give serious consideration to a proposal that lights should be fitted on the bridge of the vessel which would inform the Master whether the bow doors and, for that matter, the stern doors were closed or not. Such a warning system, if duly heeded by the Master, would have prevented this disaster. This was a suggestion which was made but seems unhappily to have been the subject of facetious comment.

Secondly, attention is drawn to the failure of the company and its representatives to report and collate information relating to previous incidents when vessels had sailed with their doors open. It appears that there were five or six such incidents between October 1983 and February 1987. Had knowledge of these repeated incidents been appreciated it should have alerted the officers of the company to the risk of disaster, but it appears that there was no person within the company who ever knew of all the incidents.

Thirdly, attention is drawn to the lack of any proper system within the company to ensure that the vessels were operated in accordance with the highest standards of safety. It is rightly urged upon us that where the result of an unsafe system is liable to be so grave, the onus on a company to ensure safe operation is correspondingly high.

At the very end of his report, Sheen J. answered the questions posed for the investigation by the Secretary of State. Question 3 was in these terms: 'Was the capsize of the "Herald of Free Enterprise" caused or contributed to by the fault of any person or persons and, if so, whom and in what respect?' The answer given to that question was: 'Yes, by the faults of the following,' and three individuals are listed. Then: '4. Townsend Car Ferries Limited at all levels from the Board of Directors through the managers of the Marine Department down to the Junior Superintendents. . . . '

[The coroner] said this: . . .

'although it is possible for several persons to be guilty individually of manslaughter, it is not permissible to aggregate several acts of neglect by different persons, so as to have gross negligence by a process of aggregation. That is a very important point of law, . . . '

No criticism is I think made of what the coroner said about manslaughter as against a personal defendant, but criticism has been made before us as to what he said about aggregation. The point has been made that a company can be guilty of manslaughter as well as an individual . . . I am, however, tentatively of opinion that on appropriate facts the *mens rea* required for manslaughter can be established against a corporation. I see no reason in principle why such a charge should not be established. . . . [F]or a company to be criminally liable for manslaughter—on the assumption I am making that such a crime exists—it is required that the *mens rea* and the *actus reus* of manslaughter should be established not against those who acted for or in the name of the company but against those who were to be identified as the embodiment of the company itself. The coroner formed the view that there was no such case fit to be left to the jury against this company. I see no reason to disagree. I would add that I see no sustainable case in manslaughter against the directors who are named either.

I do not think the aggregation argument assists the applicants. Whether the defendant is a corporation or a personal defendant, the ingredients of manslaughter must be established by proving the necessary *mens rea* and *actus reus* of manslaughter against it or him by evidence properly to be relied on against it or him. A case against a personal defendant cannot be fortified by evidence against another defendant. The case against a corporation can only be made by evidence properly addressed to showing guilt on the part of the corporation as such. On the main substance of his ruling I am not persuaded that the coroner erred."

**Applications refused**

At the inquest the jury ignored the coroner's instruction that there were no grounds for a verdict of corporate manslaughter and returned verdicts of unlawful death. Eventually, almost three years after the Zeebrugge deaths and after threats of a private prosecution, prosecutions for manslaughter were instituted against P&O (who had taken over Townsend) and seven employees of the company. At a preliminary hearing it was finally established that a company can be liable for manslaughter[74] but at the end of the prosecution case the trial judge, Turner J., directed acquittals against P&O and the five most senior employees.[75] This indicates that there was a case to be answered by the two most junior employees, Stanley, the assistant-bosun who had not closed the bow doors, and Sable, the loading officer/officer of the watch whose responsibility it was to check that the bow doors were closed. The prosecution immediately dropped all charges against

[74] *D.P.P. v P&O European Ferries (Dover) Ltd* (1991) 93 Cr.App.R.73.
[75] Unreported. Transcript: *R. v Alcindor and others* 1990 (Central Criminal Court, October 19, 1990). See Bergman, "Recklessness in the Boardroom" (1990) 140 N.L.J. 1496.

these two on the ground that it was not in the public interest to proceed against them alone. The reason for directing an acquittal against P&O and the senior managers was that it could not be proved that the risks of open-door sailing were obvious to any of them.

The collapse of this prosecution is not surprising. There was no one individual, sufficiently high in the hierarchy of P&O, who could be said to have committed the *actus reus* and *mens rea* of manslaughter. For similar reasons, the failure to secure a manslaughter conviction in the *Great Western Trains* case, discussed above, was predictable. In short, this whole approach of "humanising" companies will generally only be appropriate for small owner-managed companies where it will not be too difficult to pinpoint a senior individual with whom the company can be identified. For example, a corporate manslaughter conviction was possible in *Kite and Others*[76] where four teenagers had been drowned during a canoeing trip in Lyme Bay, because the company, OLL Ltd, was effectively a one-person company and as the trial judge put it: "Mr Kite and the company OLL, of which he is managing director, stand or fall together. One for all and all for one."[77] However, with larger companies such as P&O, it will not be easy to find a corporate officer who committed an offence that can be attributed to the company. The identification doctrine ignores the reality of modern corporate decision-making which is often the product of corporate policies and procedures rather than individual decisions.

## D. *Restructuring Corporate Criminal Liability*

The identification doctrine is inadequate to deal with the reality of decision-making in many modern companies. Accordingly, several alternative methods for the establishment of corporate culpability have been suggested.

### 1. Aggregation doctrine

In *H.M. Coroner for East Kent, ex p. Spooner* (above) the aggregation doctrine was considered and rejected.[78] Under this doctrine one aggregates all the acts and mental elements of the various relevant persons within the company to ascertain whether, aggregated together, they would amount to a crime if they had all been committed by one person. This doctrine has the advantage of recognising that in many cases it is not possible to isolate a single individual who has committed the crime with *mens rea*. This doctrine can deter companies from burying responsibility deep within the corporate structure.

However, this doctrine simply perpetuates the personification of companies myth. Instead of finding one person with whom the company can be identified (as required by the identification doctrine), one finds several people. The doctrine ignores the reality that the real essence of the wrongdoing might not be what each individual did but the fact that the company had no organisational structure or policy to prevent each individual doing what they did in a way that cumulatively

---

[76] *The Independent*, December 9, 1994.
[77] Cited in Smith and Smith, "The Company Behind Bars" *Health and Safety at Work*, February 1995, p. 10.
[78] This rejection was confirmed in *Attorney-General's Reference* (No. 2 of 1999) [2000] 2 C.App.R.207.

amounts to a crime. Indeed, in the *P&O* case it is doubtful whether the aggregation of the acts and omissions of the various personnel would have amounted to a corporate crime. The real fault in that case lay with the lack of policy and responsibility for safety within the company.

## 2. Reactive Corporate Fault

A somewhat different approach to corporate criminal liability has been proposed by Fisse and Braithwaite.

As many company structures are impenetrable to outsiders they propose that companies "activate and monitor [their own] private justice systems of corporate defendants".

### Brent Fisse and John Braithwaite, "The Allocation of Responsibility for Corporate Crime: Individualism, Collectivism and Accountability" (1988) 11 Sydney L.Rev. 468 at 511–512:

"One possible approach would be to restructure the imposition of corporate liability so as to enforce internal accountability. Where the *actus reus* of an offence is proven to have been committed by or on behalf of a corporation, the court, if equipped with a suitable statutory injunctive power, could require the company (a) to conduct its own enquiry as to who was responsible within the organisation, (b) to take internal disciplinary measures against those responsible, and (c) to return a report detailing the action taken. If the corporate defendant returned a report demonstrating that due steps had been taken to discipline those responsible then corporate criminal liability would not be imposed. If the reaction of the company was inexcusably deficient then both the company and its top managers would be criminally liable for their failure to comply with the order of the court. The range of punishments for corporate defendants would include court-ordered adverse publicity, community service, and punitive injunctive sentences ...

Where it can be proven that harm proscribed by the *actus reus* of an offence has been caused by conduct performed on behalf of a corporation, it is not unreasonable that the cost of investigating internal responsibility for that harm causing be borne by the corporate defendant rather than by taxpayers in general ... Even though sanctions available to private justice systems—fines, dismissals, demotions, shame—may be less potent than some of those available in the public arena, it seems better to have weaker sanctions hitting the right targets than stronger weapons pounding the wrong targets."[79]

There are, however, many problems with this reactive fault doctrine. What corrective measures and disciplinary actions will suffice to avoid liability? Would a formal reprimand of an employee coupled with the circulation of an internal memorandum advising staff that certain actions need to be taken in future suffice?[80] If a company fails to take sufficient steps, what offence would be committed? If the company were to be liable for established offences such as manslaughter, there would be a severe danger of "false labelling"[81] in that the established prerequisites of the crime, in terms of *actus reus* and *mens rea*, would not be made out. On the

---

[79] For a statutory model based on this proposal, see Fisse, "The Attribution of Criminal Liability to Corporations: A Statutory Model" (1991) 13 Sydney L.Rev. 277.

[80] Clarkson, "Corporate Culpability" [1998] 2 Web J.C.L.I.

[81] Sullivan, "The Attribution of Culpability to Limited Companies" [1996] C.L.J. 515 at 526.

other hand, if new special offences relating to reactive fault were to be created, there is the danger that the crimes committed by such companies will continue to be perceived as "poor cousins" to the "real criminal offences". Convicting companies of a failure to comply with a court order conveys the same message as a conviction under the Health and Safety legislation. What is needed is a more direct public shaming of the company itself for the actual harm that the company's culpable acts have caused.

### 3. Corporate *mens rea* doctrine

What is needed is a recognition that corporate policies and behaviour often depend on the organisational structure and lines of authority within the corporation with responsibility for standard procedures, such as those relating to safety, being spread throughout the company. Corporate acts and policies are not simply an aggregation of individual choices but are often the acts and policies of the company itself. A company might have "no soul to be damned, and no body to be kicked",[82] but it can be likened to "an intelligent machine"[83] which, through its corporate policy, can exhibit its own *mens rea*[84] and, therefore, the focus ought to be on the responsibility of the company itself.

### Brent Fisse, "Recent Developments in Corporate Criminal Law and Corporate Liability to Monetary Penalties" (1990) 13 UNSWLJ 1 at 15–16:

"Corporate policy is the corporate equivalent of intention, and a company that conducts itself with an express or implied policy of non-compliance with a criminal prohibition exhibits corporate criminal intentionality ... The concept of negligently failing to comply with the law is also applicable to a corporation as a collectivity. Corporations perform corporate roles in society and have collective capacities. Accordingly, they are subject to distinctly corporate standards of care.

Although it is possible to define corporate fault in terms of corporate policy and corporate negligence, the worry is that corporations will develop compliance systems that look immaculate on paper but which are not meant to be taken seriously by their personnel. One solution is to recognise that a corporation may have an implied policy of non-compliance ... There would be merit in a rule that a company is deemed to have a policy of non-compliance where the company has failed to have in place a system whereby employees could report suspected or anticipated episodes of non-compliance directly to top management."

The Law Commission has proposed a test of "management failure" to determine when a corporation should be liable for a corporate killing. This failure is defined as being "a failure to ensure safety in the management or organisation of the corporation's activities".[85] While this proposal is clearly a step in the right direction, the concept of a "management failure" is not sufficiently fleshed out by

---

[82] Coffee, " 'No Soul to Damn: No Body to Kick': an Unscandalised Inquiry into the Problem of Corporate Punishment" (1981) 79 Mich.L.Rev. 386.

[83] Dan-Cohen, *Rights, Persons, and Organisations: A Legal Theory for Bureaucratic Society* (1986), p. 49. For an argument that a company can be a culpability-bearing agent, see Clarkson, "Kicking Corporate Bodies and Damning Their Souls" (1996) 59 M.L.R. 557.

[84] Foerschler, "Corporate Criminal Intent: Towards a Better Understanding of Corporate Misconduct" (1990) 78 Cal.L.Rev. 1287 at 1303.

[85] Law Com. No. 237, *Legislating the Criminal Code: Involuntary Manslaughter* (1996) at 8.19.

the Law Commission and, by their own admission, is not designed to apply to offences requiring foresight or intention.

### C.M.V. Clarkson, "Corporate Culpability" [1998] 2 Web Journal of Current Legal Issues

"While it is perhaps easy to grasp the notion of a company being grossly negligent in that no subjective mental element is required, it is important to stress that both recklessness or intention can also be found in a company's policies, operational procedures and lack of precautions. If the corporate culture permitted or encouraged the wrongdoing, it may be easy to infer that the corporate body itself must have foreseen the possibility of the harm occurring (*Cunningham* recklessness) or that it has created an obvious and serious risk of the wrong resulting (*Caldwell/Lawrence* recklessness) or that the consequence was virtually certain to occur from which intention may be inferred (*Moloney/Hancock* intention). The important point about this approach is that it is not whether any individual within the company would have realised or foreseen the harm occurring but whether in a properly structured and organised careful company the risks would have been obvious. ... Possibly the only avenue of escape would be for a company to assert that while the risks looked objectively obvious, they had special expertise enabling them to rule out the risk (which would negate both species of recklessness and intention). In the unlikely event of this claim being believed (bearing in mind that the risk clearly did materialise), the company would (rightly) escape liability.

The major objection to the corporate *mens rea* doctrine is the difficulty of determining whether the policies and practices of a company are sufficiently defective to be adjudged blameworthy to the requisite degree. In *Herald of Free Enterprise* this could easily have been done. The company had no proper safety procedures, no director responsible for safety and had received and ignored prior warnings of open-door sailings. In other cases, however, particularly where there is no pattern of wrongdoing, it could be more difficult to identify the policies and practices as amounting to *mens rea*. One method of addressing this problem in the United States would be to inquire whether a company had a Corporate Compliance Programme which has been enforced in good faith.

A Corporate Compliance Programme (CCP) is a formal system or programme designed to ensure that all employees know the relevant laws affecting the company's operations and seeking to ensure corporate compliance with the law. ... Under the United States Sentencing Commission's Guidelines for the Sentencing of Organisations companies that commit crimes receive a significant reduction in sentence if they have implemented and enforced a CCP ... Further, the existence of a CCP may be critical in the exercise of prosecutorial discretion. The Justice Department has urged United States Attorneys to regard the presence of a CCP as a 'significant factor' in deciding whether to prosecute. What is being argued here is that such CCPs could be utilised in England and Wales as *evidence* of (lack of) corporate culpability."

Implementation of such a proposal, as well as facilitating convictions in cases such as *Herald of Free Enterprise*, could induce a change of policy by the police and the HSE in cases of death and serious injury at work. If there were a realistic prospect of conviction it might seem more worthwhile conducting fuller investigations.

### E. *Specific Corporate Offences*

One final possibility deserves consideration. In view of the difficulty in ascribing culpability to companies under the general rules of criminal law, one solution could be the creation of special corporate offences defined in a manner designed to encapsulate the distinctive nature of corporate wrongdoing. The Law Commission has proposed that a new offence of "corporate killing" be introduced into English law. This offence, which would require a management failure "falling far below what can reasonably be expected of the corporation in the circumstances",[86] would constitute a separate crime that could only be committed by companies. In this way problems associated with the ascertainment of corporate culpability, such as proof of intention or recklessness, can be overcome.

This proposal has been accepted by the Government who suggest broadening the scope of the offence to include all *undertakings*.[87] This is a concept already employed in the Health and Safety at Work etc. Act 1974 and would encompass a range of bodies which are not "corporations" such as schools, hospital trusts, partnerships and unincorporated charities: "In effect the offence of corporate killing could apply to all employing organisations. We estimate that this would mean that a total of 3.5 million enterprises might become potentially liable to the offence of corporate killing".[88]

There are several objections that can be made to this proposal. First, while the introduction of this new offence would greatly facilitate prosecutions in cases where death has been caused, the identification doctrine would continue to apply to all other cases, in particular, those where serious injury has been caused and with the high-profile problem of corporate killings being catered for, pressure for reform of the identification doctrine would be significantly reduced. Secondly, there is the danger that this offence could be perceived by prosecutors as the "easy option" and so individual managers and directors would escape prosecution. As shall be seen, the case for corporate liability is not a case for the exclusion of individual liability in appropriate cases. Thirdly, it can be argued that the introduction of a new and separate offence could lead to a marginalisation of the seriousness of such killings. The offence would not be regarded as serious as "real" manslaughter and much of the law's censuring and symbolic role would be defeated. At present, many companies that kill their employees or members of the public find themselves prosecuted under the Health and Safety at Work Act 1974. The different structure of these offences has led to a perception that these are little more than regulatory offences. Corporate crime is not "as bad" as "real" crime. The better way forward would be the recognition that companies can be culpability-bearing agents and that there is no need for special corporate offences.

On the other hand, the proposed new offence can be supported.

### C.M.V.Clarkson, "Context and Culpability in Involuntary Manslaughter: Principle or Instinct?" in Ashworth and Mitchell (eds), Rethinking English Homicide Law (2000), p. 152:

"[T]here are several reasons for endorsing the creation of a new special offence of corporate killing. First, in fair labelling terms there is something distinctive about the

---

[86] Law Com. No. 237, *ibid.*, cl. 4(1).

[87] Home Office, *Reforming the Law on Involuntary Manslaughter: The Government's Proposals* (2000).

[88] Para. 3.2.5. See Sullivan, "Corporate Killing—Some Government Proposals" [2001] Crim.L.R.31; Gobert, "Corporate Killings at Home and Abroad – Reflections on the Government's Proposals" (2002) 118 L.Q.R. 72.3.

context in which such killings occur. Corporate defendants are engaged in lawful activities that would generally be regarded as socially beneficial were they safely performed. A primary lawful motivation drives the actions. While it has become fashionable to talk of "corporate violence", in reality, like causing death by dangerous driving, such killings belong to a different family of offence. Unlike acts of violence, running a train company, for example, does not have harm of any degree to the victim as part of its rationale in acting. This is not to minimise the reprehensibility of the conduct of those whose disregard the safety of others or to suggest that significant punishments should not be imposed. It is simply to argue that the context in which the deaths have occurred is sufficiently different from the paradigmatic homicide to warrant separate appellation and treatment. Secondly, this fear of marginalisation could be misplaced. Having separate vehicular homicide offences has not resulted in trivialisation of their seriousness as can be seen by the sentences imposed in such cases. Further, concerns about the perceived lack of seriousness of the special offence are largely premised on the assumption that it will be introduced alongside the present (unreformed) offence of manslaughter, and thus would seem a "poor relative". However, if the Law Commission's proposals were accepted in toto, there would be several new offences each bearing different appellations and thus the risk of marginalisation would be reduced."

## F. *Corporate or Personal Criminal Liability*

A central question is whether the criminal law should hold *companies* accountable or whether it should rather seek to punish the culpable individuals within the company. The argument in favour of only prosecuting individuals is that it is they who are blameworthy and deserve punishment. In some cases an individual manager in order to secure promotion, for example, might implement a policy with short-term rewards but contrary to the long-term interests of the company. In such cases the company does not deserve blame and punishment. Further, it is argued that individuals within a company are the ones most amenable to deterrence. In order to deter the company itself fines would need to be huge. A company is only likely to be deterred if its expected costs exceed its expected gains. If a company anticipates making £10 million from a criminal act and the risk of apprehension is 20 per cent, it has been argued that the fine would need to be at least £50 million to have any hope of being an effective deterrent.[89] There is a further problem here with the "deterrence trap": this is where the risk of apprehension is so low that no penalty will operate as a deterrent.[90] In terms of incapacitation and rehabilitation, it could be said that it is the particular individuals who should be removed from office or disciplined or made to improve their work practices.

Finally, it is argued that punishment of a company by way of a fine amounts to punishment of innocent shareholders, creditors, employees who might be made redundant, or the public who will ultimately have to bear the burden of the fine. In short, the ones who will really suffer will be those whom the law is aiming to protect.

On the other hand, the case in favour of corporate criminal liability is formidable.

---

[89] Coffee, " 'No Soul to Damn: No Body to Kick': an Unscandalised Inquiry into the Problem of Corporate Punishment" (1981) 79 Mich.L.Rev. 386 at 389 drawing on the work of Posner, *Economic Analysis of Law* (2nd ed., 1977), p. 167.
[90] *ibid.*, at 390.

**Brent Fisse and John Braithwaite, "The Allocation of Responsibility for Corporate Crime: Individualism, Collectivism and Accountability" (1988) 11 Sydney L.Rev. 468 at 479–508:**

"In the case of organisations, individuals may be the most important parts, but there are other parts, as is evident from factories with manifest routines which operate to some extent independently of the biological agents who flick the switches. Organisations are systems … not just aggregations of individuals … Indeed, the entire personnel of an organisation may change without reshaping the corporate culture; this may be so even if the new incumbents have personalities quite different from those of the old … The fact is that organisations are blamed in their capacity as organisations for causing harm or taking risks in circumstances where they could have acted otherwise. We often react to corporate offenders not merely as impersonal harm-producing forces but as responsible, blameworthy entities. When people blame corporations they … [are not] pointing the finger at individuals behind the corporate mantle. They are condemning the fact that the organisation either implemented a policy of non-compliance or failed to exercise its collective capacity to avoid the offence for which blame attaches … We routinely hold organisations responsible for a decision when and because that decision instantiates an organisational policy and instantiates an organisational decision-making process which the organisation has chosen for itself …

Punishment directed at a corporate entity typically seeks to deter a wide range of individual associates from engaging in conduct directly or indirectly connected with the commission of an offence. Individual persons who are directly implicated in offences may be difficult or impossible to prosecute successfully, and those who influence the commission of offences indirectly may fall outside the scope of liability for complicity or other ancilliary heads of criminal liability … Companies value a good reputation for its own sake, just as do universities, sporting clubs and government agencies. Individuals who take on positions of power within such organisations, even if they as individuals do not personally feel any deterrent effects of shaming directed at their organisation, may find that they confront role expectations to protect and enhance the repute of the organisation … Another factor which tends to limit the deterrent efficacy of individual criminal liability for corporate crime is the expendability of individuals within organisations … [T]he corporation 'marches on its elephantine way almost indifferent to its succession of riders.' The risk thus arises of rogue corporations exploiting their capacity to toss off a succession of individual riders and, if necessary, to indemnify them in some way … Consider also the extreme tactic adopted by some companies of setting up internal lines of accountability so as to have a 'vice-president responsible for going to jail.' By offering an attractive sacrifice the hope is that prosecutors will feel sufficiently satisfied with their efforts to refrain from pressing charges against the corporation or members of its managerial elite …

[I]n some respects corporations may be better endowed than individuals to be the subject of responsibility. Corporations, it may be argued, have a number of advantages when it comes to rational decision-making, including access to a pool of intelligence and the resources to acquire a superior knowledge of legal and other obligations. The conclusion is thus invited that although corporations do not have a 'soul to be damned' they can deserve to be blamed …

[With regard to the argument that punishing companies amounts to punishment of innocent shareholders etc.] [f]irst, cost-bearing associates are not themselves subject to the stigma of conviction and criminal punishment—they are not convicts but corporate distributees. Secondly, employees and stockholders accede to a distributional scheme in which profits and losses from corporate activities are distributed on the basis of position in the company or type of investment rather than degree of deserved praise or blame … Thirdly, and above all, not to punish an enterprise at fault would be to allow corporations to accumulate and distribute to associates a pool of resources which does not reflect the social cost of production. Justice as fairness requires, as a minimum, that the cost of corporate offences be internalised by the enterprise."

Many large corporations have complex structures which make it difficult for outsiders to ascertain who is responsible for a particular decision. Punishing the company can trigger the most appropriate institutional response in that the company is in the best position to identify and discipline its employees. In many cases however, prosecution of individuals might be inappropriate as it ignores the corporate pressures that might have been placed upon them by the corporate structure; these pressures will often remain even after the individual has been sacrificed. It is only by punishment of the company itself that one can hope for a corporate response to the wrongdoing by the implementation of the appropriate safety procedures.

Modern companies now often promote themselves as distinct identifiable entities. Such advertising "designed to 'humanise' the company in the interests of image-building, has reinforced the anthropomorphic perception of the company in the public mind, which in turn has led to a public demand to apportion blame and to criminalise and punish companies for serious transgressions".[91] The concept of fair-labelling applies not just to offences themselves, but to whom we choose to blame for the offences committed. It is a telling fact that the relatives of the victims who died on the *Herald of Free Enterprise* were primarily interested in a prosecution of P&O and not of the individuals. Even the prosecution seemed of similar mind when it dropped the charges against the two most immediate "causers" of the sinking as soon as the judge had directed acquittals against P&O and its senior executives. Perhaps there was a realisation that the assistant bosun should never have been left in a position where the entire safety of the ferry and its passengers depended on him without any adequate system of checks or controls. The true fault lay with the company.

However, a final and critical point must be stressed here. The above argument is that companies should be capable of being held criminally liable. This does *not* mean that individuals within the company should be exempt from liability. In appropriate cases, where the individual has committed the *actus reus* with the *mens rea* of the offence, they should also be liable. Indeed, in the case of small companies, particularly "one-person-companies", imposing criminal liability on the company, in addition to the individual, is somewhat pointless. While it should always be possible in such cases, it is in relation to larger companies, such as P&O and Great Western Trains, that the case for corporate criminal liability becomes strongest.

### G. *Punishment of Companies*[92]

We saw earlier that fines imposed on companies under the Health and Safety legislation are low and could be described as little more than a "public morality tax".[93] This is one of the reasons contributing to the marginalisation of such offences. However, over the last decade the level of fines imposed has been gradually increasing, an approach endorsed by the following leading decision.

---

[91] Dunford and Ridley, "No Soul to be Damned, No Body to be Kicked: Responsibility, Blame and Corporate Punishment" (1996) 24 Int. J. Soc. L. 1 at 7.

[92] See generally, Gobert, "Controlling Corporate Criminality: Penal Sanctions and Beyond" [1998] Web J.C.L.I; Jefferson, "Corporate Criminal Liability: The Problem of Sanctions" (2001) 65 J Crim L 235.

[93] Coffee, *above*, n.89 at 407.

## R. v F. Howe & Son (Engineers) Ltd [1999] 2 Cr.App.R.(S.) 37 (Court of Appeal, Criminal Division)

A company was fined £48,000 after a conviction under the Health and Safety at Work etc. Act 1974 in a case that involved an employee being killed. The company's net profit after tax for the preceding year had been £26,969. The company appealed on the ground that the fine was excessive.

Scott Baker J.:
"In the early 90s ... the average fine in the Magistrates' courts (per offence prosecuted) for breaches of the general duties increased from £844 to £2,110 in 1992/93 and this has since risen to £6,223, but it is still less than one-third of the maximum. And almost half the fines in Magistrates' courts for these offences in 1997/98 was below one-quarter of the maximum of £20,000. In the Crown Court where the level of fine is unlimited the 1997/98 average fine per offence was £17,768.

Disquiet has been expressed in several quarters that the level of fine for health and safety offences is too low. We think there is force in this ... There has been increasing recognition in recent years of the seriousness of health and safety offences ...

[I]t is impossible to lay down any tariff or to say that the fine should bear any specific relationship to the turnover or net profit of the defendant. Each case must be dealt with according to its own particular circumstances.

[His Lordship then listed various factors, including aggravating and mitigating circumstances, that should be taken into account.] [I]t is often a matter of chance whether death or serious injury results from even a serious breach. Generally where death is the consequence of a criminal act it is regarded as an aggravating feature of the offence. The penalty should reflect public disquiet at the unnecessary loss of life. ...

Any fine should reflect not only the gravity of the offence but also the means of the offender, and this applies just as much to corporate defendants as to any other. ...

The objective of prosecutions for health and safety offences in the work place is to achieve a safe environment for those who work there and for other members of the public who may be affected. A fine needs to be large enough to bring that message home where the defendant is a company not only to those who manage it but also to its shareholders.

Mr Dixey argued in the present case that the fine should not be so large as to imperil the earnings of employees or create a risk of bankruptcy. Whilst in general we accept that submission, as the Vice President observed in argument there may be cases where the offences are so serious that the defendant ought not to be in business. That, however, is not this case. ...

In our judgment the learned judge in the present case gave inadequate weight to the financial position of the appellant. [The total fine was reduced to £22,500.]"

**Appeal allowed in part**

It is too early to assess empirically the impact of this decision. While the overall average fine for breaches of the 1974 Act has not increased since the figures cited in the above case,[94] it is clear that the average fine following a death at work has been steadily increasing—but was doing so before *Howe & Son*. For example, in the three years between 1996/97 and 1998/99 it more than doubled from £28,900 to almost £67,000.[95] In the *Great Western Trains* case a record fine of £1.5 million was imposed following the Southall train crash.

However, while this new attitude to the level of fines is to be welcomed,[96] it

---

[94] *Above*, n.72.
[95] UNISON, *Safety Last?* (2002).
[96] See also the proposals of the Sentencing Advisory Panel in relation to environmental offences (www.sentencing-advisory-panel.gov.uk/info.htm).

should be pointed out that the fine in the *Great Western Trains* case represented only 5.6 per cent of the company's profit for the preceding year.[97] Under the Powers of the Criminal Courts (Sentencing) Act 2000, section 128, the court must inquire into the financial circumstances of the offender before fixing the amount of a fine. Equality in sentencing means equality of impact. If large corporations with vast profits were to be fined according to their means (say a percentage thereof[98]) a new attitude to corporate violence and other crime might start emerging.

It remains an open question, however, whether such fines would ensure that companies revised their internal operational procedures to guard against repetition of the offence.[99] Because of these concerns and the fear that the public will ultimately have to bear the cost in terms of price rises, Coffee has advocated the imposition of "equity fines" whereby a company would be forced to issue shares to a public body (say, the Victim Compensation Fund) which would then dispose of them on the market.[1] As the company would have no need to raise immediate cash, there would be no need for consumers to bear the cost of price increases and no threat of redundancies.[2] And, as Coffee says:

> "Because the equity fine can vastly exceed the cash fine, the stock market will begin to discount the securities of those companies perceived to be vulnerable to future criminal prosecutions ... [C]orporate managers will have an incentive to institute preventive monitoring controls to forestall this decline."[3]

Releasing such shares onto the market would increase the risk of a hostile take-over. As managers gain great psychological rewards in the form of power and prestige (as well as money) from their positions of authority in the corporation, the threat of losing these benefits is regarded by managers as a traumatic experience and they will defend their positions with great zeal.[4]

One of the consequences of having "no body to kick" is that English law has simply assumed that a company has no body to incarcerate or upon which to inflict any punishment other than a fine. Such an approach displays a distinct lack of imagination. Several alternatives have been mooted and tried in other jurisdictions. For example, a community service order could be made against the company requiring it to engage in various projects. Thus a company convicted of a pollution offence could be required to clean up rivers or beaches. In imposing such orders a court could order senior management to be involved in the service: "Executive wrongdoers should not be able to delegate to employees responsibilities that are rightfully theirs ... any more than a convicted defendant should be allowed to hire

---

[97] Trotter, "Corporate Manslaughter" (2000) N.L.J. 454.

[98] Under EC anti-trust laws fines up to 10 per cent of the company's previous year's global turnover may be imposed (EC Council Reg., art. 15(2)). In 2002, Sotherby's was fined £12.9 million (6 per cent of the company's annual turnover) for an illegal price-fixing cartel (The Independent, October 31, 2002).

[99] Fisse (*above*, p. 261) makes the point that fines are inappropriate in the context of offences committed by quasi-governmental authorities as they would simply result in "some budgetary shuffling with money deducted from one arm of government passing back into general revenue" (p. 9).

[1] *Above*, n.89 at 413–424.

[2] Gobert, "Controlling Corporate Criminality: Penal Sanctions and Beyond" [1998] 2 Web J.C.L.I.

[3] *Above* n.89 at 420.

[4] *ibid.* at 412.

a substitute to serve his prison sentence".[5] However, care must be taken here to ensure that the company does not profit, in terms of publicity and reputation, from involvement in such worthwhile projects. In order to prevent this, in the United States, under federal sentencing guidelines, companies may be ordered to place adverse publicity advertisements in newspapers.[6]

An alternative sentence is corporate probation whereby companies could be forced to change those policies and procedures that allowed the offence to be committed. Courts could demand an internal restructuring of the company[7] or could appoint trustees or directors to examine the procedures of the company or to investigate who was responsible within the company. These measures, which would have to be financed by the company itself, would ensure that companies "rehabilitated themselves" and adopted whatever measures were necessary to prevent a reoccurrence of the wrongdoing. The Law Commission has put forward a similar proposal, relating to its proposed offence of corporate killing, that courts be empowered to make remedial orders under which the company would be obliged to remedy the harm caused and eliminate the cause of the harm.[8] However, a problem with this proposal is that the sanction for failing to comply with the order is a monetary penalty which means that a company could deliberately refuse to comply with the order, thus converting the remedial order into a fine.[9]

More radical alternatives include incarceration through temporary nationalisation and the appointment of public directors,[10] incarceration through "quarantine" whereby companies would be forbidden to engage in certain activities or barred from specific areas[11] or even the analogue of the death penalty, corporate dissolution.

While not necessarily advocating some of these more drastic solutions, the point is that there is a range of sentencing options that could be employed. As already stressed, nothing in this chapter should be taken as suggesting that corporate criminal liability should in all cases replace individual liability. In many cases where an individual has "gone out on a limb" it is that individual who should be prosecuted. In many cases both the company and individuals should be prosecuted.[12] Indeed, culpable persons should never be allowed to hide behind the corporate facade. Equally, however, in many cases the real fault will lie with the company and not with any individual. In such cases there should be a real possibility of a prosecution and conviction—with corporate liability no longer being dependent upon a finding of individual guilt—and with appropriate, meaningful punishment being available to reflect the true guilt of the company.

---

[5] Gobert, *above*, n.2.

[6] Gobert, *ibid.*

[7] Fisse, "Reconstructing Corporate Criminal Law: Deterrence, Retribution, Fault and Sanctions" (1983) 56 S.Cal.L.Rev. 1141, 1222. Probation is clearly more sensible in the context of offences committed by quasi-governmental bodies. See Fisse, *above*, p. 261 at 10.

[8] Law Com. No. 237, *above*, n.85 at paras 8.71–8.76.

[9] Gobert, *above*, n.89.

[10] Box, *Power, Crime and Mystification* (1983), p. 72.

[11] Meister, "Criminal Liability for Corporations that Kill" (1989–90) 64 Tulane L.R. 919 at 946.

[12] Such individuals can be liable either as principal offenders or as accessories under the general rules. There are, however, several particular provisions rendering managers liable if an offence is committed by a company with their "consent and connivance." See, for example, s.37(1) of the Health and Safety at Work etc. Act 1974.

# 3

# GENERAL DEFENCES

## I. Justification and Excuse

### A. *Introduction*

A defendant may commit the *actus reus* of an offence with the requisite *mens rea* and yet escape liability because he has a "general defence". For example, he may have intentionally killed his victim, but have been acting in self-defence because the victim had been trying to kill him. In such a case, assuming the requirements of self-defence are made out, he escapes all liability.

We have already seen that there are different ways of analysing criminal liability.[1] It could be, continuing the above example, that the defendant is regarded as having committed the *actus reus* with an appropriate *mens rea* but is afforded a defence which is a separate third element. This mode of analysis could be useful in describing the shifting burdens of proof in a criminal trial in those jurisdictions[2] where it is for the prosecution to prove beyond reasonable doubt that the defendant committed the *actus reus* with appropriate *mens rea*, but the burden then shifts to the defendant to establish on a balance of probabilities that he has a defence. This "procedural analysis" is employed in England with the defences of insanity[3] and diminished responsibility.[4] Such an approach is, however, not accurate in describing the burden of proof in other cases in England where, in relation to common law defences, the burden remains on the prosecution throughout.[5] Nor is this "procedural analysis" helpful in understanding the true bases of criminal liability: who, why and when persons should be adjudged blameworthy and held criminally responsible for their actions. Accordingly, a "substantive interpretation" tends to focus on the requirement of blameworthiness. Criminal liability is imposed on a blameworthy actor who causes a prohibited harm. If a defendant has a "general defence" he is not blameworthy and, therefore, deserves to escape criminal liability.

---

[1] *Above*, p. 83.
[2] *e.g.*, Singapore and Malaysia: see Koh, Clarkson and Morgan, *Criminal Law in Singapore and Malaysia: Text and Materials* (1989), p. 103.
[3] M'Naghten Rules, *below*, p. 374; *Bratty v Att-Gen for Northern Ireland* [1963] A.C. 386.
[4] Homicide Act 1957, s.2(2).
[5] *Woolmington v. D.P.P.* [1935] A.C. 462; see Smith and Hogan, *Criminal Law* (10th ed., 2002), p. 28.

The term "general defences" is used to convey that such defences are available to all crimes. There are some defences that are not "general" but specific to particular offences: for example, provocation is a defence only to murder, reducing liability to manslaughter. Such specific defences are dealt with later in relation to their particular offences. We have, however, chosen to deal with one specific defence, diminished responsibility, in this chapter. This is because of its close affinity to the "general defence" of insanity and it is best understood examined in that context.

Further, it must be stressed that the title "general defences" is adopted purely for expository convenience. It is patently untrue that all these defences are available to all offences. For example, duress is not available for murder and intoxication is not available for most offences. Another problematic area is the extent to which the "general defences" are available to offences of strict liability.

These general defences used to be listed as isolated sets of identifiable conditions or circumstances which prevented a defendant being convicted. However, over the last twenty years a number of attempts have been made to bring defences within an overall theoretical framework. The chief advantage of this is that it enables more rational analysis of the ways in which the law has developed or been restricted. Defences have been broadly classified into two groups: those that provide a *justification* for the defendant's conduct, and those that *excuse* his conduct.[6] More recently, commentators have reworked the category of excusatory defences and increasingly exclude from it those which amount to denials of responsibility. This latter group may be called *exemptions*.

It must be stressed, however, that the classification of defences into groups is not water-tight. This is true in two ways: the classifications themselves are still being refined and it may be difficult to locate a particular defence within just one category. "In English law this is compounded by the law's cautious insistence on having a belt as well as braces: in general no excuse is accepted into the criminal law which is not also a partial justification, and no justification is accepted which is not also a partial excuse."[7]

### Paul Robinson, "Criminal Law Defences: A Systematic Analysis" (1982) 82 Col.L.R. 199 at 213, 221, 229:

"[J]ustification defences are not alterations of the statutory definition of the harm sought to be prevented or punished by an offense. The harm caused by the justified behaviour remains a legally recognised harm which is to be avoided whenever possible. Under the special justifying circumstances, however, that harm is outweighed by the need to avoid an even greater harm or to further a great societal interest. ...

Excuses admit that the deed may be wrong, but excuse the actor. ...

Justifications and excuses may seem similar in that both are general defenses which exculpate an actor because of his blamelessness. ... The conceptual distinction remains an important one, however. Justified conduct is correct behaviour which is encouraged or at least tolerated. In determining whether conduct is justified, the focus is on the *act*, not the

---

[6] The distinction was important before 1828 as, under the common law, a killer's goods were forfeited if the killing was excusable but not if it was justifiable. In 1828 forfeiture was abolished. See further, Smith, *Justification and Excuse in the Criminal Law* (1989), p. 7. The revived interest in the distinction can largely be traced back to the publication in 1978 of Fletcher, *Rethinking Criminal Law* (1978).

[7] Gardner, "Justifications and Reasons" in Simester and Smith (eds), *Harm and Culpability* (1996), p. 122. Some commentators have found the classification so flawed that they have almost entirely abandoned it: see Simester and Sullivan, *Criminal Law: Theory and Doctrine* (2000), pp. 539–540.

actor. An excuse represents a legal conclusion that the conduct is wrong, undesirable, but that criminal liability is inappropriate because some characteristic of the actor vitiates society's desire to punish him. Excuses do not destroy blame ... rather, they shift it from the actor to the excusing condition. The focus in excuses is on the *actor*. Acts are justified; actors are excused."

Robinson's analysis has been very influential, but, as we shall see, both his description of justifications and excuses has come under fire. How does one determine whether a particular defence is justificatory or excusatory in nature?

## B. *Justification*

### Joshua Dressler, Understanding Criminal Law (1987), pp. 180–183:

"[V]arious theories of justification are espoused ...

*Moral Forfeiture*
Some moral interests ... may be forfeited as a result of morally wrong conduct. As a result of a person's improper conduct society may determine unilaterally that it will no longer recognize her interest in her life or property.

The moral-forfeiture doctrine is frequently used to explain why taking human life in self-defence or in preventing the escape of a fleeing felon is justified. Pursuant to this principle, V, an aggressor or a felon, forfeits her legal interest in the protection of her life as a result of her morally wrong conduct ... When D kills V in self-defence or in order to prevent her flight from a felony, no socially recognized harm has occurred. From the perspective of the homicide laws, the taking of V's life is viewed as no different than the killing of a fly or damage to an inanimate object.

The forfeiture principle ... is morally troubling because it involves the non-consensual loss of a valued right. When the principle is applied to the interest in human life it runs counter to the 'good and simple moral principle that human life is sacred'. A theory that treats human life as the equivalent of an inanimate object is troubling to those who believe in the sanctity of human life.

*Securing Legal and Moral Rights*
... The defendant's conduct is justified when it is determined that she had an affirmative right to protect a socially recognized interest that was threatened by the victim.

For example, when D kills or seriously injures V, a lethal aggressor, her conduct may be justified because she was enforcing a natural right of personal autonomy that V's conduct threatened. As this theory views the situation, D is a citizen protecting her interest against the outlaw, V, who seeks to take away her rights. This principle of justification does not treat V's death as socially irrelevant (as does the forfeiture doctrine); rather, it views D's conduct as affirmatively proper.

This concept is not without its critics ... Once it is determined that V has intruded on a right belonging to D—*e.g.*, the right to personal autonomy or the right to possess personal property—the theory suggests that D may use whatever force is necessary to enforce her rights, no matter how minor the intrusion on them. After all, she is in the right, and V is in the wrong, and Right should never give way to Wrong. In its unadulterated form, therefore, this justification theory may permit a disproportional response to the harm threatened.

*Superior Interest*
Conduct may be justified by a straightforward balancing of competing interests. In this view, the victim's interests are not forfeited by her prior conduct nor does the defendant

possess an unlimited right to act in enforcement of a particular interest. Pursuant to this principle the interests of D and V—and, more broadly, the interests of society in the values that they seek to enforce—are balanced. In each case there is a superior, or at least a non-inferior, interest. As long as such an interest is pursued, it is justified."

Some commentators have been of the view that "a defence is justificatory whenever it denies the objective wrongness of the act" and that "a justification is a defence, affirming that the act, state of affairs or consequences are on balance, to be socially approved, or are matters about which society is neutral".[8] However, other commentators decline to go this far.

### John Gardner, "Justifications and Reasons" in Simester and Smith (eds), Harm and Culpability (1996), pp. 107–108:

"In classifying some action as criminal, the law asserts that there are *prima facie* reasons against its performance—indeed reasons sufficient to make its performance *prima facie* wrongful. In providing a justificatory defence the law nevertheless concedes that one may sometimes have sufficient reason to perform the unlawful act, all things considered. . . .

The reasons against the action, which are the reasons for its criminalisation, may all have been defeated in the final analysis. It may have been alright for the defendant to act against them, all things considered. But it does not mean that they dropped out of the picture. That a reason is defeated does not mean that it is undermined or cancelled. It still continues to exert its rational appeal. It may indeed be a matter of bitter regret or disappointment that, thanks to the reasons which justified one's action, one nevertheless acted against the *prima facie* reasons for avoiding that action. It may even be a matter of regret or disappointment to the criminal law. The law certainly need not welcome it. But by granting a defence the law concedes that any regret or disappointment must be tolerated. . . . By granting a *justificatory* defence the law concedes that this is true by virtue of the fact that the defendant had, at the time of her *prima facie* wrongful action, sufficient reason to perform it."

According to this view it is not enough that the action may be justified on a utilitarian, balancing of interests, basis (as favoured, for example, by Robinson). It is necessary to explore the reasons the defendant had for acting. In order to have a justificatory defence the defendant's (explanatory) reasons for acting must correspond to the (guiding) reasons that exist for such actions.[9] In other words, his actual reasons for acting must be one of the accepted reasons for acting.

Whether one confines one's analysis to a balancing of interests or looks for underlying guiding reasons for permitting action, the following defences can be classified as justificatory in nature:

(a) *Self-defence.* Under any of the above theories self-defence provides a justification. The interests of the person attacked are greater than those of the attacker. The aggressor's culpability in starting the fight tips the scales in favour of the defendant.[10] Further "a rule allowing defensive action tends to inhibit aggression, or at least to restrain its continuance, as a rule forbidding defensive action would tend to promote it".[11]

[8] Williams, "The Theory of Excuses" [1982] Crim.L.R.732 at 735.
[9] Gardner, *above*, n.7, p. 111.
[10] Fletcher, *above*, n.6, p. 858.
[11] Williams, *above*, n.8, p. 739.

(b) *Necessity (Where the Harm Threatened is Greater than the Harm Caused).*
Where a lesser evil is committed in order to prevent a greater evil (*e.g.* criminal damage is caused to save the lives of 20 people), the interests of the latter outweigh the interests of the owner of the property. In the United States necessity is widely regarded as a paradigmatic example of justification.[12] This defence has only recently been admitted by English law, initially under the nomenclature "duress of circumstances". Its parameters are as yet uncertain but it is clearly not available as a defence to murder. As will be argued later, it is because of this classification of necessity as a justification that our judges, historically, showed reluctance to admit the defence at all. Perhaps if necessity had been viewed as an *excuse* only, there might have been a greater willingness to accept the defence into English law as it would have been seen as posing less threat to the established prohibitions of the criminal law. The closely related defence of duress is widely regarded as an excuse and in the leading case of *Howe*[13] the House of Lords seemed to think that the same principles applied to both. The recent "duress of circumstances" cases have a distinct excusatory flavour to them. Perhaps, then, if a fully-blown defence of necessity were to be admitted into English law it would be in an excusatory format. However, where the threatened harm is greater than the harm inflicted, the defence bears all the hallmarks, in principle, of a justification.

(c) *Public authority.* The use of force by the police, for example, in effecting an arrest is justified, the superior interest being the enforcement of the law. The same applies to acts "to prevent or terminate crime" or "to prevent or terminate a breach of the peace".[14]

(d) *Discipline.* Parents are justified in using reasonable force against their children, the superior interest being to "promote the welfare of the minor" and to prevent or punish misconduct.[15]

(e) *Consent.* Force against a person who has consented is justified, the superior interest being the value of human autonomy. Individuals are free and responsible agents and respect must be given to their right to consent to the infliction of force against them. However, in certain cases the interests of society prevail over any value attached to human automony and thus consent may not be given to certain types of force (mainly serious force such as death or grievous bodily harm, or disapproved-of-force such as sado-masochistic beatings inflicting injury).

## C. *Excuses*

A defence is excusatory when a wrongful, unjustified act has been committed, but, because of the excusing circumstances, the wrongdoer is not morally to blame for committing that act.

---

[12] Model Penal Code, s.3.02; N.Y. Penal Law, s.35.05.
[13] [1987] A.C. 417.
[14] Draft Criminal Code Bill 1989, cl. 44(1) (Law Com. No. 177).
[15] Model Penal Code, Proposed Official Draft 1962, s.308(1)(a). That this is a "superior interest" has become deeply contested. (*Tyrer* Eur.Ct. Series A. Vol. 26; *Campbell and Cosans v UK* (1980) 3 E.H.R.R. 531). *Below*, p. 321.

## Sanford H. Kadish, "Excusing Crime" (1987) 75 Cal.L.Rev. 257 at 264:

"To blame a person is to express a moral criticism, and if the person's action does not deserve criticism, blaming him is a kind of falsehood and is, to the extent the person is injured by being blamed, unjust to him. It is this feature of our everyday moral practices that lies behind the law's excuses. Excuses, then, ... represent no sentimental compromise with the demands of a moral code; they are, on the contrary, of the essence of a moral code."

According to this view an excuse destroys blame. However, the theoretical basis upon which this is done is far from agreed. "Two theories of excuses are currently popular in criminal law theory: the character theory and the capacity theory. In the former, the claim that the defendant makes is 'although I did it, I wasn't really myself'. In the latter, the claim is 'I did it but I couldn't have done otherwise. I had no real choice.'"[16] While the capacity-based approach, centred on notions of voluntariness,[17] was very influential during the latter part of the twentieth century, it has become subject to increased criticism.[18] More recently debate has focussed upon whether a character-based analysis offers a better way of understanding the role excuses play in the criminal law.

## John Gardner, "The Gist of Excuses" [1998] 1 Buffalo Criminal Law Review 575 at 575–579:

"It is often said that the criminal law judges actions, not character. That is true, but misleading. It is true that, barring certain exceptional and troubling examples, crimes are actions ... Nevertheless, the criminality of an action frequently falls to be determined, in part, according to standards of character—according to standards of courage, carefulness, honesty ... Nobody can be a thief in English law, for instance, unless she acts dishonestly. There is, to be sure, a difference between asking whether the accused acted dishonestly, and asking whether she is dishonest. She is dishonest if and only if she tends to act dishonestly. In other words, judging a person dishonest has a diachronic aspect which judging an action dishonest lacks. But apart from this diachronic aspect, the standard by which we judge a person dishonest is exactly the same standard as that by which we judge an action dishonest. It is a standard of character, a standard which bears not only on what is done, but also on the spirit in which and reason for which it is done. ...

[S]ometimes, standards of character figure in the criminal law because they are built into the definition of particular criminal offenses ... They also figure separately, however, in many of the criminal law's excusatory doctrines. ... On one familiar view, sometimes called the 'Humean' view, we should grant an excuse to somebody in respect of what he did if and only if what he did was no manifestation of his character. This view proceeds from the sound thought that excuses matter because a person's excused actions do not reflect badly on him—do not show him, personally, in a bad light. That being so, the thinking goes, an excuse must be something that blocks the path from an adverse judgment about an action to a correspondingly adverse judgment about the person whose action it is. The action is cowardly, say, but since this person does not otherwise tend towards cowardly actions, she herself is no coward. Her cowardly action is 'out of character'. And that, according to the Humean view, is the gist of excuses. But there is a good deal of confusion in this line of thought. For there is no such thing as a cowardly action which does not show its agent in a cowardly light. It is true that ... one cowardly action does not make a coward. But ... in my

[16] Tadros, "The Characters of Excuse" (2001) 21 O.J.L.S. 495.
[17] See Hart, *Punishment and Responsibility* (1968).
[18] See for example, Lacey, "Partial Defences to Homicide" in Ashworth and Mitchell (eds.), *Rethinking Homicide Law* (2000), pp.115–117; Mousourakis, *Criminal Responsibility and Partial Excuses* (1998), pp. 48–58.

cowardly action, by definition, I manifest at least the *beginnings* of a cowardly tendency ... Cowards are no more and no less than people who tend to perform cowardly actions. Their cowardly actions add up to *constitute*, not to evidence, their cowardice. Thus even if this cowardly action is my first, and is quite unprecedented, it necessarily counts constitutively and not merely evidentially against me whenever, thereafter, the question arises of whether I am a coward. And that is exactly what it means to say that my cowardly actions show me in a cowardly light. It follows that the Humean view unravels. If my excused actions do not show me in a cowardly light, they cannot, after all, be cowardly actions. That they are excused cannot therefore block the path from the judgment that I did something cowardly to the judgment that I am a coward. The excuse must intervene earlier to forestall the original judgment that this was a cowardly action. ...

So the gist of an excuse is not that the action was 'out of character', in the sense of being a departure from what we have come to expect from the person whose action it is. Quite the contrary, in fact. The gist of an excuse ... is precisely that the person with the excuse lived up to our expectations. ... [T]he question, for excusatory purposes, is obviously not whether the person claiming the excuse lived up to expectations in the predictive sense of being true to form .... The question is whether that person lived up to expectations in the *normative* sense. Did she manifest as much resilience, or loyalty, or thoroughness, or presence of mind as a person in her situation should have manifested? In the face of terrible threats, for example, did this person show as much fortitude as someone in his situation could properly be asked to show? ... The character standards which are relevant to these and other excuses are not the standards of our own characters, not even the standards of most people's characters, but rather the standards to which our characters should, minimally, conform."[19]

This assessment does not involve making broad or sweeping judgments about the individual's character as a person. Instead, the judgment, based in practice upon reasonableness, involves a specific assessment of whether the reasons upon which the action was taken correspond to the character standards to which we should conform.[20] Central to Gardner's argument is the point that those who claim excuses are not denying "responsibility" for their actions. This needs clarification because the word responsibility is ambiguous. Those who plead excusatory defences are obviously hoping to avoid responsibility in the sense associated with a conviction. However, they are not denying that they were their actions, for which there is an intelligible, rational explanation. Indeed, Gardner argues it is part of being a self-respecting person "to be able to give an intelligible rational account of herself, to be able to show that her actions were the actions of someone who aspired to live up to the proper standards ... She wants it to be the case that her actions were not truly wrongful, or if they were wrongful, that they were at any rate justified, or if they were not justified, that they were at any rate excused."[21]

It has been suggested that Gardner's gist of excuses "whilst acceptable in itself, is too narrow to provide a complete theory of excuses. ... The theory provides the defendant with an excuse only in cases on the borderline of justification".[22] Other defences, such as involuntary intoxication, fall outside this analysis but some commentators have argued that they ought to provide an excuse.[23]

---

[19] Gardner further argues (at 580–587) that one cannot distinguish the capacity to act, say with the character trait of courage, from acting courageously. One either acts courageously or not; there is no underlying capacity to act courageously that does or does not kick into operation. This view has been challenged by Tadros, "The Characters of Excuse" (2001) 21 O.J.L.S. 495 at 509–518.

[20] See further, Lacey, *ante* n.18 at 118–119.

[21] At 590.

[22] Tadros, *ante* n.19 at 496–497.

[23] On this see, Sullivan, "Making Excuses" in Simester and Smith (eds.), *Harm and Culpability* (1996).

### Victor Tadros, "The Characters of Excuse" (2001) 21 O.J.L.S. 495 at 498:

"In fact, I would suggest that there is no single gist of excuses. The criminal law is supervised by a multitude of principles. In arguing that one has an excuse, one attempts to show that whilst one's action was wrongful, the principles of the criminal law would not be served by imposing criminal liability. Excuses, then, mop up where exemptions, offence definitions and justifications would lead to convictions in inappropriate cases. That may be because the defendant came within the standards of reasonableness that the law expects. But it may also be because the defendant underwent a fundamental, and reasonable, shift in character before committing the wrongful act. Or it may be because the defendant only exhibited a vice that is an inappropriate target for criminal liability. Or it may be for some others reason, say because the defendant was, beyond her control, placed in a situation in which she was deprived of a fair opportunity to make her behaviour conform to the criminal law. In my view, that is as much as can be said for the gist of excuses."

One further issue arises. Just as we might wish to blame the intentional killer more than the negligent killer, so too we might wish to blame the provoked killer less than the unprovoked killer. In other words, there are degrees of blame that means some defences will not necessarily operate in an all or nothing fashion.

### Martin Wasik, "Partial Excuses in the Criminal Law" (1982) 45 M.L.R. 516 at 524–525:

"A more helpful model of the operation of excuses in the criminal law would involve the recognition of a 'scale of excuse', running downwards from excusing conditions, through partial excuses to mitigating excuses. Excuses towards the higher end of the scale are those where maximum moral pressure for exculpation outweighs reasons of policy and practicality for not permitting the excuse. Automatism is an example. Those towards the lower end of the scale, while they may be morally significant, are out-weighed by practical and policy considerations. A general excusing condition of good motive is an example. Partial excuses fall into the centre of this range, and exhibit a fine balance between rival considerations. The partial excuse of provocation, for example, has been said to be '... an extremely strong exculpatory claim ...' (Gross, p. 158) ... On the other hand this excusatory power should surely be weighed against the law's requirement of self-control. ...

All 'middle range' excuses may be regarded as potential partial excuses, but it is clearly not inevitable that they will turn out to be so. At a given stage in the history of criminal law, policy claims against admitting a particular excuse as an excusing condition will be seen as more or less compelling."

Despite the continued debate surrounding the underlying rationale of excuses, it is possible to identify those defences which, broadly speaking, can be classified as excuses:

(a) *Mistake.*

### Sanford H. Kadish, "Excusing Crime" (1987) 75 Cal.L.Rev. 257 at 261:

"Other mens rea requirements, on the other hand, are excuses in mens rea clothing. They are excusing conditions because they serve to deny blame for a harm done. That they are cast in the form of mens rea requirements does not change their character. ... This is why accident and mistake are excuses, despite their formal character as definitional mens rea requirements."

We have seen that there is fierce controversy over whether mistake negates a definitional element of the crime (and therefore is simply lack of *mens rea*), or whether it is a defence that previously had to be based on reasonable grounds.[24] This problem could easily be solved within the existing framework by asserting that *no* blame attaches to a person who makes a reasonable mistake (*i.e.* complete excuse), but that *some* blame attaches to the person who makes an unreasonable mistake, and he should be liable to *that* extent (*i.e.* a partial excuse).

(b) *Duress*. Duress is generally treated as an excuse rather than a justification. Some cases have identified the defence as hinging upon the morally involuntary response of the actor,[25] in other words that the defendant lacked a fair opportunity to conform to the law. It may also be explained by reference to Gardner's gist of excuses.

(c) *Provocation*. Although provocation may have originated as a justification, its transformation into a partial excuse is more or less complete. One of the attractions of pleading provocation, as opposed to diminished responsibility, is that it gives self-respecting defendants the opportunity to give an intelligible rational account of their actions rather than denying any responsibility.

(d) *Intoxication*. Again, this is generally only a partial excuse. The defendant lacks *mens rea* but because he is blamed for being so intoxicated, he is only partially excused (or for certain, generally lesser, crimes not excused at all).[26]

(e) *Necessity (Where the harm threatened is equal to the harm caused)*. As shall be seen, it is unlikely that English law affords a defence in such situations. Necessity or "duress of circumstances" as it has become known is only available as a defence when the defendant acts "proportionately in order to avoid a threat of death or serious injury"[27] and can never be a defence to a charge of murder. Accordingly, the only situations where the defence could conceivably be available in English law where the harm threatened is equal to the harm caused would be where a defendant causes serious injury to avoid threat of serious harm or (perhaps) commits what could be manslaughter to avoid a threat of death. In such cases the defence cannot be regarded as justificatory as the harm being caused is not less than the harm being threatened, but such a defence might be regarded as an excuse. We can understand the predicament of an actor who claims to have had no real choice. If the defence were ever to be allowed in the context of homicide, one might wish to treat this as only a partial excuse, *i.e.* reducing murder to manslaughter, which is the approach adopted to provocation.[28]

---

[24] *Above*, p. 184.
[25] *Below*, p. 327.
[26] Some commentators have focused upon the particular problem of "involuntary" intoxication where the defendant still has *mens rea*, to construct a variety of arguments concerning the role of defences. While such defendants would currently be found guilty, Sullivan has argued that a defence of blamelessness ought to be available, conjoining a lapse from previous good character with circumstances of destabilisation: "Making Excuses" in Simester and Smith (eds.), *Harm and Culpability* (1996), p.131. See further, Tadros, *ante* n.16 at 502–506 and Lacey, n.18 at 120—122.
[27] *Martin* (1989) 88 Cr.App.R. 343 at 346.
[28] See Commentary to Model Penal Code, Tent. Draft No. 8, 1958, pp. 8–9.

(f) *Superior orders.* Such a defence does not exist in English law. To the extent that obeying the orders of superiors is a defence in the United States, the harm done is justified on the basis that the superior interest protected is military discipline and effectiveness. The superiority of this interest is only overturned when the unlawfulness of the order is obvious. Although following this reasoning, superior orders could be tentatively classified as a justification, a better view could be that like duress, it constitutes an *excuse.* Such an approach could make the defence more "politically acceptable" and lead to its acceptance into English law. Whether this would be desirable is discussed later.

## D. *Exemptions*

While the gist of excuses may remain contested, there has been a growing acceptance of the view that excuses are not denials of responsibility. There must be a basic responsibility for one's actions for them to be amenable to excuse. However, there are other situations where the actor bears no basic responsibility for their actions. This occurs where the defendant lacks practical reasoning skills and where the actions are not amenable to intelligible rational explanation. Defences in such situations (previously categorised as excuses) are now increasingly being regarded as *exemptions.* "[T]he focus on making sense of people's actions in the light of their reasons rightly brings to the surface the important point that those whose reasoning can't be made sense of in this way, whether because of profound mental illness or infancy or sleepwalking ... are not responsible for their actions and therefore need no excuses for what they do."[29] A number of defences operate as exemptions:

(a) *Insanity.* A defendant who, because of a disease of the mind, cannot appreciate the nature and quality of her act, or cannot appreciate that it is wrong, lacks the practical reasoning skills to be found responsible for what she has done. On this basis insanity ought to act as an exemption. However, as we shall see, the wording of the *M'Naghten* Rules tends to suggest otherwise.[30]

(b) *Diminished Responsibility.* "Diminished responsibility occupies the peculiar position of a 'partial exemption'—a position which is closely related to the specific context of the mandatory life sentence for murder."[31] It is, however, based on the notion that the actions were unreasonable: "The whole point of the diminished responsibility defense is that it depends on the unreasonableness of the defendant's reactions, *i.e.* their unamenability to intelligible rational explanation."[32]

---

[29] Gardner, "The Gist of Excuses" [1998] 1 Buff. Crim.L.R. 575 at 589. For a criticism of this approach and a suggestion that it would be preferable to distinguish status excuses from non-status excuses, see Clarkson, *Understanding Criminal Law* (3rd ed., 2001) pp. 78–80.

[30] Below, p. 374.

[31] Lacey, above n.18 at 119–120.

[32] Gardner, above n.29 at 591.

(c) *Automatism.* There is some dispute as to whether automatism is a defence or whether the need for voluntariness is part of the *actus reus* requirement.[33] What is clear is that automatism shares the same rationale as other conditions which give rise to exemption from criminal liability.

(d) *Lack of Age.* Small children are not regarded as sufficiently responsible to engage in practical reasoning and, accordingly, are exempt from criminal liability when they commit a wrong.

## E. *Significance of Distinctions*

What is the point of this theoretical distinction?

The distinction between justification, excuse and exemption is the key to defining the parameters of each of the general defences. For example, approaching duress as an excuse, and not as a justification, informs one as to how its rules should be framed. Its importance as a theoretical guide, therefore, cannot be overestimated. But there is a practical utility as well. The distinction between defences has the following important consequences:

(a) Whether one is entitled to resist conduct for which the aggressor has a defence, or entitled to assist the aggressor, depends upon whether the aggressor's defence is justificatory or excusatory in nature.

### Paul Robinson, "Criminal Law Defenses: A Systematic Analysis" (1982) 82 Col.L.R. 199 at 274–275:

"Where an aggressor has a justification defence, the proper rule is clear: justified aggression should never be lawfully subject to resistance or interference. When conduct is deemed justified, it creates, by definition, a net benefit to society. The owner of a field should not be allowed to resist one who would burn it to stop a spreading fire, and others should be encouraged to assist, and not permitted to interfere.

An excused [or exempted] aggressor, on the other hand, should be subject to lawful resistance. That is, the victim of the psychotic attacker should be able lawfully to defend himself and to have others lawfully assist him in such defense. While the aggressor may be ultimately blameless, the conduct is clearly harmful. All required elements of the offense are satisfied and no justification exists."

Similar principles apply to accessories to crime. Thus in *Quick and Paddison*[34] the principal offender had a defence of automatism—an "exemption" under the above analysis. Paddison assisted him in his aggression and was held liable as an

---

[33] See *above*, pp. 87–90. See also Smith and Wilson, "Impaired Voluntariness and Criminal Responsibility: Reworking Hart's Theory of Excuses—the English Judicial Response" (1993) 13 O.J.L.S. 69 at 70–74.

[34] [1973] Q.B. 910; see also discussion of *Cogan and Leak, below,* pp. 553–556.

accessory. Had Quick's defence been justificatory in nature, say, acting reasonably to defend himself, then Paddison would have been entitled to assist him.

(b) When conduct is justified, some commentators argue that it is in effect "approved" of or, at least tolerated and there is, arguably, no need to try to prevent such conduct re-occurring. Where conduct is merely excused or exempted, however, society might wish to protect itself from repetition of such conduct and might wish to resort to coercive remedies against the defendant despite his acquittal. Thus a successful defence of insanity can lead to committment in a secure mental hospital. Lack of age is a defence to a criminal charge, but separate civil "care proceedings" may follow. Diminished responsibility exempts the actor from liability for murder, but not for manslaughter, enabling the court to take appropriate steps in relation to the defendant. So, too, intoxication is only an excuse to certain crimes—generally where there is a lesser included offence available to which it is no defence. Automatism, on the other hand, enables a defendant to escape all coercive measures, but, even here, there are suggestions that some new form of special verdict should be returned in such cases enabling a court to exercise some supervision over such a person to prevent recurrence of the involuntary action. The remaining excuses such as duress present little threat of repetition of the conduct and therefore there is no need to resort to coercive measures, but, in general, a finding of an exemption (as opposed to a justification) does alert one to the possibility of considering some form of restriction, whether criminal or civil, over the defendant.

The next two consequences of the distinction are admittedly somewhat speculative:

(c) Whether a defence is justificatory or excusatory may affect the law's response to defendants who claim to have made a mistake. Thus the law's response at present seems to be that those who make a mistake in relation to a *justification*, for example, self-defence, need only have made a genuine mistake. On the other hand, those who make a mistake in relation to an *excuse*, for example, duress, must have made a reasonable mistake to escape liability.[35]

(d) It has been suggested that the justification/excuse/exemption distinction provides the key to determining which of the general defences are available to crimes of strict liability. Justificatory defences are, but excusatory defences are not, available in such cases.[36] According to this view one could successfully plead self-defence to a strict liability offence, but could not plead intoxication or mistake to such an offence.

This view has some merit. The effect of an excusatory defence is that it destroys *blame*: the whole point of strict liability is that it is not concerned with blame. It would, therefore, be contradictory to allow excusatory defences to strict liability offences.[37] *A fortiori*, this argument would apply to exemptions. However, it is

---

[35] *Above*, pp. 197.
[36] Sornarajah, "Defences to Strict Liability Offences in Singapore and Malaysia" (1985) 27 Mal.L.R. 1.
[37] Koh, Clarkson and Morgan, *Criminal Law in Singapore and Malaysia: Text and Materials* (1989), p. 96.

submitted that this argument is unacceptable. Duress is generally regarded as an excuse. It would surely be absurd to deny the defence of duress when an actor, with a gun pointed at his head, commits a minor traffic offence. Likewise, automatism is an exemption, and it is true that it was denied as a defence to the involuntary conduct in committing strict liability offences in *Larsonneur*[38] and *Winzar v Chief Constable of Kent*.[39] These two cases have, however, been widely condemned and, it is submitted, ought not to be followed.[40] Perhaps the best way to determine what defences are available to strict liability offences is to examine each defence in turn and explore its rationale. This would then need to be contrasted with the rationale of strict liability and a decision made on a defence by defence basis as to whether each was available to offences of strict liability.[41]

(e) Where conduct is justified, some commentators suggest that the law, for conduct in those circumstances, is effectively amended.[42] A precedent is generated that others, in similar circumstances, may act in the same manner. Excuses and exemptions, on the other hand, do not constitute exceptions or modifications to the law. They simply involve an assessment that in the particular circumstances it would be unjust to hold a particular actor accountable for his actions. This distinction, perhaps, needs clearer expression.

### Paul Robinson, "Criminal Law Defenses: A Systematic Analysis" (1982) 82 Col.L.R. 199 at 245–247:

"When conduct is justified there is again nothing to condemn or punish. The defendant's conduct did not, under the circumstances, violate the prohibition of the law, and indeed may be desired and encouraged. Yet a harm or evil was inflicted, and such conduct should remain generally prohibited and condemned. Arson, for example, remains a crime even though the law may permit the burning of a field if it creates a fire break that saves an entire town, but when an actor is acquitted under a justification defense, the message to the public may be unclear, especially since the verdict of 'not guilty' gives no hint that a justification defense is at work. Thus, the condemnation and general deterrence of arson may be undercut. It might be desirable to alter the jury verdict to 'justified,' thereby acquitting the actor because his conduct caused no net harm, yet noting the continuing prohibition of arson ...

Excuses have a great potential for undercutting the condemnation and general deterrence of the harmful conduct. Even taking the objective circumstances into account, the conduct in an excuse case *does* constitute a net harm or evil that is condemned by the criminal law. Society will continue to condemn and seek to deter such conduct even in identical circumstances. It is the *actor*, not the act, which causes us to excuse. Furthermore, the explanation for acquittal of the offender is much less apparent than in cases of justification. Excuses, for the most part, rely on subjective criteria like mental illness, mistake, or subnormality. Often only a person who is aware of the evidence adduced at trial will understand that acquittal is based upon these special characteristics of the actor, not an approval or tolerance of the act.

[38] (1933) 24 Cr.App.R.74.
[39] *The Times*, March 28, 1983.
[40] Unless preceding fault could be established. See *above*, pp. 92–95.
[41] See Koh, Clarkson and Morgan (*above*, n.37 at pp. 97–98) for an illustration as to how this would work.
[42] As we have seen, other commentators, such as Gardner, would not subscribe to this view.

The limited value of a simple 'not guilty' verdict to convey the proper message accounts for some of the difficulties which have arisen in cases of excuse [such as *Dudley and Stephens*: see *below*, p. 357] ...

It may be because of this potential for misapprehension that an acquittal based on insanity is reported as a verdict of 'not guilty by reason of insanity' ...

The only sound approach is to recognize excuse defenses, but to minimize the danger of misperception of the acquittal by relying upon special verdicts—not guilty by reason of excuse—and assuring that the public understands that special message. Civil commitment and similar procedures outside the criminal justice system are available to further the goals of special deterrence and rehabilitation in the absence of condemnable culpability."

It is important to note, of course, that Robinson draws a distinction between excuses and justifications only. What we now call "exemptions" are included within the excusatory classification. However, his central message is the same. The moral message sent by an excuse or an exemption is different from that sent by justifications. This difference may be made clearer by the development of "special" verdicts. The case for this is, obviously, at its strongest in relation to exemptions. If, however, one takes the view that excuses, such as duress, are borderline justifications, the argument for a "special" verdict is very weak. Somebody who, according to Gardner's analysis, has lived up to the character standards of her role has done all that could reasonably be expected in the circumstances and should be entitled to a full and unqualified acquittal.

We are now in a position to examine the various defences.

## II. CONSENT

### A. *Introduction*

Certain crimes are defined in such a manner that they can only be committed without the victim's consent. Rape, for instance, is "sexual intercourse with a person who ... does not consent to it."[43] In such cases a defendant who claims that a person was consenting to sexual intercourse is not pleading consent as a defence, but is claiming that one of the definitional elements of the offence is missing—that the *actus reus* of the crime has not been committed.[44] A definition which provided that it was rape to engage in sexual intercourse (with a special defence to cover those cases where consent was present) would seem wrong. "The reason is that it reflects a morality that is foreign to us. We simply do not think that there is always a reason against sexual intercourse. We are much happier, therefore, with a definition of rape which includes consent in the definition of the offence rather than allowing it to operate as a separate defence that only comes into play as an after-thought once the initial prohibition has been breached."[45]

Most crimes are, however, not expressly defined in such a manner, but the consent of the "victim" may exempt the defendant from liability. The issue whether consent should be regarded as a "defence" was integral to the House of Lords

---

[43] Sexual Offences Act 1956, s.1 as amended.

[44] *D.P.P. v Morgan* [1976] A.C. 182.

[45] Shute, "The Second Law Commission Consultation Paper on Consent: Something Old, Something New, Something Borrowed: Three Aspects of the Project" [1996] Crim.L.R.684 at 690.

decision of *Brown*.[46] The majority took the view that consent should be regarded as a defence rather than as a definitional element. They then went on to conclude that it should not be available to the appellants who had been convicted of assault occasioning actual bodily harm following consensual sado-masochistic encounters. However, Lord Mustill, in the minority, approached the appeal as raising a question about the ambit of the offence rather than one involving a defence.

Normally this distinction is of little importance,[47] but in *Brown*, where the court was engaged in law-making,[48] there can be no doubt that the "defence approach" made the decision of the majority somewhat easier. While one may have doubts about the conclusion they reached, it is submitted that consent should be regarded as a defence. The defendant admits that he has committed the full *actus reus* of the offence, but claims that the consent of the "victim" justifies the wrong he would otherwise be committing. As we have seen, a justifactory defence can be explained in terms of a superior interest being upheld. In relation to consent, that superior interest is human autonomy. The foundation of the criminal law is the concept of responsibility and here it finds expression in the freedom of people to consent to what would otherwise be a criminal offence. The question is one of ascertaining what limits, if any, there are to this freedom to consent. As we shall see, consent is not a defence to all crimes. Whether it is available as a defence depends on the following matters: whether the court is sure that the recipient[49] truly consented (including whether he or she was responsible enough to make such decisions), the nature and degree of harm involved, and the rationale of consent as a defence.

### B. *The reality of consent*

**Joan McGregor, "Why When She Says No She Doesn't Mean Maybe and She Doesn't Mean Yes: A Critical Reconstruction of Consent, Sex and the Law" (1996) 2 Legal Theory 175 at 192:**

"There are a number of different ways of construing the nature and effect of consent. Consent is always given to the actions and projects of others. One common understanding of consent is that it 'authorizes' another to act in an area that is part of one's domain, *e.g.*, giving power of attorney to another. Another way of thinking about consent is that of giving 'permission' to another. Joel Feinberg said, in *Harm to Self*, 'Any act that crosses the boundaries of a sovereign person's zone of autonomy requires that person's "permission"; otherwise it is wrongful' [p. 177]. Conceiving of consent in either of these ways has

---

[46] [1994] 1 A.C. 212. See also *Kimber* (1983) 77 Cr.App.R.225 where it was implicit in the decision of the court that consent is not truly a defence.
[47] The main difference between these two modes of analysis relates to cases where the defendant mistakenly believes his victim has consented. See *above*, pp. 188–197. As to whether there is a difference in the burden of proof, see *above*, p. 270.
[48] Smith, Commentary to *Brown* [1993] Crim.L.R.585.
[49] This is the term adopted by Lord Mustill in *Brown* (*below*, p. 289), in preference to the term "victim" because of the presence of consent. It is significant that those in the majority (with the exception of Lord Jauncey) tend to refer to the consenting participant as a "victim".

normative significance, since it brings into existence new moral and legal relationships. . . . Consent must, then, be deliberate and voluntary, since its explicit purpose is to change the world by changing the structure of rights and obligations of the parties involved.

Within the sovereign zone of our domain, all others have a duty to refrain from crossing over without our permission. Consent cancels that duty, at least in regard to the specific acts consented to, and for a specified time."

To act as such a "moral transformative"[50] consent must be full and free.[51] Indeed, within the context of sexual offences, consent is to be expressly defined along these lines: "a person consents if he agrees by choice and has the freedom and capacity to make that choice".[52] However, to say that it must be informed and voluntary does not mean that every nuance is critical. Thus, the person who has intercourse because a boyfriend has declared undying love cannot later claim that the consent was invalid if it turns out that the boyfriend was lying. The person, however, who submits to intercourse rather than be beaten or killed is not regarded as having given real consent.[53]

In addition, the person must have sufficient capacity to give consent. Capacity may be lacking because of the individual's physical or mental condition. As far as medical treatment is concerned, action taken during an emergency to aid the patient may not constitute an assault even if done without consent. In theory, at least, the question is whether the patient has the capacity to consent. If, for example, a pregnant woman who needs an emergency caesarean operation has capacity to consent then her refusal ought to be respected, even if this places her life and that of her unborn child at risk.[54] In practice, however, the patient may be found to lack capacity and the operation go ahead.[55]

As far as adults with severe learning difficulties or mental disabilities are concerned, the degree of incapacity must be severe before they are not able to give consent.[56] In *Jenkins*[57] a young woman with a verbal mental age of two or three who did not understand sexual relationships, pregnancy or sexually transmitted diseases became pregnant. DNA tests on the aborted foetus (the decision being taken for her to have an abortion since she was unable to understand what had happened to her, to care for a child or give consent to an abortion) revealed that the father was a member of her residential staff. He was charged with rape but acquitted, the trial judge ruling that she had properly consented, as she simply had

---

[50] Alexander, "The Moral Magic of Consent" (1996) 2 *Legal Theory* 165.

[51] In *Brown*, Lord Templeman (at 235) sought to cast doubt on the consent of the participants, describing it as "dubious or worthless." In fact, there was some doubt as to consent in one incident only. For the rest, as Lord Slynn stated (at 281): "Astonishing though it may seem, the persons involved positively wanted, asked for, the acts to be done to them." As to the description "worthless", one is presumably to interpret this as irrelevant, rather than as casting doubt on the responsibility of the participants.

[52] Sexual Offences Bill 2003, clause 77. *Below*, p. 615.

[53] *Below*, pp. 612–616.

[54] *St.George's Healthcare Trust v S* [1998] 3 All E.R. 673. See further, Hale L.J. "A Pretty Pass: When is There a Right to Die?" (2003) 32 C.L.W.R. 1.

[55] *Re S (adult: refusal of medical treatment)* [1992] 3 W.L.R. 806.

[56] Severely subnormal women ("defectives"), however, cannot consent to sexual intercourse or indecent assault–nor in the latter case can severely subnormal men (Sexual Offences Act 1956, ss.7, 14(4), 15(3), 45, as amended by Mental Health Act 1959). See *Kimber, above*, n.46.

[57] Unreported. Central Criminal Court, January 10–12, 2000. Cited in Law Commission, *Consent in Sex Offences, A Report to the Home Office Sex Offences Review* (2000), paras 4.66–4.67.

to submit to her animal instincts to be deemed to have consented. The Law Commission has expressed the view that, whilst the law should protect the sexual autonomy of the mentally disabled and others, it should also protect the vulnerable. Rightly, it concluded that the law should be so framed that there is no capacity to consent in situations such as *Jenkins* and recommended that the need to understand the reasonably foreseeable consequences of sexual activity is fundamental to any capacity to consent to such activity.[58] The issue of the capacity of the mentally disabled also frequently arises in relation to medical treatment and will be considered further in the context of the decisions of *Bland* and *Ms B*.[59]

Incapacity may also arise because of the age of the individual. In *Howard*,[60] for example, the alleged consent of a six-year-old to attempted sexual intercourse with the defendant was deemed invalid. It was judged that she was incapable of giving real consent. Whilst transparently the right decision in that particular case, the principle that there must be informed consent by minors may not always operate so simply. A six-year-old may truthfully be said not to have attained the "age of discretion" but can the same thing be said of 12 and 13year-olds? The reality is that the "age of discretion" rests not only upon the mental and physical age of the child but also depends on the type of harm to which they have allegedly given their consent.[61] For example, in *Sutton* it was held that boys of 10, 11 and 12 could consent to their naked bodies being touched in order to indicate the pose the photographer wanted.[62] However, had the touching been held to be indecent the same consent would have been held to be invalid and the photographer would have been convicted of indecent assault.[63] In *Gillick v West Norfolk A.H.A.*[64] the court was concerned with whether contraceptive advice could be given to girls under the age of 16 without their parents' consent. The House of Lords ruled that parental rights to determine whether or not such a child should have medical treatment end "when the child achieves a sufficient understanding and intelligence to enable him or her to understand fully what is proposed."[65] This approach was followed in *R. v D.* in assessing whether a child could consent to what would otherwise be a kidnapping by one parent.[66] However, recent cases have undermined this "*Gillick*-competence" test by restricting it to cases of a child giving positive consent. "[T]he courts have held that they have power, as part of their inherent parental jurisdiction, to override the child's objections even when he does have sufficient understanding and has reached 16. They will start with a preference for

---

[58] Law Commission, above, n.57, paras 4.66–4.81. See also Law Commission, *Mental Incapacity* (Report No. 231, 1995) and clause 2 of the Draft Mental Incapacity Bill.

[59] *Below*, p. 288.

[60] [1966] 1 W.L.R. 13.

[61] The Sexual Offences Bill 2003, clause 3 will make the issue of consent irrelevant for the crime of rape where the victim is under 13 years old.

[62] [1977] 1 W.L.R. 1086. But see now the Protection of Children Act 1978, s.1(1)(a) which prohibits the taking of indecent photographs of children. See Hall, "Can Children Consent to Indecent Assault?" [1996] Crim.L.R.184 where he argues that *Sutton* was wrongly decided.

[63] By virtue of s.14(4) of the Sexual Offences Act 1956 the consent of a boy under the age of 16 is regarded as irrelevant for the purposes of determining whether there has been an indecent assault. S.15 applies the same rule to girls.

[64] [1986] 1 A.C. 112.

[65] *Per* Lord Scarman at 189. This test is approved by the Law Commission in Consultation Paper No. 139, *Consent in the Criminal Law* (1995), para. 5.21.

[66] [1984] A.C. 778.

respecting his views, but will not allow him to die, or probably suffer serious harm, through lack of treatment, especially if his illness is distorting his judgment."[67] Thus, in *Re W* a 16-year-old child suffering from anorexia nervosa refused medical treatment that would save her life. It was held that the court had the power to override her wishes even though she was "*Gillick*-competent".[68] It is probably also the case that parents can override their child's refusal of treatment.[69] Such an approach has been criticised on the basis that it is "an unattractive prospect that parents might have power to oblige a capable child to accept forcible treatment against his will and without any of the safeguards attached to legal proceedings."[70]

## C. *The nature and degree of harm*

Harm can be defined as any violation of an interest and, as we have already begun to see, there are violations of some interests to which courts will not allow consent to be given.

Whether consent will constitute a defence is ultimately a question of public policy that involves balancing the seriousness of the harm against the social utility or acceptability of the defendant's conduct. The greater the injury inflicted, the more the defendant must have some justification (in terms of social utility). Stephen J. in *Coney* held:

> "The principle as to consent seems to me to be this: When one person is indicted for inflicting personal injury upon another, the consent of the person who sustains the injury is no defence to the person who inflicts the injury, if the injury is of such a nature, or is inflicted under such circumstances, that its infliction is injurious to the public as well as to the person injured."[71]

Thus, if a defendant kills a person at that other's request, it will still be murder[72]; this will be so even though the actions could be described as "mercy-killing" and even though self-murder (suicide) is no longer a crime.[73] The Criminal Law Revision Committee has rejected the proposal that such a killing "should be a special offence removed from the law of murder and should carry a reduced sentence, the reason being that such a killing did not present a threat to public security as did murder in general".[74] However, while active euthanasia and

---

[67] Hoggett, *Parents and Children* (4th ed., 1993), p. 16.

[68] *Re W (A Minor) (Medical Treatment: Court's Jurisdiction)* [1993] Fam. 64. See further *Re R (A Minor) (Wardship: Medical Treatment)* [1992] Fam. 11; *Re J* [1992] 3 W.L.R. 521.

[69] *Re R (A Minor) (Wardship: Medical Treatment)* [1992] Fam. 11; *Re K. W and H. (Minors) (Consent to Medical Treatment)* [1993] 1 F.L.R. 845. A proper examination of this complex issue is beyond the scope of this book. See further, Murphy, "W(h)ither Adolescent Autonomy" [1992] J. Soc. Wel. and Fam. Law 529.

[70] Hoggett, *above*, n.67, p. 16

[71] (1882) 8 Q.B.D. 549.

[72] Or, possibly, manslaughter if the defendant is able to plead diminished responsibility. The House of Lords Select Committee on Medical Ethics decided that there should be no change to the substantive law relating to euthanasia, mercy-killing or complicity in suicide (Report (1993–1994) HL Paper 21–1).

[73] Suicide Act 1961, s.1.

[74] 14th Report, *Offences against the Person*, Cmnd. 7844 (1980), para. 128. The German Penal Code St.G.B. Art. 216 creates a special lesser offence of "killing on request" on the basis that the victim's consent reduces the wrongfulness of the killing. See Fletcher, pp. 332–334, where he distinguishes between voluntary, involuntary, passive and active euthanasia.

assisting suicide[75] are prohibited in this country there are an increasing number of cases in which the courts have been called upon to determine the issue of the continuance of medical treatment. In *Re B*[76] the patient had suffered an illness that left her paralyzed from the neck down and requiring the support of a ventilator to breathe. Ms B asked for the ventilator to be switched off and when the hospital refused, sought a declaration from the court that she had the capacity to make such a decision and that the hospital had been acting unlawfully in treating her in defiance of her wishes. She was found to be capable, the declaration was granted, and Ms B was moved to a hospital prepared to carry out her wishes where she died shortly afterwards.[77] In other situations, relatives or the hospital treating the patient may raise the issue of withdrawing treatment. Many of these cases have concerned babies born with severe disabilities[78] but in the case of *Bland*[79] the House of Lords was asked to make a declaration enabling life-sustaining treatment to be withdrawn from a young male patient who had been severely injured at the Hillsbrough football ground disaster in 1989. The patient had suffered catastrophic and irreversible damage to the brain, which had left him in a condition known as a persistent vegetative state. Medical opinion was agreed that there was no hope of recovery or improvement.

## Airedale N.H.S. Trust v Bland [1993] A.C. 789 (House of Lords)

Lord Goff:
"I must however stress, at this point, that the law draws a crucial distinction between cases in which a doctor decides not to provide, or to continue to provide, for his patient treatment or care which could or might prolong his life, and those in which he decides, for example by administering a lethal drug, actively to bring his patient's life to an end. . . . the former may be lawful, either because the doctor is giving effect to his patient's wishes by withholding the treatment or care, or even in certain circumstances in which . . . the patient is incapacitated from stating whether or not he gives his consent. But it is not lawful for a doctor to administer a drug to his patient to bring about his death, even though that course is prompted by a humanitarian desire to end his suffering, however great that suffering may be: see *R. v Cox* (unreported), September 18, 1992. So to act is to cross the Rubicon which runs between on the one hand the care of his living patient and on the other hand euthanasia . . .

At the heart of this distinction lies a theoretical question. Why is it that the doctor who gives his patient a lethal injection which kills him commits an unlawful act and indeed is guilty of murder, whereas a doctor who, by discontinuing life support, allows his patient to die, may not act unlawfully—and will not do so, if he commits no breach of duty to his patient? . . .

I agree that the doctor's conduct in discontinuing life support can properly be categorised as an omission . . . But in the end the reason for that difference is that, whereas the law considers that discontinuance of life support may be consistent with the doctor's duty to care for his patient, it does not, for reasons of policy, consider that it forms any part of his duty to give his patient a lethal injection to put him out of his agony."

---

[75] *R. (Pretty) v Director of Public Prosecutions (Secretary of State for the Home Department Intervening)* [2002] 1 A.C. 800. *Below*, p. 721.
[76] *Re B (Adult: Refusal of Medical Treatment)* [2002] 2 All E.R. 449.
[77] See further, Hale L.J., *above*, n.54.
[78] *Re J (A Minor) (Wardship: Medical Treatment)* [1991] 2 W.L.R. 140; *Re B (A Minor) (Wardship: Medical Treatment)* [1981] 1 W.L.R. 1421. In cases where wardship has been invoked the court is able to give consent itself.
[79] [1993] A.C. 789.

The declaration was affirmed by the House of Lords (dismissing the appeal by the Official Solicitor) on the basis that further treatment was futile and that prolonging the patient's life by medical treatment could not be said to be in his best interests. The decision was not simply based (as it would have been in the United States, for example[80]) on the principle of "substituted judgment". This is an approach which requires the court to ascertain what the patient would have wanted. Instead, in this country the concept of "substituted judgment" may be subsumed into the broader analysis of the best interests of the patient.[81] While in the United States consent is regarded as critical even in such cases, the courts in this country have rejected the idea that they have the power to give consent on behalf of an incapable adult.[82] That said, the acceptance by the House of Lords that courts ought to be involved in individual cases of withdrawal of treatment (by means of a declaration of the existing law) looks very much like the court giving consent.

In *Re A (children)(conjoined twins)*[83] the trial judge decided that the separation of the twins would be lawful, following *Bland,* because it amounted to a withdrawal of treatment. The Court of Appeal rejected this analysis. While the concerns expressed in *Bland* itself about the omission/commission distinction were echoed, the Court of Appeal was unanimous in holding that positive acts would have to be performed to save Jodie's life and thus the lawfulness of the operation had to be based on other grounds.[84] The distinction between acts and omissions continues to be of utmost importance in cases such as *Bland* where the court is effectively giving consent to the withdrawal of treatment.

But what about injuries short of death? In the absence of any social utility it is clear that consent will be no defence to really serious injuries.[85] In *Leach,*[86] for example, the "victim" organised his own crucifixion on Hampstead Heath. The defendants nailed him to a wooden cross, his hands pierced by 6 inch nails. The defendants were liable for unlawful wounding; the consent of the victim was disregarded. With regard to lesser injuries, the following leading decision establishes that one may consent to common assault which involves only minimal or no injury. It was also thought to establish that consent is not a defence where actual bodily harm occurs or where a wound is inflicted[87] unless it falls within a recognised exception such as sporting injuries.

### R. v Brown (and other appeals) [1994] 1 A.C. 212 (House of Lords)

The appellants belonged to a group of sado-masochistic homosexuals who over a 10 year period participated in the commission of acts of violence against each other, including genital torture, for the sexual pleasure engendered in the giving and receiving of pain. The

---

[80] See, *e.g. Re Quinlan* (1976) 355 A. 2d 647; *Superintendent of Belchertown State School v Saikewicz,* 370 N.E. 2d 417.

[81] See further, Wilson, "Is Life Sacred?" (1995) 17 J. of Soc. Wel. and Fam. Law 131.

[82] *Re F (Mental Patient: Sterilisation)* [1990] 2 A.C. 1; *Airedale N.H.S. Trust v Bland* [1993] A.C. 789.

[83] [2001] Fam. 147.

[84] *Below,* p. 360.

[85] *Wright* (1603) Co.Lit.f. 127 a–b; *Cato* [1976] 1 All E.R. 260 (where consent to the administration of a noxious thing likely to endanger life was no defence) and *Brown* [1994] 1 A.C. 212.

[86] *The Times,* January 15, 1969.

[87] Offences contrary to the Offences against the Person Act 1861, ss.47 and 20. Whether this applies in all cases or only cases where the harm is deliberately inflicted is discussed below, p. 296.

partner in each case consented to the acts being committed and sustained no permanent injury. The participants had code words that enabled them to indicate when the pain became excessive. The appellants were charged with assault occasioning actual bodily harm contrary to section 47, and with unlawful wounding contrary to section 20 of the Offences against the Person Act 1861. The appellants changed their pleas to guilty when the trial judge ruled that consent was no defence to such charges and subsequently appealed.

Lord Templeman:
"My Lords, the appellants were convicted of assaults occasioning actual bodily harm contrary to section 47 of the Offences against the Person Act 1861. ... The incidents which led to each conviction occurred in the course of consensual sado-masochistic encounters. The Court of Appeal upheld the convictions and certified the following point of law of general public importance:
'Where A wounds or assaults B occasioning him actual bodily harm in the course of a sado-masochistic encounter, does the prosecution have to prove lack of consent on the part of B before they can establish A's guilt under section 20 or section 47 of the Offences against the Person Act 1861?'
... In the present case each of the appellants intentionally inflicted violence upon another (to whom I refer as 'the victim') with the consent of the victim and thereby occasioned actual bodily harm or in some cases wounding or grievous bodily harm. Each appellant was therefore guilty of an offence under section 47 or section 20 of the Act of 1861 unless the consent of the victim was effective to prevent the commission of the offence or effective to constitute a defence to the charge.
In some circumstances violence is not punishable under the criminal law. When no actual bodily harm is caused, the consent of the person affected precludes him from complaining. There can be no conviction for the summary offence of common assault if the victim has consented to the assault. Even when violence is intentionally inflicted and results in actual bodily harm, wounding or serious bodily harm the accused is entitled to be acquitted if the injury was a foreseeable incident of a lawful activity in which the person injured was participating. Surgery involves intentional violence resulting in actual or sometimes serious bodily harm but surgery is a lawful activity. Other activities carried on with consent by or on behalf of the injured person have been accepted as lawful notwithstanding that they involve actual bodily harm or may cause serious bodily harm. Ritual circumcision, tattooing, ear-piercing and violent sports including boxing are lawful activities. ...
My Lords, the authorities dealing with the intentional infliction of bodily harm do not establish that consent is a defence to a charge under the Act of 1861. They establish that the courts have accepted that consent is a defence to the infliction of bodily harm in the course of some lawful activities. The question is whether the defence should be extended to the infliction of bodily harm in the course of sado-masochistic encounters. ... [This question] can only be decided by consideration of policy and public interest. ...
Counsel for some of the appellants argued that the defence of consent should be extended to the offence of occasioning actual bodily harm under section 47 of the Act of 1861 but should not be available to charges of serious wounding and the infliction of serious bodily harm under s.20. I do not consider that this solution is practicable. Sado-masochistic participants have no way of foretelling the degree of bodily harm which will result from their encounters. ...
Counsel for the appellants argued that consent should provide a defence to charges under both section 20 and section 47 because, it was said, every person has a right to deal with his body as he pleases. I do not consider that this slogan provides a sufficient guide to the policy decision which must now be made. It is an offence for a person to abuse his own body and mind by taking drugs. Although the law is often broken, the criminal law restrains a practice which is regarded as dangerous and injurious to individuals and which if allowed and extended is harmful to society generally. In any event the appellants in this case did not mutilate their own bodies. They inflicted bodily harm on willing victims. Suicide is no longer

an offence but a person who assists another to commit suicide is guilty of murder or manslaughter.[88]

The assertion was made on behalf of the appellants that the sexual appetites of sadists and masochists can only be satisfied by the infliction of bodily harm and that the law should not punish the consensual achievement of sexual satisfaction. There was no evidence to support the assertion that sado-masochist activities are essential to the happiness of the appellants or any other participants but the argument would be acceptable if sado-masochism were only concerned with sex, as the appellants contend. In my opinion sado-masochism is not only concerned with sex. Sado-masochism is also concerned with violence. The evidence discloses that the practices of the appellants were unpredictably dangerous and degrading to body and mind and were developed with increasing barbarity and taught to persons whose consents were dubious or worthless. . . .

In principle there is a difference between violence which is incidental and violence which is inflicted for the indulgence of cruelty. The violence of sado-masochistic encounters involves the indulgence of cruelty by sadists and the degradation of victims. . . . I am not prepared to invent a defence of consent for sado-masochistic encounters which breed and glorify cruelty and result in offences under sections 47 and 20 of the Act of 1861."

Lord Mustill (dissenting):

"Throughout the argument of the appeal I was attracted by an analysis on the following lines. First, one would construct a continuous spectrum of the infliction of bodily harm, with killing at one end and a trifling touch at the other. Next, with the help of reported cases one would identify the point on this spectrum at which consent ordinarily ceases to be an answer to a prosecution for inflicting harm. This could be called 'the critical level.' It would soon become plain however that this analysis is too simple and that there are certain types of special situation to which the general rule does not apply. Thus, for example, surgical treatment which requires a degree of bodily invasion well on the upper side of the critical level will nevertheless be legitimate if performed in accordance with good medical practice and the consent of the patient. Conversely, there will be cases in which even a moderate degree of harm cannot be legitimated by consent. . . .

For all the intellectual neatness of this method I must recognise that it will not do, for it imposes on the reported cases and on the diversities of human life an order which they do not possess. Thus, when one comes to map out the spectrum of ordinary consensual physical harm, to which the special situations form exceptions, it is found that the task is almost impossible, since people do not ordinarily consent to the infliction of harm. In effect, either all or almost all the instances of the consensual infliction of violence are special. . . .

Furthermore, when one examines the situations which are said to found such a theory it is seen that the idea of consent as the foundation of a defence has in many cases been forced on to the theory, whereas in reality the reason why the perpetrator of the harm is not liable is not because of the recipient's consent, but because the perpetrator has acted in a situation where the consent of the recipient forms one, but only one, of the elements which make the act legitimate. . . .

I thus see no alternative but to adopt a much narrower and more empirical approach, by looking at the situations in which the recipient consents or is deemed to consent to the infliction of violence upon him, to see whether the decided cases teach us how to react to this new challenge. . . .

[Lord Mustill concluded that the case-law left the way open for the House to determine the issue completely anew.]

As I have ventured to formulate the crucial question, it asks whether there is good reason to impress upon section 47 an interpretation which penalises the relevant level of harm irrespective of consent, *i.e.*, to recognise sado-masochistic activities as falling into a special category of acts, such as duelling and prize-fighting, which 'the law says shall not be done.' This is very important, for if the queston were differently stated it might well yield a different

---

[88] With due respect to his Lordship, it is only murder if the defendant intentionally *causes* the death of the "victim". It is manslaughter if both had intended to die and the defendant unexpectedly survives. In other circumstances the crime involved is aiding and abetting suicide (*below*, p. 721).

answer. In particular, if it were held that as a matter of law all infliction of bodily harm above the level of common assault is incapable of being legitimated by consent, except in special circumstances, then we would have to consider whether the public interest required the recognition of private sexual activities as being in a specially exempt category. This would be an altogether more difficult question and one which . . . [should be answered by Parliament] . . . I ask myself . . . whether the Act of 1861 (a statute which . . . was clearly intended to penalise conduct of a quite different nature) should in this new situation be interpreted so as to make it criminal?

[His Lordship concluded that there were insufficient grounds to do so and allowed the appeals.]"

Lord Slynn (dissenting):
"These propositions seem to me to be clear.

It is 'inherent in the conception of assault and battery that the victim does not consent:' Glanville Williams, 'Consent and Public Policy' [1962] Crim.L.R.74, 75. Secondly, consent must be full and free and must be as to the actual level of force used or pain inflicted. Thirdly, there exist areas where the law disregards the victim's consent even where that consent is freely and fully given. These areas may relate to the person (*e.g.* a child); they may relate to the place (*e.g.* in public); they may relate to the nature of the harm done. It is the latter which is in issue in the present case.

I accept that consent cannot be said simply to be a defence to any act which one person does to another. A line has to be drawn as to what can and as to what cannot be the subject of consent. . . .

[T]o be workable, it cannot be allowed to fluctuate within particular charges and in the interests of legal certainty it has to be accepted that consent can be given to acts which are said to constitute actual bodily harm and wounding. Grievous bodily harm I accept to be different by analogy with and as an extension of the old cases on maiming. Accordingly, I accept that other than for cases of grievous bodily harm or death, consent can be a defence. This in no way means that the acts done are approved of or encouraged."

**Appeal dismissed**

While this decision can only be profoundly regretted as legal moralism prevailing over human autonomy and the right of persons to express their sexuality as they see fit,[89] it did, in some respects, help to clarify the law. The majority, in their answer to the certified question, decided that consent can be a defence to common assault, but is generally no defence to an assault occasioning actual bodily harm or to an unlawful wounding. There are exceptions to this general rule based on "policy and public interest" which allow persons to consent to the infliction of actual bodily harm, wounding—and even serious bodily harm. These exceptions include activities such as surgery, tattooing, ear-piercing[90] and violent sports. However, the decision in *Brown* does leave certain questions unanswered:

1. While the House of Lords endorsed the existence of "well established exceptions", the parameters of these exceptions are far from clear.

[89] See Bibbings and Alldridge, "Sexual Expression, Body Alteration, and the Defence of Consent" (1993) 20 J. Law and Soc. 356. The appellants attempted to rely (unsuccessfully) upon the European Convention on Human Rights (most importantly, upon Article 8 which guarantees respect for private and family life) during the course of their defence. Subsequently, the European Court of Human Rights unanimously held that there had been no violation of Article 8 (*Laskey, Jaggard and Brown v The United Kingdom* (1997) 24 E.H.R.R. 39).

[90] Other forms of body-piercing, such as tongue, nose, lip, etc. may well fall within this exception if done for decoration. See *Oversby* [1991] unreported, cited in Bibbings and Alldridge, *ibid.*

## Wilson [1996] 2 Cr.App.R.241 (Court of Appeal, Criminal Division)

The defendant was convicted of assaulting his wife contrary to section 47 of the Offences Against the Person Act 1861. He admitted to the police (who had been informed by the wife's doctor) that he had used a hot knife to brand his initials on her buttocks. The judge ruled that he was bound by the decision in *Brown*. On appeal:

Russell L.J.:
"We are abundantly satisfied that there is no factual comparison to be made between the instant case and the facts of either *Donovan* and *Brown*: Mrs Wilson not only consented to that which the appellant did, she instigated it. There was no aggressive intent on the part of the appellant. On the contrary, far from wishing to cause injury to his wife, the appellant's desire was to assist her in what she regarded as the acquisition of a desirable piece of personal adornment, perhaps in this day and age no less understandable than the piercing of nostrils or even tongues for the purposes of inserting decorative jewellery.

In our judgment *Brown* is not authority for the proposition that consent is no defence to a charge under section 47 of the 1861 Act, in all circumstances where actual bodily harm is deliberately inflicted. It is to be observed that the question certified for their Lordships in *Brown* related only to a 'sadomasochistic encounter'. However, their Lordships recognised in the course of their speeches, that it was necessary that there be exceptions to what is no more than a general proposition. The speeches of [several of their Lordships] ... all refer to tattooing as being an activity which, if carried out with the consent of an adult, does not involve an offence under section 47, albeit that actual bodily harm is deliberately inflicted.

For our part, we cannot detect any logical difference between what the appellant did and what he might have done in the way of tattooing. The latter activity apparently requires no state authorisation, and the appellant was as free to engage in it as anyone else.

We do not think that we are entitled to assume that the method adopted by the appellant and his wife was any more dangerous or painful than tattooing ... [W]e are firmly of the opinion that it is not in the public interest that activities such as the appellant's in this appeal should amount to criminal behaviour. Consensual activity between husband and wife, in the privacy of the matrimonial home, is not, in our judgment, a proper matter for criminal investigation, let alone criminal prosecution. ... In this field, in our judgment, the law should develop upon a case by case basis rather than upon general propositions to which, in the changing times we live, exceptions may arise from time to time not expressly covered by authority."

**Appeal allowed**

## R. v Emmett, Case No. 9901191 ZR, The Times, October 15, 1999 (Court of Appeal, Criminal Division)

The defendant and his wife-to-be engaged in consensual sexual activity that on one occasion involved partial asphyxiation and on another occasion setting light to lighter fuel on her breast. As a result she suffered subconjunctival haemorrhages in both eyes, some bruising around her neck and a burn that at first was thought to be so serious as to require a skin graft. The offence came to light because the doctor treating the woman reported it to the police. The defendant was convicted of assault occasioning actual bodily harm. The trial judge distinguished *Wilson* and followed *Brown* in ruling that consent was no defence where the parties foresaw the risk of injuries. On appeal:

Wright J.:
"[W]e have come to the clear conclusion that the evidence in the instant case, in striking contrast to that in *Wilson*, made it plain that the actual or potential damage to which the appellant's partner was exposed in this case, plainly went far beyond that which was established by the evidence in *Wilson*. The lady suffered a serious, and what must have been, an excruciating painful burn. ... As to the process of partial asphyxiation ... while it may

now be fairly well known that the restriction of oxygen to the brain is capable of heightening sexual sensation, it is also, or should be, equally well-known that such a practice contains within itself a grave danger of brain damage or even death. ... The appellant was plainly aware of that danger. ... Accordingly, whether the line beyond which consent becomes immaterial is drawn at the point ... at which common assault becomes assault occasioning actual bodily harm, or at some higher level, where the evidence looked at objectively reveals a realistic risk of more than a transient or trivial injury, it is plain, in our judgment, that the activities involved in by this appellant and his partner went well beyond that line. ...

[The appellant argues that] the involvement of the processes of the criminal law, in the consensual activities that were carried on in this couple's bedroom, amount to a breach of Article 8 of the European Convention on Human Rights [right to respect for private and family life]. ... It seems clear to us that once the conduct of the accused person has gone beyond the permitted limit, however that is defined, in inflicting injury upon or exposing to potential risk his or her partner, in the course of sado-masochistic games whether homo- or heterosexual, so that he or she *prima facie* at least has committed an offence of a sufficient degree of seriousness, the institution of a criminal investigation and, if appropriate, criminal proceedings cannot amount to a breach of Article 8."

**Appeal dismissed**

While this decision can be welcomed, as applying the same test to different types of sexual relationships, the judgment is non-committal about the precise point at which the state may intervene in one's private sexual life. Branding one's wife with a knife is permitted (by analogy with the "exception" of tattooing[91]) but the activities in this case "went well beyond that line". Are we any closer to understanding the puzzling reliance in *Wilson* on the fact that the branding had been done as an act of affection rather than aggression? It would clearly be absurd to distinguish between acts of affection and acts committed for sexual gratification. What is the position with regard to other exceptions? Consent is a defence to sports participants who injure one another in the course of their sporting activities. Lawful sports (excluding activities such as prize-fighting) are to be encouraged: they are "manly diversions, they tend to give strength, skill and activity, and may fit people for defence, public as well as personal, in time of need".[92] In *Billinghurst* the jury was directed that rugby players consent to such force as can reasonably be expected during the game.[93] However, "off the ball" incidents are another matter. Not only may players not consent to the deliberate infliction of harm by another, but the courts will ordinarily respond to such offending by imposing a custodial sentence.[94] Where does this leave professional boxing?

"For money, not recreation or personal improvement, each boxer tries to hurt the opponent more than he is hurt himself, and aims to end the contest

---

[91] As Roberts points out, "Consent to Injury: How far Can You Go?" [1997] 113 L.Q.R. 27 at 31 there is no authority that *branding* is an exception to the general liability rule and, thus, "Russell L.J. was obliged to look for a new exception to cover Mr Wilson's handiwork."

[92] Foster, *Crown Cases* (3rd ed.), p. 260.

[93] [1978] Crim.L.R.553.

[94] See, *e.g. Birkin* [1988] Crim.L.R.855. See Grayson, *Sport and the Law* (3rd ed., 2000), where the author suggests that team managers, coaches, etc., who persistently select and encourage known violent field offenders ought also to be criminally liable as aiders and abettors. See also, McCutcheon, "Sports Violence, Consent and the Criminal Law" [1994] 45 N.I. L.Q. 267.

prematurely by inflicting a brain injury serious enough to make the defendant unconscious ... It is in my judgment best to regard this as another special situation which for the time being stands outside the ordinary law of violence because society chooses to tolerate it."[95]

There are a number of other special situations in addition to boxing where the deliberate infliction of bodily harm may be legitimated by consent. An example is the ritual circumcision of males. The cultural acceptance this form of invasive action enjoys is very different to the position of female circumcision. This latter practice is mainly performed on young girls of African origin in order to protect their virginity. "[I]ts purpose lies in the control and oppression of women and the suppression of female sexuality."[96] Such circumcisions can cause very severe injuries and have been made criminal.[97] People over the age of 16 may give consent to other forms of surgical interference. Whether it is the consent of the patient that renders the actions lawful or whether surgery forms a special category of its own is an issue which has yet to be fully resolved in the courts.[98] We know that at least one surgeon has performed amputation operations on patients suffering from the rare medical disorder of apotemnophilia which induces in its sufferers the desire to have a (healthy) limb amputated.[99] The legality of this (and its rationale) was not tested by a prosecution but a similar scenario would provide a "limit" case for the courts on the issue of consent to surgery.

Finally, there is a problem concerning "rough horseplay". In *Jones*[1] it was held that this activity which occurs "in the school playground, in the barrack-room and on the factory floor"[2] was something that persons consent to as long as there is no intention to cause injury. Because of this, a group of schoolboys in *Jones* who had thrown their victims "some 9 or 10 feet" into the air causing, in one case, a ruptured spleen which necessitated a surgical operation for its removal, had their convictions for causing grievous bodily harm quashed. In *Brown* Lord Mustill stated that the criminal law could not concern itself with such activities "provided that they do not go too far".[3] This seems to be a bully's charter.[4] It is extremely far-fetched to suggest that boys being held by several others *to prevent them running away* are genuinely consenting to being thrown into the air. To say that boys in such a situation can consent to *grievous bodily harm*, but that sado-masochists, who are genuinely consenting, cannot consent to *actual bodily harm*,

---

[95] *Per* Lord Mustill in *Brown* [1994] 1 A.C. 212 at 265. See further, Gunn and Ormerod, "The Legality of Boxing" (1995) 15 Legal Studies 181. There are a number of martial arts activities which expose the participants to just as much potential risk as boxing, often without the same strict regulatory control (Law Com. Consultation Paper No. 139 (1995), para. 1.6).

[96] Bibbings and Alldridge, *above*, n.89.

[97] The offence is punishable by up to five years' imprisonment: Prohibition of Female Circumcision Act 1985, s.1.

[98] This latter view is taken by Lord Mustill in *Brown* at 266.

[99] "News: Surgeon Amputated Healthy Legs" (2000) British Medical Journal 320. See Clarkson, *Understanding Criminal Law* (3rd ed., 2001), p. 82.

[1] (1986) 83 Cr.App.R.375. See also *Aitken* [1992] 1 W.L.R. 1006 and Law Com. Consultation Paper No. 139 (1995), paras 14.1–14.21.

[2] *Per* Lord Mustill in *Brown* at 267.

[3] At 267.

[4] The defence *may* even operate where the defendants make a drunken mistake as to the consent of the victim: see *Richardson and Irwin* [1999] 1 Cr.App.R.392. *Below*, p. 422.

provides an interesting insight into the way some of our judiciary view the world. Violence in the playground or barrack-room is what is expected and normal in the male world; it is a "manly diversion". Two men wishing to express their sexuality together and in private are not doing the sort of thing "real men" do. It is an "evil thing" and "uncivilised"[5] and cannot be the subject of valid consent.

2. An assault occasioning actual bodily harm contrary to section 47 can be inflicted intentionally or recklessly. Indeed, the defendant need not foresee any bodily harm at all as the *mens rea* is the same as that of a common assault.[6] It is unclear whether consent can *never* be a defence to section 47[7] (apart from the recognised exceptions) or whether this is limited to cases where the actual bodily harm is *deliberately* inflicted.[8] There are *dicta* supporting this latter view.[9] On the other hand, the majority all answered the certified question in the negative. This question was framed with reference to "section 20 and section 47", both of which offences can be committed recklessly. Lord Jauncey was clear that consent could never be a defence to anyone charged with either a section 47 or a section 20 offence (apart, of course, from the well-established exceptions). Further, the majority approved of the dictum of Lord Lane in *Attorney-General's Reference (No. 6 of 1980)* that it was not in the public interest that people should try to or should cause each other bodily harm (for no good reason) and that it was an assault if actual bodily harm was intended and/or caused.[10] Thus, it is possible that if actual bodily harm results, even though it is neither intended nor foreseen, consent would be negated.[11]

This would have a very significant impact upon the ambit of consent. However, this interpretation may not be the correct one. First, in *Slingsby*[12] (admittedly only a Crown Court decision), the court gave some indication that it would restrict the negation of consent to those injuries which were intentionally or recklessly inflicted and it may have been material that the court in *Emmett* stressed that the defendant was "plainly aware of the danger". Secondly, it should perhaps be stressed that the certified question in *Brown* was expressly posed in relation to woundings or actual bodily harm "in the course of a sadomasochistic encounter" and it is arguable that it is only in such cases that consent is never a defence to a section 47 charge. It is only on "public interest" grounds that consent is not a defence here and

---

[5] *Per* Lord Templeman in *Brown* at 237.

[6] *Savage; Parmenter* [1992] 1 A.C. 699. See *below*, p. 586.

[7] In *Emmett* it was stated that the issue was whether the line should be drawn between assault and section 47 "or at some higher level". See above, p. 293.

[8] Smith, Commentary on *Brown* [1993] Crim.L.R.586: "It is important to note that [the decision in *Brown*] is limited to the intentional infliction of bodily harm."

[9] Lord Templeman: "in principle there is a difference between violence which is incidental and violence which is inflicted for the indulgence of cruelty" (at 236). Lord Lowry: "If in the course of buggery . . . one participant, either with the other participant's consent or not, *deliberately* causes actual bodily harm to that other, an offence against s.47 has been committed." (at 256, emphasis added).

[10] [1981] Q.B. 715 at 719.

[11] Support for this proposition comes from the case of *Boyea* [1992] Crim.L.R.574. See further, Allen, "Consent and Assault" [1994] 58 J. Crim. Law 183.

[12] [1995] Crim.L.R.570. In this case the victim consented to intercourse during which the defendant inserted his hand into her vagina and rectum. The signet ring he was wearing caused her injuries from which she later died.

presumably the "public interest" varies with the type of case involved. For example, we are all deemed to consent to a certain degree of bodily contact in everyday life when on buses, trains and so on. It seems perfectly plausible in such a case to argue that consent can be a defence to a section 47 charge if the actual bodily harm was not deliberately caused. We all consent not only to everyday touchings but also to the risk of being pushed and jostled and perhaps injured. We certainly do not consent, however, to persons pushing us over and deliberately causing us actual bodily harm.

3. In *Attorney-General's Reference (No. 6 of 1980)* it was held that one could not consent to injuries sustained in a fight because such fighting (unless properly conducted under the Queensbury Rules) was contrary to the public interest. What if the injuries sustained in the fight were not sufficient to amount to actual bodily harm, or if the prosecution chose for other reasons to charge only with common assault? Would consent be a defence to such a charge? In *Attorney-General's Reference (No. 6 of 1980)* it was held that there could be an assault in such circumstances if actual bodily harm was "intended and/or caused".[13] If actual bodily harm is intended but not actually caused, the only possible charge is common assault. This issue is not directly addressed in *Brown* but would appear to be answered by the following, fairly typical statement by Lord Lowry that "everyone agrees that consent remains a complete defence to a charge of common assault".[14] Until this point has been resolved prosecutors are likely to avoid charging common assault in any case where consent is involved.

4. Consent is a defence to assault. How can a defendant be guilty of the offence of *assault* occasioning actual bodily harm when there can be no liability for one of the elements of the offence, namely, the assault?

## D. *Reform proposals*

The judgments of their Lordships in *Brown* prompted the Law Commission to undertake the next stage in its codification project by examining the current law relating to consent. The Commission adopts an essentially pragmatic approach and follows what it perceives to be the prevailing attitude in Parliament to questions of criminalisation,[15] that is, "paternalism softened at the edges when Parliament is confident that there is an effective system of regulatory control".[16]

### Law Commission, Consent in the Criminal Law (Consultation Paper No. 139, 1995), paras 4.47–4.51:

"4.47 We provisionally propose that the intentional causing of seriously disabling injury to another person should continue to be criminal, even if the person injured consents to such injury or to the risk of such injury.
4.48 We provisionally propose that—
(1) the reckless causing of seriously disabling injury should continue to be criminal, even if the injured person consents to such injury or to the risk of such injury; but

[13] *Above*, n.10.
[14] At 248.
[15] Para. 2.17.
[16] Para. 2.15.

(2) a person causing seriously disabling injury to another person should not be regarded as having caused it recklessly unless—
(a) he or she was, at the time of the act or omission causing it, aware of a risk that such injury would result, and
(b) it was at that time contrary to the best interests of the other person, having regard to the circumstances known to the person causing the injury (including, if known to him or her, the fact that the other person consented to such injury or to the risk of it), to take that risk.

4.49 We provisionally propose that the intentional [and reckless (4.50)] causing of any injury to another person other than seriously disabling injury . . . should not be criminal if, at the time of the act or omission causing the injury, the other person consented to injury of the type caused.

4.51 . . . 'seriously disabling injury' should be taken to refer to an injury or injuries which—
(1) cause serious distress, and
(2) involve the loss of a bodily member or organ or permanent bodily injury or permanent functional impairment, or serious or permanent disfigurement, or severe and prolonged pain, or serious impairment of mental health, or prolonged unconsciousness;
and in determining whether an effect is permanent, no account should be taken of the fact that it may be remediable by surgery.[17]

[The Law Commission then goes on to identify a number of exceptions. Persons may give consent to a higher level of harm for medical treatment and surgery. There are a number of activities (such as tattooing, sport and horseplay) where the level of harm is to stay at that permitted by the present law. Those under the age of 18 would not be able to consent to injuries intentionally caused for sexual, religious or spiritual purposes.]"

If implemented, these proposals would produce a law which would give rather more scope for the defence of consent. The Law Commission acknowledges that there are still difficulties to be resolved[18] but, beyond this, there are underlying assumptions which are not beyond challenge and to which we now return.

### E. *The rationale of consent as a defence*

An attempt to understand the basis upon which, and the extent to which, consent operates as a defence involves a consideration of liberalism, paternalism and moralism. Those issues were considered in Chapter 1 and will not be explored again here. However, two final insights may be presented.

### George P. Fletcher, Rethinking Criminal Law (1978), pp. 770–771:

"The principle that individuals are free and responsible agents informs the analysis of consent . . . Once accepted, the value of autonomy does not lend itself to being offset by competing social interests. So far as the rationale of consent is that individuals should be free to waive their rights, this capacity of waiver is not a contingent value, subject to repeated balancing against the opposing array of interests.

There is some evidence that at the fringes, however, the principle of autonomy gives way to competing social values. The prevailing view in Western legal systems is that the

---

[17] Thus the question of whether the injury is seriously disabling would have to be established in addition to grievous bodily harm in cases where consent is claimed. See, Ormerod and Gunn, "Consent—A Second Bash"[1996] Crim.L.R.694 at 701 where they argue that this is too complex, confusing and unnecessary. See further, Shute, *above*, n.45.
[18] With, for example, the concept of "horseplay"; paras 14.1–14.21.

individual has the right to take his own life or to torture himself, but he does not have the right to authorise others to do the killing or to perform a sado-masochistic beating. That there is a personal right to suffer in these cases indicates that the rationale for limiting personal autonomy is not a paternalistic governmental posture toward the victim's injuring himself. If the issue were paternalism, the government should employ sanctions as well against suicide and other forms of self-destruction.

A more convincing account of the distinction between self-injury and consenting to injury by others derives from the danger of implicating other persons in dangerous forms of conduct. The individual who kills or mutilates himself might affect the well-being of family and friends, but this result depends upon the actor's relationships with other people. In contrast, the self-destructive individual who induces another person to kill or to mutilate him implicates the latter in the violation of a significant social taboo. The person carrying out the killing or the mutilation crosses the threshold into a realm of conduct that, the second time, might be more easily carried out. And the second time, it might not be particularly significant whether the victim consents or not. Similarly, if someone is encouraged to inflict a sado-masochistic beating on a consenting victim, the experience of inflicting the beating might loosen the actor's inhibitions against sadism in general."

### David Feldman, Civil Liberties and Human Rights in England and Wales (2nd ed., 2002), p. 715–716:

"[T]o imply ... that carefully controlled, planned, and consensual violence as part of a sexual encounter has no redeeming social value, but to accept that boxing or rough and undisciplined play have social value which justifies the infliction of bodily harm, turns reality on its head. The object of respecting consent to the rough and tumble of sport (like consent to medical treatment) is primarily to protect the individual interests of the participants as they perceive them, rather than to advance any public interest. It is a recognition of individual autonomy, the right of individuals of sufficient understanding to make their own decisions about what is good for them. In principle, this should apply equally to people's sexual preferences. Indeed, it is hard to see how the interest (whether public or private) in allowing people to express their sexuality, which forms a fundamental part of people's personality, could be less important than the interest in allowing people to pursue sports. Sport is fun, but sex, for many people, is more than fun: it is a form of self-expression."

Even if one concedes that, in certain cases, consent ought not to provide a complete defence, do we blame such defendants *as much* as those who commit similar harms against their victims who are *not* consenting? Even if consent does not provide a complete justification, ought it not to provide a partial excuse so as to reduce the defendant's level of criminal liability and/or punishment?

### III. Self-defence

#### A. *Introduction*

Almost as long as the criminal law has been in existence it has consistently restricted the right of the individual to self-help; it is the function of the law to preserve law and order and protect the weak. There are, however, inevitably occasions when to depend upon the arrival of official help would be to court disaster and it would be extremely unjust if the remedy of self-help were altogether denied. The law recognises this and in certain situations deems the use of force to be lawful. It has been argued that "[t]he source of [this] right is a comparison of the competing interests of the aggressor and the defender, as modified by the important fact that the aggressor is the one party responsible for the fight. ... As the party morally at fault for threatening the defender's interests, the aggressor is entitled to lesser consideration in the balancing process."[19] The underlying rationale of defensive force may also be understood in terms of Gardner's analysis: "By granting a *justificatory* defence the law concedes that ... the defendant had, at the time of her *prima facie* wrongful action, sufficient reason to perform it."[20] While most of the rules here were developed largely to cater for situations where the defendant is acting against an aggressor, Gardner's analysis provides a more complete explanation that covers cases where self-defensive action is taken against a non-culpable person such as a small child who is inadvertently threatening the defendant's interests.

Again, as with consent, it is possible to assert that necessary defence is not truly a "defence". A defendant acting in self-defence is acting lawfully—an element of the *actus reus* is thus not established.[21] As we have seen, this method of characterisation has important implications in cases where the defendant has made a mistake, *i.e.* mistakenly thinks he needs to defend himself or others.[22] But apart from such cases, the parameters of necessary defence are constant—irrespective of whether it is regarded as a defence, or a denial of a definitional element.

As we shall see in the context of both homicide and non-fatal offences against the person, most reported violent crime is between young males, typically when they are out for the evening.[23] Violence may flare up in such situations which requires one of the parties to respond by means of self-defence. The dynamics of the interaction may not, however, be straightforward; the eventual victim may have precipitated the final outcome; the division of responsibility between them may be difficult to determine. Thus the law has developed fairly rigorous conditions before a plea based on the need to defend oneself will be accepted.

It is also true to say that the context within which these rules have been framed has been predominantly that of inter-male violence.[24] What this ignores (and what is still left largely unexposed by official statistics) is domestic violence. As with the defence of provocation,[25] the rules in relation to defensive force may make it difficult for the "battered woman" who retaliates to raise a successful plea.

## B. *The triggering conditions*

What circumstances must exist in order for an actor to be justified in acting in self-defence? It is common to state that in "defensive force justifications an

---

[19] Fletcher, *Rethinking Criminal Law* (1978), pp. 857–858. See also, Uniacke, *Permissible Killings: The Self-Defence Justification for Homicide* (1994), Chaps 4 and 5 where she rejects the argument that killings in self-defence are morally permissible because they are unintended (but merely foreseen) and argues that they are permissible because of "the moral asymmetry between the parties" (p. 229)—a development of the theory of forfeiture.

[20] Gardner, "Justifications and Reasons" in Simester and Smith (eds), *Harm and Culpability* (1996), 103 at p. 108. Above, p. 273.

[21] *Abraham* [1973] 1 W.L.R. 1270; *Williams (Gladstone)* (1984) 78 Cr.App.R.276.

[22] *Above*, p. 188.

[23] *Below*, pp. 572–573, 626–627.

[24] See O'Donovan, "Defences for Battered Women Who Kill" (1991) 18 J.L. and Soc. 219; Wells, "Domestic Violence and Self-Defence" (1990) 140 New L.J. 127; Taylor, "Provoked Reason in Men and Women: Heat of Passion Manslaughter and Imperfect Self-Defense" (1986) 33 U.C.L.A. Law Rev. 1679.

[25] *Below*, p. 682.

aggressor must present a threat of unjustified harm to the protected interest".[26]
Two points need consideration here:

**Threat of unjustified harm:**
   In the paradigmatic self-defence scenario an innocent person is attacked by an
unjustified aggressor and this triggers the right to self-defensive action. From this, it
is clear that self-defence is not a defence against justified action, for example,
against a police officer using reasonable force to make a lawful arrest. On the other
hand, as seen earlier when the significance of the distinction between justifications,
excuses and exemptions was explored, self-defence is permitted against an
exempted actor. One is entitled to defend oneself against a small child firing a gun
or an insane person wielding an axe. Such a person, while non-culpable, is still
threatening unjustified harm.

### Re A (conjoined twins: surgical separation) [2001] Fam. 147 (Court of Appeal, Civil Division)

"Jodie" and "Mary" were conjoined twins. Leaving them joined would result in the death
of both of them within six months. A separation operation would certainly result in the
death of Mary who was not capable of separate survival but would give Jodie a good
prospect of a normal life. The issue was whether such an operation would be lawful despite
the fact that it would result in the death of Mary under circumstances making the surgeons
*prima facie* liable for murder.

Ward L.J.:
"The reality here—harsh as it is to state it, and unnatural as it is that it should be
happening—is that Mary is killing Jodie. That is the effect of the incontrovertible medical
evidence and it is common ground in the case. Mary uses Jodie's heart and lungs to receive
and use Jodie's oxygenated blood. This will cause Jodie's heart to fail and cause Jodie's death
as surely as a slow drip of poison. How can it be just that Jodie should be required to tolerate
that state of affairs? One does not need to label Mary with the American terminology which
would paint her to be 'an unjust aggressor', which I feel is wholly inappropriate language for
the sad and helpless position in which Mary finds herself. I have no difficulty in agreeing that
this unique happening cannot be said to be unlawful. But it does not have to be unlawful.
The six-year-old boy indiscriminately shooting all and sundry in the school playground is
not acting unlawfully for he is too young for his acts to be so classified. But is he 'innocent'
within the moral meaning of that word? . . . I am not qualified to answer that moral question
. . . If I had to hazard a guess, I would venture the tentative view that the child is not morally
innocent. What I am, however, competent to say is that *in law* killing that six-year-old boy in
self-defence of others would be fully justified and the killing would not be unlawful. I can see
no difference in essence between that resort to legitimate self-defence and the doctors coming
to Jodie's defence and removing the threat of fatal harm to her presented by Mary's draining
her lifeblood. The availability of such a plea of quasi-self-defence, modified to meet the quite
exceptional circumstances nature has inflicted on the twins, makes intervention by the
doctors lawful."

   This view expressed by Ward L.J. raises complex issues that cannot be fully
explored here. For example, in self-defence cases, even against exempted actors
such as the small child firing a gun, the defender is acting to protect her *actual*

---

[26] Robinson, "Criminal Law Defences: A Systematic Analysis" (1982) 82 Col.L.R. 216. Alternatively, it
   may be characterised as when the reasons for acting (defensively) outweigh or defeat the normal reasons that exist against the wrongful conduct (*above*, p. 273).

bodily integrity. It has been argued that "this particular norm is inapplicable to the case of bodies that come into existence with a conjoined circulatory system".[27] How does Mary's right to life square with Jodie's "right" to have her killed? On what basis can Mary be said to have "forfeited" her right not to have force used against her?[28] Can it be argued that a "luckless" person like Mary who has become an "unjustified threat" has "opened up a gap" in her rights?[29] How can Mary be brought within the rationale of self-defence that she has "created a situation in which [her] otherwise protected interests are subject to injury because [she] has stepped outside the area where [she] can legitimately expect to remain free from interference"?[30] Probably the only way of resolving these intractable problems is by turning attention away from the person posing the unjust threat and focusing instead on the defender's normative position and whether she had sufficient reasons for her actions.[31] An alternative, and certainly easier, approach is that these cases of defensive action against a non-culpable actor should be removed from the ambit of self-defence and dealt with as cases of necessity as a majority of the judges in *Re A (Conjoined Twins: Surgical Separation)* actually did.[32]

**Protected interest:**

The "protected interests" currently recognised by the law are protection of self, protection of others, and property.[33] Overlapping these interests to a considerable extent is the further protected interest of acting in the prevention of crime.[34]

It seems only just that an innocent person who is attacked ought to be able to defend him or herself and should also be able to go to the aid of immediate family. But what if friends or even strangers are in need of help; should someone be blamed or protected if he chooses to step in? Some authorities, including *Devlin v Armstrong* suggest that there must be "some special nexus or relationship between the person relying on the doctrine to justify what he did in aid of another, and that other."[35] However, it is now clear that no such limitation exists and it makes no difference whether one is defending oneself or a complete stranger.[36] This has important implications for pub and street brawls. A fight between two people can soon escalate with persons who join in claiming that they are acting in defence of others. One may also use physical force to protect one's property.[37] As we shall see,

---

[27] Uniacke, "Was Mary's Death Murder?" (2001) Med.L.R.208 at 214.

[28] Uniacke, *Permissible Killing – the Self-Defence Justification for Homicide* (1994).

[29] Horder, "Self-Defence, Necessity and Duress: Understanding the Relationship" (1998) XI Canadian Journal of Law and Jurisprudence 143.

[30] Funk, "Justifying Justifications" (1999) 19 O.J.L.S. 631 at 637: a review article of Schopp, *Justification Defences and Justification Convictions* (1998).

[31] Gardner, *above*, n.20.

[32] *Below*, p. 360.

[33] Accordingly, this defence is sometimes termed "necessary defence", rather than "self-defence".

[34] The overlap is not complete, *e.g.* if one defends oneself against an infant's attack there is no crime. For discussion of acting in prevention of crime, see *below*, p. 307.

[35] [1972] N.I. 13 at 35–36. The relationship between Bernadette Devlin M.P., and her Londonderry constituents was held not to be a sufficient relationship.

[36] *Williams (Gladstone)* (1984) 78 Cr.App.R.276; *Tooley* (1709) 11 Mod at 250, 88 E.R. at 1020; *Prince* (1875) 2 C.C.R. at 178; *People v Keatley* [1954] I.R. 12.

[37] *Hussey* (1924) 18 Cr.App.R.160. See further, Smith, *Justification and Excuse in the Criminal Law* (1989), pp. 109–112.

however, one of the real dilemmas here is in defining how much defensive physical force one may use to protect one's property.

## C. *The Permitted response*

The law recognises the right to protect both personal and proprietary interests.[38] One can use violence to repel an attack. It is clear, however, that there are severe restrictions as to the circumstances in which one is justified in using such force. One does not have *carte blanche* to defend oneself entirely as one chooses. The law will simply not accept that it is justifiable to kill a human being in order to protect a much-loved pet guinea-pig. In order for conduct to be justified the defender must only use *such force as is necessary* to avert the attack.

In many of the leading self-defence cases the aggressor has been killed. The importance that is attached to the sanctity of life (and the corresponding need for any exception to it to be closely circumscribed) is enshrined in Article 2 of the European Convention on Human Rights.

"(1) Everyone's right to life shall be protected by law. No-one shall be deprived of his life intentionally save in execution of a sentence of a court following his conviction of a crime for which this penalty is provided by law.

(2) Deprivation of life shall not be regarded as inflicted in contravention of this article when it results from the use of force which is no more than absolutely necessary:

(a) in defence of any person from unlawful violence;

(b) in order to effect a lawful arrest or prevent the escape of a person lawfully detained."[39]

There are a number of preliminary points that need to be made in relation to Article 2. First, it deals only with the use of *fatal* force. Thus, where less defensive force is used Article 2 is of no relevance. In the interests of clarity and consistency it could be argued that the legal test for self-defence ought to be the same regardless of the level of force used so as to avoid a dual standard being applied. The use of non-lethal force is covered by Article 3 (freedom from inhuman treatment) and Article 5 (right to liberty and security of the person). It has been argued that these provisions will be interpreted so as to imply exceptions of the same type as those in Article 2(2).[40] While the attractions of having a single set of rules applying to all

---

[38] It is clear that if self-defence arises on the facts it should be put to the jury even though the defence has not been raised by the defendant (*D.P.P. v Bailey* [1995] 1 Cr.App.R.257). The judge should also explain that the prosecution has to prove beyond reasonable doubt that the defendant was not acting in self-defence (*Anderson* [1995] Crim.L.R.430).

[39] The final exception is: (c) in action lawfully taken for the purpose of quelling a riot or insurrection. Clearly, all three exceptions may be relevant when considering the defence of prevention of crime; *below*, p. 307.

[40] Ashworth, *Principles of Criminal Law* (3rd ed., 1999), p. 140. Leverick, "Is English Self-Defence Law Incompatible with Article 2 of the ECHR" [2002] Crim.L.R.347 at 360 cites cases suggesting that this has already occurred.

situations of self-defence are obvious, there could, nevertheless, be a case for employing a different (more rigorous) test in relation to fatal force given the sanctity of life.

Secondly, Article 2 refers to the "intentional" taking of life only. It has been argued that this means that the action must be taken with the "purpose" of killing and "that a person acting in order to defend themselves or others is not acting for the purpose of killing".[41] However, this view has been challenged and while the point has not been considered by the English courts since the coming into force of the Human Rights Act 1998, it does seem unlikely that such a restrictive interpretation would be compatible with decisions of the European Court.[42]

Thirdly, it has been argued that Article 2 will be confined to cases involving agents of the state.

### Richard Buxton, "The Human Rights Act and the Substantive Criminal Law" [2000] Crim.L.R.331 at 337–338:

"[U]nder Article 2 the subject has a right to have his life protected *by the state*. That obligation on the state's part is most clearly broken if ... the killing is by state agents; or possibly where state agents culpably fail to enforce protective measures. But where ... one citizen simply and unpredictably attacks another, the state, the respondent under Article 2, is only engaged if the *system* created by the state is inadequate to provide the system with protection. [I]t seems almost inconceivable that ... [the European] Court would hold that the English legal system, including the English law of self-defence, does not give adequate protection to Englishmen against the prospect of being killed by other Englishmen; and even more inconceivable that an English tribunal would feel confident enough to say that that would be the opinion of the Strasbourg Court were the issue to be considered by it."

However, the *system* of English law *has* been found wanting in relation to protecting children against excessive physical punishment[43] and one cannot confidently predict, therefore, that the law of self-defence between citizens will be safe from challenge.[44]

Finally, Article 2 only permits a killing to protect oneself or others against "unlawful violence". English domestic law allows one to act in protection of property. *If* Article 2 is extended to cases involving non-lethal force (killing in defence of property would not be protected under current English law), would Article 2 cover cases where force is used in protection of property? If not, there is again the prospect of a dual standard emerging: one set of rules for cases falling within the scope of the Convention and another set of rules for the remaining cases.

Accordingly, there is considerable uncertainty about the extent to which Article 2 will impact upon the English law of self-defence. However, the emphasis placed

---

[41] Smith, "The Use of Force in Public or Private Defence and Article 2" [2002] Crim.L.R.956 at 957 citing *Re A (Conjoined Twins: Surgical Separation)* [2001] Fam. 147 as the authority.

[42] See Leverick, *ante*, n.40 and "The Use of Force in Public or Private Defence and Article 2: A Reply to Professor Sir John Smith" [2002] Crim.L.R.961.

[43] *A v United Kingdom* (1999) 28 E.H.R.R. 603; *below*, p. 321.

[44] See Leverick, *above*, n.40 at 358–359 and Ashworth, *above*, n.40 at p. 149.

upon the sanctity of life in Article 2 and the need for force used in the exceptions to be "absolutely necessary" must raise, as we shall see, the possibility that current English law is incompatible with Article 2 in some respects.

What is meant by the current requirement of English law that the defender must only use *such force as is necessary to avert the attack*? This involves a consideration of the following issues:

(i) the necessity for *any* defensive action;
(ii) the amount of responsive force that may be used;
(iii) the duty to retreat;
(iv) the imminence of the threatened attack.

It is important to emphasise that with each of these one is ultimately balancing the competing interests of the initial aggressor and the defender, but, as the aggressor was the culpable one responsible for starting the violence, the law has tended to tip the scales in favour of the defender.

## 1. The necessity for any defensive action

It is quite clear that the person seeking to rely upon the defence must believe his action to be necessary; if he is, in reality, the aggressor seeking to disguise his status behind a smoke-screen of self-defence, the defence will not apply to him.[45]

What is the position if the response is not in fact necessary, but the defendant genuinely believes it is (because, say, he mistakenly believes he is about to be attacked)? It used to be thought that such a defendant would only escape liability if his mistake was a reasonable one.[46] In *Williams (Gladstone)*[47] however, it was held by the Court of Appeal that the defendant's mistake need not be reasonable. Instead, he had to be judged according to his view of the facts.[48] In *Oatridge* the Court of Appeal concluded that the defendant, who had been abused by her partner on previous occasions, was entitled to have her mistaken view of the incident, which led to her fatally stabbing him, considered by the jury: "the possibility of the appellant honestly believing that on this occasion the victim really was going to do what he had previously threatened—even if this was not in fact what he was going to do—was not so fanciful as to require its exclusion."[49] The Draft Criminal Law Bill 1993 also adopts this test. The amount of force the defendant may use depends on the circumstances "as he believes them to be".[50]

Self-defence is regarded as a *justificatory* defence. This, however, can only be the case where the defendant is actually acting in self-defence. Where he has made a

---

[45] The defence will not succeed if the defendant uses force which, *unknown to him*, is justified by the circumstances: *Dadson* (1850) 4 Cox C.C. 358. See Hogan, "The *Dadson* Principle" [1989] Crim.L.R.679 and Christopher, "Unknowing Justification and the Logical Necessity of the *Dadson* Principle in Self-Defence" [1995] 15 O.J.L.S. 229.

[46] *e.g. Rose* (1884) 15 Cox 540 where the defendant shot and killed his father whom he mistakenly thought was killing his mother by cutting her throat; *Albert v Lavin* [1982] A.C. 546.

[47] (1984) 78 Cr.App.R.276.

[48] This was confirmed in *Beckford* [1988] 1 A.C. 130. See *above*, p. 198 *et seq.*

[49] [1992] Crim.L.R.205 at 206.

[50] Law Commission, *Offences Against the Person and General Principles*, Law Com. No. 218 (1993), cl. 27(1).

mistake and is, therefore, attacking the interests of an innocent party, his actions cannot be *justified* as not involving any wrongdoing. But in these cases the law has decided that such a mistake negates blameworthiness and *excuses* the defendant from blame.[51] This whole approach of excusing all honest mistakes, even if unreasonable, is highly questionable.

Suppose two police officers see a man in a car. They think he is a dangerous, wanted criminal. They stop the car to arrest the man. Genuinely believing him to be a violent criminal who would shoot them to effect an escape, they beat him nearly to death with their guns. It transpires that the victim is a completely innocent man. According to *Williams (Gladstone)* the actions of the police officers must be judged according to their view of the facts. On that basis, assuming their response was not excessive, they will escape all liability.[52] They thought force was necessary; that is all that is required. Now, if their mistake was a reasonable one—if the facts were such that all reasonable police officers would similarly have thought that the man in the car was the wanted criminal and that it was necessary to use force against him—we would all have sympathy with the police officers' actions and wish to exempt them from blame and criminal liability (leaving aside, for the moment, the issue of whether their response might have been excessive). But if their mistake was an unreasonable one—if there were no reasonable grounds for thinking the man was the wanted criminal or that he would attack them—then, surely, our response is entirely different. We are now appalled at the enormity of their error. We blame the police officers for making such an unreasonable mistake—and blame them to an extent that we feel they should be made criminally accountable for their actions. In other words, the former requirement that the defendant's mistake had to be based on reasonable grounds not only mitigated the practical difficulty of proving whether the defendant actually held the belief or not, but also reflected a more fundamental attitude towards the determination of culpability.

It is in this context that Article 2 may come into play. There have been a number of decisions in which the European Court of Human Rights has held that in determining whether the killing was "absolutely necessary" the honest beliefs of the defenders must be based on "good reason".[53] This is a higher and more restrictive test than that in *Williams (Gladstone)* and reflects the status accorded to the sanctity of life by the Convention. English law, by this yardstick, accords too little priority to the protection of life and the ruling in *Williams (Gladstone)* may well be found to be incompatible with Article 2 (at the very least in relation to fatal force by state officials).

However, arguing that the approach taken in *Williams (Gladstone)* is misconceived and may be incompatible with Article 2 does not necessarily mean that the old reasonableness test should simply be resurrected. If the assessment of reasonableness is based upon typical male responses to violence, then change is necessary. What is needed is a test that is capable of taking into account the

---

[51] See further, Uniacke, *above*, n.28, Chap. 2 where she offers a more complex analysis of justification and excuse, based in part on a distinction between objective and agent-perspectival viewpoints.

[52] This is broadly what occurred in *Finch and Jardine* (Unreported, Central Criminal Court, October 12–19, 1982). See also Waddington, " 'Overkill' or 'Minimum Force' " [1990] Crim.L.R.695.

[53] *McCann v United Kingdom* (1996) 21 E.H.R.R. 97; *Andronicou v Cyprus* (1998) 25 E.H.R.R. 491; *Gul v Turkey* (2002) 34 E.H.R.R. 28.

characteristics of the defender, including, for example, prior history. The question ought to be whether it was reasonable for *that* person to have used such force in the situation. This will be considered further in the context of the next issue. In the meantime, as a result of *Williams (Gladstone)*, we are unable to distinguish between those who, when every consideration has been taken of the anguish of the situation, are still blameworthy and those whom we would wish to excuse.

## 2. The amount of responsive force that may be used

It has long been accepted that the defender may only use such force as is reasonable in the circumstances. The general rule is that the response must be proportionate to the attack.

A person acting to repel an unlawful attack is, at the same time as trying to protect himself or others, usually also acting to prevent a crime. This latter situation has been put on a statutory basis.

### Criminal Law Act 1967, section 3

"3.—(1) A person may use such force as is reasonable in the circumstances in the prevention of crime, or in effecting or assisting in the lawful arrest of offenders or suspected offenders or of persons unlawfully at large.

(2) Subsection (1) above shall replace the rules of the common law on the question when force used for a purpose mentioned in the subsection is justified by that purpose."

It could be argued that section 3 applies to all cases of necessary defence. A person acting in self-defence is usually engaged in preventing a crime, even if that is not his primary motivation in acting. However, the general view is that the common law rules of defensive force have not been effectively put on a statutory footing by virtue of section 3.[54] Not only are the express terms of section 3 restricted to prevention of crime (there was nothing in the preceding Criminal Law Revision Committee report about private defence), but also, the overlap between the two is incomplete.[55] Edmund-Davis L.J. in *McInnes*[56] endorsed this view when he stated that the law of self-defence was "similarly limited as in section 3". In other words, whilst operating along similar lines[57] it is still perfectly proper to regard as authoritative common-law decisions on necessary force.[58]

What is meant by "reasonable" and "proportionate" force here? This has always posed problems—especially in relation to the use of physical force in the defence of property. It would seem clear, for instance, that despite a common belief to the contrary, one is not at liberty to shoot dead a burglar wandering around one's house if one does not fear for one's own life. In *Martin*[59] the defendant was convicted of murder having shot a teenage burglar who broke into his isolated

---

[54] See Ashworth, "Self-Defence and the Right to Life" [1975] C.L.J. 282; Harlow, "Self-Defence, Public Right or Private Privilege" [1974] Crim.L.R.528.

[55] *Above*, n.34.

[56] (1971) 55 Cr.App.R.551.

[57] In *Clegg* [1995] 1 A.C. 482 it was indicated that the degree of force permissible was the same in both situtions.

[58] Under the Draft Criminal Law Bill 1993 the use of force to prevent crime or in protection of oneself, others or property would be dealt with by the one clause: clause 27(1), (Law Com. No. 218, 1993).

[59] [2001] 2 W.L.R. 1. See *below*, p. 311.

Norfolk farmhouse. This case attracted considerable publicity, much of it sympathetic to the defendant.[60] The difficulty is that for many persons such a degree of force is the only method by which they can protect their property. If they are not permitted to use such force, they are in effect condemned to forfeiting their property and having to rely on subsequent legal remedies for redress—remedies that will often be useless. However, the alternative is even worse. One cannot allow persons to go round inflicting death or severe personal injuries on others merely in defence of property and it seems plain that this is the view upheld by Article 2. Fatal force may be used if "absolutely necessary", but only in response to "unlawful *violence*".

English law used to insist on a fairly rigorous and objective test of reasonableness. Such an approach can be supported when one recalls that necessary defence amounts to a *justification*:

> "[C]haracterizing self-defence as justification ... involves finding that the attacker's life has become of less value *to society* than the life of the person attacked. To reach this difficult conclusion, the law must make the self-defence elements strict enough to ensure that the attacker was really the more culpable party and that there was really no reasonable alternative to killing him."[61]

However, more recent English cases have tended to favour the interests of the defender more heavily.

## Attorney-General for Northern Ireland's Reference [1977] A.C. 105 (House of Lords)

The reference arose from a case in which a soldier had been charged with murder for shooting and killing someone whom he had mistakenly thought to be a member of the I.R.A.

Lord Diplock:
"What amount of force is 'reasonable in the circumstances' for the purpose of preventing crime is, in my view, always a question for the jury in a jury trial, never a 'point of law' for the judge ...

The jury would also have to consider how the circumstances in which the accused had to make his decision whether or not to use force and the shortness of the time available to him for reflection, might affect the judgment of a reasonable man ... [The jury] should remind themselves that the postulated balancing of risk against risk, harm against harm, by the reasonable man is not undertaken in the calm analytical atmosphere of the court-room after counsel with the benefit of hindsight have expounded at length the reasons for and against the kind of degree of force that was used by the accused; but in the brief second or two which the accused had to decide whether to shoot or not and under all the stresses to which he was exposed ...

On the facts that are to be assumed for the purposes of the reference the only options open to the accused were either to let the deceased escape or to shoot at him with a service rifle. A reasonable man would know that a bullet from a self-loading rifle if it hit a human being, at any rate at the range at which the accused fired, would be likely to kill him or injure him seriously. So in one scale of the balance the harm to which the deceased would be exposed if the accused aimed to hit him was predictable and grave and the risk of its occurrence high. In the other scale of the balance it would be open to the jury to take the view that it would not be

---

[60] Yeo, "Killing in Defence of Property" (2000) N.L.J. 730 cites a poll indicating that fewer than 4 per cent of people were in favour of Martin's conviction and sentence.
[61] Creach, "Partially Determined Imperfect Self-Defense: The Battered Wife Kills and Tells Why" (1982) 34 Stan.L.R. 616, 632.

unreasonable to assess the level of harm to be averted by preventing the accused's escape as even graver—the killing or wounding of members of the patrol by terrorists in ambush and the effect of this success by members of the Provisional I.R.A. in encouraging the continuance of the armed insurrection and all the misery and destruction of life and property that terrorist activity in Northern Ireland has entailed. The jury would have to consider too what was the highest degree at which a reasonable man could have assessed the likelihood that such consequences might follow the escape of the deceased if the facts had been as the accused knew or believed them reasonably to be."

Decision of the Court of Criminal Appeal of Northern Ireland varied

## Palmer v The Queen [1971] A.C. 814 (Privy Council)

The appellant, who carried a gun, went with other men to buy ganga. During a dispute they left with the ganga without paying; during the following chase one of the pursuers was shot by the appellant, who was charged and convicted of murder, although he had claimed self-defence.

Lord Morris:
"In their Lordships' view the defence of self-defence is one which can be and will be readily understood by any jury. It is a straightforward conception. It involves no obstruse legal thought ... only common sense is needed for its understanding. It is both good law and good sense that a man who is attacked may defend himself. It is both good law and good sense that he may do, but may only do what is reasonably necessary. But everything will depend upon the particular facts and circumstances. Of these a jury can decide. It may in some cases be only sensible and clearly possible to take some simple avoiding action. Some attacks may be serious and dangerous. Others may not be. If there is some relatively minor attack it would not be common sense to permit some action of retaliation which was wholly out of proportion to the necessities of the situation. If an attack is serious so that it puts someone in immediate peril then immediate defensive action may be necessary. . . . If the attack is all over and no sort of peril remains then the employment of force may be by way of revenge or punishment or by way of paying off an old score or may be pure aggression. There may no longer be any link with a necessity of defence. Of all these matters the good sense of the jury will be the arbiter ... If there has been an attack so that defence is reasonably necessary, it will be recognised that a person defending himself cannot weigh to a nicety the exact measure of his necessary defensive action. If a jury thought that in a moment of unexpected anguish a person attacked had only done what he honestly and instinctively thought was necessary that would be most potent evidence that only reasonable defensive action had been taken. A jury will be told that the defence of self-defence, where the evidence makes the raising possible, will only fail if the prosecution show beyond doubt that what the accused did was not by way of self-defence."

Appeal dismissed

Building on dicta in *Palmer*, subsequent cases such as *Shannon*,[62] *Whyte*[63] and *Scarlett*[64] appeared increasingly to be abandoning the objective requirement. As long as the defendant *thought* he was using an appropriate amount of force, it seemed there could be no conviction. This dramatic change of approach was entirely too crude and could have led to the result that the more habituated the defendant was to violence, the more retaliatory force he was allowed to use. The Court of Appeal has now halted the trend towards a completely subjective test.

---

[62] (1980) 71 Cr.App.R.192.
[63] [1987] 3 All E.R. 416.
[64] (1994) 98 Cr.App.R.290. See also *Attorney-General's Reference (No. 2 of 1983)* [1984] 2 W.L.R. 465.

## R. v Owino [1996] 2 Cr.App.R.128 (Court of Appeal, Criminal Division)

The defendant was charged with assault occasioning actual bodily harm upon his wife. He claimed that the injuries had been caused when he had acted defensively to stop her assaulting him. He was convicted and appealed on the ground (*inter alia*) that the jury had not been properly directed on the issue of self-defence.

Collins J.:

"The essential elements of self-defence are clear enough. The jury have to decide whether a defendant honestly believed that the circumstances were such as required him to use force to defend himself from an attack or threatened attack. In this respect a defendant must be judged in accordance with his honest belief, even though that belief may have been mistaken. But the jury must then decide whether the force used was reasonable in the circumstances as he believed them to be.

*Scarlett* was a case where a landlord of a public house had been ejecting, and perfectly lawfully and properly ejecting, a drunken customer from his public house. The allegation was that he had used excessive force in the course of ejecting him so that the customer fell down the steps of the entrance to the pub and unfortunately hit his head and was killed. What . . . [Counsel for the defendant] relies upon in the case of *Scarlett* is a passage . . . where Beldam L.J., giving the judgment of the Court, said this:

'Where, as in the present case, an accused is justifed in using some force and can only be guilty of an assault if the force used is excessive, the jury ought to be directed that he cannot be guilty of an assault unless the prosecution prove that he acted with the mental element necessary to constitute his action an assault, that is "that the defendant intentionally or recklessly applied force to the person of another". Further, they should be directed that the accused is not to be found guilty merely because he intentionally or recklessly used force which they consider to have been excessive. They ought not to convict him unless they are satisfied that the degree of force used was plainly more than was called for by the circumstances as he believed them to be and, provided he believed the circumstances called for the degree of force used, he is not to be convicted even if his belief was unreasonable . . .'

The passage which we have cited could, if taken out of context, give rise to a suggestion that the submission . . . [by Counsel] is well-founded. But what, in the context, the learned Lord Justice was really saying was, in our view, this: he was indicating that the elements of an assault involved the unlawful application of force. In the context of an issue of self-defence or reasonable restraint, which was what *Scarlett* was essentially about, then clearly a person would not be guilty of an assault unless the force used was excessive; and in judging whether the force used was excessive, the jury had to take account of the circumstances as he believed them to be. That is what is clear in the first part of the sentence . . .

So far as the second half of the sentence is concerned, what we understand the learned Lord Justice to have been saying was that, in judging what he believed the circumstances to be, the jury are not to decide on the basis of what was objectively reasonable; and that even if he, the defendant, was unreasonable in his belief, if it was an honest belief and honestly held, that he is not to be judged by reference to the true circumstances. It is in that context that the learned Lord Justice talks about '[belief] that the circumstances called for the degree of force used', because clearly you cannot divorce completely the concept of degree of force and the concept of the circumstances as you believe them to be. In our judgment, that is effectively all that the learned Lord Justice was saying.

What he was not saying, in our view (and indeed if he had said it, it would be contrary to authority) was that the belief, however ill-founded, of the defendant that the degree of force he was using was reasonable, will enable him to do what he did. . . . [I]f that argument was correct, then it would justify, for example, the shooting of someone who was merely threatening to throw a punch, on the basis that the defendant honestly believed, although unreasonably and mistakenly, that it was justifiable for him to use that degree of force. That clearly is not, and cannot be, the law."

Appeal dismissed

This an important clarification of the law which quite properly discards any suggestion of an entirely subjective test. The initial aggressor, in making the attack, is culpable and deserves to forfeit some of his rights but he does not sacrifice every right. Allowing unreasonable retaliatory force to constitute a justification would be, in effect, to endorse it.

While *Owino* has been followed in the subsequent decisions,[65] a slight doubt as to the correctness of this approach has been raised by the Privy Council decision in *Shaw*[66] where it was held that the jury should take into account "the circumstances *and the danger* as the appellant honestly believed them to be". As Smith has commented, "it is not only the appellant's belief as to the facts which is relevant, but also his judgment as to the degree of danger involved".[67] However, the better position adopted in *Owino* was re-affirmed in the post-*Shaw* case of *Martin* (extracted below) where it was stated that "it cannot be left to the defendant to decide what force is reasonable to use because this would mean that even if a defendant used disproportionate force but believed he was acting reasonably he would not be guilty of any offence".

In rejecting a subjective test on this issue, English law may have done enough to avoid problems with Article 2. While the Article states that fatal force may be used only if "absolutely necessary", in practice the European Court of Human Rights has looked for a "strictly proportionate" response although there has been a degree of flexibility in interpreting this.[68] Allowances are made for the fact that decisions to use defensive force may be made in the heat of the moment under extraordinary pressure.

What is the position if the defendant's perception of the danger he is in is distorted by a mental characteristic that he possesses? We shall see later that both for the defence of duress and the partial defence of provocation the law has moved to the position that such characteristics can generally be taken into account in assessing the reasonableness of the defendant's response. Can this similarly be done when the plea is one of self-defence?

### R. v Martin [2002] 1 W.L.R. 1 (Court of Appeal, Criminal Division)

The defendant shot and killed a burglar and was convicted of murder. On appeal new medical evidence was accepted that he was suffering from a paranoid personality disorder that would have made him perceive a much greater danger to his physical safety than the average person.

Lord Woolf C.J.:
"[It has been accepted in the law of provocation that the jury is] entitled to take into account some characteristic, whether temporary or permanent, which affected the degree of control which society could reasonably expect of a defendant and which it would be unjust not to take into account.

---

[65] For example, *Armstrong-Braun* [1999] Crim.L.R.416.
[66] [2002] 1 Cr.App.R.10.
[67] [2002] Crim.L.R.140 at 142.
[68] *Andronicou v Cyprus* (1998) 25 E.H.R.R. 491. See commentary by Ashworth, [1998] Crim.L.R.823.

Is the same approach appropriate in the case of self-defence? There are policy reasons for distinguishing provocation from self-defence. Provocation only applies to murder but self-defence applies to all assaults. In addition, provocation does not provide a complete defence; it only reduces the offence from murder to manslaughter. There is also the undoubted fact that self-defence is raised in a great many cases resulting from minor assaults and it would be wholly disproportionate to encourage medical disputes in cases of that sort. … As a matter of principle we would reject the suggestion that the approach of the majority in *Smith* in relation to provocation should be applied directly to the different issue of self-defence.

We would accept that the jury are entitled to take into account in relation to self-defence the physical characteristics of the defendant. However, we would not agree that it is appropriate, except in exceptional circumstances which would make the evidence especially probative, in deciding whether excessive force has been used to take into account whether the defendant is suffering from some psychiatric condition."

### Verdict of manslaughter by reason of diminished responsibility substituted

Leaving aside the obvious absurdity of the view that medical evidence would be inappropriate in a "great many cases resulting from minor assaults" (which is tantamount to asserting that injustice is acceptable if the crime is a minor one), this approach can be supported. Unlike provocation and duress, which are classic examples of excuses, self-defence provides a justification and so there is good reason to insist that the defendant's response be reasonable without account being taken of individual characteristics. However, it is stated that the physical characteristics of the defendant can be considered. For example, if the defendant is physically handicapped or is a pregnant woman (to borrow examples from duress) and less able to escape or use lesser force, this can be taken into account in assessing whether the actions were reasonable. This approach opens up the possibility of (weaker) women being permitted a wider range of defensive action against (stronger) men.

More perplexing is the statement that mental characteristics can be taken into account "in exceptional circumstances which would make the evidence especially probative". This cannot mean that a medically recognised psychiatric condition can be considered, because Martin had such a condition and it was discounted. Nevertheless, it will not be surprising if subsequent decisions, building on this dictum, were to develop this thinking to allow, as with duress, recognised psychiatric conditions to be taken into account. As indicated earlier, however, such an approach would be inconsistent with the justificatory nature of the defence.

### 3. The duty to retreat

It can be argued that if it is possible to escape from the attack by retreating then it is unnecessary and unreasonable to use defensive force.

### Joseph H. Beale, "Retreat from a Murderous Assault" (1903) 16 Harv.L.Rev. 567 at 580–582:

"The conclusion of the courts which deny the duty to retreat is, as we have seen, more commonly rested upon two arguments: that no one can be compelled by a wrongdoer to yield his rights, and that no one should be forced by a wrongdoer to the ignominy, dishonor, and disgrace of a cowardly retreat.

As to the argument of right, the ... law does not ordinarily secure the enjoyment of rights; it grants redress for a violation of rights. ...

The argument based upon the honor of the assailed is more elusive and more difficult to answer. ... The feeling at the bottom of the argument is one beyond all law; it is the feeling which is responsible for the duel, for war, for lynching; the feeling which leads a jury to acquit the slayer of his wife's paramour; the feeling which would compel a true man to kill the ravisher of his daughter. We have outlived dueling, and we deprecate war and lynching; but it is only because the advance of civilization and culture has led us to control our feelings by our will. And yet in all these cases sober reflection would lead us to realize that the remedy is really worse than the disease. So it is in the case of killing to avoid a stain on one's honor. A really honorable man, a man of truly refined and elevated feeling, would perhaps always regret the apparent cowardice of a retreat, but he would regret ten times more, after the excitement of the contest was past, the thought that he had the blood of a fellow-being on his hands. It is undoubtedly distasteful to retreat; but it is ten times more distasteful to kill."

### Glanville Williams, Textbook of Criminal Law (1st ed., 1978), p. 461:

"[I]t seems unreasonable to require a token retreat by one who has not been involved in any kind of aggression. There is no point in requiring a token yielding away from one who is wholly to blame. The only value of a token yielding is to show a disinclination to fight on the part of a person who has previously shown that inclination."

English law used to adopt a strict approach that a "retreat to the wall" was required before extreme force could be justified.[69] Since then, however, there has been considerable amelioration of the rule. In *Julien* the law was stated thus:

"It is not, as we understand it, the law that a person threatened must take to his heels and run in the dramatic way suggested ... but what is necessary is that he should demonstrate by his actions that he does not want to fight. He must demonstrate that he is prepared to temporise and disengage and perhaps to make some physical withdrawal; and to the extent that that is necessary as a feature of the justification of self-defence, it is true, in our opinion, whether the charge is a homicide charge or something less serious."[70]

In *McInnes*[71] this was accepted as an accurate statement of the law but Edmund-Davies L.J. added that a failure to retreat is only one of the factors to be taken into account in determining the reasonableness of the defendant's conduct. This approach was confirmed in the case of *Bird*[72] and is adopted by the Draft Criminal Law Bill 1993, clause 28(8):

"The fact that a person had an opportunity to retreat before using force shall be taken into account, in conjunction with other relevant evidence, in determining whether the use of force was reasonable."[73]

Although merely one of the factors to be taken into account, this may militate against a woman who fails to leave a repeatedly violent partner being able to plead self-defence.

---

[69] Subject to certain exceptions: a person was not under a duty to retreat if he were in his own home or if it would leave his family or friends in danger.

[70] (1969) 53 Cr.App.R.407 at 411.

[71] (1971) 55 Cr.App.R.551.

[72] [1985] 1 W.L.R. 816.

[73] Law Com. No. 218, *above*, n.50, cl. 29(4).

## Katherine O'Donovan, "Defences for Battered Women Who Kill" (1991) 18 J.L. and Soc. 219 at 222, 235:

"Despite the abolition of the duty to retreat, retreat might be considered an appropriate response. In the context of killing following prolonged domestic violence the questions look rather different. There may be a history of previous retreat which, as it were, has not worked. How relevant is the previous relationship of those involved, the lack of a safe place to go, the ideology of family privacy, the presence of children? ... leaving without one's children may seem a frightening prospect. But women's own accounts reveal emotional ties to the abuser which increase the difficulty of leaving. If the legal process is to come to terms with this it will have to accept that for many women connection to others is important. In other words, women's ways of looking at relationships will have to be valued equally with those of men."

### 4. The imminence of the threatened attack

In Western films the two protagonists tend to stand at opposite ends of a dusty street, each with his fingers hovering near his holster ready to draw and fire. In such films (apart from the occasional good one) the "baddie" will draw first; the "goodie" will then follow suit; he will inevitably be the quicker on the draw and the "baddie" will be killed. The film will then end with the "goodie" looking brave and honourable. The "baddie" drew first. The "goodie" was thus fully justified in acting in self-defence. However, had the "goodie" been the one to draw first, all would have changed. A plea of anticipatory self-defence would be meaningless in a Hollywood Western. By reaching for his gun first he would have become the aggressor.

Life, however, is not lived on a Hollywood film-set and the criminal law has to reflect life as it is and mirror everyday values. Restricting rights of self-defence to purely defensive retaliation could effectively condemn some innocent persons to death or other injury. The problem may be particularly acute where a substantial difference in size and strength exists, as may well be the case when a woman is attacked by a man. In certain limited circumstances the law must permit the right to strike first. As Lord Griffiths said in *Beckford*:

"A man about to be attacked does not have to wait for his assailant to strike the first blow or fire the first shot; circumstances may justify a pre-emptive strike." [74]

The problem, however, is in defining the parameters of such a right. Allowing too much anticipatory defensive action could become a charter for vigilantism.

### Devlin v Armstrong [1971] N.I. 13 (Court of Appeal for Northern Ireland)

The defendant, during a riot in Londonderry, urged others to build barricades and throw petrol bombs at the police. She was convicted of riotous behaviour and incitement to riotous behaviour. She appealed on the basis that she thought her action necessary to prevent people being assaulted and property damaged by the police.

MacDermott L.J.:
"The plea of self-defence may afford a defence where the party raising it uses force, not merely to counter an actual attack, but to ward off or prevent an attack which he has honestly and reasonably anticipated. In that case, however, the anticipated attack must be imminent: see *R. v Chisam* (1963) 47 Cr.App.R.130 ... and the excerpt from Lord

[74] [1988] 1 A.C. 130 at 144.

Normand's judgment in *Owens v H.M. Advocate* (1946) S.C.(J.) 119 which is there quoted and which runs:

'In our opinion self-defence is made out when it is established to the satisfaction of the jury that the panel believed that he was in imminent danger and that he held that belief on reasonable grounds. Grounds for such belief may exist though they are founded on a genuine mistake of fact' ...

However reasonable and convinced the appellant's apprehensions may have been, I find it impossible to hold that the danger she anticipated was sufficiently specific or imminent to justify the actions she took as measures of self-defence."

Appeal dismissed

## Attorney-General's Reference (No. 2 of 1983) [1984] 2 W.L.R. 465 (Court of Appeal, Criminal Division)

During the rioting in Toxteth in 1981 the defendant's shop was damaged and looted. Fearing further attacks he made ten petrol bombs "to use purely as a last resort to keep them away from my shop." The expected attack never materialised. The defendant was charged with an offence under section 4 of the Explosive Substances Act 1883 which provides that: "Any person who makes or knowingly has in his possession or under his control any explosive substance, under such circumstances as to give rise to a reasonable suspicion that he is not making it or does not have it in his possession or under his control for a lawful object, shall, unless he can show that he made it or had it in his possession or under his control for a lawful object, be guilty of a felony."

At his trial the judge ruled that it was "open to a defendant to say 'my lawful object is self-defence.'" The defendant was acquitted and the Attorney-General referred the following question for consideration: "Whether the defence of self-defence is available to a defendant charged with [an] offence under section 4 of the Explosive Substances Act 1883."

Lane L.C.J.:

"[Counsel for the Attorney-General] contends that ... [self-defence] does not exist as a justification for preliminary and premeditated acts anticipatory of an act of violence by the defendant ...

[He] submits that to allow a man to justify in advance his own act of violence for which he has prepared runs wholly contrary to the principle and thinking behind legitimate self-defence and legitimate defence of property. Both are defences which the law allows to actual violence by a defendant, and both are based on the principle that a man may be justified *in extremis* in taking spontaneous steps to defend himself, others of his family and his property against actual or mistakenly perceived violent attack.

It was argued that if a plea of self-defence is allowed to section 4 of the Act of 1883, the effect would be that a man could write his own immunity for unlawful acts done in preparation for violence to be used by him in the future. Rather than that, goes on the argument, in these circumstances a man should protect himself by calling on the police or by barricading his premises or by guarding them alone or with others, but not with petrol bombs. ...

In *R. v Fegan* (1972) N.I.L.R. 80 ... [it was held that]: 'Possession of a firearm for the purpose of protecting the possessor or his wife or family from acts of violence, *may* be possession for a lawful object. But the lawfulness of such a purpose cannot be founded on a mere fancy, or on some aggressive motive. The threatened danger must be reasonably and genuinely anticipated, must appear reasonably imminent, and must be of a nature which could not reasonably be met by more pacific means.' ...

In our judgment, approaching *a priori* the words 'lawful object,' it might well seem open to a defendant to say, 'My lawful object is self-defence.' The defendant in this case said that his intentions were to use the petrol bombs purely to protect his premises should any rioters come to his shop. It was accordingly open to the jury to find that the defendant had made them for the reasonable protection of himself and his property against this danger. The fact that in manufacturing and storing the petrol bombs the defendant committed offences under

the Act of 1875 did not necessarily involve that when he made them his object in doing so was not lawful. .... The object or purpose or end for which the petrol bombs were made was not itself rendered unlawful by the fact that it could not be fulfilled except by unlawful means
....

In the Judge's summing up the threatened danger was assumed, as was the defendant's anticipation of it. Also assumed, no doubt upon the basis of the evidence led, was the imminence of the danger. What the learned Judge upon the facts of the case before him left to the jury was the reasonableness of the means adopted for the repulsion of raiders. ...

In our judgment a defendant is not left in the paradoxical position of being able to justify acts carried out in self-defence but not acts immediately preparatory to it. There is no warrant for the submission on behalf of the Attorney-General that acts of self-defence will only avail a defendant when they have been done spontaneously. There is no question of a person in danger of attack 'writing his own immunity' for violent future acts of his. He is not confined for his remedy to calling in the police or boarding up his premises.

He may still arm himself for his own protection, if the exigency arises, although in so doing he may commit other offences. That he may be guilty of other offences will avoid the risk of anarchy contemplated by the Reference. It is also to be noted that although a person may 'make' a petrol bomb with a lawful object, nevertheless, if he remains in possession of it after the threat has passed which made his object lawful, it may cease to be so. It will only be very rarely that circumstances will exist where the manufacture or possession of petrol bombs can be for a lawful object.

For these reasons the point of law referred by Her Majesty's Attorney General for the consideration of this Court is answered by saying: The defence of lawful object is available to a defendant against whom a charge under section 4 of the Act of 1883 has been preferred, if he can satisfy the jury on balance of probabilities that his object was to protect himself or his family or his property against imminent apprehended attack and to do so by means which he believed were no more than reasonably necessary to meet the force used by the attackers."

Determination accordingly

In *Georgiades*[75] the defendant was charged with possession of a firearm with intent to endanger life contrary to section 16 of the Firearms Act 1968. Police visited his flat. He came on to the balcony with a loaded shotgun and raised it to waist level before being arrested. He believed he was in danger of being attacked and had not realised his visitors were police officers. On appeal it was held that self-defence should have been put to the jury. Accordingly, his conviction was set aside and a conviction for possessing a shortened firearm without a licence contrary to sections 1 and 4 of the Firearms Act 1968 was substituted.

### Malnik v D.P.P. [1989] Crim.L.R.451 (Queen's Bench Divisional Court)

The appellant, acting as an "adviser" to X went to "visit" one J who was thought to have taken two of X's valuable cars without authority. As J was known to have a tendency to violent and irresponsible behaviour the appellant (who was accompanied by three others) armed himself with a rice flail (two pieces of wood joined by a chain which the appellant was capable of using in connection with the martial arts). He was arrested approaching J's house. He was charged with having an offensive weapon in a public place without lawful authority or reasonable excuse contrary to section 1 of the Prevention of Crime Act 1953. The appellant argued that he had a reasonable excuse for having the flail with him, namely, that he had reasonable cause to believe that he was in imminent danger of being subjected to a violent attack. The appellant was convicted and appealed.

*Held,* "dismissing the appeal, the magistrate had correctly concluded that as a matter of law the defence of reasonable excuse was not available to the appellant. The case of *Evans v*

75 [1989] 1 W.L.R. 759.

*Hughes* [in which it was held that there could be a defence to a charge of carrying an offensive weapon if there was 'an imminent particular threat affecting the particular circumstances in which the weapon was carried' [1972] 3 All E.R. 412] and *R. v Field* [one cannot drive people off the streets and compel them not to go to places where they might lawfully be because they might be subjected to an attack there—[1972] Crim.L.R.435] were distinguishable. Ordinarily, individuals could not legitimately arm themselves with an offensive weapon in order to repel unlawful violence which such individual had knowingly and deliberately brought about by creating a situation in which violence was liable to be inflicted. It was quite different where those concerned with security and law enforcement were concerned. If private citizens set out on expeditions such as this, armed with offensive weapons, the risk of unlawful violence and serious injury was great, and obvious. The policy of the law must therefore be against such conduct, which conclusion was consistent with the very narrow limits which previous decisions had imposed on the freedom of the citizen to arm himself against attack. It had been rightly concluded that the risk of violence could have been avoided and thus the need to carry weapons, by inviting the appropriate agency to repossess the cars by the usual means."

**Appeal dismissed**

Thus under the current law the requirement of imminence is enshrined. Research into battered women who kill reveals that it is this element that causes most difficulty. In Ewing's study of 100 cases of battered women who killed, he found certain features to be common: years of violence, inadequate help from the community and the police, an inability to leave the situation and a killing that anticipated further violence or followed it, but did not fit the requirement of imminence.[76] A number of cases have involved women who have waited until their husbands were asleep before killing them.[77] As the law is currently framed this removes all possibility of pleading self-defence even though it may have seemed the only way out. Other cases have concerned women who have gone to the kitchen to fetch a knife with which to respond to the attack.[78] Again this may remove the possibility of pleading self-defence and, moreover, may be deemed to be such "cooling down" time as to remove the possibility of pleading provocation.[79] The only defence available in such circumstances may be diminished responsibility. Clearly, there will be cases where that is appropriate; the condition of the woman after years of abuse may have deteriorated to such an extent that she should not be held fully responsible for her actions. But it is not at all appropriate that the male orthodoxy of fighting blows with blows should dictate the defences available.

As the law currently stands one is entitled to use defensive force in anticipation of an attack but the amount of force permissible is tested against the degree of imminence of the attack. Also, it seems that the time-scale within which pre-emptive defensive action may be taken will be stretched when, as in the above cases, no actual violence has been used. For example, while the defendant in *Attorney-General's Reference (No. 2 of 1983)* was justified in making and possessing bombs, he would not have been justified in using them until his shop was

[76] Ewing, *Battered Woman Who Kill: Psychological Self-Defence as Legal Justification* (1987).
[77] *Ahluwalia* (1993) 96 Cr.App.R.133; *below*, p. 689.
[78] *Thornton* (1993) 96 Cr.App.R.112.
[79] *Below*, pp. 689–691.

actually under attack. But as Glanville Williams has pointed out: "there is a distinction between the immediacy of the necessity for acting and the immediacy of the threatened violence. The use of force may be immediately necessary to prevent an attack in the future."[80] Moreover, as has been stated before, in determining the necessity for acting at all, one does not have to jettison the requirement of reasonableness (as *Williams (Gladstone)* has done) in order to do justice to the differing sizes and strengths of attacker and defender.

The Criminal Law Revision Committee recommended the retention of the imminence rule: "it is desirable to make it clear that a man is not allowed to take the law into his own hands by striking before self-defence becomes necessary."[81] This view was reflected in the Draft Criminal Code Bill 1989.[82] However, the latest Law Commission Report has concluded that the jury will be able to decide whether the use of pre-emptive force was reasonable without any specific reference to a requirement of imminence.[83] Accordingly, there is no reference to it in the Draft Bill. This approach has much to commend it and should, at least, raise the possibility of self-defence being available to battered women who kill.

## 5. Excessive self-defence

A successful plea of self-defence justifies the defendant's conduct and he or she goes free. Accordingly, despite an increasing flexibility in the interpretation of the rules, it nevertheless is a rigorous test to overcome. Many defendants who act in self-defence, such as the one in *Martin*, use excessive force with the result that the defence fails. Other defendants, such as the battered woman in *Ahluwalia*, who kill their violent partner while he is asleep, being fearful of violence when he awakes and knowing from past experience that their strength is inadequate to match his, will similarly fail to come within the test. Because of the excessive or premature nature of their defensive actions it is right that their conduct should not be regarded as justified. But, in terms of assessing their moral culpability, such persons are not on a par with those who cold-bloodedly kill or injure others. Their reasons for acting are understandable. It is only the execution of those actions that is unacceptable. In short, there is a strong case for excusing, or partially excusing, such actors. Where the injuries inflicted are short of death, the fact that they were acting in self-defence can be taken into account as a mitigating factor in sentencing. But where they kill, the only verdict is murder with a mandatory sentence of life imprisonment.

In an effort to circumvent such injustice, courts have increasingly allowed such persons to avail themselves of the partial defences to murder. For example, battered women who kill are being afforded defences of diminished responsibility and provocation which result in manslaughter verdicts. The defendant in *Martin* was, on appeal, also allowed a defence of diminished responsibility. But, apart from the fact that these defences do not cover all cases, this whole approach misses the point in fair labelling terms. If a person's reasons for acting are self-defensive and they are not acting *because of* an abnormality of mind or provocation, what is needed is a

---

[80] *Textbook of Criminal Law* (2nd ed., 1983), p. 503.
[81] 14th Report, *Offences Against the Person* (Cmnd.7844, 1980), para. 286.
[82] Clause 44, Law Com. No. 177 (1989).
[83] Law Com. No. 218, *above*, n.50, paras 39.6–39.7.

defence—or partial defence—that accurately explains why they are not guilty of murder. Such thinking has led to increasing calls for the introduction of a new partial defence to murder termed "excessive self-defence", which would result in a manslaughter verdict.[84]

Such a defence exists in many other jurisdictions, For example, the Australian courts used to adopt an approach that a person who killed using excessive force was not guilty of murder, but only of manslaughter.[85] He was partially excused: "the moral culpability of a person who kills another in defending himself but who fails in a plea of self-defence only because the force which he believed to be necessary exceeded that which was reasonably necessary falls short of moral culpability ordinarily associated with murder."[86] This approach recognised excessive self-defence as a partial excuse. However, the Australian courts have now abandoned this "half-way house"[87] and the House of Lords has confirmed that such an approach is not part of English law.

## R. v Clegg [1995] 1 A.C. 482 (House of Lords)

The defendant, a soldier on duty in Northern Ireland, was on patrol when he shot and killed the driver of a stolen car and his passenger. He was charged with murder of the passenger and attempted murder of the driver. The defendant claimed that he had fired four shots in self-defence. The judge accepted this defence in relation to the first three shots. However, since the fourth shot (which was a significant cause of the passenger's death) was fired after the car had passed and the soldier was thus in no further danger, the defence was rejected. The defendant was convicted of murder and appealed.

Lord Lloyd of Berwick:
"Strictly speaking, the [issue of self-defence] does not arise on the facts of the present case. Since the danger had already passed when Private Clegg fired his fourth shot, there could be no question of self-defence, and therefore no question of excessive force in self-defence. But it is convenient to deal with this issue all the same ... [His Lordship then surveyed the authorities, including *Palmer*.] In other words, there is no half-way house. There is no rule that a defendant who has used a greater degree of force than was necessary in the circumstances should be found guilty of manslaughter rather than murder. ... [S]o far as self-defence is concerned, it is all or nothing. The defence either succeeds or fails. If it succeeds, the defendant is acquitted. If it fails, he is guilty of murder. ...
[His Lordship acknowledged the weight to be given to the views of those who argued for reform and concluded] I am not averse to judges developing law, or indeed making new law, when they can see their way clearly, even when questions of social policy are involved ... But in the present case I am in no doubt that your Lordships should abstain from law-making.

---

[84] See, for example, Lacey, "Partial Defences to Homicide: Questions of Power and Principle in Imperfect and Less Imperfect Worlds" in Ashworth and Mitchell (eds), *Rethinking English Homicide Law* (2000), p. 124, 129.

[85] *McKay* [1957] V.R. 560; *Howe* [1958] 100 C.L.R. 448. There has been some support for such an approach in this country (Report of the Select Committee on Murder and Life Imprisonment, H.L. Paper 78–1, 1989, para. 89).

[86] *Viro* (1976–78) 141 C.L.R. 88 at 139, *per* Mason J.

[87] *Zecevic* (1987) 71 A.L.R. 641. See Lanham, "Death of a Qualified Defence?" (1988) 104 L.Q.R. 239.

The reduction of what would otherwise be murder to manslaughter in a particular class of case seems to me essentially a matter for decision by the legislature, and not by this House in its judicial capacity. For the point in issue is, in truth, part of the wider issue whether the mandatory life sentence for murder should still be retained."

**Appeal dismissed**

In the wake of Clegg's conviction the Government announced a review of the law relating to the use of lethal force in self-defence.

### Report of the Interdepartmental Review of the Law on the use of Lethal Force in Self-Defence or the Prevention of Crime (1996), para. 83:

"The availability of [a manslaughter] verdict might assist in a comparatively small number of cases in which, previously, the outcome had proved contentious. It might help the jury or court to meet the demands of justice where a defendant had acted sufficiently culpably to deserve a criminal conviction, yet had lacked the evil motive usually associated with murder. The review was not convinced, however, that providing an additional option of manslaughter would enable the court or jury to achieve a result which would necessarily always be seen to be just. More options required finer distinctions and judgments to be made. With more borders between cases, there could be more cases that were seen to fall unfairly on the wrong side of the borderline, this time between acquittal and conviction for manslaughter, and between conviction for murder and manslaughter."

Whether or not these reasons are regarded as convincing, the Government has not only rejected any alteration to the law of murder in this respect but has also dismissed proposals to abolish the mandatory life sentence for murder.[88] It believes that release provisions are flexible enough to deal adequately with less heinous murders. For example, Private Clegg was released after two and a half years' imprisonment.[89] New guidance for the "minimum term" (formerly known as the "tariff") to be served by murderers states that the "normal starting point" for release is 12 years' imprisonment but that where the "offender's culpability is significantly reduced", for example, because the case "involved an over-reaction in self-defence", the sentence could be reduced to 8–9 years' imprisonment.[90]

Throughout this whole section on self-defence it has been predicted that the effect of Article 2 of the European Convention on Human Rights could be to restrict somewhat the present ambit of the defence in England and Wales. If this were to occur, even fewer people would be able to avail themselves of the defence and the number of murder convictions would increase. As a result "the pressure for the introduction of a special defence may become irresistible".[91] Other jurisdictions have recognised the merits of a finer assessment of degrees of blame and it is to be hoped that English law will follow their example.

---

[88] First report, *Murder: the Mandatory Life Sentence* (H.C. 111, 1995), paras 23–27, 55–58. The Government's Reply, *Murder: the Mandatory Life Sentence* (Cm.3346, 1996); below, p. 637.

[89] Subsequently, new evidence was produced which suggested that Clegg may not have fired when the car had passed and a re–trial was ordered.

[90] *Practice Statement (Crime: Life Sentences)* [2002] 1 W.L.R.1789.

[91] Editorial, [2000] Crim.L.R.418.

## IV. Chastisement

Parents are entitled to take reasonable disciplinary measures against their children, including the use of moderate physical punishment.[92] However, this defence of "reasonable chastisement" will not protect parents from criminal prosecution for assault or more serious offences, if the force used is excessive in nature, degree or duration.[93] The law's qualified condonation of the physical punishment of children has become increasingly controversial and in recent years the debate has been fuelled by reference to Article 3 of the European Convention on Human Rights which prohibits inhuman or degrading treatment or punishment. In *A v United Kingdom*[94] a boy was beaten with a cane by his step-father-to-be. The man was subsequently acquitted of assault occasioning actual bodily harm contrary to section 47 of the Offences against the Person Act 1861, having pleaded reasonable chastisement. The boy's case was taken to the European Court of Human Rights where it was held that the United Kingdom was in breach of Article 3 for failing to protect the child from such treatment.

The Government accepted that the ruling required them to change the law to ensure that children would be protected from inhuman or degrading treatment. In 2000, it published a consultation paper in which it proposed to set out the defence of reasonable chastisement on a statutory basis.[95] Adopting the reasoning of *A v United Kingdom*, it proposed legislation instructing courts to have regard to the nature and context of the treatment, its duration, its physical and mental effects, and in some instances, the sex, age and state of health of the victim.[96] Subsequently, however, the idea of legislation was abandoned on the basis that with the implementation of the Human Rights Act 1998 courts would, in any event, have to take account of the judgment of *A v United Kingdom*.[97] In *R. v H (Assault of Child: Reasonable Chastisement)*[98] the father used a leather belt on his son as punishment for disobedience. Although the judge at first instance took the view that the considerations outlined in *A v United Kingdom* (and the Consultation Paper) would not necessarily be enough to protect the boy's rights under Article 3, the Court of Appeal stated that these were the criteria to be applied in considering the defence of reasonable chastisement.

The Government chose to clarify rather than abolish the defence of reasonable chastisement, believing "that it would be quite unacceptable to outlaw physical

---

[92] Section 1(7) of the Children and Young Persons Act 1933 provides that [the crime of wilful assault, ill-treatment or neglect in section 1(1)] does not affect the right of any parent to administer punishment to their child.

[93] *Hopley* (1860) 2 F.& F. 202.

[94] (1999) 27 E.H.R.R. 611. See also *Campbell and Cosans v United Kingdom* (1980) 3 E.H.R.R. 531 and *Costello-Roberts v United Kingdom* (1993) 19 E.H.R.R. 12.

[95] *Protecting Children, Supporting Parents: A Consultation Document on the Physical Punishment of Children* (2000).

[96] In order to constitute a breach, the ill-treatment would have to reach a minimum level of severity depending on all the circumstances identified here: para 5.3.

[97] Department of Health Press release, November 8, 2001. The Government also stated that it would keep the defence under review.

[98] [2002] 1 Cr. App.R.59; see also *A* [2001] T.L.R. 329 and Rogers, "A Criminal Lawyer's Response to Chastisement in the European Court of Human Rights" [2002] Crim.L.R.98.

punishment of a child by a parent. Nor, we believe, would the majority of parents support such a measure. It would be intrusive and incompatible with our aim of helping and encouraging parents in their role."[99] The Government was influenced by the results of a survey conducted for them in which 88 per cent of respondents believed that it was sometimes necessary to smack a naughty child.[1] Certainly, the practice of physical punishment is widespread: one long-term survey of child-rearing practices revealed that over 60 per cent of parents say that they hit their one-year-olds, that children aged four are very likely to be hit between one and six times a week and that by the age of seven 91 per cent of boys and 59 per cent of girls had been hit or threatened with an implement.[2] However, a recent survey conducted on behalf of the N.S.P.C.C. found that 58 per cent of people would support law reform if they were sure that parents would not be prosecuted for trivial smacks.[3] Moreover, the Committee on the Rights of the Child has stated that the "governmental proposals to limit rather than remove the 'reasonable chastisement' defence do not comply with the principles and provisions of the Convention [on the Rights of the Child] ... particularly since they constitute a serious violation of the dignity of the child ... Moreover, they suggest that some forms of corporal punishment are acceptable and therefore undermine educational measures to promote positive and non-violent discipline."[4]

The defence of reasonable chastisement is based on an archaic attitude that regards children as less than people. "There is an injustice and illogicality in suggesting that it is acceptable to hit children, but that it is quite unacceptable to hit others, or for adults to hit anyone else. Hitting people is wrong – and children are people too."[5] It has also been argued that it unleashes a dangerous power, that some child abuse at least is discipline that has gone too far, and that it perpetuates a cycle of violence: children who have been abused tend in turn to become abusers.[6]

Eight other European countries have acted to ban the physical punishment of children[7] and it is to be hoped that the United Kingdom can be persuaded to follow suit. In the meantime, all corporal punishment in schools has been banned by section 131 of the Schools Standards and Framework Act 1998.[8] This was confirmed in the recent decision of *Williamson v Secretary of State for Education and Employment*[9] in which it was decided that the power of parents to delegate to teachers the right to administer physical punishment at school had been removed by the legislation. The argument that the corporal punishment of children was part

[99] *Above*, n.95, para. 2.14.
[1] *ibid*, para. 2.9. Fewer than 1% of respondents thought punishment reasonable if it left marks and bruises which lasted for more than a few days.
[2] Newell, *Children are People Too* (1989), pp. 53–66. See also Smith, *A Community Study of Physical Violence to Children in the Home* (1995).
[3] N.S.P.C.C. Press release 21 March 2002: www.nspcc.org.uk.
[4] Committee on the Rights of the Child, 31st session, Report (2002), para. 35.
[5] Newell, *above*, n.2 at p. 12.
[6] Crawford, "The Defence of Discipline: the Case for Abolition" (1982) 1 Med. Law 113.
[7] Clause 43(3) of the Scottish Criminal Justice Bill 2002 which would have made the hitting of children under three *prima facie* unlawful has now been withdrawn.
[8] Amending s.548 of the Education Act 1996. This legislation applies to nursery schools as well as to those providing education for children of compulsory school age and to independent schools as well as state schools.
[9] [2003] 1 All E.R. 385.

of the religious beliefs of the applicants (teachers and parents of certain Christian schools) and therefore to be respected under Article 9 of the Human Rights Act 1998 was rejected. It is, of course, as the law stands, and as was noted by the Court of Appeal, lawful for the parents to administer physical punishment at home for misbehaviour at school as long as it is consistent with the considerations set out in *A v United Kingdom.*

## V. Duress and Necessity

### A. *Introduction*

The defence of *duress* arises where a defendant is threatened by another with death or serious injury if she does not commit a crime. For example, in *Hudson and Taylor*[10] two girls committed perjury in an unlawful wounding case in which they were the principal witnesses. When charged with perjury they claimed they had been threatened that they would be "cut up" unless they committed perjury; they had been so frightened that they had duly told the lies in court. It was held that the defence of duress should have been put to the jury. The source of the threat must be another person. This species of duress is sometimes termed "duress by threats".

The defence of *necessity* potentially arises where a defendant claims she "had" to commit the crime, not because someone was threatening her, but because something (in the shape of surrounding circumstances which may or may not have been caused by a human being) deprived her of any real alternative. In short, she is claiming she committed a crime to prevent a greater evil. For example, ten people are climbing a ladder to safety from a vessel that is sinking. One of them is so petrified that he "freezes" on the ladder and cannot be persuaded to move. Eventually, he is pushed from the ladder and dies.[11] If charged with murder the survivors would claim that their actions were necessary and that it was better for one to die so that nine could live.

The defence of duress by threats has long been recognised by English law. However, until fairly recently it was commonly thought that the defence of necessity did not exist in English law. For example, in *Buckoke v Greater London Council* it was stated (*obiter*) that the driver of a fire engine was compelled to stop at red traffic lights even though "he sees 200 yards down the road a blazing house with a man at an upstairs window in extreme peril . . . [and if he] waits for that time, the man's life will be lost".[12]

However, since the 1980s the courts have been actively extending the defence of duress to apply to a broader range of situations where the threat does not necessarily arise from other persons, but where the defendant is faced with a crisis or emergency. This extended defence has been referred to as *duress of circumstances*. For example, in *Martin*[13] the defendant drove his son to work

---

[10] [1971] 2 Q.B. 202.
[11] This seems to have happened during the sinking of the *Herald of Free Enterprise, The Times*, June 13, 1988. See *Re A (Conjoined Twins)* [2000] 4 All E.R. 961 at 1041.
[12] [1971] Ch. 655 at 668.
[13] (1989) 88 Cr.App.R.343.

(otherwise he would have been late and at risk of losing his job) because he feared his wife would commit suicide if he did not. He was afforded a defence to a charge of driving while disqualified on grounds of "duress of circumstances":

"English law does, in extreme circumstances, recognise a defence of necessity. Most commonly this defence arises as duress, that is pressure upon the accused's will from the wrongful threats or violence of another. Equally, however, it can arise from other objective dangers threatening the accused or others. Arising thus it is conveniently called 'duress of circumstances'."

## R. v Shayler [2001] 1 W.L.R. 2206 (Court of Appeal, Criminal Division)

Lord Chief Justice:
"There is no reason of principle or authority for distinguishing the two forms of duress in relation to the elements of the defence which we have identified. ... The decision in *Abdul-Hussain* provides useful clarification of the earlier three pronged definition of necessity and elaborates on the operation of the requirement of imminence. It also reflects other decisions which have treated the defence of duress and necessity as being part of the same defence and the extended form of the defence as being nothing more than different labels for essentially the same thing, see *e.g. R. v Conway* [1988] 3 All E.R. 1025 at 1029 where it was said: 'As the learned editors point out in Smith and Hogan, Criminal Law (6th ed., 1988) p. 225, to admit a defence of "duress of circumstances" is a logical consequence of the existence of the defence of duress as that term is ordinarily understood, *i.e.* "do this or else". This approach does no more than recognise that duress is an example of necessity. Whether "duress of circumstances" is called "duress" or "necessity" does not matter. What is important is that, whatever it is called, it is subject to the same limitations as the "do this or else" species of duress.' "

It would be tempting, following this, simply to regard duress, duress of circumstances and necessity as three prongs of a single broad defence. However, such an approach would be both misleading and premature for two reasons. First, as we shall see, it is true that in developing the defence of duress of circumstances the courts have largely accepted that the conditions for its application are the same as for duress by threats. We shall see, however, that the two defences are not necessarily completely identical. More significantly, however, the rationale for the application of each defence is different. Duress by threats is a classic excusatory defence: we understand the plight of the hapless person whose "will is overborne" by terrible threats. Duress of circumstances, however, has a more justificatory flavour. The defendant has committed a crime to prevent something terrible befalling herself or others: she is driven to commit the crime by force of circumstances. Despite the fact that English law has cast this defence in an excusatory mould, duress of circumstances looks more like a synonym for necessity. This brings us to the second reason for distinguishing the defences. A fully fledged defence of necessity would be far broader than the present defence of duress of circumstances. For example, it would involve a pure balancing of evils (whereas under the present law on duress of circumstances there has to be a threat of death or serious injury) and it would be a defence to all crimes (whereas duress of circumstances at present is not a defence to murder). As we shall see, it would be highly premature to regard such a broad necessity defence as having been accepted into English law.

The extent to which these are separate defences or are simply different labels for three prongs of a single defence will be explored in the following sections. As the three do not all share the same theoretical underpinnings and as they have developed differently and, to some extent, have different rules governing their applicability, they will be dealt with separately.

## B. *Duress by threats*

As seen, this is the well-established defence that is afforded to a person who is threatened with death or serious injury unless she commits a crime.

### 1. Rationale of duress by threats as a defence

#### J. F. Stephen, History of the Criminal Law of England, Vol. 2 (1883), pp. 107–108:

"Criminal law is itself a system of compulsion on the widest scale. It is a collection of threats of injury to life, liberty and property if people do commit crimes. Are such threats to be withdrawn as soon as they are encountered by opposing threats? The law says to a man intending to commit murder, If you do it I will hang you. Is the law to withdraw its threat if someone else says, If you do not do it I will shoot you? Surely it is the moment when temptation to crime is strongest that the law should speak most clearly and emphatically to the contrary. It is, of course, a misfortune for a man that he should be placed between two fires, but it would be a much greater misfortune for society at large if criminals could confer impunity upon their agents by threatening them with death or violence if they refused to execute their commands. If impunity could be so secured a wide door would be opened to collusion, and encouragement would be given to associations of malefactors, secret or otherwise. No doubt the moral guilt of a person who commits a crime under compulsion is less than that of a person who commits it freely, but any effect which is thought proper may be given to this circumstance by a proportional mitigation of the offender's punishment. These reasons lead me to think that compulsion by threats ought in no case whatever to be admitted as an excuse for crime, though it may and ought to operate in mitigation of punishment in most though not in all cases."

#### The Law Commission (Law Com. No. 83), Report on Defences of General Application (1977), para. 2.14:

"Those who favour the conclusion that duress should not afford a defence which absolves criminal liability contend that it can never be justifiable for a person to do wrong, in particular to do serious harm to another merely to avoid some harm to himself; that it is not for the individual to balance the doing of wrong against the avoidance of harm to himself. They argue that duress does not destroy the will or negative intention in the legal sense, but that it merely deflects the will so that intention conflicts with the wish; in short that it provides a motive for the wrongful act and that motive is, on general principle, irrelevant to whether a crime has been committed."

#### Abbott v The Queen [1977] A.C. 755 (Privy Council)

Lord Salmon:
"It seems incredible to their Lordships that in any civilised society, acts such as the

appellant's whatever threats may have been made to him, could be regarded as excusable or within the law. We are not living in a dream world in which the mounting wave of violence and terrorism can be contained by strict logic and intellectual niceties alone. Common sense surely reveals the added dangers to which in this modern world the public would be exposed, if the change in the law proposed on behalf of the appellant were affected. It might well ... prove to be a character for terrorists, gang leaders and kidnappers ... [If the accused were allowed to go free he would now have] gained some real experience and expertise, he might again be approached by the terrorist who would make the same threats ... [the accused] would then give a repeat performance, killing even more men, women and children. Is there any limit to the number of people you may kill to save your own life and that of your family?"

Those who oppose a defence of duress generally concede that it is a relevant matter to take into consideration in mitigation of sentence. For all crimes other than murder courts have wide discretionary powers when sentencing and in extreme cases of duress only a minimal sentence need be imposed.[14] Even for murder, the existence of duress can be taken into account in fixing the "tariff" to be served.

Thus the arguments against a general defence of duress fall broadly into two groups:

(i) the law would lose some of its deterrent effect if duress were allowed as a defence;
(ii) the defendant is morally blameworthy and, accordingly, deserves punishment. Because of the duress his blameworthiness might be *less* and so he can receive a mitigated sentence—but he is still, to some extent, morally blameworthy.

## (i) Deterrence[15]

Was Stephen correct in asserting that "it is the moment when temptation to crime is strongest that the law should speak most clearly and emphatically to the contrary"? Are the law's threats likely to serve any useful purpose to a person placed in such a perilous situation?

### Ian Dennis, "Duress, Murder and Criminal Responsibility," (1980) 96 L.Q.R. 208 at 234, 236:

"The deterrent argument is clear. If we assume that the accused acted as a reasonable man in not resisting the threat, and that both he and the reasonable man would act in the same way again whatever the attitude of the law, then the imposition of punishment cannot act as either an individual or a general deterrent. It will amount only to the useless infliction of a penalty and, on a utilitarian hypothesis, will therefore be unjustifiable ...

[A] man under pressure to kill or be killed may well reason correctly that he does, at least, gain time by ignoring the law's prohibition; the alternative of heeding the prohibition and

[14] Wasik, "Duress and Criminal Responsibility" [1977] Crim.L.R.453; Dennis, "Duress, Murder and Criminal Responsibility" (1980) 96 L.Q.R. 208 at 235–237.
[15] The other utilitarian arguments hardly seem applicable here. A person who has committed a crime because of duress does not need rehabilitation. He is also not a danger to society needing incapacitation (unless, as Lord Salmon suggested in *Abbott*, he was to be continually subjected to threats to induce him to commit crimes; this is highly unlikely—a terrorist or gang leader would be extremely foolish to use the same "agent", to whom the police were now alerted, more than once).

resisting the threat simply leads more quickly to unpleasant consequences. Secondly, if duress is to be taken into account anyway when sentence is passed, then the law's sanction for ignoring its threat is uncertain and may well not be heavy ... An appeal to the deterrent value of the law disallowing duress as a defence is thus an empty gesture; the deterrent is ineffective because it is not immediate and because it is subverted by admitting duress through the back door as evidence in mitigation."

On the other hand, "[w]e do not and we cannot know what choices may be different if the actor thinks he has a chance of exculpation on the ground of his peculiar disabilities than if he knows that he does not,"[16] and thus "[t]here is an argument for saying that we should nourish the hope, however faint, that the threat of punishment may be enough to tip the balance of decision by those who have only doubtfully sufficient fortitude to undergo martyrdom for the sake of a moral principle".[17]

Further, quite apart from general deterrence, there is the more realistic "educative" species of deterrence that "legal norms and sanctions operate not only at the moment of climactic choice but also in the fashioning of values and of character".[18] The denial of a defence of duress would strengthen values so that persons in situations of duress would be less likely to submit to the threats.

### (ii) *Moral blameworthiness*

Is the actor who submits to duress morally blameworthy and responsible for his actions so that he deserves punishment for them?

We saw in Chapter 2 that moral responsibility has been traditionally confined to those who *choose* to break the law and thus choose to become subject to criminal liability.

### H. L. A. Hart, Punishment and Responsibility (1968), pp. 22–23:

"The ... view is that of society ... *offering* individuals including the criminal the protection of the laws on terms which are fair ... because ... each individual is given a *fair* opportunity to choose between keeping the law required for society's protection or paying the penalty ...

Criminal punishment ... consists simply in announcing certain standards of behaviour and attaching penalties for deviation, making it less eligible, and then leaving individuals to choose. This is a method of social control which maximises individual freedom within the coercive framework of law in a number of different ways. ... First, the individual has an option between obeying or paying. ... Secondly, this system not only enables individuals to exercise this choice but increases the power of individuals to identify beforehand periods when the law's punishments will not interfere with them and to plan their lives accordingly."

The question in duress is whether the actor had this "fair opportunity" to choose between conforming to the law or breaking it. Where the circumstances have overwhelmed his capacity for choice, where his freedom of choice is too restricted, we do not account him blameworthy and responsible. This is what was meant by Lord Widgery C.J. in *Kray*[19] when he spoke of the accused being "so terrified that

---

[16] A.L.I., Model Penal Code, Comments (To Tent. Draft No. 10 (1960)).
[17] Williams, *Textbook of Criminal Law* (2nd ed., 1983), p. 628.
[18] *Above*, n.16.
[19] [1970] 1 Q.B. 125.

he ceased to be an independent actor" and what he meant in *Hudson and Taylor*[20] when he required that the defendant's "will" must have been "overborne"; the threats had to "neutralise the will". This does not mean that the defendant had no *mens rea*.[21] Hudson and Taylor both told their lies deliberately and intentionally. As was emphasised by Lord Hailsham in the leading case of *Howe*:

> "[An] unacceptable view is that ... duress as a defence affects only the existence or absence of mens rea. The true view is stated by Lord Kilbrandon (of the minority) in *Lynch* [1975] A.C. 653 ... at p. 703:
>
> 'the decision of the threatened man whose constancy is overborne so that he yields to the threat, is a calculated decision to do what he knows to be wrong, and is therefore that of a man with, perhaps to some exceptionally limited extent, a "guilty mind". But he is at the same time a man whose mind is less guilty than is his who acts as he does but under no such constraint.' "[22]

So the basis of the defence of duress is that the defendant did not have an effective opportunity to make a choice as to whether to commit the crime. Of course, in one sense, the defendant does make a choice, but it is only "Hobson's choice". His dilemma is to choose between two "morally unacceptable courses of action".[23] Because the external pressure is so great, in a moral sense, it "coerces" the actor into committing the crime. Fletcher describes such conduct as "morally involuntary".[24] Morally involuntary conduct is not blameworthy; the defendant does not deserve punishment.

### R. v Ruzic (2001) S.C.C. 24 (Supreme Court of Canada)

LeBel J:
"Moral involuntariness is also related to the notion that the defence of duress is an excuse ... In using the expression 'moral involuntariness', we mean that the accused had no 'real' choice but to commit the offence. This recognizes that there was indeed an alternative to breaking the law, although in the case of duress that choice may be even more unpalatable—to be killed or physically harmed ...
Punishing a person whose actions are involuntary in the physical sense is unjust because it conflicts with the assumption in criminal law that individuals are autonomous and freely choosing agents. It is similarly unjust to penalize an individual who acted in a morally involuntary fashion. This is so because his acts cannot realistically be attributed to him, as his will was constrained by some external force ... [T]he accused's agency is not implicated in her doing. In the case of morally involuntary conduct, criminal attribution points not to the accused but to the exigent circumstances facing him, or to the threats of someone else."

In England this view has been largely[25] accepted—primarily on the ground that it would be unjust or unfair to punish in such circumstances.

---

[20] [1971] 2 Q.B. 202.
[21] As was suggested by Lord Goddard C.J. in *Bourne* (1952) 36 Cr.App.R.125.
[22] [1987] 1 A.C. 417; see also Lord Bridge's similar comments in *Howe* at 436.
[23] Horder, "Occupying the Moral High Ground? The Law Commission on Duress" [1994] Crim.L.R.334 at 340–341.
[24] Fletcher, *Rethinking Criminal Law* (1978), p. 803.
[25] With the exception of murder, attempted murder and some forms of treason.

## D.P.P. v Lynch [1975] A.C. 653 (House of Lords)

Lord Morris:

"[I]t is proper that any rational system of law should take fully into account the standards of honest and reasonable men. By those standards it is fair that actions and reactions may be tested. If then someone is really threatened with death or serious injury unless he does what he is told to do is the law to pay no heed to the miserable, agonising plight of such a person? For the law to understand not only how the timid but also the stalwart may in a moment of crisis behave is not to make the law weak but to make it just. In the calm of the court-room measures of fortitude or of heroic behaviour are surely not to be demanded when they could not in moments for decision reasonably have been expected even of the resolute and the well disposed ...

The law must, I think, take a common sense view. If someone is forced at gun-point either to be inactive or to do something positive—must the law not remember that the instinct and perhaps the duty of self-preservation is powerful and natural? I think it must. A man who is attacked is allowed within reason to take necessary steps to defend himself. The law would be censorious and inhumane which did not recognise the appalling plight of a person who perhaps suddenly finds his life in jeopardy unless he submits and obeys."

Does recognising "the appalling plight" of the defendant reduce itself to taking motive into account? Norrie points out, "If 'doing justice' to a Lynch means taking into account his motives, it is unclear why 'doing justice' to everyone else means ignoring theirs."[26] Motive is generally irrelevant under the criminal law—because the law seeks to set an objective standard of behaviour—yet there can be no doubt that motives other than the threat of death or serious harm may be compelling. Indeed, as we shall see, this was one of the factors involved in the resistance of English Law to the defence of necessity. However, as far as duress is concerned it has to be recognised that it is a "concession to human frailty"[27] which is available only when the threats are extreme. It is thus best viewed as an excuse rather than a justification.[28] The defendant has done wrong; he has violated the interests of an innocent person, but because of his appalling predicament, he is excused from blame.[29]

## 2. Parameters of the defence

In what circumstances may a defendant break the law but escape liability because of duress? Or, to put it another way, when will conduct be regarded as "morally involuntary"? When will the circumstances be such that we will not account the defendant blameworthy for her actions?

### Hyman Gross, A Theory of Criminal Justice (1979), p. 276:

"Sometimes people are forced to do what they do. When what they are forced to do is wrong it seems that the compulsion ought to count in their favour. After all, we say, such a

---

[26] Norrie, *Crime, Reason and History* (1993), p. 166.

[27] *Howe* [1987] 1 A.C. 417; *Shepherd* (1988) 86 Cr.App.R.47.

[28] There are elements of a justificatory defence, however. In Lord Hailsham's speech in *Howe*, for example, he spoke of the defendant possibly regarding his choice "as the lesser of two evils". In other words, the defendant claims to have done the *right* thing (or, at least, the only reasonable thing) in the circumstances; this is a justificatory claim. The Law Commission rejected the notion of a balancing of harms approach; *below*, p. 33. But see further, Horder, "Autonomy, Provocation and Duress" [1992] Crim.L.R.706; McAuley, "Beckford and the Criminal Law Defences" (1990) 41 N.I.L.Q. 158.

[29] Kadish, "Excusing Crime" (1987) 75 Cal.L.Rev. 257; *cf.* Smith, "Must Heroes Behave Heroically?" [1989] Crim.L.R.622.

person wasn't free to do otherwise—he couldn't help himself, not really. No claim to avoid blame appeals more urgently to our moral intuitions, yet none presents more problems of detail. There are times, after all, when we ought to stand firm and run the risk of harm to ourselves instead of taking a way out that means harm for others. In such a situation we must expect to pay the price if we cause harm when we prefer ourselves, for then the harm is our fault even though we did not mean it and deeply regret it. But how shall the line be drawn to separate cases in which the constraint is sufficiently powerful to make blame inappropriate from cases in which constraint is simply a challenge to avoid harm to oneself as best one can while doing no harm to others? A line too far in either direction means injustice, for it is not right to allow with impunity harming that should have been avoided, nor is it right to punish for harm whose avoidance cannot reasonably be expected."

### John Gardner, "The Gist of Excuses" (1998) 1 Buffalo Criminal Law Review 575 at 578–579:

"The gist of an excuse ... is precisely that the person with the excuse lived up to our expectations ... in the *normative* sense. Did she manifest such resilience, or loyalty, or thoroughness, or presence of mind as a person in her situation should have manifested? In the face of terrible threats, for example, did this person show as much fortitude as someone in his situation could properly be asked to show? ... The character standards which are relevant to these and other excuses are not the standards of our own characters, nor even the standards of most people's characters, but rather the standards to which our characters should, minimally, conform."

Essentially the attribution of blame involves a moral judgment relating, *inter alia*, to our expectations of how people should act in certain situations. This inevitably involves a comparison between the defendant's response and how we imagine *we*, or other "ordinary people", would respond in that situation. If we perceive that ordinary people would have responded as the defendant did, then we do not blame the defendant for his actions. But if we perceive that ordinary people would have withstood the threats, then we legitimately blame the defendant for his failure to do so.

This test provides us with the key to answering the following questions concerning the parameters of the defence of duress.

### (i) *Threat of death or serious harm*

In making our moral judgment as to whether to blame the defendant, we would surely wish to compare the crime committed with the nature of the threats to which the defendant was exposed. Suppose a defendant had been threatened that his house would be burnt to the ground if he did not steal a tin of beans from the local supermarket. We would not blame a defendant who committed such a crime. Suppose a defendant who had access to the water supply of London was threatened with death or serious bodily harm if he did not place a deadly poison in the water supply. If he poisoned the water and 10,000 people died (as he knew they would), we would blame him for his actions because the harm he caused was so much greater than the harm threatened. This "balancing of harms" approach ought not to operate in a rigid mechanistic manner, but it is a useful aid to our moral judgment as to whether to blame the defendant.[30] This is broadly the approach of the Model Penal Code which states that any "use of, or a threat to use, unlawful

[30] Fletcher, *Rethinking Criminal Law* (1978), p. 804.

force against his person[31] or the person of another, which a person of reasonable firmness in his situation would have been unable to resist"[32] will afford a defence of duress. Lord Wilberforce flirted with this notion in *Lynch* when he said that "[n]obody would dispute that the greater the degree of heinousness of the crime, the greater and less resistable must be the degree of pressure, if pressure is to excuse".[33] In *Howe* Lord Hailsham said he "believe[d] that some degree of proportionality between the threat and the offence must, at least to some extent, be a prerequisite of the defence under the existing law".[34]

English law, however, is committed to the view that only threats of death or serious harm will suffice for a defence of duress.[35] If the threats are less terrible they should be matters of mitigation only.[36]

What is meant be serious harm here? Must this be serious physical harm or will serious psychological harm suffice? For the purposes of offences against the person, the term "grievous bodily harm" has been interpreted to include serious psychological harm.[37] Such an approach was rejected in *Baker and Wilkins*[38] but *Shayler*[39] seems to support the view that a threat of serious psychological harm can suffice as it is stated that "protection of the physical *and mental* well-being of a person from serious harm is still being required". Of course, where the threat is one of serious psychological harm, it will be difficult (but not impossible) to satisfy the test, to be explored shortly, that the threat must be one of imminent harm.

The threat must be extraneous to the offender. In *Rodger and Rose*[40] it was held that the defence of duress of circumstances was not available to a charge of breaking prison where the defendants claimed that if they had not escaped, they would have committed suicide.

### The Law Commission, Working Paper No. 55, Defences of General Application (1974), paras 16, 17:

"16 ... We have considered whether a defence of duress could be framed in terms of the balancing of one harm against another, permitting it to be raised only when the harm to be inflicted upon the defendant is greater than the harm which he is obliged to do. For various reasons, however, we regard this as impracticable. In the first place, if the defence was so framed it would follow that where the defendant, to save his own life, imperilled the lives of more than one other person, the defence would be unavailable. ...

Secondly, a test involving the concept of balance of harms cannot, it seems to us, operate satisfactorily where the offences involved are of an entirely different character. There is, for example, no sensible means of weighing a threat of severe injury to the person against an enforced disclosure of information contrary to the Official Secrets Act which might lead to a danger to national security. Our provisional conclusion is, therefore, that in defining the

---

[31] Threats to property are suprisingly not included. The commentary (to Tent. Draft No. 8 (1958)) points out that threats to property are covered by the necessity defence in s.3.02.

[32] A.L.I., Model Penal Code, Proposed Official Draft (1962), s.2.09(1).

[33] [1975] A.C. 653 at 681.

[34] [1987] 1 A.C. 417 at 432–433.

[35] *Hudson and Taylor* [1971] 2 Q.B. 202; *D.P.P. v Lynch* [1975] A.C. 653; *Conway* [1988] 3 W.L.R. 1238; *Martin* [1989] 1 All E.R. 652; *D.P.P. v Davis*; *D.P.P. v Pittaway* [1994] Crim.L.R.600.

[36] Law Com. No. 83, *Report on Defences of General Application* (1977), para. 2.18.

[37] *Ireland; Burstow* [1998] A.C. 147.

[38] [1997] Crim.L.R.497.

[39] [2001] 1 W.L.R. 2206.

[40] [1998] 1 Cr.App.R.143.

kind of threats which are the subject of duress, it must be borne in mind that the basic justification of the defence is that it is a concession to human infirmity in situations of extreme peril.

17. This conclusion leads us to take the provisional view that duress ought for the future to be available only in cases where the threat is a threat of death or of serious injury."

This conclusion is confirmed in Clause 25(1) of the Draft Criminal Law Bill 1993. As it is largely accepted that it is the task of the criminal law to set objective standards of behaviour, it is hardly surprising that the defence of duress should be so closely circumscribed. It is only when the threats are extreme that the law can allow individual motive to be an excuse. This does, however, lead to anomalies in the law.[41] The Criminal Damage Act 1971 states that the fact that the defendant acted in order to protect property belonging to himself or another may be a lawful excuse for damage caused.[42]

### (ii) *Multiple threats*

In *Valderrama-Vega*[43] the defendant was threatened with the disclosure of his homosexuality, was under financial pressure and received threats of death or serious harm. The first two are incapable of amounting to duress but the court held that the jury was entitled to look at the cumulative effect of all of the threats. It was wrong to direct the jury that the threat of death or serious injury had to be the sole reason for him committing the crime. In *Ortiz*,[44] however, a direction that the threat to life be the sole threat was upheld, although the court also thought the use of the word "solely" should normally not be included. The special feature of *Ortiz* appears to have been the possibility of the defendant's actions also being motivated by the large amount of money he was making from dealing in cocaine and on that basis the authority of *Valderrama-Vega* is to be preferred.[45]

### (iii) *Stipulated crime*

Duress by threats is a defence where the defendant is threatened with death or serious injury unless he commits a particular, stipulated crime. What is the position if there is no link between the threat and the offence committed? In *Cole*[46] the defendant robbed two building societies and claimed that he had done so to pay off a debt to moneylenders who had hit him with a baseball bat and had threatened him and his family. The Court of Appeal held that the defence of duress is only available if the threats are directed at the offence committed. In this case the

---

[41] Padfield, "Duress, Necessity and the Law Commission" [1992] Crim.L.R.778 at 782. See also *Shortland* [1996] 1 Cr.App.R.116 where it was held that the defence of marital coercion under the Criminal Justice Act s.47 is quite distinct from duress and not confined to threats of physical harm.

[42] s.5(2)(b). *Cf. Baker and Wilkins* [1997] Crim.L.R.497. See Clause 28(2)(e) of the Draft Criminal Code Bill 1992, Law Com. No. 122 (1992).

[43] [1985] Crim.L.R.220.

[44] (1986) 83 Cr.App.R.173.

[45] See also *Bell* [1992] Crim.L.R.176.

[46] [1994] Crim.L.R.582.

moneylenders had not stipulated that he commit robbery in order to meet their demands and there was, therefore, an insufficient nexus between the threat and the offence.

As we shall see, for the newly-developed defence of "duress of circumstances" there is no requirement that the defendant commit a stipulated crime. For example, in *Martin*[47] the evil to be averted was his wife committing suicide; the crime committed was driving while disqualified. There was no link between them. There are two views that can be adopted in relation to this. First, while duress and duress of circumstances are largely identical in the conditions for their application, there are differences and this is one of them. Secondly, if they are in reality two "prongs" of the same defence, simply bearing different labels to describe the different situations involved, it could be that *Cole* should no longer be regarded as good law. If a person's will is so overborne by terrible threats that his actions become "morally involuntary", it hardly seems material that he commits a crime other than the one stipulated.

### (iv) Belief in threat; steadfastness: subjective or objective

There are two issues here. First, what is the position if the defendant thinks he has been threatened with death or serious injury but a reasonable man in his situation would not have interpreted the threat thus? Secondly, what is the position if the defendant is terrified by the threats and duly commits a crime, but the reasonable man would have "stood his ground" and not committed the crime? As the following two extracts demonstrate, these two questions are often dealt with jointly. However, as each raises rather different issues they will be dealt with separately after the extracts.

### The Law Commission No. 83, Defences of General Application (1977), paras 2.27, 2.28:

"2.27. The defence of duress is essentially a concession to human weakness in the face of an overwhelming threat of harm by another, and it is therefore right that so far as possible the criteria to be applied should be subjective. It should be sufficient, provided always that there is a threat of harm, that the defendant believes that the threat is of death or serious personal injury and believes that there is no way of avoiding or preventing the threatened harm other than by committing the offence. That a reasonable person would not have so believed may be relevant in testing the defendant's evidence as to his own belief but it should not of itself disentitle the defendant to the defence.

2.28. It may be said that the whole test as to whether the requirements of duress exist should be subjective, but we feel that this would create too wide a defence. Serious personal injury can cover a wide range of threatened harm, and if the defence is to be available even in respect of the most serious offences, it would be unsatisfactory in the final event to dispense with some objective assessment of whether the defendant could reasonably have been expected to resist the threat. The solution which is adopted by section 2.09(1) of the American Law Institute's Model Penal Code is to provide that the threat of unlawful force (which is left undefined) must be that 'which a person of reasonable firmness in his situation would have been unable to resist.' Whether the words 'in his situation' comprehend more than the surrounding circumstances, and extend to characteristics of the defendant himself, it is difficult to say, and for that reason we would not recommend without qualification the adoption of that solution. We think that there should be an objective element in the

---

[47] (1989) 88 Cr.App.R.343.

requirements of the defence so that in the final event it will be for the jury to determine whether the threat was one which the defendant in question could not reasonably have been expected to resist. This will allow the jury to take into account the nature of the offence committed, its relationship to the threats which the defendant believed to exist, the threats themselves and the circumstances in which they were made, and the personal characteristics of the defendant. The last consideration is, we feel, a most important one. Threats directed against a weak, immature or disabled person may well be much more compelling than the same threats directed against a normal healthy person."

## R. v Graham (1982) 74 Cr.App.R.235 (Court of Appeal, Criminal Division)

The appellant, a practising homosexual, lived in a flat with his wife and another homosexual man, K, in a *ménage à trois*. The appellant was taking drugs for anxiety which made him more susceptible to bullying. K was a violent man and was jealous of the appellant's wife. One night after the appellant and K had been drinking heavily K put a flex round the wife's neck, pulled it tight and then told the appellant to take hold of the other end of the flex and pull on it. The appellant did so for about a minute. The wife was killed as a result of the pressure of the flex on her neck. The appellant was charged with murder, as was K, who pleaded guilty. The appellant pleaded not guilty and in evidence said that he had complied with K's demand to pull on the flex only because of his fear of K. The Crown conceded that it was open to the appellant to raise the defence of duress and did not seek to contend that the defence was not available to a principal to murder. In directing the jury on the defence, the judge posed two questions for the jury: (i) the subjective question of whether the appellant took part in the killing because he feared for his life or personal safety as a result of K's words or conduct, and (ii) if so, the objective question of whether, taking into account all the circumstances, including the appellant's age, sex, sexual propensities and other personal characteristics, and his state of mind and the drink and drugs he had taken, it was reasonable for the appellant, because of fear of K, to take part in killing his wife. The judge further stated that the test of reasonableness in that context was whether, having regard to those circumstances, the appellant's behaviour reflected the degree of self-control and firmness of purpose to be expected from a person in today's society. The appellant was convicted of murder. He appealed against conviction.

Lord Lane C.J.:

"[T]he direction appropriate ... [to the first question] should have been in these words: 'Was this man at the time of the killing taking part because he held a well-grounded fear of death [or serious physical injury] as a result of the words or conduct on the part of King?' The bracketed words may be too favourable to the defendant. The point was not argued before us.

... [Counsel for the appellant] contends that no second question arises at all; the test is purely subjective. He argues that if the appellant's will was in fact overborne by threats of the requisite cogency, he is entitled to be acquitted and no question arises as to whether a reasonable man, with or without his characteristics, would have reacted similarly ...

[Counsel for the Crown], on the other hand, submits that such dicta as can be found on the point are in favour of a second test; this time an objective test. ...

As a matter of public policy, it seems to us essential to limit the defence of duress by means of an objective criterion formulated in terms of reasonableness. Consistency of approach in defences to criminal liability is obviously desirable. Provocation and duress are analogous. In provocation the words or actions of one person break the self-control of another. In duress the words or actions of one person break the will of another. The law requires a defendant to have the self-control reasonably to be expected to the ordinary citizen in his situation. It should likewise require him to have the steadfastness reasonably to be expected of the ordinary citizen in his situation. So too with self-defence, in which the law permits the use of no more force than is reasonable in the circumstances. And, in general, if a mistake is to excuse what would otherwise be criminal, the mistake must be a reasonable one.

It follows that we accept [counsel for the Crown's] submission that the direction in this case was too favourable to the appellant. The Crown having conceded that the issue of duress was open to the appellant and was raised on the evidence, the correct approach on the facts of this case would have been as follows: (1) Was the defendant, or may he have been, impelled to act as he did because, as a result of what he reasonably believed King had said or done, he had good cause to fear that if he did not so act King would kill him or (if this is to be added) cause him serious physical injury? (2) If so, have the prosecution made the jury sure that a sober person of reasonable firmness, sharing the characteristics of the defendant, would not have responded to whatever he reasonably believed King said or did by taking part in the killing? The fact that a defendant's will to resist has been eroded by the voluntary consumption of drink or drugs or both is not relevant to this test.

We doubt whether the Crown were right to concede that the question of duress ever arose on the facts of this case. The words and deeds of King relied on by the defence were far short of those needed to raise a threat of the requisite gravity. However, the Crown having made the concession, the judge was right to pose the second objective question to the jury. His only error lay in putting it too favourably to the appellant."

**Appeal dismissed**

## (a) Belief in threat

According to *Graham* the defendant must *reasonably* believe he has been threatened with death or serious injury ("the first question"). It is interesting that Lord Lane asserts that "consistency of approach in defences to criminal liability is obviously desirable" yet in the self-defence case of *Williams (Gladstone)*[48] he ruled that the defendant had to be judged according to the facts as he believed them to be. *Graham* has been approved by the House of Lords in *Howe*[49] and has been followed in some subsequent cases.[50] However, in *Martin (D.P.)*[51] an analogy was drawn between duress and self-defence and it was held, following *Williams (Gladstone)*, that the defence of duress will be available if the defendant honestly believes that he has been threatened with death or serious injury even if that belief is not reasonable. This is in line with the proposals contained in the Draft Criminal Law Bill 1993 that a person acts under duress if "he knows or believes" that a threat of the requisite gravity has been made.[52] This subjective approach adopted in *Martin (D.P.)* is in accord with the recent House of Lords decisions on mistake which affirm that it is the defendant's honest belief that is material.[53]

The better approach is that adopted in *Graham*. As argued earlier,[54] while mistakes as to justifications (such as self-defence) need only be honest, mistakes as to excuses (such as duress) should have to be reasonable as well. While this argument could potentially be problematic when applied to duress of circumstances which contains elements of a justificatory nature, the fact remains that the English courts have treated duress of circumstances as being an excuse. If excuses are to exempt defendants from liability, they should be plausible—*i.e.* reasonable—excuses.[55]

---

[48] (1984) 78 Cr.App.R.276; see also Alldridge, "Developing the Defence of Duress" [1986] Crim.L.R.433.

[49] [1987] 1 A.C. 417.

[50] For example, *D.P.P. v Davis; D.P.P. v Pittaway* [1994] Crim.L.R.600.

[51] [2000] 2 Cr.App.R.42.

[52] Law Commission No. 218 (1993), cl 25(2).

[53] *B (A Minor) v D.P.P.* [2000] 2 A.C. 428; *R. v K* [2002] 1 A.C. 462.

[54] *Above*, p. 197.

[55] In *Cairns* [1999] 2 Cr.App.R.137, a duress of circumstances case, it was emphasised that the defendant must reasonably believe there was a threat of death or serious injury.

## (b) Steadfastness

It is clear from *Graham* ("the second question") that the defendant must display reasonable steadfastness or bravery. This was also confirmed in *Howe*. The test is that the threats must be such that a person of reasonable firmness *sharing the characteristics of the defendant* would have given way to the threats. There have been a number of cases in which the courts have struggled to distinguish relevant characteristics from those which should be ignored.[56] In *Emery*, for example, the Court of Appeal held that medical evidence about "learned or dependent helplessness" was rightly admitted in determining whether the defendant, charged with cruelty to a child, could have withstood threats from the child's father.[57] The following case has attempted to synthesise the principles which have emerged.

### R. v Bowen [1996] 2 Cr.App.R.157 (Court of Appeal, Criminal Division)

The defendant was charged with obtaining services by deception. He claimed that he had been forced to do so, having been accosted by two men who threatened him and his family with petrol-bombing if he did not obtain the goods. He was convicted and appealed on the ground that his abnormal suggestibility and vulnerability (low I.Q. was added at the appeal stage) were relevant characteristics not put to the jury as affecting his ability to withstand the threats.

Stuart-Smith L.J.:
"[T]he question remains, what are the relevant characteristics of the accused to which the jury should have regard in considering the second objective test? This question has given rise to considerable difficulty in recent cases. It seems clear that age and sex are, and physical health or disability may be, relevant characteristics. But beyond that it is not altogether easy to determine from the authorities what others may be relevant ...
[His Lordship then surveyed the case-law.]
What principles are to be derived from these authorities? We think they are as follows:
    (1) The mere fact that the accused is more pliable, vulnerable, timid or susceptible to threats than a normal person are not characteristics with which it is legitimate to invest the reasonable/ordinary person for the purpose of considering the objective test.
    (2) The defendant may be in a category of persons who the jury may think less able to resist pressure than people not within that category. Obvious examples are age, where a young person may well not be so robust as a mature one; possibly sex, though many women would doubtless consider they had as much moral courage to resist pressure as men; pregnancy, where there is added fear for the unborn child; serious physical disability, which may inhibit self protection; recognised mental illness or psychiatric condition, such as post traumatic stress disorder leading to learned helplessness.
    (3) Characteristics which may be relevant in considering provocation, because they relate to the nature of the provocation, itself will not necessarily be relevant in cases of duress. Thus homosexuality may be relevant to provocation if the provocative words or conduct are related to this characteristic; it cannot be relevant in duress, since there is no reason to think that homosexuals are less robust in resisting threats of the kind that are relevant in duress cases.
    (4) Characteristics due to self-induced abuse, such as alcohol, drugs or glue-sniffing, cannot be relevant.

---

[56] *Hegarty* [1994] Crim.L.R.353 (evidence of emotional instability and a grossly elevated neurotic state inadmissible); *Horne* [1994] Crim.L.R.584 (evidence that unusually pliable and vulnerable to pressure inadmissible); *Hurst* [1995] 1 Cr.App.R.82 (evidence of possible effects upon defendant of child abuse as a child inadmissible) and *Flatt* [1996] Crim.L.R.576 (evidence of drug addiction excluded as a self-induced condition not a characteristic).

[57] (1993) 14 Cr.App.R.(S.) 394. The condition is also known as post-traumatic stress disorder. The defendant was convicted but her sentence reduced on appeal from four years to 30 months.

(5) Psychiatric evidence may be admissible to show that the accused is suffering from some mental illness, mental impairment or recognised psychiatric condition provided persons generally suffering from such condition may be more susceptible to pressure and threats and thus to assist the jury in deciding whether a reasonable person suffering from such a condition might have been impelled to act as the defendant did. It is not admissible simply to show that in the doctor's opinion an accused, who is not suffering from such illness or condition, is especially timid, suggestible or vulnerable to pressure and threats. Nor is medical opinion admissible to bolster or support the credibility of the accused.

(6) Where counsel wishes to submit that the accused has some characteristic which falls within (2) above, this must be made plain to the judge. The question may arise in relation to the admissibility of medical evidence of the nature set out in (5). If so, the judge will have to rule at that stage. There may, however, be no medical evidence, or, as in this case, medical evidence may have been introduced for some other purpose, *e.g.* to challenge the admissibility or weight of a confession. In such a case counsel must raise the question before speeches in the absence of the jury, so that the judge can rule whether the alleged characteristic is capable of being relevant. If he rules that it is, then he must leave it to the jury.

(7) In the absence of some direction from the judge as to what characteristics are capable of being regarded as relevant, we think that the direction approved in *Graham* without more will not be as helpful as it might be, since the jury may be tempted, especially if there is evidence, as there was in this case, relating to suggestibility and vulnerability, to think that these are relevant. In most cases it is probably only the age and sex of the accused that is capable of being relevant. If so, the judge should, as he did in this case, confine the characteristics in question to these.

How are these principles to be applied in this case? [Counsel for the Crown] accepts, rightly in our opinion, that the evidence that the appellant was abnormally suggestible and a vulnerable individual is irrelevant. But she submits that the fact that he had, or may have had, a low I.Q. of 68 is relevant since it might inhibit his ability to seek the protection of the police. We do not agree. We do not see how low I.Q., short of mental impairment or mental defectiveness, can be said to be a characteristic that makes those who have it less courageous and less able to withstand threats and pressure."

Appeal dismissed

## Buchanan and Virgo, "Duress and Mental Abnormality" [1999] Crim.L.R.517 at 529–530:

"Diagnosis in psychiatry .... [has moved] to an 'atheoretical' approach. Less emphasis is placed on causative factors, pathological changes or abnormalities of process underlying each disorder and more emphasis is placed on symptoms and signs. This change presents two related problems for the law as it relates to duress. The first is that, as a result, psychiatric conditions are now 'recognised' according to different criteria than was previously the case and these criteria cannot be relied upon to identify a group of people whose ability to withstand threats is reduced. The second is that if an atheoretical approach is adopted, psychiatric conditions cannot be said to 'cause' any aspect of behaviour because they themselves comprise no more or less than various aspects of behaviour.

It follows that the test .... in *Bowen* .... is unworkable and needs to be reformulated. There are two options. ... Second, ... The crucial question would then be whether the defendant could reasonably be expected to have resisted the threat given his or her mental condition. It would not matter that the condition could not be described as recognized."

This second option is not dissimilar to that proposed by the Draft Criminal Law Bill 1993 whereby the threat must be "one which in all the circumstances (including any of his personal circumstances that affect its gravity) he cannot reasonably be expected to resist" (clause 25(2)).[58] (It is taken as axiomatic that a person should not be able to rely upon his intoxication as a relevant circumstance.) This clause makes the proposed test less stringent than that accepted in *Graham*. The Law Commission are not convinced that "a person's 'characteristics' can be distinguished in the way that the *Graham* test appears to contemplate. Relative timidity, for example, may be an inseparable aspect of a total personality that is in turn part cause and part product of its possessor's life situation; and thus may itself be one of the 'circumstances' in the light of which the pressure represented by the duress is to be assessed".[59]

Clearly, one would not wish to blame someone who, by virtue of his age or sex, for example, was unable to withstand a threat that might have been ineffective against another. But what of other characteristics, such as timidity or nervousness? As we saw with self-defence, if these are taken into account, the question that arises is whether the test is in any real way objective. Some commentators have argued that this sweeps "away almost every legal requirement of moral scrutiny of D's choice ... [and is an] over-hasty abolition of the common law's objectivism".[60] However, it must be remembered that the Law Commission's approach is different from an unquestioning acceptance of the defendant's submission to threats. The reaction of the defendant still has to be a reasonable one for *that* defendant.

Finally, one must ask whether this steadfastness rule or the requirement of a reasonable response serves any useful purpose. Bearing in mind that duress can only be pleaded if there has been a threat of death or serious injury and that it is not a defence to murder, when would it ever be unreasonable to give in to such grave threats?

### K.J.M.Smith, "Duress and Steadfastness: In Pursuit of the Unintelligible" [1999] Crim.L.R.363 at 370, 375:

"Is it being maintained that, when faced with a belief in the threat of death or serious harm, the question is, *should* that defendant have capitulated bearing in mind their personal characteristics? In other words, does the reasonable steadfastness test envisage some defendants of strong emotional or physical disposition who will be denied a defence of duress and who must not choose self-preservation? ... [N]o coherent function can be assigned to the steadfastness requirement ...

[T]he presence of a steadfastness test deflects attention away from legitimate defence conditions relating to the neutralization or avoidance of threats ... [T]he steadfastness requirement cannot coherently relate to anything other than the distinct conditions that defendants take all reasonable opportunities to escape from or neutralize an aggressor's threat."

### (v) *Imminence of threat*

It is generally stated that the defence of duress is only available if there is a threat of *immediate* harm. Thus in *Gill*[61] the defendant was threatened with personal violence if he did not steal his employer's lorry. It was held *obiter* that he probably

---

[58] Law Com. No. 218 (1993).

[59] Law Com. Consultation Paper No. 122, *Legislating the Criminal Code: Offences Against the Person and General Principles* (1992), para. 18.11.

[60] Horder, "Occupying the Moral High Ground? The Law Commission on Duress" [1994] Crim.L.R.334 at 341.

[61] (1963) 47 Cr.App.R.166. See also *Cole* [1994] Crim.L.R.582.

could not have pleaded duress because there had been a period of time during which he could have raised the alarm and wrecked the whole enterprise. As Lord Morris said in *Lynch*:

> "[The question is whether] a person the subject of duress could reasonably have extricated himself or could have sought protection or had what has been called a 'safe avenue of escape'."[62]

This approach can be supported. We would blame someone who had a reasonable opportunity to raise the alarm and wreck the criminal enterprise,[63] but we would not blame someone who had no such opportunity. What is the position if the defendant has an opportunity to seek help but fears that police protection will be ineffective?

### R. v Hudson and Taylor [1971] 2 Q.B. 202 (Court of Appeal, Criminal Division)

(The facts are set out, *above*, p. 323.)

Widgery L.J.:

"In the present case the threats ... were likely to be no less compelling, because their execution could not be effected in the court room, if they could be carried out in the streets of Salford the same night ...

[Counsel for the Crown] ... submits on grounds of public policy that an accused should not be able to plead duress if he had the opportunity to ask for protection from the police before committing the offence and failed to do so. The argument does not distinguish cases in which the police would be able to provide effective protection, from those when they would not, and it would, in effect, restrict the defence of duress to cases where the person threatened had been kept in custody by the maker of the threats, or where the time interval between the making of the threats and the commission of the offence had made recourse to the police impossible ...

In the opinion of this court it is always open to the Crown to prove that the accused failed to avail himself of some opportunity which was reasonably open to him to render the threat ineffective, and that upon this being established the threat in question can no longer be relied on by the defence. In deciding whether such an opportunity was reasonably open to the accused the jury should have regard to his age and circumstances, and to any risks to him which may be involved in the course of action relied upon."

### The Law Commission, Working Paper No. 55, Defences of General Application (1974), para. 20:

"We recognise that effective protection may not be continuously available; yet it seems to us that a defendant subject to this kind of threat must always be under a duty at least to seek that protection in order to reduce the possibility of its execution and failure to do so through fear of the consequences ought properly to be a factor in mitigation rather than a complete defence."[64]

In *Hudson and Taylor* the threats could have been reported to the police, but the two young girls, aged 17 and 19, were convinced that the police protection would be ineffective. Are we to blame them for their failure to seek official protection? It would appear that their response was typical of the response of most ordinary girls

---

[62] [1975] A.C. 653 at 668.
[63] Ashworth, "Reason, Logic and Criminal Liability" (1975) 91 L.Q.R. 102 at 104.
[64] See also Law Com. No. 83, paras 2.29–2.31.

of that age faced with such a predicament. It would be absurd to assert that the defence of duress would only be available to them if there had been a sniper sitting in court ready to execute his threats immediately. These views were echoed by Lord Griffiths in *Howe*:

"if duress is introduced as a merciful concession to human frailty it seems hard to deny it to a man who knows full well that any official protection he may seek will not be effective to save him from the threat of death under which he has acted."[65]

In *Heath*[66] the defence was denied to a defendant who had "more than one avenue of escape open to him". (He could have gone to the police or his parents.) In *Baker and Ward*[67] it was held that the test was whether a reasonable person would have gone to the police.

## R. v Abdul-Hussain and others (1998) (No. 9707785, Lawtel) (Court of Appeal, Criminal Division)

The defendants, a group of Iraqis, highjacked a Sudanese aeroplane. They feared they would be killed if returned to Iraq.

Rose V.P.:
"[Counsel for the appellants submitted that] [a]lthough there must be a nexus between the threat of death or serious injury and the criminal act, this nexus arises ... from imminent peril not immediate threat or 'a virtually spontaneous reaction'. Imminent means impending threateningly, hanging over one's head, ready to overtake one, coming on shortly. Immediate means without intermediary, proximate, nearest, next. Spontaneous, means voluntarily, without thought or premeditation, without external stimulus ...
[W]e derive the following propositions from the relevant authorities: ...
4. The peril must operate on the mind of the defendant at the time when he commits the otherwise criminal act, so as to overbear his will, and this is essentially a question for the jury
...
5. But the execution of the threat need not be immediately in prospect ... [Some previous authorities did not have] the advantage of argument, as to the distinction between imminence, immediacy and spontaneity which has been addressed to us ...
6. The period of time which elapses between the inception of the peril and the defendant's act, and between that act and execution of the threat, are relevant but not determinative factors for a judge and jury in deciding whether duress operates ...
7. All the circumstances of the peril, including the number, identity and status of those creating it, and the opportunities (if any) which exist to avoid it are relevant, initially for the judge, and, in appropriate cases, for the jury, when assessing whether the defendant's mind was affected as in 4 above ...
8. As to 6 and 7, if Anne Frank had stolen a car to escape from Amsterdam and been charged with theft, the tenets of English law would not, in our judgment, have denied her a defence of duress of circumstances, on the ground that she should have waited for the Gestapo's knock on the door ...

[65] [1987] A.C. 417 at 433.
[66] [2000] Crim.L.R.109.
[67] [1999] 2 Cr.App.R.335.

In our judgment, although the judge was right to look for a close nexus between the threat and the criminal act, he interpreted the law too strictly in seeking a virtually spontaneous reaction. He should have asked himself, in accordance with *Martin* [see p. 351], whether there was evidence of such fear operating on the minds of the defendants at the time of the hijacking as to impel them to act as they did."

This passage was approved in *Shayler*. Both these decisions, dealing with duress of circumstances, confirmed that that the rules for duress by threats and duress of circumstances are the same. Nevertheless, it does appear that the operation of the imminence rule is context-sensitive and that the more one slides along the continuum from duress to duress of circumstances and through to necessity, the less rigorous this requirement becomes. This is because in cases of duress by threats the rationale for the excuse is that the defendant's "will has been overborne" whereas at the other extreme (necessity) the defendant is making a more rational choice. It was stressed in *Re A (Conjoined Twins),*[68] a classic case of necessity, that the principle is "one of necessity, not emergency". In this case the death of both twins was not an immediate or even imminent prospect; they could both well have lived for many months. However, as their deaths within that period were a certainty, a severance operation that would kill the weaker twin was a necessity.

(vi) *Threats to others*

### The Law Commission, Working Paper No. 55, Defences of General Application (1974), para. 18:

"[W]e consider that no limitation should be placed upon the persons against whom the threat may be made. Obviously, a threat of imminent death, for example, to the defendant's wife or children ought to suffice for the defence[69]; but it is not, in our view, possible to maintain with confidence that it should not apply also in the case of threats to a friend[70] of the defendant nor, indeed, to someone he does not know. No rational dividing line is discernible in this context."

"Duress of circumstances" cases have indicated that the threat can be to the defendant or "some other person",[71] and the Draft Criminal Law Bill 1993 provides that the threat must be to the defendant "or another".[72]

### R. v Shayler [2001] 1 W.L.R. 2206 (Court of Appeal, Criminal Division)

The defendant, a former member of MI5, was charged with breaching the Official Secrets Act 1989, s.1(1) by disclosing deficiencies in the MI5. He claimed that it was necessary to do so because if MI5 continued to operate in this manner it would inevitably create a danger to the public. He was convicted and appealed.

Woolf C.J.:
"It is also necessary to consider in greater detail the nature of the responsibility and the category of persons to whom the defendant must owe the responsibility for the purposes of

---

[68] [2001] Fam.147.
[69] *Ortiz* (1986) 83 Cr.App.R.173: threats to wife and child sufficed; *K* (1984) 148 J.P.410: implicit threat to mother sufficed.
[70] *Wright* [2000] Crim.L.R.510: threat to boyfriend sufficed.
[71] *Conway* [1988] 3 All E.R. 1025; *Martin* [1989] 1 All E.R. 652.
[72] Law Com. No. 218 (1993), clause 25(2)(a).

the defence. Mr Shayler contends that, as a member of the government secret services, he owed a responsibility to the general public at large. His acts were necessary to protect a yet to be identified group from among the public for whose protection MI5 had responsibilities who would inevitably suffer because of MI5's incompetence. . . .

So in our judgment the way to reconcile the authorities to which we have referred is to regard the defence as being available when a defendant commits an otherwise criminal act to avoid an imminent peril of danger to life or serious injury to himself or towards somebody for whom he reasonably regards himself as being responsible. That person may not be ascertained and may not be identifiable. However, if it is not possible to name the individuals beforehand, it has at least to be possible to describe the individuals by reference to the action which is threatened would be taken which would make them victims absent avoiding action being taken by the defendant. The defendant has responsibility for them because he is placed in a position where he is required to make a choice whether to take or not to take the action which it is said will avoid them being injured. Thus if the threat is to explode a bomb in a building if defendant does not accede to what is demanded the defendant owes responsibility to those who would be in the building if the bomb exploded."

**Appeal dismissed**[73]

As this bomb example demonstrates, most endangered strangers can be brought within the test as being persons for whom the defendant "reasonably regards himself as being responsible" provided they can be identified in a general way: for example, persons in a building. On the facts of *Shayler* itself, it was stated that "if it is possible to identify the members of the public at risk this will only be by hindsight. This creates difficulty over the requirement of responsibility".

Where the threat is directed against the defendant, his family or others to whom a direct responsibility is owed, one can legitimately describe the defendant's conduct as being "morally involuntary" and excusable. But where strangers are involved, it is questionable whether a defendant should be permitted to, say, cause grievous bodily harm to one stranger in order to save another stranger from grievous bodily harm (especially as there must always be a chance, however small, that the threat will not be carried out). This is in effect allowing the defendant to choose between the two strangers. How is he to assess their relative "worth"? Of course, in many cases the harm to be inflicted by the defendant will be much less than that threatened against the stranger and in such situations it ought certainly to be an excuse that the defendant committed his crime to save the third party from, at least, serious injury.

### (vii) *Defendant placing himself in a position where he might be open to threats*

A defendant who joins a criminal association (whether terrorist, gangster or otherwise) which could force him to commit crimes can be blamed for his actions. In joining such an organisation fault can be laid at his door and his subsequent actions described as blameworthy. This is the approach adopted by English law which denies the defence of duress to such a person.

---

[73] On appeal, the House of Lords declined to discuss these issues on the basis that the facts were "not within measurable distance of affording him a defence of necessity or duress of circumstances" (*Shayler* [2002] 2 All E.R. 477 at 491).

## R. v Sharp [1987] 1 Q.B. 853 (Court of Appeal, Criminal Division)

The appellant joined a gang of robbers, knowing they used firearms. He participated in a robbery upon a sub-post office but claimed he had been forced to as one of the other robbers had threatened to kill him if he did not carry through the plan. He was convicted of manslaughter and appealed.

Lord Lane C.J.:
"No one could question that if a person can avoid the effects of duress by escaping from the threats, without damage to himself, he must do so. In other words if there is a moment at which he is able to escape, so to speak, from the gun being held at his head by Hussey, or the equivalent of Hussey, he must do so. It seems to us to be part of the same argument, or at least to be so close to the same argument as to be practically indistinguishable from it, to say that a man must not voluntarily put himself in a position where he is likely to be subjected to such compulsion ...

[I]n our judgment, where a person has voluntarily, and with knowledge of its nature, joined a criminal organisation or gang which he knew might bring pressure on him to commit an offence and was an active member when he was put under such pressure, he cannot avail himself of the defence of duress."

**Appeal dismissed**

## R. v Baker and Ward [1999] 2 Cr.App.R.335 (Court of Appeal, Criminal Division)

The defendants were drug dealers. They got into debt with their suppliers who threatened them with violence and instructed them to rob a store. Their defence to a charge of robbery was that they were acting under duress. They were convicted and appealed.

Roch L.J.:
"In some situations, the evidence may be so clear that the judge will be entitled to rule that the defence is not open to the accused, for example, where the accused has joined a terrorist organisation or a gang of armed robbers...

In another type of case, the accused, although not joining a gang or organisation, may have involved himself in criminal activities which bring him into contact with other criminals in circumstances where the accused knew or was aware that if he defaulted in fulfilling his role or in discharging obligations he assumed in relation to the other criminals he would be subjected to such compulsion. Drug dealing on a scale which is significant could be such a case. The present case was a case in which it was appropriate to leave to the jury the question whether the accused had voluntarily put themselves in a position where they were likely to be subjected to duress. The defence of duress will not be available to an accused in this situation if he is aware that there is a risk of pressure by way of violence or threats of death or violence to him or a member of his immediate family being brought to bear upon him. The purpose of the pressure has to be to coerce the accused into committing a criminal offence of the type for which he is being tried. If the accused had no reason to anticipate such pressure, then they would be entitled to rely upon duress."

**Appeal allowed**

The test here would appear to be a subjective one. The defendant must be aware of the risks when involving himself with the criminal enterprise.[74] But what of the person who ought to know he is likely to be exposed to threats? Duress is an excuse and, on principle, there ought to be a plausible—or reasonable—excuse for the actions. The basis of the rule here is that a defendant has no plausible excuse and is

[74] *Ali* [1995] Crim.L.R.303.

blameworthy if he associates with such criminal enterprises or organisations. If the risks of violence were obvious, even though he gave no thought to them, there is a strong case for denying the defence.[75] However, despite the dictum in *Baker and Ward* that the defence would only be available if the defendant "had no reason" to anticipate threats, the weight of authority favours a subjective approach.

What is the position if the defendant, when joining or associating with the criminal group, does foresee the risk of serious violence but does not anticipate he might be ordered to commit a crime. This issue is unresolved. In *Baker and Ward* it was stated that the defendant "has to be aware of the risk that the group might try to coerce him into committing criminal offences *of the type* for which he is being tried". This approach was also adopted in Z.[76] On the other hand, some cases have held that it is only necessary that the defendant expose himself to unlawful violence: "the fact that the defendant did not foresee that he might be required under the threat of violence to commit crimes was irrelevant".[77]

### (viii) *Length of time after threats*

The defendant can only rely upon the defence as long as the threat is operative. In *D.P.P. v Davis; D.P.P. v Pittaway*[78] both defendants were charged separately with driving with excess alcohol, contrary to section 5(1)(a) of the Road Traffic Act 1988. Both pleaded duress. However, on appeal by way of case stated, the Divisional Court held (on a number of grounds) that there was no evidence of duress. In particular, the fact that one of the defendants had driven for two miles without any suggestion that he was being pursued and that the other had decided to drive off after a five minute pause in which no threat had materialised meant that duress could not apply.[79]

### (ix) *Crimes to which duress is a defence*

If the defendant's conduct can be described as being "morally involuntary", and if we are satisfied that we do not blame the defendant for his actions, because ordinary people would have responded in the same way, it follows that he ought to have a defence to any crime. However, English law adopts the view that duress is a defence to all crimes *except* murder, attempted murder[80] and treason.[81] In *Lynch* the House of Lords decided that duress was a defence to an accessory to murder but in *Abbott* the Privy Council ruled that it was not a defence to the principal offender (the one who actually does the killing) of murder. In *Howe*[82] the House of Lords

---

[75] Under the Draft Criminal Law Bill 1993, cl.25(4), the defence is not available to a person who has knowingly and without reasonable excuse exposed himself to the risk of a threat (Law Com. No. 218, 1993).

[76] [2003] *The Times*, March 26.

[77] *Harmer* [2002] Crim.L.R.401. See also *Heath* [2000] Crim.L.R.109.

[78] [1994] Crim.L.R.600.

[79] See *Pommell* [1995] 2 Cr.App.R.607; *Bell* [1992] Crim.L.R.176; *Jones* [1990] R.T.R. 33 and *Tomkinson* [2001] R.T.R. 583 where similar reasoning was applied in duress of circumstances cases.

[80] *Gotts* [1992] 2 A.C. 412.

[81] "Prosecutions for treason are virtually confined to the circumstances of war. Perhaps in war even the private citizen is expected to cast himself in a heroic mould." (Williams, *Textbook of Criminal Law* (2nd ed., 1983), p. 627). There are, however, dicta in *Lynch* to the effect that duress could in some circumstances be a defence to treason. See, for example, Lord Morris at 672.

[82] [1987] 1 A.C. 417.

held that duress was not a defence to murder, irrespective of the degree of participation.

## D.P.P. v Lynch [1975] A.C. 653 (House of Lords)

The appellant was ordered to drive members of the IRA in Northern Ireland to a place where they intended to kill, and did kill, a policeman. The appellant claimed that he was convinced that he would be shot if he did not obey. He was convicted of murder, the trial judge holding that the defence of duress was not available to an accessory to murder. The Court of Criminal Appeal in Northern Ireland dismissed his appeal.

Lord Morris:
"It may be that the law must deny such a defence to an actual killer, and that the law will not be irrational if it does so.

Though it is not possible for the law always to be worked out on coldly logical lines there may be manifest factual differences and contrasts between the situation of an aider and abettor to a killing and that of the actual killer. Let two situations be supposed. In each let it be supposed that there is a real and effective threat of death. In one a person is required under such duress to drive a car to a place or to carry a gun to a place with knowledge that at such place it is planned that X is to be killed by those who are imposing their will. In the other situation let it be supposed that a person under such duress is told that he himself must there and then kill X. In either situation there is a terrible agonising choice of evils. In the former, to save his life, the person drives the car or carries the gun. He may cling to the hope that perhaps X will not be found at the place or that there will be a change of intention before the purpose is carried out or that in some unforeseen way the dire event of a killing will be averted. The final and fatal moment of decision has not arrived. He saves his own life at a time when the loss of another life is not a certainty. In the second (if indeed it is a situation likely to arise) the person is told that to save his life he himself must personally there and then take an innocent life. It is for him to pull the trigger or otherwise personally to do the act of killing. There, I think, before allowing duress as a defence it may be that the law will have to call a halt. May there still be force in what long ago was said by Hale?
'Again, if a man be desperately assaulted, and in peril of death, and cannot otherwise escape, unless to satisfy his assailant's fury he will kill an innocent person then present, the fear and actual force will not acquit him of the crime and punishment of murder, if he commit the fact; for he ought rather to die himself, than kill an innocent.' (*Hale's Pleas of the Crown*, Vol. 1, p. 51.)"

Appeal allowed: new trial ordered

## Abbott v The Queen [1977] A.C. 755 (Privy Council)

The appellant was ordered by one Malik to kill a girl. He claimed he was afraid that if he did not obey he and his mother would be killed. He dug a hole for the body and held the girl while she was stabbed by another man. She was left dying in the hole while the appellant and others filled in the hole. Both the trial judge and the Court of Appeal of Trinidad and Tobago held that duress was not available as a defence.

Lord Salmon (delivering the majority judgment of their Lordships):
"Counsel for the appellant has argued that the law now presupposes a degree of heroism of which the ordinary man is incapable and which therefore should not be expected of him and that modern conditions and concepts of humanity have rendered obsolete the rule that the actual killer cannot rely on duress as a defence. Their Lordships do not agree. In the trials of those responsible for wartime atrocities such as mass killings of men, women or children, inhuman experiments on human beings, often resulting in death, and like crimes, it was invariably argued for the defence that these atrocities should be excused on the ground that they resulted from superior orders and duress: if the accused had refused to do these dreadful things, they would have been shot and therefore they should be acquitted and allowed to go

free. This argument has always been universally rejected. Their Lordships would be sorry indeed to see it accepted by the common law of England."

Lord Wilberforce and Lord Edmund-Davies dissenting:
"If the Crown is right, there is no let-out for any principal in the first degree, even if the duress be so dreadful as would be likely to wreck the morale of most men of reasonable courage, and even were the duress directed not against the person threatened but against other innocent people (in the present case, the appellant's mother) so that considerations of mere self-preservation are not operative. That is indeed 'a blueprint for heroism': *S. v Goliath*, 1972 (3) S.A. 1 ...

The question that immediately arises is whether any acceptable distinction can invariably be drawn between a principal in the first degree to murder and one in the second degree, with the result that the latter *may* in certain circumstances be absolved by his plea of duress, while the former may never even advance such a plea.

The simple fact is that *no* acceptable basis of distinction has even now been advanced. ...

*Lynch* having been decided as it was, the most striking feature of the present appeal is the lack of any indication, in the judgment of the majority, *why* a flat declaration that in no circumstances whatsoever may the actual killer be absolved by a plea of duress makes for sounder law and better ethics. In truth, the contrary is the case. For example ... no one can doubt that our law would today allow duress to be pleaded in answer to a charge, under section 18 of the Offences against the Person Act 1861, of wounding with intent. Yet, here again, should the victim die after the conclusion of the first trial, the accused when faced with a murder charge would be bereft of any such defence. It is not the mere lack of logic that troubles one. It is when one stops to consider why duress is *ever* permitted as a defence even to charges of great gravity that the lack of any moral reason justifying its *automatic* exclusion in such cases as the present becomes so baffling—and so important. ...

To hold that a principal in the first degree in murder is never in any circumstances to be entitled to plead duress, whereas a principal in the second degree may, is to import the possibility of grave injustice into the common law."

Appeal dismissed

## R. v Howe and Others [1987] 1 A.C. 417 (House of Lords)

Two appellants, Howe and Bannister, participated with others in torturing, kicking, punching and sexually abusing a man. The man was then strangled to death by one of the others. These events were repeated on a second occasion but this time it was Howe and Bannister who themselves killed the victim by strangling him with a shoelace. The appellants claimed that they had acted under duress at the orders of and through fear of one Murray. At their trial the judge, following *Lynch* and *Abbott*, directed the jury that duress could be a defence to the first killing where the appellants were only accessories, but not to the second killing where the appellants were the principal offenders. The Court of Appeal held this was correct. They appealed to the House of Lords.

Lord Hailsham of St Marylebone L.C.:
"In general, I must say that I do not at all accept in relation to the defence of murder it is either good morals, good policy or good law to suggest, as did the majority in *Lynch* and the minority in *Abbott* that the ordinary man of reasonable fortitude is not to be supposed to be capable of heroism if he is asked to take an innocent life rather than sacrifice his own. Doubtless in actual practice many will succumb to temptation, as they did in *Dudley and Stephens*. But many will not, and I do not believe that as a 'concession to human frailty' the former should be exempt from liability to criminal sanctions if they do. I have known in my own lifetime of too many acts of heroism by ordinary human beings of no more than

ordinary fortitude to regard a law as either 'just or humane' which withdraws the protection of the criminal law from the innocent victim and casts the cloak of its protection upon the coward and the poltroon in the name of a 'concession to human frailty'.

I must not, however, underestimate the force of the arguments on the other side. . . .

A long line of cases . . . establish duress as an available defence in a wide range of crimes, some at least, like wounding with intent to commit grievous bodily harm, carrying the heaviest penalties commensurate with their gravity. To cap this, it is pointed out that at least in theory, a defendant accused of this crime under section 18 of the Offences against the Person Act 1861, but acquitted on the grounds of duress, will still be liable to a charge of murder if the victim dies . . . I am not, perhaps, persuaded of this last point as much as I should. It is not simply an anomaly based on the defence of duress. It is a product of the peculiar *mens rea* allowed on a charge of murder which is not confined to an intent to kill. . . .

I . . . believe that some degree of proportionality between the threat and the offence must, at least to some extent, be a prerequisite of the defence under existing law. Few would resist threats to the life of a loved one if the alternative were driving across the red lights or in excess of 70 m.p.h. on the motorway. But, . . . it would take rather more than the threat of a slap on the wrist or even moderate pain or injury to discharge the evidential burden even in the case of a fairly serious assault. In such a case the 'concession to human frailty' is no more than to say that in such circumstances a reasonable man of average courage is entitled to embrace as a matter of choice the alternative which a reasonable man could regard as the lesser of two evils. Other considerations necessarily arise where the choice is between the threat of death or *a fortiori* of serious injury and deliberately taking an innocent life. In such a case a reasonable man might reflect that one innocent human life is at least as valuable as his own or that of his loved one. In such case a man cannot claim that he is choosing the lesser of two evils. Instead he is embracing the cognate but morally disreputable principle that the end justifies the means. . . .

During the course of argument it was suggested that there was available to the House some sort of half way house between allowing these appeals and dismissing them. The argument ran that we might treat duress in murder as analogous to provocation, or perhaps diminished responsibility, and say that, in indictments for murder, duress might reduce the crime to one of manslaughter. I find myself quite unable to accept this. The cases show that duress, if available and made out, entitles the accused to a clean acquittal, without, it has been said, the 'stigma' of a conviction. . . . [The suggestion] is also contrary to principle. Unlike the doctrine of provocation, which is based on emotional loss of control, the defence of duress, as I have already shown, is put forward as a 'concession to human frailty' whereby a conscious decision, it may be coolly undertaken, to sacrifice an innocent human life is made as an evil lesser than a wrong which might otherwise be suffered by the accused or his loved ones at the hands of a wrong doer."

Lord Griffiths:

"It is therefore neither rational nor fair to make the defence dependent upon whether the accused is the actual killer or took some other part in the murder. . . .

I am not troubled by some of the extreme examples cited in favour of allowing the defence to those who are not the killer such as a woman motorist being highjacked and forced to act as getaway driver or a pedestrian being forced to give misleading information to the police to protect robbery and murder in a shop. The short, practical answer is that it is inconceivable that such persons would be prosecuted; they would be called as the principal witnesses for the prosecution.

As I can find no fair and certain basis upon which to differentiate between participants to a murder and as I am firmly convinced that the law should not be extended to the killer, I would depart from the decision of this House in *Director of Public Prosecutions for Northern Ireland v Lynch* and declare the law to be that duress is not available as a defence to a charge of murder, or to attempted murder. I add attempted murder because it is to be remembered that the prosecution have to prove an even more evil intent to convict of attempted murder than in actual murder.

. . . This leaves, of course, the anomaly that duress is available for the offence of wounding with intent but not to murder if the victim dies subsequently. But this flows from the special regard that the law has for human life, it may not be logical but it is real and has to be accepted.

[Lords Bridge, Brandon and Mackay agreed that duress should never be a defence to murder irrespective of the defendant's degree of participation. In addition to the above concerns over the special value accorded human life and the difficulty in drawing moral and legal distinctions between perpetrators and accomplices, the House felt there were three further reasons justifying their approach:

(1) if duress were to be made a defence to the perpetrator of murder, that should be done by Parliament, not the courts; the Law Commission (Law Com. No. 83) recommended ten years previously that duress should be a defence to the principal offender of murder; Parliament's failure to enact this recommendation is an indication that they have rejected the proposal.
(2) The defence of duress is imprecisely defined and extending it to murder would cause too much uncertainty;
(3) administrative remedies such as not prosecuting, use of parole and the royal prerogative would ensure that no injustice was perpetrated.]"

**Appeals dismissed**

## R v Gotts [1992] 2 A.C. 412 (House of Lords)

The defendant, aged 16, seriously injured his mother with a knife. In his defence to a charge of attempted murder he claimed that his father had threatened to shoot him unless he killed his mother. The judge ruled that such evidence was inadmissible since duress was not a defence to such a charge. The defendant pleaded guilty but then appealed.

Lord Jauncey:
"It is agreed that there is no English authority which deals directly with the availability of the defence of duress to a charge of attempted murder, but [Counsel for the appellant] ... submitted that this is so because it has long been recognised that the defence of duress is available in respect of all crime except murder and treason ...

My Lords, I share the view of Lord Griffiths that 'it would have been better had [the development of the defence of duress] not taken place and that duress had been regarded as a factor to be taken into account in mitigation' ... *R. v Howe* ... At the time of the earlier writings on duress as a defence, offences against the person were much more likely to have involved only one or two victims. Weapons and substances capable of inflicting mass injury were not readily available to terrorists and other criminals as they are in the reputedly more civilised times in which we now live. While it is not now possible for this House to restrict the availability of the defence of duress in those cases where it has been recognised to exist, I feel constrained to express the personal view that given the climate of violence and terrorism which ordinary law-abiding citizens now have to face Parliament might do well to consider whether the defence should continue to be available in the case of all very serious crimes. ... The reason why duress has for so long been stated not to be available as a defence to a murder charge is that the law regards the sanctity of human life and the protection thereof as of paramount importance. Does that reason apply to attempted murder as well as to murder? As Lord Griffiths pointed out [in *Howe*] ... an intent to kill must be proved in the case of attempted murder but not necessarily in the case of murder. Is there logic in affording the defence to one who intends to kill but fails and denying it to one who mistakenly kills intending only to injure? ...

It is of course true that withholding the defence in any circumstances will create some anomalies but I would agree with Lord Griffiths (*R. v Howe*) that nothing should be done to undermine in any way the highest duty of the law to protect the freedom and lives of those who live under it. I can therefore see no justification in logic, morality or law in affording to an attempted murderer the defence which is withheld from a murderer. The intent required of an attempted murderer is more evil than that required of the murderer and the line which divides the two is seldom, if ever, of the deliberate making of the criminal. A man shooting to kill but missing a vital organ by a hair's breadth can justify his action no more than can the man who hits the organ. It is pure chance that the attempted murderer is not a murderer. . . .

For the foregoing reasons I have no doubt that the Court of Appeal reached the correct decision and that the appeal should be dismissed."

**Appeal dismissed**[83]

Is duress a defence to conspiracy and incitement to murder? Although the point has not been authoritatively decided, it was stated by the Court of Appeal in *Gotts* that there was "a legitimate distinction to be drawn" between these crimes and attempted murder because they are a "stage further away from the completed offence than is the attempt".[84] Thus, while the defence is not available to murder or attempted murder (or treason) it is available to these other serious crimes as well as manslaughter, causing grievous bodily harm with intent contrary to section 18 of the Offences against the Person Act 1861 and arson intending or being reckless as to whether life is endangered contrary to section 1(2) of the Criminal Damage Act 1971.[85] As Lord Lowry stressed in his dissenting speech in the House of Lords, such anomalies are bound to result unless the defence is extended or denied to all crimes.[86] The view espoused by Lord Jauncey that duress ought to be only a matter of mitigation in sentencing rather than a defence to serious crimes is one that needs to be resisted for the reasons explored at the beginning of this section.

What is disappointing about these decisions is the lack of attention paid to the theoretical basis of the defence. In *Gotts*, the House concentrated upon whether early writings established duress as a defence to attempted murder and then on its relationship to the crime of murder. At no time did they address fully why duress is a defence.[87] Prior to *Gotts*, *Howe* had already been roundly condemned as requiring unrealistic heroism.[88] Heroism might be a desirable quality but it is unduly harsh to sentence someone to life imprisonment for failing to achieve such heights. The criminal law should rest content if its exhortations induce persons to act reasonably. It seems an odd and an unjust law that can proclaim that the defendant has acted perfectly reasonably but is guilty of murder. And it is simply no answer to assert that injustice will be avoided by the use of administrative discretion, whether by the prosecution or the Parole Board. The whole thrust in recent criminal law thinking is against granting too much discretion to those administering the criminal justice system. Further, these platitudes have been heard before in other areas of criminal law—and been blatantly ignored.[89]

---

[83] The defendant was sentenced to three years' probation, so clearly some recognition was taken of his plight.

[84] (1991) 92 Cr.App.R.269 at 276.

[85] *ibid.* at 273.

[86] [1992] 2 A.C. 412 at 441.

[87] See Gardiner, "Duress in Attempted Murder" (1991) 107 L.Q.R. 389 at 391; Gardiner, "Duress in the House of Lords" (1992) 108 L.Q.R. 349.

[88] Smith and Hogan, *Criminal Law* (10th ed. 2002), pp. 255–256; Alldridge, "Duress, Murder and the House of Lords" (1988) 52 J.Crim.L.186; Milgate, "Duress and the Criminal Law: Another About Turn by the House of Lords" [1988] C.L.J. 61; Dennis, "Developments in Duress" (1987) 51 J.Crim.L.463; Walters, "Murder under Duress and Judicial Decision-making in the House of Lords" (1988) 8 L.S. 61.

[89] See the prosecution that was brought in *Anderton v Ryan* [1985] A.C. 560—exactly the sort of case in which The Law Commission (Law Com. Working Paper No. 102) had predicted that a prosecution would never be brought.

The better view is that duress should be an *excuse* to all crimes. What the defendant has done remains wrong but we can understand his predicament and excuse him. Given the severe threats, his actions are in effect morally involuntary. Perhaps if the majority in *Abbott* had realised this they might have produced a different result. Instead they seemed to think they were dealing with a justificatory defence when they spoke of duress bringing the defendant's act "within the law".[90] Lord Mackay in *Howe* spoke of a defendant subject to duress having a "right" to commit a crime.[91] This is simply not so. With excusatory defences one has no "right" to commit crimes. One is simply excused from blame: "To acquit him on grounds of duress is merely to sympathise, understand, commiserate with what he did."[92] In the light of these criticisms, and bearing in mind the fact that the defence is not available to members of terrorist groups, the Law Commission has recommended that the defence of "duress by threats" be available to all offences.[93]

## C. Duress of Circumstances

As seen earlier, until fairly recently it was clear that no general defence of necessity existed in English law. However, starting in the 1980s, the judiciary has been actively developing this area of law in a way that "can be likened to the overnight growth of a mushroom".[94] Rather than simply introducing or developing a new full-blown defence of necessity, the courts have chosen to expand the defence of duress by threats to cover what is termed "duress of circumstances". While often describing the defence as "necessity or duress of circumstances"[95] or even as "duress of necessity"[96] the courts have been careful to ensure that the new defence of "duress of circumstances" has largely followed the contours of the existing defence of duress by threats. By emphasising the similarities between the two defences and, importantly, imposing similar rigorous restraints upon the defence, judges have been able to overcome their reluctance to admit a defence of necessity into English law.

The emergence of this defence occurred "more or less by accident".[97] In *Willer*[98] the defendant was charged with reckless driving when he drove on a pavement to escape from a gang of youths. It was held that regardless of whether necessity had been established or was available, the defence of "duress of circumstances" was applicable.[99] "Duress of circumstances" was also considered in the case of *Conway*, another case of reckless driving.[1] The defendant pleaded that he had to make off in

---

[90] At 766; see Fletcher, *Rethinking Criminal Law* (1978), p. 832.
[91] At 456; see Walters, *above*, n.88 at p. 72.
[92] Katz, *Bad Acts and Guilty Minds* (1987), p. 65.
[93] Law Commission No. 218 (1993), paras 30.1–31.8. Horder is critical of this proposal and offers an alternative: that duress should not be extended to those killings which are *directly* intended and are thus inexcusable (*above*, n.60, pp. 339–340).
[94] Elliott, "Necessity, Duress and Self-Defence" [1989] Crim.L.R.611 at 612.
[95] *Abdul-Hussain, above*, p. 340.
[96] *Cairns* [1999] Cr.App.R.137.
[97] Smith and Hogan, *Criminal Law* (10th ed., 2002), p. 263.
[98] (1986) 83 Cr.App.R.225.
[99] See also *Denton* (1987) 131 S.J. 476.
[1] (1989) 88 Cr.App.R.159. See Alldridge, "Duress, Duress of Circumstances and Necessity" (1989) 139 N.L.J. 911.

his car when approached by two men (who were in fact police officers) because his passenger was fearful of an attack. In saying that the defence of duress of circumstances should have been put to the jury, the Court of Appeal indicated that it was immaterial whether the defence was called necessity or duress. In *Bell*[2] the Queen's Bench Divisional Court referred to the defence that was available to the defendant who had driven with excess alcohol in his blood in order to escape attackers as "duress/necessity".

## R. v Martin (1989) 88 Cr.App.R.343 (Court of Appeal, Criminal Division)

The defendant was charged with driving whilst disqualified under section 99(b) of the Road Traffic Act 1972. The facts appear from the judgment.

Simon Brown J.:
"The circumstances which the appellant desired to advance by way of defence of necessity were essentially these. His wife has suicidal tendencies. On a number of occasions before the day in question she had attempted to take her own life. On the day in question her son, the appellant's stepson, had overslept. He had done so to the extent that he was bound to be late for work and at risk of losing his job unless, so it was asserted, the appellant drove him to work. The appellant's wife was distraught. She was shouting, screaming, banging her head against a wall. More particularly, it is said she was threatening suicide unless the appellant drove the boy to work.

The defence had a statement from a doctor which expressed the opinion that 'in view of her mental condition it is likely that Mrs Martin would have attempted suicide if her husband did not drive her son to work.'

The appellant's case on the facts was that he genuinely, and he would suggest reasonably, believed that his wife would carry out that threat unless he did as she demanded. Despite his disqualification he therefore drove the boy. He was in fact apprehended by the police within about a quarter of a mile of the house.

Sceptically though one may regard that defence on the facts … the sole question before this court is whether those facts, had the jury accepted they were or might be true, amounted in law to a defence. … As it was, such a defence was pre-empted by the ruling. Should it have been?

In our judgment the answer is plainly not. The authorities are now clear. Their effect is perhaps most conveniently to be found in the judgment of this court in *R. v Conway*. The decision reviews earlier relevant authorities.

The principles may be summarised thus. First, English law does, in extreme circumstances, recognise a defence of necessity. Most commonly this defence arises as duress, that is pressure on the accused's will from the wrongful threats or violence of another. Equally however it can arise from other objective dangers threatening the accused or others. Arising thus it is conveniently called 'duress of circumstances'.

Secondly, the defence is available only if, from an objective standpoint, the accused can be said to be acting reasonably and proportionately in order to avoid a threat of death or serious injury.

Thirdly, assuming the defence to be open to the accused on his account of the facts, the issue should be left to the jury, who should be directed to determine these two questions: first, was the accused, or may he have been, impelled to act as he did because as a result of what he reasonably believed to be the situation he had good cause to fear that otherwise death or serious physical injury would result? Second, if so, would a sober person of reasonable firmness, sharing the characteristics of the accused, have responded to that

---

[2] [1992] Crim.L.R.176. See also *Jones* [1990] R.T.R. 33 at p. 339.

situation by acting as the accused acted? If the answer to both those questions was Yes, then the jury would acquit; the defence of necessity would have been established. ...

We see no material distinction between offences of reckless driving and driving whilst disqualified so far as the application and scope of this defence is concerned. Equally we can see no distinction in principle between various threats of death; it matters not whether the risk of death is by murder or by suicide or indeed by accident. One can illustrate the latter by considering a disqualified driver being driven by his wife, she suffering a heart attack in remote countryside and he needing instantly to get her to hospital.

It follows from this that the judge quite clearly did come to a wrong decision on the question of law, and the appellant should have been permitted to raise this defence for what it was worth before the jury."

**Appeal allowed. Conviction quashed**

## Pommell [1995] 2 Cr.App.R.607 (Court of Appeal, Criminal Division)

The defendant was found by police at 8 a.m. at home in bed with a loaded sub-machine gun. He was charged with possession of a firearm, contrary to section 5(1)(a) of the Firearms Act 1968. In his defence he pleaded that he had taken the gun from someone the night before to prevent that person shooting some people who had killed a friend. He claimed that he had intended to take the gun to the police in the morning. He was convicted, the judge ruling that his failure to go to the police immediately robbed him of the defence of necessity.

Kennedy L.J.:

"There is an obvious attraction in the argument that if A finds B in possession of a gun which he is about to use to commit a crime, and if A is then able to persuade B to hand over the gun so that A may hand it to the police, A should not immediately upon taking possession of the gun become guilty of a criminal offence. ...

The strength of the argument that a person ought to be permitted to breach the letter of the criminal law in order to prevent a greater evil befalling himself or others has long been recognised ... but it has, in English law, not given rise to a recognised general defence of necessity, and in relation to the charge of murder, the defence has been specifically held not to exist (see *Dudley and Stephens*). Even in relation to other offences, there are powerful arguments against recognising the general defence ... [His Lordship then cited the Canadian decision of *Perka et al. v R.* (1985) 13 D.L.R. 1 where the court thought that a general defence would make the law too subjective, would enable illegal acts to be validated on the basis of expediency and would invite courts to second guess the Legislature.]

However, that does not really deal with the situation where someone commendably infringes a regulation in order to prevent another person from committing what everyone would accept as being a greater evil with a gun. In that situation it cannot be satisfactory to leave it to the prosecuting authority not to prosecute ...

It was, as it seems to us, to meet this difficulty that the limited defence of duress of circumstances has been developed in English law in relation to road traffic offences. ... Professor Sir John Smith has written:

'All the cases so far have concerned road traffic offences but there are no grounds for supposing that the defence is limited to that kind of case. On the contrary, the defence, being closely related to the defence of duress by threats, appears to be general, applying to all crimes except murder, attempted murder and some forms of treason.' See [1992] Crim.L.R.176.

We agree. ...

That leads us to the conclusion that in the present case the defence was open to the appellant. ... That leaves the question as to his continued possession of the gun thereafter. ... In our judgment, a person who has taken possession of a gun in circumstances where he has the defence of duress by circumstances must 'desist from committing the crime as soon as he reasonably can' (Smith and Hogan (7th ed.) p. 239) ... However, the situation does not seem to us to have been sufficiently clear cut [to remove the defence] ... in the present case."

**Appeal allowed. Retrial ordered**

This approach has been followed in numerous other decisions[3] where it has been emphasised that both species of duress are governed by the same principles, which were canvassed above. Importantly, this means that the defence is not available to murder, attempted murder and certain forms of treason. However, the rather different nature of the defences has involved some inevitable divergence in the application of the two defences. For example, as already seen, for duress by threats there must be a link between the threat and the crime whereas for duress of circumstances there is no such requirement.

In reality, duress of circumstances covers situations that are termed "necessity" in other jurisdictions. However, necessity is widely regarded as a *justificatory* defence. On that basis, duress of circumstances could logically be regarded similarly as a justification. However, by building on the blocks of duress by threats, the courts have been able to develop duress of circumstances as an excusatory defence.[4] It is recognised that the defendant has done wrong but we do not think it appropriate, because of his plight, to blame him. This means that a defendant can only be excused if he is able to satisfy stringent requirements: his will must be overborne by threats of death or serious bodily harm.

Such an approach leaves no scope for a claim that actions were justified and that the defendant's will was not overborne. Indeed, recognition of the defence of excusatory necessity may leave the development of justificatory necessity perpetually in the shadows. The Law Commission has proposed statutory endorsement of the defence of duress of circumstances.

### Draft Criminal Law Bill, 1993 (Law Commmission No. 218), clause 26:

"(1) No act of a person constitutes an offence if the act is done under duress of circumstances.
(2) A person does an act under duress of circumstances if—
(a) he does it because he knows or believes that it is immediately necessary to avoid death or serious injury to himself or another, and
(b) the danger that he knows or believes to exist is such that in all the circumstances (including any of his personal characteristics that affect its gravity) he cannot reasonably be expected to act otherwise."[5]

### D. *Necessity*

The defence of necessity is well-established in other jurisdictions and applies to situations where a defendant chooses to commit a crime in order to avert a greater evil. For example, in the Missouri decision of *State v Green*[6] the defendant committed the crime of escaping from prison in order to avoid being raped.

[3] For example, *Cairns, above,* n.96 and *Abdul-Hussain, above,* p.34.
[4] Padfield, "Duress, Necessity and the Law Commission" [1992] Crim.L.R.778.
[5] This defence would be available to all crimes—even murder—as with duress by threats (Law Com. Consultation Paper No. 122 (1992), para. 19.9, confirmed in Law Com. No. 218 (1993), para. 35.10). In contrast, the earlier draft bill had excluded the defence from the crimes of attempted murder and murder (Law Com. No. 143 (1985), cl. 43(3)(a)).
[6] 470 S.W.2d 565 (1971).

## 1. Distinction between necessity and duress of circumstances

All the cases on duress of circumstances, considered above, concern situations of necessity and we have seen that many recent cases use the terms "duress of circumstances" and "necessity" interchangeably as simply being "different labels for essentially the same thing".[7]

There are, however, important differences between the two defences. Necessity is widely regarded in other jurisdictions as a justificatory defence whereas, as seen, the defence of duress of circumstances has been viewed as an excuse by English law. This difference in theoretical approach has important consequences for the rules governing each defence.

First, duress of circumstances is a defence only when there has been a threat of death or serious injury. With an excusatory defence, the essence of which involves the defendant's will being overborne and the actions being morally involuntary, one can perhaps understand the view that this will only be so if the threat is truly awesome as in the case of a threat of death or serious injury. With a justificatory defence, however, the emphasis is on the actor making a choice between two evils and pursuing the lesser of them. So, with necessity the threat need not be of death or serious injury. The essence of the defence is that it involves a balancing of evils. The threat can take any form but the crime committed by the defendant must involve a lesser evil.

Secondly, with duress of circumstances the threat must be "imminent" in the sense of being operative on the mind of the defendant and overbearing her will. With necessity, the principle is one of "necessity, not emergency".[8] A rational choice is made to avert a greater evil that will necessarily occur even if it would be some time before it occurs.

Thirdly, the cases on duress of circumstances have allowed certain aspects of the vulnerability of the defendant to be taken into account; the test is whether the reasonable person, sharing the same characteristics as the defendant, would have given in to the threats. This is an appropriate test for determining whether a person should be excused because *their* will was overborne. With necessity, the focus is on the balancing of evils and not on the particular defendant's condition. There should be no scope for making allowance for the defendant's condition or vulnerability.

Finally, duress of circumstances is not a defence to murder, attempted murder or certain forms of treason. With necessity the focus is on the balancing of evils and judging the choices of the defendant. In principle, necessity ought to be a defence when the defendant kills one person in order to save the lives of more than one person.

---

[7] *Shayler, above,* p. 324.
[8] *Re A (Conjoined Twins)* [2001] Fam.147.

## 2. The traditional approach of English law

Until the development of duress of circumstances in the 1980s, it was commonly thought that a defence of necessity did not exist in English law.[9] In *O'Toole*[10] and *Wood v Richards*[11] an ambulance driver and a police officer respectively were involved in car accidents while rushing to answer emergency calls. Both were convicted of road traffic offences, necessity being no defence[12] In *Kitson*[13] a passenger woke up drunk in a car to find it running downhill; he steered the car on to a grass verge to avoid a possible accident; he was convicted of driving while under the influence of drink; the defence of necessity was not even raised. And in *Southwark L.B.C. v Williams* where defendants in dire need of housing accommodation entered empty houses owned by the local authority, it was held that the defence of necessity did not apply. Lord Denning M.R. stated:

"If homelessness were once admitted as a defence to trespass, no one's house could be safe. Necessity would open a door which no man could shut. It would not only be those in extreme need who would enter. There would be others who would imagine that they were in need, or would invent a need, so as to gain entry."[14]

And Edmund-Davis L.J. held:

"[T]he law regards with the deepest suspicion any remedies of self-help, and permits those remedies to be resorted to only in very special circumstances. The reason for such circumspection is clear—necessity can very easily become simply a mask for anarchy."[15]

However, later in the same case Edmund-Davis L.J. stated:

"[I]t appears that all the cases where a plea of necessity has succeeded are cases which deal with an urgent situation of imminent peril; for example, the forcible feeding of an obdurate suffragette, . . . or performing an abortion to avert a grave threat to the life, or . . . health of a pregnant young girl who had been ravished in circumstances of great brutality."[16]

This apparent recognition of the defence of necessity in extreme cases demonstrates that there has never been a blanket condemnation of it in all guises and in all situations. The following two situations require separate consideration.

### (i) *Medical treatment*

Edmund-Davies L.J. spoke of the forced feeding of suffragettes and emergency abortions being defended on the basis of necessity. More recently, one

---

[9] *Dudley and Stephens* is usually cited to support this proposition. It has been argued that the facts of that case did not disclose a true case of necessity: Smith and Hogan, *Criminal Law* (10th ed., 2002), pp. 271–272; Williams, *Textbook of Criminal Law* (2nd ed., 1983), p.606, but it is submitted that the overall tenor of the judgement indicates that Lord Coleridge was simply not prepared to accept necessity as a defence to murder. In any event, the House of Lords in Howe (below, p. 359) interpreted the case in this way.

[10] (1971) 55 Cr.App.R.206.

[11] [1977] Crim.L.R.295.

[12] *cf. Johnson v Phillips* [1976] 1 W.L.R. 65 where necessity was accepted as a basis for *convicting* a defendant.

[13] (1955) 39 Cr.App.R.66.

[14] [1971] Ch. 734 at 744.

[15] *ibid*. at 745–746.

[16] *ibid*. at 746.

interpretation of the case of *Gillick*[17] is that it involved a "hidden" defence of necessity. The doctor who prescribes contraceptive advice or treatment to a girl under the age of 16 does not commit the offence of aiding and abetting underage sexual intercourse if he does so (*inter alia*) in the belief that unless she receives it her physical or mental health would be likely to suffer.[18]

In *F. v Berkshire Health Authority*[19] it was held that doctors were justified in carrying out a sterilisation operation upon a woman who was incapable of giving informed consent because of her mental handicap. Lord Goff's argument was based upon necessity; there was a grave risk of her becoming pregnant if she was not sterilised and it was agreed that such a condition would have a very disturbing impact upon her.[20]

What is significant about this development is that necessity is not used to excuse wrongful conduct but to justify conduct as the *right* thing to do. "[T]here is no question of the defence depending on the actor's resistance being overcome."[21] An example given by Lord Goff during his speech makes this clear: "a man who seizes another and forcibly drags him from the path of an oncoming vehicle, thereby saving him from injury or even death, commits no wrong".[22]

The Draft Criminal Law Bill 1993 recognises this underdeveloped justificatory defence in clause 36(2) by explicitly retaining "any distinct defence of necessity" at the same time as it codified duress by threats and duress of circumstances.[23]

### (ii) *Statutory defences that are in substance necessity*

Some statutes expressly provide defences that are in substance defences of necessity. For example, fire-engines, police and ambulances are exempted from observing the speed limit in certain circumstances,[24] and in specified circumstances they may treat a red traffic light as a warning to give way.[25] In such cases it is not possible to plead a general defence of necessity. The only possible defence is under the regulation itself.[26] Another important statutory example is that in order to protect property that is in immediate need of protection, it is permissible to destroy the property of another person.[27] Further, many statutes contain phrases such as "unlawful", "without lawful excuse" or "without reasonable excuse" which may be construed to cover situations in which a defence of necessity might be appropriate: for example, sections 8–10 of the old Forgery Act 1913 prohibited the

---

[17] [1986] A.C. 112.
[18] Smith, *Justification and Excuse in the Criminal Law* (1989), pp. 64–68. Smith argues that there are many other "concealed defences" in the criminal law (pp. 61–72).
[19] [1990] 2 A.C. 1.
[20] To similar effect, see *R. v Bournewood Community and Mental Health NHS Trust, ex parte L (Secretary of State for Health intervening)* [1999] A.C. 458.
[21] Law Com. Consultation Paper No. 122, *Legislating the Criminal Code: Offences Against the Person and General Principles* (1992), para. 19.5.
[22] [1990] 2 A.C. 1 at 74.
[23] Law Com. No. 218 (1993).
[24] Road Traffic Regulation Act 1984, s.87.
[25] Traffic Signs Regulations and General Directions (SI 1981 No. 859), reg. 34(1)(b).
[26] *D.P.P. v Harris* [1995] 1 Cr.App.R.170. In such cases, if there is a threat of death or serious injury, duress of circumstances can be pleaded (*Backshall* [1999] Cr.App.R.35).
[27] Criminal Damage Act 1971, s.5(2)(b).

possession of forged bank notes "without lawful authority or excuse".[28] In *Wuyts*[29] it was held that if the defendant's sole purpose in retaining possession of the notes was to hand them to the police, it would have been a "lawful excuse".[30]

### (iii) *Necessity in relation to homicide*

One of the greatest handicaps to the development of a general defence of necessity has been that the issue has usually arisen in homicide cases where "there is always a corpse, casting a shadow across the proceedings".[31]

## R. v Dudley and Stephens (1884) 14 Q.B.D. 273 (Queen's Bench Division)

The two defendants, with a third man and a 17 year old boy, were cast away on the high seas in an open boat, 1,600 miles from land. They drifted in the boat for 20 days. When they had been eight days without food and six days without water, and fearing they would all die soon without some sustenance, the defendants killed the boy, who was likely to die first. The men ate his flesh and drank his blood for four days. They were then rescued by a passing vessel and were subsequently charged with murder. The jury found the facts of the case in a special verdict and the case was referred to the Queen's Bench Division for its decision.

Lord Coleridge C.J.:

"[T]he prisoners put to death a weak and unoffending boy upon the chance of preserving their own lives by feeding upon his flesh and blood after he was killed, and with a certainty of depriving *him* of any possible chance of survival. The verdict finds in terms that: 'if the men had not fed upon the body of the boy, they would *probably* have not survived ...' and that 'the boy, being in a much weaker condition, was *likely* to have died before them'. They might possibly have been picked up next day by a passing ship; they might not have been picked up at all; in either case it is obvious that the killing of the boy would have been an unnecessary and profitless act. It is found by the verdict that the boy was incapable of resistance, and, in fact, made none ...

[I]t is admitted that the deliberate killing of this unoffending and unresisting boy was clearly murder, unless the killing can be justified by some well-recognised excuse admitted by the law. It is further admitted that there was in this case no such excuse, unless the killing was justified by what has been called 'necessity.' But the temptation to the act which existed here was not what the law has ever called necessity. Nor is this to be regretted. Though law and morality are not the same, and though many things may be immoral which are not necessarily illegal, yet the absolute divorce of law from morality would be of fatal consequence, and such divorce would follow if the temptation to murder in this case were to be held by law an absolute defence of it. It is not so. To preserve one's life is generally speaking, a duty, but it may be the plainest and the highest duty to sacrifice it. War is full of instances in which it is a man's duty not to live, but to die. ....

It is not needful to point out the awful danger of admitting the principle which has been contended for. Who is to be the judge of this sort of necessity? By what measure is the comparative value of lives to be measured? Is it to be strength, or intellect, or what? It is plain that the principle leaves to him who is to profit by it to determine the necessity which will justify him in deliberately taking another's life to save his own. In this case the weakest, the youngest, the most unresisting was chosen. Was it more necessary to kill *him* than one of the grown men? The answer be, No ...

It must not be supposed that, in refusing to admit temptation to be an excuse for crime, it is forgotten how terrible the temptation was; how awful the suffering; how hard in such trials

---

[28] See now Forgery and Counterfeiting Act 1981, s.16(2).
[29] [1969] 2 Q.B. 474.
[30] For a full discussion of the circumstances when a statute can be construed to cover situations of necessity, see Glazebrook, "The Necessity Plea in English Criminal Law" [1972] C.L.J. 87.
[31] Alldridge, "Duress, Duress of Circumstances and Necessity" (1989) 139 N.L.J. 911.

to keep the judgment straight and the conduct pure. We are often compelled to set up standards we cannot reach ourselves, and to lay down rules which we could not ourselves satisfy. But a man has no right to declare temptation to be an excuse, though he might himself have yielded to it, nor allow compassion for the criminal to change or weaken in any manner the legal definition of the crime. It is therefore our duty to declare that the prisoners' act in this case was wilful murder."

**Judgment for the Crown. Sentence of death, later commuted to six months' imprisonment**

## B. N. Cardozo, "Law and Literature" from Selected Writings (1947), p. 390:

"Where two or more are overtaken by a common disaster, there is no right on the part of one to save the lives of some by the killing of another. There is no rule of human jettison. Men there will often be who, when told that their going will be the salvation of the remnant, will choose the nobler part and make the plunge into the waters. In that supreme moment the darkness for them will be illuminated by the thought that those behind will ride to safety. If none of such mould are found aboard the boat, or too few to save the others, the human freight must be left to meet the chances of the waters. Who shall choose in such an hour between the victims and the saved? Who shall know when masts and sails of rescue may emerge out of the fog?"

## United States v Holmes 26 Fed. Cas. 360 (1842) (Circuit Court, Eastern District, Pennsylvania)

The defendant along with eight other seamen and 32 passengers were in an overcrowded lifeboat. Fearing that the boat would sink he threw 16 passengers overboard. The crew were directed " 'not to part man and wife, and not to throw over any women.' There was no other principle of selection." The next morning the survivors in the boat were all rescued.

Baldwin C.J. directing jury:
"[M]an, in taking away the life of a fellow being, assumes an awful responsibility to God, and to society; and that the administrators of public justice do themselves assume that responsibility if, when called on to pass judicially upon the act, they yield to the indulgence of misapplied humanity. It is one thing to give a favourable interpretation to evidence in order to mitigate an offence. It is a different thing, when we are asked, not to extenuate, but to justify, the act ... [T]he case does not become 'a case of necessity', unless all ordinary means of self-preservation have been exhausted. The peril must be instant, over-whelming, leaving no alternative but to lose our own life, or to take the life of another person ...
[He then held that the seamen should have been sacrificed first as they were not in an equal position with the passengers as 'the sailor is bound ... to undergo whatever hazard is necessary to preserve the boat and the passengers'. As between equals the decision as to who should be sacrificed should be made by drawing lots.]
When the solution has been made by lots, the victim yields of course to his fate, or, if he resists, force may be employed to coerce submission. Whether or not 'a case of necessity' has arisen, or whether the law under which death has been inflicted have been so exercised as to hold the executioner harmless, cannot depend on his own opinion; for no man may pass upon his own conduct when it concerns the rights and especially, when it affects the lives, of others. ... [H]omicide is sometimes justifiable; and the law defines the occasions in which it is so. The transaction must, therefore, be justified to the law ...
[The jury returned a verdict of guilty. The defendant who had already been confined in jail for several months was sentenced to six months imprisonment with hard labour and fined $20. The penalty was subsequently remitted.]"

## American Law Institute, Model Penal Code, Tent. Draft No. 8 (1958), Comments to Art. 3, pp. 8–9:

"It would be particularly unfortunate to exclude homicidal conduct from the scope of the defense ... For recognising that the sanctity of life has a supreme place in the hierarchy of values, it is nonetheless true that conduct which results in taking life may promote the very value sought to be protected by the law of homicide. Suppose, for example, that the actor has made a breach in a dike, knowing that this will inundate a farm, but taking the only course available to save a whole town. If he is charged with homicide of the inhabitants of the farm house, he can rightly point out that the object of the law of homicide is to save life, and that by his conduct he has effected a net saving of innocent lives. The life of every individual must be assumed in such a case to be of equal value and the numerical preponderance in the lives saved compared to those sacrificed surely establishes an ethical and legal justification for the act. So too a mountaineer, roped to a companion who has fallen over a precipice who holds on as long as possible but eventually cuts the rope, must certainly be granted the defense that he accelerated one death slightly but avoided the only alternative, the certain death of both.

... [T]he evil sought to be avoided [must] be a greater evil than that sought to be protected by the law defining the offense. For the result is that the defense would not be available to a defendant who killed A to save B, in circumstances where had he done nothing B would have been killed and A saved, assuming, of course, that there was not ... aggression on either's part ... Nor would the defense be available to one who acted to save himself at the expense of another, as by seizing a raft when men are shipwrecked ... In all ordinary circumstances lives in being must be assumed, as we have said, to be of equal value, equally deserving the protection of the law."

*Dudley and Stephens* has, more recently, received judicial confirmation.

## R. v Howe [1987] 1 A.C. 417 (House of Lords)

(For facts see, p. 346)

Lord Hailsham L.C.:
"[I]f we were to allow this appeal [against a conviction for murder on the basis of duress], we should, I think, also have to say that *Dudley and Stephens* was bad law. There is, of course, an obvious distinction between duress and necessity as potential defences; duress arises from the wrongful threats of violence of another human being and necessity arises from any other objective dangers threatening the accused. This, however, is in my view a distinction without a relevant difference, since on this view duress is only that species of the genus of necessity which is caused by wrongful threats. I cannot see that there is any way in which a person of ordinary fortitude can be excused from the one type of pressure on his will rather than the other."

Lord Hailsham's view is that because the defences of duress and necessity are so similar, neither is available to the person who kills. This could be regarded as implicit acknowledgment of the existence of a defence of necessity to crimes other than murder, attempted murder and certain forms of treason. Perhaps it was *dicta* such as these that permitted the rapid development of the defence of duress of circumstances.

All the above extracts rightly treat necessity as a justificatory defence. In *Dudley and Stephens*, Lord Coleridge expressed the view that a defence of necessity would alter "the legal definition of the crime" which would only be the case if it acted as justificatory defence. This approach raises the intractable problem discussed in *Dudley and Stephens* and in *Holmes* of having to decide whose lives should be sacrificed. Perhaps the law might have developed in a different direction if the defendants in *Dudley and Stephens* had been viewed as pleading an excuse. It was not a case of the lives of the three men being superior to that of the cabin-boy. However, given that their lives were of equal value, due consideration should have been given to the awfulness of the situation they were in. The fact that their sentences were so rapidly commuted gives further strength to this argument. Indeed, it has been said that the pardon had been arranged well in advance of the sentences being passed.[32]

The shadow of *Dudley and Stephens* has long hung over English law. In 1974 the Law Commission proposed that a general defence of necessity be introduced into English law.[33] However, three years later it rejected the idea, going so far as to say that if a defence of necessity already existed at common law, it should be abolished. It felt that allowing such a defence to a charge of murder could effectively legalise euthanasia in England. For "human rights" reasons it would not be prepared to see necessity covering a situation where "an immediate blood transfusion must be made in order to save an injured person: the only one who has the same blood type as the injured refuses to give blood. Can he be overpowered and the blood taken from him?[34] Instead, the Draft Criminal Code Bill 1993 proposed a statutory formulation of duress of circumstances, cast as an excuse, but applying to all offences.

### 3. Emergence of a new defence?

By the turn of the century, English law thus appeared fairly settled. Whatever the nomenclature, necessity had been let in the back door under the guise of duress of circumstances and was viewed as an excuse with the implications discussed earlier, including the fact that it was not a defence to murder, attempted murder and certain forms of treason. This tranquillity was shattered by the following decision.

### Re A (Conjoined Twins: Surgical Separation) [2001] Fam.147 (Court of Appeal, Civil Division)

"Jodie" and "Mary" were conjoined twins. Leaving them joined would result in the death of both of them within six months. A separation operation would certainly result in the death of Mary who was not capable of separate survival but would give Jodie a good prospect of a normal life. The parents objected to the operation and an application was made to the High Court and then to the Court of Appeal for a declaration, *inter alia*, that the operation would be lawful despite the fact that it would result in the death of Mary under circumstances making the surgeons prima facie liable for murder.

Ward L.J.:
"The first important feature is that the doctors cannot be denied a right of choice if they are under a duty to choose. They are under a duty to Mary not to operate because it will kill Mary, but they are under a duty to Jodie to operate because not to do so will kill her... What then is the position where there is a conflict of duty? ...Wilson J, ... in *Perka v The Queen* (1984) 13 DLR (4th) 1, 36 [stated]:

---

[32] Katz, *Bad Acts and Guilty Minds* (1987), p. 27.
[33] Working Paper No. 55 (1974), para. 57.
[34] Law Commission No. 83 (1977), para. 4.27.

'the ethical considerations of the 'charitable and the good' must be kept analytically distinct from duties imposed by law. Accordingly, where necessity is invoked as a justification for violation of the law, the justification must, in my view, be restricted to situations where the accused's act constitutes the discharge of a duty recognised by law. The justification is not, however, established simply by showing a conflict of legal duties. The rule of proportionality is central to the evaluation of a justification premised on two conflicting duties since the defence rests on the rightfulness of the accused's choice of one over the other.'

So far I agree... In [these] circumstances it seems to me that the law must allow an escape through choosing the lesser of the two evils. The law cannot say, "Heads I win, tails you lose." Faced as they are with an apparently irreconcilable conflict, the doctors should be in no different position from that in which the court itself was placed in the performance of its duty to give paramount consideration to the welfare of each child. The doctors must be given the same freedom of choice as the court has given itself and the doctors must make that choice along the same lines as the court has done, giving the sanctity of life principle its place in the balancing exercise that has to be undertaken. The respect the law must have for the right to life of each must go in the scales and weigh equally but other factors have to go in the scales as well. For the same reasons that led to my concluding that consent should be given to operate, so the conclusion has to be that the carrying out of the operation will be justified as the lesser evil and no unlawful act would be committed."

Brooke L.J.:
"I have described how in modern times Parliament has sometimes provided 'necessity' defences in statutes and how the courts in developing the defence of duress of circumstances have sometimes equated it with the defence of necessity. They do not, however, cover exactly the same ground. In cases of pure necessity the actor's mind is not irresistibly overborne by external pressures. The claim is that his or her conduct was not harmful because on a choice of two evils the choice of avoiding the greater harm was justified....

I have considered very carefully the policy reasons for the decision in *R. v Dudley and Stephens* supported as it was by the House of Lords in *R. v Howe*. These are, in short, that there were two insuperable objections to the proposition that necessity might be available as a defence for the *Mignonette* sailors. The first objection was evident in the court's questions: who is to be the judge of this sort of necessity? By what measure is the comparative value of lives to be measured? The second objection was that to permit such a defence would mark an absolute divorce of law from morality. In my judgment, neither of these objections are dispositive of the present case. Mary is, sadly, self-designated for a very early death. Nobody can extend her life beyond a very short span.... [With regard to the second objection] all that a court can say is that it is not at all obvious that this is the sort of clear-cut case, marking an absolute divorce from law and morality, which was of such concern to Lord Coleridge CJ and his fellow judges.

There are sound reasons for holding that the existence of an emergency in the normal sense of the word is not an essential prerequisite for the application of the doctrine of necessity. The principle is one of necessity, not emergency...

If a sacrificial separation operation on conjoined twins were to be permitted in circumstances like these, there need be no room for the concern felt by Sir James Stephen that people would be too ready to avail themselves of exceptions to the law which they might suppose to apply to their cases, at the risk of other people's lives. Such an operation is, and is always likely to be, an exceptionally rare event...

According to Sir James Stephen there are three necessary requirements for the application of the doctrine of necessity: (i) the act is needed to avoid inevitable and irreparable evil; (ii) no more should be done than is reasonably necessary for the purpose to be achieved; (iii) the evil inflicted must not be disproportionate to the evil avoided. Given that the principles of modern family law point irresistibly to the conclusion that the interests of Jodie must be preferred to the conflicting interests of Mary, I consider that all three of these requirements are satisfied in this case."

Robert Walker L.J.:

"Duress of circumstances can therefore be seen as a third or residual category of necessity, along with self-defence and duress by threats. I do not think it matters whether these defences are regarded as justifications or excuses. Whatever label is used, the moral merits of the defence will vary with the circumstances....

In the absence of parliamentary intervention the law as to the defence of necessity is going to have to develop on a case by case basis... I would extend it, if it needs to be extended, to cover this case. It is a case of doctors owing conflicting legal, and not merely social or moral, duties. It is a case where the test of proportionality is met, since it is a matter of life and death, and on the evidence Mary is bound to die soon in any event. It is not a case of evaluating the relative worth of two human lives, but of undertaking surgery without which neither life will have the bodily integrity, or wholeness, which is its due. It should not be regarded as a further step down a slippery slope because the case of conjoined twins presents an unique problem."

The full implications of this decision have yet to be worked out. The narrower interpretation is that this is an extension of the "medical necessity" principle discussed above. Ward L.J. limited his judgment to cases where there was a conflict between a doctor's duties. A doctor is under a legal duty to do what is best for a patient. Here there were conflicting duties owed to the twins and, in exercising their duty, the doctors had to make a choice of the lesser of two evils. Even this narrower interpretation involves a significant extension of the law in that it allows doctors to kill their patients in these tightly-defined circumstances.

The bolder interpretation is that adopted by Lord Brooke which can be seen as endorsing a true defence of necessity cut free from its theoretical links to duress. Many of the examples of necessity he cites and discusses extend beyond medical necessity and suggest a wider role for the defence. However, when dealing with necessity as a defence to murder, he was careful to limit his judgment to the killing of those already "designated for death". This means that a defendant cannot choose (by whatever criterion) to throw four people off a boat to their death in order to save ten others: those four people have not been designated for death. Similarly, on the facts of *Dudley and Stephens* there would still not be a defence of necessity. While the cabin-boy was the weakest and most likely to die first, they could all have been rescued. He was not designated for death.

However, in clear situations this interpretation would allow necessity as a defence to murder. For example, if after a car crash a driver and passenger were seriously injured but it was clear that the driver was dying with no prospect of recovery but the passenger's life could be saved, it could be open to paramedics or other emergency services personnel to kill the driver in cutting her loose if that was the only means by which they could get to the passenger in time to save his life. Professor Sir John Smith uses an even more telling example: "Following the destruction of the World Trade Centre in New York by hijacked aircraft it now appears to be recognized that it would be lawful to shoot down the plane, killing all the innocent passengers and crew if this were the only way to prevent a much greater impending disaster. Even if duress cannot be a defence to murder, it seems quite clear that necessity can."[35]

---

[35] Smith and Hogan, *Criminal Law* (10th ed., 2002), pp. 273–274.

## VI. *Superior Orders*

We have seen that the defence of duress can be rationalised on the basis that the defendant lacked effective and real choice in committing the crime; he was forced by someone else to do something he was loath to do. In the same way, a subordinate may assert that he was forced by duty and loyalty to a superior to obey an order which leads him into conflict with the criminal law. Following this analogy it would seem that superior orders should constitute an *excuse*. The inferior has done wrong but is excused from blame. It is, however, clear that there is no such defence as superior orders in English law. Lord Salmon in the duress case of *Abbott*[36] said that the idea of such a defence "has always been universally rejected" and Lord Hailsham took a similar position in *Howe*.[37] In *Yip Chiu-Chang*[38] it was held that a person, who acted as an undercover agent to break a drug ring in Hong Kong, could be guilty of conspiring to traffic in dangerous drugs. The Privy Council confirmed that there was no general defence of superior orders as "neither the police, nor customs, nor any other members of the executive"[39] had any power to alter the terms of the Hong Kong Ordinance that made the export of heroin unlawful even though the court acknowledged that what the defendant had done was courageous and from the best of motives. In *Clegg*, the House of Lords held that the soldier would not be entitled to be acquitted by virtue of superior orders as "no such general defence [is] known to English law".[40] While such an approach might be uncontroversial in civil situations, the matter is not free from dispute in relation to military situations where it may be argued that the claims of duty, especially in war-time, are so strong as to warrant some kind of defence of superior orders.[41]

## McCall v McDowell, 1 Abb 212 Fed Cas. No. 8673 (1867) (Circuit Court of California)

Deaty J.:
"I cannot but think that the law should excuse the military subordinate when acting in obedience to the orders of his commander. Otherwise he is placed in the dangerous dilemma of being liable in damages to a third party[42] for obedience of an order or to the loss of his commission and disgrace for disobedience thereto[43] ... The first duty of a soldier is obedience, and without this there can be neither discipline nor efficiency in an army. If every subordinate officer and soldier were at liberty to question the legality of the orders of the commander ... the camp would be turned into a debating school, where the precious moment for action would be wasted in wordy conflicts between the advocates of conflicting opinions."

---

[36] [1976] 3 W.L.R. 462 at 469.
[37] [1987] A.C. 417 at 427.
[38] [1995] 1 A.C. 111.
[39] At 118.
[40] [1995] 1 A.C. 482 at 498.
[41] As no similar justification exists in civil situations it is not proposed to discuss superior orders further in that context.
[42] Or subject to a criminal charge.
[43] The soldier may claim further that he would have been shot for disobedience (Nazi war criminals included this in their defence), thereby pleading duress.

There have been numerous cases[44] in the United States which have attempted to recognise the "practical dilemma"[45] of the soldier by striking a balance between total immunity and total liability.

## United States v Calley 22 U.S.M.C.A. 534 (1973) (US Court of Military Appeals)

Lieutenant Calley was a platoon leader engaged in sweeping out the enemy in part of Vietnam. He was charged with the premeditated murder of 22 infants, children, women and old men. His defence was that he was acting under the direct orders of his commanding officer; he had been told that under no circumstances were they to leave Vietnamese alive as they passed through the villages. He was to "waste them."

Quinn J.:
"[There is] ample evidence from which to find that Lieutenant Calley directed and personally participated in the intentional killing of men, women and children who were unarmed and in the custody of soldiers ... [T]he uncontradicted evidence is that ... they were offering no resistance. In his testimony, Calley admitted he was aware of the requirement that prisoners be treated with respect ... he knew that the normal practice was to interrogate villagers, release those who could satisfactorily account for themselves and evacuate the suspect among them for further examination. ...

We turn to the contention that the [trial] judge erred in his submission of the defense of superior orders to the court [by framing the instructions thus]: '[I]f you find that Lieutenant Calley received an order directing him to kill unresisting Vietnamese within his control ... that order (as a matter of law) would be an illegal order. A determination that an order is illegal does not, of itself, assign criminal responsibility to the person following the order for acts done in compliance with it. ... [such] acts of a subordinate ... are excused and impose no criminal liability upon him unless the superior's order is one which a man of ordinary sense and understanding would, under the circumstances, know to be unlawful, or if the order in question is actually known to the accused to be unlawful.' ...

[Defence counsel urged that this was too high a standard for soldiers who may not be persons of ordinary sense and understanding; they argued for a lower test of 'commonest understanding'] ... [W]hether Lieutenant Calley was the most ignorant person in the United States Army in Vietnam or the most intelligent, he must be presumed to know that he could not kill the people involved here ... [the order was] so palpably illegal that whatever conceptual difference there may be between a person of 'commonest understanding' and a person of 'common understanding,' that difference could not have had any impact on a court."

Decision of the Court of Military Review affirmed[46]

This test of "palpable illegality" has been followed elsewhere. In the South African case of *Banda and others*[47] it was held that the defence was not available where the orders were "manifestly and palpably illegal and that a reasonable man in the circumstances of the soldier would know them to be".[48] The English approach of

---

[44] *United States v Kinder* (1953) A.C.M. 7321, 14 C.M.R. 742, *United States v Quarles* 350 US II (1955). Both cases arose from incidents in the Korean War.

[45] Brownlee, "Superior Orders—Time for a New Realism" [1989] Crim.L.R.395 at 396.

[46] In the *New York Times*, April 10, 1971, Marshall Burke argued that to hold Calley personally accountable was unjust; it was the whole nation that was accountable and ought to push for the end of the war. Goldstein argued against this view: "if future wars must be fought, there [must] be some expectation that each participant will abide by minimum standards of conduct which a law of crimes is designed to maintain." ("The Meaning of Calley" *The New Republic*, Vol. 194, No. 19, pp. 13–14.)

[47] (1990) (3) S.A. 466.

[48] At 494.

denying the existence of a defence of superior orders has been condemned as inappropriate and unrealistic.

### Ian D. Brownlee, "Superior Orders—Time For a New Realism?" [1989] Crim.L.R.396 at 411:

"It is inappropriate because the harm it is aimed at remedying, namely the abuse of executive fiat, is being perpetrated, if at all, by the superiors at various levels who have committed him to that situation. It is unrealistic because it requires the individual soldier to be able to make decisions on legal niceties in situations where sometimes his or her military competence and perhaps even instinct for physical survival will compel instant obedience. The strict 'no-defence' position is predicated upon assumptions about constitutional law and the possible consequences of allowing such a defence which cannot be demonstrated in practice. ... On the contrary, therefore, it is submitted that courts should be allowed to decide the bona fides of such a defence on the basis that military orders which are not manifestly illegal may give rise to a mistake of law ... [which should be relevant]. It is in this way that the interests of justice both for the individual soldier and for the wider civil society in which, increasingly, the soldier is becoming involved, will best be served."

Given recent judicial pronouncements against superior orders (and both duress and duress of circumstances as defences to murder) it seems most unlikely that any change will take place. Moreover, there must remain grave doubts as to the wisdom of introducing a defence that would allow soldiers to kill innocent persons deliberately and claim that their actions were excused.

## VII. Involuntary Conduct

### A. *Introduction*

The need for voluntary conduct, and the philosophical problems associated with the meaning of terms such as "voluntary" and "involuntary", have already been examined.[49] A claim of involuntariness is a "denial of authorship"[50] and "it is only where defendants are agents and not mere causers of harm that they are to be regarded as responsible for causing that harm".[51] The object of this section is to examine the implications and consequences of a finding that conduct is involuntary.

If conduct is involuntary there is no *actus reus* (and certainly no *mens rea*). This indicates that the defendant should be exempted completely from criminal liability. For example, in the Australian case of *Cogden*[52] a woman, in a somnambulistic state, dreaming that her daughter was being attacked by ghosts, spiders and North

---

[49] *Above*, p. 87.
[50] Ashworth, *Principles of Criminal Law* (3rd ed., 1999), p. 101.
[51] Horder, "Pleading Involuntary Lack of Capacity" (1993) 52 C.L.J. 298 at 300.
[52] (1950) unreported. See Morris, "Somnambulistic Homicide: Ghosts, Spiders and North Koreans" V *Res Judicatae* 29.

Korean soldiers, axed her to death. She was acquitted on the ground that her actions were not voluntary. Because a finding of involuntariness can potentially lead to a complete acquittal (with the danger that the conduct could be repeated), English courts have approached the problem of involuntariness with great circumspection and have adopted a restrictive approach as to when there should be a complete exemption from liability. This caution has manifested itself in three ways.

### 1. Narrow Definition of Involuntariness

The criminal law has adopted a narrow interpretation of "involuntary conduct". Not only is this because of the possibility of a complete acquittal, but also because of the difficulty of distinguishing a genuine claim from a fraudulent one. In *Bratty v Attorney-General for Northern Ireland*[53] it was acknowledged that pleading a blackout is one of the first refuges of a guilty conscience and is a popular excuse.[54] Accordingly, the law has tended to the view that there is a continuum of involuntariness ranging from complete absence of consciousness, through persons acting in a confused or semi-conscious manner, to those who actually know what they are doing but claim that their actions were morally involuntary because their will was overborne and they were forced to act as they did. The courts, in determining where to draw the line on this continuum, have been strongly influenced by the context, nature and dangerousness of the behaviour.[55] In cases where the defendant is engaged in a particularly dangerous activity, such as driving a car, the law has adopted a strict stance that only a complete absence of consciousness will exempt from liability. In *Broome v Perkins*[56] the defendant, when charged with driving without due care and attention, claimed to be in a hypoglycaemic condition. He was acquitted at first instance on the basis that his conduct was involuntary. However, an appeal by case stated resulted in a direction to the magistrates to convict. It was held that his actions were only automatic at intervals; at times "the respondent's mind must have been controlling his limbs (from the evidence) and thus he was driving".

### J.C. Smith, Commentary to Broome v Perkins [1987] Crim.L.R.272:

"The defendant was held not to be in a state of automatism throughout his journey because, from time to time, he apparently exercised conscious control over his car veering away from other vehicles so as to avoid a collision, braking violently when approaching the back of another vehicle and so on. This is a very harsh decision, resulting in the conviction of a person who appears to have suffered a misfortune, not to have been at fault in any real sense and to have behaved most responsibly by going to the police and saying that he believed he must have been involved in a road accident."

Despite this view, the same approach was adopted in *Attorney-General's Reference (No. 2 of 1992)*[57] where it was held that conduct was only involuntary if there was a total loss of voluntary control. In this case, the defendant, a lorry driver,

---

[53] [1963] A.C. 386.
[54] Citing Stable J. in *Cooper v McKenna* [1960] Q.L.R. 406 at 419.
[55] Clarkson, *Understanding Criminal Law* (3rd ed., 2001), p. 37.
[56] [1987] Crim.L.R.271.
[57] (1993) 97 Cr.App.R.429.

crashed into a broken-down vehicle parked on the hard shoulder of a motorway and killed two people. Experts described the defendant's condition as "driving without awareness".[58] Whilst not asleep, "the driver's capacity to avoid a collision ceased to exist because of repetitive stimuli experienced on straight flat featureless motorways could induce a trance-like state". However, the expert acknowledged that this amounted to reduced or imperfect awareness and, accordingly, the Court of Appeal ruled that this could not amount to involuntary conduct.

As shall be seen, however, when defendants are engaged in less widely-practised dangerous activities, the courts have been less insistent upon a complete absence of consciousness or control and have allowed conduct that is only "semi-conscious" to be classed as involuntary.

## 2. Preceding Fault

The rationale for requiring voluntary conduct is that there can be no authorship or responsibility for involuntary conduct and, accordingly, blame is inappropriate. It is not a person's fault if she is attacked and, in a state of concussion, causes a harm to another. Punishment is not deserved and no deterrent goals can be achieved by holding such a person criminally liable. In some situations, however, it might be the defendant's own fault that the state of involuntariness was brought about. In such cases, the courts, conscious of the fact that the defendant is not only blameworthy in precipitating the involuntariness but could do it again, have been careful to ensure that criminal liability is not evaded.

In *Quick and Paddison*[59] the defendant, a diabetic, was charged with an assault that occurred during a hypoglycaemic episode. This arose from eating too little and drinking too much alcohol after having taken insulin. It led to an aggressive outburst and an impairment of consciousness. Lawton L.J. stated that: "a self-induced incapacity will not excuse ... nor will one which could have been reasonably foreseen as a result of either doing, or omitting to do something, as, for example, taking alcohol against medical advice after using certain prescribed drugs, or failing to have regular meals while taking insulin."[60]

So, while "accidental" hypoglycaemia could have secured an acquittal, Quick's abuse of his body meant that he could be blamed for the ensuing hypoglycaemic episode. Although the conviction was actually reversed on appeal (on the basis that the issue of involuntariness should have been left to the jury), it was made clear that self-induced involuntariness will not provide a defence to crimes of basic intent.[61]

What, however, is meant by preceding fault in this context? Must the defendant know that her conduct will cause the involuntary conduct or is it sufficient that the reasonable person would know this? In *Quick and Paddison* the question was whether the incapacity could reasonably have been foreseen. In *Bailey*[62] the defendant was a diabetic who had not taken sufficient food after a dose of insulin to combat its effects. It was held (somewhat controversially) that it was not common knowledge amongst diabetics that such failure could lead to aggressive, dangerous

[58] At 431.
[59] [1973] 1 Q.B. 910.
[60] *ibid.* at 922.
[61] For the meaning of this term, see *below*, pp. 411–420.
[62] [1983] 1 W.L.R. 760.

or unpredictable behaviour. Accordingly, it could not be inferred that the defendant knew of the risks and he should not be penalised for his lack of knowledge.[63] One way of reconciling these cases would be to restrict the operation of the rule in *Quick and Paddison* to cases involving alcohol and drugs because it is so widely known that intoxicants can have such an effect[64] and, because of the statistical correlation between intoxication and crime, policy demands that no relief from criminal liability be afforded to intoxicated persons. Such an approach is arguably supported by *Hardie*[65] where it was held that a defendant who took Valium could escape liability for subsequent involuntary conduct because it was not known to the defendant, nor generally known, that Valium could cause unpredictability and aggressiveness. The essence of the *Quick and Paddison* principle is that one can legitimately blame a person who, through his own fault, causes his own involuntary conduct. When such fault is established, the requirement of voluntariness is dispensed with—largely because that requirement is only there to protect the faultless.[66] The question whether one can only blame those who knew of the risks they were running or whether blame is appropriate because the risks were obvious and they ought to have appreciated them raises broadly the same issues as were canvassed in relation to the concept of recklessness.[67]

It is important that there be precision in locating the act alleged to be involuntary. The rule that preceding fault negates automatism could be employed in driving cases where the driver falls asleep or suffers some form of attack that could have been predicted.[68] However, where the driver has previously had similar attacks, the act of driving can in itself amount to dangerous driving. In *Marison*[69] the defendant suffered a hypoglycaemic episode while driving; he lost control of the car and caused the death of another driver. It was held that even though the defendant had become an automaton at the moment of the accident, this was not a case of automatism. Being aware that he might have a hypoglycaemic attack while driving meant that the driver was "in a dangerously defective state due to diabetes". The offence of dangerous driving had already been committed before the attack occurred.

### 3. Cause of Involuntariness

Bearing in mind the central point that a finding of involuntariness can lead to a complete acquittal, the courts have been anxious to investigate the cause of the involuntary conduct. If the cause of the involuntary conduct is something internal to the defendant—a disease of the mind—then clearly there is the potential danger that the involuntary conduct could be repeated. Society could need protection from such persons. Accordingly, where the defendant is suffering from a disease of the

---

[63] The appeal was in fact dismissed because of insufficient evidence that the defendant's actions had been involuntary.

[64] *Allen* [1988] Crim.L.R.698.

[65] (1984) 80 Cr.App.R.157. See *below*, p. 410.

[66] See further, Smith and Wilson, "Impaired Voluntariness and Criminal Responsibility" (1991) 3 O.J.L.S. 69.

[67] *Above*, pp. 143–172.

[68] See *Kay v Butterworth* (1947) 173 L.T. 191; *Hill v Baxter* [1958] 1 Q.B. 277.

[69] [1996] Crim.L.R.909.

mind the involuntary conduct is described as insane automatism. Such an insane defendant, while escaping formal criminal liability, nevertheless receives a special verdict of "not guilty by reason of insanity" whereupon the courts have power to restrain the person. On the other hand, if the cause of the involuntary conduct is something external to the defendant—such as a blow on the head—there is little chance of repetition; the defendant is not dangerous. Such cases are described as non-insane automatism—or simply automatism—and the defendant is afforded a complete acquittal. Given this critical distinction between insanity and automatism, one way in which the courts can reduce the number of defendants, such as the sleep-walking Mrs Cogden, escaping all liability is to expand the category of insanity thereby reducing the scope of the defence of automatism. For example, as we shall see, sleep-walking was traditionally regarded by English law (as it was in *Cogden*) as automatism. Today it has been reclassified as an instance of insanity.

The distinction between insanity and automatism is thus one of fundamental importance and each will be considered in turn.

## B. *Insanity*

### 1. Introduction

The defence of insanity brings into sharp focus many of the issues discussed in previous chapters and has been the source of more debate and heart-searching than almost any other area of criminal law.[70]

Requiring a jury to decide whether a person accused of a crime is to be punished as criminal or "treated" as insane forces two major questions to the surface. The first addresses itself to the premise upon which the sane individual is punished. We have seen in Chapter 2 that inherent in the criminal justice system is a view of people as responsible agents. Individuals possess freedom of will and can choose one course of action rather than another. If they step outside the limits of legal action we are, therefore, justified in imposing blame and punishment. By the same argument we cannot blame people who do not have this ability to choose or control their actions.[71] The insanity defence thus seeks to distinguish the responsible from those lacking responsibility. The difficulty lies in determining where the line between sanity and responsibility on the one hand, and insanity and irresponsibility on the other hand, is to be drawn. It has been increasingly argued that absolute states of sanity and insanity rarely (if ever) exist; instead there are shades of sanity. This attitude towards sanity and responsibility has expressed itself in a number of forms. For some commentators it has necessitated a more rigorous approach to the search for the crucial dividing line. For them the question of ascertaining who is responsible has been made more important, not less. The same doubt has, however, led others to demand that the insanity defence (or the concept

---

[70] This is despite the fact that there are only about nine findings of insanity per year (Mackay and Kearns, "More Fact(s) about the Insanity Defence" [1999] Crim.L.R.714).

[71] Gross, *A Theory of Criminal Justice* (1979), pp. 298–305, points out that three contentions may be involved. It may, first, be thought that it is wrong in these situations to punish the accused *for being sick*, or, secondly, that it is wrong to punish someone for what he does *as a result of being sick*, or, lastly, that it is cruel to add to the suffering of someone who is sick: in other words, that it is wrong to punish someone *when he is sick*.

of responsibility itself) be abolished.[72] As we shall see, however, where the insanity defence has been abolished or amended as in some of the states in the United States, it has been in response to criticisms other than those concerning the principle of responsibility.[73]

Secondly, how are the traditional objectives of punishment, which largely assume responsibility, affected when it comes to the punishment of the insane?

### Abraham Goldstein, The Insanity Defense (1967), pp. 11–15:

"At the present time, the objectives of the criminal law are ordinarily said to be retribution, deterrence and rehabilitation. ... The *retributive* function building on the widely held feeling that the criminal owes the community a measure of suffering comparable to that which he has inflicted ... channelled the anger of victims (and of their friends) lest they ... [sought] revenge. But to do so, it was necessary to make a criminal conviction sufficiently consequential to satisfy those who were inclined to feel retributive ... A corollary of this, however, was the feeling that so serious a sanction ought not to be imposed in situations in which the initial impulse to anger was likely to give way, even among victims, to feelings of compassion. These were situations in which the offender seemed so obviously different from most men that he could not be blamed for what he had done. Even under a retributive theory, therefore, an insanity defense was needed to trace in outline those who could not be regarded as blameworthy. ...

Under the *deterrent* theory ... the primary function of criminal law is to move men to conform to social norms, particularly those which cannot be left entirely to informal processes of social control or to those of the civil law. This is accomplished by announcing in a criminal code what conduct is prohibited and how much of a sanction of imprisonment or fine will be visited upon those who ignore the prohibition. Such a system can be effective only with men who can understand the signals directed at them by the code, who can respond to the warnings, and who feel the significance of the sanctions imposed upon violators. ... If a man cannot make the calculations or muster the feelings demanded of him by the theory, he is classed as insane. He lacks the requisite degree of intelligence, reasoning power and foresight of consequence. If he were held criminally responsible he would be made to suffer harsh sanctions without serving the purpose of individual deterrence.

It would still be possible, however, to conceive that such a man might serve the ends of general deterrence ... [but] the examples are likely to deter only if the person who is not involved in the criminal process regards the lessons as applicable to him. He is likely to do so only if he identifies with the offender and with the offending situation. This feat of identification is difficult enough to achieve under ordinary circumstances ... it is probably hopeless if the deterrent example is so different from most men that the crime can be attributed to the difference. ...

The third view of the insanity defense ... tends to view deviant behaviour as psychological maladjustment, the product of forces beyond the individual's control; he is less to be blamed than to be helped to restore the balance between him and his background or his environment. The tacit assumption is that a paternal state can put him right by psychotherapy or by judicious social planning, if only the 'helping' professions are provided with the resources to do the job. ... This 'mental health' image has unquestionably captured the imagination of the reformers and has been propagated almost as a faith. ...

Because it is widely assumed that 'blame' plays a critical role in maintaining individual responsibility and social order, the insanity defense continues to be regarded as exceptional. It becomes the occasional device through which an offender is found to be inappropriate for

[72] *Below*, p. 388.
[73] *Below*, p. 387.

the social purposes served by the criminal law. He is too much unlike the man in the street to permit his example to be useful for the purposes of deterrence. He is too far removed from normality to make us angry with him. But because he is sick rather than evil, society is cast as specially responsible for him and obligated to make him better."

A final preliminary point needs to be considered. Is the insanity defence really a "defence" at all? The issue of insanity is invariably included in discussions of defences to crime, yet this classification is not without its difficulties. To assert that a defendant has a defence to crime has connotations that may or may not prove to be applicable to the case of insanity. Three matters, in particular, require consideration.

(a) Is insanity regarded as a general exempting condition or as a specific excuse to a particular wrongful act? According to the analysis of defences at the start of this chapter, insanity should be perceived as akin to the general defence of infancy and act as an exemption. The defendant lacks *capacity-responsibility* for her "wrongful" actions and thus requires no excuse. This incapacity may well be demonstrated in many ways other than the particular act. However, this analogy does not sit well with the wording of the legal test for insanity. As we shall see, the M'Naghten Rules link the mental condition of the accused causally to the prohibited *act*. In other words, it appears to focus upon *attribution-responsibility*. Our inclusion of insanity as an exemption, therefore, is, in part, based upon the way it ought to operate and serves to highlight in advance one of the many flaws of the current test.[74]

(b) Is insanity a true defence or does it negate a definitional element? Support for the view that it performs this latter function comes from the argument that prior to the statutory creation of the special verdict, a finding of insanity would lead to a complete acquittal at common law.[75] Indeed, it has been argued further that this would still be true today of defendants pleading insanity in the magistrates' courts.[76] However, it may be that conclusions about whether insanity negates *mens rea* are best drawn once the M'Naghten Rules have been explored.

(c) In view of the consequences of a finding of insanity, can it really be said that it is a "defence"? The result of a successful plea of insanity is the special verdict of not guilty by reason of insanity.[77] As Goldstein has stated: "In virtually every state a successful insanity defense does not bring freedom with it. Instead it has become the occasion for either mandatory commitment to a mental hospital or for an exercise of discretion by the court regarding the advisability of such commitment."[78] In this country, as a result of the Criminal Procedure (Insanity and Unfitness to Plead) Act 1991, we have moved from the first position Goldstein describes to the second, with the

---

[74] See Tadros, "Insanity and the Capacity for Criminal Responsibility" (2000) 5 Edinburgh Law Review 325 for an analysis of the significance of the difference between capacity and attribution responsibility.
[75] Criminal Lunatics Act 1800. White, "Insanity Defences and the Magistrates' Courts" [1991] Crim.L.R.501 at 502.
[76] *ibid.* R. v *Horseferry Road Magistrates Court, ex p. K* [1996] 2 Cr.App.R.574 confirms that it is still possible to raise the insanity defence at summary trial. See further, comment by Smith, [1997] Crim.L.R.132; White and Bowen, "Insanity Defences in Summary Trials" [1997] 61 J.Crim.L. 198.
[77] Criminal Procedure (Insanity) Act 1964, s.1.
[78] Goldstein, *The Insanity Defence* (1967), p. 19.

exception of the crime of murder, for which mandatory commitment still results. It can be argued, therefore, that the "defence" is merely a way of substituting one method of state control for another. The state may not hold the defendant responsible for her actions but still retains the right to dispose of her as it thinks fit.

## 2. The Law

### (1) *Fitness to plead*

There is little point in going through the ritual of a criminal trial if the defendant is unable to comprehend what is happening.

### R. A. Duff, Trials and Punishments (1986), pp. 27, 263–264:

"[W]hat is crucial here (apart from considerations of past deserts or of future consequences) is the offender's capacity to understand and respond to her imprisonment as a *punishment*: if she is now so disordered that she lacks this capacity she is not fit to be punished, whether or not she committed an offence which merited punishment, and whether or not imprisonment would be the most efficient way of protecting others against her. For punishment aims and must aim, if it is to be properly justified, to *address* the offender as a rational and responsible agent: if she cannot understand what is being done to her, or why it is being done, or how it is related as a punishment to her past offence, her punishment becomes a travesty ...

This means that an offender who is fit to be punished ... must be capable not only of grasping the fact that what is being done to her is done because she has broken the law, but also of grasping and responding to its moral meaning and purpose as a punishment. She must have the capacity and the potential for the kind of penitential redemption which punishment aims to induce: which means she must already have some concern, which punishment may reawaken and strengthen, for the values which she has flouted, or at least that she has some moral concerns which would enable her to come, through her punishment, to understand and care for the values which the law embodies."[79]

Accordingly, before there can be a trial, a defendant must be found "fit to plead".[80] The earliest criteria employed by the courts to determine this were that the defendant had to be able to understand the charge, challenge jurors, and follow evidence.[81] It has been pointed out that these criteria developed in relation to defendants who were deaf and dumb rather than defendants who were mentally ill and thus the test concentrated upon ability to communicate and intelligence (because at the time deaf mutes were widely regarded as mental defectives). "Because the focus was on mental deficiency ... delusions, disorders of mood and other features common to mental illness which were clearly relevant to the notion of unfitness to plead ... had no role in the concept ... regardless of how they might impinge on a defendant's chances of having a fair trial."[82] To these early criteria was then added the requirement that the defendant be able to instruct counsel.[83]

---

[79] See further, Mackay, *Mental Condition Defence in the Criminal Law* (1995), pp. 216–219.
[80] The issue of fitness may be raised by the prosecution or the defence or by the judge. On the origins of the concept of fitness to plead, see Grubin, "What Constitutes Fitness to Plead?" [1993] Crim.L.R.748.
[81] *Dyson* (1831) 7 C. & P. 305; *Pritchard* (1836) 7 C. & P. 303. *Podola* [1960] 1 Q.B. 325 decided that the burden of proof rests upon the defence if they raise the issue of fitness.
[82] Grubin, above, n.80 at 753.
[83] *Davies* (1853) C.L.C. 326.

What is significant about this development was that it arose from a case dealing with a mentally ill defendant and emphasis was not placed upon ability to communicate or intelligence but upon the capacity of the defendant properly to instruct his counsel. Since then, however, this distinction has been lost and for the last 150 years the test has concentrated upon cognitive ability.

Important reforms have taken place. The Criminal Procedure (Insanity and Unfitness to Plead) Act 1991 has substantially altered the consequences of a finding of unfitness or "disability". Where the jury finds that the defendant is under a disability but that he has not done the act or omission charged, they "shall return a verdict of acquittal as if on the count in question the trial had proceeded to a conclusion".[84] The defendant goes free.

The alternative is for the jury to find that the defendant is under a disability but did the act or omission charged. In *Antoine* the House of Lords ruled that this requires the jury to find that the *actus reus* is established only.[85] It overruled the previous decision of *Egan* in which the Court of Appeal had held that the *mens rea* of the offence need also be established.[86] While the interpretation favoured by the House of Lords accords with that of Parliament in debates during the passage of the 1991 Act, the level of protection for unfit defendants has been reduced.[87] However, the general rule that only the *actus reus* need be proved is subject to qualification. Where, for example, the unfit person participated in the offence as a secondary party rather than as the principal, it will be necessary to refer to the basis of secondary liability. Thus, the jury will have to be satisfied that the unfit person participated with knowledge of the activities of the principal offender and surrounding circumstances before he can be held to have "done the act or omission charged".[88] Where the jury comes to the conclusion that the person did the act or omission the judge now has the same flexible powers of disposal as follow from a finding of insanity.[89]

Research has shown that the judges have responded positively to this increased flexibility and there is also evidence that, after years of decline, the use of the plea has increased since the implementation of the 1991 Act.[90] At the same time as its use has been increasing, however, the 1991 Act has been subject to a fundamental challenge. In *H*[91] it was argued that the procedure to establish whether the person has done the act or omission is to all intents and purposes a procedure to determine a criminal charge and thus ought to attract the protection provided in Article 6 (the right to a fair trial) of the European Convention on Human Rights. This protection was absent because the defendant, being unfit to plead, could not give instructions and participate fully in his defence.[92] The House of Lords rejected this claim,

---

[84] S.2 of the Criminal Procedure (Insanity and Unfitness to Plead) Act, substituting a new s.4A(4) to the Criminal Procedure (Insanity) Act 1964.

[85] [2001] 1 A.C. 340. See also *Attorney-General's Reference (No. 3 of 1998)* [1999] 2 Cr.App.R.214.

[86] [1998] 1 Cr. App.R.121.

[87] See further, Mackay and Kearns, "The Trial of the Facts and Unfitness to Plead" [1997] Crim.L.R.644.

[88] *Martin* [2003] EWCA Crim 357.

[89] Murder is an exception. *Below*, p. 383.

[90] Mackay and Kearns, *above*, n.87 and Mackay and Kearns, "An Upturn in Unfitness to Plead? Disability in Relation to the Trial Under the 1991 Act" [2000] Crim.L.R.532.

[91] [2003] All E.R. (D) 293.

[92] See further, *T v United Kingdom* [2002] 2 All E.R. 1024.

holding that the procedure lacked the essential features of the criminal process and that it would be highly anomalous if a procedure introduced to protect those unable to defend themselves at trial was to be found incompatible with the Convention. However, while section 4A may now be safe from Human Rights challenge, the criteria by which fitness is judged have remained unchanged and it is likely that the flaws in the procedure will become increasingly apparent if the trend towards greater reliance upon it continues.[93]

### (ii) *Insanity as a "defence"*

In many of the most extreme cases the defendant will not be found fit to stand trial.[94] Accordingly, the insanity defence is usually reserved for problematic and borderline cases.

Before examining the test for insanity it should be noted that, exceptionally, the burden of proof rests with the defendant to show on a balance of probabilities that he was insane at the time of the act[95] and that it is for the judge to determine whether a defence raised by the defendant is, in fact, one of insanity. The question of reverse burdens of proof has become deeply problematic with the implementation of the European Convention on Human Rights. The issue is whether placing the burden of proof upon the defendant contravenes the presumption of innocence protected by Article 6(2). While the point has yet to be tested in relation to insanity, one indication of the way in which courts may now approach reverse burdens of proof is given by the decision of *Kebeline*[96] where it was suggested by the House of Lords that these might be re-interpreted as imposing an evidential burden upon the defendant only rather than the probative burden.

### (a) The M'Naghten Rules

### M'Naghten's Case (1843) 10 C & F, 200, 8 Eng. Rep. 718

The defendant was indicted for the murder of Edward Drummond, Secretary to the Prime Minister, Sir Robert Peel. The defence introduced evidence of the defendant's insanity,

---

[93] Grubin, "What Constitutes Fitness to Plead" [1993] Crim.L.R.748 at 749. A further problem relates to hysterical amnesiacs who can recall nothing of the crime they are alleged to have committed. According to *Podola* [1960] 1 Q.B. 325 they will be found fit to plead.

[94] At the other end of the spectrum there will be significant numbers of defendants who will be held responsible for their actions, but whose sentences will include psychiatric treatment. See, for example, Allen, *Justice Unbalanced* (1987).

[95] *Woolmington v D.P.P.* [1935] A.C. 462 at 475–476. The same is true for diminished responsibility: Homicide Act 1957 s.2(2). There are difficulties with this exception. For example, if a defendant pleads (simple) lack of *mens rea* the burden of proof rests with the prosecution to prove beyond reasonable doubt that he did have *mens rea*; however, if the defendant adds that the absence of *mens rea* was due to a disease of the mind the burden then shifts to the defendant. If the defendant pleads automatism the burden will only shift in cases of insane automatism. See further, Jones, "Insanity, Automatism and the Burden of Proof on the Accused" [1995] 111 L.Q.R. 475.

[96] *R. v Director of Public Prosecutions, ex parte Kebeline* [1999] 3 W.L.R. 972. The case, decided prior to the Human Rights Act 1998, dealt with reverse burdens of proof under the Prevention of Terrorism Act 1989 which the Divisional Court found to be in flagrant breach of Article 6(2). The House of Lords took a much more qualified approach, arguing that each instance of the reverse burden would have to be considered on its own merits and that would include how the burden operated in practice. For a fuller discussion of this issue, see pp. 234–235.

particularly his obsession with certain morbid delusions. The presiding judge, Lord Tindal C.J., directed the jury in the following terms: "The question to be asked is whether ... the prisoner had or had not the use of his understanding, so as to know that he was doing a wrong and wicked act." The jury returned a verdict of not guilty by reason of insanity. The furore occasioned by the verdict led to the whole issue of insanity being debated in the House of Lords. As a result, five questions were put to the judges of the day; the answers to questions two and three form the basis of the "M'Naghten Rules" by which lack of criminal responsibility is tested.

Lord Tindal C.J.:
"Your lordships are pleased to inquire of us, secondly, 'What are the proper questions to be submitted to the jury, where a person alleged to be afflicted with insane delusion respecting one or more particular subjects or persons, is charged with the commission of a crime (murder, for example), and insanity is set up as a defence?' And, thirdly, 'In what terms ought the question to be left to the jury as to the prisoner's state of mind at the time when the act was committed?' And as these two questions appear to us to be more conveniently answered together, we have to submit our opinion to be, that the jurors ought to be told in all cases that every man is to be presumed to be sane, and to possess a sufficient degree of reason to be responsible for his crimes, until the contrary be proved to their satisfaction; and that *to establish a defence on the ground of insanity, it must be clearly proved that, at the time of the committing of the act, the party accused was labouring under such a defect of reason, from disease of the mind, as not to know the nature and quality of the act he was doing; or, if he did know it, that he did not know he was doing what was wrong.* The mode of putting the latter part of the question to the jury on these occasions has generally been, whether the accused at the time of doing the act knew the difference between right and wrong: which mode, though rarely, if ever, leading to any mistake with the jury, is not, as we conceive, so accurate when put generally and in the abstract, as when put with reference to the party's knowledge of right and wrong in respect to the very act with which he is charged. If the question were to be put as to the knowledge of the accused solely and exclusively with reference to the law of the land, it might tend to confound the jury, by inducing them to believe that an actual knowledge of the law of the land was essential in order to lead to a conviction; whereas the law is administered upon the principle that every one must be taken conclusively to know it, without proof that he does know it. If the accused was conscious that the act was one which he ought not to do, and if the act was at the same time contrary to the law of the land, he is punishable; and the usual course therefore has been to leave the question to the jury, whether the party accused had a sufficient degree of reason to know that he was doing an act that was wrong: and this course we think is correct, accompanied with such observations and explanations as the circumstances of each particular case may require." (Emphasis added)

Although the essence of the M'Naghten Rules may be simply stated—it asks whether the defendant knew what he was doing at the time the crime was committed—certain of the phrases used in the formulation of the rules have been subject to much judicial (and academic) interpretation.

One can envisage the M'Naghten Rules as a series of hurdles over which the defendant must jump in order to be excused liability.

The defendant must, first, be suffering from a *"disease of the mind"*. This phrase

"initially seems to have attracted no judicial scrutiny ... However, the development of the automatism defence changed this. For suddenly the courts were confronted by the fact that a successful defence based on 'unconscious involuntary action' could result in an unqualified acquittal. For obvious social defence reasons this fact began to worry the courts and in order to restrict the availability of such acquittals the judiciary began to develop a complex body of law built upon the phrase 'disease of the mind'."[97]

The case of *Kemp*[98] (where the defendant suffered from arteriosclerosis which induced a state of unconsciousness during which he attacked his wife with a hammer) makes it clear that the condition of the brain is irrelevant. The test is not necessarily whether there is some damage to that physical entity (although the mental disease may have a physical origin) but, more widely, whether the mental faculties of reason, understanding and memory are impaired or absent. This approach has been affirmed by the House of Lords.

### R. v Sullivan [1984] A.C. 156 (House of Lords)

The defendant was charged with inflicting grievous bodily harm, contrary to section 20 of the Offences against the Person Act 1861, after he had attacked Payne, his friend, during the post-ictal stage of an epileptic seizure. The trial judge ruled that this amounted to insanity rather than automatism; consequently the defendant changed his plea to guilty to the lesser offence of assault occasioning actual bodily harm. He then appealed against conviction on the basis that he should have been allowed to raise the issue of automatism.[99]

Lord Diplock:
"The M'Naghten Rules have been used as a comprehensive definition for this purpose by the courts for the last 140 years. Most importantly, they were so used by this House in *Bratty v Attorney-General for Northern Ireland* [1963] A.C. 386. That case was in some respects the converse of the instant case. Bratty was charged with murdering a girl by strangulation. He claimed to have been unconscious of what he was doing at the time he strangled the girl and he sought to run as alternative defences non-insane automatism and insanity. The only evidential foundation that he laid for either of these pleas was medical evidence that he might have been suffering from psychomotor epilepsy which, if he were, would account for his having been unconscious of what he was doing. No other pathological explanation of his actions having been carried out in a state of automatism was supported by evidence. The trial judge first put the defence of insanity to the jury. The jury rejected it; they declined to bring in the special verdict. Thereupon, the judge refused to put to the jury the alternative defence of automatism. His refusal was upheld by the Court of Criminal Appeal of Northern Ireland and subsequently by this House.

The question before this House was whether, the jury having rejected the plea of insanity, there was any evidence on non-insane automatism fit to be left to the jury. The *ratio decidendi* of its dismissal of the appeal was that the jury having negatived the explanation that Bratty might have been acting unconsciously in the course of an attack of psychomotor epilepsy, there was no evidential foundation for the suggestion that he was acting unconsciously from any other cause.

In the instant case, as in *Bratty*, the only evidential foundation that was laid for any finding by the jury that Mr Sullivan was acting unconsciously and involuntarily when he was kicking Mr Payne, was that when he did so he was in the post-ictal stage of a seizure of psychomotor epilepsy. The evidential foundation in the case of Bratty, that he was suffering from psychomotor epilepsy at the time he did the act with which he was charged, was very weak and was rejected by the jury; the evidence in Mr Sullivan's case, that he was so suffering when he was kicking Mr Payne, was very strong and would almost inevitably be accepted by a properly directed jury. It would be the duty of the judge to direct the jury that if they did accept that evidence the law required them to bring in a special verdict and none other. The

[97] Mackay, *Mental Condition Defences in the Criminal Law* (1995), p. 97.
[98] [1957] 1 Q.B. 399.
[99] For an informative discussion of the medical background to this case, see Eastman, "Defending the Mentally Ill" in Mackay and Russell (eds), *Psychiatry and the Criminal Law* (1986).

governing statutory provision is to be found in section 2 of the Trial of Lunatics Act 1883. This says 'the jury *shall* return a special verdict ...'

My Lords, I can deal briefly with the various grounds on which it has been submitted that the instant case can be distinguished from what constituted the *ratio decidendi* in *Bratty v Attorney-General for Northern Ireland*, and that it falls outside the ambit of the M'Naghten Rules.

First, it is submitted the medical evidence in the instant case shows that psychomotor epilepsy is not a disease of the mind, whereas in *Bratty* it was accepted by all the doctors that it was. The only evidential basis for this submission is that Dr Fenwick said that in medical terms to constitute a 'disease of the mind' or 'mental illness,' which he appeared to regard as interchangeable descriptions, a disorder of brain functions (which undoubtedly occurs during a seizure in psychomotor epilepsy) must be prolonged for a period of time usually more than a day; while Dr Taylor would have it that the disorder must continue for a minimum of a month to qualify for the description 'a disease of the mind.'

The nomenclature adopted by the medical profession may change from time to time; Bratty was tried in 1961. But the meaning of the expression 'disease of the mind' as the cause of 'a defect of reason' remains unchanged for the purposes of the application of the M'Naghten Rules. I agree with what was said by Devlin J. in *R. v Kemp* that 'mind' in the M'Naghten Rules is used in the ordinary sense of the mental faculties of reason, memory and understanding. If the effect of a disease is to impair these faculties so severely as to have either of the consequences referred to in the latter part of the rules, it matters not whether the aetiology of the impairment is organic, as in epilepsy, or functional, or whether the impairment itself is permanent or is transient and intermittent, provided that it subsisted at the time of commission of the act. The purpose of the legislation relating to the defence of insanity, ever since its origin in 1800, has been to protect society against recurrence of the dangerous conduct. The duration of a temporary suspension of the mental faculties, of reason, memory and understanding, particularly if, as in Mr Sullivan's case, it is recurrent, cannot on any rational ground be relevant to the application by the courts of the M'Naghten Rules, though it may be relevant to the course adopted by the Secretary of State, to whom the responsibility for how the defendant is to be dealt with passes after the return of the special verdict 'not guilty by reason of insanity.'

To avoid misunderstanding I ought perhaps to add that in expressing my agreement with what was said by Devlin J. in *Kemp*, where the disease that caused the temporary and intermittent impairment of the mental faculties was arteriosclerosis, I do not regard that learned judge as excluding the possibility of non-insane automatism (for which the proper verdict would be a verdict of 'not guilty') in cases where temporary impairment (not being self-induced by consuming drink or drugs) results from some external physical factor such as a blow on the head causing concussion or the administration of an anaesthetic for therapeutic purposes. ... The instant case, however, does not in my view afford an appropriate occasion for exploring possible causes of non-insane automatism. ...

My Lords, it is natural to feel reluctant to attach the label of insanity to a sufferer from psychomotor epilepsy of the kind to which Mr Sullivan was subject, even though the expression in the context of a special verdict of 'not guilty by reason of insanity' is a technical one which includes a purely temporary and intermittent suspension of the mental faculties of reason, memory and understanding resulting from the occurrence of an epileptic fit. But the label is contained in the current statute, it has appeared in this statute's predecessors ever since 1800. It does not lie within the power of the courts to alter it. Only Parliament can do that. It has done so twice; it could do so once again.

Sympathise though I do with Mr Sullivan, I see no other course open to your Lordships than to dismiss this appeal."

**Appeal dismissed**

## R. v Burgess [1991] 2 W.L.R. 1206 (Court of Appeal, Criminal Division)

The defendant attacked his friend, Miss Curtis, with a bottle and then a video-recorder, finally putting a hand round her throat. The defendant claimed that he was acting unconsciously in that he had been sleep-walking and was thus entitled to be acquitted as a non-insane automaton. The trial judge ruled that the jury had to decide whether the defendant was acting consciously or whether he was not guilty by reason of insanity. The jury returned the latter verdict against which the defendant appealed.

Lord Lane C.J.:
"Where the defence of automatism is raised by the defendant, two questions fall to be decided by the judge before the defence can be left to the jury. The first is whether a proper evidential foundation for the defence of automatism has been laid. The second is whether the evidence shows the case to be one of insane automatism, that is to say, a case which falls within the M'Naghten Rules, or one of non-insane automatism. ...

There can be no doubt but that the appellant on the basis of the jury's verdict, was labouring under ... such a defect of reason as not to know what he was doing when he wounded Miss Curtis. The question is whether that was from 'disease of the mind' ...

The appellant plainly suffered from a defect of reason from some sort of failure (for lack of a better term) of the mind causing him to act as he did without conscious motivation. His mind was to some extent controlling his actions which were purposive rather than the result of muscular spasm, but without his being consciously aware of what he was doing. Can it be said that that 'failure' was a *disease* of the mind rather than a defect or failure of the mind not due to disease? That is the distinction, by no means easy to draw, upon which this case depends, as others have depended in the past.

One can perhaps narrow the field of enquiry still further by eliminating what are sometimes called the 'external factors' such as concussion caused by a blow on the head. There were no such factors here. Whatever the cause may have been, it was an internal cause.

[His Lordship then cited the case of *Sullivan*]

What help does one derive from the authorities as to the meaning of 'disease' in this context? Lord Denning in *Bratty v Attorney-General for Northern Ireland* [1963] A.C. 236, 412 said:

... 'It seems to me that any mental disorder which has manifested itself in violence and is prone to recur is a disease of the mind. At any rate it is the sort of disease for which a person should be detained in hospital rather than be given an unqualified acquittal.'

It seems to us that if there is a danger of recurrence that may be an added reason for categorising the condition as a disease of the mind. On the other hand, the absence of the danger of recurrence is not a reason for saying that it cannot be a disease of the mind. Subject to that possible qualification, we respectfully adopt Lord Denning's suggested definition.

There have been several occasions when during the course of judgments in the Court of Appeal and the House of Lords observations have been made, obiter, about the criminal responsibility of sleep-walkers, where sleep-walking has been used as a self-evident illustration of non-insane automatism. For example in the speech of Lord Denning, from which we have already cited an extract, appears this passage, at p. 409:

'No act is punishable if it is done involuntarily: and an involuntary act in this context—some people nowadays prefer to speak of it as "automatism"—means an act which is done by the muscles without any control by the mind, such as a spasm, a reflex action or a convulsion; or an act done by a person who is not conscious of what he is doing, such as an act done whilst suffering from concussion or whilst sleep-walking. The point was well put by Stephen J. in 1889: "Can anyone doubt that a man who, though he might be perfectly sane, committed what would otherwise be a crime in a state of somnambulism, would be entitled to be acquitted? And why is this? Simply because he would not know what he was doing." ' ...

We accept of course that sleep is a normal condition, but the evidence in the instant case indicates that sleep-walking, and particularly violence in sleep, is not normal. ... [I]n none of the other cases where sleep walking has been mentioned, so far as we can discover, has the court had the advantage of the sort of expert medical evidence which was available to the judge here.

One turns then to examine the evidence upon which the judge had to base his decision ... Dr d'Orban in examination-in-chief said ... [that]:

'Burgess's actions had occurred during the course of a sleep disorder.'

He was asked, 'Assuming this is a sleep associated automatism, is it an internal or external factor?' Answer: 'In this particular case, I think that one would have to see it as an internal factor.'

Then in cross-examination: Question: 'Would you go so far as to say that it was liable to recur?' Answer: 'It is possible for it to recur, yes.' Finally, in answer to a question from the judge, namely, 'Is this a case of automatism associated with a pathological condition or not?' Answer: 'I think the answer would have to be yes, because it is an abnormality of the brain function, so it would be regarded as a pathological condition.'

Dr Eames in cross-examination agreed with Dr d'Orban as to the internal rather than the external factor. He accepted that there is a liability to recurrence of sleep-walking. He could not go so far as to say that there is no liability of recurrence of serious violence but he agreed with the other medical witnesses that there is no recorded case of violence of this sort recurring.

It seems to us that on this evidence the judge was right to conclude that this was an abnormality or disorder, albeit transitory, due to an internal factor, whether functional or organic, which had manifested itself in criminality. It was a disorder or abnormality which might recur, though the possibility of it recurring in the form of serious violence was unlikely. Therefore since this was a legal problem to be answered on legal principles, it seems to us that on those principles the answer was as the judge found it to be."

**Appeal dismissed**

These two cases are highly significant. They bear witness to the continued development of the distinction between internal and external causes as a basis for determining whether a particular condition is a "disease of the mind". It has long been recognised that psychomotor epilepsy is a disease of the mind but *dicta*, at least, had placed sleep-walking into the category of non-insane automatism. What *Burgess* does is to draw the internal/external factor analysis to its logical conclusion in this respect. Given that sleep-walking has been described as a "near cousin" of epilepsy[1] and given also the medical evidence called in this case, it seems the court had little choice but to decide that sleep-walking should be perceived as arising from some internal factor. Despite efforts to show that what caused the defendant's suspension of mental faculties was his falling asleep (a perfectly normal occurrence),[2] *Burgess* in this respect is unimpeachable.

However, this distinction between internal and external causes is fundamentally flawed. We are forced to conclude that epileptics (0.5 per cent of the population) will be regarded as insane if they commit offences during epileptic fits, as will sleep-walkers. The same is true of some diabetics. Diabetics can experience hyperglycaemic episodes (triggered by too much blood sugar and caused by the diabetic condition itself) or hypoglycaemic episodes (too little blood sugar, arising from the combination of diabetes, insulin, food (or lack of it) and possibly alcohol). In *Quick and Paddison*[3] the court distinguished these two conditions holding that a transitory malfunctioning of the mind caused by *hypoglycaemia* due to external factors (for example, the taking of insulin) is non-insane automatism entitling the defendant to an acquittal. On the other hand, in *Hennessy*[4] it was held that *hyperglycaemia* gave rise to insane automatism. In this case the defendant was charged with taking a conveyance and with driving while disqualified. His defence

---

[1] Eastman, *ibid.*
[2] Mackay, "Sleepwalkers are Not Insane" (1992) 55 M.L.R. 714 at 718.
[3] [1973] Q.B. 910. See also *Bailey* [1983] 1 W.L.R. 760.
[4] [1989] 1 W.L.R. 287.

was that at the relevant time he had failed to take his proper dose of insulin due to stress, anxiety and depression and this caused the ensuing state of hyperglycaemia. The Court of Appeal accepted the *Quick and Paddison* distinction between hyper- and hypoglycaemia and rejected the defence argument that stress, anxiety and depression were factors that could count as external for the purposes of non-insane automatism. The court added that they constituted a state of mind that was prone to recur and lacked the feature of novelty or accident traditionally associated with non-insane automatism.

The result of these decisions is that we are left with a law under which some diabetics will be able to secure a complete acquittal while others will be regarded as insane. Such a position is absurd. Moreover, the harshness of these categorisations is hardly tempered by telling defendants (and their families), as Lord Diplock does in *Sullivan* and echoed by Lord Lane in *Burgess*, that the label "insanity" is merely a technical one.

The key to evaluating these cases depends upon whether the concept "disease of the mind" requires anything more than a finding that the cause is an internal one. In particular, we need to know whether there is any requirement that the internal cause be associated with violence. Lord Denning in *Bratty* stated that "any mental disorder which has manifested itself in violence and is prone to recur is a disease of the mind".[5] This was cited with approval in *Sullivan* but in *Burgess* Lord Lane said that "the absence of the danger of recurrence is not a reason for saying that it cannot be a disease of the mind". It was this that enabled his Lordship to state that the defendant in the instant case could be said to have a disease of the mind despite the fact that the experts could point to no reported incident of a sleep-walker being repeatedly violent. This modification of *Bratty* flies in the face of Lord Diplock's statement in *Sullivan* that "the purpose of the legislation relating to the defence of insanity, ever since its origin, has been to protect society against dangerous conduct". However, this social defence argument could not withstand rigorous scrutiny even before *Burgess*. For example, how can one say that epileptics are more dangerous than diabetics having a hypoglycaemic episode? Can mental disorders that do not manifest themselves in violence, for example, kleptomania, never be diseases of the mind? Nevertheless, despite such weaknesses the social defence argument did have a valuable limiting function. As a result of *Burgess* all that "disease of the mind" seems to mean is any internal factor that has, on one occasion at least, manifested itself in criminality.

This discussion demonstrates that the internal/external factor distinction is unable to bear the weight of distinguishing insanity from non-insane automatism. It highlights the failure of the insanity test (and perhaps, any insanity test) to come to terms with the issue of the responsibility of the individual defendant on the one hand, and the protection of the public (and the defendant himself) against harm on the other. We shall return to this question later, once the remaining elements of the test of insanity, and the proposals for reform thereof, have been considered.

Assuming that the defendant is suffering from a disease of the mind, the next hurdle to be overcome is that this disease of the mind must induce a "defect of reason". The reasoning ability of the defendant must be affected; it is not enough

[5] *Bratty v Attorney-General for Northern Ireland* [1963] A.C. 386 at 412.

that he simply failed to use powers of reasoning which he had.[6] This aspect of the insanity test is classically illustrative of one of the basic premises of responsibility in law: guilt cannot be adduced in the absence of the *capacity* to reason.

Having passed over the initial hurdles, the defendant may be brought within the ambit of the special verdict if either of two further conditions are satisfied. First, the defendant must not know "the nature and quality of his acts". Kenny provides a vivid example of this: "The madman who cuts a woman's throat under the idea that he is cutting a loaf of bread"[7] does not know the nature and quality of his acts. Alternatively, it must be established that the defendant does not know that his actions are "wrong". The case of *Windle*[8] decided that this means knowledge that the acts are *legally* (and not merely morally) wrong. It is often thought that this limb adds very little to the insanity test, yet research has shown that it is this part of the test that is very commonly used to secure a special verdict.[9] For example, in one case

> "a 22 year old male attempted to kill his parents because he believed that they were to be tortured and that he must kill them in order that they would die in a humane way. Two psychiatrists stated that while he knew the nature and quality of the act of stabbing his parents, he did not know that what he was doing was wrong ... His mind was plagued with delusional perceptions which confused his rational thinking to the extent that the wrongness of his act would not have been a consideration."[10]

The research also shows that a broad-brush approach is taken to this requirement. Little effort is made to distinguish between cases where the defendant does not know his actions were legally wrong and those where there is a lack of knowledge that the actions are morally wrong.[11] "In so doing, it may be argued that psychiatrists in many respects are adopting a common sense or folk psychology approach and that the courts by accepting this interpretation are, in reality, expanding the scope of the M'Naghten Rules."[12]

The courts have made it plain from *M'Naghten* onwards that they regard all these questions as legal ones for their determination. Medical evidence is, in theory, just that—evidence from which decisions can be made. However, there can be little doubt that a large part of the decision-making can rest with the medical expert. Under section 1 of the Criminal Procedure (Insanity and Unfitness to Plead) Act 1991 no verdict of not guilty by reason of insanity can be returned except on the written or oral evidence of two or more registered medical practitioners (at least one of whom has to be approved under section 12 of the Mental Health Act 1983). The reasons advanced for the introduction of this requirement are of interest. In some cases insanity verdicts had been returned without any medical evidence to support the plea.[13] Clearly, giving so little weight to the role of experts was

---

[6] *Clarke* [1972] 1 All E.R. 219.
[7] Kenny, *Outlines of Criminal Law* (17th ed.), p. 76.
[8] [1952] 2 Q.B. 826.
[9] Mackay and Kearns, "More Fact(s) about the Insanity Defence" [1999] Crim.L.R.714.
[10] Mackay, *above*, n.97, p. 104.
[11] *ibid.*
[12] Mackay and Kearns, "More Fact(s) about the Insanity Defence" [1999] Crim.L.R.714 at 723.
[13] Mackay, "Fact and Fiction about the Insanity Defence" [1990] Crim.L.R.247 at 251; Baker, "Human Rights, M'Naghten and the 1991 Act" [1994] Crim.L.R.84 at 86.

unsatisfactory. The position now, however, is that experts are called upon to do too much *if* the issue is a legal one. Medical experts may not be asked baldly: "Do you think this person is insane?" (the word would be of no medical significance in any event) but they may well be asked: "Do you think this defendant has a disease of the mind?" This intermingling of medical and legal concepts is fraught with danger and the situation is not likely to be improved by the decision in *Burgess* where, despite stating that the issues involved were legal ones, considerable reliance was placed upon the expert's statement that the defendant's condition was pathological. Further, not only may medical experts fundamentally disagree amongst themselves about a particular diagnosis but they may, if their sympathies are engaged with their "patient", distort the evidence to fit the "manifest absurdity of the M'Naghten test".[14] One possibility is that it was because neither the judiciary nor the medical experts seemed wholly convinced about their role in the adjudication process that section 1 was passed. It has been argued that it is an "effort to ensure greater congruence between the evidence necessary for a person to be found not guilty by reason of insanity and that necessary for long term detention under the Mental Health Act 1983 on grounds of mental disorder".[15] If this argument is correct then it would help to rebut a challenge that the M'Naghten Rules contravene the European Convention on Human Rights.[16] It is by no means clear, however, that section 1 was meant to be anything more than a procedural change and the Draft Criminal Code expressly rejects the assimilation of the two concepts on the basis that the definition of mental disorder under the Mental Health Act 1983 is too wide and was designed for different purposes.[17]

As matters stand, even if medical experts and judges are clear in their own minds about their respective roles, juries appear to have little role to play in most cases. Research has revealed that in 86 per cent of cases there was agreed expert evidence and the jury was simply directed (with both prosecution and defence agreement) to return a verdict of not guilty by reason of insanity.[18]

### (b) Criminal Procedure (Insanity and Unfitness to Plead) Act 1991

Before the 1991 Act the result of a finding of "not guilty by reason of insanity" was mandatory commitment to such hospital as directed by the Home Secretary (commonly a special hospital such as Ashworth, Rampton or Broadmoor) without limitation of time. Not unnaturally, defendants faced with this possibility, when their plea had originally been not guilty (because of non-insane automatism), decided in a number of instances to change their pleas to guilty; indeed, Sullivan did precisely this. Whilst research supports the view that defendants do not spend as

---

[14] Royal Commission on Capital Punishment, Cmnd.8932 (1953), p. 104.
[15] Fennell, "The Criminal Procedure (Insanity and Unfitness to Plead) Act 1991" (1992) 55 M.L.R. 547 at 549.
[16] *Below*, p. 385. See further, Baker, *above*, n.13.
[17] Law Com. Report No. 177 (1989), paras 11.26–11.28.
[18] Mackay and Kearns, *above*, no.9.

long in hospital as they might fear,[19] this forced change of plea was clearly unacceptable. Further, given the diversity of cases brought within the concept of "disease of the mind" by the development of the internal/external factor analysis, there was a pressing need for this to be reflected in the methods of disposal available to the court. It was profoundly unsatisfactory that judges could not make an order that distinguished between the treatment appropriate for an epileptic and a diabetic and a schizophrenic.

The Criminal Procedure (Insanity and Unfitness to Plead) Act 1991 enables the court to do this in all cases other than those of murder.[20] It answers the criticisms of medical experts such as Eastman who have taken the view that it "is only the mandatory commitment to hospital which results from insanity which has, teleologically, given rise to the judicial need to construct artificial mental definitions which go towards the verdict".[21]

### Criminal Procedure (Insanity and Unfitness to Plead) Act 1991, section 3:

"For section 5 of the [Criminal Procedure (Insanity) Act] 1964 Act there shall be substituted the following section—
5.—(1) This section applies where—
(a) a special verdict is returned that the accused is not guilty by reason of insanity; or
(b) findings are recorded that the accused is under a disability and that he did the act or made the omission charged against him.
(2) Subject to subsection (3) below, the court shall either—
(a) make an order that the accused be admitted, in accordance with the provisions of Schedule 1 [to this Act], to such hospital as may be specified by the Secretary of State; or
(b) where they have the power to do so by virtue of section 5 of that Act, make in respect of the accused such one of the following orders as they think most suitable in all the circumstances of the case, namely—
   (i) a guardianship order within the meaning of the Mental Health Act 1983;
   (ii) a supervision and treatment order within the meaning of Schedule 2 [of the Act]; and
   (iii) an order for his absolute discharge.
(3) Paragraph (b) of subsection (2) above shall not apply where the offence to which the special verdict or findings relate is an offence the sentence for which is fixed by law."[22]

It should be stressed that this section does nothing to alter the M'Naghten Rules themselves.[23] Indeed, it seems likely that by removing mandatory commitment reform may now be less likely than ever. Despite their limited nature, however, these reforms are welcome and, in cases other than murder, it seems that the

---

[19] Mackay, "Fact and Fiction about the Insanity Defence" [1990] Crim.L.R.247 at 251–255 and Mackay, *above*, n.96, pp. 104–105. For those detained under hospital orders with restriction orders there was a right to apply to a Mental Health Review Tribunal for discharge *within* six months of the making of the order. It is unclear if this right still exists for those who after the Act are so detained, or whether a right will only arise *after* the lapse of six months: see, Fennell, "The Criminal Procedure (Insanity and Unfitness to Plead) Act" (1992) 55 M.L.R. 547 at 554.

[20] s.5(3) Criminal Procedure (Insanity) Act 1964, as substituted by section 3 of the Criminal Procedure (Insanity and Unfitness to Plead) Act 1991.

[21] Eastman, *above*, n.99 at 24.

[22] It is unclear whether there is any right of appeal against a particular disposition since it would not appear to be an appeal against "sentence" under the Criminal Appeal Act 1968: see further, Fennell, *above*, n.15.

[23] There is an argument, canvassed earlier, that section 1 of the Act does effect a change. *Above*, p. 382.

judiciary have embraced the new flexibility[24] and that, an increase in the use of the insanity plea is occurring. For those charged with murder, the position remains unchanged; such defendants will generally continue to plead diminished responsibility[25] and may, therefore, run the risk of the prosecution introducing the defence of insanity with its consequent mandatory hospital order.

### (c) Proposals for reform

It is possible to support the M'Naghten Rules.

### American Law Institute, Model Penal Code Tent. Draft. No. 4 (1955), comments to S 4.01, pp. 156–157:

"The traditional M'Naghten rule resolves the problem solely in regard to the capacity of the individual to know what he was doing and to know that it was wrong. Absent these minimal elements of rationality, condemnation and punishment are obviously both unjust and futile. They are unjust because the individual could not, by hypothesis, have employed reason to restrain the act; he did not and he could not know the facts essential to bring reason into play. On the same ground, they are futile. A madman who believes that he is squeezing lemons when he chokes his wife or thinks that homicide is the command of God is plainly beyond reach of the restraining influence of law; he needs restraint but condemnation is entirely meaningless and ineffective. Thus the attacks on the M'Naghten rule as an inept definition of insanity or as an arbitrary definition in terms of special symptoms are entirely misconceived. The rationale of the position is that these are cases in which reason can not operate and in which it is totally impossible for individuals to be deterred. Moreover, the category defined by the rule is so extreme that to the ordinary man the exculpation of the person it encompasses bespeaks no weakness in the law. He does not identify such persons and himself; they are the world apart."[26]

However, more commonly, the M'Naghten Rules have been subjected to intense criticism.

### Report of the Committee on Mentally Abnormal Offenders (Butler Committee), Cmnd.6244 (1975), pp. 217–219:

"18.5 Almost throughout their existence the M'Naghten Rules have been criticised, generally as being based on too limited a concept of the nature of mental disorder. The Royal Commission on Capital Punishment in 1953 noted that the interpretation of the rules by the courts had been broadened and stretched to make them fit particular cases, to the point where 'the gap between the natural meaning of the law and the sense in which it is commonly applied has for so long been so wide, it is impossible to escape the conclusion that an amendment of the law, to bring it into closer conformity with the current practice, is long overdue.' The Royal Commission pointed out that many offenders who know what they are doing and that it is wrong are nevertheless undoubtedly insane and should not be held responsible for their actions. Another serious difficulty lies in the outmoded language of the rules which gives rise to problems of interpretation. It is unclear, for example, whether the

---

[24] Mackay's research revealed that in the first year of operation of the Act, in none of the six special verdict cases was a restriction order imposed; *above*, n.97, p. 107.

[25] Mackay and Kearns, "More Fact(s) about the Insanity Defence" [1999] Crim.L.R.714.

[26] See also Devlin, "Mental Abnormality and the Criminal Law" in St. J. MacDonald (ed.), *Changing Legal Objectives* (1963).

reference to the knowledge of the accused of the nature and quality of his act should be taken to cover the whole mental element in crime or some narrower concept. Similarly the nineteenth century term 'disease of the mind' raises the question whether the rules are intended to cover severe subnormality, neurosis or psychopathy.

18.6 But the main defect of the M'Naghten test is that it was based on the now obsolete belief in the pre-eminent role of reason in controlling social behaviour. It therefore requires evidence of the cognitive capacity, in particular the knowledge and understanding of the defendant at the time of the act or omission charged. Contemporary psychiatry and psychology emphasise that man's social behaviour is determined more by how he has learned to behave than by what he knows or understands. For many years a number of mental disorders differing in their clinical characteristics have been recognised and distinguished from one another. In some disorders the patient's beliefs are so bizarre or his change of mood is so profound and inexplicable, or he is so changed in manner and conduct, that his condition can only be described as alien, or mad. In such cases it is accepted opinion in civilised countries that he should not be held responsible for his actions.

18.7 Strictly interpreted the M'Naghten Rules would provide that mentally disordered defendant with very limited protection. Just as a person must generally be very mad indeed not to know what he is doing (the nature and quality of his act) when he is killing a man or setting fire to a building, so he must be very mad not to know that these acts attract the unfavourable notice of the police (his knowledge of wrong). For example, if a psychotic patient kills a person whom he believes to be putting thoughts into his mind, or kills him and gives as a reason that the victim is spying on him, or simply kills him because he has an overpowering urge to do so, the M'Naghten Rules, strictly interpreted, will not give him a defence if he admits that he knew that he was killing a man and that murder was a crime.

18.8 The M'Naghten Rules are in part linked with the *mens rea* doctrine, in recognising that evidence of disease of the mind may have the effect of negativing a mental element of the crime. The 'knowledge of wrong' test is not an application of the ordinary rules of *mens rea*, however. 'Wrong' has been held to mean 'legally wrong' and a sane defendant cannot set up a defence of ignorance of the criminal law. Knowledge of the law is hardly an appropriate test on which to base ascription of responsibility to the mentally disordered. It is a very narrow ground of exemption since even persons who are grossly disturbed generally know that murder and arson instances, are crimes. It might seem at first sight more attractive to have regard to the defendant's appreciation of what is morally wrong, but the problems in a test to the mentally disordered would be very great. 'Knowledge of wrong,' as included in M'Naghten, is not therefore a satisfactory test of criminal responsibility."

In addition to these criticisms, there is a further problem with the M'Naghten Rules. There is a very real possibility that they could be found to be incompatible with Article 5 of the European Convention on Human Rights. This provision protects the right of individuals to "liberty and security of person" and deprivation of this right has to be "in accordance with a procedure prescribed by law". Further, "persons of unsound mind" can only be detained where proper account of objective medical expertise has been taken. This has been interpreted to mean that there must be a strong relationship between legal and medical criteria used to assess those who are insane.[27] The potential for being found in breach is strongest in relation to defendants who currently fall within the M'Naghten Rules because of, say, epilepsy or diabetes (which results in hyperglycaemia). In these cases the gap between medical and legal criteria is enormous. However, Article 5 would only be

[27] *Winterwerp v The Netherlands* (1979) 2 E.H.R.R. 387. See further, Sutherland and Gearty, "Insanity and the European Court of Human Rights" [1992] Crim.L.R.418.

breached if, after having been found not guilty by reason of insanity, an order depriving the individual of liberty were to be made. If, as seems likely in such cases, non-custodial orders were made, there would be no breach.

Although the 1991 Act has, therefore, rendered one form of challenge less likely, murder still results in mandatory commitment and this may be in contravention of Article 5. Further, although section 1 states that no person can be found not guilty by reason of insanity unless two doctors have given evidence, the weight to be given to this evidence is unspecified. Certainly it is not binding because, as we have seen, the test of insanity is regarded as a legal one. The result may be again that M'Naghten contravenes the Convention.[28]

Further reform has been proposed. The Butler Committee on Mentally Abnormal Offenders[29] reported in 1975 that major reform was necessary but this Report has been ignored by successive governments. The Law Commission has also recommended reform.

### Draft Criminal Code Bill (1989) (Law Com. No. 177), clauses 35–36:

"35.—(1) A mental disorder verdict shall be returned if the defendant is proved to have committed an offence but it is proved on the balance of probabilities (whether by the prosecution or by the defendant) that he was at the time suffering from severe mental illness or severe mental handicap.

(2) Subsection (1) does not apply if the court or jury is satisfied beyond reasonable doubt that the offence was not attributable to the severe mental illness or severe mental handicap.

36. A mental disorder verdict shall be returned if—

(a) the defendant is acquitted of an offence only because, by reason of evidence of mental disorder or a combination of mental disorder and intoxication, it is found that he acted or may have acted in a state of automatism, or without the fault required for the offence, or believing that an exempting circumstance existed; and

(b) it is proved on the balance of probabilities (whether by the prosecution or by the defendant) that he was suffering from mental disorder at the time of the act."

These proposals, which are mainly based on the Butler Committee's recommendations, would constitute a significant improvement on the present law.[30] The new verdict of not guilty by reason of mental disorder would not only build upon recent reforms by not leading to mandatory commitment[31] but the new label would also avoid the offensive stigma that surrounds a finding of insanity. Because of these changes mental disorder has been defined[32] so that it would not be possible to distinguish between the epileptic, the diabetic and the defendant with a

---

[28] Indeed, this view was accepted in Jersey at first instance (Mackay and Gearty, "On Being Insane in Jersey—the case of *Attorney-General v Jason Prior*" [2001] Crim.L.R.560). However, the appeal court disagreed (Mackay, "On Being Insane in Jersey Part Two—the Appeal in *Jason Prior v Attorney-General*" [2002] Crim.L.R.728).

[29] Cmnd.6244 (1975).

[30] See further, Wasik, "Codification: Mental Disorder and Intoxication under the Draft Criminal Code" (1986) 50 J.Crim.L. 393. For an earlier defence of the Butler proposals see Dell, "Wanted; An Insanity Defence that can be Used" [1983] Crim.L.R.431. But see the *Report of the Committee on the Penalty for Homicide* (1993), p. 33 where the proposals found little support among some psychiatrists.

[31] The Draft Code does not address the issue of disposal in detail although the drafters were clearly committed to flexible powers of disposal (paras 11.34–11.36). Clause 39 provides for the drafting of a Schedule concerning such powers. Whether this would merely reflect the reforms contained in the 1991 Act or whether flexibility would also extend to murder is unclear.

[32] In Clause 34.

brain tumour: "(i)f any of these conditions causes a state of automatism in which the sufferer commits what would otherwise be an offence of violence, his acquittal should be on evidence of 'mental disorder' ".[33] If these proposals were enacted the possibility of a challenge under the European Convention on Human Rights would certainly be lessened[34] but the reforms, welcome though they be, may not do enough to satisfy critics. The model adopted is still one of social defence and it still results in, for example, epileptics being dealt with in the same way as those who are mentally ill.[35]

In contrast to England where reform proposals have been left on the shelf, the United States has witnessed a remarkable series of reforms. Initially, based upon the formula of the Model Penal Code,[36] the insanity laws were widened to include those who could not control their actions (sometimes referred to as irresistible impulse). The inclusion of this volitional limb in the test was never without its critics: some believed that the test was too broad and others argued that it was simply not possible to identify those who could not control their actions. These doubts, particularly as voiced by the anti-crime, pro-victim lobby, were fuelled by the highly controversial acquittal of John Hinckley on the ground of insanity, after he had attempted to murder President Reagan.[37] The insanity defence was thought to have been blatantly misused with expensive defence lawyers hoodwinking juries into false acquittals. It was also said that dangerous persons were being given early release from psychiatric detention after having been "cured", only to commit further serious crimes.[38]

In fact, evidence fails to support either of these criticisms of the operation of the defence.[39] In reality, just as in this country, the insanity defence in the United States is very rarely used and even more rarely successful.[40] However, the combination of myth and valid criticism led to rapid and widespread reform. In some states reform has done nothing more than change the description of the verdict to "not responsible by reason of insanity" on the basis that public reaction to the Hinckley verdict was based upon a misunderstanding.[41] A number of states have shifted the burden of proof from the prosecution to the defence to prove that the defendant was insane. The fact that in the District of Columbia, unlike in England, the prosecution had to prove that Hinckley was sane was thought to be one of the main reasons he was acquitted.[42] Sometimes, in addition to this change, the standard of

---

[33] Draft Criminal Code (1989), Law Com. No. 177, p. 224.

[34] But not eliminated: it is unclear, for example, whether mandatory commitment would be retained in the case of murder and the weight to be given to medical evidence remains problematic.

[35] For a recent critique (relating to Scottish law), based upon capacity-responsibility, see Tadros, "Insanity and the Capacity for Criminal Responsibility" [2000] Edinburgh Law Review 325.

[36] The American Law Institute, Model Penal Code, Proposed Official Draft, 1962, s.4.01 was approved by statute in 29 states and all federal courts by 1982.

[37] *USA v Hinckley* Criminal No. 81, 306 US Dt. Ct. for the District of Columbia, 525 F. Supp. 1342, Nov. 17, 1981.

[38] Brooks, "The Merits of Abolishing the Insanity Defense" (1985) 477 *The Annals* 125 at 126.

[39] Steadman, "Empirical Research on the Insanity Defense" (1985) 477 *The Annals* 58; Perlin, *The Jurisprudence of the Insanity Defense* (1994).

[40] National Advisory Commission, *Myths and Realities: A Report of the National Commission on the Insanity Defense* (1983).

[41] For example, Indiana: Ind. Stat. 35–36–2–3, s.3(3).

[42] About two-thirds of those states which accept the insanity defence now place the burden of proof upon the defendant, normally by a preponderance of the evidence (Mackay, *above*, n.97, p. 117).

proof has also been raised.[43] Other states have abandoned the "capacity to conform" test in a remarkable return to a modernised version of the M'Naghten Rules.[44] Other states have introduced new verdicts of "guilty but mentally ill" as alternatives to the existing verdict.[45] However, as we shall see, a few states have been much more radical and have rejected the insanity defence altogether.[46]

### (d) Should the insanity defence be retained?

There are critics who would still be profoundly dissatisfied even if reforms of the type indicated above were to take place. It is their belief that the insanity defence ought to be completely abolished. Most, although not all, of these attacks have taken place in the United States and the reasoning behind them embraces arguments of principle about the concept of responsibility as well as mistaken assessments of the danger to which the public are exposed by abuse of the insanity defence.

### (1) *Procedural criticisms*

There are very real problems of procedure in this area: expert evidence often conflicts, trials may be long, the difficulty of sifting through the evidence to assess accountability is immense, but, as Fletcher points out, "it is curious to argue from these problems to the conclusion that the defence ought to be abolished. Would anyone wish to abolish the defence of duress because it might be difficult to establish whether the accused was fairly capable of resisting pressure exerted against him?"[47]

### (2) *Therapeutic criticisms*

### A. W. B. Simpson, "The Butler Committee's Report: The Legal Aspects" (1976) 16 Brit.J.Criminol. 175 at 176:

"If one takes the central recommendation of the Butler Committee on the disposal of mentally disordered 'offenders'[48]—'the guiding principle in disposal of mentally disordered offenders by the courts is that they should be sent wherever they can best be given the treatment they need: generally treatment by the health services is appropriate'—one cannot but be struck by the incongruity of involving criminal courts in the matter at all. What are

---

[43] For example, in Arizona the defendant must prove insanity by "clear and convincing evidence" (Ariz. Rev. Stat. An. S.13–502(b) (1984)).

[44] Federal law was changed by the Insanity Reform Act 1984 (see Title 18 of the United States Code). In relation to state law see, for example, California Penal Code (supp. 1987), s.25(b). Research has shown that such revised tests have had little impact upon the number of successful insanity pleas: Steadman *et al.*, *Before and After Hinckley: Evaluating Insanity Defense Reform* (1993), p. 142. Alaska has gone even further. A defendant will only have a defence where "as a result of a mental disease or defect, [he or she was unable] to appreciate the nature and quality of that conduct" (Alaska Stat. 12.47.010(a)). However, it seems that the abolition of the second limb of the M'Naghten rules has been compensated for by a broad interpretation of the retained first limb: *Patterson v State*, 708 P.2d 712 (Alaska App. 1985).

[45] The additional verdict was introduced to give juries a choice and to reduce the number of acquittals on the basis of insanity. Research suggests that it has made very little impact upon the success rate of insanity pleas overall but that the success rate for violent crimes has declined: Steadman *et al.*, *above*, n.39, p. 114. See further, Mackay, *above*, n.69, pp. 118–121.

[46] *Below*, p. 392.

[47] *Rethinking Criminal Law* (1978), p. 845.

[48] Adopted in the Draft Criminal Code, *above*, n.33.

red judges doing performing functions which, in the case of measles or mumps, we assign to general practitioners and supporting medical staff? It is as if a doctor, lighting on a case where a patient contracted a chill whilst stealing, took to prescribing aspirins and six months in the local prison.

This fundamental incongruity makes it extremely difficult, and perhaps impossible, to produce a set of recommendations designed to adapt a penal system to a task utterly out of character with the nature of such a system."

### (3) *Criminal Law v Mental Health Powers*

Commentators have increasingly voiced doubts about the uneasy mixture of the criminal law and its objectives with the power of courts under Mental Health legislation to confine dangerous people to hospitals. Some critics of the insanity defence have argued that discussion of mental disorder should be limited to the issue of *mens rea*. If the mental condition of the defendant negated the *mens rea* required for the offence, then no further criminal questions could arise—the defendant would be entitled to an acquittal. There would, however, remain the separate issue of civil commitment.

### J. Goldstein and J. Katz, "Abolish the 'Insanity Defense'—Why Not?" (1963) 72 Yale L.J. 853 at 854–855, 862–864, 865:

" 'Insanity,' however formulated, has been considered a defense. An evaluation of such a defence rests on first identifying a need for an exception to criminal liability. Unless a conflict can be discovered between some basic objective of the criminal law and its application to an 'insane' person, there can be no purpose for 'insanity' as a defence. Until a purpose is uncovered, debates about the appropriateness of any insanity defence formula as well as efforts to evaluate various formulae with respect to the present state of psychiatric knowledge are destined to continue to be frustrating and fruitless. ...

In enunciating yet another formula for insanity, the Court of Appeals for the Third Circuit in *United States v Currens* (1961) (290 F.2d 751, 773, (3d Cir. 1961)) contaminates its thinking by confusing and merging the inherently incompatible concepts of 'insanity' as a defense to a crime with 'insanity' as evidence to cast doubt on a material element of an offense. It suggests ... in *Durham*, that some relationship exists between the insanity defence and *mens rea*, a material element of every major crime.

And the court criticized the *Durham*[49] and *M'Naghten* formulae because:

'They do not take account of the fact that an "insane" defendant commits the *crime* not because his mental illness causes him to do a certain prohibited act but because the totality of his personality is such, because of mental illness, that he has lost the capacity to control his acts in the way that the normal individual can and does control them. If this effect has taken place he must be found not to possess the guilty mind, the *mens rea*, necessary to constitute his prohibited act *a crime*.' (at p. 774).

At this point the court by the force of its own reasoning *should* have been led to say:

'Without the essential element of *mens rea*, there is no crime from which to relieve the defendant of liability and consequently, since no crime has been committed, there is no need for formulating an insanity defence.'

But instead the court actually concludes:

'We are of the opinion that the following (insanity) formula most nearly fulfills the objectives just discussed. ...'

The court uses the word 'crime' first to mean 'dangerous conduct' and then, without alerting itself to the shift, to mean technically the establishment beyond doubt of each material element of an offence. With this sleight of thought the court shifts focus from

---

[49] (1954) 214 F.2d 862. The test formulated in this case was that the defendant was not criminally responsible if his actions were the product of mental disease or mental defect.

'insanity' as a *defense* to conduct 'otherwise criminal' to insanity as *evidence* to negate an element essential to categorizing the accused's conduct 'criminal.'

In announcing a new formula for the insanity defence, the court fails to recognize that there is no need for such a defence to remove criminal liability since it has concluded that no crime is established once mental illness (however defined) has cast doubt on *mens rea* (however defined). Conceptually, at least, outright acquittal would result and instructions to the jury would reflect a time, pre-*M'Naghten*, when evidence of mental condition, like any other relevant evidence, was used to cast doubt on a material element of the crime. . . .

In our efforts to understand the suggested relationship between 'insanity' and '*mens rea*' there emerges a purpose for the 'insanity defense' which, though there to be seen, has remained of extremely low visibility. That purpose seems to be obscured because thinking about such a relationship has generally been blocked by unquestioning and disarming references to our collective conscience and our religious and moral traditions. Assuming the existence of the suggested relationship between 'insanity' and '*mens rea*,' the defence is not to absolve of criminal responsibility 'sick' persons who would otherwise be subject to criminal sanction. Rather, its real function is to authorize the state to hold those 'who must be found not to possess the guilty mind *mens rea*,' even though the criminal law demands that no person be held criminally responsible if doubt is cast on any material element of the offense charged. . . .

What this discussion indicates, then, is that the insanity defense is not designed, as is the defence of self-defense, to define an exception to criminal liability, but rather to define for sanction and exception from among those who would be free of liability. It is as if the insanity defense were prompted by an affirmative answer to the silently posed question: 'Does *mens rea* or any essential element of an offense exclude from liability a group of persons whom the community wishes to restrain?' If the suggested relationship between *mens rea* and 'insanity' means that 'insanity' precludes proof beyond doubt of *mens rea* then the 'defense' is designed to authorize the holding of persons who have committed no crime. So conceived, the problem really facing the criminal process has been how to obtain authority to sanction the 'insane' who would be excluded from liability by an overall application of the general principles of the criminal law.

Furthermore, even if the relationship between insanity and '*mens rea*' is rejected, this same purpose re-emerges when we try to understand why the consequence of this defense, unlike other defenses, is restraint, not release."

### Norval Morris, Madness and the Criminal Law (1982), pp. 31–32, 61–64:

"It is the overarching theme of this book that injustice and inefficiency invariably flow from any blending of the criminal-law and mental health powers of the state. Each is sufficient unto itself to achieve a just balance between freedom and authority; each has its own interested constituency; when they are mixed together, only the likelihood of injustice is added. . . .

My belief is that practice and scholarship have been led astray by the following ambivalent and corruptive reaction: though he has done a criminal act, being mentally abnormal he is less guilty in moral terms; St. Peter may indeed hold him morally faultless or at least less blameworthy and so should we; but also he is different from the rest of us, strange and probably more dangerous, and therefore, since he has committed a crime, we had better for his sake and ours separate him from the community or prolong his separation, for his treatment and our protection. We are at the same time more forgiving and more fearful, less punitive and more self-protective; we wish to have it both ways. . . .

[From this position Morris goes on to attack the notion that we seek to identify the truly responsible by means of an insanity defence]. [The central issue is] the question of fairness, the sense that it is unjust and unfair to stigmatize the mentally ill as criminals and to punish them for their crimes. The criminal law exists to deter and to punish those who would or who would choose to do wrong. If they cannot exercise choice, they cannot be deterred and it is a moral outrage to punish them. The argument sounds powerful but its premise is weak.

Choice is neither present nor absent in the typical case where the insanity defense is currently pleaded; what is at issue is the degree of freedom of choice on a continuum from the hypothetically entirely rational to the hypothetically pathologically determined—in states of consciousness neither polar condition exists.

The moral issue sinks into the sands of reality. Certainly it is true that in a situation of total absence of choice it is outrageous to inflict punishment; but the frequency of such situations to the problems of criminal responsibility becomes an issue of fact in which tradition and clinical knowledge and practice are in conflict. The traditions of being possessed of evil spirits, of being bewitched, confront the practices of a mental health system which increasingly fashions therapeutic practices to hold patients responsible for their conduct. And suppose we took the moral argument seriously and eliminated responsibility in those situations where we thought there had been a substantial impairment of the capacity to choose between crime and no crime (I set aside problems of strict liability and of negligence for the time being). Would we not have to, as a matter of moral fairness, fashion a special defense of gross social adversity? The matter might be tested by asking which is the more criminogenic, psychosis or serious social deprivation? ...

[A]t first blush, it seems a perfectly legitimate correlational and, I submit, causal inquiry, whether psychosis, or any particular type of psychosis, is more closely related to criminal behaviour than, say, being born to a one-parent family living on welfare in a black inner-city area. And there is no doubt of the empirical answer. Social adversity is grossly more potent in its pressure toward criminality, certainly toward all forms of violence and street crime as distinct from white-collar crime, than is any psychotic condition. As a factual matter, the exogenous pressures are very much stronger than the endogenous.

But the argument feels wrong. Surely there is more to it than the simple calculation of criminogenic impact. Is this unease rationally based? I think not, though the question certainly merits further consideration. As a rational matter it is hard to see why one should be more responsible for what is done to one than for what one is. Yet major contributions to jurisprudence and criminal-law theory insist that it is necessary to maintain the denial of responsibility on grounds of mental illness to preserve the moral infrastructure of the criminal law. For many years I have struggled with this opinion by those whose work I deeply respect, yet I remain unpersuaded. Indeed, they really don't try to persuade, but rather affirm and reaffirm with vehemence and almost mystical sincerity the necessity of retaining the special defense of insanity as a moral prop to the entire criminal law.[50]

And indeed I think that much of the discussion of the defense of insanity is the discussion of a myth rather than of a reality. It is no minor debating point that in fact we lack a defense of insanity as an operating tool of the criminal law other than in relation to a very few particularly heinous and heavily punished offenses. There is not an operating defense of insanity in relation to burglary or theft, or the broad sweep of index crimes generally; the plea of not guilty on the ground of insanity is rarely to be heard in city courts of first instance which handle the grist of the mill of the criminal law—though a great deal of pathology is to be seen in the parade of accused and convicted persons before these courts. As a practical matter we reserve this defense for a few sensational cases where it may be in the interest of the accused either to escape the possibility of capital punishment (though in cases where serious mental illness is present, the risk of execution is slight) or where the likely punishment is of a sufficient severity to make the indeterminate commitment of the accused a preferable alternative to a criminal conviction. Operationally the defense of insanity is a tribute, it seems to me, to our hypocrisy rather than to our morality.

To be less aggressive about the matter and to put aside anthropomorphic allegations of hypocrisy, the special defense of insanity may properly be indicted as producing a morally unsatisfactory classification on the continuum between guilt and innocence. It applies in practice to only a few mentally ill criminals, thus omitting many others with guilt-reducing

---

[50] Morse, "Retaining a Modified Insanity Defence" (1985) 477 The Annals 137 at 139–140 argues that the case for a defence of "social adversity or disadvantage" is misconceived. It may well be a powerful cause of *criminal* behaviour but has nothing to do with rationality.

relationships between their mental illness and their crimes; it excludes other powerful pressures on human behaviour, thus giving excessive weight to the psychological over the social. It is a false classification in the sense that if a team of the world's most sensitive and trained psychiatrists and moralists were to select from all those found guilty of felonies and those found not guilty by reason of insanity any given number who should not be stigmatized as criminals, very few of those found not guilty by reason of insanity would be selected."

Morris concludes that the mentally disordered are entitled to be held responsible for their actions, but that their condition may be relevant in sentencing and might result in mitigation on grounds of less moral blameworthiness, or aggravation because of constituting a danger to the public.

### (4) *Denial of responsibility*

#### Baroness Wootton, Crime and the Criminal Law (2nd ed., 1981), pp. 90–91:

"At a more fundamental level, acceptance of mental disorder as diminishing or *eliminating* criminal responsibility demands an ability to get inside someone else's mind so completely as to be certain whether he has acted wilfully or knowingly, and also to experience the strength of the temptations to which he is exposed. This, I submit, is beyond the competence of even the most highly qualified expert. Psychiatrists may uncover factors in patients' backgrounds (often in terms of childhood experience) by which they profess to 'explain' why one individual has an urge to strangle young girls and another to rape elderly women: but these 'explanations' are merely predictive of the *likelihood* of such behaviour occurring. ...

I submit, therefore, that the present law, under which offenders must be classified as either mentally disordered or criminally responsible for their actions not only produces anomalies but attempts the impossible. ... In the end it would seem that for practical purposes we are brought to the paradoxical conclusion that, if a person's crimes are by ordinary standards only moderately objectionable, he should be regarded as wicked and liable to appropriate punishment, but if his wickedness goes beyond a certain point (when we cannot comprehend how anyone could commit such a crime) it ceases to be wickedness at all and becomes a medical condition."

At least some of Baroness Wootton's arguments would be supported by those who have secured wide-ranging reform of the insanity laws in the United States following the acquittal of John Hinckley.[51] Indeed, some states have become so disenchanted with the insanity defence that, rather than amend it, they have completely abolished it.[52] Where this reform has taken place, the trend has been to restrict the role of insanity to one of determining whether the defendant lacked the necessary mental state for the definition of the crime. If for this reason the defendant cannot be convicted of an offence, then automatic civil commitment follows.

The effect of this is, of course, to make *mens rea* even more important and this aspect of reform of the insanity defence would have found no favour at all with Baroness Wootton. Her view (explored earlier in connection with the desirability

[51] *Above*, n.37.
[52] Montana (Mont. Code s.46–14–102 (1985)), Idaho (Idaho Code 18–207 (1986 Supp.)) and Utah (Utah Code Ann. ss.77–35–21 (1986 Supp.)). See, further, Mackay, *Mental Condition Defences in the Criminal Law* (1995), pp. 123–131.

of strict liability[53]), was that the entire assessment of responsibility was a futile one and that questions relating to the mental state of the defendant ought to be reserved for the post-conviction, sentencing stage.

In complete contrast to Baroness Wootton we may examine the views of Szasz, a psychologist who embraces so whole-heartedly the concept of responsibility that he feels everyone ought to be regarded as sane and accountable for their actions.

### T. S. Szasz, "The Myth of Mental Illness" (1960) 15 American Psychologist 113 at 115–118:

"[A] currently prevalent claim [is that] ... mental illness is just as 'real' and 'objective' as bodily illness. ... This is a confusing claim since it is never known exactly what is meant by such words as 'real' and 'objective.' I suspect, however, that what is intended by the proponents of this view is to create the idea in the popular mind that mental illness is some sort of disease entity, like an infection or a malignancy. If this were true, one could *catch* or *get* a 'mental illness,' one might *have* or harbour it, one might transmit it to others, and finally one could get rid of it. In my opinion there is not a shred of evidence to support this view. To the contrary, all the evidence is the other way and supports the view that what people now call mental illnesses are for the most part communications expressing unacceptable ideas, often framed, moreover in an unusual idiom. ...

[T]he diversity of human values and the methods by means of which they may be realized is so vast ... that they cannot fail but lead to conflicts in human relations. Indeed, to say that human relations at all levels from mother to child, through husband and wife, to nation and nation—are fraught with stress, strain and disharmony is, once again, making the obvious explicit. ... I submit that the idea of mental illness is now being put to work to obscure certain difficulties which at present may be inherent—not that they need be unmodifiable—in the social intercourse of persons. If this is true, the concept functions as a disguise; for instead of calling attention to conflicting human needs, aspirations and values, the notion of mental illness provides an amoral and impersonal 'thing' (an illness) as an explanation for *problems in living*. We may recall in this connection that not so long ago it was devils and witches who were held responsible for men's problems in social living. The belief in mental illness, as something other than man's trouble in getting along with his fellow man, is the proper heir to the belief in demonology and witchcraft. Mental illness exists or is 'real' in exactly the same sense in which witches existed or were 'real.'

... The myth of mental illness encourages us, moreover, to believe in its logical corollary: that social intercourse would be harmonious, satisfying and the secure basis of a good life were it not for the disrupting influences of mental illness. The potentiality for universal human happiness, in this form at least, seems to me but another example of the I-wish-it-were-true type of fantasy. I do believe that human happiness or well-being on a hitherto unimaginably large scale, and not for a select few, is possible. This goal could be achieved, however, only at the cost of many men, and not just a few being willing and able to tackle their personal, social and ethical conflicts. This means having the courage and integrity to forgo waging battles on false fronts, finding solutions for substitute problems— for instance, fighting the battle of stomach acid and chronic fatigue instead of facing up to a marital conflict. ...

My argument [is] ... limited to the proposition that mental illness is a myth, whose function it is to disguise and thus render more palatable the bitter pill of moral conflicts in human relations."

One final insight might be considered.

---

[53] *Above*, p. 240.

## D. L. Rosenhan, "On being Sane in Insane Places" (1973) 179 Science 250 at 250–258:

"If sanity and insanity exist, how shall we know them?

The question is neither capricious nor itself insane. However much we may be personally convinced that we can tell the normal from the abnormal, the evidence is simply not compelling. It is commonplace, for example, to read about murder trials wherein eminent psychiatrists for the defense are contradicted by equally eminent psychiatrists for the prosecution on the matter of the defendant's sanity. More generally, there are a great deal of conflicting data on the reliability, utility and meaning of such terms as 'sanity,' 'insanity,' 'mental illness' and 'schizophrenia' ... what is viewed as normal in one culture may be seen as quite aberrant in another. Thus, notions of normality and abnormality may not be quite so accurate as people believe they are ... [this] in no way questions the fact that some behaviours are deviant or odd.

[Rosenhan then goes on to describe the nature of the research he had undertaken; 8 sane people gained secret admission to 12 different hospitals, all complained that they had heard voices, saying in particular, 'thud,' 'hollow and empty.' In all other respects (save their name and if necessary their profession) the pseudo-patients told the truth about their feelings, their background, and their present lives. The aim of the research was to ascertain whether and how the sane people would be detected. If they were, it would be some support at least for the view that sanity and insanity are distinct enough to be recognised wherever they occur. *All* the pseudo-patients were admitted to hospital, whereupon they ceased simulating any symptoms of abnormality but behaved as they 'normally' behaved.]

Despite their public 'show' of sanity, the pseudo-patients were never detected. Admitted, except in one case, with a diagnosis of schizophrenia each was discharged after hospitalisation of between 7 to 52 days, with a diagnosis of schizophrenia 'in remission.' The label 'in remission' should in no way be dismissed as a mere formality, for at no time during any hospitalisation had any question been raised about any pseudo-patients' simulation. Nor are there any indications in hospital records that the pseudo-patients status was suspect. Rather, the evidence was strong that once labelled schizophrenic, the pseudo-patient was stuck with that label. If the pseudo-patient was to be discharged, he must naturally be 'in remission'; but he was not sane, nor in the institutions' view, had he ever been sane. ...

The facts of the matter are that we have known for a long time that diagnoses are often not useful or reliable, but we have nevertheless continued to use them. We now know that we cannot distinguish insanity from sanity. It is depressing to consider how that information will be used.

Not merely depressing but frightening. How many people, one wonders are sane but not recognised as such by our psychiatric institutions? How many have been needlessly stripped of their privileges of citizenship, from the right to vote and drive to that of handling their own accounts? How many have feigned insanity in order to avoid the criminal consequences of their behaviour, and conversely, how many would rather stand trial than live interminably in a psychiatric hospital—but are wrongly thought to be mentally ill? ... The label sticks, a mark of inadequacy forever.

Finally, how many patients might be 'sane' outside psychiatric hospital but seem insane in it—not because craziness resides in them, as it were, but because they are responding to a bizarre setting."[54]

---

[54] Rosenhan, himself one of the researchers, describes the depersonalisation that took place in the wards, "At times, depersonalisation reached such proportions that pseudo-patients had the sense that they were invisible, or at least unworthy of account. ... A nurse unbuttoned her uniform to adjust her brassiere in the presense of an entire ward of viewing men. One did not have the sense that she was being seductive. Rather, she didn't notice us." The pseudo-patients found themselves trying to assert some individuality, some link with their "real" lives to fight off the depersonalisation. The implication is that the other patients might respond similarly with outbreaks of personality which will then be seen as indicative of their need for treatment.

How are we to respond to arguments such as these? Do they constitute a persuasive case for abolition that "trumps" the arguments addressed in the introductory discussion of this defence? Fletcher, for example, remains unconvinced.

### George P. Fletcher, Rethinking the Criminal Law (1978), p. 846:

"The criminal law expresses respect for the autonomy of the sane as much as it shows compassion for the insane. The line between the two may shift over time. Our theories of sanity may change. But the line remains. If the criminal law is to be an institution expressing respect as well as compassion, its institutions must be able both to punish the guilty and excuse the weak. These two sentiments depend on each other. Compassion is possible only so far as punishment is the norm. Punishing wrongdoing is possible only so far as we have a concept of accountability for wrongdoing. Respect for autonomy and compassion for the weak are too important to our culture to be easily shaken by the skeptics."

## C. *Automatism*

In the two preceding sections we have seen that non-insane automatism (commonly termed simply "automatism") entitles a defendant to a complete acquittal and that, fearful of allowing too many such acquittals, the law has rigorously circumscribed the parameters of the defence of automatism. This has been achieved, in particular, by insisting that the defendant be blameless in causing the state of automatism and by adopting a broad definition of "disease of the mind" to ensure that in many cases, where there is the slightest risk of repetition of the conduct, the defendant is adjudged insane giving the courts power to make orders in relation to that person.

There have been two main consequences of this restrictive approach. First, the number of situations in which automatism can be successfully pleaded are few and far between. Apart from hypoglycaemia, already discussed, it would appear that it is only in cases involving isolated incidents of an external cause prompting the involuntary behaviour that the defence will be available. Examples would include physical compulsion (for example, being pushed over so as to injure another) and reflex actions of external origin (for example, reflexive movements while being attacked by a swarm of bees[55]). More problematic is involuntary action caused by a blow. Clearly a physical blow which causes concussion will qualify here. But, in some cases, there might be a less immediate connection between the "blow" and the automatic behaviour. In *T*[56] the defendant, on a charge of robbery and assault causing actual bodily harm, claimed that she had been raped three days previously and that this caused her to suffer from post-traumatic stress disorder with the result that she was in a state of psychogenic fugue rendering her actions automatic. At her trial it was ruled that she was entitled to have this defence put to the jury as one of non-insane automatism. (The jury convicted her.) It is, however, extremely doubtful whether the law would extend this to purely non-physical psychological "blows" such as receiving a shock or distressing news. In such a situation it has been held that the ensuing behaviour has its source in the internal psychological or emotional condition of the defendant thus rendering the case one of insanity.[57] Such

---

[55] *Hill v Baxter* [1958] 1 Q.B. 277.
[56] [1990] Crim.L.R.256.
[57] *Rabey* [1980] S.C.R. 513 (Canada).

distinctions are, however, difficult to sustain. It seems unlikely that the post-traumatic stress disorder in *T* was purely the product of the physical impact of the rape; presumably it was the psychological shock thereof that produced this state. Given the law's reluctance to expand the category of automatism, it seems unlikely that the approach adopted in *T* would be approved if tested in the appellate courts.

Another problematic cause of "involuntary" behaviour is hypnotism. There are *dicta* in *Quick*[58] to the effect that this could give rise to automatism. On the other hand, it seems unlikely that the courts would go so far as to hold that "brainwashing" can lead to automatic behaviour.[59] Such a holding would be dangerously close to concluding that a person's unfortunate upbringing should exempt him or her from criminal liability.

The second consequence of the courts' restrictive interpretation of automatism and expansive interpretation of insanity has been to force many defendants to plead guilty. The defendants in both *Sullivan* and *Hennessy*, discussed earlier, changed their pleas to guilty as soon as it was ruled that their defence was, in reality, one of insanity. These cases were both decided before the Criminal Procedure (Insanity and Unfitness to Plead) Act 1991 at which time all defendants found not guilty by reason of insanity faced mandatory indefinite commitment. The reforms effected in the 1991 Act are producing a slow increase in the use of the plea in non-murder cases; thus it would appear that the fear which induced defendants to change their plea is dissipating as the courts show their willingness to use the more flexible powers given to them under the 1991 Act.[60] However, mandatory commitment is still the only disposal available in murder cases. Such defendants very rarely plead insanity; instead, they rely upon diminished responsibility and many of these cases are dealt with by a guilty plea. The situation remains, therefore, that some defendants, who might properly be found to lack responsibility for their actions, are being found guilty.

There is a great deal of dissatisfaction with the present response of the law to the problem of automatism. Along with proposals to modify the insanity defence have come suggested reforms of the law of non-insane automatism.

### Draft Criminal Code Bill 1989 (Law Com. No. 177), clause 33:

"(1) A person is not guilty of an offence if—
  (a) he acts in a state of automatism, that is, his act—
    (i) is a reflex, spasm, or convulsion; or
    (ii) occurs while he is in a condition (whether of sleep, unconsciousness, impaired consciousness or otherwise) depriving him of effective control of the act; and
  (b) the act or condition is the result neither of anything done or omitted with the fault required for the offence nor of voluntary intoxication."

As the examples in the Draft Criminal Code make clear, this provision would still be denied to the epileptic and hyperglycaemic diabetic who would be dealt with under the mental disorder provisions.[61] The diabetic in a hypoglycaemic state would, however, be protected, as would (unlike the present position) the

---

[58] [1973] 1 Q.B. 910.
[59] Clarkson, *Understanding Criminal Law* (3rd ed., 2001), p. 40.
[60] Mackay and Kearns, "More Fact(s) About the Insanity Defence" [1999] Crim.L.R.714 at 716.
[61] Draft Criminal Code Bill 1989 (Law Com. No. 177), examples to cl.36.

sleep-walker *if* the sleep-walking episode was not a feature of an underlying condition and, therefore, not prone to recur.[62]

Finally, we need to examine whether this whole approach is sound. Should automatism provide a complete defence?

The result may be open to doubt at two levels.

### (i) Psychiatry's view of the automaton's true state of mind

### David Henderson and R. D. Gillespie, A Textbook of Psychiatry (7th ed., 1950), pp. 125, 191:

"A *somnambulism* is a general automatism occurring in the course of, and interrupting, normal sleep. In this condition the patient rises from sleep, disregards the ordinary significance of his environment and those in it, and behaves as if he were living in an environment conjured up by himself. If spoken to, not brusquely, he may reply in terms of the phantasy which he is enacting. If roughly stimulated, he may regain full consciousness, or pass into a trance state of immobility, muscular flaccidity and total lack of response of any kind. Patients in somnambulic states have sometimes met with unfortunate accidents, *e.g.* scalding, or even death from drowning. ...

During the somnambulism the patient commonly lives through a vivid experience, little or not at all related to his surroundings, and therefore hallucinatory in character. By talking to him, not insistently, but in a persuasive attempt to enter into his experience, the patient may be got to describe the nature of the experience while he is still in the somnambulistic state. Although such patients appear to be 'walking in their sleep' they are not really asleep. Their perceptions are often acute."

### Robert W. White, The Abnormal Personality (1948), pp. 203–205, 288:

"A colour-sergeant was carrying a message, riding his motorcycle through a dangerous section of the front. All at once it was several hours later and he was pushing his motorcycle along the streets of a coastal town nearly a hundred miles away. In utter bewilderment he gave himself up to the military police, but he could tell absolutely nothing of his long trip. The amnesia was ultimately broken by the use of hypnosis. The man then remembered that he was thrown down by a shell explosion, that he picked up himself and his machine, that he started straight for the coastal town, that he studied signs and asked for directions in order to reach this destination.

It is clear, in this case, that the amnesia entailed no loss of competence. The patient's actions were purposive, rational, and intelligent. The amnesia rested only on his sense of personal identity. The conflict was between fear, suddenly intensified by his narrow escape and duty to complete the dangerous mission. The forgetting of personal identity made it possible to give way to his impulse toward flight, now irresistible, without exposing himself to the almost equally unbearable anxiety associated with being a coward, failing his mission, and undergoing arrest as a deserter. When he achieved physical safety the two sides of the conflict resumed their normal proportions and his sense of personal identity suddenly returned. ...

Hypnotism makes a very strong appeal to a man's delight in the marvellous and his desire for omnipotence. So strong is this appeal that many people would rather not be told that hypnotic phenomena are measurable and that they can be explained by straightforward psychological principles. It is more fun to believe that every vestige of the response to pain can be wiped out, or that suggested blindness produces the equivalent of real blindness, than

---

[62] *ibid.* cl.34. See also the comments on the proposed code by Mackay in "Craziness and Codification— Revising the Automatism and Insanity Defences" from Dennis (ed.), *Criminal Law and Justice* (1987), pp. 112–118.

to regard these as limited, measurable changes in the usual organisation of behaviour. As a result of this secret joy in magic and omnipotence, there has tended to be a large and important constant error in all thinking about the nature of hypnotism. This error is the belief that the *hypnotist, rather than the subject produces the phenomena.* The trouble began with Mesmer, who believed that he possessed a peculiar magnetic force which could be directed into his patient's bodies. It continued in those theories which represented the subject as a helpless automaton whose will, body and muscles were given over completely to the operator's whims and wishes. It continues today in the minds of those hypnotists who believe that the subject does not know what is going on, that you can fool him with statements which do not in the least fool an onlooker, that you can divide him up into dissociated pockets and hold private conversation with different parts of him. We should always bear in mind that the subject is still a person, even though he is participating in an unusual experiment and entering an unusual state. He has not become a fool, and it is he who produces the hypnotic behaviour.

… [There have been] various experimental investigations in which hypnotized persons were given suggestions to perform criminal acts. These experiments laboured under one great disadvantage. As it was not known whether the subjects would carry out the suggestions, the 'criminal acts' had to be arranged so that a really dangerous outcome was impossible. Rubber daggers and wooden pistols were used, the subjects being assured that they were real weapons. The outcome of all these earlier experiments can be condensed in a single illustration, amusingly described by Janet:

'A number of persons of importance, magistrates and professors, had assembled in the main hall of the Salpetriere museum to witness a great seance of criminal suggestions. Witt, the principal subject, thrown into the somnambulist state, had under the influence of suggestion displayed the most saguinary instincts. At a word or sign, she had stabbed, shot and poisoned; the room was littered with corpses. The notables had withdrawn, greatly impressed, leaving only a few students with the subject, who was still in the somnambulist state. The students, having a fancy to bring the seance to a close by a less bloodcurdling experiment, made a very simple suggestion to Witt. They told her that she was now quite alone in the hall. She was to strip and take a bath. Witt, who had murdered all the magistrates without turning a hair was seized with shame at the thought of undressing. Rather than accede to the suggestion, she had a violent fit of hysteria.' (P. Janet, *Psychological Healing* (1925), Vol. 1, p. 184.)

This example exposes the fallacy that has ruined so much experimental work with hypnotism: the notion that the subject is a helpless fool who has no idea that he is being deceived. It points unmistakably to the conclusion that hypnotized persons will not carry out suggested acts which are repugnant to them—not when they think the consequences are real."

If one accepts the above psychiatric evidence, what should be the law's response to a defendant who, while under a hypnotic influence, commits a crime? Do you agree that such persons should have a complete defence as "the dependency and helplessness of the hypnotised subject are too pronounced",[63] and that many persons are saved from being criminals by the force of their inhibitions which hypnotism removes?

*(ii) That even if insanity is not an issue, the public interest may not be served by a complete acquittal.*

Even those who would not go so far as to accept psychiatry's view of autonomic acts have sometimes expressed concern that certain automatons have been given absolute acquittals.

[63] A.L.I. Model Penal Code, Tent. Draft. No. 4 (1955), Comments to s.2.01 at p. 122.

## R. Cross, "Reflections on Bratty's Case" (1962) 78 L.Q.R. 236 at 238–239:

"Although they are still comparatively rare, pleas of non-insane automatism are becoming increasingly frequent, and questions may be legitimately raised concerning the sufficiency of the courts' powers. Is it right that someone who has been acquitted on the ground of non-insane automatism should inevitably go free? In *R. v Charlson* (1955) 29 Cr.App.R.37 the accused was acquitted on various charges of causing grievous bodily harm to his son because he acted in a state of automatism which may have been due to a cerebral tumour. It is only natural to feel the deepest sympathy for the accused in such a case, but it is equally natural to question the propriety of an unqualified acquittal. One way of dealing with such problems would be to give the judge powers in all cases of a successful plea of automatism, insane or non-insane, to order the detention of the accused pending a medical inquiry, after which the appropriate order could be made."

A similar approach to that advocated by Cross is to be found in the Scottish case of *H.M. Advocate v Fraser.*[64] In this sleepwalking case it was made a condition of discharge that the defendant should not sleep in the same room with anyone else. We have seen that as a result of *Sullivan*, epileptics, sleepwalkers, those suffering from arteriosclerosis and diabetics during hyperglycaemic episodes, may all now be regarded as insane. It has been argued that this is inappropriate for two main reasons. First, in the case of murder mandatory commitment still results. For these defendants, pleading automatism is a high risk venture. Secondly, there is an undeniable stigma attached to a finding of insanity. The Draft Criminal Code would rename the special verdict. However, it is doubtful whether the proposed term "mental disorder" is neutral enough to have the desired effect.[65] Two options, therefore, could be considered. One could continue to include some automatons within the "special verdict" but demedicalise the test and label, or one could deal with all automatons outside the special verdict but qualify the acquittal as and when necessary by appropriate orders. Clearly there would be problems in empowering courts to make appropriate orders in these cases, for example, such orders would probably be incompatible with Article 5 of the European Convention on Human Rights.[66] However, if constructed in such a manner as to ensure compatability with the Convention, such an approach might well be preferable to including such automatons within the definition of insanity.

## VIII. Diminished Responsibility

### A. *Introduction*

The "defence" of diminished responsibility is not a general defence and, strictly, ought to be discussed elsewhere in this book, since, like provocation, it operates only as a defence to murder,[67] reducing liability to manslaughter. However, it will be discussed at this stage, rather than in the context of homicide, for two important reasons.

---

[64] (1878) 4 Couper 70. But see now *Carmichael v Boyle* [1985] S.L.T. 399.
[65] Griew argues that public education would be necessary. "Let's Implement Butler on Mental Disorder and Crime" [1984] C.L.P. 47 at 52. We would tend to agree with Mackay that this is unlikely to be successful: *above*, n.52, p. 115.
[66] Baker, "Human Rights, M'Naghten and the 1991 Act" [1994] Crim.L.R.84 at 90.
[67] *Campbell* [1997] Crim.L.R.495 confirms that it does not apply to attempted murder.

First, the partial defence raises problems of responsibility similar to those raised by the insanity defence, and secondly, the practical effect of the availability of the defence of diminished responsibility has been to decrease resort to the insanity plea.[68] Recent research indicates that this is still the case; however it is also clear that the plea of diminished responsibility is itself in decline for reasons which, as yet, are not entirely clear.[69]

## B. *The Problem*

### Royal Commission on Capital Punishment, Cmnd.8932 (1949–1953), para. 411:

"It must be accepted that there is no sharp dividing line between sanity and insanity, but that the two extremes of 'sanity' and 'insanity' shade into one another by imperceptible gradations. The degree of individual responsibility varies equally widely; no clear boundary can be drawn between responsibility and irresponsibility. The existence of degrees of responsibility has been recognised in ... [other] legal systems. ... The acceptance of the doctrine of diminished responsibility would undoubtedly bring the law into closer harmony with the facts."

The doubts that have led many to argue for the abolition of the insanity defence[70] have here been used to justify a half-way house; some device, it was felt, was needed to reflect the view that where there was less responsibility there ought to be less punishment. Such acceptance of partial responsibility would enable the courts to do what, after all discussion of responsibility was ended, they really desired: to avoid the fixed penalty for murder by convicting the killer of manslaughter instead. For all other crimes which do not carry a fixed penalty, a partial defence was unnecessary. The lesser degree of responsibility could be reflected at the sentencing stage by "less punishment".

## C. *The Solution*

### Homicide Act 1957, section 2

"(1) Where a person kills or is a party to the killing of another, he shall not be convicted of murder if he was suffering from such abnormality of mind (whether arising from a condition of arrested or retarded development of mind or any inherent causes or induced by disease or injury) as substantially impaired his mental responsibility for his acts and omissions in doing or being a party to the killing. ...
(3) ... [he] shall be liable instead to be convicted of manslaughter."[71]

---

[68] Diminished responsibility is significantly easier to prove than insanity (although it may be getting harder, *below*, p. 405); indeed, recent research shows that less than 15 per cent of cases go before a jury. The overwhelming majority of cases are dealt with by means of guilty pleas with unanimous medical evidence; Mackay, "Diminished Responsibility and Mentally Disordered Killers" in Ashworth and Mitchell (eds), *Rethinking English Homicide Law* (2000), p. 62.

[69] The number of diminished responsibility pleas peaked in 1979 at 109 but by 1997/98 had fallen by over 50 per cent to 47. See Mackay, *ibid.*

[70] *Above*, p. 388.

[71] *Antoine* [2001] 1 A.C. 340 decided that once a defendant has been found unfit to plead she cannot go on to plead diminished responsibility (to avoid indefinite mandatory commitment) because the trial terminates. Since the defendant is no longer liable to be convicted of murder the defence in section 2 cannot arise.

The plea is raised by the defence on whom, as with insanity, the burden rests. Attempts to argue that this contravened Article 6(2) of the European Convention on Human Rights which guarantees the presumption of innocence were rejected outright by the Court of Appeal in *Lambert, Ali and Jordan*.[72] Following *dicta* in *Kebeline*[73] the court argued that the Convention did not prevent exceptions to the normal burden of proof provided an appropriate balance was struck between the general interest of the community and the protection of the rights of the individual. Since section 2 established a defence (and not an ingredient to an offence) if the defendant did not wish to rely on it she was not required to prove anything. "The change in the law brought about by section 2 was of benefit to those who were in a position to take advantage of it."

In evidence to the Butler Committee[74] members of the judiciary suggested that section 2 of the Homicide Act embodies a concept which is easier to grasp than define and that normally it requires the defendant to show "recognisably abnormal mental symptoms".[75] The Court of Appeal has stated that it is rarely helpful to a jury to read them section 2 in its entirety and that judges should focus upon the elements relevant to the particular facts of the case.[76] In general, the courts "have shown no willingness to delve into the meaning of section 2. ... Rather, the judiciary have instead been content to permit the diminished plea to operate in a largely pragmatic manner."[77]

Nevertheless, some attempt has to be made to understand the section. The requirements of the section may be broken down thus: there must be an *abnormality of mind* arising from one of the *bracketed causes* (arrested or retarded development of mind or any inherent causes or induced by disease or injury) and it must result in *substantial impairment of mental responsibility*.

The key phrases have caused considerable problems. "Abnormality of mind" is extremely vague; the concept has only been slightly clarified by the case of *Byrne*.[78] The appellant strangled and then mutilated a girl. It was alleged that he suffered from violent perverted sexual desires which he found difficult or impossible to control. He was, in fact, described as a sexual psychopath. In the course of his judgment (allowing the appeal) Lord Parker C.J. defined "abnormality of mind" thus:

"[it is] a state of mind so different from that of ordinary human beings that the reasonable man ... would term it abnormal. It appears to us wide enough to cover the mind's activities in all its aspects, not only the perception of physical acts and matters, and the ability to form a rational judgment as to whether the act

---

[72] [2001] 1 W.L.R. 211. The subsequent appeal to the House of Lords did not deal with diminished responsibility. The prosecution may raise the plea if the defendant is pleading insanity: *Campbell* (1987) 84 Cr.App.R.255.

[73] *R. v Director of Public Prosecutions, ex parte Kebeline* [1999] 3 W.L.R. 972.

[74] *Report of the Committee on Mentally Abnormal Offenders*, Cmnd.6244 (1975).

[75] *ibid.*, p. 242, para. 19.4.

[76] *Sanderson* (1994) 98 Cr.App.R.325.

[77] Mackay, *Mental Condition Defences in the Criminal Law* (1995), pp. 184–185. See also, Griew, "Reducing Murder to Manslaughter: Whose Job" (1986) 2 J. of Medical Ethics 18.

[78] (1960) 44 Cr.App.R.246.

was right or wrong, but also the ability to exercise will-power to control physical acts in accordance with that rational judgment."[79]

As the evidence to the Butler Committee suggested, this interpretation still leaves the meaning of "abnormality of mind" somewhat imprecise. It is a quasi-legal, quasi-medical formula that can satisfy no-one.

The abnormality of mind must have been caused by one of the conditions listed in brackets in section 2. In *Sanderson*[80] it was held that "any inherent cause" covers functional mental illness such as paranoid psychosis from which the defendant in this case suffered. It is in relation to this condition that the vexed problem of the psychopathic offender arises. Some psychiatrists are prepared to state that psychopathy may be due to inherent causes; others feeling that it may be due to mishandling in childhood, are not. If the former view is held then psychopathic offenders who fall outside the M'Naghten Rules may have a partial defence to a charge of murder. Some commentators are sceptical about whether the label "psychopath" has any meaning at all. Another problem arises with reactive depression: as the name implies, it arises from outside influences and so can hardly be described as an "inherent cause". For example, since this more restrictive interpretation adopted in *Sanderson*, it may be that certain cases of reactive depressive mental illness, such as that caused by the trauma and distress associated with caring for a terminally ill relative, may not be regarded as being an "inherent cause".[81] This would have important implications for "mercy-killers" who had previously been brought within the ambit of the defence.[82] For example, in *Price*[83] a father placed his severely handicapped son on a river and watched him float away; he was convicted of manslaughter on the basis of diminished responsibility.

What is the meaning of the phrase "induced by disease or injury"? In *Sanderson* it was held that this refers to organic or physical injury or disease of the body, including the brain. The court, however, declined to decide that "disease" within section 2 was synonymous with "disease of the mind" within the M'Naghten Rules. It has been held that alcoholism may amount to an "injury".[84] However, for policy reasons the courts consistently uphold the distinction between alcoholism and mere intoxication (by whatever means). In *Dietschmann*[85] the House of Lords held that where a defendant pleads diminished responsibility resulting from the combination of mental abnormality and intoxication the jury should be satisfied that, despite the drink, the defendant's mental abnormality substantially impaired his mental responsibility for his fatal acts.[86] Finally, as we shall see, "battered woman's syndrome" has been classed as a "disease" for the purposes of section 2.

The final key phrase "substantial impairment of mental responsibility" has also given rise to interpretative difficulties.

---

[79] In *Seers* (1984) 79 Cr.App.R.261, the Court of Appeal held that the jury should have been directed in these terms, without the "unhelpful" addition of the description of diminished responsibility as "partial or borderline insanity".

[80] (1994) 98 Cr.App.R.325.

[81] Mackay, "The Abnormality of Mind Factor in Diminished Responsibility" [1999] Crim.L.R.117 at 121–123.

[82] Between 1982 and 1991 there were 22 homicide cases involving mercy-killing with a murder verdict being returned in one case only: Ashworth, *Principles of Criminal Law* (3rd ed., 1999), p. 295.

[83] *The Times*, December 2, 1971.

[84] *Tandy* [1988] Crim.L.R.308.

[85] [2003] 1 All E.R. 897.

[86] An extract from this case appears below at p. 429.

### Report of the Committee on Mentally Abnormal Offenders (Butler Committee) Cmnd.6244 (1975), para. 19.5:

" 'Mental responsibility', a phrase not to be found elsewhere in any statute, has created difficulties both for doctors and jurors. It is either a concept of law or a concept of morality; it is not a clinical fact relating to the defendant. 'Legal responsibility' means liability to conviction (and success in a defence of diminished responsibility does not save the defendant from conviction of manslaughter); 'moral responsibility' means liability to moral censure (but moral questions do not normally enter into the definition of a crime). It seems odd that psychiatrists should be asked and agree to testify as to legal and moral responsibility. It is even more surprising that courts are prepared to hear that testimony. Yet psychiatrists commonly testify to impaired 'mental responsibility' under section 2. Several medical witnesses pointed out to us that the difficulty is made worse by the use of the word substantial.[87] The idea that ability to conform to the law can be measured is particularly puzzling."

The difficulty described in this passage is illustrative of the central problem with section 2: the compromise it achieves between medical and legal issues leaves neither side on safe ground. Neither medical experts nor the jury can satisfactorily answer the questions demanded of them. Indeed, the process has been described by psychiatrists as "an expensive farce" and a "blot on psychiatric practice".[88] What has happened is the familiar story of medical experts being made to determine the issue of responsibility.[89] Evidence suggests that, in the past at least, medical experts do not even refer to the bracketed causes specified in section 2 in many cases.[90] If this practice continues it may well be that many persons, such as mercy-killers, could still be able to utilise the defence. In short, they (with the collusion of judges and juries) have simply stretched the interpretation of section 2 to cover cases where a conviction of murder is thought to be inappropriate. We have seen that persons suffering from reactive depressions and alcoholism, as well as mercy-killers have been brought within the ambit of the defence. Women suffering from pre-menstrual syndrome[91] have also been included as have, most importantly, psychopaths and persons acting under "irresistible impulse".[92]

One particular category of cases deserves special consideration and that is battered women who have killed their partners after suffering abuse for, sometimes, many years. Such defendants have, at first sight at least, three options.

---

[87] The intention of the Act was the juries would undertake the task of assessing the substantiality of the impairment. *Cf. Gittens* [1984] Q.B. 698, and *Atkinson* [1985] Crim.L.R.314. As this latter case shows, this task can be a very difficult one.

[88] *Report of the Committee on the Penalty for Homicide* (1993), p. 33.

[89] Although juries can reject medical evidence (*Walton v The Queen* [1977] 3 W.L.R. 902) there must be evidence justifying their refusal: *Matheson* [1958] 1 W.L.R. 474 and *Vernege* [1982] 1 W.L.R. 293. If there is no such evidence the conviction for murder may be quashed and one of manslaughter substituted.

[90] Mackay, *above*, n.68 at p.120, citing Dell, *Murder into Manslaughter* (1984), p. 39.

[91] *Reynolds*, April 23, 1988 (C.A.). For discussion of this and other cases of P.M.T. (including that of *Smith (Sandie)* [1982] Crim.L.R.531), see Edwards, "Mad, Bad or Pre-Menstrual?" (1988) 138 N.L.J. 456.

[92] Traditionally excluded from the M'Naghten Rules, because of the difficulty of distinguishing the unresistable from the unresisted impulse. Such a person will have a partial defence here if he was either unable to conform or experienced substantially more difficulty in conforming to the law than an ordinary man; the jury should approach this question in "a broad common-sense way" because it is not one, given the present state of medical knowledge, that can be solved scientifically (*Byrne, above*, n.78).

Self-defence, provocation or diminished responsibility may be pleaded in answer to a charge of murder. As the law stands, however, self-defence is unlikely to be available in practice. Until recently, provocation was also unlikely to succeed. For example in *Ahluwalia*,[93] the defendant was beaten and threatened with death for over 10 years before she poured petrol over her husband whilst he was asleep and then set light to him. At her trial she pleaded provocation (or alternatively lack of *mens rea*) but was found guilty of murder. The Court of Appeal, however, very exceptionally, permitted medical evidence that was not brought before the court at the trial to be admitted at the appeal stage. On the basis of the evidence of her depressive condition her conviction was quashed; at the re-trial a plea of manslaughter on the basis of diminished responsibility was accepted and she was sentenced to 40 months imprisonment (exactly the amount she had already served).[94] Forcing such defendants to resort to diminished responsibility has been severely criticised.

### Katherine O'Donovan, "Defences for Battered Women Who Kill" (1991) 18 J.L. and Soc. 219 at 229–230:

"So why not advise those who kill following cumulative violence to plead diminished responsibility? One answer is that such a plea avoids placing the issue of justification before the court. If the accused wishes to vindicate her conduct, a plea of diminished responsibility alienates her from a claim to have acted justly. Instead of proposing herself as a legal subject responsible for her actions, she denies this and proposes abnormality of mind. This prevents attention being given to cumulative violence and appropriate responses. Instead, the focus is on her mental state at the time of what is acknowledged as a crime. Her personality, characteristics, and problems are on trial.

A second answer is that a plea of diminished responsibility enables the labelling of the woman who makes it as crazy or incapable, or both. There is a contradiction here if the defendant wants to appear as active in dealing with the abuse she has suffered, and yet, as abnormal. If abnormality is over-emphasised, she may find that the outcome of the trial is not probation, but incarceration in an institution for persons designated 'mental.'

A third answer is that, although a diminished responsibility plea enables an individual woman to excuse her action in an acceptable legal form, it does nothing for battered women as a group. It is, of course, of the nature of criminal charges that they are brought against individuals. However, unless a challenge is presented to the current law on self-defence and provocation, change cannot occur."

More recently, however, the landmark House of Lords decision in *Smith*[95] has opened the door to battered women being able to plead provocation. For example, in *Smith (Jocelyn)*[96] a battered woman who had killed her husband had failed at her trial with both the partial defences of provocation and diminished responsibility. On appeal (after *Smith*) a conviction for manslaughter on grounds of provocation was substituted. It was pointed out that, unlike the earlier law, it could actually be easier now to plead provocation than diminished responsibility. For diminished responsibility one of the bracketed causes must be established, for example, that

---

[93] (1993) 96 Cr.App.R.133.

[94] See also *Hobson* [1998] 1 Cr.App.R.31 where the Court of Appeal ordered a retrial on the basis that the issue of "Battered Women's Syndrome" (added to the British Classification of Mental Diseases after her trial but prior to the appeal) should have been put to the jury.

[95] [2001] A.C. 146. *Below*, p. 701.

[96] [2002] EWCA Crim 2671.

the woman was suffering from battered women's syndrome and that this amounts to a disease. Since *Smith* the jury is permitted to take into account "everything" in determining whether the defence of provocation is established: "more minor symptoms are relevant to provocation, when they may not be to diminished responsibility." As a result of these developments, it could well be that there will be an even greater decline in the use of diminished responsibility as a partial defence.

What is the outcome of a successful plea of diminished responsibility if widely divergent cases are going to be brought within its protection? Simply because the conviction is for manslaughter rather than murder does not ensure lenient treatment. A finding of mental imbalance does not automatically entail a hospital order under section 37 of the Mental Health Act 1983 although this is now imposed in approximately 40 per cent of diminished responsibility cases.[97] The use of imprisonment has increased to over one third of cases although life sentences are rare.[98] The Court of Appeal in *Chambers*[99] felt that a sentence of life imprisonment could only be imposed where the defendant constituted a danger to the public for an unpredictable length of time (and where a hospital order was not deemed appropriate). Determinate sentences of imprisonment can be imposed where there is no proper basis for a hospital order, but where the defendant's degree of responsibility is not minimal. The residual cases "which have been felt to merit sympathetic consideration have resulted in more lenient disposal".[1] The case of *Price*[2] is typical. In passing sentence the judge told the father that he would be required to "undergo treatment as a doctor may prescribe for the next few weeks or so"; in such cases a community rehabilitation order with requirement as to treatment may be felt to be the most appropriate sentence.

### D. *Should the partial defence of diminished responsibility be retained?*

Those who attack the diminished responsibility defence often do so on the same grounds as the insanity defence has been criticised.[3] However, the concept of diminished responsibility has also been subject to more specific criticism. As we have seen, this defence operates on the premise of a half-way house of responsibility. It is this that has caused other commentators some misgivings.

Sparks[4] feels that the concept of diminished responsibility rests on a mistaken view of the relationship between mental disorder and criminal liability. In any discussion of this relationship, two questions are involved:

---

[97] Mackay, *above*, n.77, p. 182. The court may attach a "restriction order" (Mental Health Act 1983, s.41) to the hospital order. This prevents the offender being transferred to another hospital, given leave of absence or discharged without the Home Secretary's consent.

[98] In 1999/2000 3 of the 24 defendants convicted under s.2 received life sentences in comparison with 18 out of 87 in 1981; *Crime in England and Wales*, Supplementary volume (2003).

[99] [1983] Crim.L.R.688. The court also laid down guidelines as to when hospital orders or supervision orders would be appropriate. In *Fairhurst* [1996] 1 Cr.App.R.(S.) 242, for example, the Court of Appeal substituted a hospital order with a restriction order unlimited in time for the life sentence imposed by the trial judge.

[1] Butler Committee on Mentally Abnormal Offenders, Cmnd.6244, para. 19.7.

[2] *Above*, n.83.

[3] Hart, *Punishment and Responsibility, Essays in the Philosophy of Law* (1968), pp. 202–209.

[4] Sparks, "Diminished Responsibility in Theory and Practice" (1964) 27 M.L.R. 9 disagreeing fundamentally with the reasoning in the Royal Commission on Capital Punishment, *above*, p. 400.

(1) was the accused mentally abnormal, and

(2) could the accused in that condition help committing his crime?

One cannot deduce the answer to the second question merely by reference to the first; the illness may be completely unrelated to the conduct. If that is the case, it is not at all unfair to punish: "to say that we are less willing to blame such a man if he does something wrong, surely does not mean: we are willing to blame him less, if he does something wrong."[5] Moreover, if there is a connection between the mental abnormality and the crime committed because he could not help committing the crime in that condition, he ought to be excused all punishment. He is not responsible at all; the concept of a half-way house is, therefore, devoid of substance.

This reasoning can be contrasted with that of the Royal Commission on Capital Punishment. If the latter is found to be more persuasive and diminished responsibility is to be seen as more than "a device for circumventing the embarrassments that flow from a mandatory sentence",[6] is there any justification for restricting the operation of the defence to murder only?[7] The force of this argument, however, was not accepted by the Criminal Law Revision Committee in its 14th Report and has not been incorporated into the Draft Code. Instead it is proposed that diminished responsibility should continue to be a partial defence to murder only.

### Draft Criminal Code Bill 1989 (Law Com. No. 177), clause 56:

"(1) A person who but for this section, would be guilty of murder is not guilty of murder if, at the time of his act, he is suffering from such mental abnormality as is a substantial enough reason to reduce his offence to manslaughter.

(2) In this section 'mental abnormality' means mental illness, arrested or incomplete development of mind, psychopathic disorder, and any other disorder or disability of mind, except intoxication."

### IX. Intoxication

### A. *Background*

A significant proportion of criminal offences are committed by persons who are drunk.

---

[5] *ibid.* at p. 16.

[6] Dell, "Diminished Responsibility Reconsidered" [1982] Crim.L.R.809 at 814, and *Murder into Manslaughter* (1984).

[7] In several European countries (France, Italy and Belgium) the defence operates more widely. The Butler Committee's preference was for the abolition of the mandatory life sentence for murder and with it the device of diminished responsibility. Failing acceptance of that recommendation it favoured a rewording of the defence (still applicable only to murder) so that psychiatrists would have a firmer medical basis upon which to testify (pp. 244–248, paras 19.8–19.21). It was this latter view that was adopted by the Criminal Law Revision Committee (14th Report, *Offences Against the Person*, Cmnd.7844 (1980), paras 76, 91–93). See further, Mackay *above*, n.68 at p. 81.

## John E. Hodge, "Alcohol and Violence" in Pamela J. Taylor (ed.), Violence in Society (1993), pp. 129–130:

"*Assault*
There is clear evidence of a consistent association with alcohol use in cases of assault . . . Meyer *et al* found that approximately two-thirds of perpetrators of police assault had been drinking just prior to the assault, while in a large study in which data on over 10,000 inmates of American prisons were reviewed, just under two-thirds of those convicted of assault were found to have been drinking at the time of the offence.

*Homicide*
Lindquist found that two-thirds of the offenders and approximately half their victims had been intoxicated at the time of the offence . . .

*Rape*
The use of alcohol by rapists and their victims also seems fairly well established. Shupe found 50 per cent of men arrested for rape had been drinking, and 45 per cent could be described as intoxicated . . .

*Domestic violence*
Pizzey found that alcohol had been involved in about 40 per cent of cases of battered wives and children seeking refuge from domestic violence. Other studies have tended to find rates of alcohol involvement of about 50 per cent."

Research into crimes of violence in Bristol has confirmed this pattern: "we came to regard cases in which drink was *not* a factor as rather remarkable."[8]

The above research is not necessarily claiming that the consumption of alcohol *caused* the criminal acts, but that there is a strong association between the two. Why is this so?

## John E. Hodge, "Alcohol and Violence" in Pamela J. Taylor (ed.), Violence in Society (1993), pp. 132–134:

"*Moral theory*
Probably the first was the pre-scientific 'moral theory' which held that drinking loosens moral restraints, with the result that individuals who drink lose personal control and, as a result, engaged in immoral behaviours, including violence. While this theory has little scientific validity, it is still popular . . . Labelling alcohol as the culprit provides a convenient scapegoat for violent acts.

*Disinhibition theory*
[B]ehavioural constraints are loosened by the pharmacological action of alcohol, and violence then results. However, the theory appears to imply that aggression is a natural state which is normally held in check . . . which can be released by the pharmacological effects of alcohol. . . . [However], there is little evidence that aggression or violence is a normal human state . . . Sobell and Sobell suggested that alcohol may directly act on the inhibitory control of the cerebral cortex over the lower brain centres and thus disinhibit aggressive urges. However, no empirical evidence has been obtained which either supports or refutes this hypothesis.

*Stimulation theory*
[S]ome . . . have suggested that alcohol may directly stimulate aggression in individuals who may in some way be more biologically sensitive to its effects. A particular example of this is the theory of pathological intoxication, which suggests that a small proportion of

[8] Cretney and Davis, *Punishing Violence* (1995), p. 26.

individuals are particularly prone to become excessively aggressive under the influence of alcohol ...

*Other factors which may explain the relationship between alcohol and violence*
... The first is the simple physiological effects of alcohol, such as impaired reaction time. It seems unlikely, though, that these effects will lead directly to violence, although it is possible that poor co-ordination may result in a more extreme violent outcome that was perhaps the original intention. Similarly, Pernanen's hypothesis that cognitive impairment may be important in understanding the relationship between alcohol and violence has little supportive evidence ... [There are other] situational and psychological variables ... which help explain the association between alcohol and violence. One of these is the drinking situation itself. In this case, it is fairly clear that situations do influence the association between violence and alcohol. Alcohol use in some situations (for example, at football matches) is more likely to be associated with violence than in others (for example, party going). Cultural factors would also appear to be associated with the levels of violence after drinking ...
One major factor ... is the individual's expectancy of the outcome of drinking. If, as seems likely, there is a generally held belief that violence and alcohol are associated, this is likely to affect both the behaviour of the drinker and the interpretations of his/her behaviour by observers."

The problem for the criminal law is one of determining what importance should be attached to the intoxication (whether by drink or drugs or both) of a defendant who might claim either that she would never have committed the crime but for her drunkenness which loosened her inhibitions, or, alternatively, that she was so drunk that she did not know what she was doing and thus lacked *mens rea*. An example of the latter claim can be seen from *Lipman*[9] where the defendant, a drug addict, while on an L.S.D. "trip" had the illusion of descending to the centre of the earth and being attacked by snakes. In his attempt to fight off these reptiles he struck the victim (also a drug addict on an L.S.D. "trip") two blows on the head causing haemorrhage of the brain and crammed some eight inches of sheet into her mouth causing her to die of asphyxia. He claimed to have had "no knowledge of what he was doing and no intention to harm her". A similar example can be found in the Scottish case of *Brennan v H.M. Advocate*[10] where the defendant consumed between 20 and 25 pints of beer, a glass of sherry and a quantity of the drug L.S.D. He then stabbed his father to death with a knife. In both these cases the defendant claimed that because of drunkenness he was unable to foresee the consequences of his actions and so lacked *mens rea*.

The law here is faced with a dilemma. On the one hand, strict principle suggests that defendants such as Lipman and Brennan lack *mens rea*, or perhaps did not even "act" and, accordingly, should escape criminal liability. On the other hand, particularly given the statistics on the close connection between crime and alcohol, the law is concerned with protecting the public (and deterrence) and cannot allow drunk persons to escape criminal liability and punishment. In short, there is a clash between principle and policy and, while the law has tried to achieve some sort of compromise, inevitably it has been policy that has prevailed.

[9] [1970] 1 Q.B. 152.
[10] (1977) S.L.T. 151.

## B. *Drunken intent*

As the above cases make clear, the law is *not* concerned with a defendant who has several (or many) drinks that merely "loosen her up" and remove her inhibitions. If at the time of the crime she knows what she is doing, it is irrelevant that she would not have committed the crime, but for the drinks she has consumed. It was stressed in *Sheehan and Moore* that "a drunken intent is nevertheless an intent".[11]

Equally, the law is not concerned with persons who claim that they would not have committed the crime had they not been intoxicated. The loss of self-control was the defendant's fault. At the time of the crime she knew what she was doing and so must be held fully responsible.

Accordingly, the only cases in which the criminal law might become involved so as to allow intoxication to afford any excuse are those where the defendant is so intoxicated as to lack *mens rea* or to be in a state of automatism. It is not a matter of whether the defendant was *capable* of forming *mens rea*. It is a question of whether *mens rea* was, in fact, formed.[12]

However, even in such cases the law is unwilling to allow drunk persons to escape criminal liability and draws a distinction between voluntary and involuntary intoxication, the general rule being that drunkenness is only a complete defence in the latter situation. With voluntary intoxication drunkenness is usually no defence at all, but in certain cases is allowed to operate as a partial excuse reducing the level of criminal liability and punishment.

## C. *Meaning of voluntary intoxication*

### Report of the Committee on Mentally Abnormal Offenders (Butler Committee) Cmnd.6244 (1975), para. 18.56:

" 'Voluntary intoxication' would be defined to mean intoxication resulting from the intentional taking of drink or a drug knowing that it is capable in sufficient quantity of having an intoxicating effect; provided that intoxication is not voluntary if it results in part from a fact unknown to the defendant that increases his sensitivity to the drink or drug. The concluding words would provide a defence to a person who suffers from hypoglycaemia, for example, who does not know that in that condition the ingestions of a small amount of alcohol can produce a state of altered consciousness, as well as to a person who has been prescribed a drug on medical grounds without warning of the effect it may produce."

The present law does not appear to go quite as far as the above proposal. In *Allen*[13] the defendant claimed that he had not realised that wine he had drunk had a high alcohol content. It was held that where an accused knows he is drinking alcohol it is irrelevant whether he knows the precise nature or strength of the alcohol. It was a clear case of voluntary intoxication.

---

[11] [1975] 1 W.L.R. 739; in *Stubbs* (1989) 88 Cr.App.R.53 it was stated that the intoxication needed to be "very extreme".
[12] *Pordage* [1975] Crim.L.R.575; *Cole* [1993] Crim.L.R.300; *Hayes* [2002] EWCA Crim 1945.
[13] [1988] Crim.L.R.698.

## R. v Hardie (1984) 80 Cr.App.R.157 (Court of Appeal, Criminal Division)

Parker L.J.:

"The problem is whether ... [the taking of] valium ... should properly be regarded as self-induced intoxication ...

There can be no doubt that the same rule applies both to self-intoxication by alcohol and intoxication by hallucinatory drugs, but this is because the effects of both are well-known and there is therefore an element of recklessness in the self-administration of the drug ...

In the present instance the defence was that the valium was taken for the purpose of calming the nerves only, that it was old stock and that the appellant was told it would do him no harm. There was no evidence that it was known to the appellant or even generally known that the taking of valium in the quantity taken would be liable to render a person aggressive or incapable of appreciating risks to others or have other side effects such that its self-administration would itself have an element of recklessness. It is true that valium is a drug and it is true that it was taken deliberately and not taken on medical prescription, but the drug is, in our view, wholly different in kind from drugs which are liable to cause unpredictability or aggressiveness. It may well be that the taking of a sedative or soporific drug will, in certain circumstances, be no answer, for example in a case of reckless driving, but if the effect of a drug is merely soporific or sedative the taking of it, even in some excessive quantity, cannot in the ordinary way raise a *conclusive* presumption against the admission of proof of intoxication for the purpose of disproving *mens rea* in ordinary crimes, such as would be the case with alcoholic intoxication or incapacity or automatism resulting from the self-administration of dangerous drugs."

Thus, the fact that the court thought that the drug was non-dangerous was highly significant. The Law Commission regarded it as unsatisfactory that the courts should have to determine whether a drug is dangerous or not on a case by case basis.[14] Its approach was to define intoxication and the circumstances in which it would be held to be involuntary.[15] However, the latest Government proposals have chosen, instead, to define voluntary intoxication and have, significantly, inserted a provision that intoxication is presumed to be voluntary.

### Draft Offences Against the Person Bill 1998, clause 19:

"(3) A person is voluntarily intoxicated if—
(a) he takes an intoxicant otherwise than properly for a medicinal purpose,
(b) he is aware that it is or may be an intoxicant, and
(c) he takes it in such a quantity as impairs his awareness or understanding.
(4) An intoxicant, although taken for a medicinal purpose, is not properly so taken if—
(a) the intoxicant is not taken on medical advice, and the taker is aware that the taking may result in his doing an act or making an omission capable of constituting an offence of the kind in question, or
(b) the intoxicant is taken on medical advice, but the taker fails then or afterwards to comply with any condition forming part of the advice and he is aware that the failure may

---

[14] Law Com., *Legislating the Criminal Code: Intoxication and Criminal Liability* (Law Com. No. 229, 1995), para. 5.42. See also, Mackay, *Mental Condition Defences in The Criminal Law* (1995), pp. 153–157.

[15] Draft Criminal Law (Intoxication) Bill, clause 4.

result in his doing an act or making an omission capable of constituting an offence of the kind in question.

(5) Intoxication must be presumed to have been voluntary unless there is adduced such evidence as might lead the court or jury to conclude that there is a reasonable possibility that the intoxication was involuntary.

(6) An intoxicant is any alcohol, drug or other thing which, when taken into the body, may impair the awareness or understanding of the person taking it.

(7) A person must be treated as taking an intoxicant if he permits it to be administered to him."

## D. *Law on Voluntary Intoxication*

### 1. Specific and basic intent

In the leading case of *Majewski*[16] the House of Lords confirmed a long line of authority[17] that drunkenness could only be a defence to crimes of "specific intent" and not to crimes of "basic intent".[18]

This distinction caused little problem at first. A rough list was drawn up by judges: for example, murder and section 18 of the Offences against the Person Act 1861 were deemed to be crimes of specific intent while manslaughter and section 20 of the Offences against the Person Act 1861 were held to be crimes of basic intent. This distinction was a purely functional one aimed at achieving a "compromise between the rigors of denying the relevance of intoxication and allowing it to undercut all liability".[19] Intoxication was, in effect, taken into account as a mitigating factor. Drunken defendants charged with murder and section 18 could instead be convicted of manslaughter and section 20 respectively. What did the terms "specific" and "basic" intent mean? The true answer was, of course: nothing. They were like elephants—the courts knew them when they saw them (*i.e.* they knew when a defendant's liability could be reduced without escaping all punishment)—but they could not be defined. Difficulties started arising when judges began trying to define these concepts. Attempting to define terms designed to provide maximum flexibility for policy considerations was always going to be problematic.

Several views started emerging. For example, Lord Simon in *Majewski* equated specific intent with "direct" intent (*i.e.* aim or purpose): "the prosecution must in general prove that the purpose for the commission of the act extends to the intent expressed or implied in the definition of the crime".[20] This view, however, never won judicial support and instead the "ulterior intent test" was the first to gain

---

[16] [1977] A.C. 443.

[17] *D.P.P. v Beard* [1920] A.C. 479; *Att-Gen for Northern Ireland v Gallagher* [1963] A.C. 349; *Bratty v Att-Gen for Northern Ireland* [1963] A.C. 386.

[18] For crimes requiring specific intent intoxication will be part of all the evidence that the jury must consider in determining whether the prosecution has established that the defendant had the necessary *mens rea* (earlier *dicta* in *Beard* [1920] A.C. 479 that the onus of proof is on the defendant cannot now be relied upon). If the issue of intoxication emerges as a material factor at the trial, the judge should direct the jury on it, even if the defendant does not himself raise the issue: *Bennett* [1995] Crim.L.R.877; *Groark* [1999] Crim.L.R.669; *Hayes* [2002] EWCA Crim 1945.

[19] Fletcher, *Rethinking Criminal Law* (1978), p. 849.

[20] [1977] A.C. 443 at 479.

broad acceptance. Under this view crimes of specific intent are crimes where the *mens rea* of the offence extends beyond the *actus reus*, while in crimes of basic intent the *mens rea* goes no further than extending to the elements of the *actus reus* itself. An example will illustrate this distinction. Assault is a crime of basic intent: the *actus reus* is causing apprehension of immediate force; the *mens rea* is an intention (or recklessness) to cause such apprehension; no *mens rea* extending beyond the *actus reus* is required. But assault with intent to resist arrest[21] is a crime of specific intent: the *actus reus* is the same as that of common assault, namely, causing apprehension of immediate force; the *mens rea* is two-fold—there must be the *mens rea* of the assault *and in addition* there must be an intent to resist arrest. This additional intention does not relate to anything in the *actus reus* of the crime; it extends beyond the *actus reus*; the crime is thus one of specific intent.

However, an alternative view was also expressed in *Majewski*,[22] and endorsed in the subsequent House of Lords decision of *Caldwell*, namely, the "recklessness test". According to this, drunkenness can only be a defence to crimes that require proof of intention (such as murder and section 18), and it cannot be a defence to crimes that can be committed recklessly (such as manslaughter and section 20).

## R. v Caldwell [1982] A.C. 341 (House of Lords)

(The facts are set out *above*, p. 147)
(Criminal Damage Act 1971, s.1(2):
"A person who without lawful excuse destroys or damages any property, whether belonging to himself or another—(a) intending to destroy or damage any property or being reckless as to whether any property would be destroyed or damaged; and (b) intending by the destruction or damage to endanger the life of another or being reckless as to whether the life of another would be thereby endangered; shall be guilty of an offence.")

Lord Diplock:
"As respects the charge under section 1(2) the prosecution did not rely upon an actual intent of the respondent to endanger the lives of the residents but relied on his having been reckless whether the lives of any of them would be endangered. His act of setting fire to it was one which the jury were entitled to think created an obvious risk that the lives of the residents would be endangered; and the only defence with which your Lordships are concerned is that the respondent had made himself so drunk as to render him oblivious of that risk. If the only mental state capable of constituting the necessary *mens rea* for an offence under section 1(2) were that expressed in the words 'intending by the destruction or damage to endanger the life of another', it would have been necessary to consider whether the offence was to be classified as one of 'specific' intent for the purposes of the rule of law which this House affirmed and applied in *R. v Majewski* [1977] A.C. 443; and this it plainly is. But this is not, in my view, a relevant inquiry where 'being reckless as to whether the life of another would be thereby endangered' is an alternative mental state that is capable of constituting the necessary *mens rea* of the offence with which he is charged.

The speech of Lord Elwyn-Jones L.C. in *R. v Majewski* ... is authority that self-induced intoxication is no defence to a crime in which recklessness is enough to constitute the necessary *mens rea*. The charge in *Majewski* was of assault occasioning actual bodily harm and it was held by the majority of the House, approving *R. v Venna* [1976] Q.B. 421, 428, that recklessness in the use of force was sufficient to satisfy the mental element in the offence of assault. Reducing oneself by drink or drugs to a condition in which the restraints of reason and conscience are cast off was held to be a reckless course of conduct and an integral part of

---

[21] Offences against the Person Act 1861, s.38, as amended.
[22] [1977] A.C. 443 at 475 (Lord Elwyn-Jones).

the crime. The Lord Chancellor accepted at p. 475 as correctly stating English law the provision in section 2.08(2) of the American Model Penal Code:

'When recklessness establishes an element of the offence, if the actor, due to self-induced intoxication, is unaware of a risk of which he would have been aware had he been sober, such unawareness is immaterial.'

So in the instant case, the fact that the respondent was unaware of the risk of endangering the lives of residents in the hotel owing to his self-induced intoxication would be no defence if that risk would have been obvious to him had he been sober.

My Lords, the Court of Appeal in the instant case regarded the case as turning on whether the offence under section 1(2) was one of 'specific' intent or 'basic' intent. Following a recent decision of the Court of Appeal by which they were bound, *R. v Orpin* [1980] 1 W.L.R. 1050, they held that the offence under section 1(2) was one of 'specific' intent in contrast to the offence under section 1(1) which was of basic intent. This would be right if the only *mens rea* capable of constituting the offence were an actual intention to endanger the life of another. For the reasons I have given, however, classification into offences of 'specific' and 'basic' intent is irrelevant where being reckless as to whether a particular harmful consequence will result from one's act is a sufficient alternative *mens rea*".

Lord Edmund-Davis (dissenting):

"Something more must be said ... having regard to the view expressed by my noble and learned friend, Lord Diplock, ... that the speech of Lord Elwyn-Jones L.C. in *R. v Majewski* 'is authority that self-induced intoxication is no defence to a crime in which recklessness is enough to constitute the necessary *mens rea*'. It is a view which, with respect, I do not share. In common with all the noble and learned Lords hearing that appeal, Lord Elwyn-Jones L.C. adopted the well-established (though not universally favoured) distinction between basic and specific intents. *R. v Majewski* ... related solely to charges of assault, undoubtedly an offence of basic intent, and the Lord Chancellor made it clear that his observations were confined to offences of that nature. ... My respectful view is that *Majewski* accordingly supplies no support for the proposition that, in relation to crimes of specific intent (such as section 1(2)(b) of the Act of 1971) incapacity to appreciate the degree and nature of the risk created by his action which is attributable to the defendant's self-intoxication is an irrelevance. The Lord Chancellor was dealing simply with crimes of basic intent, and in my judgment it was strictly within that framework that he adopted the view expressed in the American Penal Code ... and recklessness as an element in crimes of specific intent was, I am convinced, never within his contemplation.

For the foregoing reasons, the Court of Appeal were in my judgment right in quashing the conviction under section 1(2)(b) and substituting a finding of guilty of arson contrary to section 1(1) and (3) of the Act of 1971. It follows, therefore, that I agree with learned counsel for the respondent that the certified point of law should be answered in the following manner:

Yes, evidence of self-induced intoxication can be relevant both to (a) whether the defendant *intended* to endanger the life of another, and to (b) whether the defendant *was reckless* as to whether the life of another would be endangered, within the meaning of section 1(2)(b) of the Criminal Damage Act 1971.

My Lords, it was recently predicted that 'There can hardly be any doubt that *all* crimes of recklessness except murder will not be held to be crimes of basic intent within *Majewski*': see *Glanville Williams, Textbook of Criminal Law*, p. 431. That prophecy has been promptly fulfilled by the majority of your Lordships, for, with the progressive displacement of 'maliciously' by 'intentionally' or 'recklessly' in statutory crimes, that will surely be the effect of the majority decision in this appeal. That I regret, for the consequence is that, however grave the crime charged, if recklessness can constitute its *mens rea* the fact that it was committed in drink can afford no defence. It is a very long time since we had so harsh a law in this country."

**Appeal dismissed**

An example will illustrate the difference between this "recklessness test" and the "ulterior intent test". The charge in *Caldwell* was section 1(2) of the Criminal

Damage Act 1971, namely, destroying or damaging any property intending or
being reckless as to whether the life of another would be thereby endangered.
According to the "ulterior intent test" this would be a crime of specific intent as the
*mens rea* (intention or recklessness as to whether life would be endangered) extends
beyond the *actus reus* (destroying or damaging property). According to the
"recklessness test", however, this is a crime of basic intent (as was held in *Caldwell*)
because it is a crime that can be committed recklessly.

After *Majewski* and *Caldwell* one point remains unresolved. In *Majewski* Lord
Elwyn-Jones L.C. used this "recklessness test" to identify crimes of basic and
specific intent. To Lord Diplock in *Caldwell* the inquiry involves two stages. If the
crime can only be committed intentionally, *then* one needs to ask whether it is a
crime of specific intent, using the "ulterior intent test". He stated that if section 1(2)
had required intention (only) then "it would have been necessary to consider
whether the offence was to be classified as one of 'specific' intent". But where the
crime can be committed recklessly "this is not, in my view, a relevant inquiry":
drunkenness can be no defence to such crimes.

It is uncertain which of these two views prevails and, in any event, perhaps the
point is of little practical importance as most offences that require intention only
are, in fact, also crimes of ulterior intent (for example, theft, robbery and attempt).
However, there is abundant precedent that murder and section 18 are crimes of
specific intent. As neither of these is generally[23] a crime of ulterior intent, perhaps
the better view is the simple "recklessness test": drunkenness is a defence to crimes
that can only be committed intentionally.

Whilst the House of Lords has endeavoured to distinguish specific and basic
intent, those applying the law suggest that it has caused little difficulty in practice.
The Law Commission acknowledges the importance of this perspective but states
that the lack of general agreement on the test "must inevitably lead to uncertainty,
wasted court time and the unnecessary incurring of legal costs when a new offence
is introduced, since, until the matter is decided by the courts, it will not be possible
to ascertain into which category it falls".[24] This may be to overstate the lack of
certainty in the current law.

On the basis of both precedent and the judicial pronouncements concerning the
specific/basic intent distinction it would appear that the following cannot be
committed recklessly and are crimes of specific intent, thus allowing drunkenness
to operate as a defence.

[i] *murder*: there is no doubt that intoxication is a defence to the crime of murder;
the defendant will instead be found guilty of the lesser included offence of
manslaughter.[25] This rule can now be reconciled with the "recklessness test" as
since *Moloney* and *Hancock* it is clear that murder is a crime of intention; it cannot
be committed recklessly. However, this coincidence between principle and policy is

[23] *Below*, p. 415.
[24] Law Com. No. 229, *above*, n.14, para. 3.27. For example, in *D.P.P. v Kellet* [1994] Crim.L.R.916 the
   court had to decide whether s.1(7) of the Dangerous Dogs Act 1991 created an offence of basic or
   specific intent. It was held to be the former.
[25] *Beard* [1920] A.C. 479; *Gallagher* [1963] A.C. 349; *Majewski* [1977] A.C. 443.

little more than chance. For many years preceding *Moloney* and *Hancock* murder was a crime that arguably could be committed recklessly,[26] yet during this time it was never doubted that murder was nevertheless a crime of specific intent. The policy reasons underlying this were clear. In murder cases there was always the possibility of a manslaughter conviction operating as a safety-net. Drunken defendants would not escape liability completely so it was "safe" to deem murder to be a crime of specific intent. This had the further advantage that it enabled the judge to avoid the imposition of the mandatory sentence for murder.[27] Drunken killers were blameworthy and deserved punishment, but they were, perhaps, not always as blameworthy as deliberate murderers. Conviction for manslaughter allowed the judge flexibility to assess the degree of blameworthiness and punish appropriately.

[ii] *section 18*: The crime of wounding or causing grievous bodily harm with intent to cause grievous bodily harm or with intent to resist apprehension is a crime that cannot be committed recklessly. Drunkenness can be a defence but the defendant will be convicted of the lesser basic intent offence of section 20, an offence that can be committed recklessly.[28] However, if one applied Lord Diplock's two-stage test from *Caldwell* there could be a problem here. While wounding with intent to cause grievous bodily harm, and wounding or causing grievous bodily harm with intent to resist apprehension, are clearly crimes of ulterior intent, the same cannot be said of causing grievous bodily harm with intent to cause grievous bodily harm. Smith and Hogan argue that it depends on the precise charge and the state of mind that has to be proved in the particular case.[29] Thus if the charge is causing grievous bodily harm with intent to cause grievous bodily harm, drunkenness will be no defence. This view, however, is not consistent with the better "recklessness test" and is not supported by authority which suggests that section 18 is *always* a specific intent offence.[30]

[iii] *theft*[31]: this is a crime of intention; it is also a crime of ulterior intent. For the same reasons, obtaining property by deception contrary to section 15 of the Theft Act 1968 would probably be held to be a crime of specific intention.

[iv] *robbery*[32]: again, recklessness will not suffice here and it is a crime of ulterior intent.

[26] This was certainly a plausible interpretation of *Hyam* [1975] A.C. 55.
[27] Sellers, "Mens Rea and the Judicial Approach to 'Bad Excuses' in the Criminal Law" (1978) 41 M.L.R. 245 at 261. This approach was endorsed by the Criminal Law Revision Committee, 14th Report. See *below*, p. 431.
[28] *Pordage* [1975] Crim.L.R.575; *Majewski* [1977] A.C. 443; *Bailey* [1983] 1 W.L.R. 760; *Davis* [1991] Crim.L.R.469.
[29] *Criminal Law* (10th ed., 2002), p. 244.
[30] It is conceded that in none of these cases (*above*, n.28) was the charge causing grievous bodily harm with intent to cause grievous bodily harm. By analogy, the Smith and Hogan argument is weakened by the decision in *Fotheringham* (*below*, p. 416) which suggests that crimes either are, or are not, ones of specific intent irrespective of what mental element has to be proved in the particular case.
[31] Theft Act 1968, s.1. *Ruse v Reed* [1949] 1 K.B. 377; Lord Salmon in *Majewski* [1977] A.C. 443 at 482.
[32] Theft Act 1968, s.8.

[v] *burglary*: while recklessness as to whether entry to a building as a trespasser will suffice, such entry must be accompanied by an intention (only) to commit a listed offence.[33] It would thus appear to be a crime of specific intent, passing the "recklessness test". It is also a crime of ulterior intent.

[vi] *handling stolen goods*: In *Durante*[34] it was accepted that this was an offence of specific intent. This is not an offence of intention at all. The *mens rea* stipulated by section 22 of the Theft Act 1968 is that the defendant must act dishonestly and must know or believe that the goods are stolen. It is difficult to see any reason why this should be regarded as a crime of specific intent. It could, however, be argued that, as the requirement of "dishonestly" does not correlate exactly with the *actus reus* requirements, this is a crime of ulterior *mens rea*, albeit not ulterior intent.

[vii] *attempt*: only intention suffices; further, it is a crime of ulterior intent.[35]

[viii] *assault with intent to resist arrest*: as with burglary, while one of the elements, the assault, may be committed recklessly, there must be a further intention to resist arrest.

[ix] *indecent assault*: in *Court*[36] it was held that where the manner and circumstances of an assault are ambiguous (slapping the buttocks of a 12 year-old girl outside her shorts), it would only be an indecent assault if the defendant had an indecent intention or purpose. In *C*[37] it was held that where an assault was unequivocally indecent (inserting fingers into a child's vagina) indecent assault was a crime of basic intent. It is thus possible[38] that where the act is ambiguous and the prosecution has to prove an indecent purpose, indecent assault is a crime of specific intent to which drunkenness would be a defence. The defendant would instead be found guilty of common assault.

It must be emphasised that this list does not purport to be exhaustive.

Most other offences are crimes of basic intent to which drunkenness is no defence. The most prominent on this list are the following: manslaughter, section 20, section 47 and common assault. Occasionally, a statute specifically provides that intoxication cannot be a defence: the Public Order Act 1986 is an example of this.[39] It is also widely accepted that rape is a crime of basic intent.

## R. v Fotheringham (1989) 88 Cr.App.R.206 (Court of Appeal, Criminal Division)

The appellant and his wife went out for the evening leaving a 14 year-old girl to babysit. The wife (probably in the appellant's absence) told the girl to sleep in the matrimonial bed.

---

[33] Theft Act 1968, s.9.

[34] [1972] 3 All E.R. 962.

[35] In *Durante (ibid.) endeavouring* to obtain money on a forged instrument was accepted as a crime of specific intent; this is analogous to an *attempt* to commit a crime.

[36] [1989] A.C. 28

[37] [1992] Crim.L.R.642.

[38] Smith, Commentary on C [1992] Crim.L.R.643.

[39] s.6(5).

On returning home the appellant got into the matrimonial bed and had sexual intercourse with the girl without her consent. The wife appeared and the intercourse ceased. The appellant was charged with rape but claimed that because of drunkenness, he had mistaken the girl for his wife. He admitted that he would not have made this mistake if he had been sober. The judge directed the jury to disregard the appellant's self-induced intoxication in considering whether there were reasonable grounds for his believing that he was having sexual intercourse with a consenting woman, namely, his wife. The appellant was convicted and appealed.

Watkins L.J.:
"The point of law ... [is] whether it is a defence to a charge of rape ... that a defendant, as a result of self-induced intoxication, has an honest but mistaken belief that he was having conjugal relations ...

Counsel had to recognise, as in fact he did, that where the issue in rape is consent, a defendant's self-induced intoxication is not a relevant matter which a jury are entitled to take into account in deciding whether there were reasonable grounds for the defendant's belief that the woman consented—see *Woods* (1982) 74 Cr.App.R.312. Likewise he had to face the law, which is that 'self-induced intoxication is no defence to a crime in which recklessness is enough to constitute the necessary *mens rea*'—see ... [*Caldwell* where Lord Diplock refers to *Majewski*] where it was held that rape is a crime of basic intent to which self-induced intoxication is no defence ...

[The appellant's argument] clearly runs counter to authority, which is that in rape self-induced intoxication is no defence, whether the issue be intention, consent or, as here, mistake as to the identity of the victim. We do not doubt that the public would be outraged if the law were to be declared to be otherwise."

**Appeal dismissed**

Rape is clearly a crime that can be committed recklessly insofar as section 1(1)(b) states that knowledge or recklessness *as to consent* will suffice. But in *Fotheringham* the mistake was not as to consent but as to whether the defendant was having unlawful sexual intercourse. (As the law then stood, if it had been his wife the sexual intercourse would have been lawful.) It is widely assumed that the defendant must *intend* to have sexual intercourse.[40] What was never decided, before the reforms to the law of rape in 1994, was whether there had to be an intention to have *unlawful* sexual intercourse (*i.e. knowledge* that it was not his wife) or whether recklessness as to the element sufficed. If the former view was correct, the defendant would have lacked *mens rea* in respect of an element which could not be satisfied by recklessness. On this basis drunkenness should have been a defence. This interpretation would mean that *any* element of a crime can be satisfied by proof of recklessness, the crime is always one of basic intent. Acceptance of this view would necessitate a reassessment of the list of crimes of specific intent presented above. In particular, burglary, indecent assault and assault with intent to resist arrest would all have to be regarded as crimes of basic intent because in each of them one element can be satisfied by proof of recklessness.

The alternative interpretation is that, consistent with the general principle, recklessness as to a surrounding circumstance (in this case, the "unlawfulness" requirement) suffices and, accordingly, his drunkenness as to this element is irrelevant. Since the abolition of the "marital rape exemption" this particular point

---

[40] Smith and Hogan, *Criminal Law* (10th ed., 2002), p. 244.

is no longer of practical importance but the broader issue still remains. What is the position if a defendant intends to indecently assault a woman in the vaginal area without penetrating her, but, because of his drunkenness, he does penetrate her? Strict principle might suggest that as this element of the crime can only be committed intentionally, drunkenness ought to be a defence. However, it is almost inconceivable that any court would engage in such an analysis. Policy would almost certainly prevail here and so it can be concluded, with some confidence, that, irrespective of the nature of the mistake, rape is always a crime of basic intent.

What is the rationale of this "recklessness test"? In *Majewski* Lord Elwyn-Jones L.C. said:

"If a man of his own volition takes a substance which causes him to cast off the restraints of reason and conscience, no wrong is done to him by holding him answerable criminally for any injury he may do while in that condition. His course of conduct in reducing himself by drugs and drink to that condition in my view supplies the evidence of *mens rea*, of guilty mind certainly sufficient for crimes of basic intent. It is a reckless course of conduct and recklessness is enough to constitute the necessary *mens rea* in assault cases ... The drunkenness is itself an intrinsic, an integral part of the crime, the other part being the evidence of the unlawful use of force against the victim. Together they add up to criminal recklessness."[41]

There were two problems with this approach. Suppose a defendant starts drinking at 8pm and by 10pm is no longer aware of his actions. At 11pm he commits the *actus reus* of the crime. The *mens rea* of the crime (getting so drunk which is a reckless thing to do) precedes the *actus reus*. There is no coincidence of *actus reus* and *mens rea*, and as Dashwood points out:

"It might be argued that the carry-over of *mens rea* in the present situation would correspond to that in the famous cases of *Thabo-Meli* and *Church* [above, pp. 180–184] where the immediate cause of death was not the attack upon the victim but the measures taken to dispose of what was believed to be a dead body. However, an important distinction is that in these cases the attack and the disposal of the supposed corpse represented successive steps in a single criminal transaction, the later act being consciously linked in the mind of the accused with the earlier act; such an analysis would not apply to the case of misconduct following reckless intoxication."[42]

The second problem with Lord Elwyn-Jones' approach is that recklessness does not exist in the abstract. One has to be reckless as to a particular consequence. Thus under the subjective test of recklessness it should have been necessary to establish that when the defendant was getting drunk (the recklessness) he foresaw the possibility of his committing the crime.

It is quite clear that the courts were less concerned with fine arguments such as these than with ensuring that a fair and just solution (in terms of balancing the competing interests of protection of society and the rights of the defendant) was achieved. As Lord Simon said:

---

[41] [1977] A.C. 443 at 474–475. In *Kingston* [1995] 2 A.C. 355 at 369 Lord Mustill stated that he was not required to decide how this rationalisation (or that of the defendant being estopped from relying on his self-induced in capacity) stood up to attack.

[42] Dashwood, "Logic and the Lords in Majewski" [1977] Crim.L.R.532, 591 at 540.

"One of the prime purposes of the criminal law, with its penal sanctions, is the protection from certain proscribed conduct of persons who are pursuing their lawful lives. Unprovoked violence has, from time immemorial, been a significant part of such proscribed violence. To accede to the argument on behalf of the appellant would leave the citizen legally unprotected from unprovoked violence where such violence was the consequence of drink or drugs having obliterated the capacity of the perpetrator to know what he was doing or what were its consequences."[43]

Lord Diplock, in *Caldwell*, was able to avoid these problems by re-casting recklessness in an objective mould. If the risks would have been obvious to an ordinary person at the time of drinking, then the defendant *is* reckless *as to the particular consequence*; it is irrelevant whether the defendant, because of intoxication, foresaw the risk himself.

However, as we have seen, the *Caldwell*-recklessness test has not been applied throughout English law and, particularly in the non-fatal offences against the person, the subjective *Cunningham*-recklessness test continues to apply. It is here that the clash between principle and policy is most marked. When subjective *mens rea* correlates with ordinary people's notions of fault or blameworthiness (say, cases of sober mistakes or accidents) it can be employed. When it does not (as in cases of drunken violence), the concept of subjective *mens rea* has to be jettisoned. The true basis of *mens rea* is the attribution of blame, which might, or might not, coincide with a defendant's state of mind. Blame is attributed to persons who render themselves insensible through drink or drugs and then commit a crime. As Lord Russell in *Majewski* said:

"*Mens rea* has many aspects. If asked to define it in such a case as the present I would say that *the element of guilt or moral turpitude* is supplied by the act of self-intoxication reckless of possible consequences."[44]

Such views were endorsed by Lord Simon in *Majewski*:

"*Mens rea* is therefore on ultimate analysis the state of mind stigmatised as wrongful by the criminal law which, when compounded with the relevant prohibited conduct, constitutes a particular offence. There is no juristic reason why mental incapacity brought about by self-induced intoxication, to realise what one is doing or its probable consequences should not be such a state of mind stigmatised as wrongful by the criminal law."[45]

These rules received the following endorsement in 1980.

### Criminal Law Revision Committee, 14th Report, Offences Against the Person, Cmnd.7844, (1980), paras 267, 270:

"267(1): ... evidence of voluntary intoxication should be capable of negating the mental element in murder and the intention required for the commission of any other offence; and

(2) in offences in which recklessness constitutes an element of the offence, if the defendant owing to voluntary intoxication had no appreciation of a risk which he would have appreciated had he been sober, such lack of appreciation is immaterial ...

[43] *Majewski* [1977] A.C. 443 at 476.
[44] *ibid.* at 498 (Emphasis added).
[45] [1977] A.C. 443 at 478.

270. The test in (2) above is formulated in such a way as to require the court to take into consideration any particular knowledge or any other personal characteristics of the defendant, as for example backwardness. Thus in a case where a gun is discharged killing or injuring another a jury might consider that many people could have made a mistake about the risk. But if the defendant was familiar with fire-arms the jury may find that he would have appreciated the risk if he had been sober. For similar reasons it would be unjust that a subnormal person should be judged on the same basis as one of average intelligence."

## 2. A partial defence?

As we have seen, the courts have been loath to admit intoxication as a complete defence to a criminal charge as the defendant is clearly at fault in reducing himself to such a level of intoxication. But as such a defendant is not aware of his actions at the time of the crime, his position is analogous to that of a reckless wrongdoer—who deserves punishment but, possibly, not to the same extent as the intentional wrongdoer. Thus the compromise was developed that intoxication would be a defence to those crimes of intention where there was a lesser included offence for which the defendant could be convicted. Thus intoxication has the practical effect of reducing murder to manslaughter[46] and of reducing section 18 to section 20. The Californian Penal Code expressly incorporates this compromise that intoxication can only reduce liability to an offence of a lower species or degree.[47]

However, despite this underlying rationale of the defence of drunkenness, it is clear that intoxication can sometimes operate as a complete defence in English law. As Lord Russell stated in *Majewski*:

"special intent cases are not restricted to those crimes in which the absence of a special intent leaves available a lesser crime embodying no special intent, but embraces all cases of special intent even though no alternative lesser criminal charge is available."[48]

The crime of theft is just such a case. Intoxication is a defence to a charge of theft,[49] although there is no lesser included offence of which the defendant can be convicted.

This sudden reassertion of principle is somewhat anomolous and, while there are dicta supporting this approach, it is unlikely that the courts actually will take this step and allow a complete defence in such circumstances.[50]

## 3. Drunken mistake

In most cases a drunken defendant will claim that a mistake has been made with the result that *mens rea* is missing. For example, there will be a claim that there was no intention to kill; the drunken defendant thought he was shooting at a tree stump. Such a plea will be dealt with under the rules canvassed above. There is evidence that drink can cause persons to make mistakes of a somewhat different nature. One effect of alcohol can be to lead the drinker to interpret the words and actions of

---

[46] See Clarkson, "Drunkenness, Constructive Manslaughter and Specific Intent" (1978) 41 M.L.R. 478.
[47] Cal. Penal Code, Art. 22; Fletcher, *Rethinking Criminal Law*, (1978), pp. 848–849.
[48] [1977] A.C. 443 at 499.
[49] *Above*, n.31.
[50] A common circumstance is that of "stealing" a vehicle whilst drunk. Even if the defendant was drunk enough to be afforded a defence to a charge of theft, he would still be liable for the offence of taking and driving away, contrary to s.12 of the Theft Act 1968.

others as threatening, thereby increasing "defensive activity".[51] In other words, a drunken person may act violently, mistakenly believing himself to be under attack.[52] What is the position where such a person makes a mistake as to a "defence"? The view now taken by the English courts is that such a drunken mistake, however genuinely believed, is no defence to a criminal charge—not even to crimes of specific intent.

## R. v O'Grady [1987] 1 Q.B. 995 (Court of Appeal, Criminal Division)

The appellant woke from a drunken stupor to find his equally drunken friend hitting him. In order to defend himself he retaliated with several blows and then returned to sleep. He awoke to find his friend dead. He was convicted of manslaughter and appealed on the ground that the judge had misdirected the jury as to the law of mistake.

Lord Lane C.J.:
"We have come to the conclusion that where the jury are satisfied that the defendant was mistaken in his belief that any force or the force which he in fact used was necessary to defend himself and are further satisfied that the mistake was caused by voluntarily induced intoxication, the defence must fail. We do not consider that any distinction should be drawn on this aspect of the matter between offences involving what is called specific intent, such as murder, and offences of so called basic intent, such as manslaughter. Quite apart from the problem of directing a jury in a case such as the present where manslaughter is an alternative verdict to murder, the question of mistake can and ought to be considered separately from the question of intent ...

This brings us to the question of public order. There are two competing interests. On the one hand the interest of the defendant who has only acted according to what he believed to be necessary to protect himself, and on the other hand that of the public in general and the victim in particular who, probably through no fault of his own, has been injured or perhaps killed because of the defendant's drunken mistake. Reason recoils from the conclusion that in such circumstances a defendant is entitled to leave the Court without a stain on his character. ...

We have therefore come to the conclusion that a defendant is not entitled to rely, so far as self-defence is concerned, upon a mistake of fact which has been induced by voluntary intoxication."

**Appeal dismissed**

This was followed in the similar murder case of *O'Connor*[53] where it was held that a drunken mistake as to the need for self-defensive action was to be ignored by the jury. However, in murder cases the drunkenness of the defendant could be taken into consideration in determining whether the defendant had the necessary specific intent (and on this basis a verdict of manslaughter was substituted).

These cases suggest that if a defendant mistakenly acts in self-defence and is drunk the mistake will be ignored—even if the mistake is not attributable to the

---

[51] Gustafson and Kallinen, "Changes in the Psychological Defence System as a Function of Alcohol Intoxication in Men" (1989) 84 B.J. Addict. 1515.
[52] Cretney and Davis, *above*, n.8, p. 27.
[53] [1991] Crim.L.R.135.

drunkenness, and, perhaps, even if it is a perfectly reasonable mistake. This is surely absurd. If a person makes the sort of mistake that he would have made when sober—*i.e.* a reasonable mistake—he should be entitled to a defence even if he is intoxicated because in such circumstances the intoxication is irrelevant. It is only where a mistake has been made *because of* intoxication that policy considerations dictate the strict approach adopted in the above cases.

There is a further problem with these cases. Why should intoxication be critical in deciding whether there is *mens rea* in relation to an element of the offence, but be totally discounted when deciding whether a defendant thought he was acting in self-defence? We saw earlier that it is not always easy to decide whether a mistake has been made as to a definitional element or as to a defence element[54] and it seems irrational that criminal liability should be dependent on such a classification. It is difficult to see any material distinction in culpability between a defendant who makes a drunken mistake about the *actus reus* and one who makes a similar mistake concerning a defence element.[55]

The already deeply unsatisfactory nature of the law in relation to drunken mistake has been compounded by the decision of *Richardson and Irwin*.[56] In this case the defendants, who were students, dropped the victim from a balcony causing him to be seriously injured. The Court of Appeal held that their drunken mistake that the victim was consenting to this "horseplay" could be a defence to inflicting grievous bodily harm contrary to section 20 of the Offences Against the Person Act 1861. Whether one adopts the general rule that intoxication is no defence to basic intent crimes (of which section 20 is undoubtedly one) or one adopts the rule in *O'Grady* that all drunken mistakes are irrelevant, the defendants ought to have been convicted. The authority of this decision must be in serious doubt.

Finally, there are certain statutes that expressly provide that a defendant has a defence if he holds a particular belief. For example, the Criminal Damage Act 1971, section 5(2) provides that a person has a defence (or a "lawful excuse" as per section 1(1)) to a charge of criminal damage if he believed that he had the consent of the person entitled to give consent and section 5(3) provides that "it is immaterial whether a belief is justified or not if it is honestly held". What is the position where a defendant only holds such a belief because of his drunkenness?

### Jaggard v Dickinson [1981] Q.B. 527 (Queen's Bench Divisional Court)

The appellant while drunk broke two windows and damaged a curtain in another person's house. She honestly believed that the house belonged to a friend who would have consented to her breaking in and causing the damage.

Mustill J.:
"Her defence is founded on the state of belief called for by section 5(2). True, the fact of the appellant's intoxication was relevant to the defence under section 5(2), for it helped to explain what would otherwise have been inexplicable, and hence lent colour to her evidence about the state of her belief. This is not the same as using drunkenness to rebut an inference

[54] *Above*, p. 188.
[55] The Law Commission takes the view that the law relating to drunken mistake "cannot sensibly be reconciled with the general law on intoxication and recommends bringing them into line": Law Com. No. 229, *Legislating the Criminal Code: Intoxication and Criminal Liability* (1995), paras 7.1–7.15.
[56] [1999] 1 Cr.App.R.392.

of intention or recklessness. Belief, like intention or recklessness, is a state of mind: but they are not the same states of mind.

Can it nevertheless be said that, even if the context is different, the principles established by *R. v Majewski* ... ought to be applied to this new situation? If the basis of the decision in *R. v Majewski* had been that drunkenness does not prevent a person from having an intent or being reckless, then there would be grounds for saying that it should equally be left out of account when deciding on his state of belief. But this is not in our view what *R. v Majewski* decided. The House of Lords did not conclude that intoxication was irrelevant to the fact of the defendant's state of mind, but rather that, whatever might have been his actual state of mind, he should for reasons of policy be precluded from relying on any alteration in that state brought about by self-induced intoxication. ... But these considerations do not apply to a case where Parliament has specifically required the court to consider the defendant's actual state of belief, not the state of belief which ought to have existed. It seems to us that the court is required by section 5(3) to focus on the existence of the belief, not its intellectual soundness; and a belief can be just as much honestly held if it is induced by intoxication as if it stems from stupidity, forgetfulness or inattention. ...

Parliament has specifically isolated one subjective element, in the shape of honest belief, and has given it separate treatment, and its own special gloss in section 5(3). This being so, there is nothing objectionable in giving it special treatment as regards drunkenness, in accordance with the natural meaning of the words."

**Appeal allowed**

This whole approach does seem distinctly odd. Where a defendant causing criminal damage makes a drunken mistake, his entire criminal liability depends on the precise form of his mistake. For instance, if he makes a mistake and thinks the property is his own, he will be liable as drunkenness is no defence to a charge of criminal damage. If, however, because of his drunkenness he believes that the owner would consent to the damage to the property, then section 5(3) applies and, as in *Jaggard v Dickinson*, the defendant will escape liability.

It is interesting to compare section 5(3) with section 8 of the Criminal Justice Act 1967. In *Majewski* Lord Elwyn-Jones held that drunkenness could not be taken into account under section 8:

> "Its purpose and effect [section 8] was to alter the law of evidence about the presumption of intention to produce the reasonable and probable consequences of one's acts. It was not intended to change the common law rule. In referring to 'all the evidence' it meant all the *relevant* evidence. But if there is a substantive rule of law that in crimes of basic intent, the factor of intoxication is irrelevant (and such I hold to be the substantive law), evidence with regard to it is quite irrelevant."[57]

It has been commented that it "is difficult to see that section 5(3) performs any different function in relation to lawful excuse than section 8 of the Criminal Justice Act 1967 performs in relation to intention and recklessness."[58] If evidence of drunkenness is irrelevant to an ascertainment of intention or foresight, it is difficult to understand why it is relevant to determining whether one believes another has consented to his property being damaged.[59]

---

[57] At 475–476.
[58] Wells, "Swatting the Subjectivist Bug" [1982] Crim.L.R.209.
[59] The Law Commission finds no justification for the anomalous result and recommends that the same rules apply to both statutory and general defences: Law Com. No. 229, *above*, n.55, paras 7.16–7.18.

## E. *Involuntary intoxication*

Where a defendant is reduced to a state of intoxication through no fault of her own (because, for example, her drinks were "laced"), she cannot be "blamed" for her actions and will accordingly have a defence to any criminal charge. However, this protection extends only to the defendant who is so intoxicated that she does not form *mens rea*.

## R. v Kingston [1995] 2 A.C. 355 (House of Lords)

The appellant, his drink having been laced with drugs, indecently assaulted a 15-year-old boy. He was convicted after the judge directed the jury that they should acquit if they found that he was so affected by the drugs that he lacked intent, but to convict if he had intent. The defendant appealed, claiming that he would not have committed the offence but for the drugs. The Court of Appeal upheld his appeal on the basis that the "operative fault" was not his. The Crown appealed to the House of Lords.

Lord Mustill:
"[T]he general nature of the case is clear enough. In ordinary circumstances the respondent's paedophiliac tendencies would have been kept under control, even in the presence of the sleeping or unconscious boy on the bed. The ingestion of the drug (whatever it was) brought about a temporary change in the mentality or personality of the respondent which lowered his ability to resist temptation so far that his desires overrode his ability to control them. Thus we are concerned with a case of disinhibition. . . .

On these facts there are three grounds on which the respondent might be held free from criminal responsibility. First, that his immunity flows from general principles of the criminal law. Secondly, that this immunity is already established by a solid line of authority. Finally, that the court should, when faced with a new problem acknowledge the justice of the case and boldly create a new common law defence.

It is clear . . . that the Court of Appeal adopted the first approach. The decision was explicitly founded on general principle . . . :

'the law recognises that, exceptionally, an accused person may be entitled to be acquitted if there is a possibility that although his act was intentional, the intent itself arose out of circumstances for which he bears no blame.' . . .

My Lords, with every respect I must suggest that no such principle exists or, until the present case, had ever in modern times been thought to exist. Every offence consists of a prohibited act or omission coupled with whatever state of mind is called for by the statute or rule of the common law which creates the offence. In those offences which are not absolute the state of mind which the prosecution must prove to have underlain the act or omission—the 'mental element'—will in the majority of cases be such as to attract disapproval. The mental element will then be the mark of what may properly be called a 'guilty mind'. . . . [His Lordship then surveyed cases both here and in other jurisdictions and concluded that there was no basis] for holding that the defence relied upon is already established by the common law, any more than it can be derived from general principles. Accordingly I agree with the analysis of Professor Griew, *Archbold News*, May 28 1993, pp. 4–5:

'What has happened is that the Court of Appeal has recognised a new *defence* to criminal charges in the nature of an exculpatory excuse. It is precisely because the defendant acted in a prohibited way with the intent (the *mens rea*) required by the definition of the offence that he needs this defence.' . . .

To recognise a new defence of this type would be a bold step. . . . I can only say that the defence runs into difficulties at every turn. In point of theory, it would be necessary to reconcile a defence of irresistible impulse derived from a combination of innate drives and external disinhibition with the rule that irresistible impulse of a solely internal origin (not necessarily any more the fault of the offender) does not in itself excuse although it may be a symptom of disease of the mind . . . Equally, the state of mind which founds the defence superficially resembles a state of diminished responsibility ... On the practical side there are serious problems ...

My Lords, the fact that a new doctrine may require adjustment of existing principles to accommodate it ... is not of course a ground for refusing to adopt it, if that is what the interests of justice require. Here, however, justice makes no such demands, for the interplay between the wrong done to the victim, the individual characteristics and frailties of the defendant, and the pharmacological effects of whatever drug may be potentially involved can be far better recognised by a tailored choice from the continuum of sentences available to the judge than by the application of a single yea-or-nay jury decision.

... I consider that both the ruling and the direction of the judge were correct."

**Appeal allowed**

Many commentators condemned the Court of Appeal decision in *Kingston* as surprising, dangerous and contrary to principle[60] and favour the narrower view of blame adopted by the House of Lords. However, others have argued that a new exculpatory defence should be developed for circumstances such as those in *Kingston*. Many persons might have secret urges to commit criminal acts but blame is inappropriate if they exercise control and restraint. If the only reason their inhibitions are removed is because someone else has secretly laced their drink, they are no longer able to evaluate their actions[61] and should not be blamed. It has been suggested that such a defence, if it were to be afforded, should depend upon an assessment whether the conduct was "out of character".[62] This would involve comparing the defendant's "settled" character with the defendant's intoxicated character. If the involuntary intoxication "destabilises" his character so that he commits an offence he should have an excuse.[63] Such an approach, however, is perceived by others to be blaming a person for what he is rather than what he has done. Apart from difficulties of proof (for example, establishing whether or not Kingston had abused children on previous occasions), the fact is that the evidence established on this occasion that Kingston only gave way to his desires because of the unforeseen actions of a third party. The real blame should be directed at that third party. Where a person commits a crime because of threats by another, we blame that other person and allow the defendant a defence of duress. We do not enquire whether the actions were "out of character". The same approach should be adopted to those whose inhibitions are removed by the secret acts of others.

It is a theme of this book that criminal liability should generally only be imposed upon blameworthy actors who caused prohibited harms. *Mens rea*, as traditionally defined, is an indicator of blame. However, as seen in this chapter, we do sometimes blame persons without *mens rea*: when they voluntarily become intoxicated. Similarly, we ought not to blame some actors, such as Kingston, even though they do have *mens rea*. As the Court of Appeal put it: "the law should exculpate him because the operative fault is not his".[64] This lack of fault should be reflected by the

[60] For example, Smith [1993] Crim.L.R.784; Griew, *Archbold News*, May 28, 1993.
[61] Horder, "Pleading Involuntary Lack of Capacity" (1993) 52 C.L.J. 298. See also, Smith and Clements, "Involuntary Intoxication, the Threshold of Inhibition and the Instigation of Crime" [1995] 46 N.I.L.Q. 210.
[62] See Sullivan, "Involuntary Intoxication and Beyond" [1994] Crim.L.R.272 and Wilson, "Involuntary Intoxication: Excusing the Inexcusable" [1995] 1 *Res Publica* 25.
[63] Sullivan, "Making Excuses" in Simester and Sullivan (eds), *Harm and Culpability* (1996), p. 131. See also Tadros, "The Characters of Excuse" [2001] 21 O.J.L.S. 495 at 502–506.
[64] *Kingston* (1993) 97 Cr.App.R.401.

creation of a new defence. Lacey, for example, has argued for the creation of a new defence of "blocked evaluation" which, rather than operating on the basis of lapse of character, could be thought of in "terms of temporary lapses of normal conditions of agency, given that the lapse is of the kind which removes or seriously undermines the normal reasoning process."[65] Such a defence might not only be available to those defendants (with *mens rea*) pleading involuntary intoxication.[66] The House of Lords, has, however, rejected any such approach and, clinging to orthodoxy, proclaimed that Kingston must be liable as he acted with *mens rea* and no established defence was applicable. It must be seriously doubted whether this severing of the link between moral fault and blame can be justified.

It is unfortunate that the Law Commission decided not to extend its deliberations to encompass the rule in *Kingston*[67] and it is most unlikely that its proposed definition of involuntary intoxication would have been of assistance to such a defendant.[68] The latest Government proposals in the Draft Offences Against the Person Bill 1998 are similarly unlikely to encompass defendants such as Kingston. Whilst the intoxicant was clearly administered without his consent, because he acted with *mens rea* "his awareness or understanding" would not be impaired.[69]

### F. *"Dutch courage" intoxication*

Where a person deliberately reduces himself to a state of intoxication to give himself "Dutch courage" to commit a crime, his intoxication will not be a defence even to crimes that can only be committed with a specific intention. He is to be "blamed" to the same extent as the person who intentionally commits a crime. As Lord Denning stated in *Gallagher*:

> "If a man, whilst sane and sober, forms an intention to kill ... and then gets himself drunk so as to give himself Dutch courage to do the killing ... he cannot rely on his self-induced drunkenness as a defence to a charge of murder, nor even as reducing it to manslaughter ... the wickedness of his mind before he got drunk is enough to condemn him, coupled with the act which he intended to do and did do."[70]

### Law Commission Report No. 229, Legislating the Criminal Code, Intoxication and Criminal Liability (1995), paras 6.51–6.52:

> "[T]he situation is far-fetched in the extreme ... Lord Denning was concerned with the defendant who becomes intoxicated *in order to give himself courage to carry out his intention*—not in the hope that he will lose all control of his actions but will nevertheless somehow happen to do the very thing that he lacks the courage to do while conscious. If his purpose is to give himself 'Dutch courage' rather than to turn himself into an automaton, we

---

[65] "Partial Defences to Homicide" in Ashworth and Mitchell (eds), *Rethinking English Homicide Law* (2000), p. 107 at p. 120. See also Sullivan, *above*, n.63 and Tadros, *above*, n.63.

[66] Lacey discusses whether it could be used in situations of mercy-killing, for example, where the extreme distress or despair edges out the normal processes of reasoning; *ibid.*, at pp. 123–125.

[67] Law Com. No. 229, *above*, n.55, paras 1.7–1.8.

[68] Cl. 5. While this definition includes "impairment of control" it seems clear that the Law Commission did not envisage this phrase extending to cases such as *Kingston*: para. 1.9.

[69] *Above*, p. 410.

[70] [1963] A.C. 349.

do not think it right that he should be regarded, *at the time when he causes the consequence he desires*, as intending that consequence. He cannot fairly be deemed to have had, at that later time, the intention that he in fact had when he became intoxicated ... We have considered whether to propose a special rule for the case of the person who becomes intoxicated in order to turn himself into an automaton, hoping that while in that state he will commit the *actus reus* of an offence requiring intention; but we have concluded that such a rule would be of no practical value. ...[I]t is almost inconceivable that the case envisaged could ever arise; certainly we are unaware of any such case."

## G. *Intoxication can cause insanity or diminished responsibility*

Drunkenness can cause a disease of the mind sufficient to bring the defendant within the insanity rules.[71] It can cause, for example, a *delirium tremens*. However, the defence is rarely successful in England. In *Burns*[72] a psychiatrist testified that Burns had a disease of the mind because his brain was damaged by alcohol with the result that on the occasion of the alleged crime he was suffering from "amnesia in the sense that the thing does not register at the time because the brain function is impaired" which meant that Burns did not know what he was doing, or that it was wrong. It was accepted that this defence could result in an insanity verdict, but the jury rejected the psychiatric evidence and concluded that Burns knew what he was doing.

Perhaps with the new greater flexibility in sentencing options upon a finding of "not guilty by reason of insanity", insanity caused by drunkenness will be pleaded more often in future. In *Bromley*[73] the defendant suffered from brain damage which could motivate him into violence upon consuming a small quantity of alcohol. On a charge of attempted rape it was held that the drink had made him temporarily insane. Pursuant to the court's new powers[74] he was given an absolute discharge.

Can alcoholism amount to a disease of the mind for the purposes of the insanity defence? This issue is problematic because the medical and sociological literature is still divided as to whether alcoholism is a disease or learned behaviour.

## Julia Tolmie, "Alcoholism and Criminal Liability" (2001) 64 M.L.R. 688 at pp. 689–708:

"[These] two competing conceptualisations of the phenomenon ... can be labelled the 'disease model' and the 'habit model' ...

[T]he disease model views alcoholism as an abnormal mental condition, whereas the habit model views alcoholics as involved in normal human processes but making bad choices ... [S]ome disease models of alcoholism view the condition as involving a total loss of control over drinking, whereas *some* disease models and *all* habit models view an alcoholic's control over their drinking as impaired rather than totally lost. ... The model of criminal responsibility that purportedly underpins the criminal justice system is premised on the

[71] *Davis* (1881) 14 Cox C.C. 563; *Beard* [1920] A.C. 479; *Gallagher* [1963] A.C. 349.
[72] (1974) 58 Cr.App.R.364.
[73] (1992) 142 New.L.J. 116 (Winchester Crown Court)
[74] s.5(2)(b)(iii) of the Criminal Procedure (Insanity) Act 1964, as substituted by the Criminal Procedure (Insanity and Unfitness to Plead) Act 1991.

notion that people have free will and rationality. ... Intoxication can impair one's capacity for choice on a number of ... levels. However, even if it has, as a matter of public policy the defendant is often not exonerated in spite of that impairment. It is considered that their choice to get dangerously intoxicated in the first place is sufficiently morally culpable to supply criminal responsibility in spite of their lack of choice at the time of the crime. The condition of alcoholism is interesting because it challenges this assumption. Unlike other people who choose to get drunk, alcoholics belong to a category of people who have impaired choice around even the decision to get intoxicated.

How the defendant's alcoholism should shift the normal calculation of criminal liability based on their intoxication differs depending on the model of alcoholism that one adopts. For example, if one views alcoholism as a habit that has impaired the defendant's choices to drink but still left them with choice, it is extremely difficult to argue that there should be reduced criminal liability based on the condition. On the other hand if one views alcoholism as an abnormal mental condition which either totally deprives the defendant of the choice to drink, or leaves them with both an impaired choice and disordered thinking around what degree of choice they do have, then there is a strong argument for taking into account the alcoholic's intoxication when considering their criminal liability. ...

If a history of alcoholism produces an independent and recognised pathological condition then it is uncontroversial that this can form the foundation of an insanity defence. Thus delirium tremens and alcohol withdrawal psychosis can be the basis of a successful insanity defence. What is not so clear is whether alcoholism *per se*, along with states of intoxication which result from it, can form the basis of the insanity defence. ...

Once again the strongest argument for alcoholism forming the foundation of the insanity defence applies if the disease model of alcoholism is adopted. ... On the other hand, if the habit model of alcoholism is adopted then there is little argument for alcoholism forming the foundation of an insanity defence. ...

So from a policy point of view it appears to make the most sense to treat an alcoholic defendant within the auspices of the criminal justice system, releasing them if treatment is successful and they are likely to be reintegrated as a contributing and functional member of the community, but requiring them to serve out the standard sentence for their crime if they are not treatable at that point in time. There are two ways of achieving this result.

The first is to deal with the alcoholic's condition at the point of trial and impose treatment in the place of punishment as a matter of liability rather than sentence. Insanity is a defence that effectively achieves this result. ... The second way of dealing with the issue is to hold an alcoholic fully responsible for the crimes that they have committed and then deal with their condition as a sentencing issue."

Although the matter is unresolved in English law, the better approach would be to follow the lead provided in the United States[75] and regard alcoholism as capable of amounting to a disease of the mind—bearing in mind that a defence of insanity will not succeed in such cases unless the other rigourous requirements of the M'Naghten Rules have been satisfied.

Can intoxication give rise to a defence of diminished responsibility? In *Tandy*[76] it was indicated that alcoholism could bring a defendant within the scope of section 2 of the Homicide Act 1957 (i) "if the alcoholism had reached the level at which her brain had been injured by the repeated insult from intoxicants so that there was gross impairment of her judgment and emotional responses"[77]; and (ii) if "the appellant's drinking had become involuntary, that is to say she was no longer able to resist the impulse to drink". It has been argued that the court "effectively required a defendant who wants to base a defence of diminished responsibility on

[75] Salzman v United States, 405 F.2d 358 (1968).
[76] (1988) 87 Cr.App.R.45.
[77] See also *Inseal* [1992] Crim.L.R.35.

their alcoholism to demonstrate a *total* impairment of control *at all times* around alcohol. What this means is that the court was setting a requirement that even the most chronic alcoholic will find difficult to meet".[78] The decision appears to be inconsistent with section 2 which requires only a substantial, and not total, impairment of mental responsibility.[79]

It is clear that the transient effect of drink or drugs is insufficient.[80] However, more problematic is the situation where the defendant pleads mental abnormality but is also heavily intoxicated at the time of the offence.

## R. v Dietschmann [2003] 1 All E.R. 897 (House of Lords)

The defendant was suffering from a mental abnormality (an adjustment disorder which was a depressed grief reaction to a bereavement) but was also heavily intoxicated at the time of the killing.

Lord Hutton:
"The policy of the criminal law in respect of persons suffering from mental abnormality is to be found in the words of section 2. . . . [A] brain-damaged person who is intoxicated and who commits a killing is not in the same position as a person who is intoxicated, but not brain-damaged, and who commits a killing . . . I consider that the jury should be directed along the following lines:

'Assuming that the defence have established that the defendant was suffering from mental abnormality as described in section 2, the important question is: did that abnormality substantially impair his mental responsibility for his acts in doing the killing? You know that before he carried out the killing the defendant had had a lot to drink. Drink cannot be taken into account as something which contributed to his mental abnormality and to any impairment of mental responsibility arising from that abnormality. But you may take the view that both the defendant's mental abnormality and drink played a part in impairing his mental responsibility for the killing and that he might not have killed if he had not taken drink. If you take that view, then the question for you to decide is this: has the defendant satisfied you that, despite the drink, his mental abnormality substantially impaired his mental responsibility for his fatal acts, or has he failed to satisfy you of that? If he has satisfied you of that, you will find him not guilty of murder but you may find him guilty of manslaughter.' "

While this is clearly in line with other policy decisions in relation to intoxication this is not an easy exercise for the jury. The fact that the defendant is intoxicated is not to be taken into account. The jury must focus on the pre-existing abnormality of mind and assess whether that abnormality substantially impaired his mental responsibility. But, given the fact that the drink may also have "played a part in impairing his mental responsibility",[81] it is surely far-fetched to expect a jury to be able to discriminate between the two causes of impairment. The short answer is that juries will continue to do what they normally do when dealing with diminished responsibility in the minority of cases where there is not a guilty plea and simply accept the views of the medical experts.[82] The practical importance of this decision

---

[78] Tolmie, *above*, p.427 at 699.
[79] *ibid.* at 700.
[80] *Di Duca* (1959) 43 Cr.App.R.167; *Fenton* (1975) 119 S.J. 695.
[81] *Dietschmann* [2003] 1 All E.R. 897.
[82] *Above*, p. 402.

is that it confirms that drunken defendants with mental abnormalities are not barred from pleading diminished responsibility.

## H. *Reform of the law*

### Law Commission Report No. 229, Legislating the Criminal Code, Intoxication and Criminal Liability (1995), paras 5.4–5.6:

"5.4. First, conflicting views as to the exact implications of *Majewski*, and in particular the lack of any satisfactory criteria for drawing the crucial distinction between crimes of basic and of specific intent, meant that the law was complicated and difficult to explain.

5.5 Secondly, the *Majewski* principle operates through tchnical rules of law which have been developed piecemeal by the courts. As a result, the policy which lies behind the rules, namely the protection of the public from those who commit violent or harmful acts when intoxicated, is being implemented in an erratic and unprincipled manner. This is particularly apparent in the way the rules are applied to defences based on a mistaken belief.

5.6. Thirdly, the *Majewski* approach gives rise to practical difficulties, because it is not clear whether evidence of the defendant's intoxication can be treated as *equivalent* to the mental state required for the offence, or whether the jury should ignore *only* the fact of the defendant's intoxication and consider whether he would have had the necessary awareness had he not been intoxicated."

### George P. Fletcher, Rethinking Criminal Law (1978), pp. 847–848:

"His fault in rendering himself non-responsible at the time of the violent act is constant, whether he commits a burglary, a rape, or a murder. To bring the scope of his liability into line with his culpability in getting drunk, the law seeks a compromise. There has to be some accommodation between (1) the principle that if someone gets drunk, he is liable for the violent consequences, and (2) the principle that liability and punishment should be graded in proportion to actual culpability.

German law and American law reveal two different approaches to reconciling these conflicting principles. German law includes intoxication along with mental illness as a basis for denying the capacity to be held accountable for a wrongful act. Deference to the conflicting principle of liability for the risk implicit in getting drunk is found in a special section of the Code, which is here translated in full:

§323a(1) Whoever intentionally or negligently becomes intoxicated through the use of alcohol or other intoxicating substances is punishable up to five years in prison, if while in that intoxicated condition he commits a wrongful act and if by virtue of the intoxication is not responsible for that act (or his non-responsibility is a possibility).

(2) In no event may the punishment be greater than that for the wrongful act committed in the state of intoxication.

The concept of negligence underlying this provision is negligence as to the risk of committing a crime while intoxicated. If the suspect takes adequate precautions against committing a crime while intoxicated, there is no negligence. If, for example, he hires someone to supervise his conduct while he is intoxicated and the hired person unexpectedly fails to restrain him, there would be a good case against liability. If he gets drunk in a bar and while in a state of non-responsibility he throws a bottle at a valuable mirror, he is not punished for the wrongful act of intentionally destroying the property of another; rather he is punished for the wrongful act of creating a risk that he would behave non-responsibly and intentionally destroy property. . . .

[T]he theory of the provision is not simply that he negligently take the risk that he might do some harm. The requirement of a wrongful act while intoxicated is an important limitation.

Indeed the limitation suggests that the theory underlying the provision is not simply one of negligently endangering other persons. If risk-taking were the essence of the crime, there would be no concern about the wrongfulness of the intoxicated act and indeed it would be hard to explain why the subsequent act should be required at all."

Over the past few decades English law reform bodies have vacillated between proposals to modify *Majewski* and the more radical proposal of abolishing *Majewski* and replacing it with a separate offence.

### Criminal Law Revision Committee, 14th Report, Offences Against the Person, Cmnd.7844 (1980), paras 259–264:

"259. ... What calls for punishment is getting intoxicated and when in that condition behaving in a way which society cannot, and should not, tolerate. An offence which covers this situation must make some reference to the harm caused, and cannot be expressed simply in terms of getting dangerously intoxicated, however gross the intoxication may have been. Furthermore, the harm needs to be identified to some extent: the drunken man who on arrest punches a police officer should not be labelled with the same offence as the alcoholic who kills a child when trying to interfere with her sexually. It is doubtful whether any solution to the problem based solely upon legal principle would be generally acceptable. Policy has to be taken into account. ...

260. The Butler Committee considered offences committed while voluntarily intoxicated (paragraphs 18.51–18.59 of their report), and they proposed the creation of a strict liability offence where a person while voluntarily intoxicated does an act (or makes an omission) that would amount to a dangerous offence if it were done or made with the requisite state of mind for that offence. Their proposal is that the offence should not be charged in the first instance. On indictment the jury would be directed to find on this offence in the event of intoxication being successfully raised as a defence to the offence originally charged ... On this proposal the jury would have no option but to convict of the dangerous intoxication offence. On conviction of the offence on indictment the maximum penalty suggested is one year's imprisonment for a first offence or three years' imprisonment for a second or subsequent one; on summary trial the maximum sentence of imprisonment would be six months.

261. One of the defects in the Butler Committee proposal is, in our opinion, the problem of the nomenclature of the offence. A conviction of the Butler Committee offence would merely record a conviction of an offence of committing a dangerous act while intoxicated. This is insufficient. The record must indicate the nature of the act committed, for example whether it was an assault or a killing. It would be unfair for a defendant who has committed a relatively minor offence while voluntarily intoxicated to be labelled as having committed the same offence as a defendant who has killed. The penalty suggested is also in our opinion insufficient to deal with serious offences such as killings or rapes while voluntarily intoxicated by drink or drugs.

262. Professors Smith and Glanville Williams support the proposal of a separate offence because in the first place they consider it to be a fundamental principle that a person should not be convicted of an offence requiring recklessness when he was not in fact reckless. In such a case the verdict of the jury and the record of the court do not represent the truth. Secondly, they think it important that the verdict of the jury should distinguish between an offender who was reckless and one who was not because that is relevant to the question of sentence. ...

The majority of us feel, however, that [the Smith and Williams proposal for a special offence carrying the same punishment as the complete offence] would also create problems. The separate offence would add to the already considerable number of matters which a jury often has to consider when deciding whether the offences charged have been proved, and some of us feel that the separate offence would make the jury's task even more difficult than it is at present in some cases. ... It seems likely moreover, that if the separate offence is created there would be many more trials in which defendants would raise the issue of drunkenness, ... [M]any defendants might seek to plead to the special offence rather than the offence charged, either because they might prefer to be convicted of the special offence rather than the offence charged (as for example rape), or because the special offence might tend to be regarded as a less serious offence. ... We also consider that it is artificial and undesirable to have a separate offence for which conviction is automatic but which carries the same maximum penalty as the offence for which a defendant would have been convicted but for the lack of proof of the required mental element due to intoxication. It is also important to consider the public reaction to the creation of a separate offence: we are of the opinion that they would be confused by it."

The majority of the Criminal Law Revision Committee accordingly rejected the proposal for a special intoxication offence and instead recommended a codification of the law, endorsing the "recklessness test" discussed above, namely, that intoxication should never be a defence to crimes that can be committed recklessly; it could at most negative the mental element of intention required for the commission of an offence. This proposal was reproduced by the Draft Criminal Code Bill 1989, clause 22.[83]

Such an approach, however, was not without its critics.

### Andrew Ashworth, "Intoxication and General Defences" [1980] Crim.L.R.556 at 558–560:

"[M]any people drive whilst intoxicated without infringing any other rules of the road, and yet the criminal law does not hesitate to strike at the risk-creation involved in drunken driving, without waiting for the risk to materialise. Indeed, for that offence complete intoxication is not required and a certain blood/alcohol concentration suffices, and for controlled drugs mere possession attracts criminal liability. A prohibition on alcohol would be unworkable; yet, since drinking oneself into a state of intoxication involves voluntarily casting off 'the restraints of reason and conscience,' should the law not go further than the summary offences of public drunkenness and make intoxication itself a serious crime, as a kind of inchoate offence? The Committee might well use the following arguments against this. First, it might be possible to construct a statistical argument that only a minority of totally intoxicated persons actually cause harm whilst in that condition.[84] Secondly, the social effects of criminalising intoxication would be more widely resented than the prohibition on driving with excess alcohol. But thirdly, when an intoxicated person does cause harm, the balance is tilted in favour of criminal liability. Whilst it might be oppressive to punish all intoxicated persons (even though no harm is caused) on the basis that they have voluntarily created a risk, a law which reserves that punishment for those intoxicated persons who do cause harm cannot be reproached with sacrificing individual liberty to a statistical possibility. If he has caused harm, the risk has materialised. Thus a higher value is set upon popular conceptions of liberty (perhaps because alcohol fulfils a social want, and because wider criminalisation might bring a style of law enforcement which would unduly infringe other liberties) than upon the benefits to society in general and to victims in particular of a peremptory requirement that citizens should not so intoxicate themselves as to lose control over their behaviour.

*The Appropriate Label for the Offence*
The Committee agree that a principal defect of the Butler recommendation was the proposed label: a single offence of being dangerously intoxicated would lump together the intoxicated child killer and the drunken brawler (paras 259, 261). Why exactly do the Committee object to this? ...
What is the nature of 'the offender's fault' in intoxicated harm-doing? His fault lies in rendering himself insensible and uncontrolled."

---

[83] Law Com. No. 177 (1989).
[84] Ed.: Less than 1 per cent of intoxicated persons involve themselves in serious criminal activity (Mitchell (1988) *Int. Journal of Law and Psychiatry*, 77 at 89).

In 1993 the Law Commission published a Consultation Paper in which, after examining the possible options for change, it provisionally recommended the abolition of *Majewski* and the creation of a new special offence.[85] However, these proposals were subjected to severe criticism. Some respondents opposed the very notion of a separate offence (for example, on the basis that defendants would inevitably perceive it as a chance to be convicted of a less serious offence and that the suggested criterion of substantial impairment was flawed, adding to the length of trials[86]), while others so qualified the Law Commission's proposal that it "would largely defeat its purpose".[87] The Law Commission has, therefore, done a dramatic *volte face* and now recommends that the present law be codified in an amended form.

### Law Commission Report No. 229, Legislating the Criminal Code, Intoxication and Criminal Liability (1995), paras 6.6–6.7:

"6.6 We ... have concluded that the best way of codifying the present law, whilst avoiding the problems inherent in the present distinction between offences of specific and basic intent, is to confine the *Majewski* principle, broadly speaking, to offences for which proof of recklessness (or awareness of risk) is sufficient. ...

6.7 This policy *may* represent the present law, although it is difficult to state this with any certainty. ... [I]t has the advantages of simplicity and clarity, both matters of great importance in any system of criminal law. Finally, this change in the law will have a negligible practical effect in relation to crimes already judicially categorised as being of basic or specific intent, since most crimes designated as being of basic intent are capable of reckless commission."

This recommendation has been substantially adopted in the latest Government proposals.

### Draft Offences Against the Person Bill 1998, clause 19:

"(1) For the purposes of this Act a person who was voluntarily intoxicated at any material time must be treated—
(a) as having been aware of any risk of which he would have been aware had he not been intoxicated, and
(b) as having known or believed in any circumstances which he would have known or believed in had he not been intoxicated."

The Law Commission's approach, now endorsed by government, has been criticised.

---

[85] Law Com. Consultation Paper No. 127, *Intoxication and Criminal Liability* (1993).
[86] Law Com. No. 229, *above*, n.55, paras 5.8–5.13.
[87] *ibid.* para. 5.14.

Jeremy Horder, "Sobering Up? The Law Commission on Criminal Intoxication"
[1995] 58 M.L.R. 534 at 535–536:

"Despite the radical change of direction since the Consultation Paper, one thing has not changed in the Commission's final Report. This is, ironically, the attitude of uncomprehending hostility towards the common law's attempt to express, in its division of crimes between those of basic and of specific intent, the very distinctions between offences on which the Commission's new proposals are broadly based. Despite the views of those working in the criminal justice system that the current law works *fairly*, as well as without difficulty, the Commission makes little effort to discern any deeper principles underlying the common law that might explain why its rules can be regarded as fair. They endorse the view that 'the designation of crimes as requiring, or not requiring, specific intent is based on no principle at all' (3.27; 5.36). How is it, then, that the Commission has thought it right to track the designation so closely in its own proposals? For the kinds of *mentes reae* mentioned in clause 1(2), allegations of which may be met by leading evidence of voluntary intoxication, bear a striking resemblance to the *mentes reae* of crimes of specific intent, allegations of which can presently be rebutted by such evidence at common law.

The answer is that the Commission regards the case for restricting the ability of a defendant to deny *mens rea* through pleading voluntary intoxication as founded on pure and simple policy considerations. They side with J.C. Smith in taking the view that 'the real reason for punishing [the defendant, by applying *Majewski*] is the outrage that would quite reasonably be felt if serious injury caused to an innocent person by a drunk were to go unpunished' (5.23). In a sense, thus, the Commission's proposals are purely defensive. The main bulk of the provisions are designed to fend off public criticism rather than to provide a principled basis on which the law can operate. If this is true (as it seems to be), then to allow evidence of voluntary intoxication to negative *mens rea* in *any* crime, particularly a serious crime of violence, looks perverse. ... By allowing a concern for policy to dominate its thinking, the Commission simply clears the way for a Government obsessed with 'crime control' to take that concern to its logical conclusion, which is that the Commission's proposals should be ignored and voluntary intoxication should make no impact whatsoever on criminal liability. Yet this is the very conclusion the Commission and its consultees thought most undesirable."[88]

## X. LACK OF AGE

### A. *Introduction*

Crime (particularly less serious forms of crime) is predominantly a youthful phenomenon. Both official statistics and self-report studies confirm that the peak age of offending is in mid-teens and that most such offenders (particularly females) will "grow out of crime".[89] The response of the criminal justice system to crime by

---

[88] See also, Gough, "Intoxication and Criminal Liability" (1996) 112 L.Q.R. 335; O'Leary, "Lament for the Intoxication 'Defence'" [1997] 48 N.I.L.Q. 152 and Gough "Surviving without *Majewski* [2000] Crim.L.R.719.

[89] See further, Cavadino and Dignan, *The Penal System* (3rd ed., 2002), pp. 284–285; Flood-Page, Campbell, Harrington and Miller, *Youth Crime: Findings from the 1998–99 Youth Lifestyles Survey* (Home Office Research Study No. 209) (2000); East and Campbell, *Aspects of Crime: Young Offenders 1999* (www.homeoffice.gov.uk/rds/pdfs/aspects-youngoffs.pdf).

children has fluctuated sharply and has been fundamentally affected by political considerations. The pendulum has swung between a punitive approach (which holds a child responsible as if an adult) and one based upon considerations of welfare. As part of an ever-changing uneasy balance between the two, the law does take some account of the different stages of childhood. Of course, in reality the process of maturation is a gradual one, with a child becoming more and more aware of his or her place in the order of things.[90] The criminal law is rather less subtle than this: it recognises that very young children should not be held responsible for their actions and, thus, there is a blunt cut-off age below which they will be excused liability.

The age of criminal responsibility is currently set at 10.[91] This is considerably lower than many other European countries but is not the lowest: for example, Scotland sets the age of criminal responsibility at 8 and Ireland at 7.[92] There was also a transitional phase between the ages of 10–14 during which time the child used to be presumed to be "*doli incapax*". Only if the prosecution could rebut the presumption by proof that the child knew what he or she was doing was seriously or gravely wrong and not merely naughty or mischievous could the child be held criminally responsible for his or her actions.[93] Although entirely sound in relation to the underlying principles of the criminal law, the presumption increasingly came under fire as illogical, lacking in common-sense, out-dated, a serious disservice to the law and unnecessary. In *C v D.P.P.* the House of Lords urged that the presumption be subject to "parliamentary investigation, deliberation and legislation".[94] This advice was followed and section 34 of the Crime and Disorder Act 1998 states that "[t]he rebuttable presumption of criminal law that a child aged 10 or over is incapable of committing an offence is hereby abolished." Strictly speaking, this section abolishes the *presumption* only and it has been persuasively argued that it is still open to a child between the ages of 10–14 to show that *she* did not understand that what she had done was seriously wrong.[95] However, while this may well be the proper construction of the section, it appears to have been interpreted as having abolished the defence of *doli incapax* entirely for children aged 10 and over. It is regrettable that such a significant change in the law's approach to the criminal responsibility of children should have been achieved in such an ambiguous manner.

This reform is a very significant part of a policy which over the last twenty years or so has sought to make children—even very young children—increasingly liable for their actions.[96] Despite the fact that only a small number of very young children

---

[90] Civil law reflects this by reference to the test of "*Gillick*-competence": *Gillick v West Norfolk and Wisbech Area Health Authority* [1986] A.C. 112.

[91] Children and Young Persons Act 1933, s.50 as amended by Children and Young Persons Act 1963, s.16. At common law the age of criminal responsibility was 7. The Children and Young Persons Act 1969, s.4, raised the age of responsibility to 14 but this was never implemented.

[92] See Penal Affairs Consortium, *The Doctrine of Doli Incapax* (1995) and Justice, *Children and Homicide* (1996).

[93] *C. v D.P.P.* [1996] A.C. 1.

[94] At 40.

[95] Walker, "The End of an Old Song" (1999) 149 N.L.J. 64.

[96] Without a corresponding increase in emphasis upon the rights of natural justice such as those pertaining to the trial of adults (Freeman, "The Rights of Children When They Do Wrong" (1981) 21 Brit. J. Criminol. 210).

are brought before the courts[97] and that the 1980s saw considerable successes in diverting children away from custody and from the courts by use of formal cautioning etc.,[98] the perception has grown that children are out of control. Concerns about the use of multiple cautions[99] and the perceived growth in both the prevalence and gravity of young children's crime, fed, in part, by the highly-publicised killing of James Bulger by two ten-year-olds[1] have led to a flurry of punitive initiatives. "In the space of only five years the young person in the arms of the criminal law has been largely reconstructed within the 'little adult' imagery of the Victorian era."[2]

## B. *Below the age of 10*

Children below this age are irrebuttably presumed to be incapable of committing crime. Care proceedings may be brought if it is thought that the child "is suffering or is likely to suffer significant harm and that the care given to him is not what it would be reasonable to expect a parent to give, or the child is beyond parental control".[3] These proceedings are entirely civil and decisions are based upon the welfare of the child.[4] However, the Crime and Disorder Act 1998 has introduced parenting orders, curfew orders and child safety orders for children under the age of 10.[5]

## C. *Above the age of 10*

Between the ages of 10–13 offenders are categorised as children and between 14–17 inclusive as young persons.[6] The sentencing options available to the youth court[7] depend upon this categorisation. A further, transitional category, referred to

---

[97] The number of children aged 10 or 11 appearing in courts is on the increase. In 1989, 330 such children were sentenced for indictable offences, while in 1999 the figure was 602: East and Campbell, *above*, n.89, p. 47.

[98] Cavadino and Dignan, *above*, n.87 at pp. 292–297.

[99] Ss.61 and 62 of the Crime and Disorder Act 1998 replaced cautioning with a statutory scheme in which the police give a young offender a police reprimand followed by a final warning in the event of re-offending. See further, Home Office, *Tackling Youth Crime* (1997), paras 49–70.

[1] In *R. v Secretary of State for the Home Department, ex parte Venables*; *R. v Secretary of State for the Home Department, ex parte Thompson* [1997] 3 All E.R. 97 the House of Lords (by a 3/2 majority) held that the Home Secretary had acted unlawfully in setting a tariff of 15 years' imprisonment for the boys. It was confirmed that a sentence of detention under Her Majesty's pleasure (Children and Younger Persons Act 1933, s.53(1)) is not equivalent to a life sentence imposed upon an adult convicted of murder. See also *T and V v United Kingdom* [2000] 30 E.H.R.R. 121. On the issue of child homicides (and their scarcity) see, Justice, *Children and Homicide* (1996) and Cavadino, *Children Who Kill* (1996) and McDiarmid, "Children who Murder" [2000] Crim.L.R.547.

[2] Rutherford, "Young People and the Penal System" (1997) 147 N.L.J. 771 at 772. In addition to other changes identified in this section, the government has, for example, introduced secure training centres for 12–14 year olds by the Criminal Justice and Public Order Act 1994 and has extended the range of Children and Young Persons Act 1933, s.53(1).

[3] Children Act 1989, s.31(2).

[4] Care orders in criminal proceedings were abolished by the Children Act 1989, Sched. 12, para. 23, adding s.12AA to the Children and Young Persons Act 1969.

[5] Ss.8–15, at the application of the local authority.

[6] s.68, Sched. 8, Criminal Justice Act 1991.

[7] Criminal Justice Act 1991, s.70(1). The youth court hears all cases involving young offenders except where the offence is homicide, or where the child is charged jointly with an adult or there is other adult involvement in the crime.

in the preceding White Paper[8] as "near adults" has been included in the young person category. The courts are given additional sentencing powers for 16–17 year olds whose maturity warrants such treatment. Courts must "have regard to the welfare of the child or young person"[9] but as this is not the only consideration, the court may find persuasive, for example, the need to protect the public.[10]

### XI. SUNDRY DEFENCES

In addition to the general defences discussed in this chapter there are numerous other defences which are beyond the scope of this book. Such defences are more specific: it is, for example, a defence to a charge of unlawful possession of a firearm to show reasonable excuse or lawful authority.[11] Likewise it is a defence to the offence of failing to provide a specimen of breath or blood or urine (for the purposes of the offence of driving or being in charge of a vehicle with a blood/alcohol concentration above the prescribed limit) to show a reasonable excuse.[12] Another example of a specific defence is that a police officer may use such force as is reasonable in effecting a lawful arrest.[13]

---

[8] *Crime, Justice and Protecting the Public*, Cm. 965 (1990), para. 8.16.
[9] Children and Young Persons Act 1933, s.44(1) as amended.
[10] For the range of sentencing options available to the courts see, Cavadino and Dignan, n.89 at pp. 284–304.
[11] Firearms Act 1968, s.17.
[12] Road Traffic Act 1988, s.7(6).
[13] Criminal Law Act 1967, s.3(1).

# 4

# CAUSATION

---

## Commonwealth v Welansky, 316 Mass. 383, 55 N.E. 2d 902 (1944) (Supreme Judicial Court of Massachusetts)

On the evening of November 28, 1942 a fire broke out at the New Cocoanut Grove, a nightclub in Boston. The fire quickly spread throughout the crowded premises. Panic resulted and nearly 500 people died of burns, smoke inhalation, or injuries suffered in the attempt to escape. Who caused the death of these people?[1] There were several candidates for blame:

### 1. The waiter, Stanley Tomaszewski

A prankster had turned off a light bulb set in a decorative palm tree. A bartender ordered Stanley, a sixteen year old boy, to light the bulb. He got a stool, lit a match in order to see the bulb and turned the bulb in its socket. The flame of his match ignited the artificial palm tree which in turn speedily ignited a low cloth ceiling near it. Did Stanley cause the death of the 500 victims? Initially he was blamed by the local press, but as other "scapegoats" were found, he was exonerated from blame and treated with "near adulation" and started receiving "fan letters." But for the next 28 years Stanley received abusive telephone calls in the middle of the night and his life was threatened "hundreds of times by people who blame me for the fire."[2]

### 2. The prankster

The prankster who turned off the light bulb was also blamed initially in the press, but as his identity was never discovered, his condemnation was shortlived. Can he be said to have caused the death of the victims?

---

[1] The ensuing discussion of *Welansky* is drawn from the report of the case itself, from Veltford and Lee, "The Cocoanut Grove Fire: A Study in Scapegoating," Journal of Abnormal and Social Psychology, XXXVIII (No. 2 clinical supp.; 1943) 138 at 141–154, and from Goldstein, Dershowitz and Schwartz, *Criminal Law: Theory and Process* (1974), pp. 833–837.

[2] *The Boston Globe*, December 28, 1970, p. 10 col. 3. See Goldstein *et al.*, p. 836.

3. *Public officials*

The week before, the Fire Department had inspected the Cocoanut Grove and approved it as safe, despite the fact that there was a lack of adequate fire-exits and that highly inflammable materials were used throughout the nightclub and, in particular, in the decorative palm tree and in the low cloth ceiling. Did the particular fire inspector cause the deaths?

The local press also blamed other public officials. They condemned the Fire Commissioner on the basis that he was responsible for his subordinate's performance of duty. They castigated a Captain in the Police Department who was inside the club at the time of the fire on inspection duties for not enforcing the law against over-crowding. Even the mayor was blamed for appointing such "negligent" and "lax" heads of departments and because he had taken no action to adopt a new building code that had been in the hands of the City Council for the previous four years. Did any of these public officials cause the deaths?

4. *The owners*

The nightclub was owned and run by Barnett Welansky. In decorating and equipping the club he had used defective wiring and installed the inflammable decorations. There were insufficient exit doors and some of these doors were kept locked. At the time of the fire Barnett Welansky was confined in hospital with a serious illness—his brother James Welansky and an employee, Jacob Goldfine, "assumed some of [his] duties at the night club, but made no change in methods."[3] To what extent can it be said that the death of the victims was caused by Barnett Welansky or by his two delegates?

*The result*

Barnett Welansky and his two delegates were charged with the crime of manslaughter. The two delegates were acquitted by the jury, but Barnett Welansky was convicted of manslaughter and sentenced to a term of imprisonment of not less than twelve years and not more than fifteen years. Welansky's appeal was dismissed. Thus both the trial court and the Supreme Judicial Court of Massachusetts clearly found that Barnett Welansky caused the death of the victims of the fire. After serving three years of his sentence, Welansky, who was suffering from terminal cancer and was not expected to live for more than another year, was granted a full and complete pardon by the Governor of Massachusetts.

It is interesting to contrast the views expressed in two of the many letters addressed to the Governor prior to his granting a pardon.

(i) "If Welansky was guilty of manslaughter in connection with the terrible deaths resulting from the Cocoanut Grove fire, then it was a technical guilt and nothing more. Certainly, in those circumstances, the sentence that was imposed upon him by the court was much too severe . . . It may well be true that in appropriate cases, such as criminals whom the public would have a right to fear if they were released, that the criminal's health should not be taken into consideration, but in this particular case where there was no intention to do harm in the first place, but through a succession of misfortunes a man has been found guilty of manslaughter only from a technical point of view and not otherwise, [he is deserving of a pardon.]"[4]

(ii) "I vehemently oppose any pardon for Barnett Welansky whose criminal reconstruction of the Cocoanut Grove building sacrificed 492 human beings. I am a close relative of one of the victims. This horrible holocaust was a civic disgrace. It would become even more unspeakable were this man to be freed. In his petition for premature freedom, Welansky claims illness—says he wants to spend the rest of his days with his family. I recall

---

[3] *Welansky* 55 N.E. 2d 902 at 905.
[4] Letter by F. Lichtenstein, cited in Goldstein (*above*, n.1), p. 835.

492 persons (one in particular) who wanted to live out their lives with their families. *They are dead*. He also disclaims guilt because he was at home the night of the fire.

Guiltless? He *accepted guilt* when he criminally flouted the building laws in callously renovating his nightclub and did *not* have the work done according to the plans which he had had okayed.

He evaded the law when he employed a young fellow to do some electrical wiring and *knew* that his worker did not have the proper license to do this work. Has it been *absolutely proven* that faulty wiring *did not* cause this fire? Although he was not present he *knew* that his illegally reconstructed club was open for public attendance the night of the fire.

Governor Tobin, consider the fact of locked exits in a place of public patronage. Hundreds died because a locked exit barred their way to the street's safety. These facts are on public record. They also are hideous facts burning deeply into the hearts of hundreds of heartbroken families."[5]

### H. Veltford and G. Lee, "The Cocoanut Grove Fire: A Study in Scapegoating." Journal of Abnormal and Social Psychology, XXXVIII (No. 2 clinical supp; 1943), 138:

"The people [of Boston] felt some person or persons must be held responsible; attaching responsibility to mere laws or to the *panic* provided neither sufficient outlet for their emotions nor opportunity for punishment ...

Significantly, newspapers and public alike overlooked the fact that the panic created by the fire must have been largely responsible for the great loss of life. In spite of statements by officials immediately after the fire, the people were not ready to accept the fact that 'the Boston tragedy was due in part to a psychological collapse.' To the extent that they ignored this fact, the blame that the newspapers and public placed on various persons involved in the fire was disproportionate to their responsibility."

### Sally Lloyd-Bostock, "The Ordinary Man, and the Psychology of Attributing Causes and Responsibility" (1979) 42 M.L.R. 143 at 155–156:

"Walster ('Assignment of Responsibility for an Accident' (1963) 3, 1 Journal of Personality and Social Psychology, 73–79) ... found that people attributed more responsibility for an accident (in which a car parked unbraked ran down a hill) as the severity of the consequence increased. She formulated a version of what has become known as 'the defensive attribution hypothesis.' Chance happenings over which the individual has no control (and, hence, no responsibility) are threatening. Therefore, when faced with an accident with serious consequences, an individual will seek to attribute responsibility to somebody in order to protect himself from acknowledging that the accident could happen to anyone, including himself. The need to protect himself in this way will increase with increasing severity of outcome ...

Often more than one kind of responsibility may be attributed in relation to the same event. For example, a *Sunday Times* article (April 13, 1977) after describing at some length the circumstances surrounding the collision between two jumbo jets at Santa Cruz airport in Tenerife, concluded by attributing responsibility—'Blame for the world's worst aviation tragedy will no doubt be apportioned in time. One name will certainly not feature in any official inquest however: Antonio Cubillo. It is he who, no matter how indirectly, must shoulder responsibility for what happened at Santa Cruz.' (Cubillo was leader of the movement which claimed responsibility for a bomb at Las Palmas airport. As a result of the bomb, aircraft, including those in the accident, were diverted to Santa Cruz, overloading the airport.) This illustrates a number of interesting things about reactions to disasters and attributing responsibility for them in newspapers. The writers recognise that it will differ from other attributions, and that Antonio Cubillo's causal contribution will in other contexts be insufficient grounds. It is a non-legal attribution of responsibility, but even if

---

[5] Letter by K. Denehy, cited in Goldstein (*above*, n.1), pp. 835–836.

nobody quarrelled with it in this context, it is clearly not *the* everyday answer to the question 'who is responsible for the crash?,' nor does it exemplify *the* common-sense principles on which questions about remoteness of causes, etc. are decided.

The fact that everyday judgments are related to everyday purposes and consequences must be a major limitation on the usefulness of comparisons between legal and ordinary common-sense notions of cause and fault."

## II. Approaches to Causation

In such cases how does the law determine which of several candidates actually caused the result? How far does the chain of causation extend? Welansky did not start the fire. Why was he liable for the resultant deaths? If the waiter had deliberately started the fire, would Welansky still have been liable or would the chain of causation have then been broken? While attempts have been made to discover a metaphysical rationale for the law's rules on causation,[6] the more usual approach is that legal doctrines are shaped by other considerations and do not map metaphysical causal reality.[7] What are these other considerations?

There are three approaches that can be adopted in relation to the problem of causation.

### A. *"Policy" Approach*

There are no underlying general *principles* of causation. Judges simply resort to considerations of "policy" to determine whether a particular defendant caused the specified harm.

### H. L. A. Hart and Tony Honoré, Causation in the Law (2nd ed., 1985), pp. 103–104:

"For writers of the first school 'policy' is just a name for an immense variety of considerations which do weigh and should weigh with courts considering the question of the existence or extent of responsibility. No exhaustive enumeration can be given of such factors and no general principles can be laid down as to how a balance should be struck between them. Policy, on this interpretation, is atomized: the courts must focus attention on the precise way in which harm has eventuated in a particular case, and then ask and answer, in a more or less intuitive fashion, whether or not on these particular facts a defendant should be held responsible. The court's function is to pass judgments acceptable to society for their time and place on these matters, and general policies can never take the place of judgment. Edgerton says, 'It neither is nor should be possible to extract rules which cover the subject (of legal cause) and are definite enough to solve cases ... The solution ... depends upon a balancing of considerations which tend to show that it is or is not reasonable or just to treat the act as the cause of the harm ... these considerations are indefinite in number and in value and incommensurable' ('Legal Cause,' (1924) U.Pa.L.R. 211)."

Norrie argues that any "principles" that might exist require "constant supplementation by 'policy' considerations to reach decisions in individual cases" because causation can only be explained by taking into account the social context within which people act.[8]

---

[6] Moore, "Causal Intervention" (2000) 88 Cal.L.R. 827.
[7] Morse, "The Moral Metaphysics of Causation and Results" (2000) 88 Cal.L.R. 879.
[8] "A Critique of Criminal Causation" (1991) 54 M.L.R. 685 at 701.

In holding that Welansky caused the death of the victims of the Cocoanut Grove fire, were the judges (and jury) simply giving effect to their conceptions of justice, expediency, or "policy"? In deciding who to prosecute, are prosecutors to be guided by the same considerations of "policy"? Is such an *ad hoc* approach acceptable? It must be remembered that, apart from crimes of strict liability, criminal liability does not necessarily follow from a finding that causation is established. Some *mens rea* or culpability must also be found to exist. If policy considerations are to affect legal decisions, should they not be reserved for the *mens rea* assessment, or is it unrealistic to divorce policy considerations from any one aspect of a crime?

## B. *Mens Rea Approach*

There are two strands to the argument here. The first is that causation will generally be established if the defendant has *mens rea*. It is often stated that an intended consequence can never be too remote.[9] Because recklessness (or gross negligence) could be attributed to Welansky, causation could be established. The alternative analysis (theoretically quite different, but similar in effect) is that because of the doctrine of *mens rea* and the test of responsibility, principles of causation are unnecessary in the criminal law. Any factual cause can be held to be the legal cause because actual liability will be limited to those who have *mens rea*. "Under the modern conception of *mens rea* no hardship can result from any finely drawn investigation of causes, since the more remote the cause the greater the difficulty of proving that the accused person intended or realised what the effect of it would be."[10] In *Welansky* the prankster's action of switching off the light bulb was *a* cause of the fire and subsequent deaths, but as *mens rea* could never be attributed to him, there was no point in prosecuting him. On the other hand, because Welansky was blameworthy he was prosecuted and convicted. Under these views all the "real work" is done by the doctrine of *mens rea*. Either the rules on causation are shaped by the existence of *mens rea*, or, alternatively, no rules on causation are necessary. All that is needed, in either case, is a simple proposition that the defendant's act must have been *a* cause in the sense that without it the ultimate harm would not have occurred (known as the *sine qua non* rule or "but for" causation: *but for* the prankster turning off the bulb, the fire would never have started and the patrons would not have died).

There are problems with these approaches. How can they be adopted when dealing with crimes of strict liability? Clearly, the first view that causation is only established if there is a "blamable" cause[11] is problematic. Particularly when dealing with strict liability offences, the courts have tended to emphasise that whether causation is established is a question of fact and not law.[12] It has been argued that this amounts to an invitation to juries and magistrates only to find

---

[9] Ashworth, *Principles of Criminal Law* (3rd ed., 1999), p. 126.

[10] Turner, *Kenny's Outlines of Criminal Law* (19th ed., 1966), pp. 20–21. See *Royall v The Queen* (1991) 65 A.L.J.R. 451, *per* McHugh J., discussed in Shute, "Causation: Foreseeability *v* Natural Consequences" (1992) 55 M.L.R. 584.

[11] Williams, *Textbook of Criminal Law* (2nd ed., 1983), p. 381.

[12] *National Rivers Authority v Yorkshire Water Services Ltd* [1994] 4 All E.R. 274; *Alphacell v Woodward* [1972] A.C. 854.

causation established if the defendant was blameworthy: "By delegating the question of causation to the finders of fact, the courts are able to avoid the rigours of strict liability. The device allows both courts and Parliament to bury their heads in the sand, and to avoid any reassessment of the role of strict liability in criminal law. The courts undermine the rigidity of the strict liability rules by allowing juries to introduce a judgmental or culpability element into their decision-making on causation".[13] However, in *Environment Agency v Empress Car Co. (Abertillery) Ltd*[14] it was expressly stated that causation may be established even though the defendant did not intend the harm and was not even negligent; any other approach would defeat the object of strict liability legislation. Under the second view, causation would be established on a simple "but for" basis in all cases regardless of how far removed the act was from the result. Such an approach would be unacceptable and does not represent the law. While it is arguable that causation is more easily established in cases of strict liability, it is nevertheless clear that legal rules of causation do exist. As stated in *Environment Agency v Empress Car Co. (Abertillery) Ltd*: "while liability is strict ... it is not an absolute liability in the sense that all that has to be shown is that the polluting matter escaped from the defendant's land."[15] In *Alphacell v Woodward*[16] it was indicated that causation depended on a "proper attribution of responsibility". While "responsibility" in this context should not be confused with culpability, it is clear that more than "but for" causation needs to be established.

Even in cases where *mens rea* is established, there are problems with these approaches to causation. The result would be that Welansky, because he had *mens rea* (as defined in that case) would still have been liable even if the waiter, Stanley, had deliberately started the fire with the intention of killing everyone in the nightclub. Would such a result be acceptable? If these views are correct, is it right that *all* liability should turn on such a nebulous and elusive concept as *mens rea*? Might it not be better to clarify and strengthen the rules on causation which could lead to a diminution of the importance of the doctrine of *mens rea*?

## C. *Quest for General Principles*

Not satisfied with the above approaches, attempts have been made to formulate general principles of causation that could be applicable in all cases. Two of these attempted formulations will be presented:

(1) Hart and Honoré's principles derived from our common-sense notions of causation; and
(2) The Draft Criminal Code's "restatement" of the present law.

### 1. Hart and Honoré's principles of causation

Events do not have single "causes", but only occur when there is a combination of a complex set of conditions. We might identify the dropping of a lighted cigarette

---

[13] Padfield, "Clean Water and Muddy Causation: Is Causation a Question of Law or Fact, or Just a Way of Allocating Blame?" [1995] Crim.L.R.683 at 692–693.
[14] [1999] 2 A.C. 22. See also *Southern Water Authority v Pegrum and Pegrum* [1989] Crim.L.R.442.
[15] [1999] 2 A.C. 22 at 33. See *below*, p. 460.
[16] [1972] A.C. 854.

in a waste-paper basket as the cause of a fire but in reality this leads to a fire only if certain other conditions are satisfied: there must be oxygen in the air; there must be combustible material in the waste-paper basket, and so on. Each of these conditions is equally necessary if a fire is to be started. How are we to select one of this complex set of conditions as the cause?

## H. L. A. Hart and Tony Honoré, Causation in the Law (2nd ed., 1985), pp. 29, 33–34, 42, 77–80, 326, 340–341:

"Human action in the simple cases, where we produce some desired effect by the manipulation of an object in our environment, is an interference in the natural course of events which *makes a difference* in the way these develop ... Common experience teaches us that, left to themselves, the things we manipulate, since they have a 'nature' or characteristic way of behaving, would persist in states or exhibit changes different from those which we have learnt to bring about in them by our manipulation. The notion that a cause is essentially something which interferes with or intervenes in the course of events which would normally take place, is central to our commonsense concept of cause. ...

[I]n distinguishing between causes and conditions two contrasts are of prime importance. These are the contrasts between what is abnormal and what is normal in relation to any given thing or subject-matter, and between a free deliberate human action and all other conditions. ...

### (a) *Abnormal and normal conditions*

... In the case of a building destroyed by fire 'mere conditions' will be factors such as the oxygen in the air, the presence of combustible material or the dryness of the building. ... These factors are, of course, just those which are present alike both in the case where such accidents occur and in the normal cases where they do not; and it is this consideration that leads us to reject them as the cause of the accident, even though it is true that without them the accident would not have occurred ... : such factors do not 'make the difference' between disaster and normal functioning, as ... the dropping of a lighted cigarette [does] ...

### (b) *Voluntary action*

... [A] voluntary human action intended to bring about what in fact happens, and in the manner in which it happens, has a special place in causal inquiries; not so much because this, if present among a set of conditions required for the production of the effect, is often treated as the cause (though this is true), but because, when the question is how far back a cause shall be traced through a number of intervening causes, such a voluntary action very often is regarded both as a limit and also as still the cause even though other later abnormal occurrences are recognized as causes ...

[However in certain cases even when an actor intends to achieve a result (and that result occurs), the chain of causation between the actor's conduct and the result might be broken.]

### *Tracing consequences*

... A hits B who falls to the ground stunned and bruised by the blow; at that moment a tree crashes to the ground and kills B. A has certainly caused B's bruises but not his death ...

The connexion between A's action and B's death ... would naturally be described in the language of *coincidence*. 'It was a coincidence: it just happened that, at the very moment when A knocked B down, a tree crashed at the very place where he fell and killed him.' ... We speak of a coincidence whenever the conjunction of two or more events in certain spatial or temporal realtions (1) is very unlikely by ordinary standards and (2) is for some reason significant or important, provided (3) that they occur without human contrivance and (4) are independent of each other. ...

In the present case the fall of the tree just as B was struck down within its range satisfies the four criteria for a coincidence which we have enumerated. First, though neither event was of a very rare or exceptional kind, their conjunction would be rated very unlikely judged by the standards of ordinary experience. Secondly, this conjunction was causally significant for it was a necessary part of the process terminating in B's death. Thirdly, this conjunction was not consciously designed by A; had he known of the impending fall of the tree and hit B with the intention that he should fall within its range B's death would not have been the result of any coincidence. A would certainly have caused it. The common-sense principle that a contrived conjunction cannot be a coincidence is the element of truth in the legal maxim (too broadly stated even for legal purposes) that an intended consequence cannot be too 'remote'. Fourthly, each member of the conjunction in this case was independent of the other; whereas if B had fallen against the tree with an impact sufficient to bring it down on him, this sequence of physical events, though freakish in its way, would not be a coincidence and in most contexts of ordinary life, as in the law, the course of events would be summarized by saying that in this case, unlike that of the coincidence, A's act was the cause of B's death, since each stage is the effect of the preceding stage. Thus, the blow forced the victim against the tree, the effect of this was to make the tree fall and the fall of the tree killed the victim.

One further criterion in addition to these four must be satisfied if a conjunction of events is to rank as a coincidence and as a limit when the consequences of the action are traced ... An abnormal *condition* existing at the time of a human intervention is distinguished both by ordinary thought and, with a striking consistency, by most legal systems from an abnormal event or conjunction of events subsequent to that intervention; the former, unlike the latter, are not ranked as coincidences or 'extraneous' causes when the consequences of the intervention come to be traced. Thus A innocently gives B a tap over the head of a normally quite harmless character, but because B is then suffering from some rare disease the tap has, as we say, 'fatal results'. In this case A has caused B's death though unintentionally. The scope of the principle which thus distinguishes contemporaneous abnormal conditions from subsequent events is unclear; but at least where a human being initiates some physical change in a thing, animal, or person, abnormal physical states of the object affected, existing at the time, are ranked as part of the circumstances in which the cause 'operates'. In the familiar controlling imagery these are part of 'the stage already set' before the 'intervention'.

... Just how unlikely must a conjunction be to rank as a coincidence, and in the light of what knowledge is likelihood to be assessed? The only answer is: 'very unlikely in the light of the knowledge available to ordinary men.'

... [S]o in criminal law courts have often limited responsibility by appealing to the causal distinctions embedded in ordinary thought, with their emphasis on voluntary interventions and abnormal or coincidental events as factors negativing responsibility.

*Voluntary conduct*

The free, deliberate, and informed intervention of a second person, not acting in concert with the first, and intending to bring about the harm which in fact occurs or recklessly courting it, is normally held to relieve the first actor of criminal responsibility. One must distinguish, however, the situation where the first actor's conduct was sufficient in the existing circumstances to bring about the harm ( ... the case for holding the first actor responsible despite the voluntary intervention of the second is naturally much stronger) ... from that where it was not sufficient without the intervention of the second actor ( ... here most decisions relieve the first actor of responsibility) ...

*Abnormality*

The basic principle here is that a physical state or event, even if subsequent to the act of the defendant, does not negative causal connection if it is normal or usual in the context.

In criminal as in civil law a conjunction of events amounting to a coincidence is held to negative causal connection."

A central problem with this analysis is that everything depends on one's definition of "normal", "abnormal" and "voluntary". As Norrie says:

"Thus, individuals are held to be causes until something abnormal intervenes, but what is abnormal depends upon social perception, and therefore upon a socio-political label being stuck upon it. Similarly, causation stretches as far as the new voluntary act of a third party, but what is meant by voluntary can be as narrow or as broad as one likes, depending upon how much one is prepared to recognise the social character of the lives of individuals."[17]

## 2. Draft Criminal Code

### Draft Criminal Code Bill 1989 (Law Com. No. 177), clause 17:

"(1) Subject to subsections (2) and (3), a person causes a result which is an element of an offence when—
(a) he does an act which makes a more than negligible contribution to its occurrence; or
(b) he omits to do an act which might prevent its occurrence and which he is under a duty to do according to the law relating to the offence.
(2) A person does not cause a result where, after he does such an act or makes such an omission, an act or event occurs—
(a) which is the immediate and sufficient cause of the result;
(b) which he did not foresee, and
(c) which could not in the circumstances reasonably have been foreseen.
(Clause 17(3) states that subject to exceptions 'a person who procures, assists or encourages another to cause a result that is an element of an offence does not himself cause that result so as to be guilty of the offence as a principal.')"

### III. THE LAW'S RESPONSE

In order to establish causation for the purposes of criminal liability it is necessary that there be both factual and legal causation. Most of the cases have concerned homicide and offences against the person and so discussion here will be primarily (but not exclusively) limited to these areas. The problems of causation in relation to omissions, aiding and abetting and obtaining property by deception are discussed when dealing with those topics.

### A. *Factual causation*

The defendant's actions must be a *sine qua non* (or "but for" cause) of the result. "But for" the defendant striking the victim, she would not have died. In *White*[18] the defendant put cyanide in his mother's drink with intent to kill her. She had a heart attack and died before she had drunk any of the poisoned mixture. The defendant had not caused her death. His actions were not even a "but for" cause of her death.

### B. *Legal causation*

We have seen, however, that there may be a wide range of "but for" causers. For example, in *Welansky*, the waiter, the prankster and Welansky all satisfied this test. The law, in selecting those who are causally responsible, insists that the defendant's actions be the "operative",[19] "substantial",[20] "beyond the *de minimus* range",[21] or

---

[17] "A Critique of Criminal Causation" (1991) 54 M.L.R. 685 at 692.
[18] [1910] 2 K.B. 124.
[19] *Malcherek & Steel* (1981) 73 Cr.App.R.173.
[20] *Smith* [1959] 2 Q.B. 35; *Mitchell* [1983] 2 W.L.R. 938.
[21] *Cato* [1976] 1 W.L.R. 110; *Notman* [1994] Crim.L.R.518.

"proximate",[22] cause of the prohibited consequence; they must "contribute significantly" to the result.[23] The problem with these terms is their elasticity. They can be made as broad or narrow as one likes and essentially take one no further in the quest for principles of causation.

Before examing the cases, it might be helpful to set out some preliminary propositions.

1. The defendant's actions need not be the medical cause of the result. In *McKechnie*[24] the defendant hit the victim over the head with a television set. These injuries prevented doctors operating on the victim's duodenal ulcer. The medical cause of death was a burst duodenal ulcer. The defendant was nevertheless held to have legally caused that death.

2. The result need not be the direct consequence of the defendant's physical actions. For example, one can cause death or other injury by fright or shock without touching one's victim. For example, in *Watson*[25] a burglar entered a house and verbally abused the elderly householder who died of a heart attack shortly afterwards. The burglar was held to have caused the death of the householder.

3. The defendant must "take his victim as he finds him". In *Hayward*[26] the defendant chased his wife into the street. She fell down and he kicked her arm. She died. Medical evidence established that she had a persistent thyrus gland and such persons could die from a combination of fright or strong emotion and physical exertion. The defendant was convicted of manslaughter.

4. The defendant's actions need not be the sole cause of the consequence. In several of the medical cases, shortly to be discussed, the defendant attacked a victim who then received negligent treatment. As stated in *Cheshire*: "the accused's acts need not be the sole cause or even the main cause of death, it being sufficient that his acts contributed significantly to that result".[27] In such cases it is possible for both the original attacker and the doctors to be found to have caused the death.

5. A *novus actus interveniens* will break the chain of causation. A *novus actus interveniens* is an intervening act or event that takes over as the new "operative" cause, relegating the defendant's actions to the realms of the history of the case. In all the cases to be examined there was some act or event or omission that occurred after the defendant had acted and which had the potential to break the chain of causation. This can be the act of a third party, an act of the victim or a natural event. In these cases the problem is whether this intervening act or event is so significant as to become the new *sole* cause of the result.

## 1. Act of third party

It will be recalled that, according to Hart and Honoré, causation cannot be traced through the voluntary action of a third party. For example, if I stab my

---

[22] Hart and Honoré, p. 4.
[23] *Pagett* (1983) 75 Cr.App.R.279.
[24] (1992) 94 Cr.App.R.51.
[25] [1989] 1 W.L.R. 684. See also *Towers* (1874) 12 Cox C.C. 530 and *Hayward* (1908) 21 Cox C.C. 692. For a medical explanation of how one can frighten someone to death, see Busuttil and McCall Smith, "Fright, Stress and Homicide" (1990) 54 J.Crim.L. 257.
[26] (1908) 21 Cox C.C. 692.
[27] (1991) 93 Cr.App.R.251.

victim who is lying in the street dying and you come along and shoot the victim killing her instantly, your action will break the chain of causation. However, if you merely kick the victim, accelerating death by a matter of seconds, your "voluntary action" will not break the causal chain. The issue is one of determining the circumstances in which the voluntary action of a third party will be so significant as to break the causal chain. In several of the leading cases it has been action on the part of doctors that has been alleged to be a *novus actus interveniens*.

## R. v Smith [1959] 2 Q.B. 35 (Courts Martial Appeal Court)

During a fight in a barracks the appellant twice stabbed the victim, Private Creed, with a bayonet. He appealed against his conviction for murder on the ground *inter alia* that the summing up by the judge-advocate on the question of causation was defective.

Lord Parker C.J. (delivering the judgment of the Court):
"The second ground concerns a question of causation. The deceased man in fact received two bayonet wounds, one in the arm and one in the back. The one in the back, unknown to anybody, had pierced the lung and caused haemorrhage. There followed a series of unfortunate occurrences. A fellow-member of his company tried to carry him to the medical reception station. On the way he tripped over a wire and dropped the deceased man. He picked him up again, went a little further, and fell apparently a second time, causing the deceased man to be dropped on to the ground. Thereafter he did not try a third time but went for help, and ultimately the deceased man was brought into the reception station. There, the medical officer, Captain Millward, and his orderly were trying to cope with a number of other cases, two serious stabbings and some minor injuries, and it is clear that they did not appreciate the seriousness of the deceased man's condition or exactly what had happened. A transfusion of saline solution was attempted and failed. When his breathing seemed impaired, he was given oxygen and artificial respiration was applied, and, in fact, he died after he had been in the station about an hour, which was about two hours after the original stabbing. It is now known that, having regard to the injuries which the man had in fact suffered, his lung being pierced, the treatment that he was given was thoroughly bad and might well have affected his chances of recovery. There was evidence that there is a tendency for a wound of this sort to heal and for the haemorrhage to stop. No doubt his being dropped on the ground and having artificial respiration applied would halt or at any rate impede the chances of healing. Further, there were no facilities whatsoever for blood transfusion, which would have been the best possible treatment. There was evidence that, if he had received immediate and different treatment, he might not have died. Indeed, had facilities for blood transfusion been available and been administered, Dr Camps, who gave evidence for the defence, said that his chances of recovery were as high as 75 per cent.
In these circumstances Mr Bowen [counsel for the appellant] urges that not only was a careful summing-up required but that a correct direction to the court would have been that they must be satisfied that the death of Private Creed was a natural consequence and the sole consequence of the wound sustained by him and flowed directly from it. If there was, says Mr Bowen, any other cause, whether resulting from negligence or not, if, as he contends here, something happened which impeded the chance of the deceased recovering, then the death did not result from the wound. The court is quite unable to accept that contention. It seems to the court that if at the time of death the original wound is still an operating cause and a substantial cause, then the death can properly be said to be the result of the wound, albeit that some other cause of death is also operating. Only if it can be said that the original wounding is merely the setting in which another cause operates can it be said that the death does not result from the wound. Putting it in another way, only if the second cause is so overwhelming as to make the original wound merely part of the history can it be said that the death does not flow from the wound. ...
Mr Bowen placed great reliance on ... *Jordan* ... The court is satisfied that *Jordan's* case was a very particular case depending on its exact facts. ...

In the present case ... : a man is stabbed in the back, his lung is pierced and haemorrhage results; two hours later he dies of haemorrhage from that wound; in the interval there is no time for a careful examination, and the treatment given turns out in the light of subsequent knowledge to have been inappropriate and, indeed, harmful. In those circumstances no reasonable jury or court could, properly directed, in our view possibly come to any other conclusion than that the death resulted from the original wound. Accordingly, the court dismisses this appeal."

Appeal dismissed

## R. v Jordan (1956) 40 Cr.App.R.152 (Court of Appeal, Criminal Division)

The appellant stabbed the deceased who died some days later in hospital. Jordan, who had been convicted of murder, sought to adduce further medical evidence on appeal to the effect that the wound was not the cause of death.

Hallet J.:
"There were two things other than the wound which were stated by these two medical witnesses to have brought about death. The stab wound had penetrated the intestine in two places, but it was mainly healed at the time of death. With a view to preventing infection it was thought right to administer an antibiotic, terramycin.

It was agreed by the two additional witnesses that that was the proper course to take, and a proper dose was administered. Some people, however, are intolerant to terramycin, and Beaumont was one of those people. After the initial doses he developed diarrhoea, which was only properly attributable, in the opinion of those doctors, to the fact that the patient was intolerant to terramycin. Thereupon the administration of terramycin was stopped, but unfortunately the very next day the resumption of such administration was ordered by another doctor and it was recommenced the following day. The two doctors both take the same view about it. Dr Simpson said that to introduce a poisonous substance after the intolerance of the patient was shown was palpably wrong. Mr Blackburn agreed.

Other steps were taken which were also regarded by the doctors as wrong—namely, the intravenous introduction of wholly abnormal quantities of liquid far exceeding the output. As a result the lungs became waterlogged and pulmonary oedema was discovered. Mr Blackburn said that he was not surprised to see that condition after the introduction of so much liquid, and that pulmonary oedema leads to broncho-pneumonia as an inevitable sequel, and it was from broncho-pneumonia that Beaumont died.

We are disposed to accept it as the law that death resulting from any normal treatment employed to deal with a felonious injury may be regarded as caused by the felonious injury ... It is sufficient to point out here that this was not normal treatment. Not only one feature, but two separate and independent features, of treatment were, in the opinion of the doctors, palpably wrong and these produced the symptoms discovered at the post-mortem examination which were the direct and immediate cause of death, namely, the pneumonia resulting from the condition of oedema which was found ...

We feel no uncertainty at all that, whatever direction had been given to the jury and however correct it had been, the jury would have felt precluded from saying that they were satisfied that death was caused by the stab wound."

Conviction quashed

## R. v Cheshire (1991) 93 Cr.App.R.251 (Court of Appeal, Criminal Division)

The appellant shot the deceased in the leg and stomach. As part of his treatment in hospital a tracheotomy tube was placed in his windpipe. Some two months later, at a time when his wounds were no longer threatening his life, his windpipe became obstructed and he died. This was due to a narrowing of the windpipe where the tracheotomy had been performed—a rare but not unknown complication. At the appellant's trial for murder evidence was given that the medical treatment had been negligent. The trial judge directed the jury that only recklessness, and not negligence, could break the causal chain. He was convicted of murder and appealed.

Beldam L.J.:
"[Causation] is a question of fact for the jury, but it is a question of fact to be decided in accordance with legal principles explained to the jury by the judge ...

In the criminal law the jury ... will we think derive little assistance from figures of speech more appropriate for conveying degrees of fault or blame in questions of apportionment ... [W]e think such figures of speech are to be avoided in giving guidance to a jury on the question of causation. ...

[W]hen the victim of a criminal attack is treated for wounds or injuries by doctors or other medical staff attempting to repair the harm done, it will only be in the most extraordinary and unusual case that such treatment can be said to be so independent of the acts of the accused that it could be regarded in law as the cause of the victim's death to the exclusion of the accused's acts ...

[T]he accused's acts need not be the sole cause or even the main cause of death it being sufficient that his acts contributed significantly to that result. Even though negligence in the treatment of the victim was the immediate cause of his death, the jury should not regard it as excluding the responsibility of the accused unless the negligent treatment was so independent of his acts, and in itself so potent in causing death, that they regard the contribution made by his acts as insignificant.

It is not the function of the jury to evaluate competing causes or to choose which is dominant provided they are satisfied that the accused's acts can fairly be said to have made a significant contribution to the victim's death. We think the word 'significant' conveys the necessary substance of a contribution made to the death which is more than negligible ...

[W]e think that the judge erred when he invited the jury to consider the degree of fault in the medical treatment rather than its consequences, [but] we consider that no miscarriage of justice has actually occurred. Even if more experienced doctors than those who attended the deceased would have recognised the rare complication in time to have prevented the deceased's death, that complication was a direct consequence of the appellant's acts, which remained a significant cause of his death."

**Appeal dismissed**

## R. v Mellor [1996] 2 Cr.App.R.245 (Court of Appeal, Criminal Division)

The appellant was charged with the murder of an elderly man who, after being attacked, died in hospital two days later. It was alleged that negligence by the hospital staff broke the chain of causation. The appellant was convicted and appealed.

Schiemann L.J.:
"The immediate cause of death was broncho-pneumonia which, upon the evidence, was brought on directly by the injuries inflicted by the appellant. Those injuries were certainly the cause of death. Probably if the appellant had been administered sufficient oxygen in time, the broncho-pneumonia would not have been fatal, and therefore the failure to administer sufficient oxygen could be regarded as a cause of death. It was asserted on behalf of the appellant, and supported by expert evidence, that the failure to administer sufficient oxygen in time amounted to negligence or incompetence ...

In homicide cases, where the victim of the alleged crime does not die immediately, supervening events will occur which are likely to have some causative effect leading to the victim's death; for example, a delay in the arrival of the ambulance, a delay in resuscitation, the victim's individual response to medical or surgical treatment, and the quality of medical, surgical and nursing care. Sometimes such an event may be the result of negligence or mistake or bad luck. It is a question of fact and degree in each case for the jury to decide, having regard to the gravity of the supervening event, however caused, whether the injuries inflicted by the defendant were a significant cause of death.

The onus on the Crown is to make the jury sure that the injuries inflicted by the defendant were a significant cause of death. However, the Crown have no onus of establishing that any supervening event was not a significant cause of death or that there was no medical negligence in the deceased's treatment.

... In appropriate cases the jury can be told that there may be a number of significant causes leading to a victim's death. So as long as the Crown proves that the injuries inflicted by the defendant were at least a significant, if not the only, cause of death that will be sufficient to prove the nexus between injury and death ...

In our judgment, it is undesirable in most cases for juries to be asked to embark upon the question of whether medical negligence as a significant contributory cause of death has been negatived because it diverts the jury from the relevant question, namely, has the accused's act contributed significantly to the victim's death?"

**Appeal dismissed**

The effect of these decisions is that the actions of medical practitioners will (almost) never break the causal chain. It is irrelevant that the doctors were negligent or even reckless. It will require a "most extraordinary and unusual case" (*Cheshire*) for this to occur. Perhaps *Jordan* was such a case. The original wound had almost healed and had become part of the background. The victim was effectively killed by the administration of a drug to which he was known to be allergic. However, even on these facts subsequent cases have been careful to confine *Jordan* as being a "very exceptional"[28] case. Indeed, it is difficult to see that *Jordan* is really different from some of the other cases. In *Smith* the victim's treatment was "thoroughly bad". In *Jordan* it was "palpably wrong". In *Smith* the victim had a 75 per cent chance of recovery had he received proper medical treatment. In *Jordan* the victim's wounds had almost healed. Hart and Honoré argue that abnormal contingencies constitute a "coincidence" and break the chain of causation. It is difficult to see that the treatment in *Jordan* was an abnormal contingency, but that this was not the case in *Smith*. Of course, it could be argued that the victim in *Jordan* died from the drugs prescribed by the doctors whereas in *Smith* he died from loss of blood caused by the stab wound inflicted by the defendant. This cannot be the explanation. The victim in *Cheshire* did not die from his wounds. He died because the doctors inserted a tracheotomy tube in his windpipe and were negligent in their subsequent treatment. Why was this not an abnormal contingency?

The picture that starts to emerge is that Hart and Honoré's "abnormal contingency" and "coincidence" are hollow concepts that can be interpreted as the courts see fit. In short, all these "principled tests" provide no more than a veil under which decisions are ultimately based on policy considerations. With a National Health Service hard pressed for funds the courts are not going to start exempting violent assailants from liability because their victims did not receive the best treatment—except in what can be regarded as very exceptional cases such as *Jordan*.

An alternative way of looking at these cases, is that the doctors were simply performing their duty to their patients and so their actions cannot count as

---

[28] *Malcherek; Steel* (1981) 73 Cr.App.R.173.

sufficiently free or voluntary to break the causal chain. This approach was explicitly followed in the following two cases.

## R. v Latif [1996] 2 Cr.App.R.92 (House of Lords)

The defendant was charged with importing controlled drugs into the country. In fact, the drugs were knowingly brought in by a customs officer acting with a paid informer, Honi.

Lord Steyn:
"The general principle is that the free, deliberate and informed intervention of a second person, who intends to exploit the situation created by the first, but is not acting in concert with him, is held to relieve the first actor of criminal responsibility. For example, if a thief had stolen the heroin after Shahzad delivered it to Honi, and imported it into the United Kingdom, the chain of causation would plainly have been broken. The general principle must also be applicable to the role of the customs officers in this case. They acted in full knowledge of the content of the packages. They did not act in concert with Shahzad. They acted deliberately for their own purposes whatever those might have been. In my view consistency and legal principle do not permit us to create an exception to the general principle of causation to take care of the particular problem thrown up by this case."

**Appeal dismissed (as defendants were guilty of an attempt to commit the offence)**

Much the same approach has been applied where the third party intervention has come from other public officials, such as the police, performing their duties.

## R. v Pagett (1983) 76 Cr.App.R.279 (Court of Appeal, Criminal Division)

The appellant shot at police officers who were attempting to arrest him for various serious offences. He had a girl with him and against her will used her body to shield himself from any retaliation by the officers. The officers returned the appellant's fire; three of their bullets hit the girl; she died from these wounds. The appellant was convicted of manslaughter and appealed to the Court of Appeal.

Goff L.J.:
"[One of the] specific points raised on behalf of the appellant ... [was that] the learned judge ... ought to have held that the appellant had not in the circumstances of this case caused the death of the deceased. The learned judge, in directing himself upon the law, ought to have held that where the act which immediately resulted in a fatal injury was the act of another party, albeit in legitimate self-defence, then the ensuing death was too remote or indirect to be imputed to the original aggressor ...

[I]t was pressed upon us by [counsel for the appellant] that there either was, or should be, a ... rule of English law, whereby, as a matter of policy, no man should be convicted of homicide (or, we imagine, any crime of violence to another person) unless he himself, or another person acting in concert with him, fired the shot (or, we imagine, struck the blow) which was the immediate cause of the victim's death (or injury).

No English authority was cited to us in support of any such proposition, and we know of none. So far as we are aware, there is no such rule in English law; and ... we can see no basis in principle for any such rule in English law. ...

In our judgment, the question whether an accused person can be held guilty of homicide, either murder or manslaughter, of a victim the immediate cause of whose death is the act of another person must be determined on the ordinary principles of causation. ...

In cases of homicide, it is rarely necessary to give the jury any direction on causation as such ... Even where it is necessary to direct the jury's minds to the question of causation, it is usually enough to direct them simply that in law the accused's act need not be the sole cause, or even the main cause, of the victim's death, it being enough that his act contributed significantly to that result. Occasionally, however, a specific issue of causation may arise. One such case is where although an act of the accused constitutes a *causa sine qua non* of (or necessary condition for) the death of the victim, nevertheless the intervention of a third person may be regarded as the sole cause of the victim's death, thereby relieving the accused of criminal responsibility. Such intervention, if it has such an effect, has often been described by lawyers as a *novus actus interveniens*. ...

Professors Hart and Honoré, *Causation in the Law* ... consider the circumstances in which the intervention of a third person, not acting in concert with the accused, may have the effect of relieving the accused of criminal responsibility. The criterion which they suggest should be applied in such circumstances is whether the intervention is voluntary, *i.e.* whether it is 'free, deliberate and informed.' We resist the temptation of expressing the judicial opinion whether we find ourselves in complete agreement with that definition; though we certainly consider it to be broadly correct and supported by authority. Among the examples which the authors give of non-voluntary conduct, which is not effective to relieve the accused of responsibility, are two which are germane to the present case, *viz.* a reasonable act performed for the purpose of self-preservation, and an act done in performance of a legal duty.

There can, we consider, be no doubt that a reasonable act performed for the purpose of self-preservation, being of course itself an act caused by the accused's own act, does not operate as a *novus actus interveniens*. If authority is needed for this almost self-evident proposition, it is to be found in such cases as *Pitts* (1842) C & M 284, and *Curley* (1909) 2 Cr.App.R. 96. In both these cases, the act performed for the purpose of self-preservation consisted of an act by the victim in attempting to escape from the violence of the accused, which in fact resulted in the victim's death. In each case it was held as a matter of law that, if the victim acted in a reasonable attempt to escape the violence of the accused the death of the victim was caused by the act of the accused. Now one form of self-preservation is self-defence; for present purposes, we can see no distinction in principle between an attempt to escape the consequences of the accused's act, and a response which takes the form of self-defence. Furthermore, in our judgment, if a reasonable act of self-defence, against the act of the accused causes the death of a third party we can see no reason in principle why the act of self-defence, being an involuntary act caused by the act of the accused, should relieve the accused from criminal responsibility for the death of the third party. ...

The principles which we have stated are principles of law. ... It follows that where, in any particular case, there is an issue concerned with what we have for convenience called *novus actus interveniens*, it will be appropriate for the judge to direct the jury in accordance with these principles.

... [I]t is for the judge to direct the jury with reference to the relevant principles of law relating to causation, and then to leave it to the jury to decide, in the light of those principles, whether or not the relevant causal link has been established."

**Appeal dismissed**

The Law Commission is currently re-examining its proposals on causation and it is thought likely that it will propose a test that causation will be broken by the free, deliberate and informed intervention of another party. Such a test works well when the intervening actor intentionally commits the offence, as occurred in *Latif*. However, when the intervening party is only acting negligently, as were the police in *Paggett*[29] and the doctors in some of the medical cases, and where the actions can, at most, be described as "morally involuntary", one is still left with the intractable problem of defining voluntariness. For instance, the "palpably wrong" treatment by the doctors in *Jordan* was, nevertheless, action performed by doctors carrying

---

[29] Some 10 years later the deceased girl's mother was awarded damages against the police for their negligent handling of the siege (*The Guardian*, December 4 and 5, 1990).

out their moral and legal duties to their patient. Under the test approved in *Latif*, their actions could presumably count as "involuntary" and so the chain of causation would not be broken.

## 2. Act of victim

### (i) *Victim escaping*

### R. v Roberts (1972) 56 Cr.App.R.95 (Court of Appeal, Criminal Division)

A girl who was a passenger in the appellant's car injured herself by jumping out of the car while it was in motion. Her explanation was that the appellant had made sexual advances to her and was trying to pull her coat off. The appellant was convicted of an assault occasioning actual bodily harm. He appealed on the ground *inter alia* that causation had not been established.

Stephenson L.J.:
"The test is: Was it the natural result of what the alleged assailant said and did, in the sense that it was something that could reasonably have been foreseen as the consequence of what he was saying or doing? As it was put in one of the old cases, it had got to be shown to be his act, and if of course the victim does something so 'daft,' in the words of the appellant in this case, or so unexpected, not that this particular assailant did not actually foresee it but that no reasonable man could be expected to foresee it, then it is only in a very remote and unreal sense a consequence of his assault, it is really occasioned by a voluntary act on the part of the victim which could not reasonably be foreseen and which breaks the chain of causation between the assault and the harm or injury."

*Appeal dismissed*

### R. v Mackie (1973) 57 Cr.App.R.453 (Court of Appeal, Criminal Division)

A three year old boy whom the appellant was looking after fell downstairs while running away in fear of being ill-treated by the appellant. The boy died. The appellant appealed against conviction for manslaughter.

Stephenson L.J.:
"The victim was a child of three and regard must be had to his age in considering whether his reaction was well-founded or well-grounded on an apprehension of immediate violence (in the language of the old cases appropriate to adults) and therefore reasonably to be expected ... [T]he issue is whether the boy 'over-reacted' in a way which the appellant could not reasonably be expected to have foreseen was another. ... At the end of the summing-up the judge came back to these questions in suggesting what the vital points might be: 'First, was the boy in fear of Mackie? Secondly, did that cause him to try to escape? Thirdly, if he was in fear, was that fear well-founded?'"

*Appeal dismissed*

### R. v Williams and Davis (1992) 95 Cr.App.R.1 (Court of Appeal, Criminal Division)

The appellants gave a lift to a hitch-hiker and allegedly tried to rob him. The hitch-hiker jumped from the moving car (travelling about 30 mph) and died from head injuries caused by falling into the road. The appellants were convicted of manslaughter and appealed.

Stuart-Smith L.J.:
"There must be some proportionality between the gravity of the threat and the action of the deceased in seeking to escape from it ... [T]he deceased's conduct ... [must] be

something that a reasonable and responsible man in the assailant's shoes would have foreseen ... [T]he nature of the threat is of importance in considering both the foreseeability of harm to the victim from the threat and the question whether the deceased's conduct was proportionate to the threat, that is to say that it was within the ambit of reasonableness and not so daft as to make it his own voluntary act which amounted to a novus actus interveniens and consequently broke the chain of causation. It should of course be borne in mind that a victim may in the agony of the moment do the wrong thing ...

The jury should consider two questions: first, whether it was reasonably foreseeable that some harm, albeit not serious harm, was likely to result from the threat itself; and, secondly, whether the deceased's reaction in jumping from the moving car was within the range of responses which might be expected from a victim placed in the situation which he was. The jury should bear in mind any particular characteristic of the victim and the fact that in the agony of the moment he may act without thought and deliberation ...

In our judgment the failure of the judge to give any direction on causation was a misdirection and the conviction on this count must be quashed.

**Appeals allowed**

In *Corbett*[30] the defendant assaulted a drunk, mentally-handicapped man who, in the course of running away, fell into a gutter where he was struck by a passing car and killed. The Court of Appeal approved the trial judge's direction that the issue was whether the victim's reaction was within the foreseeable range and, in assessing this, they had to decide whether this was something that might be expected as a reaction of somebody in that state. While the test of foreseeability allows account to be taken of the victim's situation and characteristics, this is not true of defendants. In *Marjoram*[31] it was stated that the test of reasonable foresight is purely objective and so no account could be taken of the age or sex or any other characteristics of the defendant—otherwise, where two defendants with different characteristics acted together, one might be held to have caused the result but not the other.

It was the approach adopted in these cases that led to the Draft Criminal Code Bill 1989 formulation that an intervening act will only break the causal chain if it "could not in the circumstances reasonably have been foreseen". The cases are also explicable in terms of Hart and Honoré's analysis in that the actions of the victims were not very unlikely or abnormal (a synonym for reasonably foreseeable) and, in the circumstances, were hardly the result of voluntary action. The fear of the victims in these cases was such that they had no real choice but to do as they did.

### (ii) *Drugs supplied to victim*

What is the position if the defendant supplies drugs to another who injects herself and dies? Will the act of self-injection constitute a voluntary intervening act, breaking the chain of causation? In *Kennedy*[32] this view was rejected and it was held that the supplier could be regarded as having caused the death of the person self-injecting the drugs. However, this approach has since been disapproved.

[30] [1996] Crim.L.R.594.
[31] [2000] Crim.L.R.372.
[32] [1999] Crim.L.R.65.

## R. v Dias [2001] 2 Cr.App.R.96 (Court of Appeal, Criminal Division)

The defendant supplied heroin to the victim who injected himself and died. The defendant appealed against conviction.

Keene LJ:

"Assistance and encouragement is not to be automatically equated with causation. Causation raises questions of fact and degree. The recipient does not have to inject the drug which he is encouraged and assisted to take. He has a choice. It may be that in some circumstances the causative chain will still remain. That is a matter for the jury to decide.... It may seem to some that there is morally not a great deal between this situation where A hands B a syringe containing a drug such as heroin, with death resulting, and that where A injects B with his consent with the contents of the syringe. But the vital difference (and this is why causation cannot be assumed) is that the former situation involves an act of B's taken voluntarily and leading to his death."

**Appeal allowed**

This approach is preferable to that adopted in *Kennedy* which collapsed the distinction between secondary parties and principal offenders. The *Dias* reasoning is consistent with the Hart and Honoré thesis, likely to be supported by the Law Commission, that the voluntary act of injection relieves the supplier of drugs of causal responsibility. This approach, however, is not consistent with the reasonable foresight test favoured by cases such as *Roberts*. If one supplies drugs to another it is clearly reasonably foreseeable that the person will take the drugs. However, as suggested above, in the context of escaping from an assailant, reasonably foreseeable actions by the victim can be regarded as involuntary. But, as stated in *Roberts*: if "the victim does something so 'daft' ... that no reasonable man could be expected to foresee it ... then it is really occasioned by a voluntary act on the part of the victim."

However, this possible reconciliation of the two approaches reveals a deeper problem. Whether conduct can be regarded as "involuntary" is a somewhat elusive matter. In *Dias* it was stated that a recipient of drugs "has a choice". This cannot be true in many cases. If a drug addict, deprived of drugs, injects the drugs supplied, it seems implausible to argue that this is the product of a free, informed and voluntary choice.

Perhaps, this issue is best resolved in the manner suggested by the Law Commission that, irrespective of general principles, a person who procures, assists or encourages another to commit a crime is not to be regarded as having caused that crime.[33]

### (iii) *Other victim action (or inaction)*

There have been cases where the victim has refused medical treatment and consequently died. Such cases have been treated as manifestations of the principle that one must "take one's victim as one finds him". In *Hayward*[34] and *McKechnie*[35] it was held that if a victim had a physical weakness (a thyrus gland and a duodenal ulcer respectively) which hastened death following an assault, the defendant could

[33] Law Com. No. 177, Draft Criminal Code Bill 1989, cl.17(3).
[34] (1908) 21 Cox C.C. 692.
[35] (1992) 94 Cr.App.R.51.

not claim a break in causation merely because a healthy victim might not have died. In the following cases this principle has been applied to the psychological condition of the victim. The defendant must "take his victim as he finds him in mind as well as in body".

## R. v Blaue (1975) 61 Cr.App.R.271 (Court of Appeal, Criminal Division)

The appellant stabbed a woman piercing her lung. She refused to have a blood transfusion as it was contrary to her religious beliefs as a Jehovah's Witness. The surgeon advised her that without the transfusion she would die. Medical evidence established that with the transfusion she would have survived. She died and the appellant was convicted of manslaughter (on grounds of diminished responsibility). He appealed on the ground that causation was not established.

Lawton L.J.:
"Maule J.'s direction to the jury reflected the common law's answer to the problem. He who inflicted an injury which resulted in death could not excuse himself by pleading that his victim could have avoided death by taking greater care of himself. See Hale, *Pleas of the Crown* (1800 ed.) pp. 426–428. The common law in Sir Matthew Hale's time probably was in line with contemporary concepts of ethics. A man who did a wrongful act was deemed *morally* responsible for the natural and probable consequences of that act. [Counsel for the appellant] ... asked us to remember that since Sir Matthew Hale's day the rigour of the law relating to homicide has been eased in favour of the accused. It has been—but this has come about through the development of the concept of intent, not by reason of a different view of causation ...

The physical cause of death in this case was the bleeding into the pleural cavity arising from the penetration of the lung. This had not been brought about by any decision made by the deceased girl but by the stab wound.

[Counsel for the appellant] ... tried to overcome this line of reasoning by submitting that the jury should have been directed that, if they thought the girl's decision not to have a blood transfusion was an unreasonable one, then the chain of causation would have been broken. At once the question arises—reasonable by whose standards? Those of Jehovah's Witnesses? Humanists? Roman Catholics? Protestants of Anglo-Saxon descent? The man on the Clapham omnibus? But he might well be an admirer of Eleazar who suffered death rather than eat the flesh of swine ... or of Sir Thomas More who, unlike nearly all his contemporaries, was unwilling to accept Henry VIII as Head of the Church in England. Those brought up in the Hebraic and Christian traditions would probably be reluctant to accept that these martyrs caused their own deaths.

As was pointed out to ... [counsel for the appellant] in the course of argument, two cases, each raising the same issue of reasonableness because of religious beliefs, could produce different verdicts depending on where the cases were tried. ... It has long been the policy of the law that those who use violence on other people must take their victims as they find them. This in our judgment means the whole man, not just the physical man. It does not lie in the mouth of the assailant to say that his victim's religious beliefs which inhibited him from accepting certain kinds of treatment were unreasonable. The question for decision is what caused her death. The answer is the stab wound. The fact that the victim refused to stop this end coming about did not break the causal connection between the act and death."[36]

**Appeal dismissed**

Other cases have concerned victims who, in a state of anguish or fear as a result of the defendant's attack, have committed suicide. In the American case of *Lewis*[37]

---

[36] See also *Holland* (1841) 2 Mood. & R. 351 where a victim, who could have recovered, ignored medical advice and died two weeks later; the original assailant was held to have caused the death.
[37] 124 Cal. 551, 57 Pac. 470 (1889).

the defendant shot the deceased in the abdomen—a wound that would have caused death in an hour. The deceased, however, cut his own throat and died within five minutes. The court conceded that the defendant would nevertheless be liable if the self-inflicted knife wound could be causally connected to the defendant's gunshot wound, *i.e.* if it was self-inflicted because of grief or pain or through a desire to shield the defendant. Temple J. stated:

> "But, if the deceased did die from the effect of the knife wound alone, no doubt the defendant would be responsible, if it was made to appear … that the knife wound was caused by the wound inflicted by the defendant, in the natural course of events. If the relation was causal, and the wounded condition of the deceased was not merely the occasion upon which another cause intervened, not produced by the first wound, or related to it in other than in a causal way, then defendant is guilty of a homicide. But, if the wounded condition only afforded an opportunity for another unconnected person to kill, the defendant would not be guilty."

*Lewis* is a decision from the United States. Would it be followed here? In *Bunn*[38] the defendant hit the victim on the head with a snooker cue. This allegedly led to mental illness and three and a half months later the victim committed suicide. The defendant was charged with murder but the prosecution abandoned its case on the ground that "no jury could be sure beyond a reasonable doubt that the death … was caused by the blow". In *Prudom*[39] an intensive armed search was mounted in Yorkshire against Prudom who had killed two policemen. After a search lasting several days Prudom was cornered by police who warned that they were about to open fire. Prudom shot himself in the head. At the coroner's inquest a verdict was returned that Prudom had taken his own life; the actions of the police had not caused his death. At another coroner's inquest[40] it was held that builders had unlawfully killed a man who hanged himself after he had been cheated into paying £4,000 for building work worth only a fraction of that price.

### R. v Dear [1996] Crim.L.R.595 (Court of Appeal, Criminal Division) (Lexis Transcript, March 14, 1996)

The appellant slashed the victim repeatedly with a Stanley knife. The victim died two days later. The defence was that the deceased committed suicide either by reopening his wounds or, the wounds having reopened themselves, by failing to take steps to stop the bleeding. The trial judge directed the jury that causation was established if the victim did what he did because of the wounds and would not have done so unless he had been wounded. The chain of causation would only be broken if the victim acted only for some reason unconnected to the attack on him, for example, shame at his own prior conduct (it was alleged that the victim had sexually interfered with the appellant's daughter). The appellant was convicted of murder and appealed.

[38] *The Times*, May 11, 1989.
[39] *The Times*, October 8, 1982, p. 2.
[40] *The Times*, June 14, 1996.

Rose L.J.:

"[Counsel for the appellant argues that] 'voluntary' suicide ... is a novus actus interveniens. A suicide where the deceased can be taken to know and understand the nature of his act, and thus exercise a choice, is a novus actus, even if it follows upon an attack upon the victim. ...

[E]ven assuming that there was evidence of suicide, through shame or some other reason unrelated to the defendant's conduct ... this did not ... render inaccurate ... the direction which the judge gave on causation ...

The correct approach in the criminal law is ...: were the injuries inflicted by the defendant an operating and significant cause of death? That question, in our judgment, is necessarily answered, not by philosophical analysis, but by common sense according to all the circumstances of the particular case.

In the present case the cause of the deceased's death was bleeding from the artery which the defendant had severed. Whether or not the resumption or continuation of that bleeding was deliberately caused by the deceased, the jury were entitled to find that the defendant's conduct made an operative and significant contribution to the death."

**Appeal dismissed**

Smith has commented on this case that if "the wounds were effectively healed when D took the Stanley knife to himself, it is not so clear that the wounds were an operating and substantial cause of death. Arguably, it was then the same as if he had cut his throat or blown his brains out".[41]

"Victim condition" cases such as *Blaue* are straightforward applications of Hart and Honoré's "abnormal condition" exception. The "abnormality" of the victim does not break the chain of causation. The "suicide" cases are more difficult and appear irreconcilable other than on a policy basis. Was it not for policy reasons that the police were held not to have caused Prudom's death, while the opposite result was reached in *Lewis* and *Dear* where the victims similarly took their own lives?

There is a problem in these cases where the defendant is held to take his victim as he finds him. In *Blaue* the victim's physical or mental condition is counted as an "abnormal condition" and thus unable to rank as a coincidence. But in the cases of victims escaping from attackers, such as *Roberts* and *Mackie*, the victim's psychological make-up that might have induced flight from the defendant is disregarded and insistence is placed on such actions being reasonable, likely or foreseeable. But what if the victim, because of, say, a pre-existing neurotic condition, grossly over-reacts to a minor assault? Under the *Blaue* principle the defendant must take his victim as he finds her and causation is established. Under the *Roberts* principle such a victim's action could be viewed as "daft" and so break the causal chain. How can this divergence of approach be explained? It has been suggested that the issue in all such cases be determined by whether the victim's act was "voluntary".[42] If the victim's suicide or leaping from a moving car was voluntary it breaks the chain of causation as "[i]n the view of many theorists, the attribution of a harm cannot be traced past a voluntary intentional act that brings it about".[43] This was the solution adopted in *Pagett* and *Latif* for determining whether the actions of a third person constituted a *novus actus interveniens*. It is submitted that a better (and certainly simpler) approach is to allow the central principle of reasonable foresight or expectation to prevail. However, in

---

[41] [1996] Crim.L.R.596.
[42] Hart and Honoré, p. 326; Fletcher, *Rethinking Criminal Law* (1978), p. 365.
[43] Fletcher, *ibid.*

ascertaining whether the victim's response is reasonable, account should be taken of any particular idiosyncracies of the victim. Thus in *Roberts* the girl was "normal". The question is simply whether her response was reasonable. In *Blaue* the issue is whether it is reasonably foreseeable that a Jehovah's Witness would refuse a blood transfusion. This was the approach approved in *Williams and Davis* where it was held that, in assessing whether the victim's response in jumping out of the car was reasonably foreseeable one had to bear in mind "any particular characteristic of the victim". In *Corbett* the issue was whether the reaction of a victim "in that state" was foreseeable. This test enables the victim's condition or characteristics to be taken into account, while imposing some limit to the chain of causation.

### 3. Causation and Strict Liability

Strictly speaking, there is no reason why the rules on causation should be any different for offences of strict liability. Mindful, however, of the purpose of such offences, the courts have adopted a somewhat broader approach.

### Environment Agency v Empress Car Co. (Abertillery) Ltd [1999] 2 A.C. 22 (House of Lords)

The appellant company maintained a diesel oil tank on its premises. An outlet from the tank was governed by a tap which had no lock. An unknown person (probably a vandal) opened the tap causing the oil to run into a river. The company was convicted of causing polluting matter to enter controlled waters contrary to section 85(1) of the Water Resources Act 1991.

Lord Hoffman:
"[O]ne cannot give a commonsense answer to a question of causation for the purpose of attributing responsibility under some rule without knowing the purpose and scope of the rule ...

What, therefore, is the nature of the duty imposed by s.85(1)? ... It is immediately clear that the liability imposed is strict: it does not require mens rea in the sense of intention or negligence. Strict liability is imposed in the interests of protecting controlled waters from pollution. ...

... [T]o frame the question as 'who or what caused the result under consideration' is wrong and distracting, because it may have more than one right answer. The question is whether the defendant caused the pollution. How is foreseeability a relevant factor to consider in answering this question? ... [T]he question is not whether the consequences ought to have been foreseen; it is whether the defendant caused the pollution. And foreseeability is not the criterion for deciding whether a person caused something or not. People often cause things which they could not have foreseen.

The true commonsense distinction is, in my view, between acts and events which, although not necessarily foreseeable in the particular case, are in the generality a normal and familiar fact of life, and facts or events which are abnormal and extraordinary ... There is nothing unusual about people putting unlawful substances into the sewage system and the same, regrettably, is true about ordinary vandalism. So when these things happen, one does not say: that was an extraordinary coincidence, which negatived the causal connection between the original act of accumulating the polluting substance and its escape ... On the other hand, the example I gave of the terrorist attack would be something so unusual that one would not regard the defendant's conduct as having caused the escape at all. ...

I shall try to summarise the effect of this discussion ...

(2) The prosecution need not prove that the defendant did something which was the *immediate* cause of the pollution: maintaining tanks, lagoons or sewage systems full of

noxious liquid is doing something, even if the immediate cause of the pollution was lack of maintenance, a natural event or the act of a third party.

(3) When the prosecution has identified something which the defendant did, the justices must decide whether it caused the pollution. They should not be diverted by questions like 'What was the cause of the pollution?' or 'Did something else cause the pollution?' because to say that something else caused the pollution (like brambles clogging the pumps or vandalism by third parties) is not inconsistent with the defendant having caused it as well.

(4) If the defendant did something which produced a situation in which the polluting matter could escape but a necessary condition of the actual escape which happened was also the act of a third party or a natural event, the justices should consider whether the act or event should be regarded as a normal fact of life or something extraordinary. If it was in the general run of things a matter of ordinary occurrence, it will not negative the causal effect of the defendant's acts, even if it was not foreseeable that it would happen to that particular defendant or take that particular form. If it can be regarded as something extraordinary, it will be open to the justices to hold that the defendant did not cause the pollution.

(5) The distinction between ordinary and extraordinary is one of fact."

**Appeal dismissed**

This was followed in *Environment Agency v Brook plc*[44] where it was held that leakage of pollution caused by a latent fault in a seal was a rare but ordinary fact of life. Although the bursting of the seal was unforeseeable, it was not an extraordinary event breaking the causal chain.

In one respect this approach is no different from that adopted in other cases where *mens rea* is a requirement of the offence. An "extraordinary" intervening act, like a "daft and unexpected" one (*Roberts*) amounts to a "coincidence" and breaks the causal chain. However, what is different is that causation can be established despite the voluntary intervention of a third party (the vandal) and the rejection of the *Roberts* test of reasonable foresight.

While this decision has received a hostile reception by some commentators,[45] it is perhaps understandable in policy terms. Many offences are deliberately made ones of strict liability to ensure that persons and companies take every precaution to prevent the harm occurring; this includes taking steps to prevent deliberate interventions by third parties. The reasoning in this decision is likely to be limited to strict liability offences where a person is subject to a legal duty to guard against the harm that is caused, albeit by another.[46] However, given the criticisms of strict liability offences, it must be questionable whether such a relaxation of the rules on causation for such offences is justifiable.

## IV. Conclusion

It is interesting that, leaving aside the medical and strict liability judgments, many of the problem cases discussed above involved constructive manslaughter,[47] which is a species of crime where no *mens rea* is required as to the final result. The other leading case, *Roberts*, involved section 47 of the Offences against the Person Act

---

[44] *The Times*, March 26, 1998.
[45] Simester and Sullivan, *Criminal Law Theory and Doctrine* (2000), pp. 88–90.
[46] *ibid.*
[47] The defendant was convicted of murder in *Dear*. In *Blaue* the conviction was for manslaughter by diminished responsibility.

1861 which, as another constructive crime, also does not require *mens rea* as to the result. This tends to lend some credence to the view that principles of causation are subservient to those of *mens rea*. Where there is clear *mens rea* as to the result, problems of causation will not be allowed to intrude. (*Dear* is an exception here.) But, where one is dealing with constructive crime, the job cannot be left to *mens rea* and it is in this area that "principles", such as they are, have started emerging. However, even in these, and certainly in the other cases, it would be a mistake to ignore the role of policy: for example, the policy of not allowing medical treatment to break the chain of causation or the policy of respecting a victim's religious beliefs in *Blaue*.

It must be remembered that most of the defendants in the above cases could have been charged with, or found guilty of, lesser offences. Pagett was convicted of possession of a firearm, kidnapping and attempted murder. McKechnie was charged, in the alternative, with causing grievous bodily harm with intent. Blaue could have been convicted of attempted murder, Hayward of assault, and so on. Welansky could have been found guilty of a violation of safety regulations. Policy considerations dictated that they all be blamed and punished for something, but the question is what were the policy considerations that dictated they be found liable for homicide offences, as opposed to these lesser offences? It is interesting how much importance has been attached to the resulting harm as opposed to the more immediate "wrongdoing" of the defendant. Whether this approach is justifiable is one of the main themes of the next chapter to which we now turn.

# 5

# INCHOATE OFFENCES

---

## I. Introduction

An inchoate crime is one that is "committed by doing an act with the purpose of effecting some other offence".[1] It is committed when the defendant takes certain steps towards the commission of a crime. There are three main inchoate offences in English law—attempt, conspiracy and incitement—and the nature of the requisite steps that need be taken varies with each. With attempt the defendant must have tried to commit the offence and have got relatively close to achieving the objective. With conspiracy at least two people must have agreed to commit a crime. With incitement the defendant must have tried to persuade another to commit a crime.

An inchoate offence is one that is "relative to the offence-in-chief".[2] It consists of actions falling short of the consummated crime. It is thus not a crime existing in the abstract. One cannot be charged with "conspiracy" or "attempt". The indictment must be drafted with reference to the complete offence, for example, conspiracy to murder or attempt to steal.

There are many other offences in English law that might be thought of as inchoate in the sense that they penalise conduct that might be preparatory to the commission of other offences—for example, possession of firearms.[3] These offences are, however, "crimes in themselves" and are charged as such without reference to any further offence. Such offences could be described as precursor offences or endangerment offences.

Both inchoate and precursor offences share a common element. No harm is caused, in the ordinary sense of the word; no person need be injured; no proprietary interest is damaged. A crucial question, therefore, running through the analysis of such offences will be: how can one justify the existence of these offences and how should they be punished in comparison with the complete offence?

---

[1] Williams, *Textbook of Criminal Law* (2nd ed., 1983), p. 402.
[2] Fletcher, *Rethinking Criminal Law* (1978), p. 132.
[3] Firearms Act 1968, ss.16–22.

463

## II. ATTEMPT

### A. *Criminology of Attempts*

**Editorial "The Criminology of Attempts" [1986] Crim.L.R.769:**

"In recent years the law of criminal attempts has been one of the most discussed areas of the criminal law. ... Over the same period there has also been an increasing criminological interest in the prevention of crime, which has manifested itself in the publication of various Home Office Research Studies on crime prevention, with many of the studies based on experiments undertaken in different areas of the country. Both the Home Office and the police have been placing more emphasis on the taking of measures to prevent crime, and few would argue with the general proposition that successful prevention is preferable to *post hoc* efforts to reform or deter offenders. If the crime prevention movement has had any success, then one might expect that more criminal endeavours are ending in failure—to be precise, that the proportion of offences which are mere attempts rather than completed crimes is increasing. Has this happened?

The present structure of the annual criminal statistics does not permit such inferences, since the statistical categories are not apt, but there is now some interesting material from the two sweeps of the British Crime Survey. ... [S]ome 11,000 households were asked about offences which had been committed against them or their members in the previous year, and it has thus been possible to obtain a realistic estimate of how many crimes are actually committed each year rather than relying on police figures of the offences recorded by them. Home Office Research Bulletin no. 21 (1986), at pages 10–13, discusses the British Crime Survey findings on attempted burglaries, an area in which crime prevention has received considerable publicity. The general finding is that only about half of all burglaries or attempts are reported to the police, but when the figures were examined further it was found that two-fifths of all burglaries are unsuccessful attempts to gain entry. Only about 20 per cent of attempts are ever reported to the police,[4] and therefore the proportion coming through the courts is much smaller. It is speculated that about half of the attempts failed because of the level of security, and that the proportion of attempts has increased in recent years."

### B. *Should there be a Law of Attempt?*

Generally, criminal liability is imposed upon a *blameworthy* actor who causes a prohibited *harm*.

We have seen that an important (and often decisive) indicator of blame is the existence of *mens rea*. With attempts, this element is clearly satisfied. The person who attempts to commit an offence clearly has the *mens rea* of that full offence.[5] But no harm has been caused in the usual sense of the word: for instance, the victim has not died or has not lost any property. Are we justified in imposing criminal liability upon an actor who has caused no such harm?

---

[4] The reporting rate for some attempted burglaries is much higher for some types of premises than for others; for example, it is 80 per cent for retail premises and 53 per cent for manufacturing premises (Mirrlees-Black and Ross, *Crime Against Retail Premises in 1993* (H.O.R.S. No. 26) (1995); *Crime Against Manufacturing Premises in 1993* (H.O.R.S. No. 27) (1995)).

[5] Indeed, as shall be seen, this *mens rea* will often have to be of a *greater* degree than that required for the completed offence.

There are two quite distinct ways of answering this question—both leading to the conclusion that criminal liability *should* be imposed for attempts:

1. Where a crime is attempted, there *is* a harm, namely, a threat to security. We all have rights to bodily and proprietary security. An attempt to commit a crime represents a danger to these rights. Our right to security has been infringed. This infringement of our rights constitutes, in itself, a harm that the criminal law seeks to punish. Gross expresses the point well:

> "Where there is only attempt liability, the conduct itself may usefully be regarded as a second order harm: in itself it is the sort of conduct that normally presents a threat of harm; and that, by itself, is a violation of an interest that concerns the law. The interest is one in security from harm and merely presenting a threat of harm violates that security interest."[6]

2. In utilitarian terms, criminal liability for attempts may be justified in the absence of any harm. A person who attempts to commit a crime is dangerous and needs restraining. Such a person is also in need of rehabilitation and punishment for individual deterrence, otherwise she might try to commit the crime again being more careful the next time. It is, however, doubtful whether punishment for general deterrence purposes will suffice here: people who attempt crimes, by definition, aim at success; if punishment for the complete crime is an ineffective deterrent, nothing is gained by punishment for an attempt to commit the crime. There is also a final important utilitarian justification here: the police should be given every encouragement to prevent crime, not simply to detect it. On this basis the police should be empowered to arrest, and the C.P.S. to prosecute, for attempts to commit crimes.

Of course, whenever utilitarian arguments such as these are raised, we find ourselves faced with the same central question: while utilitarian considerations might explain the *purpose* of punishment, are we ever justified in punishing exclusively for such reasons? Or may we only punish offenders who *deserve* punishment? If the latter, then we are back to our starting point that, generally, punishment is only deserved where there is a combination of blame and harm. However this is not a cast-iron rule. With crimes of strict liability, the law is prepared to dispense with the element of blame in imposing liability. It could be that with crimes of attempt, the utilitarian arguments for punishment are so strong that we are prepared to dispense with the element of harm, and assert that punishment is justified (*i.e.* deserved) on the basis of the blame element alone.

Thus under either of these explanations it is possible to justify the existence of a law of attempt. The contours of such a law will vary, however, depending on which of the two views is accepted. This is because the first view focuses on attempts as threats to people's interests in security from interference. Thus unless the attempter gets near to completing the crime (and, generally, unless the crime is possible), no interests are threatened and criminal liability is not justified. But the emphasis in the second view is on the *mens rea* of the attempter: if he has the requisite *mens rea*, he need not get near to committing the complete offence (and, generally, it will be

[6] Gross, *A Theory of Criminal Justice* (1979), p. 125.

irrelevant whether the crime is possible). The tensions between these two approaches and their impact upon the law will be explored further when we examine the *actus reus* of attempt.

Can there be an attempt to commit all crimes? Section 1(4) of the Criminal Attempts Act 1981 provides that there can only be criminal liability for attempts to commit "any offence which, if it were completed, would be triable ... as an indictable offence".[7] This includes offences "triable either way".[8]

Criminal liability for attempts to commit summary offences was excluded because there is "no social need to extend the punishment of attempt outside the class of serious crime. The amount of time spent considering complicated questions would be out of all proportion to the advantage accruing from allowing the law to intervene at an early stage."[9] It is submitted that such an approach is justifiable.[10] With attempts, criminal liability is imposed in the absence of any direct harm (other than a threat to security). When dealing with serious offences we are arguably justified in dispensing with the requirement of harm. But when dealing with the lesser summary offences which pose less of a threat to security, we should insist on harm actually occurring as a prerequisite to any criminal liability.

It has been suggested that we do not need a *general* law of attempt. Each substantive offence could be defined, or redefined, so as to include attempts to commit that offence.[11] For instance, the crime of handling stolen goods is defined by section 22 of the Theft Act 1968 in the following terms:

"(1) A person handles stolen goods if ... he ... receives the goods, or ... undertakes or assists in their retention, removal, disposal or realisation ..., *of if he arranges to do so.*"

Arranging to receive stolen goods is part of the substantive offence. Without this provision many such arrangements would have constituted attempts to commit the offence. If all offences were defined in a comparable manner, a general law of attempt would be unnecessary. Such an approach, however, poses immense problems. First, is it realistic to expect that *all* criminal offences could be defined (and all existing offences redefined) so as to include attempts within their definition? Secondly, and most importantly, if, as will be suggested in the next section, attempts are to be regarded as less serious than completed offences, we surely do not wish to collapse the distinction between the two. One way of avoiding this would be to increase the number of separate offences of ulterior intent, such as assault with intent to rob.[12] This would have the advantage of fair labelling[13]—

---

[7] Section 1(4) also excludes liability for attempted (a) conspiracy; (b) aiding, abetting, counselling, procuring or suborning an offence; and (c) offences under section 4(1) (assisting offenders) or section 5(1) (accepting or agreeing to accept consideration for not disclosing information about an arrestable offence) of the Criminal Law Act 1967. There can be liability for an attempt to incite an offence (*Goldman* [2001] Crim.L.R.822).

[8] An offence is an "indictable offence" even if it is one, such as low value criminal damage, that has to be proceeded with as if it were triable only summarily (*R. v Bristol Masgistrates' Court, ex p.E* [1999] Crim.L.R.161).

[9] H.C.Deb., Vol. 2, ser. 6, cols. 214 (1981).

[10] *Contra*, Law Commission Working Paper No. 50 *Inchoate Offences* (1973), para. 109.

[11] Glazebrook, "Should we have a Law of Attempted Crime?" (1969) 85 L.Q.R. 28.

[12] Theft Act 1968, s.8(2).

[13] For an example of where an ulterior intent crime might have played such a role, see *Geddes* [1996] Crim.L.R.894; *below* p. 489.

accurately reflecting what the defendant did—but it would lead to a plethora of offences. Ulterior intent crimes have their place but a general law of attempt, separate from the complete crime, is still needed for reasons of fair labelling and punishment.[14]

## C. *Punishment of Attempts*

### Criminal Attempts Act 1981, section 4(1)

"A person guilty ... of attempting to commit an offence shall—

(a) if the offence attempted is murder or any other offence the sentence for which is fixed by law, be liable on conviction on indictment to imprisonment for life; and

(b) if the offence attempted is indictable but does not fall within paragraph (a) above, be liable on conviction on indictment to any penalty to which he would have been liable on conviction on indictment of that offence; and

(c) if the offence attempted is triable either way, be liable on summary conviction to any penalty to which he would have been liable on summary conviction of that offence."

### California Penal Code, § 664. Attempts; punishment (as amended, 1997)

"Every person who attempts to commit any crime, but fails, or is prevented or intercepted in its perpetration shall be punished, where no provision is made by law for the punishment of those attempts, as follows:

(a) If the crime attempted is punishable by imprisonment in the state prison, the person guilty of such attempt shall be punished by imprisonment in the state prison for one-half the term of imprisonment prescribed upon a conviction of the offense so attempted. However, ... if the crime attempted is any other one in which the maximum sentence is life imprisonment or death, the person guilty of the attempt shall be punished by imprisonment in the state prison for five, seven or nine years. ...

(b) If the crime attempted is punishable by imprisonment in a county jail, the person guilty of the attempt shall be punished by imprisonment in a county jail for a term not exceeding one-half the term of imprisonment prescribed upon a conviction of the offense attempted.

(c) If the offense so attempted is punishable by a fine, the offender convicted of that attempt shall be punished by a fine not exceeding one-half the largest fine which may be imposed upon a conviction of the offense attempted."

The completed crime of theft carries a maximum of seven years' imprisonment in England and attempted theft can similarly be punished, on conviction on indictment, up to this maximum of seven years. But in California, if theft there carried a presumptive penalty of seven years imprisonment in the state prison, attempted theft would carry a presumptive penalty of three and a half years' imprisonment. This divergence of approach raises the fundamental question: should attempts be punished to the same, or to a lesser, extent as the completed crime? On what basis can either of these approaches be rationalised?

### James Brady, "Punishing Attempts" (1980) 63 The Monist 246 at 247–250:

#### "2. *Equal harm*

"... According to Becker ('Criminal Attempt and the Law of Crimes', Philosophy and Public Affairs, Vol. 3 (Spring, 1974): pp. 262–294), we need to distinguish between the

---

[14] Horder, "Crimes of Ulterior Intent" in Simester and Smith, *Harm and Culpability* (1996), pp. 153–172.

private harm done to the individual, which, of course, is different in the case of attempts and completions, and the 'social' harm to which the criminal law is mainly addressed. The harm which is the concern of the criminal law is that which disrupts social stability and arouses self-defensive reactions within persons in the society. One's assurance that one will not be interfered with is perceived to be threatened equally by an attempt on others and by completed crimes. Thus, in general, attempts and completed crimes are equal in what Becker calls their 'social volatility'; the *criminal* harm is the same. ...

However ... his claim ... is unfounded. The fear, resentment, and apprehension occasioned when harm, in its ordinary sense, occurs does appear to be different than when, even by accident, no harm occurs. These attitudes seem to be what Becker has in mind when he talks of the 'social volatility' of conduct. Therefore, on Becker's own theory we should, *contra* his position, treat attempts differently ...

### 3. *Equal dangerousness*

A more plausible claim than the argument that attempts and the completed crime do not differ in the harm done, is the claim that, in general, attempts pose no less danger to the legally protected interest than does the completed crime. If the general purpose in punishing is to prevent harm, the law should identify, at the earliest feasible moment, the dangerous individual who is likely to cause harm. In such a theory, conduct might be required before such intervention is justifiable, but the primary function of the conduct requirement would be evidentiary, serving as proof of the intent which is an index to the dangerousness of the offender.

If the dangerousness of the offender is the key element in grading offenses, then it follows that two equally dangerous offenders should be treated the same. If there is no difference in dangerousness between the successful offender and the person who fails to cause harm because he is prevented by some external circumstance, the law should treat them equally. Being equally dangerous, they are equally in need of treatment and reform.

There is, of course, the chance that the person who attempts a crime might be deterred from completing it if he were to receive a more severe penalty for the successful crime than if the penalty for attempts and the completed crime are the same. If he is already liable to the full penalty for the attempt, then he has no motive to desist from completing the crime. But this does not provide an argument, under an equal dangerousness theory, for punishing attempts, in general, less than the completed crime. To take care of these special, and probably rare cases, it would seem to be better to provide, as the Model Penal Code does, an affirmative defense of abandonment or, renunciation of purpose. Such a defense is a defense to the crime of attempt.[15] If the defendant is successful in proving the defense, he receives no punishment at all. Thus, the offender has an even greater motive for not carrying out his purpose than if the law merely provided an across-the-board reduction in punishment for attempts.

[But if this] equal dangerousness argument were to be followed consistently, crimes of unequal culpability should also be treated the same. The focus of a dangerousness approach is on the characteristics of a person which identify him as presenting a threat of harm to society. Negligent or reckless offenders may pose as much of a continuing threat of harm and may require as much treatment and reform to 'neutralize' their dangerousness as the intentional offender. Thus, if we accept the equal dangerousness rationale for punishing attempts, it would appear that we should also accept the premise that offenses should not be ranked according to culpability elements such as intention, recklessness, and negligence. We could, of course, simply accept this conclusion that intentional offenses should be classified as being of the same criminal 'degree' as reckless or negligent offenses where there is reason to believe that there is no difference in the dangerousness of the offender. But this would entail a radical reform of the criminal law; indeed, to follow a dangerous rationale consistently would be, in effect, to abolish the system of control now known as the criminal law and substitute a system of treatment and prevention. ...

---

[15] This is the position in the United States, but as shall be seen, not under English law.

## 4. *Equal culpability*

... [This] assumes that the sole determining factor in assessing the degree of blame in attempts is the person's intention. If the offender has done everything in his power to carry out his intention to cause harm and fails through some fortuity, then he should be considered as culpable as if he had succeeded. The first version holds, moreover, that cases of attempts other than the extreme case should also be ranked equally with the extreme case and with the completed offense. After all, what difference in intent is discernible between a person who is apprehended before he has taken the last step towards the commission of the offense, if we are convinced that he had the intention or the 'fixed' intention to commit the offense, and one who has taken that step in furtherance of his intent? On this view, how can there be any difference in culpability between the person apprehended while 'lying in wait', or at an even earlier stage of preparation, and the person who shoots but misses? Under this version, punishment for attempts should be the same whenever we are satisfied that intent or 'fixed' intent is present, the conduct requirement serving as evidence of that intent."

## Andrew Ashworth, "Belief, Intent and Criminal Liability" in J. Eekelaar and J. Bell (eds), Oxford Essays in Jurisprudence (1987), pp. 16–17:

"Is A, who shoots at X intending to kill him but misses because X unexpectedly moves, any less culpable than B, who shoots at Y intending to kill him and does so? An external description of both sets of events would probably not suggest that they have 'done' the same thing, whereas an account which paid more attention to the actor's point of view and to matters which lay within the actor's control would suggest that they both intended and tried, to the same extent, to do the same thing. The argument here is that, because of the element of uncertainty in the outcome of things which we try to do, it would be wrong for assessments of culpability to depend on the occurrence or non-occurrence of the intended consequences. 'Success or failure ... makes no difference at all to [an agent's] moral status in relation to his original act. His original act, strictly considered, was simply his trying and *that* is what moral assessment must concern itself with' (Winch, *Ethics and Action*, 1972, p. 139) ... Moral blame and criminal liability should be based so far as possible on choice and control, on the trying and not on what actually happened thereafter.

What are the reasons for wishing to reduce the influence of chance upon criminal liability? It cannot be doubted that luck plays a considerable part in everyday events. Actual results also play a considerable part in judgments of others, and tend to dominate assessments in such fields as business, sport, and education. Those who try hard but are unsuccessful often receive less recognition than those who achieve goals (no matter how little effort they put into it). But these are not moral assessments of the individuals or their characters. If one turns to moral and social judgments, it is doubtful whether outcomes should be proper criteria. It may be desirable overall to have fewer bad outcomes and more good outcomes in society, but that does not lead to the conclusion that moral praise and blame should be allocated solely according to result. Indeed, a bad outcome stemming from a good intent may be a better predictor of good outcomes than a good outcome born of a bad intent. From time to time we may praise someone for producing a good result, even though it was not what he was trying to do, but this is more a reflection of our pleasure at the outcome than an assessment of his conduct and character. If we turn to blaming, is it not unacceptable to blame people for causing results irrespective of whether they were caused intentionally, negligently, or purely accidentally? Blaming is a moral activity which is surely only appropriate where the individual had some choice or control over the matter. For this reason the criminal law should seek to minimize the effect of luck upon the incidence and scale of criminal liability."

A relatively common view is that punishment for attempts should depend upon the dangerousness of the defendant's actions; this is measured by determining how imminent the threatened harm is and by examining the reason for failure.

## Sir Rupert Cross and Andrew Ashworth, Cross: The English Sentencing System (3rd ed., 1981), pp. 154–155:

"[T]he question whether an attempt should be punished less severely than the completed crime is largely dependent on the reason why the attempt failed. If it failed because the attempter voluntarily abandoned the attempt, he should be punished less because he is less wicked or needs less deterring. If it failed because of his incompetence, either in executing his design clumsily or in choosing a method which, owing to his failure to appreciate the true facts, proved to be impossible, he may be punished less on the ground that he represents less of a social danger than successful criminals. If it failed because of someone's intervention before he had done all he set out to do, he may be treated more leniently than the successful criminal: his wickedness may be less, since (as Blackstone said) it takes more wickedness to carry through a plan than to conceive it, and it may be desirable (on a utilitarian view) to mark each stage of an attempt by a portion of punishment in order to deter the attempter from pursuing his criminal design to its conclusion. There remain difficulties, however, with cases ... where the attempter has done all the acts he intended and has failed to produce the planned result. ... On principle ... there is no distinction in point of either wickedness or social danger between the successful criminal and the unsuccessful attempter in this last class. Chance may well be the only explanation of why one attempt succeeded and the other failed, and a sound sentencing policy should take little notice of a factor which lies outside the offender's control. He should be judged on the basis of what he intended to do, believed he was doing or knowingly risked."

Gross pushes the argument to its logical conclusion by asserting:

"In some cases, then, attempt liability will be as extensive as liability for the completed crime, and may even be greater, for sometimes, even though harm does not occur, the conduct of the accused was more dangerous than in a case in which harm does occur. In other cases of attempt the conduct is less dangerous and so liability is less extensive."[16]

It is our submission that it can *never* be justifiable to impose greater punishment for an attempt than for the completed crime. Indeed, it is our submission that attempts should *always* be punished to a lesser extent than the completed crime. This is because the paradigm of criminal liability is the combination of blame and harm and the absence of one of these should be reflected by no, or, at most, less punishment. In relation to the law of attempt there is no harm (or, at most, second-order harm) and, therefore, punishment should be lower than for the completed crime. The reasons why this should be the case need to be explored. Why should the causing of harm be regarded as so significant?

## Michael Davis, "Why Attempts Deserve Less Punishment than Complete Crimes" 5 Law & Phil. (1986) 1 at 28–29:

"Someone who attempts a crime but fails to do the harm characteristic of success still (ordinarily) risks doing that harm. He deserves punishment for risking that harm because

---

[16] *Theory of Criminal Justice, above,* at n.6, at p. 425. For a criticism of Gross's views, see Brady, "Punishing Attempts" (1980) 63 *The Monist* 246 at 251–255.

even risking such harm is an advantage the law abiding do not take. He deserves less punishment for the attempt than he would for the complete crime because being able to risk doing harm is not as great an advantage as being able to do it. To attempt murder is, for example, not worth as much as to succeed. The successful murderer has the advantage of having done what he set out to do. The would-be murderer whose attempt failed has only had the *chance* to do what he set out to do. The difference is substantial."

## J. C. Smith, "The Element of Chance in Criminal Liability" [1971] Crim.L.R.63 at 69–72:

"Ought we then to get rid of the element of harm and base liability purely on fault? . . .

Even the most ardent advocate for the re-introduction of capital punishment did not—so far as I know—want it for *attempted* murder as well as murder. Yet the only difference between the attempt and the full offence is that in the latter the harm which it is the object of the law to prevent is caused, in the former it is not; but it seems to be generally accepted that this justifies a difference in the gravity of the offence and the punishment which may be imposed. . . .

[This] suggests that great significance is still attached to the harm done, as distinct from the harm intended or foreseen. Perhaps the significance of the harm done derives from our emotional reaction to the acts of others. If one of my small boys, not looking what he is doing, throws a stone which just misses the dining room window, I shall be very cross with him; but if the stone breaks the dining room window, I shall be absolutely furious. His behaviour is just as bad and just as dangerous in the one case as in the other; but my indignation is much greater in the case where he has caused the harm than in that where he has not. . . .

Stephen J. thought . . . there was nothing irrational in basing liability on the harm done:
'If two persons are guilty of the very same act of negligence, and one of them causes thereby a railway accident, involving the death and mutilation of many persons, whereas the other does no injury to anyone, it seems to me that it would be rather pedantic than rational to say that each had committed the same offence, and should be subjected to the same punishment. . . . Both certainly deserve punishment, but it gratifies a natural public feeling to choose out for punishment the one who actually has caused great harm, and the effect in the way of preventing a repetition of the offence is much the same as if both were punished.' "

## H. L. A. Hart, Punishment and Responsibility (Essays in the Philosophy of Law) (1968), p. 131:

"It is pointed out that in some cases the successful completion of a crime may be a source of gratification, and, in the case of theft, of actual gain, and in such cases to punish the successful criminal more severely may be one way of depriving him of these illicit satisfactions which the unsuccessful have never had . . .

My own belief is that this form of retributive theory appeals to something with deeper instinctive roots than the last mentioned principle. Certainly the resentment felt by a victim actually injured is normally much greater than that felt by the intended victim who has escaped harm because an attempted crime has failed."

## James Brady, "Punishing Attempts" (1980) 63 The Monist 246 at 255:

"[F]eelings of guilt and remorse are significantly different in the case where one has actually caused harm than in the case where, acting with the same intent, one has not been the cause of harm. Feelings of guilt and remorse do vary in degree when one has, for example, through reckless driving caused a death and where one has acted with equal recklessness but there has been no victim. In this case, as with the unsuccessful attempt, there is a kind of 'space' in which the person is allowed to express relief that he has not been the cause of harm."

Thus the occurrence of harm plays a crucial role in the shaping and assessing of moral responsibility.

### R. A. Duff, Criminal Attempts (1996), pp. 351–352, 354:

"Our moral responses to an agent and her action, including such responses as blame or reproach, are commonly conditioned partly by her action's actual outcome; rather than seeing this as a regrettably irrational infection of our moral judgments of culpability by our natural concerns for actual outcomes, we should recognise it as an appropriate structuring of the moral responses of people living a human social life. ... [This involves] portraying moral blame as a social, communicative response to another's wrongdoing: an attempt to communciate to him, to persuade him to accept, an adequate moral understanding of the implications of what he has done ... On a communicative conception of punishment, the punishment which an offender receives should itself aim to communicate to her an appropriate understanding of the wrong that she did: to give forceful and symbolic expression to the message which her conviction itself aimed to communicate. ... One who tried but failed to do some criminal harm should ... understand and repent the wrong that she did; if she attempted to commit a serious crime, that wrong was itself serious. Our understanding of her wrongdoing is, however, conditioned by its failure: we are relieved that she has failed. If she is to come to an adequate moral understanding of what she has done, she must therefore come to share that relief ...

If the law ignored actual outcomes at the stage of conviction or of sentencing, it would in effect be saying that it does not matter whether the defendant actually caused harm, actually killed his victim, or actually damaged another's property."

Before ending this section it is perhaps worth pausing to consider briefly the concept of "blame" as applied in the field of attempts, and to question the assumption that the blameworthiness of those who attempt and those who succeed is necessarily the same. It is a prerequisite of criminal liability for attempts that the attempter intends to commit the criminal offence. But while many attempters *appear for legal purposes* to possess this necessary intention, closer examination reveals that this might not necessarily be so. As Menninger has written: "[T]he failure to achieve success ... is apt to express accurately the mathematical resultant of component wishes—conscious and unconscious—acting as vectors."[17] And Freud wrote that: "Errors ... are not accidents; they are serious mental acts; they have their meaning; they arise through the concurrence—perhaps better, the mutual interference—of two different intentions."[18]

### Stephen J. Schulhofer, "Harm and Punishment: A Critique of Emphasis on the Results of Conduct in the Criminal Law" (1974) 122 University of Pennsylvania Law Review 1497 at 1590:

"A slightly different dimension is added by psychological theories concerning the interplay between conscious and unconscious intentions. Freud argued that divergence

---

[17] *Man against Himself* (1938), p. 22.
[18] *A General Introduction to Psychoanalysis* (1958), p. 48.

between an actor's conscious purpose and the results he actually achieves will often be explained by an unconscious intention to further a different purpose. A defendant who attempted to shoot his victim but missed may, of course, have failed because of his inherent lack of skill or because the victim suddenly moved away. But he also may have failed because an unconscious desire not to kill interfered with his conscious purpose, causing him to aim poorly and miss a shot that would have given him no difficulty under other circumstances. And even the first group of explanations is not inconsistent with the possibility that the defendant's intention was ambivalent. If the defendant had always been a poor shot, his decision not to choose a weapon better suited to his talents may have been influenced by an unconscious intention that the plan fail; similarly, the victim may be lucky enough to move out of the way only because the defendant waited unnecessarily long before firing. Even if success is prevented only by police intervention at the last moment, it cannot always be said that the defendant's intention was unequivocal; he may have purposely, though unconsciously, chosen to execute his plan at a time when apprehension was especially likely."

However, while many attempts might have failed as a result of the attempter exercising internal control at the unconscious level (and thus arguably deserving less punishment), it is clear that in some cases the attempt only fails as a result of factors lying outside the attempter's control, namely, chance. Even in that respect it has already been argued that attempts ought *on principle* to be punished to a lesser extent that the completed crime.

It is difficult to establish sentencing levels for attempts because the statistics only cover attempted murder. In 2000, the average sentence for attempted murder was about eight years' imprisonment.[19]

In most of these, and other, attempt cases it ought to be borne in mind that the sentence is reflecting not just the "pure attempt" but the fact that there has usually been very serious injury caused (in attempted murder cases) or severe fear and degradation (in attempted rape cases). Further, in some attempted theft cases it seems that the court is sentencing defendants as "professional pickpockets". The fact that there is only evidence to support a charge of attempt is effectively ignored.[20] One of the few reported cases where there was no other injury, fear or distress (at least at the time of the crime) is *Cooper* where the defendant attempted to rape a drunk girl who was largely unaware of what was happening. A sentence of eighteen months youth custody was imposed on appeal.[21] Had the crime been completed the defendant would have received a sentence more in the region of the three years' youth custody originally imposed.

A final question remains: should it be left to the judiciary to exercise a broad discretion and impose lesser sentences for attempts? Surely it is incumbent upon the law to perform its symbolic function of indicating *how seriously* it regards offences, by grading them (with appropriate penalties) in terms of their gravity. If this latter solution were adopted, there would have to be a clear articulation of the exact bases upon which attempts are punished, and a rational assessment of just how seriously attempts are regarded in comparison with completed crimes. It is to be hoped that

---

[19] Home Office, *Criminal Statistics England and Wales, Supplementary Tables* (vol. 2, 2000). This average excludes those who were given life sentences.
[20] *Daniel* (1988) 10 Cr.App.R.(S.) 341.
[21] *Cooper* (1988) 10 Cr.App.R.(S.) 325.

this is a matter to which the Sentencing Advisory Panel will turn its attention to in due course.

## D. *The Law*

### 1. Mens rea

Section 1(1) of the Criminal Attempts Act 1981 provides that the defendant must act "with intent to commit an offence".

### Merrit v Commonwealth, 164 Va. 653, 180 S.E. 395 (1935) (Supreme Court of Appeals of Virginia)

"[W]hile a person may be guilty of murder though there was no actual intent to kill, he cannot be guilty of an attempt to commit murder unless he has a specific intent to kill ... A common example, illustrating this principle is: 'If one from a house-top recklessly throw a billet of wood upon the sidewalk where persons are constantly passing, and it fall upon a person passing by and kill him, this would be by the common law murder. But if, instead of killing, it inflicts only a slight injury, the party could not be convicted of an assault with intent to commit murder.' (*Moore v State*, 18 Ala. 532) ...

When we say that a man attempted to do a given wrong, we mean that he intended to do it specifically; and proceeded a certain way in the doing. The intent in the mind covers the thing in full; the act covers it only in part.

... To commit murder, one need not intend to take life; but to be guilty of an attempt to murder, he must so intend. It is not sufficient that his act, had it proved fatal, would have been murder."

In *Whybrow*[22] the defendant constructed a device and administered an electric shock to his wife while she was taking a bath. The Court of Appeal held that while an intention to kill *or to cause grievous bodily harm* would suffice for the completed crime of murder, for attempted murder an intention to kill was necessary. This was because for attempted murder "the intent becomes the principal ingredient of the crime". In *O'Toole*[23] the defendant was charged with attempted arson (causing criminal damage by fire). It was held that while recklessness would suffice for the completed offence,[24] there had to be intention for the attempted offence.

If the complete crime can be committed recklessly or negligently, why does this same *mens rea* not suffice for an attempt to commit the crime?

### R. v Mohan [1976] Q.B. 1 (Court of Appeal, Criminal Division)

James L.J.:

"In our judgment it is well established law that intent (*mens rea*) is an essential ingredient of the offence of attempt ...

An attempt to commit crime is itself an offence. Often it is a grave offence. Often it is as morally culpable as the completed offence which is attempted but not in fact committed. Nevertheless it falls within the class of conduct which is preparatory to the commission of a crime and is one step removed from the offence which is attempted. The court must not strain to bring within the offence of attempt, conduct which does not fall within the

---

[22] (1951) 35 Cr.App.R.141. See also *Pond* [1984] Crim.L.R.164.
[23] [1987] Crim.L.R.759.
[24] Criminal Damage Act 1971, s.1(2).

well-established bounds of the offence. On the contrary, the court must safeguard against extension of those bounds save by the authority of Parliament."

## Donald Stuart, "Mens Rea, Negligence and Attempts" [1968] Crim.L.R.647 at 656, 658–659, 661–662:

"Many writers rely heavily on the fact that the word 'attempt' refers to an endeavour or an effort to commit a crime. It is argued that there cannot be an attempt unless the defendant was trying to commit the crime and that, in legal terms, this necessarily means that there must have been an intention of the 'purpose' type to commit the crime. Even Howard (*Australian Criminal Law* (1965) 253) says:

'Attempt implies purpose. To say that D is attempting to do something means that he is acting with the purpose of accomplishing that which he is said to be attempting. There is no disagreement that purpose must be proved for conviction of attempts but different views have been expressed on the scope of the purpose.'

It is, however, difficult to see why there is such magic in the popular meaning of the word 'attempt' but not in the words 'murder', 'assault' or 'rape'—crimes for which recklessness is now sufficient *mens rea*. . . .

Do any of the theories of punishment offer an explanation of why it is that only direct intention will suffice in these cases of attempt? . . . It is difficult to challenge Professor Hart's (*Punishment and Responsibility*, p. 127) assertion that

'No calculation of the efficacy of deterrence or reforming measures, and nothing that would ordinarily be called retribution seems to justify this distinction. In the attempt case, for example, the variant where the intention is indirect seems equally wicked, equally harmful, and equally in need of discouragement by the law.' . . .

There seems, furthermore, to be every reason to apply the full notion of *mens rea* (embracing intention and recklessness) . . . to attempts. . . .

If a fanatical punter contrives to half-sever the stirrup on the saddle of the favourite horse before a race he would be guilty of recklessly assaulting the jockey if the stirrup broke during the race and the jockey fell and was trampled. If, however, the mischief was unearthed before the race was run the punter should surely be guilty of recklessly attempting an assault even though he was aiming, not to injure the jockey, but merely to stop the horse from winning.
. . .

Further there is much to be said for . . . [the] suggestion that a negligent attempt to commit a crime of negligence should be punished. Negligence is a failure to measure up to a standard and if this failure occurs or is stopped short of the completed offence there seems to be no reason of policy why it should escape punishment. This would lead to the view, at present widely rejected, that it is possible to attempt to commit the crime of involuntary manslaughter. If a pharmacist is grossly negligent in making up a prescription and the patient dies as a result of taking the dosage on the bottle the pharmacist is clearly guilty of manslaughter. Surely the policy considerations which dictate such a conviction apply equally if, through chance, the negligent error is discovered before any damage is done. There seems to be every reason for a verdict of attempted manslaughter.

If, in the Code of the Brave New World, the codifiers are prepared to cast off the traditional misplaced fear of liability based on negligence, there is, then, a strong case for declaring that the mental element for an attempt may consist in the mental element—here including negligence—required for the completed crime."

Such an approach is surely unacceptable. Apart from the semantic argument that it is linguistic nonsense to speak of someone attempting to commit a crime unless she is trying to commit that crime, there is a more important argument of principle. With attempts we are punishing in the absence of any harm (or "first order harm"). While such an approach can be justified, it is surely only permissible when dealing with the highest degree of blame. Exceptions to the paradigm of criminal liability involve extensions of liability and should be rigidly controlled. As attempt is essentially a crime of *mens rea*, with the *actus reus* performing only a secondary or subsidiary role, only the clearest form of *mens rea* should suffice, namely, intention.

This latter reasoning was given statutory force by section 1(1) of the Criminal Attempts Act 1981. It is now clear that even for attempting a crime of strict liability, the defendant must intend to produce the prohibited consequence.[25]

What meaning is to be attributed to the word "intention" in section 1(1)? In *Mohan*[26] it was held that this involved "proof of specific intent, a decision to bring about, in so far as it lies within the accused's power, the commission of the offence which it is alleged the accused attempted to commit, no matter whether the accused desired that consequence of his act or not". This was approved, after the coming into force of the Criminal Attempts Act 1981, in *Millard and Vernon*[27] where it was stated that a direct or purposive intention was required. Intention had to bear its "ordinary meaning", namely, that the defendant must have "decided, so far as in him lay, to bring about" the result. It would, of course, be possible (albeit messy) for intention to bear different meanings in different contexts and for direct intent to be required here as the concept of an "attempt" connotes trying or meaning to achieve a result. However, the courts seem now to have rejected such an approach holding that "intention" bears the same meaning, whether for a completed crime or an attempt.

### R. v Pearman (1984) 80 Cr.App.R.259 (Court of Appeal, Criminal Division)

Stuart-Smith J:

"We see no reason why the passing of the 1981 Act should have altered the law as to what is meant by the word 'intent'. The purpose of the Act was to deal with other matters rather than the content of the word 'intent'. We can see no reason why the judgment of the court in that case [*Mohan*] should not still be binding upon this court.

The words of James L.J. [in *Mohan*] which he used at the end of that passage, namely 'no matter whether the accused desired that consequence of his act or not', are probably designed to deal with a case where the accused has, as a primary purpose, some other object, for example, a man who plants a bomb in an aeroplane, which he knows is going to take off, it being his primary intention that he should claim the insurance on the aeroplane when the freight goes down into the sea. The jury would not be put off from saying that he intended to murder the crew simply by saying that he did not want or desire to kill the crew, but that was something that he inevitably intended to do. Similarly, for example, a man who is cornered by the police when he is in a car may have the primary purpose of simply escaping from that situation. If he drives straight at the police officers at high speed, a jury is likely to conclude that he intended to injure a police officer and maybe cause him serious grievous bodily harm."

### R. v Walker and Hayles (1990) 90 Cr.App.R.226 (Court of Appeal, Criminal Division)

The defendants threw the victim from a third floor balcony. At their trial for attempted murder the judge directed the jury that they had to be sure that the defendant intended and tried to kill. The jury asked for clarification and the judge directed them in *Moloney/Hancock* terms that if

---

[25] This was probably the position at common law: *Gardner v Akeroyd* [1952] 2 Q.B. 743; *cf. Collier* [1960] Crim.L.R.204. It should, however, be borne in mind that most strict liability offences are summary offences which cannot be attempted.

[26] [1976] Q.B. 1.

[27] [1987] Crim.L.R.393.

(1) there was a very high degree of probability that the victim would be killed, and
(2) the defendant knew there was such a high risk, then
(3) they were entitled to draw the inference that the defendants intended to kill.

The defendants appealed against this direction.

Lloyd L.J.:
"By the use of the word 'entitled' [the recorder] was making it sufficiently clear to the jury that the question whether they drew the inference or not was a question for them ... [He was not] equating foresight with intent ... He was perfectly properly saying that foresight was something from which the jury could infer intent. He was treating the question as part of the law of evidence, not as part of the substantive law of attempted murder ...

[I]n the great majority of cases of attempted murder, as in murder, the simple direction will suffice, without any reference to foresight. In the rare case where an expanded direction is required in terms of foresight, courts should continue to use virtual certainty as the test, rather than high probability."

**Appeals dismissed**

This case must now be read in the light of *Woollin* under which an inference of intention can only be drawn if the consequence is foreseen as virtually certain (or, under the alternative interpretation, foresight of a virtual certainty is intention). Following this, it now seems tolerably clear now that the concept "intention" bears the same meaning here as elsewhere in the criminal law.[28]

What *mens rea* is required with regard to relevant surrounding circumstances? The position at common law appears to have been that while the consequence had to be intended, recklessness with regard to circumstances would suffice for attempt, provided such recklessness would suffice for the completed offence.[29] Thus if a defendant, being reckless as to whether his first wife was alive, were about to go through a second marriage ceremony, he could be convicted of attempted bigamy. The 1981 Act draws no distinction between consequences and circumstances,[30] but simply states that the defendant must act "with intent to commit an offence". Despite the wording of this statute, the common law approach has now been confirmed.

## R. v Khan [1990] 2 All E.R. 783 (Court of Appeal, Criminal Division)

The appellant attempted to have sexual intercourse with a non-consenting girl, but failed. The trial judge directed the jury that recklessness as to whether the girl consented was sufficient for attempted rape. The appellant appealed on this point.

---

[28] Clause 20 of the Draft Offences against the Person Bill 1998 states that, for the law of attempt, a person acts with intent with respect to a result if it is his purpose to cause it, or if he knows it would occur in the ordinary course of events if he were to succeed in his purpose of causing some other result.
[29] *Pigg* (1982) 74 Cr.App.R.352; Williams, *Textbook of Criminal Law* (2nd ed., 1983), p. 409; Buxton, "Inchoate Offences: Incitement and Attempt" [1973] Crim.L.R.656 at 661–664.
[30] Such a distinction was drawn by the Law Commission Working Paper, No. 50 and by the original Government Bill, but not by the Law Commission's Final Report, No. 102.

Russell L.J.:

"The only difference between the two offences is that in rape sexual intercourse takes place whereas in attempted rape it does not, although there has to be some act which is more than preparatory to sexual intercourse. Considered in that way, the intent of the defendant is precisely the same in rape and in attempted rape and the mens rea is identical, namely an intention to have intercourse plus a knowledge of or recklessness as to the woman's absence of consent. No question of attempting to achieve a reckless state of mind arises; the attempt relates to the physical activity; the mental state of the defendant is the same. A man does not recklessly have sexual intercourse, nor does he recklessly attempt it. Recklessness in rape and attempted rape arises not in relation to the physical act of the accused but only in his state of mind when engaged in the activity of having or attempting to have sexual intercourse.

If this is the true analysis, as we believe it is, the attempt does not require any different intention on the part of the accused from that for the full offence of rape. We believe this to be a desirable result which in the instant case did not require the jury to be burdened with different directions as to the accused's state of mind, dependent on whether the individual achieved or failed to achieve sexual intercourse.

We recognise, of course, that our reasoning cannot apply to all offences and all attempts. Where, for example as in causing death by reckless driving or reckless arson, no state of mind other than recklessness is involved in the offence, there can be no attempt to commit it.

In our judgment, however, the words 'with intent to commit an offence' to be found in s.1 of the 1981 Act mean, when applied to rape, 'with intent to have sexual intercourse with a woman in circumstances where she does not consent and the defendant knows or could not care less about her absence of consent'. The only 'intent', giving that word its natural and ordinary meaning, of the rapist is to have sexual intercourse. He commits the offence because of the circumstances in which he manifests that intent, ie when the woman is not consenting and he either knows it or could not care less about the absence of consent."

**Appeal dismissed**

It is possible to support such an approach. If recklessness as to surrounding circumstances suffices for the complete offence it should also suffice for an attempt, as "the *mens rea* of the complete crime should be modified only in so far as it is necessary in order to accommodate the concept of attempt."[31] The Criminal Code Bill endorses this view:

"[A]n intention to commit an offence is an intention with respect to all the elements of the offence other than fault elements, except that recklessness with respect to a circumstance suffices where it suffices for the offence itself."[32]

The approach adopted in *Khan* was followed in *Attorney-General's Reference (No. 3 of 1992)*[33] where it was held that on a charge of attempted arson contrary to section 1(2) of the Criminal Damage Act 1971 it was sufficient to prove an intention to cause damage by fire and that the defendant was reckless as to whether life would thereby be endangered. It was stated that for an attempt "it must be shown that the defendant intended to achieve that which was missing from the full offence". In *Khan* what was missing was sexual intercourse. In *Attorney-General's Reference (No. 3 of 1992)* what was missing was damage to property. Intention must be proved in relation to these missing elements but beyond that only the same *mens rea* as for the full crime need be proved.

---

[31] Smith and Hogan, *Criminal Law* (10th ed., 2002), p. 330.
[32] Law Com. No. 177, clause 49(2). An earlier Law Commission Paper (No. 102, 1980) stated that an intention as to every element of the offence was required (although in practice knowledge of surrounding circumstances would suffice to establish the necessary intent (No. 102, 1980, para. 2.15).
[33] (1994) 98 Cr.App.R.383.

However, *Khan* and *Attorney-General's Reference (No.3 of 1992)* are distinguishable from each other. *Khan* was clearly dealing with a surrounding circumstance: whether the woman was consenting. In *Attorney-General's Reference (No.3 of 1992)* the offence element of "whether the life of another would be thereby endangered" can be viewed as a consequence.[34] Under section 1(2) two consequences need to be achieved: damage to property and a state of affairs perceived to be life-threatening by an ordinary prudent person. While intention is required for the first consequence (damage to property) because that was what was "missing", recklessness with regard to the second consequence (creating a life-threatening situation) suffices. This marks an important extension of the law and it has been argued that the ratio of *Attorney-General's Reference (No.3 of 1992)* should be confined to "state-of-affairs consequences that do not comprise realised harms".[35]

The above analysis demonstrates that it can be difficult to draw a clear distinction between consequences and circumstances. For example, it could be argued that section 1(2) required the causing of criminal damage to be committed in the circumstances of it being life-endangering. It is highly inappropriate to make criminal liability hinge on such fine distinctions that have no bearing on culpability. Accordingly, it is submitted that the better view is that recklessness should not suffice even for clear circumstances such as those in *Khan*. For surrounding circumstances, knowledge (the general equivalent to intention when dealing with surrounding circumstances) should be required. The 1981 Act specifies that the defendant must act "with intent to commit an offence". This view is reinforced by considerations of principle. Attempt is essentially a crime of *mens rea*. Given this, there is a strong case that it ought to be restricted to those who act with intent in relation to all the elements of the offence.

A final problem remains: will a so-called "conditional intention" suffice for attempt? If a defendant opens a suitcase, intending to steal its contents "on condition they are of some value", can he or she be convicted of attempted theft?

### The Law Commission (Law Com. No. 102) Attempt . . . , 1980, Appendix E, " 'Conditional Intent' and R. v Husseyn":

"3. [Theft-related offences] all have two features in common—
(i) each requires proof that the accused 'intended to steal' at the time when he committed the *actus reus* of the offence;
(ii) none requires proof that anything has in fact been stolen.

4. In delivering the judgment of the Court of Appeal in the attempted theft case of *R. v Husseyn*, Lord Scarman stated ((1978) 67 Cr.App.R.131, at p. 132) 'it cannot be said that one who has it in mind to steal only if what he finds is worth stealing has a present intention to steal'.

5. This simple statement, taken by itself and out of context, was the origin of the difficulties. It gave rise to the doctrine that 'conditional intent' in the sense of 'intending to steal whatever one might find of value or worth stealing' was not a sufficient mental element in these theft-related offences; the prosecution must aver and prove that at the time of attempting, entering as a trespasser, etc., the accused had a settled intention to steal some particular and specified object existing or believed by him to exist in his target area.

---

[34] Smith and Hogan, *Criminal Law* (10th ed., 2002), p. 331.
[35] Simester and Sullivan, *Criminal Law: Theory and Doctrine* (2000), p. 303.

6. In such a form, the doctrine was obviously capable of mischievous results. In particular, it excluded from criminal liability the large majority of sneak thieves and burglars who conduct their operations 'on spec'. Without knowing what a handbag, a package left in a car, or a house contains, they nevertheless proceed in the hope or expectation that they will find something of value or worth stealing there, and intend, in that event, to steal it. As Geoffrey Lane L.J. pungently remarked (*R. v Walkington* [1979] 1 W.L.R. 1169, 1179), after setting out the reasoning that led to the acquittal of one burglar, 'a reading of that would make the layman wonder if the law had taken leave of its senses. ... Nearly every prospective burglar could no doubt truthfully say that he only intended to steal if he found something in the building worth stealing.'

7. Unfortunately, several factors obscured the clarity of the issue. As reported, *R. v Husseyn* gave no indication that the charge of attempted theft in that case had related to specific identifiable objects, and although Lawton L.J. did stress that the indictment in the subsequent case of *R. v Hector* ((1978) 67 Cr.App.R.224) also charged attempted theft of particular objects, the report was headed 'Whether conditional intention enough', a phrase not used in the judgment. So it was not realised that Lord Scarman's statement related only to the facts of the case before him or that the decision in both cases rested on the basic rule of criminal pleading that an allegation that the accused attempted to steal a particular item involves proof that that item was what he intended to steal; in such a case it is not enough to show that he intended to steal whatever he found worth stealing. ...

8. Whatever the reasons, within a few months of the decision in *R. v Husseyn*, submissions that 'conditional intent is not enough' were being accepted by magistrates and Crown Court judges in all these theft-related offences, causing frustration and perplexity to prosecuting authorities and bringing the criminal law into disrepute.

9. Study of the relevant indictments and transcripts convinced us that, once the complications mentioned in paragraph 7 had been cleared out of the way, the matter could be put right without recourse to legislation and that the appropriate way to proceed was by way of Attorney General's References to the Court of Appeal under section 36 of the Criminal Justice Act 1972. ...

10. The two References were decided by the Court of Appeal as *Attorney General's References (Nos 1 and 2 of 1979)* ([1979] 3 W.L.R. 577) on June 18, 1979 and together with the ancillary judgments of the same judges sitting as a Divisional Court in *Scudder v Barrett* and *Miles v Clovis* ([1979] 3 W.L.R. 591), restore clarity and common sense to the law. Where the accused's state of mind is that of intending to steal whatever he may find worth stealing in his target area, there is no need to charge him with attempting to steal specific objects. In appropriate cases of attempted theft a charge of attempting to steal some or all of the contents of (for example) a car or a handbag will suffice. In cases where the substantive offence does not require anything to be stolen, it is not necessary to allege more than 'with intent to steal'. The important point is that the indictment should correctly reflect that which it is alleged the accused did and that the accused should know with adequate detail what he is alleged to have done (at 590). The result, in the Commission's view, is that it is now possible to state with confidence that in cases where an intention to steal anything of value or worth stealing accurately reflects the accused's state of mind at the time of the actus reus, this is sufficient to constitute 'an intention to steal' and applies equally to all the theft-related offences."

The law on this point is unaffected by the Criminal Attempts Act 1981, which abolishes "the offence of attempt at common law" (s.6(1)). These developments on "conditional intention" are best regarded as part of the "common law of intention"; some of the important decisions on this point were not delivered in the context of attempted crime at all.[36] It is simply that the point is of particular importance when dealing with attempts.

[36] *Greenhof* [1979] Crim.L.R.108, *Bozickovic* [1978] Crim.L.R.686 and *Walkington* [1979] 1 W.L.R. 1169 were all decisions on burglary.

## 2. Actus reus

(i) *Act must be more than merely preparatory*

### Criminal Attempts Act 1981, section 1(1):

"If, with intent to commit an offence to which this section applies, a person does an act which is more than merely preparatory to the commission of the offence, he is guilty of attempting to commit the offence."

This is similar to the common law rule as laid down by Baron Parke in *Eagleton* that:

"[S]ome act is required ... Acts remotely leading towards the commission of the offence are not to be considered as attempts to commit it; but acts immediately connected with it are."[37]

Suppose a defendant wakes up one morning and decides to kill his wife by poisoning her. He walks to a shop where he purchases some rat poison. He returns home and adds the poison to the whisky in his whisky decanter. That evening he offers his wife a drink of whisky; she accepts. He pours the poisoned whisky into a glass and hands it to her. She starts drinking the whisky. At what point in this chain of actions could he be said to have done an act which was "more than merely preparatory to the commission of the offence"? When he handed her the whisky? When he put the poison in the decanter? When he purchased the poison?

Questions such as these cannot be answered in a jurisprudential vacuum; they, and all the contours of the law of attempt, can only be determined by reference to the underlying justification (and policy) of the law of attempt. Thus if attempts are viewed as being threats to people's interests in security from interference (the "second order harm" discussed earlier), one ought to insist on the attempter getting near to completing the crime. Until he has got near to committing the complete crime, the wife's interests in security from interference are not threatened. On the other hand, if the law of attempt is justified on the utilitarian bases canvassed above, then the emphasis is on the *mens rea* of the attempter and liability can be imposed at a much earlier stage in the chain of actions. Of course, such an approach still does not tell us exactly when the husband has done enough to threaten the wife's interests; or when his *mens rea* is sufficiently manifest to justify the imposition of criminal liability for attempt, but adoption of one or other of these views does provide an important indication of *how* to try to answer the question.

Fletcher and Duff suggest another approach, not dissimilar in its effect.

### George P. Fletcher, Rethinking Criminal Law (1978), pp. 138–139:

"The critical question ... is the elementary issue whether the act of attempting is a distinct and discernible element of the crime of attempting. To say that the act is a distinct element is to require that the act conform to objective criteria defined in advance. The act must evidence attributes subject to determination independently of the actor's intent. In short, there must be features of the attempt as palpable as the death of the victim in homicide or a trespassory taking in larceny. We shall refer to the set of arguments favoring this approach as the

[37] (1855) Dears C.C. 515 at 538.

'objectivist' theory of attempts. Though the term 'objective' may have a different connotation in some contexts, we shall use the term to mean a legal standard for assessing conduct that does not presuppose a prior determination of the actor's intent.

The opposing school is appropriately called 'subjectivist', for it dispenses with the objective criteria of attempting. The act of execution is important so far as it verifies the firmness of the intent. No act of specific contours is necessary to constitute the attempt, for any act will suffice to demonstrate the actor's commitment to carry out his criminal plan.

As we delve more deeply into objectivist and subjectivist theories of liability for criminal attempts, we shall discover that objectivists tend to favor a minimalist approach, subjectivists, a maximalist approach to liability. ... [T]his means that objectivists tend to draw the line of liability as close as possible to consummation of the offense and tend, further, to be sympathetic to claims of impossibility as a bar to liability. This combination of views generates a minimalist approach to liability. Subjectivists, in contrast, tend to push back the threshold of attempting and reject the relevance of impossibility—a stance that yields a maximalist net of liability. In turning to a more detailed study of objectivist and subjectivist theories, we should keep in mind that the watershed between them is the question whether the act of attempting is a distinct element of liability."

Thus there are two competing theories underlying the law of attempt. First, the "objectivist" theory requires the defendant to have come sufficiently close to committing the crime for his conduct to generate apprehension and thus amount to a "second order harm". Duff supports this objectivist approach because, by insisting that conduct comes close to the actual commission of the offence, one is affording intending criminals an opportunity to abandon their criminal enterprise. By doing this, even if we think it unlikely she will desist, we are according the person respect as a responsible agent "who is in principle susceptible to rational persuasion".[38] Secondly, there is the "subjectivist" theory which stresses the mental element of the defendant: if she has *mens rea* she is dangerous and needs restraining. Liability can accordingly be imposed at a much earlier stage (which will facilitate the task of the police and other law enforcement agencies). The only conduct required would be some action that would be corroborative of this intention. The tensions between these two theories is demonstrated by a consideration of the various "tests" employed by English law in its effort to demarcate how much action is required for the *actus reus* of attempt.

### (a) The Common Law

Until 1981 the common law flirted with various tests. One of these was the "equivocality test" under which a defendant had to take sufficient steps towards the crime for his actions clearly and unequivocally to indicate that his purpose was to commit the crime.[39] This was clearly in accord with the "second order harm" view and the objectivist theory. The defendant had to get sufficiently close to committing the offence for his actions to be "manifestly criminal ... [and] unnerving to the community".[40] This test was eventually abandoned because a defendant could be on the point of committing a crime (for example, about to break into a car) but the actions could still be equivocal (for example, was he going to steal the car or vandalise it?).

---

[38] *Criminal Attempts* (1996), p. 388.
[39] *Davey v Lee* [1968] 1 Q.B. 366, 371.
[40] Fletcher, *Rethinking Criminal Law* (1978), pp. 142–144.

An alternative test, suggested by the Law Commission, was the "substantial step test" where the focus was on whether the defendant had taken a substantial step towards the crime, for example, reconnoitering the place contemplated for a burglary.[41] This test, consistent with the subjectivist theory of attempts because the focus was on the action only having to be sufficient to provide evidence of the defendant's intention, was never adopted as it would have amounted to casting the net of liability far too wide in the sequence of actions.[42]

Another test was Stephen's "series of acts" test under which it was necessary to determine whether the defendant had committed an act which was one of a series of acts that would lead to the crime if it were not interrupted. This test was also of little utility: it was too imprecise and could have led to the imposition of liability at an intolerably early state.

The test finally adopted by the common law[43] was the "proximity test". The defendant's actions had to be proximate to the completed offence in the sense of being "immediately and not merely remotely, connected"[44] with the completed offence. In *Robinson* a jeweller, who had insured his stock against burglary, hid the jewellery, tied himself up, called for help and represented to the police that his premises had been burgled. His object was to obtain policy money from his insurance company. It was held that his actions were still merely preparatory; they were "only remotely connected with the commission of the full offence, and not immediately connected with it".[45] He would have needed to have communicated with the insurance company before an attempt could be committed. In *Stonehouse* Lord Diplock stated that in order to have passed the threshold of proximity, the defendant must have "crossed the Rubicon and burnt his boats".[46] All the cases confirming this test emphasised that the defendant had to get very close to committing the offence; in some cases such as *Robinson* it appeared that the defendant would only be liable if he had committed the last act dependent upon himself—although from other cases it is clear that the proximity test did not demand as a matter of law that the defendant go so far.[47] This proximity test was very much in tune with Fletcher's objectivist theory of attempts: the emphasis was on the objective acts and not on the intentions of the defendant.

### (b) Criminal Attempts Act 1981

Section 1(1) states that the defendant must do "an act which is more than merely preparatory to the commission of the offence". Is this different in any way from the proximity test developed by the common law?

---

[41] Law Com. Working Paper No. 50, *Inchoate Offences* (1973), para. 75.

[42] Law Com. No. 102 (1980), para. 2.32. For a plea for the introduction of the test, see Williams, "Wrong Turnings in the Law of Attempt" [1991] Crim.L.R.416.

[43] History is in the process of being rewritten with cases since the 1981 Act suggesting that it is not clear which test was applied at common law. However, two House of Lords decisions, *Haughton v Smith* [1975] A.C. 476 and *Stonehouse* [1978] A.C. 55 made it plain that the proximity test was the favoured one.

[44] *Jones v Brooks* (1968) 52 Cr.App.R.614 at 616; *Davey v Lee* [1968] 1 Q.B. 366 at 371, approved in *Haughton v Smith* (*ibid.*).

[45] [1915] 2 K.B. 342 at 349.

[46] *Above*, n.43.

[47] Again, post-1981 Act cases are rewriting history by suggesting that the proximity test was synonymous with a last act test. It was not. See, *e.g. Harris* (1976) 62 Cr.App.R.28.

One view is that no real change in the law was intended by the enactment of section 1(1). The government, in the course of the parliamentary proceedings, took the view that the law on this matter was not being altered.[48] The Law Commission, whose Report led to the legislation, felt that it was "undesirable to recommend anything more complex than a rationalisation of the present law".[49] Under *Eagleton* the common law always distinguished between preparatory and non-preparatory acts and non-preparatory acts were simply called "proximate" acts.

However, the Law Commission at the same time did recommend abandoning the phrase "proximate" as its literal meaning was "nearest, next before or after ... [and] thus would clearly be capable of being interpreted to exclude all but the 'final act' ".[50] The Law Commission disapproved of such an approach and felt that the new terminology could open the door to conviction in cases such as *Robinson*. If the Act had not altered the law, reference to the common law cases would presumably be permissible. However, the leading cases since the Act have stressed that discussion of the old cases is impermissible, suggesting that a new test for the *actus reus* of attempts is being evolved. Further, it can be argued that a change in the law has been brought about by the insertion of the word "merely". Unlike the position at common law, not all preparatory acts are excluded; only *merely* preparatory acts do not suffice.[51] Indeed, in *Tosti*[52] it was stated that the defendants "had committed acts which were preparatory, but not merely so".

Before examining the cases it is important to stress that the ultimate decision here is one for the jury. Section 4(3) of the Criminal Attempts Act 1981 provides:

> "Where ... there is evidence sufficient in law to support a finding that he did an act falling within [section 1(1)] ..., the question whether or not his act fell with that subsection is a question of fact."

So the judge, using the law about to be outlined, must decide whether there is sufficient evidence that the defendant *could* come within the law of attempt, and then, if so, it must be left to the jury to decide whether the acts did or did not come within the definition of the *actus reus* provided in section 1(1). Not only will this lead to inconsistency of jury verdicts, with one jury deciding that a defendant like Robinson did commit the *actus reus* of attempt while another jury decides that he did not, but also it involves the jury having to decide what is essentially a matter of law. Whether certain acts satisfy certain legislative criteria ("more than merely preparatory") so as to amount in law to a crime, is a question of law which ought to be left to the judges to develop.[53]

The following is the leading case which has been cited in most subsequent decisions.

---

[48] Dennis, "The Criminal Attempts Act 1981" [1982] Crim.L.R.379.
[49] Law Com. No. 102 (1980), para. 2.47.
[50] *ibid.* para. 2.48.
[51] Smith and Hogan, *Criminal Law* (10th ed., 2002), p. 335.
[52] [1997] Crim.L.R.746.
[53] See further, Williams, *above*, n.29.

## R. v Gullefer (1990) 91 Cr.App.R. 356 (Court of Appeal, Criminal Division)

During a race at a greyhound racing stadium the appellant climbed on to the track in front of the dogs and attempted to distract them by waving his arms. His efforts were only marginally successful and the stewards decided it was unnecessary to declare "no race". The appellant told the police he had attempted to stop the race because the dog on which he had staked £18 was losing. He had hoped for a no-race declaration and the recovery of his stake. He was convicted of attempted theft and appealed on the ground that his acts were not "sufficiently proximate to the completed offence of theft to be capable of comprising an attempt to commit theft".

Lane L.C.J.:
"The first task of the court is to apply the words of the Act of 1981 to the facts of the case. Was the appellant still in the stage of preparation to commit the substantive offence, or was there a basis of fact which would entitle the jury to say that he had embarked on the theft itself? Might it properly be said that when he jumped on to the track he was trying to steal £18 from the bookmaker?

Our view is that it could not properly be said that at that stage he was in the process of committing theft. What he was doing was jumping on to the track in an effort to distract the dogs, which in its turn, he hoped would have the effect of forcing the stewards to declare 'no race', which would in turn give him the opportunity to go back to the bookmaker and demand the £18 he had staked. In our view there was insufficient evidence for it to be said that he had, when he jumped on to the track, gone beyond mere preparation ...

[His Lordship considered the common law proximity test and Stephen's 'series of acts' test.]

It seems to us that the words of the Act of 1981 seek to steer a midway course. They do not provide, as they might have done, that the *Eagleton* test is to be followed, or that, as Lord Diplock suggested, the defendant must have reached a point from which it was impossible for him to retreat before the actus reus of an attempt is proved. On the other hand the words give perhaps as clear a guidance as is possible in the circumstances on the point of time at which *Stephen's* 'series of acts' begin. It begins when the merely preparatory acts come to an end and the defendant embarks upon the crime proper. When that is will depend of course upon the facts in any particular case."

**Appeal allowed**

Lord Lane clearly thought he was pushing back the point at which liability could be imposed. In adopting his "midway course" he rejected the "Rubicon test". But what else was there left for the defendant to do? Assuming his efforts had been successful and the race declared void, all that remained for him to do was to claim his refund which would have been his last act, comparable to Robinson filing a claim with his insurance company. Accordingly, the approach adopted in *Gullefer* looks indistinguishable from that adopted in the much-criticised common law decision of *Robinson*.

## R. v Rowley (1992) 94 Cr.App.R.95 (Court of Appeal, Criminal Division)

The appellant left notes in public places offering money and presents to boys. These notes, which were not indecent in themselves and did not contain any propositions, were designed to lure boys for immoral purposes. He was convicted of attempted incitement of a child under the age of 14 years to commit an act of gross indecency and appealed.

Taylor L.J.:
"Here the notes relied upon went no further than to seek to meet with the boy or boys in question. In our judgment this could not be regarded as more than a preparatory act, even on the assumption that the ultimate intention of the appellant was gross indecency. Incitement

to commit gross indecency would require a proposition to be made for that specific purpose. A letter sent by an accused inviting a boy to commit gross indecency which did not reach him would be an attempted incitement. *Ransford* (1874) 31 L.T. 488, was such a case. It involved a letter sent to a boy at school, the letter being intercepted and handed to the school authorities. That was an attempt because the accused had done all he could towards inciting the boy to commit an unnatural offence. Here, however, the note went no further than to seek to engineer a preliminary meeting. No proposition or incitement to the offence had emanated from the appellant. At most he was preparing the ground for an attempt. Accordingly, in our judgment, there was no evidence upon which he could be convicted. We are wholly sympathetic to the need perceived by the prosecuting authorities to take action in the circumstances of this case, but in our judgment the evidence was not capable of supporting the charges laid."

**Appeal allowed[54]**

The notion that there would be an intervening "preliminary meeting" lies at the heart of this decision, but, in fact, seems unlikely. In reality, what else was there left for the defendant to do in this case? If he had met the boys and said anything suggestive, he would have committed the full offence of incitement. Lord Taylor's example of the non-arriving letter is a classic instance of a defendant having performed the last act there was for him to do. Again, it appears that the 1981 Act has not effected any change to the law.

## R. v Jones (1990) 91 Cr.App.R.351 (Court of Appeal, Criminal Division)

The appellant, a married man, had an affair with a woman who then started a relationship with another man, Foreman. When she refused to resume their association the appellant applied for a shotgun certificate and three days later bought some guns. He shortened the barrel of one of them and test fired it twice. Three days later he told his wife he was going to Spain to work on their chalet and left home dressed normally for work. He then changed into a disguise of overalls and a crash helmet with the visor down. He waited outside a school where Foreman dropped his daughter off and then jumped into the rear seat and asked Foreman to drive on. They drove to a grass verge where the appellant took the loaded sawn-off shotgun from a bag and pointed it at Foreman at a range of some 10–12 inches and said: "You are not going to like this." The safety catch of the shotgun was in the on position. Foreman grabbed the end of the gun and after a struggle managed to throw it out of the window and escape. The appellant was convicted of attempted murder and appealed on the ground that he had not yet committed the actus reus of this offence.

Taylor L.J.:
"[At his trial the defence had argued] that since the appellant would have had to perform at least three more acts before the full offence could have been completed, i.e. remove the safety catch, put his finger on the trigger and pull it, the evidence was insufficient to support the charge ...
The 1981 Act is a codifying statute. It amends and sets out completely the law relating to attempts and conspiracies. In those circumstances the correct approach is to look first at the natural meaning of the statutory words, not to turn back to earlier case law and seek to fit some previous test to the words of the section ... [He then cited *Gullefer* with approval.] We respectfully adopt those words. We do not accept ... [the] contention that section 1(1) of the 1981 Act in effect embodies the 'last act' test derived from *Eagleton*. ...

[54] For a similar decision, see *Nash* [1999] Crim.L.R.308.

[T]he 1981 Act followed a report from the Law Commission [No. 102] [which] states:
'... the definition must cover those instances where a person has to take some further step to complete the crime, assuming that there is evidence of the necessary mental element on his part to commit it; for example, when the defendant has raised the gun to take aim at another but has not yet squeezed the trigger ...'

Clearly, the draftsman of section 1(1) must be taken to have been aware of ... the Law Commission's report. The words 'an act which is more than merely preparatory to the commission of the offence' would be inapt if they were intended to mean 'the last act which lay in his power towards the commission of the offence.' ... Clearly his actions in obtaining the gun, in shortening it, in loading it, in putting on his disguise, and in going to the school could only be regarded as preparatory acts. But, in our judgment, once he had got into the car, taken out the loaded gun and pointed it at the victim with the intention of killing him, there was sufficient evidence for the consideration of the jury on the charge of attempted murder."

**Appeal dismissed**

It ought to be stressed again that, despite the comments in the above case, the common law was not rigidly committed to any "last act" doctrine. While it was necessary to get close to committing the offence, many defendants were convicted at common law who still had several acts to perform.[55] Jones would almost certainly have been liable for attempt at common law.

## R. v Campbell (1991) 93 Cr.App.R.350 (Court of Appeal, Criminal Division)

The appellant planned to rob a sub-post office. He drove a motorbike to near the post office, parked it and approached, wearing a disguise of sun glasses and a crash helmet, although he later placed the sunglasses in his pocket. He was carrying an imitation gun and a threatening note which he planned to pass to the cashier in the sub post office. He was walking down the street and when one yard from the post office door, police, who had been tipped off, grabbed the appellant and arrested him. He was convicted of attempted robbery and appealed.

Watkins L.J.:
"[His Lordship repeated the *Gullefer* test that the 1981 Act was steering a 'midway course' and that preparatory acts ended when the defendant 'embarks on the crime proper'. He endorsed the stance in *Jones* that judges 'should stick to the definition of an attempt in the Act itself' and that it was 'wholly unnecessary' to refer to the common law.]

Looking at the circumstances here it was beyond dispute that the appellant, at the material time, was carrying an imitation firearm which he made no attempt to remove from his clothing. He was not, as he had done previously that day, wearing, as a form of disguise, sunglasses. It was not suggested that he had, in the course of making his way down the road ..., moved towards the door of the post office so as to indicate that he intended to enter that place.

In order to effect the robbery it is equally beyond dispute it would have been quite impossible unless obviously he had entered the post office, gone to the counter and made some kind of hostile act—directed, of course, at whoever was behind the counter and in a position to hand him money. A number of acts remained undone and the series of acts which

---

[55] See *above*, n.47.

he had already performed—namely, making his way from his home ..., dismounting from the cycle and walking towards the post office door—were clearly acts which were, in the judgment of this court, indicative of mere preparation ... If a person, in circumstances such as this, has not even gained the place where he could be in a position to carry out the offence, it is extremely unlikely that it could ever be said that he had performed an act which could be properly said to be an attempt."

**Appeal allowed**

There can only be an attempt when the defendant has "embarked on the crime proper" and in this case it is suggested that the defendant could have embarked on the crime of robbery when he entered the sub-post office. Robbery involves the use of force or threatened force.[56] It is difficult to see how someone who has entered a post office, but has not yet reached the counter or issued any threats can be said to have embarked on the crime of robbery. Clearly, the court in *Campbell* was adopting a more flexible approach to the notion of "embarking on the crime proper". This flexibility was reinforced in the following case.

## Attorney-General's Reference (No. 1 of 1992) (1993) 96 Cr.App.R.298 (Court of Appeal, Criminal Division)

The defendant, walking a girl home (both of them drunk), pulled her behind a hedge, forced her to the ground and lay on top of her. She lost consciousness. He then dragged her up some nearby steps to a shed. The girl, who had resumed consciousness, was crying and trying to scream. The defendant had lowered his trousers and interfered with her private parts but had not actually attempted penetration because his penis was flaccid. He claimed he was unable to have intercourse ''cause I was drunk, so I couldn't, could I?' The trial judge directed an acquittal because there was no evidence of an actual physical attempt at penetration. The Attorney-General referred the following point of law for the opinion of the Court of Appeal: "Whether, on a charge of attempted rape, it is incumbent upon the prosecution, as a matter of law, to prove that the defendant physically attempted to penetrate the woman's vagina with his penis."

Taylor L.C.J.:
"The words [in the 1981 Act] are not to be interpreted so as to re-introduce either of the earlier common law tests. Indeed one of the objects of the Act was to resolve the uncertainty those tests created ...

It is not, in our judgment, necessary, in order to raise a prima facie case of attempted rape, to prove that the defendant with the requisite intent had necessarily gone as far as to attempt physical penetration of the vagina. It is sufficient if there is evidence from which the intent can be inferred and there are proved acts which a jury could properly regard as more than merely preparatory to the commission of the offence. For example, and merely as an example, in the present case the evidence of the young woman's distress, of the state of her clothing, and the position in which she was seen, together with the respondent's acts of dragging her up the steps, lowering his trousers and interfering with her private parts, and his answers to the police, left it open to a jury to conclude that the respondent had the necessary intent and had done acts which were more than merely preparatory. In short that he had embarked on committing the offence itself."

**Opinion accordingly**

Clearly, when the defendant is trying to commit the offence, that is, trying to penetrate the woman, he can be said to have embarked on the crime. However,

---

[56] Theft Act 1968, s.8.

in this case it is stated that even prior to that the defendant can be held to have "embarked on the crime proper". This decision is understandable in both common sense and policy terms in that the defendant had progressed relatively far in the series of acts that might have culminated in penetration: in particular, he had lowered his trousers and interfered with her private parts. However, in *Patnaik*[57] it was held that it was unnecessary for the defendant to have removed any clothing or to have done "some unequivocal sexual act". In this case the defendant had not undone any of his clothing and had not indecently disarranged the woman's clothing or intimately touched her. It was held that pushing her over a wall, straddling her legs and attempting to kiss her amounted to sufficient evidence to go to the jury that his acts were more than merely preparatory to the crime of rape: "the threshold was essentially a matter for the judge's judgment of the facts of the case".

Such an approach renders the test of "embarking on the crime" useless. The defendant in *Patnaik* had clearly embarked on the crime of indecent assault in trying to kiss the woman and, in his other actions, had committed several complete offences. It is not easy to see, however, that he had embarked on the crime of rape.

The difficulty of applying this test is revealed by a consideration of two final cases, not involving attempted rape. In *Griffin*[58] a mother planning to abduct her children and take them out of the country, bought ferry tickets to Ireland and went to the childrens' school and told the teacher she had come to take them to the dentist. These actions were held to constitute an attempt to abduct children. The full offence here, under the Child Abduction Act 1984, section 1(1), is only committed if the child is taken or sent out of the U.K. The court rejected an argument that the mother would at least have had to had the children in her custody and have embarked on the journey. In *Geddes*[59] the defendant, with no legitimate purpose for being there, was seen on school premises, equipped with a knife, lengths of rope and masking tape. Whilst the court was in little doubt (from all the evidence) as to his intention, they found his actions to be merely preparatory to the crime of false imprisonment. The defendant had not made any contact with a child and it could not be said that he had "actually tried to commit the offence in question".[60]

It is, of course, inevitable that fine distinctions have to be drawn in determining liability for attempt but as a result of these cases it is virtually impossible to predict at what stage the defendant will have passed beyond the point of mere preparation and have "embarked on the crime proper".

Finally, it ought perhaps to be emphasised that, apart from *Gullefer*, all the above cases concerned attempts to commit offences against the person. In *Qadir and Khan*[61] it was stated that because attempted killing or wounding concentrates on a particular moment, acts earlier in time are more likely to be merely preparatory. On the other hand, with attempts to commit offences involving

[57] LTL 1/2/2000, unreported (2000).
[58] [1993] Crim.L.R.515.
[59] [1996] Crim.L.R.894.
[60] As Smith points out in his commentary (at p. 896) there was no precursor or ulterior intent crime (such as going equipped with intent to kidnap) with which the defendant could be charged.
[61] *Archbold News*, November 17, 1997.

deception or evasion then there is more likely to be a "stratagem carried on over a period of time" and thus the moment of embarkation on the crime "may be quite remote in time from its final outcome".

### (c) Conclusion

It is almost impossible to extract any clear principles from the cases interpreting section 1(1). Three points can be stated with confidence, although quite where they lead and what they mean in real cases is another matter.

[i] The courts are striving at some sort of half-way house between the old proximity test and Stephen's "series of acts" tests. The problem with this is that it is impossible to find a "midway" point between proximity (which meant different things to different judges) and something completely unascertainable (which is all that can be said for Stephen's test). In short, talk about a "midway" point is empty rhetoric disguising the court's desire to give themselves maximum flexibility.

[ii] The "Rubicon test" has been abandoned.[62] A defendant need not have reached the point of no-return. Similarly, the fact that he has reached such a point will not necessarily indicate that his actions are more than merely preparatory. When a defendant climbs on to a race track in front of racing dogs and waves his arms at the animals it would surely be permissible to assert that he has "crossed the Rubicon and burnt his boats". This is what the defendant did in *Gullefer* and yet it was insufficient for liability.

[iii] The test now appears to be whether the defendant has "embarked on the crime proper". The defendant must have started committing the crime. He must be "on the job".[63] Such a test works well when applied to some cases. In *Boyle and Boyle*[64] the defendants had broken down a door in their effort to commit burglary. Burglary requires an *entry* as a trespasser. To break down a door means that you have embarked on the process of securing entry to the building and can clearly be said to have embarked on committing the crime. This approach was extended in *Tosti*[65] where it was held that a defendant who was merely examining a padlock (having hidden oxyacetylene equipment behind a hedge) was liable for attempted burglary. Similarly, in *Toothill*[66] it was held that a defendant who knocked at the proposed victim's door was in the "executory stage of his plan" and liable for attempted burglary.

A theme uniting many of the cases where there has been liability for attempt is that there has been a "confrontation" with the victim or the property[67] whereas in the cases where acts have been held to be merely preparatory there has been no such confrontation. For example, in *Geddes* the defendant had not met any of the children; in *Gullefer* the defendant had not confronted the bookmakers from whom he was charged with attempted theft. But confrontation can be no more than

---

[62] It was never a "test" in the sense that the proximity test was. It was one method for establishing whether the proximity test had been satisfied. Had it ever been a "test" gunmen would not have been guilty of attempted murder until they had pulled the trigger.

[63] Smith and Hogan, *Criminal Law* (10th ed., 2002), p. 335, citing Rowlatt J. in *Osborn* (1919) 84 J.P. 63.

[64] (1987) 84 Cr.App.R.270.

[65] [1997] Crim.L.R.746.

[66] [1998] Crim.L.R.876.

[67] Clarkson, *Understanding Criminal Law* (3rd ed., 2001), p. 24.

evidence that acts are more than merely preparatory. In an attempted rape scenario, a man might confront a woman and pull her arm. Even under the broadest approach adopted above, this could never amount to acts more than merely preparatory to the crime of rape.

As the above cases demonstrate, in many instances this test is problematic and appears to be little more than yet another smoke-screen behind which policy can dictate when liability should be imposed.

### (ii) *Abandonment*

What is the position if a defendant, with intention to commit the complete offence, does an act which is more than merely preparatory, but then decides to abandon the criminal enterprise? Can there still be liability for an attempt to commit the crime?

## Le Barron v State, 32 Wis. 2d 294; 145 N.W. 2d 79 (1966) (Supreme Court of Wisconsin)

Currie C.J.:
"Was the evidence adduced sufficient to prove the finding of defendant guilty beyond a reasonable doubt of the crime of attempted rape? ...

[The defendant accosted a woman and took her to a deserted coal shack.] He then forced her into the shack and up against the wall. As she struggled for her breath he said, 'You know what else I want', unzipped his pants and started pulling up her skirt. She finally succeeded in removing his hand from her mouth, and after reassuring him that she would not scream, told him she was pregnant and pleaded with him to desist or he would hurt her baby. He then felt of her stomach and took her over to the door of the shack, where in the better light he was able to ascertain that, under her coat, she was wearing maternity clothes. He thereafter let her alone and left after warning her not to scream or call the police, or he would kill her."

**Conviction affirmed**

Should such a defendant be guilty of attempted rape? Would it make any difference if, instead of discovering the woman was pregnant, the defendant had simply been struck by remorse and had desisted saying: "I won't do it; God has stayed my hand"?[68]

It is clear that there is no "defence" of abandonment in English law.

## Haughton v Smith [1975] A.C. 476 (House of Lords)

Lord Hailsham:
"First [the defendant] may simply change his mind before committing any act sufficiently

[68] See *People v Graham*, 176 App.Div. 38, 162 N.Y.S., 334 (1916).

overt to amount to an attempt. Second, he may change his mind, but too late to deny that he had got so far as an attempt ... In the first case no criminal attempt is committed. At the relevant time there was no *mens rea* since there had been a change of intention, and the only overt acts relied upon would be preparatory and not immediately connected with the completed offence. In the second case there is both *mens rea* and an act immediately connected with the completed offence. ... It follows that there is a criminal attempt."

## The Law Commission (Law Com. No. 102), Attempt ... (1980):

"2.132. There is no authority to suggest that withdrawal from an attempt to commit an offence may at present be raised as a defence. Any interruption of the defendant's acts, whether or not due to his voluntary desistance, is not material to whether there has been an attempt, although it might show that there was not the *mens rea* necessary for liability. As the Working Party pointed out, an attempt is committed as soon as there are proximate acts accompanied by the necessary intent; thus even though withdrawal might result in the completed offence not being committed, it could not undo the fact that at some stage the defendant would have committed the inchoate offence. ... In favour of the defence was the suggestion that it could operate as an inducement to one who had embarked upon criminal conduct to desist from the completion of the offence by enabling him to raise a complete defence to criminal charges. On the other hand, it was suggested that, since the principal justification for provision of inchoate offences lay in the opportunity they gave for intervention by the police at an early stage in criminal activity, there would be an inherent contradiction in providing a defence when that activity had already reached a stage sufficiently advanced to warrant such intervention. The social danger already manifested by the defendant's conduct made it appropriate that any effort he might make to nullify its effects should instead be reflected by mitigation of penalty.

2.133. ... We believe that provision of a defence could only be justified if there were decisive arguments in its favour; particularly in the context of attempt, the defence could raise difficulties for law enforcement authorities still greater than those which already exist in deciding where the law may impose criminal sanctions. ...

For these reasons we do not recommend any defence of withdrawal in relation to attempt."

Such a defence, however, is widely accepted in the United States.

## American Law Institute, Model Penal Code, Proposed Official Draft, s.5.01(4):

"*Renunciation of criminal purpose*. When the actor's conduct would otherwise constitute an attempt ... it is an affirmative defence that he abandoned his effort to commit the crime or otherwise prevented its commission, under circumstances manifesting complete and voluntary renunciation of his criminal purpose. ...

Within the meaning of this Article, renunciation of criminal purpose is not voluntary if it is motivated, in whole or in part, by circumstances, not present or apparent at the inception of the actor's course of conduct, which increase the probability of detection or apprehension or which make more difficult the accomplishment of the criminal purpose. Renunciation is not complete if it is motivated by a decision to postpone the criminal conduct until a more advantageous time or to transfer the criminal effort to another but similar objective or victim."

Should English law follow this lead and allow for such a defence?

## Martin Wasik, "Abandoning Criminal Intent" [1980] Crim.L.R.785 at 787–788, 790–794:

"It is clear that the *voluntary* nature of the abandonment is an essential requirement for the success of any excuse in this area. ... [T]wo reasons [are put forward] for the central importance of the requirement of voluntariness. Sometimes it is argued that voluntary desistance provides clear evidence that the actor lacked the resolve to carry out the crime, and hence was not truly dangerous, and sometimes it is said that voluntary desistance is a 'good act' which somehow compensates for or erases the initial criminal act, thus making an acquittal appropriate.[69]

... One argument in favour of excusing the defendant who renounces a criminal purpose is in terms of negation of *mens rea*. According to Glanville Williams (*Criminal Law: The General Part* (1961), pp. 620–621) '... where the accused has changed his mind, it would only be just to interpret his previous intention where possible as only half-formed or provisional, and hold it to be an insufficient *mens rea* ...' ... Any [such] suggestion ... would greatly undermine the law of attempt. There must be few cases where the defendant would not accept the need to give up the attempt in certain circumstances ... [Also] the problems of proof would be considerable. ... In the leading Australian case on this topic, *Page* ([1933] V.L.R. 351), Mann A.C.J. emphasised the problems of proof involved in accepting such an excuse to crime. It

'... would seem to involve the necessity, in almost every case of an unsuccessful attempt to commit a crime, of determining whether the accused desisted from sudden alarm, from a sense of wrongdoing, from failure of resolution, or from any other cause. In the great majority of attempts to commit a crime the persons concerned desist because of causes affecting their volition ...'

... [W]hat other reasons exist for allowing [the excuse] to relieve the defendant of responsibility? First, it is argued that any dangerousness of character is negatived by clear evidence of abandonment ... It *may* follow from the fact that the course of conduct can no longer be regarded as dangerous that the defendant can be regarded as being no longer dangerous, but this is surely not a necessary inference from the abandonment of one attempt. The dangerousness of the conduct and the dangerousness of the actor are closely related concepts, but they are not identical. It might be that the defendant could experience profound remorse from coming very close to the commission of a criminal offence, and thus never seek to commit one again. ... An acceptance of abandonment as an excuse would ... show that the psychological barrier had not been crossed. Under English law, as we have seen, such late abandonment could not amount to an excuse because a proximate act has already been committed. On the other hand such questions of individual psychology and relative dangerousness are the very stuff of mitigation and sentencing policy. ...

The second reason often advanced for allowing a defence of withdrawal is one of legal policy. It is claimed that since it is a prime purpose of the criminal law to prevent the occurrence of harm, it makes sense to provide a reasonable inducement for the attempter to desist before any real harm is done. ... The importance of the argument turns upon how realistic it is. How likely is it that a man who is sufficiently far along the path towards committing a criminal offence, that he would be guilty of an attempt if stopped, and who then decides not to commit it, would change his mind again and decide to carry on, since he realises he is guilty of the attempt anyway? The argument is far-fetched.[70] ...

It has been strongly argued, then, that mitigation is not enough in cases of voluntary abandonment and that 'No argument of deterrence, reformation or prevention seems to require the punishment of one who is truly repentant and has done no harm.' It may be

---

[69] If this latter view is adopted, must the abandonment be prompted by a commendable motive? *Cf.* Fletcher, *Rethinking Criminal Law* (1978), pp. 193–194.

[70] *cf.* Wechsler, "The Treatment in Inchoate Crimes in the Model Penal Code ... " (1961) 61 Col.L.R. 571 at 617–618: "It is possible, of course, that the defense of renunciation of criminal purpose may add to the incentives to take the first steps towards crime. Knowledge that criminal endeavours can be undone with impunity may encourage preliminary steps that would not be undertaken if liability inevitably attached to every abortive criminal undertaking that proceeded beyond preparation. But this is not a serious problem. ... [A]ny consolation the actor might draw from the abandonment defense would have to be tempered with the knowledge that the defence would be unavailable if the actor's purposes were frustrated by external forces before he had an opportunity to abandon his efforts."

conceded that in a case of 'perfect' voluntary and complete abandonment, this argument is irrefutable. On a retributive view, punishment would be in accordance with bad intent, so on withdrawal the reason for punishment is removed. D's own change of heart perhaps rules out the need for preventative or reformative measures. Individual or general deterrence may also be out of place on the 'economy of threats' argument that punishing a man who has a good moral excuse will not serve to deter him or anyone else. In such a clear case punishment, and perhaps even the stigma of a conviction, seems inappropriate. . . .

[Wasik, nevertheless, concludes that abandonment should only be relevant in mitigation of sentence.]"

### R. A. Duff, Criminal Attempts (1996), pp. 395–396:

"Consider a paradigmatically 'voluntary' abandonment, by someone who at the last minute repents his criminal enterprise because she sees that it is wrong. . . . [E]ven if we should place on the defendant the onus of adducing evidence that her abandonment was voluntary, it should be seen as negating an essential element of the offence. It turns what would otherwise have been a criminal attempt into something that is not after all a criminal attempt. Her conduct takes its character as a criminal attempt from its relationship to the complete offence which she intends to commit: it counts as an attempt because it is directed towards that offence. Once she abandons the attempt, though, it ceases to be one . . . She had been trying to commit an offence (she embarked on the attempt): but in the end she did not try (but fail) to commit it . . .

The obvious objection to this account is that the intending rapist, murderer, or wounder who voluntarily abandons his attempt at the last moment has already attacked his victim, even if he aborted the attack himself . . . Surely he should not be able to escape all criminal liability by his abandonment? . . . [W]e should retain a narrow general law of attempts, supplemented (when necessary) by more specific offences capturing particularly wrongful kinds of conduct which fall outside its scope."

Thus, Duff's objectivist account would not necessarily lead to the complete acquittal of those who abandon their attempts (as they would be guilty of other offences) but would restrict the crime of attempt itself. Is such an approach preferable to that of the current law's reliance upon judicial discretion at the sentencing stage?

### (iii) *Impossibility*

### (a) Introduction
Can there be criminal liability for attempting the impossible? If a defendant shoots at his victim trying to kill her but unknown to him the victim has had a heart attack and is already dead, can the defendant be liable for attempted murder?

Before exploring the present law, it is helpful briefly to outline the position at common law before the enactment of the Criminal Attempts Act 1981.

### (b) The common law
The common law utilised a three-fold classification:

### 1. *Legal impossibility:*
This is where the defendant performs all the physical actions he intends to perform, but, unknown to him, what he has done does not amount to a crime. For example, he intends to steal an umbrella but unknown to him, the umbrella turns out to be his own.

In *Haughton v Smith*[71] the defendant was charged with attempting to handle stolen goods contrary to section 22 of the Theft Act 1968. The defendant had actually handled the goods but, unknown to him, they were not stolen goods.[72] The House of Lords unanimously held that there could be no liability for attempt in such circumstances. Lord Hailsham stated:

"there must be an overt act of such a kind that it is intended to form and does form part of a series of acts which would constitute the actual commission of the offence if it were not interrupted. In the present case the series of acts would never have constituted and in fact did not constitute an actual commission of the offence, because at the time of the handling the goods were no longer stolen goods."[73]

Lord Reid:

"The crime is impossible in the circumstances, so no acts could be proximate to it ... [H]e took no step towards the commission of a crime because there was no crime to commit."[74]

Lord Morris:

"His belief that the goods were stolen did not make them stolen goods. ... To convict him of attempting to handle stolen goods would be to convict him not for what he did but simply because he had had a guilty intention."[75]

### 2. *Physical impossibility:*

This is where it is physically impossible for the defendant to commit the complete crime, whatever means she adopts. For example, she intends to pick a pocket and places her hand in the victim's pocket, but it is empty; there is nothing to steal. In *Partington v Williams* it was held that there could be no liability in such cases because the commission of the substantive offence was, in the circumstances, impossible.[76]

The House of Lords in *D.P.P. v Nock*,[77] a conspiracy case, considered *obiter* "the proper limits" of *Haughton v Smith* and attempts to commit the impossible, and held that liability depended on the manner in which the particular indictment was framed. If, in an attempted theft case, the indictment was limited to an attempt to steal specific property or property from a specific place, then if the property was not there, the *actus reus* of the complete crime, namely, the appropriation of the

---

[71] [1975] A.C. 476.

[72] The goods had been stolen, but when the police commandeered the van in which the goods were travelling, the goods ceased to be "stolen" by virtue of section 24(3) of the Theft Act 1968 as they had been "restored to lawful custody".

[73] At 92.

[74] At 499–500.

[75] At 501.

[76] (1975) 62 Cr.App.R.220. The Divisional Court considered itself bound by *Haughton v Smith* which is not technically correct as the cases were dealing with different categories of impossibility.

[77] [1978] A.C. 979.

*specific* property belonging to another, would be incapable of proof. The defendant would escape liability. On the other hand, if the indictment alleged an attempt to steal from the person generally, then the pickpocket who put his hand in an empty pocket could be liable for attempted theft. This would be a mere "transient frustration". The crime would still be possible; the pickpocket, if undetected, would continue her attempts until successful.

This purported limitation of the *Haughton v Smith* principle does not stand up to close analysis. First, it ignores the immense difficulties involved in proving the requisite general intent to continue until the crime is eventually completed successfully, and, secondly, it overlooks the necessity to prove that the defendant's actions were proximate to the complete offence.

This whole approach towards attempts to commit the physically impossible caused other problems. What was meant by an empty pocket or an empty box? What if the pocket contained only a dirty handkerchief or a broken match? Was the test of emptiness a purely objective one, or was it relative to the defendant, namely, whether there something there that she would (or might) have stolen? For instance, the Law Commission[78] cite an unreported case in which a suitcase full of luggage was effectively held to be "empty" because it contained nothing the defendant wanted. In *Bayley and Easterbrook*[79] the defendants opened a box hoping to steal from it; the box contained "a Pammex Model 60 rail and flange lubricator"—a valuable article, but useless to the defendants so they returned the box and its contents. Their conviction for "attempting to steal the contents of a box belonging to the British Railways Board" was upheld, but as Smith points out:

> "It is clear then that the defendants were convicted of attempting to steal not the actual contents but something, unidentified, that was not in the box. ... Apart from the Pammex Model 60 rail and flange lubricator, this was an empty box. The presence of those articles was clearly totally irrelevant. They were of no more significance than, say, pieces of straw in which they had been packed."[80]

### 3. *Impossibility through ineptitude*

This is where the crime is impossible in the circumstances because of the defendant's ineptitude, inefficiency or his adoption of insufficient means. For example, he tries to force open a door with a jemmy, but the jemmy is too weak ever to open the door. Here the common law took a different approach from that adopted in relation to the above two categories of impossibility and held that there could be criminal liability for attempt. The reasoning was that such crimes were not really "impossible" because the crime *was* possible with different means. The defendant could open the door; he simply needed to fetch and use a stronger jemmy.[81]

In *Farrance*[82] the defendant had been convicted of attempting to drive with a blood alcohol concentration above the prescribed limit contrary to section 6(1) of

---

[78] Law Com. No. 102 (1980), para. 2.62.
[79] [1980] Crim.L.R.503.
[80] [1980] Crim.L.R.504. On this problem, see generally, Williams, "Three Rogues' Charters" [1980] Crim.L.R.263.
[81] *Haughton v Smith* [1975] A.C. 476 at 500.
[82] (1977) 67 Cr.App.R.136.

the Road Traffic Act 1972. The clutch of his car had burnt out so that she could not drive the car. The Court of Appeal upheld his conviction on the ground that a burnt out clutch was only an impediment to the commission of a crime similar to the inadequate burglar's tool or the poisoner's insufficient dose. In the Brunei case of *Zainal Abidin b Ismail*[83] the defendant's impotence prevented him from raping a woman. This was regarded as an instance of impossibility by ineptitude and the defendant was convicted of attempted rape.

Holding that there could be liability in these cases, but not in cases of attempting the physically impossible, posed immense problems. Suppose a defendant fired his gun at a victim who was out of range. Was this ineptitude or physical impossibility? Did it matter whether the victim was only just out of range or miles out of range? Or suppose that a defendant tried to kill his victim with a weak solution of poison; this was presumably ineptitude, but what if the solution was so weak that it could cause no harm at all? Or if the solution was entirely innocent, as where water was administered in mistake for cyanide? At what point did ineptitude become transformed into impossibility?

### (c) Criminal Attempts Act 1981

#### Criminal Attempts Act 1981, section 1:

"(2) A person may be guilty of attempting to commit an offence to which this section applies even though the facts are such that the commission of the offence is impossible.
(3) In any case where—
(a) apart from this subsection a person's intention would not be regarded as having amounted to an intent to commit an offence; but
(b) if the facts of the case had been as he believed them to be, his intention would be so regarded,
then, for the purposes of subsection (1) above, he shall be regarded as having had an intent to commit that offence.
(4) This section applies to any offence which, if it were completed, would be triable in England and Wales as an indictable offence. ...."

Section 1(2) provides that there can be liability for attempting the impossible, irrespective of the category of impossibility. Section 1(3) purports to confirm the self-evident proposition that where a person believes the facts to be such that she would be committing a crime, she is to be regarded as having the necessary intention to commit the offence. This means that a defendant who intends to handle a particular radio believing it to be stolen, when in fact it is not stolen, cannot argue that she intended to handle a "non-stolen radio". Section 1(3) makes it plain that if she believed the radio was stolen, she intended to handle a "stolen radio". This provision is actually completely redundant. Intention relates purely to a defendant's subjective state of mind. An intention to handle a stolen radio is just that: an intention to handle a radio believed to be stolen. The objective status of the goods (stolen or not stolen) has no bearing upon the defendant's intention.

These provisions represent a clear and emphatic victory for the "subjectivist" theory of attempts where emphasis is placed on the intention of the defendant and

[83] [1987] 2 M.L.J. 741. For a discussion of this case, see Clarkson, "Rape: Emasculation of the Penal Code" [1988] 1 M.L.J. cxiii.

the firmness of that intention. However, the House of Lords was initially not prepared to accept such blatant subjectivism and, in an extraordinary judgment, declared that the statute would lead to "asinine" results and proceeded to subvert the legislation from its original purpose.

## Anderton v Ryan [1985] A.C. 560 (House of Lords)

The defendant was convicted of dishonestly attempting to handle a stolen video recorder. She had purchased the recorder believing it was stolen and had confessed this to police investigating a burglary at her home. There was however no evidence that the recorder had been stolen and it therefore had to be treated as if it were not stolen. She appealed against her conviction.

Lord Bridge:

"Does section 1 of the Act of 1981 create a new offence of attempt where a person embarks on and completes a course of conduct which is objectively innocent, solely on the ground that the person mistakenly believes facts which, if true, would make that course of conduct a complete crime? If the question must be answered affirmatively it requires convictions in a number of surprising cases: the classic case ... of the man who takes away his own umbrella from a stand, believing it not to be his own and with intent to steal it; the case of the man who has consensual intercourse with a girl over 16 believing her to be under that age; the case of the art dealer who sells a picture which he represents to be and which is in fact a genuine Picasso, but which the dealer mistakenly believes to be a fake.

The common feature of all these cases, including that under appeal, is that the mind alone is guilty, the act is innocent. I should find it surprising that Parliament, if intending to make this purely subjective guilt criminally punishable, should have done so by anything less than the clearest express language, and, in particular, should have done so in a section aimed specifically at inchoate offences.

... [S]ection 1(1) and (4) of the Act of 1981 provide a statutory substitute for the common law offence of attempt ...

It is sufficient to say of subsection (2) that it is plainly intended to reverse the law ... that the pickpocket who puts his hand in an empty pocket commits no offence. Putting the hand in the pocket is the guilty act, the intent to steal is the guilty mind, the offence is appropriately dealt with as an attempt, and the impossibility of committing the full offence for want of anything in the pocket to steal is declared by the subsection to be no obstacle to conviction ...

It seems to me that subsections (2) and (3) are in a sense complementary to each other. Subsection (2) covers the case of a person acting in a criminal way with a general intent to commit a crime in circumstances where no crime is possible. Subsection (3) covers the case of a person acting in a criminal way with a specific intent to commit a particular crime which he erroneously believes to be, but which is not in fact, possible. Given the criminal action, the appropriate subsection allows the actor's guilty intention to be supplied by his subjective but mistaken state of mind, notwithstanding that on the true facts that intention is incapable of fulfilment. But if the action is throughout innocent and the actor has done everything he intended to do, I can find nothing in either subsection which requires me to hold that his erroneous belief in facts which, if true, would have made the action a crime makes him guilty of an attempt to commit that crime."

**Appeal allowed**

## C. M. V. Clarkson, Understanding Criminal Law (3rd. ed., 2001), p. 167:

"This distinction between 'objectively innocent' acts on the one hand and 'criminal' or 'guilty' acts on the other is particularly interesting. It would appear that a 'criminal' or 'guilty' act is one that looks *manifestly criminal*. (This cannot refer to actual crimes. The defendant stabbing the pillow believing he is stabbing his victim commits no offence if it is his own bedding and pillow that he is damaging. Yet Lord Roskill clearly held that there would be liability for attempt in such a situation.) Fletcher (1978) states that 'manifestly criminal' activities must exhibit at least the following essential features. First, the criminal act must manifest, on its face, the actor's criminal purpose. And secondly, the conduct should be 'of a type that is unnerving and disturbing to the community as a whole'. These requirements are clearly satisfied in the pickpocket and defendant stabbing the pillow cases. The actions manifest the defendant's unlawful purpose and are 'unnerving and disturbing' to the community. This requirement of manifest criminality is, of course, one that lays emphasis on *harm*, albeit of a second-order nature. It insists that actions infringe another's security interests; they must seemingly pose real and objective threats of harm.

On the other hand, 'objectively innocent' activities such as those of Mrs Ryan or the defendant having sexual intercourse with the 16-year-old girl believing her to be under 16 pose no threat of harm to anyone. Nobody's security interests are being violated thereby. At most, he is manifesting a generalised dangerousness, in the sense that he has shown that he could perhaps commit the crime at another time and place. If criminal liability were to be imposed in such cases it would be in the complete absence of any degree of harm, however defined. On this basis it can be suggested that the House of Lords in *Anderton v Ryan* (1985), despite blatantly ignoring Parliament's intentions and creating confused distinctions, did lend its weight to the view ... that the causing of harm is an essential prerequisite in the general formula for the construction of criminal liability."

In one of the most dramatic about-turns in English law, the House of Lords within months overruled itself and held that there could be criminal liability in all cases of attempting the impossible.

## R. v Shivpuri [1987] A.C. 1 (House of Lords)

The defendant thought he was dealing in prohibited drugs but it transpired that the substance in his possession was only snuff or similarly harmless vegetable matter. He was convicted of attempting to be knowingly concerned in dealing with prohibited drugs, contrary to section 1(1) of the Criminal Attempts Act 1981 and section 170(1)(b) of the Customs and Excise Management Act 1979. He appealed against his conviction.

Lord Bridge:

"[T]he first question to be asked is whether the appellant intended to commit the offences of being knowingly concerned in dealing with and harbouring drugs of Class A or Class B with intent to evade the prohibition on their importation. Translated into more homely language the question may be rephrased, without in any way altering its legal significance, in the following terms: did the appellant intend to receive and store (harbour) and in due course pass on to third parties (deal with) packages of heroin or cannabis which he knew had been smuggled into England from India? The anwer is plainly yes, he did. Next, did he in relation to each offence, do an act which was more than merely preparatory to the commission of the offence? The act relied on in relation to harbouring was the receipt and retention of the packages found in the lining of the suitcase. The act relied on in relation to dealing was the meeting at Southall station with the intended recipient of one of the packages. In each case the act was clearly more than preparatory to the commission of the *intended* offence; it was not and could not be more than merely preparatory to the commission of the *actual* offence, because the facts were such that the commission of the actual offence was impossible. Here then is the nub of the matter. Does the 'act which is more than merely preparatory to the commission of the offence' in section 1(1) of the Act of 1981 (the *actus reus* of the statutory offence of attempt) require any more than an act which is more than merely preparatory to the commission of the offence which the defendant intended to commit? Section 1(2) must surely indicate a negative answer; if it were otherwise, whenever the facts were such that the commission of the actual offence was impossible, it would be impossible to prove an act more than merely preparatory to the commission of that offence and subsections (1) and (2) would contradict each other.

This very simple, perhaps over simple, analysis leads me to the provisional conclusion that the appellant was rightly convicted of the two offences of attempt with which he was charged. But can this conclusion stand with *Anderton v Ryan?* ...

Running through Lord Roskill's speech and my own in *Anderton v Ryan* is the concept of 'objectively innocent' acts which, in my speech certainly, are contrasted with 'guilty acts'.

I am satisfied on further consideration that the concept of 'objective innocence' is incapable of sensible application in relation to the law of criminal attempts. The reason for this is that any attempt to commit an offence which involves 'an act which is more than merely preparatory to the commission of the offence' but for any reason fails, so that in the event no offence is committed, must ex hypothesi, from the point of view of the criminal law, be 'objectively innocent'. What turns what would otherwise, from the point of view of the criminal law, be an innocent act into a crime is the intent of the actor to commit an offence. ... A puts his hand into B's pocket. Whether or not there is anything in the pocket capable of being stolen, if A intends to steal, his act is a criminal attempt; if he does not so intend, his act is innocent. A plunges a knife into a bolster in a bed. To avoid the complication of an offence of criminal damage, assume it to be A's bolster. If A believes the bolster to be his enemy B and intends to kill him, his act is an attempt to murder B; if he knows the bolster is only a bolster, his act is innocent. These considerations lead me to the conclusion that the distinction sought to be drawn in *Anderton v Ryan* between innocent and guilty acts considered 'objectively' and independently of the state of mind of the actor cannot be sensibly maintained.

Another conceivable ground of distinction which was to some extent canvassed in argument, both in *Anderton v Ryan* and in the instant case, though no trace of it appears in the speeches in *Anderton v Ryan*, is a distinction which would make guilt or innocence of the crime of attempt in a case of mistaken belief dependent on what, for want of a better phrase, I will call the defendant's dominant intention. According to the theory necessary to sustain this distinction, the appellant's dominant intention in *Anderton v Ryan* was to buy a cheap video recorder; her belief that it was stolen was merely incidental. Likewise in the hypothetical case of attempted unlawful sexual intercourse, the young man's dominant intention was to have intercourse with the particular girl; his mistaken belief that she was under 16 was merely incidental. By contrast, in the instant case, the appellant's dominant intention was to receive and distribute illegally imported heroin or cannabis.

Whilst I see the superficial attraction of this suggested ground of distinction, I also see formidable practical difficulties in its application. By what test is a jury to be told that a defendant's dominant intention is to be recognised and distinguished from his incidental but mistaken belief? But there is perhaps a more formidable theoretical difficulty. If this ground of distinction is relied on to support the acquittal of the appellant in *Anderton v Ryan*, it can only do so on the basis that her mistaken belief that the video recorder was stolen played no significant part in her decision to buy it and therefore she may be acquitted of the intent to handle stolen goods. But this line of reasoning runs into head-on collision with section 1(3) of the Act of 1981. The theory produces a situation where, apart from the subsection, her intention would not be regarded as having amounted to any intent to commit an offence. Section 1(3)(b) then requires one to ask whether, if the video recorder had in fact been stolen, her intention would have been regarded as an intent to handle stolen goods. The answer must clearly be yes, it would. If she had bought the video recorder knowing it to be stolen, when in fact it was, it would have availed her nothing to say that her dominant intention was to buy a video recorder because it was cheap and that her knowledge that it was stolen was merely incidental. This seems to me fatal to the dominant intention theory.[84]

I am thus led to the conclusion that there is no valid ground on which *Anderton v Ryan* can be distinguished. I have made clear my own conviction ... that the decision was wrong."

**Appeal dismissed**

---

[84] For a discussion of this dominant intention theory, see p. 504.

# The Law Commission (Law Com. No. 102), Attempt ... (1980), paras 2.96–2.98:

"2.96. We think it would be generally accepted that if a man possesses the appropriate *mens rea* and commits acts which are sufficiently proximate to the *actus reus* of a criminal offence, he is guilty of attempting to commit that offence. Where, with that intention, he commits acts which, if the facts were as he believed them to be, would have amounted to the *actus reus* of the full crime or would have been sufficiently proximate to amount to an attempt, we cannot see why his failure to appreciate the true facts should, in principle, relieve him of liability for the attempt. We stress that this solution to the problem does not punish people simply for their intentions. The necessity for proof of proximate acts remains. The fact that the impossibility of committing the full crime reduces the social danger is adequately reflected in the generally milder penalty which an attempt attracts instead of that for the full offence. And even if it is conceded that there may be some reduction in the social danger in cases of impossibility, it has to be borne in mind that a certain social danger undoubtedly remains. Defendants in cases such as *Haughton v Smith* and *Nock and Alsford* are prepared to do all they can to break the criminal law even though in the circumstances their attempts are doomed to failure; and if they go unpunished, they may be encouraged to do better at the next opportunity. Finally, if the solution under consideration is accepted, it makes it possible to dispense with the doctrine of 'inadequate means' and with stained efforts to catch those who might otherwise escape by resort to broadly drawn indictments and an 'inferred general intention'.

2.97. If it is right in principle that an attempt should be chargeable even though the crime which it is sought to commit could not possibly be committed, we do not think that we should be deterred by the consideration that such a change in our law would also cover some extreme and exceptional cases in which a prosecution would be theoretically possible. An example would be where a person is offered goods at such a low price that he believes that they are stolen, when in fact they are not; if he actually purchases them, upon the principles which we have discussed he would be liable for an attempt to handle stolen goods. Another case which has been much debated is that raised in argument by Bramwell B. in *R. v Collins* (1864) 9 Cox C.C. 497. If A takes his own umbrella, mistaking it for one belonging to B and intending to steal B's umbrella, is he guilty of attempted theft? Again, on the principles which we have discussed he would in theory be guilty but in neither case would it be realistic to suppose that a complaint would be made or that a prosecution would ensue. On the other hand, if our recommendations were formulated so as to exclude such cases, then it might well be impossible to obtain convictions in cases such as *Haughton v Smith*, where a defendant handles goods which were originally stolen, intending to handle stolen goods, but where, unknown to him, the goods had meanwhile been restored to lawful custody. Another example of possible difficulty which has been suggested is where a person in the erroneous belief that he can kill by witchcraft or magic takes action such as sticking pins into a model of his enemy—intending thereby to bring about his enemy's death. Could that person be charged with attempted murder? It may be that such conduct could be more than an act of mere preparation on the facts as the defendant believes them to be; and in theory, therefore, it is possible that such a defendant could be found guilty. In the ordinary course, we think that discretion in bringing a prosecution will be sufficient answer to any problems raised by such unusual cases; but even if a prosecution ensued, it may be doubted whether a jury would regard the acts in question as sufficient to amount to an attempt.

2.98. A possible difficulty of another kind which we have considered is the distinction which it will be necessary to draw between impossibility arising from misapprehension as to the facts and impossibility arising from a misapprehension of the law in situations which at first sight appear to be similar. As we have seen, if the defendant believes, because of a mistake of law, that certain conduct constitutes an offence when it is not, he should not be liable for attempt if he acts in accordance with his intent. For example, the defendant intends to smuggle certain goods through the customs in the belief that they are dutiable; under the relevant law those goods are in fact not dutiable. He has made no mistake as to the nature of the goods; his error is solely one of law, and if he imports them he should not be liable for an attempt improperly to import goods without paying duty, since he had no intent to commit an offence known to the law.[85] The position is different if the defendant is asked while abroad to smuggle into the country goods which he is assured by the person making the request are goods which are actually dutiable, but which are not in fact dutiable because they are not what he believes them to be. Here the defendant's error arises solely from his misapprehension as to the nature of the goods; it is a pure error of fact. He has every intention of committing an offence on the facts as he believes them to be, and if he succeeds in importing the goods or in getting sufficiently close to his objective, he must be liable for an attempt upon the principles which we have been considering. Fine as the distinction appears to be in these cases it is one which is in our view vital to make."

Supporters of the objective theory of attempts tend to reject such reasoning and assert that such "subjectivism" amounts to little more than punishing people for their guilty intentions. The Law Commission conceded the absurdity of there being liability in situations where a person buys legitimate goods but at such a low price that she thinks (wrongly) that they are stolen. It concluded that prosecutions would never be brought in such cases. Yet it was broadly similar on facts that a prosecution was brought in *Anderton v Ryan* forcing the House of Lords to adopt some highly innovative techniques to ensure an acquittal.

However, even the hardened "objectivist" concedes the necessity for liability in certain obvious cases. The problem is in isolating such situations.

### George P. Fletcher, Rethinking Criminal Law (1978), pp. 149–150, 152–154, 161–163, 165–166:

"It is agreed by all supporters of an objectivist approach to attempts that there should be no liability in the case of shooting at a tree stump with the intent to kill. Yet the courts have found liability in closely related situations. ... [A] Missouri court convicted on a charge of attempted murder for shooting at the bed where the intended victim usually slept. (*State v Mitchell*, 170 Mo. 633, 71 S.W. 175 (1902)). ... Shooting at the intended victim's bed and aiming a gun manifest the intent to kill. In shooting at a tree stump, in contrast, there is nothing in the facts to indicate that an attempt is under way. According to objectivist theory, attempting is not just an event of inner experience. It is an effort in the real world to accomplish one's objective. Therefore, when the act is aptly related to that actor's objective, the courts perceive a manifest attempt to commit an offense. Yet when the act is objectively unrelated to the intent, as in the case of shooting at a tree stump, judges and theorists properly balk at positing an act of attempting. The notion of aptness here is obviously closely related to the principle of manifest criminality. ...

[T]he problem of aptness is one of assessing whether in the long run the type of conduct involved is likely to produce harm. If the type of conduct would produce harm in the long run, then the defendant's act is apt and a punishable attempt, even though it is impossible under the circumstances. ...

The principle that inapt efforts should be exempt from liability readily explains why the courts do not discern an act of attempting in the giving of an innocuous substance as an intended poison or abortifacient.

---

[85] This is illustrated by *Taaffe* [1984] 1 A.C. 539, where the defendant, believing that the importation of currency was prohibited, tried to smuggle several packages of what he (wrongly) believed was currency into the country. Although this made his actions "morally reprehensible", he could not be guilty of an attempt to commit any crime—there is no such crime. He had made a classic mistake of law, which was "irrelevant". See *above*, p. 204. See also p. 190.

The difficult problem in these cases is drawing the distinction between giving the intended victim an innocuous substance and giving him too small a dosage of a noxious poison. It is the distinction between trying to kill by putting sugar in his coffee and trying to kill by administering a harmless dosage of cyanide. In the latter cases, the courts have been willing to convict, and as a result we are put to the challenge to explain why sugar makes the attempt inapt but a harmless dosage of cyanide makes it apt. As we discovered in our analysis of the shooting cases, the standard of aptness does not apply to isolated events, but rather to types or classes of acts. Apt attempts belong to a class of acts that are likely to generate harm. If the class is defined as administering a dosage of cyanide or other deadly poison, there is no doubt that the class of acts is likely to generate harm, and therefore we can regard every instance of the class as an apt attempt. ...

[Dealing with the empty pocket cases] there is nothing inapt about these efforts. They are well calculated to provide a thief's income, even if it turns out that in the particular situation the bounty is not there. ...

[However for other cases, for example, cases such as *Haughton v Smith*, Fletcher suggests an alternative theory—'the test of rational motivation'.] The thesis is this: mistaken beliefs are relevant to what the actor is trying to do if they affect his incentive in acting. They affect his incentive if knowing of the mistake would give him a good reason for changing his course of conduct. ... Suppose the accused engages in sexual intercourse with a girl he takes to be under the age of consent; in fact, she is over age. Is he guilty of attempted statutory rape? In the normal case it would not be part of the actor's incentive that the girl be underage (again, one could imagine a variation in which the youth of the girl did bear upon the actor's motivation). If he is just as happy to have intercourse with a girl over age, then his mistake would not bear on his incentive and it would be incorrect to describe his act as trying to have intercourse with a girl under the age of consent. ... The thesis is that there should be liability in a case of impossibility only if the actor fails in his purpose. ... The only way to determine whether the actor is attempting an act that includes a particular circumstance, X, is to inquire: what would the actor do if he knew that X was not so? If he would behave in precisely the same way, we cannot say that his mistaken belief in X bears on his motivation; and if it does not, we cannot say that he is attempting to act with reference to X. ...

If applied to the cases of shooting at stumps and 'poisoning' with sugar, the test of rational motivation leads to convictions where the standard of aptness would favour an acquittal. It is obviously part of the actor's system of incentives that he believe the stump to be a person, or the dosage to be sufficient to kill. If told of the truth, he would presumably change his plans. So far as the standard of incentive is controlling, the person shooting at the stump is undoubtedly attempting to kill. The problem is whether the test of aptness should prevail over the theory of rational motivation in cases involving assaults on the core interests protected by the criminal law. ...

One reason to believe that the principle of aptness is indispensable in a comprehensive theory of attempt liability is that there is no other way to solve one case in which virtually everyone agrees that there should be no liability. That is the case of nominal efforts to inflict harm by superstitious means, say by black magic or witchcraft. The consensus of Western legal systems is that there should be no liability, regardless of the wickedness of intent, for sticking pins in a doll or chanting an incantation to banish one's enemy to the nether world.[86] Against the background of the fears and taboos prevailing in modern Western society, objectivist theorists take these cases to be inapt attempts, therefore exempt from punishment. Yet the theory of rational motivation points in the direction of liability. If the intending party knows the truth about black magic (namely, that it does not work), he would have a good reason to change his plan of attack. To account for the consensus favouring an

[86] cf. *The Times*, October 12, 1983: "Aborigines in the West Australian town of Roebourne say they will use traditional methods to punish a local policeman who, they say, was responsible for the death of an Aboriginal youth in police custody more than a week ago. They say they will 'sing' him to death. The ceremony, equivalent to an execution, is carried out only rarely. Anthropologists have documented many Aboriginal deaths after such ceremonies. Mr Mick Lee, the stepfather of the boy, said 'When someone is sung to death by Aboriginal lawmen, he dies in two days. Black or white, all the same.' "

exemption in this type of case, we need the principle of aptness to offset the implications of the competing theory of rational motivation.

The problem that remains to be resolved is determining the relative scope of these two competing theories."

Duff supports an approach broadly similar to Fletcher's theory of rational motivation. Under his view Mrs Ryan did not intend to handle a stolen video recorder as that played no motivational part in her conduct; her actions were not directed towards handling stolen goods; the fact that the goods were stolen was merely a side-effect.[87] Both these approaches are similar to the "dominant intention" theory rejected in *Shivpuri*. The problem with these theories is that they boil down to making liability dependent on motive. This is problematic in evidential terms and questionable in moral terms.[88] Further, as Fletcher points out, it leads to liability in the shooting at the tree-stump case. Duff rejects liability in such cases on the ground that the attack "fails so radically to engage with the world that it does not even amount to a failed attack". Fletcher's theory of aptness would similarly resolve some of these issues, but the real problem with his analysis is the failure to spell out the exact circumstances in which the theory of aptness is applicable and those in which it is appropriate to apply the theory of rational motivation.

English law has rejected the dominant intention (rational motivation) theory. The theory of aptness is broadly similar to the "objectively innocent" *v* "guilty acts" approach approved in *Anderton v Ryan*. This was rejected in *Shivpuri*. It is, of course, extremely difficult to capture these notions in a practicable statutory formulation.[89] However, it must remain questionable whether English law has adopted the right solution in ignoring these important considerations of principle and imposing liability in all these situations and then relying on prosecutorial discretion to avoid injustice.

## III. CONSPIRACY

### A. *Introduction*

Conspiracy is an inchoate crime because, like attempt, it penalises steps towards the commission of a crime. In the case of conspiracy, an *agreement* is the essence of the offence. The agreement may be to murder someone, to import cocaine into this country, to take millions of pounds from a pension fund or to publish names and information about prostitutes. The law on conspiracy has been described as "the least systematic, the most irrational branch of English penal law".[90] Whilst some

---

[87] Duff, *Criminal Attempts* (1996), pp. 378–379.
[88] For a discussion of the role of motive in assessing intention, see pp. 130–134.
[89] Duff, *Criminal Attempts* (1996), p. 384.
[90] *D.P.P. v Bhagwan* (1972) A.C. 60 at 79. The development of conspiracy from a narrowly circumscribed crime of agreeing falsely to accuse another to one where agreeing to do any unlawful act fell within its ambit, and its use, in particular, against the early trade union movement has been well documented; see Robertson, *Whose Conspiracy?* (1974); Hazell, *Conspiracy and Civil Liberties* (1974), pp. 13–19, Sayre; "Criminal Conspiracy" (1922) 35 Harv.L.R. 402; Spicer, *Conspiracy* (1981).

reform has taken place since that statement was made, it is still the case that in terms of its rationale, its content and its use, the crime of conspiracy is highly suspect.

## B. *Should there be a Law of Conspiracy?*

### Richard Card, "Reform of the Law of Conspiracy" [1973] Crim.L.R.674 at 675–676:

"It may be asked whether it is desirable that criminal liability should attach to persons who, albeit at the time of the agreement intend to carry it out, never get beyond the stage of agreement. To take an extreme case, suppose that there is a bare agreement, the details remaining to be agreed, and that the next day the parties withdraw from their agreement; is this really conduct deserving of punishment?

It must be admitted that in practice a conviction for conspiracy in such a case will not generally be possible because of the difficulty of proving the agreement. Convictions for conspiracy usually depend on inferences from overt acts said by the prosecution to have been performed in pursuance of the agreement. In practical terms liability often arises by virtue of overt acts done in pursuance of the agreement . . . In such cases, . . . the offence of conspiracy would seem to be in part redundant. If these further acts constitute an attempt the conspirators who commit them can be convicted of attempt (to which any other conspirator would be an accomplice). On the other hand, if the further acts are insufficient to constitute an attempt, the punishment of the conspirators, both those who committed the overt acts and those who did no more than enter the agreement, can only be justified on the basis that it is the combination of persons which aggravates their conduct and produces liability. . . .

It is merely suggested that criminal liability should not attach to those who merely agree, . . . where no further steps are taken to effect it. Such a rule has been adopted in part in the Model Penal Code of the American Law Institute. Article 5.03 provides:

'*Overt Act*. No person may be convicted of conspiracy to commit a crime, other than a felony of the first or second degree, unless an overt act in pursuance of such conspiracy is alleged and proved to have been done by him or by a person with whom he conspired.'

Conspiracy has another rationale besides that of 'nipping crime in the bud'. This is that it is an appropriate offence to charge where a series of crimes have been committed at different times by different people pursuant to a prior agreement. The series of crimes may be so large that there would be great difficulty in indicting for all of them. In addition, each offence taken on its own may be relatively trivial but the gravity of the conduct of those involved greatly increased by viewing their acts as part of a larger criminal enterprise. These matters can be dealt with at present by the use of a conspiracy charge. Such situations may well warrant the creation of a crime which specifically deals with such completed criminal enterprises but, it is submitted, they do not justify the continued existence of a crime where liability is based on agreement and no more.

If it was accepted that there should no longer be a crime of conspiracy based on mere agreement to commit a crime, it is submitted that the criminality of acts done pursuant to that agreement (which did not result in the commission of a substantive offence) should be dealt with by the law of attempt."

### Phillip Johnson, "The Unnecessary Crime of Conspiracy" (1973) 61 Cal.L.Rev. 1137 at 1157–1158:

"Conspiracy is also an inchoate or preparatory crime, permitting the punishment of persons who agree to commit a crime even if they never carry out their scheme or are apprehended before achieving their objective. . . .

The Model Penal Code commentary offers perhaps the most carefully stated justification for a doctrine of conspiracy that 'reaches further back into preparatory conduct than attempt':

*First*: The Act of agreeing with another to commit a crime, like the act of soliciting, is concrete and unambiguous; it does not present the infinite degrees and variations possible in the general category of attempts. The danger that truly equivocal behaviour may be misinterpreted as preparation to commit a crime is minimized; purpose must be relatively firm before the commitment involved in agreement is assumed.

*Second*: If the agreement was to aid another to commit a crime or it otherwise encouraged its commission, it would establish complicity in the commission of the substantive offense. … It would be anomalous to hold that conduct which would suffice to establish criminality, if something else is done by someone else is insufficient if the crime is never consummated. This is a reason, to be sure, which covers less than all the cases of conspiracy, but that it covers many is the point.

*Third*: In the course of preparation to commit a crime, the act of combining with another is significant both psychologically and practically, the former since it crosses a clear threshold in arousing expectations, the latter since it increases the likelihood that the offense will be committed. Sharing lends fortitude to purpose. The actor knows, moreover, that the future is no longer governed by his will alone; others may complete what he has had a hand in starting, even if he has a change of heart."

### Abraham Goldstein, "Conspiracy to Defraud the United States" (1959) 68 Yale L.J. 405 at 414:

"More likely, empirical investigation would disclose that there is as much reason to believe that a large number of participants will increase the prospect that the plan will be leaked as that it will be kept secret; or that the persons involved will share their uncertainties and dissuade each other as that each will stiffen the other's determination."

### Note, "The Conspiracy Dilemma: Prosecution of Group Crimes or Protection of Individual Defendants" (1948) 62 Harv.L.Rev. 276 at 283–284:

"Several factors, seldom articulated by the courts, seem to underlie this concept of the unique criminality of group action. Basic is the increased danger to the public welfare and safety that exists in the combination of united wills to effect a harmful object, as contrasted with the menace of the criminal purpose of a single individual. Reliance on the co-operation of co-conspirators and the intent to support and aid them in the future increases the likelihood of criminal conduct on the part of individual conspirators. And it is more difficult to guard against the antisocial designs of a group of persons than those of an individual. Thus, the crucial importance of the conspiracy weapon stems from its effectiveness in reaching organized crime. The advantages of division of labor and complex organization characteristic of modern economic society have their counterparts in many forms of criminal activity. Manufacture or importation and distribution of contraband goods, for example, often demands a complicated organization. The interrelations of the parties in schemes to defraud may be highly complex. Except for the conspiracy device, society would be without protection until the criminal object is actually executed or at least sufficiently approached to become indictable as an attempt; and even then often only the actual perpetrator and perhaps his immediate accessories could be reached. Through the conspiracy dragnet, all participants in gang operations, the catspaw and his principal, those who contribute from afar as well as the immediate actors can be punished often before the evil design has fully matured into the criminal act."

The arguments for retaining a crime of conspiracy can thus be grouped into three main strands:

1. The prevention of crime: if this is regarded as the main objective (and according to the Law Commission it is[91]) then it would seem to follow as a matter of inexorable logic that the agreement should be to do something that would be *criminal* if completed. As we shall see, the Criminal Law Act 1977 has only partially succeeded in reducing conspiracy to this formula. Moreover, if this is the main objective then its justification depends to a major degree on the ambit of the law of attempt. If English law had adopted the substantial step test[92] for determining the extent of action required for an attempt, this justification for conspiracy would have largely collapsed as in most cases the only evidence of the agreement will be overt acts that could have satisfied the substantial step test. However, as this test has not been adopted by English law, which requires the defendant to have done acts that are more than merely preparatory to the commission of the offence, there clearly is some need, in crime prevention terms, for a crime of conspiracy.

   Finally, the fact that large numbers of conspiracy charges are brought *after* the crime has been completed tends to cast further doubt on the notion of prevention.[93]

2. The "full story" rationale: a conspiracy charge enables numbers of crimes, which may or may not be serious in themselves, to be brought before the court in their "true" light. It enables larger numbers of those involved to be held responsible. However, this largely ignores the role of the law relating to complicity and may lead to the conspiracy charge being abused.[94]

3. The "general danger" rationale: that people working in concert with one another are more dangerous than lone actors. Not only are they able to commit more complex crimes but they will be more likely to carry out their intentions. The least one can say in response to this is that it is unproven. More fundamentally, it is this argument which enabled conspiracy to develop so as to embrace an agreement with others to do an act, such as trespass, which was not in itself criminal. Few would now wish to defend conspiracy on this basis.[95]

One has to conclude that conspiracy is used as more than an inchoate crime. The reality is that its use, when the crime has been completed, brings substantial advantages for the prosecution. Not only does it provide them with another chance of securing a conviction where the evidence relating to the completed crime is doubtful, but there are evidential benefits as well.[96]

[91] Law Com. No. 76, *Conspiracy and Criminal Law Reform* (1976), para. 1.5.
[92] *Above*, p. 483.
[93] There is no bar under English law to bringing conspiracy charges when the offence has been completed (they do not "merge"), but it is bad practice: Practice Direction [1977] 2 All E.R. 540. The prosecution has to justify to the judge the inclusion of the conspiracy count and if the judge is not satisfied then the prosecution has to elect to proceed with either the conspiracy or the substantive count.
[94] In *Barrett and Sheehan* [1996] Crim.L.R.495, for example, the court felt that the evidence fell far short of establishing a single conspiracy extending over two years to burgle houses. As Smith comments (at p. 497) the idea was "utterly far-fetched".
[95] Law Com. No. 76, *Conspiracy and Criminal Law Reform* (1976), para. 1.9.
[96] The normal rule of evidence, for example, that prevents the statements of one co-defendant being used against another does not apply in conspiracy trials.

As with attempts, a conspiracy, if charged when the offence has not been completed, causes no actual harm. Bearing in mind our discussion of the rationale of the law of attempt, the following questions present themselves:

(1) Do conspiracies pose a "second order" harm—in the sense of posing a threat to security? or
(2) Is the blameworthiness of a conspirator so great as to justify dispensing with the requirement of harm which is normally required for the imposition of criminal liability? Or are there (and can there ever be) sufficient utilitarian arguments to justify dispensing with the requirement of harm?

## C. *Punishment of Conspiracies*

At common law the punishment of those convicted of conspiracy was at the discretion of the court.[97] In the case of those conspiracies which now fall within section 1 of the Criminal Law Act 1977, punishment is limited to the maximum sentence for the complete crime which the defendants conspired to commit.[98] In the case of common law conspiracies to defraud the maximum sentence has been reduced to 10 years.[99]

### Sir Rupert Cross and Andrew Ashworth, Cross; The English Sentencing System (3rd ed., 1981), p. 156:

"Conspiracies might, however, be regarded as more serious crimes than attempts. Indeed, at common law it was held in *Verrier v Director of Public Prosecutions* ([1967] 2 A.C. 195) that some conspiracies might call for a greater punishment than could be imposed for the completed offence. Although s.3 of the Criminal Law Act now prohibits courts from exceeding the statutory maximum for the completed offence in conspiracy cases, a court still might wish to visit conspirators with more severe punishment than it would mete out to an individual committing the completed offence, whilst keeping within the statutory maximum. The argument is that the nature of the offence is exceptionally changed by the co-operation of large numbers in its commission, because of the greater chance of the occasioning of alarm and of the use of force. In fraud cases, the co-operation of different people in different places may facilitate both the execution and the concealment of the design. These considerations go to show that any offence, whether inchoate or completed, which is committed by a number of people acting in concert may be viewed as presenting a greater social danger than the same offence committed by an individual. On general deterrent grounds the sentence for 'group' offences may therefore be longer. Sentences for rape by gangs are on this account higher than those for rape by an individual."

Consider, again, the discussion of the punishment for attempts and the significance of harm. Surely those considerations have even greater force here if what is being punished is an agreement (that goes no further) to commit a crime, especially since the "dangerousness of collaboration argument" carries less weight now. If, on the other hand, the court is dealing with a conspiracy where the crime has been completed (or where it has failed) there are different concerns. For evidential reasons the prosecution may fail to prove the complete crime but manage

---

[97] This is still true in relation to the imposition of fines by the Crown Court (Criminal Law Act 1977, s.3(1)).
[98] *ibid.* s.3(3).
[99] Criminal Justice Act 1987, s.12.

to secure a conviction for conspiracy. If the crime is the *agreement*, tempting though it might be to look beyond it in sentencing, this would amount to punishing somebody for something that has not been proven.

## D. *The Law*

### 1. Types of conspiracy

At common law a conspiracy was an agreement between two or more persons "to do an unlawful act, or to do a lawful act by unlawful means".[1] Thus it was not necessary to prove that there was an agreement to commit a crime; agreements to commit other "unlawful acts", such as fraud, some torts or corruption of public morals, clearly sufficed. For instance, in *Kamara v D.P.P.*[2] an agreement to commit the tort of trespass to land, if accompanied by an intention to inflict more than merely nominal damage, was held to be a criminal conspiracy. Of course, it was virtually impossible to justify making it a crime to agree to do something that if actually done by one person acting alone would not have been criminal. Accordingly, the Criminal Law Act 1977 sought to limit conspiracy primarily to agreements to commit crimes. However, fearing that gaps might be created, and pending a comprehensive review of the law of fraud, obscenity and indecency, section 5 preserved certain common law conspiracies. We are thus left with the following rather unsatisfactory situation:

(1) There are agreements to commit a crime. These are termed statutory conspiracies and are governed by the provisions of section 1 of the Criminal Law Act 1977;

(2) There are common law conspiracies governed by the old common law rules. Under section 5 of the Criminal Law Act 1977, two species of common law conspiracy have been preserved. These are conspiracy to defraud and conspiracy to corrupt public morals or outrage public decency. Commentators have been saying since 1977 that these retentions were designed to be temporary. Indeed, the Law Commission has now proposed (25 years after the 1977 Act) the abolition of the crime of conspiracy to defraud.[3] Until that proposal is implemented, this common law conspiracy continues to exist and be utilised.

### 2. Common law conspiracies

#### (i) *Conspiracy to defraud*

Section 5(2) of the Criminal Law Act 1977 provides that common law rules continue to apply "so far as relates to conspiracy to defraud".Two issues need to be addressed: the relationship between this common law conspiracy and statutory conspiracy and the width of this offence.[4]

[1] *Malcahy* (1868) L.R. 3 H.L. 306.
[2] [1974] A.C. 104.
[3] Law Commission No. 276, *Fraud* (2002).
[4] For further details of conspiracy to defraud, see Smith (A. T. H.), *Property Offences* (1994), Chap. 19.

(a) **Relationship to statutory conspiracy.** Common law conspiracies to defraud will usually involve agreements to commit crimes. At one stage the House of Lords took the view that any conspiracy which involved an agreement to commit a crime had to be dealt with under the Criminal Law Act 1977 rather than the common law.[5] This caused the prosecution considerable difficulties with both indictments and convictions for common law conspiracy being quashed when belatedly it was realised that the agreement was to commit an offence. The position now is that defendants may be charged with either offence in such cases.[6]

(b) **Width of the offence.** In *Scott v Metropolitan Police Commr.*, the leading case on conspiracy to defraud, the House of Lords stated: "[I]t is clearly the law that an agreement by two or more by dishonesty to deprive a person of something which is his or to which he is or would be or might be entitled and an agreement by two or more by dishonesty to injure some proprietary right of his, suffices to constitute the offence of conspiracy to defraud."[7]

The following points need to be made in relation to this definition:

As indicated above, it embraces agreements to do an act which would not be an offence if completed. The Law Commission has provided an extensive list of conduct that can be prosecuted only as conspiracy to defraud.[8] Some examples are: (i) deception which obtains a benefit which does not amount to property, services or any of the other benefits defined in the Theft Acts, for example, obtaining confidential information; (ii) deception which does not obtain a gain, or cause a loss, but which prejudices another's financial interests; (iii) deception for a non-financial purpose; (iv) deception to gain a temporary benefit; (v) making a secret gain or causing a loss by abusing a position of trust or fiduciary duty; (vi) obtaining services by giving false information to a machine; (vii) "fixing" an event on which bets have been placed.

No element of deception is required in order for the offence to be committed. In *Scott*, for example, the defendant agreed with employees of cinema owners temporarily to remove films so that he could make pirate copies which could be distributed commercially. There was no deception played on the owners who were unaware of what was happening. The House of Lords rejected the idea that deception was a necessary ingredient of the offence. There must, of course, be dishonesty. However, the offence is so broad that many activities that would otherwise be legitimate can become fraudulent if the conduct is regarded as dishonest. As the Law Commission point out: "In a capitalist society, commercial life revolves around the pursuit of gain for oneself and, as a corollary, others may lose out, whether directly or indirectly. Such behaviour is perfectly legitimate. It is only the element of 'dishonesty' which renders it a criminal fraud."[9]

There is no requirement that actual economic loss be involved as long as the victim's economic interests are put at risk.[10] "If the interests of some other

[5] *Ayres* [1984] A.C. 447.
[6] Criminal Justice Act 1987, s.12. Guidelines on when to charge conspiracy to defraud are contained within the *Code for Crown Prosecutors*.
[7] [1975] A.C. 819 at 840.
[8] Law Commission No. 276, *Fraud* (2002), paras 4.5–4.59.
[9] *ibid.*, para. 3.6
[10] *Allsop* (1976) 64 Cr.App.R.29.

person—the economic or proprietary interests of some other person are imperilled, that is sufficient to constitute fraud even though no loss is actually suffered and even though the fraudsman himself did not desire to bring about any loss."[11]

Theoretically, at least, the agreed offence needs to be one that will be committed by the parties to the agreement,[12] yet in practice it appears to be irrelevant that third parties will effect the defrauding.[13]

It now seems settled that there need be no intent to defraud in the sense of intending to cause another economic loss. The Privy Council has held that it is sufficient if the conspirators have dishonestly agreed to do something "which they realise will or may deceive the victim into so acting, or failing to act, that he will suffer economic loss or his economic interests will be put at risk".[14] The defendants may not wish to harm the victim (they may even think they are acting with the best of motives)[15] but if they intend to bring about the state of affairs realising that the victim's interests could be put at risk, they will be guilty.

Finally, conspiracy to defraud is not limited to situations where economic loss is involved or risked. It is also a conspiracy to defraud to agree dishonestly to deceive a public official into acting contrary to his public duties.[16]

The Law Commission has concluded that the common law offence of conspiracy to defraud is "so wide that it offers little guidance on the difference between fraudulent and lawful conduct"[17] and that it should be abolished and replaced by two new statutory offences—one of fraud, and one of obtaining services dishonestly.[18] Of course, there could be liability for a conspiracy to commit one of these new offences, but they would become statutory conspiracies.

### (ii) *Conspiracy to corrupt public morals or outrage public decency*

Section 5(3) of the Criminal Law Act 1977 provides that the common law rules continue to apply to conspiracies to corrupt public morals or outrage public decency provided that the object of the agreement does not amount to a crime. At the time it was unclear whether outraging public decency and corrupting public morals were criminal offences in their own right although the Law Commission was of the view that they probably were.[19] The issue must now be regarded as settled in relation to outraging public decency. In *Gibson*[20] the defendant exhibited earrings made from freeze-dried human foetuses of three or four months gestation. His conviction for the offence of outraging public decency was upheld. In *Rowley*[21]

---

[11] *Wai Yu-Tsang* [1992] 1 A.C. 269 (trial judge's direction approved on appeal by the Privy Council). See also *Adams* [1995] 2 Cr.App.R.295.

[12] The rule contained in s.1(1)(a) is meant to be a restatement of the common law.

[13] *Hollinshead* [1985] A.C. 975.

[14] *Wai Yu-Tsang* [1992] 1 A.C. 269 at 280.

[15] As in the case of *Wai Yu-Tsang* where one of the conspirators thought he was acting in the defrauded bank's best interests by trying to prevent a run on it.

[16] *Wai Yu-Tsang* (*ibid.*); *Moses and Ansbro* [1991] Crim.L.R.617; *D.P.P. v Withers* [1975] A.C. 842; *Board of Trade v Owen* [1957] A.C. 602; *Welham v D.P.P.* [1961] A.C. 103.

[17] Law Commission No. 276, *Fraud* (2002), para. 1.6.

[18] These proposals are discussed in Ch. 9.

[19] Law Com. No. 76 (1976), paras 3.21–3.24.

[20] (1990) 91 Cr.App.R.341, following the decision of *Knuller v D.P.P.* [1973] A.C. 435.

[21] (1992) 94 Cr.App.R.95.

the defendant left notes in public places inviting boys to meet him and offering money for unexplained (though alleged to be immoral) purposes. His conviction for the offence of outraging public decency (and attempted incitement of a child under the age of 14 to commit an act of gross indecency) was quashed on the basis that the offence had not been made out, but no doubts were expressed about the existence of the offence. Given these developments it is submitted that charges of conspiracy to outrage public decency should be brought under the Criminal Law Act 1977 as statutory conspiracies.

The position is still unclear with regard to conspiracy to corrupt public morals. The House of Lords decision of *Shaw v D.P.P.*, in which the defendant agreed to (and did) publish a "Ladies' Directory" advertising information about named prostitutes, affirmed the existence of the offence of conspiracy to corrupt public morals.[22] It did not resolve the issue of whether there is a substantive offence of corrupting public morals.[23]

Where does this leave us? Where the agreement involves a criminal offence (for example, under the Obscene Publications Act 1959) statutory conspiracy should be charged rather than conspiracy to corrupt public morals. There may well be gaps, however, where no criminal offence is involved and conspiracy to corrupt public morals currently occupies this space. This could be supported provided its use was confined to circumstances which "the jury might find to be destructive to the very fabric of society"[24] rather than being used for conduct which, by current standards of ordinary decent people, is mildly offensive. On the other hand, it is extremely difficult to justify the criminalisation of an agreement to do something which, if actually done, would not be criminal.

## 3. Statutory conspiracy

(i) *Definition*

### Criminal Law Act 1977, section 1[25]:

"(1) Subject to the following provisions of this Part of this Act, if a person agrees with any other person or persons that a course of conduct shall be pursued which, if the agreement is carried out in accordance with their intentions, either—
  (a)  will necessarily amount to or involve the commission of any offence or offences by one or more of the parties to the agreement, or
  (b)  would do so but for the existence of facts which render the commission of the offence or any of the offences impossible,
he is guilty of conspiracy to commit the offence or offences in question.

(2) Where liability for any offence may be incurred without knowledge on the part of the person committing it of any particular fact or circumstance necessary for the commission of the offence, a person shall nevertheless not be guilty of conspiracy to commit that offence by virtue of subsection (1) above unless he and at least one other party to the agreement intend

---

[22] [1962] A.C. 220. *Shaw* is an important decision for a further reason. Lord Simmonds, in particular, seemed to be of the view that the judiciary had a residual power to create new criminal offences to deal with new situations. This view was firmly rejected in the subsequent decision of *Knuller (above*, n.20).

[23] Although this was the view of the Court of Criminal Appeal, the House of Lords did not decide this point. The case of *Gibson (above*, n.20) lends some support to the view that there is an offence of corrupting public morals.

[24] *Per* Lord Simon in *Knuller* at 491.

[25] As amended by the Criminal Attempts Act 1981.

or know that that fact or circumstances shall or will exist at the time when the conduct constituting the offence is to take place."

## (ii) *Agreement*

There must be an agreement between at least two persons. There must have been a meeting of minds; decisions must have been communicated between the parties.[26]

There must, of course, be at least two parties to the agreement. However, section 2(2)(a) provides that a husband and wife cannot be liable for conspiracy, if they are the only parties to the agreement[27];[27] this is a policy provision aimed at exempting marital confidences from the ambit of the criminal law. The Act also provides that a person cannot be liable for conspiracy if the only other party to the "agreement" is a person under the age of criminal responsibility (section 2(2)(b)) or is the intended victim of the offence (section 2(2)(c)). It would thus appear that there *can* be liability if the defendant conspired with any other person having a defence (say insanity) other than the above, provided that such person was capable of reaching an *agreement* with the defendant.[28] Where a defendant and others are charged with conspiracy and those others are acquitted, section 5(8) provides that the defendant may nevertheless be convicted "unless under all the circumstances of the case his conviction is inconsistent with the acquittal of the other person or persons in question".[29] This is sensible. There may be evidence admissible against the defendant that he conspired with A and B, but that evidence might not be admissible against A or B. Alternatively, it might be clear that he conspired with either A or B, but it is not certain which one it was. A and B must be given the benefit of the doubt and acquitted, but there is no reason why the defendant, whose guilt is beyond doubt, should be offered the same indulgence.[30]

## (iii) *Object of agreement*

There must be an agreement that:

(a) a course of conduct be pursued
(b) which if carried out in accordance with their intentions
(c) will necessarily amount to (or involve) a crime.

**(a) Course of conduct be pursued:** The phrase "course of conduct" here does not refer purely to physical actions, but must be taken to include intended consequences—in short, the plan. This point is best illustrated with an example. Suppose two persons agree to place a bomb under another's car and detonate the bomb so as to kill the owner. The physical course of conduct agreed to, namely, the physical actions of planting the bomb, will not necessarily amount to the crime because the bomb may never go off. But if the *plan* is carried out according to their

---

[26] *Scott* (1979) 68 Cr.App.R.164. See, generally, Orchard, "Agreement in Criminal Conspiracy" [1974] Crim.L.R.297 at 335.

[27] This confirms the common law decision of *Mawji* [1957] A.C. 126. See *Chrastny (No. 1)* [1992] 1 All E.R. 189.

[28] This confirms the common law decision of *Duguid* (1906) 75 L.J. K.B. 470.

[29] This was already the position at common law in relation to separate trials (*D.P.P. v Shannon* [1975] A.C. 717), but reverses the common law position in relation to joint trials (*Thompson* (1851) 16 Q.B. 832; *Coughlan* (1977) 64 Cr.App.R.11).

[30] See *Longman and Cribben* (1980) 72 Cr.App.R.121; *Roberts* [1985] Crim.L.R.218. But see *Ashton* [1992] Crim.L.R.667 and commentary thereto.

intentions, the bomb will explode and the owner of the car will be killed. This necessarily amounts to a crime; killing someone in such circumstances is murder.

To say that the agreed course of conduct includes the planned consequences is also a limiting qualification. Only planned consequences can be included within the agreed course of conduct. Thus, as stated in *Siracusa*,[31] an agreement to cause grievous bodily harm is not sufficient to support a charge of conspiracy to murder even though it is sufficient to support a charge of murder itself. The planned course of conduct only extends as far as causing grievous bodily harm. In *Siracusa* it was held that although a person smuggling heroin could be convicted of a substantive offence if he thought he was smuggling cannabis, the same was not true on a conspiracy charge: "the essence of the crime of conspiracy was the agreement and, in simple terms, one did not prove an agreement to import heroin by proving an agreement to import cannabis."[32] The basis of this decision is that heroin and cannabis are different class drugs, involving separate offences. In *Broad*[33] it was held to be immaterial that one conspirator thought heroin was to be produced while the other thought it would be cocaine. Both are Class A drugs; they had agreed to commit the same offence. It is further submitted that planned consequences mean intended consequences. If arson is planned between conspirators who are reckless as to whether anyone is killed during their fire, the death of those persons is not part of their plan. One does not plan for and intend an event possibly happening. Intention here, of course, should bear the same meaning as in other areas of law—bearing in mind that such intention may be inferred or established from foresight of a consequence as virtually certain.

The planned course of conduct also includes (and only includes) *intended or known* surrounding circumstances.[34] Although section 1(2) uses the term "intend or know", it is submitted that "know" here must be interpreted to mean "believe". If parties conspire to handle stolen goods, they can never *know* those goods are stolen—but it should suffice that they *believe* that they are stolen.

**(b) If carried out in accordance with their intentions:** What is the position if the parties' intentions are equivocal? For example, they might agree to burgle a house if a window has been left open. The better view here is that the "plan" is a plan to burgle a house (albeit subject to a condition) and if that plan is carried out it will necessarily amount to a crime.

### R. v Reed [1982] Crim.L.R.819 (Court of Appeal, Criminal Division)

"In the first [example], A and B agree to drive from London to Edinburgh in a time which can be achieved without exceeding the speed limits, but only if the traffic which they encounter is exceptionally light. Their agreement will not necessarily involve the commission of any offence, even if it is carried out in accordance with their intentions, and they do arrive from London to Edinburgh within the agreed time. Accordingly the agreement does not constitute the offence of statutory conspiracy or indeed of any offence.

---

[31] (1989) 90 Cr.App.R.340.

[32] This was confirmed in *Taylor* [2002] Crim.L.R.205.

[33] [1997] Crim.L.R.666.

[34] Section 1(2). On its actual wording section 1(2) appears to be limited to crimes of strict liability. It must, however, *a fortiori* apply to crimes of full *mens rea*. It would be truly paradoxical if greater *mens rea* were required for conspiracies to commit crimes of strict liability than for other conspiracies.

In the second example, A and B agree to rob a bank, if when they arrive at the bank it seems safe to do so. Their agreement will necessarily involve the commission of the offence of robbery if it is carried out in accordance with their intentions. Accordingly, they are guilty of the statutory offence of conspiracy."

## R. v Jackson [1985] Crim.L.R.442 (Court of Appeal, Criminal Division)

The appellants agreed to shoot their friend, W, in the leg if he was convicted of a burglary for which he was being tried. They thought this would provide mitigation. W was shot and permanently disabled. The appellants appealed against their conviction for conspiracy to pervert the course of justice on the ground that their agreement did not necessarily involve the commission of a crime, as everything depended on a contingency (W's conviction for burglary) which might not have taken place.

*Held*, "[P]lanning was taking place for a contingency and if that contingency occurred the conspiracy would necessarily involve the commission of an offence. 'Necessarily' is not to be held to mean that there must inevitably be the carrying out of an offence. It means, if the agreement is carried out in accordance with the plan, there must be the commission of the offence referred to in the conspiracy count."

**Appeal dismissed**

In *Hadhmaill*[35] the defendant, a member of the I.R.A., agreed to a bombing campaign if the cease-fire in Northern Ireland ended. This was held to be sufficient intention for the crime of conspiracy.

The approach adopted in all these cases is defensible. Virtually all agreements are conditional. It is implicit in most agreements to commit a crime that the actions will only be carried out if there is not the metaphoric "policeman at one's elbow" at the scene of the crime.

The plan must be carried out "in accordance with their intentions". What does this mean? What is the position of a person who agrees to the commission of a crime and agrees to supply tools for the crime but who thereafter has no interest in what happens and indeed thinks the planned crime is over-ambitious and will never be committed? Or, what is the position of a plain-clothes police officer who, with a view to entrapping the others, "agrees" to a plan to commit a crime, but actually intends to prevent the crime at the last moment? In short, must each conspirator intend that the crime actually be carried out?

## R. v Anderson [1986] A.C. 27 (House of Lords)

The defendant agreed for a fee to supply diamond wire to cut through bars in order to enable another person, Andaloussi, to escape from prison. He claimed that he only intended to supply the wire and then go abroad. He believed the plan could never succeed. He

---

[35] [1996] Crim.L.R.509.

appealed against his conviction for conspiring with others to effect the release of one of them from prison claiming that as he did not intend or expect the plan to be carried out, he lacked the necessary *mens rea* for the offence of conspiracy.

Lord Bridge:
"[I]t is not necessary that more than one of the participants in the agreed course of conduct shall commit a substantive offence. It is, of course, necessary that any party to the agreement shall have assented to play his part in the agreed course of conduct, however innocent in itself, knowing that the part to be played by one or more of the others will amount to or involve the commission of an offence.

... The heart of the submission for the appellant is that in order to be convicted of conspiracy to commit a given offence ... the party charged should not only have agreed that a course of conduct shall be pursued which will necessarily amount to or involve the commission of that offence by himself or one or more other parties to the agreement, but must also be proved himself to have intended that that offence should be committed. Thus, it is submitted here that the appellant's case that he never intended that Andaloussi should be enabled to escape from prison raised an issue to be left to the jury, who should have been directed to convict him only if satisfied that he did so intend. ...

I am clearly driven by consideration of the diversity of roles which parties may agree to play in criminal conspiracies to reject any construction of the statutory language which would require the prosecution to prove an intention on the part of each conspirator that the criminal offence or offences which will necessarily be committed by one or more of the conspirators if the agreed course of conduct is fully carried out should in fact be committed.

... In these days of highly organised crime the most serious statutory conspiracies will frequently involve an elaborate and complex agreed course of conduct in which many will consent to play necessary but subordinate roles, not involving them in any direct participation in the commission of the offence or offences at the centre of the conspiracy. Parliament cannot have intended that such parties should escape conviction of conspiracy on the basis that it cannot be proved against them that they intended that the relevant offence or offences should be committed.

There remains the important question whether a person who has agreed that a course of conduct will be pursued which, if pursued as agreed, will necessarily amount to or involve the commission of an offence is guilty of statutory conspiracy irrespective of his intention, and, if not, what is the *mens rea* of the offence. I have no hesitation in answering the first part of the question in the negative. There may be many situations in which perfectly respectable citizens, more particularly those concerned with law enforcement, may enter into agreements that a course of conduct shall be pursued which will involve commission of a crime without the least intention of playing any part in furtherance of the ostensibly agreed criminal objective, but rather with the purpose of exposing and frustrating the criminal purpose of the other parties to the agreement. To say this is in no way to encourage schemes by which police act, directly or through the agency of informers, as agents provocateurs for the purpose of entrapment. That is conduct of which the courts have always strongly disapproved. But it may sometimes happen, as most of us with experience in criminal trials well know, that a criminal enterprise is well advanced in the course of preparation when it comes to the notice either of the police or of some honest citizen in such circumstances that the only prospect of exposing and frustrating the criminals is that some innocent person should play the part of an intending collaborator in the course of criminal conduct proposed to be pursued. The *mens rea* implicit in the offence of statutory conspiracy must clearly be such as to recognise the innocence of such a person, notwithstanding that he will, in literal terms, be obliged to agree that a course of conduct be pursued involving the commission of an offence. ...

... [B]eyond the mere fact of agreement, the necessary *mens rea* of the crime is, in my opinion, established if, and only if, it is shown that the accused, when he entered into the agreement, intended to play some part in the agreed course of conduct in furtherance of the criminal purpose which the agreed course of conduct was intended to achieve. Nothing less will suffice; nothing more is required.

Applying this test to the facts which, for the purposes of the appeal, we must assume, the appellant, in agreeing that a course of conduct be pursued that would, if successsful, necessarily involve the offence of effecting Andaloussi's escape from lawful custody, clearly intended, by providing diamond wire to be smuggled into the prison, to play a part in the agreed course of conduct in furtherance of that criminal objective. Neither the fact that he intended to play no further part in attempting to effect the escape, nor that he believed the escape to be impossible, would, if the jury had supposed they might be true, have afforded him any defence."

**Appeal dismissed**

One of the major reservations underlying all the inchoate offences is that no harm (first order) has been caused. How do we justify the invocation of the criminal law? We saw that (apart from arguments of there being a second order harm) the main case for criminalisation was on grounds of blameworthiness. With attempted crime the absence of harm is compensated by a requirement that the defendant intend the complete offence; the highest degree of blame is required. An examination of section 1 of the Criminal Law Act 1977 should lead one to a similar conclusion in relation to conspiracy. One would have thought that no one could be convicted of an offence if he did not intend the consequences comprising the offence. *Anderson* refutes this view with the result that a defendant can be guilty of a serious criminal offence when there has been no conduct beyond a bare agreement and where the defendant never intended that the offence be carried out.

Subsequent decisions have appeared to share this concern and have not all followed *Anderson*. In *McPhillips*[36] a defendant was acquitted of conspiracy to murder because he intended to give a warning before a bomb was exploded. It was held that he could only be liable if he had intended that the plan be carried out. *Anderson* was distinguished on the fairly unconvincing ground that in that case there had been no intention of frustrating the plan. In *Edwards*[37] the Court of Appeal stated that the trial judge had been right to direct the jury that the defendant could only be guilty of conspiring to supply amphetamine if he had intended to supply amphetamine. *Anderson* was again distinguished in the following Privy Council decision.

### Yip Chiu-Cheung v The Queen [1995] 1 A.C. 111 (Privy Council)

The defendant was convicted of conspiracy to traffic in heroin contrary to common law and the Hong Kong Dangerous Drugs Ordinance. He appealed on the basis that his co-conspirator, Needham, (who had not been prosecuted) was an under-cover drugs enforcement agent who had had no intention that the crime would be committed.

Lord Griffiths:
"[I]t was submitted that the trial judge and the Court of Appeal were wrong to hold that Needham, the undercover agent, could be a conspirator because he lacked the necessary *mens rea* or guilty mind required for the offence of conspiracy. It was urged upon their

[36] (1990) 6 BNIL (Northern Ireland).
[37] [1991] Crim.L.R.45.

Lordships that no moral guilt attached to the undercover agent who was at all times acting courageously and with the best of motives in attempting to infiltrate and bring to justice a gang of criminal drug dealers. In these circumstances it was argued that it would be wrong to treat the agent as having any criminal intent, and reliance was placed upon a passage in the speech of Lord Bridge of Harwich [in *Anderson* above]; but in that case Lord Bridge was dealing with a different situation from that which exists in the present case. There may be many cases in which undercover police officers or other law enforcement agents pretend to join a conspiracy in order to gain information about the plans of the criminals, with no intention of taking any part in the planned crime but rather with the intention of providing information that will frustrate it. It was to this situation that Lord Bridge was referring in *R. v Anderson*. The crime of conspiracy requires an agreement between two persons to commit an unlawful act with the intention of carrying it out. It is the intention to carry out the crime that constitutes the necessary *mens rea* for the offence. As Lord Bridge pointed out, the undercover agent who has no intention of committing the crime lacks the necessary *mens rea* to be a conspirator.

The facts of the present case are quite different. ... Needham intended to commit that offence by carrying the heroin through the customs and on to the aeroplane bound for Australia. ... Naturally, Needham never expected to be prosecuted if he carried out the plan as intended. But the fact that in such circumstances the authorities would not prosecute the undercover agent does not mean that he did not commit the crime albeit as part of a wider scheme to combat drug dealing."

**Appeal dismissed**

This decision is, of course, of persuasive authority only and, strictly, applies only to the common law offence of conspiracy. However, it restates the right principle and is the approach that should be adopted. What the defendant in *Anderson* should have been charged with was aiding and abetting the conspiracy; he was not a conspirator himself.[38]

On the facts of *Anderson* there were two or more other conspirators who did intend the offence to be committed, and, although the House of Lords does not seem to have regarded this as significant, it is submitted that this is crucial for a conviction under section 1. If this were not so, one could have a situation where there was a "conspiracy which no one intends to carry out [which would be] an absurdity, if not an impossibility".[39] The better solution is that advocated by the Draft Criminal Code (below) that it is necessary for the accused and at least one other party to the agreement to intend that the offence be committed.

In addition to these difficulties, *Anderson* creates a further problem. Lord Bridge refers to the requirement that each conspirator must have "assented to play his part in the agreed course of conduct". It has never been part of the crime of conspiracy that all conspirators need to agree to play an active role. "This novel addition to the common law may place the godfathers of criminal conspiracies even further beyond the reach of the criminal justice system."[40]

**(c) Necessarily amount to (or involve) a crime:** We have already examined the meaning of "necessarily". It does not matter whether the actual conduct will in fact amount to a crime. What matters is whether the plan, if successfully carried out,

---

[38] One can aid and abet any offence, common law or statutory, unless expressly excluded by statute (*Jefferson*[1994] 1 All E.R. 270).

[39] Smith and Hogan, *Criminal Law*(10th ed., 2002), p. 299.

[40] Fitzpatrick, "Variations on Conspiracy" (1993) 143 N.L.J. 1180. See also *Siracusa* (1989) 90 Cr.App.R.340, where the Court of Appeal tried (unsuccessfully) to repair the damage.

will do so. It therefore follows that it is irrelevant whether the crime is even possible. As shall be seen, this is confirmed by section 1(1)(b) of the Criminal Law Act 1977.

What is meant by "amount to or involve the commission of any offence or offences by one or more of the parties to the agreement?" In *Hollinshead*[41] the Court of Appeal held that this meant that one of the parties had to intend to commit the offence as a principal offender. This means that there cannot be a conspiracy to aid and abet an offence.[42]

### Draft Criminal Code Bill 1989 (Law Com. No. 177), clause 48:

"(1) A person is guilty of conspiracy to commit an offence or offences if—
(a) he agrees with another or others that an act or acts shall be done which, if done, will involve the commission of the offence or offences by one or more of the parties to the agreement; and
(b) he and at least one other party to the agreement intend that the offence or offences shall be committed.
(2) For the purpose of subsection (1) an intention that an offence shall be committed is an intention with respect to all the elements of the offence (other than fault elements), except that recklessness with respect to a circumstance suffices where it suffices for the offence itself."

### (iv) *Impossibility*

At common law the House of Lords in *Nock*[43] followed *Haughton v Smith*[44] and held there could be no liability for a conspiracy to commit the impossible. This decision has now been reversed by the amendment to section 1(1) which clearly states that there can be liability even though there exist facts which render the commission of the offence impossible. Thus if two defendants agree to kill X, but unknown to them X is already dead, they can nevertheless still be liable for criminal conspiracy. This provision is, however, limited to statutory conspiracies. The result is somewhat anomalous: there can be liability for a statutory conspiracy to commit the impossible, but no liability for similar common law conspiracies. In relation to statutory conspiracies, the question must be asked again: when defendants have done no more than *agree* to commit a crime, and when it is quite impossible in any event for that crime to be committed, are we justified in imposing criminal liability?

### (v) *Repentance*

If a conspirator repents and withdraws immediately after the agreement has been reached, it would appear that he is still guilty of conspiracy.[45] In the light of the material on repentance in the law of attempt,[46] should not a defendant who never gets further than agreeing to commit a crime, and who never does anything in pursuance of that agreement—indeed, who positively disassociates himself from

---

[41] [1985] 1 All E.R. 850.
[42] The House of Lords in *Hollinshead* left this point open. See Smith and Hogan, *Criminal Law* (10th ed., 2002), p. 306 for an argument that the House of Lords did effectively hold that there can be no agreement to aid and abet an offence.
[43] [1978] A.C. 979.
[44] [1975] A.C. 476.
[45] Wasik, *above*, p. 492 at 788; *Barnard* (1979) 70 Cr.App.R.28.
[46] *Above*, pp. 491–492.

it—be entitled to a defence? Given the decreasing weight attached to the "dangerousness of collaboration" argument, it seems unlikely that this would justify liability in such cases.

### (vi) *Jurisdiction*

One of the justifications offered in support of conspiracy is that it is necessary to fight organised crime and, increasingly, organised crime involves trading in drugs. It is, therefore, likely that such conspiracies (and, with growing mobility, others as well) will contain an international element. More recently, there has been significant concern over international conspiracies to commit terrorist acts.

The position now is clear. If the agreement is made in this country to commit a crime in this country (such as the importation of controlled substances) then no problems of jurisdiction arise. If the agreement is made abroad the conspiracy is indictable in this country even though no overt act takes place here before the defendants are caught.[47]

The reverse situation, where there is an agreement in this country to commit a crime abroad, is dealt with by section 1A of the Criminal Law Act 1977.[48] English courts will have jurisdiction over any conspiracy to commit a crime abroad. The agreed acts must be a crime in the country where they are to take place and must constitute an offence under English law were they to be committed here. This provision, aimed at terrorist organisations in England planning crimes abroad, is of wide effect and covers agreements to commit any crime abroad, no matter how trivial it might be.

### IV. INCITEMENT

#### A. *Introduction*

The crime of incitement[49] is a common law inchoate offence[50] whereby the defendant persuades or encourages another to commit a crime.[51] When tried on indictment[52] it is an offence punishable with a fine and imprisonment at the discretion of the court; a greater penalty could thus be imposed for incitement than for the actual commission of the substantive offence.

---

[47] It was formerly the case that some such overt act needed to be proved: *D.P.P. v Doot* [1973] A.C. 807. However, both the Privy Council in *Liangsiriprasert v US Government* (1991) 92 Cr.App.R.77 and the Court of Appeal in *Sanson* [1991] Crim.L.R.126 have rejected this.

[48] Inserted by the Criminal Justice (Terrorism and Conspiracy) Act 1998, s.5(1).

[49] Sometimes known as "solicitation," particularly in the United States.

[50] Statute sometimes prohibits certain specific incitements—for example, incitement to racial hatred contrary to section 18(1) of the Public Order Act 1986. These are generally not true inchoate offences in the sense of being steps on the way to the commission of a crime: there is no substantive crime of "racial hatred". See also incitement to sedition contrary to section 3 of the Aliens Restriction (Amendment) Act 1919; Incitement to Disaffection Act 1934, ss.1, 2; causing disaffection (inciting disaffection amongst members of the police force) contrary to section 53 of the Police Act 1964.

[51] Jurisdiction extends to inciting another person in this country to commit certain sexual offences abroad as long as the act is an offence in the country in which it is committed (Sexual Offences (Conspiracy and Incitement) Act 1996).

[52] An incitement to commit a summary offence is only triable summarily (Magistrates' Courts Act 1980, s.45(1)) and the defendant cannot be punished to a greater extent than he would have been liable to on summary conviction of the complete offence (Magistrates' Courts Act 1980, s.45(3)).

## B. *Rationale and Punishment of Incitement*

### Wayne R. LaFave and Austin W. Scott, Criminal Law (2nd ed., 1986), pp. 488–489:

"One view is that a mere solicitation to commit a crime, not accompanied by agreement or action by the person solicited, presents no significant social danger. It is argued, for example, that solicitation is not dangerous because the resisting will of an independent agent is interposed between the solicitor and commission of the crime which is his object. Similarly, it is claimed that the solicitor does not constitute a menace in view of the fact that he has manifested an unwillingness to carry out the criminal scheme himself. There is not the dangerous proximity to success which exists when the crime is actually attempted, for, 'despite the earnestness of the solicitation, the actor is merely engaging in talk which may never be taken seriously'. (1 National Commission of Reform of Federal Criminal Laws, Working Papers 370 (1970)).

On the other hand, it is argued 'that a solicitation is, if anything, more dangerous than a direct attempt, because it may give rise to that cooperation among criminals which is a special hazard. Solicitation may, indeed, be thought of as an attempt to conspire. Moreover, the solicitor, working his will through one or more agents, manifests an approach to crime more intelligent and masterful than the effort of his hireling.' (Wechsler, Jones and Korn, . . . 61 Colum.L.Rev. 571 (1961)). It is noted, for example, that the imposition of liability for criminal solicitation has proved to be an important means by which the leadership of criminal movements may be suppressed.

Without regard to whether it is correct to say that solicitations are more dangerous than attempts, it is fair to conclude that the purposes of the criminal law are well served by inclusion of the crime of solicitation within the substantive criminal law. Providing punishment for solicitation aids in the prevention of the harm which would result should the inducements prove successful, and also aids in protecting the public from being exposed to inducements to commit or join in the commission of crimes. As is true of the law of attempts, the crime of solicitation (a) provides a basis for timely law enforcement intervention to prevent the intended crime, (b) permits the criminal justice process to deal with individuals who have indicated their dangerousness, and (c) avoids inequality of treatment based upon a fortuity (here, withholding of the desired response by the person solicited) beyond the control of the actor.

Objections to making solicitation a crime . . . are sometimes based upon the fear that false charges may readily be brought either out of a misunderstanding as to what the defendant said or for purposes of harassment. This risk is inherent in the punishment of almost all inchoate crimes, although it is perhaps somewhat greater as to the crime of solicitation in that the crime may be committed merely by speaking."

Consider again our earlier discussion of the rationale and punishment of attempts and conspiracies.[53] Bearing in mind that if the person incited agrees to commit the crime there will be a criminal conspiracy and so incitement amounts to no more than an attempted conspiracy (an offence abolished by section 1(4) of the Criminal Attempts Act 1981), can one really justify the existence of the offence of incitement? Such persons clearly have indicated some degree of dangerousness and it is obviously desirable to deter people from encouraging others to commit crime, but, unlike attempt, inciters are far removed from the complete crime; their actions are not *manifestly* dangerous; they constitute no "second order" harm; and, unlike conspiracy, there is no "dangerousness of combination" argument that can justify the existence of the offence. In short, given the reasons why the law does not punish

[53] *Above,* pp. 464–474; 505–509.

guilty intentions alone but insists upon a manifestation of those intentions, is not the crime of incitement pushing back the threshold of criminal liability too far? And even if the crime could be justified, surely for the same reasons, it could *never* be justifiable to impose the same sentence (let alone a greater one) as for the completed crime.


### C. The Law


In *D.P.P. v Armstrong*[54] it was stated that the following was an accurate definition of incitement.


### Draft Criminal Code Bill 1989 (Law Com. No. 177), clause 47:

"A person is guilty of incitement to commit an offence or offences if—
  (a) he incites another to do or cause to be done an act or acts which, if done, will involve the commission of the offence or offences by the other; and
  (b) he intends or believes that the other, if he acts as incited, shall or will do so with the fault required for the offence or offences."


### 1. Actus reus

The *actus reus* of the crime of incitement is the act of persuading, encouraging or commanding another to commit a crime. In *Fitzmaurice*[55] it was held that the necessary "element of persuasion" was satisfied by a "suggestion, proposal or request [that] was accompanied by an implied promise of reward". The initiative need not come from the inciter. In *Goldman*[56] the defendant responded to an advertisement and ordered videotapes of young girls. It was held that this could be an incitement because the videos would not be sent except in response to an order. The fact that the initiative had come from the incitee advertising its wares "was nothing to the point".

In *R.R.B. v Applin*[57] Lord Denning stated that: "a person may 'incite' another to do an act by threatening or by pressure, as well as by persuasion." The incitement can take any form (words or deeds). It may be addressed to a particular person or group of persons or to the public at large. In *Marlow*[58] it was held that publishing a book on the cultivation and production of cannabis amounted to incitement to commit an offence, contrary to section 19 of the Misuse of Drugs Act 1971.[59] The solicitation must be communicated to the person being incited, but if the communication fails (*e.g.* letter failing to reach incitee) there can be liability for attempted incitement.[60]

[54] [2000] Crim.L.R.379.
[55] [1983] 1 All E.R. 189, 192.
[56] [2001] Crim.L.R.822.
[57] [1973] 1 Q.B. 815, 825; *Evans* [1986] Crim.L.R.470.
[58] [1997] Crim.L.R.897.
[59] See also *Most* (1881) 7 Q.B.D. 244. and *Invicta Plastics v Clare* [1976] R.T.R. 251.
[60] *Chelmsford Justices, ex p. Amos* [1973] Crim.L.R.437.

If the person incited agrees to commit the crime, both are liable for conspiracy. If the incitee actually commits the crime, the inciter will be liable as an accessory to the complete offence.

## 2. Mens rea

The inciter must intend that as a result of his persuasion, the incitee will bring about the crime. The inciter must believe that the person incited will have the *mens rea* necessary for the offence. In *Armstrong*[61] the defendant encouraged a man who, unknown to him, was really a police officer, to supply him with pornography involving children. It was held that as long as the defendant believed the other would have *mens rea*, there could be liability for incitement. It was not necessary that there be "parity of *mens rea*" between the two. The fact that the police officer never had any intention of supplying the pornographic material was immaterial. If, however, the inciter knows that the incitee has no *mens rea* (assuming the complete crime requires *mens rea*) there can be no incitement; he is not inciting a crime.[62] If such an incitee actually committed the crime, the inciter could be liable as a principal offender acting through an innocent agent.[63]

## 3. Impossibility

In *McDonough*[64] it was held that there could be liability for an incitement to commit the impossible. This was approved *obiter* by the House of Lords in *Nock*.[65] However, doubt has been cast on the correctness of this proposition.

### R. v Fitzmaurice [1983] Q.B. 1083 (Court of Appeal, Criminal Division)

The appellant was asked by his father to find someone to rob a woman on her way to a bank by snatching wages from her. The appellant, believing the robbery was to take place, approached B, who was unemployed and in need of money, and encouraged him to take part in the proposed robbery. In fact the proposed robbery was a fiction invented by the father to enable him to collect reward money from the police for providing false information about a false robbery. The appellant was convicted of inciting B to commit robbery by robbing a woman near the bank. He appealed against the conviction, contending that at common law incitement to commit an offence could not be committed where it was impossible to commit the offence incited, and that, since the proposed robbery of the woman was fictitious, it was impossible to commit that robbery.

Neill J.:
"It is to be observed that the omission of the crime of incitement from the Criminal Attempts Act 1981 followed the recommendations of the Law Commission in their Report [Law Com. No. 102, 1980] ... The Law Commission explained the omission of incitement from the draft bill on the basis that in their view the House of Lords in *D.P.P. v Nock* was prepared to distinguish the law relating to incitement from that relating to attempts: see paras 4.2 to 4.4. ...

We have come to the conclusion that ... Lord Scarman's speech [in *Nock*] does not support the proposition that cases of incitement are to be treated quite differently at common law from cases of attempt or conspiracy. ... The explanation of *McDonough's*

---

[61] [2000] Crim.L.R.379.
[62] *Curr* [1968] 2 Q.B. 944. Cf. *Whitehouse* [1977] Q.B. 868 and *Pickford* [1995] 1 Cr.App.R.420.
[63] *Below*, p. 530.
[64] (1962) 47 Cr.App.R.37.
[65] [1978] A.C. 979.

case, as it seems to us, is that though there may have been no stolen goods or no goods at all which were available to be received at the time of the incitement, the offence of incitement to receive stolen goods could nevertheless be proved because it was not impossible that at the relevant time in the future the necessary goods would be there.

In our view, therefore, the right approach in a case of incitement is the same as that which was underlined by Lord Scarman in *D.P.P. v Nock* when he considered the offence of conspiracy. In every case it is necessary to analyse the evidence with care to decide the precise offence which the defendant is alleged to have incited . . .

In our view . . . [this is] the correct approach at common law to any inchoate offence. It is necessary in every case to decide on the evidence what was the course of conduct which was (as the case may be) incited or agreed or attempted. In some cases the evidence may establish that the persuasion by the inciter was in quite general terms whereas the subsequent agreement of the conspirators was directed to a specific crime and a specific target. In such cases where the committal of the specific offence is shown to be impossible it may be quite logical for the inciter to be convicted even though the alleged conspirators (if not caught by s.5 of the Criminal Attempts Act 1981) may be acquitted. On the other hand, if B and C agree to kill D, and A standing beside B and C, though not intending to take any active part whatever in the crime, encourages them to do so, we can see no satisfactory reason, if it turns out later that D was already dead, why A should be convicted of incitement to murder whereas B and C at common law would be entitled to an acquittal on a charge of conspiracy. The crucial question is to establish on the evidence the course of conduct which the alleged inciter was encouraging.

We return to the facts of the instant case. Counsel for the appellant submitted that the 'crime' which Bonham and the two Browns were being encouraged to commit was a mere charade. The appellant's father was not planning a real robbery at all and therefore the appellant could not be found guilty of inciting the three men to commit it. In our judgment, however, the answer to counsel's argument is to be found in the facts which the Crown proved against the appellant. As was made clear by counsel on behalf of the Crown, the case against the appellant was based on the steps he took to recruit Bonham. At that stage the appellant believed that there was to be a wage snatch and he was encouraging Bonham to take part in it. As counsel put it: 'The appellant thought he was recruiting for a robbery not for a charade.' It is to be remembered that the particulars of offence in the indictment included the words 'by robbing a woman at Bow.' By no stretch of the imagination was that an impossible offence to carry out and it was that offence which the appellant was inciting Bonham to commit.

For these reasons, therefore, we are satisfied that the appellant was rightly convicted. The appeal is dismissed."

**Appeal dismissed**

It is ironic (to put it mildly) that so soon after the Criminal Attempts Act 1981 declared that there could be liability for attempt or conspiracy to commit the impossible, this decision should hold that in some cases there would be no liability for incitement to commit the impossible. The irony is heightened by recalling that the reason incitement was not included in the Criminal Attempts Act 1981 was because it was assumed that *McDonough* (as approved in *Nock*) had already clearly established that there could be liability in such cases.

We are thus left in the absurd situation that there can be liability for attempting the impossible and for statutory conspiracies to commit the impossible—but there can be no liability in such situations[66] for common law conspiracies or incitement. Such diversity of approach is indefensible.

---

[66] As explained in *Nock* and *Fitzmaurice*, which only apply to "the most complete impossibility" (Williams, *Textbook of Criminal Law* (2nd ed., 1983), p. 440).

## V. ENDANGERMENT OFFENCES

### R. A. Duff, "Intentions Legal and Philosophical" (1989) 9 O.J.L.S. 76 at 86:

"What harms should the criminal law aim to prevent? Death, bodily injury and the loss of property may seem to be three obvious 'primary harms' (each primary harm will generate a range of 'secondary harms', which take their character as harms from their relation to a primary harm; if death is a primary harm, then being subjected to the threat, risk or fear of death is a secondary and derivative harm); ...

Though these harms are initially identified without reference to human actions as their causes, the criminal law, as a set of sanction-backed prohibitions, can help to prevent them by prohibiting and thus preventing actions which cause them. It can do this in various ways: by directly prohibiting actions which cause such harms ('killing', 'wounding and causing grievous bodily harm', 'damaging or destroying property' or 'depriving another of his property'); by prohibiting actions which are likely to cause such harms, under descriptions which refer directly to those harms ('attempting to kill'; 'reckless driving', defined in terms of the creation of an 'obvious and serious risk of causing physical injury'; or 'causing danger to the lieges by culpable recklessness'); by prohibiting conduct which is likely to cause such harms, but under descriptions which make no *direct* reference to those harms ('driving with excess alcohol in the blood,' or offences under s.19 and s.20 of the Firearms Act 1968)."

The terms "endangerment offences" or "precursor offences" are used here to describe the latter type of criminal offence. These are offences that are complete in themselves and not dependent upon proof that any further offence was intended. However, the main rationale for penalising such conduct is similar to that for the inchoate offences. They are usually conceived of as being steps to the commission of further offences. People who carry offensive weapons in public places could well use those weapons. As Bazelon J. reasoned in *Benton v United States*,[67] such possession gives "rise to sinister implications".

English law abounds with a wide variety of such offences. There are many offences of possessing prohibited articles, such as possessing explosives,[68] firearms,[69] or counterfeiting tools.[70] The object of the legislation prohibiting such possession is "frequently to prevent the articles being used for criminal purposes".[71] The Criminal Attempts Act 1981, s.9, creates the offence of interfering with vehicles; such conduct again has "sinister implications" as being indicative that theft or a similar offence is likely to be committed.

In the United States many states have general offences of "reckless endangerment". Section 211.2 of the Model Penal Code provides the following definition of such an offence:

"A person commits a misdemeanour if he recklessly engages in conduct which places or may place another person in danger of death or serious bodily injury. Recklessness and danger shall be presumed where a person knowingly points a firearm at or in the direction of another, whether or not the actor believed the firearm to be loaded."[72]

---

[67] 232 F.2d 341 at 344–345 (D.C. Cir. 1956).
[68] Explosive Substances Act 1883, s.4(1).
[69] Firearms Act 1968, ss.16–22.
[70] Forgery and Counterfeiting Act 1981, s.17.
[71] Williams, *Textbook of Criminal Law* (2nd ed., 1983), p. 446.
[72] In Australia many states have separate endangerment offences relating to death and to serious injury. See Lanham, "Danger Down Under" [1999] Crim.L.R.960.

English law has no such general counterpart, preferring to focus instead on specific areas of risk-creation, such as dangerous driving[73], or driving with a high blood-alcohol level or criminal damage "intending ... or being reckless as to whether the life of another would be thereby endangered".[74] Further, acts of reckless endangerment can often be punished for what they are in reality; the defendant can be convicted for a precursor offence such as unlawful possession of a firearm but punished more severely because of the risks created. For instance, in *Pennifold and Naylor*[75] the defendants toured a residential area with a ·22 rifle, shooting into lighted rooms; no one was injured. They were convicted of a number of offences, mainly relating to possession of a firearm. The trial judge imposed a sentence of 10 years' imprisonment on one of the defendants. The Court of Appeal confirmed that this was "a reckless and disgraceful episode and someone might have been killed", but for other reasons reduced the sentence to three years.[76]

In evaluating these precursor offences it is important to remember that, unlike the inchoate offences, they are all complete crimes in themselves, each carrying its own penalty. Indeed, if they are indictable offences, there may be liability for attempting to commit them, or for conspiracy or incitement to commit them. Can one ever justify liability for an inchoate offence, when the offence-in-chief is itself only a precursor offence?

With these offences there is a harm, albeit a second-order harm. For example, the harm involved in unauthorised possession of a firearm or other offensive weapons is the violation of society's interests in security and freedom from alarm. Firearms are inherently dangerous and their widespread, unlicensed possession could lead to an increase in their usage. Whether conduct that has the potential for causing harm is criminalised depends on balancing the seriousness of the possible harm and the likelihood of its occurrence against the social value of the conduct. So, possession of firearms is prohibited while possession of other dangerous weapons with greater social value, such as kitchen knives, is not criminalised.[77]

Following this reasoning, it is possible to justify the existence of these offences on the basis of there being a secondary harm. However, it is disturbing that many of these offences are ones of strict liability. For example, in *Hussain*[78] the defendant was convicted of possessing a firearm which he believed was his son's toy. With attempts, the second-order harm has to be backed up by "first degree blameworthiness" in the form of intention. With precursor offences, such as

---

[73] Road Traffic Act 1988, s.2.

[74] Criminal Damage Act 1971, s.1(2). See also Explosive Substances Act 1883, s.2 (offence to cause an explosion likely to endanger life or property). For a list of offences under the Offences Against the Person Act 1861 involving danger to life or bodily harm, see Criminal Law Revision Committee, 14th Report, *Offences Against the Person*, Cmnd.7844, (1980) paras 192–214. See generally, Smith (K. J. M.), "Liability for Endangerment: English *Ad Hoc* Pragmatism and Amercian Innovation" [1983] Crim.L.R.127.

[75] [1974] Crim.L.R.130.

[76] It is interesting, in the light of our analysis of the importance of harm being caused, that the Court of Appeal added that "if someone had been killed a sentence approaching 10 years might have had to be considered". Presumably in such a case the defendant would have been facing charges of, at least, manslaughter.

[77] See, generally, von Hirsch, "Extending the Harm Principle: 'Remote' Harm and Fair Imputation" in Simester and Smith (eds), *Harm and Culpability* (1996).

[78] (1981) 47 Cr.App.R.143. See also *Bradish* [1990] Crim.L.R.723; *Waller* [1991] Crim.L.R.381; *Steele* [1993] Crim.L.R.298.

possession of a firearm, the second-order harm need be accompanied by no blameworthiness at all. This hardly seems justifiable. In such cases there ought to be a "due-diligence defence" to enable defendants such as Hussain to escape liability.

A final question remains about the English *ad hoc* approach. There appears to be no particular reason why certain dangerous activities have been criminalised by English law, but not others. For example, why is reckless endangerment a criminal offence (carrying a maximum punishment of life imprisonment) when the defendant is damaging another's property but no offence at all when he is engaged in some other activity?[79] While the American solution would have the advantage of eliminating these anomalies, there is nevertheless some merit (albeit unintentional) to the English approach. Having separate precursor offences enables one to focus on the wrongdoing and the risks involved to determine the appropriate level of liability and punishment. For example, dangerous driving and recklessly endangering life while damaging another's property involve different wrongs with different degrees of culpability and risk and ought not to be collapsed into a single broad offence. Retaining them as separate precursor offences enables them to "fulfil the educative or 'fair warning' function of singling out situations which carry a particular risk of danger".[80]

---

[79] Ashworth, *Principles of Criminal Law* (3rd ed., 1999), p. 317.
[80] *ibid.*

# 6

# PARTICIPATION IN CRIME

## I. Introduction

So far in our analysis of the criminal law we have assumed that only one defendant is involved, and we have considered that person's liability for acting alone. This may well be the case but it is also likely that at some stage either in the planning or commission of the crime other persons have become involved.[1] They may have supplied tools, information, advice, kept a look-out or even instigated the crime. In the case of *Slack*,[2] for example, the defendant helped in a burglary with robbery in mind. One of those involved killed the occupant. Not only was the killer (the principal offender) convicted of murder but so too was Slack. The help or encouragement may range from the indispensable to that which makes little difference. In *Giannetto*,[3] for example, the court stated that a husband saying "Oh goody" in response to being told that another person intended to kill his wife would make him liable for the subsequent murder. Thus the approach taken by English law is to make those who help in the commission of offences liable for the full crime. Such secondary offenders (also known as accessories) are "liable to be tried, indicted and punished"[4] as if they had committed the crime themselves. This means, for example, that a defendant who assisted another to rape a woman (say, by blocking any entrance to the room) is guilty of rape, even though he never touched the woman. Unlike the inchoate offences, there is no crime of "aiding and abetting rape" or any other offence. References to "aiding and abetting rape" or other offences are simply a short-hand way of describing *how* the defendant came to be liable for the offence. Another consequence of this approach is that an accessory can plead common law defences such as duress or self-defence or provocation.[5] Also, it means accessories are sentenced as if they were principals in cases where fixed or automatic sentences apply.[6] Whether it is appropriate to

---

[1] Between 1990 and 2000, 22 per cent of murders and 15 per cent of involuntary manslaughters involved multiple parties (Weston, *Criminal Complicity: A Comparative Analysis of Homicide Liability*, 2002, PhD thesis, University of Wales, Swansea).

[2] [1989] Q.B. 775.

[3] [1997] 1 Cr.App.R.1 at 13.

[4] s.8 Accessories and Abettors Act 1861, as amended by Sched. 12 of the Criminal Law Act 1977. It is also possible to aid and abet a summary offence: Magistrates' Courts Act 1980, s.44.

[5] *Marks* [1998] Crim.L.R.676. Although the partial defence of provocation is provided for in s.3 of the Homicide Act 1957, it is still essentially a common law defence.

[6] *Attorney-General's Reference (No.71 of 1998) (Anderson)* [1999] 2 Cr.App.R.(S.) 369.

regard all of those involved in crimes as equally blameworthy is a question which can only be considered once the law has been examined. But what needs to be explored now is *how* the law is able to come to a conclusion that such parties are guilty of the same offence as the principal offender.

There are two stumbling-blocks to the imposition of full liability: in *Slack*, where the defendant was not even present in the room when the killing took place, it is difficult to say that his conduct *caused* the killing and, also, he lacked the *mens rea* of murder. Thus whatever links the defendant with the crime, it cannot be the same *actus reus* and *mens rea* as that required for the killer. The question then becomes one of ascertaining what the different requirements are.

Present English law on participation is committed to the principle of *derivative liability*. The liability of the secondary party derives from, and is dependent on, the commission of an offence by the principal offender. Unlike the law of attempt where the focus is forward-looking on the defendant's actions and endeavours towards the commission of a crime, accessorial liability is backwards-looking. A crime must have been committed. The issue is one of determining which persons participated sufficiently in that crime to be held liable for it. How is one to determine whether there has been "sufficient participation"?

### K. J. M. Smith, A Modern Treatise on the Law of Complicity (1991), p. 5:

"[I]t is tempting to view complicity as a shadow variety of principal liability, following as far as possible, both its *actus reus* and *mens rea* contours. As a starting-point, paradigmatic principal liability could be taken as involving a voluntary actor, with appropriate fault, engaging in harmful conduct or causing harm. An equivalence or parallel liability theory of complicity would demand a variable level of culpability as dictated by the principal offence's fault requirements. Such a shadowing process would, though, require the accessory's mental state to be an amalgam of purpose, perception, etc. in respect of both his own and the principal's actions. Paralleling the requirements of principal liability becomes even more difficult in respect of the principal's *actus reus*. While there is some level of plausibility in maintaining that an accessory must have a similar level of mental culpability to the perpetrator, this is not possible in respect of *actus reus* demands. Whether the principal offence is one based on the actor's conduct or the result of such conduct, the accessory's involvement (depending on the offence) cannot always be that stipulated by the offence's definition."

As the secondary party is fully liable for the offence committed, logic dictates that there should be a high degree of *mens rea* as well as a substantial contribution (*actus reus*) towards the offence. However, because the accessory's liability is based not only on his own acts, but also on his involvement or participation in the offence committed by another, the *actus reus* and *mens rea* required for secondary liability have to be assessed, not in isolation, but also in relation to the *actus reus* and *mens rea* of the principal offender.

Hardly surprisingly, this task of specifying the appropriate level of contribution and the required mental element for the accessory has proved highly problematic. This has led to calls for a rethinking of accessorial liability with the focus being more on the accessory's actions of helping and encouraging. One would concentrate on the culpable acts of participation without any necessary causal effect on the principal's actions or their outcome. Participation alone serves as potent evidence of an accomplice allying or associating himself with the principal's criminal venture."[7] Such a doctrine could be based upon similar rationales to those used for inchoate offences: participation is culpable because it increases the risk of crime or by itself amounts to a "sufficiently strong manifestation of the criminal's proclivities to warrant punishment".[8] The Law Commission has endorsed this latter way of thinking, but taken it further and proposed abolishing the present structure of the law, based on derivative liability, and, instead, advocates converting the law to an inchoate model with the creation of specific offences of assisting and encouraging crime.[9] These proposals have yet to be enacted.

## II. The Law

### A. *Principal Offenders*

Despite the fact that all parties to a crime may, by virtue of section 8 of the Accessories and Abettors Act 1861, be tried, indicted and punished in the same way,[10] it is necessary to distinguish between the principal offender and secondary parties.[11] The principal offender is usually described as the one whose act is the most immediate cause of the *actus reus*.[12] It is the principal offender who shoots and kills the victim in a crime of murder or who snatches the bag in the crime of theft or robbery. Clearly, there may be more than one principal offender: two or more defendants may fatally stab a victim.

There is one exception to the rule that the principal offender is the one whose act is the most immediate cause of the *actus reus*. Where a defendant acts through an intermediary who is an "innocent agent" because, for example, he is below the age of criminal responsibility, it will be the instigator who will be regarded as the principal offender. The same result will apply if the defendant acts through someone who has no *mens rea*, as in the situation where the agent is instructed to put what is described as a harmless substance into someone's food, which the defendant knows will kill.[13]

### B. *Secondary Parties*

#### 1. Distinct modes of participation?

The liability of secondary parties is governed by section 8 of the Accessories and Abettors Act 1861:

---

[7] Smith (K.J.M.), *A Modern Treatise on the Law of Complicity* (1991), p. 6.

[8] *ibid.*

[9] Law Commission Consultation Paper No. 131, *Assisting and Encouraging Crime* (1993), para. 2.18.

[10] Until 1967, principals were known as principals in the first degree and secondary parties as principals in the second degree if they were present at the crime and accessories if they were not. The Criminal Law Act 1967 effectively abolished the need for that distinction to be drawn.

[11] Not least because strict liability does not extend to accessories (*Callow v Tillstone* (1900) 8 L.T. 411). Even if a principal can be convicted without proof of *mens rea*, secondary parties must act with the requisite mental element.

[12] Smith and Hogan, *Criminal Law* (10th ed., 2002), p. 142.

[13] See *Stringer* (1992) 94 Cr.App.R.13 where the defendant, a business manager of a company, signed false invoices with the intention that innocent company employees would pass them for payment. When the company's bank account was duly debited, the defendant was convicted of theft of the money involved, through innocent agents.

"whosoever shall aid, abet, counsel or procure the commission of any indictable offence ... shall be liable to be tried, indicted and punished as a principal offender."

The Law Commission has pointed out that prior to 1975 "the received view was that the particular words used in section 8 [aid, abet, counsel or procure] ... had no special implications, and certainly were not to be taken in their literal or natural meaning as coercing any particular conclusion as to the type of conduct that amounts in law to complicity".[14] In that year, however, the Court of Appeal stated that:

"We approach s.8 of the 1861 Act on the basis that the words should be given their ordinary meaning, if possible. We approach the section on the basis also that if four words are employed here 'aid, abet, counsel or procure', the probability is that there is a difference between each of those four words and the other three, because, if there were no difference, then Parliament would be wasting time in using four words where two or three would do."[15]

It is, however, extremely difficult to give these archaic words their "ordinary meaning". At a simplistic level, "aid" means help or assistance. While "abet" is generally regarded as largely synonymous with "aid", there have been suggestions that while "aid" is a neutral term, "abet" suggests wrongdoing: "'abet' clearly imports *mens rea*, which 'aid' may not".[16] "Counsel" suggests advice or encouragement while "procure" means "produce by endeavour".[17] This terminology was, perhaps, apt before 1967 when a distinction had been drawn between those present at the crime (aiders and abetters) and those not present (counsellors and procurers).[18] However, this distinction is no longer part of the law and in more recent years it has become clear that, with the possible exception of "procure", these words are mere synonyms for helping and encouraging.[19]

That there is no critical distinction between these terms is emphasised by the fact that it is possible for an indictment to be framed in language which embraces all four terms[20] or for the defendant to be charged with committing the crime without any reference to the terms in section 8.[21] While the House of Lords in *Maxwell*[22] stressed that it was desirable that the true nature of the case against the defendant should be made clear in the indictment, it appears this recommendation is "universally ignored".[23] There is no legal obligation to make such a specification and a failure to spell out the precise role of a person in an enterprise is not a breach of Article 6 of the European Convention on Human Rights.[24]

---

[14] Law Commission Consultation Paper No. 131, *Assisting and Encouraging Crime* (1993), para. 2.10.

[15] *Attorney-General's Reference (No. 1 of 1975)* [1975] Q.B. 773 at 779.

[16] *D.P.P. for Northern Ireland v Lynch* [1975] A.C. 653 at 698.

[17] *Attorney-General's Reference (No.1 of 1975)* [1975] Q.B. 773.

[18] *Above*, n.10.

[19] For example, in *Attorney-General v Able* [1984] Q.B. 795 all the words were regarded as synonyms for "helping".

[20] As in *Blakely, Sutton v D.P.P.* [1991] Crim.L.R.763.

[21] *Forman and Ford* [1988] Crim.L.R.677. This avoids prosecution problems where uncertainty exists as to who is the principal.

[22] (1979) 68 Cr.App.R.128.

[23] *Taylor, Harrison and Taylor* [1998] Crim.L.R.582.

[24] *Mercer* [2001] EWCA Crim 638. Art. 6(3)(a) states that everyone charged with a criminal offence has the right to be informed "in detail, of the nature and cause of the accusation against him".

To conclude, therefore, it is almost certain that no real conceptual distinctions can be drawn between most of the terms. Between them they embrace conduct which encourages or influences the principal offender or helps him in the commission of the crime. Accordingly, the following analysis of the law will not focus on its antiquated terminology but will concentrate on the different ways in which persons can be said to participate in the commission of a crime. However, as there might still be some justification for regarding procuring as distinct, this form of complicity is discussed later in the chapter.

## 2. Causation

English law on participation in crime is theoretically underpinned by the doctrine of derivative liability. As seen, this means accessories are held responsible for the result (the crime) that occurs. Unlike an inchoate model of liability, the focus is not simply on their contribution. If they are being blamed for the end result, it would follow logically that their actions should have had a role in *causing* that result. This view has support. Smith (K.J.M.) argues that a "broad causal account of complicity offers the most internal coherence alongside the greatest consistency with general principles of criminal responsibility that touch and concern complicity"[25] and that "it has always been implied in the concept of complicity that an accessory's involvement (whether as an 'assister' or 'encourager') did make some difference to the outcome".[26]

However, causation is difficult to establish here because of the central principle that a causal chain is generally broken by voluntary, willed human action. In participation cases this means that the voluntary, willed actions of the principal offender would normally be regarded as breaking the causal chain. As Kadish says:

"Causation applies where results of a person's actions happen in the physical world. Complicity applies where results take the form of another person's involuntary action. Complicity emerges as a separate ground of liability because causation doctrine cannot satisfactorily deal with results that take the form of another's voluntary action."[27]

English law has largely accepted this latter view.

### R. v Calhaem [1985] 1 Q.B. 808 (Court of Appeal, Criminal Division)

The defendant, Mrs Calhaem, was infatuated with her solicitor. She was charged with the murder of a woman who was having an affair with her solicitor. She had instructed one Zajac to commit the murder. He pleaded guilty to the murder but said in evidence that up to the point when he went berserk and killed the woman, he had come to a decision not to go through with the plan. The defendant appealed against her conviction for murder on the basis that counselling required a substantial causal connection between the acts of the counsellor and the commission of the offence and that none existed on the facts.

Parker L.J.:
"We must therefore approach the question raised on the basis that we should give to the word 'counsel' its ordinary meaning, which is as the judge said, 'advise', 'solicit', or

---

[25] Smith (K.J.M.), *A Modern Treatise on the Law of Complicity* (1991), p. 7.

[26] *ibid.* at 246.

[27] Kadish, "Complicity, Cause and Blame: A Study in the Interpretation of Doctrine" (1985) 73 Cal.L.Rev. 324 at 327. See also, Williams, "Complicity, Purpose and the Draft Code—I" [1990] Crim.L.R.4 at 6.

something of that sort. There is no implication in the word itself that there should be any causal connection between the counselling and the offence. It is true that, unlike the offence of incitement at common law, the actual offence must have been committed and by the person counselled. To this extent there must clearly be, first, contact between the parties, and secondly, a connection between the counselling and the murder. Equally, the act done must, we think, be done within the scope of the authority or advice, and not, for example, accidentally when the mind of the final murderer did not go with his actions. For example, if the principal offender happened to be involved in a football riot in the course of which he laid about him with a weapon of some sort and killed someone, who, unknown to him, was the person whom he had been counselled to kill, he would not, in our view, have been acting within the scope of his authority; he would have been acting entirely outside it, albeit what he had done was what he had been counselled to do.

We see, however, no need to import anything further into the meaning of the word."

**Appeal dismissed**

From this, it is clear that liability is not restricted to situations where there is a causal relationship between the accessory's and principal's acts.[28] This was underlined in *Giannetto*[29] where the court was of the view that liability would follow if a husband merely said "Oh goody" to a plan *already in existence* to kill his wife.[30] In such a case it cannot be asserted that the accessory's acts made any causal contribution to the end result. Indeed, going further, it is possible that one could aid a crime without the principal even being aware that assistance is being provided. It is, of course, difficult to see how a crime could be "counselled" without there being any measure of consensus but the same is not necessarily true of "aiding".[31]

However with regard to "procuring", it has been held that causation is necessary[32] although consensus is not required. This, again, underlines the need for procuring to be dealt with separately.

### 3. Assistance and encouragement

While the following are not distinct legal categories, it is useful, for purposes of exposition, to group the types of assistance and encouragement that may be provided as follows:

### (i) *Unplanned presence at the crime*

Generally, being present[33] when a crime is committed does not, of course, implicate one in the crime. But what if a fight starts in a pub and those present start to "egg on" the participants? The following is the leading decision on this point.

---

[28] The position is different with regard to procuring.

[29] [1997] 1 Cr.App.R.1.

[30] See further, Smith, "Criminal Liability of Accessories: Law and Law Reform" (1997) 113 L.Q.R. 453 at 458. See also *Attorney-General v Able* [1984] 1 Q.B. 795 where it was stated that it "does not make any difference" whether the person counselled would have acted anyway.

[31] Smith and Hogan, Criminal Law (10th ed., 2002), pp. 146–147. One may certainly procure an offence without the principal's knowledge.

[32] *Attorney-General's Reference (No. 1 of 1975)* [1975] Q.B. 773.

[33] The term "presence" is broadly interpreted so as to include, for example, the look-out person standing outside: *Betts and Ridley* (1930) 22 Cr.App.R.148.

## R. v Clarkson (1971) 55 Cr.App.R.445 (Courts-Martial Appeal Court)

The defendant was convicted of aiding and abetting the rape of a woman in an army barracks. He and another defendant, Carroll, appealed.

Megaw L.J.:
"[T]he presence of those two appellants in the room where the offence was taking place was not accidental in any sense and it was not by chance, unconnected with the crime, that they were there. Let it be accepted that they entered the room when the crime was committed because of what they had heard, which indicated that a woman was being raped, and they remained there.

*Coney* (1882) 8 Q.B.D. 534 decides that non-accidental presence at the scene of the crime is not conclusive of aiding and abetting. . . .

What has to be proved is stated by Hawkins J. in a well-known passage in his judgment in *Coney* at p. 557 of the report. What he said was this:

'. . . In my opinion, to constitute an aider and abettor some active steps must be taken by word, or action, with the intent to instigate the principal, or principals. Encouragement does not of necessity amount to aiding and abetting, it may be intentional or unintentional, a man may unwittingly encourage another in fact by his presence, by misinterpreted words, or gestures, or by his silence, or non-interference, or he may encourage intentionally by expressions, gestures, or actions intended to signify approval. In the latter case he aids and abets, in the former he does not. It is no criminal offence to stand by, a mere passive spectator of a crime, even of a murder. Non-interference to prevent a crime is not itself a crime. But the fact that a person was voluntarily and purposely present witnessing the commission of a crime, and offered no opposition to it, though he might reasonably be expected to prevent and had the power so to do, or at least to express his dissent, might, under some circumstances, afford cogent evidence upon which a jury would be justified in finding that he wilfully encouraged and so aided and abetted. But it would be purely a question for the jury whether he did so or not.'

It is not enough, then, that the presence of the accused person has, in fact, given encouragement. It must be proved that he intended to give encouragement; that he *wilfully* encouraged. In a case such as the present, more than in many other cases where aiding and abetting is alleged, it was essential that that element should be stressed; for there was here at least the possibility that a drunken man with his self-discipline loosened by drink, being aware that a woman was being raped, might be attracted to the scene and might stay on the scene in the capacity of what is known as a voyeur; and, while his presence and the presence of others might in fact encourage the rapers or discourage the victim, he himself, enjoying the scene or at least standing by assenting, might not intend that his presence should offer encouragement to rapers and would-be rapers or discouragement to the victim; he might not realise that he was giving encouragement; so that, while encouragement there might be, it would not be a case in which, to use the words of Hawkins J., the accused person 'wilfully encouraged'.

A further point is emphasized in passages in the judgment of the Court of Criminal Appeal in *Allan* [1965] 1 Q.B. 130, at 135 and 138. That was a case concerned with participation in an affray. On page 135 the Court said this:

'In effect, it amounts to this: that the judge thereby directed the jury that they were in duty bound to convict an accused who was proved to have been present and witnessing an affray, if it was also proved that he nursed an intention to join in if help was needed by the side he favoured and this notwithstanding that he did nothing by words or deeds to evince his intention and outwardly played the role of a purely passive spectator. It was said that, if that direction is right, where A and B behave themselves to all outward appearances in an exactly similar manner, but it be proved that A had the intention to participate if needs be, whereas B had no such intention, then A must be convicted of being a principal in the second degree to the affray, whereas B should be acquitted. To do that, it is objected, would be to convict A on his thoughts, even though they found no reflection in his action.' . . .

From that it follows that mere intention is not in itself enough. There must be an intention to encourage; and there must also be encouragement in fact in cases such as the present case."

Appeal allowed[34]

In *Tait*[35] the Court of Appeal confirmed that both an intention to encourage and encouragement in fact must be established. Fletcher, however, has questioned the necessity for such a psychological effect on the principal: "After all, whether the aid is actually rendered is fortuitous; the actor is equally culpable and his dangerousness is equally great if the perpetrator never receives the aid."[36] Such an argument rationalises complicity in the same way as inchoate offences—in terms of endangerment or risk—and points to a participation theory of complicity.[37] However, while causal explanations of complicity have been generally rejected by English law (except in relation to procuring), it would seem that in these cases of unplanned presence at the scene of the crime, the law's insistence upon actual encouragement does manifest vestiges of a causal theory of complicity. This can best be explained by looking at the problem from another perspective. If, in these cases, liability were imposed in the absence of actual encouragement, this would be tantamount to punishing persons for an omission to act in situations where there was no pre-existing duty to act.

(ii) *Failure to exercise control*

Exceptionally, presence without intended and actual encouragement may give rise to liability if the defendant has a right to control the actions of the principal offender. If, for instance, the owner of a vehicle sits in the passenger seat and does nothing whilst the principal offender behind the wheel drives dangerously, his omission may inculpate him.[38] Perhaps because visions of owners grabbing the steering wheel from the dangerous driver (and exacerbating the situation) arose before the judges' eyes, the rule of control being the legal equivalent of actual encouragement is now regarded as *evidence* only that the owner may have encouraged the commission of the crime.[39] In *Alford Transport Ltd*[40] it was held that actual presence at the scene of the crime was not necessary. Where a transport manager or the managing director of a company who had a right to control the actions of its employees deliberately refrained from exercising control, it could be inferred that there was positive encouragement. The *mens rea* of this species of complicity will be considered later.

---

[34] See also *Wilcox v Jeffrey* [1951] 1 All E.R. 464 and *Bland* [1988] Crim.L.R.41.

[35] [1993] Crim.L.R.538.

[36] *Rethinking Criminal Law* (1978), p. 679.

[37] See *below*, p. 551 for the recommendations of the Law Commission on the proposed offence of encouraging crime under which the principal would need to be aware of the encouragement but need not be affected by it: para. 4.163(2).

[38] *Du Cros v Lambourne* [1907] 1 K.B. 40; *cf. Harris* [1964] Crim.L.R.54 where the supervisor of a learner-driver was convicted as accessory to the learner-driver's traffic offences because he knowingly failed to take steps to stop them.

[39] *Cassady v Morris (Reg.) (Transport)* [1975] R.T.R. 470; *Forman and Ford* [1988] Crim.L.R.677.

[40] [1997] 2 Cr.App.R.326.

### (iii) *Counselling*

Counselling normally (although not invariably) refers to help given before the commission of the crime. It may take a wide variety of forms but includes advice, encouragement or the supply of information or equipment. The *mens rea* of counselling is discussed below.

### (iv) *Joint unlawful enterprise*

Where two or more people embark on a joint unlawful enterprise, for example a burglary or an attack on someone, the law has long adopted the view that all the parties should be liable for the direct and agreed consequences of that joint enterprise. However, problems arise when the principal offender goes beyond what was agreed. For example, in *Slack*[41] the defendant handed a knife to the principal offender during a burglary so that he could threaten the occupier if she started screaming. While the defendant was out of the room, the principal offender stabbed and killed the occupier. Is the accessory guilty of murder in such a case?

### R. v Powell and Another; R. v English [1999] 1 A.C. 1 (House of Lords)

In the first appeal Powell and Daniels went with another man to a drug dealer's house to purchase drugs. The drug dealer was shot dead when he came to the door. The Crown case was that if the other man fired the gun, Powell and Daniels were guilty of murder because they knew the other man was armed with a gun and realised he might use it to kill or cause really serious injury to the drug dealer. They were convicted of murder and appealed.

In the second appeal, English and another man took part in a joint enterprise to attack and cause injury with wooden posts to a police officer. During the attack the other man used a knife and stabbed the officer to death. English had no knowledge that the other man was carrying a knife but was convicted of murder on the basis that he realised there was a substantial risk that the other man might kill or cause really serious injury to the police officer with the wooden post. He appealed.

Lord Hutton:
"[T]he two questions certified for the opinion of the House are as follows:
'(i) Is it sufficient to found a conviction for murder for a secondary party to a killing to have realised that the primary party might kill with intent to do so or with intent to cause grievous bodily harm or must the secondary party have held such an intention himself?
(ii) Is it sufficient for murder that the secondary party intends or foresees that the primary party would or may act with intent to cause grievous bodily harm, if the lethal act carried out by the primary party is fundamentally different from the acts foreseen or intended by the secondary party?' ...
My Lords, I consider that there is a strong line of authority that where two parties embark on a joint enterprise to commit a crime, and one party foresees that in the course of the enterprise the other party may carry out, with the requisite *mens rea*, an act constituting another crime, the former is liable for that crime if committed by the latter in the course of the enterprise ...
In *R. v Anderson and Morris* [1966] 2 Q.B. 110 the primary party (Anderson) killed the victim with a knife. The defence of the secondary party (Morris) was that even though he may have taken part in a joint attack with Anderson to beat up the victim, he did not know that Anderson was armed with a knife ...
In delivering the judgment of the Court of Appeal Lord Parker C.J. accepted the principle [that] ...
'... where two persons embark on a joint enterprise, each is liable for the acts done in pursuance of that joint enterprise, that that includes liability for unusual consequences if

[41] [1989] Q.B. 775.

they arise from the execution of the agreed joint enterprise but (and this is the crux of the matter) that if one of the adventurers goes beyond what has been tacitly agreed as part of the common enterprise, his co-adventurer is not liable for the consequences of that unauthorised act. Finally, he says it is for the jury in every case to decide whether what was done was part of the joint enterprise, or went beyond it and was in fact an act unauthorised by that joint enterprise.'

As a matter of strict analysis there is ... a distinction between a party to a common enterprise contemplating that in the course of the enterprise another party may use a gun or knife and a party tacitly agreeing that in the course of the enterprise another party may use such a weapon. In many cases the distinction will in practice be of little importance because as Lord Lane C.J. observed in *R. v Wakely* with reference to the use of a pickaxe handle in a burglary, 'forseeability that the pickaxe handle might be used as a weapon of violence was practically indistinguishable from tacit agreement that the weapon should be used for that purpose'. Nevertheless, it is possible that a case might arise where a party knows that another party to the common enterprise is carrying a deadly weapon and contemplates that he may use it in the course of the enterprise, but whilst making it clear to the other party that he is opposed to the weapon being used, nevertheless continues with the plan. In such a case, it would be unrealistic to say that, if used, the weapon would be used with his tacit agreement. However, it is clear from a number of decisions ... that as stated by the High Court of Australia in *McAuliffe v R.* (1995) 130 A.L.R. 26 at 30 ... 'the scope of the common purpose is to be determined by what was contemplated by the parties sharing that purpose'. Therefore, when two parties embark on a joint criminal enterprise one party will be liable for an act which he contemplates may be carried out by the other party in the course of the enterprise even if he has not tacitly agreed to that act.

The principle ... was applied by the Privy Council in *Chan Wing-siu v R.* [1985] A.C. 168 at 175 in the judgment delivered by Sir Robin Cooke, who stated:

'The case must depend rather on the wider principle whereby a secondary party is criminally liable for acts by the primary offender of a type which the former foresees but does not necessarily intend. That there is such a principle is not in doubt. It turns on contemplation or, putting the same idea in other words, authorisation, which may be express but is more usually implied. It meets the case of a crime foreseen as a possible incident of the common unlawful enterprise. The criminal culpability lies in participating in the venture with that foresight.' ...

In *Hui Chi-ming v R.* [1992] 1 A.C. 34 at 53 the Privy Council [agreed and] ... Lord Lowry stated:

'The appellant's second point relies on Sir Robin Cooke's use of the word "authorisation" as a synonym for contemplation ... Their Lordships consider that Sir Robin Cooke used this word ... to emphasise the fact that mere foresight is not enough: the accessory, in order to be guilty, must have foreseen the relevant offence which the principal may commit *as a possible incident of the common unlawful enterprise* and must, with such foresight, still have participated in the enterprise. The word "authorisation" explains what is meant by contemplation, but does not add a new ingredient ...'

In *McAuliffe v R.* the High Court of Australia has recently stated that the test for determining whether a crime falls within the scope of a joint enterprise is now the subjective test of contemplation and the court stated:

'... each of the parties to the arrangement or understanding is guilty of any other crime falling within the scope of the common purpose which is committed in carrying out that purpose ... [I]n accordance with the emphasis which the law now places upon the actual state of mind of an accused person, the test has become a subjective one and the scope of the common purpose is to be determined by what was contemplated by the parties sharing that purpose.'

There is therefore a strong line of authority that participation in a joint criminal enterprise with foresight or contemplation of an act as a possible incident of that enterprise is sufficient to impose criminal liability for that act carried out by another participant in the enterprise. ...

I consider that Lord Parker C.J. [in *Anderson and Morris*] applied the test of foresight when he stated:

'It seems to this court that to say that adventurers are guilty of manslaughter when one of them has departed completely from the concerted action of the common design and has suddenly formed an intent to kill and has used a weapon and acted in a way which no party to that common design could suspect is something which would revolt the conscience of people today.' ...

In reliance upon *R. v Moloney* and *R. v Hancock* Mr Feinberg, on behalf of the appellants Powell and Daniels, submitted to this House ... that as a matter of principle there is an anomaly in requiring proof against a secondary party of a lesser *mens rea* than needs to be proved against the principal who commits the *actus reus* of murder. If foreseeability of risk is insufficient to found the *mens rea* of murder for a principal then the same test of liability should apply in the case of a secondary party to the joint enterprise. Mr Feinberg further submitted that it is wrong for the present distinction in mental culpability to operate to the disadvantage of a party who does not commit the *actus reus* and that there is a manifest anomaly where there is one test for a principal and a lesser test for a secondary party ...

My Lords, I recognise that as a matter of logic there is force in the argument ... But the rules of the common law are not based solely on logic but relate to practical concerns and, in relation to crimes committed in the course of joint enterprises, to the need to give effective protection to the public against criminals operating in gangs ...

A further consideration is that, unlike the principal party who carries out the killing with a deadly weapon, the secondary party will not be placed in the situation in which he suddenly has to decide whether to shoot or stab the third person with intent to kill or cause really serious harm. There is, in my opinion, an argument of considerable force that the secondary party who takes part in a criminal enterprise (for example the robbery of a bank) with foresight that a deadly weapon may be used, should not escape liability for murder because he, unlike the principal party, is not suddenly confronted by the security officer so that he has to decide whether to use the gun or knife or have the enterprise thwarted and face arrest. This point has been referred to in cases where the question has been discussed whether in order for criminal liability to attach the secondary party must foresee an act as more likely than not or whether it suffices if the secondary party foresees the act only as a possibility.

In *Chan Wing-siu v R.* counsel for the Crown submitted:

'Regard must be had to public policy considerations. Public policy requires that when a man lends himself to a criminal enterprise knowing it involves the possession of potentially murderous weapons which in fact are used by his partners with murderous intent, he should not escape the consequences to him of their conduct by reliance upon the nuances of prior assessment of the likelihood that such conduct will take place. In these circumstances an accomplice who knowingly takes the risk that such conduct might, or might well, take place in the course of that joint enterprise should bear the same responsibility for that conduct as those who use the weapons with the murderous intent.'
...

Therefore, for the reasons which I have given I would answer the [first] certified question of law ... by stating that ... it is sufficient to found a conviction for murder for a secondary party to have realised that in the course of the joint enterprise the primary party might kill with intent to do so or with intent to cause grievous bodily harm ...

... The problem raised by the second certified question is [whether] there will be liability for murder on the part of the secondary party if he foresees the possibility that the other party in the criminal venture will cause really serious harm by kicking or striking a blow with a wooden post, but the other party suddenly produces a knife or a gun, which the secondary party did not know he was carrying, and kills the victim with it.

[Counsel] for the appellant ... [argued that] where the primary party kills with a deadly weapon, which the secondary party did not know that he had and therefore did not foresee his use of it, the secondary party should not be guilty of murder. He submitted that to be guilty under the principle stated in *Chan Wing-siu v R.* the secondary party must foresee an act of the type which the principal party committed, and that in the present case the use of a knife was fundamentally different to the use of a wooden post.

My Lords, I consider that this submission is correct . . .

Accordingly, in the appeal of English, I consider that the direction of the learned trial judge was defective . . . [because] he did not qualify his direction on foresight of really serious injury by stating that if the jury considered that the use of the knife by Weddle was the use of a weapon and an action on Weddle's part which English did not foresee as a possibility, then English should not be convicted of murder. As the unforeseen use of the knife would take the killing outside the scope of the joint venture the jury should also have been directed, as the Court of Appeal held in *R. v Anderson and Morris*, that English should not be found guilty of manslaughter.

. . . However, I would wish to make this observation: if the weapon used by the primary party is different to, but as dangerous as, the weapon which the secondary party contemplated he might use, the secondary party should not escape liability for murder because of the difference in the weapon, for example, if he foresaw that the primary party might use a gun to kill and the latter used a knife to kill, or vice versa.

. . . [With regard to] the degree of foresight required to impose liability . . . the secondary party is subject to criminal liability if he contemplated the act causing the death as a possible incident of the joint venture, unless the risk was so remote that the jury take the view that the secondary party genuinely dismissed it as altogether negligible.

. . . I consider that the test of foresight is a simpler and more practicable test for a jury to apply than the test of whether the act causing the death goes beyond what had been tacitly agreed as part of the joint enterprise. Therefore, in cases where an issue arises as to whether an action was within the scope of the joint venture, I would suggest that it might be preferable for a trial judge in charging a jury to base his direction on the test of foresight rather than on the test set out in the first passage in *R. v Anderson and Morris* [above, p. 536]. But in a case where, although the secondary party may have foreseen grievous bodily harm, he may not have foreseen the use of the weapon employed by the primary party or the manner in which the primary party acted, the trial judge should qualify the test of foresight . . . in the manner stated by Lord Parker C.J. in the second passage in *R. v Anderson and Morris* [above, p. 537)."

Lord Steyn:

"I would reject the argument that the accessory principle *as such* imposes a form of constructive liability. The accessory principle requires proof of a subjective state of mind of the part of a participant in a criminal enterprise, *viz* foresight that the primary offender might commit a different and more serious offence. Professor Sir John Smith explained how the principle applies in the case of murder ((1997) 113 L.Q.R. 453 at 464):

'Nevertheless, as the critics point out it is enough that the accessory is reckless, whereas, in the case of the principal, intention must be proved. Recklessness whether death be caused is a sufficient *mens rea* for a principal offender in manslaughter, but not murder. The accessory to murder, however, must be proved to have been reckless, not merely whether death might be caused but whether murder might be committed; *he must have been aware, not merely that death or grievous bodily harm might be caused, but that it might be caused intentionally, by a person whom he was assisting or encouraging to commit a crime.* Recklessness whether murder be committed is different from, and more serious than, recklessness whether death be caused by an accident.' (My emphasis.)

. . . [There is an] argument that it is anomalous that the secondary party can be guilty of murder if he foresees the possibility of such a crime being committed while the primary can only be guilty if he has an intent to kill or cause really serious injury. Recklessness may suffice in the case of the secondary party but it does not in the case of the primary offender. The answer to this supposed anomaly, and other similar cases across the spectrum of criminal law, is to be found in practical and policy considerations. If the law required proof of the specific intention on the part of a secondary party, the utility of the accessory principle would be gravely undermined. It is just that a secondary party who foresees that the primary offender might kill with the intent sufficient for murder, and assists and encourages the primary offender in the criminal enterprise on this basis, should be guilty of murder. He ought to be criminally liable for harm which he foresaw and which in fact resulted from the crime he assisted and encouraged. But it would in practice almost invariably be impossible for a jury to say that the secondary party wanted death to be caused or that he regarded it as virtually certain. In the real world proof of an intention sufficient for murder would be well nigh impossible in the vast majority of joint enterprise cases. Moreover, the proposed change in the law must be put in context. The criminal justice system exists to control crime. A prime function of that system must be to deal justly but effectively with those who join with others in criminal enterprises. Experience has shown that joint criminal enterprises only too readily escalate into the commission of greater offences. In order to deal with this important social problem the accessory principle is needed and cannot be abolished or relaxed."

**Powell and Daniels' appeals dismissed. English's appeal allowed**

From this decision it is clear that an accessory will only be liable for acts done within the scope of the joint unlawful enterprise. Each party to a joint unlawful enterprise is liable for any act done pursuant to that venture. Where there is a shared joint enterprise, each member of the group assumes responsibility for the actions of other members of the group. However, one is only a "member of a group" with regard to "group actions", that is, acts done in accordance with the joint enterprise. If the principal offender departs from the joint enterprise in a material manner, for example, produces a gun and kills, when the enterprise was to beat the victim with sticks, the defendant escapes liability.

How does one determine the scope of the joint enterprise? In *Hui Chi-ming* this was defined as the "contemplated area of guilty conduct" and in *McAuliffe* as being "determined by what was contemplated by parties sharing that purpose". Both decisions were approved in *Powell*. Accordingly, if two parties embark on a burglary and one contemplates that the other might have a knife, the joint enterprise is burglary armed with a knife. The joint enterprise is defined by reference to the type of activity and the degree of dangerousness involved. Lord Hutton stated that if the weapon used was different to, but just as dangerous as, the contemplated weapon, for example, a gun as opposed to a knife, the act would still be within the joint enterprise.

### R. v Greatrex [1999] 1 Cr.App.R.126 (Court of Appeal, Criminal Division)

A group of youths, including the defendant, were violently kicking a victim when the principal offender produced a bar or spanner and struck the victim killing him. The defendant was convicted of murder and appealed.

Beldam L.J.:
"In deciding whether the actions of one participant are so fundamentally different the jury will have regard to all the circumstances and of course where one participant unknown to the others is carrying a lethal weapon such as a knife or revolver and uses it in a way which indicates that his actions go entirely beyond actions which were foreseen by the others, that is cogent evidence that what was done was substantially different from actions within the common purpose. ... Whilst it would have been open to the jury to conclude that the shod foot is as much a weapon as a bar, and equally dangerous in the sense of being capable of inflicting really serious injury and so not beyond the contemplation or foresight of Greatrex when he joined in the attack, it was for the jury to decide whether that was so or whether the

actions of Bates in using the bar were not foreseen by Greatrex at the time when the fatal blow was struck and so were outside the combined purpose. ...

As these questions were not left to the jury, we consider that the conviction of Greatrex cannot be upheld."

**Appeal of Greatrex allowed**

In *Powell; English* Lord Hutton was of the view was that a gun was intrinsically more dangerous than a stick or post. However, it is not simply the nature of the weapon that matters. It is the use to which it is to be put that determines the scope of the enterprise. In *Bamborough*[42] there was a joint enterprise to inflict violence. The accessory knew the principal offender had a gun but thought it was unloaded and believed it would only be used to pistol-whip the victim. The victim was initially beaten with the gun but then the principal offender shot and killed the victim. It is submitted that, after *Powell*, this act of shooting the victim would not be within the scope of the joint enterprise.[43] Using a gun to pistol-whip someone is equivalent to using a stick or a blunt instrument. The use of the gun to shoot someone is a qualitatively different use of the weapon. Lord Hutton supported this view when, in referring to the Northern Ireland case of *Gamble*,[44] he stated that if the enterprise was to "kneecap" a victim with a gun but the principal offender deliberately shot the victim in the head, the issue was "more debatable" but he agreed with the trial judge in *Gamble* that the accessory in such a case would not be guilty of murder.

In most cases of group violence involving fighting there has seldom been planning. As stated in *Greatrex*: "as the participants rush to take part in the attack, they give no thought to the means by which they will overwhelm the victim nor do they have any particular foresight whether one or other of them may in the course of the ensuing violence pick up or use any weapon which may conveniently come to hand." In *Uddin*[45] it was held that the scope of an unlawful enterprise can change if, after the production of an unforeseen weapon, the others continue with their attack:

"If in the course of the concerted attack a weapon is produced by one of the participants and the others knowing that he has it in circumstances where he may use it in the course of the attack participate or continue to participate in the attack, they will be guilty of murder if the weapon is used to inflict a fatal wound."

While the ratio of *Powell* only extends to murder, the principle underlying this case is broader and applies to all crimes. This is particularly true of its analysis of the *mens rea* of accessories.

### 4. Mens rea of accessories

#### (i) *Introduction*

The extracts from the above cases (*Clarkson* and *Powell; English*) considered not only the extent of conduct required for accessorial liability (*actus reus*) but also the

---

[42] [1996] Crim.L.R.744.
[43] In *Bamborough* it was held, under the law as it then stood, that this was within the joint enterprise.
[44] [1989] N.I. 268.
[45] [1998] 2 All E.R. 744.

*mens rea* needed by the accessory. In assessing the following section, reference should again be made to these cases.

Accessorial liability involves a "two-fold structure".[46] The accessory who is assisting or encouraging the crime must have *mens rea* in relation to his own conduct. For example, in *Clarkson* it was said there must be an "intention to encourage". It is implicit in the notion of counselling that one can only encourage or influence another to do something if it is one's intention to encourage. With joint enterprise cases, participation in the enterprise is deemed to be intentional assistance. However, because the accessory is liable for the crime committed by the principal (as opposed to being simply liable for his own acts of encouragement, etc.), the accessory also needs *mens rea* in relation to that crime. This could take the form of *mens rea* with respect to the acts of the principal and its consequences or it could involve *mens rea* in relation to the mental state of the principal. This section is concerned with these latter forms of *mens rea*.

The common theme of all these forms of assistance and encouragement is that the accessory is knowingly and deliberately providing help to a criminal enterprise. The point has already been made that no real conceptual distinctions can be drawn between most of the terms. Arguably, therefore, it is irrelevant whether the accessory is described as a party to a joint unlawful enterprise or a counsellor. Nothing should hinge upon the term adopted in a particular case. The judgment in *Powell; English* can certainly be read as applying to all cases of consensual accessorial liability. Other cases confirm this approach. In *Rook*,[47] for example, the accessory helped plan the crime but failed to turn up for the execution of the crime. A person who provides advice and helps plan a crime in advance traditionally has been described as a counsellor. Equally, such a person can be regarded as a party to a joint enterprise, albeit one who was absent from the actual scene of the crime—and this was how the case was dealt with. Similarly, in *Reardon*,[48] which was a classic case of counselling in that a knife was provided by an accessory who was not involved in any enterprise with the principal offender, the joint unlawful enterprise principles established in *Powell; English* were applied.

While this approach of treating all accessories as subject to the same *mens rea* rules would appear to represent the present law,[49] the matter is not beyond doubt[50] and Lord Hutton, in answering the certified questions in *Powell; English*, did limit himself to cases arising "in the course of the joint enterprise". For this reason, and for simplicity of exposition, the *mens rea* requirement in joint unlawful enterprises will be examined separately from that requirement in other cases.

---

[46] Law Commission Consultation Paper No. 131, *Assisting and Encouraging Crime* (1993), para. 2.49.

[47] (1993) 97 Cr.App.R.327.

[48] [1999] Crim.L.R.392.

[49] Virgo, "Clarifying Accessorial Liability" (1998) 57 C.L.J. 13 at 15: "It is to be hoped that in future joint enterprise liability can be treated simply as a historical footnote and not as a distinct part of accessorial liability". See also *Marks* [1998] Crim.L.R.676 and Sir John Smith's commentary that: "it is unfortunate that the phrase 'joint enterprise' has been given a special status for which there is no proper foundation" (at 677).

[50] Simester and Sullivan, *Criminal Law: Theory and Doctrine* (2000) at 212: "There is a distinct doctrine of joint enterprise."

(ii) *Joint unlawful enterprise*

*Powell* affirms that an accessory who foresees a risk that the principal offender might, with the *mens rea* of murder, kill the victim is liable for murder even if he did not want this result to occur and might even have urged the principal offender not to kill. He has joined an enterprise knowing this could occur and, for policy reasons, is held responsible for the foreseen result. Even though the crime of murder requires an intention to kill or cause grievous bodily harm, the accessory need only foresee a risk of the principal offender committing murder. While at first glance this looks like classic *Cunningham* recklessness, it must be stressed that mere foresight of death or grievous bodily harm (which would be such recklessness) does not suffice. The accessory must foresee the possibility of the principal offender *intentionally* killing or causing grievous bodily harm. What degree of risk must the accessory foresee? Lord Hutton's answer was plain. The defendant need only foresee the principal acting in such a manner as a "possible incident" of the venture unless the risk was so remote that the jury believe the accessory had "genuinely dismissed it as altogether negligible".

It is worth repeating that the principle in *Powell* applies to all crimes that can be committed by accessories and not just to murder. Thus, for example, if the principal were charged with constructive manslaughter, a crime which only requires that the defendant commit an unlawful act (say, a battery) which is objectively likely to cause some physical injury, the accessory will also be liable for manslaughter if he foresees a risk that the principal offender might intentionally or recklessly (the *mens rea* of battery) hit the victim.

There are problems with the *Powell* principle. In the *English* appeal the joint enterprise was to inflict blows with wooden posts. What would have been the position if the victim had died from blows inflicted by the posts but the accessory had not foreseen that result? If the principal offender (unknown to the defendant) inflicted the blows with intent to kill or cause grievous bodily harm and was convicted of murder, would the defendant escape all liability for the death? It is unfortunate that a definitive answer is not given to this by the House of Lords' decision (although it is certainly possible to interpret it as affirming this). However, both policy and principle would suggest that the answer should be no. The first stage would be for the jury to find that the act was within the scope of the joint unlawful enterprise. Precise liability should then be determined by the defendant's *mens rea*. The accessory lacks the *mens rea* for murder as defined by *Powell* but clearly satisfies all the requirements for constructive manslaughter and should be liable for that offence.

This was the approach adopted in the pre-Powell case of *Stewart and Schofield*[51] where the joint unlawful enterprise was to rob a shop while armed with a scaffolding bar to inflict only moderate injury. The principal offender, motivated by racial hatred, beat the victim to death. This act was found to be within the scope of the joint unlawful enterprise and the principal was liable for murder. The accessory, who had not foreseen this result, was nevertheless liable for constructive manslaughter. This approach was adopted in the following post-*Powell* case.

---

[51] [1995] 1 Cr.App.R.441.

## R. v Gilmour [2000] 2 Cr.App.R.407 (Court of Appeal of Northern Ireland)

The defendant drove the principal offenders to a house knowing that it was going to be petrol-bombed. Three people died in the fire. The defendant was convicted of murder. On appeal, it was found that the defendant had not realised the principals intended to inflict grievous bodily harm. He thought they intended to start a fire to put the occupants in fear and intimidate them. Accordingly, the murder conviction was quashed. The issue then was whether he could be found guilty of manslaughter.

Carswell L.C.J.:

"The appellant foresaw that the principals would carry out the act of throwing a petrol bomb into the house, but did not realise that in so doing they intended to kill or do grievous bodily harm to the occupants... The line of authority represented by such cases as *Anderson* and *Morris*, approved in *R. v Powell and English*, deals with situations where the principal departs from the contemplated joint enterprise and perpetrates a more serious act of a different kind unforeseen by the accessory. In such cases it is established that the accessory is not liable at all for such unforeseen acts. It does not follow that the same result should follow where the principal carries out the very act contemplated by the accessory, though the latter does not realise that the principal intends a more serious consequence from the act.

We do not consider that we are obliged by authority to hold that the accessory in such a case must be acquitted of manslaughter as well as murder. The cases in which an accessory has been found not guilty both of murder and manslaughter all concern a departure by the principal from the *actus reus* contemplated by the accessory, not a difference between the parties in respect of the *mens rea* of each. In such cases the view has prevailed that it would be wrong to hold the accessory liable when the principal committed an act which the accessory did not contemplate or authorise. We do not, however, see any convincing policy reason why a person acting as an accessory to a principal who carries out the very deed contemplated by both should not be guilty of the degree of offence appropriate to the intent with which he so acted."

**Appeal allowed; verdict of guilty of manslaughter substituted**

This approach was followed again in *Day*[52] where it was stated that if the accessory only foresees some harm in the course of a joint attack, but does not foresee the "murderous state of mind" of the principals, he can be convicted of manslaughter while the principals are convicted of murder. In such a case where the principals have "larger intentions" than the accessory, "there is no reason why the participants should not be convicted and sentenced appropriately as their several states of mind dictate."

The situation is different when, unlike the above cases, the principal offender's acts take him outside the scope of the joint enterprise. This is what happened in the *English* appeal. The House of Lords indicated that English fully deserved punishment for the attack but as he had already spent a number of years in detention, no further consideration was given to the matter. However, in quashing his conviction, the House of Lords did not substitute a manslaughter verdict and, indeed, indicated that he should not be liable for manslaughter. Despite this, even

---

[52] [2001] Crim.L.R.984.

in this situation there is a strong argument that the accessory should be liable for manslaughter. The defendant in the *English* appeal could easily have been charged with assault or conspiracy to commit an aggravated assault, but the principle of fair labelling surely dictates that he should have been liable for manslaughter. While he was no longer a party to a murderous joint enterprise, he was, at the very least, a party to a joint enterprise involving a battery which was objectively likely to cause some physical harm. He should have been convicted of constructive manslaughter.[53]

A further problem is that it appears from *Powell* that even if the defendant does foresee the principal offender will kill with the *mens rea* of murder, he will escape liability (for murder) if the principal offender uses a weapon taking him outside the scope of the joint unlawful enterprise. If, in the *English* appeal, the accessory had foreseen that the principal offender might beat the officer to death with a wooden post, he would escape liability if the principal offender killed with a gun. There can be no justification for such an approach. While, of course, a gun is intrinsically more dangerous than a wooden post, nevertheless, if the defendant has foreseen the principal offender murdering the victim, it is difficult to see why the method of killing, or the instrument used, should make such a fundamental difference.

Finally, one must question whether their Lordships were right to conclude that while the principal offender is only guilty of murder if he intended to kill or cause grievous bodily harm, the secondary party, who might not even have been present at the scene of the crime, is guilty of murder on the basis of merely foreseeing a risk that the principal offender might commit murder. While it has been held not to be contrary to Article 6 of the European Convention on Human Rights for an accessory to be convicted of murder with a lesser *mens rea* than the principal offender,[54] the question still remains whether this is the right approach in terms of principle and policy.

The argument in favour of the *Powell* approach is that this is not holding the accessory liable for murder by recklessness; it is not enough that the accessory foresees death or grievous bodily harm. If the accessory knows that the principal offender might kill with the *mens rea* of murder "he becomes a participant in an intentional offence".[55] Because of the dangerousness of collaborative ventures and group violence, policy dictates that anyone who goes along with a venture knowing that murder might occur (and not just a killing), ought to be counted a murderer when that very crime is committed. On the other hand, it can be argued that an accessory should not be guilty of the same offence as the principal offender if he has a lesser *mens rea*. As has been said: "Since the act and cause requirements of accomplice liability are so minimal, and since ... an accomplice [can be punished] the same as the perpetrator of the substantive offence, the *mens rea* requirement becomes more significant. Accomplice liability hinges upon the *mens rea* element."[56] It is accordingly submitted that in such cases the extent of the

---

[53] Clarkson, "Complicity, *Powell* and Manslaughter" [1998] Crim.L.R.556. *Cf.* Smith, [1998] Crim.L.R.232.

[54] *Concannon* [2002] Crim.L.R.213.

[55] Smith [1998] Crim.L.R.49. See also Smith, "Criminal Liability of Accessories: Law and Law Reform" (1997) 113 L.Q.R. 453.

[56] Mueller, "The Mens Rea of Accomplice Liability" (1988) 61 South. Calif.L.R.2169 at 2172.

accessory's liability should be dependent upon *mens rea*. If the accessory *intends* death or grievous bodily harm (bearing in mind that intention can be inferred in cases where the consequence is foreseen as virtually certain) a murder verdict is appropriate. However, if the accessory only foresees a risk that the principal will cause death with the requisite *mens rea* of murder, this is only a species of recklessness and the accessory should only be convicted of manslaughter.[57] It is a matter of regret that the House of Lords has firmly rejected such a view.

(iii) *Counselling*

Before *Powell* it was relatively clear that it was only necessary to prove that the accessory knew that the offence was to be committed. It was enough that he foresaw a real or substantial risk of the principal committing the offence.[58] The leading, and much cited, case is *N.C.B. v Gamble*[59] where a weigh-bridge operator, in the course of his job, issued a ticket to a driver leaving the colliery premises, knowing that the lorry was over-loaded. The Coal Board (as the weigh-bridge operator's employer) was convicted of being an accessory to the offence of using a lorry on the road with a load weighing more than that permitted.[60] It was held that the only *mens rea* required was knowledge of the circumstances rendering the act criminal. Devlin J. concluded that:

"an indifference to the result of crime does not of itself negative abetting. If one man deliberately sells to another a gun to be used for murdering a third, he may be indifferent about whether the third man lives or dies and interested only in the cash profit to be made out of the sale, but he can still be an aider and abettor."[61]

This approach has been criticised by Williams:

"It seems a strong thing to hold that a man who is simply pursuing his ordinary and lawful vocation, and takes no special steps to assist illegalities, becomes involved as a party to crime committed by the customer merely because he realises that his customer will be enabled by what he himself does to commit such a crime."[62]

On the other hand, it is possible to defend the approach adopted in *Gamble*. If the defendant knows that a crime is to be committed, why should he be allowed to shelter behind a shield that he was "just doing his job"? Legitimate business enterprise should not be permitted to extend to the knowing provision of tools for the commission of crime.

The *Gamble* rule applies to cases of complicity where one person has the right to control the actions of another.[63] The central question, however, is whether these rules have been affected by *Powell*. *Gamble*, and its progeny, states that the defendant must foresee the risk of the crime occurring. For example, when supplying a gun to the principal offender, the accessory must foresee the risk of the victim being killed. This is classic *Cunningham* recklessness. *Powell*, however,

[57] This used to be the position in English law. See, *e.g. Reid* (1975) 62 Cr.App.R.109.
[58] *Rook* (1993) 97 Cr.App.R.327.
[59] [1959] 1 Q.B.11. See also *D.P.P. v Lynch* [1975] A.C. 653.
[60] Contrary to the Motor Vehicles (Construction and Use) Regulations, 68 and 104, 1955.
[61] [1959] 1 Q.B.11 at 23.
[62] *Textbook of Criminal Law* (2nd ed., 1983), p. 342.
[63] *Alford Transport Ltd* [1997] 2 Cr.App.R.326.

rules that the accessory, to be liable for murder, must foresee the risk of the principal offender killing *with the mens rea of murder*. These two formulations are not the same. An accessory might foresee the risk of a principal killing "accidentally" when the gun was only being used to frighten but not foresee the principal deliberately killing.

While the answer to this problem is not clear, the better view is that the *Powell* rule should apply in all cases. As argued earlier, it is impossible in practice, and pointless in principle, to draw sharp distinctions between counsellors and parties to joint unlawful enterprises. Returning to the case of *Rook*[64] there seems no difference in culpability whether the defendant is classed as a counsellor or a member of a joint unlawful enterprise. In an area of law renowned for its complexity, there would be much to be gained from the development of a single rule applicable to most cases of complicity. It is to be hoped that, to the extent that there is a difference between *Powell* and *Gamble*, the former decision will be followed.

One final question remains. To what extent must the accessory know the details of the principal's intended offence? Is it enough that he knows that some sort of property offence is being planned or does he need to have a fair idea of when or how or where? In the case of *Bainbridge*[65] it was held that as long as the defendant was aware of the type of offence to be committed, that would be enough to incriminate him. The "type of offence" formula was not without difficulties (establishing, for example, whether one offence was of a similar type to another) and so the issue was re-examined by the House of Lords in the following case.

### Maxwell v D.P.P. for Northern Ireland (1979) 68 Cr.App.R.128 (House of Lords)

Lord Scarman:
"I think *Bainbridge* ... was correctly decided. But I agree with counsel for the appellant that in the instant case the Court of Criminal Appeal in Northern Ireland has gone further than the Court of Criminal Appeal for England and Wales found it necessary to go in *Bainbridge*. It is not possible in the present case to declare that it is proved, beyond reasonable doubt, that the appellant knew a bomb attack upon the Inn was intended by those whom he was assisting. It is not established, therefore, that he knew the particular type of crime intended. The Court, however, refused to limit criminal responsibility by reference to knowledge by the accused of the type or class of crime intended by those whom he assisted. Instead, the Court has formulated a principle which avoids the uncertainties and ambiguities of classification. The guilt of an accessory springs, according to the Court's formulation, 'from the fact that he contemplates the commission of one (or more) of a number of crimes by the principal and he intentionally lends his assistance in order that such a crime will be committed': *per* Sir Robert Lowry C.J. 'The relevant crime', the Lord Chief Justice continues, 'must be within the contemplation of the accomplice and only exceptionally would evidence be found to support the allegation that the accomplice had given the principal a completely blank cheque'.

The principle thus formulated has great merit. It directs attention to the state of mind of the accused—not what he ought to have in contemplation, but what he did have: it avoids definition and classification, while ensuring that a man will not be convicted of aiding and abetting any offence his principal may commit, but only one which is within his

---

[64] *Above*, p. 542.
[65] [1960] 1 Q.B. 129.

contemplation. He may have in contemplation only one offence, or several: and the several which he contemplates he may see as alternatives. An accessory who leaves it to his principal to choose is liable, provided always the choice is made from the range of offences from which the accessory contemplates the choice will be made. Although the court's formulation of the principle goes further than the earlier cases, it is a sound development of the law and in no way inconsistent with them. I accept it as good judge-made law in a field where there is no statute to offer guidance."

*Maxwell* left one question unresolved. Does the accessory continue to be liable for the crimes of the principal so long as they continue to be on his "shopping list" of crimes? One could imagine the well-worn and well-used jemmy being the source of endless liability for the supplier of it. There is nothing in the law as it presently stands, which prevents the accessory being implicated every time the tool is used for one of the "shopping list" crimes—although it does not appear to have been a problem in practice.[66]

Assuming the earlier argument, that *Powell* applies in all such cases, is accepted, these cases must be read in the light of that decision. When *Maxwell* states that "the crime" must be within the contemplation of the accessory, this must be interpreted literally as meaning that the accessory must foresee the principal offender committing the crime with the appropriate *mens rea*.

## 5. Procuring

### Attorney-General's Reference (No. 1 of 1975) [1975] Q.B. 773 (Court of Appeal, Criminal Division)

The defendant surreptitiously laced a friend's drinks with double measures of spirits when he knew his friend would be driving home. He was charged with aiding, abetting, counselling and procuring the offence of driving with an excess quantity of alcohol in the blood under section 6(1) of the Road Traffic Act 1972. The reference concerned the question of whether there had to be a shared intention between the parties or encouragement of the offence.

Lord Widgery C.J.:
"Of course it is the fact that in the great majority of instances where a secondary party is sought to be convicted of an offence there has been a contact between the principal offender and the secondary party. Aiding and abetting almost inevitably involves a situation in which the secondary party and the main offender are together at some stage discussing the plans which they may be making in respect of the alleged offence, and are in contact so that each knows what is passing through the mind of the other.

In the same way it seems to us that a person, who counsels the commission of a crime by another, almost inevitably comes to a moment when he is in contact with the other, when he is discussing the offence with that other and when, to use the words of the statute, he counsels the other to commit the offence.

The fact that so often the relationship between the secondary party and the principal will be such that there is a meeting of minds between them caused the trial judge in the case from which this reference is derived to think that this was really an essential feature of proving or establishing the guilt of the secondary party and, as we understand his judgment, he took the view that in the absence of some sort of meeting of minds, some sort of mental link between the secondary party and the principal, there could be no aiding, abetting or counselling of the offence within the meaning of the section.

[66] Under the Law Commission's proposals the problem would cease to exist because liability would be for the initial act of assistance or encouragement rather than for the principal's crime.

So far as aiding, abetting and counselling is concerned we would go a long way with that conclusion. It may very well be, as I said a moment ago, difficult to think of a case of aiding, abetting or counselling when the parties have not met and have not discussed in some respects the terms of the offence which they have in mind. But we do not see why a similar principle should apply to procuring. We approach section 8 of the Act of 1861 on the basis that the words should be given their ordinary meaning, if possible. We approach the section on the basis also that if four words are employed here, 'aid, abet, counsel or procure', the probability is that there is a difference between each of those four words and the other three, because, if there were no such difference, then Parliament would be wasting time in using four words where two or three would do. Thus, in deciding whether that which is assumed to be done under our reference was a criminal offence we approach the section on the footing that each word must be given its ordinary meaning.

To procure means to produce by endeavour. You procure a thing by setting out to see that it happens and taking the appropriate steps to produce that happening. We think that there are plenty of instances in which a person may be said to procure the commission of a crime by another even though there is no sort of conspiracy between the two, even though there is no attempt at agreement or discussion as to the form which the offence should take. In our judgment the offence described in this reference is such a case.

If one looks back at the facts of the reference: the accused surreptitiously laced his friend's drink. This is an important element and, although we are not going to decide today anything other than the problem posed to us, it may well be that, in similar cases where the lacing of the drink or the introduction of the extra alcohol is known to the driver, quite different considerations may apply. We say that because, where the driver has no knowledge of what is happening, in most instances he would have no means of preventing the offence from being committed. If the driver is unaware of what has happened, he will not be taking precautions. He will get into his car seat, switch on the ignition and drive home and, consequently, the conception of another procuring the commission of the offence by the driver is very much stronger where the driver is innocent of all knowledge of what is happening, as in the present case where the lacing of the drink was surreptitious.

The second thing which is important in the facts set out in our reference is that, following and in consequence of the introduction of the extra alcohol, the friend drove with an excess quantity of alcohol in his blood. Causation here is important. You cannot procure an offence unless there is a causal link between what you do and the commission of the offence, and here we are told that in consequence of the addition of this alcohol the driver, when he drove home, drove with an excess quantity of alcohol in his body.

Giving the words their ordinary meaning in English, and asking oneself whether in those circumstances the offence has been procured, we are in no doubt that the answer is that it has. It has been procured because, unknown to the driver and without his collaboration, he has been put in a position in which in fact he has committed an offence which he never would have committed otherwise."

**Opinion accordingly**

This case was followed a number of years later by another, more bizarre, case of lacing. In *Blakely, Sutton*[67] the defendants laced the principal's tonic water with vodka. They intended to tell him before he left to drive home so that he would stay the night. In other words, they gave him the alcohol so that he would *not* drive. Unfortunately, the principal left before they could tell him and was subsequently found to be over the legal limit when breathalysed. The defendants' evidence ensured that the principal was given an absolute discharge to the charge of

---

[67] [1991] Crim.L.R.763.

drink-driving but they were then charged with "aiding, abetting, counselling, procuring and commanding" that offence. In fact, as only procuring was alleged, the case proceeded on this footing. They appealed against their conviction, the questions being whether procuring could be committed recklessly and, if so, whether this included inadvertent recklessness.

The answer to the second question was a definite "no". However, the Court of Appeal was more tentative in its response to the first question. It was stated that it "must, at least, be shown that the accused contemplated that his act would or might bring about or assist the commission of the principal offence: he must have been prepared nevertheless to do his own act, and he must have done that act intentionally." But it was further stated that in relation "to those accused only of procuring and perhaps also those accused only of counselling and commanding, it might be . . . that it was necessary to prove that the accused intended to bring about the principal offence". The appeal was allowed.

It is submitted that if one accepts that to procure is "to produce by endeavour" then it is impossible to avoid the conclusion that intention is required and that there is some merit in continuing to regard procuring in this way. Take the example of the generous host who makes drink available for her guests but leaves them to decide whether they will drink, walk home or drive. If charged with procuring the principal's offence of drunken driving, then, following *Attorney-General's Reference (No. 1 of 1975)*, she should be acquitted. But, if procuring can be satisfied by mere contemplation, then generous hosts (and publicans) could be convicted. Does this satisfactorily identify those who are truly deserving of blame?[68]

However, *Attorney-General's Reference (No. 1 of 1975)* is not inviolate. The view that each of the terms in section 8 has a separate meaning is already much discredited. Clearly, therefore, one could discard the particular meaning given to "procuring". Indeed, this view has been expressed by the Law Commission.[69] Under its proposals, complicity in crime would fall within the two inchoate offences of assisting or encouraging. However, the Law Commission recognises that cases with facts such as those in *Attorney-General's Reference (No. 1 of 1975)* or *Blakely, Sutton* (where the principal is unaware not only of the "help" but also of doing the act which constitutes the offence) do not fit easily into either concept. The Law Commission concludes that a special offence of procurement limited to strict liability cases (because this is where the "rare" problem cases have arisen) would resolve the matter.[70]

## 6. Reform Proposals: Assisting and Encouraging Crime

The Law Commission proposals represent a radical rethink of the law relating to complicity. The terms "aid, abet, counsel or procure" would be jettisoned as would

---

[68] It is accepted that Lord Widgery himself in *Attorney-General's Reference* suggested that the problem of the generous host should be resolved by reference to cases on the supply of tools, etc., for use in a crime: *i.e.* liability based upon awareness rather than intention. However, as seen, such cases should now be read subject to the principles established in *Powell; English*.
[69] Law Commission Consultation Paper No. 131, *Assisting and Encouraging Crime* (1993), para. 4.11.
[70] *ibid.*, paras 4.192–4.197.

the derivative principle of liability for the full offence. Instead, two new inchoate offences would be created: assisting crime and encouraging crime. This latter offence would replace the existing inchoate offence of incitement. Basic definitions of the proposed offences are contained in the Consultation paper.

### Law Commission Consultation Paper, No. 131, Assisting and Encouraging Crime (1993), paras 4.99, 4.163:

"*4.99* ...
(1) A person commits the offence of assisting crime if he
    (a) knows or believes that another ('the principal') is doing or causing to be done, or will do or cause to be done, acts that do or will involve the commission of an offence by the principal; and
    (b) knows or believes that the principal, in so acting, does or will do so with the fault required for the offence in question; and
    (c) does any act that he knows or believes assists or will assist the principal in committing the offence.
(2) Assistance includes giving the principal advice as to [how to] commit the offence, or as to how to avoid detention or apprehension before or during the commission of the offence.[71]

*4.163* ...
(1) A person commits the offence of encouraging crime if he
    (a) solicits, commands or encourages another ('the principal') to do or cause to be done an act or acts which, if done, will involve the commission of an offence by the principal; and
    (b) intends that that act or those acts should be done by the principal; and
    (c) knows or believes that the principal, in so acting, will do so with the fault required for the offence in question.
(2) The solicitation, command or encouragement must be brought to the attention of the principal, but it is irrelevant to the person's guilt whether or not the principal reacts to or is influenced by the solicitation, command or encouragement."[72]

The Law Commission's analysis of complicity as consisting of either encouraging or assisting is to be welcomed. Such reform would remove many of the uncertainties and inadequacies of the current law. However, there is much less support for the radical proposal to abandon derivative liability.[73] Whether this is

---

[71] Provisions also make it clear that a person does not assist in the commission of an offence if all he does is to fail to prevent (or impede) the commission of the offence; a person will be guilty if he knows or believes an offence is to be committed even if he does not know the time or place, etc.; he is also guilty if he knows or believes that the principal intends to commit one of a number of offences and does any act that he knows or believes will assist the principal in committing whichever of those offences the principal in fact intends (addressing the "shopping-list" problem): para. 4.99.

[72] Further provisions establish that the defendant need not know the identity of the principal, nor have any particular principal or group of principals in mind, provided that he intends his communication to be acted on by any person to whose attention it comes (thus covering cases where, for example, there is a general incitement to commit a crime in a newspaper article); defendants can be convicted of the new offence if they encourage an offence without intending that it should be committed at a specific time or place: para. 4.163.

[73] See Smith, "Criminal Liability of Accessories: Law and Law Reform" (1997) 113 L.Q.R. 453 at 463 and Smith (K.J.M.), "The Law Commission Consultation Paper on Complicity: (1) A Blueprint for Rationalisation" [1994] Crim.L.R.239 at 250.

too big a price to pay for the introduction of clarity into the law is examined in the final section of this chapter.


## III. The Limits of Accessorial Liability


### A. *No Principal Offender*

As we have seen, complicity is currently a form of derivative liability. It presupposes the existence of a crime. "There is one crime and that it has been committed must be established before there can be any question of criminal guilt or participation in it."[74] In *Dias*[75] the defendant supplied heroin to the victim who injected himself and died. It was held that as there is "no offence of self-manslaughter" the defendant could not be guilty as a secondary party.

This simple proposition requires qualification:

(a) The principal may be acquitted through lack of evidence or because of some procedural defect that applies to her. Secondary parties may nevertheless be convicted if the evidence shows clearly that there was a crime.

(b) The principal may be acquitted and the court can apply the doctrine of innocent agency to justify the conviction of the secondary party. In such a case the secondary party is in fact deemed to be the principal offender.

(c) In situations where the doctrine of innocent agency is inapplicable but where the *actus reus* has been committed, the accessory may be convicted even though the principal offender is acquitted because of lack of *mens rea* or the existence of a defence.

The relationship between the last two propositions needs to be examined.


### R. v Bourne (1952) 36 Cr.App.R.1251 (Court of Criminal Appeal)

The defendant terrorised his wife into committing buggery with a dog. He was convicted of aiding and abetting his wife to commit buggery with a dog. He appealed.

Lord Goddard C.J.:
"I am willing to assume for the purpose of this case ... that if this woman had been charged herself with committing the offence, she could have set up the plea of duress, not as showing that no offence had been committed, but as showing that she had no *mens rea* because her will was overborne by threats of imprisonment or violence so that she would be excused from punishment.... [T]he offence of buggery ... depends on the act, and if an act of buggery is committed, the felony is committed.

---

[74] Turner, *Russell on Crime* (12th ed., 1964), p. 128; affirmed in *Surujpaul v R.* [1958] 3 All E.R. 300 at 301.
[75] [2001] EWCA Crim 2986.

... The evidence was ... that he caused his wife to have connection with a dog, and ... he is guilty, whether you call him an aider and abettor or an accessory, as a principal in the second degree."

Appeal dismissed

## R. v Cogan and Leak [1976] Q.B. 217 (Court of Appeal, Criminal Division)

Leak compelled his wife to have sexual intercourse with Cogan, who believed that she consented. As Cogan's conviction was quashed on the strength of his belief, it became necessary to decide whether Leak's conviction as aider and abettor could stand.

Lawton L.J.:
"Leak's appeal against conviction was based on the proposition that he could not be found guilty of aiding and abetting Cogan to rape his wife if Cogan was acquitted of that offence as he was deemed in law to have been when his conviction was quashed. ... [A]s was said by this court in *R. v Quick* [1973] Q.B. 910, 923, when considering this kind of problem:

'The facts of each case ... have to be considered and in particular what is alleged to have been done by way of aiding and abetting.'

The only case which counsel for Leak submitted had a direct bearing on the problem of Leak's guilt was *Walters v Lunt* [1951] 2 All E.R. 645. In that case the respondents had been charged under the Larceny Act 1916, s.33(1), with receiving from a child aged seven years, certain articles knowing them to have been stolen. In 1951 a child under eight years was deemed in law to be incapable of committing a crime: it followed that at the time of receipt by the respondents the articles had not been stolen and that the charges had not been proved. That case is very different from this because here one fact is clear—the wife had been raped.

Cogan had had sexual intercourse with her without her consent. The fact that Cogan was innocent of rape because he believed that she was consenting does not affect the position that she was raped.

Her ravishment had come about because Leak had wanted it to happen and had taken action to see that it did by persuading Cogan to use his body as the instrument for the necessary physical act. In the language of the law the act of sexual intercourse without the wife's consent was the *actus reus*; it had been procured by Leak who had the appropriate *mens rea*, namely his intention that Cogan should have sexual intercourse with her without her consent. In our judgment it is irrelevant that the man whom Leak had procured to do the physical act himself did not intend to have sexual intercourse with the wife without her consent. Leak was using him as a means to procure a criminal purpose. ...

Had Leak been indicted as a principal offender, the case against him would have been clear beyond argument. Should he be allowed to go free because he was charged with 'being aider and abettor to the same offence'? If we are right in our opinion that the wife had been raped (and no one outside a court of law would say that she had not been), then the particulars of offence accurately stated what Leak had done, namely he had procured Cogan to commit the offence. This would suffice to uphold the conviction. We would prefer, however, to uphold it on a wider basis. In our judgment convictions should not be upset because of mere technicalities of pleading in an indictment. Leak knew what the case against him was and the facts in support of that case were proved. But for the fact that the jury thought that Cogan in his intoxicated condition might have mistaken the wife's sobs and distress for expressions of her consent, no question of any kind would have arisen about the form of pleading. By his written statement Leak virtually admitted what he had done. As Judge Chapman said in *R. v Humphreys* [1965] 3 All E.R. 689, 692:

'It would be anomalous if a person who admitted to a substantial part in the perpetration of a misdemeanour as aider and abettor could not be convicted on his own admission merely because the person alleged to have been aided and abetted was not or could not be convicted.'

In the circumstances of this case it would be more than anomalous: it would be an affront to justice and to the common sense of ordinary folk. It was for these reasons that we dismissed the appeal against conviction."

**Appeal dismissed**

Two main arguments were advanced in *Cogan and Leak*. The first concerned the doctrine of innocent agency. It is quite clear that crimes may be committed through an innocent agent but to employ it in *Cogan and Leak* would be to stretch the doctrine to implausible lengths. Even if one accepts the abuse of language involved in saying that Leak raped his wife when he committed no such act against her, Williams has demonstrated the fundamental flaw with its use in this context:

"The decision was rendered possible by the fact that the defendant happened to be a man. Rape can only be perpetrated by a man; the statute says so ... if the duress is applied by a woman it would need an even greater degree of hawkishness than that displayed by the court in *Cogan* to call her a constructive man. Yet it is highly illogical that a man can commit rape through an innocent agent when a woman cannot."[76]

Fletcher adds that cases of innocent agency or "perpetrator-by-means" ought to be restricted to situations where "the party behind the scenes in fact dominates and controls his agent".[77] Finally, if the doctrine was thought to be applicable in *Cogan and Leak* it is difficult to see why it was not invoked in *Bourne*.

If the doctrine of innocent agency is, therefore, inappropriate in some circumstances, an alternative basis for liability has to be found. This can be derived from the assertion by Lawton L.J. that it was clear that "the wife had been raped" and that Leak had procured the rape (a similar view is implicit in *Bourne*). However, a finding of rape could only follow if both *actus reus* and *mens rea* were established and the argument is, thus, of doubtful validity. However, it has been refined and developed in subsequent cases. In *Millward*[78] it was held that the defendant could be liable for procuring a driving offence provided there is an *actus reus* even though the principal offender is acquitted.[79] There are doubts about whether there was an *actus reus* on the facts of *Millward*[80] but the principle itself appears to be gaining momentum.

### D.P.P. v K and B [1997] 1 Cr.App.R.36 (Court of Appeal, Criminal Division)

Two girls, aged 14 and 11, were alleged to have procured the rape of another girl by the principal offender, a boy (never traced) aged between 10 and 14. The magistrates acquitted the girls on the basis (*inter alia*) that the prosecution had failed to rebut the presumption of *doli incapax* in relation to the boy. The prosecution appealed by way of case stated.

Russell L.J.:
"In my judgment, the decision of the magistrate in this appeal cannot be supported. There is no doubt whatever that 'W' was the victim of unlawful sexual intercourse without her

[76] *Textbook of Criminal Law* (2nd ed., 1983), p. 371.
[77] Fletcher, *Rethinking Criminal Law* (1978), pp. 665–667. Cf. *Stringer* (1992) 94 Cr.App.R.13.
[78] [1994] Crim.L.R.527.
[79] *Wheelhouse* [1994] Crim.L.R.756 followed *Millward* although it was unnecessary to do so on the facts since the doctrine of innocent agency applied.
[80] See, for example, commentary to *Loukes* [1996] Crim.L.R.341 at 343.

consent; such was not disputed. The *actus reus* was proved. The respondents procured the situation which included the sexual intercourse. It would, in my view, be singularly unattractive to find that because of the absence of a mental element on the part of the principal, the procurers could thereby escape conviction when, as the magistrate found, K and B had the requisite *mens rea* namely, the desire that rape should take place and the procuring of it.

In my judgment, neither authority nor common sense nor justice compels this Court to support the finding of the magistrates."

Appeal allowed

Two points must be stressed. First, there must be an *actus reus*. If there is no *actus reus*, the secondary party cannot be found liable. So, for example, in *Loukes*,[81] a case involving causing death by dangerous driving,[82] the principal was acquitted because there was insufficient evidence that he knew of the dangerous condition of the vehicle or that it was so obvious that he ought to have known (an objective standard of driving). There was, therefore, no evidence of dangerous driving on his part, and thus no *actus reus*. In such circumstances the defendant, whose business it was to oversee the condition of the vehicles, could not be convicted of procuring the offence.

The underlying ratonale of these developments can be accepted in relation to the procuring of offences where, as we have seen, it is causation and not consensus that is material and the principal need not even be aware that a crime is being committed. However, the application of the principle in cases such as *Loukes* is more questionable. In this case, and in *Roberts and George*,[83] the offence of causing death by dangerous driving was described as being a strict liability offence. Because there was insufficient evidence of dangerous driving by the principal offender, there was no *actus reus*. However, this offence could be regarded as one of negligence. Culpability is required in that the driving must be dangerous.[84] According to this latter analysis, there was an *actus reus* in these cases and the procurer, assuming his *mens rea* was established, should have been liable.

The second point to stress is that the principle that the accessory can be liable if there is an *actus reus* has only been applied in cases of procuring. Assuming the *Powell* principle does extend to all other situations of complicity, it is difficult to see how, in principle, an accessory could be liable if the principal offender is not liable. Under *Powell* the accessory must realise that there is a risk the principal offender will commit the offence with the *mens rea* of that offence. The accessory's liability is, thus, dependent upon that of the principal.

This does, at first sight, seem anomalous. There appears to be one rule for procuring and another for other forms of complicity. This is compounded when one considers that the prosecution does not even have to specify the form of complicity in the charge. However, the problem may not, in fact, be as significant as it seems. If the accessory does have the appropriate *mens rea* and the crime is committed by a principal offender who lacks *mens rea* or who has a defence such as

---

[81] [1996] 1 Cr.App.R.444; see also *Thornton v Mitchell* [1940] 1 All E.R. 339 and *Roberts and George* [1997] Crim.L.R.209.
[82] Contrary to the Road Traffic Act 1988, ss.1 and 2A (as amended by the Road Traffic Act 1991).
[83] [1997] Crim.L.R.209.
[84] Smith, Commentary to *Roberts and George, ibid.*, at 211.

duress, the situation would almost certainly be regarded as one of procuring or innocent agency. Liability could then be imposed under the above principles.

## B. *Accessory can be Guilty of Graver Offence than the One Committed*

Until the following decision in *Howe* the law was that if the principal had the *mens rea* of one offence, such as manslaughter, it was not possible for an accessory not present at the scene of the crime to be guilty of the graver offence of murder.[85] The reason for this rule was "that one could [not] say that that which was done can be said to be done with the intention of the defendant who was not present at the time". Without, it must be said, much discussion of the merits or demerits of this approach, the law has now changed.

### R. v Howe [1987] 1 A.C. 417 (House of Lords)

(The facts and a fuller extract appear, *above*, p. 346.)

Lord Mackay of Clashfern:
"I turn now to the second certified question [whether a secondary party can be convicted of murder despite the conviction of the principal for manslaughter] ... I am of the opinion that the Court of Appeal reached the correct conclusion upon it as a matter of principle.
Giving the judgment of the Court of Appeal Lord Lane C.J. said [1986] Q.B. 626, 641–642:
'The judge based himself on a decision of this court in *R. v Richards*. The facts in that case were that Mrs Richards paid two men to inflict injuries on her husband which she intended should "put him in hospital for a month". The two wounded the husband but not seriously. They were acquitted of wounding with intent but convicted of unlawful wounding. Mrs Richards herself was convicted of wounding with intent, the jury plainly, and not surprisingly, believing that she had the necessary intent, though the two men had not. She appealed against her conviction on the ground that she could not properly be convicted as accessory before the fact to a crime more serious than that committed by the principals in the first degree. The appeal was allowed and the conviction for unlawful wounding was substituted. The court followed a passage from *Hawkins' Pleas of the Crown*, vol. 2. c. 29, para. 15: "I take it to be an uncontroverted rule that [the offence of the accessory can never rise higher than that of the principal]; it seeming incongruous and absurd that he who is punished only as a partaker of the guilt of another, should be adjudged guilty of a higher crime than the other."
James L.J. delivering the judgment in *R. v Richards* said: "If there is only one offence committed, and that is the offence of unlawful wounding, then the person who has requested that offence to be committed, or advised that that offence be committed, cannot be guilty of a graver offence than that in fact which was committed." The decision in *R. v Richards* has been the subject of some criticism ... Counsel before us posed the situation where A hands a gun to D informing him that it is loaded with blank ammunition only and telling him to go and scare X by discharging it. The ammunition is in fact live, as A knows, and X is killed. D is convicted only of manslaughter, as he might be on those facts. It would seem absurd that A

[85] *Richards* [1974] Q.B. 776.

should thereby escape conviction for murder. We take the view that *R. v Richards* was incorrectly decided, but it seems to us that it cannot properly be distinguished from the instant case.'

I consider that the reasoning of Lord Lane C.J. is entirely correct and I would affirm his view that where a person has been killed and that result is the result intended by another participant, the mere fact that the actual killer may be convicted only of the reduced charge of manslaughter for some reason special to himself does not, in my opinion in any way, result in a compulsory reduction for the other participant."

Appeal dismissed

It has been pointed out[86] that in neither *Howe* nor *Richards* was any real attempt made to understand the theoretical underpinnings of the two positions. Since it has long been possible to convict those present at the scene of the crime of a more serious offence than the principal, at one level, *Howe* merely reflects the increasing trend of regarding presence as not determinative of anything. However, it is a departure "from orthodox complicity theory that insists on the parties' sharing in liability for *one* offence".[87] In other words, this may be a departure from derivative liability similar to that in cases such as *Cogan*. Further, despite all the criticism of *Richards* there may have been a sound principle underlying it: that of control. Mrs Richards lacked control over the principal offender and should not have been guilty of a more serious offence despite her greater *mens rea*. We will return to this issue in the final section of this chapter.

## C. Withdrawal of Accessories

A withdrawal from a criminal enterprise may amount to a claim that there is no *actus reus* or *mens rea* of complicity. For example, a person may lend a gun to the principal offender to commit murder, but later take the gun back. If the principal offender shoots the victim with a different gun, the original provider of the gun will not be liable as there will be no *actus reus* of complicity.[88] However, in other cases the accessory's involvement might clearly satisfy the *actus reus* and *mens rea* requirements of complicity but there might be a "withdrawal" before the commission of the offence.[89] This latter scenario is exemplified by the following leading case.

## R. v Becerra and Cooper (1975) 62 Cr.App.R.212 (Court of Appeal, Criminal Division)

Becerra broke into a house with Cooper and another. They intended to steal but Becerra gave a knife to Cooper which he was to use if anyone interrupted them. Lewis, an upstairs

---

[86] Smith (K.J.M.), *A Modern Treatise on the Law of Complicity* (1991), p. 130.

[87] Law Commission Consultation Paper No. 131, *Assisting and Encouraging Crime* (1993), para. 2.38. See also Smith (K.J.M.), *ibid.*, pp. 127–133.

[88] Smith (K.J.M.), "Withdrawal in Complicity: A Restatement of Principles" [2001] Crim.L.R.769.

[89] Smith (*ibid.*) argues that the nature and scope of a withdrawal defence should depend on the rationale for having such a defence: whether it is an incentive for the accessory to desist or whether it is evidence of the accessory's lack of (or diminished) culpability or future dangerousness.

tenant, came to investigate the noise, at which Becerra said "There's a bloke coming. Let's go", and jumped out of a window. As he ran away Cooper stabbed and killed Lewis with the knife. Becerra was convicted with Cooper of murder, and appealed.

Roskill L.J.:

"It was argued in the alternative on behalf of Becerra, that even if there were this common design, ... nonetheless Becerra had open to him a second line of defence, namely that ... —whatever Cooper did immediately before and at the time of the killing of Lewis, Becerra had by then withdrawn from that common design and so should not be convicted of the murder of Lewis, even though the common design had previously been that which I have stated. ...

It is necessary, before dealing with that argument in more detail, to say a word or two about the relevant law. [Roskill L.J. then cited a decision of the Court of Appeal of British Columbia in *Whitehouse (alias Savage)* (1941) 1 W.W.R. 112, at pp. 115 and 116.] 'Can it be said on the facts of this case that a mere change of mental intention and a quitting of the scene of the crime just immediately prior to the striking of the fatal blow will absolve those who participate in the commission of the crime by overt acts up to that moment from all the consequences of its accomplishment by the one who strikes in ignorance of his companion's change of heart? I think not. After a crime has been committed and before a prior abandonment of the common enterprise may be found by a jury there must be, in my view, in the absence of exceptional circumstances, something more than a mere mental change of intention and physical change of place by those associates who wish to dissociate themselves from the consequences attendant upon their willing assistance up to the moment of the actual commission of that crime. I would not attempt to define too closely what must be done in criminal matters involving participation in a common unlawful purpose to break the chain of causation and responsibility. That must depend upon the circumstances of each case but it seems to me that one essential element ought to be established in a case of this kind. Where practicable and reasonable there must be timely communication of the intention to abandon the common purpose from those who wish to dissociate themselves from the contemplated crime to those who desire to continue in it. What is "timely communication" must be determined by the facts of each case but where practicable and reasonable it ought to be such communication, verbal or otherwise, that will serve unequivocal notice upon the other party to the common unlawful cause that if he proceeds upon it he does so without the further aid and assistance of those who withdraw. The unlawful purpose of him who continues alone is then his own and not one in common with those who are no longer parties to it nor liable to its full and final consequences.' ...

In the view of each member of this Court, that passage, if we may respectfully say so, could not be improved upon and we venture to adopt it in its entirety as a correct statement of the law which is to be applied in this case. ...

We therefore turn back to consider the direction which the learned judge gave in the present case to the jury and what was the suggested evidence that Becerra had withdrawn from the common agreement. The suggested evidence is the use by Becerra of the words 'Come on let's go', coupled, ... with his act in going out through the window. The evidence, as the judge pointed out, was that Cooper never heard that nor did the third man. But let it be supposed that that was said and the jury took the view that it was said.

On the facts of this case, in the circumstances then prevailing, the knife having already been used and being contemplated for further use when it was handed over by Becerra to Cooper for the purpose of avoiding (if necessary) by violent means the hazards of identification, if Becerra wanted to withdraw at that stage, he would have to 'countermand,' to use the word that is used in some of the cases or 'repent' to use another word so used, in some manner vastly different and vastly more effective than merely to say 'Come on, let's go' and go out through the window.

It is not necessary, on this application, to decide whether the point of time had arrived at which the only way in which he could effectively withdraw, so as to free himself from joint responsibility for any act Cooper thereafter did in furtherance of the common design, would be physically to intervene so as to stop Cooper attacking Lewis, as the judge suggested, by interposing his own body between them or somehow getting in between them or whether some other action might suffice. That does not arise for decision here. Nor is it necessary to decide whether or not the learned judge was right or wrong, on the facts of this case, . . . [to say] 'and at least take all reasonable steps to prevent the commission of the crime which he had agreed the others should commit'. It is enough for the purposes of deciding this application to say that under the law of this country as it stands, and on the facts (taking them at their highest in favour of Becerra), that which was urged as amounting to withdrawal from the common design was not capable of amounting to such withdrawal. Accordingly Becerra remains responsible, in the eyes of the law, for everything that Cooper did and continued to do after Becerra's disappearance through the window as much as if he had done them himself."

**Appeal dismissed**

Acordingly, there must be, at least, a "timely communication" of the decision to withdraw. This was confirmed in *Rook*[90] where the appellant tried to disassociate himself from the planned murder by simply not being around when the others came to collect him on the way to the crime. "[T]he appellant never told the others that he was not going ahead with the crime. His absence on the day could not possibly amount to 'unequivocal communication' of his withdrawal . . . he had made it quite clear to *himself* that he did not want to be there on the day. But he did not make it clear to the others." However, in *Mitchell and King*[91] it was held that the requirement of communication of withdrawal only applies in cases of pre-planned violence and not to cases of spontaneous violence, although in these latter cases it would be more difficult evidentially to establish withdrawal if there had been no communication.

In some cases, depending on the circumstances, it may be that timely communication alone is not enough and that some further action is required. In *Rook*, for example, the Court of Appeal stated that a suggestion that "a declared intent to withdraw from a conspiracy to dynamite a building is not enough, if the fuse has been set; he must step on the fuse" went too far. "It may be enough that he should have done his best to step on the fuse." Presumably in such cases "some form of correlation [should] exist between the nature or form of the defendant's complicitous behaviour and the nature or form of his required exculpatory action. In crude terms: the greater the extent of inculpatory behaviour the more demanding will be the price of exculpation".[92]

The proposals of the Law Commission which, as has been stated, transform complicity into two inchoate offences, accept pragmatic arguments favouring a defence of withdrawal. In the case of the crime of assistance it is proposed that the defendant must take all reasonable steps to prevent the commission of the crime.[93] With the crime of encouragement, either taking reasonable steps or countermanding the encouragement would suffice.[94]

[90] (1993) 97 Cr.App.R.327. See also *Grundy* [1977] Crim.L.R.543, where the party also sought (successfully) to withdraw before the commission of the crime (some two weeks hence); see also *Croft* (1944) 29 Cr.App.R.169, *Whitefield* (1984) 79 Cr.App.R.36 and *Baker* [1994] Crim.L.R.444.
[91] [1999] Crim.L.R.496.
[92] Smith, *above*, n.88 at 776.
[93] Law Commission Consultation Paper No. 131, *Assisting and Encouraging Crime* (1993), para. 4.136.
[94] *ibid.* para. 4.169. See further, Smith (K.J.M.), "The Law Commission Consultation Paper on Complicity: (1) A Blueprint for Rationalisation" [1994] Crim.L.R.239 at 247–249.

## D. *Victims Cannot Be Accessories*

### R. v Whitehouse [1977] Q.B. 868 (Court of Appeal, Criminal Division)

The defendant pleaded guilty to two charges of inciting his 15-year-old daughter to commit incest with him and was sentenced to two years' imprisonment. He appealed against the sentence but the Court of Appeal granted leave to appeal against conviction on the basis that he might have pleaded guilty to an offence unknown to the law.

Scarman L.J.:

"Is there such an offence known to the law? The difficulty arises from two features of the law. ... First, at common law the crime of incitement consists of inciting another person to commit a crime ... [secondly] ... a woman under the age of 16 cannot commit the crime of incest. But, says the Crown, a man can commit incest, and so they go on to make their submission that a girl of 15 can aid and abet him to do so.

There is no doubt of the general principle, namely that a person, provided always he or she is of the age of criminal responsibility, can be guilty of aiding or abetting a crime even though it be a crime which he or she cannot commit as a principal in the first degree. ...

But what if the person alleged to be aiding and abetting the crime is herself the victim of the crime? This poses the short question with which this appeal is concerned. ...

The important matters in our judgment are these. First this girl, aged 15, belongs to a class which is protected, but not punished, by sections 10 and 11 of the Sexual Offences Act 1956, and secondly the girl is alleged to be the victim of this notional crime. The whole question has an air of artificiality because nobody is suggesting either that the father has committed incest with her or that she has aided and abetted him to commit incest upon her. What is suggested is that the father has committed the crime of incitement because by his words and conduct he has incited her to do that which, of course, she never has done.

The question in our judgment is determined by authority. It is, strictly speaking, persuasive authority only because it deals with a different Act of Parliament, but it is a decision by a strong court which has declared a principle which is as applicable to the statutory provision with which we are concerned as to that with which that case was concerned. The case is *R. v Tyrrell* [1894] 1 Q.B. 710. ...

Lord Coleridge C.J. in giving judgment said, at p. 712:

'The ... Act was passed for the purpose of protecting women and girls against themselves. At the time it was passed there was a discussion as to what point should be fixed as the age of consent. That discussion ended in a compromise, and the age of consent was fixed at 16. With the object of protecting women and girls against themselves the Act of Parliament has made illicit connection with a girl under that age unlawful; if a man wishes to have such illicit connection he must wait until the girl is 16, otherwise he breaks the law; but it is impossible to say that the Act, which is absolutely silent about aiding or abetting, or soliciting or inciting, can have intended that the girls for whose protection it was passed should be punishable under it for the offences committed upon themselves.' ...

In our judgment it is impossible, as a matter of principle, to distinguish *R. v Tyrrell* from the present case. Clearly the relevant provisions of the Sexual Offences Act 1956 are intended to protect women and girls. Most certainly, section 11 is intended to protect girls under the age of 16 from criminal liability, and the Act as a whole exists, in so far as it deals with women and girls exposed to sexual threat, to protect them. The very fact that girls under the age of 16 are protected from criminal liability for what would otherwise be incest demonstrates that this girl who is said to have been the subject of incitement was being incited to do something which, if she did it, could not be a crime by her. ...

We have therefore come to the conclusion, with regret, that the indictment does not disclose an offence known to the law because it cannot be a crime on the part of this girl aged 15 to have sexual intercourse with her father, though it is of course a crime, and a very serious crime, on the part of the father. There is here incitement to a course of conduct, but that course of conduct cannot be treated as a crime by the girl. Plainly a gap or lacuna in the protection of girls under the age of 16 is exposed by this decision."

**Appeal allowed**[95]

---

[95] See also *Congdon* (1990) 140 N.L.J. 1221.

The extent of the protection afforded by these cases is uncertain and interpretative difficulty surrounds the notion of "victim". For example, in *Pickford*[96] the Court of Appeal applied the principle of *Tyrell* to a case where the husband forced his wife and step-son to commit incest. The court, somewhat controversially, took the view that section 11 of the Sexual Offences Act 1956 (prohibiting incest by a woman with certain male relatives) exists, in part, to protect certain potential victims, such as the boy in this case.[97] Since the boy was the victim of the crime, the step-father could not be guilty of inciting the child to commit incest. However, he could be guilty of inciting the mother to commit incest with her son.

Similarly, the notion of "victim" appeared to take on different meanings in *Brown*.[98] Prior to the prosecution 26 people were cautioned for aiding and abetting offences against themselves.[99] It thus seems that the passive participants in the sado-masochistic activities in *Brown* were not "victims" for the purpose of the protection afforded by the rules on accessorial liability but, of course, were regarded as "victims" for the purpose of assessing the criminal liability of the principal offender.[1]

The Law Commission has recommended that, in the case of the proposed crime of assistance this "defence" be extended to cover those whose conduct is "inevitably incidental" to the commission of an offence and where that conduct is not made criminal by that offence.[2]

## E. *Accomplices and Transferred Malice*

### David Lanham, "Accomplices and Transferred Malice" (1980) 96 L.Q.R. 110 at 110–111:

"An accomplice (A) instigates a principal offender (PO) to commit a specific crime. PO commits a crime of the same description but against a different victim or subject-matter or in a different manner. In what circumstances is A criminally liable for the crime committed by PO? The law in this area has become incoherent for two reasons. First, opinions differ on the nature of the link required between A and the crime actually committed. There are four theories running through the authorities. First, the direct consequences theory. Under this theory it is enough that the crime committed by PO flows directly from PO's attempt to commit the crime suggested. The second theory is the probable consequence theory. A is liable only if the crime actually committed is a probable consequence of the crime suggested by A. This has been held to mean that A is liable if he ought to have foreseen the likelihood of the crime actually committed by PO. The third theory is that of recklessness. A will be liable only if he actually foresees the possibility that the crime actually committed will occur. Finally, there is the express authority theory. A will be liable only if he has expressly authorised the crime which is actually committed.

---

[96] [1995] 1 Cr.App.R.420.
[97] The court also held that the (now repealed) presumption of criminal incapacity only applied to offences committed by, rather than against, boys under the age of 14.
[98] [1994] 1 A.C. 212.
[99] *The Guardian*, February 8, 1992.
[1] Bibbings and Alldridge, "Sexual Expression, Body Alteration, and the Defence of Consent" (1993) 20 J.L. and Soc. 356 at 364.
[2] *Above*, n.93, para. 4.103.

These four approaches would be enough in themselves to lead to confusion but the law is complicated still further by the fact that some authorities appear to apply different principles to different aspects of the problem. While the problem is basically one of transferred malice, the situations requiring the transfer can arise in various different ways. First, PO may attempt to harm the right victim (X) but harm another (V) by accident. Secondly, he may believe that V is X and so harm the wrong victim by mistake. Thirdly, he may do more harm than A ordered, *e.g.* injuring V (an unintended victim) as well as X (the intended victim). Fourthly, he may deliberately depart from A's orders and injure V even though he knows that V is not X. Fifthly, he may commit the crime ordered by A against the correct victim but at a different time, place or in a different manner from that ordered or advised by A. Finally, he may commit the crime ordered but against the wrong subject-matter."

Authority on this problem is scarce with most of the controversy revolving around the following case.

### R. v Saunders and Archer (1573) 2 Plowden 473; 75 E.R. 706 (Warwick Assizes)

Saunders wished to kill his wife so that he could marry another woman. He explained his plans to Archer who advised him to kill her by poison. Archer bought the poison and gave it to Saunders to give to his wife. Saunders mixed the poison with two pieces of roasted apple and gave it to his wife. After tasting it the wife handed the rest of the apple to Eleanor, their three year old daughter. Saunders, on seeing this, merely said that "apples were not good for such infants" but when his wife persisted he simply watched his daughter eat the apple and did nothing "lest he be suspected". The daughter died of the poison. Saunders was found guilty of murder but the question remained as to the liability of Archer.

Lord Dyer C.J.:
"But the most difficult point in this case . . . was whether or not Archer should be adjudged accessory to the murder. For the offence which Archer committed was the aid and advice which he gave to Saunders, and that was only to kill his wife, and no other, for there was no parol communication between them concerning the daughter, and although by the consequences which followed from the giving of the poison by Saunders the principal, it so happened that the daughter was killed, yet Archer did not precisely procure her death, nor advise him to kill her, and therefore whether or not he should be accessory to this murder which happened by a thing consequential to the first act, seemed to them to be doubtful. For which reason they thought proper to advise and consider of it until the next gaol delivery, and in the meantime to consult with the justices in the term. . . . [It was finally agreed] that they ought not to give judgment against the said Alexander Archer, because they took the law to be that he could not be adjudged accessory to the said offence of murder, for that he did not assent that the daughter should be poisoned, but only that the wife should be poisoned, which assent cannot be drawn further than he gave it, for the poisoning of the daughter is a distinct thing from that to which he was privy, and therefore he shall not be adjudged accessory to it; and so they were resolved before this time."

The judges took two years to decide that Archer was not liable as accessory to the crime of murder.[3] Many times that number of years have been spent interpreting this decision. A narrow interpretation of the case suggests that secondary parties will not be liable if the principal *deliberately* chooses another victim; effectively this is what Saunders did. He chose to let a different victim die, rather than step in to prevent it. On the other hand, if Saunders had not been present when his daughter ate the apple, he would not have deliberately changed the plan and the doctrine of transferred malice could apply and Archer would have been liable. The first case to

---

[3] Even then, his release was not immediately ordered; he was kept in prison until he could purchase his pardon.

arise on similar facts in recent times is *Leahy*.[4] In this case, where a deliberate wounding of a different victim took place, the defendant was held not to have aided and abetted the principal's offence. The Draft Criminal Code Bill 1989 echoed this interpretation with a proposal that the accessory be liable where the intended offence takes place on an unintended victim or property, but not liable for "an offence intentionally committed by the principal in respect of some other person or thing".[5]

A broader, more positive, interpretation of *Saunders and Archer* is that the accomplice will only be liable if he expressly authorises or foresees the harm which occurs. In *Reardon*[6] the principal offender shot two victims who were carried into the garden of a bar. The principal offender returned to the bar and asked for a knife because one of the victims was still alive. The defendant handed over a knife. The principal offender stabbed both victims to death. It was held that the defendant would be liable if he foresaw the type of act the principal offender committed. He "would have foreseen at least the strong possibility that if [the principal] found that the other deceased was still breathing and alive, he might use the knife in the same way, and therefore that was an act by [the principal offender] of a type which the appellant had foreseen even though he might not necessarily have intended that use." Of course, this whole problem would disappear if the Law Commission's proposals were implemented, since liability would no longer be based upon the offence committed by the principal.

## IV. Conclusion

We have seen that underpinning the present law are two assumptions. The first is that complicity is a form of derivative liability—there is only one offence, that of the principal—and the second is that accessories are as blameworthy as principal offenders. They are liable to the same extent and deserve comparable punishment.

We have already seen that the first of these assumptions has come under attack by the Law Commission whose reform proposals would set complicity liability adrift from its ancient anchor. Liability instead would be based upon endangerment or risk theory. An inchoate crime approach to complicity does follow logically if the main focus is upon helping. Moreover, despite the fact that the provisions are fairly elaborate, the law would, in fact, be simpler than at the present. However, there are difficulties with this approach:

"An inchoate (or endangerment) based form of complicity, by focusing mainly on the defendant's mental culpability, would avoid the problems associated with causal contribution. However, unless an unwavering attachment to subjectivistic notions of culpability is held to and the *causing* of harm denied relevance, where a secondary party *has* been demonstrably instrumental in bringing about a certain proscribed consequence it could be claimed that inchoate liability understates or incompletely represents the full degree of criminal culpability."[7]

---

[4] [1985] Crim.L.R.99.
[5] Clause 27(5), (Law Commission No. 177), (1989).
[6] [1999] Crim.L.R.392.
[7] Smith (K.J.M.), *A Modern Treatise on the Law of Complicity* (1991), p. 134, n.164.

Others have come to a similar conclusion. Smith has argued that "it is not hard to believe that any judge will willingly ignore ... [the eventual outcome, say, killings] in sentencing, or that there would not be public outrage if he did. Why? Because, of course, we feel strongly that D is *responsible* for those deaths. If we are going to punish him because he bears that responsibility, we are going to punish him for homicide; and if we are going to punish him for homicide, then he ought to be charged with, and convicted of, homicide".[8] He concludes that we cannot afford to dispense with accessorial liability.

Secondly, it is necessary to question the assumption that accessories are as blameworthy as principal offenders and deserve comparable punishment. At a superficial level, of course, the rationale for this is obvious: the accessory's role may have greatly facilitated the commission of the crime; he "may sometimes be more guilty than the perpetrator. Lady Macbeth was worse than Macbeth."[9] English law currently allows for maximum flexibility: where the contribution of the secondary party is greater than that of the principal he can receive greater punishment, where the contribution is minor, he can receive less punishment.

The Law Commission, while rethinking the theoretical basis of accessorial liability, nevertheless proposes that the maximum penalty for complicity should be the same as that for the principal crime in which the defendant becomes involved. Differences in culpability should be left to the court's discretion as occurs with other inchoate offences.[10]

However, this approach can be challenged. The primary question is to determine whether, in principle, accessories should be punished to the same, or to a lesser, extent than principal offenders. This question can only be satisfactorily answered by reference to the possible theoretical underpinnings of complicity liability and, more widely, of the criminal law.

It should now be apparent (particularly from the chapter on inchoate offences) that a basic theme of this book is that criminal liability ought generally to be imposed only when a blameworthy actor has caused a specified harm. This is only a general proposition, not a necessary rule. Thus, as we have seen, one *might* be justified in imposing criminal liability in the absence of blameworthiness (as in crimes of strict liability) or in the absence of obvious harm, or "first order harm" (as with inchoate offences). But where one of these elements is missing and liability is nevertheless justified, the equation ought only to be balanced by imposing *less* criminal liability. This model provides the key for the structuring of all criminal offences and ascertaining appropriate levels of punishment. Thus there can be degrees of blameworthiness (for instance, intentionally causing harm being regarded as worse than recklessly causing harm), and, of course, there are degrees of harm (for instance, killing one's victim is worse than injuring her). The correlation of the degree of blameworthiness with the degree of harm ought to

---

[8] "Criminal Liability of Accessories: Law and Law Reform" (1997) 113 L.Q.R. 453 at 461.
[9] Williams, *Textbook of Criminal Law* (1st ed., 1978), p. 287; see also Smith, "A Note on Duress" [1974] Crim.L.R.349 at 351, cited with approval by Lord Edmund-Davies in *Lynch v D.P.P.* [1975] A.C. 653 at p. 709. Lord Simon in *Lynch* and Lords Wilberforce and Edmund-Davies in *Abbott* [1977] A.C. 755, all opined that no distinction could be based on the degree of participation in a crime.
[10] Law Com. Consultation Paper No. 131, *Assisting and Encouraging Crime* (1993), para. 4.190.

provide a fairly precise level of criminal liability with appropriate level(s) of punishment.

How does accessorial liability fit into such a model of criminal liability and punishment? The answer is clear. If an accessory is less blameworthy or causes less harm than the principal offender, then he deserves less criminal liability. If he is *both* less blameworthy *and* causes less harm, then he deserves *even less* criminal liability and punishment. So the central questions become:

1. Is the accessory less blameworthy, and/or
2. Does he cause less harm than the principal offender?

## 1. Blameworthiness

We have seen that an important indicator of blame is the *mens rea* of the defendant.[11] The liability of the accessory is derivative; it stems from the offence committed by the principal. "Since the source of culpability as an accessory is not the offence definition, there is no logical imperative that the mental element for an accessory should be the same as that required for a principal."[12] As we have seen, the courts appear now to have accepted this proposition, but not its implications. If it were accepted that the concept of *mens rea* presupposes a capacity to control one's actions and to choose between alternative courses of conduct, then the implications become clear. An accessory lacks control over the principal offender; he cannot make choices for that principal. (If he could we should classify him as a principal acting through an innocent agent, or as a co-principal.) The principal is "always the dominant party in the transaction. In criminal schemes, the principal is the actor-on-stage, who makes the final determination whether to commit the discrete criminal act."[13] The principal can have the *mens rea* of the actual offence because of his hegemony and control. The accessory, at most, has choice and control over his *own actions, namely, his acts of assistance or encouragement.* Once it is realised that this *mens rea* of the accessory is not the *mens rea* of the offence itself, that it is, in a sense, a step removed from the offence, we can then focus on the real question: is this *mens rea* of assisting as reprehensible as the *mens rea* of the principal who actually commits the offence? The answer to this question must be delayed until we have considered the next problem.

## 2. Causing harm

Except in cases of procuring, an accessory, by definition, does not cause the ultimate harm. He contributes to the crime by his assistance or encouragement, but he does not actually cause the ultimate harm if it is inflicted by a responsible principal. So, in *Lynch v D.P.P.*,[14] for example, Lynch drove some I.R.A. gunmen to a place where they killed a policeman. By his driving, Lynch assisted in the commission of the crime, but his actions clearly did not "cause" the death of the policeman. Indeed, the rules of accessorial liability only exist because such an

---

[11] For present purposes, it will be assumed that there are no other indicators of blame involved, or that these are constant as between principal offender and accessory.

[12] Dennis, "The Mental Element For Accessories" in Smith (ed.), *Essays in Honour of J. C. Smith* (1986), p. 40.

[13] Fletcher, *Rethinking Criminal Law* (1978), p. 656.

[14] [1975] A.C. 653.

accessory does not cause the prohibited harm; if he did, he would be a principal offender (or co-principal) and such rules would be unnecessary.[15]

## David Lanham, "Accomplices, Principals and Causation" (1980) 12 Melbourne University Law Review 490 at 510–511:

"*Assistance or permission*: neither assistance nor permission should be sufficient to amount to cause. If this is all that can be proved against A, it seems plain that the main motivation for the deed has come from B or elsewhere. Assistance or permission may be enough to make A liable as a secondary party where the other conditions for such liability have been met but they should not be sufficient to make A a principal on the basis of causation. . . .

*Advice or counselling*: These should arguably be enough where A knows the facts which make B's conduct criminal and B does not. They should not amount to causation where B knows that his conduct is criminal. In this latter situation it is reasonable to regard B, the immediate actor, as the principal offender and to relegate A's position to that of secondary party."

So causation is not established in such cases. But why is this so? Mrs Richard's actions, in arranging for her husband to be beaten up badly enough to "put him in hospital for a month", were clearly *a* cause of her husband's ultimate injuries.[16] Why can they not be regarded as the *legal* cause? Unless one adopts the "policy approach" or the "*mens rea* approach" to causation the answer would appear to be as follows: an accessory cannot cause that over which he has no control[17] and the causal link cannot be traced through the actions of a responsible actor.[18] Mrs Richards caused the principal to act,[19] but, by being a responsible actor not subject to the control or dominance of Mrs Richards, the principal's actions broke the chain of causation between Mrs Richards' actions and the injuries sustained by her husband. The principal caused the injuries.

In some cases, particularly those of aiding and abetting, it might be difficult even to establish that the accessory's actions were *a* cause of the ultimate harm. Thus in *State v Tally*[20] it was stated:

"The assistance given, however, need not contribute to the criminal result in the sense that, but for it, the result would not have ensued. It is quite sufficient if it facilitated a result that would have transpired without it. It is quite enough if the aid merely renders it easier for the principal actor to accomplish the end intended

---

[15] But see Smith (K.J.M.), *above*, n.7, pp. 54–93 where he explores causation's role in complicity and concludes that "narrowing complicity's coverage to cases of provable causal contribution . . . would offer a basis of liability which was more intuitively appealing and morally consistent (with that of a principal)" (p. 90).

[16] *Above*, p. 556.

[17] Fletcher, *Rethinking Criminal Law* (1978), p. 656; Lanham, p. 506.

[18] *Above*, pp. 444–445.

[19] Hart and Honoré would dispute even this. Where the actions of the principal offender are fully voluntary "it will not strictly be correct to say that the instigator has caused the principal to act as he does". They argue however that the actions of the principal "may, in a sense, be described as the *consequence* of the instigator"—this they describe as a different variety of causal connection. (*Causation in the Law* (2nd ed., 1985), p. 381.)

[20] (1894) 102 Ala. 25.

by him and the aider and abettor, though in all human probability the end would have been attained without it."[21]

However, even though the accessory does not cause the ultimate harm, it is clear that he does cause a "harm", namely, the harm of assisting or encouraging the principal offender. The harm involved in assisting or encouraging other criminals, like the "harm" in endangerment offences, is quite different from the ultimate harm actually inflicted and does not necessarily deserve the same level of criminal liability and punishment.

### 3. Lesser liability and punishment

An accessory causes a different harm from the principal (the harm of assisting or encouraging a criminal act); she has a different *mens rea* from the principal (the *mens rea* of assisting or encouraging). On this basis one can support the Law Commission's proposals for the creation of new offences of assisting and encouraging crime. But there is still a critical question to be faced: is this different *mens rea* and harm less reprehensible than the *mens rea* and harm caused by the principal? If so, then this lesser blameworthiness and/or lesser harm caused should result in a lesser level of criminal liability and punishment.

There is one context in which the courts have had to face questions similar to these and that is in relation to whether the defence of duress should be made available to an accessory to murder, but withheld from the principal. In the case of *Lynch v D.P.P.*[22] the House of Lords held that duress was a defence to an accessory to murder. In *Abbott*[23] the Privy Council held that duress was no defence to a principal offender to murder. Lord Morris in *Lynch v D.P.P.* felt there was a material difference between the role of the principal and that of the accessory. An accessory "may cling to the hope that perhaps X will not be found at the place or that there will be a change of intention before the purpose is carried out or that in some unforeseen way the dire event of a killing will be averted. *The final and fatal moment of decision has not arrived.* He saves his own life at a time when the loss of another life *is not a certainty*. … [But the principal offender] must personally there and then take an innocent life. It is for him to pull the trigger or otherwise personally to do the act of killing."[24]

*Lynch* has now been overruled by the decision of *Howe*,[25] partly on the basis of finding the weight of previous authority to have been against extending the defence of duress to any party to murder, but also partly as a disavowal of there necessarily being a distinction between the killer and her side-kick:

> "I can, of course see that as a matter of commonsense one participant in a murder may be considered less morally at fault than another. The youth who hero-worships the gang-leader and acts as a look-out man whilst the gang enter a jeweller's shop and kill the owner in order to steal is an obvious example. In the

---

[21] Hart and Honoré, *above*, n.19: "When the participant merely assists he neither 'causes' the principal to act nor does the latter act 'in consequence' of his assistance. Probably the assistance need not even be a *sine qua non* of success" (p. 388).

[22] [1975] A.C. 653.

[23] [1977] A.C. 755.

[24] Emphasis added; the opposite view was expressed by Lords Wilberforce and Edmund-Davies, dissenting in *Abbott*.

[25] [1987] 1 A.C. 417.

eyes of the law they are all guilty of murder, but justice will be served by requiring those who did the killing to serve a longer period in prison before being released on licence than the youth who acted as look-out. However, it is not difficult to give examples where more moral fault may be thought to attach to a participant in murder who was not the actual killer; I have already mentioned the example of a contract killing, when the murder would never have taken place if a contract had not been placed to take the life of the victim. Another example would be an intelligent man goading a weakminded individual into a killing he would not otherwise commit."[26]

Are these arguments convincing? Or do the views of Lord Morris in *Lynch* reflect the way most people think?[27] The accessory who provides assistance or encouragement is clearly blameworthy, but not as blameworthy as the principal who actually pulls the trigger, stabs with the knife or takes the property. It is the principal who is the dominant party who has to make the final decision to commit the crime. It is the principal who is in control and has the power to choose whether to commit the crime or not.[28] In moral terms this surely makes his actions "worse" than those of the accessory. The principal is "tainted",[29] contaminated by being the direct instrument of the crime; he is the one with the "blood on his hands". The accessory is likewise tainted or contaminated—but for what he has done, namely his lesser role of assistance or encouragement. Of course, it does not follow that all secondary parties should be treated the same. One might wish to distinguish between different classes of accessories in terms of their liability and punishment. The actions of the instigator or master-mind behind the crime are generally more reprehensible than those of an accessory simply assisting the principal at the scene of the crime; the causal contribution of such an instigator towards the ultimate crime is certainly greater; he may thus deserve greater punishment. Accordingly, Ashworth has suggested a general guideline that accessories should receive no more than half the sentence of the principal, but would allow variation where the accessory's role is unusually influential or very minor.[30]

These ideas are recognised by German law which provides that punishment for an accessory be reduced as follows:

"1. Instead of life imprisonment, the punishment is imprisonment for not less than three years.

2. In cases of prescribed terms of imprisonment, the maximum term may be reduced to three-fourths of the prescribed maximum. The same reduction applies to monetary penalties.

---

[26] At 444–445.

[27] The respondents to a survey on public opinion by Robinson and Darley, "Objectivist Versus Subjectivist Views of Criminality: A Study in the Role of Social Sciences in Criminal Law Theory" (1998) 18 O.J.L.S. 409 assigned significantly less liability (and punishment) to accomplices compared to the perpetrators of crime.

[28] The "weakminded individual" cited by Lord Griffiths (*above*, n.26), either has this ability to choose, or, if not, should have a partial defence available to him, or even be able to plead lack of *mens rea*.

[29] Fletcher, *Rethinking Criminal Law* (1978), pp. 345–347.

[30] Ashworthy, *Principles of Criminal Law* (3rd ed., 1999), p. 428.

3. The minimum term of imprisonment is mitigated as follows:
   A. From a minimum of ten or five years to a minimum of two years.
   B. From a minimum of three or two years to a minimum of six months.
   C. From a minimum of one year to a minimum of three months.
   D. In other cases the statutory minimum is retained."[31]

Even if not all the ideas expressed in this section are fully accepted, it is nevertheless hoped that one fact has clearly emerged. Rules of criminal liability should not be rationalised or reformed in a vacuum. This should only be done by reference to a coherent theory of criminal liability, and such a theory should only be constructed by ultimate reference to the punishment to be meted out to offenders.

---

[31] StGB Art. 49(1). See Fletcher, p. 650.

# 7

# NON-FATAL OFFENCES AGAINST THE PERSON

────────────

## I. Offences Against the Person (Non-Sexual)

### A. *The Extent and Context of Violence*

There are many varied explanations as to why people commit crimes of violence: biological theories, psychoanalytic and other socialisation theories, and various sociological theories.[1] Discussion of these is beyond the scope of this book. However, an understanding of the law is assisted by an appreciation of the context in which violence occurs and the extent to which the law is utilised as a response to violence.

Offences of violence comprise a relatively small proportion of recorded crime. For example, in 2001/02 such offences accounted for 15 per cent of all offences recorded by the police.[2] Of these violent offences, the most common is the least serious one, which is common assault. Figure 1 shows the breakdown of these offences.

However, the official total figure of 812,954 offences does not reveal the true extent of violence, often called the "dark figure of crime". This is because large numbers of violent incidents are never reported to the police. The British Crime Survey, which is based on interviews with members of 40,000 households, reveals that only 45 per cent of violent incidents are reported to the police.[3] Many of these unreported incidents would be common assaults, often involving fights at school and in and around pubs and clubs when little serious injury has been caused. However, it would be a mistake to conclude that there was a clear correlation between seriousness of injury and the reporting of such offences. Many serious attacks resulting in stab wounds, broken cheekbones, noses and ribs are also not reported.[4]

---

[1] For a good overview of these explanations, see Jones, *Understanding Violent Crime* (2000) and Levi and Maguire, "Violent Crime" in Maguire, Morgan and Reiner, *The Oxford Handbook of Criminology* (3rd ed., 2002).

[2] Simmons *et al, Crime in England and Wales 2001/02* (2002), p. 7. This figure includes homicides and sexual offences.

[3] Kershaw *et al, The 2001 British Crime Survey* (2001).

[4] Clarkson, Cretney, Davis and Shepherd, "Assaults: the Relationship between Seriousness, Criminalisation and Punishment" [1994] Crim.L.R.4.

Figure 1

Jon Simmons and colleagues, Crime in England and Wales 2001/02 (Home Office Statistical Bulletin, 2002), p. 47

Police recorded and BCS violence broken down by offence, 2001/02

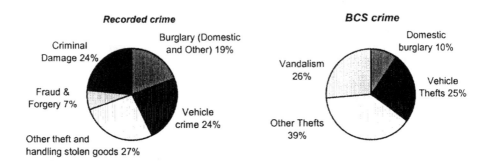

There are various reasons, apart from the triviality of the incident and injury, why offences are not reported. Factors associated with the decision not to report include: an assessment that the police will not be able to do anything about it; the victim's habituation to violence; an unwillingness to have their own conduct exposed to scrutiny; hostility towards the police; fear of reprisal; and the impact such reporting might have upon continuing relationships with the assailant and others.[5] The British Crime Survey 2001 found that the main reason for not reporting violent crime (in 49 per cent of cases) was that the victim considered the issue as a private matter best dealt with by themselves.[6] This last reason helps explain why cases of domestic violence are reported even less frequently than other cases,[7] although the difference in reporting rates between the official statistics and the British Crime Survey is no longer as great as it was.

A further important factor to consider is that, even if the violent incident has been reported to the police, they may not record it because they regard the alleged offence as too trivial or perhaps disbelieve the person reporting the crime especially if that person comes from a section of society perceived as unreliable as witnesses.[8] It has been estimated that 60 per cent of all offences of violence reported to the police are not recorded with only 10 per cent of reported common assaults ending up in the police records.[9] Further, even if an offence is recorded it may be under a different classification, such as drunk and disorderly conduct or criminal damage.[10] And, of course, the fact that a crime has been recorded does not mean that it will be

---

[5] *ibid.*
[6] *Above*, n.3.
[7] Simmons *et al*, above, n.2, Table 3.06.
[8] Jones, *Understanding Violent Crime* (2000), p. 16.
[9] Kershaw *et al*, *The 2001 British Crime Survey* (2001), p. 12.
[10] Jones, Maclean and Young, *The Islington Crime Survey* (1986), p. 61.

followed by a prosecution. In many cases the CPS will refuse to prosecute mainly on the basis of the unreliability of the victim/witness or their unwillingness to testify.

In recent years research has begun to focus on the characteristics of the victims of crime. One of the most significant factors affecting the risk of violence is that of ethnic origin. Since separate records were kept, the number of racial assaults has been increasing every year. According to the British Crime Survey, persons of Afro-Caribbean and Pakistani origin were almost twice as likely to be assaulted as others; 27 per cent of Afro-Caribbean and 37 per cent of Asian respondents felt there was a racial motive to attacks on them.[11] Concern over such assaults, fuelled by media coverage of a few high-profile cases, led to the enactment of the Crime and Disorder Act 1998 increasing the maximum sentence for most of the offences against the person where the offence is "racially aggravated".[12] Fear after September 11 that there could be an increase in attacks on members of religious groups led to the Anti-terrorism, Crime and Security Act 2001 making similar increases in maximum sentence where the offence is "religiously aggravated".[13]

Women are more likely to be victims of crime than they are to be offenders and are more likely than men to be assaulted by someone they know. As Cretney and Davis say: "Assaults are overwhelmingly perpetrated by men. Men in public use violence against other males, whom they may not know. In private they assault women, whom they *do* know."[14] It has been estimated that 75 per cent of assaults against women are likely to be in their own home or that of the suspect as opposed to 35 per cent for male victims.[15]

Overall, males, especially those aged between 16 and 24, are most likely to be the victims of violence. Much of this violence is associated with the lifestyles of the persons concerned. Younger people are more likely to go to pubs and clubs and other places of entertainment where alcohol is consumed and spend some time on the streets at night, these factors being well-documented predictors of victimisation.[16] Many such cases involve fighting where there might have been victim precipitation of the assault. The reporting and prosecution rate for such violence is particularly low.[17]

It is often stated that society is becoming more violent but the extent to which this is true is difficult to measure. Certainly, if one takes one's lead from the official statistics, it can be seen that crimes of violence rose by 34 per cent from 1998/99 to 2001/02.[18] (a faster rate of growth than the overall rate). However, whilst the debate about the influence of the media, and lack of "discipline" on the part of parents and teachers alike rumbles on, there is evidence that rises may be due, in part at least, to changes in reporting rates and police recording practices. According to the British Crime Survey, crimes of violence in fact declined by 22 per cent from

---

[11] Mirrlees-Black, Mayhew and Percy, *The 1996 British Crime Survey* (1996).
[12] ss.25, 26. This applies to common assault and ss.47 and 20 of the Offences against the Person Act 1861.
[13] s.39.
[14] Cretney and Davis, *Punishing Violence* (1995), p. 18.
[15] *Information on the Criminal Justice System (Digest 2)* (1993), p. 14.
[16] Cretney and Davis, *above*, n.14, pp. 23–32.
[17] *ibid.* p. 39.
[18] Simmons *et al*, *Crime in England and Wales 2001/02* (2002), p. 48.

1997 to 2001/02.[19] Society has always been violent and, even if violent crime is increasing, a solution is unlikely to be found in increases to the maximum sentences available to the courts. Sentencing in this area is traditionally tough and so, rather than attributing any rise to the failure of courts to reflect society's disapproval, much more searching and unpalatable questions have to be asked about the structure of the society in which we live.

## B. *The Law*

### 1. Introduction

There are many offences involving personal violence, ranging from "mainstream" offences such as causing grievous bodily harm, through kidnapping and administering poison to those such as assaulting a clergyman in the execution of his duties. The main offences, which are mostly statutory, will be considered as these represent an ideal forum for considering how the law deals with the various configurations of degrees of harm and levels of *mens rea*. The offences are ranked in some sort of hierarchy of seriousness: the extent to which this ordering is based on principle will emerge as the offences are examined. As we shall see, they range from "the merest touching of another in anger",[20] to injuries which fall only just short of death. Because several of the offences contain the basic element of assault, and as it constitutes the lowest rung in the hierarchy of seriousness, this will be examined first.

### 2. Common Assault and Battery

The terms "common assault", "assault" and "battery" are often used interchangeably by laymen and even lawyers. This terminological confusion which causes "angels [to] prepare to dance on needles and legal pedants [to] sharpen their quill pens"[21] is compounded by statute. Section 39 of the Criminal Justice Act 1988 refers to "common assault and battery" as two separate offences while section 40(3) refers only to a "common assault". In *Lynsey*[22] it was held that this latter phrase includes a battery and in *Ireland; Burstow*[23] it was held that the term "assault" in section 47 of the Offences against the Person Act 1861 includes both a common assault and battery.

It is thus clear that there are two separate crimes[24]: common assault and battery. While these are both statutory offences,[25] the statute contains no definition and one has to turn to the common law to discover their constituent elements.[26] A common assault is putting someone in fear of immediate force; a battery is the actual infliction of force on a person. To avoid confusion in this book, the term "assault"

---

[19] *Above*, n.15.
[20] *Cole v Turner* (1705) 6 Mod. 149, 87 E.R. 907.
[21] *Lynsey* [1995] 2 Cr.App.R.667 at 671.
[22] *ibid.*
[23] [1998] A.C. 147 at 161. See also *Taylor; Little* (1992) 95 Cr.App.R.28.
[24] *Taylor; Little, ibid.*
[25] Criminal Justice Act 1988, s.39; *Taylor; Little, ibid.*
[26] In *Haystead v Chief Constable of Derbyshire* [2000] Cr.App.R.339 it was stated that while charges refer to s.39 "in truth, common assault . . . remains a common law offence" (at 340).

is used in its broad generic sense as encompassing either of these specific crimes and the two specific offences will be referred to as "technical assault" and "battery".

Both these offences are only triable summarily (in the magistrates' court) and subject to a maximum penalty of six months' imprisonment.[27] These offences are in practice used in many cases where more serious injury has resulted and one of the more serious charges could have been brought. For example, the C.P.S. generally does not charge defendants with the more serious offence of assault occasioning actual bodily harm (section 47) unless there are aggravating circumstances, preferring to charge either assault or battery. This is because the case then has to be heard in the magistrates' court instead of the crown court (the defendant has a right of election with section 47); the C.P.S. perceives this as being quicker and cheaper, more likely to result in conviction and, particularly in the context of domestic violence, involving a less onerous task for the victim/witness.[28]

## (i) *Technical Assault*

This offence is committed when the defendant intentionally or recklessly causes the victim to apprehend imminent force.

**(a) Actus reus** The defendant must do something to make the victim apprehend imminent force. It is often stated that the victim must fear an immediate attack. This latter formulation, while descriptive of most situations of technical assault, is deceptive for two reasons. First, the victim need not be placed in "fear" in the sense of being frightened; he might be confident of his ability to repel the attack. He is nevertheless assaulted as he is made to apprehend the force. Secondly, he need not apprehend an "attack" in the sense of a severe measure of aggressive or destructive force; he need only apprehend any degree of force, which, as we shall see, in some circumstances need amount to little more than an unlawful touching.

Can the threat to use force be of any nature or form? While it has always been clear that physical gestures such as shaking a fist or pointing a gun at the victim would suffice, there used to be doubt whether mere words could constitute an assault. This issue has been resolved in the following decision.

### R. v Ireland; R. v Burstow [1998] A.C. 147 (House of Lords)

In the first appeal the defendant made repeated silent telephone calls, mostly at night, to three women. Sometimes, he resorted to heavy breathing. As a result, the women suffered psychiatric illness. He was charged with assault occasioning actual bodily harm, contrary to section 47 of the Offences against the Person Act 1861. One of the issues on appeal was whether such conduct could amount to an assault.

Lord Steyn:
"The proposition that a gesture may amount to an assault, but that words can never suffice, is unrealistic and indefensible. A thing said is also a thing done. There is no reason why something said should be incapable of causing an apprehension of immediate personal

---

[27] Under the Crime and Disorder Act 1998 (as amended) if the offence is "racially or religiously aggravated" it can be tried on indictment and carries a maximum term of two years' imprisonment (s.26(3)).
[28] Cretney and Davis, "Prosecuting Domestic Assault: Victims Failing Courts, or Courts Failing Victims" (1997) 36 *Howard Journal of Criminal Justice* 146.

violence, *e.g.* a man accosting a woman in a dark alley saying 'come with me or I will stab you'. I would, therefore, reject the proposition that an assault can never be committed by words."

Lord Hope of Craighead:
"[I]t is not true to say that mere words or gestures can never constitute an assault. It all depends on the circumstances . . . The words or gestures must be seen in their whole context.

In this case the means which the appellant used to communicate with his victims was the telephone. While he remained silent, there can be no doubt that he was intentionally communicating with them as directly as if he was present with them in the same room. But whereas for him merely to remain silent with them in the same room, where they could see him and assess his demeanour, would have been unlikely to give rise to any feelings of apprehension on their part, his silence when using the telephone in calls made to them repeatedly was an act of an entirely different character. He was using his silence as a means of conveying a message to his victims. This was that he knew who and where they were, and that his purpose in making contact with them was as malicious as it was deliberate. In my opinion silent telephone calls of this nature are just as capable as words or gestures, said or made in the presence of the victim, of causing an apprehension of immediate and unlawful violence."

**Appeals dismissed**

Another rule has long been beyond doubt: words may negate an assault. In *Tuberville v Savage*[29] the defendant placed his hand on his sword hilt and told the victim: "If it were not assize-time, I would not take such language from you." This was held not to be an assault. The words accompanying the action (of placing the hand on the sword) clearly demonstrated that because the assize judge was in town, the defendant was *not* going to use his sword. There could thus be no apprehension of immediate force. This case must be carefully distinguished from cases involving a conditional threat, such as *Read v Coker*[30] where it was held to be an assault to threaten to break the victim's neck if he did not leave the premises. In such a case there *is* a threat to use immediate force; the victim *does* apprehend immediate force and the onus is on him to do something to avert that force. If the rule were otherwise it would mean there could be no assault where a robber says "Your money or your life"; such a position would be intolerable.

Another point to be considered is the stance that law takes in relation to empty threats. For example, a victim might be threatened with a toy gun or an unloaded gun. Understandably, the law regards this fact as immaterial as long as the victim is made to fear an attack[31]; after all, the victim cannot be expected to know whether the threat is real or not.

The victim must apprehend the immediate use of force. It is a serious gap in the law that it is no offence whatsoever to tell someone that you intend to break both their legs the next day rather than there and then.[32] One of the provisions in the Draft Offences Against the Person Bill 1998 is that the existing offence of threatening to kill should be extended to include non-immediate threats to cause serious injury.[33] One of the consequences of this present gap has been the

[29] (1669) 1 Mod.Rep. 3; 86 E.R. 684.
[30] (1853) 13 C.B. 850. See also *Ansell v Thomas* [1974] Crim.L.R. 31.
[31] *Lodgen v D.P.P.* [1976] Crim.L.R. 121; *St. George* (1840) 9 C. & P. 483; 173 E.R. 921.
[32] See, generally, Alldridge, "Threats Offences—A Case for Reform" [1994] Crim.L.R.176.
[33] Clause 10 (Home Office, *Violence: Reforming the Offences Against the Person Act 1861* (1998)).

development by the courts of a rather generous interpretation of "immediacy". In *Smith v Chief Superintendent, Woking Police Station*[34] it was held that a woman had been assaulted when she saw a man looking through her closed bedsitting room window at night. Although he was outside her room and would have had to break or force open her window and climb in before he could have actually inflicted violence upon her, it was held that she had apprehended a sufficiently immediate application of force. In *R. v Horseferry Road Magistrates' Court, ex p. Saidatan*[35] it was stated that "immediate" (for purposes of section 4 of the Public Order Act 1986) "connotes proximity in time and proximity in causation; that it is likely that violence will result within a reasonably short period of time and without any other intervening occurrence". This problem of immediacy is of particular importance in cases where the defendant makes silent or verbally threatening telephone calls.

### R. v Ireland; R. v Burstow [1998] A.C. 147 (House of Lords)

Lord Steyn:
"That brings me to the critical question whether a silent caller may be guilty of an assault. The answer to this question seems to me to be 'Yes, depending on the facts'. It involves questions of fact within the province of the jury. After all, there is no reason why a telephone caller who says to a woman in a menacing way 'I will be at your door in a minute or two' may not be guilty of an assault if he causes his victim to apprehend immediate personal violence. Take now the case of the silent caller. He intends by his silence to cause fear and is so understood. The victim is assailed by uncertainty about his intentions. Fear may dominate her emotions, and it may be the fear that the caller's arrival at her door may be imminent. She may fear the *possibility* of immediate personal violence. As a matter of law the caller may be guilty of an assault: whether he is or not will depend on the circumstance and in particular on the impact of the caller's potentially menacing call or calls on the victim. Such a prosecution case under section 47 may be fit to leave to the jury. And a trial judge may, depending on the circumstances, put a commonsense consideration before jury, namely what, if not the possibility of imminent personal violence, was the victim terrified about? I conclude that an assault may be committed in the particular factual circumstances which I have envisaged."

**Appeals dismissed**

This decision is best understood in the context of events leading up to the appeal. For at least two years prior to the House of Lords' judgment the media had been conducting a high-profile campaign against stalking.

### Home Office, Stalking—The Solutions: A Consultation Paper (1996)

"1.2 Stalking ... can be broadly described as a series of acts which are intended to, or in fact, cause harassment to another person.
1.4 Stalkers can have a devastating effect on the lives of their victims, who can be subjected to constant harassment at home, in public places, and at work, to the extent that they can feel that they are no longer in control of their lives ...
1.5 The motives for stalking are complex, but cases typically arise from situations where a stalker believes that they are loved by, or that a relationship exists with, the victim, or in

[34] (1983) 76 Cr.App.R.234.
[35] (1991) 92 Cr.App.R.257.

which a stalker is trying to resurrect, or seek revenge for, a relationship with the victim which has broken down ... Occasionally, the activity is directed towards celebrities who the stalker would like to befriend ...
1.6 The methods employed by stalkers can take many forms ... [such as] making obscene telephone calls, using abusive and threatening language, or committing acts of violence ... However, frequently stalkers do not overtly threaten their victims but use behaviour which is ostensibly routine and harmless and therefore not caught by existing laws. But even apparently innocuous behaviour, such as following someone down the street, or sending them flowers, can be intimidating if it is persistently inflicted on a victim against their will. This is one of the defining characteristics of stalking: irrespective of the nature of its component acts, stalking can be distressing and threatening to a victim because of its sheer, oppressive persistence.
1.8 ... The National Anti-Stalking and Harassment campaign (NASH) report that over 7,000 victims of stalking telephoned their helpline between January 1994 and November 1995. Stalking affects both women and men, although NASH estimates that about 95 per cent of victims are women."

There were already several laws, both civil and criminal, in existence capable of being utilised against many stalkers. For example, section 43(1) of the Telecommunications Act 1984 makes it an offence to make an indecent, obscene or menacing telephone call or persistently to use a telephone to cause annoyance, inconvenience or needless anxiety. Section 1(1) of the Malicious Communications Act 1988 prohibits the sending of an indecent, offensive or threatening letter with the intention of causing distress or anxiety to the recipient. However, both these are only summary offences carrying a maximum of six months' imprisonment—a sentence perceived to be inadequate for the serious and persistent stalker such as Ireland who was sentenced to three years' imprisonment upon conviction for an offence contrary to section 47 of the Offences against the Person Act 1861. Sections 4, 4A and 5 of the Public Order Act 1986 can also be utilised against persons who stalk their victims in public. For example, under section 4A an offence is committed if a person intentionally causes harassment, alarm or distress by using threatening, abusive or insulting words or behaviour. Again, the maximum penalty for this offence is six months' imprisonment. In *Johnson*[36] a person who made numerous obscene telephone calls to several different women was convicted of the common law offence of public nuisance. This, however, involved somewhat stretching the law of public nuisance which had previously been thought to involve activities having an indiscriminate impact on members of the public.[37]

Responding to the media clamour for more effective criminal laws against stalking, the Government responded by enacting the Protection from Harassment Act 1997 which introduced two criminal offences of harassment. Section 1 creates the offence of pursuing a course of conduct (on at least two occasions) which amounts to harassment of another and which the defendant knows or ought to know amounts to harassment. This offence carries a maximum penalty of six months' imprisonment. The emphasis in this crime is upon the stalker's conduct and pursuit of the victim and not upon an impending attack on the victim. Section 4(1) creates the more serious offence of pursuing a course of conduct (on at least

---

[36] (1996) 2 Cr.App.R.434.
[37] Allen, "Look Who's Stalking: Seeking a Solution to the Problem of Stalking" [1996] 4 Web J.C.L.I. 182.

two occasions) which causes another to fear, on at least two occasions, that violence *will* be used against him. The defendant will be liable if he knows or ought to know that his course of conduct will cause the other so to fear on each of those occasions. The maximum penalty is five years' imprisonment.

The Protection from Harassment Act 1997 was not in force at the time of the *Ireland* prosecution and, in any event, Lord Steyn described it as "not ideally suited" to deal with the case before him where the victim only feared that violence *might* be used against her. Under the Act there has to be fear that violence *will* be used. It was against this background that the appeal in *Ireland* was heard. Lord Steyn commenced his judgment by outlining the "significant social problem" of harassment of women by repeated silent telephone calls and immediately pronounced it was "self-evident" that the criminal law had to be capable of dealing with the problem. His stance was clear. If the law of assault had to be stretched beyond all previously recognised limits, then so be it. Ireland's appeal was doomed from the start. However, as shall be explained, the law has not been radically altered and conviction of similar telephone callers in the future will be no simple matter.

As seen in the *Ireland* extract above, Lord Steyn accepted the basic definition of an assault involving the apprehension of imminent personal violence—with "violence" meaning physical violence. The only extension of the law was his ruling that the victim need only fear the *possibility* of immediate personal violence. She needs only fear that "the caller's arrival at her door may be imminent". On the facts of the particular appeal, the House of Lords was able to side-step the problem of immediacy on the basis that Ireland had pleaded guilty at this trial.[38] In other cases, however, this problem will not be easily overcome. If a victim has received hundreds of phone calls and none of them have been followed by "the caller's arrival at her door", it will be extremely difficult to establish that the victim genuinely feared the possibility of immediate personal violence. In *D.P.P. v Ramos*[39] it was held that it was "the state of mind of the victims which is crucial rather than the statistical risk of violence actively occurring within a short space of time". Nevertheless, the more incidents that have not been followed up by violence, the less plausible the claimed apprehension becomes. Further, even in extreme cases where the seriousness of the threats increases, such as *Cox*[40] where after "hundreds of incidents" the caller told the victim that before she went on holiday, she was "going to her death", it is going to be no less difficult to establish that she feared *there and then* the possibility of immediate personal violence—as opposed to fearing violence at some time and at some place in the future. These difficulties were conceded by Lord Steyn when he concluded: "I nevertheless accept that the concept of an assault involving immediate personal violence as an ingredient of the section 47 offence is a considerable complicating factor in bringing prosecutions under it in respect of silent telephone callers and stalkers. That the least serious of the ladder of offences is difficult to apply in such cases is unfortunate."

---

[38] See Lord Steyn at 163 and Lord Hope at 167.
[39] [2000] Crim.L.R.768.
[40] [1998] Crim.L.R.810.

A similar unduly broad approach was adopted by the Court of Appeal in *Constanza*[41] (a case decided a few months before, and not referred to in, *Ireland*). This case involved a stalker who made repeated silent telephone calls and sent 800 letters culminating in two further letters which the victim interpreted as clear threats. It was held that the assault was committed when the victim read these latter letters as there was a "fear of violence at some time *not excluding the immediate future*". This is similar to Lord Steyn's test that the victim need only fear the possibility of immediate personal violence. This is surely going too far. While the recipient of a telephone call might conceivably fear that the call is from a nearby call-box or mobile phone and that the caller will be at her door "in a minute or two",[42] it seems inconceivable that she would apprehend such *immediate* violence upon receipt of a letter.

This whole approach adopted by the House of Lords is misguided and involves stretching the existing concept of assault beyond its expansion limit. The central problem with these cases is that they have failed to capture the essence of the wrongdoing involved.[43] Lord Steyn comes close when he posed the right question: "what ... was the victim terrified of?" However, his answer—"imminent personal violence"—misses the point for most cases. The recipient of silent or menacing telephone calls is not generally afraid that the caller will arrive soon at the front door to inflict violence upon her. The fear is more likely to be one of future physical violence, future harassment and similar future calls increasing her tension and anxiety. In short, the relentless pressure combined with fear of the unknown causes continuing psychological trauma. The Court of Appeal in *Ireland*[44] recognised this by reformulating an assault as the apprehension of immediate violence with "violence" including psychological damage. In the Court of Appeal Swinton Thomas L.J. stated: "when a telephone call is made by the appellant and the victim lifts the telephone and then knows that the man is telephoning them yet again, they will be apprehensive of suffering the very psychological damage from which they did suffer, namely palpitations, difficulty in breathing, cold sweats, anxiety, inability to sleep, dizziness, stress and the like ... [T]he fact that the violence is inflicted indirectly, causing psychological harm, does not render the act to be any less an act of violence."

This view was expressly rejected by Lord Hope in the House of Lords[45] and with it goes the hope of many convictions in such cases for offences involving an assault. The Protection from Harassment Act 1997 and the other lesser offences discussed above now seem the most realistic way in most cases of securing a conviction against those who make menacing telephone calls.

---

[41] [1997] 2 Cr.App.R.492.
[42] *Ireland* at 162.
[43] Horder ("Reconsidering Psychic Assault" [1998] Crim.L.R.392) argues that the essential wrong in assault is causing fear: "a psychic assault is the sensory and contemporaneous experience that induces a fear of physical interference—whether or not to be inflicted immediately—being done by the threatener" (at 401).
[44] [1996] 3 W.L.R. 657.
[45] At 165.

(b) **Mens rea** The defendant must intentionally or recklessly cause his victim to apprehend the infliction of immediate force.[46] Thus if he intends to alarm his victim, or is reckless thereto, the *mens rea* requirement is satisfied, even if he never intended to carry out the threat.

What is meant by recklessness here? In *D.P.P. v K*[47] it was held that the *Caldwell* meaning applied. However, this was disapproved in *Spratt*[48] where it was held that the subjective *Cunningham* test of recklessness applied. The House of Lords, in the leading case of *Savage; Parmenter*,[49] did not deal with this issue. However, as a substantial portion of the judgment was devoted to stressing that "maliciously" in section 20 was different from recklessness and *therefore* could bear a subjective meaning, the logical inference could be that it was assumed that recklessness here bears its more objective *Caldwell* meaning.[50] On the other hand, the House of Lords has since accepted that recklessness has a variable meaning in the criminal law,[51] and the failure of the House of Lords to deal with the issue probably indicates an acceptance that the *Spratt* line of cases represents the law and that *Cunningham* recklessness is required.[52]

(ii) *Battery*

A battery is the intentional or reckless infliction of unlawful personal force by one person upon another. While a technical assault is the *threatening* of such force, a battery is the actual infliction of the force.

(a) **Actus reus** The defendant must inflict unlawful personal force. What is meant by "force" in this context?

### Wilson v Pringle [1986] 2 All E.R. 440 (Court of Appeal, Civil Division)

Croom-Johnson L.J.:

"In our view the authorities lead to the conclusion that in a battery there must be an intentional touching or contact in one form or another of the plaintiff by the defendant. That touching must be proved to be a hostile touching. That still leaves unanswered the question, when is a touching to be called hostile? Hostility cannot be equated with ill-will or malevolence. It cannot be governed by the obvious intention shown in acts like punching, stabbing or shooting. It cannot be solely governed by an expressed intention, although that may be strong evidence. But the element of hostility, in the sense in which it is now to be considered, must be a question of fact for the tribunal of fact. . . .

Although we are all entitled to protection from physical molestation, we live in a crowded world in which people must be considered as taking on themselves some risk of injury (where it occurs) from the acts of others which are not in themselves unlawful."

---

[46] *Venna* [1976] Q.B. 421.

[47] (1990). The Court of Appeal in *Savage* [1991] 2 W.L.R. 418 adopted a similar view.

[48] [1990] 1 W.L.R. 1073. This same view was adopted in *Nash* [1991] Crim.L.R. 768 and by the Court of Appeal in *Parmenter* [1991] 2 W.L.R. 418.

[49] [1992] 1 A.C. 699.

[50] Clarkson, "The Law Commission Report on Offences against the Person and General Principles: (1) Violence and the Law Commission" [1994] Crim.L.R. 324 at 329–330.

[51] *Reid* (1992) 95 Cr.App.R.393.

[52] This point was conceded on appeal in *Haystead v Chief Constable of Derbyshire* [2000] 2 Cr.App.R.339.

This was approved by the House of Lords in *Brown*.[53] Lord Jauncey, however, unhelpfully added that if the defendant's actions are unlawful they are necessarily hostile. Thus because it is unlawful to cause injuries in the course of sado-masochistic activities, the element of hostility is satisfied. Such circular reasoning defies explanation. To say that injuries are inflicted with hostility when they have been consented to is to deprive the word "hostility" of any meaning. A better approach was adopted by Lord Mustill, dissenting in *Brown*, who stated that hostility was not a crucial matter in determining guilt or innocence, "although its presence or absence may be relevant when the court has to decide as a matter of policy how to react to a new situation".[54]

Three further matters need consideration. First, a battery involves the application of physical force upon the victim. Actual touching is not necessary. For example, in *Lynsey*[55] there was a battery when the defendant spat in the face of a police officer. However, the force must be physical. In *Ireland; Burstow* it was held that silent telephone calls resulting in psychiatric injury could not constitute a battery.[56]

Secondly, a battery cannot be committed by omission. However, we have already seen that although courts are reluctant to base liability in this area on omissions alone they are prepared to use devices that achieve substantially similar results.[57]

The third issue is whether the force need be applied directly. Is it necessary, for example, that the defendant physically come into contact with the victim with his fist, spittle or some weapon? Older authorities[58] suggest that this was indeed the case (although "direct" was interpreted with a certain amount of flexibility). However, the case of *Martin*[59] can be read as dispensing with the requirement of direct force. In this case the defendant barred the exit to a theatre with an iron bar, turned off the lights and shouted "fire". Some people subsequently were injured when they were crushed against the exit in the panic to escape. The defendant was convicted under section 20 of the Offences against the Person Act 1861 of *inflicting* grievous bodily harm (an offence then thought to require proof of an assault).

The decision of *Wilson*,[60] however, interpreted *Martin* somewhat differently as supporting the view that "to inflict" grievous bodily harm under section 20 does not necessitate an assault taking place. On the issue of whether an assault itself necessitates direct force, Lord Roskill in *Wilson* approved a passage from the Australian decision of *Salisbury*[61] where a distinction was drawn between "directly and violently" inflicting a harm (an assault) and inflicting harm that was "not itself

---

[53] [1994] 1 A.C. 212. See also *Cole v Turner* (1705) 6 Mod, 149, 87 E.R. 907; *Collins v Wilcock* [1984] 1 W.L.R. 1172; *Faulkner v Talbot* [1981] 1 W.L.R. 1528. On the issue of the amount of everyday contact to which we are deemed to consent, see *Sutton* [1977] 3 All E.R. 476.
[54] *ibid.* at 261.
[55] [1995] 2 Cr.App.R.667.
[56] [1998] A.C. 147 at 161.
[57] See *Fagan v Metropolitan Police Commissioner* [1969] 1 Q.B. 439, *above*, p. 182.
[58] See Williams, *Textbook of Criminal Law* (2nd ed., 1983), p. 179 where he cites authorities such as *Scott v Sheppherd* (1773) W. Black 892.
[59] (1881) 8 Q.B.D. 54.
[60] [1984] A.C. 242.
[61] [1976] V.R. 452 at 461.

a direct application of force to the body of the victim, [but] does directly result in force being applied violently to the body of the victim" (not an assault). The House of Lords in *Savage; Parmenter*, albeit *obiter* endorsed this approach in holding that there would be no assault in cases like *Martin* or where a defendant had interfered with the breaking mechanism of a car thereby causing an accident and injuries to the driver. Further, in *Ireland; Burstow*[62] Lord Hope stated that a battery could not be committed over the telephone because there was no physical contact between the defendant and the victim.

On the other hand, the following case clearly suggests that a battery can be committed even if the force is applied indirectly.[63]

### D.P.P. v K (a minor) (1990) 91 Cr.App.R.23 (Queen's Bench Divisional Court)

The defendant, a 15-year-old schoolboy, was carrying out an experiment using concentrated sulphuric acid in a chemistry class at school when he splashed some of the acid on his hand. He was given permission to go to the toilet to wash it off and without his teacher's knowledge, took a test-tube of the acid with him to test its reaction on some toilet paper. While he was in the toilet he heard footsteps in the corridor and in a panic poured the acid into a hot air drier to conceal it. He returned to his class intending to return later to remove it and wash out the drier. Before he could do so another pupil used the drier. Acid squirted onto his face causing a permanent scar. The defendant was charged with assault occasioning actual bodily harm but was acquitted because he had not intended to harm anyone. The prosecution appealed by way of case stated.

Parker L.J.:
"[I]n my judgment there can be no doubt that if a defendant places acid into a machine with the intent that it shall, when the next user switches the machine on, be ejected onto him and do him harm there is an assault when the harm is done. The position was correctly and simply stated by Stephen J. in *R. v Clarence* (1888) 22 Q.B.D. 23 at 45, where he said:
'If a man laid a trap for another into which he fell after an interval, the man who laid it would during the interval be guilty of an attempt to assault, and of an actual assault as soon as the man fell in.'
This illustration was also referred to by Wills J. in the same case in relation to s.20 of the 1861 Act. Wills J. there also referred to *R. v Martin* (1881) 8 Q.B.D. 54, saying:
'The prisoner in that case did what was certain to make people crush one another, perhaps to death, and the grievous bodily harm was as truly inflicted by him as if he had hurled a stone at somebody's head.'
In the same way a defendant who pours a dangerous substance into a machine just as truly assaults the next user of the machine as if he had himself switched the machine on."

**Appeal allowed**

In *Haystead v Chief Constable of Derbyshire*[64] the defendant punched a woman who was holding a child. The child fell from her arms and hit his head on the floor. The main argument on appeal was whether there could be a battery when force was indirectly applied. In a highly ambiguous judgment it was indicated that this "may

---

[62] [1998] A.C. 147 at 165.
[63] For a view that this case was decided *per incuriam* and that a battery does require a direct physical attack, see Hirst, "Assault, Battery and Indirect Violence" [1999] Crim.L.R.557.
[64] [2000] 2 Cr.app.R.339.

well be" so, but it was unnecessary to decide as, on the facts, there was a direct application of force even though there was no physical contact with the child: "[dropping] the child was entirely and immediately the result of the appellant's action in punching her. There is no difference in logic or good sense between the facts of this case and one where the defendant might have used a weapon to fell the child to the floor."

## (b) Mens rea

### R. v Venna [1976] Q.B. 421 (Court of Appeal, Criminal Division)

James L.J.:
"In our view the element of mens rea in the offence of battery is satisfied by proof that the defendant intentionally or recklessly applied force to the person of another....

We see no reason in logic or in law why a person who recklessly applies physical force to the person of another should be outside the criminal law of assault. In many cases the dividing line between intention and recklessness is barely distinguishable. This is such a case. In our judgment ... this ground of appeal fails."

As with technical assault, the meaning of recklessness here has not been authoritatively determined. The same arguments as above apply here with the prevailing consensus being that recklessness bears its "subjective" *Cunningham* meaning.

### (iii) *Punishment*

A common assault is punishable upon summary conviction by a fine of up to (currently) £5,000 and/or six months' imprisonment. The offence is no longer triable upon indictment.[65] The Magistrates' Association Sentencing Guidelines provide that the guideline consideration for magistrates is: "is it serious enough for a community penalty?"[66]

If the common assault is "racially or religiously aggravated", the maximum sentence is two years' imprisonment.[67] An offence is racially or religiously aggravated if the offender demonstrates or is motivated (wholly or partially) by racial or religious hostility.[68] For such offences the guideline for magistrates is: "is it so serious that only custody is appropriate?"[69]

## 3. Aggravated Assaults

The more serious offences of violence are commonly termed "aggravated assaults" although, as we shall see, for some of these offences it is not necessary to prove the existence of an assault.

---

[65] Criminal Justice Act 1988, s.39. Exceptionally, common assault can still be tried on indictment if it is founded on the same facts as an indictable offence which is charged, or if it forms part of a series of offences of a similar character to an indictable offence charged. (Criminal Justice Act 1988, s.40.)

[66] The Magistrates' Association, *Sentencing Guidelines* (2000).

[67] Crime and Disorder Act 1998, s.29, as amended by the Anti-terrorism, Crime and Security Act 2001, s.39.

[68] *ibid.*, s.28.

[69] *Above*, n.66.

(i) *Assault occasioning actual bodily harm*

### Offences against the Person Act 1861, section 47:

"Whosoever shall be convicted on indictment[70] of any assault occasioning actual bodily harm shall be liable ... to be imprisoned for any term not exceeding five years."

(a) **Actus reus** Three conditions need to be satisfied here. First, there must be an "assault". This means there must be either a technical assault or a battery.[71] Secondly, this assault must "occasion" or *cause* actual bodily harm. For example, in *Roberts*[72] the defendant tried to pull a girl's coat off in a moving car. She jumped out of the car and was injured. Here there clearly was a common assault and she had suffered actual bodily harm. The sole issue in this case was whether causation had been established.[73] Where it is alleged that the actual bodily harm has been caused by a technical assault (as opposed to a battery) it must be established that it was the apprehension of imminent force—as opposed to general fear and upset—that caused the actual bodily harm.[74]

Thirdly, the assault must cause "actual bodily harm". With regard to physical injuries this includes "any hurt or injury calculated to interfere with health or comfort".[75] In *Chan-Fook*[76] it was held that the words "actual bodily harm" were ordinary words generally requiring no elaboration: "The word 'harm' is a synonym for injury. The word 'actual' indicates that the injury (although there is no need for it to be permanent) should not be so trivial as to be wholly insignificant."

Accordingly, as long as it is not "wholly insignificant", almost any injury will suffice and indeed may simply be inferred from the facts of the case as in *Taylor v Granville*.[77] The evidence established that the defendant had struck the victim in the face and it was held that bruising must, at the least, have been thereby caused; such a finding clearly fell within the definition of actual bodily harm. This demonstrates the ease with which a common assault (punishable by a maximum of 6 months' imprisonment) can be transformed into an offence punishable by up to five years' imprisonment. However, as seen earlier, the C.P.S. only tends to bring prosecutions for section 47 in cases where there are aggravating circumstances.[78]

What is the position where the defendant's conduct causes psychiatric illness? Previously the test of "any hurt or injury calculated to interfere with health or comfort" was thought to include hysterical and nervous conditions and shock. This position has now been qualified.

---

[70] The offence is also triable summarily by virtue of the Magistrates' Court Act 1952, s.19, Sched. 1 and punishable by a maximum of six months' imprisonment or £5,000 fine, or both.

[71] *Ireland; Burstow* [1998] A.C.147 at 161.

[72] (1972) 56 Cr.App.R.95.

[73] See p. 454.

[74] Smith, Commentary to *Cox* [1998] Crim.L.R.810.

[75] *Miller* [1954] 2 Q.B. 282.

[76] [1994] 1 W.L.R. 689.

[77] [1978] Crim.L.R. 482. *Cf. Reigate Justices, ex p. Counsell* (1984) 148 J.P. 193.

[78] *Taylor*; *Little* (1992) 95 Cr.App.R.28.

## R. v Ireland; R. v Burstow [1998] A.C. 147 (House of Lords)

In *Ireland* the victims of repeated silent telephone calls suffered psychiatric illness. The defendant was charged with an assault occasioning actual bodily harm under section 47. In *Burstow* the victim of an eight-month campaign stalking suffered from severe depressive illness. The defendant was charged with unlawfully and maliciously inflicting grievous bodily harm contrary to section 20 of the Offences against the Person Act 1861. Both were convicted and appealed.

Lord Steyn:
"The appeals under consideration do not involve structural injuries to the brain such as might require the intervention of a neurologist. One is also not considering either psychotic illness or personality disorders ... The case was that they developed mental disturbances of a lesser order, namely neurotic disorders. For present purposes the relevant forms of neurosis are anxiety disorders and depressive disorders. Neuroses must be distinguished from simple states of fear, or problems in coping with everyday life. Where the line is to be drawn must be a matter of psychiatric judgment. But for present purposes it is important to note that modern psychiatry treats neuroses as recognisable psychiatric illnesses ... [N]eurotic illnesses affect the central nervous system of the body, because emotions such as fear and anxiety are brain functions ...

[I]n *Chan-Fook* the Court of Appeal squarely addressed the question whether psychiatric injury may amount to bodily harm under section 47 of the 1861 Act ... Hobhouse L.J. stated:
'The first question ... is whether the inclusion of the word "bodily" in the phrase "actual bodily harm" limits harm to harm to the skin, flesh and bones of the victim ... The body of the victim includes all parts of the body, including his organs, his nervous system and his brain. Bodily injury therefore may include injury to any of those parts of his body responsible for his mental and other faculties.'
In concluding that 'actual bodily harm' is capable of including psychiatric injury Hobhouse L.J. emphasised that—
'it does not include mere emotions such as fear or distress or panic nor does it include, as such, states of mind that are not themselves evidence of some identifiable clinical condition.'
He observed that in the absence of psychiatric evidence a question whether or not an assault occasioned psychiatric injury should not be left to the jury ...

In my view the ruling in [*Chan-Fook*] was based on principled and cogent reasoning and it marked a sound and essential clarification of the law. I would hold that 'bodily harm' in ss.18, 20 and 47 must be interpreted so as to include recognisable psychiatric illness."

In *Morris*[79] the conviction of a stalker, who had allegedly caused his victim to suffer pains, sleeplessness, tension and fear of being alone, was quashed because the trial judge had allowed the issue of whether the assault had occasioned psychiatric injury to be left to the jury without expert evidence. Even with respect to her physical pains, psychiatric evidence should have been adduced to testify that they were the result of the defendant's non-physical attack.

(b) **Mens rea** Section 47 makes no express reference to any *mens rea* requirement, but it is settled that liability is established if the defendant has the *mens rea* of common assault.

---

[79] [1998] 1 Cr.App.R.386.

## R. v Savage; D.P.P. v Parmenter [1992] 1 A.C. 699 (House of Lords)

In the first appeal, the appellant, Mrs Savage, threw a pint glass full of beer over Miss Beal. The glass slipped out of her hand, broke, and a piece of it cut Miss Beal's wrist. Savage was convicted of unlawful wounding contrary to section 20 of the 1861 Act. The Court of Appeal partially allowed her appeal substituting a verdict of assault occasioning actual bodily harm contrary to section 47 of the Act. She appealed to the House of Lords.

Lord Ackner:
"[Mrs Savage assaulted Miss Beal when she threw beer over her. Her actions also caused actual bodily harm, the cut wrist.] Was the offence thus established or is there a further mental state that has to be established in relation to the bodily harm element of the offence? Clearly the section, by its terms, expressly imposes no such requirement. Does it do so by necessary implication? It uses neither the word 'intentionally' or 'maliciously'. The words 'occasioning actual bodily harm' are descriptive of the word 'assault', by reference to a particular kind of consequence ...
[His Lordship then discussed *Roberts* (*above*, p. 454) where it was held that] once the assault was established, the only remaining question was whether the victim's conduct was the natural consequence of that assault. The word 'occasioning' raised solely a question of causation, an objective question which does not involve inquiring into the accused's state of mind. In *R. v Spratt* [1990] 1 W.L.R. 1073 McCowan L.J. said, at p. 1082:
'However, the history of the interpretation of the Act of 1861 shows that, whether or not the word 'maliciously' appears in the section in question, the courts have consistently held that the mens rea of every type of offence against the person covers both actual intent and recklessness, in the sense of taking the risk of harm ensuing with foresight that it might happen.'
McCowan L.J. then quotes a number of authorities for that proposition ... [However] none of the cases cited were concerned with the mental element required in s.47 cases. Nevertheless, the Court of Appeal in *R. v Parmenter* [1991] 2 W.L.R. 408 preferred the decision in *R. v Spratt* [1990] 1 W.L.R. 1073 to that of *R. v Savage* [1991] 2 All E.R. 220 because the former was 'founded on a line of authority leading directly to the conclusion there expressed'.
My Lords, in my respectful view, the Court of Appeal in *Parmenter* were wrong in preferring the decision in *Spratt's* case. The decision in *Roberts's* case was correct. The verdict of assault occasioning actual bodily harm may be returned upon proof of an assault together with proof of the fact that actual bodily harm was occasioned by the assault. The prosecution are not obliged to prove that the defendant intended to cause some actual bodily harm or was reckless as to whether such harm would be caused."

**Appeal in R. v Savage dismissed**

There is thus no requirement that the defendant foresee actual bodily harm. All that is required is that he or she have the *mens rea* of the assault, namely, intention or recklessness to cause force or apprehension of force. Recklessness here bears the same meaning as in assault. The effect is that section 47 is a constructive crime of "half mens rea" where the *mens rea* requirement does not correspond with the *actus reus*.

It is unfortunate that the House of Lords should reach a decision such as this with no reasoning at all. The result is that the degree of moral culpability required for section 47 and for assault is the same despite the maximum penalties for the two offences being five years' and six months' imprisonment respectively. Surely, before reaching such a conclusion we are entitled to expect their Lordships to tell us why *Roberts* was correct but *Spratt* and *Parmenter* (Court of Appeal) were wrong.

(c) **Punishment** The maximum punishment is five years' imprisonment. The offence is triable either way. If a defendant is tried on indictment in the Crown Court the jury can no longer return an alternative verdict of guilty of assault unless such a charge is specifically included in the indictment in the circumstances permitted by section 40 of the Criminal Justice Act 1988.[80] As seen earlier, many offences that could have been charged under section 47 are in fact charged as common assault, ensuring trial in the Magistrates' Court. The Magistrates' Association Sentencing Guidelines (2000) provide that the guideline consideration for magistrates is: "are magistrates' sentencing powers appropriate?" If the offence is "racially or religiously aggravated" the maximum penalty is increased to seven years' imprisonment.[81]

(ii) *Malicious wounding and inflicting grievous bodily harm*

### Offences against the Person Act 1861, section 20

"Whosoever shall unlawfully and maliciously wound or inflict any grievous bodily harm upon any other person, either with or without any weapon or instrument, shall be guilty of [an offence punishable up to a term not exceeding five years' imprisonment]."

(a) **Actus reus** There must be a wounding or infliction of grievous bodily harm. A *wound* necessitates that the continuity of the whole skin be broken.[82] Given medical advances it is highly questionable whether minor wounds, for example, a slight cut, should form the basis for so serious a charge. *Grievous bodily harm* means nothing more technical than "really serious bodily harm".[83] This can include really serious psychological harm.[84] This is a question of fact to be determined by the jury which means that one jury could find that, say, a broken thumb was grievous bodily harm while another jury could decide it was not.

The grievous bodily harm has to be "inflicted". Until 1983 the word "inflict" was generally interpreted[85] to mean that it was necessary to prove that there had been an assault (a technical assault or a battery). Section 20 was truly an "aggravated assault". For example, in *Clarence*[86] the defendant, knowing he was suffering from venereal disease, had sexual intercourse with his wife and communicated the disease to her. It was held that because of the wife's consent there had been no battery and, accordingly, he could not be liable under section 20. However, the House of Lords in *Wilson*[87] held that while most cases of inflicting

---

[80] *Mearns* [1990] 3 W.L.R. 569.
[81] Crime and Disorder Act 1998, s.29, as amended by the Anti-terrorism, Crime and Security Act 2001, s.39.
[82] Both the dermis and the epidermis must be broken (*Moriarty v Brooks* (1834) 6 C. & P. 684). Thus a scratch or break to the outer skin is not sufficient if the inner skin remains intact (*M'Loughlin* (1838) 8 C. & P. 635), nor is an internal rupture of blood vessels (*J.C.C.C. (A minor) v Eisenhower* (1984) 78 Cr.App.R.48).
[83] *D.P.P. v Smith* [1961] A.C. 290. It has been held that it is not necessary to include the word "really" in the summing up to the jury (*Saunders* [1985] Crim.L.R. 230; *Janjua; Choudury* [1999] 1 C.App.R.91).
[84] *Ireland; Burstow* [1998] A.C. 147.
[85] *Clarence* (1888) 22 Q.B.D. 23; *Halliday* (1889) 61 L.T. 701; *Lewis* [1970] Crim.L.R. 647 and *Cartledge v Allen* [1973] Crim.L.R. 530.
[86] (1888) 22 Q.B.D. 23.
[87] [1984] A.C. 242.

grievous bodily harm would involve an assault, this was not a prerequisite. There could be an infliction of grievous bodily harm contrary to section 20 without an assault being committed. This same reasoning was applied in *Savage; Parmenter* to cases of unlawful wounding where, although it would require "quite extraordinary facts", one can have an unlawful wounding for the purposes of section 20 without the necessity of proving an assault.

It was, however, implicit in *Wilson* that one could only "inflict" grievous bodily harm if there were a direct or indirect application of force to the victim's body. This view has now been challenged.

### R. v Ireland; R. v Burstow [1998] A.C. 147 (House of Lords)

The facts are given above at p. 585.

Lord Steyn:

"Counsel argued that the difference in wording [between 'causing' in s.18 and 'inflicting' in s.20] reveals a difference in legislative intent: inflict is a narrower concept than cause. This argument loses sight of the genesis of ss.18 and 20 [as the various sections in the 1861 Act were taken from different Acts passed at different times] ... The difference in language is therefore not a significant factor.

Counsel for Burstow then advanced a sustained argument that an assault is an ingredient of an offence under section 20 ... Counsel's argument can only prevail if one may supplement the section by reading it as providing 'inflict *by assault* any grievous bodily harm'. Such an implication is, however, not necessary. On the contrary, section 20, like section 18, works perfectly satisfactorily without such an implication. I would reject this part of counsel's argument.

But counsel had a stronger argument when he submitted that it is inherent in the word 'inflict' that there must be a direct or indirect application of force to the body ... [I]n *Mandair* [1995] 1 A.C. 208 at 215 Lord Mackay of Clashfern L.C. observed ...: 'In my opinion ... the word "cause" is wider or at least not narrower than the word "inflict".' ... I regard this observation as making clear that in the context of the 1861 Act there is no radical divergence between the meaning of the two words.

... [With regard to *R. v Clarence*] it must be accepted that in a case where there was direct physical contact the majority ruled that the requirement of infliction was not satisfied. This decision was never overruled. It assists counsel's argument. But it seems to me that what detracts from the weight to be given to the dicta in *R. v Clarence* is that none of the judges in that case had before them the possibility of the inflicting, or causing, of psychiatric injury. The criminal law has moved on in the light of a developing understanding of the link between the body and psychiatric injury. In my judgment *R. v Clarence* no longer assists.

The problem is one of construction. The question is whether as a matter of current usage the contextual interpretation of 'inflict' can embrace the idea of one person inflicting psychiatric injury on another. One can without straining the language in any way answer that question in the affirmative. I am not saying that the words cause and inflict are exactly synonymous. They are not. What I am saying is that in the context of the 1861 Act one can nowadays quite naturally speak of inflicting psychiatric injury. Moreover, there is internal contextual support in the statute for this view. It would be absurd to differentiate between ss. 18 and 20 in the way argued. ... The interpretation and approach should so far as possible be adopted which treats the ladder of offences as a coherent body of law."

Lord Hope of Craighead:

"[*R. v Wilson*, referring with approval to *R. v Salisbury*, does] not wholly resolve the issue which arises in this case, in the context of grievous bodily harm which consists only of psychiatric injury.

The question is whether there is any difference, in this context, between the word 'cause' and the word 'inflict' ... [F]or all practical purposes there is, in my opinion, no difference between these two words. [He then cited *Mandair* (above) with approval.] But I would add that there is this difference, that the word 'inflict' implies that the consequence of the act is something which the victim is likely to find unpleasant or harmful. The relationship between cause and effect, when the word 'cause' is used, is neutral. It may embrace pleasure as well as pain. The relationship when the word 'inflict' is used is more precise, because it invariably implies detriment to the victim of some kind.

In the context of a criminal act therefore the words 'cause' and 'inflict' may be taken to be interchangeable. As the Supreme Court of Victoria held in *R. v Salisbury*, it is not a necessary ingredient of the word 'inflict' that whatever causes the harm must be applied directly to the victim. It may be applied indirectly, so long as the result is that the harm is caused by what has been done. In my opinion it is entirely consistent with the ordinary use of the word 'inflict' in the English language to say that the appellant's actions 'inflicted' the psychiatric harm from which the victim has admittedly suffered."

**Appeals dismissed**

While it is now clear that no assault is necessary for section 20 and that the injury may be caused directly or indirectly, two matters deserve mention. First, strictly speaking, the ratio of this case extends only to the infliction of psychiatric injury. Indeed, Lord Steyn stated that *Clarence* did not assist because that case was not concerned with psychiatric injury and Lord Hope limited his comments to cases involving psychiatric injury. However, such an interpretation cannot be accepted. Lord Steyn expressly answered the certified question, which referred to *all* cases under section 20, in the affirmative.

Secondly, Lord Steyn was careful to state that he was "not saying that the words cause and inflict are exactly synonymous. They are not." The only hint as to what the difference might be is provided by Lord Hope when he stated that the word inflict "implies that the consequence of the act is something which the victim is likely to find unpleasant or harmful". This is extraordinary. The word "harmful" here must refer to the victim subjectively interpreting the injury as harmful because objectively there must, of course, be grievous bodily harm; the word thus adds nothing to the word "unpleasant". Taken literally, this seems to suggest that sado-masochistic activities such as those in *Brown*[88] cannot be prosecuted under section 20 because the victims do not find their injuries unpleasant and do not suffer "detriment". On the contrary, they find the pain and injury pleasant and to their benefit as an expression of their sexuality. While, for rather different reasons,[89] such an approach could be welcomed, these dicta can hardly be taken to cast doubt on the well-established principles laid down in *Brown*. It follows that the difference between the words "cause" in section 18 and "inflict" in section 20 remains something of a mystery.

In view of these difficulties it would be best to adopt the strict interpretation of *Ireland; Burstow* that it only applies to cases involving psychiatric injury and so an application of force is still required in cases involving physical injuries.

The broader implications of the decision in *Ireland; Burstow* are disturbing. The fact that psychiatric injury can constitute grievous bodily harm combined with the fact that no assault, nor any direct or indirect application of force, is required for

[88] [1994] 1 A.C. 212.
[89] *Above*, pp. 23, 292.

section 20 raises the potential for liability in situations far removed from those traditionally associated with section 20. For example, if I fail a student's essay with the result that she suffers a psychiatric illness, I have committed the *actus reus* of section 20, and if I know of her mental instability and foresee her sustaining some psychiatric injury, I have *mens rea* and could be liable. This is removing section 20 too far from its paradigm. While one can understand that the seriousness of psychiatric illnesses can be such that it is perhaps justifiable to conclude that they are the equivalent of serious bodily harm, liability for section 20 should be limited to cases where there has been an assault or the application of some force. This, however, is not the law since *Ireland; Burstow*.

Where a defendant has been charged with a section 20 offence, it has long been possible for a jury, where they were not satisfied that all the elements of section 20 had been proven, to return a verdict of guilty of section 47 as this was a "lesser included offence",[90] that is, all the elements of the lesser offence, section 47 (an assault causing actual bodily harm), were included in the greater offence, section 20 (an assault causing grievous bodily harm). However, if the greater offence, section 20, no longer requires proof of an assault, how could the jury convict of section 47 which does require an assault? Lord Roskill in *Wilson* answered this by stating that while it was not necessarily so, most section 20 cases would involve an assault. "Inflicting" therefore impliedly *includes* "inflicting by assault" and therefore section 47 could be a lesser included offence. This was endorsed in *Savage; Parmenter*. Such an approach is not surprising. Without the power to convict of lesser offences many defendants would have escaped liability altogether. However, the result is that in some cases a defendant can be convicted of an offence (section 47) when one of the elements of that offence (an assault) has not been proved to exist. Given the broad interpretation of assault in *Ireland* this is unlikely to be a common occurrence. However, as the appeal in *Burstow* itself demonstrates, there can be cases, particularly concerning stalking, when grievous bodily harm is inflicted without an assault. Further, serious injury can be inflicted without an assault in cases where a disease (say gonorrhoea or AIDS) is transmitted as a result of consensual sexual intercourse; because of consent there would be no battery. Such situations demonstrate that it is not always appropriate to stretch the present offences against the person to cover inappropriate cases. In cases of stalking, utilisation of the Protection from Harassment Act 1997 will generally be more appropriate.

With regard to AIDS and other serious diseases, the central offences of violence under the Offences Against the Person Bill 1998 do not require an assault and specific provision is made in clauses 1 and 15 for the intentional transmission of serious diseases.[91]

**(b) Mens rea** The *mens rea* element of section 20 is supplied by the inclusion of the word "maliciously" within the section. In the case of *Cunningham*,[92] where the

---

[90] Criminal Law Act 1967, s.6(3). Of course, s.47 is not actually a lesser offence as it carries the same maximum penalty as s.20. It is nevertheless treated as a lesser offence in sentencing practice.
[91] See p. 596.
[92] [1957] 2 Q.B. 396.

charge concerned the malicious administrating of a noxious thing under section 23 of the Act, the Court of Criminal Appeal interpreted "maliciously" to mean that the defendant had to foresee the particular kind of harm that might be done and that he nevertheless went on to take the risk of it occurring. It was held that the defendant had to foresee that the victim might inhale gas which the defendant knew was, or might be, noxious. In other words, the crime was one of "full *mens rea*", where the *mens rea* "matched" or corresponded with the *actus reus*.

Since then, however, this principle has been considerably whittled away. In *Mowatt*[93] it was held that it was unnecessary for the defendant to foresee a wound or grievous bodily harm. It was enough that some physical harm, albeit of a minor character, was foreseen.

These cases were, of course, decided before *Caldwell*. As it had long been common to use the terms "maliciously" and "recklessly" as synonymous, the question arose whether the "objective" test of recklessness introduced in *Caldwell* applied to "maliciously" in section 20. This point was considered in the following leading decision, as was the question whether the defendant needed to foresee wounding or grievous bodily harm or whether it was enough that he foresaw merely some physical harm.

### R. v Savage; D.P.P. v Parmenter [1992] 1 A.C. 699 (House of Lords)

In the second appeal, the appellant roughly handled his baby son causing injuries to the bony structures of the legs and the forearm. He was convicted of inflicting grievous bodily harm contrary to section 20 of the 1861 Act. The Court of Appeal quashed his conviction on the basis that he did not realise that his handling of the child would cause injury. The Crown appealed to the House of Lords.

Lord Ackner:
"3. *In order to establish an offence under section 20 of the Act, must the prosecution prove that the defendant actually foresaw that his act would cause harm, or is it sufficient to prove that he ought so to have foreseen?* ...

[In *Cunningham* Bryne J.] accepted as accurate the following statement of the law as set out by Professor Kenny in his *Outlines of Criminal Law*, 1st ed. (1902):
'In any statutory definition of a crime, malice must be taken not in the old vague sense of wickedness in general but as requiring either (1) an actual intention to do the particular kind of harm that in fact was done; or (2) recklessness as to whether such harm should occur or not (*i.e.* the accused has foreseen that the particular kind of harm might be done and yet has gone on to take the risk of it). ....'

[In *Mowatt* it was stated that]
'the word "maliciously" does import upon the part of the person who unlawfully inflicts the wound or other grievous bodily harm an *awareness* that his act may have the consequence of causing some physical harm to some other person ...'

Mr Sedley submitted that in *Caldwell's* case your Lordships' House could have followed either of two possible paths to its conclusion as to the meaning of 'recklessly' in the Act of 1971. These were: (a) to hold that *Cunningham* (and *Mowatt*) were wrongly decided and to introduce a single test, wherever recklessness was an issue; or (b) to accept that *Cunningham*, (subject to the *Mowatt* 'gloss' to which no reference was made), correctly states the law in relation to the Offences against the Person Act 1861, because the word 'maliciously' in that statute was a term of legal art which imported into the concept of recklessness a special restricted meaning, thus distinguishing it from 'reckless' or 'recklessly'

---

[93] [1967] 1 Q.B. 421.

in modern 'revising' statutes then before the House, where those words bore their then popular or dictionary meaning.

I agree with Mr Sedley that manifestly it was the latter course which the House followed. Therefore in order to establish an offence under section 20 the prosecution must prove either the defendant intended or that he actually foresaw that his act would cause harm.

4. *In order to establish an offence under section 20 is it sufficient to prove that the defendant intended or foresaw the risk of some physical harm or must he intend or foresee either wounding or grievous bodily harm?*

It is convenient to set out once again the relevant part of the judgment of Diplock L.J. in *R. v Mowatt* ...

'In the offence under section 20 ... for ... which [no] specific intent is required, the word "maliciously" does import ... an awareness that his act may have the consequence of causing some physical harm to some other person. That is what is meant by "the particular kind of harm" in the citation from Professor Kenny. It is quite unnecessary that the accused should have foreseen that his unlawful act might cause physical harm of the gravity described in the section, *i.e.* a wound or serious physical injury. *It is enough that he should have foreseen that some physical harm to some person, albeit of a minor character, might result.*' (Emphasis in original.)

Mr Sedley submits that this statement of the law is wrong. He contends that properly construed, the section requires foresight of a wounding or grievous bodily harm. ...

The contention is apparently based on the proposition that as the actus reus of a section 20 offence is the wounding or the infliction of grievous bodily harm, the mens rea must consist of foreseeing such wounding or grievous bodily harm. But there is no such hard and fast principle. To take but two examples, the actus reus of murder is the killing of the victim, but foresight of grievous bodily harm is sufficient and indeed, such bodily harm, need not be such as to be dangerous to life. Again, in the case of manslaughter, death is frequently the unforeseen consequence of the violence used.

The argument that as section 20 and section 47 have both the same penalty, this somehow supports the proposition that the foreseen consequences must coincide with the harm actually done, overlooks the oft repeated statement that this is the irrational result of this piece-meal legislation. The Act 'is a rag-bag of offences brought together from a wide variety of sources with no attempt, as the draftsman frankly acknowledged, to introduce consistency as to substance or as to form': Professor Smith in his commentary on *R. v Parmenter* [1991] Crim.L.R.43.

If section 20 was to be limited to cases where the accused does not desire but does foresee wounding or grievous bodily harm, it would have a very limited scope. The mens rea in a section 20 crime is comprised in the word 'maliciously'. As was pointed out by Lord Lane C.J., giving the judgment of the Court of Appeal in *R. v Sullivan* ... ([1981] Crim.L.R.46), the 'particular kind of harm' in the citation from Professor Kenny was directed to 'harm to the person' as opposed to 'harm to property'. Thus it was not concerned with the degree of the harm foreseen. It is accordingly in my judgment wrong to look upon the decision in *Mowatt* as being in any way inconsistent with the decision in *Cunningham*.

My Lords, I am satisfied that the decision in *Mowatt* was correct and that it is quite unnecessary that the accused should either have intended or have foreseen that his unlawful act might cause physical harm of the gravity described in section 20, *i.e.* a wound or serious physical injury. It is enough that he should have foreseen that some physical harm to some person, albeit of a minor character, might result."

**Appeal in D.P.P. v Parmenter allowed in part and conviction of assault occasioning actual bodily harm substituted**

This decision has been welcomed by prosecutors in that it clarifies previously uncertain law. This is true, but at what price?

First, subjective foresight is required for section 20. This can be defended, but it is difficult to see why this should be so when criminal damage only requires proof of

*Caldwell* recklessness. Is it the policy of the law to favour property over persons making convictions in the former cases easier?[94]

Secondly, was the House of Lords justified in holding that the defendant need only foresee *some harm*? If the defendant only foresees some harm resulting, but is then convicted and punished for ensuing serious harm, is this not making liability and punishment dependent on luck? Horder argues that one should distinguish between "pure" luck and making one's own luck and in the latter situation "by doing something intended to harm V, D changes her own normative position, making the bad luck of V's serious injury her (D's) own. There is nothing inappropriate in holding D criminally liable for the serious injury actually inflicted, if there was any risk of such injury resulting from D's intended conduct."[95] Issues such as these were, however, not considered by the House of Lords. No serious attempt to justify its position was made. Simply pointing out that anomalies also exist in other areas of law is not a justification, nor is it enough for them metaphorically to shrug their shoulders by stating that the 1861 Act is simply "a rag-bag of offences" with no consistency. Such platitudes reinforce the need for statutory intervention—a matter to be dealt with shortly.

(c) **Punishment** The maximum penalty is five years' imprisonment, the same penalty as section 47, and under the Magistrates' Association Sentencing Guidelines (2000) the guideline is, as with section 47: "are magistrates' sentencing powers appropriate?" This is irrational and distorts any structure of offences based on seriousness. In practice, however, it is perceived as the more serious offence and in the Crown Court longer prison sentences (on average) are imposed for section 20.[96]

If the offence is "racially or religiously aggravated" the maximum penalty is increased to seven years' imprisonment.[97]

(iii) *Wounding and causing grievous bodily harm with intent*

### Offences against the Person Act 1861, section 18

"Whosoever shall unlawfully and maliciously by any means whatsoever wound or cause any grievous bodily harm to any person, with intent ... to do some grievous bodily harm to any person, or with intent to resist or prevent the lawful apprehension or detainer of any person, shall be guilty of [an offence and shall be liable ... to imprisonment for life]."

(a) **Actus reus** The terms "wound" and "grievous bodily harm" bear the same meaning as in section 20. "Cause", however, has never been held to imply that the injury need be the result of a common assault. Until the decision of *Wilson*[98] it was,

---

[94] For further argument on this, see *below*, p. 596.
[95] "A Critique of the Correspondence Principle" [1995] Crim.L.R. 759 at 765. See also Gardner, "Rationality and the Rule of Law in Offences against the Person" [1994] C.L.J. 502 at 508–509.
[96] Moxon, *Sentencing Practice in the Crown Court* (H.O.R.S. No. 103) (1988).
[97] Crime and Disorder Act 1998, s.29, as amended by the Anti-terrorism, Crime and Security Act 2001. For sentencing guidelines, see *Saunders* (2000) 1 Cr.App.R.458.
[98] [1984] A.C. 242.

therefore, true to say that "cause" was wider than "inflict" with the paradoxical result that it was easier to prove the *actus reus* of the more serious offence, section 18, than that of section 20. In *Mandair*[99] the House of Lords held that "causing" was "wider or at least not narrower than the word 'inflict'". This statement was approved in *Ireland*; *Burstow* where it was added that there was "no radical divergence between the meaning of the two words". Accordingly, on a section 18 charge the jury can instead convict a defendant of an offence contrary to section 20. Research reveals that only 23 per cent of offenders indicted under section 18 are eventually convicted of that offence, with most of the remainder being convicted of lesser offences, particularly section 20.[1]

**(b) Mens rea** Two *mens rea* elements are contained within section 18; the offence must be committed "maliciously" and "with intent".

1. *Maliciously.* In order to appreciate the significance of this term in section 18, it is necessary to dismantle the section to find the possible charges contained within it. If one is charged with maliciously causing grievous bodily harm with intent to cause grievous bodily harm, then *Mowatt*[2] is right in suggesting that the word maliciously adds nothing that is not already present in the requirement of intent.

On the other hand, if the defendant is charged with maliciously causing grievous bodily harm with intent to resist or prevent arrest, the inclusion of the term malicious may be crucial. If, for example, the defendant intends only to resist arrest and has no state of mind at all in relation to the possibility of harm, he cannot be convicted because he is not malicious. He must, at least, foresee the possibility of some harm.[3]

2. *With intent.* The defendant must either intend grievous bodily harm or intend to resist arrest.

It has been held that "intent" here bears the same meaning as in *Nedrick*.[4] Whether the House of Lords decision in *Woollin* apples to crimes other than murder is a moot point discussed elsewhere.[5] The better view is that *Woollin* (to the extent that it may have modified *Nedrick*) should apply to section 18. It would be unfortunate if intention in "intention to cause grievous bodily harm" bore different meanings for section 18 and for murder. It is perhaps because of the difficulty of establishing this requisite intention that so few of those indicted under section 18 are actually convicted of the offence. The cases in which offenders are finally convicted under section 18 tend to be those where there is some objective evidence of premeditation, such as when a weapon has been taken to the scene of the crime.[6]

---

[99] [1995] 1 A.C. 208.
[1] Genders, "Reform of the Offences Against the Person Act: Lessons from the Law in Action" [1999] Crim.L.R.689.
[2] [1967] 1 Q.B. 421.
[3] *Morrison* (1989) 89 Cr.App.R.17.
[4] *Purcell* (1986) 83 Cr.app.R.45.
[5] See p. 135.
[6] Genders, *above*, n.1.

**(c) Punishment** Section 18 carries a maximum sentence of life imprisonment. With the maximum penalty set so high no "racially or religiously aggravated" category of this offence was introduced. In practice the vast majority of sentences fall well below this maximum with the normal sentencing bracket being in the range of three to eight years' imprisonment although greater sentences are imposed in particularly grave cases.[7]

## C. *Evaluation*

It is obvious that something needs to be done about the present structure of non-fatal offences against the person. What precisely is needed?

The present structure of these offences, both in terms of substance and penalty structure, is little short of chaotic. Given the large difference in penalty, it is highly anomalous that the same *mens rea* suffices for both common assault and section 47 and that the difference in harm caused in these two offences need only be slight.[8] Section 20 is supposed to be a far more serious offence than section 47,[9] yet both carry the same maximum penalty. Both section 18 and section 20 cover the same harm—grievous bodily harm; can the difference in their maximum penalties (life imprisonment and five years' imprisonment respectively) be justified exclusively in terms of their differing *mens rea* requirements?

It is clear that both the substance of these offences and their scale of punishments must be restructured so as to represent a true hierarchy of seriousness. Failure to do this "might either confuse moral judgments or bring the law into disrepute, or both".[10] Further, "principles of justice or fairness between different offenders require morally distinguishable offences to be treated differently and morally similar offences to be treated alike".[11]

How should this relative seriousness of the offences be determined? The present unhappy distinction between offences rests on a confused conjunction of *mens rea* and harm done. Law reform efforts in England have been mainly aimed at achieving a more rational combination of these two elements. Drawing on the work of the Law Commission,[12] the Government has published a Consultation Document containing a Draft Bill with the following provisions.

### Home Office, Violence: Reforming the Offences Against the Person Act 1861, Draft Offences Against the Person Bill 1998:

"1(1) A person is guilty of an offence if he intentionally causes serious injury to another. (Max: life imprisonment)

2(1) A person is guilty of an offence if he recklessly causes serious injury to another. (Max: seven years' imprisonment)

---

[7] Blackstone's *Criminal Practice* (2001), p. 181.

[8] This situation has been exacerbated by the decision in *Brown* [1994] 1 A.C. 212 where it was held that consent could be a defence to common assault but not to assault occasioning actual bodily harm.

[9] Cavadino and Wiles, "Seriousness of Offences: The Perceptions of Practitioners" [1994] Crim.L.R. 489.

[10] Hart, *Law, Liberty and Morality* (1963), p. 36.

[11] *ibid.* p. 37.

[12] Law Commission No. 218, *Legislating the Criminal Code: Offences against the Person and General Principles* (1993).

3(1) A person is guilty of an offence if he intentionally or recklessly causes injury to another. (Max: five years' imprisonment)

4(1) A person is guilty of an offence if—

(a) he intentionally or recklessly applies force to or causes an impact on the body of another, or

(b) he intentionally or recklessly causes the other to believe that any such force or impact is imminent.

(2) No such offence is committed if the force or impact, not being intended or likely to cause injury, is in the circumstances such as is generally acceptable in the ordinary conduct of daily life and the defendant does not know or believe that it is in fact unacceptable to the other person. (Max: six months' imprisonment)

10(1). A person is guilty of an offence if he makes to another a threat to cause the death of, or serious injury to, that other or a third person, intending that other to believe that it will be carried out. (Max: ten years' imprisonment)

15(1) In this Act 'injury' means—

(a) physical injury, or

(b) mental injury.

(2) Physical injury does not include anything caused by disease but (subject to that) it includes pain, unconsciousness and any other impairment of a person's physical condition.

(3) Mental injury does not include anything caused by disease but (subject to that) it includes any impairment of a person's mental health.

(4) In its application to section 1 this section applies without the exceptions relating to things caused by disease.

[The Bill contains a definition of both intention (cl. 14(1)) and recklessness (cl. 14(2)), the latter being defined in terms of subjective awareness (*Cunningham* recklessness).]"

Such a restructuring represents an improvement on the present law. It does, however, raise several important questions. First, the only forms of blameworthiness codified are intention and subjective recklessness. No provision is made for *Caldwell* recklessness. Might there not be some situations involving *Caldwell* recklessness when punishment (at a lesser level) is appropriate?:

"The fact that D consciously and without justification decided to run a risk indicates his indifference or thoughtlessness. But thoughtlessness and indifference can equally well exist without advertence. Thus when a man lights his garden bonfire, he does not generally advert to the inevitable risk that he will kill many insects who will perish in the flames. Such inadvertence is not culpable. But what are we to say of the man who, as in *Caldwell*, sets a hotel on fire without adverting to the risk that the guests may be burned? Such inadvertence indicates a shocking state of mind—one that cares as little for human beings as for insects."[13]

Secondly, the distinction between intention and recklessness is thought to be so significant as to justify a maximum of life imprisonment for intentionally causing serious injury as opposed to seven years' imprisonment for recklessly causing serious injury. This is because there is "a definite moral and psychological difference between the two offences which it is appropriate for the criminal law to reflect".[14] But when it comes to causing lesser injuries, these concerns have

---

[13] Stannard, "Subjectivism, Objectivism and the Draft Criminal Code" (1985) 100 L.Q.R. 540 at 551. See, further, Clarkson, *above*, n.50 at 329–331.

[14] Law Commission, *above*, n.12, para. 8.3, citing the Criminal Law Revision Committee, 14th Report, *Offences against the Person* (1980), para. 152.

evaporated into thin air and no distinction is drawn between intention and recklessness. It seems odd that the difference in moral blame between intention and recklessness should be regarded as sufficiently significant to warrant such a huge difference in sentencing maxima for serious injury and yet simply be dismissed as inconsequential for lesser injuries.

Thirdly, there is the problem of defining injury. "Injury" includes pain. A slap across the face hurts; it causes pain. If that is so (and the defendant becomes liable for an offence carrying a maximum of five years' imprisonment), it would appear that assault will only cover the most trivial cases of force being applied. The Law Commission decided not to exclude minor injuries arguing, inter alia, that the level of injury would be taken into account by prosecutors in deciding the level of charge. However, research has revealed that the seriousness of the injury does not play a significant role in the decision to charge and prosecute.[15] The definition of "injury" includes "impairment of a person's mental health". The Law Commission felt that this would cover serious mental injury, such as post-traumatic stress disorder that is a medically recognised illness, but will exclude mere anxiety or distress.[16] It is regrettable that minor physical injuries were not similarly excluded.

Fourthly, the Bill only draws a distinction between serious injury and injury and leaves the former undefined. In the United States the Model Penal Code has defined "serious injury" as "bodily injury which creates a substantial risk of death or which causes serious, permanent disfigurement, or protracted loss or impairment of the function of any bodily member or organ".[17] Is there not a case for drawing more precise distinctions in the hierarchy of offences between different levels of injury? For instance, should we not distinguish between serious injury which is of a temporary nature (such as a broken limb) and that which is permanently crippling or disfiguring?[18]

A final question needs to be asked: must the restructuring of these offences be based *entirely* on new combinations of *mens rea* and harm? Could not other factors also be utilised in informing our moral assessments (to be translated into legal judgments) of the relative seriousness of offences.

Gardner[19] rejects the Law Commission's view that the structure of these offences should be restricted to variations in the configuration of *mens rea* and resulting harm as this "does not capture all that is interesting, or rationally significant, about the wrong".[20] What matters is the *wrong* involved and not just the harm caused and "the wrong is that of bringing the harm about in that way. In morality, as in law, it matters how one brings things about."[21] For instance, he argues that sections 20 and 47 are neither more serious nor less serious than each other, but rather each belongs to its "own family of offences"[22]: section 20 is a crime of violence; section

---

[15] Clarkson, Cretney, Davis and Shepherd, "Assaults: The Relationship between Seriousness, Criminalisation and Punishment" [1994] Crim.L.R. 4.

[16] Law Com. *above*, n.12, paras. 15.26–15.29. This result has now been broadly achieved by *Ireland* [1997] 4 All E.R. 225.

[17] Proposed Official Draft, s.210.0(3).

[18] Clarkson, *above*, n.50 at 327–328.

[19] "Rationality and the Rule of Law in Offences against the Person" [1994] C.L.J. 502.

[20] At 511.

[21] At 505.

[22] At 507.

47 is a crime of assault which is "not a crime of violence. Its essential quality lies in the invasion by one person of another's body space."[23] Drawing an analogy with the Theft Acts where theft, obtaining by deception, false accounting, making off without payment etc. are differentiated, not by the harm done (the same property might have been lost), but by the different mode of wrongdoing, he points to lesser known provisions of the 1861 Act where distinctions are drawn between different modes of violence. For instance, "Section 21 deals with choking, suffocating, or strangling; section 22 deals with the use of stupefacients and overpowering substances, sections 23 and 24 with poisoning, section 26 with starving and exposing to the elements; sections 28 to 30 deal with burning, maiming, disfiguring and disabling by use of explosives" and so on. Such offences, he claims "are notable for the moral clarity with which they are differentiated".[24]

In much the same vein, Horder argues that in terms of fair labelling the Law Commission's recommendations amount to "a slide into the vice of moral vacuity".[25] There are "important qualitative moral distinctions" between deliberately punching someone hard and breaking his nose and castrating a person; these distinctions should be marked in the offence committed.[26]

It could be possible to structure offences not only by the degree and type of harm involved, but also by *how* the harm is caused. In the United States, the Model Penal Code provides that the use of a deadly weapon aggravates the seriousness of the offence. For example, an "aggravated assault" is committed when serious bodily injury is caused with *mens rea*; this same offence is committed when a deadly weapon is used if mere bodily injury results.[27]

Such an approach, however, can only be accepted if there is something *morally significant* (as opposed to just different) about the method by which the harm is caused or morally significant about the type of harm caused (broken nose or castration). This test of morally significant wrongness is arguably satisfied when a deadly weapon, particularly a firearm, is used:

> "In general it is fair to say that firearms can be more lethal than other weapons or methods, that they put the victim at greater disadvantage, and that often their use (where there is forearmament) is evidence of premeditation ... Firearms tend to put victims in a terrible state of fear."[28]

Similarly, there is an argument that the use of torture involves a significant wrong justifying the separate existence of such an offence. The willingness of the torturer to inflict such pain (along with whatever injury is caused) demonstrates greater culpability. The actual pain caused (along with the actual injury) constitutes a morally significant harm.

One could go even further and argue that other factors such as the identity of the victim or defendant or the motive underlying the crime could significantly mark out

---

[23] At 507–508.

[24] At 515.

[25] "Rethinking Non-Fatal Offences against the Person" (1994) 14 O.J.L.S. 335 at 340.

[26] At 342.

[27] American Law Institute, Model Penal Code (Proposed Official Draft) 1962, s.211.1(2). This provision has been substantially adopted by a number of states—*e.g.* N.H. §§ 631: 1, 2; N.J. § 2C: 12–1; Pa.tit. 18 §§ 2701, 2702; S.D. §§ 22–18–1.–1.1; Vt.tit. 13 §§ 1023 to 1024.

[28] Ashworth, *Sentencing and Penal Policy* (1983), p. 166.

the wrong involved. Some examples of this are canvassed in the next chapter when homicide offences are evaluated. Two examples will suffice here. First, one crime where the identity of the victim aggravates the seriousness of an offence is assault on a police constable contrary to section 51 of the Police Act 1964.[29] As Ashworth states:

> "Submission of citizens to lawful authority is an important part of social order: assaulting a law enforcement officer is therefore morally worse than assaulting a private citizen, *ceteris paribus*, because of the implied rejection of the authority of the law itself."[30]

While there are probably equally clear deterrent reasons underlying the existence of this offence, it nevertheless serves as a useful illustration of the point.

Secondly, there is the new offence in the Crime and Disorder Act 1998 of racially or religiously[31] aggravated assault. Taking the former as an example, the distinctive wrong here is that the assault is not simply against a person as an individual but constitutes an attack on him as a member of a racial group. Not only is injury caused to the individual, but the assault also expresses hatred or contempt of an entire racial group. The victim is particularly vulnerable. The normal assault-prevention mechanisms commonly employed (looking away; doing nothing to precipitate the assault) are worthless if one is attacked simply because of one's race. This distinctive wrong needs to be marked out by a separate offence with a different sentencing maximum.

A major problem with this whole approach is that it can lead to over-specificity. One could be left with a bewildering array of offences—the vice of "particularism"[32]—each marking a separate wrong but with a failure to distinguish the offences *in terms of seriousness*. Fair labelling involves not only capturing the essential wrong involved but also communciating the relative seriousness of that wrongdoing.[33] Despite its internal incoherence, the present structure of offences against the person does represent a reasonably well-understood hierarchy of seriousness. Perhaps the best way forward is through a recognition that the true criterion for assessing appropriate levels of criminal liability should be a combination of blame and harm. *Mens rea* need not be the only indicator of blame. While we might rightly choose to blame the intentional actor more than the reckless one, we might also choose to blame the torturer or the racist attacker more than other assailants. Similarly, the notion of harm need not merely be defined by reference to the degree of injury caused. It has already been argued that permanent serious injury ought to be distinguished from temporary serious injury (castration is more serious than a broken nose). In assessing the appropriate level of harm, the

---

[29] See also: assaulting a clergyman in the discharge of his duties (Offences against the Person Act 1861, s.36); assaulting a magistrate in the exercise of his duty concerning the preservation of a vessel in distress or a wreck (s.37). These offences would be abolished under the Draft Criminal Code, in line with the thinking of the Criminal Law Revision Committee that the victim's identity should generally be relevant to sentencing only and not to the definition of the offence (14th Report, para. 162).

[30] *Above*, n.28, pp. 158–159.

[31] Inserted by the Anti-terrorism, Crime and Security Act 2001, s.39.

[32] Horder, *ante*, n.25, at 338.

[33] Gardner does not accept that fair labelling is concerned with marking relative seriousness between offences. See, further, Clarkson, *Understanding Criminal Law* (2001), p. 186.

threat or risk of injury needs to be taken into account. If no actual injury occurs (as with attempts) an appropriate discount should be made as there will be a lesser impact on the victim.[34] On this basis, perhaps technical assault should be rated as less harmful than a battery. Similarly, extra threat or risk could be regarded as aggravating the level of harm. Whatever the level of actual injury caused, the use of a firearm is necessarily more dangerous and poses the risk of death and should be regarded as an aggravating factor.

This suggested approach has two advantages. First, it concentrates the mind into an assessment of whether the different wrong involved is indeed morally significant, as opposed to being just different. Only if it can be regarded as aggravating the level of culpability of the defendant or the level of harm caused can it legitimately be taken into account.[35] Secondly, by a conjunction of these more finely-tuned elements, a true hierarchy of seriousness can be revealed. It is important that individual criminal offences communicate the essence of the wrongdoing involved. It is equally important that the relative seriousness of such offences be communciated and that the criminal law as a whole convey a morally-informative set of messages.

## II. Sexual Offences

### A. *Introduction*

There are a large number of offences that proscribe certain forms of sexual behaviour. They vary widely in the type of harm encompassed, from the very serious (such as rape) to the less significant (such as indecent exposure). Even within a particular offence, for example, indecent assault, the conduct may range from the life-threatening to little more than touching. Many of these offences have been placed on a statutory footing, but developments have taken place in such a piece-meal fashion that the latest reform proposals condemned the law as "archaic, incoherent and discriminatory"[36]. This section will focus upon the crime of rape to illustrate these difficulties but reference will be made, where appropriate, to other sexual offences.

### 1. The level of offending

It is extremely difficult to assess the extent of offending in this area. What is clear is that, whether one is talking about consensual but unlawful under-age sexual intercourse, incest, indecent assault or rape, the official statistics reveal only a tiny proportion of offending. According to such statistics, 9,008 female rapes and 735 male rapes were recorded in 2001/02.[37] This represents a staggering increase over

[34] Von Hirsch and Jareborg, "Gauging Criminal Harm: A Living-Standard Analysis" (1991) 11 O.J.L.S. 1.
[35] It is arguable that these various factors should rather be taken into account at the sentencing stage. See, further, Clarkson, *above*, n.33 at 186.
[36] *Protecting the Public, Strengthening Protection Against Sexual Offenders and Reforming the Law on Sexual Offences* (Cm.5668, 2002), para. 8.
[37] www.homeoffice.gov.uk/rds/sexoffend1.html.

the 240 rapes recorded in total for the year 1947.[38] Whilst some of this continued increase may be explicable in terms of increasing levels of violence, much more is due to an increased willingness to report rape as well as changes to recording practices.[39] However, very substantial problems remain. Whilst the reporting and recording rates for rape have gone up, the level of offending in society is still undoubtedly much greater and the level of convictions for rape has actually fallen.

(i) *The dark figure of offending*

Over the last two decades research has done much to shed some light, generally, on the dark figures of crime. However, until very recently the British Crime Surveys have not proved to be a useful source of information about the incidence of sexual violence in society.[40] The 2000 British Crime Survey estimated that 61,000 women had been victims of rape in the previous 12 months.[41] This finding echoes smaller scale research conducted over the last 20 years or so into sexual violence against women, which suggests that only between 10 and 25 per cent of offences are reported to the police.[42] In *Ask Any Woman*, 17 per cent of the respondents to a questionnaire said they had been raped and a further 20 per cent said they had been a victim of attempted rape. One in seven married women said they had been forced into sex against their will by their husbands; indeed, this was the most common form of rape identified in the survey.[43]

Victim surveys, as well as providing an insight into the amount of crime, also enable a picture to be built up about the way crime, and the fear of crime, affects people's lives. All the evidence supports the view that women's lives and freedom of movement are curtailed by the fear of violence and, in particular, the fear of rape. The 1988 British Crime Survey revealed that one in five women felt "very unsafe" when walking outside at night,[44] and in the earlier 1984 survey half of the respondents said they would always be accompanied if they went out at night.[45] So real are women's fears that some taxi firms now guarantee women drivers to their customers. For many, in other words, there is a self-imposed curfew—an interesting concept given that they are not the criminals. It is sometimes said that these fears are exaggerated out of all proportion; indeed, the newspaper report which gave details of the 1988 British Crime Survey was headed "Women too wary of violent attack".[46] Given the low level of offending revealed by that survey,

---

[38] Cambridge Department of Science Report, *Sexual Offences*, (1957), p. 12.

[39] Male rape could not be recorded as such until 1995 when the legal definition of rape was changed, *below*, p. 610. Povey, Nicholas and Ellis, *Crime in England and Wales: Quarterly Update* (2003) state sexual offences increased by 26% in 2001/02 but that the introduction of National Crime Recording Standards in April 2002 would have had an impact on this figure.

[40] See further, Temkin, *Rape and the Legal Process* (2nd ed., 2002), pp. 16–17.

[41] Myhill and Allen, *Rape and Sexual Assault of Women: The Extent and Nature of the Problem—Findings from the British Crime Survey* (Home Office Research Study No. 237, 2002).

[42] Male rape is probably even more under-reported. See further, McMullen, *Male Rape* (1990); King and Hezey, *Male Victims of Sexual Assault* (1992) and Hillman, "Medical and Social Aspects of Sexual Assault of Males: A Survey of 100 Victims" (1990) British Journal of General Practice 502.

[43] Hall, *Ask Any Woman: A London Inquiry into Rape and Sexual Assault* (1985). See also, Kelly, *A Research Review on the Reporting, Investigation and Prosecution of Rape Cases* (2002). See *below*, p. 609 for discussion of the former marital rape bar.

[44] Mayhew, Elliot and Dowds, *The 1988 British Crime Survey* (1989).

[45] Hough and Mayhew, *Taking Account of Crime* (1985), p. 40.

[46] *The Sunday Correspondent*, September 17, 1989.

perhaps this is none too surprising, but, as the other studies above show, their fears may be based on fairly solid ground.

There is one last insight provided by victim studies that needs to be considered: why are rape and other sexual assaults so under-reported? As far as rape is concerned, the most frequently cited reasons revolve around the unsympathetic and even hostile treatment victims fear they will receive, first, at the hands of the police—at a time when they are at their most vulnerable—and then by the courts.[47] Victims may well be put off reporting when they know that defence barristers or the defendant may take them, stage by detailed stage, through the offence.[48] Both male and female victims have likened this to being raped again.[49] In addition, male victims may well decline to report through a fear of being thought gay or a feeling that as men they should have been able to repel the aggressor. Further, victims of incest and marital rape are often put under severe emotional, as well as physical, pressure not to report. In short, it would be dangerously wrong to assume that generally the crime is not reported because it had no serious or lasting impact upon the victim.

### (ii) *From reporting to conviction*

Even if a rape is reported, the chances of securing a conviction are low and have become lower. Recording rates have become higher and the proportion of these that are subsequently no-crimed has declined.[50] However, just because a complaint reaches this point in the criminal justice system does not mean that a prosecution will be brought. Clearly, there will be cases where no suspect is found[51] but more frequently the police will take "no further action" against the suspect (because the complainant withdraws the allegation or there is insufficient evidence) or the CPS will decide not to prosecute (predominantly on evidential grounds).[52] The proportion of cases reaching court has declined substantially: in 1985, 31 per cent

---

[47] See Temkin, *above*, n.40, pp. 3–4, 17–19. Research examining the treatment of victims by the police suggests that whilst real improvements have been made police practice is not uniformly good. See Temkin, "Reporting Rape in London: A Qualitative Study" (1999) 38 Howard J. of Criminal Justice 17; Temkin, "*Plus ca Change*. Reporting Rape in the 90's" (1997) 37 Brit. J.Criminol. 507.

[48] See further, Temkin, "Prosecuting and Defending Rape: Perspectives from the Bar"(2000) 27 J. of Law and Society 219.

[49] A statement made by, for example, Julia Mason who in 1996 was cross-examined for six days by the defendant, Ralston Edwards (who wore the same clothes that he had worn on the night of the attack). He was later given two life sentences. Partly as a consequence of the outcry surrounding this trial, the automatic right of defendants to conduct their own defence was ended: Youth Justice and Criminal Evidence Act 1999, s.34. See further, Temkin, *above*, n.40, pp. 320–324; Stewart, Dobbin and Gatowski, "'Real Rapes' and 'Real Victims': The Shared Reliance on Common Cultural Definitions of Rape" [1996] IV *Feminist Legal Studies* 159 and Rumney "Male Rape in the Courtroom: Issues and Concerns" [2001] Crim.L.R.205.

[50] Home Office guidance (Circular 69/1986) states that "no-criming is only appropriate where the complainant retracts completely and admits to fabrication". As a consequence of this, one study showed that no-criming fell from 45% to 25% between 1985–96, but that some cases were still being no-crimed on the basis of insufficient evidence: Harris and Grace, *A Question of Evidence? Investigating and Prosecuting Paper in the 1990's* (Home Office Research Study No. 196, 1999). See also, Gregory and Lees, *Policing Sexual Assault* (1999), pp. 60–66.

[51] In Harris and Grace's study, (*ibid.*), p. 15, 15% of crimed rapes overall were undetected, but 66% of the cases involving strangers were undetected, meaning that in practice these were the least likely type of rapes to be prosecuted.

[52] *ibid.* pp. xi–xii. See also, Temkin, *above* n.40, pp. 22–25; Gregory and Lees, pp. 68–78.

of cases initially recorded as rape resulted in an offender appearing for trial at Crown court; by 1997 the percentage was down to 19 per cent.[53] Of those cases reaching court, some will result in acquittals and a significant number will be dealt with by means of guilty pleas to lesser charges. In 1997, the percentage of those convicted or cautioned for rape was 9 per cent in comparison with 24 per cent in 1985.[54] In 2001, (in which, as noted above, almost 10,000 male and female rapes were recorded) there were 559 convictions for female rape and 53 convictions for male rape.[55] What is clear is that as well as the proportion of rape cases reaching court having declined, the nature of the cases has changed as well. Many more now involve people who were known to each other (either as acquaintances or intimates) prior to the incident which led to the complaint. However, while it might be tempting to use this to explain low conviction rates, caution has to be exercised. The category "acquaintance" rape includes those who have met within the previous 24 hours and may even include a complainant who was stopped by her assailant to give directions.[56] Such cases are hardly any different from stranger rape cases and mean that there can be no straightforward explanation for low conviction rates based on prior relationship. The presence or absence of violence may well be as significant as any prior relationship.[57]

## 2. Rape in context

Whether the crime involves so-called date rape, rape by a stranger or by a partner or friend, the rhetoric of the law and its reality can only be truly understood against the backdrop of societal attitudes to women and rape generally.

### Allison Morris, Women, Crime and Criminal Justice (1987), pp. 165–181:

"Most of us believe we know what rape is, but our knowledge is derived from social not legal definitions. 'True' rape in popular imagination involves the use of weapons, the infliction of serious injury and occurs in a lonely place late at night. The 'true' rapist is over-sexed, sexually frustrated or mentally ill, and is a stranger. The 'true' rape victim is a virgin (or has had no extra-marital affairs), was not voluntarily in the place where the act took place, fought to the end and has bruises to show for it. . . . [T]he reason [other] kinds of situations are not seen as rape is the strength of the assumptions we hold about rape. . . . I will now examine some of these assumptions. . . .

*'Rape is impossible'*
. . . [Some] criminologists have argued that to force a woman into intercourse is an impossible task in most cases if the woman is conscious and extreme pain is not inflicted. These beliefs have become part of rape folklore (. . . 'a woman with her skirt up can run faster than a man with his trousers down' and the like) and embedded in the practice of criminal justice professionals. . . .

*'Women want to be raped'*
This assumption has its roots in Freudian beliefs about the masochistic nature of female sexuality . . . rape is believed to dominate women's sexual fantasies. . . .

---

[53] *ibid.*, p. 51.
[54] *ibid.*
[55] *Criminal Statistics, England and Wales 2001* (Cm.5696), p. 50.
[56] In Harris and Grace's study (*above*, n.50), of the194 cases concerning acquaintances 102 had met during this period.
[57] *ibid.* and see further, Temkin, *above*, n.40, pp. 25–30.

*' "No" means "Yes"*

Nineteenth-century women—or, at least ladies—were seen as asexual and presumed not to enjoy sex. Whereas they were passive and submitted (rather than consented) to the sex act, men were viewed as the aggressors and the initiators, and as having sexual needs. These beliefs have resonances today. ... Men are expected to make advances (otherwise the woman thinks she is unattractive) and women are expected to be sexually attractive and, at the same time, both coy and flirtatious. They are expected to play hard to get, to need to be seduced. ... A judge in a recent rape trial in Cambridge told the jury that women sometimes say 'no' when they mean 'yes' and to remember the expression 'stop it. I like it'.[58] ...

*' "Yes" to one, then "yes" to all.'[59]*

*'The victim was asking for it'*

In essence, this assumption implies that the victim should not have dressed like that (*e.g.* with no bra), behaved like that (*e.g.* hitch-hiked), gone to places like that (*e.g.* singles' bars). ... Amir, in his study of rape, developed the notion of victim precipitation. His definition is both extremely broad and stresses the offender's interpretation of the victim's behaviour, not the victim's. 'The victim actually—or so it was interpreted by the offender—agreed to sexual relations but retracted ... or did not resist strongly enough when the suggestion was made by the offender.' The term applies also to cases in which the victim enters vulnerable situations charged sexually. (*Patterns in Forcible Rape* (1971), p. 266). Earlier, he seems to define any form of female behaviour as rape-precipitating. ... Despite this, only 19 per cent of the rapes in Amir's sample could be so 'explained'. ...

*'Rape is a cry for vengeance'*

... Standard legal texts on evidence and procedure ... warn of the danger of women contriving false charges of sexual offences. And as recently as 1984, the Criminal Law Revision Committee prefaced its report on sex offences with the words that 'by no means every accusation of rape is true' (15th Report, Sexual Offences, Cmnd.9213, p. 5). ...[60]

*'Rape is a sexual act'*

... The popular conception now is that rape is sexually motivated: this is most apparent in accounts offered to excuse rape. Smart and Smart (*Women, Sexuality and Social Control* (1978), pp. 98–99) provide examples of this from media coverage of rape:

'The pregnancy of B's wife may have been one of the reasons for his committing the offence.'

'R attacked her five days before his wife gave birth to their first child.' "

Sexual gratification, however, may not be the major reason for rape. As Brownmiller says "the penis is deployed as a weapon",[61] and research conducted amongst convicted rapists suggests that the desire to dominate and humiliate the rape victim (often coupled with revenge motives) features most commonly.[62] In

---

[58] See further Lees, *Ruling Passions: Sexual Violence, Reputation and the Law* (1997), pp. 75–78 and Schulhofer, *Unwanted Sex: The Culture of Intimidation and the Failure of the Law* (1998), pp. 47–68.

[59] For discussion of the extent to which evidence of past sexual experience can be introduced, see pp. 612–613.

[60] This distrust of complainants resulted in the development of rules of corroboration. It was not until 1994 that it ceased to be mandatory to give a warning as to the danger of uncorroborated evidence: *below*, p. 612.

[61] Brownmiller, *Against Our Will* (1975), p. 11.

[62] Queen's Bench Foundation, *Rape—Prevention and Resistance* (1976), p. 80; *contra* Amir, *Patterns in Forcible Rape* (1971), p. 131 who concluded, without much supportive evidence, that strong sexual emotion was the dominant motive.

furtherance of this motive the attractiveness of the victim is not a vital ingredient, although it is a paradox in a society demanding its females to make themselves attractive that if the rape victim has done so, she may well be condemned for it. Whilst most rape victims are young,[63] what matters more than physical appearance is vulnerability. As one rape victim said, "what I exuded that night was not sexuality ... but vulnerability ... I, by virtue of my size and gender ... was recognisable to the rapist as easy game and an exemplary target for his generalised misogyny".[64]

It has often been asserted that rapists are pathological individuals; they are "victims of a disease from which many of them suffer more than their victims"[65]; they are "sexual psychopaths". Whilst there are undoubtedly rapists who are psychologically disturbed, more recent research has shown how rare this is.[66] The better view, it is submitted, is that rape is about inequalities of power, whether the victim is female or male. The stereotypical rape is depicted as an act committed by a stranger, probably outside the home, at night and where violence is employed. In reality, most victims know their assailants and the home may well be the location for rape.[67]

Much attention has been focused recently on two different types of rape, both of which have been contrasted with the supposed paradigm of stranger rape. The first is that of relationship rape. It has been suggested that this is a less serious form of sexual assault than stranger rape.[68] In contrast, however, one may point to accounts of rape given by those who have been or are in relationships with their assailant:

"Linda, 41, has to walk with crutches after being violently raped and battered by her husband. ... Her husband began attacking her when she was pregnant. ... The rapes began after her son was born. ... 'He used to tell me that I was supposed to enjoy it—he actually thought women liked being raped. He said it was what all his mates talked about at work. In the end I just hated him. Sex could never be normal—how can you like someone who's beating you up and telling you you should be liking it?' "[69]

The second type is that of "date-rape", perhaps better described as acquaintance rape.[70] There have been a number of cases both in the United States and this country where defendants have been acquitted of rape charges brought as a consequence of

[63] The ages most at risk were between 16–25 in Harris and Grace's study (*above*, n.50, p. 7) But studies do report ranges between 1 and 82 years (Brownmiller, *above*, n.61, p. 272).
[64] Anonymous letter to *The Observer*, January 10, 1982.
[65] Karpman, *The Sexual Offender and his Offenses*, (1954), p. 482.
[66] For example, Smithyman in Parsonage (ed.), *Perspectives on Victimology* (1979), pp. 99–120. See also Howard League Working Party, *Unlawful Sex* (1985), pp. 47 *et seq.*
[67] In Harris and Grace's study (*above*, n.50), 88% of victims were, at least, acquainted with the suspect and that the offence took place in either their joint home or the victim's home in 35% of cases. Research for Channel 4's *Dispatches* programme (1994) found that 6 out of 7 women knew the person who raped them. A study by King of male victims of rape found that the majority of men knew the person who was attacking them (*The Independent*, July 3, 1997).
[68] Williams, "Rape is Rape" (1992) 142 N.L.J. 11.
[69] *The Independent*, February 23, 1990.
[70] The phrase, date-rape is thought to have been coined by American psychologist, Mary Koss, in 1985 but it can be argued that the very description belittles the seriousness of the offence.

allegedly non-consensual intercourse at parties, etc. As with marital rape, these cases have brought into sharp focus many of the assumptions which may be implicit in relationships between men and women. Does a man who buys a woman a meal have a right to have intercourse with her? Does a woman who gets drunk at a party ask for it? If she cries rape afterwards is it because she is ashamed or did not enjoy it? Do women lie about rape? Has feminism taught young women that all men are rapists[71] or have men yet to catch up mentally with the changing rules of sexual encounters?

No one has a right to expect sex on the basis of favours or persuasions and the idea that men can be so biologically carried away that they are unable to stop is a poorly disguised historical excuse for an exercise of male power. But neither are women weak creatures who cannot take responsibility for their actions; they can read the signs that indicate that the situation may be about to escalate; if she says she is not interested it is rape to persist.

### 3. What is rape?

Many of the issues highlighted above have had very significant consequences for the shape the law has taken (for example, in relation to the concept of consent) as well as how it has operated in practice. However, before turning to that discussion, it is important to try to identify the "essence" of rape. Rape and other sexual offences, such as indecent assault, are sometimes associated with gross violence. For some, rape is always and essentially a crime of violence. One effect of this could be that the offence should be defined so that rape only occurs where the victim has shown physical resistance.[72] However, it is not true that all "rapes" are accompanied by violence.[73] Does this mean that there has been no rape? One answer increasingly given is that rape is a crime against sexual autonomy and that what matters is whether there was consent. There are difficulties with both approaches. Perceiving rape as a crime of violence makes for a relatively straightforward offence but ignores the dynamics of sexual relationships and enables husbands, partners and "date-rapists" to deny that what they do is rape. However, making consent the pivotal concept has proved to be deeply problematic. Nevertheless, if one conceives of a hypothetical scenario as Gardner and Shute do, in which the victim is unconscious, unharmed and never learns that sexual intercourse (with a condom) has taken place, it is still right to state that the victim has been raped. Indeed, this "pure" case of rape enables one to identify what they describe as "the wrongness of rape":

"Rape, in the pure case, is the sheer use of a person. ... Rape is humiliating even when unaccompanied by further affronts because the sheer use of a person, and

---

[71] Mackinnon, *Toward a Feminist Theory of the State* (1989) p. 174 argues that it is difficult for women to distinguish between rape and intercourse under current conditions of male dominance.

[72] In the United States many of the states have removed the requirement that the woman show utmost resistance but still define rape as non-consensual and forced sexual intercourse: see, West, "A Comment on Consent, Sex and Rape" (1996) 2 *Legal Theory* 232.

[73] See Temkin, *above*, n.40, pp. 167–168.

in that sense the objectification of a person, is a denial of their personhood. It is literally dehumanizing."[74]

Because rape is the sheer use of a person as an object there is no case for its being subdivided into more or less serious offences depending upon whether a relationship or acquaintance existed between the victim and the offender.

## 4. Sentencing

Rape is punishable by a maximum sentence of life imprisonment and it is now almost axiomatic that if the defendant is convicted, he will serve a period of immediate imprisonment. The sentencing guideline case of *Billam*,[75] makes it clear that custodial sentences of five years will be the normal sentence for rape without aggravating features and that only in the most exceptional circumstances will a non-custodial sentence be imposed.[76] There is evidence that *Billam* has had the effect of lengthening sentences overall for rape and its general approach was confirmed recently in the decision of *Millberry, Morgan, and Lackenby*.[77] However, *Billam* pre-dated changes to the law relating to male rape, anal rape and the removal of the marital rape exemption and gave little guidance in cases of relationship rape, except to state that "the victim's sexual experience ... [is] irrelevant." Despite this, courts have often used the fact that the parties have or have had a relationship as a mitigating factor.[78] This ignores the growing body of research which highlights the traumatic effect of rape by someone known to the victim where the abuse of trust involved may cause lasting harm.[79] The Sentencing Advisory Panel has taken these issues on board:

"[T]he Panel proposes that the Court of Appeal should make a clear statement to the effect that the starting point for sentence is that cases of 'relationship rape' and 'acquaintance rape' are to be treated as being of equal seriousness to cases of 'stranger rape' with the sentence increased or reduced, in each case, by the presence of specific aggravating or mitigating factors. ...

---

[74] "The Wrongness of Rape" in Horder (ed.), *Oxford Essays in Jurisprudence* (2000), p. 205. *Contra* Simester and Sullivan, *Criminal Law: Theory and Doctrine* (2000), p. 403 who regard this as a peripheral rather than core example of rape. For them, the psychological trauma (with physical injury, unwanted pregnancy, infection) are very much part of our conception of rape and mean that rape is appropriately characterised as a form of violence as well as a wrong of disregard of the victim's autonomy.

[75] (1986) 8 Cr.App. R.(S.) 48.

[76] As, for example, in the case of *Taylor* (1983) 5 Cr.App. R.(S.) 241, where the defendant was found to be mentally retarded.

[77] [2002] EWCA Crim 2891; [2003] Crim.L.R.207.

[78] The first case post-*Billam* to do so was *Berry* (1988) 10 Cr.App. R.(S.) 13. In *M* (1995) 16 Cr.App. R.(S.) 770 the Court of Appeal indicated that a distinction could be drawn between cases where an estranged husband forces his way into the wife's home and those where the husband was still living in the same house and occupying the bed with consent. The Court of Appeal has approved this distinction in *Millberry, Morgan and Lackenby* but also indicated that today the sentence of three years would not be reduced to 18 months as in the original appeal. See also *Attorney-General's Reference (No. 24 of 1999)* [2000] 1 Cr.App. R.(S.) 275.

[79] See Rumney, "When Rape Isn't Rape: Court of Appeal Sentencing Practice in Cases of Marital and Relationship Rape" [1999] 19 O.J.L.S. 243; Warner, "Sentencing in Cases of Marital Rape: Towards Changing the Male Imagination" [2000] 20 Legal Studies 592 and Easteal, *Rape, Law Reform and Australian Culture* (1998).

[T]he same guidelines should apply in principle to male and female rape, with factors relevant to only one gender (such as pregnancy resulting from the rape of a woman) taken into account on a case by case basis. ... [T]he new guidelines should make it clear that there is no inherent distinction for sentencing purposes, between anal and vaginal rape."

The Court of Appeal has largely accepted this advice in *Millberry, Morgan and Lackenby*. In doing so, however, the door has been left open for previous attitudes to creep back in:

"Where, for example, the offender is the husband of the victim there can, but not necessarily, be mitigating features that clearly cannot apply to a rape by a stranger. On the other hand ... because of the existence of a relationship the victim can feel particularly bitter about an offence of rape, regarding it as a breach of trust. This may, in a particular case, mean that looking at the offence from the victim's point of view, the offence is as bad as a 'stranger rape'. The court has the task of balancing any circumstances of mitigation against the aggravating circumstances. In drawing the balance it is not to be overlooked, when considering 'stranger rape', the victim's fear can be increased because her assailant is an unknown quantity. Is he a murderer as well as a rapist? In addition, there is the fact ... that when a rape is committed by a stranger in a public place, not only is the offence horrific to the victim it can also frighten other members of the public."

The acceptance of the Panel's advice looks somewhat grudging. As already discussed, looking at it from "the victim's point of view" relationship rape can clearly be as bad as stranger rape. It would appear that generalisations about the seriousness of different types of rape have yet to be fully abandoned.

The average sentence for rape by an adult offender was 7 years 4 months in 2000. 57 per cent of sentences fell within the 5–10 years range but 10 per cent were given life sentences.[80] Section 109 of the Powers of the Criminal Courts (Sentencing) Act 2000 provides for automatic life sentences for those convicted of a second relevant sexual offence (rape, attempted rape or unlawful sexual intercourse with a girl under the age of 13).[81]

## B. *The Law*

### Sexual Offences Act 1956, section 1

"(1) It is an offence for a man to rape a woman or another man.
  (2) A man commits rape if—
    (a) he has sexual intercourse with a person (whether vaginal or anal) who at the time of the intercourse does not consent to it; and
    (b) at the time he knows that the person does not consent to the intercourse or is reckless as to whether that person consents to it."

---

[80] *Millberry, Morgan and Lackenby*, above, n.77.
[81] See *Offen* [2000] 2 All ER 154; *Kelly No.2* [2002] 1 Cr.App. R.(S.) 85 and *Richards* [2002] 2 Cr..App. R.91.

This definition, enacted in 1994,[82] removes many of the anomalies of the previous law.

## 1. Introduction

### (i) Rape within marriage

The reformed offence no longer contains the phrase "unlawful". Historically, this was taken to refer to intercourse outside marriage. The origin of this understanding or rule (whether one regards it as one or the other was a part of the debate, as we shall see) lay not in a statute or a case but in the writings of Sir Matthew Hale:

> "But the husband cannot be guilty of a rape committed by himself upon his lawful wife, for by their mutual matrimonial consent and contract the wife hath given herself in this kind unto her husband, which she cannot retract."[83]

For the following 200 years, Hale's analysis was unquestioningly accepted. Husbands who used force could, of course, be charged with an offence of violence[84] but there was a bar to charges of rape. This marital immunity began to erode, however, from 1949 onwards. In a succession of cases the courts held that where the parties were no longer bound in law to live together (because, for example, a separation order had been made) the husband would be guilty of rape if he had non-consensual sexual intercourse with his wife.[85]

At the same time as these developments began to extend protection to some wives, other cases illustrated "the contortions to which judges have found it necessary to resort in the face of the fiction of implied consent to sexual intercourse".[86] For example, in *Caswell*[87] the court held that pulling one's wife's head down on to one's penis was an assault if done against her will, but that forcing her to commit fellatio was no offence at all since husbands could not be guilty of indecent assault.

This erosion or circumvention of the rule became a full scale attack in the House of Lords decision of *R*.[88] Lord Keith of Kinkel held that whatever status Hale's proposition might have had, the common law had to evolve in the light of changing social, economic and cultural developments. He stated that the notion that "by marriage a wife gives her irrevocable consent to her husband under all circumstances and irrespective of her health and how she happens to be feeling at the time ... [is] in modern times ... quite unacceptable".[89] He believed that "it is clearly unlawful to have sexual intercourse with any woman without her consent,

---

[82] By the Criminal Justice and Public Order Act 1994, s.142.

[83] History of the Pleas of the Crown (1736) Vol. 1 at p. 629.

[84] He could also be guilty of rape as an aider and abetter: see, *e.g. Cogan and Leek* [1976] Q.B. 217, *above*, p. 553.

[85] *Clarke* (1949) 33 Cr.App. R.216; *Miller* [1954] 38 Cr.App. R.1; *O'Brien (Edward)* [1974] 3 All E.R. 663; *Steele* (1977) 66 Cr.App. R; *Roberts* [1986] Crim.L.R.188. But see *Sharples* [1990] Crim.L.R.198.

[86] *Per* Lord Keith in *R*. [1992] 1 A.C. 598 at 620.

[87] [1984] Crim.L.R.111.

[88] [1992] 1 A.C. 598.

[89] At 616.

and that the use of the word [unlawful] adds nothing ... [T]here are no rational grounds for putting the suggested gloss on the word, and it should be treated as mere surplusage in this enactment."[90]

Although most commentators have warmly welcomed this result[91] there were doubts as to whether the House of Lords was entitled to act in the way it did. It has been described it as "blatant" judicial law-making[92] and the decision was open to allegations of retrospectivity. The matter is now beyond doubt. First, the European Court of Human Rights decided that the decision had not contravened Article 7 of the European Convention on Human Rights.[93] Secondly, the reform in 1994 has placed the ruling in *R.* upon a solid statutory footing.

### (ii) Male rape

Although it has become increasingly common to talk about the phenomenon of male rape, the law traditionally dealt with non-consensual anal intercourse as buggery. However, the changes made in 1994 providing that intercourse may be anal or vaginal and that the victim may be male or female, mean that this is now rape.[94] The law has thus moved towards gender-neutrality (although the move is not complete since legally only males are capable of committing the offence). This reform was controversial. It has been argued that it ignores the reality of rape: "It is still men who are raping and women who are being raped."[95] It has also been claimed that gender-specific laws "raise unique and important issues of male and female power. It invokes the differences in male and female ways of understanding force and consent and each other."[96] However, these views are not shared by all commentators.

### Philip Rumney and Martin Morgan-Taylor, "Recognizing the Male Victim: Gender Neutrality and the Law of Rape" (1997) 26 Anglo-American Law Review 198 at 219–234:

"[T]he acts of vaginal and anal penetration are too similar to warrant separate legal classification ... The motives of the assailant ... would appear to be similar for the penetrative acts in question, irrespective of the sex of the victim ... Indeed, it is argued ... that male rape is an act of violence, committed to assert power, rather than being primarily sexually motivated. ... [T]he trauma and consequences of rape are similar for both men and women. In addition to any physical injury, victims may suffer serious psychological trauma as a consequence of rape. Both male and female victims appear to suffer similar psychological reactions after rape ...

---

[90] At 622–623.

[91] The most notable exception being Williams in "Rape is Rape" (1992) 140 N.L.J. 11 where he identifies what he describes as four "powerful" reasons why rape by husbands (and cohabitees) should be distinguished from that by strangers.

[92] Giles, "Judicial Law-Making in the Criminal Court" [1992] Crim.L.R.407 at 408.

[93] It ruled that Article 7 which prohibits retrospectivity did not prevent judicial clarification and development of case-law provided that the development could reasonably have been foreseen: *C.R. v The United Kingdom; S.U. v The United Kingdom* [1996] 1 F.L.R. 434.

[94] Buggery is now confined to consensual anal intercourse with a person under the age of 18: Sexual Offences Act 1956, s.12 as amended by the Criminal Justice and Public Order Act 1994, s.143.

[95] Nafine, "Possession: Erotic Love in the Law of Rape" [1994] 57 M.L.R. 10 at 24. On this, see further, Schulhofer, *Unwanted Sex: The Culture of Intimidation and the Failure of the Law* (1998), pp. 47–68.

[96] Estrich, "Rape" [1986] 95 Yale L.J. 1086 at 1149.

It is therefore argued that the consequences of either vaginal or anal rape are not sufficiently dispersive to justify an exclusionary gender specific approach to rape, and that, on the evidence, the new law is wholly justifiable."

The latest reform proposals to sexual offences[97] continue the trend towards gender-neutral offences but draw back from completing the process in that rape will continue to be defined so as to be committed by men only.[98] These proposals are discussed in the following sections.

## 2. Actus reus

### (i) Sexual intercourse

This may be either vaginal or anal. It is clear that full sexual intercourse need not take place for rape to occur; the slightest degree of penetration of the vagina or the anus with the penis suffices.[99] Thus, the rubbing of the entrance to the vagina with the penis causing ejaculation is not rape, nor is oral sex (fellatio). Similarly, penetration of the vagina or anus with inanimate objects is not rape. In such circumstances indecent assault is frequently charged.[1] However, this offence (which is widely regarded as anachronistic) carries a maximum of 10 years' imprisonment only and may inadequately reflect the gravity of what has taken place. Two decades ago, the Criminal Law Revision Committee recommended that the definition of rape should not be extended to cover any of these acts. In their view, "the concept of rape, as a distinct form of criminal misconduct, is well established in popular thought and corresponds to a distinctive form of wrongdoing".[2] The most recent reform proposals, however, propose widening the definition of rape so as to include penetration of the mouth by the penis because this is perceived to be as "horrible, as demeaning and as traumatising as other forms of penile penetration".[3] The gravity of penetration of the body by inanimate objects is recognised, not by defining it as rape, but by the creation of a new offence of sexual assault by penetration, punishable by a maximum of life imprisonment.[4] To this extent, rape continues to be a gender-specific offence whilst sexual assault is not.

### (ii) Lack of consent

It is the element of lack of consent that transforms sexual intercourse into rape. Indeed, as the majority of victims know their assailant, the issue of consent is, in

[97] *Protecting the Public: Strengthening Protection Against Sex Offenders and Reforming the Law on Sexual Offences*, Cm.5668, (2002).
[98] For a critique of this recommendation, see Rumney, "The Review of Sex Offences and Rape Law Reform: Another False Dawn?" [2001] 64 M.L.R. 890 at 894–898.
[99] *People (Att-Gen) v Dermody* [1956] I.R. 32; Sexual Offences (Amendment) Act 1976, s.7(2).
[1] Sections 14 and 15 of the Sexual Offences Act 1956. An indecent assault is an assault in circumstances of indecency; see *Court* [1989] A.C. 28. The offence of gross indecency with another man (s.13) may also be used.
[2] 15th Report, *Sexual Offences* (1984), para. 45. Rumney, *above*, n.98 at 896 challenges the assumption that the public have a clear view about the crime of rape, for which, as he states, no evidence is provided.
[3] Home Office, *Setting the Boundaries: Reforming the Law on Sexual Offences* (2000), para. 2.8.4; see also *Protecting the Public*, (Cm.5668, 2002), para. 40, and Sexual Offences Bill 2003, s.1(1).
[4] *Protecting the Public*, para. 44. There would be a separate, lesser offence of sexual assault to cover non-penetrative behaviour (para. 45). See Sexual Offences Bill 2003, clauses 3 and 5.

many rape trials, the pivotal issue. What needs to be established? The answer in theory is clear; lack of consent is required and not positive dissent.[5] Thus, if a woman is so drunk that she is unable to communicate her unwillingness to have sexual intercourse she is to be regarded as not having consented.[6] However, in reality, there are profound evidential and conceptual difficulties with this rule.

1. English law no longer defines rape as sexual intercourse by force. It thus absolves the victim from having to make a show of resistance. However, it is clear that in the absence of marks or injuries the victim may find it very hard for her story to be believed.[7] Evidentially, there is real pressure on the rape victim to struggle and further endanger herself. Moreover, although changes to legislation mean judges are no longer obliged to warn the jury of the dangers of accepting the victim's uncorroborated story, they have discretion still to do so.[8] The myth of the lying, vengeful woman or frightened, pregnant girl is what really underpinned the corroboration warning and it is to the credit of the Court of Appeal that it has shown "its unequivocal support for the policy and purpose of the legislation".[9]

One further related question bears examination at this point. The prosecution in seeking to show that the victim did, in fact, consent to sexual intercourse may wish to adduce evidence of prior relationships with the defendant or with other men. This question assumes great importance in cases where the victim claims to have been a virgin. May evidence of this type be introduced at the trial?

### Zsuzsanna Adler, "Rape—the Intention of Parliament and the Practice of the Courts" (1982) 45 M.L.R. 664 at 666–667:

"Before 1976, the defence in a rape trial were free to cross-examine about any prior sexual behaviour, whether with the defendant or anyone else. Her experience with a third party was thought to be relevant to her credibility: the law of evidence seemed to reflect an assumption that women involved in rape cases were likely to be untruthful as a direct result of their sexual 'immorality' ... [It] gave the defence a virtually unconstrained licence to sling sexual mud ...

The Advisory Group on the Law of Rape ... expressed particular anxiety about the humiliation and distress suffered by complainants during cross-examination and argued that the procedure was in need of urgent reform. 'We have reached the conclusion that the previous sexual history of the alleged victim with third parties is of no significance so far as credibility is concerned, and is only rarely likely to be relevant to the issues directly before the jury.' (Report of the Advisory Council on the Law of Rape, 1975, para. 131.)"

As a result of such reasoning, section 2 of the Sexual Offences (Amendment) Act 1976 gave the trial judge complete discretion as to whether general or specific past history and reputation of the victim might be introduced.[10] However, studies of the

---

[5] *Lang* (1975) 62 Cr.App. R.50; *Olugboja* (1981) 73 Cr.App. R.344.

[6] *Malone* [1998] 2 Cr.App. R.454.

[7] There are higher conviction rates for those rapes where violence has been used (Harris and Grace, *above*, n.50).

[8] Criminal Justice and Public Order Act 1994, s.32 .

[9] Temkin, *Rape and the Legal Process* (2nd ed., 2002), p. 263.

[10] In Adler's study, the defence applied for leave in 40 per cent of cases and were successful (in part or wholly) in some 75 per cent of applications. Adler believes that any scheme based on judicial discretion controlling sexual history evidence is doomed to fail, because judges will have to fall back on their own beliefs and attitudes (*Rape on Trial* (1987), p. 154).

case law on this point concluded that the Court of Appeal was far too ready to allow evidence to be admitted[11] and the report *Speaking up for Justice* concluded that there was "overwhelming evidence that the ... practice in the courts [was] unsatisfactory and that the existing law [was] not achieving its purpose".[12] As a consequence, a new, much tighter, scheme governing sexual history evidence has been introduced[13] although this too has attracted criticism, with some commentators arguing that only a complete ban will solve the problem.[14] Moreover, the new scheme has already run into difficulties in the courts and a declaration of incompatability with Article 6 (the right to a fair trial) was only avoided by the House of Lords placing the most strained construction on the section.[15] As a result there have already been calls for its reform.[16]

2. The statute may define rape as intercourse without consent, but this is not an unproblematic concept. What is consent and what do we mean when we say that someone has consented to sex? There have been numerous attempts to answer these questions, both philosophically and legally.[17] A starting point might be a focus on the notion of free choice: consent involves a voluntary decision taken by someone who has control over what follows. This is not uncontroversial. Some feminists, such as MacKinnon, have argued that any attempt to distinguish rape from sexual intercourse on the basis of choice and thus consent is naïve. In a society in which women are socialised to passive receptivity, where sex is something men do to women, there is no clear distinction that can be drawn.[18]

### S. Schulhofer, Unwanted Sex: The Culture of Intimidation and the Failure of the Law (1998), pp. 56–57:

"MacKinnon's far-reaching claims about cultural pressure have opened many eyes to the multiple constraints on women's freedom to make independent sexual choices. At the same time, by collapsing the distinctions *between* kinds of sexual pressure, feminism of this sort doesn't advance the effort to draw workable legal lines. Sometimes this strand of feminism

---

[11] Temkin, "Sexual History Evidence—the Ravishment of Section 2" [1993] Crim.L.R.3. See also, McColgan, "Common Law and the Relevance of Sexual History Evidence" [1996] 15 O.J.L.S. 275, and Durston, "Cross-examination of Rape Complainants: Ongoing Tensions between Conflicting Priorities of the Criminal Justice System" (1998) 62 J.Crim.L. 91.

[12] Home Office, *Speaking Up for Justice: Report of the Interdepartmental Working Group on the Treatment of Vulnerable and Intimidated Witnesses in the Criminal Justice System* (1998), para. 9.64.

[13] Youth Justice and Criminal Evidence Act 1999, ss.41–43.

[14] Others have, conversely, commented that the provisions are so tightly drawn so as to prevent the court hearing evidence which is relevant. See further, Birch, "A Fairer Deal for Vulnerable Witnesses" [2000] Crim L.R.223; Kibble, "The Sexual History Provisions: Charting a Course Between Inflexible Legislative Rules and Wholly Untrammelled Judicial Discretion?" [2000] Crim.L.R.274.

[15] *R. v A (No. 2)* [2001] 2 W.L.R. 1546. See Spencer, "'Rape Shields' and the Right to a Fair Trial" (2001) 60 C.L.J. 26. See also, *R. v T* [2002] 1 All E.R. 683.

[16] McEwan, "The Rape Shield Askew? *R. v A*" [2001] 5 International J. of Evidence and Proof 267.

[17] See, for example, Alexander, "The Moral Magic of Consent" (1996) 2 *Legal Theory* 165; McGregor, "Why When She Says No She Doesn't Mean Maybe and Doesn't Mean Yes" (1996) 2 *Legal Theory* 175; Estrich, *Real Rape* (1987); Dripps, "Beyond Rape: An Essay on the Difference Between the Presence of Force and the Absence of Consent" (1992) 92 Colum.L.R. 1780; Temkin, *Rape and the Legal Process* (2nd ed. 2002); MacKinnon, *Towards a Feminist Theory of the State* (1989); Lees, *Ruling Passions: Sexual Violence, Reputation and the Law* (1997); Gardner and Shute, "The Wrongness of Rape" in Horder (ed.), *Oxford Essays in Jurisprudence* (2000).

[18] MacKinnon, *Towards a Feminist Theory of the State* (1989).

even seems to impede the legal reform effort, because it tends to obliterate differences between the kinds of pressure that society will inevitably tolerate and the kinds that it might plausibly forbid ... The refusal of some leading theorists to draw moral distinctions among the many forms of pressure women face maintains a certain purism for these feminist projects, but it vastly oversimplifies the give-and-take of social power in a complex, imperfect, but not uniformly oppressive society."

It is obvious that not all sexual choices are completely freely made and yet consent may well have been given. An individual's choice may be constrained for all sorts of reasons: it may be a desire to avoid the row that will follow if sex is not forthcoming; a need for cash; a need to keep one's job; a fear of being beaten or killed. If a person says "yes" in any of these scenarios—or if she permits intercourse after persuading the assailant to wear a condom[19]—is this consent real? The difficult task for the law has been to determine which such constraints operate to nullify consent and which do not. As long as rape is viewed predominantly as a crime of violence the answer is relatively unproblematic. Traditionally, therefore, only threats of death or serious harm vitiate an apparent consent. However, the more rape is perceived as an offence against sexual autonomy, the more the wrong is perceived to be the objectification of a person, the more open-ended become the types of constraints which may nullify consent.[20]

In *Olugboja*[21] the victim had intercourse with the defendant after his companion had raped her and her friend. The defendant claimed that these circumstances did not nullify her consent since only a threat of death or serious harm would suffice. The Court of Appeal held that, using the "ordinary meaning" of the word, the victim could not be said to have consented to sexual intercourse. The court held that there is a difference between the state of mind of real consent and that of mere submission. The difference between the two is a matter of degree and it is for the jury to decide which side of the line a particular sequence of events falls. For example, a jury would almost inevitably decide that a wife who "reluctantly acquiesces" to intercourse to avoid a sulking husband has, nevertheless, consented.

### Simon Gardner, "Appreciating Olugboja" [1996] 16 Legal Studies 275 at 278–280:

"On the one hand, then, the reasoning in *Olugboja* appeals to the ordinary meaning of consent, in order to see off the argument that consent has a special legal meaning whereby ... only certain forms of pressure qualify to negate it. On the other hand, that reasoning asserts that consent in its ordinary meaning is a state of mind, and that a person can be said to possess that state of mind notwithstanding that she feels pressured, so long as her feelings are on the right side of the point at which consent turns into submission.

There is some difficulty about this. We have only the court's word for it that the ordinary meaning does follow those lines. The ordinary meaning may just as well follow the approach of the legal rule contended for by the defendant. ... It appears, then, that we should read the court's invocation of the ordinary meaning of consent as a rhetorical device ... the court appears in reality to be making law. Once one has come to terms with the disingenuity

---

[19] In 1992, in Texas, a grand jury refused to indict a man who had broken into a house at night, held a knife to a woman's throat and then had intercourse with her on the ground that, because she had begged him to put on a condom, she had consented: *The Washington Post*, October 31, 1992.

[20] See Gardner, "Appreciating Olugboja" [1996] 16 *Legal Studies* 275 at 277–282.

[21] [1982] Q.B. 320.

involved, there is little to cavil at this. . . . [T]he handling of consent in *Olugboja* displays a particularly acute form of the prevailing modern perception, that the offence of rape should protect sexual autonomy, as distinct from other kinds of interest such as freedom from aggression."

The jury is entrusted with the task of rejecting those constraints on, or invasions of, autonomy that are insufficiently serious to transform the incident into rape. Some may be thought to be so trivial that they fall outside the regulation of the law altogether; others may be more appropriately dealt with by the offence of procuring sexual intercourse by threats.[22] There are difficulties with *Olugboja*. To talk in terms of "reluctant acquiescence" may be confusing, rather than illuminating, since could it not also be said that the victim with a knife to her throat reluctantly acquiesces? The distinction between mere submission and real consent may not be able to bear close scrutiny[23] but, nevertheless, the flexibility of this approach has its strengths. One intuitively senses the distinction the court strives to make.

However, the approach taken in *Olugboja* has been rejected by law reform proposals because it had "led to confusion and [risked] very different conclusions being drawn on similar facts in different cases".[24] Instead, in order to be clear and unambiguous,[25] it has been recommended that consent should be defined as free agreement and a non-exhaustive list of circumstances, in which consent is presumed to be absent, drawn up.[26]

## Sexual Offences Bill 2003, clauses 77 and 78:

### "77 'Consent'
For the purposes of this Part, a person consents if he agrees by choice, and has the freedom and capacity to make that choice.

### 78 Presumptions about the absence of consent
    (1) If in proceedings for an offence to which this section applies it is proved that the defendant did the relevant act, that any of the circumstances specified in subsection 3 existed, and that the defendant knew that those circumstances existed—
        (a) the complainant is to be taken not to have consented to the relevant act unless sufficient evidence is adduced to raise an issue as to whether the complainant consented; and
        (b) the defendant is to be taken not to have believed that the complainant consented unless the defendant proves that he did believe it . . .
    (3) The circumstances referred to in subsection (1) are that—
        (a) any person was, at the time of the relevant act or immediately before it began, using violence against the complainant or causing the complainant to fear that immediate violence would be used against him;

---

[22] Sexual Offences Act 1956, s.2. However, as Temkin notes (*above*, n.40, p. 101) in practice this offence is very rarely prosecuted.

[23] In *McAllister* [1997] Crim.L.R.233 the jury asked for a definition of the difference between the two. Edwards argues that *Olugboja* has been marginalised and that in cases of similar psychological duress and entrapment, in the absence of threats, and where the parties were acquainted, the CPS would be most unlikely to prosecute: *Sex and Gender in the Legal Process* (1996), p. 340.

[24] *Setting the Boundaries* (2000), para. 2.2.3.

[25] *Protecting the Public* (Cm.5668, 2002), para. 30.

[26] Law Commission, *Consent in Sexual Offences* (2000); *Setting the Boundaries* (2000); *Protecting the Public*, (Cm.5668, 2002).

(b) any person was, at the time of the relevant act or immediately before it began, causing the victim to fear that violence was being used, or that immediate violence would be used, against another person;

(c) the complainant was, and the defendant was not, unlawfully detained at the time of the relevant act;

(d) the complainant was asleep or otherwise unconscious at the time of the relevant act;

(e) because of the complainant's physical disability, the complainant would not have been able at the time of the relevant act to communicate to the defendant whether the complainant consented."[27]

While the circumstances in which consent will be considered to be absent are not restricted to either the use or threat of violence, the list omits an original proposal that consent should also be considered to be absent where a person has submitted because of threats or fear of serious detriment of any type.[28] Clause 78 is proving to be highly controversial with judges, in particular, and may not survive in its current form.[29]

3. Just as consent induced by fear of violence is not regarded as real consent, neither is consent which is given under certain fundamental mistakes, brought about by the deceit of the defendant, regarded as real. In *Clarence*[30] Stephen J. identified two such kinds of fundamental mistake, the first as to the identity of the actor and the second as to the nature of the act. As far as the first kind of mistake is concerned, the (amended) Sexual Offences Act 1956, s.1(3) states that a man also commits rape "if he induces a married woman to have sexual intercourse with him by impersonating her husband". The limitations of such a provision are all too obvious. What of the man who impersonates the victim's boyfriend? In *Elbekkay*[31] the sleepy and drunk victim had intercourse with a man who got into her bed, thinking that it was her boyfriend. The moment she discovered her mistake, she reacted violently, punching the defendant and cutting him with a knife. The Court of Appeal, in confirming that this was rape stated: "How could we conscientiously hold that it is rape to impersonate a husband in the act of sexual intercourse, but not if the person impersonated is merely, say, the long-term, live-in lover ... The vital point about rape is that it involves the absence of consent. That absence is equally crucial whether the woman believes that the man she is having sexual intercourse with is her husband or another." The court thus adopted the approach to consent taken in *Olugboja* and also echoed the words of Lord Keith of Kinkel in *R.* that the common law was capable of evolving as times changed. However much one might agree with the removal of the anomaly, the fact that the statutory reform

---

[27] In addition, children under 13 are deemed incapable of giving consent to any form of sexual activity. Thus, clause 2 of the Bill states that it is rape for a person to intentionally penetrate the vagina, anus or mouth of another person and the other person is under 13. The issue of consent simply does not arise.

[28] As recommended by *Setting the Boundaries*, para. 2.10.9 and *Protecting the Public*, para. 31. While the list does not purport to be exhaustive, since section 2 of the 1956 Act is due to be repealed by the Sexual Offences Bill it appears that protection will actually be lessened in circumstances where intercourse is obtained by threats as to employment etc. The Rape Federation Crisis has urged the Government to rethink this.

[29] Amendments have been tabled to omit virtually all of clause 78 (except clause 78(4)) from the Bill.

[30] (1888) 22 Q.B.D. 23.

[31] [1995] Crim.L.R.163.

of 1994 so recently re-enacted section 1(3) without extension to other impersonations means that there are problems with the status of the decision of *Elbekkay*.[32]

The second type of fundamental mistake induced by fraud goes to the very nature of the act. In *Flattery*[33] the defendant induced a woman to submit to intercourse by maintaining the deception that he was performing a surgical operation. He was convicted of rape. This was followed in the not dissimilar case of *Williams*[34] where the defendant, who was a singing-master, had intercourse with one of his pupils aged 16. She made no resistance as she believed his claim that he was merely improving her breathing. He too was convicted. The principle upon which both cases were decided was made clear by the trial judge in *Williams* and approved by Lord Hewart C.J. on appeal:

"The law has laid it down that where a girl's consent is procured by the means which the girl says the prisoner adopted, that is to say, where she is persuaded that what is being done to her is not the ordinary act of sexual intercourse but is some medical or surgical operation in order to give her relief from some disability from which she is suffering, then it is rape although the actual thing that was done was done with her consent, because she never consented to the act of sexual intercourse. She was persuaded to consent to what he did because she thought it was not sexual intercourse and because she thought it was a surgical operation."[35]

The courts have generally declined to extend the ambit of the law of rape to cases other than those involving these two types of fundamental mistake.

### Linekar [1995] Q.B. 250 (Court of Appeal, Criminal Division)

The complainant worked occasionally as a prostitute. One night she was approached by the defendant and had sexual intercourse with him for the agreed fee of £25. The defendant then made off without paying. The defendant was later convicted of rape. On appeal:

Morland J.:

"Moving to more recent times, there is the highly persuasive authority of *Papadimitropoulos v The Queen* (1957) 98 C.L.R. 249, a decision of the High Court of Australia. . . . The facts of that case were that the complainant believed that she had gone through a marriage with the appellant. In the judgment of the court, the court said: . . .

'To say that in the present case the facts which the jury must be taken to have found amount to wicked and heartless conduct on the part of the applicant is not enough to establish that he committed rape. To say that in having intercourse with him she supposed that she was concerned in a perfectly moral act is not to say that the intercourse was without her consent. To return to the central point; rape is carnal knowledge of a woman without her consent: carnal knowledge is the physical fact of penetration; it is consent to that which is in question; such a consent demands a

---

[32] Smith and Hogan, *Criminal Law* (10th ed., 2002), p. 468 argue that the courts are likely to treat the re-enactment of this sub-section as the governmental and parliamentary blunder that it is and carry on as if it does not exist.

[33] (1877) 2 Q.B.D. 410.

[34] [1923] 1 K.B. 340.

[35] *ibid.* at 347.

perception as to what is about to take place, as to the identity of the man and the character of what he is doing. But once the consent is comprehending and actual the inducing causes cannot destroy its reality and leave the man guilty of rape.'

Respectfully applying those dicta to the facts of the present case, the prostitute here consented to sexual intercourse with the appellant. The reality of that consent is not destroyed by being induced by the appellant's false pretence that his intention was to pay the agreed price of £25 for her services. Therefore, he was not guilty of rape."

**Appeal allowed**

Whilst the defendant might have committed an offence under section 3 of the Sexual Offences Act 1956 of procuring a woman by false pretences or false representations to have sexual intercourse, he did not commit rape.[36] However, this approach, followed for many years by the courts, has been shaken by the decision of *Tabussum*.[37] In this case, concerning indecent assault but raising the issue of consent, the court took the view that the victims, who had consented to breast examinations for what they thought was a medical research, would never have done so had they known that the defendant was not medically qualified. It was held that they had consented to the nature of the act but not to its quality—and that accordingly there was no real consent. This new distinction has been criticised as "highly suspect" and increasing the need for statutory reform.[38]

The Sexual Offences Bill 2003 states that a person will be conclusively presumed not to consent to sexual activity where they have been intentionally deceived as to the nature or purpose of the act or the defendant intentionally induced the complainant to consent by impersonating a person known personally to the complainant.[39] An example given in the explanatory notes to the Bill is where the defendant intentionally tells the victim that digital penetration of her vagina is necessary for medical reasons when in fact it is for his sexual gratification.

Does a defendant in such cases deserve to be labelled a rapist? When a victim (married or not) has knowingly consented to the defendant's penetration will she suffer the same degree of emotional and psychological trauma as in other rape cases? Should the crime, and label, "rape" be reserved for those cases where there is non-consensual penetration?[40]

### 3. Mens rea

The *mens rea* of the crime of rape is defined by section 1(2)(b) of the Sexual Offences Act 1956.[41] In addition to intending to have sexual intercourse the defendant must *know* that the person is not consenting, or be *reckless* as to whether he or she is consenting. This is a statutory endorsement of the law as laid down by

---

[36] See further, Reed, "An Analysis of Fraud Vitiating Consent in Rape Cases" (1995) 59 J.Crim.L. 310.
[37] [2000] Crim.L.R.686.
[38] Commentary to *Tabussum* at 688.
[39] Clause 78 (7) and (8).
[40] In *Kaitamaki* (1985) 79 Cr.App. R.251 the Privy Council held that a man could be guilty of rape, despite having penetrated the woman with her consent, if he continued sexual intercourse after a stage when he realised that she was no longer consenting. Sexual intercourse was held to be a continuing act which only ended with withdrawal of the penis. See also *Cooper and Schaub* [1994] Crim.L.R. 531. Clearly a woman must have a right to terminate sexual intercourse—but should the man who fails to desist be guilty of rape? Might not a lesser level of criminal liability be more appropriate in such cases?
[41] As amended by the Sexual Offences (Amendment) Act 1976, s.6(A).

the House of Lords in *Morgan*.[42] Prior to *Morgan* a defendant's belief that the woman was consenting had to be based on reasonable grounds. The House of Lords dispensed with this requirement; if the defendant honestly believed the woman was consenting, he lacked *mens rea*.[43]

The House of Lords did, however, emphasise that the reasonableness of the defendant's belief would be taken into account by the jury when deciding whether he could possibly have entertained such a belief. This evidential proposition was enshrined in the Sexual Offences (Amendment) Act 1976, s.1(2):

> "It is hereby declared that, if at a trial for a rape offence the jury has to consider whether a man believed that a woman was consenting to sexual intercourse, the presence or absence of reasonable grounds for such a belief is a matter to which the jury is to have regard, in conjunction with any other relevant matters, in considering whether he so believed."

It is important to remember that *Morgan* was decided, and the Sexual Offences (Amendment) Act 1976 enacted, at a time when recklessness bore only its "subjective" meaning: the defendant had actually to be aware that there was a risk the woman was not consenting. Subsequently, the House of Lords in *Caldwell* and *Lawrence* redefined the concept of recklessness so as to encompass a failure to consider an obvious risk and initially it seemed as if this interpretation would be applied to the *mens rea* of rape.[44] However, mirroring developments elsewhere in the criminal law, the *Caldwell/Lawrence* definition of recklessness has since been rejected.

### R. v Satnam and Kewal (1984) 78 Cr.App.R.149 (Court of Appeal, Criminal Division)

The appellants were convicted of raping a young girl. They appealed on the ground that there had been a misdirection as to the meaning of recklessness for the purposes of rape.

Bristow J.:

"The question of law is whether, in directing the jury as to the state of mind of the appellants in 'reckless' rape, the judge should have left to the jury the question whether they genuinely though mistakenly believed that the victim was consenting to sexual intercourse; and whether the judge was right to direct them that it was sufficient, in order to prove recklessness, if it was obvious to an ordinary observer that she was not consenting. . . .

Any direction as to the definition of rape should therefore be based upon section 1 of the 1976 Act and upon *R. v Morgan*, without regard to *R. v Caldwell* or *R. v Lawrence* which were concerned with recklessness in a different context and under a different statute.

The word 'reckless' in relation to rape involves a different concept to its use in relation to malicious damage or, indeed, in relation to offences against the person. In the latter cases the foreseeability, or possible foreseeability, is as to the consequences of the criminal act. In the case of rape the foreseeability is as to the state of mind of the victim.

---

[42] [1976] A.C. 182. This case is discussed, *above*, pp. 191–193.
[43] In *Taylor* (1985) 80 Cr.App. R.327, *Haughian* (1985) 80 Cr.App. R.334 and *Adkins* [2000] 2 All E.R. 185 the courts held that it was unnecessary to give detailed guidance on mistaken belief in all cases. Where the conflict of evidence is acute, once the jury decides that the victim's account is truthful, there is no room for such a belief on the part of the defendant.
[44] See *Pigg* [1982] 1 W.L.R. 762.

A practical definition of recklessness in sexual offences was given in *R. v Kimber* [1983] 1 W.L.R. 1118, where [Lawton L.J. said] ... '... his attitude to her was one of indifference to her feelings and wishes. This state of mind is aptly described in the colloquial expression, "couldn't care less." In law this is recklessness.'

In summing-up a case of rape, which involves the issue of consent, the judge should, in dealing with the state of mind of the defendant, first of all direct the jury that before they could convict of rape the Crown had to prove either that the defendant knew the woman did not want to have sexual intercourse, or was reckless as to whether she wanted to or not. If they were sure he knew she did not want to they should find him guilty of rape knowing there to be no consent. If they were not sure about that, then they would find him not guilty of such rape and should go on to consider reckless rape. If they thought he might genuinely have believed that she did want to, even though he was mistaken in his belief, they would find him not guilty. In considering whether his belief was genuine, they should take into account all the relevant circumstances (which could at that point be summarised) and ask themselves whether, in the light of those circumstances, he had reasonable grounds for such a belief. If, after considering those circumstances, they were sure he had no genuine belief that she wanted to, they would find him guilty. If they came to the conclusion that he could not care less whether she wanted to or not, but pressed on regardless, then he would have been reckless and could not have believed that she wanted to, and they would find him guilty of reckless rape."

**Appeals allowed**

While expressly rejecting the *Caldwell/Lawrence* test of recklessness, holding that a "couldn't care attitude" can amount to recklessness is coming close to an objective test because a person could have such an attitude because he failed to consider obvious risks (*Caldwell* recklessness). However, it is clear that section 1(2) of the Sexual Offences Amendment Act 1976 does endorse a subjective test. How does this fit with a "couldn't care less attitude" satisfying the test of reckless rape?

### R. v Adkins [2000] 2 All E.R.185 (Court of Appeal, Criminal Division)

Roch L.J.:

"[Counsel] is wrong in his primary submission that whenever the issue of consent arises there must be a direction as to honest belief. Such a direction need only be given when the evidence in the case is such that there is room for the possibility of a genuine mistaken belief that the victim was consenting ... [T]he jury should not be subjected to unnecessary and irrelevant directions. Similarly, it is only when the issue of honesty arises on the evidence that the requirements of s 1(2) of the 1976 Act apply. We also reject the alternative submissions. The question of honest belief does not necessarily arise where reckless rape is in issue. The defendant may have failed to address his mind to the question whether or not there was consent, or be indifferent to whether there was consent or not, in circumstances where, had he addressed his mind to the question, he could not genuinely have believed that there was consent."

A test that recklessness can be satisfied by a failure to consider the risk or indifference as to the risk of the complainant not consenting bears the hallmarks of *Caldwell* recklessness. Under *Caldwell*, if a person genuinely believes there is no risk because he has ruled it out, he will fall into the lacuna and not be reckless. Section 1(2) is similar in effect. If the defendant genuinely believes that there is consent, he will escape liability. The reasonableness or otherwise of this belief is only of evidential importance.

Section 1(2) is drafted in terms of "belief": "whether a man believed that a woman was consenting". It is possible to argue that this provision only applies to the *knowledge* species of *mens rea* in section 1(1)(b) on the basis that "know" is generally interpreted in criminal law to mean "believe" and so the provision should not apply to the recklessness limb of the provision. However, the better view, supported by the above decision, is that the definition of "belief" in section 1(2) applies to both knowledge and recklessness in section 1(1)(b).

This broader interpretation raises the deeper issue of the exact basis upon which criminal liability ought to be based. *Should* the law require that any belief as to the victim's consent be based on reasonable grounds?

## J. C. Smith, Commentary on D.P.P. v Morgan [1975] Crim.L.R.717 at 719:

"As Lord Hailsham said, [in *Morgan*] the question for the House was one of great academic importance in English law. The question of principle received a very satisfactory answer. The case may be taken to establish that, once it is settled that the definition of a crime requires intention or recklessness with respect to particular elements of an offence, a mistake of fact whether reasonable or not, which is inconsistent with that intention or recklessness is also incompatible with the guilt of the accused and must lead to his acquittal. In the present case the trial judge had stressed to the jury that the *mens rea* of rape was an intention not merely to have intercourse with a woman, but an intention to have intercourse with a woman *without her consent*. Yet he went on to tell the jury that they could convict if the accused believed, without reasonable grounds, that the woman was consenting. This, as Lord Cross pointed out, was to present the jury with two incompatible alternatives. Lord Hailsham said, 'Once one has accepted, what seems to me abundantly clear, that the prohibited act in rape is non-consensual sexual intercourse, and that the guilty state of mind is an intention to commit it, it seems to me to follow as a matter of inexorable logic that there is no room either for a "defence" of honest belief or mistake, or of a defence of honest and reasonable mistake. Either the prosecution proves its case or it does not.' ...

The first question, in every case, is, of course, what *mens rea* does the definition of the crime in question require? The present case decides that in rape the *mens rea* is an intention to have intercourse with a woman without her consent or an intention to have intercourse with a woman being indifferent (reckless) whether she consents or not. ... The present case decides nothing about the *mens rea* of any other crime. It does decide, it is submitted, that, as a matter of general principle, once it is settled that the crime in question requires an element of intention or recklessness any mistake, whether reasonable or not, which is inconsistent with that intention or recklessness requires an acquittal. This conclusion appears, perhaps, to be so obvious that it is absurd to make a fuss about it. It is, as Lord Hailsham says, a 'matter of inexorable logic.'"

## Criminal Law Revision Committee, 15th Report, Sexual Offences, Cmnd.9213 (1984):

"2.37 ... Sexual intercourse on the part of a man is in general a deliberate course of conduct (although drugs or drink may affect his awareness of his actions). As the Policy Advisory Committee said ... sexual intercourse is 'an act which can be a fundamental means of expressing love for another; and to which as a society we attach considerable value.' Sexual intercourse is an intimate act between man and woman, and a man is expected to have regard to the question whether the woman is consenting to the act or not.

2.38 Where the man knows that the woman is not consenting he should clearly be guilty of rape. The mental element in rape must, however, go wider than that. It should also be rape if he is aware of a possibility, however slight, that she may not be consenting but he persists regardless. ...

2.40 If however, the defendant was mistaken in his belief that the woman was consenting, he should not be liable to conviction for rape, even if he had no reasonable grounds for his belief. None of us would wish to extend the offence of rape to such a case. This would in effect turn rape into a crime of negligence, an approach which was rejected by the majority of their Lordships in *Morgan*, a decision endorsed by Parliament in 1976. ...
    2.41 We recommend, therefore, that the mental element in rape should cover:
    (a) the man who knew that the woman was not consenting, and
    (b) the man who either was aware that she might not be consenting or did not believe that she was consenting."

### T. Pickard, "Culpable Mistakes and Rape: Relating Mens Rea to the Crime" (1980) 30 University of Toronto Law J. 75 at 77, 83:

"There can be no doubt that it is a major harm for a woman to be subjected to non-consensual intercourse notwithstanding that the man may believe he has her consent. There can be little doubt that the cost of taking reasonable care is insignificant compared with the harm which can be avoided through its exercise: indeed, the only cost I can identify is the general one of creating some pressure towards greater explicitness in sexual contexts. To accept an honest but unreasonable belief in consent as a sufficient answer in these circumstances is to countenance the doing of a major harm that could have been avoided at no appreciable cost. Therefore, in terms of simple balancing of interest, it is sound policy to require reasonable care, given the capabilities of the actor. It is true, of course, that not all sound policies can be appropriately pursued through the use of criminal law. But considering the disparate weights of the interests involved, a failure to inquire carefully into consent constitutes, in my view, such a lack of minimal concern for the bodily integrity of others that it is good criminal policy to ground liability on it. ... I accept that in many instances, particularly where inadvertence is involved, mistaken wrongdoing may not be bad enough to deserve criminal sanction. But a major part of my effort is to show that there are different kinds of mistakes. In rape, we are dealing not with the kind of mistake that results from the complexity of our endeavours and inevitable human frailty, but with an easily avoided and self-serving mistake produced by the actor's indifference to the separate existence of another. When the harm caused is so great, it seems clear to me that making such a mistake is sufficiently culpable to warrant criminal sanction."

### Setting the Boundaries: Reforming the Law on Sexual Offences (2000), paras. 2.13.1–2.13.2:

"2.13.1 The question of honest, albeit mistaken, belief in consent, is used as a defence in court, and rouses strong passions in [commentators and reformers]. ...
    2.13.2 This issue is often discussed in theoretical terms: for instance, in terms of rape, the extent to which criminality depends on the state of mind of the accused, and whether or not he should be found guilty of a crime that he did not intend to commit. The law at present does not require the reasonableness of a defendant's belief to be tested (although other tests are possible) so making it possible for a defendant to claim he held a completely irrational but honest belief in the consent of the woman: if this is upheld, he must be acquitted. In terms of subjectivist legal principle this is right. In terms of social policy, it makes some very large assumptions. By allowing the belief of the accused to be paramount, the law risks saying to a victim/survivor who feels violated and betrayed that they were not really the victim of a crime, and that what they thought, said or did was immaterial. It is seen to validate male assumptions that they can assume consent without asking. It is an issue that utterly divides opinion."

Arguments such as those raised by Pickard have steadily gained ground over subjectivist arguments in recent years. In 1995, the Law Commission took the view that there might be good reasons for departing from a subjectivist approach in relation to rape.[45] Subsequent reports have developed this although different strategies have been proposed.[46] The latest proposals are contained in the Sexual Offences Bill 2003 and give the strongest support yet for an objective approach. This is true in two contexts. In clause 1(2) the defendant will be liable for rape (having committed the *actus reus*) if he does not believe that the victim (B) consents "whether because he knows that B does not consent, *gives no thought to whether B consents*, or otherwise."[47] This is broadly similar to the interpretation adopted in *Satnam* and in *Adkins*, discussed above. However, far more significant is the provision in the Bill relating to honest belief. Clause 1(3) states that a person (A) will be committing rape if (having committed the *actus reus*):

"(a) a reasonable person would in all the circumstances doubt whether B consents; and

(b) A does not act in a way that a reasonable person would consider sufficient in all the circumstances to resolve such doubt."[48]

### C. Evaluation

Despite the reforms of 1994, the law of rape has continued to evoke controversy. There is still much cause for concern in the response of the criminal justice system. The decline in the prosecution and conviction rate is alarming. Even if a case does proceed to trial the complainant may be exposed to the most humiliating of cross-examination (by defence barristers if not, now, by the defendant himself), the new scheme to prevent previous sexual history being introduced may already be in need of reform and it is too early to tell whether the latest sentencing guideline case will improve sentencing practice in the context of relationship and acquaintance rape.

In relation to the substantive law there have been considerable improvements but there is no doubt that the further reforms proposed need to be implemented. It is absolutely right that no truck has been given to the idea that there should be different levels of rape depending upon whether there was or had been a relationship between the complainant and the defendant. Any such view, based upon the paradigm of the stranger/violent rape, is built upon a false premise. Not only are most victims likely to know their assailant, but strangers do not have exclusive dominion over the use of violence. With or without violence, relationship or acquaintance rape may destroy the possibility of future relationships. If the wrong in rape is the objectification of a person then those who are made to have sexual intercourse without consent by people they know are raped.

---

[45] Consultation Paper No. 139, *Consent in the Criminal Law*, paras 7.7–7.24. However, in their Policy Paper to *Setting the Boundaries*, the Law Commission reasserted its commitment to the defence of honest belief, subject to two qualifications: that the defence would be unavailable if the belief arose from self-induced intoxication and the judge would be required to direct the jury to have regard to whether the defendant, pleading honest belief, had sought to ascertain consent (Vol. 2, Appendix C).

[46] See *Setting the Boundaries*, paras 2.12–2.13.14; *Protecting the Public*, paras 32–34.

[47] Our emphasis.

[48] In addition, by virtue of clauses 78(5) and (6) where the *only* evidence of the defendant's belief as to consent is what has been said or done by a third party, the defendant will be conclusively presumed to have acted unreasonably.

The *actus reus* of rape has already been broadened to include anal penetration but the question is whether it should be extended further. This, in turn, opens up the broader issue of whether the current division of sexual offences is the most appropriate. The arguments for extending rape to cover penile penetration of the mouth are convincing and have now been accepted by reform bodies. In addition, there is overdue recognition of the gravity of other forms of penetrative sexual assault by the proposal to create a new offence of assault by penetration, punishable by a maximum of life imprisonment. There can be no doubt, hearing evidence from victims, that the trauma and harm involved in these assaults can be as bad as that involved in rape. Whether such penetrative assaults should be included within a broadened definition of rape, as has been done in some other jurisdictions, is a controversial matter. On the one hand, there is the view that if the wrong is the objectification of a person one should not distinguish between penetration by the penis and penetration by an inanimate object. On the other hand, there is the argument that, for fair labelling reasons, rape should be limited to penetration by the penis.[49]

With regard to the *mens rea* of rape the rule that the defendant need only make an honest mistake about the victim's consent—and that reasonableness is evidentially important only—is highly questionable, to say the least. If personal property is protected to the extent that the unthinking risk-taker is punished, then the person should be entitled to the same protection. Most people, after all, would rate harm to the person more seriously than harm to property. Moreover, the moral judgment that holds such defendants not blameworthy is, as we have seen, suspect. In addition, the difficulty of proving that some defendants did not have an honest belief may be one of the factors contributing to the low conviction rate. Thus the proposals contained in the Sexual Offences Bill are to be welcomed. As Gardner and Shute argue, those who wish to have sexual intercourse ought to be "astute" to the consent of the other person.[50]

Some commentators on the rape laws of the United States have concluded that the laws are inherently defective; because they have their origins in a patriarchal society, reform attempts will inevitably be half-baked.[51] According to this view we ought to start again from contemporary liberal and feminist first principles regarding women's equal interests in and rights to sexual autonomy and physical security. This has led some commentators to argue, as we have seen, that the law of rape ought to jettison the troublesome concept of consent from the definition (and use force instead) since in an unequal society no woman is in a position to consent freely. This position asserts that "consent is no more than a notion men conveniently employ to characterise women's submission as the product of free choice".[52] Indeed, if views such as "No can mean yes if I persist long enough" linger

---

[49] For further argument on this point, see Clarkson, *Understanding Criminal Law* (3rd ed., 2001), p. 198.

[50] *Above*, n.17, p. 206, 213.

[51] Dripps, "Beyond Rape" (1992) 92 Colum.L.Rev. 1780; West, "Legitimating the Illegitimate: A Comment on Beyond Rape" (1993) 93 Colum.L.Rev. 1442; Dripps, "More on Distinguishing Sex, Sexual Assault: A Reply to Professor West" (1993) 93 Colum.L.Rev. 1460.

[52] Sherwin, "Infelicitous Sex" (1996) 2 *Legal Theory* 209 at 214.

in the minds of defendants and even judges, a woman's consent (or lack of it) is meaningless anyway.

As noted earlier, views such as these have been profoundly important in changing attitudes, but it is submitted that any redefinition of rape in terms of force rather lack of consent would bring its own, arguably much greater, dangers. Developing and refining the concept of consent is the way forward, not least because it does encapsulate the "wrongness" of rape. This is not to under-estimate the difficulty with either the proper definition of consent or with the question of how consent is communicated. Those jurisdictions in which "free agreement" has been adopted have not seen a significant increase in conviction rates[53]; cultural attitudes are slow to change; human communication is fraught with the potential for ambiguity and violence is likely to remain an important factor in securing a conviction. However, ultimately, the offence of rape should serve to protect sexual integrity and autonomy.

[53] See further, Rumney, "The Review of Sex Offences and Rape Law Reform: Another False Dawn?" [2001] 64 M.L.R. 890 at 908–909.

# 8

# HOMICIDE

---

## I. INTRODUCTION

### A. *The Level of Offending*

Violent crime generally accounts for about 15 per cent of offences recorded by the police; within that, homicide, that is, murder, manslaughter and infanticide, accounts for only 0.1 per cent of offences committed. In 2001/02, for example, of the 32,350 more *serious* offences of violence, 886 were initially recorded as homicide.[1] Whereas official statistics only reveal part of the picture of offending for many offences, for homicide, by virtue of the very nature of the offence, the data is likely to be almost entirely accurate.

As with other offences, more homicide appears to be taking place: over the last twenty years the average annual increase has been 1.6 per cent. However, two points have to be borne in mind when interpreting these figures. First, because there are so few offences, the variations that may occur annually look large in percentage terms. For example, 58 of the deaths recorded in 2000/01 were Chinese nationals who were collectively suffocated in a lorry *en route* into the United Kingdom. Secondly, there is evidence that despite the current trend, historically, there are now fewer killings recorded as homicides than in earlier centuries: "homicide rates were three times higher in the thirteenth century than the seventeenth, three times higher in the seventeenth than the nineteenth, and in London they were twice as high in the early nineteenth century as they are now".[2]

### B. *Homicide in Context*

Males are most likely to be both the victims and offenders in homicide. Overall, 70 per cent of homicide victims in 2000/01 were male and 86 per cent of persons

---

[1] Home Office, *Crime in England and Wales 2001/02*, Table 3.04.
[2] Gurr, "On the History of Violent Crime in Europe and America" in Graham and Gurr (eds), *Violence in America* (1979), p. 356.

indicted for homicide were male. At first glance this seems to portray a picture similar to that encountered with non-fatal offences against the person of young males inflicting violence on each other. However, closer analysis of the official statistics reveals a different picture: that homicide is predominantly "domestic" in nature. The victim is likely to have known the killer. In 2000/01, for example, 71 per cent of female victims were killed by persons they knew, 59 per cent of whom were current or former spouses, cohabitants or lovers and 28 per cent were other members of their family (mostly parents). In the same year, men were killed by people they knew in only 42 per cent of cases; of these killings 8 per cent were by current or former spouses, cohabitants or lovers and 29 per cent were other members of the family (again, mostly parents). In short, fewer women were killed by strangers than men and women were killed by a far higher proportion of cohabitants/lovers than men.[3]

Of all killings by "acquaintances", 48 per cent took place during a quarrel or loss of temper; with killings by strangers, 20 per cent took place during a quarrel or loss of temper. Out of all homicides, only 11 per cent were committed in furtherance of theft or gain.[4]

All this data is of importance[5] and relevance to the way the law responds, particularly in relation to the development of the partial defences of provocation and diminished responsibility and the general defence of self-defence. Over the past 20 years much has been learned about the extent of domestic violence in some women's lives that eventually leads them to kill. What has emerged is that much law, for example, relating to self-defence and provocation, is based upon a male typology of anger and violence and that women who kill are more likely to be dealt with "as mad rather than bad".[6] Increased understanding of such issues has been a driving force behind developments in the law relating to provocation and is currently an important factor informing the debate on the parameters of the law relating to self-defence.

The official statistics also reveal another important fact. Children under one year of age are most at risk of homicide. For example, in 2000/01 there were 82 children under one-year-old killed per million population in that age group, compared with 23 persons per million for the 16 to 30 age group (the next highest band).[7] While this figure is much lower than it previously was when women had little access to birth control or abortion and faced harsh penalties for giving birth to illegitimate children, the figure is nevertheless significant enough to be, at least, a factor in the debate as to whether infanticide should be retained as a separate offence or whether many of such killings should be brought within the ambit of the defence of diminished responsibility.

[3] Home Office, *Criminal Statistics: England and Wales 2000* (2001), Table 4.4.
[4] *ibid.*, Table 4.5.
[5] The finding that males are responsible for the majority of homicides has led to research exploring the relationship of masculinity to violence. See, for example, Alder and Polk, "Masculinity and Child Homicide" [1996] 36 Brit. J. Criminol. 396.
[6] There is also a continuing debate as to whether women defendants are treated more or less leniently than men. One argument is that because they "betray" their stereotypical role they are likely to be dealt with more harshly. See Bandelli, "Provocation from the Home Office" [1992] Crim.L.R. 716 for an illustration of how difficult it is to unravel the arguments and statistics.
[7] Above, n.3, Table 4.6

What is it that makes a person resort to such extremes of violence?

Some writers have explored the interaction between victim and offender. "Murder and assault are not one-sided, mechanical activities, with offenders simply acting out aggressive dispositions and victims serving as mere instigators or passive foils. Rather, they are products of a dynamic interchange. The opponents establish and escalate conflict, reject peaceful or mildly aggressive means for resolving it, and turn to massive force as an effective, perhaps mutually agreed-upon method."[8] The official statistics lend considerable support to this interpretation.

However, as seen with offences against the person, there are many broader explanations: biological, psychological and sociological.[9] While an exploration of these theories is beyond the scope of this book, that is not to deny their importance in the construction of the law of homicide—for example, in informing the debate on the offence of infanticide and the limits of the defences of self-defence and provocation.

Homicide is regarded as the most serious offence. Our revulsion against it is embedded deep within us and our reactions to certain killings may be extreme. The following extract attempts to explain the underlying significance of homicide.

### George P. Fletcher, Rethinking Criminal Law (1978), pp. 235–236, 341:

"What makes homicide unique is, among other things, the uniqueness of causing death. While all personal injuries and destruction of property are irreversible harms, causing death is a harm of a different order. Killing another human being is not only a worldly deprivation; in the Western conception of homicide, killing is an assault on the sacred, natural order. In the Biblical view, the person who slays another was thought to acquire control over the blood—the life force—of the victim ...

Though we are inclined today to think of homicide as merely the deprivation of a secular interest, the historical background of desecration is essential to an adequate understanding ... of the current survival of many historic assumptions. For example, consent is not a defense to homicide, as it is in cases of battery and destruction of property. The reason is that the religious conception of human life still prevails against the modern view that life is an interest that the bearer can dispose of at will ...

There are three prominent starting places for thinking about criminal liability. In the pattern of manifest criminality, the point of departure is an act that threatens the peace and order of community life. In the theory of subjective criminality, the starting place is the actor's intent to violate a protected legal interest. In the law of homicide, the focal point is neither the act nor the intent, but the fact of death. This overpowering fact is the point at which the law begins to draw the radius of liability. From this central point, the perspective is: who can be held accountable, and in what way, for the desecration of the human and divine realms? The question is never where to place the point of the legal compass, but how far the arc should sweep in bringing in persons to stand responsible for the death that has already occurred."

This special significance attached to the causing of death is exemplified by the existence of the special offence of causing death by dangerous driving while there is no offence of causing, for example, serious injury by dangerous driving. Similarly,

---

[8] Luckenbill, "Murder and Assault" in Meier, *Major Forms of Crime* (1984), p. 32.
[9] Some of these theories look to the structure of the society in which the offender is placed, claiming to be able to identify sub-cultures of violence, where a system of values supports the use of violence. See generally the references cited at p. 570., n. 1.

the Law Commission's proposals in relation to a new offence for corporations is limited to corporate killings. Also, the Law Commission, while generally committed to a subjectivist approach to liability, is prepared to recognise the significance of death by accepting liability based on inadvertence in such cases.[10]

The task of this chapter is to determine who should be swept within the arc of liability for homicide and to assess the bases upon which we grade the liability of such persons. This necessarily raises the question of why we grade homicide offences, and whether we should continue to do so.

In England there are three categories of homicide: murder, manslaughter (of which there are several species) and infanticide. Although not classified as homicide by the official statistics, there are further similar offences of "vehicular homicide" which will also be explored in this chapter. We shall examine each in turn before asking whether such categorisation serves any useful purpose.

## II. ACTUS REUS OF MURDER AND MANSLAUGHTER

Both these forms of homicide share a common *actus reus*. Historically, this was "unlawfully killing a reasonable person who is in being and under the King's Peace, the death following within a year and a day".[11]

However, the year and a day rule, developed at a time when medical science was primitive, had increasingly been the subject of criticism and in 1994 the Law Commission recommended its abolition.

### The Law Commission, The Year and a Day Rule in Homicide (Consultation Paper No. 136, 1994), para. 6.19:

"Our reasons for advocating the abolition of the rule are:
(a) That the rule appears to have become rooted in substantive law by way of a historical accident, rather than through any deliberate policy.
(b) That with the advance of modern medical science it is possible to ascertain the cause of death and in particular to point to a specific cause which may have arisen some years earlier.
(c) That in consequence the rule operates to prevent convictions when the cause of death can be **shown** to be a wrongful act which occurred more than a year and a day before the death. In cases where the prosecution cannot satisfy the burden of proving causation there would be no problem because the defendant would then be acquitted.
(d) The rule gives an almost complete immunity to people who would have been guilty of gross negligence manslaughter if the victim had died within a year and a day of the infliction of injury.
(e) That in many cases the rule leads to convictions for lesser crimes than are appropriate, typically, attempted murder or causing grievous bodily harm with or without intent, merely because the victim lived for more than a year and a day after the injury, for example, because he was kept on a life support machine.
(f) That following on from the previous point, we have referred to instances which show that in some cases, the rule may lead to unacceptably low sentences being imposed. An example is the substitution of a conviction for dangerous driving, which has a maximum

---

[10] Law Commission, *Legislating the Criminal Code: Involuntary Manslaughter* (Law Com. No.237) (1996), para.4.23.
[11] Coke, 3 Inst. 47.

of two years' imprisonment, for the more serious offence of causing death by dangerous driving, which has a maximum sentence of 10 years' imprisonment.

(g) That experience in Scotland has shown that a criminal justice system can operate fairly and effectively without the rule.

(h) That, in cases where there is a delay between the initiating act and the injury inflicted, it is uncertain when the time period should start to run, which might cause problems if ever such a case came before the courts."

The recommendation was implemented by the Law Reform (Year and a Day Rule) Act 1996, section 1 which abolishes the rule for all purposes. However, because of concerns about prosecutions being brought many years after the infliction of injury, section 2 requires the consent of the Attorney-General to proceedings against a person for a fatal offence[12] if the injury alleged to have caused the death was sustained more than three years before the death occurred.[13]

The remaining elements of the *actus reus* are unaffected by the reform:

1. "*unlawfully*": some killings, such as those in self-defence, may be justified and therefore lawful;

2. "*killing*": the act (or omission) of the defendant must have killed the victim; it must have been the legal cause of the death of the victim. Causation must be established;

3. "*a reasonable person who is in being*": the victim must be a human being who was alive at the time of the defendant's actions. This raises problems outside the scope of this book as to the precise moment when life begins and ends. In view of developments with heart transplant operations and life support machines the problem of determining the exact moment of death has assumed some importance in recent years.

According to English law a foetus is not a human being for the purposes of the law of homicide. However, it is possible for a charge of manslaughter to be brought against a defendant who causes injury to a mother carrying a child in utero if that child is born alive and then subsequently dies from the injuries.[14] If a miscarriage is intentionally procured, and is not a lawful abortion within the terms of the Abortion Act 1967, s.1, the procurer will be guilty of the offence of criminal abortion.[15] There is also a separate offence of child destruction covering cases of destroying a foetus that is capable of being born alive.[16] A pregnancy that has lasted 24 weeks provides *prima facie* proof that the foetus is capable of being born alive.[17]

---

[12] This term is defined in s.2(3) as murder, manslaughter, infanticide or any other offence of which one of the elements is causing a person's death, or the offence of aiding, abetting, counselling or procuring a person's suicide.

[13] This abolition of the year and a day rule, coupled with a procedural safeguard, is preferable to the solution adopted in some other jurisdictions, such as California, where the time limit has been extended to three years and a day (Cal. Penal Code, s.194).

[14] In *Attorney-General's Reference (No. 3 of 1994)* [1998] A.C. 245 the House of Lords held it was not possible for the defendant to be guilty of murder where the injury was caused to the mother whilst the child was in utero. Their Lordships did not accept the idea that a foetus could be treated as part of the mother's body in the same way as, for example, an arm. As far as unlawful act manslaughter was concerned, however, liability is not negatived by the fact that the death of the child is caused as a consequence of injury to the mother rather than as a consequence of direct injury to the foetus. See pp. 185 and 664.

[15] Offences Against the Person Act 1861, s.58.

[16] Infant Life (Preservation) Act 1929, s.1.

[17] *ibid.* s.1(2). Human Fertilisation and Embryology Act 1990, s.37(1)(a).

Both these offences—criminal abortion and child destruction—carry the same maximum penalty as manslaughter, namely, life imprisonment;

4. "*under the King's Peace*": all human beings are under the "Queen's" peace except an alien enemy "in the heat of war, and in the actual exercise thereof"[18];

## III. MURDER

Murder is committed when a defendant commits the *actus reus* of homicide with *malice aforethought*. Murder is the most heinous form of homicide carrying the severest penalty in English law—mandatory life imprisonment. The law reserves this category of homicide for those who kill with the most blameworthy state of mind, known technically as "malice aforethought".[19] Defining the parameters of murder is thus primarily[20] a task of defining malice aforethought, the *mens rea* of murder.

### A. History

The term "malice aforethought" originally[21] bore its literal meaning and it would only be murder if the defendant had thought out, planned or premeditated the killing. In the fifteenth and sixteenth centuries an intentional homicide "on the sudden" was not murder but manslaughter. However, it soon became clear that this was too narrow a definition for murder. Other types of homicide were just as reprehensible and deserving of the ultimate penalty. Accordingly, the judges started expanding the concept "malice aforethought" and dispensing with the requirement of a premeditated intent, until by the mid-seventeenth century it was clear that malice aforethought could be established in any of the following ways.

**1. Intent to kill.** The development that an intent to kill, without premeditation, sufficed for murder was initially achieved by resorting to the fiction that where there was a sudden killing without provocation, the defendant must have planned the killing and thus the requisite "aforethought" was inferred. Before long, however, judges had abandoned this fictitious reasoning and were clearly stating that malice aforethought was present whenever there was an intent to kill.[22]

**2. Intent to cause grievous bodily harm.** This has long been established as a form of malice aforethought.[23] In *Vickers*[24] the Court of Appeal confirmed that this was an

---

[18] Hale, 1 P.C. 433.

[19] This phrase was described in *Moloney* [1985] A.C. 905 at 920 as "anachronistic and now wholly inappropriate".

[20] In certain cases, such as where there is adequate provocation, a killing can be committed with malice aforethought but, because of the circumstances of the killing, the crime is reduced to voluntary manslaughter. See *below*, p. 682.

[21] For a full discussion of the earliest development of the term "malice aforethought," and of the separation of murder from manslaughter in the late fifteenth century, see Sayre, "Mens Rea" (1932) 45 Harv.L.Rev. 974; Moreland, *The Law of Homicide* (1952), pp. 1–16 (and references cited therein) and Horder, "Two Histories and Four Hidden Principles of *Mens Rea*" (1997) 113 L.Q.R. 95 at 100–109.

[22] Moreland, *ibid.*, Ch. 1; Perkins, "A Re-examination of Malice Aforethought" (1934) 43 Yale L.J. 537.

[23] For a full historical discussion, see *Hyam* [1975] A.C. 55 and *Cunningham* [1982] A.C. 566.

[24] [1957] 2 Q.B. 664.

independent species of malice aforethought and not merely a particular example of the felony-murder rule (intentionally causing grievous bodily harm was a felony and thus if death resulted would have been murder under the felony-murder rule). In *D.P.P. v Smith*[25] the House of Lords held that the words "grievous bodily harm" must bear their ordinary natural meaning: "Bodily harm needs no explanation, and 'grievous' means no more and no less than 'really serious.'" This species of malice aforethought is often called "implied malice".

**3. Constructive malice.** This covered two situations:

(i) *killing a police officer while resisting arrest.* Initially this extension to the law was rationalised as being an intentional killing. By strained reasoning it was inferred that the killer must have thought the matter over and determined to kill rather than be taken into custody. However, with the development of the term malice aforethought as a technical phrase with several meanings, efforts to rationalise this extension ceased and it became clearly accepted as a separate species of malice aforethought. The only intention that had to be proved was an intention to resist arrest by force.

(ii) *killing in the course of committing a felony: the felony-murder rule.* Until 1967 crimes were classified as either felonies or misdemeanours,[26] the former being the more serious offences.

Attempts to rationalise the extension of the concept of malice aforethought to cover felony-murders can be based on the fiction that the killer must have intended to kill rather than be unsuccessful in the commission of the felony. However, an alternative analysis by Horder suggests that the felony-murder rule was part of a "coherent larger picture",[27] namely the development of a concept of "malice" based upon the notion that a defendant crossed the threshold for criminal liability if his actions were "wrongfully directed" at the victim, irrespective of whether the actual results were intended or even foreseen. According to Horder, the gradual restriction of the felony-murder rule, in cases such as *Serné*[28] where Sir James Stephen held that it applied only if the felony was "known to be dangerous to life, and likely in itself to cause death", demonstrates the development of a principle of proportionality.[29]

The felony-murder rule still flourishes today in the United States where one of its main rationales is that it is a deterrent to the commission of felonies that create a risk of death. Accordingly, it is generally limited to felonies that are "inherently dangerous". This is sometimes achieved by a statutory limitation of the doctrine to those felonies perceived (normally) to involve danger to human life. In Colorado, for example, the only felonies that qualify for an application of the felony-murder

---

[25] [1961] A.C. 290 at 334.
[26] Or as treason. The Criminal Law Act 1967, s.1 abolished this distinction and substituted the present classification of crimes as being either arrestable offences or non-arrestable offences (s.2).
[27] *Above*, n.21.
[28] (1887) 16 Cox C.C. 311.
[29] "The proportionality principle ... permits criminal liability for harm done to an interest beyond that which was intended or foreseen, but ... restricts such liability to instances where the harm done was not disproportionate to the harm intended." (p. 96).

rule are arson, robbery, burglary, kidnapping, escape from prison and sexual assaults (or attempts to commit these crimes).[30] In other states it is left to the courts to determine whether a particular felony is "inherently dangerous".[31]

Other restrictions have been placed on the felony-murder rule in the United States. Thus in many cases a strict causation requirement is imposed that the felon's act must "directly" cause the death of the victim.[32] Also, the underlying felony must be "independent" of the killing, *i.e.* it must include an element which is not an element of murder.[33] Thus assault and battery is not independent of the killing since all the elements of this crime are included in murder. But robbery is independent of the killing because it includes an element (theft) which is not an element of murder.[34] A final restriction on the felony-murder rule has been achieved by placing a restrictive interpretation on the time period surrounding the felony upon which liability for murder can be based.[35]

The result of all these limitations is that most persons convicted under the felony-murder rule could be regarded as grossly reckless as to the causing of death. The Model Penal Code in the United States recognised this by proposing the abolition of the felony-murder rule *per se*, but providing instead that the commission of a listed dangerous felony should raise a presumption of the requisite "recklessness... [and] extreme indifference to the value of human life" required for murder.[36]

Such persons would almost certainly have been liable for murder in England under the loose *Hyam* test of murder.[37] However, English law has now attempted to limit the crime of murder to intentional killings and to classify killings by excessive risk-taking as manslaughter (subject to the preservation of the grievous bodily harm rule). Thus the felony-murder rule and the other species of constructive malice, killing an officer while resisting arrest, were abolished by the Homicide Act 1957, section 1, and *Hyam* has been judicially laid to rest by the House of Lords in *Moloney*[38] and *Hancock*.[39]

**D.P.P. v Smith.** Before turning to the present law of murder and the meaning of malice aforethought today, it is necessary to mention one final development already discussed in a different context.[40] The House of Lords in *D.P.P. v Smith*[41] in 1960 effectively laid down an objective test of malice aforethought in holding that a defendant would be guilty of murder if he or she intended to do an act where death or grievous bodily harm was the natural and probable result. Condemnation of this

---

[30] Colo.Rev.Stat.Ann. s.18–3–102(1)(b).
[31] Some courts make this determination on an abstract basis without reference to the particular facts of the case (*e.g. Morales* 49 Cal.App. 3d 134, 122 Cal.Rptr. 157 (1975)). Other courts prefer to consider whether the particular defendant's commission of the felony was inherently dangerous (*e.g. State v Chambers* 524 S.W. 2d 826 (Mo. 1975)).
[32] *Commonwealth v Redline*, 391 Pa. 486, 137 A.2d 472 (1958).
[33] *People v Ireland*, 70 Cal. 2d 522, 450 P.2d 580, 75 Cal.Rptr. 188 (1969).
[34] *People v Burton*, 491 P.2d 793 (Cal. 1971).
[35] *People v Walsh*, 186 N.E. 422 (N.Y. 1933); *Parson v State* 222 A.2d 326 (Del. 1966).
[36] S.210.3(1)(b), see *below*, p. 646.
[37] See *below*, p. 643.
[38] [1985] A.C. 905.
[39] [1986] A.C. 455.
[40] *Above*, p. 211.
[41] [1961] A.C. 290.

decision resulted in the enactment of section 8 of the Criminal Justice Act 1967.[42] The House of Lords in *Hyam* has confirmed that as a result of section 8, the test of malice aforethought is clearly the subjective one of determining the actual state of mind of the defendant. Further, the Privy Council in *Frankland*[43] has held that the objective test never accurately represented English law and that *D.P.P. v Smith* was wrong.

## B. *Present Law*

The *mens rea* of murder can now be simply stated.
 The defendant must either:
 1. intend to cause death, or
 2. intend to cause grievous bodily harm.

This, of course, does not solve the central problem of determining the meaning of intention. The leading decisions on intention are *Moloney*, *Hancock*, *Nedrick* and *Woollin*, which are extracted and discussed in Chapter 2 and to which reference should be made. Whether these cases lay down an appropriate test is discussed later.[44]

These cases have, however, removed one problem. In *Hyam*[45] it was held that foresight of death or grievous bodily harm as a (highly) probable consequence of one's actions was sufficient to constitute the mental element for murder. It was uncertain whether this amounted to a separate head of malice aforethought apart from intention—or whether this was an alternative and broad way of defining intention itself. It is now clear that there is no head of malice aforethought apart from the two intention tests listed above—and it is also clear that the concept intention cannot be given such a broad meaning.

The validity of the grievous bodily harm rule would appear to be beyond doubt as a result of the House of Lords decision of *Cunningham*. Prior to that it had been argued that the grievous bodily harm rule was simply a sub-species of the felony-murder rule and was thus also abolished by the Homicide Act 1957. This view, endorsed by a minority in *Hyam*, was rejected in *Cunningham*. It had further been argued in *Hyam* that the reason for the grievous bodily harm rule was that in the last century, because of the poor state of medical knowledge and experience, persons sustaining such injuries were likely to die; such a rationale was unacceptable today with the advances in medical knowledge. If transplanting the grievous bodily harm rule into modern times it would need qualifying so that only grievous bodily harm which endangered life should come within the *mens rea* of murder. This argument was similarly rejected.

### R. v Cunningham [1982] A.C. 566 (House of Lords)

Lord Hailsham:
 "I ... genuflect before the miracles of modern surgery and medicine, though I express some doubt whether these may not have been offset to some extent by the increased lethal

---

[42] See *above*, p. 212.
 [43] [1988] Crim.L.R.117.
 [44] *Below*, pp. 642–650.
 [45] [1975] A.C. 55.

characteristics of modern weaponry (particularly in the fields of automatic weaponry, explosives and poisons), and the assistance to criminality afforded by the automobile, the motorway and international air transport. I also take leave to doubt whether in the case of injuries to the skull in particular or indeed really serious bodily harm in general these advances have made the difference between inflicting serious bodily harm and endangering life sufficiently striking as to justify judicial legislation on the scale proposed. But, more important than all this, I confess that I view with a certain degree of scepticism the opinion expressed in *R. v Hyam* ... that the age of our ancestors was so much more violent than our own that we can afford to take a different view of 'concepts of what is right and what is wrong that command general acceptance in contemporary society'. ..."

Lord Edmund-Davies:

"[T]he view I presently favour is ... that there should be no conviction for murder unless an intent to kill is established, the wide range of punishment for manslaughter being fully adequate to deal with all less heinous forms of homicide. I find it passing strange that a person can be convicted of murder if death results from, say, his intentional breaking of another's arm, an action which, while undoubtedly involving the infliction of 'really serious harm' and, as such, calling for severe punishment, would in most cases be unlikely to kill. And yet, for the lesser offence of attempted murder, nothing less than intent to kill will suffice. But I recognise the force of the contrary view that the outcome of intentionally inflicting serious harm can be so unpredictable that anyone prepared to act so wickedly has little ground for complaint if, where death results, he is convicted and punished as severely as one who intended to kill.

So there are forceful arguments both ways. And they are arguments of the greatest public consequence, particularly in these turbulent days when, as the Lord Chancellor has vividly reminded us, violent crimes have become commonplace. Resolution of that conflict cannot, in my judgment, be a matter for your Lordships' House alone. It is a task for none other than Parliament. ..."

Whether this grievous bodily harm rule should be retained is discussed later.

## C. *Penalty for Murder*

The Murder (Abolition of the Death Penalty) Act 1965 abolished capital punishment for murder and substituted a sentence of mandatory life imprisonment. The judge has no discretion as to sentence. A convicted murderer must be sentenced to imprisonment for life.[46]

However, convicted murderers seldom remain in prison for the duration of their lives. They can be released from prison on "licence". This means that the offender does not regain absolute liberty. The licence is subject to conditions: for example, requiring supervision by a probation officer. All such persons released on licence are liable to be recalled to prison at any time during the rest of their lives should there be a breach of the conditions of licence or should their conduct indicate that there is a risk of a serious offence being committed. Until it was declared incompatible with the European Convention on Human Rights the following was the procedure adopted for determining when murderers could be released on licence.

When passing a sentence of mandatory life imprisonment the trial judge is empowered to recommend a minimum period that should be served for retribution and general deterrence before the offender can be considered for release. This is

---

[46] Such a sentence is not incompatible with either Art. 3 or Art.5 of the European Convention on Human Rights (*Lichniak; Pyrah* [2002] 4 All E.R.1122).

known as the "tariff". This advice is passed to the Lord Chief Justice who can review the tariff taking into account the need for uniformity in particular classes of case. Until 2002, this advice was then passed to the Home Secretary who made the final tariff decision determining how long the convicted murderer should remain in prison (again, to meet the requirements of retribution and general deterrence) before being eligible for consideration for release on licence. In some 95 per cent of cases the Home Secretary accepted the judicial recommendation but he had the power to lengthen or reduce the period of the tariff and he did so in 5 per cent of cases.[47]

When the tariff period had been served, the Home Secretary could refer the case to the Parole Board who could recommend release on licence but this recommendation had to be accepted by the Home Secretary, after consultation with the Lord Chief Justice together with the trial judge if available.[48] This meant that in reality the final decision as to the length of time served in prison was made by the Home Secretary. In certain high-profile cases, most notably that of Myra Hindley, successive Home Secretaries repeatedly refused to allow the Parole Board to consider release on licence.

In *R. (on the application of Anderson) v Secretary of State for the Home Department*[49] it was held by the House of Lords that the imposition of a sentence was an integral part of the trial and that fixing a tariff was legally indistinguishable from imposing any other sentence. Article 6(1) of the European Convention on Human Rights guarantees defendants the right to a fair trial by an independent and impartial tribunal. "Independent" means "independent of the parties to the case and also of the executive".[50] As the Home Secretary was not an independent tribunal, his fixing the tariff was incompatible with Article 6(1) of the Convention.

Accordingly, the fixing of tariffs was to have become entirely a matter for the trial judge although that decision could be appealed by the defendant or be the subject of an Attorney-General's Reference.[51] The Sentencing Advisory Panel had already, prior to the decision in *Anderson*, submitted evidence to the Court of Appeal on the setting of minimum terms in murder cases.[52] This advice was largely accepted in *Practice Statement (Crime: Life Sentences)*.[53] However, even before these guidelines had been laid down the Home Secretary announced that legislation would be introduced establishing "a clear set of principles within which the judges will fix minimum tariffs in the future".[54] A late amendment to the Criminal Justice Bill 2003 proposes putting such principles on a statutory basis. If implemented these "tariffs" would be significantly harsher than those laid down judicially and would include provision for "life means life" in the most serious cases.

---

[47] Memorandum submitted by the Home Office to the Second Report of the Home Affairs Committee, *Murder: the Mandatory Life Sentence* (Session 1995–96, Paper 412) (1996), p. xxii.

[48] Crime (Sentences) Act 1977, s.29.

[49] [2002] 4 All E.R.1089 following the European Court decision in *Stafford v UK* (2002) 13 BHRC 260.

[50] *V v UK* (2000) 30 E.H.R.R. 121.

[51] *McBean* [2002] 1 Cr.App.R.(S.) 98.

[52] Sentencing Advisory Panel, *Annual Report 2001/02*, Appendix E: it is suggested that there should be a "middle starting point" (12 or 14 years) and also lower and higher starting points for cases where the offender's culpability is significantly reduced (for example, overreacted in self-defence) or exceptionally high (for example, a contract killing).

[53] [2002] 1 W.L.R. 1789. See further, below p. 732.

[54] Home Office, *Press Release*, 25 November, 2002.

The setting of tariffs means that the sentencing of murderers is not dissimilar to the sentencing of other offenders. But there are important differences, quite apart from the former involvement of the Home Secretary. First, there is never a right to release on parole. The Parole Board must judge whether it is safe to release the murderer. Secondly, the released murderer is always on licence and liable to recall to prison. These differences raise the fundamental question whether the mandatory sentence of life imprisonment for murder should be retained.[55]

### Report of the Advisory Council on the Penal System, Sentences of Imprisonment (A Review of Maximum Penalties), (1978), paras 235–244:

"235. .... [If] life imprisonment should remain the penalty for murder and manslaughter ... [t]here remains the specific question whether life imprisonment should continue to be the *mandatory* penalty for murder, or whether it should become the *maximum* penalty, thus permitting the imposition of determinate sentences of any length for the offence. ...

236. The mandatory penalty of life imprisonment was substituted for the death penalty by the Murder (Abolition of Death Penalty) Act 1965. The Government at that time supported the new penalty essentially on two grounds: that murder was a unique offence and should be marked by a unique penalty; and that to permit determinate sentencing for the offence could be risky, since there might be cases in which the Home Secretary would have to release a prisoner who had served a determinate sentence, less remission, even though he might feel that it was unsafe to do so.

237. One of the arguments of those who believe that murder merits a unique penalty is that the mandatory life sentence reflects the retributive view that anyone who murders another must place his life at the disposal of the State to the extent that both his release and his liberty to remain at large will always be subject to executive decision. This view is usually associated with the argument that to sentence murderers in the same way as other offenders would be to devalue murder as an offence and to reduce the deterrent effect of the existing penalty.

238. Another argument in favour of the mandatory element is that acts of murder can arouse a good deal of public passion and indignation which would attract more than usual interest to apparent discrepancies in sentencing decisions and tend to bring the administration of justice into undesirable public controversy. This, it is argued, would be likely to cause particular difficulty in what are considered the less culpable types of homicide, where a judge might think it appropriate to pass a shorter sentence than in a bad case of, for instance, robbery, but would immediately become susceptible to the accusation that the courts care more for property than for lives.

239. It is also argued that the absence of the mandatory element in the penalty for murder might actually lead (as the result of public attitudes to the crime of murder) to a situation in which the least dangerous of murderers might remain in custody longer as a result of relative determinate sentencing than they would have done if sentenced to life imprisonment. A related objection to the abolition of the mandatory sentence is that it would lead to over-long sentences in very serious cases. ...

243. .... [W]e see a number of positive arguments to justify the abolition of the mandatory element in the penalty for murder. The Criminal Law Revision Committee rightly recognised that the main advantage to be derived from the mandatory life sentence is its flexibility in providing the releasing authorities with the freedom to gauge the public interest and the needs of the offender throughout the period of his imprisonment and after release. The prison service and the Parole Board can take account of continuing observation of the

---

[55] See also Criminal Law Revision Committee, 14th Report, *Offences Against the Person*, Cmnd.7844, paras 42–74; Criminal Law Revision Committee, 12th Report, *Penalty for Murder*, Cmnd.5184; *Report of the Committee on the Penalties for Homicide* (Scottish Home and Health Department), Cmnd.5137; *Report of the Committee on the Penalty for Homicide* (Chairman: Lord Lane), Prison Reform Trust (1993).

prisoner's development in prison and the Board can monitor his behaviour while on licence and, if necessary, recall him without recourse to the courts. These are powerful considerations in favour of the indeterminacy implicit in the life sentence. We do not, however, consider that they necessarily imply that the life sentence must be imposed indiscriminately on every person convicted of murder. Where the nature of the offence connotes dangerousness and there is evidence of a likely continued threat that it will be repeated, the life sentence may be the appropriate, indeed the only wise, sentence to pass. But for some murderers we think that there are strong reasons for giving courts the power to pass fixed terms of imprisonment.

244. Although murder has been traditionally and distinctively considered the most serious crime, it is not a homogeneous offence but a crime of considerable variety. It ranges from deliberate cold-blooded killing in pursuit of purely selfish ends to what is commonly referred to as 'mercy killing'. Instead of automatically applying a single sentence to such an offence, ... sentences for murder should reflect this variety with correspondingly variable terms of imprisonment or, in the exceptional case, even with a non-custodial penalty ... [We] cannot believe that the problems of predicting future behaviour at the time of conviction are inherently more difficult in a murder case than in any other case where there is a measure of instability, or that judges are any less able to make predictions or to assess degrees of culpability in murder cases than in any others. ... [Further] efforts to alleviate the harshness of the mandatory penalty, [provocation and diminished responsibility] have led to complications in legal proceedings for which we believe there can be no proper justification."

## House of Lords, Report of the Select Committee on Murder and Life Imprisonment (Session 1988–89, H.L. Paper 78), 1989, paras 108B–118:

"108B. The counter-arguments [against retention of the mandatory sentence] are as follows:

(i) Not all murders are 'uniquely serious' ... Some cases of murder will be less grave than some cases of attempted murder, or of manslaughter, or of causing grievous bodily harm with intent. The organisation JUSTICE has examined in some detail over 200 cases over the last 30 years and concluded that the circumstances giving rise to murder vary infinitely so that the relative heinousness of the crime covers the whole spectrum from the tragic mercy killing to the most sadistic type of sex murder of young children.

(ii) The definition of murder is not and, if the Committee's recommendations are accepted, will not be confined to intentional killings ... All murderers receive the same sentence whether they are intentional killers or not. If the intentional and unprovoked killings are to be regarded as 'uniquely serious' the definition of murder ought to be limited to such killings ...

(iv) The alleged 'unique' quality of a life sentence for murder is undermined by the availability of that sentence for other offences. ...

111B(i) Many murderers are not generally dangerous. This was asserted by Dr Thomas who pointed out that, during a ten-year period when 6,000 persons convicted of homicide (including manslaughter) were at large, only six persons previously convicted of murder committed a second murder—and several of these were committed in prison ...

(ii) The opinion of the Lord Chief Justice is that the problem of dangerousness arises in a more acute form in relation to offences other than murder. Rapists and arsonists may be much more likely to commit the same sort of offences than a murderer; and they are dealt with by passing a life sentence or a sentence which is somewhat longer than would have been necessary without the element of risk ...

113A. The abolition of the mandatory sentence would present peculiarly difficult sentencing problems for the trial judge. Because the sentence has always been fixed in law there are no precedents to guide the judge in imposing a determinate sentence for murder: ...

113B. The counter argument is that the Court of Appeal would soon establish appropriate principles of sentencing for murder as it has for other offences ...

114A. The mandatory life sentence is, or may be, a valuable deterrent ...

114B. The counter argument is that the fact that the life sentence is mandatory actually reduces any deterrent value a life sentence may have. It dilutes what should be the awe-inspiring nature of the life sentence. Because many murderers receive unnecessary life sentences, the average time served is reduced, giving credence to the common belief that 'life' means nine years . . .[56]

117. Finally, the Committee were impressed by the argument put forward by Victim Support, that the existence of the mandatory life sentence led to inappropriate verdicts of manslaughter. Many families of murder victims felt that 'somebody being charged and found guilty of murder does imply and represent an appropriate recognition of the crime that has actually happened' . . .

*Opinion of the Committee*
118. The Committee agree with the majority of their witnesses that the mandatory life sentence for murder should be abolished."

However, despite the very substantial body of opinion endorsing this view, two Home Affairs Committee Reports[57] have concluded that, although the issue was "exceptionally finely balanced", the mandatory life sentence ought to be retained:

"This reflects a concern for public safety, and doubts about whether there is a satisfactory solution to the problem of how to protect the public from clearly dangerous prisoners who would have to be released at the end of a determinate sentence."[58]

The Committee also suggested that there was more flexibility in the mandatory life sentence than appears at first sight, and believed that many of the perceived drawbacks of the current arrangements could be rectified by a number of reforms, including changes to the way in which the tariff is set.[59] As seen above, the Home Secretary's involvement in the setting of tariffs and in authorising release on parole has been held to be incompatible with the European Convention on Human Rights and new legislation setting a framework for the setting of tariffs is proposed. It is clear that the abolition of the mandatory life sentence is not currently on the political agenda.

### D. *Evaluation*

Apart from criticism of the mandatory penalty of life imprisonment for murder, there are two further criticisms of the present law.
(1) Criticism of the grievous bodily harm rule.
(2) Criticism of the *Woollin* test of intention.

### 1. The grievous bodily harm rule

There are arguments in favour of the retention of the grievous bodily harm rule as a species of malice aforethought. If a defendant intends *really* serious bodily

---

[56] In fact, in 1997, the "average" term served by lifers was just over 14 years (Cullen and Newell, *Murderers and Life Imprisonment* (1999), p. 21). See also Wasik, "Sentencing in Homicide" in Ashworth and Mitchell (eds), *Rethinking English Homicide Law* (2000), pp. 174–183.

[57] Home Affairs Committee, *Murder: the Mandatory Life Sentence* (First Report) (Session 1995–96, Paper 111) (1995); *Murder: the Mandatory Life Sentence* (Second Report) (Session 1995–96, Paper 412) (1996).

[58] First Report, p. xxxv.

[59] First Report, p. xxxvi; Second Report, pp. vii–ix. JUSTICE, which continues to press for the abolition of the mandatory life sentence provides further evidence in support of the proposed reforms: see, *Sentenced For Life* (1996).

harm to another there is always a probability that death may result from such injuries. Most defendants would know this. Thus people who intend to cause grievous bodily harm have chosen to run a risk of endangering life. They are as dangerous and as blameworthy as those who actually intend to kill. Their excessive risk-taking as to the death should render them liable for murder.

### Criminal Law Revision Committee, Working Paper on Offences Against the Person, 1976, para. 29:

"It is argued that a person who inflicts serious injury on another intentionally must know that by so doing there is a real chance that his victim will die and if death results it is right that he should be convicted of murder. There is force also in the argument that a person who is minded to use violence in achieving an unlawful purpose may take more care to refrain from inflicting serious injury if he knows that he may be convicted of murder if his victim dies. A few of our members are in favour of an intent to cause serious injury, simpliciter, remaining a sufficient intent in murder."

### The Law Commission, Imputed Criminal Intent (Director of Public Prosecutions v Smith), 1965, para. 13:

"13. The main arguments in favour of retaining the intent to inflict grievous bodily harm as an alternative to the intent to kill in murder are as follows:
(a) It is in accord with the general sense of justice of the community that a man who causes death by the intentional infliction of grievous bodily harm, although not actually intending to kill, should not only be punished as severely as a murderer, but should be treated in law as a murderer.
(b) Grievous bodily harm is a relatively simple concept which can be readily explained to a jury. Any attempt to define 'grievous bodily harm' as, for example, 'harm likely to endanger life,' or further to require that the accused should *know* that the harm inflicted is likely to endanger life, would make the judge's direction more difficult for the jury to follow.
(c) It is true that, with the suspension of the death sentence, a person who kills while intending to inflict grievous bodily harm could, if such an offence were only manslaughter, receive as a maximum the same sentence, namely life imprisonment, as that which would remain obligatory for murder. But the judge might face practical difficulties in such a case of manslaughter in ascertaining the intent to inflict grievous bodily harm, which he would require to know in order to fix the appropriate sentence. These difficulties would be most acute if the prosecution had accepted pleas of not guilty of murder but guilty of manslaughter, when the judge would have to rely on depositions; but they would also exist to some extent where the accused had been tried on a count of murder but had been found guilty of manslaughter, in which event the judge would have heard the evidence in the case, but would have no verdict of the jury on the question whether the killing followed an act intended to inflict grievous bodily harm."

Despite the approval of the grievous bodily harm rule in *Hyam* and *Cunningham*, it has been the subject of severe judicial criticism.

### Attorney-General's Reference (No. 3 of 1994) [1998] A.C. 245 (House of Lords)

Lord Mustill:
"Murder is widely thought to be the gravest of crimes. One could expect a developed system to embody a law of murder clear enough to yield an unequivocal result on a given set

of facts, a result which conforms with apparent justice and has a sound intellectual base. This is not so in England, where the law of homicide is permeated by anomaly, fiction, misnomer and obsolete reasoning. One conspicuous anomaly is the rule which identifies the 'malice aforethought' (a doubly misleading expression) required for the crime of murder not only with a conscious intention to kill but also with an intention to cause grievous bodily harm. ... Many would doubt the justice of this rule, which is not the popular conception of murder and ... no longer rests on any intellectual foundation ... [I]t is, I think, right to recognise that the grievous bodily harm rule is an outcropping of old law from which the surrounding strata of rationalisations have weathered away."

Despite this attack, Lord Mustill recognised that there was no ground upon which the House of Lords could abolish so established a rule. However, law reform bodies have also rejected the grievous bodily harm rule in its present form.

### The Law Commission, Imputed Criminal Intent (Director of Public Prosecutions v Smith), 1965, paras 15, 18:

"15. The main arguments for changing the present law, which prescribes intent to inflict grievous bodily harm as an alternative to the intent to kill in murder, are as follows:
  (a) Murder is commonly understood to mean the intentional killing of another human being; and, unless there are strong reasons which justify a contrary course, it is generally desirable that legal terms should correspond with their popular meaning.
  (b) To limit intent in murder to the intent to kill is not to disregard the very serious nature of causing death by the infliction of grievous bodily harm, but, since the suspension of the death sentence, if such an offence were to be treated as manslaughter only, it could nevertheless be punished by a maximum penalty as severe as the penalty prescribed for murder, namely, imprisonment for life. ...
  (d) Furthermore, a man should not be regarded as a murderer if he does not *know* that the bodily harm which he intends to inflict is likely to kill. ... If there is any special deterrent effect in the label 'murder' as distinguished from manslaughter, it should be attached to an act done with intent to inflict bodily harm which the accused knows is likely to kill. ...
18. ...
  (a) So long as a distinction between murder and manslaughter is to be maintained, there must be a defensible criterion for distinguishing between them. In our view the essential element in murder should be willingness to kill, thereby evincing a total lack of respect for human life."

### Criminal Law Revision Committee, Working Paper on Offences Against the Person, 1976, para. 29:

"29. ... The majority of us ... think that if an intent to cause serious injury is to remain part of the mens rea of murder, it should be limited in some way so that it is related more closely to the fact of death. Some of us take the view that the law should distinguish between a person who, although intending to cause serious injury, inflicts it in such a way that death is not likely to result and the person who intentionally causes serious injury in such a way that death is likely to be caused. These members hope that such a distinction might deter a person from causing serious injury with the likelihood of death resulting. Other members think that the distinction should depend on whether or not the offender realised at the time that he might well cause death."

The Draft Criminal Code followed this last proposal and recommended modification of the grievous bodily harm rule so that it would only be murder in such cases should when the defendant acts "intending to cause serious personal harm and being aware that he may cause death."[60]

In the United States the Model Penal Code recommended that no express significance be accorded to an intent to cause grievous bodily harm, but that such cases should be subsumed under the standards of extreme recklessness (murder)[61] or recklessness (manslaughter).[62] Thus the fact that the defendant intended to cause serious injury would simply become a relevant consideration in determining whether he acted with "extreme indifference to the value of human life" (murder) or "recklessly" with respect to the death of another (manslaughter). While many states have given effect to this recommendation,[63] others continue to specify "intent to cause serious injury" as sufficing for murder (generally murder in the second degree). Many of these latter states however define "serious bodily injury" in a manner relating it to the death. Thus in Texas, for instance, it is murder if one "intends to cause serious bodily injury and commits an act clearly dangerous to human life that causes the death of an individual".[64]

On the other hand, four states (Connecticut, Delaware, Kentucky and New York) have taken the significant step of declaring that killing "with intent to cause serious physical injury" only constitutes manslaughter—and the serious physical injury must "to a reasonable person in the defendant's situation, knowing the facts known to the defendant, seem likely to cause death"[65] or, as in the other three states, " 'serious physical injury' means physical injury which creates a substantial risk of death, or which causes serious disfigurement, serious impairment of health or serious loss or impairment of the function of any bodily organ".[66]

Is a defendant who takes such a clear risk as to death so much less culpable or blameworthy as to deserve liability for manslaughter only? Perhaps this question cannot be fully answered until the *Woollin* test of intention has been considered.

## 2. Woollin test of intention

As we have seen, the House of Lords in *Moloney* and *Hancock* ruled that there must be an *intention* to kill or cause grievous bodily harm. These decisions overruled *Hyam* in which it had been held that the *mens rea* of murder could be *satisfied* by proof that the defendant foresaw death or grievous bodily harm as a likely consequence.

It ought perhaps to be emphasised that in overruling *Hyam* the House was overruling what had in reality been the law for at least a hundred years. It is true that there had long been a tendency before *Hyam* to assert that, because murder was the most serious crime in the land, it could only be committed intentionally.

[60] Law Commission No. 177, Draft Criminal Code Bill 1989, cl. 54(1). This proposal was endorsed by the House of Lords Select Committee on Murder and Life Imprisonment (Session 1988–89, H.L. Paper 78) (1989), para. 71.

[61] Section 210.2(1)(b).

[62] Section 210.3(1)(a).

[63] *e.g.* North Dakota (N.D. Cent. Code ss.12.1–16–01(1)(b)).

[64] Tex. Penal Code Ann. s.19.02(b)(2).

[65] Del. Code Ann. tit. 11, s.11–632(2).

[66] Conn.Gen.Stat.Annot. s.53a–3(4); Kentucky (Ky.Rev.Stat., s.500.080(15)) and New York (N.Y. Penal Law, s.10.00(10)) have similar definitions.

This however was "really a sort of hypocrisy stemming from the days of captial punishment: a desire to pretend to the public that the law only hanged people for intentional killing, while at the same time hanging people who were felt to deserve hanging whether they killed intentionally or not".[67] Some of their Lordships in *Hyam* were prepared to admit openly that murder was not a crime of intention alone—alternative states of mind could suffice. But the others, desirous of clinging to the false notion that murder was a crime of intention, were forced to place expansive interpretations on the concept of intention so as to encompass the alternative state of mind approved by the others.

Following *Woollin*, there is some uncertainty as to the meaning of intention.[68] One interpretation of this decision is that foresight of a virtual certainty is an alternative species of intention. The other interpretation is that intention remains undefined but the jury is entitled to find intention only where there is such foresight of a virtual certainty. But, while they are "entitled" to find such intention, equally they are entitled to find that the defendant did not intend death or grievous bodily harm.

Under this latter interpretation, where intention is not defined and the jury is allowed "moral elbow-room" to decide whether the defendant deserves to be labelled a murderer, the hypocrisy of the past century is continued. Murder is a "crime of intention", but maximum flexibility is retained by not defining the concept.

### Alan Norrie, "After *Woollin*" [1999] Criminal Law Review 532 at 542–543

"[T]he five recent murder/intention cases ... can be divided into two groups of two, with one case, *Hancock*, left by itself. In the first group come *Moloney* and *Woollin*. Both involved domestic killings in which there was evidence of a lack of moral *animus* between the killer and his victim. Moloney felt affection for his stepfather. Woollin had seemingly never harmed his baby before. In both cases the use of the symbolic label 'murder', not to mention the mandatory life sentence, probably seemed inappropriate ... [I]t is not unreasonable to assume the judges felt some moral sympathy for the accused in these cases ...

Judges are in a sense like Everyman in that they too participate in a moral community ... What Everyman might achieve by considering first the nature of Woollin's relationship with his child or Moloney's with his father as the irreducible moral context of judgment, the judges must achieve, ventriloquially, as it were, through the law of indirect intention ...

Then take *Hyam* and *Nedrick*, both cases involving the introduction of inflammable materials through letterboxes ... [This] represents ... a pattern of manifest wrongdoing which may not yet be reflected in the intentions of the accused. Mrs Hyam may genuinely have only intended to frighten, but the action carries with it its own intrinsic dangers. There is also no redeeming aspect in the moral relationship between the parties, indeed the fact that it was the other woman's young daughters that died exacerbates the moral view of Hyam's actions ... *Hancock* ... occupies a third moral position in which the accused were probably regarded as lacking in the kind of malice evinced in *Hyam*, but still not regarded with the same sympathy as the accused in *Moloney* or *Woollin*.
(Norrie goes on to point out that while Nedrick in fact escaped liability for murder he was nevertheless convicted of manslaughter and a 15 year prison sentence was imposed—in effect, what he would have served on a murder conviction.)"

---

[67] Gordon, "The Mental Element in Crime," (1971) 16 J.L.S.S. 282 at 285.
[68] See pp.127–143.

Such an approach is, however, a recipe for unpredictability and opens the door to irrelevant factors being taken into consideration. Fair labelling requires an open acknowledgment of what forms of killing are murder. In order to determine this, two questions present themselves for consideration. Was the House of Lords in *Moloney* and *Hancock* justified in overruling *Hyam* and so narrowing the *mens rea* of murder? Secondly, if so, did they go far enough? Should not the crime of murder have been restricted to those who *directly* intend to kill (or cause grievous bodily harm)?

The argument for limiting the *mens rea* of murder to a *direct* intention is a two-fold one. Murder is the most serious crime under English law and carries the most severe penalty. It should be reserved for the worst cases which are directly intended killings. In such cases the defendant has acted with a degree of control and deliberation that enhances his responsibility for the outcome of his actions and affects our judgment of him as a moral agent. He is not simply showing indifference to the value of human life; he is actually taking positive and purposeful steps towards the ending of the life of another. This evil aim marks him out as more blameworthy. Also, a person who is trying to achieve a result is usually more likely to succeed than someone who merely foresees that result as a by-product of his actions, and can thus perhaps be regarded as more blameworthy than one who engages in conduct with a lesser chance of harm.

Secondly, such an approach avoids all problems of having to draw fine lines on the continuum of risk-taking—for example, distinguishing between foresight of the virtually certain (murder) and foresight of the extremely probable (manslaughter).

The argument against such a strict limitation is that it would unduly restrict the crime of murder and that many persons, such as the bomber on the aeroplane wanting the insurance money, deserve to be brought within the category of murder. This raises the question as to whether there is a moral distinction between one who wants death to result and one who foresees death as virtually certain—or one who merely foresees death as likely.[69] In short, should murder be expanded beyond intent (as currently understood) to kill (or cause grievous bodily harm)? Should cases of gross recklessness be included within the crime of murder?

### Criminal Law Revision Committee, 14th Report, Offences Against the Person, Cmnd.7844 (1980), paras 19–31:

"19. It is the mental element in murder which distinguishes it from involuntary manslaughter. . . . [W]e need to define the mental element which will distinguish the gravest from the less grave homicides. . . . It is important that the definition of murder should, so far as possible, ensure that those convicted of murder will be deserving of the stigma. Too wide a law of murder would not only be unjust but would also tend to diminish the stigma to which we . . . attach value.

20. In our opinion the mental element of murder is too broadly stated in *Hyam*. . . . [The C.L.R.C. then went on to reject the grievous bodily harm rule as it stands at present.]

---

[69] See *above*, pp. 138–143, for further argument on this point.

*Should all reckless killings be murder?*

23. We considered whether to propose a definition of murder in terms of intentional or reckless killing, but it seems to us such a wide offence that it could not be called murder. It would include many killings that are now manslaughter and would not be generally thought to be murder. A builder who uses a method of construction which he knows might, in some circumstances, be dangerous to life, might be guilty of an unlawful homicide if a fatal accident results; but it would be wrong to hold him guilty of the same offence as the deliberate killer and for him to be subject to a mandatory sentence of life imprisonment. . . .

*Should killing with a high degree of recklessness be murder?*

24. If reckless conduct causing death is not enough to make a man guilty of murder, why should there not be a conviction for that offence if the defendant knows that there is a high probability or even a mere probability or a serious risk that death will be caused? . . . What is a high probability? Or a mere probability? Or a serious risk? Some may think that there is a probability if death is more likely than not to result—the 3 to 2 odds on chance—and that there is a high probability if the odds are shorter (but how much shorter?). Others may think that there is a probability when the odds are much longer. Should a man who kills another while playing an adaptation of 'Russian roulette' be guilty of murder if he knows there is a bullet in one of the six chambers of the revolver? Or in two, three, four or five chambers? It has been suggested that, since the outcome of death is so serious, knowledge of a statistically small risk of causing death could be held to be knowledge of probability and even high probability. We do not accept that suggestion, but the fact that it can be made confirms our opinion as to the unsatisfactory nature of the formula.

25. We appreciate that it is difficult to draw the line between what we recommend should be the meaning of intention and the high probability test mentioned in *Hyam*. To confine intention to wanting a particular result to happen would be too rigid . . .

*Should killing ever be murder when death is not intended?*

28. We think that murder should be extended beyond intentional killing in one respect. There is one category of reckless killing where we believe there would be general agreement that the stigma of murder is well merited. That is where the killer intended unlawfully to cause serious bodily injury and knew that there was a risk of causing death. The intention to cause serious bodily injury puts this killing into a different class from that of a person who is merely reckless, even gravely reckless. The offender has shot, stabbed or otherwise seriously injured the victim, and the circumstances are so grave that the jury can find that he must have realised that there was a risk of causing death. . . . To classify this particular type of risk-taking as murder does not involve the danger of escalation to cases of recklessness in general, since it is tied specifically to circumstances in which the defendant intended to inflict serious injury.

*Recommendations*

31. We therefore conclude that it should be murder:
(a) if a person, with intent to kill, causes death and
(b) if a person causes death by an unlawful act intended to cause serious injury and known to him to involve a risk of causing death.

In addition, if Parliament favours . . . [a further] provision . . . we recommend that it should be on the following lines: that it should be murder if a person causes death by an unlawful act intended to cause fear (of death or serious injury) and known to the defendant to involve a risk of causing death."

## Draft Criminal Code Bill 1989, (Law Com. No. 177), clause 54(1):

"A person is guilty of murder if he causes the death of another—
(a) intending to cause death; or
(b) intending to cause serious personal harm and being aware that he may cause death."

It should be recalled that this Bill defined intention as including oblique intention: a person acts intentionally with respect to a result when "he acts either in order to bring it about or being aware that it will occur in the ordinary course of events".[70]

There are serious problems with any approach based on foresight of a probability of a consequence occurring.[71] In this respect the demise of *Hyam* is to be welcomed. However, the Draft Criminal Code Bill, in that it endorses a concept of "oblique intention" and links the grievous bodily harm rule to an awareness that death "may" result, is to be treated with caution. This is preserving one species of risk-taking. It is difficult, however, to see why the other forms of risk-taking are not regarded as equally reprehensible. Surely, being grossly reckless as to *death* is at least on a par morally with intending serious injury and being aware that one "may" cause death—especially if "may" covers knowledge that there is a *chance*, albeit a minute one, of death resulting.[72]

Alternative approaches are possible and deserve consideration.

### American Law Institute, Model Penal Code, Proposed Official Draft, 1962:

"Section 210.3 *Murder*
(1) ... [C]riminal homicide constitutes murder when:
   (a) it is committed purposely or knowingly; or
   (b) it is committed recklessly under circumstances manifesting extreme indifference to the value of human life. Such recklessness and indifference are presumed if the actor is engaged or is an accomplice in the commission of, or an attempt to commit, or flight after committing or attempting to commit robbery, rape or deviate sexual intercourse by force or threat of force, arson, burglary, kidnapping or felonious escape.
   [Under s.210.3 it is manslaughter when a criminal homicide is 'committed recklessly'.]"

Thus under the Mode Penal Code formulation the distinction between murder and manslaughter is a distinction between extreme recklessness and recklessness.

Critics of this formulation ask: When does "reckless" become "extremely reckless"? "It is like drawing the weight line between a 'big bear' and an 'extremely big bear' ",[73] and the Criminal Law Revision Committee has stated:

"It seems to us that, apart from the adjective 'extreme', this formula merely restates a requirement of recklessness as to causing death in somewhat emotive terms. Everyone who recklessly causes death must by definition manifest indifference to the value of human life; at least, he is indifferent to the extent of being willing to run the risk of extinguishing life in the particular circumstances. ... [W]e do not think that an adjective like 'extreme' is a satisfactory way of excluding from the law of murder cases of risk-taking that ought not to be included. We conclude that recklessness alone, of whatever degree, should not be

---

[70] Cl 18(b)(ii).
[71] Such tests cannot be defined exclusively by reference to mathematical probabilities. See further, the previous edition of this book at pp. 648–649.
[72] Clarkson and Keating, "Codification: Offences against the Person under the Draft Criminal Code" (1986) 50 J.Crim.L. 405.
[73] Moreland, "A Re-examination of the Law of Homicide in 1971: The Model Penal Code", (1971) 59 Ky.L.J. 788, 828 at 798.

a sufficient mental element for murder. Murder should be limited, insofar as a definition can do so, to the worst cases, and, other things being equal, to kill a person by taking an unreasonable risk of doing so, wicked though it is, is not as bad as intentionally to kill another."[74]

The commentary to the Model Penal Code argues, on the other hand, that some reckless homicides are as reprehensible as deliberate homicides and thus need to be classed as murder:

"Since risk, however, is a matter of degree and the motives for risk creation may be infinite in variation, some formula is needed to identify the case where recklessness should be assimilated to purpose or knowledge. The conception that the draft employs is that of extreme indifference to the value of human life. The significance of purpose or knowledge is that, cases of provocation apart, it demonstrates precisely such indifference. Whether recklessness is so extreme that it demonstrates similar indifference is not a question that, in our view, can be further clarified; it must be left directly to the trier of the facts. If recklessness exists but is not so extreme, the homicide is manslaughter."[75]

Such a test is not dissimilar to one commonly employed in the United States that it is murder "when the circumstances attending the killing show an abandoned and malignant heart",[76] or if the killing is committed "under circumstances which show utter disregard for human life".[77]

### Robert Goff, "The Mental Element in the Crime of Murder" (1988) 104 L.Q.R. 30 at 54–58:

"It is on the element commonly known as 'wicked recklessness' that I now wish to concentrate. Sheriff Gordon comments:
'Recklessness is . . . not so much a question of gross negligence as of wickedness. Wicked recklessness is recklessness so gross that it indicates a state of mind which is as wicked and depraved as the state of mind of a deliberate killer.' (*The Criminal Law of Scotland* (2nd ed., 1978) at pp. 735–736) . . .
Now we may not be too happy about the use of the word 'wicked,' which is perhaps rather emotive; but the concept is clear enough—it is the fact that the accused did not care whether the victim lived or died—which can be epitomised as indifference to death.
I think it important to observe that the principle so stated does not necessarily involve a conscious appreciation of the risk of death at the relevant time. This is of importance, because we can think of many cases in which it can be said that the accused acted regardless of the consequences, not caring whether the victim lived or died, and yet did not consciously appreciate the risk of death in his mind at the time—for example, when a man acts in the heat of the moment, as when he lashes out with a knife in the heat of a fight; or when a man acts in panic, or in blind rage. These circumstances may explain why the man has gone to the extent of acting as he did, not caring whether the victim lived or died; but I cannot see that the fact

---

[74] 14th Report, *Offences Against the Person*, Cmnd.7844, para. 26.
[75] Commentary to 9th Tent. Draft, p. 29.
[76] Cal. Penal Code, s.188.
[77] Wis.Stat.Ann. s.940.02(1).

that, in consequence, he did not have the risk of death in his mind at the time should prevent him from being held guilty of murder, and this indeed appears to be the position in Scots law . . .

*Cases of intention to cause grievous bodily harm.* As I see it, adoption of the concept of 'wicked recklessness' provides a far more just solution than does this form of intent, and indeed renders it surplus to requirements . . .

So it looks as though the concept of 'wicked recklessness' works well in practice. Moreover, having regard to the reactions of judges and juries in some of the decided cases, it appears to produce results which conform to their feelings. It has another advantage, because, with this as an alternative, intention to kill can be confined to its ordinary meaning—did the defendant mean to kill the victim? We do not have to try to expand intention by artificial concepts such as oblique intention. Furthermore, in directing juries on intention to kill, judges should not have to embark on complicated dissertations about foresight of consequences and such like. With the alternative of 'wicked recklessness' open to them, the jury in *Hancock* (the case of the striking miners) should not have been puzzled if they had been told to ask themselves the simple questions—did the defendants mean to kill? Or did they act totally regardless of the consequences, indifferent whether anybody in the convoy died or not?"

The advantage of such a proposal is that it attempts to capture the moral difference between murder and manslaughter, rather than concentrating on the form of the distinction.

The distinction between murder and manslaughter should be based on a policy of discrimination between "ethically extremely blameworthy attitudes on the part of the offender toward the life he took on the one hand and attitudes which are considerably less blameworthy on the other".[78] The distinction need not necessarily be drawn in cognitive terms (what the defendant intended or foresaw). Rather, as Lord Goff suggests above, it could depend on a moral judgment of the defendant's actions. Such judgment must reflect community values which can be represented by the jury. Again, a problem with this approach is the inherent uncertainty and unpredictability involved—although in the United States a certain jurisprudence has grown up around the concept of "a depraved and malignant heart". For example, use of a dangerous weapon can be indicative of such "depravity", whereas use of a motor car with its greater social utility can be a pointer in the opposite direction.[79] The test is also more likely to be satisfied where the defendant's acts create a grave risk to human life generally as opposed to merely risking the life of an individual.[80]

There are, however, problems with such a test which would not "mean much to a cardiologist".[81]

### People v Phillips, 64 C.2d 574; 51 Cal.Rptr. 225, 414 P.2d 353 (Supreme Court of California)

Tobriner J.:

"The [direction to the jury] of the 'abandoned and malignant heart' could lead the jury to equate the malignant heart with an evil disposition or a despicable character; the jury, then,

---

[78] Mueller, "Where Murder Begins" (1960) 2 New Hamps B.J. 214 at 217. *Contra*, Williams, "The *Mens Rea* for Murder" (1989) 105 L.Q.R. 387.
[79] *People v Phillips*, 64 C.2d 574; 51 Cal.Rptr. 255; 414 P.2d 353.
[80] *McCormack v State*, 431 So. 2d 1336 (Ala. Crim.App.1982).
[81] *Windham v State*, 602 So. 2d 798 (Miss. 1992).

in a close case, may convict because it believes the defendant a 'bad man.' We should not turn the focus of the jury's task from close analysis of the facts to loose evaluation of defendant's character....

The instruction in terms of 'abandoned and malignant heart' contains a further vice. It may encourage the jury to apply an objective rather than a subjective standard in determining whether the defendant acted with conscious disregard of life, thereby entirely obliterating the line which separates murder from involuntary manslaughter."[82]

Wilson, in a similar vein, has suggested an expansion of the law of murder so that it would cover "what it is about the 'murderer' which we find so appalling. Murderers, in the focal sense, show themselves to be a peculiar kind of person, uncomprehended by civilized society. Shooting into a train carries a small risk but it is a type of risk-taking which causes us to question the shooter's humanity." However, to avoid the vagueness associated with the Scottish "wicked recklessness" and American "depraved-heart" approaches, he suggests that there is a distinct wrong involved in cases where death results from an attack. The nature of the "attack" necessary for murder can be defined with some precision.

### William Wilson, "Murder and the Structure of Homicide" in Ashworth and Mitchell (eds), *Rethinking English Homicide Law* (2000), pp. 38–45:

"I shall argue for an extended fault element to take into account two forms of risk-taking ... each involv[ing], as does GBH-murder, a purposive attack upon a victim's corporal interests ...

*1. Intending to Expose Someone to Mortal Danger*
... What distinguishes Messrs Hyam and other risk-takers as murderers ... is that the point of their action is victim-centred or, for want of a better expression, 'aimed at' a victim. Looked at another way, which indicates how distinct in terms of moral responsibility the two attitudes are, the (merely) reckless killer acts despite the risk of death. Mrs Hyam ... act[ed] because of it. If there was no risk to life attending their conduct they would not have acted in the way they did; they would have changed their behaviour. Taking the risk thus structures their conduct ... [T]he proposed refined mental element ... [is] an intention to expose someone to mortal danger. As such it would neatly accommodate cases provided for by the American depraved-heart doctrine without succumbing to its emotionalism and conceptual vagueness ...

*2. Risk-Taking in the Course of Violent Crime.*
... A proposal for elevating recklessness above the ordinary is to tie risk-taking constitutive of murder into particularly heinous contexts such as the commission of dangerous felonies. In a number of jurisdictions a criminal context aggravates an intentional killing. There is no obvious reason why such a context should not also aggravate a reckless killing such that it is 'pushed' through a higher 'threshold' of blame ... (Wilson then considers some hypothetical examples, such as a rape victim being thrown into a river to destroy evidence of the rapist's involvement.) Each of these cases involves the defendant in an activity which already involves an attack upon the physical interests of another. It is submitted that it should not be

---

[82] For example, in *People v Roe* 74 N.Y. 2d 20, 542 N.E. 2d 610 (1989) it was stated that the defendant's subjective mental state was not relevant for a finding of depraved indifference murder; the test was whether the defendant's conduct objectively created a very substantial risk of death.

necessary to show further either an intention to cause serious injury or a specific intention to expose the victim to the risk of death. His willingness 'to go the extra distance' should suffice for murder.

The main problem here is in circumscribing the 'unholy' context ... The simplest way of doing so, and one which would dovetail satisfactorily with GBH-murder, is to require the unlawful object to be the commission of a crime ordinarily involving an attack on or threat to the autonomy or bodily integrity of another or to involve hostile activity in evading capture or lawful arrest ... A tentative proposal follows:

Criminal homicide also constitutes murder when—
    1(a) death results from the reckless exposure of another to a serious risk of death; and
      (b) D. acted either
       (i) for the purpose of resisting arrest; or
       (ii) in the execution of and for the purpose of executing any specified offence, or for the purpose of evading capture or detection following the commission or attempted commission of such offence.
      (c) The specified offences are robbery, serious sexual assault, torture, whether or not serious injury was thereby effected or intended, abduction."

The problem with this approach is that, as we shall see, persons who kill while committing dangerous, unlawful acts are guilty of manslaughter. Therefore, all that would distinguish murder (under Wilson's proposal) from manslaughter in these cases is that for murder the death must result from "the reckless exposure of another to the serious risk of death". This seems little different to the Scottish test of "wicked recklessness" advocated by Lord Goff.

## 3. Conclusion

As long as murder is retained as a separate crime, it must be reserved for the "worst", "most reprehensible" killings. Emotive tests such as those involving criteria of depravity or wantonness must be rejected; judgments must relate to people's actions, not to their characters. The better view is that the Draft Criminal Code's proposed test is inadequate in that *only* the mental state of the defendant is considered—whether it be intention or a requisite degree of foresight. The better view is that the test of "worst" or "most reprehensible" can only be determined by reference to current community values as to which killings are morally the most blameworthy. In assessing this, the mental element of the defendant will usually be of primary importance—but not of exclusive importance. Arguably there can be room for a consideration of other important factors, such as the circumstances or methods of the killing[83] and the social utility, if any, of the actions causing death. Such factors are excluded from consideration under the Draft Criminal Code's tests but, as we have seen, the concept of recklessness does allow, to some extent, for a consideration of such factors.[84] It is clear that recklessness *simpliciter* is too broad a concept to isolate the "worst" killings. What is needed is a test that can isolate killings by *gross* recklessness. Of the formulations considered in this chapter, perhaps the Model Penal Code's definition of murder (which is not dissimilar from Wilson's proposals) comes closest to allowing room for a wide-ranging assessment of the morality of the deed.

[83] See *below*, pp. 731–732.
[84] See *above*, pp. 169–172.

Or, perhaps, distinguishing murder from manslaughter is such an impossible task that we ought to abandon the effort and simply merge the two crimes into one offence of unlawful homicide. We shall return to consider this possibility after the remaining categories of homicide have been investigated.

## IV. MANSLAUGHTER

The crime of manslaughter is committed when a defendant commits the *actus reus* of homicide but the killing is not sufficiently blameworthy to warrant liability for murder. This will be so in two situations:

1. where the defendant does not have the necessary mental element for murder (malice aforethought), but can nevertheless be regarded as blameworthy to some extent (involuntary manslaughter); or

2. where the defendant does possess the necessary malice aforethought for murder, but has killed under certain specific circumstances which the law regards as mitigating the seriousness of the offence (voluntary manslaughter).

The lesser blameworthiness is reflected by an avoidance of both the label and stigma of murder and the mandatory penalty of life imprisonment imposed for murder. The maximum penalty for the crime of manslaughter is life imprisonment, enabling the judge to impose any sentence up to that maximum to reflect the appropriate degree of culpability of the defendant.[85]

### A. *Involuntary Manslaughter*

"[O]f all crimes manslaughter appears to afford most difficulties of definition, for it concerns homicide in so many and so varying conditions."[86]

This is because manslaughters range from killings just short of murder to killings only just above the accidental. This can be represented diagrammatically[87]:

| | A | | B | |
|---|---|---|---|---|
| MURDER | MANSLAUGHTER | | ACCIDENTAL KILLINGS | |

In assessing the parameters of the crime of manslaughter, attention must be focused on two questions:

(a) How is manslaughter distinguished from murder (A)? Despite the minimal discussion of manslaughter in *Woollin* and the other leading cases, the House of Lords, in defining the parameters of the crime of murder was, in essence, focusing on the distinction between murder and manslaughter. The point at which this line was drawn was considered above.

---

[85] Offences against the Person Act 1861, s.5.
[86] *Andrews v D.P.P.* [1937] A.C. 576, *per* Lord Atkin. These difficulties extend through to the sentencing stage. See, for example, *Cawthorne* [1996] 2 Cr.App.R(S) 445; *Byrne* [2003] 1 Cr.App.R.(S) 68. There is no guideline sentencing decision on manslaughter because of the breadth of the offence.
[87] Justifiable killings have not been included in this diagram.

(b) How is manslaughter distinguished from accidental or non-culpable killings (B)? What factors make a killing sufficiently blameworthy to justify liability for manslaughter as opposed to liability for some lesser offence or no liability at all? It is this question that requires close consideration in this section.

During the last 20 years or so, the law of involuntary manslaughter has been the subject of very considerable change. It is now common to assert that it takes three forms:

(1) (Subjective) reckless manslaughter;

(2) Gross negligence manslaughter;

(3) Constructive or unlawful act manslaughter.

It should be stressed at the outset that these are not three separate crimes. Indeed, there is no discreet crime of "involuntary manslaughter" in the sense that one is charged with or convicted of the offence. The term "involuntary manslaughter" is simply a convenient label to describe those residual unlawful killings not otherwise specifically catered for by the law and the culpability necessary for the offence can be established in one of the above three ways.

### 1. (Subjective) Reckless manslaughter

Where the defendant subjectively foresees a risk of death or serious injury (but the degree of foresight fails to come within the *Woollin* test of intention required for murder), there will be liability for manslaughter.[88] As the law of murder has been progressively narrowed with tighter tests of intention, so this category of manslaughter has been correspondingly broadened to occupy the "area vacated by murder".[89] There is little specific authority on this species of manslaughter because in practice such cases are usually dealt with as constructive manslaughter.[90] This category also covers cases where the defendant is charged with murder but the jury convict of manslaughter[91] or the appellate courts substitute a verdict of manslaughter[92] or where the defendant pleads guilty to manslaughter having a plea of not guilty to murder accepted.[93]

### 2. Gross negligence manslaughter

Most manslaughter cases involve the commission of an unlawful act, usually an assault,[94] and so constructive manslaughter is easier to establish. Accordingly, gross negligence manslaughter is utilised where the defendant is engaged in a *prima facie* lawful activity, such as treating a patient or taking care of an aged aunt, from which death results. Mere negligence does not suffice for manslaughter: gross negligence must be established. The classic statement on gross negligence is that of Lord Hewitt C.J. in *Bateman* that:

---

[88] Law Commission, *Legislating the Criminal Code: Involuntary Manslaughter* (Law Com. No. 237) (1996), para. 5.15. The existence of this category of manslaughter was confirmed in *Lidar* LTL 12/11/99.

[89] JC Smith, Commentary to *Adomako* [1994] Crim.L.R.758 at 759.

[90] Law Com. No. 237, para. 2.27.

[91] See, for example, *Kime* [1999] 2 Cr.App.R.(S.) 3.

[92] See for example, *Woollin* [1999] 1 Cr.App.R.8.

[93] See, for example, *Jackson* [1999] 2 Cr.App.R.(S.) 77.

[94] In a survey of 56 involuntary manslaughter sentencing cases there was no unlawful act in only five cases (Clarkson, "Context and Culpability in Involuntary Manslaughter: Principle or Instinct?" in Ashworth and Mitchell (eds), *Rethinking English Homicide Law* (2000).

"in order to establish criminal liability the facts must be such that, in the opinion of the jury, the negligence of the accused went beyond a mere matter of compensation between the subjects and showed such disregard for the life and safety of others as to amount to a crime against the state and conduct deserving of punishment."[95]

For a period it was thought that this basis of manslaughter had been subsumed into *Lawrence* recklessness manslaughter.[96] However, in the following case, the House of Lords jettisoned *Lawrence* in the context of manslaughter and reverted to the test of gross negligence.

## R. v Adomako [1995] 1 A.C. 171 (House of Lords)

The defendant was an anaesthetist in an eye operation which involved paralysing the patient. During the operation a tube became disconnected from the ventilator. The defendant became aware that something was wrong four and a half minutes after the disconnection when an alarm sounded. However, the checks he carried out failed to reveal the disconnection. The patient suffered a cardiac arrest and died. The defendant was convicted of manslaughter and appealed. His appeal was dismissed by the Court of Appeal. He appealed to the House of Lords.

Lord Mackay of Clashfern, L.C.:
"For the prosecution it was alleged that the appellant was guilty of gross negligence in failing to notice or respond appropriately to obvious signs that a disconnection had occurred and that the patient had ceased to breathe. In particular the prosecution alleged that the appellant had failed to notice at various stages during the period after disconnection and before the arrest either occurred or became inevitable that the patient's chest was not moving, the dials on the mechanical ventilating machine were not operating, the disconnection in the endotracheal tube, that the alarm on the ventilator was not switched on and that the patient was becoming progressively blue. Further the prosecution alleged that the appellant had noticed but failed to understand the significance of the fact that during this period the patient's pulse had dropped and the patient's blood pressure had dropped.

Two expert witnesses gave evidence for the prosecution. Professor Payne described the standard of care as 'abysmal' while Professor Adams stated that in his view a competent anaesthetist should have recognised the signs of disconnection within 15 seconds and that the appellant's conduct amounted to 'a gross dereliction of care'.

On behalf of the appellant it was conceded at his trial that he had been negligent. The issue was therefore whether his conduct was criminal ...

The jury convicted the appellant of manslaughter ... The Court of Appeal (Criminal Division) dismissed the appellant's appeal against conviction but certified that a point of law of general public importance was involved in the decision to dismiss the appeal, namely: 'in cases of manslaughter by criminal negligence not involving driving but involving a breach of duty is it a sufficient direction to the jury to adopt the gross negligence test ... [as in *Bateman*] without reference to the test of recklessness as defined in *R. v Lawrence (Stephen)*?' ...

[Counsel for the appellant] criticised the concept of gross negligence which was the basis of the judgment of the Court of Appeal submitting that its formulation involved circularity, the jury being told in effect to convict of a crime if they thought a crime had been committed and that accordingly using gross negligence as the conceptual basis for the crime of

[95] (1925) 19 Cr.App.R.8.
[96] *Seymour* [1983] 2 A.C. 493.

involuntary manslaughter was unsatisfactory and the court should apply the law laid down in *Seymour* generally to all cases of involuntary manslaughter or at least use this as the basis for providing general applicability and acceptability.

I begin with *Rex v Bateman*, and the opinion of Lord Hewart C.J., where he said:

'In expounding the law to juries on the trial of indictments for manslaughter by negligence, judges have often referred to the distinction between civil and criminal liability for death by negligence. The law of criminal liability for negligence is conveniently explained in that way. If A has caused the death of B by alleged negligence, then, in order to establish civil liability, the plaintiff must prove (in addition to pecuniary loss caused by the death) that A owed a duty to B to take care, that that duty was not discharged, and that the default caused the death of B. To convict A of manslaughter, the prosecution must prove the three things above mentioned and must satisfy the jury, in addition, that A's negligence amounted to a crime. In the civil action, if it is proved that A fell short of the standard of reasonable care required by law, it matters not how far he fell short of that standard. The extent of his liability depends not on the degree of negligence, but on the amount of damage done. In criminal court, on the contrary, the amount and degree of negligence are the determining question. There must be *mens rea*.'

Later he said:

'In explaining to juries the test which they should apply to determine whether the negligence, in the particular case, amounted or did not amount to a crime, judges have used many epithets, such as "culpable", "criminal", "gross", "wicked", "clear", "complete". But, whatever epithet be used and whether an epithet be used or not, in order to establish criminal liability the facts must be such that, in the opinion of the jury, the negligence of the accused went beyond a mere matter of compensation between subjects and showed such disregard for the life and safety of others as to amount to a crime against the state and conduct deserving punishment.' ...

Next I turn to *Andrews v Director of Public Prosecutions* [1937] A.C. 576 which was a case of manslaughter through the dangerous driving of a motor car. ... Lord Atkin said:

'... Simple lack of care such as will constitute civil liability is not enough: for purposes of the criminal law there are degrees of negligence: and a very high degree of negligence is required to be proved before the felony is established. Probably of all the epithets that can be applied "reckless" most nearly covers the case. It is difficult to visualise a case of death caused by reckless driving in the connotation of that term in ordinary speech which would not justify a conviction for manslaughter: but it is probably not all-embracing, for "reckless" suggests an indifference to risk whereas the accused may have appreciated the risk and intended to avoid it and yet shown such a high degree of negligence in the means adopted to avoid the risk as would justify a conviction. If the principle of *Bateman's* case is observed it will appear that the law of manslaughter has not changed by the introduction of motor vehicles on the road. Death caused by their negligent driving, though unhappily much more frequent, is to be treated in law as death caused by any other form of negligence: and juries should be directed accordingly.'

In my opinion the law as stated in these two authorities is satisfactory as providing a proper basis for describing the crime of involuntary manslaughter. Since the decision in *Andrews* was a decision of your Lordships' House, it remains the most authoritative statement of the present law which I have been able to find ... On this basis in my opinion the ordinary principles of the law of negligence apply to ascertain whether or not the defendant has been in breach of a duty of care towards the victim who has died. If such breach of duty is established the next question is whether that breach of duty caused the death of the victim. If so, the jury must go on to consider whether that breach of duty should be characterised as gross negligence and therefore as a crime. This will depend on the seriousness of the breach of duty committed by the defendant in all the circumstances in which the defendant was placed when it occurred. The jury will have to consider whether the extent to which the defendant's conduct departed from the proper standard of care incumbent upon him, involving as it must have done a risk of death to the patient, was such that it should be judged criminal.

It is true that to a certain extent this involves an element of circularity, but in this branch of the law I do not believe that is fatal to its being correct as a test of how far conduct must depart from accepted standards to be characterised as criminal. This is necessarily a question of degree and an attempt to specify that degree more closely is I think likely to achieve only a spurious precision. The essence of the matter which is supremely a jury question is whether having regard to the risk of death involved, the conduct of the defendant was so bad in all the circumstances as to amount in their judgment to a criminal act or omission. ...

My Lords, in my view the law as stated in *R. v Seymour* should no longer apply since the underlying statutory provisions on which it rested have now been repealed by the Road Traffic Act 1991. It may be that cases of involuntary motor manslaughter will as a result become rare but I consider it unsatisfactory that there should be any exception to the generality of the statement which I have made, since such exception, in my view, gives rise to unnecessary complexity. ...

I consider it perfectly appropriate that the word 'reckless' should be used in cases of involuntary manslaughter, but as Lord Atkin put it 'in the ordinary connotation of that word'. Examples in which this was done, to my mind, with complete accuracy are *R. v Stone [and Dobinson]* [1977] Q.B. 354 and *R. v West London Coroner, ex p. Gray* [1988] Q.B. 467.

In my opinion it is quite unnecessary in the context of gross negligence to give the detailed directions with regard to the meaning of the word 'reckless' associated with *R. v Lawrence*. ...

For these reasons I am of the opinion that this appeal should be dismissed and that the certified question should be answered by saying:

'In cases of manslaughter by criminal negligence involving a breach of duty, it is a sufficient direction to the jury to adopt the gross negligence test set out by the Court of Appeal in the present case following *Rex v Bateman* and *Andrews v Director of Public Prosecutions* and that it is not necessary to refer to the definition of recklessness in *R. v Lawrence*, although it is perfectly open to the trial judge to use the word "reckless" in its ordinary meaning as part of his exposition of the law if he deems it appropriate in the circumstances of the particular case.' "

**Appeal dismissed**

Following this, there are three conditions to be satisfied for this type of manslaughter:

1. the defendant must owe a duty of care to the victim;
2. the defendant must breach that duty;
3. the breach must amount to gross negligence.

The first requirement that there be a "duty of care" has the potential to cause confusion. It is simply not helpful to import civil concepts into this area of the criminal law. Fortunately, the following decision emphatically states that concepts such as "duty of care" and "breach" do not bear the same meaning in the criminal law as under the law of tort.

### R. v Wacker [2003] 1 Cr.App.R.22 (Court of Appeal, Criminal Division)

The appellant attempted to smuggle illegal Chinese immigrants into the country in a lorry. On arrival at Dover one of the containers have found to contain the dead bodies of most of the immigrants. The appellant was convicted of 58 offences of manslaughter and appealed.

Kay L.J.:

"[Counsel for the appellant] submitted that the first question to be decided was whether applying 'the ordinary principles of the law of negligence', the appellant owed to those in the container a duty of care. He submitted that one of the general principles of the law of negligence, known by the Latin maxim of *ex turpi causa non oritur actio*, was that the law of negligence did not recognise the relationship between those involved in a criminal enterprise as giving rise to a duty of care owed by one participant to another. ...

We venture to suggest that all right minded people would be astonished if the propositions being advanced on behalf of the appellant correctly represented the law of the land. The concept that one person could be responsible for the death of another in circumstances such as these without the criminal law being able to hold him to account for that death even if he had shown not the slightest regard for the welfare and life of the other is one that would be unacceptable in civilised society ...

[I]t is clear that the criminal law adopts a different approach to the civil law in this regard [because] ... the very same public policy that causes the civil courts to refuse the claim points in a quite different direction in considering a criminal offence. The criminal law has as its function the protection of citizens and gives effect to the state's duty to try those who have deprived citizens of their rights of life, limb or property. It may very well step in at the precise moment when civil courts withdraw because of this very different function. The withdrawal of a civil remedy has nothing to do with whether as a matter of public policy the criminal law applies. The criminal law should not be disapplied just because the civil law is disapplied. It has its own public policy aim which may require a different approach to the involvement of the law.

Further, the criminal law will not hesitate to act to prevent serious injury or death even when the persons subjected to such injury or death may have consented to or willingly accepted the risk of actual injury or death. By way of illustration, the criminal law makes the assisting another to commit suicide a criminal offence and denies a defence of consent where significant injury is deliberately caused to another in a sexual context (*Brown* [1994] 1 A.C. 212). The state in such circumstances has a overriding duty to act to prevent such consequences.

[W]e can see no justification for concluding that the criminal law should decline to hold a person as criminally responsible for the death of another simply because the two were engaged in some joint unlawful activity at the time or, indeed, because there may have been an element of acceptance of a degree of risk by the victim in order to further the joint unlawful enterprise. Public policy, in our judgment, manifestly points in totally the opposite direction."

**Appeal dismissed**

If the civil law is (rightly) not to be employed here, it is difficult to see what the *Adomako* requirement of "duty of care" actually means—especially as it is clear we all owe a duty to other persons not to expose them to a risk of death. Possibly the requirement of a "duty of care" has most significance for the law relating to manslaughter by omission. The Law Commission argues that *Adomako* may have changed the law by restricting the scope of duties to act in criminal cases by equating it with that of tort where, generally, liability does not flow if a defendant abandons an effort to care for someone (unless, he causes harm through his own incompetence).[97] For example, the defendants in *Stone and Dobinson* might not have been liable in tort. It would, however, be extremely surprising if Lord Mackay's comments were interpreted as (inadvertently) altering the relatively established body of criminal law rules relating to omissions.

Whether these civil law concepts are given any meaning or not, it is clear that the critical requirement for this type of manslaughter is that there has been gross negligence. The rejection of *Lawrence* means that there is no longer any scope for

---

[97] Law Commission, *Legislating the Criminal Code: Involuntary Manslaughter* (Law Com. No. 237, 1996), paras 3.12–3.13. The Law Commission concludes that the language of tort is best avoided.

an argument that the defendant ruled out the risks. The test is simply one of determining how far the standard of behaviour of the defendant departs from accepted standards and this is "supremely a jury question". The jury must assess whether, having regard to the risk of death, the conduct was so bad in all the circumstances as to be criminal.

This unanimous decision of the House of Lords in *Adomako* (which applies irrespective of the method of killing[98]) has received a mixed response.[99] There are substantial problems with the decision.

First, the test to be employed by juries is circular. They should find the defendant's actions criminal (manslaughter) if they think the conduct falls so far below proper standards of care that it should be judged criminal. This amounts to leaving questions of law to the jury as it is for them to decide whether the conduct amounts to a crime. Further, no guidance is given as to how far below accepted standards of behaviour the defendant's conduct must fall other than that the conduct must be "so bad" in all the circumstances as to warrant criminalisation as manslaughter. This absence of any legally defined criteria renders the law highly uncertain and increases the chances of inconsistency of verdicts.

Secondly, it is perhaps unclear what type of risk is required. While Lord Mackay refers to the "risk of death", his approval of other authorities such as *Bateman* ("disregard for life and safety"), *Stone* ("disregard of danger to the health and welfare of the infirm person") and *R. v West London Coroner, ex p. Gray* ("obvious and serious risk to the health and welfare") suggests that a risk of something less than death will suffice. However, Lord Mackay twice emphasised that the risk must be one of death and this view has now been judicially confirmed.[1] In this respect (assuming that a risk of death will be required) the decision in *Adomako* is to be welcomed. Under *Lawrence* and its progeny[2] all that was required was that the defendant create an obvious and serious risk of *injury*. For a crime as serious as manslaughter, this was casting the net of liability too wide.

Finally, the decision effectively increases the number of mental elements employed by the criminal law. There is (subjective) recklessness, inadvertent recklessness and, in the context of manslaughter only, gross negligence. Not only is this accumulation regrettable but the relationship between the three concepts is unclear. Lord Mackay endorses the use of the phrase "recklessness" in involuntary manslaughter cases, if appropriate in the circumstances of the particular case, as long as it is given its "ordinary meaning". This is meant to exclude *Caldwell* and *Lawrence* recklessness but little further guidance is given. Its use in the decision of *Stone and Dobinson*,[3] for example, is described as completely accurate.

---

[98] See *below*, p. 677 for the effect of *Adomako* on so-called motor manslaughter.

[99] Smith, [1994] Crim.L.R.758; Virgo, "Reconstructing Manslaughter on Defective Foundations" [1995] C.L.J. 14 at 15. See also, Leigh, "Liability for Inadvertence: A Lordly Legacy" [1995] 58 M.L.R. 457; Gardner, "Manslaughter by Gross Negligence" (1995) 111 L.Q.R. 22.

[1] *Singh* [1999] Crim.L.R.582: *Lewin v C.P.S.* [2002] EWHC 1049 (Admin.).

[2] *Goodfellow* (1986) 83 Cr.App.R.23.

[3] [1977] Q.B. 354.

## Attorney-General's Reference (No. 2 of 1999) [2000] Q.B. 796 (Court of Appeal, Criminal Division)

Rose LJ:
"Can a defendant be properly convicted of manslaughter by gross negligence in the absence of evidence as to that defendant's state of mind? . . . [This] must be answered, Yes. Although there may be cases where the defendant's state of mind is relevant to the jury's consideration when assessing the grossness and criminality of his conduct, evidence of his state of mind is not a prerequisite to a conviction for manslaughter by gross negligence. The *Adomako* test is objective, but a defendant who is reckless as defined in *R. v Stone, R. v Dobinson* may well be the more readily found to be grossly negligent to a criminal degree."

These comments do not help clarify the law. In certain cases a reference to recklessness could be appropriate where there is advertence or a "could not care less" attitude on the part of the defendant. However, the approval of *Stone and Dobinson* suggests that in such cases foresight of a lesser risk than death (namely, "disregard of danger to the health and welfare of the infirm person") might suffice. Where, however, there is inadvertence, as in *Adomako* itself, references to recklessness seem misplaced. It is unfortunate that the opportunity to clarify these issues has been lost and one is left contemplating possible interpretations.[4]

What is clear is that the risk of inconsistent verdicts has increased and that *Adomako* has not removed the need for reform.

### 3. Constructive manslaughter

As a corollary of the felony-murder rule, the law developed a misdemeanour-manslaughter rule whereby it was manslaughter to kill in the course of committing a misdemeanour. The obvious rigours of such a rule were soon mitigated, and this species of manslaughter survived the abolition of the felony-murder rule and abolition of the distinction between felonies and misdemeanours. The present law may be stated in the following terms:

(i) The defendant must commit an unlawful act; and
(ii) The unlawful act must be dangerous, namely, it must expose the victim to the risk of some bodily harm resulting therefrom.

### (i) *The unlawful act*

Not all unlawful acts will suffice for constructive manslaughter. Three limitations upon the earlier rule have been developed:

(a) The unlawful act must constitute a crime. A tort or other civil wrong will not suffice. In *Franklin*,[5] Field J. ruled that "the mere fact of a civil wrong committed by one person against another ought not to be used as an incident which is a necessary step in a criminal case. I have a great abhorrence of constructive crime."

Further, if the defendant would have a defence (say, self-defence) to the unlawful act, then there is no "crime" for the purposes of constructive manslaughter.[6]

(b) The act must be criminal for some other reason than that it has been negligently performed. For example, driving a car is a lawful act; driving that car

---

[4] See further, Gardner, "Manslaughter by Gross Negligence" [1995] 111 L.Q.R. 22 and Leigh, "Liability for Inadvertance: A Lordly Legacy" [1995] 58 M.L.R. 457.
[5] (1883) 15 Cox C.C. 163.
[6] *Scarlett* (1994) 98 Cr.App.R.290.

negligently is a criminal offence. Such a crime will not suffice for constructive manslaughter. In *Andrews v D.P.P.* Lord Atkin held:

"There is an obvious difference in the law of manslaughter between doing an unlawful act and doing a lawful act with a degree of carelessness which the legislature makes criminal. If it were otherwise a man who killed another while driving without due care and attention would *ex necessitate* commit manslaughter."[7]

(c) It is doubtful whether an omission will suffice for constructive manslaughter. In *Lowe* it was held that the mere fact that a parent was guilty of the statutory offence of wilful neglect of a child, did not make that parent liable for manslaughter if the child died in consequence of the neglect.

### R. v Lowe [1973] Q.B. 702 (Court of Appeal, Criminal Division)

Phillimore L.J. said:

"Now in the present case the jury negatived recklessness. How then can mere neglect amount to manslaughter? The court feels that there is something inherently unattractive in a theory of constructive manslaughter. It seems strange that an omission which is wilful solely in the sense that it is not inadvertent and the consequences of which are not in fact foreseen by the person who is neglectful should, if death results, automatically give rise to an indeterminate sentence instead of the maximum of two years which would otherwise be the limit imposed.

We think that there is a clear distinction between an act of omission and an act of commission likely to cause harm. Whatever may be the position with regard to the latter it does not follow that the same is true of the former. In other words, if I strike a child in a manner likely to cause harm it is right that, if the child dies, I may be charged with manslaughter. If, however, I omit to do something with the result that it suffers injury to health which results in its death, we think that a charge of manslaughter should not be the inevitable consequence, even if the omission is deliberate."[8]

Apart from these three limitations it would appear that any unlawful act will suffice. It is irrelevant whether that act previously constituted a felony or a misdemeanour. In practice, however, the majority of constructive manslaughter cases are based on some form of assault as the unlawful act. In a survey of 56 manslaughter sentencing appeals, 51 of the cases involved the commission of an unlawful act. Of these, only five cases did not involve an attack amounting to at least a common assault.[9]

### R. v Lamb [1967] 2 Q.B. 981 (Court of Appeal, Criminal Division)

Lamb, in jest, with no intention of doing any harm, pointed a revolver at his best friend who was similarly treating the incident as a joke. He knew there were two bullets in the chambers but as neither bullet was in the chamber opposite the barrel he did not foresee any danger. He pulled the trigger; this rotated the cylinder and placed a bullet opposite the barrel so that it was struck by the striking pin. The bullet was fired and the friend killed. Three experts agreed that Lamb's mistake was natural for somebody unfamiliar with the way the revolver mechanism worked. Lamb was convicted of manslaughter and appealed.

[7] [1937] A.C. 576 at 585.

[8] [1973] Q.B. 702 at 709. In stating that manslaughter should not be the *inevitable* consequence Phillimore L.J. was presumably conceding that, while an omission will not suffice for constructive manslaughter, it can form the basis of a manslaughter conviction if there has been gross negligence or recklessness as discussed above.

[9] Clarkson, *above*, n.94.

Sachs J.:

"The trial judge took the view that the pointing of the revolver and pulling of the trigger was something which could of itself be unlawful even if there was no attempt to alarm or intent to injure.

It was no doubt on that basis that he had before commencing his summing-up stated that he was not going to 'involve the jury in any consideration of the niceties of the question whether or not the' action of the 'accused did constitute or did not constitute an assault': and thus he did not refer to the defence of accident or the need for the prosecution to disprove accident before coming to a conclusion that the act was unlawful.

Mr Mathew, [counsel for the Crown] however, had at all times put forward the correct view that for the act to be unlawful it must constitute at least what he then termed 'a technical assault.' In this court moreover he rightly conceded that there was no evidence to go to the jury of any assault of any kind. Nor did he feel able to submit that the acts of the defendant were on any other ground unlawful in the criminal sense of that word. Indeed no such submission could in law be made: if, for instance, the pulling of the trigger had had no effect because the striking mechanism or the ammunition had been defective no offence would have been committed by the defendant.

Another way of putting it is that *mens rea*, being now an essential ingredient in manslaughter (compare *Andrews v Director of Public Prosecutions* and *R. v Church*) that could not in the present case be established in relation to the first ground except by proving that element of intent without which there can be no assault.

It is perhaps as well to mention that when using the phrase 'unlawful in the criminal sense of that word' the court has in mind that it is long settled that it is not in point to consider whether an act is unlawful merely from the angle of civil liabilities. That was first made clear in *R. v Franklin* ...

The whole of that part of the summing-up which concerned the first ground was thus vitiated by misdirections based on an erroneous concept of the law ...

[Sachs J. went on to rule that, while an appropriately directed jury could have convicted Lamb of manslaughter by gross negligence, the jury had not been so directed and so the verdict could not stand].

**Appeal allowed**

This case can be contrasted with that of *Larkin*[10] where the defendant brandished a razor at a man in order to terrify him. His mistress fell against the razor, cut her throat and died. Larkin's conviction for manslaughter was upheld. In this case, unlike *Lamb*, there was clearly an unlawful act, namely, an assault by intentionally terrifying the man.[11]

In *Jennings*[12] it was held that it was necessary to identify the unlawful act. In this case the Crown had relied on the offence of carrying an offensive weapon, contrary to the Prevention of Crimes Act 1953, s.1, but, as it had not been proved that the knife was an offensive weapon, there was no unlawful act for the purposes of constructive manslaughter.

In the earlier case of *Cato*[13] the defendant injected his friend, at the friend's request, with a mixture of heroin and water. The friend died. The unlawful act here

---

[10] (1942) 29 Cr.App.R.18.

[11] *cf. Arobieke* [1988] Crim.L.R.314 where a conviction for manslaughter was quashed on the basis of lack of an unlawful act. The victim, terrified of the defendant, had run away and electrocuted himself. The defendant had, however, done no more than look for the victim which was insufficient to amount to an assault.

[12] [1990] Crim.L.R.588.

[13] (1976) 62 Cr.App.R.41.

was administering a noxious thing contrary to section 23 of the Offences against the Person Act 1861. Lord Widgery CJ, however, indicated *obiter* that while it is not an offence to take prohibited drugs (as opposed to possessing or supplying such drugs), there was, nevertheless, an unlawful act of "injecting the deceased with a mixture of heroin and water which at the time of the injection and for the purposes of the injection the accused had unlawfully taken into his possession". Similarly, in *Kennedy*[14] it was held that self-injection by the deceased of heroin was an unlawful act. However, in *Dias* this approach, which amounts to little more than manufacturing an unlawful act as and when needed for the purposes of constructive manslaughter, was disapproved. In this case the deceased was supplied with heroin and injected himself and died. It was held that there was no offence of injecting oneself with prohibited drugs.[15] The only unlawful act in such situations is the supply of prohibited drugs—which, as seen earlier,[16] gives rise to problems of causation where the deceased self-injects.

### (ii) *The unlawful act must be dangerous*

It is clear that constructive manslaughter requires more than simply an unlawful act which causes death. The unlawful act must be a dangerous one, in the sense that it must expose the victim to the risk of some bodily harm resulting therefrom. The fact that an act is unlawful does not necessarily mean that it is dangerous. The requirement of dangerousness is a separate matter requiring proof.[17]

### R. v Church [1966] 1 Q.B. 59 (Court of Criminal Appeal)

The appellant knocked a woman unconscious. On failing to revive her he threw her into a river where she drowned. He appealed against his conviction for manslaughter on the ground of a misdirection by the trial judge.

Edmund-Davies L.J.:
"In the judgment of this court [the trial judge's direction on unlawful act manslaughter] ... was a misdirection. It amounted to telling the jury that, whenever any unlawful act is committed in relation to a human being which resulted in death there must be, at least, a conviction for manslaughter. This might at one time have been regarded as good law: ... But it appears to this court that the passage of years has achieved a transformation in this branch of the law and, even in relation to manslaughter, a degree of *mens rea* has become recognised as essential. ... [T]he conclusion of this court is that an unlawful act causing the death of another cannot, simply because it is an unlawful act, render a manslaughter verdict inevitable. For such a verdict inexorably to follow, the unlawful act must be such as all sober and reasonable people would inevitably recognise must subject the other person to, at least, the risk of some harm resulting therefrom, albeit not serious harm. ...

[However the trial judge's direction was not sufficiently defective to warrant quashing the conviction; further, the defendant might have been convicted on grounds of criminal negligence.]"

**Appeal dismissed**

---

[14] [1999] Crim.L.R. 65.
[15] [2002] 2 Cr.App.R.96. This approach was approved in *Richards* [2002] E.W.C.A. Crim 3175 and in *Rodgers* [2003] E.W.C.A. Crim 945. In the latter case it was held that holding a tourniquet on the arm of a person injecting himself with heroin was "playing a part in the mechanics of the injection" which was a criminal offence under s.23.
[16] *Above*, p. 456.
[17] *Scarlett* (1994) 98 Cr.App.R.290.

## D.P.P. v Newbury [1977] A.C. 500 (House of Lords)

The appellants, two boys aged 15, pushed part of a paving stone off the parapet of a railway bridge. The stone struck an oncoming train, went through the glass window of the driver's cab and killed a guard who was sitting next to the driver. The boys were convicted of manslaughter. The Court of Appeal dismissed their appeal but certified the following point of law: "Can a defendant be properly convicted of manslaughter, when his mind is not affected by drink or drugs, if he did not foresee that his act might cause harm to another?"

Lord Salmon:
"In *R. v Larkin*, Humphreys J. said:
'Where the act which a person is engaged in performing is unlawful, then if at the same time it is a dangerous act, that is, an act which is likely to injure another person, and quite inadvertently the doer of the act causes the death of that other person by that act, then he is guilty of manslaughter.'
I agree entirely ... that that is an admirably clear statement of the law which has been applied many times. It makes it plain (a) that an accused is guilty of manslaughter if it is proved that he intentionally did an act which was unlawful and dangerous and that that act inadvertently caused death and (b) that it is unnecessary to prove that the accused knew that the act was unlawful or dangerous. This is one of the reasons why cases of manslaughter vary so infinitely in their gravity. They may amount to little more than pure inadvertence and sometimes to little less than murder. ...
The test is still the objective test. In judging whether the act was dangerous the test is not did the accused recognise that it was dangerous but would all sober and reasonable people recognise its danger. ..."

Lord Edmund-Davies:
"My Lords, for the reasons developed in the speech of my noble and learned friend, Lord Salmon, I concur in holding that these appeals against conviction should be dismissed.
*R. v Church*, which the learned trial judge adopted for the purpose of his direction to the jury, marked no new departure in relation to the offence of involuntary manslaughter. In so far as the charge was based on the commission of an unlawful act causing death, the Court of Criminal Appeal was there concerned to demolish the old notion (which the direction to the jury in that case was thought to have resurrected) that, whenever *any* unlawful act is committed in relation to a human being which causes his death, there must at least be a conviction for manslaughter. ...
I would respectfully say that Widgery L.J. (who was a member of the court in *R. v Church*) was perfectly correct in observing in *R. v Lipman* [1970] 1 Q.B. 152, 159 that, 'The development recognised by *R. v Church* relates to the *type* of act from which a charge of manslaughter may result, not in the intention (real or assumed) of the prisoner.'
But, in so far as *R. v Church* has been regarded as laying down that for the proof of manslaughter in such circumstances what is required is no more than the *intentional* committing of an unlawful act of the designated type or nature, it followed a long line of authorities which the court there cited. ... Accordingly, if *R. v Church* was wrong, so was its long ancestry.
I believe that *R. v Church* accurately applied the law as it then existed. I believe, further, that, since it was decided, nothing has happened to change the law in relation to the constituents of involuntary manslaughter caused by an unlawful act. The Criminal Justice Act 1967 has certainly effected no such change, for, as I sought to show in *R. v Majewski* [1977] A.C. 443, section 8 thereof has nothing to do with *when* intent or foresight or any other mental state has to be established, but simply *how* it is to be determined where such determination is called for."

**Appeal dismissed**

It is not entirely clear what the unlawful act was that formed the basis of the manslaughter charge and conviction in *Newbury*. Was it criminal damage, common assault or the offence of "endangering the safety of any person conveyed upon a railway" contrary to the Offences against the Person Act 1861, s.34? Since *Jennings*[18] it is necessary for the prosecution to identify the wrongful act. As one is dealing here with what is often termed "unlawful act manslaughter," the requirement that the unlawful act be specified is to be welcomed.

In *Watson*[19] it was held that the "sober and reasonable" bystander was to be endowed with whatever knowledge the defendant possessed. In this case the defendant and another burgled an elderly man's house and verbally abused him. The victim was suffering from a serious heart condition and died an hour and a half later. It was held that the unlawful act, the burglary, lasted throughout the time the appellant was on the premises and during that time the defendant must have become aware of the victim's frailty and age. The question then was whether a sober and reasonable bystander, armed with this knowledge, would have recognised that the burglary was likely to expose that elderly man to the risk of some harm. In *Ball*,[20] however, it was emphasised that the sober and reasonable bystander could *not* be endowed with any mistaken belief held by the defendant. In this case the defendant fired at his victim thinking his gun contained blanks (he kept live and blank cartridges together and had grabbed a handful when picking up his gun). Such an act was unquestionably dangerous from the required objective point of view.

In *Dawson*[21] it was held that the unlawful act must expose the victim to the risk of some physical harm. Shock or pure emotional disturbance produced by terror would not suffice. However, there could be liability for manslaughter if it was likely that the shock would cause a physical injury, for example, cause a heart attack.[22]

(iii) *The unlawful act need not be directed at the victim*

It used to be thought that because the unlawful act must expose the victim to the risk of some bodily harm, it had to be aimed at that victim.

### R. v Dalby (1982) 74 Cr.App.R.348 (Court of Appeal, Criminal Division)

The appellant, who had obtained Diconal tablets upon prescription, unlawfully supplied his friend, O'Such, with some of the tablets (this was the unlawful act, namely, an offence contrary to section 4(1) of the Misuse of Drugs Act 1971). The friend injected himself intravenously with the tablets and later died. He appealed against his conviction for manslaughter.

Waller L.J.:

"The difficulty in the present case is that the act of supplying a scheduled drug was not an act which caused direct harm. It was an act which made it possible, or even likely, that harm

[18] *Above*, n.12.
[19] [1989] 1 W.L.R. 684.
[20] [1989] Crim.L.R.730.
[21] (1985) 81 Cr.App.R.23.
[22] *Williams* [1992] 2 All E.R. 183 at 191.

would occur subsequently, particularly if the drug was supplied to somebody who was on drugs. In all the reported cases, the physical act has been one which inevitably would subject the other person to the risk of some harm from the act itself. In this case, the supply of drugs would itself have caused no harm unless the deceased had subsequently used the drugs in a form and quantity which was dangerous ...

In the judgment of this Court, the unlawful act of supplying drugs was not an act directed against the person of O'Such and the supply did not cause any direct injury to him. The kind of harm envisaged in all the reported cases of involuntary manslaughter was physical injury of some kind as an immediate and inevitable result of the unlawful act, *e.g.*, a blow on the chin which knocks the victim against a wall causing a fractured skull and death, or threatening with a loaded gun which accidentally fires, or dropping a large stone on a train (*D.P.P. v Newbury*) or threatening another with an open razor and stumbling with death resulting (*Larkin*).

In the judgment of this Court, where the charge of manslaughter is based on an unlawful and dangerous act, it must be directed at the victim and likely to cause immediate injury, however slight."

**Appeal allowed**

This approach has subsequently been disapproved. In *Mitchell*[23] it was held that the only issue in such cases was one of causation and that in *Dalby* there had been "no sufficient link between Dalby's wrongful act (supplying the drug) and his friend's death".

## Attorney-General's Reference (No. 3 of 1994) [1998] A.C. 245 (House of Lords)

For facts see *above*, p. 185.

Lord Hope:
"[It is not] necessary, in order to constitute manslaughter, that the death resulted from an unlawful and dangerous act which was done with the intention to cause the victim to sustain harm. This is because it is clear from the authorities that, although the defendant must be proved to have intended to do what he did, it is not necesssary to prove that he knew that his act was unlawful or dangerous. So it must follow that it is unnecessary to prove that he knew his act was likely to injure the person who died as a result of it. All that need be proved is that he intentionally did what he did, that the death was caused by it and that, applying an objective test, all sober and reasonable people would recognise the risk that some harm would result. ... [Certain cases] suggest that the defendant cannot be found guilty of this crime unless his unlawful and dangerous act was directed at the person who was the ultimate victim of it. I am not persuaded that ... [this] proposition is borne out by the authorities. In *R. v Mitchell* ... [it] was rejected ...

In this case the act which had to be shown to be an unlawful and dangerous act was the stabbing of the child's mother. There can be no doubt that all sober and reasonable people would regard that act .. as dangerous. It is plain that it was unlawful as it was done with the intention of causing her injury. As the defendant intended to commit that act, all the ingredients necessary for *mens rea* in regard to the crime of manslaughter were established, irrespective of who was the ultimate victim of it. ... The question, once all the other elements are satisfied, is simply one of causation."

**Reference answered accordingly**

Following this decision, it seems clear that generally there is no requirement that the act be aimed at the victim and the issue is one of causation. Subsequent, and more recent, cases make no reference to any such requirement. Nevertheless, some

---

[23] (1983) 76 Cr.App.R.293.

commentators support the requirement that the act should be aimed at the victim on the grounds that the approach in *Dalby* "at least introduces a subjective element. ... An act can only be 'directed at the victim' if there is an intention so to direct it" and because the "second qualification stated, that the act must be likely to cause immediate injury also seems to be new, significant and appropriate."[24] There is also a further reason to support the *Dalby* requirement that the unlawful act should be directed at the victim. As will be seen in the following section on the rationale and reform of the law, there is much criticism of the law of constructive manslaughter. One view to be explored is that, if constructive manslaughter is to be maintained in any form, it should be limited to cases where the unlawful act comprises an attack on a victim.[25] This requirement of an attack necessarily means that the unlawful act must be directed at the victim. This view, however, does not represent the current law.

## 4. Rationale and reform

Evaluation of the law of involuntary manslaughter raises two fundamental, but connected, issues. First, where a person has been unlawfully killed, when is a charge of manslaughter—as opposed to some lesser endangerment offence—appropriate? In answering this question it is clear that the law is strongly influenced by the context in which the killing took place. Most killings occur as a result of unlawful risk-creating activity such as careless or dangerous driving, breaches of the Health and Safety at Work etc Act 1974, or criminal attacks such as assaults. With respect to the first two categories, the most common response is for the prosecution to be brought in relation to the underlying dangerous activity. For example, defendants will simply be charged with breaches of the Health and Safety legislation and the fact that death occurred will only be considered, if at all, at the sentencing stage.

### Glanville Williams, Textbook of Criminal Law (1st ed., 1978), pp. 245–247:

"No one has studied how people become selected for the privilege of being prosecuted for manslaughter. Here are some more grisly figures. In 1976 there were 582,825 deaths in England and Wales from all causes, including the following (provisional figures).

| | |
|---|---|
| Motor vehicle accidents | 5,834 |
| Accidents in factories | 427 |
| Accidents in the construction industries | 182 |
| Other accidents (home, rail, air, etc.) | 8,817 |

Some of these fatalities must have been caused by the negligence of other persons, often (one may imagine) criminal in degree. If the culprits are charged at all, it is almost invariably with some more specific offence than manslaughter. Negligent drivers are proceeded against for a driving offence, and the outcome is generally lenient, even where death has been

[24] J.C. Smith, [1982] Crim.L.R.440.
[25] Clarkson, "Context and Culpability in Involuntary Manslaughter: Principle or Instinct" in Ashworth and Mitchell (eds), *Rethinking English Homicide Law* (2000).

caused. Fatal 'accidents' at work are charged as summary offences under the relevant legislation, if a breach has occurred. The average fine for all infractions (fatal or not) in factories and the construction industries in 1975 was £75; and the usual fine in fatal cases was not much higher: say about £200. Since the proceedings are almost invariably against companies, the individuals at fault are in effect shielded from liability. Inspectors regard it as their sole duty to bring a charge under the relevant legislation, not the more serious and cumbrous charge at common law. Similarly, when a man is killed at a poisonous waste tip, those responsible are likely to be brought to court under the Deposit of Poisonous Waste Act 1972 rather than for manslaughter. When a child is killed, by neglect or even by assault, the charge brought by the local authority or by the National Society for the Prevention of Cruelty to Children is a minor one under the Children and Young Persons Act, or other legislation, though very occasionally the police intervene to make it manslaughter.

Can it be, therefore, that the few people who are indicted for negligent manslaughter each year generally suffer this fate only because there happens to be no other offence covering the case? It is noticeable that this was so with … Lamb (unless Lamb happened not to possess a certificate for his gun).

Evidently thinking little of the law of manslaughter as an effective schoolmaster for clots, Parliament has proliferated offences aimed at preventing accidents. An astonishing example is the Children and Young Persons Act 1933, s.11 as amended.

'If any person who has attained the age of 16 years, having the custody, charge or care of any child under the age of 12 years, allows the child to be in any room containing an open fire grate or any heating appliance liable to cause injury to a person by contact therewith not sufficiently protected to guard against the risk of his being burnt or scalded without taking precautions against that risk, and by reason thereof the child is killed or suffers serious injury, he shall on summary conviction be liable to a fine not exceeding £10.'

This is a perfect example of the simple belief that any social ill can be cured, or anyway alleviated, by passing a law against it."

Whether the context of the killing is sufficiently material to warrant separate criminalisation is a matter considered elsewhere.[26]

Secondly, in those cases where a charge of manslaughter is brought, the law here raises, yet again, the fundamental question of what importance should be attached to the actual harm done. If a defendant has acted with gross negligence, or has committed an unlawful act, why should he not simply be punished for that gross negligence or for that unlawful act? Why should he be punished for the more serious crime of manslaughter merely because his actions cause death—if that death was not within his range of contemplation? Take *Larkin* for example. He committed an unlawful act, an assault. Why was he not simply punished for that unlawful act? Why should he be guilty of the much more serious offence of manslaughter merely because his drunk mistress happened to fall against his razor? Was not his blameworthiness the same, whether she fell against the razor or whether she fell to the ground, missing his razor and not injuring herself?

## H. Wechsler, "The Challenge of a Model Penal Code" (1952) 65 Harv.L.Rev. 1097 at 1106–1107:

"From the preventive point of view, the harmfulness of conduct rests upon its tendency to cause the injuries to be prevented far more than on its actual results; results, indeed, have meaning only insofar as they may indicate or dramatize the tendencies involved. Reckless driving is no more than reckless driving if there is a casualty and no less if by good fortune nothing should occur. Actual consequences may, of course, arouse resentments that have

[26] With regard to corporate killings, see pp. 262–263; with regard to vehicular killings, see pp. 673–676.

bearing on the proper sanction. But if the criminality of conduct is to turn on the result, it rests upon fortuitous considerations unrelated to the major purpose to be served by declaration that behaviour is a crime. . . .

A major issue to be faced, therefore, is whether penal law ought to be shaped to deal more comprehensively with risk creation, without reference to actual results."

## Criminal Law Revision Committee, 14th Report, Offences against the Person, 1980, Cmnd.7844, paras 120–121, 124:

"120 . . . Suppose that A strikes B and gives him a bleeding nose; B, unknown to A, is a haemophiliac and bleeds to death. Or, A strikes B who falls and unluckily hits his head against a sharp projection and dies. Or A chases B with the object of chastising him; B runs away, trips and falls into a river in which he drowns. In each of these cases, although A is at fault and is guilty of an assault or of causing injury, his fault does not extend to the causing of death or to the causing of serious injury which he did not foresee and in some cases could not reasonably have foreseen. In our opinion, they should not be treated as manslaughter because the offender's fault falls too far short of the unlucky result. So serious an offence as manslaughter should not be a lottery. . . . [T]here seems to be no reason for calling it manslaughter. Indeed, the name is positively objectionable for several reasons, among which are the fact that it gives a false idea of the gravity of the defendant's moral offence and that there is always the possibility that it may receive a punishment going beyond that appropriate to the assault.

121 The second instance is causing death by an act of gross negligence. Evidence of this will often be sufficient to enable the jury to draw an inference of recklessness as to the causing of death or serious injury, in which case the act will amount to manslaughter under our recommendation. . . . But sometimes the jury may not be able to find more than that the defendant was extremely foolish; and although the foolishness may amount to gross negligence we do not think that it should be sufficient for manslaughter in the absence of advertence to the risk of death or serious injury. It seems that in fact prosecutions falling exclusively under this heading of manslaughter are very rare."

There is, however, another view that weight should be attached to the resulting harm in assessing the extent of criminal liability. The fact that death has been caused is, under this view, crucial in justifying increased liability and punishment.

## C. M. V. Clarkson and H. M. Keating, "Codification: Offences against the Person under the Draft Criminal Code" (1986) 50 J.Crim.L. 405 at 422–423:

"Criminal liability cannot and should not be based exclusively on mental elements. The significance of the harm caused, in this case, death, is critical in the construction of criminal liability. We do not judge people solely on the basis of the quality of their actions and their exertions, but also by the *results* of those actions. The fact that a person's negligent or unlawful actions have resulted in the death of a human being totally alters our moral judgment; it arouses resentment in society (quite apart from the bitterness and pain caused to the relatives and friends of the deceased). Imagine a workman high on a building who negligently tosses a brick to the street below where it strikes and kills a passer-by. The response of the C.L.R.C. . . . is that this death is 'pure chance.' It is simply 'bad luck.' The workman's actions must be judged *totally* on the basis of his *subjective mens rea*.

It is strongly submitted that this view is unacceptable. Those observing the above incidents would respond with horror. The workman has *killed* the passer-by. His actions were not just dangerous, that is, likely to cause danger. The danger has materialised and someone lies dead. This resultant harm makes its mark and leaves a lasting impression. If the workman tried to run away, we would chase him and attempt his detention."

## George P. Fletcher, Rethinking Criminal Law (1978), pp. 474, 476, 478, 481–482:

"It is important to see that the problem arises in cases of negligent as well as intentional wrongdoing. If negligent risk-taking issues in death, the actor might be liable for manslaughter; but if nothing happens, the negligent risk-taker is not liable at all. If she were reckless in creating the risk, she might be liable in some jurisdictions for the newly framed offence of 'reckless endangerment.' Again we confront the question why, if the risk-creating act is the same, the fortuitous accrual of harm should matter in the assessment of punishment. . . .

One argument is that the purpose of the criminal law is to prevent external harm; wrongdoing should consist, therefore, in the causing of external harm. . . .

A good defense of the objective theory requires a return to the harm-oriented theory of homicide. If one sees an act causing death as an evil, then it follows that wrongdoing—at least in homicide cases—consists in causing harm. . . . [W]e should recall that causing death was treated as an evil by virtue of the taint implicit in taking human life. . . .

If is often argued that the occurrence of harm fulfils an important evidentiary function. If the actor has succeeded in killing, he is more likely to have actually intended the death. If a reckless driver causes harm, he is more likely to have been truly reckless . . .

A totally different approach begins with the observation that persons who inadvertently cause harm feel greater remorse than those who have 'close calls.' If a reckless driver goes into a skid and collides with another car, he is likely to feel different from another driver, equally reckless, whose car merely slides into an embankment. If an assassin aims, shoots and hits her intended victim, she is likely to feel different about her act than she would if the bullet has gone astray. Feelings of guilt, and remorse are appropriate when harm is done, but if all is the same after as before the act, there would be nothing to be remorseful about, and the actor's feelings of guilt would make us wonder why he wanted to suffer inappropriate anguish. Feelings of remorse and guilt are closely connected with causing harm, for these feelings are part of a broader pattern of human interaction. The notions of causing harm, injuring others, feeling guilt and making amends are all part of the patterns by which human relationships are disturbed and then restored. The notion of guilt cannot be lifted out of context and fitted to cases where there is merely a risk of harm, but no concrete impact on the lives of others."

## CMV Clarkson, "Context and Culpability in Involuntary Manslaughter: Principle or Instinct" in Andrew Ashworth and Barry Mitchell, Rethinking English Homicide Law (2000), pp. 154–155, 158–160:

"Grossly careless killings

. . . The Law Commission has long been committed to subjectivism in the criminal law on the basis that criminal liability and punishment should be linked to moral guilt which involves blaming only those who have chosen to cause harm in the sense of intending or knowing that harm could occur. However, while such cognition clearly does involve moral guilt, it is not obvious that moral guilt **must** be linked to cognition. We can blame people for making choices even when the possibility of harm is not in the forefront of their minds. As Duff has argued: a failure to consider obvious risks to others demonstrates an attitude of indifference. Assuming the person is capable of foresight, failing to recognise obvious risks when choosing to act demonstrates that s/he regards them as unimportant or "couldn't care less". Students almost never forget a final exam; some students forget tutorials. Exams are of critical importance and care is taken not to oversleep etc.; attendance at tutorials, to some students, is not important and careful precautions (setting the alarm clock etc.) are not taken.

Such uncaring indifference could be condemned even more strongly than the choices of the classically subjective risk-taker who recognises a small chance of a risk occurring, hopes it will not materialise, but nevertheless goes ahead and acts. This indifference is a state of mind, albeit an affective one rather than a cognitive one.

In many situations Duff's account is "easy". For example, the boorish man who assumes that all women would consent to intercourse with him clearly demonstrates indifference when having intercourse without consent. But some cases are "harder". Horder, ("Gross Negligence and Criminal Culpability" (1997) 47 University of Toronto Law Journal 495) has argued that there are two forms of gross negligence: indifference and a great departure from expected standards. However, assuming a capacity to choose otherwise had all the relevant facts been brought to the actor's attention, the latter is better regarded as evidence of the former. For example, doctors because of their training and rules of conduct regarding their profession are expected to act in the best interests of their patients and achieve a basic level of competence. If, through inattentiveness or tiredness, they make a slight error (not a **great** departure from expected standards) we would probably not conclude that their actions demonstrated uncaring indifference sufficient for criminal liability. But where there is a gross or substantial departure from **expected** standards (bearing in mind that what is expected could vary depending on working conditions) indifference (given the doctor's situation) can more easily be inferred. The fact that s/he is overworked by a stretched NHS will not serve to exculpate. Unless so tired as to be an effective automaton the doctor chose to act knowing of the fatigue. While the primary motivation in acting might be concern for the care of the patient, ultimately other secondary concerns (career prospects, willingness to obey superior's orders etc.) prevailed thereby demonstrating an attitude of indifference to the patient's interests. For instance, the conduct and attitude of the anaesthetist in *Adomako* was described by an expert witness as "a gross dereliction of care". Such a choice can be condemned (although we might also wish to blame others for putting the doctor in such a situation). . . .

*Killings resulting from dangerous unlawful acts:*

. . . It is my argument that in appropriate cases the requisite culpability can be found in the circumstances/context in which the defendant acted without any necessary correspondence to the death. The notion that culpability can be established without the fault element corresponding to the prohibited harm is hardly a novel one in English law. For example, cases on intoxication clearly establish that the requisite culpability lies in the excessive consumption of drink or drugs . . .

However, once one has severed the connection between fault and result, the problem is one of identifying what sort of fault should suffice for manslaughter. It is submitted that when death has been caused departure from the paradigm is permissible as long as the actions are within the same family of offence, namely violence. The essential point about constructive manslaughter is that the defendant has chosen to engage in criminal, dangerous activity: usually violence. Such a person is deliberately engaging in a morally different course of action compared to those who act lawfully and inadvertently cause death. As Horder puts it:

'The fact that I *deliberately* wrong V arguably changes my normative position *vis a vis* the risk of adverse consequences of that wrongdoing to V, whether or not foreseen or reasonably foreseeable . . . if . . . my unlawful act is meant to wrong V . . . its deliberateness changes my relationship with the risk of adverse consequences stemming therefrom.' ("A Critique of the Correspondence Principle in Criminal Law" [1995] Crim.L.R.759.)

This change in normative position is, of course, morally interesting. But is it enough for the fault element for manslaughter? The answer is yes—provided the change in normative position is one involving an attack upon the victim. The moral quality of a deliberate attack upon a person brings the assailant within the family of violence. A defendant who attacks another and risks injury cannot complain when criminal liability is imposed in relation to injuries—even death—resulting from the attack. Horder distinguishes between "pure luck" (where a fortuitous result unconnected to one's endeavours occurs) and "making one's own luck" (where the consequence is directly connected to one's endeavours). Where a death results from an unlawful attack on a victim, the defendant "by directing [his/her] efforts towards harming V" is responsible for the bad luck that s/he has created.

Take, for example, the case of *Williams* ([1996] 2 Cr.App.R.(S) 72) which is a classic example of the sort of constructive manslaughter objected to by the Law Commission and many commentators. The defendant gave a young woman two pushes and one slap. As a result she fell back, caught her head on a wall-mounted heater, damaged her neck and died. Sacks J., in substituting a sentence of two-and-a-half years' imprisonment, agreed with the trial sentencing judge that this death was "in a sense, accidental" but stressed that "we do bear well in mind that this was an assault on a woman" and that he "set about her ... with terrible consequences". Such, admittedly rather generalised, statements are an acceptance of the above proposition that when the defendant, instead of merely quarrelling with the woman as he had been, chose to attack her, he deliberately changed his normative stance to become a violent actor who should bear responsibility for the consequences of his violence. His actions were simply not of the same moral order as those of a person who swears at a woman who in distress turns away and hits her head on a wall-heater and dies.

This line of reasoning, however, suggests that it is only those who attack their victims in the sense of **assaulting** them **intending or foreseeing some injury** who alter their normative position relevantly to bring themselves within the family of violence. From this it follows that not every unlawful act should suffice for constructive manslaughter as it does under the present law (as long as it is dangerous). Accordingly, there should be no liability for manslaughter in some of the well-known cases such as *Newbury* and the drug-injection or drug-supply cases such as *Cato*. Such offenders have of course engaged in actions of a certain moral quality and there might indeed be risks of adverse consequences flowing from their wrongdoing. They could possibly be liable for killing by gross carelessness. But, by not attacking their victims, they have not chosen to embark on a violent course of action. They have departed too far from the family of violence: the connection between their fault and the death is too tenuous.

From this it follows that some sort of constructive manslaughter should be retained but only unlawful acts of personal violence involving at least a common assault with intention or foresight of some injury should suffice ... "

The Law Commission, in a Consultation Paper in 1994[27] was critical of the (then) law on gross negligence manslaughter and was of the view that constructive manslaughter should be completely abolished. However, it is Final Report in 1996[28] the Commission conceded that the arguments in favour of gross negligence were formidable—where the harm risked was very serious, namely, death or serious injury: "We may plead that we trod on the snail inadvertently: but not on the baby—you ought to look where you are putting your great feet".[29] Secondly, in response to strong comments favouring retention, in some form, of constructive manslaughter, the Law Commission included a modified form of unlawful act manslaughter in its proposals. In 2000, the Home Office largely accepted these recommendations and, in place of the present broad offence of manslaughter, proposed the creation of new separate offences.

## Home Office, Reforming the Law on Involuntary Manslaughter: The Government's Proposals (2000)

### Draft Involuntary Homicide Bill
"1. (1) A person who by his conduct causes the death of another is guilty of reckless killing if—

---

[27] Law Commission, Consultation Paper No. 135, *Involuntary Manslaughter* (1994).
[28] Law Com. No. 237 (1996).
[29] Para. 4.23, citing Austin, "A Plea for Excuses" in *Proceedings of the Aristotelian Society*, New Series, vol. 57 (1956–7), 1.

(a) he is aware of a risk that his conduct will cause death or serious injury; and
(b) it is unreasonable for him to take that risk having regard to the circumstances as he knows or believes them to be.
(2) A person guilty of reckless killing is liable on conviction on indictment to imprisonment for life.

2. (1) A person who by his conduct causes the death of another is guilty of killing by gross carelessness if—
   (a) a risk that his conduct will cause death or serious injury would be obvious to a reasonable person in his position;
   (b) he is capable of appreciating that risk at the material time; and
   (c) either—
       (i) his conduct falls far below what can reasonably be expected of him in the circumstances; or
       (ii) he intends by his conduct to cause some injury or is aware of, and unreasonably takes, the risk that it may do so.
   (2) there shall be attributed to the person referred to in subsection (1)(a) above—
   (a) knowledge of any relevant facts which the accused is shown to have at the material time; and
   (b) any skill or experience professed by him.
   (3) In determining for the purposes of subsection (1)(c)(i) above what can reasonably be expected of the accused regard shall be had to the circumstances of which he can be expected to be aware, to any circumstances shown to be within his knowledge and to any other matter relevant for assessing his conduct at the material time.
   (4) Subsection (1)(c)(ii) above applies only if the conduct causing, or intended to cause, the injury constitutes an offence.
   (5) A person guilty of killing by gross carelessness is liable on conviction on indictment to imprisonment for a term not exceeding [*] years.
[* The Law Commission had felt unable to make a recommendation as to the maximum sentence for this offence but, by analogy with causing death by dangerous driving, mooted the possibility of 10 years' imprisonment as the maximum penalty.[30]]"

Offences should be defined with sufficient specificity to capture what is morally significant about them and should be structured to reflect a hierarchy of seriousness. The creation of the above two separate offences would be a significant improvement on the present over-broad offence of involuntary manslaughter. It is, however, arguable that these proposals do not go far enough. Clause 2(1)(c)(ii) (read with clause 2(4)) represents a modified form of constructive manslaughter. However, it has been subsumed into the offence of killing by gross carelessness and it must still be shown that it was obvious from the defendant's conduct that there was a risk that death or serious injury would be caused. For the reasons suggested above it is not obvious why, in cases of an attack on the victim, this extra requirement should be imposed. Indeed, it is possible to argue further that such cases of attack leading to death should be regarded as separate and more serious offences than other killings by gross negligence. These latter killers are normally engaged in lawful activities, often simply performing their job. Causing injury is not part of their reason for acting. The moral culpability of those who choose to

---

[30] Law Com. No. 237, para. 5.51.

engage in a violent attack is aggravated by their crossing a moral threshold and engaging in violence. Fair labelling suggests that this difference in the context and culpability associated with the killing should be marked by a separate offence.

## B. *Vehicular Homicide*

There are three species of vehicular homicide in English law: causing death by dangerous driving; causing death by careless driving while under the influence of drink or drugs and causing death by aggravated vehicle-taking. In *Government of USA v Jennings*[31] it was held that causing death by reckless driving (the predecessor of causing death by dangerous driving) was no more than a particular species of manslaughter. In cases where persons are killed by motor vehicles the prosecution has a choice. It can either charge the defendant with one of these statutory offences or it can charge with manslaughter.[32] In *Adomako*, Lord Mackay stated that the decision of *Seymour*[33] no longer applies. This latter case concerned the relationship between "motor-manslaughter" and killing by reckless driving and decided that the word reckless bore the same meaning in both offences although a prosecution for manslaughter should be reserved for the worst cases. Although, strictly speaking, Lord Mackay's discussion of vehicular homicide was *obiter*, it seems clear now that whatever the method of killing, the test of gross negligence is to be applied if a manslaughter charge is brought. The jury, having regard to the risk of death involved, should consider whether the conduct of the defendant was so bad in all the circumstances as to amount to a criminal act or omission. Lord Mackay acknowledges that, as a consequence of this, cases of involuntary motor manslaughter will become rare.

## 1. Causing death by dangerous driving

(a) *Introduction*
    Section 1 of the Road Traffic Act 1988, as amended by the Road Traffic Act 1991, provides as follows:

> "A person who causes the death of another person by driving a mechanically propelled vehicle dangerously on a road or other public place is guilty of an offence."

The offence is triable only on indictment and is punishable by a maximum penalty of 10 years' imprisonment.[34]
    Before 1977 the offence covered causing death by reckless or dangerous driving. In 1977 it was narrowed to causing death by reckless driving.[35] The *Lawrence* test

---

[31] [1983] 1 A.C. 624.
[32] In 1996 charging standards were introduced, agreed upon by the police and CPS, in an attempt to improve consistency in charging practices across the country and reduce the number of occasions in which charges are subsequently amended. See [1996] Crim.L.R.458.
[33] [1983] 1 A.C. 493.
[34] The Criminal Justice Act 1993, s.67(1), increased the maximum penalty from five to 10 years. An amendment to the Criminal Justice Bill 2003 proposes to increase the maximum penalty to 14 years' imprisonment
[35] Criminal Law Act 1977, s.50(1).

of recklessness, as qualified in *Reid*, applied. In 1991 this was abolished and replaced by the new offence of causing death by dangerous driving. Why did this occur?

### Department of Transport and Home Office, Road Traffic Law Review Report (The North Report) (1988), para. 5.8:

"5.8 ... There is a general ... view that, ... the test in *Lawrence* is too subjective. It is said that the more subjective the test, and the further removed from an objective assessment of the standard of driving, the harder it is to provide cogent evidence of the commission of the offence and that this deters the bringing of prosecutions for reckless driving in serious instances of bad driving ...

There is criticism that the test in *Lawrence* allows a defendant to exculpate himself by admitting that, in retrospect, his driving created an obvious risk but by showing also that he did at the time apply his mind to the question of the existence of the risk and (foolishly perhaps) concluded that there was none ...

The *Lawrence* test can also be interpreted as being too wide in scope ... [as including cases] when the behaviour involved was no more than mere thoughtless incompetence."

(b) *Rationale of law*

Why is it necessary to have a special offence? Why are such persons not simply charged with manslaughter? Is it less blameworthy to kill another with a motor vehicle than with some other instrument?

### Sir Brian MacKenna, "Causing Death by Reckless or Dangerous Driving: a Suggestion" [1970] Crim.L.R.67:

"By 1955–56 it was clear to all that prosecutions for motor manslaughter were a failure: juries just would not convict. Different reasons were assigned for their perversity ... 'The very word "manslaughter" is ugly and is associated in the minds of most people with brawls and sordid offences of various kinds. A jury is therefore reluctant to convict of this offence a person who is obviously very decent, and about whom the jury may think "there but for the grace of God, go I" ' (Mr. Molson, *Hansard*, H.C. Vol. 534, Cols. 782–783). For those who favoured this diagnosis the remedy seemed obvious: a new offence of causing death by reckless driving ... punishable by a maximum of five years imprisonment."

### Sally Lloyd-Bostock, "The Ordinary Man, and the Psychology of Attributing Causes and Responsibility" (1979) 42 M.L.R. 143 at 156–157:

"[It has been pointed out] that the more relevant a particular type of accident becomes to the perceiver, the more he is forced to find ways of avoiding acknowledging that he could be blamed for, as distinct from just injured in, such an accident. He may therefore be expected to attribute less blame in accidents which are situationally relevant to himself. For example, a motorist may be more lenient in his judgment about someone involved in a road accident. As well as situational relevance, a misfortune may be personally relevant, *i.e.* the actor or victim may be similar to the perceiver. Similarity to oneself has often been found to relate to empathy and liking and to a tendency to judge another's actions more leniently ... [Another possibility is that where] the judger can identify with an actor and his act, he is more likely to perceive the situation as if he were himself the actor and hence assign less personal responsibility."

Not only are manslaughter charges extremely rare when death has been caused by a motor vehicle, but so are charges of causing death by dangerous driving.

In 2000 there were 3,108 persons killed on the roads[36] yet in that year only 206 people were charged with causing death by dangerous driving.[37] This has led to some calls for the total abolition of the special offence: prosecutions should simply be brought under section 2 of the Road Traffic Act 1988 for dangerous driving, punishable by a maximum of two years' imprisonment. The argument is that prosecutors would be more willing to charge with this offence; in the worst cases a manslaughter prosecution could always be brought.

### Criminal Law Revision Committee, 14th Report, Offences Against the Person, Cmnd.7844 (1980), para. 142:

"We consider that the fact that death occurs in motoring cases should not enable a graver charge than reckless driving to be preferred unless the facts are that the full mental element appropriate to manslaughter can be proved. The real mischief where that mental element cannot be proved is the very bad driving, and the fact that it causes death should be treated as no more than an aggravating factor of that road traffic offence for sentencing purposes in appropriate cases."

This is the simple view that it is the bad driving that is reprehensible and the defendant should be blamed for that. The fact that death has been caused is "chance" and should be irrelevant in terms of substantive criminal liability.[38] This approach was not adopted by the North Report nor accepted by the Government.

### Department of Transport and Home Office, Road Traffic Law Review Report (The North Report) (1988), paras 6.5–6.9, 6.23–6.27:

6.5 ... The detailed arguments for abolishing the offence [causing death by reckless driving] (excluding the argument that all such cases should be charged as manslaughter) included the following:

there is a danger that the existence of the offence would be seen as downgrading cases where there is *no* death or injury;

it is improper to create greater liability based on consequences which may to a degree be fortuitous, resulting for example from the non-availability at the time of medical help or the presence of a pedestrian who happens to be struck;

although the offence is not unique in the fact that its seriousness depends on the results of unintended conduct (the whole of involuntary manslaughter being so based), it is desirable to limit the number of such instances;

why should the road user continue to be singled out as the only kind of person whose act causing death constitutes a separate offence?

it is wrong, in England and Wales, to have a complete overlap with the offence of manslaughter;

the law takes no account of injury short of death as a constituent element of an offence;

the maximum sentence of two years' imprisonment for reckless driving is adequate in the vast majority of reckless driving cases involving death; and if the case is very bad, then manslaughter or culpable homicide should be charged.

---

[36] *Road Accidents Great Britain, 2001: The Casualty Report* (2001).
[37] *Criminal Statistics, England and Wales 2000* (Supplementary Tables, Vol. 2).
[38] Such an approach was adopted in *Krawec* [1985] 149 J.P. 709 but disapproved in *Simmonds* [1999] 2 Cr.App.R.(S) 218. See further, Clarkson, *Understanding Criminal Law* (3rd ed., 2001), pp. 158–163.

6.6 The arguments in favour of retaining a causing death offence concentrated more on practicality and on public expectations of the law. They included the following:

it is generally accepted in the law that consequences can affect the nature of an offence, as may be illustrated by the different offences of murder and attempted murder, and murder where there is no intent to kill but where there is intent to cause grievous bodily harm which has resulted in death;

the public sense of justice requires that the very bad driver who has killed should be guilty of a more serious offence;

the seriousness of the offence (and penalty) is desirable in order to have a deterrent effect;

juries are reluctant to convict of manslaughter in most causing death cases. Death should be singled out for special treatment because it is the most serious consequence of a criminal act, and so doing would exemplify the concern of the law for the sanctity of life;

though logic might suggest that consequences should be irrelevant, public opinion is strongly in favour of the retention of such an offence;

the case for the retention of an offence of causing death by bad driving is strong if there is no longer a complete overlap with the offence of manslaughter or culpable homicide;

outside the motoring sphere, reckless acts may amount either to no offence at all or, if death happens to result, to manslaughter or culpable homicide; so consequences should be no less relevant in the road traffic context;

if someone drives so badly as to be reckless, the consequences are not 'fortuitous,' for the driver has created a real risk of death or injury;

if there continues to be some overlap between causing death by reckless driving and manslaughter, it would be strange to be able to take consequences into account in the latter but not in the former ...

6.9 Taking all these arguments into consideration, we have concluded that, on balance, an offence of causing death by very bad driving, however defined, should be retained. Two main factors have influenced our thinking. To abolish the offence in the absence of compelling reasons for doing so would mean that some cases of very bad driving were not dealt with with appropriate seriousness. Repeal of section 1 would be seen as a down-grading of bad driving as a criminal activity. This is not a message which we wish to convey. Secondly, though logic might pull us towards arguments in favour of abolition, neither English nor Scots law in fact relies entirely on intent as the basis for offences. There seems to be a strong public acceptance that, if the consequence of a culpable act is death, then this consequence should lead to a more serious charge being brought than if death had not been the result. We concur with this view. We recommend that a separate causing death offence be retained, but that it be reformulated in terms consistent with our recommended very bad driving offence.

6.27 We have considered carefully the merits of recommending the introduction of injury related offences, taking account of the disquiet expressed over conduct which maims but does not kill. We recognise that some very serious injuries are caused by bad drivers, and that these can in many respects be considered to be as bad as causing a death. We have, however, concluded that the arguments in favour of the injury offences ... are not sufficiently compelling to outweigh the disadvantages of extending consequence linked offences to injuries as well as to death. The special emphasis which society places on the wrong created by causing a death justifies the retention of an offence from which death results, but we do not recommend the introduction of new offences based on the causing of injury."

It has recently been proposed that the current offence of causing death by dangerous driving should be extended to include severe injuries as this would "recognise the suffering and impact that severe and permanent injuries have both on the victim and their family".[39] If the causing of a consequence is to be taken into account in structuring offences, it is logical that serious injury as well as death should be catered for. However, as the North Report, extracted above, recognises, the causing of death has a special significance that perhaps needs to be singled out by the law.

(c) *The law*

### Road Traffic Act 1988 (as amended by the Road Traffic Act 1991), section 2A:

"2A. Meaning of dangerous driving.

(1) For the purposes of sections 1 and 2 above a person is to be regarded as driving dangerously if (and, subject to subsection (2) below, only if)—

(a) the way he drives falls far below what would be expected of a competent and careful driver, and

(b) it would be obvious to a competent and careful driver that driving in that way would be dangerous.

(2) A person is also to be regarded as driving dangerously for the purposes of sections 1 and 2 above if it would be obvious to a competent and careful driver that driving the vehicle in its current state would be dangerous.

(3) In subsections (1) and (2) above 'dangerous' refers to danger either of injury to any person or of serious damage to property; and in determining for the purposes of those subsections what would be expected of, or obvious to, a competent and careful driver in a particular case, regard shall be had not only to the circumstances of which he could be expected to be aware but also to any circumstances shown to have been within the knowledge of the accused.

(4) In determining for the purposes of subsection (2) above the state of a vehicle, regard may be had to anything attached to or carried on or in it and to the manner in which it is attached or carried."

### The Road User and The Law (The Government's Proposals for Reform of Road Traffic Law) Cm.576 (1989), paras 2.6–2.9:

"2.6 There are already helpful precedents in Scottish case law which it is intended to follow in formulating the new section 2 offence. It will have two ingredients:

(a) a standard of driving which falls far below that expected of a competent and careful driver; and

(b) the driving must carry a potential or actual danger of phsyical injury or serious damage to property.

2.7 *The standard of driving* will be judged in absolute terms, taking no account of factors such as inexperience, age or disability (though such factors are relevant in sentencing). It is not intended that the driver who merely makes a careless mistake of a kind which any driver might make from time to time should be regarded as falling *far* below the standard expected of a competent and careful driver.

2.8 The *danger* must be one which a competent and careful driver would have appreciated or observed. It means any danger of injury (however minor) to a person, or of serious damage to property. It will not be necessary to establish that any person or property was actually endangered. It will be sufficient for the prosecution to establish that a competent and careful driver would have appreciated that some person or property might be endangered by the accused's manner of driving.

---

[39] Department for Transport, Local Government and the Regions, *Dangerous Driving and the Law*, Road Safety Research Report No. 26 (2002). See Cunningham, "Dangerous Driving A Decade On" [2002] Crim.L.R.945.

2.9 The requirements will be met if the state of the vehicle driven is such that a competent and careful driver would not drive at all. They will not be met simply by the physical condition of the driver, which will be dealt with by the proposed amendment to the offence of driving while unfit. However, if an unfit driver drives dangerously as defined above he will be guilty of the reformulated reckless driving offence, and his unfitness will not be an excuse."

The emphasis is thus on the objective nature of the driving rather than on the defendant's state of mind.[40] However, one element of subjectivity is imported. Under section 2A(3) if the defendant knows of circumstances rendering the driving dangerous (for example, a defect in the car)—even though the driving was not obviously dangerous—such knowledge can be imputed to the competent and careful driver.

What is the difference between this test of dangerous driving and that required for gross negligence manslaughter as laid down in *Adomako* (apart from the fact that causing death by dangerous driving can only be committed on a road or other public place whereas manslaughter can be committed anywhere)? The most important distinction is that for manslaughter the driving must have involved a *risk of death*: it must be "not only dangerous but inherently life-threatening".[41] However, given the potential danger of all motor vehicles, "measuring the risk to determine whether it was one of death or one of mere physical injury is surely a near impossible task, given that death did in fact occur".[42] A second possible difference is that for manslaughter the defendant's driving must have fallen below "the minimum acceptable", whereas for the statutory offence the standard is "far below what would be expected of a competent and careful driver".[43] While this seems to suggest that the standard of driving must be worse for manslaughter, the reality is that in most cases, no matter how bad the driving, the police, and especially the C.P.S., prefer to charge the statutory offence as being easier to obtain a conviction.

### (d) *Sentencing*

For many years the leading sentencing guideline judgment here was *Boswell*.[44] However, following advice from the Sentencing Advisory Panel,[45] new guidelines have been issued.

### R. v Cooksley and others [2003] EWCA Crim 996 (Court of Appeal, Criminal Division)

Woolf L.C.J.:

"[W]e do not dissent from the Panel's view that culpability must be the dominant factor when assessing as precisely as possible just where in the level of serious crimes the particular offence comes.

The Panel sets out a series of aggravating and mitigating factors . . . We adopt them but stress that they should not be regarded as an exhaustive statement of the factors. In addition

---

[40] *Collins* [1997] Crim.L.R.578.

[41] Brownlee and Seneviratne, "Killing with Cars after Adomako: Time for Some Alternatives" [1995] Crim.L.R.389.

[42] Cunningham, "The Reality of Vehicular Homicide: Convictions for Murder, Manslaughter and Causing Death by Dangerous Driving" [2001] Crim.L.R.679.

[43] *ibid*.

[44] (1984) 79 Cr.App.R.277.

[45] Sentencing Advisory Panel, *Sentencing in Cases of Causing Death by Dangerous Driving* (2002).

it is important to appreciate that the significance of the factors can differ. There can be cases with three or more aggravating factors, which are not as serious as a case providing a bad example of one factor. They are as follows:

**Aggravating Factors**
'*Highly culpable standard of driving at time of offence*
- (a) the consumption of drugs (including legal medication known to cause drowsiness) or of alcohol, ranging from a couple of drinks to a "motorised pub crawl";
- (b) greatly excessive speed; racing; competitive driving against another vehicle; "showing off";
- (c) disregard of warnings from fellow passengers;
- (d) a prolonged, persistent and deliberate course of very bad driving;
- (e) aggressive driving (such as driving much too close to the vehicle in front, persistent inappropriate attempts to overtake, or cutting in after overtaking);
- (f) driving while the driver's attention is avoidably distracted, *e.g.* by reading or by use of a mobile phone (especially if hand-held);
- (g) driving when knowingly suffering from a medical condition which significantly impairs the offender's driving skills;
- (h) driving when knowingly deprived of adequate sleep or rest;
- (i) driving a poorly maintained or dangerously loaded vehicle, especially where this has been motivated by commercial concerns.

*Driving habitually below acceptable standard*
- (j) other offences committed at the same time, such as driving without ever having held a licence; driving while disqualified; driving without insurance; driving while a learner without supervision; taking a vehicle without consent; driving a stolen vehicle;
- (k) previous convictions for motoring offences, particularly offences which involve bad driving or the consumption of excessive alcohol before driving.

*Outcome of offence*
- (l) more than one person killed as a result of the offence (especially if the offender knowingly put more than one person at risk or the occurrence of multiple deaths was foreseeable);
- (m) serious injury to one or more victims, in addition to the death(s).

*Irresponsible behaviour at time of offence*
- (n) behaviour at the time of the offence, such as failing to stop, falsely claiming that one of the victims was responsible for the crash, or trying to throw the victim off the bonnet of the car by swerving in order to escape;
- (o) causing death in the course of dangerous driving in an attempt to avoid detection or apprehension;
- (p) offence committed while the offender was on bail.'

**Mitigating Factors**
'(a) a good driving record;
- (b) the absence of previous convictions;
- (c) a timely plea of guilty;
- (d) genuine shock or remorse (which may be greater if the victim is either a close relation or a friend);
- (e) the offender's age (but only in cases where lack of driving experience has contributed to the commission of the offence); and
- (f) the fact that the offender has also been seriously injured as a result of the accident caused by the dangerous driving.'

**Starting Points**

We have set out four *starting points*; no aggravating circumstances—12 to 18 months; intermediate culpability—2 to 3 years; higher culpability—4 or 5 years and most serious culpability—6 years or over. We make clear that *starting points* only indicate where a person sentencing should start from when seeking to determine what should be the appropriate sentence. There is, however, a danger in relation to the higher *starting points* of the sentencer, if he is not careful, double accounting. The sentencer must be careful not to use the same aggravating factors to place the sentence in a higher category and then add to it because of the very same aggravating features.

In making our recommendations as to *starting points*, we have made the allowance we consider appropriate for the fact that those who commit offences of dangerous driving which result in death are less likely, having served their sentence, to commit the same offence again. Apart from their involvement in the offence which resulted in death, they can be individuals who would not otherwise dream of committing a crime. They, unlike those who commit crimes of violence, also do not intend to harm their victims."

Research into 91 reported sentencing appeal cases between 1994 and mid–1999 revealed that even in the very worst cases, a sentence in excess of five years' imprisonment was only confirmed or imposed in five cases, the highest sentence being seven years' imprisonment.[46] In these cases there were aggravating features and the offences were regarded as extremely serious yet it is rare for sentences approaching the maximum to be imposed.[47] One can only wonder how often the most serious culpability starting point of six years or over will be utilised. Given this sentencing reality it seems odd that the Government is proposing in the Criminal Justice Bill 2003 to increase the maximum penalty for this offence to 14 years' imprisonment.

Such sentencing patterns raise critical questions relating to "motor manslaughter". When would such a charge be appropriate? When would a sentence of more than ten (or 14) years' imprisonment be deserved? One might think that this would only be so in cases like *Seymour*[48] where the defendant uses a motor vehicle as an offensive weapon, in much the same way as a gun might be used. In such cases, however, a murder charge could often be brought—yet seldom is.[49] In the case of *Gault*,[50] for example, the defendant argued with a woman, with whom he had a stormy relationship, before slowly running his car over her, causing injuries from which she died. He was, exceptionally, charged with murder and, alternatively, manslaughter and with causing death by driving without due care and attention, when under the influence of drink or drugs (see below). He was, however, acquitted of murder by direction of the judge. He pleaded guilty to manslaughter and was sentenced to nine years' imprisonment for manslaughter

---

[46] Clarkson, "Context and Culpability in Involuntary Manslaughter: Principle or Instinct?" in Ashworth and Mitchell (eds), *Rethinking English Homicide Law* (2000). This pattern has been repeated since then with only a further four sentences of more than five years' imprisonment being upheld in reported cases.

[47] One case in which the maximum penalty was imposed is *Noble* [2002] EWCA Crim 1713 where the defendant was convicted of six different offences of causing death by dangerous driving arising from a single incident and there were numerous other aggravating factors.

[48] [1983] 1 A.C. 493.

[49] In 2000 there were 3,108 persons killed on the roads (*above*, n.36). In the year 2000/01 people were charged with either murder or manslaughter using a motor vehicle as the instrument. (*Criminal Statistics, England and Wales 2000*, Cm.5312). See, generally, Cunningham, "The Reality of Vehicular Homicide: Convictions for Murder, Manslaughter and Causing Death by Dangerous Driving" [2001] Crim.L.R.679.

[50] [1996] R.T.R. 348.

and four years for the statutory offence. On appeal against sentence the Court of Appeal took the view that the "cap of the fixed period which exists in relation to the statutory offences does not exist in relation to the common law offence of manslaughter" and that it could, therefore, take a different approach when sentencing for manslaughter. On the facts, it was thought appropriate to do so because of the element of hostility. Despite this, the court then reduced the sentence for manslaughter to six years (in good part because of the guilty plea).[51]

Why is it that society seems to show such tolerance to those who kill with their cars? As Spencer concludes:

"But unless we agree with Peter Simple's mythical J. Bonnington Jagworth that it is part of the British motorist's birthright to wipe out any more primitive road user who offends him, there is no case whatever for lenity towards those who run pedestrians and cyclists over on purpose. They deliberately attack defenceless people with lethal weapons, and they deserve to be punished accordingly. If a car is a lethal weapon which several million inhabitants of this country normally take around with them for lawful purposes, much as the Tudor Englishman used to carry his sword, and attack other people with an impulse rather than with premeditation, that is no reason for treating these cases the less seriously."[52]

## 2. Causing Death by Careless Driving when under the Influence of Drink or Drugs

### Road Traffic Act 1988, section 3A (as amended by the Road Traffic Act 1991):

"3A. *Causing death by careless driving when under influence of drink or drugs.*
(1) If a person causes the death of another person by driving a mechanically propelled vehicle on a road or other public place without due care and attention, or without reasonable consideration for other persons using the road or place, and—
  (a) he is, at the time when he is driving, unfit to drive through drink or drugs, or
  (b) he has consumed so much alcohol that the proportion of it in his breath, blood or urine at that time exceeds the prescribed limit, or
  (c) he is, within 18 hours after that time, required to provide a specimen in pursuance of section 7 of this Act, but without reasonable excuse fails to provide it, he is guilty of an offence.
(2) For the purposes of this section a person shall be taken to be unfit to drive at any time when his ability to drive properly is impaired.
(3) Subsection (1)(b) and (c) above shall not apply in relation to a person driving a mechanically propelled vehicle other than a motor vehicle."

This offence is punishable by a maximum of 10 years' imprisonment.[53] Why was it introduced?

---

[51] The court also thought it wrong in principle to impose a separate penalty for the statutory offence. In another of the comparatively rare manslaughter convictions, the Court of Appeal increased the sentence from three years' imprisonment to four years and three months' imprisonment (*Attorney-General's Reference (No. 14 of 2001)* [2002] 1 Cr.App.R.(S.) 25.).

[52] Spencer, "Motor Vehicles as Weapons of Offence" [1985] Crim.L.R.29 at 40–41.

[53] Increased from five to 10 years by the Criminal Justice Act 1993, s.67(1). The Criminal Justice Bill 2003 proposes increasing the maximum penalty to 14 years' imprisonment.

## Department of Transport and Home Office, Road Traffic Law Review Report (The North Report) (1988), paras 6.18–6.23:

"Our consultation identified a strongly held view ... that bad drivers who have been drinking and who cause death are frequently dealt with too leniently. Under present legislation a driver who is over the prescribed alcohol limit ... and whose driving causes an accident in which someone is killed may often be charged with only an alcohol or drugs offence, or with this offence coupled with one of careless driving ... [P]rosecuting authorities will, we are told, often settle for a drink driving charge as being easier to prove ... [There is a] growing concern among the public over drinking and driving and in particular over drinking drivers who kill. There is understandable revulsion that innocent lives can be lost in such a fashion. We share these anxieties ... [T]he availability of such a specific offence would be of real value in further marking out the dangers to the community of drinking and driving ...

[One] alternative might be to have an absolute offence of killing someone while driving with more than the legal limit of alcohol in the body or while unfit to drive through drink or drugs ... Under such an offence it would be enough to prove involvement by a drinking driver in an accident where a person was killed ... [T]here are problems with this type of approach. There is no doubt that drivers should not take so much alcohol as to put them over the legal limit; but it is easy to visualise circumstances where an accident leading to a death may have occurred and yet the drinking driver was not in any way to blame. Where, for example, a drunken pedestrian dashes out in front of a car in circumstances such that no driver could have avoided him, it would seem unduly harsh to charge the driver not only with the drink offence but also with a new causing death offence.

The final possibility which we have considered is that of an offence in which two elements would have to be proved. The first would be that the driver was over the legal alcohol limit or unfit to drive through drink or drugs; the second that there had been a level of bad driving amounting at least to driving without due care. By including a requirement to prove that some legally bad driving had occurred, such a formulation would protect from prosecution for this new offence drivers who had indeed been over the alcohol limit or who were otherwise unfit but the standard of whose driving had had no part in causing the death."

Like causing death by dangerous driving, this offence eschews the view that the focus ought to be solely on the quality of the driving. As in so many areas of criminal law, the degree of resulting harm is critical in determining the extent of liability and punishment.

In *Cooksley and others*[54] it was held that the sentencing guidelines laid down for causing death by dangerous driving should also be applied to causing death by careless driving when under the influence of drink.

### 3. Causing Death by Aggravated Vehicle-Taking

Section 12 of the Theft Act 1968 makes it an offence for any person to take any conveyance without the consent of the owner. The *mens rea* of the offence is that the defendant must know that the conveyance has been taken without authority. This offence was introduced to deal with the problem of "joy-riding" where an intention to permanently deprive the other of the car, as required for theft, cannot be established.

The Aggravated Vehicle-Taking Act 1992, section 1(1), inserting section 12A of the Theft Act 1968, created a new offence of aggravated vehicle-taking covering situations where the taken vehicle is driven dangerously or causes injury to any person or damage to any property. This offence is punishable by a maximum of two

---

[54] [2003] EWCA Crim 996.

years' imprisonment but under section 12A(4) if death is caused, the maximum punishment is increased to five years' imprisonment.[55]

The death that is caused must be "owing to the driving of the vehicle". This is a straightforward matter of causation. It is unnecessary to prove that the driving was bad or that the driver was in any way culpable.[56] This is a clear example of constructive crime. If one commits crime A (taking a conveyance) one becomes automatically liable for crime B if the specified consequence (death) occurs. The object of the statute is simply to increase the penalty for joy-riders who cause death.

In comparison with the other two categories of vehicular homicide, this offence is not extensively utilised. In 2000, 185 people were sentenced for causing death by dangerous driving, 53 were sentenced for causing death by careless driving while under the influence of alcohol or drugs while only nine people were sentenced for aggravated vehicle-taking.[57]

### C. Voluntary Manslaughter

A defendant who possesses malice aforethought may, when charged with murder, be convicted of the lesser crime of manslaughter if he satisfies one of three mitigating criteria. At common law there was only one such mitigating criterion: killing under provocation. Two further partial defences have been added by statute: diminished responsibility[58] and killing in pursuance of a suicide pact.[59] The term voluntary manslaughter is nothing more than a convenient label for these forms of killing.[60]

### 1. Provocation

#### (i) Introduction

In *Duffy*[61] a young woman killed her husband after having been savagely beaten by him; in *Camplin*[62] a 15-year-old boy who had been buggered killed his assailant; in *Bedder*[63] a man, who knew himself to be impotent, stabbed to death a prostitute who had jeered at him and kicked him in the groin after he had unsuccessfully tried to have intercourse with her. All claimed that they had been provoked into losing their self-control and killing their "victims".

Do we wish to blame such persons for their actions and hold them criminally responsible? If we can envisage situations in which violence of this sort would be a natural response to their suffering, how is our understanding of their plight to be reflected in the law? By no punishment? By less punishment?

---

[55] The Criminal Justice Bill 2003 proposes increasing the maximum sentence to 14 years' imprisonment.
[56] *Marsh* [1997] 1 Cr.App.R.67.
[57] Sentencing Advisory Panel, *Sentencing in Cases of Causing Death by Dangerous Driving* (2002).
[58] Homicide Act 1957, s.2.
[59] *ibid.*, s.4.
[60] It has been commented that this group excludes a number of possible defences, such as duress, which might be regarded as similarly compelling: see, Lacey, "Partial Defences to Homicide: Questions of Power and Principle in Imperfect and Less Imperfect Worlds" in Ashworth and Mitchell (eds), *Rethinking English Homicide Law* (2000), p. 107.
[61] [1949] 1 All E.R. 932.
[62] [1978] A.C. 705.
[63] (1954) 38 Cr.App.R.133.

The law has traditionally accepted claims of provocation affecting liability in one area only. Provocation may reduce murder to manslaughter[64] because it is felt unjust to subject the defendant to the full rigour of a conviction for murder—in other words, the courts wish to avoid the mandatory life sentence. A conviction for manslaughter, on the other hand, gives the courts the necessary flexibility to impose whatever sentence is deemed appropriate.[65] Provocation is not a defence to any other crime as no other serious offence in England carries a fixed penalty. For other crimes provocation can be taken into account as a mitigating factor, lessening the severity of the sentence.

(ii) *The Rationale of the Law's Response*

It seems, therefore, that the law regards the actions of the provoked defendant as less blameworthy, but not free from blame. What is the basis of this approach? As we shall see, the answer to this question is far from straightforward and the controversy which has surrounded recent developments in the law relating to provocation is in no small part due to this.

(a) One possible rationale of the law's response is that in weighing the competing interests of the eventual victim against those of the defendant it decides that the victim, by participating in the chain of events is to *some* extent responsible for his own demise. The victim, therefore, loses some of his claim to be protected by the law.

This interplay of victim and offender raises fundamental legal issues of responsibility.

## M. E. Wolfgang, "Victim-Precipitated Criminal Homicide" (1957) 48 Journal of Criminal Law, Criminology and Police Science, pp. 2–3:

"Primary demonstration of physical force by the victim, supplemented by scurrilous language, characterizes the most common victim-precipitated homicides. All of [the] ... slayings (below) that were listed by the Philadelphia Police as criminal homicides, none of the offenders was exonerated by a coroner's inquest, and all of the offenders were tried in criminal court.

A husband accused his wife of giving money to another man, and while she was making breakfast, he attacked her with a milk bottle, then a brick and finally a piece of concrete. Having had a butcher knife in hand, she stabbed him during the fight. ...

During a lover's quarrel, the male (victim) hit his mistress and threw a can of kerosene at her. She retaliated by throwing the liquid on him, and then tossed a lighted match in his direction. He died from the burns.

A drunken husband, beating his wife in their kitchen, gave a butcher's knife to her and dared her to use it on him. She claimed that if he should strike her once more, she would use the knife, whereupon he slapped her in the face and she fatally stabbed him."

---

[64] In *Marks* [1998] Crim.L.R.676 the Court of Appeal accepted that the defence of provocation was available to an accomplice to murder.

[65] See Horder, "Sex, Violence and Sentencing in Domestic Provocation Cases" [1989] Crim.L.R.546. Reviewing domestic provocation killings, Horder concludes that, despite judicial statements that a custodial sentence will almost always be necessary, for such killings they are almost unusual.

## J. E. Conklin, Criminology (1981), pp. 302–304:

"Victim precipitation of a crime means that the person who suffers eventual harm from a crime may play a direct role in causing the crime to be perpetrated. For example, the homicide victim may be the first to use force. ... About one murder in four is victim precipitated, although one study found that 38 per cent of a sample of murders were caused in part by the victim. ... There is a continuum from deliberate provocation by the victim, to some involvement by the victim, to little or no victim contribution. ... One study has examined the social interaction between offender and victim prior to the commission of murder. In about half of the seventy murders there was a prior history of hostility or even physical violence between the parties to the crime. This study found that homicides were not one-sided events in which a passive victim was attacked by the murderer. In fact, in nearly two thirds of the murders the victim initiated the interchange, the offender stated his intent to harm the victim and the offender killed the victim."

Victim studies bring an awareness of how close in reality may be the plea of self-defence and the plea of provocation. With a successful plea of self-defence, however, the claims of the defendant totally supersede those of the apparent victim, resulting in acquittal. But with a defence of provocation, even if the response to that provocation is reasonable, the defendant is still held to be blameworthy to some extent and thus guilty of manslaughter. Yet he may, in some 25 per cent of cases[66] be the true victim of the whole affair. Could one not argue that in such cases the apparent victim has no claim at all to the law's protection and that the defendant ought to be regarded as blameless? And in cases where the victim has played a part and *non-fatal* injuries have been sustained, should the law reflect this by holding the defendant less *responsible* rather than merely mitigating the severity of the sentence?

Viewed in this light one could regard provocation as a partial justification for the defendant's actions and a historical analysis of the defence affords considerable support for this. The common-law defence of provocation is of ancient origin but "it emerged in recognisably modern form in the late 17th and early 18th centuries. It comes from a world of Restoration gallantry in which gentlemen ... acted in accordance with a code of honour which required insult to be personally avenged by instant angry retaliation ... To show anger 'in hot blood' for a proper reason by an appropriate response was not only permissible but the badge of a man of honour. The human frailty to which the defence of provocation made allowance was the possibility that the man of honour might overreact and kill when a lesser retaliation would have been appropriate. Provided that he did not grossly overreact in the extent or manner of his retaliation, the offence would be manslaughter."[67] Thus, an important feature of the law at this time was that of proportionality.[68]

(b) However, while it may well be that for at least some of its history the defence of provocation was a partial justification,[69] the law, by the 19th century had already begun to shift in emphasis. Rather than focusing upon the rightfulness of anger,

---

[66] Wolfgang, "Victim Precipitated Criminal Homicide" (1957) 48 J. of Criminal Law, Criminology and Police Science 1.

[67] *Smith* [2001] 1 A.C. 146 at 159–160 *per* Lord Hoffmann, drawing upon the work of Horder, *Provocation and Responsibility* (1992).

[68] See further, Gough, "Taking the Heat out of Provocation" [1999] 19 O.J.L.S. 481.

[69] See Ashworth, "The Doctrine of Provocation" [1976] C.L.J. 292; Alldridge, "The Coherence of Defences" [1983] Crim.L.R.665.

judges "preferred to look upon provocation as something which temporarily deprived the accused of his reason"[70] and were concerned with whether there had been a loss of control. However, as we shall see, this loss of control had to manifest itself in a particular way: extreme anger.[71] This trend continued and the law, especially since the Homicide Act 1957, s.3, now seems to regard the defence as a "partial excuse". The law is no longer solely concerned with the victim-offender relationship. Provocation may now be pleaded even if the victim was not the provoking agent[72] (in other words, was entirely innocent in the affair). The victim need no longer commit an "unlawful act"[73]; indeed, the victim may be far too young to appreciate the quality of his actions at all.[74] In short, the thrust of the inquiry has shifted from the victim (and his provocative acts) to the defendant (and his loss of self-control)[75] and the rationale of the defence is "compassion for human infirmity."[76] As in the cases of diminished responsibility and duress, the law recognises that people are not in perfect control of their emotions and actions, particularly when subject to great pressure.

### George P. Fletcher, Rethinking Criminal Law (1978), pp. 246–247:

"The primary source of difficulty in the analysis of provocation derives from the failure of the courts and commentators to face the underlying normative issue whether the accused may be fairly expected to control an impulse to kill under the circumstances. Obviously there are some impulses such as anger and even mercy ... that we do expect people to control. If they fail to control these impulses and they kill another intentionally, they are liable for unmitigated homicide or murder. The basic moral question in the law of homicide is distinguishing between those impulses to kill as to which we as a society demand self-control, and those as to which we relax our inhibitions."

This basic moral question continues to cause difficulty partly because we may not be conceptualising the rationale of the defence in the most helpful way. It may be that the underlying rationale of the defence still contains elements of both excuse and justification. Currently, the law requires that the defendant lost control and this is most commonly categorised as an excusatory element. Further, it also insists that he or she did so in circumstances in which a reasonable person might well have done the same. It has been suggested that this retains an element of justification in the defence[77] (although it could be argued that this is no more than to ensure that

---

[70] *Smith* [2001] 1 A.C. 146, *per* Lord Hoffmann at 160.

[71] *Below*, p. 688

[72] *e.g. Davies* [1975] Q.B. 691. The requirement in s.3 that the provocation result from "things done or said" does, however, suggest that human activity must be involved: the defendant could not plead, for example, that he was provoked by bad weather.

[73] See Alldridge, *above*, n.69.

[74] As in *Doughty* (1986) 83 Cr.App.R.319, *below*, p. 686.

[75] See, generally, on this transmutation of provocation from a partial justification to a partial excuse, Alldridge, *above*, n.69 at 669–672.

[76] *Hayward* (1908) 21 Cox C.C. 692 at 694, *per* Lord Tindal C.J.

[77] See further, Ashworth, "The Doctrine of Provocation" [1976] C.L.J. 292; Horder, "Autonomy, Provocation and Duress" [1992] Crim.L.R.706 at 707–711; Horder, *Provocation and Responsibility* (1992).

the excuse offered is plausible). However, another suggestion is that a loss of control should be perceived as justified because it is not only natural, but right to become angry in some circumstances. However, unlike the early law of provocation this version does not lead to the defendant's actions being justified:

> "[T]hat one has been provoked is not an insufficient reason to kill, it is no reason whatsoever. If the defendant is to have a conviction reduced from murder to manslaughter, it is only because she has a partial excuse for killing."[78]

Finally, although analysing provocation in terms of its incomplete transformation to a partial excuse may help to explain some of the twists and (sometimes wrong) turns the defence has taken in the name of human frailty, once the current law has been examined the question will be posed whether an alternative approach could offer a better way forward for the defence or whether the defence is so flawed that it should be abolished.

## (iii) *The Law*

### Homicide Act 1957, section 3

"Where on a charge of murder there is evidence on which the jury can find that the person charged was provoked (whether by things done or by things said or by both together) to lose his self-control, the question whether the provocation was enough to make a reasonable man do as he did shall be left to be determined by the jury; and in determining that question the jury shall take into account everything both done and said according to the effect which, in their opinion, it would have on a reasonable man."

It has been held that the words "provoked" and "provocation" are to be given their ordinary meaning, unaffected by any technical legacies from the pre-1957 common law as to what may or may not constitute provocation.

### R. v Doughty (1986) 83 Cr.App.R.319 (Court of Appeal, Criminal Division)

The defendant was convicted of the murder of his 17-day-old son. He had had to look after both his wife (after a caesarian operation) and the baby since their return from the hospital. The baby was extremely restless and cried persistently. The defendant, agreed to have been a conscientious father who had done his best, finally tried to stop the crying by placing a cushion over the baby's head and then kneeling on it. The trial judge refused to allow the baby's crying immediately prior to the killing to go to the jury as evidence of provocation. The defendant appealed against the conviction.

Stocker L.J.:
"The learned [trial] judge said: . . . 'In my judgment the perfectly natural episodes or events of crying and restlessness by a 17-day-old baby does not constitute evidence of provocation in relation to the first subjective question. Put another way, the crying and restlessness of a

---

[78] Tadros, "The Characters of Excuse" [2001] 21 O.J.L.S. 495 at 508.

17-day-old baby cannot be utilised as being provocative to enable the defendant to raise the defence of provocation. Though provocation can be constituted by conduct or words which are not unlawful, provocation cannot be founded, in my judgment, on the perfectly natural episodes or events arising in the life of a 17-day-old baby. It is notorious that every baby born cries, that every baby can at times be burdensome. . . . I think that the episodes or events in the life of the baby of 17 days old could not have been in the mind of Parliament when section 3 became the law. The words of section 3, I quote: "Whether by things done or words said or by both together"—are not, in my judgment, apposite to embrace the perfectly ordinary, certain, and natural episodes or events in the life of a 17-day-old baby. Further, common law directions cannot be construed as including these natural and certain episodes that occur in the life of every baby of days old. Finally, I think civilised society dictates that the natural episodes occurring in the life of a baby only days old have to be endured and cannot be utilised as the foundation of subjective provocation to enable his killer to escape a conviction for murder.'

We appreciate the reasons which the learned judge gave for reaching the conclusion that he did, but we are unable to construe section 3 in such a light. The first sentence of section 3 reads: 'Where on a charge of murder there is evidence on which the jury can find that the person charged was provoked . . . to lose his self-control.' There is no doubt, and it is not in dispute, that there was here evidence upon which the appellant was—I use the word loosely 'provoked' to lose his self-control. . . . .

The reasoning which the learned judge gave, understandable though it was, involves, in our view, adding in to section 3 words which are not there, presumably by way of restriction. It is accepted by Mr Klevan [for the Crown] that there was evidence which linked causally the crying of the baby with the response of the appellant. Accordingly, in our view, it seems inevitable that that being so the section is mandatory and requires the learned judge to leave the issue of the objective test to the jury.

Mr Klevan also referred us to what might, in shorthand, be called the 'floodgates proposition', that if the learned judge's direction was wrong it opens up the possibility that in any case in which there is a battered baby allegation and the baby dies, the argument based on provocation may be raised. We feel that even if that submission was right it could not be allowed to dissuade us from putting a construction on section 3 which, in our view, its wording plainly constrains. We also feel that reliance can be placed upon the common sense of juries upon whom the task of deciding the issue is imposed by section 3 and that common sense will ensure that only in cases where the facts fully justified it would their verdict be likely to be that they would hold that a defendant's act in killing a crying child would be the response of a reasonable man within the section. That matter is, in our view, imposed by Parliament upon the jury, not upon a judge, and the common sense of juries can be relied upon not to bring in perverse verdicts where the facts do not justify the conclusion.

In our view, therefore, though fully understanding his reasons, we are of the view that the learned judge was wrong in not leaving the issue of provocation to the jury."

**Appeal allowed in part**
**Conviction of manslaughter substituted**[79]

As this case makes clear, once there is evidence of provocation in a "loose" sense, the issue must be put to the jury:

"It is now well established that even if the defence do not raise the issue of provocation, and even if they would prefer not to because it is inconsistent with and will detract from the primary defence, the judge must leave the issue to the jury to

---

[79] For criticism of this case, see Horder, "The Problem of Provocative Children" [1987] Crim.L.R.655. He argues that cases where children are the provokers "pose difficulties that go to the root of the rationale for the doctrine of provocation" (at 661), because the courts seem to concentrate exclusively on provocation as a partial excuse. His view is that provocation is still a partial justification; the victim is to some extent "asking for it". But, as he rightly argues, a baby cannot be said to have enough responsibility to be "asking for it".

decide if there is evidence which suggests that the accused may have been provoked; and this is so even if the evidence of provocation is slight or tenuous in the sense that the measure of the provocative acts or words is slight."[80]

Of course, there has to be *some* evidence: in *Acott*[81] it was stated that a speculative possibility that there may have been provocation should not lead the judge to direct the jury to consider it. Welcome though this statement is, together with the fact that there must have been some human action upon which the plea is based, there are, nevertheless, grounds for concern. The (strong) word "provoked" appears to have been reduced, by its "loose" interpretation, to mere causation.[82] It is then left to the jury, as is increasingly the case in the criminal law, to decide for themselves the merits of the claim. It is arguable that an important preliminary element of the defence has been lost[83] in the understandable judicial desire to make concessions to "human frailty".

Once the issue of provocation has been put to the jury, they then have to satisfy themselves as to two questions:

**a. Subjective loss of self-control** The law will partially excuse the defendant who has "lost self-control". No matter how severe the provocation, if the defendant is in control at the time of the killing, there is no evidence upon which the defence can be based.[84] This is meant to exclude from the ambit of the defence planned or revenge killings and in the majority of cases where a sudden killing follows on from a highly provocative incident it will more or less be assumed that the defendant had lost control. However, in some cases it will be more problematic and the case-law is disappointing in explaining what "loss of self-control" means. The cases refer to the defendant not being "master of his own understanding",[85] although beyond using phrases such as "snapping", or "exploding into anger", little further attention is generally paid to this element.[86] It does not mean that it is necessary for the defendant to have "gone berserk"[87]: such an extreme (and rare) condition might even be inconsistent with a finding that the defendant acted with an intention to kill.[88] In *Richens*[89] it was stressed that there does not need to be a complete loss of

---

[80] *Stewart* [1996] 1 Cr.App.R.229. See also *Cox* [1995] 2 Cr.App.R.513; *Baillie* [1995] 2 Cr.App.R.31 and *Dhillon* [1997] Crim.L.R.295

[81] [1997] 2 Cr.App.R.94. See also, *Kromer* [2002] EWCA 1278.

[82] In which case, as Smith points out, the requirement that circumstances alone cannot amount to provocation appears "to look a little thin": Smith and Hogan, *Criminal Law* (10th ed., 2002), p. 366.

[83] See Allen, "Provocation's Reasonable Man: A Plea for Self-Control" [2000] J.of Crim.L.216 at 230 and Macklem and Gardner, "Provocation and Pluralism" [2001] 64 M.L.R. 815 at 817–820.

[84] As, in *Cocker* [1989] Crim.L.R.740 where the undeniably provocative behaviour of his terminally ill wife did *not* cause the defendant to lose control (as it could have done) but led him *calmly* to accede to her requests to die.

[85] *Per* Tindal C.J. in *Hayward* (1833) 6 C. & P. 157, 159, repeated in *Ahluwalia* (1993) 96 Cr.App.R.133 at 138 by Taylor L.C.J.

[86] Horder, *Provocation and Responsibility* (1992), p. 109; Ashworth, *Principles of Criminal Law* (3rd ed., 1999), pp. 276–277.

[87] Horder, *ibid.*, pp. 101–102.

[88] It is sometimes claimed (*Holmes* [1946] A.C. 588) that provocation negates malice aforethought. Both *Lee Chun-Chuen* [1963] A.C. 220 and the Royal Commission on Capital Punishment, Cmd.8932 (1953), at p. 51, point out that this is wrong if it means that the prosecution do not have to establish *mens rea*. If it did, one would not need a special defence of provocation. See also Horder, "Autonomy, Provocation and Duress" [1992] Crim.L.R.706 at 712–715.

[89] (1994) 98 Cr.App.R.43.

control so that the defendant does not know what he is doing; what is required is that the defendant be so angry as to be unable to restrain himself.

Thus, loss of self-control is equated with anger and not with fear or despair or other strong emotions. The person who kills through terror of what may happen to them is traditionally excluded from the ambit of the provocation defence if this terror does not express itself in anger.

This concept of anger requires further consideration. Horder has suggested that loss of self-control is one of the forms that anger may take.[90] For example, a lecturer may be so enraged by a late-comer to her lecture that her response is to take out a gun and shoot the unfortunate student. Taking this sequence of events apart, the late arrival of the student leads to a judgment being made by the lecturer that wrong has been done to her. This generates anger in the form of loss of control so that the lecturer responds "impetuously", without stopping to determine the appropriate response to the provocative event. She is so carried away that she does not pause to reflect that a verbal rebuke might have suited the occasion rather better.[91]

If, as Horder suggests, the modern law of provocation is based upon such a conception of anger, one can see why the law insisted that the loss of self-control be "sudden and temporary".[92] However, what *precisely* does the phrase "sudden and temporary" (added without the support of precedent in *Duffy*)[93] mean? Does it mean that the response must be more or less immediate? Courts have often stated that the more time "to cool down", the less likely it is that the defendant can be regarded as acting in anger, and the more likely it is that it will be seen as "planned" or "revenge".[94] However, in recent years the requirement that there be a sudden and temporary loss of control has been re-examined in cases of cumulative provocation.

### R. v Ahluwalia (1993) 96 Cr.App.R. 133 (Court of Appeal, Criminal Division)

The defendant, who had endured 10 years of violence and humiliation from her husband, threw petrol in his bedroom and set it alight. He sustained severe burns and died six days later. She was charged and convicted of murder. On appeal, it was argued that the direction that there be a sudden and temporary loss of control was wrong.

Taylor L.C.J.:
"This is a tragic case which has aroused much public attention. ...

*The appellant's case at trial*:
The appellant did not give evidence. No medical evidence was adduced on her behalf. Her case was that she had no intention either of killing her husband or of doing him really serious

---

[90] *Above*, n.86, pp. 72–110. The other form Horder identifies is that of "anger as outrage" which has been lost to modern law: see further, *ibid.*, pp. 59–71.

[91] Despite the clear over-reaction in this example, it will not necessarily be the case that a hasty reaction is an excessive one. See further, Horder, *above*, n.86, pp. 107–109.

[92] *Duffy* [1949] 1 All E.R. 932.

[93] Ashworth, *above*, n.86, p. 276.

[94] The issue may be withdrawn from the jury if the delay is considerable. See, for example, *Ibrams, Gregory* (1982) 74 Cr.App.R.154 in which the Court of Appeal upheld the withdrawal of the defence from the jury in the case of two appellants who had delayed several days before retaliating.

harm, only to inflict some pain on him. Provocation was a secondary line of defence. To support it, reliance was placed upon the whole history of ill-treatment throughout the marriage, culminating on the night in the deceased's refusal to speak to her, his threat to use the hot iron upon her, his threat to beat her the next morning if she did not provide him with money and his clear indication that he wished the marriage to end. ...

*Sudden and temporary loss of self-control*:

The classic definition of provocation in law is that given by Devlin J. ... and which was approved by this Court in *Duffy* [1949] 1 All E.R. 932. He said:

'Provocation is some act, or series of acts done (or words spoken) ... which would cause in any reasonable person and actually causes in the accused, a sudden and temporary loss of self-control, rendering the accused so subject to passion as to make him or her for the moment not master of his or her own mind.' ...

The phrase 'sudden and temporary loss of self-control' encapsulates an essential ingredient of the defence of provocation in a clear and readily understandable phrase. It serves to underline that the defence is concerned with the actions of an individual who is not, at the moment when he or she acts violently, master of his or her own mind. [Counsel for the appellant] Mr Robertson suggested that the phrase might lead the jury to think that provocation could not arise for consideration unless the defendant's act followed immediately upon the acts or words which constituted the alleged provocation. ...

Nevertheless, it is open to the judge, when deciding whether there is any evidence of provocation to be left to the jury and open to the jury when considering such evidence, to take account of the interval between the provocative conduct and the reaction of the defendant to it. Time for reflection may show that after the provocative conduct made its impact on the mind of the defendant, he or she kept or regained self-control. The passage of time following the provocation may also show that the subsequent attack was planned or based on motives, such as revenge or punishment, inconsistent with the loss of self-control and therefore with the defence of provocation. In some cases, such an interval may wholly undermine the defence of provocation; that, however, depends entirely on the facts of the individual case and is not a principle of law.

Mr Robertson referred to the phrase 'cooling off period' which has sometimes been applied to an interval of time between the provocation relied upon and the fatal act. He suggests that although in many cases such an interval may indeed be a time for cooling and regaining control so as to forfeit the protection of the defence, in others the time lapse has an opposite effect. He submits ... that women who have been subjected frequently over a period to violent treatment may react to the final act or words by what he calls a 'slow-burn' reaction rather than by immediate loss of self-control.

We accept that the subjective element in the defence of provocation would not as a matter of law be negatived simply because of the delayed reaction in such cases, provided that there was at the time a 'sudden and temporary loss of self-control' caused by the alleged provocation. However, the longer the delay and the stronger the evidence of deliberation on the part of the defendant, the more likely it will be that the prosecution will negative provocation.

In the present case, despite the delay after the last provocative act or words by the deceased, and despite the appellant's apparent deliberation in seeking and lighting the petrol, the trial judge nevertheless left the issue of provocation to the jury. His references to 'sudden and temporary loss of self-control' were correct in law. He did not suggest to the jury that they should or might reject the defence of provocation because the last provocative act or word of the deceased was not followed immediately by the appellant's fatal acts.

We consider that the learned judge's direction was in accordance with the well established law and cannot be faulted.

Mr Robertson's argument in support of this ground of appeal amounted in reality to an invitation to this court to change the law. We are bound by the previous decisions of this court to which reference has been made, unless we were convinced that they were wholly wrong. Where a particular principle of law has been re-affirmed so many times and applied so generally over such a long period, it must be a matter for Parliament to consider any change. There are important considerations of public policy which would be involved should provocation be re-defined so as possibly to blur the distinction between sudden loss of self-control and deliberate retribution.[95]

[The court felt, however, that the defendant ought to have an opportunity to plead diminished responsibility.]"

**Appeal allowed.**
**Conviction quashed. Retrial ordered[96]**

The acceptance in *Ahluwalia* that a delayed reaction may still amount to killing under provocation was followed in *Baille*.[97] In this case the defendant, enraged, went to the attic to fetch a gun, drove two miles to the victim's house (stopping en route to fill up with petrol and having an accident on the way) and then killed the victim. The Court of Appeal concluded that although there might be difficulties with the defence of provocation succeeding, it should still have been left to the jury to determine. Thus, "sudden" should not be equated with "immediate" and treating delay as a matter of evidence rather than rule of law could open the door to the defence of provocation becoming available to more battered women who kill.[98] If this is the case, the chances of a manslaughter conviction rather than one of murder will be considerably greater, since at the moment such defendants are unlikely to succeed with a plea of self-defence, and they should not be placed in the position of having to plead diminished responsibility unless their debilitated mental condition makes this truly the appropriate plea. However, although it is now widely accepted that the current test of sudden and temporary loss of self-control is based upon a male typology of anger,[99] changing it may not be straightforward.[1]

There is little difficulty in those cases of cumulative provocation where there is an immediate trigger, even if it is trivial, to a loss of control that is sudden and temporary.[2] Courts are now more willing to look at the whole history of mistreatment in judging the nature of the provocation.[3] But what if there is no immediate trigger? It was this problem that the counsel in *Ahluwalia*[4] confronted by asking the court to consider so-called "slow-burn" anger. Such rage in women is to be regarded as "legally and morally equivalent to the paradigmatic male 'snapping'."[5] The question then is whether the person who kills during a state of

---

[95] The other point of appeal, relating to the objective requirement, is dealt with *below*, p. 701.

[96] At the re-trial a plea of guilty to manslaughter on the basis of diminished responsibility was accepted. Ahluwalia was sentenced to 40 months' imprisonment; this was the period she had already served.

[97] [1995] 2 Cr.App.R.31.

[98] Nicolson and Sanghvi, "Battered Women and Provocation: The Implications of *R. v Ahluwalia*" [1993] Crim.L.R.728 at 731.

[99] See, *e.g.* O'Donovan, "Defences For Battered Women Who Kill" (1991) 18 J.L. and Soc. 219.

[1] One can compare the *Ahluwalia* case with that of *Singh*, *The Times*, January 30, 1992, for example. In this latter case the defendant who *had* lost self-control was found guilty of manslaughter on the basis of provocation, after killing his wife "who had a sharp and persistent tongue".

[2] For a detailed discussion of cumulative provocation see Wasik, "Cumulative Provocation and Domestic Killing" [1982] Crim.L.R.29.

[3] See, for example, the judgment of Taylor L.C.J. in *Ahluwalia* (1993) 96 Cr.App.R.133 at 141. Recent decisions have emphasised that "guidance, in the form of a careful analysis" of the history should be given to the jury so that the full significance of events can be understood: *Humphreys* [1995] 4 All E.R. 1009 and *Stewart* [1996] 1 Cr.App.R.229.

[4] See also *Thornton* (1993) 96 Cr.App.R.112; *Thornton (No. 2)* [1996] 2 Cr.App.R.108. At Thornton's retrial she was convicted of manslaughter and sentenced to five years' imprisonment.

[5] Nicolson and Sanghvi, *above*, n.98 at 737.

slow-burn anger can really be said to be acting without self-control. This is going to be extremely difficult to establish evidentially and, arguably, amounts to abandoning not only the "sudden and temporary" element but also the entire requirement that there be a "loss of self-control".

### Jeremy Horder, Provocation and Responsiblity (1992), p. 190:

"Ironically, until the hardening of attitudes towards loss of self-control from the time of *Duffy* onwards, no real extension or relaxation of the law would have been required to incorporate such 'slow-burn' cases within the scope of the defence. The root of the trouble and misunderstanding has been the recent failure to recognise that the law's conception of anger has never always been loss of self-control alone, but has historically included outrage. Someone who acts in outrage acts on a principle of retributive justice, and may not be responding to a proximate triggering event in quite the way a tennis player responds to an opponent's shot with a 'reflex' volley. The person who boils up when her long-term violent abuser is asleep in his chair may well be acting out of provoked outrage, despite the absence of immediate provocation. Such a person's anger would historically have fallen within the scope of the defence. What is required is a restatement of this legal position, through substitution of references to provoked angry retaliation in place of references to provoked loss of self-control in the Homicide Act 1957, section 3."[6]

In contrast to Horder, who feels that the courts should return to their earlier, broader conception of anger, their Lordships in *Ahluwalia* took the view that any change to the principles governing provocation would have to come from Parliament. It is unfortunate, but understandable, that the law as stated in *Duffy* is felt to be too deeply entrenched for judicial amendment. However, the case for change is compelling. Whilst the law's insistence upon a loss of self-control may rightly serve to exclude revenge killings from the defence it has done so in a way which has focused attention on one form of emotional disturbance only.[7] Why should anger continue to receive special consideration? Just because one can trace the law back to much earlier notions of outraged honour does not mean that anger should continue to be a privileged emotion, especially when it has become so muddled with loss of self-control. Put simply, why should someone who kills out of (uncontrolled) anger be regarded today as morally more excusable than someone who kills through fear or despair of what has happened or may happen to them?[8] The most recent House of Lords' decision on provocation, *Smith*[9] appears to recognise this with Lord Hoffmann stating:

"There are people (such as battered wives) who would reject any suggestion that they were 'different from ordinary human beings' but have undergone experiences which, without any fault or defect of character on their part, have affected their powers of self-control. *In such cases the law now recognises that the emotions which may cause loss of self-control are not confined to anger but may include fear and despair* (our emphasis)."[10]

---

[6] See also, Horder, "Provocation and Loss of Self-Control" (1992) 108 L.Q.R. 191. Despite putting the case persuasively for extension of the law, Horder then goes on to call for the abolition of the defence. *Below*, pp. 718–719.

[7] And, moreover, has done so in a way which removed the 17th and 18th century's common-law tradition of proportionality: see, *above*, p. 684 and more generally, Gough, "Taking the Heat out of Provocation" [1999] 19 O.J.L.S. 481.

[8] One answer could be that given above, (*above*, p. 684) that, in fact, anger continues to be privileged because loss of control is justified by anger rather than excused.

[9] [2001]1 A.C. 146.

[10] At 168.

One needs to be cautious here. Lord Hoffmann made this point in a case in which the subjective issue of loss of control was not part of the appeal and where the argument rested upon the nature of the objective element (and, in particular, whether the objective standard of self-control varied depending on the defendant) and none of the other speeches in *Smith* go this far. Indeed, Lord Millett reaffirmed that the requirement for a sudden and temporary loss of self-control is the source of the difficulty battered women face in pleading provocation.

Whether there is still a need for reform, therefore, and the shape any such change might take, is a question to which we shall return once the second limb of the test has been considered.

**b. The reasonable man test** It is not sufficient to show that the defendant lost control. There is also, by virtue of section 3, "the question [of] whether the provocation was enough to make a reasonable man do as he did ... and in determining that question the jury shall take into account everything both done and said according to the effect which, in their opinion, it would have on a reasonable man."

Whether this amounts to a partial justification is, as already discussed, open to question.[11] We now need to consider the difficulties the courts have faced with the concept of the "reasonable man" who kills under provocation:

### State v Hoyt, 128 N.W. 2d 645, 21 Wis. 2d 284 (1964) (Supreme Court of Wisconsin)

Wilkie J.:

"The 'reasonable man' concept in the law generally has two distinct meanings. There is the statistical concept under which the reasonable man does what most people do in fact under the circumstances. Yet if this is the meaning of the test, it is clear that as a matter of fact a great majority of people will never commit murder no matter how violently provoked by another. A consistent application of this test, viewing the reasonable man as the statistical factual norm would, in effect read ... [the defence] ... out of existence.

However, in other contexts there is the ethical concept under which the reasonable man functions as the person the law *expects* everyone to be, regardless of whether a majority, in fact, fall short of the *moral* normal in actual conduct. To take this view of the reasonable man for the purposes of the provocation test would propel courts and juries into the strange task of deciding when a person, taken as the ethical ideal, would commit murder. This may well result in reading ... [the partial defence] out of existence. The person we expect people to be like would not solve his problems by murder. If we conclude that an ethical ideal—that person whom all others aspire to emulate—would be driven to kill under the circumstances of a given case, logically the verdict should be not guilty, not morally blameworthy to any degree. ...

The basic question is whether [the defendant] ... is as culpable as a person who kills solely for self-aggrandizement or out of sheer malevolence. To answer this question, we must place ourselves emphatically in the actual situation in which the defendant was placed, a situation which may be relatively unique. Therefore, an inquiry into what most people would do in such circumstances cannot be completely determinative of the issue. The test cannot be wholly objective or wholly subjective. ... The victim's conduct must be such that we conclude that the feeling and conduct of the defendant can be understood sympathetically,

[11] *Above*, pp. 684–686.

albeit not condoned. The trier-of-fact must be able to say: although I would have acted differently, and I believe most people would have acted differently, I can understand why this person gave way to the impulse to kill."

The courts have managed to evade the real question (a moral question) of whether the defendant could be expected to control the impulse to kill, by constructing the reasonable man test, which has been used in provocation cases since the 19th century.[12] Prior to the Homicide Act 1957, judges were able to control the test in two ways. Firstly, they could withdraw the issue from the jury on the basis that there was no evidence on which the jury could find that a reasonable man would have been provoked, and secondly, they were able to keep the test objective. In other words, the courts excluded from the reasonable man any of the characteristics of the defendant which might have had an impact on why, and the extent to which, he was provoked.

Thus, in *Bedder*[13] the House of Lords held that the fact that the defendant was impotent should be ignored in assessing whether his killing of the prostitute who had taunted him (as well as hitting and kicking him) was something a reasonable man might have done. The courts were loath to include any unusual physical characteristic for fear of "not knowing where to draw the line".[14] The extent to which the common law was changed by section 3 has only become clear in recent years:

### D.P.P. v Camplin [1978] A.C. 705 (House of Lords)

(The facts appear from the judgment of Lord Diplock)

Lord Diplock:
"The respondent, Camplin, who was 15 years of age, killed a middle-aged Pakistani, Mohammed Lal Khan, by splitting his skull with a chapati pan, a heavy kitchen utensil like a rimless frying pan. At the time the two of them were alone together in Khan's flat. At Camplin's trial for murder before Boreham J. his only defence was that of provocation so as to reduce the offence to manslaughter. According to the story that he told in the witness box but which differed materially from that which he had told to the police, Khan had buggered him in spite of his resistance and had then laughed at him. Whereupon Camplin had lost his self-control and attacked Khan fatally with the chapati pan. ...

The point of law of general public importance involved in the case has been certified as being:
'Whether, on the prosecution for murder of a boy of 15, where the issue of provocation arises, the jury should be directed to consider the question, under section 3 of the Homicide Act 1957 whether the provocation was enough to make a reasonable man do as he did by reference to a "reasonable adult" or by reference to a "reasonable boy of 15." '
...

[In] *Bedder v D.P.P.* ....the Court of Criminal Appeal had approved the summing-up [of the trial judge to ignore the issue of importance] when they said...:
'... no distinction is to be made in the case of a person who, though it may not be a matter of temperament is physically impotent, is conscious of that impotence, *and therefore*

---

[12] From the dicta of Keating J. in *Welsh* (1869) 11 Cox C.C. 336 at 339 who stated that provocation would be sufficient if it was "something which might naturally cause an ordinary and reasonably minded man to lose his self-control and commit such an act."

[13] *Bedder v D.P.P.* [1954] 1 W.L.R. 1119. For facts, see *above*, p. 682.

[14] Fletcher, *Rethinking Criminal Law*, (1978) p. 249; see also *Holmes* [1946] A.C. 588 and the Royal Commission on Capital Punishment, Cmd.8932, paras 139–145 where some reluctance to close the door completely was expressed before agreeing with judicial evidence that this should be done.

*mentally liable to be more excited unduly* if he is "twitted" or attacked on the subject of that particular infirmity.'

This statement, for which I have myself supplied the emphasis, was approved by Lord Simonds L.C. speaking on behalf of all the members of this House who sat on the appeal; but he also went on to lay down the broader proposition that:

'It would be plainly illogical not to recognise an unusually excitable or pugnacious temperament in the accused as a matter to be taken into account but yet to recognise for that purpose some unusual physical characteristic, be it impotence or another.'

... My Lords, ... section [3] ... was intended to mitigate in some degree the harshness of the common law of provocation ... [I]t brings about two important changes in the law. The first is it abolishes all previous rules of law as to what can or cannot amount to provocation and in particular the rule of law that ... words unaccompanied by violence could not do so. Secondly it makes clear that if there was any evidence that the accused himself at the time of the act which caused the death in fact lost his self-control in consequence of some provocation however slight it might appear to the judge, he was bound to leave to the jury the question, which is one of opinion not of law, whether a reasonable man might have reacted to that provocation as the accused did....

Although it is now for the jury to apply the 'reasonable man' test, it still remains for the judge to direct them what, in the new context of the section, is the meaning of this apparently inapt expression ...

As I have already pointed out, for the purposes of the law of provocation the 'reasonable man' has never been confined to the adult male. It means an ordinary person of either sex, not exceptionally excitable or pugnacious, but possessed of such powers of self-control as everyone is entitled to expect that his fellow citizens will exercise in society as it is today. A crucial factor in the defence of provocation from earliest times has been the relationship between the gravity of provocation and the way in which the accused retaliated, both being judged by the social standards of the day. When Hale was writing in the seventeenth century, pulling a man's nose was thought to justify retaliation with a sword; when *Mancini v D.P.P.* ... was decided by this House, a blow with a fist would not justify retaliation with a deadly weapon. But so long as words unaccompanied by violence could not in common law amount to provocation the relevant proportionality between provocation and retaliation was primarily one of degrees of violence. Words spoken to the accused before the violence started were not normally to be included in the proportion sum. But now that the law has been changed so as to permit of words being treated as provocation, even though unaccompanied by any other acts, the gravity of verbal provocation may well depend on the particular characteristics or circumstances of the person to whom a taunt or insult is addressed. To taunt a person because of his race, his physical infirmities or some shameful incident in his past may well be considered by the jury to be more offensive to the person addressed, however equable his temperament, if the facts on which the taunt is founded are true than it would be if they were not. It would stultify much of the mitigation of the previous harshness of the common law in ruling out verbal provocation as capable of reducing murder to manslaughter if the jury could not take into consideration all those factors which in their opinion would effect the gravity of taunts and insults when applied to the person to whom they are addressed. So to this extent at any rate the unqualified proposition accepted by this House in *Bedder v D.P.P.* ... that for the purposes of the 'reasonable man' test any unusual physical characteristics of the accused must be ignored requires revision as a result of the passing of the Act of 1957.

That he was only 15 years of age at the time of the killing is the relevant characteristic of the accused in the instant case. It is a characteristic which may have its effects on temperament as well as physique. If the jury think that the same power of self-control is not to be expected in an ordinary, average or normal boy of 15 as in an older person, are they to treat the lesser powers of self-control possessed by an ordinary, average or normal boy of 15 as the standard of self-control with which the conduct of the accused is to be compared?

It may be conceded that in strict logic there is a transition between treating age as a characteristic that may be taken into account in assessing the gravity of the provocation addressed to the accused and treating it as a characteristic to be taken into account in determining what is the degree of self-control to be expected of the ordinary person with whom the accused's conduct is to be compared. But to require old heads on young shoulders is inconsistent with the law's compassion of human infirmity to which Sir Michael Foster ascribed the doctrine of provocation more than two centuries ago. The distinction as to the purposes for which it is legitimate to take the age of the accused into account involves considerations of too great nicety to warrant a place in deciding a matter of opinion, which is no longer one to be decided by a judge trained in logical reasoning but by a jury drawing on their experience of how ordinary human beings behave in real life.

There is no direct authority prior to the Act of 1957 that expressly states that the age of the accused could not be taken into account in determining the standard of self-control for the purposes of the reasonable man test—unless this is implicit in the reasoning of Lord Simonds L.C. in *Bedder*. ... The Court of Appeal distinguished the instant case from that of *Bedder* on the ground that what it was there said must be ignored was an unusual characteristic that distinguished the accused from ordinary normal persons, whereas nothing could be more ordinary or normal than to be aged 15. The reasoning in *Bedder* would, I think, permit of this distinction between normal and abnormal characteristics, which may affect the powers of self-control of the accused; but for reasons that I have already mentioned the proposition stated in *Bedder* requires qualification as a consequence of changes in the law affected by the Act of 1957. To try to salve what can remain of it without conflict with the Act could in my view only lead to unnecessary and unsatisfactory complexity in a question which has now become a question for the jury alone. In my view *Bedder*, like *Mancini* ... and *Holmes*, ... ought no longer to be treated as an authority on the law of provocation.

In my opinion a proper direction to a jury on the question left to their exclusive determination by section 3 of the Act of 1957 would be on the following lines. The judge should state what the question is using the very terms of the section. He should then explain to them that the reasonable man referred to in the question is a person having the power of self-control to be expected of an ordinary person of the sex and age of the accused, but in other respects sharing such of the accused's characteristics as they think would affect the gravity of the provocation to him; and that the question is not merely whether such a person would in like circumstances be provoked to lose his self-control but also whether he would react to the provocation as the accused did."[15]

Appeal dismissed

The model direction appears to make two things clear. First, not all characteristics of the defendant have to be taken into account by the court and secondly, in determining which characteristics to include, a distinction needs to be drawn. Lord Diplock broadly adopts Ashworth's argument that "the proper distinction ... is that individual peculiarities which bear on the gravity of the provocation should be taken into account, whereas individual peculiarities bearing on the accused's level of self-control should not."[16] Thus, the fact that a defendant is impotent may be highly relevant if the defendant is claiming to have been taunted about his impotence, but is irrelevant in determining the level of self-control he should possess. However, Lord Diplock makes an exception to this in the model direction. Two characteristics are deemed to be relevant to the standard of self-control which may be expected of a defendant: age and sex. Age (or, rather, lack of age) is included because "to require old heads on young shoulders is

---

[15] In *Burke* [1987] Crim.L.R.336, it was held unnecessary for the judge to use the *exact* words of this direction but that the *full substance* of them must be made clear. In this case it was held that being a churchgoer was a relevant characteristic to be put to the jury in assessing a reaction to sexual harassment.

[16] "The Doctrine of Provocation" [1976] C.L.J. 292 at 300. See also, Williams, *Textbook of Criminal Law* (2nd ed., 1983) p. 540 where a similar argument is made.

inconsistent with law's compassion of human infirmity". The reason why this concession was also extended to sex has never been made clear.[17]

Unfortunately, Lord Diplock's speech is not free from ambiguity. While endorsing a distinction between characteristics which affect the gravity of the provocation and characteristics which affect the power of self-control he, nevertheless, added that this was of "too great nicety" for the jury whose task it is to determine whether the defendant was provoked. Be that as it may, acceptance of the distinction lies at the core of the decision of the House of Lords in *Morhall* and of the Privy Council in *Luc Thiet Thuan*.

### R. v Morhall [1996] 1 A.C. 90 (House of Lords)

The defendant stabbed the deceased during a fight, which had followed persistent taunts by the deceased and others, about the defendant's addiction to glue-sniffing. The defendant was convicted of murder and his appeal to the Court of Appeal was dismissed. It was held that a self-induced addiction to glue-sniffing brought on by voluntary and persistent abuse of solvents was wholly inconsistent with and repugnant to the concept of the reasonable man and could not, therefore, be included as a characteristic.

Lord Goff:
"The Court of Appeal gave leave to appeal to your Lordships' House, certifying that the following point of law of general public importance was involved in the decision:
'When directing a jury on provocation under section 3 of the Homicide Act 1957, and explaining to them in accordance with the model direction of Lord Diplock in *R. v Camplin* ... should the judge exclude from the jury's consideration characteristics and past behaviour of the defendant at which the taunts are directed, which in the judge's view are inconsistent with the concept of the reasonable man?' ...
[The issue] is whether the defendant's addiction to glue sniffing should have been taken into account as affecting the gravity of provocation.
Judging from the speeches in *R. v Camplin*, it should indeed have been taken into account. Indeed, it was a characteristic of peculiar relevance, since the words of the deceased which were said to constitute provocation were directed towards the defendant's shameful addiction to glue sniffing and his inability to break himself of it. Furthermore, there is nothing in the speeches in *R. v Camplin* to suggest that a characteristic of this kind should be excluded from consideration. On the contrary, ... Lord Diplock spoke of the jury taking into consideration 'all those factors' which would affect the gravity of the taunts or insults when applied to the defendant. Likewise, Lord Simon of Glaisdale said ...
'in determining whether a person of reasonable self-control would lose it in the circumstances, the entire factual situation, which includes the characteristics of the accused, should be considered.'
Even so the Court of Appeal felt that the defendant's addiction to glue-sniffing should be excluded because it was a characteristic which was repugnant to the concept of the reasonable man. It seems to me, with all respect, that this conclusion flows from a misunderstanding of the function of the so-called 'reasonable person test' in this context. In truth the expression 'reasonable man' or 'reasonable person' in this context can lead to misunderstanding. Lord Diplock described it (in *R. v Camplin* ...) as 'an apparently inapt expression'. This is because the reasonable person test is concerned not with ratiocination, nor with the reasonable man whom we know so well in the law of negligence (where we are concerned with reasonable foresight and reasonable care), nor with reasonable conduct generally. The function of the test is only to introduce, as a matter of policy, a standard of self-control which has to be complied with if provocation is to be established in law: ... Lord Diplock himself spoke of 'the reasonable or ordinary person', and indeed

---

[17] The Australian decision of *Masciantonio v R.* (1995) 69 A.L.J.R. 598 decided that age was the only factor relevant to the issue of self-control.

to speak of the degree of self-control attributable to the ordinary person is (despite the express words of the statute) perhaps more apt, and certainly less likely to mislead, than to do so with reference to the reasonable person. The word "ordinary" is in fact the adjective used in criminal codes applicable in some other common law jurisdictions (as in New Zealand) ... Indeed, by exploiting the adjective 'reasonable' it is easy to caricature the law as stated in section 3 of the Act of 1957 by talking of the test of, for example, the reasonable blackmailer or, nowadays perhaps, the reasonable glue-sniffer; indeed, the sting of the caricature is derived from the implication that the adjective 'reasonable' refers to a person who is guided by reason or who acts in a reasonable manner. This is however misleading. In my opinion it would be entirely consistent with the law as stated in section 3 of the Act of 1957, as properly understood, to direct the jury simply with reference to a hypothetical person having the power of self-control to be expected of an *ordinary* person of the age and sex of the defendant, but in other respects sharing such of the defendant's characteristics as they think would affect the gravity of the provocation to him. ...

[I]n an appropriate case, it may be necessary to refer to other circumstances affecting the gravity of the provocation to the defendant which do not strictly fall within the description 'characteristics', as for example the defendant's history or the circumstances in which he is placed at the relevant time. ... At all events in the present case, when the judge turned to the second and objective inquiry, he was entitled to direct the jury that they must take into account the entire factual situation (and in particular the fact that the provocation was directed at a habitual glue sniffer taunted with his habit) when considering the question whether the provocation was enough to cause a man possessed of an ordinary man's power of self control to act as the defendant did.

However, the point can be taken further. Among the characteristics stated to be excluded from consideration on the approach favoured by the Court of Appeal is that of being a paedophile. But suppose that a man who has been in prison for a sexual offence, for example rape, has after his release been taunted by another man with reference to that offence. It is difficult to see why, on ordinary principles, his characteristic or history as an offender of that kind should not be taken into account as going to the gravity of the provocation ...

In truth, the mere fact that a characteristic of the defendant is discreditable does not exclude it from consideration, as was made plain by Lord Diplock in *R. v Camplin* when, he referred to a shameful incident in a man's past as a relevant characteristic for present purposes. ...

Of course glue-sniffing (or solvent abuse), like indulgence in alcohol or the taking of drugs, can give rise to a special problem in the present context, because it may arise in more than one way. First, it is well established that, in considering whether a person having the power of self-control to be expected of an ordinary person would have reacted to the provocation as the defendant did, the fact (if it be the case) that the defendant was the worse for drink at the time should not be taken into account, even though the drink would, if taken by him, have the effect of reducing an ordinary person's power of self-control. It is sometimes suggested that the reason for this exclusion is that drunkenness is transitory and cannot therefore amount to a characteristic. But I doubt whether that is right. Indeed some physical conditions (such as eczema) may be transitory in nature and yet can surely be taken into account if the subject of taunts. In *R. v Camplin*, Lord Simon of Glaisdale considered that drunkenness should be excluded as inconsistent with the concept of the reasonable man in the sense of a man of ordinary self-control; but it has to be recognised that, in our society, ordinary people do sometimes have too much to drink. I incline therefore to the opinion that the exclusion of drunkenness in this context flows from the established principle that, at common law, intoxication does not of itself excuse a man from committing a criminal offence, but on one or other of these bases it is plainly excluded. At all events it follows that, in a case such as the present, a distinction may have to be drawn between two different situations. The first occurs where the defendant is taunted with his addiction (for example, that he is an alcoholic, or a drug addict, or a glue-sniffer), or even with having been intoxicated (from any cause) on some previous occasion. In such a case, however discreditable such condition may be, it may where relevant be taken into account as going to the gravity of the provocation. The second is the simple fact of the defendant being intoxicated—being drunk, or high with drugs or glue—at the relevant time, which may not be so taken into account, because that, like displaying a lack of ordinary self-control, is excluded as a matter of policy. Although the distinction is a fine one, it will, I suspect, very rarely be necessary to explain it to a jury. ... The present case may therefore be compared with *R. v Newell*, in which the defendant's chronic alcoholism was excluded from consideration because 'it had nothing to do with the words by which it is said that he was provoked'. ...

It follows from what I have said that I am, with all respect, unable to accept the reasoning, or the conclusion, of the Court of Appeal. ... In my opinion, the judge should have directed the jury to take into account the fact of the defendant's addiction to glue-sniffing when considering whether a person with the ordinary person's power of self-control would have reacted to the provocation as the defendant did."

**Appeal allowed**

## Luc Thiet Thuan v R. [1997] A.C. 131 (Privy Council)

The defendant and another man went to the flat of his ex-girlfriend to collect money which he said she owed him. She taunted him about her new boyfriend and his own sexual inadequacy. The defendant lost control and stabbed her repeatedly. At his trial he relied upon diminished responsibility and provocation. Two experts for the defence gave evidence that the defendant suffered from brain damage which could make it difficult for him to control his impulses. He was convicted of murder by the Hong Kong court and appealed to the Privy Council on the basis that the jury should have been directed to have regard to the defendant's brain damage when considering whether a reasonable man having the characteristics of the defendant would have reacted to the provocation as he did.[18]

Lord Goff:
"[T]heir Lordships return to the interpretation placed on the English statute in *R. v Camplin* ... for guidance in answering the question posed for their consideration in the present case. Their conclusion is that, on the principles there stated, there is no basis upon which mental infirmity on the part of the defendant which has the effect of reducing his powers of self-control below that to be expected of an ordinary person can, as such, be attributed to the ordinary person for the purposes of the objective test in provocation.

First of all, for mental infirmity of the defendant so to be taken into account would be inconsistent with the statute as interpreted in *R. v Camplin*, in which it was held that the reasonable man referred to in the statute means a person having the power of self-control to be expected of an ordinary person. But their Lordships wish to state that, in so holding, they are not simply treating the matter as one of literal application of the principle stated in *R. v Camplin*. That principle is, in their respectful opinion, well-founded in law. It is widely accepted that section 3 of the Act of 1957 is not a codifying Act, but an amending Act which expressly recognised and retained the objective test as established in the common law subject to the amendments provided for in the section. Having regard to the principles of common law then applicable, the intention must, as Professor Ashworth has convincingly demonstrated in his article ['The Doctrine of Provocation' [1976] C.L.J. 292 at 299–300], have been that individual peculiarities of the defendant affecting his power of self-control should not, as such, be taken into account for the purposes of the objective test. Moreover an indication of the problems involved in so taking mental infirmity into account is provided by *R. v Raven* [1982] Crim.L.R.51, which was concerned with the trial for murder of a man whose physical age was 22 years, but whose mental age was only nine years. The Recorder of London directed the jury that, in considering the objective test in provocation, they should attribute to the reasonable man the retarded development and mental age of the defendant. It is scarcely surprising that Professor Birch, in her commentary on the report, should have expressed the opinion ... that 'putting oneself in the position of a reasonable 22-year-old

[18] The Hong Kong Homicide Ordinance, s.4 is defined in identical terms to s.3 of the Homicide Act 1957.

with a mental age of nine is a tremendously difficult feat' [see [1982] Crim.L.R.51 at 52]. Even greater problems would arise if the defendant's argument was to be accepted in the present case, in which event the jury should have been directed to attribute to the reasonable man, *i.e.* a man having the ordinary man's power of self-control, the defendant's brain damage, with the consequent impairment of that power ...

It is, of course, consistent with Lord Diplock's analysis in *R. v Camplin* ... and indeed with the decision of the House of Lords in *R. v Morhall*, that mental infirmity of the defendant, if itself the subject of taunts by the deceased, may be taken into account as going to the gravity of the provocation as applied to the defendant. ... But this is a far cry from the defendant's submission that the mental infirmity of the defendant, impairing his power of self-control should as such be attributed to the reasonable man for the purposes of the objective test ...

But their Lordships wish to add that the recognition by the legislature of the defence of diminished responsibility gives a defendant suffering from abnormality of mind the opportunity to establish a defence upon which a very wide interpretation has been placed by the courts and which, if proved, has like provocation the effect of reducing to manslaughter what would otherwise be murder. ...

Their Lordships wish to add, as a footnote, that it may be open to a defendant to establish provocation in circumstances in which the act of the deceased, though relatively unprovocative if taken in isolation, was the last of a series of acts which finally provoked the loss of self-control by the defendant and so precipitated his extreme reaction which led to the death of the deceased."

**Appeal dismissed**

The combined effect of the decisions of *Morhall* and *Luc Thiet Thuan* appears to be the following:

1. Provocation is a defence which attempts to make concessions to "human frailty" but is addressed to those defendants who "are in a broad sense mentally normal".[19] The (wide) partial defence of diminished responsibility exists for those defendants who kill while suffering from an abnormality of mind.[20]

2. In cases where there is a real connection between the provocation and the characteristic relied upon by the defendant (and in many cases it will be appropriate to talk in terms of the provocation being aimed at the characteristic) there appears to be almost no limit to the sorts of characteristics which may be considered, however "shameful" that characteristic might seem.

3. In some cases the facts will require the jury to draw a distinction between matters which go to the powers of self-control of the defendant (where only age and sex are permitted to vary the ordinary standard demanded) and those which affect the gravity of the provocation. If one takes, for example, an alcoholic defendant who is taunted about his alcoholism, jury members will have to separate in their own minds the issue of the current intoxicated state of the defendant (which has to be ignored as a matter of policy and which would go to the issue of self-control) from the characteristic of alcoholism (which they may consider). Thus, the question is whether an alcoholic having the same degree of self control as the person of similar age and sex would have reacted as the defendant did to taunts about his condition.[21]

[19] Ashworth, *above*, n.86 at 314.
[20] There is some evidence that defendants may have a better chance of a conviction for manslaughter (rather than murder) if they plead both provocation and diminished responsibility: see Mackay, "Pleading Provocation and Diminished Responsibility Together" [1988] Crim.L.R.411. See further, *Roberts* [2002] LTL24/2/2002.
[21] See further, Horder, "Provocation's 'Reasonable Man' Reassessed" (1996) 112 L.Q.R. 35.

This is a difficult distinction and it is not altogether surprising that there is a strong line of Court of Appeal decisions which, in an attempt to do justice to the individual defendant, has blurred the distinction.[22] In *Thornton (No. 2)* Lord Taylor C.J. stated:

"A defendant, even if suffering from ... [Battered Woman Syndrome], cannot succeed in relying on provocation unless the jury consider she suffered or may have suffered a sudden and temporary loss of self-control at the time of the killing. That is not to say that Battered Woman Syndrome has no relevance to the defence of provocation. The severity of such a syndrome and the extent to which it may have affected a particular defendant will no doubt vary and is for the jury to consider. But it may be relevant in two ways. First, it may form an important background to whatever triggered the *actus reus*. A jury may more readily find there was a sudden loss of control triggered by even a minor incident if the defendant had endured abuse over a period, on the 'last straw' basis. Secondly, depending on the medical evidence, the syndrome may have affected the defendant's personality so as to constitute a significant characteristic relevant ... to the second question the jury has to consider in relation to provocation."[23]

In *Humphreys*[24] the Court of Appeal held that it was appropriate to take into account abnormal immaturity and attention-seeking by wrist-slashing in determining whether a reasonable person in the defendant's situation would have lost self-control and in *Dryden*[25] the court concluded that the defendant's obsessive nature and eccentric character should have been specifically left to the jury to consider.

Surprisingly, given the existence of both *Morhall* and *Luc Thiet Thuan* these Court of Appeal decisions were approved by the House of Lords in its latest decision.

### R. v Smith [2001] 1 A.C. 146 (House of Lords)

The defendant killed his friend in an argument over tools. At his trial for murder he raised three defences: (a) lack of intention to cause death or really serious harm; (b) provocation; (c) diminished responsibility. In relation to provocation, the defendant's case was that he was suffering from serious clinical depression and that as a result of three incidents involving the deceased (particularly the respondent's belief that the deceased had stolen his tools) he had been so provoked as to lose his self-control and to kill him.

The trial judge ruled that severe depressive illness was not a matter for the jury to take into account in deciding whether an ordinary man sharing the respondent's characteristics would have lost his self control. In his summing up he told the jury that a depressive state was a characteristic to be taken into account when dealing with the gravity of the provocation but that the fact that the depressive illness might have affected his powers of self-control was

---

[22] Relying, in part, on the dissenting speech of Lord Steyn in *Luc Thiet Thuan*.
[23] [1996] 2 Cr.App.R.108 at 116 following *Ahluwalia* (1993) 96 Cr.App.R.133. See also *Hobson* [1998] 1 Cr.App.R.31.
[24] [1995] 4 All E.R. 1008.
[25] [1995] 4 All E.R. 987. See also *Campbell (No.2)* [1997] Crim.L.R.227 and *Parker* [1997] Crim.L.R.760.

irrelevant. He was convicted of murder. The Court of Appeal allowed the appeal on the direction as to provocation but rejected the other grounds of appeal. The court gave leave to appeal and certified the following question:

"Are characteristics other than age and sex, attributable to a reasonable man, for the purpose of section 3 of the Homicide Act 1957, relevant not only to the gravity of the provocation to him but also to the standard of self-control to be expected?"

Lord Hoffmann:

"2. *The defence of provocation.*

[T]he common law of provocation was tolerably well settled. First, the provocation had to be such as to temporarily deprive the person provoked of the power of self-control, as a result of which he committed the unlawful act which caused death. Secondly, the provocation had to be such as would have made a reasonable man act in the same way. These two requirements are commonly called the subjective and objective elements of the defence respectively....

Section [3 of the Homicide Act 1957] plainly changed the law in two ways. First, it provided that if there was evidence that the accused was provoked to lose his self-control (the subjective element) then the question of whether the objective element was satisfied had to be left to the jury. The judge was not entitled, as he could at common law, to withdraw the issue from the jury if he thought there was no evidence upon which a jury could reasonably consider that the objective element might have been satisfied. Secondly, the jury could for this purpose take into account 'everything both said and done.' This removed any legal restriction on the kind of acts that could amount to provocation ...

The question which came before the House in *Reg. v Camplin* was whether by implication the section had also changed a third common law doctrine. This was the rule in *Bedder* which required the 'reasonable person' to be devoid of any particular characteristics.... The House decided that since provocation by words was frequently directed at some characteristic of the accused, such as his past behaviour, disabilities or race, the change in the law which allowed such taunts or insults to constitute provocation would be ineffectual if the accused had to be assumed to lack such a characteristic. It was therefore decided that, at least for the purpose of considering the gravity of the provocation, the reasonable man should normally be assumed to share the relevant characteristics of the accused. Whether the decision went further and allowed the jury to take into account characteristics of the accused which affected his powers of self-control is the chief question in this appeal ... It can however be said that *Camplin* allowed at least one such characteristic to be taken into account, namely, the youth of the accused....

The extent to which matters affecting the power of self-control should be taken into account divided the Judicial Committee of the Privy Council in *Luc Thiet Thuan v The Queen*. The majority, in an opinion given by Lord Goff of Chieveley, decided that in principle the actual characteristics of the accused were relevant only to the gravity of the provocation. The only characteristics of the accused which could be attributed to the reasonable person for the purpose of expressing a standard of self-control were his or her age and sex....

6. *The construction of section 3.*

... [O]ne has to conclude that the concept of the reasonable man as a touchstone of the objective element could not have been intended to stay the same.

The reasons are to be found in both the other changes expressly made by the section. The first, namely the admission of words as a legitimate source of provocation..... It was this reason which received the main emphasis in *Camplin*. But the other change, in the respective roles of judge and jury, was equally important...

[T]he jury was given a normative as well as a fact-finding function. They were to determine not merely whether the behaviour of the accused complied with some legal standard but could determine for themselves what the standard in the particular case should be. In this way they could, as the Royal Commission said, 'give weight to factors personal to the prisoner' in cases in which it appeared unjust not to do so.

It follows, in my opinion, that it would not be consistent with section 3 for the judge to tell the jury as a matter of law that they should ignore any factor or characteristic of the accused in deciding whether the objective element of provocation had been satisfied. That would be to trespass upon their province . . . If, therefore, the purpose of section 3 was to legitimate the normative role of the jury and free their consciences from the burden of having to give a perverse verdict in order to do justice, it must have had a corresponding effect upon the nature of the directions they were to be given by the judge. . . . But that did not mean that he was required to leave the jury at large and without any assistance in the exercise of their normative role. He could tell the jury that the doctrine of provocation included the principle of objectivity and that they should have regard to that principle in deciding whether the act in question was sufficiently provocative to be acceptable as a partial excuse. . . .

### 7. *D.P.P. v Camplin* [1978] A.C. 705.

[Lord Hoffman drew their] Lordships' attention to the following points:

(1) Lord Diplock says that youth may be taken into account because the principle of compassion to human infirmity, as a jury drawing on their experience may apply it, requires one to do so. He does not say that the same principle of compassion is incapable of applying to any other characteristics which a jury might on similar grounds think should be taken into account. It would have been easy for him to have said that youth was for this purpose unique.

(2) Lord Diplock expressly rejects the distinction between the effect of age on the gravity of the provocation and on the power of self-control on the grounds that it is 'of too great nicety' for application by a jury. Again, there is nothing to suggest that this comment is not equally true of other characteristics. . . .

(3) If age were to be the only case in which a particular characteristic could be taken into account as relevant to the expected power of self-control, it would be necessary to explain why it should be so singled out. The High Court of Australia, in *Stingel v The Queen* (1990) 171 C.L.R. 312, 330, said that it was because age is a normal characteristic: 'the process of development from childhood to maturity is something which, being common to us all, is an aspect of ordinariness.' This explanation was embraced by Lord Goff of Chieveley in *Luc Thiet Thuan v The Queen*. It had, as I have said, been relied upon in *Camplin* by the Court of Appeal to distinguish *Bedder*. But the distinction between normal and abnormal characteristics was expressly rejected by Lord Diplock. He said that:

'The reasoning in *Bedder* would, I think, permit of this distinction between normal and abnormal characteristics, which may affect the powers of self-control of the accused; but for reasons that I have already mentioned the proposition stated in *Bedder* requires qualification as a consequence of the changes in the law effected by the Act of 1957. To try to salve what can remain of it without conflict with the Act could in my view only lead to unnecessary and unsatisfactory complexity in a question which has now become a question for the jury alone.'

My Lords, the important passage which I have cited from Lord Diplock's speech provides in my view no support for the theory, widely advanced in the literature, that he was making a clear distinction between characteristics relevant to the gravity of the provocation and characteristics relevant to the power of self-control, with age (and possibly sex) as arbitrary exceptions which could be taken into account for the latter purpose. This interpretation depends principally upon [the model direction, above p. 696] . . .

The references to age and sex have been taken to mean that in all cases these are the only matters which should be mentioned as relevant to the question of self-control. It seems to me clear, however, that Lord Diplock was framing a suitable direction for a case like *Camplin* and not a one-size-fits-all direction for every case of provocation. A jury would be puzzled about why they were being asked to pay particular attention to the age and sex of the defendant if he was an ordinary adult. A number of writers and judges have thought that Lord Diplock was wrong to include the sex of the accused (see, for example, *Stingel v The Queen*) and if the direction had been intended to be of general application, I would agree. But in my view Lord Diplock was only drawing attention to the fact that the hormonal development of male adolescents is different from that of females.

Finally, my Lords, I draw attention to the concluding sentence of Lord Diplock's speech, in which he summed up why he thought it would be wrong to direct the jury that they were not entitled to take into account the youth of the accused. It was because:

'So to direct them was to impose a fetter on the right and duty of the jury which the Act accords to them to act upon their own opinion on the matter.'

This, in my view, goes to the heart of the matter and is in accordance with the analysis of the effect of section 3 which I have made earlier in my speech. The jury is entitled to act upon its own opinion of whether the objective element of provocation has been satisfied and the judge is not entitled to tell them that for this purpose the law requires them to exclude from consideration any of the circumstances or characteristics of the accused.

### 8. *The gravity of provocation/self-control distinction.*

Although *D.P.P. v Camplin* does not in my opinion provide authoritative support for the distinction between gravity of provocation and powers of self-control, it has been adopted in ....[a number of jurisdictions and supported by academic writings]. It must therefore be considered on its own merits.

The theoretical basis for the distinction is that provocation is a defence for people who are, as Professor Ashworth put it, "in a broad sense mentally normal:" see [1976] C.L.J. at p. 312. If they claim that they had abnormal characteristics which reduced their powers of self-control, they should plead diminished responsibility. There is a clear philosophical distinction between a claim that an act was at least partially excused as normal behaviour in response to external circumstances and a claim that the actor had mental characteristics which prevented him from behaving normally . . .

The difficulty about the practical application of this distinction in the law of provocation is that in many cases the two forms of claim are inextricably muddled up with each other . . .

Besides these practical difficulties in explaining the distinction to the jury, I think it is wrong to assume that there is a neat dichotomy between the 'ordinary person' contemplated by the law of provocation and the 'abnormal person' contemplated by the law of diminished responsibility. The Act of 1957 made a miscellany of changes of the law of homicide which can hardly be described as amounting to a coherent and interlocking scheme. Diminished responsibility as defined in section 2 . . . is a general defence which can apply whatever the circumstances of the killing and was introduced because of what was regarded as the undue strictness of the defence of insanity. Provocation is a defence which depends upon the circumstances of the killing and section 3 was introduced, as I have suggested, to legitimate the consideration by juries of 'factors personal to the prisoner'. If one asks whether Parliament contemplated that there might be an overlap between these two defences, I think that the realistic answer is that no one gave the matter a thought. But the possibility of overlap seems to me to follow inevitably from consigning the whole of the objective element in provocation to the jury. If the jury cannot be told that the law requires characteristics which could found a defence of diminished responsibility to be ignored in relation to the defence of provocation, there is no point in claiming that the defences are mutually exclusive.

There are in practice bound to be cases in which the accused will not be suffering from 'abnormality of mind' within the meaning of section 2 ('a state of mind so different from that of ordinary human beings that the reasonable man would term it abnormal': *Reg. v Byrne* [1960] 2 Q.B. 396, 403) but will nevertheless have mental characteristics (temporary or permanent) which the jury might think should be taken into account for the purposes of the provocation defence. The boundary between the normal and abnormal is very often a matter of opinion . . .

There is, however, one really serious argument in favour of the distinction between characteristics affecting the gravity of the provocation and characteristics affecting the power of self-control. This is the claim that, despite all its difficulties of application, it is the only way to hold the line against complete erosion of the objective element in provocation. The purpose of the objective element in provocation is to mark the distinction between (partially) excusable and inexcusable loss of self-control. As Lord Diplock said in *D.P.P. v Camplin*, the conduct of the accused should be measured against 'such powers of self-control as everyone is entitled to expect that his fellow citizens will exercise in society as it is today'. If there is no limit to the characteristics which can be taken into account, the fact that the accused lost self-control will show that he is a person liable in such circumstances to lose his self-control. The objective element will have disappeared completely.

My Lords, I share the concern that this should not happen. For the protection of the public, the law should continue to insist that people must exercise self-control. A person who flies into a murderous rage when he is crossed, thwarted or disappointed in the vicissitudes of life should not be able to rely upon his anti-social propensity as even a partial excuse for killing ... Male possessiveness and jealousy should not today be an acceptable reason for loss of self-control leading to homicide ... So, it is suggested, a direction that characteristics such as jealousy and obsession should be ignored in relation to the objective element is the best way to ensure that ... [defendants claiming this] cannot rely upon the defence ...

### 10. Guiding the jury

... The effect of section 3 is that once the judge has ruled that there is evidence upon which the jury can find that something caused the accused to lose self-control ...he cannot tell the jury that the act in question was incapable of amounting to provocation. But that no longer involves any decision by the judge that it would be rational so to decide. For example, in *Reg. v Doughty* the Court of Appeal held that the judge had been wrong to direct the jury that the crying of a 17–day old baby, which had caused its father to kill it by covering its head with cushions and kneeling on them, could not constitute a provocative act. Section 3 said that the jury were entitled to take into account 'everything both done and said'. I respectfully think that this construction of the Act was correct. But that does not mean that the judge should tell the jury that the crying of the baby was, in the traditional language, capable of amounting to provocation. This would give the jury the impression that the judge thought it would be rational and in accordance with principle to hold that the crying of the baby constituted an acceptable partial excuse for killing it. The point about section 3 is that it no longer matters whether the judge thinks so or not. He should therefore be able simply to tell the jury that the question of whether such behaviour fell below the standard which should reasonably have been expected of the accused was entirely a matter for them. He should not be obliged to let the jury imagine that the law now regards anything whatever which caused loss of self-control (whether an external event or a personal characteristic of the accused) as necessarily being an acceptable reason for loss of self-control.

### 11. The reasonable man

The main obstacle to directing the jury in a way which does not give such a false impression is the highly artificial way in which courts and writers have attempted to marry two discordant ideas: first, the old formula that the provocation must have been such as to cause a 'reasonable man' to act in the same way as the accused and, secondly, the rule in section 3 that no circumstances or characteristics should be excluded from the consideration of the jury. They have done so by telling the jury that certain characteristics are to be 'attributed' to the reasonable man. By such a combination, they have produced monsters like the reasonable obsessive, the reasonable depressive alcoholic and even ...the reasonable glue-sniffer. Nor does it elucidate matters to substitute 'ordinary' for 'reasonable'. Quite apart from the question of whether the jury can understand what such concepts mean, it is bound to suggest to them that obsession, alcoholism and so forth are not merely matters which they are entitled in law to take into account but that, being 'attributed' to the reasonable man, they are qualities for which allowances must be made. ... [T]he concept of the 'reasonable man' has never been more than a way of explaining the law to a jury; an anthropomorphic image to convey to them, with a suitable degree of vividness, the legal principle that even under provocation, people must conform to an objective standard of behaviour which society is entitled to expect. ... In referring to 'the reasonable man' section 3 invokes that standard. But I do not think that it was intended to require judges always to use that particular image ... [Moreover] the value of the image has been hopelessly compromised by the Act of 1957 ... [I]t seems to me now, since *Camplin*, impossible to avoid giving the jury a misleading, not to say unintelligible, account of the law when particular characteristics, sometimes highly unusual and even repulsive, are welded onto the concept of the reasonable man. . . .

I do emphasise that what has been rendered unworkable is not the principle of objectivity which (subject to the changes noted in *Camplin*) section 3 was plainly intended to preserve, but a particular way of explaining it. I am not suggesting that your Lordships should in any way depart from the legal principle embodied in section 3 but only that the principle should be expounded in clear language rather than by the use of an opaque formula.

In my opinion, therefore, judges should not be required to describe the objective element in the provocation defence by reference to a reasonable man, with or without attribution of personal characteristics. They may instead find it more helpful to explain in simple language the principles of the doctrine of provocation. First, it requires that the accused should have killed while he had lost self-control and that something should have caused him to lose self-control. For better or for worse, section 3 left this part of the law untouched. Secondly, the fact that something caused him to lose self-control is not enough. The law expects people to exercise control over their emotions. A tendency to violent rages or childish tantrums is a defect in character rather than an excuse. The jury must think that the circumstances were such as to make the loss of self-control sufficiently *excusable* to reduce the gravity of the offence from murder to manslaughter. This is entirely a question for the jury. In deciding what should count as a sufficient excuse, they have to apply what they consider to be appropriate standards of behaviour; on the one hand making allowance for human nature and the power of the emotions but, on the other hand, not allowing someone to rely upon his own violent disposition. In applying these standards of behaviour, the jury represent the community and decide, as Lord Diplock said in *Camplin*, what degree of self-control 'everyone is entitled to expect that his fellow citizens will exercise in society as it is today'. The maintenance of such standards is important. As Viscount Simon L.C. said more than 50 years ago in *Holmes v D.P.P.* [1946] A.C. 588, 601, 'as society advances, it ought to call for a higher measure of self-control'.

The general principle is that the same standards of behaviour are expected of everyone, regardless of their individual psychological make-up. In most cases, nothing more will need to be said. But the jury should in an appropriate case be told, in whatever language will best convey the distinction, that this is a principle and not a rigid rule. It may sometimes have to yield to a more important principle, which is to do justice in the particular case. So the jury may think that there was some characteristic of the accused, whether temporary or permanent, which affected the degree of control which society could reasonably have expected of *him* and which it would be unjust not to take into account. If the jury take this view, they are at liberty to give effect to it.

I do not wish to lay down any prescriptive formula for the way in which the matter is explained to the jury. I am sure that if judges are freed from the necessity of invoking the formula of the reasonable man equipped with an array of unreasonable 'eligible characteristics', they will be able to explain the principles in simple terms. Provided that the judge makes it clear that the question is in the end one for the jury and that he is not seeking to 'impose a fetter on the right and duty of the jury which the Act accords to them', the guidance which he gives must be a matter for his judgment on the facts of the case . . .

13. *Conclusion.*

In my opinion the judge should not have directed the jury as a matter of law that the effect of Smith's depression on his powers of self-control was 'neither here nor there'. They should have been told that whether they took it into account in relation to the question of whether the behaviour of the accused had measured up to the standard of self-control which ought reasonably to have been expected of him was a matter for them to decide . . . I would dismiss the appeal."

Lord Clyde:
"[I]f the appellant is correct, it seems to me that there would be a serious risk of injustice being done in some cases where the homicide is due to provocation but the condition of the accused falls short of a mental abnormality. While I fully recognise the importance of not

allowing the effects of a quarrelsome or choleric temperament to serve as a factor which may reduce the crime of murder to one of manslaughter, nevertheless I consider that justice cannot be done without regard to the particular frailties of particular individuals where their capacity to restrain themselves in the face of provocation is lessened by some affliction which falls short of a mental abnormality. It does not seem to me that it would be just if in assessing their guilt in a matter of homicide a standard of behaviour had to be applied to people which they are incapable of attaining. I would not regard it as just for a plea of provocation made by a battered wife whose condition falls short of a mental abnormality to be rejected on the ground that a reasonable person would not have reacted to the provocation as she did. The reasonable person in such a case should be one who is exercising a reasonable level of self-control for someone with her history, her experience and her state of mind. On such an approach a jury should be perfectly capable of returning a realistic answer and thus achieve a verdict which would fairly meet any peculiarities of the particular case consistently with the recognition of the importance of curbing temper and passion in the interest of civil order . . .

It may be thought that the introduction of the reasonable man to this area of the law has added unnecessary obscurity to what ought to be a matter of relative simplicity; but he has been perpetuated in the formulation of the statutory provision. All the greater care is needed to secure that he does not lead the law into wonderland.

There is then a potential tension between the requirement of society that people should restrain their natural passions and the law's compassion for those who under the stress of provocation temporarily lose their self-control. This is not solved by recourse to the concept of the reasonable man. That concept may indeed make the solution the more elusive . . .

Even those who are sympathetic with what may be described as an objective approach have to recognise that at its extreme it is unacceptable. So a concession is made for considerations of the age and sex of the accused. But then the problem arises why consideration should not be given to other characteristics. Some groups of people may be seen to be by nature more susceptible to provocation than others. Some races may be more hot-blooded than others. Nor do age or gender necessarily carry with them unusual levels of self-control or the lack of it. The problem is to identify where in the middle ground between these two extremes the line is to be drawn. It seems to me that the standard of reasonableness in this context should refer to a person exercising the ordinary power of self-control over his passions which someone in his position is able to exercise and is expected by society to exercise. By position I mean to include all the characteristics which the particular individual possesses and which may in the circumstances bear on his power of control other than those influences which have been self-induced. Society should require that he exercise a reasonable control over himself, but the limits within which control is reasonably to be demanded must take account of characteristics peculiar to him which reduce the extent to which he is capable of controlling himself. Such characteristics as an exceptional pugnacity or excitability will not suffice. Such tendencies require to be controlled. Section 3 requires that the accused should have made reasonable efforts to control himself within the limits of what he is reasonably able to do. This is not to destroy the idea of the reasonable man nor to reincarnate him; it is simply to clothe him with a reasonable degree of reality. But as the statute prescribes, the matter comes to be one of the circumstances of the case and the good sense of the jury. Although the statute expressly refers to a reasonable man it does not follow that in directing a jury on provocation a judge must in every case use that particular expression. The substance of the section may well be conveyed without necessarily importing the concept of a reasonable man."

[Lord Slynn also dismissed the appeal, stating that justice demanded that the defendant's characteristics be taken into account in relation to both the issue of loss of self-control and the gravity of the provocation.]

Lord Millett:

"Diminished responsibility and provocation are both partial defences to a charge of murder. They have the effect of reducing the offence to manslaughter. But there the similarity ends . . .

Although the defences are distinct, they may of course overlap, for a person with diminished responsibility may be provoked to lose his self-control and react in the same way as any one else. Accordingly, a jury may have to consider both defences, as they did in this case. But they are distinct defences nevertheless, for each has a necessary element which is absent from the other. The defence of diminished responsibility requires proof of diminished responsibility resulting from mental abnormality but not of provocation or loss of self-control. The defence of provocation requires disproof of loss of self-control induced by provocation but not of diminished responsibility or mental abnormality. Their underlying rationales are also very different. In the one case the jury are invited to say: 'You can't really call it murder: the poor man wasn't fully responsible for his actions.' The defence is the response of a civilised society to inadequacy. In the other, they are typically invited to say: 'You can't really call it murder. It was at least partly the victim's fault. Any one of us might have reacted in the same way if we had been in the defendant's shoes.' The defence is often described as a concession to human frailty. . . .

These requirements make up what has been described as the subjective element of the defence. But there is an additional requirement: the provocation must have been sufficient to cause a reasonable man to react in the same way. This is usually described as the objective element . . . [S]ome objective test of the sufficiency of the provocation was necessary if the requirement that the accused must have been provoked to lose his self-control was to be preserved. Otherwise, loss of self-control alone would be sufficient, for the accused could always say that he was provoked by *something*. Accordingly the objective element was retained and henceforth provided the sole test of the sufficiency of the provocation. There must be something said or done which the jury considers might provoke a reasonable man to react in the same way as the accused . . .

In the present case . . . the Court of Appeal ruled [that the trial judge] should have directed the jury that in his case 'the reasonable man' meant a man with the powers of self-control of a person suffering from such an illness; *i.e.* a person with less than normal powers of self-control. . . .

[T]his approach requires the accused to be judged by his own reduced powers of self-control, eliminates the objective element altogether and removes the only standard external to the accused by which the jury may judge the sufficiency of the provocation relied on. By introducing a variable standard of self-control it subverts the moral basis of the defence, and is ultimately incompatible with a requirement that the accused must not only have lost his self-control but have been provoked to lose it; for if anything will do this requirement is illusory. It is also manifestly inconsistent with the terms of section 3. It makes it unnecessary for the jury to answer the question which section 3 requires to be left to them, *viz.* whether the provocation was enough to make a reasonable man do as the accused did. It becomes sufficient that it made the accused react as he did. It substitutes for the requirement that the jury shall take into account everything both done and said according to the effect which in their opinion it would have on a reasonable man a different requirement by reference to the effect which it actually had on the accused. These tests are in truth no tests at all . . .

I think that the law has taken a wrong turning. It is time to restore a coherent and morally defensible role to the defence, and one which juries can understand. This can be achieved if it is recognised that the function of the 'reasonable man' is merely to provide an external standard by which the sufficiency of the provocation to bring about the defendant's response to it can be judged . . .

In the present case I consider that Judge Coombe's summing up was sound and in accordance with law, and that it contained no material irregularity. The jury (not surprisingly) were unimpressed with the defence of provocation. They may well have taken the view that there was none. They must have taken the view that such provocation as there was, if any, was insufficient to cause an ordinary person to lose his self-control. I would allow the appeal and restore the conviction for murder."

Lord Hobhouse of Woodborough:

"The second question is what is called the 'objective' question. . . . This question itself contains two elements. The first is the assessment of the gravity of the provocation. The second is the assessment how a reasonable man would react to provocation of that gravity. The second element involves applying a standard of self-control. Essential to the understanding of the authorities and the issue on this appeal is the distinction between these two elements. It is well established and not in dispute that in assessing the gravity of the provocation everything both said and done must be taken into account and that this inevitably involves taking into account any peculiarity of the defendant which affects that gravity. What is in dispute on this appeal is whether in applying the standard of self-control the jury should apply a qualified standard to reflect the respondent's lack of capacity to exercise ordinary self-control. . . .

My Lords, in this speech . . . I consider that . . . English law does not require that the jury be directed to visualise an ordinary (reasonable) man with abnormal (unreasonable) mental characteristics. . . .

*Anthropomorphism etc:*
[T]he view of English law relied upon by the respondent on this appeal is a recent phenomenon . . . [but] the seeds from which it has sprung can be detected further back. A root cause is the inveterate (and not wholly unmeritorious) tendency of common lawyers to anthropomorphise concepts. Thus the test of liability in negligence was explained by reference to 'the man on the Clapham omnibus'. When the phrase 'reasonable man' (coming from 19th Century cases such as *Reg. v Welsh* (1869) 11 Cox 336) is used in s.3, the common lawyer immediately tries to visualise and define some physical human being with identified characteristics (apparently both reasonable and unreasonable) whereas what the phrase is doing is identifying a concept, a standard of self-control. This standard is, as Lord Diplock . . . said in *Reg. v Camplin* those 'powers of self-control as everyone is entitled to expect his fellow citizens will exercise in society as it is today' . . .

It is the anthropomorphic thinking and the artificialities to which it has given rise which have pervaded the more recent judgments of the Court of Appeal. . . . If judges are encouraged or required to sum up to juries in artificial and self-contradictory anthropomorphic terms, it is no wonder that people are confused and critical. One can compare that with the simple and clearly understandable language used by Judge Coombe in the present case which is minimally anthropomorphic. Indeed, there is no complaint that the language of Judge Coombs was in any way obscure or incomprehensible. The complaint is that the jury will have understood his direction too well and therefore have excluded a factor in the respondent's favour which, it is said, they ought to have taken into account.

There have been other contributory factors to which I will have to draw attention in the course of this speech. They include a recurringly expressed sentiment that the function of the law of provocation is to show mercy for inadequates. . . . This theme disregards that since then the concept of a reasonable standard of self-control has been developed in direct contradiction of such sentiments . . . and the answer given by the Legislature, was to introduce into the English law of homicide the special defence of diminished responsibility. The absence of a consideration of the significance of s.2 of the Act of 1957 is a striking feature of most of the judgments on s.3.

*Construing the 1957 Act in its Context: Diminished Responsibility:*
. . . The Act of 1957 was an amending act. It changed the existing law. . . . Sections 2 and 3 have clear inter-relation. They both deal with factors which may affect the responsibility of the defendant for the killing. The premise upon which they both proceed is that the defendant has killed or been a party to the killing and has had the *mens rea* requisite to the crime of murder. Sections 2 and 3 provide defences which reduce what would otherwise have been murder to manslaughter, thus disapplying the mandatory sentences applicable to murder. . . .

The subject matter of . . . section [2] and the special defence to murder which it provides is expressly 'abnormality of mind' and consequential impairment of mental responsibility for the *actus reus*. It is a provision which covers any kind of abnormality of mind provided that it is relevant and sufficient substantially to impair the defendant's responsibility. It is thus a provision which expressly addresses and provides for such matters as brain damage and depressive illness. . . .

The striking thing about the present and similar cases is that the defendant is either unwilling to rely upon s.2 or, having done so, fails to satisfy the jury and wishes then to adopt a strained construction of s.3 in order to escape the burden of proof and introduce vaguer concepts not contemplated by either section. The present case has only come before the Court of Appeal and your Lordships' House because the jury, having heard the evidence and having been properly directed upon the law, rejected the defence under s.2. They were not satisfied that whatever degree of depressive illness the respondent was suffering from was such as substantially to impair his mental responsibility for the killing, that is to say, the actual killing with which he was charged taking into account the circumstances in which it occurred.

This is important because there seems in some quarters to be an implicit assumption that the assessment by a jury under s.2 is inadequate properly to allow for the defendant's abnormality of mind in relation to any killing which was contributed to by provocation. There is no reason to make this assumption. Further, it is contrary to the drafting of s.2 and to sections 2 and 3 read together. The brain-damaged man has an abnormality of the mind. If it is of sufficient severity, in the opinion of the jury, to impair substantially his mental responsibility for killing his provoker, he will be found guilty of manslaughter, not murder, even if his action was not that of a reasonable man (indeed, one could say, *because* his action was not that of a reasonable man).

If the defendant is merely someone with a personality disorder, for example an exceptionally violent or immoral disposition, he will not be able to rely on s.2, nor will he be able to rely on s.3 if his response to the provocation was disproportionate. This is all in accord with the specific policy of the Act and the ordinary principles of criminal responsibility. Similarly, if the defendant suffered from an abnormality but the jury do not consider it to be sufficient substantially to impair his responsibility, he will not have a defence under s.2. This simply reflects the policy of the statute and it would be contrary to that policy to extend s.3 to give him the defence advisedly denied him by s.2.

One of the errors that have bedevilled some of the recent judicial statements in this part of the English law of homicide is the failure to take account of the interaction of sections 2 and 3 and appreciate that they not only show that the strained construction of s.3 is wrong but also that the perceived injustice which the strained construction is designed to avoid is in fact covered by an application of s.2 in accordance with its ordinary meaning. Section 2 is of course capable of applying in any situation and those situations include a killing by a defendant who has killed after losing his self-control. A defendant in this situation can contend that his conduct was not abnormal and require the prosecution to satisfy the jury that his loss of self-control was not the result of provocation or his response to it was not that of a reasonable man. Or, he can contend and seek to satisfy the jury on the balance of probabilities that he had an abnormality of the mind which in the circumstances substantially reduced his mental responsibility for what he did. A defendant can of course place both contentions before the jury, as the respondent did in this case. The jury can then return a verdict of manslaughter on the one or the other basis. But it is always open to the jury to conclude (as no doubt the jury did in the present case) that the defendant's response was objectively disproportionate and that his abnormality of mind did not suffice to impair his mental responsibility for what he had done. . . .

*Reg. v Camplin:*
. . . When the alteration [to s.3] was made so as to enable provocation to be by words alone, inevitably peculiarities of the defendant became relevant. Physical provocation may affect all those subjected to it in a broadly similar way (except for the one-legged man who loses his crutch) and the reasonable man test was simpler to apply. But provocative words causing loss of self-control are far more likely to be specific to the defendant and his characteristics and will usually leave all others unmoved. How then, it is asked, can one answer the second question taking into account everything said 'according to the effect it would have on a reasonable man'? In *Reg. v Morhall* the difficulty was caused by the fact that the defendant was a glue-sniffer who killed the man who was nagging him about his glue-sniffing. It is said, rhetorically, how can one have a reasonable glue-sniffer? It is a contradiction in terms just as is the idea of a reasonable drunkard.

The answer is that the role of the second question is being misunderstood. Its purpose is, as previously stated, to provide a standard of ordinary self-control so as to compare the reaction of the defendant as he was in fact provoked to lose his self-control with the reaction of a person with ordinary powers of self-control to provocation of equal gravity. Its purpose is not to create for the jury some impossible self-contradictory chimera designed ultimately to displace the concept of reasonableness altogether. . . .

Lord Diplock stressed that s.3 recognised and retained the dual test for provocation. He also confirmed his agreement with Lord Simon of Glaisdale that evidence is not admissible upon the second question. He then stated the meaning of the phrase 'reasonable man' for the purposes of the law of provocation:

'It means an ordinary person of either sex, not exceptionally excitable or pugnacious' but possessed of such powers of self-control as everyone is entitled to expect that his fellow citizens will exercise in society as it is today.'

. . . He was clearly of the view that the word 'reasonable' was still to be treated as a synonym for ordinary or normal. . . .

As I have emphasised, his formulation [in the model direction] is based upon the assumption of the possession of ordinary powers of self-control and it is only *in other respects* that the defendant's abnormal characteristics are to be taken into account. It is also loyal to the drafting of s.3 which is concerned with the *effect* the provocation would have on the reasonable/ordinary man. . . .

*Conclusion:*

The law, as provided in s.3 of the Act of 1957 and held in the authorities down to *Luc Thiet*, establishes that the constituents of provocation are:

(a) The defendant must have been provoked (whether by things done or by things said or by both together) to lose his self-control and kill or do whatever other act is alleged to render him guilty of murder. (b) This is a factual question upon which all relevant evidence is admissible including any evidence which tends to support the conclusion that the defendant either may have or did not lose his self-control. (c) If the jury conclude that the defendant may have been provoked to lose his self-control and do as he did, the jury should, as an exercise of judgment, but taking into account all the evidence, form a view as to the gravity of the provocation for the defendant in all the circumstances. (d) Finally, the jury should decide whether in their opinion, having regard to the actual provocation (a and b above) and their view as to its gravity (c above), a person having ordinary powers of self-control would have done what the defendant did. If some elaboration of the word 'ordinary' is thought necessary, it should be along the lines advised by Lord Diplock and used by Judge Coombe in the present case. The phrase 'reasonable man' although used in the section is better avoided as not assisting the understanding of the criterion 'ordinary powers of self-control'. The word 'characteristics' should be avoided altogether in relation to (d). It is not used in the section. It is alien to the objective standard of ordinariness and experience has shown that it is a persistent source of confusion. Where relevant the age or gender of the defendant should be referred to since they are not factors which qualify the criterion of ordinariness. But language which qualifies or contradicts such ordinariness must be avoided. It is the standard of ordinary not an abnormal self-control that has to be used. It is the standard which conforms to what everyone is entitled to expect of their fellow citizens in society as it is. . . .

It is not acceptable to leave the jury without definitive guidance as to the objective criterion to be applied. The function of the criminal law is to identify and define the relevant legal criteria. It is not proper to leave the decision to the essentially subjective judgment of the individual jurors who happen to be deciding the case. Such an approach is apt to lead to idiosyncratic and inconsistent decisions. The law must inform the accused, and the judge must direct the jury, what is the objective criterion which the jury are to apply in any exercise of judgment in deciding upon the guilt or innocence of the accused. Non-specific criteria also create difficulties for the conduct of criminal trials since they do not set the necessary parameters for the admission of evidence or the relevance of arguments. . . .

The appeal should be allowed. The direction of the Judge was appropriate to the issues at the trial. The conviction was not unsafe."

**Appeal dismissed**

Thus, by a majority of 3/2 the House of Lords has decided that aspects[26] of the defendant which affect her ability to exercise control should be considered. They may be told that certain traits are unacceptable reasons for loss of self-control, such as pugnacity, male possessiveness, obsession and jealousy[27] but beyond this juries should be directed to assess whether the defendant's behaviour had measured up to the standard of self-control which ought reasonably to be expected of her. The distinction between characteristics, which affect powers of self-control and those which affect the gravity of the provocation is lost and the transformation of provocation from partial justification to excuse has been taken to a new dimension. Whilst some commentators have given a highly qualified welcome to the decision on the basis that it enables more defendants to avoid the mandatory life sentence,[28] most have been deeply critical.

### John Gardner and Timothy Macklem, "Compassion without Respect? Nine Fallacies in R. v Smith" [2001] Crim.L.R.623 at 625:

"In making this superficially liberal ruling, the House of Lords was attempting to deal in one fell swoop with a range of pressures to which the law has been subject in the last decade or so. They were exercised not only by the immediate problem of whether and how to accommodate mental illness in the provocation defence. They also had in mind a variety of indirectly related and somewhat overlapping problems associated with the alleged maleness of the 'reasonable man' standard and its alleged insensitivity to cultural difference. The question of law before them hence resolved itself into the following broader question: How are we to make room, within the standard of the reasonable man in section 3, for the fact of human diversity? The answer favoured by the majority was the simplest answer of all: make the standard fit the person. Allow the jury to hear everything that might conceivably help them to be more understanding of the reactions of the person in the dock before them, and allow them (but not require) them to make corresponding relaxations in the applicable standard of self-control."[29]

Smith has written:
"Who was right? The reasoning of the minority, Lords Millett and Hobhouse, is completely convincing. The majority is shown to have misinterpreted the most important case, *Camplin*, and other authorities, to have brushed aside the effect of the unanimous recent decision of the House in *Morhall* and to have given insufficient weight to the context of section 3 of the Homicide Act, notably that it follows, and should be read in the light of, section 2, diminished responsibility."[30]

In the pursuit of individual justice the majority of their Lordships have dramatically diluted the ethical standard of the law of provocation. How realistic is it to expect a jury, armed with the knowledge that the defendant possessed a characteristic which may well have had an impact on his power of self-control, to decide that the loss of control was unreasonable? Instead of judging the defendant

---

[26] It no longer matters whether a condition is so permanent as to constitute a "characteristic": it is part of the factual background to be included.

[27] Self-induced intoxication continues to be excluded for policy reasons. See, for a post-*Smith* example, *Pearce* [2001] 1 W.L.R. 1553.

[28] See, for example, Virgo, "Provocation: Muddying the Waters" [2001] 60 C.L.J. 23.

[29] See further, Gardner and Macklem, *above*, n.83 at 824–827.

[30] [2000] Crim.L.R.1004 at p.1005.

by the standard of the reasonable man (as required by the wording of section 3) they are judging the defendant against himself.[31]

The reasoning and impact of the decision need to be evaluated further. At the root of all four of the decisions over which their Lordships have presided have been two key considerations: the contested distinction between matters which affect self-control and those which affect the gravity of the provocation, and the role of the partial defence in making concessions to human frailty.

*1. The self-control/gravity of provocation distinction*
Of the four decisions, there are two where this distinction is upheld (*Luc Thiet Thuan* and *Morhall*), one which rejects it (*Smith*) and one, *Camplin*, which is relied upon by the others as proof of their argument. The weight of academic argument, as we have seen, favours the maintenance of the distinction although, as with the judiciary, views are not unanimous. Norrie has argued that the distinction is not one that can be sustained:

**Alan Norrie, "From Criminal Law to Legal Theory: The Mysterious Case of the Reasonable Glue Sniffer [2002] 65 M.L.R. 538 at 548–550:**

"It suggests that we can draw a line between matters that are provocative and persons who are provocable. However, this is not necessarily the case. For someone like the impotent man in *Bedder*, the taunt concerning his impotence is more *provocative*, and therefore he is more *provocable*, because of his impotence. We cannot appreciate his 'provocability' without knowing of the gravity, the particular 'provocativeness', of the taunt to him. If the law is to do justice to his particular situation, it has to recognise that he is more 'provocable' than the average person precisely because of the characteristic at which the provocation is aimed: precisely because it is more 'provocative' to him. Once this is conceded, however, there is no logical reason why any characteristic which would make him more provocable should not equally be taken into account. In short, if 'provocativeness' depends upon 'provocability', then provocability is the issue. But if the subjective provocability of the accused is ultimately what is at stake, then it becomes harder to deny the relevance of *any* characteristic, whether it is the direct subject of the provocation or not. ...

*Smith* is therefore both correct in its elucidation of the law and woefully inadequate in its ability to provide any control on the characteristics that are to be taken into account in determining the result of a provocation plea. All that is of real interest to it is whether the individual was in psychological control; all the moral issues about which characteristics should be taken into account are lost ...

The core of the law has shifted from the question of how *morally provocative* the provocation was to the accused to how *psychologically provocable* the accused was and ought to be in the circumstances of the provocation. In moving from justification to excuse, provocation has moved from a matter of *moral judgment* to *psychological fact*."[32]

According to this view, *Smith* has merely taken the law to its logical conclusion (even though that conclusion leaves the law without a "moral cap"). Clearly, there are some characteristics which have such an impact upon the defendant that the distinction is difficult to sustain. One could imagine a scenario where someone who

---

[31] Gardner and Macklem argue that the distinction drawn in *Smith* between one's capacity to exercise self-control and one's actual self-control is an empty one: "To lack self-control is to lack the capacity for self-control." "Compassion without Respect? Nine Fallacies in *R. v* Smith" [2001] Crim.L.R.623 at 626.

[32] Stannard argues, *contra*, that Lord Hoffmann has restored the moral question to the law of provocation: the jury have to decide whether the circumstances were such as to make the loss of self-control sufficiently excusable to reduce the gravity of the offence from murder to manslaughter: "Towards a Normative Defence of Provocation on England and Ireland" [2002] 66 J. of Crim.L. 528 at 537.

has, say, the debilitating skin condition, psoriasis, (and in *Morhall* Lord Goff suggested that the condition of eczema might be taken into consideration if the subject of taunts) may not only be subjected to painful taunts about the condition but, also, because of the effect of the condition upon their well-being and temper, finds it more difficult than the "ordinary" person to control their response to the taunts. How should the law respond to this particular manifestation of human frailty? *Smith* enables every aspect to be considered—the jury can look at the whole picture and they might well feel considerable sympathy for the plight of such a defendant. Presumably this would still be the case if the defendant were to be taunted about something completely unrelated to his skin condition.

But what of others scenarios where there are no obvious underlying causes for the defendant's bad-temper. Are the jury to look at the whole picture here too? Absolutely not. The majority make it clear that certain characteristics, such as bad temper, a tendency to violent rages or tantrums, a violent disposition, drunkenness, exceptional pugnacity or excitability are to be ignored in order to preserve the objective test in section 3. These are defects of character that we are required to control; indeed, as society advances it is entitled to expect higher standards of self-control from its citizens.[33] Yet, it may not always be easy to distinguish situations where there is an underlying cause (excuse) which may be considered from those where there is none. Moreover, it is uncertain whether the list of excluded characteristics is more extensive: male possessiveness, and obsession may also have to be ignored[34]. These do not (at least directly) relate to the issue of self-control but are more general flaws of character. The question is not only why these should be singled out but also whether other trial judges will feel tempted to add other unsavoury characteristics to the list. There seems to be no reliable basis for doing so.[35] And, finally, what if the defendant is known to be particularly phlegmatic—should she be judged against a higher standard of control?[36]

Artificial though the distinction between characteristics affecting self-control and those affecting the gravity of the provocation may be in some cases, it performed an important function. Either the distinction needs to be restored, harsh though that may seem in some cases (although the defence of diminished responsibility can provide some amelioration) or, given the problems with the law prior to *Smith*, a preferable solution may be to consider more radical reform.

### 2. *A concession to human frailty*

Most of the relaxation of the law of provocation is justified by reference to a desire to make allowances for human frailty. Clearly, a law which judges people by a standard they cannot possibly meet looks like an unjust law (although this

---

[33] See *Suratan, Humes, Wilkinson (Attorney-General's References Nos 74, 95 and 118 of 2002)* [2002] EWCA Crim 2982 where the issue was defined as whether the loss of self-control was reasonable in all the circumstances bearing in mind society's advancement of social discipline.

[34] This is contested: Lord Hoffmann excludes male obsessiveness, whereas Lord Clyde approved of *Dryden* [1995] 4 All E.R. 987 in which the defendant's obsessiveness was held to be a relevant characteristic. In the recent decision of *Weller* [2003] EWCA Crim 815 it was held that jealousy could not be excluded from the jury's consideration. See also, *R. (on the application of Farnell) v The Criminal Cases Review Commission* [2003] EWHC 835.

[35] Why should male obsessiveness etc. be excluded while addiction to glue-sniffing included? (Clarkson, *Understanding Criminal Law* (3rd ed., 2001) p. 125).

[36] See further, Gardner and Macklem, *above*, n.83 at 624.

argument seems to have been ignored, for example, in the context of the non-availability of the defence of duress to murder).[37] *Smith,* was, for example, welcomed by some women's groups for acknowledging the plight of women who, after an abusive relationship, killed their tormentor and as a "liberalisation of the law."[38] The law has rightly been criticised in the past for its response to women who kill: self-defence may not be available, neither may provocation because of the loss of self-control element and the requirement of reasonableness. Accordingly, such women may be forced to plead diminished responsibility in inappropriate circumstances to avoid the mandatory life sentence. There is no doubt that the relaxation of the law has, in good part, been framed by reference to the plight of such women (often discussed in the context of BWS—battered women's syndrome). However, accepting that the law has traditionally failed to provide an appropriate defence for women who kill after abuse should not lead us blindly to accept the solution adopted in *Smith.* Opening up the defence to those who may be thought to have a strong case (in other words, are *morally* deserving) creates its own problems:

### Donald Nicolson and Rohit Sanghvi, "Battered Women and Provocation: The Implications of R. v Ahluwalia" [1993] Crim.L.R.728 at 733–734:

"At first glance, this development seems to be a step forward. Battered women will no longer be judged by the same standards as 'ordinary' women... Nevertheless, BWS suffers from serious problems. ...

[W]hereas BWS is useful in explaining the reasonableness of the general behaviour of battered women, it is not well-suited (at least as presently developed and applied) to establish the reasonableness of her killing in provocation, nor that it took place during a sudden loss of self-control ...

But even if BWS is developed to address the pertinent issues, it will always actively shift the emphasis from the reasonableness of the defendant's actions to her personality in a way which confirms existing gender stereotypes, silences battered women and conceals society's complicity in domestic violence ... BWS suggests reliance on personal incapacity."[39]

Gardner and Macklem argue that one of the reasons such defendants dislike having to plead diminished responsibility is that it denies their status as fully-fledged human beings. They wish to come within the provocation defence because, traditionally, it accorded them this status: they were treated as "creatures whose lives are rationally intelligible even when they go off the rails, and who can therefore give a rationally intelligible account of how they came to do so." What *Smith* has done by bringing the standard of self-control down to the individual's

---

[37] *Above,* p. 357.

[38] See, "Fear is the new defence for women who kill", *The Times,* July 28, 2000, quoted in Burton, "Intimate Homicide and the Provocation Defence – Endangering Women? *R. v Smith*" [2001] 9 Feminist Legal Studies 247 at 251.

[39] See further, O'Donovan, "Defences for Battered Women Who Kill" (1991) 18 J.L. and Soc. 219 and Nicholson, "Telling Tales: Gender Discrimination, Gender Construction and Battered Women Who Kill" [1995] 2 *Feminist Legal Studies* 185. Dressler argues that the patholcolisation effect of BWS evidence occurs even in jurisdictions where self-defence has been extended to women who kill after abuse: Dressler, "Battered Women Who Kill Their Sleeping Tormentors: Reflections on Maintaining Respect for Human Life while Killing Moral Monsters" in Shute and Simester (eds), *Criminal Law Theory: Doctrines of the General Part* (2002).

level is to take this option away from defendants.[40] "The plea of provocation then becomes merely euphemistic: It is really a defence of diminished responsibility by another name, with a more positive public relations spin."[41]

These are by no means the only problems: in relaxing the defence in the way *Smith* has done, the *less* deserving may also be included. Without the distinction above, all human frailty (apart from jealousy etc.) falls to be included and, paradoxically, in an arena when it is still much more common for males to be defendants in homicide cases,[42] there can be no guarantees that the main beneficiaries of the relaxation of the law will not be men who kill women.[43]More broadly, "the provocation defence cannot discriminate between excusable violence and blind prejudice."[44]

All of these problems point to fundamental flaws in the law of provocation. The courts have sought to take a compassionate view of human frailty while endeavouring to maintain the test of reasonableness. The problems inherent in the reasonable man test raise fundamental questions about its appropriateness in this area of law and whether fundamental changes are needed. However, before examining any possible reform we may well wish to consider another dimension; we may conclude that it was reasonable to retaliate, but question the particular mode of retaliation chosen by the defendant. Dealing with this problem in pre-1957 days was relatively straightforward.

## Mancini v D.P.P. [1942] A.C. 1 (House of Lords)

The appellant had stabbed a member of a club of which he was manager with a sharp dagger-knife.

Viscount Simon L.C.:

"It is not all provocation that will reduce the crime of murder to manslaughter. Provocation, to have that result, must be such as temporarily deprives the person provoked of the powers of self-control, as the result of which he commits the unlawful act which causes death. ... The test to be applied is that of the provocation of the reasonable man ... it is of particular importance ... to take into account the instrument with which the homicide was effected, for to retort, in the heat of passion induced by provocation, by a simple blow, is a

---

[40] *Above*, n.31 at p. 627. The authors go on to consider the question of whether what defendants are aspiring to is a justification for their actions: pp. 627–629.

[41] Gardner and Macklem, *above*, n.83 at 827.

[42] See further, Wells, "Provocation: the Case for Abolition" in Ashworth and Mitchell (eds), *Rethinking English Homicide Law* (2000) p. 93.

[43] In *Suratan, Humes, Wilkinson (Attorney-General's References Nos 74, 95 and 118 of 2002)* [2002] EWCA Crim 2982 the Court of Appeal opined that there was no reason to suppose that *Smith* would lead to an increase in manslaughter verdicts in domestic cases or otherwise. The case also stated that there should be no distinction in the way the courts approached sentencing in cases where men have killed women or visa versa and that it was not a distinct aggravating feature in provocation cases that the victim is the offender's spouse or partner.

[44] *Above*, n.42, p. 95. See also, Howe, "Provoking Polemic-Provoked Killings and the Ethical Paradoxes of the Post-modern Feminist Condition" [2002] 10 Feminist Legal Studies 39. Both articles examine recent Australian cases, and in particular, the development of the "homosexual advance defence" (HAD) as part of their critique.

very different thing from risking use of a deadly instrument like a concealed dagger. In short, the mode of resentment must bear a reasonable relationship to the provocation if the offence is to be reduced to manslaughter."

The status of this "rule of law" was in some doubt as a result of section 3. It was not at all clear whether the words "whether the provocation was enough to make a reasonable man do as he did" meant, simply, "make a reasonable man kill" or "make a reasonable man kill in the manner used by the defendant." Williams has argued that "the Homicide Act is ambiguous, but it can be read as affirming a rule of reasonable relationship to the mode of killing (what we may call a modal reasonable relationship rule)."[45]The better view, however, is that the reasonable relationship test is no longer a rule of law but it is still evidence for the jury to take into account in their task of determining what a reasonable man would have done in the situation; the more excessive the response, the more the jury will be inclined to decide that the reasonable man would not have responded similarly.[46]This will, on occasions, involve the jury in having to decide whether it can ever be reasonable to kill in response to purely verbal provocation.

**c. Reform or abolition?** We are unlikely to have heard the last word on the law of provocation. At the very least we may see a developing case-law on what aspects of the defendant's personality (alongside excitability, jealousy etc.) the judge is going to invite, although not command, the jury to ignore. We may also see a challenge to *Smith* on the basis that far too little notice was taken of the earlier decision of *Morhall* and that *Camplin* was misinterpreted. But if change is necessary—and it is argued here that it is—what shape should it take? Simply returning to the law pre-*Smith* would satisfy few; the law had already lost its way by then. One option is to try to improve the provocation defence.

Does the formulation adopted by the Model Penal Code or the recommendations of the Criminal Law Revision Committee provide a more satisfactory basis for judging provocation?

### American Law Institute, Model Penal Code, Proposed Official Draft (1962):

"Section 210.3.
(1) Criminal homicide constitutes manslaughter when: ... b) a homicide which would otherwise be murder is committed under the influence of extreme mental or emotional disturbance for which there is reasonable explanation or excuse. The reasonableness of such explanation or excuse shall be determined from the viewpoint of a person in the actor's situation under the circumstances as he believed them to be."

### American Law Institute, Model Penal Code, Tentative Draft No. 9 (1959) Comments, pp. 47–48:

"Though it is difficult to state a middle ground between a standard which ignores all individual peculiarities and one which makes emotional distress decisive regardless of the

---

[45] *Textbook of Criminal Law* (2nd ed., 1983), p. 543.
[46] *Walker* [1969] 1 W.L.R. 311; *Phillips* [1969] 2 A.C. 130; *Brown* [1972] 2 Q.B. 299; *Davies* [1975] Q.B. 691.

nature of its cause, we think that such a statement is essential. ... We submit that the formulation in the draft affords sufficient flexibility to differentiate between those special features in the actor's situation which should be deemed material for purposes of sentence and those which properly should be ignored ...

There will be room, of course, for interpretation of the breadth of meaning carried by the word 'situation,' precisely the room needed in our view. There will be room for argument as to the reasonableness of the explanations or excuses offered; we think again that argument is needed in these terms. The question in the end will be whether the actor's loss of self-control can be understood in terms that arouse sympathy enough to call for mitigation in the sentence. That seems to us the issue to be faced."

The Criminal Law Revision Committee in 1980 recommended changes that would bring the English law on provocation much closer to that adopted by the Model Penal Code.

### Criminal Law Revision Committee, Offences Against the Person, 14th Report, Cmnd.7844 (1980), paras 81–83:

"81. Our principal recommendation is that the law of provocation should be reformulated and in place of the reasonable man test the test should be that provocation is a defence to a charge of murder if, on the facts as they appeared to the defendant, it can reasonably be regarded as a sufficient ground for the loss of self-control leading the defendant to react against the victim with a murderous intent. This formulation has some advantage over the present law in that it avoids reference to the entirely notional 'reasonable man' directing the jury's attention instead to what they themselves consider reasonable—which has always been the real question.

82. A number of commentators queried one detail of the suggestions made in the Working Paper, namely that provocation would be sufficient if, on the facts as they appeared to the accused, it constituted a reasonable excuse for the loss of self-control on his part. They did not like the phrase 'a reasonable excuse': they preferred 'a reasonable explanation' because there could never be a reasonable excuse for taking another's life. We found this rather difficult to resolve. We accepted the criticisms made of the word 'excuse' but remained of the opinion that 'explanation' was not a suitable word either. We finally decided that 'a sufficient ground for the loss of self-control' would be an easier phrase for juries to understand and apply.

83. ... [We] recommend that the defendant should be judged with due regard to all the circumstances, including any disability, physical or mental, from which he suffered."[47]

Reform along these lines would not be far removed from the position we have reached as a result of *Smith*. However, section 3 would be repealed and its associated case-law no longer the nightmare that it has become. However, does the suggested reform go far enough to silence the critics and does it tackle the moral issue highlighted by Fletcher that the question is whether the defendant could be expected to control his impulse to kill?

---

[47] The Draft Criminal Code (Law Commission No. 177 (1989)) reformulates this in clause 58(b): "the provocation is, in all the circumstances (including any of his personal characteristics that affect its gravity), sufficient ground for the loss of self-control".

## George P. Fletcher, Rethinking Criminal Law (1978), pp. 513–514:

"The obvious difference between the irascible man and the impotent man is that, absent a documentable psychological impediment, we properly expect people to control their anger as we expect them to control greed and jealousy. Therefore persons who are irascible, greedy or given to jealousy hardly warrant preferential treatment in the assessment of their conduct. These are character traits for which people are properly held accountable, not excused. Yet no one is to be blamed for impotence, and therefore it is a feature of the defendant that must be considered in assessing whether he was adequately provoked by taunting or teasing related to his impotence."

As we saw in the earlier discussion of loss of self-control, Horder is critical of the over-reliance of the law on the test of anger as loss of self-control. He offers a test of "provoked angry retaliation" in its place.[48] However, while this would address the more obvious difficulties of the male typology of anger currently in place in the test, he is ultimately critical of the entire defence of provocation: "[T]he vast majority of killers are male. Even in the domestic context, men are much more likely to have been the serious aggressors whether they are ultimately killers or victims. These grim facts might at one time have been regarded as part of the natural order of things which it is the function of the law to reflect. One must now ask whether the doctrine of provocation, under the cover of an alleged compassion for human infirmity, simply reinforces the conditions in which men are perceived and perceive themselves as natural aggressors, and in particular *women's* natural aggressors. Unfortunately, the answer to that question is yes."[49] The common causes of angry male violence are attacks upon their self-worth in the context of their possessiveness—particularly sexual—of their partners and wives. There are deeply entrenched double standards which result in men, who, for example, kill after discovering their wives in bed with another, being treated leniently. Others have responded that these defects constitute a compelling argument for reform rather than abolition.[50] Horder's call for abolition of the defence goes further, however. He questions the ethical status of a law that enables the angry infliction of retaliatory suffering to result in partial exoneration. It is one thing to feel anger—so angry that you want the victim to suffer; it is quite another to go on to inflict that suffering yourself.[51]

### (iv) *Conclusion*

If one decides that, rather than abolish the test, there is a case for an amended test of provocation, the crime of murder with its mandatory life sentence is obviously one area where it can be usefully employed. But this raises two further questions. First, would the defence still be desirable if the mandatory life sentence were

---

[48] *Above*, p. 692.

[49] Horder, *Provocation and Responsibility* (1992), p. 192. See further, Wells, "Battered Woman Syndrome and Defences to Homicide" (1994) 14 *Legal Studies* 266.

[50] Sullivan, "Anger and Excuse: Reassessing Provocation" (1993) 13 O.J.L.S. 421 at 426.

[51] Horder's analysis is a philosophical one. He acknowledges that the psychological dimension is largely ignored. The physiological evidence is also disputed. See, for example, Brett, "The Physiology of Provocation" [1970] Crim.L.R.634 and Williams, *Textbook of Criminal Law* (1st ed., 1978), p. 483.

abolished? The Criminal Law Revision Committee, although evenly divided on the question of whether the fixed penalty ought to be abolished, thought that there would still be a good case for the partial defence even if it were.[52] If that is the case, is there, secondly, any justification for restricting the operation of the defence to the crime of murder? There will obviously be instances in lesser crimes where people will act as they do because of severe stress and provocation. Should the law give formal recognition to this? The Criminal Law Revision Committee has recommended that the partial defence be extended to attempted killings,[53] but not to other crimes.[54] The only justification for this refusal in the light of their attitude towards the fixed penalty must be that murder "is a crime standing out from all others".[55] Is this sufficient justification to warrant the denial of the partial defence to other defendants who act under stress?

If, however, the law of provocation is beyond redemption and Horder is certainly not alone in advocating abolition,[56] one could repeal it without replacement although, while the mandatory life sentence continues, some might baulk at this. But consideration could be given to another possibility. If all trace of justification has been removed from the defence which now excuses those who kill under severe emotional disturbance, do we need a new, broader partial defence, freed from phrases like "loss of self-control", that encompasses defendants who kill under duress, use excessive self-defence as well as what today would be regarded as killing under provocation?[57]

### 3. Diminished responsibility

Where a defendant is suffering from "diminished responsibility" she will have a partial defence to murder and will instead be convicted of manslaughter—again giving the court the necessary flexibility as to sentence.

Although it is only a defence to murder and is thus not a general defence, because of its close nexus to the defence of insanity, the partial defence of diminished responsibility has been discussed in the chapter on general defences.[58]

---

[52] This was endorsed by House of Lords, *Report of the Select Committee on Murder and Life Imprisonment*. (Session 1988–89, H.L. Paper 78), 1989, para. 83. Wasik, "Partial Excuses in the Criminal Law" (1982) 45 M.L.R. 516 argues from this that there is now room for partial defences to develop a life of their own in the criminal law, overcoming the traditional reluctance to find a place for them in the orthodox division of excusing conditions (such as infancy) and mitigating circumstances (those taken into account in sentencing only). The Law Commission, in evidence to the C.L.R.C., proposed a general defence of extenuating circumstances to a charge of murder (including provocation), dependent on the abolition of the fixed penalty; the C.L.R.C. rejected the proposal: para. 80. See also Wells, "The Death Penalty for Provocation" [1978] Crim.L.R.662.

[53] Para. 98. See now Draft Criminal Code, Law Com. No. 177 (1989), cl. 61.

[54] C.L.R.C. Working Paper (1976), para. 109.

[55] 14th Report, para. 84.

[56] See also Wells, *above* r.42.

[57] See further, Lacey, "Partial Defences to Homicide: Questions of Power and Principle in Imperfect and less Imperfect Worlds" in Ashworth and Mitchell (eds), *Rethinking English Homicide Law* (2000), p. 107. For further critiques and other suggestions for reform, see Allen, "Provocation's Reasonable Man: A Plea for Self-Control" [2000] 64 J. of Crim.L. 216 at 240–244 and Williams, "Provocation and Killing With Compassion" [2001] 65 J. of Crim.L. 149.

[58] *Above*, p.399.

## 4. Killing in pursuance of a suicide pact

### Homicide Act 1957, section 4

"(1) It shall be manslaughter, and shall not be murder, for a person acting in pursuance of a suicide pact between him and another to kill the other or be a party to the other being killed by a third person ...

(3) For the purposes of this section 'suicide pact' means a common agreement between two or more persons having for its object the death of all of them, whether or not each is to take his own life, but nothing done by a person who enters into a suicide pact shall be treated as done by him in pursuance of the pact unless it is done while he has the settled intention of dying in a pursuance of the pact."

The law acts with some clemency towards a defendant who survives a suicide pact when he had intended to die himself. Such clemency does not, however, extend to other situations. If the agreement to "kill and then die" is merely a front for murder where the defendant has no intention of killing himself, then he will be convicted of murder. This will be the case even if the deceased consented to die and even if, furthermore, it can be described as a mercy-killing. It is, therefore, thought to be more blameworthy to kill in such situations than where a suicide pact exists. The basis of this distinction in blameworthiness must lie in the "settled intention" of the defendant to die himself. Perhaps it is felt that the person killed would not have consented had he not been aware of the intention of the other; more probably, however, the consent of the "victim" is still irrelevant and the partial defence represents "a concession to human frailty". It recognises with compassion the state of despair of one who would kill and then die himself.[59] Or could it be that this is a remnant of the Biblical historical origins of the law of homicide—that he who kills intending to die himself immediately thereafter does not "acquire the [same] control over the blood—the life force—of the victim"[60]—and therefore deserves less punishment?

This distinction in blameworthiness will be further enhanced if the Draft Criminal Code is brought into effect. This states that suicide pact killing is a separate offence, punishable by a maximum of seven year's imprisonment.[61]

Killing in pursuance of a suicide pact is distinguished from the separate crime of aiding and abetting suicide.

### Suicide Act 1961, section 2

"A person who aids, abets, counsels or procures the suicide of another or an attempt by another to commit suicide, shall be liable on conviction on indictment to imprisonment for a term not exceeding 14 years."

It has been pointed out that "[t]he distinction between ... [complicity in suicide and manslaughter by suicide pact] ... may be very fine. If D and P agree to gas themselves and D alone survives, it appears that he will be liable under the Homicide Act if he turned on the tap and under the Suicide Act if P did".[62]

---

[59] In *Dunbar v Plant* [1997] 3 W.L.R. 1261 it was stated that the public interest does not generally call for the survivor of a suicide pact to be prosecuted.

[60] Fletcher, *above*, n.14, p. 236.

[61] Law Com. No. 177, (1989) cl. 62, implementing the proposals of the Criminal Law Revision Committee.

[62] Smith and Hogan, *Criminal Law* (10th ed., 2002), p. 395.

The distinction is currently of importance in terms of punishment. Killing in pursuance of a suicide pact is punishable as manslaughter by a maximum of life imprisonment, while aiding and abetting suicide is punishable by a maximum of 14 years' imprisonment. The Draft Criminal Code recognises the strength of the point made above by proposing to make both offences subject to a seven year maximum sentence.[63]

The consent of the D.P.P. is required before a prosecution may be brought under the Suicide Act 1961. In *R. (on the application of Pretty) v D.P.P.*,[64] the first case on assisted suicide to reach the House of Lords, it was held that the D.P.P. is unable to give an undertaking to people that they will not be prosecuted if they assist their spouse to commit suicide—even if that spouse, by virtue of their incurable condition, is unable to carry out their wishes themselves.[65]

## V. Infanticide

### Infanticide Act 1938, section 1

"(1) Where a woman by any wilful act or omission causes the death of her child being a child under the age of twelve months, but at the time of the act or omission the balance of her mind was disturbed by reason of her not having fully recovered from the effect of giving birth to the child or by reason of the effect of lactation consequent upon the birth of the child, then, notwithstanding that the circumstances were such that but for this Act the offence would have amounted to murder, she shall be guilty of ... infanticide, and may for such offence be dealt with and punished as if she had been guilty of the offence of manslaughter of the child."

Infanticide is similar to voluntary manslaughter in that it is effectively a partial defence to murder. It has especially close links with the partial defence of diminished responsibility and, indeed, there is some question as to whether infanticide is redundant given the existence of this wider defence. When introduced in this form,[66] however, infanticide was seen by many as a welcome solution to juries' reluctance to convict distressed women of the murder of their babies—with the consequence they would be sentenced to death. One of the reasons for the welcome the crime of infanticide received was that it avoided the hypocrisy of passing a death sentence that all in authority (at least) knew would not be carried out; the sentence of death would invariably be commuted to one of life

---

[63] *Above*, n.53, clause 63.

[64] [2002] 1 All E.R. 1

[65] Mrs Pretty brought her case under a number of the Articles of the Human Rights Act 1998: Articles 2, 3, 8,9,14. It was decided that section 2 of the Suicide Act 1961 was not incompatible with the Human Rights Act 1998. See generally, Freeman, "Death, Dying and the Human Rights Act 1998 (1999) 52 CLP 218.

[66] The Infanticide Act 1922, s.5 (1), first made a finding of manslaughter instead of murder possible if "at the time of the act or omission [in killing her *newly-born* child] she had not fully recovered from the effect of giving birth to such child". For an account of the history of infanticide before that date, see, Langer, "Infanticide: A Historical Survey" (1974) 1 Hist. of Childhood Quarterly 353; Jones, *Women Who Kill* (1991), pp. 45–60 and Jackson, *New-born Child Murder, Women, Illegitimacy and the Courts of Eighteenth-Century England* (1996).

imprisonment by the Royal Prerogative of Mercy. Since 1849 no mother had been executed for the murder of her own child under the age of one year.[67]

Whilst useful, therefore, in giving effect to both judicial and societal desire to express understanding for and sympathy with the defendant's plight, the medical basis upon which infanticide has rested since the twentieth century[68] has never been beyond doubt. It is estimated that about half of new mothers experience "baby blues" in the first few days after giving birth and that in about 10 per cent of cases more severe depressions result. The most severe forms of psychiatric illnesses of postpartum psychosis and psychotic depression are thought to be much less common but do exist. Medically, therefore, it can be argued that there is a case for a special defence (although no one is suggesting that all these women are likely to kill their children).[69] However, the most serious cases would certainly fall within the newer defence of diminished responsibility. Moreover, there are clear problems with both the terminology employed in the Infanticide Act and its use in practice.

### The Report of the Committee on Mentally Abnormal Offenders (Butler Committee), Evidence of the Governor and Staff of Holloway Prison, Cmnd.6244 (1975), para. 19.24:

"The disturbance of the 'balance of mind' that the Act requires can rarely be said to arise directly from incomplete recovery from the effects of childbirth and even less so from the effects of lactation.[70]

Infanticide due to puerperal psychotic illness is rare. The type of killing where the child is killed immediately after birth and which is usually associated with illegitimate concealed pregnancies is also very uncommon. Most cases of child murder dealt with by the courts as infanticide are examples of the battered child syndrome in which the assault has had fatal consequences and the child is aged under 12 months. A combination of environmental stress and personality disorder with low frustration tolerance are the usual aetiological factors in such cases and the relationship to 'incomplete recovery from the effects of childbirth or lactation' specified in the Infanticide Act is often somewhat remote. The Act is nevertheless nearly always invoked in cases of maternal filicide when the victim is aged under 12 months, in order to reduce the charge from murder to manslaughter. The illogical operation of the Act is illustrated by the fact that an exactly similar type of case where the victim happened to be over the age of 12 months can no longer be dealt with as infanticide."

This illogicality is reinforced by the lack of any mitigating provision to protect the woman who does not succeed in killing her child. She may be charged with attempted murder or wounding with intent. The Criminal Law Revision Committee has stated that the particular drafting of section 1 of the Infanticide Act

---

[67] Royal Commission on Capital Punishment (1953), Cmd. 8932, p. 11.

[68] It was not until 1922 that infanticide was framed with reference to the medical effects of childbirth; previously it had been more concerned with social conditions and moral values. Originally, for example, infanticide applied only to the killing of illegitimate children and was more concerned with the concealment of death (which acted as a presumption of guilt to murder) rather than the death itself (21 Jac. 1, c. 27, 1623).

[69] Maier-Katkin and Ogle, "A Rationale for Infanticide Laws" [1993] Crim.L.R.903 at 906–909.

[70] West in *Murder followed by Suicide* (1955) found no significant connection between women who killed their children and this period of time. In a more recent survey of cases of infanticide it was found that psychiatric experts made no reference in their reports to the effects of lactation and often had to be prompted to refer to the effects of childbirth: Mackay, "The Consequences of Killing Very Young Children" [1993] Crim.L.R.21 at 29.

1938 makes the charging of *attempted infanticide* impossible.[71] Despite this, in the case of *K. A. Smith*,[72] the trial judge accepted a plea of guilty to attempted infanticide. Whilst the means by which this was done are suspect—the section seems much more like a partial defence to murder than anything else—the result is admirable. Such a woman in these circumstances is trying to commit infanticide and the law should recognise this. Further, if found guilty of attempted murder she may be sentenced to imprisonment.[73] The woman who is convicted of infanticide (which, like attempted murder and wounding with intent, carries a maximum sentence of life imprisonment) is almost never sent to prison—and presumably this would also be true of attempted infanticide. The sentence is almost always one of probation.[74] In more serious cases of imbalance the woman may be made subject to a hospital order and committed to her local hospital.

The Draft Criminal Code recognises the present anomaly: attempted infanticide would become the appropriate charge where a woman in such circumstances fails to kill her child.[75]

One might also wish to add that if the current use of the defence rests much more on the effects of child-rearing than on childbirth, then is it not also illogical that the defence is open to mothers only? Clearly, fathers may be subject to similar pressures. As the law stands such defendants will have to plead diminished responsibility or provocation.[76] Mackay's research leads him to conclude that "as far as females were concerned, these were viewed as tragic cases which the prosecution was prepared to deal with leniently, while the males, although avoiding murder convictions, were considered much more culpable".[77] Such defendants are very likely to be sentenced to prison.[78]

### Is infanticide redundant?

Given the disputed medical basis of the statute and the illogical limitations it imposes, the Butler Committee on Mentally Abnormal Offenders[79] decided that infanticide could be subsumed in the partial defence of diminished responsibility. Not only would the limitations to 12 months and to the mother be abolished, but they concluded that there would be little difficulty in establishing the necessary medical evidence for a finding of diminished responsibility. However, the Criminal Law Revision Committee was opposed to any such reform.

---

[71] 14th Report, *Offences Against the Person*, Cmnd.7844 (1980), para. 113.

[72] [1983] Crim.L.R.739.

[73] See Walker, Crime and Insanity in England (1968).

[74] In 2001 there were only 5 convictions for infanticide (*Criminal Statistics, England and Wales 2001* (Cm.5695). See also Mackay, *above*, n.70 at 23. This is supported by Wilczynski and Morris, "Parents Who Kill Children" [1993] Crim.L.R.31 at 35, but see also Wilczynski, "Images of Women Who Kill Their Infants: The Mad and the Bad" (1991) 2 Women and Criminal Justice 71.

[75] Law Commission No. 177, (1989) cl. 6 (2)

[76] As in the case of *Doughty* (1986) 83 Cr.App.R.319, *above*, p.686.

[77] Mackay, Mental Defence Conditions in the Criminal Law (1995), p. 211.

[78] Mackay, *ibid* at 30. However, the position may be somewhat complicated by the fact that the male defendants in the survey tended to have previous convictions whilst female defendants did not.

[79] Cmnd.6244, paras 19.22, 19.26.

## Criminal Law Revision Committee, 14th Report, Offences against the Person, Cmnd.7844 (1980):

"102. . . . . [W]e are not, with respect to the Butler Committee, satisfied that the offence of manslaughter by diminished responsibility could cover all such cases as does infanticide at present. Nor are we satisfied that the kinds of disturbances of mind which now lead to an infanticide verdict would in all cases be regarded as a mental disorder within section 4 of the Mental Health Act 1959. There would be the possibility, if the offence of infanticide were abolished, that in a case where a conviction for infanticide would today result, the defendant would be convicted of murder. Naturally in such a case counsel and medical witnesses would strain the interpretation of the law on diminished responsibility to ensure that a verdict of manslaughter was returned, but we would not wish to make a recommendation that puts too great a strain upon the professional consciences of expert witnesses.

104. A second reason why infanticide should not be merged with manslaughter but should continue to be a separate offence is that it is an offence for which imprisonment is rarely an appropriate sentence and for which a life sentence, the maximum for manslaughter, is never likely to be imposed. We are satisfied that the maximum penalty for infanticide should be no more than 5 years' imprisonment."

Their finding in paragraph 102 is supported by Mackay's survey of infanticide cases. Whilst there were a few cases where either statute could have been employed, there were many where the psychiatric evidence could not support a finding of diminished responsibility. Mackay continues: "the overall impression gained from an examination of the psychiatric reports which were used in support of infanticide leaves little room to doubt that the criteria within the 1938 Act were being used primarily as a legal device for avoiding the mandatory penalty and thus ensure that leniency could be shown in appropriate cases".[80] It can be argued, of course, as the Criminal Law Revision Committee intimated, that if the 1938 provisions were not there experts would stretch the evidence to fit the test of diminished responsibility. This would still be a gamble, however, and might result in some cases which are currently dealt with as infanticide being dealt with as murder.[81]

Despite the fact that the present basis of the offence is outmoded, it would seem desirable that this additional protection should be afforded to unbalanced women who kill. If the Draft Criminal Code is brought into effect there will be a welcome reduction in the maximum sentence from life to five years' imprisonment.[82] Protection will be substantially extended; however, it will still only be available to those who kill during the child's first year of life.[83] Mackay suggests that the age of five "might be a realistic solution for any newly formulated infanticide offence".[84] However, although the evidence supports the view that women will receive lenient

---

[80] *Above*, n.70 at 29. See also, Mackay, *above*, n.77 at p. 210.

[81] An alternative possibility is that abolition would bring about an increase in the number of cases in which it is decided not to bring prosecutions. This is already relatively common, for example, where the defendant is very young and the offence is an attempt to conceal the pregnancy and birth: Mackay, *above*, n.70 at 30. See also Wilczynski and Morris, *above*, n.74.

[82] Law Com. No. 177 (1989), cl. 64, incorporating the recommendation of the C.L.R.C., 14th Report, para. 106.

[83] *ibid.* implementing the recommendations of the C.L.R.C., para. 108.

[84] Mackay, *above*, n.77, p. 213.

treatment, there is a price to pay. The offence of infanticide (as with diminished responsibility) helps to perpetuate notions of "mad not bad" criminal women.

## VI. The Structure of Homicide Offences

In England there are several categories of homicide. The main distinction is between murder and involuntary manslaughter, a distinction resting on the presence or absence of a mental element, malice aforethought. However, murder is also distinguished from voluntary manslaughter, this distinction being based either on the mental condition of the defendant (diminished responsibility), or on the circumstances of the killing (provocation and suicide pacts). There are two other main species of homicide: infanticide, which refers specifically to the death of a particular type of victim (child under one year of age); and vehicular homicide[85] which refers to death being caused in a particular manner.

In this section we shall be concerned with four questions:

1. Why do we distinguish between different categories of homicide?
2. Do we distinguish between these categories with sufficient particularity?
3. On what basis ought such distinctions to be made?
4. Should we abolish these categories and replace them with a single offence of unlawful homicide?

### A. *Rationale of Distinction between Different Categories of Homicide*

Homicides range from cold-blooded, malicious killings to killings not far removed from accidents or killings where there are severe mitigating circumstances, such as provocation. It is necessary to differentiate between these homicides in terms of their perceived seriousness. This differentiation is useful for two purposes:

(a) Different penalties can be attached for the different categories of homicide. Thus the fact that murder is perceived as being far more serious than manslaughter is clearly reflected in the sentence: capital punishment before 1965 and mandatory life imprisonment since then, as opposed to a *maximum* of life imprisonment for manslaughter. Similarly, the fact that the crime of causing death by dangerous driving is perceived as being less serious than other unlawful homicides can be reflected by its sentence of a maximum of 10 years' imprisonment.

(b) Differentiating between homicide offences emphasises the different stigma attached to each and enables us to differentiate between different kinds of moral wrong. For example, the label "murder" emphasises the special stigma attached to that crime. One of the main purposes of the criminal law and punishment is its symbolic value in communicating messages to the public as to what is permissible or not. Different labels are used for different crimes to communicate the degree of rejection of the specific crime. The label "murder" is used to emphasise the

---

[85] The former offence of causing death by reckless driving was held to be a species of manslaughter in *Govt. of USA v Jennings* [1983] 1 A.C. 624.

"dreadfulness"[86] and the "uniquely horrible [nature of the] crime".[87] Also, it may have a significant deterrent value.[88] Abolishing the label "may appear to have the effect of lessening the seriousness of taking life".[89] Similar arguments may be put forward to explain why we retain the label "manslaughter" and treat separately the offences of infanticide and vehicular homicide.

### T. Morris and L. Blom-Cooper, A Calendar of Murder (Criminal Homicide in England since 1957) (1964), pp. 271–272:

"[W]anton murder is dramatically defined as the most dreadful of crimes, a view which has been upheld by the laws and customs of civilised societies down the ages. The act of murder occupies a unique place in the feelings of men in that it falls into a class of actions the results of which are irreversible. . . . Around the notion of death a whole series of institutional beliefs and practices have arisen creating a sense of social balance in which the realisation of mortality is incorporated into the fabric of human experience; only thus is death made tolerable.

The act of murder disturbs this balance. It accelerates the inevitable in a way which profoundly unsettles the delicate equilibrium which social institutional devices have achieved, and arouses in individuals the most deep-seated unconscious fears and anxieties . . .

Murder produces a sense of profound social shock—heightened in our own society by dissemination of the details through modern mass media. It can normally be relieved only by some highly dramatic act on the part of the community towards the offender. In days gone by this act was the public imposition of capital punishment; latterly . . . the criminal trial and the dramatisation of its preliminaries may be gradually taking its place. . . . Clearly, it is the special character of murder, the attendant sensationalism of the re-enactment of the killing with its actual risk of imitation, which wide advertisement brings in its trial, that gives murder its quintessential quality—a crime apart."

### B. *Greater Specificity*

Given the above views, another question presents itself. Does English law distinguish with sufficient precision between different homicides? Many would assert that it does not. Murder and manslaughter, in particular, are far too broad, each encompassing too many different types of conduct, circumstances and offenders—in short, too many different degrees of "heinousness". Murders, for example, vary widely: they cover planned, cold-blooded killings, deliberate killings with torture all the way down to killings only marginally qualifying as intentional under *Woollin*. They cover people who coldly kill for no reason, down through all the different motivations and explanations to mercy killings, where an anguished defendant kills a loved one to end their suffering. Manslaughters, too, cover a vast field: they range from conduct just short of murder to just above the non-criminal category of justifiable or accidental death. Is not each crime, each label, covering too vast a field?

When the English common law was introduced into the United States, these points were taken. The English categories of murder and manslaughter were each

---

[86] *La Fontaine* 11 A.L.R. 507 at 535, *per* Jacobs J.
[87] Cross, "Penal Reform in 1965 . . ." [1966] Crim.L.R.184 at 189.
[88] C.L.R.C., Working Paper on Offences against the Person, 1976, para. 7.
[89] *ibid.*

seen to be too broad to serve any useful purpose. In particular, it was felt to be wrong for the death penalty to apply to all murders. The crime of murder should be divided into categories with the death penalty only applying to the "worst". In 1794 the pioneering Pennsylvania Code divided murder into two degrees, with the death penalty only applying to first degree murder. Similarly, manslaughters were divided into different degrees, each degree carrying a separate penalty. This approach has been widely adopted with the result that both murder and manslaughter are now divided into degrees or categories in most states. In addition, the majority of states have yet further homicide offences, apart from murder and manslaughter, such as reckless homicide, negligent homicide and vehicular homicide.

## Arizona Rev.Stat.Ann. (Amended 1983)

"13–1102 Negligent Homicide
A person commits negligent homicide if with criminal negligence such person causes the death of another person. [4.5 years[90]]
13–1103 Manslaughter
A person commits manslaughter by:
1. Recklessly causing the death of another person; or
2. Committing second degree murder (13–1104) upon a sudden quarrel or heat of passion resulting from adequate provocation by the victim; or
3. Intentionally aiding another to commit suicide; or
4. Committing second degree murder (13–1104) while being coerced to do so by the use or threatened immediate use of unlawful deadly physical force upon such person or a third person which a reasonable person in his situation would have been unable to resist; or
5. Knowing or recklessly causing the death of an unborn child at any stage of its development by any physical injury to the mother of such child which would be murder if the death of the mother had occurred. [9.25 years]
13–1104 Second Degree Murder
A person commits second degree murder if without premeditation:
1. Such person intentionally causes the death of another person; or
2. Knowing that his conduct will cause death or serious physical injury, such person causes the death of another person; or
3. Under circumstances manifesting extreme indifference to human life, such person recklessly engages in conduct which creates a grave risk of death and thereby causes the death of another person. [16 years]
13–1105 First Degree Murder
(a) A person commits first degree murder if:
1. Intending or knowing that the person's conduct will cause death, such person causes the death of another with premeditation; or
2. Acting either alone or with one or more other persons such person commits or attempts to commit ... sexual assault ..., molestation of a child ..., [specified] narcotics offences ..., kidnapping ..., burglary ..., arson of an occupied structure ..., robbery ..., escape ..., and in the course of and in furtherance of such offence or immediate flight from such offence, such person or another person causes the death of any person.[91]
3. Intending or knowing that the person's conduct will cause death to a law enforcement officer, the person causes the death of a law enforcement officer who is in the line of duty.
(b) Homicide, [as defined in paragraph 2 above] requires no specific mental state other than what is required for the commission of any of the enumerated felonies. [Death or life

---

[90] This and the ensuing presumptive penalties are increased where the offender has two or more prior felony convictions or commits the offence with a deadly weapon (s.13–604).
[91] Details of each of these felonies have been omitted.

imprisonment depending on presence or absence of specified aggravating and mitigating circumstances.]

[Note: All the above penalties are presumptive penalties that a defendant will receive in the absence of aggravating or mitigating circumstances. Thus, for example, 16 years is the presumptive penalty for second degree murder, but this may be increased or reduced by six years depending on aggravating or mitigating circumstances.[92]]"

Vehicular homicide is a separate offence in 28 states. In some states, for example Colorado, criminally negligent homicide and vehicular homicide co-exist as separate offences (in addition to manslaughter and two degrees of murder).[93]

There is a major problem with such precise gradations of homicide offences. It assumes that one can isolate those factors or criteria that *always* makes a homicide more or less reprehensible. Let us take the deliberation/premeditation formula as an example. In most states in the United States the "worst" murders, first degree murders, are reserved for deliberate and premeditated killings. One can perhaps understand the rationale behind such provisions, namely that it "reflect[s] a belief that one who meditates an intent to kill and then deliberately executes it is more dangerous, more culpable or less capable of reformation than one who kills on sudden impulse; or that the prospect of the death penalty is more likely to deter men from deliberate than from impulsive murder".[94] There are, however, severe problems with such an approach:

(a) It is almost impossible to distinguish between a "premeditated" and a "merely intentional" killing. In the United States most statutes have defined "intention" in terms of "conscious objective". If something is your objective, that, of necessity, means you have made a decision to bring about that objective. The making of that decision must, by definition, involve premeditation and deliberation. As Cardozo J. put it:

"... an intent to kill is always deliberate and premeditated. ... There can be no intent unless there is a choice, yet by the hypothesis, the choice without more is enough to justify the inference that the intent was deliberate and premeditated ... [such statutes are] framed along the lines of a defective and unreal psychology."[95]

(b) A "purely impulsive" murder may be just as, if not more, reprehensible than the cold-blooded, premeditated killing. The American Law Institute has stated:

"Prior reflection may reveal the uncertainties of a tortured conscience rather than exceptional depravity. The very fact of a long internal struggle may be evidence that the homicidal impulse was deeply aberrational and far more the product of extraordinary circumstances than a true reflection of the actor's normal character."[96]

---

[92] Ariz.Rev.Stat.Ann. s.13–1103(B); s.13–604.
[93] Colo.Rev.Stat.Ann. ss.18–3–101—18–3–106.
[94] *Bullock v US*, 122 F. 2d 213 (D.C. Cir. 1941).
[95] Cardozo, "What Medicine Can Do for Law," in *Law and Literature and other Essays and Addresses* (1930), pp. 99–100.
[96] American Law Institute, Model Penal Code and Commentaries, Part II (1980), p. 127.

And as Stephen put it:

> "As much cruelty, as much indifference to the life of others, a disposition at least
> as dangerous to society, probably even more dangerous, is shown by sudden as
> by premeditated murders. The following cases appear to me to set this in a clear
> light. A, passing along the road, sees a boy sitting on a bridge over a deep river
> and, out of mere wanton barbarity, pushes him into it and so drowns him. A man
> makes advances to a girl who repels him. He deliberately but instantly cuts her
> throat. A man civilly asked to pay a just debt pretends to get the money, loads a
> rifle and blows out his creditor's brains. In none of these cases is there
> premeditation unless the word is used in a sense as unnatural as 'aforethought',
> in 'malice aforethought'; but each represents even more diabolical cruelty and
> ferocity than that which is involved in murders premeditated in the natural sense
> of the word."[97]

(c) Many premeditated killings are clearly not the most reprehensible. Mercy
killings, for example, are invariably premeditated killings, yet they are generally
regarded as far less blameworthy than most other types of killings. A good example
of this is to be found in the United States case of *Repouille v United States*.[98] In this
case the defendant's son was aged 13, had been bedridden since infancy and was
described as an "incurable imbecile" who could not walk or talk; he had been blind
for five years. The defendant had spent all his savings on an operation for the child
but his condition had not improved. The defendant began to talk of putting the boy
out of his misery and one day soaked a rag with chloroform and applied it to the
boy's face, while he lay in his bed, until he died. This was a clear case of a planned,
premeditated killing which would be first degree murder. Yet the jury convicted the
defendant of second degree manslaughter and requested sentencing leniency. The
judge suspended execution of a five year sentence and placed the defendant on
probation. Commenting on this, Learned Hand J. stated:

> "... the jury ... did not feel any moral repulsion at his crime. Although it was
> inescapably murder in the first degree, not only did they bring in a verdict that
> was flatly in the face of the facts and utterly absurd—for manslaughter in the
> second degree presupposes that the killing was not deliberate—but they coupled
> even that with a recommendation which showed that in substance they wished to
> exculpate the offender. Moreover, it is also plain, from the sentence which he
> imposed, that the judge could not have seriously disagreed with their
> recommendation."

A case such as this highlights the total inadequacy of the premeditation/
deliberation formula in that it has not succeeded in isolating the worst killings.
Categories of homicide become meaningless if they do not reflect common views of
reprehensibility.

### C. *Basis of Distinctions*

Given the inadequacy of the deliberation/premeditation formula, what of the other
bases utilised to distinguish between homicide offences? Can such offences be
graded exclusively in terms of different mental elements?

---

[97] Stephen, 3 *History of the Criminal Law* (1883), p. 94.
[98] 165 F. 2d 152 (2d Cir. 1947).

### Kentucky Revised Statutes 1996

"507–020 Murder

(1) A person is guilty of murder when:
- (a) With intent to cause the death of another person, he causes the death of such person or of a third person ... [unless defendant acted under extreme ... otional disturbance].
- (b) [U]nder circumstances manifesting extreme indifference to human life, he wantonly[99] engages in conduct which creates a grave risk of death to another person and thereby causes the death of another person.

507–030 Manslaughter in the First Degree

(1) A person is guilty of manslaughter in the first degree when:
- (a) With intent to cause serious physical injury to another person, he caused the death of such person or of a third person; or
- (b) [extreme emotional disturbance].

507–040 Manslaughter in the Second Degree

(1) A person is guilty of manslaughter in the second degree when ... he wantonly causes the death of another person.

507–050 Reckless Homicide

(1) A person is guilty of reckless homicide when, with recklessness he causes the death of another person."

Such fine distinctions are surely impracticable. Even if they could be justified philosophically they would not be meaningful to a jury. In England the Criminal Law Revision Committee proposed important reforms in the law of homicide which were adopted by the Draft Criminal Code.[1] These proposals proceed on an assumption, apparently felt to be so obvious as not even to need articulation, that the only way to distinguish murder from manslaughter is to specify different mental elements for each.

In the previous chapter on non-fatal offences against the person it was argued that appropriate levels of criminal liability and punishment ought to be fixed by reference to a combination of *blame* and harm, and that "blame" could involve a consideration of other factors in addition to *mens rea*. Thus, as we saw, we might blame someone more because of the method or circumstances of the crime—*e.g.* torturing the victim. In homicide the harm is, of course, constant; the victim is dead. There is, however, no particular reason why the blame element giving rise to different offence categories, *must* be limited to a consideration of the mental element of the defendant.

Indeed, a glance at other jurisdictions reveals that classifications of homicide offences could be made to depend on a variety of other factors. The identity of the victim, for instance, could be regarded as the key factor distinguishing two homicides with identical mental states.[2] In Arizona dangerous crimes against children carry greater penalties than when committed against adults: for example, the presumptive penalty for second degree murder against an adult is 16 years'

---

[99] Section 501.020(3) defines "wantonly": "... consciously disregards a substantial and unjustifiable risk. ... The risk must be of such a nature and degree that disregard thereof constitutes a gross deviation from the standard of conduct that a reasonable person would observe in the situation ...."

[1] Law Com. No. 177, 1989, paras 14.5–14.14.

[2] Such a proposal was considered and rejected by the Criminal Law Revision Committee in relation to assaults (14th Report, para. 162).

imprisonment but against a child it is 20 years' imprisonment.[3] In France there has long been a separate crime of parricide where a parent or grandparent is killed.[4] In Louisiana it is first degree murder to kill intentionally a fireman or a peace officer engaged in the performance of his duties.[5] Or, it could be the identity of the killer that is regarded as decisive as in New York where it is first degree murder if the murderer was confined in prison.[6]

Alternatively, the categorisation could be made to depend on the method and circumstances of the killing. In Louisiana it is first degree murder to kill after being offered anything of value for the killing,[7] and in Idaho it is first degree murder to kill by torturing a victim to death.[8] In many states in the United States it is a first degree murder to kill by using poison.[9]

Such an approach would not be totally alien to English law where the identity of the victim and the killer are highly relevant for the crime of infanticide, and the method and circumstances of the killing are equally relevant for the crime of causing death by dangerous driving.

Moving away from homicide offences, we have already seen that assaulting a police constable contrary to section 51 of the Police Act 1964 is regarded as "worse" than assaulting other persons; and the method of committing a crime is crucial in distinguishing between many property offences, for example, whether the property was obtained by theft or deception.

An objection to such an approach might be that it would be impossible to achieve agreement as to what factors rendered a killing more or less reprehensible. Yet in the United States there is a surprising measure of uniformity among the 50 states as to this. Typical of the factors widely regarded there as aggravating a murder are: killing with poison; killing with explosives; killing while in prison or escaping from prison; killing after being paid to kill; intentionally killing while committing certain crimes such as robbery, kidnapping or rape; killing a prospective witness in a criminal trial; killing a police officer, fireman or judge; if the defendant has previously been convicted of murder; killing a hostage or kidnap victim; if the circumstances of the killing are particularly heinous, atrocious or cruel. And factors widely regarded as mitigating the seriousness of a homicide are: adequate provocation; diminished responsibility; if the victim consented to or participated in his own killing; duress; if the defendant was an accessory and his participation was relatively minor.

In England there have been several proposals in the House of Commons over the last two decades that the death penalty be restored for certain aggravated classes of murder. These were murder resulting from an act of terrorism, murder of a police officer in the course of his duties, murder of a prison officer in the course of his duties, murder by shooting or causing an explosion, and murder in the course or furtherance of theft. All these proposals were rejected. It is important to emphasise

---

[3] Ariz.Rev.Stat.Ann., s.13–604.01(A).
[4] Code Penal, Art. 299.
[5] La.Rev.Stat., s.14.30(2).
[6] N.Y. Penal Law, s.125.27(1)(a)(iv).
[7] La.Rev.Stat., s.14.30(4).
[8] Idaho Code, s.18–4003(a).
[9] For example, California (Cal. Penal Code, s.189).

that what was rejected was capital punishment; the possibility of distinguishing between murders was still open. Although now incompatible with the European Convention on Human Rights,[10] the Home Secretary previously adopted the policy that certain categories of murderers (those who have killed police or prison officers, terrorist killings, murder during robbery or the sadistic or sexual murder of children) would not be released on parole until the expiry of at least 20 years.[11]

More recently, the Sentencing Advisory Panel has issued guidance to the Court of Appeal on the setting of "minimum terms" in murder cases.[12] This advice has been accepted in *Practice Statement (Crime: Life Sentences)*.[13] Under this guidance there are (effectively) three "starting points" which can then be varied by the presence of aggravating or mitigating circumstances. Lower starting point murders include those where the offender suffers from diminished capacity, was provoked or overreacted in self-defence, and where the offence was a mercy killing. These cases should attract minimum terms in the region of 8–9 years. The "normal" starting point for cases involving "the killing of an adult victim, arising from a quarrel or loss of temper between two persons known to each other" will be twelve years. Higher starting point cases include professional or contract killings, politically motivated killings, killings for gain (in the course of a burglary or robbery), killings to defeat the ends of justice (such as killing a witness), where the victim was providing a public service or was a child[14] or otherwise vulnerable or was targeted because of their religious or sexual orientation, where the killing was racially aggravated, where there is evidence of sadism, gratuitous violence or sexual maltreatment, humiliation or degradation of the victim before the killing, where extensive and/or multiple injuries were inflicted on the victim before death, or where the offender committed multiple murders. The starting point in such cases is 15–16 years. These starting points can be adjusted for aggravation or mitigation. Aggravating factors include planned killings, use of a weapon, concealment of the body and the previous record of the offender. Mitigating factors include an intention to cause grievous bodily harm rather than an intention to kill, spontaneity and lack of pre-meditation, the age of the offender, clear evidence of remorse or contrition and a timely plea of guilty.[15]

The above possible bases of distinction relate to murder. Any restructuring of homicide offences in English law would need to go further and consider a subdivision of the present broad offence of manslaughter as has been proposed by the Law Commission[16] and the relationship between these offences and the other

---

[10] *Above*, p. 636.

[11] This policy had been held to be lawful, even though it involved the Home Secretary binding himself in advance to exercise his discretion according to a set policy. (*Findlay v Secretary of State for the Home Department* [1985] A.C. 318.)

[12] Sentencing Advisory Panel, *Annual Report 2001–2002*, Appendix E.

[13] [2002] 1 W.L.R. 1789.

[14] A survey of public opinion found the killing of children to be the most serious form of homicide (Mitchell, "Further Evidence of the Relationship Between Legal and Public Opinion on the Law of Homicide" [2000] Crim.L.R.814).

[15] The Criminal Justice Bill 2003 proposes placing a significantly harsher version of these "starting points" (including "life means life" for the most serious cases) on a statutory basis.

[16] *Above*, pp. 670–671. See Clarkson, "Context and Culpability in Involuntary Manslaughter: Principle or Instinct" in Ashworth and Mitchell (eds), *Rethinking English Homicide Law* (2000).

homicide offences such as infanticide and vehicular homicide and other proposed offences such as corporate killing.

The danger of such an approach is that it runs the risk of over-specificity: too many offences could be morally confusing. The central issue is one of determining when there are sufficiently sound reasons to justify marking moral differences by the creation of separate offences. This in turn raises the almost intractable problem of determining which moral differences are so significant that they need to be reflected at the substantive offence level as opposed to being matters that can be taken into account at the sentencing level.[17]

### D. *Unlawful Homicide—A Single Offence*

Should English law abandon any such thoughts of further categorisation, indeed abandon its existing categories of homicide offences, and replace them with a single offence of unlawful homicide?

In *Hyam v D.P.P.* Lord Kilbrandon said:

"There does not appear to be any good reason why the crimes of murder and manslaughter should not both be abolished, and the single crime of unlawful homicide substituted; one case will differ from another in gravity, and that can be taken care of by variation of sentences downwards from life imprisonment."[18]

The following arguments can be adduced in favour of the introduction of a single offence of unlawful homicide:

1. Murder varies so widely both in character and in culpability that the judge ought to have a discretion as to sentence.

### Royal Commission on Capital Punishment, Report, Cmd.8932 (1953), para. 21:

"The crime [of murder] may be human and understandable, calling more for pity than for censure, or brutal and callous to an almost unbelievable degree. It may have occurred so much in the heat of passion as to rule out the possibility of premeditation, or it may have been well prepared and carried out in cold blood. ... The motives, springing from weakness as often as from wickedness, show some of the basest and some of the better emotions of mankind, cupidity, revenge, lust, jealousy, anger, fear, pity, despair, duty, self-righteousness, political fanaticism; or there may be no intelligible motive at all."

The argument is that not all these persons deserve the label "murder" with its mandatory life sentence.

---

[17] Difficulties such as these led the Home Affairs Committee to reject any division of murder into degrees (*Murder: the Mandatory Life Sentence*(First Report, 1995)).

[18] [1975] A.C. 55 at 98. A similar proposal was made by the New Zealand Law Reform Committee but has not been implemented (*Report on Culpable Homicide*, 1976, pp. 3–4).

2. Since the abolition of the death penalty, there is no longer the same need to draw a distinction between murder and manslaughter. One can receive the same penalty now for manslaughter as for murder. With the sentencing justification for the distinction largely gone, one is forced to ask: is the labelling justification (that one needs to retain the special label "murder" for the "worst" killings) sufficient to outweigh all the problems involved in drawing the distinction?

### M. D. Farrier, "The Distinction between Murder and Manslaughter in its Procedural Context" (1976) 39 M.L.R. 414 at 428:

"[T]here is an undeveloped hypothesis that criminal labelling in general is functional for society in that it lays down the limits of tolerable behaviour by revealing in a stark form the type of behaviour which is not to be tolerated. Thus Erikson ('Notes on the Sociology of Deviance' in Scheff, T.J., ed., *Mental Illness and Social Processes*, pp. 299–303) regards the transactions taking place between deviant persons and agencies of control as boundary maintaining mechanisms which mark the outer limits of acceptable conduct and assert how much diversity can be contained within the system before it begins to lose its distinctive structure. It would be extremely difficult to justify the distinction drawn in *Hyam* on this basis, given its nebulous nature and its probable lack of meaning to those not versed in the myseries of the law. Indeed, although it might be true that this kind of argument would justify the existence of a distinct homicide label as compared merely with one encompassing the broad area of conduct relating to violence to the person, any further division within the sub-category of homicide would have to be a very sharp one if it was going to have any meaning for the social audience and be capable of implementation by a jury."

3. Since the abolition of the death penalty and because of the difficulty in defining the "intention" necessary for murder, the distinction between murder and manslaughter appears to be dying a natural death. In many cases where a murder conviction could probably have been obtained, prosecutors are content to charge with manslaughter, or accept pleas of guilty to manslaughter. This saves much time and expense and indicates that prosecutors, at least, are often willing to rely on judges exercising their sentencing discretion reasonably. Thus, for example, in the Iranian Embassy siege case[19] the prosecution accepted a plea of guilty to manslaughter in a fairly clearly-cut case of murder; the defendant was promptly sentenced to life imprisonment, the same sentence he would have received after a long, expensive trial resulting in a murder conviction. Similar considerations, coupled with a desire to shield the relatives of victims from hitherto unrevealed details, prompted the prosecution in *Sutcliffe* (the so-called Yorkshire Ripper case)[20] to agree to a plea to manslaughter (the judge declined to accept such a plea). If there were a single offence of unlawful homicide, one would avoid the present anomalous situation of some prosecutors accepting lesser pleas, while other prosecutors insist on pursuing a murder charge.

Further, juries appear unwilling to convict of murder except in clear cases as this is tying the judge's hands as to sentence. By returning verdicts of manslaughter in many cases, they are allowing the judge to take all the circumstances into account before imposing an appropriate sentence. Lord Denning has said that "in many cases which are in law plainly murder, juries return verdicts of manslaughter,

[19] *The Times*, May 8, 1981, p. 1, Col. 2.
[20] *The Times*, April 30, 1981, p. 1, Col. 1.

because they do not think the death sentence is appropriate".[21] Such a practice seems to have survived the abolition of the death penalty. In *Repouille v US*,[22] a case described as "inescapably first degree murder", the jury, quite perversely, returned a verdict of second degree murder enabling the judge to impose a suspended sentence. If the law is in a strait-jacket, judges, prosecutors and juries will start ignoring the law. If this starts happening too extensively, should not the law be changed?

4. A single offence of unlawful homicide would mean that life imprisonment would be restricted to the worst cases. Such persons would actually remain in prison for a substantial period of time. This would increase public confidence in the life sentence. At the moment many people receive the mandatory life sentence for murder who arguably do not deserve it. Justice is achieved by the Parole Board releasing such persons on licence after a relatively short period of time. The message communicated to the public is "Murderer Released After One Year in Prison" or the over-simplistic "Life Means Twelve Years."[23] Any utility in the special label "murder" is soon devalued by such practices.

### Report of the Advisory Council on the Penal System, Sentences of Imprisonment: A Review of Maximum Penalties, 1978, para. 255:

"[L]ife imprisonment would be reserved for those cases where both the gravity of the offence and the instability of the offender suggested that an indeterminate sentence was necessary for the protection of the public. The effect of this would probably be a presumption that any murderer given a life sentence should remain in custody longer than most of those given fixed sentences; the Parole Board ... would be bound to take account of the length of determinate sentences when deciding on release from life imprisonment and this, because life imprisonment would be restricted to the worst cases, would mean that the period served would be substantially longer than the average period at present. This, in our opinion, would increase, rather than diminish, public confidence in the life sentence."

5. Partial defences, such as provocation and diminished responsibility—and the special offence of infanticide—exist mainly to alleviate the harshness of the mandatory penalty for murder and give the judge a discretion to take all the circumstances into account in fixing sentence.

### Baroness Wootton, Crime and Penal Policy: Reflections on Fifty Years Experience (1978), p. 143:

"[D]iminished responsibility seems to come perilously near to merely providing a means of escape from the life sentence for murder, in circumstances where, if this sentence was not mandatory, it might be held that there were grounds for mitigation. In other instances, however, the terms of Section 2 are stretched to a point at which (again clearly as a method of mitigation) the offender, far from suffering from any diminution of responsibility, appears to have acted from excessively responsible motives. Thus, in 1960 a retired Army officer became increasingly worried as he realised that his baby son was a mongol. He therefore

---

[21] Royal Commission on Capital Punishment, Cmd.8932 (1953), para. 27.
[22] *Above*, n.98.
[23] 12.6 years was the average time served by life sentence prisoners released over the last decade. Home Office, *Prison Statistics: England and Wales 1996* (Cm.3732) p. 122. For those released in 2000 the figure had increased to 14.3 years (Sentencing Advisory Panel *Annual Report 2001–02*, Appendix E).

read up all that he could find about mongolism and came to the conclusion that the kindest course would be to do away with the child. So he smothered it, and immediately informed the police. Although it might be thought that this action was morally wrong, it would be difficult to argue that it was not responsibly motivated. Nevertheless, in a successful Section 2 defence, a sentence of 12 months' imprisonment was imposed."

The creation of a single offence would mean that the somewhat artificial rules on provocation, diminished responsibility, infanticide and suicide pacts could be abandoned.[24] These matters could then simply be treated as mitigating factors relevant to sentencing.

What are the arguments against the introduction of a single offence of unlawful homicide?

### Criminal Law Revision Committee, Working Paper on Offences against the Person, 1976:

"5. To have a single offence of homicide, combining murder with a lesser offence of manslaughter, would mean that the jury's verdict would leave the judge with no guidance as to the gravity of the offence. In the absence of any new provision introducing a system of special verdicts, the judge would have to assess, in deciding what penalty to impose, whether intent to kill or a less serious degree of criminality amounting to what is now manslaughter had been proved. If the accused pleaded not guilty, the facts of the case would come out in the evidence, but the verdict of the jury would be confined to the issue of guilt or innocence of the offence of homicide. The judge would be left to decide, for example, whether the provocation alleged in mitigation (with the merger of murder and manslaughter, provocation would be a matter of mitigation only) existed in fact. If the accused pleaded guilty to homicide, the judge would have even less material on which to decide such questions since he would not have had the benefit of hearing detailed evidence. Thus the offence of homicide would apply to a very wide range of circumstances, varying in their degree of gravity, and the judge would be left to determine the true nature of the offence without the assistance of the jury. The majority of us think that the argument discussed in this paragraph is a very strong one; a minority of members, however, consider that it is overstated.

6. To have a single offence of homicide covering such a wide range of acts would make a conviction of the offence relatively uninformative in that it would be used to describe the most heinous case of murder and the least serious case of manslaughter. Although the Committee's proposals about the existing offence of manslaughter would reduce the scope of the single offence of homicide (combining murder and manslaughter), it would still be a wide-ranging offence classifying under the same head both a person who killed under provocation or while suffering from diminished responsibility and a person who killed deliberately without any provocation and not suffering from any mental disorder.

7. To abolish the offence of murder as such, although retaining it as part of a wider offence of homicide, may appear to have the effect of lessening the seriousness of taking life. We think that, in the public's mind, there is a stigma attaching to a conviction of murder and that this rightly emphasises the seriousness of the offence and may have a significant deterrent value ...

8. ... [T]he majority of us see advantages in the mandatory sentence and think that there is a need for a special penalty for the most serious cases of homicide in order to reassure the public and also for the purposes of prevention and deterrence."[25]

---

[24] Of course, it does not follow that these defences would *have* to be abolished. See Mackay, "Diminished Responsibility and Mentally Disordered Offenders" in Ashworth and Mitchell, *Rethinking English Homicide Law* (2000), pp. 80–81.

[25] Similar views were expressed by Lord Hailsham in *Cunningham* [1982] A.C. 566 at 580.

There is a further objection to the suggested new offence of unlawful homicide. Such a proposal would result in a substantial increase of judicial discretion in sentencing. In Chapter 1 the dangers of such discretion were considered. Over the past two decades there has been a strong movement away from judicial discretion in sentencing which ought to lead to a more precise classification of offences. It can only be a retrograde step to propose reforms to the substantive law that would involve an *increase* in judicial discretion in sentencing.

A possible compromise solution could be the introduction of a single offence of unlawful homicide together with clear sentencing guidelines for the new offence. Building on the work already done by the Sentencing Advisory Panel in relation to the length of tariffs in murder cases, guidelines could be established as to the appropriate level of sentence in all homicide cases. Such guidelines would not be limited by the present straight-jacket of existing offence categories but could concentrate on the true issue: given the mental element of this defendant and given the context and circumstances of this killing, including the presence or absence of aggravating and mitigating circumstances, what penalty should be imposed? This could well involve a separate sentencing hearing after the primary ascertainment of criminal liability.

## 9

# OFFENCES AGAINST PROPERTY

---

## I. Introduction

There is a wide variety of offences against property in English law, for example, theft, robbery, burglary, offences involving deception and fraud, taking a motor vehicle or other conveyance without authority, abstracting electricity, blackmail, handling stolen goods, forgery, criminal damage—and many more.

### A. *The level of offending*

So widespread are these offences that people are more likely to be the victim of a property offence than of any other kind of crime. In 2001/02 offences against property accounted for 82 per cent of all recorded crime. Of this, 41 per cent was theft and handling offences; 16 per cent was burglary and 19 per cent was criminal damage.[1] However, official figures only deal with those offences which are recorded and thus information about the extent of many forms of property crime is not accurate. British Crime Surveys (where victims are asked to give details of offences against them) have attempted to shed some light upon the dark figure of crime. The 2001 British Crime Survey estimates that only 33 per cent of all property crime is reported to the police and then recorded by them (see Table 1). Reporting and recording rates vary considerably by type of offence. For instance, 90 per cent of vehicle thefts are reported (largely for insurance reasons) and, of these, 78 per cent are recorded. However, for theft from a person only 35 per cent are reported of which only 40 per cent are recorded; thus, overall a mere 14 per cent of such thefts appear in the official statistics.[2]

---

[1] Simmons *et al*, *Crime in England and Wales 2001/02* (2002), p. 27.
[2] Kershaw *et al*, *The 2001 British Crime Survey* (2001), pp. 17–20.

Table 1

### Kershaw et al, The 2001 British Crime Survey (2001)
### Table 2.1: Crimes estimated by the British Crime Survey and recorded by the Police in 2000

|  | Police (000s) | BCS (000s) | % BCS reported | % recorded of reported | % recorded of all BCS |
|---|---|---|---|---|---|
| Vandalism | 481 | 2,608 | 34% | 54% | 18% |
| All comparable property crime (acquisitive crime) | 1,553 | 4,689 | 51% | 65% | 33% |
| Burglary | 409 | 1,063 | 66% | 59% | 38% |
| Attempts and no loss | 106 | 660 | 55% | 30% | 16% |
| Burglary with loss | 303 | 403 | 84% | 90% | 75% |
| All vehicle thefts | 938 | 2,619 | 49% | 73% | 36% |
| Thefts from vehicles | 478 | 1,626 | 47% | 63% | 29% |
| Thefts of vehicles | 235 | 337 | 90% | 78% | 70% |
| Attempted vehicle theft | 224 | 656 | 33% | [100%] | 34% |
| Bicycle theft | 119 | 377 | 54% | 58% | 31% |
| Theft from the person | 88 | 629 | 35% | 40% | 14% |

The reasons for the differences between the official and the unofficial figures are not hard to identify. For example, the value of the property involved may be perceived by the victim (and the police) as being too trivial to proceed; the cost and inconvenience of taking action may make some victims reluctant to proceed; it may be impossible to identify offenders (as will be the case with much shoplifting); the behaviour may not be seen by even the victim as truly criminal (as may be the case with the problem of bad cheques); and, in some cases, the victim may never even learn of his loss.

The cost of property crime is vast. For instance, it has been estimated that fraud in the United Kingdom financial community results in losses of up to nearly £14 billion a year. In 1998 fraud linked to plastic payment cards amounted to £135 million.[1-3]

There is thus a wide diversity of offences thrown together under the umbrella of property offences. The harm done may vary from damage that endangers life, through robbery and "professional" theft to behaviour that lies at the very fringes of criminality. There is no typical offender (although the chances of it being a young male are even higher than for other types of offences). The public imagination may conjure up images of Fagin, Bill Sikes or Ronald Biggs and those large scale professional crimes that capture the news headlines but, although professional criminals do exist, there also exists a vast army of occasional criminals: the opportunist burglar, the shoplifter, the juvenile joy-rider, the naive passer of dud cheques, and the "respectable" employee who takes advantage of his employer's

[1-3] Barclay and Tavares, *Information on the Criminal Justice System in England and Wales: Digest 4* (1999).

trust to embezzle funds. Property offences encompass crime that could be described as violent[4] to crime that could be labelled as white-collar crime.[5]

## B. *The sociological background*

### 1. Why do people commit property offences?

Given the diversity of property offenders and offences, it is not surprising that there exists a multiplicity of theories attempting to account for such criminality. Some attempts have tried to establish links between economic conditions and the rate of property offending. Overall conclusions are difficult to draw and any causal relationship is unlikely to be straight-forward. However, a study at the beginning of the 1990s, looking back over 12 years, found that increases in property offending were most marked during periods when spending power was reduced.[6]

Other theories are dependent upon the drawing of a distinction between utilitarian and non-utilitarian crime. Merton, for example, in his theory of anomie,[7] saw crime as an unorthodox route to achieving the American Dream of monetary wealth in a society that held out this goal to all as achievable but at the same time savagely restricted legitimate means of obtaining the goal. In such a society where the emphasis was all upon success and not on the means of achieving success, there was pressure upon individuals to take whatever route would transform them from plough-boys to presidents. Crime was strictly utilitarian. Cohen, on the other hand, emphasised the non-utilitarian nature of much juvenile property crime.[8] He believed that as a result of school failure in a system that was inherently middle-class and, therefore, stacked against them, working-class boys would respond by inverting the norms of their parent culture. They would reject the values of working hard and having respect for other people's property and behave in a way that showed their commitment to opposite values. By doing this they would thereby set standards that they were capable of achieving. Delinquency was thus an attempt to disassociate themselves from a culture that had doomed them to fail; the characteristic crimes engaged in would be stealing and then throwing away or acts of small-scale vandalism.

Other theorists have concentrated not so much on the delinquent act itself, but on the way in which society responds to it. This argument runs counter to deterrence reasoning in that here it is claimed that by "dramatising the evil"[9] and acting repressively against it by legal sanctions, criminality is exacerbated. By

---

[4] Robbery, although a violent offence, is described as a property offence because the violence is incidental to the main aim, the acquisition of property.

[5] This term was invented by Sutherland in *White-Collar Crime* (1949) to illuminate crime committed not by young working-class males but by persons of apparent respectability in the course of their employment. There now exists a wealth of literature on this subject. See, for example, Nelkin, "White Collar Crime" in Maguire, Morgan and Reiner, *The Oxford Handbook of Criminology* (3rd ed., 2002) and Levi, *Regulating Fraud* (1987).

[6] Field, *Trends in Crime and their Interpretation: A Study of Recorded Crime in Post-war England and Wales* (H.O.R.S. No. 119) (1991).

[7] *Social Theory and Social Structure* (3rd ed., 1968).

[8] *Delinquent Boys: The Culture of the Gang* (1955).

[9] Tannenbaum's term for societal reaction: (*Crime and the Community* (1938)), laid the foundations from which developed modern day labelling theory. For a detailed criticism of such theories, see, Downes and Rock, *Understanding Deviance* (2nd ed., 1995), pp. 187–214 and Jones, *Criminology* (2nd ed., 2001), pp. 192–195.

acting to prevent further crime or by labelling a deviant/delinquent act as criminal, society actually creates a criminal. Evidence exists on both sides of this evergreen debate but it must be admitted that the labelling perspective is of particular significance in shaping penal policy towards young offenders. Many commentators regard some juvenile delinquency as quite a normal feature of growing up. It is in the best interests of everyone, therefore, not to be too heavy-handed in the treatment of such offenders, to avoid as much as possible the stigmatising effect of court appearances and the like.[10] To ignore this is to risk a phase in the juvenile's life becoming a permanent feature.[11]

Despite this criticism of the way in which delinquency can be amplified, most such theories do not attack the framework of the criminal law or the criminal justice system in any fundamental sense. Both mainstream criminologists and labelling theorists accept the existence of laws protecting property. This represents a consensus view of society; there is a shared sense of right and wrong. Conflict criminology attacks this view and suggests that whilst the notion of consensus might be appropriate for simple societies, complex, industrial, multi-racial and multi-cultural societies such as those in Great Britain and the United States are dominated by conflict instead. The important task for such theorists is to describe the process by which some members of society consistently have their interests protected at the expense of others.

### Steven Box, Power, Crime and Mystification (1983), p. 10:

"The criminal law sees only some types of property deprivation as robbery or theft; it excludes, for example, the separation of consumers and part of their money that follows manufacturers' malpractices or advertisers' misrepresentations; it excludes shareholders losing their money because managers behaved in ways which they thought would be to the advantage of shareholders even though the only tangible benefits accrued to the managers … it excludes the *extra* tax citizens, in this or other countries, have to pay because: (i) corporations and the very wealthy are able to employ financial experts at discovering legal loopholes through which money can be safely transported to tax havens; (ii) Defence Department officials have been bribed to order more expensive weaponry systems or missiles in 'excess' of those 'needed'; (iii) multinational drug companies charge our National Health Services prices which are estimated to be at least £50 millions in excess of alternative supplies. If an employee's hand slips into the governor's pocket and removes any spare cash, that is theft; if the governor puts his hand into the employees' pockets and takes their spare cash, *i.e.* reduces wages, even below the legal minimum, that is the labour market operating reasonably. To end the list prematurely and clarify the point, the law of theft includes, in the words of that anonymous poet particularly loved by teachers of 'A' level economic history, 'the man or woman who steals the goose from off the common, but leaves the greater villian loose who steals the common from the goose.' "

From this beginning came the development of radical criminology where crime was seen as the inevitable by-product of a society divided into classes by capitalism. Offenders might be forced to commit crime by the laws designed to protect the

---

[10] The well-established practice of cautioning young offenders (especially first-time property offenders) was put on a statutory footing by the Crime and Disorder Act 1998. Sections 65 and 66 establish a new system of reprimands and warnings, and restrictions have been imposed on the use of multiple cautions.

[11] Research, however, suggests that the notion of "growing out of crime" may be more true for female than male offenders (Graham and Bowling, *Young People and Crime* (1995)).

ruling classes, either as a means of survival or as part of the struggle to be free from repression. Emphasis was placed on crime committed by the powerful and their relative immunity from prosecution. The resolution of the conflict is seen in terms of the elimination of capitalism; with this would come the end of all crime not based on biological or psychological factors.[12]

Despite the insight offered into modern society, radical criminology has fared badly at the hands of its critics. Cross-cultural studies, for example, have shown that high working-class crime rates are not necessarily a feature of capitalist societies.[13] Crime surveys in this country have made it clear that it is the working-classes who more frequently suffer both victimisation and repeat victimisation and that the laws are protective of them as well as the despised bourgeoisie.[14] Radical criminology has also been accused of taking no account of gender, despite the fact that women are often the poorest members of society. Moreover, and overwhelmingly, radical criminology ignores the fact that most crime is inter-group rather than intra-group: crimes by the powerful against the powerful and crimes by the working-classes against the working-classes. The notion of classes at war, therefore, cannot be sustained by the empirical evidence any more than there is evidence that absolute deprivation leads automatically to crime. However, there is a stronger case that crime can be the result of relative deprivation.[15]

Some theorists have responded to such criticisms by continuing to stress the importance of a critical approach to the search for causes of the crime problem. Others, however, have effectively abandoned that search and have focused attention on ways, for example, in which the impact of crime may be reduced by crime prevention and community safety measures.[16] Whilst this approach has been subject to criticism itself, there is little doubt that the resulting crime surveys are a rich source of information about crime, and property crime in particular. What is learnt may well have implications for substantive criminal law as well as, for example, policing.

If it transpires that much property crime is being dealt with non-legally then there may be a case[17] for the decriminalisation of some offences at the fringes of criminality.

---

[12] See, *e.g.*, Taylor, Walton and Young, *The New Criminology* (1973).

[13] *e.g.* Clinard, *Cities with Little Crime: The Case of Switzerland* (1978).

[14] As well as the British Crime Surveys, 1982–2001, see also more localised surveys: *e.g.* Jones, Maclean, Young, *The Islington Crime Survey* (1986) and, generally, Koffman, *Crime Surveys and Victims of Crime* (1996). For similar findings in other countries, see *e.g.* the President's Commission on Law Enforcement and the Administration of Justice, *Crime and its Impact: an Assessment* (1967).

[15] See further, Young, "Recent Paradigms in Criminology" in Maguire, Morgan and Reiner, *The Oxford Handbook of Criminology* (2nd ed., 1997).

[16] See Pease, "Crime Reduction" in Maguire, Morgan and Reiner, *The Oxford Handbook of Criminology* (3rd ed., 2002).

[17] *Post*, pp. 854–855.

## 2. Societal attitudes towards property offences

### J. Hepburn, Occasional Property Crime, in R. Meier (ed.), Major Forms of Crime (1984), pp. 88–89:

"Among the earliest criminal laws were those pertaining to property. In a highly stratified society, especially one with a capitalistic economy, power and status depend to a large degree on the economic resources a person accumulates. Consequently, there generally is a strong, negative public reaction to property offenses in the United States. The reaction is particularly strong against armed robbery, mugging, and arson, because these offenses combine loss of property with a potential for physical harm to the victim. Residential burglary, which violates the sanctity of the home, also generates a strong condemnation. In contrast, the public outcry against shoplifting, vandalism, and other 'petty' forms of property crime is least vocal.

The magnitude of the public's reaction to property offenses does not seem to be associated with the amount of financial loss involved. Compared to the multimillion-dollar losses which result from corporate crime and organized crime, the losses incurred by occasional property crimes are quite small . . .

Armed robbery netted a total of $339 million in property loss, for example, while the total loss due to burglary was $3 billion. According to the FBI, the total cost of all Part I property offenses was slightly over $10 billion. In comparison, the annual cost to the public of faulty goods, monopolistic practices, and other corporate crimes has been estimated at between $174 and $231 billion . . . Furthermore, the financial losses due to the criminal activities of organized crime are estimated to be upwards of $50 billion annually . . . Despite the greater loss due to corporate and organized crime, these crimes receive less public condemnation than the more traditional property crimes.

The public's reaction to property crimes is reflected in the legal reaction taken by law enforcement agencies. Police agencies are largely reactive; they respond to the crimes that are brought to their attention by citizens. Legislators also are responsive to their constituency's concern with property crimes. As a result, a significant amount of the time, money, and energy of law enforcement agencies is directed toward ordinary property crimes. Increased police patrols are justified on the (false) assumption that they reduce the opportunity for crime and increase the risk of arrest. Merchants and residents are advised by the police of various 'target-hardening' tactics, such as exterior lighting and barred windows, designed to reduce the opportunity for crime. Prosecutors and legislators champion the view that more severe legal penalties are needed to deter crime.

Although the public and legal reaction to property crimes in general is rather severe, the reaction to those who are occasional offenders tends to be more restrained. Compared to other offenders processed routinely by the courts, the occasional offender is (1) less likely to have a criminal record of prior arrests and convictions, (2) more likely to have been charged with a minor offense, (3) more respectable, as defined in terms of employment history, residential stability, and family relationships, and (4) more repentant. As a result of these characteristics of the offender and the offense, the occasional offender is treated less harshly by the criminal justice system. The prosecutor's office is less likely to file initial charges against the offender. If it does, there is a strong probability that the offender will be diverted from prosecution to some special restitution-oriented program or that the charges will be dismissed before trial. Should the offender be convicted, a prison sentence is most unlikely."

British Crime Surveys (1982–2001) are a useful source of information about public attitudes towards property offences, in two main contexts. First, such surveys have a great deal to say about the sorts of crime that people are most anxious about and the steps they take to reduce their vulnerability. Fear of being "mugged" is a commonly expressed concern; for some people this may cause them to avoid going out at night at all if it can be avoided, for others it might (especially in the case of women) mean never going out alone. Fear of burglary might cause some to support neighbourhood watch schemes. Fear of having their computers used for fraud might cause executives to spend large amounts of money on security systems and security experts.

Secondly, such surveys are a valuable means of ascertaining what the public thinks about sentencing practices in relation to property offences. Generally, public opinion polls reveal a punitive approach to sentencing[18] but it appears that "people overestimate the leniency of the courts".[19] Further, there is evidence that while some victims of crime may have a generalised preference for tough sentences, their views as to what should happen in their own case may appear lenient in comparison.[20] Other research concludes that most victims have no idea at all about the sentence which should be imposed: "As far as the justice of their case is concerned, they have suffered a lobotomy".[21]

Even in abstract terms, the attitudes expressed in such surveys are not always in favour of stiffer penalties. Where the offence is perceived as less serious, there may be considerable support for non-custodial alternatives to imprisonment. One in 12 of the respondents in the second British Crime Survey favoured the use of informal police warnings for shoplifters over the age of 25 with previous convictions.[22] This raises once again the issue whether some offences are properly the concern of the criminal law.

## C. *The Legal Background*

Discussion so far makes it clear that the structure of property offences is very different from the offences against the person already covered. With the latter, the seriousness of the injury was critical in the structuring of offences and concomitant levels of punishment: for example, causing death is more serious than causing grievous harm, which in turn is worse than causing actual bodily harm—and so on. Offences against property, however, are not structured in such a clear manner. It is not possible to follow the same pattern in structuring liability because of the difficulty in measuring the "harm" done. One possible method here is by assessing the value of the property involved. English law, however, has eschewed such an approach at least at a substantive level and instead has chosen to distinguish property offences by the method of taking or dealing with the property. According to this approach, deceiving someone into agreeing to part with his property (obtaining property by deception) is treated differently from coercing someone with threats into parting with property (blackmail). Whether each grouping is sufficiently precise and/or meaningful is a matter to be returned to after an examination of the offences themselves.

Another distinctive feature of the offences against property is that they are mainly statutory and largely found in modern statutes, in particular, the Theft Act

---

[18] Mayhew, Elliott and Dowds, *The 1988 British Crime Survey* (1989), p. 43. See also Walker and Hough (eds), *Public Attitudes to Sentencing* (1988), pp. 203–217.

[19] Mayhew *et al.*, *ibid.*, p. 43. This finding was confirmed by Walker and Hough (eds.), *ibid*, pp. 185–202.

[20] Shapland, Willmore and Duff, *Victims in the Criminal Justice System* (1985).

[21] Cretney and Davis, *Punishing Violence* (1995), pp. 156–157. This research examined victims of assault but there is no reason to suppose victims of property crimes have a clearer view.

[22] *Above*, n.18, p. 44.

1968, the Theft Act 1978, the Criminal Damage Act 1971 and the Forgery and Counterfeiting Act 1981. These statutes are somewhat distinctive in that they approximate to a code. Most English statutes consolidate, amend or add to the pre-existing law. The approach here is different. Take, for instance, the Theft Act 1968. This Act swept away all the previous law on the subject, creating entirely new law dealing with most forms of dishonest dealings with property. As English law enters an era possibly culminating in a codification of the whole of the criminal law,[23] it becomes particularly important and interesting to see how our courts have handled these areas of law.

Before examining the property offences themselves two important preliminary points must be made.

The Criminal Law Revision Committee, in putting forward its proposals[24] which largely became the Theft Act 1968, wished to avoid the technicality and complexity of the old law under the Larceny Acts and, accordingly, deliberately tried to frame as much of the legislation as possible in ordinary "simple" language capable of being easily understood by the layman. Accordingly, many key concepts (for example, "dishonesty") were inserted in the legislation without definition. The courts could, of course, have developed their own legal definitions of such concepts but have instead preferred to leave the meaning of such words to the jury, as questions of fact. The jury are ordinary people; they know what ordinary words mean—and do not need judges to explain their meaning to them. This approach, leading to a lack of fixed standards and inconsistency, has proved highly controversial, as will be seen in this chapter.

The second preliminary issue in some ways completely contradicts the above point. Offences against property deal with interference with other persons' rights or interests in property. One is free to do as one likes with one's own property. It is therefore always necessary to ascertain that there is some other person who has some right or interest in the property. For instance, in *Corcoran v Whent*[25] a defendant ate a meal in a hotel restaurant and left without paying. In order to determine his liability for theft it became necessary to determine whether at the time he decided not to pay (after he had eaten the food), the food (in his stomach) belonged to anyone else! If it belonged to himself he could commit no crime as he would not be interfering with anyone else's rights or interests in property.[26]

But how is one to determine whether anyone else has such proprietary right or interest in the property? There is a whole body of law—the law of property, contract and quasi-contract—devoted to answering such questions. The Theft Act 1968, for example, uses many technical legal terms such as "trespasser",[27] "proprietary right or interest",[28] "trust",[29] etc. As these terms are undefined it would appear reasonable that they be assigned their established civil law meaning.

---

[23] Law Commission Working Paper, No. 143, *Codification of the Criminal Law* (1985).

[24] Criminal Law Revision Committee, Eighth Report, *Theft and Related Offences*, Cmnd.2977 (1966).

[25] [1977] Crim.L.R.52.

[26] The defendant's conviction for theft was quashed. Once he had eaten the food he could not "deal with it" and it was no longer property "belonging to another". This would now be dealt with as making off without payment under s.3 of the Theft Act 1978.

[27] s.9.

[28] s.5(1).

[29] s.5(2).

Such an approach would, however, fly in the face of the philosophy that words in such legislation be assigned their ordinary meaning by ordinary people, the jury. There is some force in such an approach. Civil law meanings of words need adaptation to the purposes of the criminal law, for instance, to accommodate the normal requirement of *mens rea*. Further, the criminal law ought to reflect everyday values and "the way we live". Who better to reflect such values than those "everyday folk", the jury? This appears to be the prevailing articulated view. In *Morris*,[30] one of the leading House of Lords decisions on theft, Lord Roskill was highly critical of the approach that relied on the civil law meaning of concepts. For instance, whether a contract was void or voidable, was "so far as possible" not a relevant question in relation to the law of theft.

As will be seen, however, courts are not always prepared to jettison established legal meanings and replace them with "ordinary meanings". (What is the ordinary meaning of those ordinary words, "trust" or "equitable interest"?) Accordingly, one of the fascinations of this area of law is to observe the lurchings along the tightrope as the English courts try to achieve an impossible balance between these two competing and irreconcilable approaches.

A thorough consideration of all property offences is not possible, even in a book of this size. Accordingly, the enquiry will be limited to those offences that tell us most about the purposes and structures of this area of law. The main offences to be considered will be theft and the various deception offences in both the Theft Act 1968 and Theft Act 1978. Brief consideration will also be given to the offences of robbery, burglary, handling stolen goods and making off without payment.

## II. THEFT

### A. *Extent and Context*

Theft offences account for 41 per cent of all recorded crime in England and Wales.[31] However, as already seen, such official figures do not reveal the dark figure of crime. Many thefts are simply not reported or recorded. Whereas a high proportion of thefts of motor vehicles are reported (because of the value of vehicles and for insurance purposes), the picture of theft *from* vehicles and shoplifting is rather different. In relation to thefts from motor vehicles, the 2001 British Crime Survey estimates that 30 per cent of such offences are reported and recorded.[32] In relation to shoplifting (a particularly difficult crime to observe) the percentage is certainly lower than that. Astor's research concluded, for example, that one in 15 people stole goods from stores with store detectives noticing only about one per cent of those.[33] It has been estimated that of those detected only about 20 per cent of customer thefts are reported.[34] Such research renders almost meaningless the official figure of recorded thefts from shops of 293,080 in 2000/01.[35] It also means

---

[30] [1984] A.C. 320.
[31] Simmons *et al*, *Crime in England and Wales 2001/02* (2002), P. 27.
[32] Kershaw *et al*, *The 2001 British Crime Survey* (2001), pp. 17–19.
[33] Astor, "Shoplifting Survey," *Security World*, Vol. 8, Part 3, (1971), pp. 3–4.
[34] Mirrlees-Black and Ross, *Crime Against Retail Premises in 1993* (H.O.R.S. No. 26) (1995), p. 4.
[35] *Criminal Statistics, England and Wales 2000* (2001), p. 54.

that despite the fact that the average value of goods taken tends to be small in shoplifting offences, only very rough estimates about overall losses can be given. In 1993 it was thought that losses through customer theft cost retail premises about £200m.[36]

Under-reporting occurs, as we have seen, for a variety of reasons, but it does reflect to some extent the degree of seriousness with which the offence is regarded. Vehicle thefts, for instance, were viewed seriously in the 2001 British Crime Survey and were almost always reported. These surveys also enable assessments of seriousness to be made on the basis of the penalties chosen by respondents for a variety of offences. In relation to car thefts 23 per cent of the respondents thought that prison was the appropriate penalty for 25-year-old offenders with previous convictions, in comparison with 12 per cent who felt it to be the appropriate penalty for shoplifting. One might be tempted to conclude from this, and the lower rate of reporting of theft from shops, that this crime is regarded less seriously than other forms of theft. The development of the term "shoplifting" may even be seen as evidence of this, separating this form of activity from "theft". But any such conclusions would have to be highly qualified. The relationship between reporting and seriousness is by no means a perfect one. Sexual crimes, for example, are rated highly seriously, yet are grossly under-reported. In other words, there are other reasons for not reporting an offence other than an attitude as to its seriousness.[37] Despite this, it is probably the case that shoplifting is regarded as a comparatively minor offence: the amount involved will generally be small; the victim of the offence may be perceived as being a large, impersonal organisation able to absorb the loss; and there may even be at times a "there but for the grace of God ..." sentiment. All this does not, of course, amount to an argument for the decriminalisation of "shoplifting"—but it may well be an argument for the creation of a separate lesser offence.[38]

### B. *The Legal Background*

Prior to the Theft Act 1968, what is now the crime of theft was dealt with by three separate offences: larceny, embezzlement and fraudulent conversion. Each of these offences and the distinction between them was technical and highly complex. Further, the offences were felt to be defective in that certain conduct that would ordinarily be regarded as stealing did not come within the definitions of the offences.

### Criminal Law Revision Committee, Eighth Report, Theft and Related Offences, Cmnd.2977 (1966), paras. 33, 60:

"33. The committee generally are strongly of opinion that larceny, embezzlement and fraudulent conversion should be replaced by a single new offence of theft. The important element of them all is undoubtedly the dishonest appropriation of another's property—the treating of 'tuum' as 'meum'; and we think it not only logical, but right in principle, to make

---

[36] Mirrlees-Black and Ross, *above*, n.34, p. 3.
[37] Clarkson, Cretney and Davis, "Assaults: the Relationship between Seriousness, Criminalisation and Punishment" [1994] Crim.L.R.4.
[38] *Below*, pp. 854–856.

this the central element of the offence. In doing so the law would concentrate on what the accused dishonestly achieved or attempted to achieve and not on the means—taking or otherwise—which he used in order to do so. This would avoid multiplicity of offences …

60. We recommend that the maximum penalty for stealing should be 10 years' imprisonment in all cases."

This proposal was accepted by section 7 of the Theft Act 1968 but in 1991 the penalty was reduced to a maximum of seven years' imprisonment.[39] It is interesting to compare this with the sentencing reality of today where, in 2000, 22 per cent of those convicted of theft or handling stolen goods were given absolute or conditional discharges, 23 per cent were fined and 32 per cent were given community sentences. Of the 20 per cent given custodial sentences, the average length of such sentences, for males over 21, was 2.3 months (in the Magistrates' Court) and 11 months (in the Crown Court).[40]

## C. *The Law*

### 1. Definition

### Theft Act 1968, section 1(1)

"A person is guilty of theft if he dishonestly appropriates property belonging to another with the intention of permanently depriving the other of it; and 'thief' and 'steal' shall be construed accordingly."

The maximum penalty for this offence is seven years' imprisonment.[41]

In *Lawrence*[42] it was stressed by the House of Lords that this definition involves several elements, all of which must be proved to coincide before liability can be imposed. Each of these elements is defined, wholly or partially, in the ensuing sections of the Theft Act 1968 as follows:

section 2: dishonesty
section 3: appropriation
section 4: property
section 5: belonging to another
section 6: intention of permanent deprivation.

We shall deal first with the *actus reus* elements, namely, appropriation of property belonging to another—before turning to the *mens rea* elements, dishonesty and intention of permanent deprivation.

### 2. Appropriation

### Theft Act 1968, section 3

"(1) Any assumption by a person of the rights of an owner amounts to an appropriation, and this includes, where he has come by the property (innocently or not) without stealing it, any later assumption of a right to it by keeping or dealing with it as owner.

[39] Criminal Justice Act 1991, s.26.
[40] *Criminal Statistics, England and Wales 2000* (2001). One per cent were given a suspended sentence and one per cent were dealt with otherwise.
[41] Theft Act 1968, s.7, as amended by the Criminal Justice Act 1991, s.26.
[42] *Lawrence v Metropolitan Police Commissioner* [1972] A.C. 626.

(2) Where property or a right or interest in property is or purports to be transferred for value to a person acting in good faith, no later assumption by him of rights which he believed himself to be acquiring shall, by reason of any defect in the transferor's title, amount to theft of the property."

## Criminal Law Revision Committee, Eighth Report, Theft and Related Offences, 1966, Cmnd.2977, paras 34–35:

"34. We hope, and believe, that the concept of 'dishonest appropriation' will be easily understood even without the aid of further definition. But there is a partial definition of 'appropriates' in ... (section) 3(1) ... It seems to us natural to refer to the act of stealing in ordinary cases as 'appropriation'. We see no reason why the word should seem strange for more than a short time ...

35. There is an argument for keeping the word 'converts' because it is well understood. But it is a lawyers' word, and those not used to legal language might naturally think that it meant changing something or exchanging property for other property. 'Appropriates' seems altogether a better word."

An appropriation is an *assumption of the rights of an owner*. But what are the rights of an owner?

## F. H. Lawson and Bernard Rudden, The Law of Property (1982), pp. 8–9:

"The main elements (of ownership) are (a) the right to make physical use of a thing; (b) the right to the income from it, in money, in kind, or in services; and (c) the power of management, including that of alienation. Thus the owner of a car may drive it, hire it out, or sell it. And of course within these areas he may do the same things more generously: take the children for a drive, lend it to a friend, give it away."

In short, as Roman law used to put it, an owner has the right to "use, enjoy and abuse" his property as he sees fit.[43] An owner of property may keep it, sell it, give it away or destroy it. *Assuming* the rights of owner is laying claim to be in such a position. The method of acquiring the property is not important. There does not have to be a taking or removal although this is, of course, what occurs in the paradigmatic theft. The second part of section 3(1) makes this clear. If the owner accidentally leaves a book in the defendant's room there can be an appropriation the moment the defendant decides to keep the book. At this point he will be assuming a right to the book by keeping or dealing with it as owner, despite the fact he originally came by the property quite innocently.

This last point leads directly to the central problem in the interpretation of an "appropriation". When the book has been accidentally left in the defendant's room he assumes the right of an owner the moment he *decides* to keep it. At this point he is exercising one of the rights of ownership. But if it were held that this amounted to an appropriation this would mean that there could be a theft by a defendant who has done nothing *wrong*—other than have a blameworthy state of mind. Following this logic, a defendant in a supermarket who places goods in a trolley but who has a secret intention of stealing them will be guilty of theft. He has decided not to pay for the goods and to make off with them as and when he sees fit. The argument runs that this is treating the goods as one's own and is thus an appropriation.

---

[43] This is subject, of course, to numerous restrictions aimed at protecting the interests of others.

# Lawrence v M.P.C. [1972] A.C. 626 (House of Lords)

Occhi, an Italian visitor who spoke little English, arrived in England at Victoria station and asked the defendant, Lawrence, a taxi driver, to take him to an address in Ladbroke Grove. The defendant informed Occhi that it was a long way and would be expensive. (In reality the correct fare would have been about 10s. 6d. [52½p].) Occhi got into the taxi and offered a £1 note. Lawrence said that this was not enough and, with Occhi holding out his wallet for him, helped himself to a further £6 from the wallet. He then drove Occhi to his destination. The defendant was convicted of the theft of the approximate sum of £6 contrary to section 1(1) of the Theft Act 1968 and appealed against his conviction.

Viscount Dilhorne:
"Mr Occhi, when asked whether he had consented to the money being taken, said that he had 'permitted' . . . It may well be that when he used the word 'permitted', he meant no more than that he had allowed the money to be taken. It certainly was not established at the trial that he had agreed to pay to the appellant a sum far in excess of the legal fare for the journey and so had consented to the acquisition by the appellant of the £6.
The main contention of the appellant in this House and in the Court of Appeal was that Mr Occhi had consented to the taking of the £6 and that, consequently, his conviction could not stand. In my opinion, the facts of this case to which I have referred fall far short of establishing that Mr Occhi had so consented.
Prior to the passage of the Theft Act 1968, which made radical changes in and greatly simplified the law relating to theft and some other offences, it was necessary to prove that the property alleged to have been stolen was taken 'without the consent of the owner' (Larceny Act 1916, section 1(1)).
These words are not included in section 1(1) of the Theft Act, . . .
I see no ground for concluding that the omission of the words 'without the consent of the owner' was inadvertent and not deliberate, and to read the subsection as if they were included is, in my opinion, wholly unwarranted. Parliament by the omission of these words has relieved the prosecution of the burden of establishing that the taking was without the owner's consent. That is no longer an ingredient of the offence . . .
That there was an appropriation in this case is clear. Section 3(1) states that any assumption by a person of the rights of an owner amounts to an appropriation. Here there was clearly such an assumption. . . .
Belief or the absence of belief that the owner had with such knowledge consented to the appropriation is relevant to the issue of dishonesty, not to the question whether or not there has been an appropriation. That may occur even though the owner has permitted or consented to the property being taken. So proof that Mr Occhi had consented to the appropriation of £6 from his wallet without agreeing to paying a sum in excess of the legal fare does not suffice to show that there was not dishonesty in this case. There was ample evidence that there was."

**Appeal dismissed**

Following this decision there can be an appropriation even though the victim is consenting to hand over the property. Thus the shopper who places the goods in the supermarket trolley can be held to appropriate the goods at that stage. The only thing that distinguishes the legitimate shopper from the thief is the mental state of the latter.

In 1984 the House of Lords in *Morris* cast doubt on this proposition by holding that the defendant must have done something objectively wrong for there to be an appropriation. As we shall see, however, this case (and its progeny) is no longer good authority.

### R. v Morris, Anderton v. Burnside [1984] A.C. 320 (House of Lords)

Two defendants took goods from a shelf in a supermarket and removed the proper price labels, and replaced them with labels from cheaper goods. The goods, bearing their incorrect price labels were presented at the check-out counter. One defendant was arrested before, and the other after, paying for the goods. The appeals were heard together.

Lord Roskill:
"It is to be observed that the definition of 'appropriation' in section 3(1) is not exhaustive ...

The starting point ... must, I think, be the decision of this House in *R. v Lawrence* ... [in which] Viscount Dilhorne also rejected the argument that even if [the] four elements were all present there could not be theft within the section if the owner of the property in question had consented to the acts which were done by the defendant. That there was in that case a dishonest appropriation was beyond question and the House did not have to consider the precise meaning of that word in section 3(1).

Mr Denison submitted that the phrase in section 3(1) 'any assumption by a person of *the rights*' (my emphasis) 'of an owner amounts to an appropriation' must mean any assumption of '*all* the rights of an owner.' Since neither respondent had at the time of the removal of the goods from the shelves and of the label switching assumed *all* the rights of the owner, there was no appropriation and therefore no theft. Mr Jeffreys for the prosecution, on the other hand, contended that *the* rights in this context only meant *any* of the rights. An owner of goods has many rights—they have been described as 'a bundle or package of rights'. Mr Jeffreys contended that on a fair reading of the subsection it cannot have been the intention that every one of an owner's rights had to be assumed by the alleged thief before an appropriation was proved and that essential ingredient of the offence of theft established.

My Lords, if one reads the words 'the rights' at the opening of section 3(1) literally and in isolation from the rest of the section, Mr Denison's submission undoubtedly has force. But the later words 'any later assumption of a right' in subsection (1) and the words in subsection (2) 'no later assumption by him of rights' seem to me to militate strongly against the correctness of the submission. Moreover the provisions of section 2(1)(a) also seem to point in the same direction. It follows therefore that it is enough for the prosecution if they have proved in these cases the assumption by the respondents of *any* of the rights of the owner of the goods in question, that is to say, the supermarket concerned, it being common ground in these cases that the other three of the four elements ... [of theft] had been fully established.

My Lords, Mr Jeffreys sought to argue that any removal from the shelves of the supermarket, even if unaccompanied by label switching, was without more an appropriation. In one passage in his judgment in Morris's case, the learned Lord Chief Justice appears to have accepted the submission, for he said [1983] Q.B. 587, 596:
'it seems to us that in taking the article from the shelf the customer is indeed assuming one of the rights of the owner—the right to move the article from its position on the shelf to carry it to the check-out.'
With the utmost respect, I cannot accept this statement as correct. If one postulates an honest customer taking goods from a shelf to put in his or her trolley to take to the checkpoint there to pay the proper price, I am unable to see that any of these actions involves any assumption by the shopper of the rights of the supermarket. In the context of section 3(1), the concept of appropriation in my view involves not an act expressly or impliedly authorised by the owner but an act by way of adverse interference with or usurpation of those rights. When the honest shopper acts as I have just described, he or she is acting with the implied authority of the owner of the supermarket to take the goods from the shelf, put them in the trolley, take them to the checkpoint and there pay the correct price, at which moment the property in the goods will pass to the shopper for the first time. ...

If, as I understand all your Lordships to agree, the concept of appropriation in section 3(1) involves an element of adverse interference with or usurpation of some right of the owner, it is necessary next to consider whether that requirement is satisfied in either of these cases. As I have already said, in my view mere removal from the shelves without more is not an appropriation. Further, if a shopper with some perverted sense of humour, intending only to create confusion and nothing more both for the supermarket and for other shoppers, switches labels, I do not think that that act of label switching alone is without more an appropriation, though it is not difficult to envisage some cases of dishonest label-switching which could be. In cases such as the present, it is in truth a combination of these actions, the removal from the shelf and the switching of the labels, which evidences adverse interference with or usurpation of the right of the owner. Those acts, therefore, amount to an appropriation and if they are accompanied by proof of the other three elements to which I have referred, the offence of theft is established. Further, if they are accompanied by other acts such as putting the goods so removed and re-labelled into a receptacle, whether a trolley or the shopper's own bag or basket, proof of appropriation within section 3(1) becomes overwhelming. ...

I would answer the certified questions in this way:

'There is a dishonest appropriation for the purposes of the Theft Act 1968 where by the substitution of a price label showing a lesser price on goods for one showing a greater price, a defendant either by that act alone or by that act in conjunction with another act or other acts (whether done before or after the substitution of the labels) adversely interferes with or usurps the right of the owner to ensure that the goods concerned are sold and paid for at that greater price.'

I would dismiss these appeals."

**Appeals dismissed**


This requirement that the defendant must do acts objectively inconsistent with the rights of the owner is consistent with what Fletcher calls the "theory of manifest criminality". We saw when examining the law of attempts how this theory leads to an "objectivist orientation", with insistence that the acts must come close to the completed crime so as to be manifestly dangerous and a threat to security. This was the theory endorsed by the House of Lords in *Anderton v Ryan*[44] where a distinction was drawn between "objectively innocent" acts on the one hand and "criminal" or "guilty" acts on the other.

Fletcher states that "manifestly criminal" activities must exhibit at least the following essential features. First, the criminal act must manifest, on its face, the actor's criminal purpose. And secondly, the conduct should be "of a type that is unnerving and disturbing to the community as a whole".


### George P. Fletcher, Rethinking Criminal Law (1978), pp. 82–89:

"The principle of manifest criminality supported the expansion of the law to include all acts of taking that conformed to the shared paradigms of stealthful and forcible taking. A guest sneaking out with his host's dining utensils looked as much like a thief as any then punished. So, too, the customer that runs from the store with the shopkeeper chasing after him ... The purpose of raising an issue of *animus* was to challenge the authenticity of appearances. Someone who looked like a thief in the act of taking might not have been one in fact ... The primary inquiry was the act of larceny (theft), and only in extraordinary cases might there have been a dispute about whether someone who acted like a thief had the 'spirit' or *animus* of a thief. Thus the law was structured so as to render intent a subsidiary issue. It was a basis for defeating the implications of the primary element of acting manifestly like a

---

[44] [1985] A.C. 567.

thief ... Routine business transactions, deliveries and takings by consent do not bear this imprint of larceny, and therefore ... lack the features of manifest thievery ... The value implicitly protected in the pattern of manifest criminality is the privacy of criminal suspects. Judges may not enquire about the accused's mental state, self-control and culpability unless they find preliminarily that the accused's conduct meets an objective standard of liability. The objective standard is the manifestly criminal act."

The approach adopted in *Morris* can be seen as consistent with the "harm principle": conduct should only be criminalised to prevent the causing of harm, albeit of a "second-order" nature,[45] to others. The defendant by doing something manifestly observable as wrong, for example, switching price labels, is doing something that is a threat to the security of the store; the interests of the store have been violated and they have sustained a "second-order harm". This approach stands in sharp contrast to "protectionalist criminology"[46] sustained by the utilitarian philosophies of punishment. Where the main interest is the protection of the property of others, then whatever measures are necessary to effect such protection become acceptable, even if this means imposing liability at an early stage when a defendant has done nothing observably wrong. If an individual has a blameworthy state of mind, then for deterrent, incapacitative and rehabilitative reasons she needs punishment.

The operation of the *Morris* principle can best be seen by applying it to the facts of several cases on theft.

In *Eddy v Niman*[47] the defendant, intending to steal goods from a store, took them from a shelf and placed them in the provided receptacle. He was not liable for theft because he had done nothing manifestly wrong. He was doing precisely what the store expected all its customers to do, namely, place goods in a receptacle provided by the store.

In *Skipp*[48] the defendant, posing as a genuine haulage contractor, obtained instructions and collected two loads of oranges and onions to be delivered from London to Leicester. He had the intention of stealing the goods from the outset but only after loading them did he actually make off with them. It was held that he did not appropriate the goods when he loaded them because at that stage he was not doing anything inconsistent with the owner's rights. The appropriation occurred when the goods were "diverted from their true destination". In *Fritschy*[49] the defendant, acting under the instructions of the owner, collected a quantity of krugerrands in London to deliver them to Switzerland. All along he had a secret intention to steal the coins, which he did in Switzerland. The Court of Appeal held that there was no appropriation in England because the defendant had acted with the owner's authority at that stage. The coins were only appropriated in Switzerland where the defendant committed the acts that amounted to an adverse interference with the owner's rights.

These cases were, of course, difficult to reconcile with *Lawrence*. The House of Lords in *Gomez* strongly confirmed *Lawrence*, disapproved much of *Morris* and

---

[45] *above*, p. 465.
[46] Fletcher, *Rethinking Criminal Law* (1978), p. 101.
[47] (1981) 73 Cr.App.R.237.
[48] [1975] Crim.L.R.114.
[49] [1985] Crim.L.R.745.

overruled *Skipp* and *Fritschy*. In doing so much reliance was placed on the following decision.


## Dobson v General Accident Fire and Life Assurance Corp. PLC [1989] 3 W.L.R. 1066 (Court of Appeal, Civil Division)

The plaintiff had a home insurance policy with the defendant which covered him against loss by "theft". He advertised a Rolex watch and diamond ring for sale for £5,950. The goods were purchased by a rogue using a stolen building society cheque which was worthless. The plaintiff claimed under his insurance policy and the question was whether there had been a "theft".

Parker L.J.:
"On the basis of *R. v Lawrence* ... the facts of the present case appear to establish that the rogue assumed all the rights of an owner when he took or received the watch and ring from the plaintiff. That he did so dishonestly and with the intention of permanently depriving the plaintiff of it are matters beyond doubt ...
After anxious consideration I have reached the conclusion that whatever *R. v Morris* did decide it cannot be regarded as having overruled the very plain decision in *R. v Lawrence* that appropriation can occur even if the owner consents and that *R. v Morris* itself makes it plain that it is no defence to say that the property passed under a voidable contract ...
I would therefore dismiss the appeal."

Bingham L.J.:
"I do not find it easy to reconcile ... [*Lawrence*] with the reasoning of the House in *R. v Morris*. Since, however, the House in *R. v Morris* considered that there had plainly been an appropriation in *Lawrence's* case, this must (I think) have been because the Italian student, although he had permitted or allowed his money to be taken, had not in truth consented to the taxi driver taking anything in excess of the correct fare. This is not a wholly satisfactory reconciliation, since it might be said that a supermarket consents to customers taking goods from its shelves only when they honestly intend to pay and not otherwise. On the facts of the present case, however, it can be said, by analogy with *Lawrence's* case, that although the plaintiff permitted and allowed his property to be taken by the rogue, he had not in truth consented to the rogue becoming owner without giving a valid draft drawn by the building society for the price. On this basis I conclude that the plaintiff is able to show an appropriation sufficient to satisfy s.1(1) of the 1968 Act when the rogue accepted delivery of the articles."

*Appeal dismissed*


## R. v Gomez [1993] A.C. 442 (House of Lords)

The appellant, an assistant manager of an electrical goods shop, lied to the manager of the store that two cheques were valid, with the result that £16,000 worth of goods were supplied to a rogue. The appellant and the rogue were convicted of theft. Their appeal was allowed by the Court of Appeal (Criminal Division). The Crown appealed to the House of Lords.

Lord Keith of Kinkel (with whom Lord Jauncey of Tullichettle and Lord Slynn of Hadley agreed):
"Lord Roskill was undoubtedly right [in *Morris*] ... that the assumption by the defendant of any of the rights of an owner could amount to an appropriation ... But there are

observations [from his speech] ... that I must regard as unnecessary ... and as being incorrect. In the first place, it seems to me that the switching of price labels on the article is in itself an assumption of one of the rights of the owner, whether or not it is accompanied by some other act such as removing the article from the shelf and placing it in a basket or trolley. No one but the owner has the right to remove a price label from an article or to place a price label upon it. If anyone else does so, he does an act, as Lord Roskill puts it, by way of adverse interference with or usurpation of that right. This is no less so in the case of the practical joker figured by Lord Roskill than in the case of one who makes the switch with dishonest intent. The practical joker, of course, is not guilty of theft because he has not acted dishonestly and does not intend to deprive the owner permanently of the article. So the label switching in itself constitutes an appropriation and so to have held would have been sufficient for the dismissal of both appeals. On the facts of [Morris] ... it was unnecessary to decide whether ... the mere taking of the article from the shelf and putting it in a trolley or other receptacle amounted to the assumption of one of the rights of the owner, and hence an appropriation. There was much to be said in favour of the view that it did, in respect that doing so gave the shopper control of the article and the capacity to exclude any other shopper from taking it. However, Lord Roskill expressed the opinion that it did not, on the ground that the concept of appropriation in the context of section 3(1) 'involves not an act expressly or impliedly authorised by the owner but an act by way of adverse interference with or usurpation of those rights'.

While it is correct to say that appropriation for purposes of section 3(1) includes the latter sort of act, it does not necessarily follow that no other act can amount to an appropriation and in particular that no act expressly or impliedly authorised by the owner can in any circumstances do so. Indeed, *R. v Lawrence* is a clear decision to the contrary since it laid down unequivocally that an act may be an appropriation notwithstanding that it is done with the consent of the owner. It does not appear to me that any sensible distinction can be made in this context between consent and authorisation. ...

[His Lordship then cited extensively from *Dobson* agreeing with Parker L.J. but finding Bingham's L.J.'s suggested reconciliation of *Morris* with *Lawrence* to be unsound.]

The actual decision in *Morris* was correct, but it was erroneous, in addition to being unnecessary for the decision, to indicate that an act expressly or impliedly authorised by the owner could never amount to an appropriation. There is no material distinction between the facts in *Dobson* and those in the present case. In each case the owner of the goods was induced by fraud to part with them to the rogue. *Lawrence* makes it clear that consent to or authorisation by the owner of the taking by the rogue is irrelevant. The taking amounted to an appropriation within the meaning of section 1(1) of the Act of 1968. *Lawrence* also makes it clear that it is no less irrelevant that what happened may also have constituted the offence of obtaining property by deception under section 15(1) of the Act. ...

The decision in *Lawrence* was a clear decision ... which had stood for 12 years when doubt was thrown upon it by obiter dicta in *Morris*. *Lawrence* must be regarded as authoritative and correct, and there is no question of it now being right to depart from it ...

In my opinion ... [*Skipp* and *Fritschy*] were inconsistent with *Lawrence* and were wrongly decided."

Lord Browne-Wilkinson:

"The fact that Parliament used that composite phrase—'dishonest appropriation'—in my judgment casts light on what is meant by the word 'appropriation'. The views expressed (obiter) by this House in *Morris* that 'appropriation' involves an act by way of adverse interference with or usurpation of the rights of the owner treats the word appropriation as being tantamount to 'misappropriation'. The concept of adverse interference with or usurpation of rights introduces into the word appropriation the mental state of both the owner and the accused. So far as concerns the mental state of the owner (did he consent?), the Act of 1968 expressly refers to such consent when it is a material factor: see section 2(1)(b), 11(1), 12(1) and 13. So far as concerns the mental state of the accused, the composite phrase in section 1(1) itself indicates that the requirement is dishonesty.

For myself, therefore, I regard the word 'appropriation' in isolation as being an objective description of the act done irrespective of the mental state of either the owner or the accused.

It is impossible to reconcile the decision in *Lawrence* (that the question of consent is irrelevant in considering whether there has been an appropriation) with the views expressed in *Morris*, which latter views in my judgment were incorrect."

Lord Lowry (dissenting):
"The ordinary and natural meaning of 'appropriate' is to take for oneself, or to treat as one's own, property which belongs to someone else. The primary dictionary meaning is 'to take possession of, take to oneself, especially without authority', and that is in my opinion the meaning which the word bears in section 1(1). The act of appropriating property is a one-sided act, done without the consent or authority of the owner. And, if the owner consents to transfer property to the offender or to a third party, the offender does not appropriate the property, even if the owner's consent has been obtained by fraud ...

Coming now to section 3, the *primary* meaning of 'assumption' is 'taking to oneself', again a unilateral act, and this meaning is consistent with subsections (1) and (2). To use the word in its secondary, neutral sense would neutralise the word 'appropriation', to which assumption is here equated, and would lead to a number of strange results. Incidentally, ... 'the rights' may mean '*all* the rights', which would be the normal grammatical meaning, or (less probably, in my opinion) 'any rights' see *R. v Morris* ...

[His Lordship then considered the Eighth Report of the Criminal Law Revision Committee which led to the enactment of the Theft Act 1968 and concluded that the Committee rejected the idea of making theft cover the old offence of obtaining by false pretences which became obtaining property by deception under section 15 of the Theft Act 1968.]

The Crown say that section 15 merely describes a particular type of theft and that all stealing by means of deception can be prosecuted under section 1 just as well as under section 15. I would point out that section 15 covers what were formerly two offences, obtaining by false pretences (where the ownership of the property is transferred by the deceived victim) and theft (or larceny) by a trick (where the possession of the property passes, but not the ownership). In the former case, according to the interpretation which I prefer, the offender does not *appropriate* the property, because the ownership (in colloquial terms, the property) is transferred with the owner's consent, albeit obtained by deception. In the latter case the offender does appropriate the property because, although the owner has handed over *possession* by consent (which was obtained by deception), he has not transferred the property (that is, the ownership) and the offender, intending to deprive the owner permanently of his property, appropriates it, not by taking possession, but by the unilateral act, adverse to the owner, of treating as his own and taking to himself property of which he was merely given *possession*. Thus, the kind of obtaining by deception which amounts to larceny by a trick and involves appropriation *could* be successfully prosecuted under section 1, but the old false pretences type of obtaining by deception could not. ...

I would respectfully agree with [Lord Roskill's description in *Morris*] ... in relation to dishonest actions, of appropriation as involving an act by way of adverse interference with or usurpation of the owner's rights, but I believe that the less aggressive definition of appropriation which I have put forward fits the word as used in an honest sense in section 2(1) as well as elsewhere in the Act ... [He then expressly declined to discuss whether *Morris* itself was really an example of theft.]

[T]here was no theft [in *Dobson*] because the property passed with the fraudulently obtained consent of the owner and the buyer was guilty of obtaining by deception in the false pretences sense ...

It is true that *Morris* contains no disapproval or qualification of *Lawrence*, but, in my view, the main statements of principle in these cases cannot possibly be reconciled and the later case therefore must not be regarded as providing any support for the earlier ...

[In the Court of Appeal in the present case] Lord Lane C.J. said:
'... We therefore conclude that there was a de facto, albeit voidable, contract between the owners and Ballay [one of Gomez's associates]; that it was by virtue of that contract that Ballay took possession of the goods; that accordingly the transfer of the goods to him was

with the consent and express authority of the owner and that accordingly there was no lack of authorisation and no appropriation ...'

I respectfully agree ... [and] would dismiss the Crown's appeal."

**Appeal allowed**

## R. v Hinks [2001] 2 A.C. 241 (House of Lords)

The defendant made friends with a man of limited intelligence. She regularly accompanied him to his building society where he made withdrawals from his account amounting to a total of about £60,000 which was deposited in the defendant's account. A consultant psychiatrist gave evidence that the man was naive and trusting and had no idea of the value of his assets or the ability to calculate their value, and that, although he was capable of making the decision to divest himself of money, it was unlikely he could make that decision alone. The defendant was convicted of theft of the money withdrawn from his account. The Court of Appeal dismissed her appeal. She appealed to the House of Lords.

Lord Steyn:

"The certified question before the House is as follows: 'Whether the acquisition of an indefeasible title to property is capable of amounting to an appropriation of property belonging to another for the purposes of section 1(1) of the Theft Act 1968.' In other words, the question is whether a person can 'appropriate' property belonging to another where the other person makes him an indefeasible gift of property, retaining no proprietary interest or any right to resume or recover any proprietary interest in the property. ...

[I]t is immaterial whether the act was done with the owner's consent or authority. It is true of course that the certified question in *Gomez* referred to the situation where consent had been obtained by fraud. But the majority judgments do not differentiate between cases of consent induced by fraud and consent given in any other circumstances. The ratio involves a proposition of general application. *Gomez* therefore gives effect to section 3(1) of the Act by treating 'appropriation' as a neutral word comprehending 'any assumption by a person of the rights of an owner'. If the law is as held in *Gomez*, it destroys the argument advanced on the present appeal, namely that an indefeasible gift of property cannot amount to an appropriation.

Counsel for the appellant submitted in the first place that the law as expounded in *Gomez* and *Lawrence* must be qualified to say that there can be no appropriation unless the other party (the owner) retains some proprietary interest, or the right to resume or recover some proprietary interest, in the property. Alternatively, counsel argued that 'appropriates' should be interpreted as if the word 'unlawfully' preceded it. Counsel said that the effect of the decisions in *Lawrence* and *Gomez* is to reduce the *actus reus* of theft to 'vanishing point'. He argued that the result is to bring the criminal law 'into conflict' with the civil law. Moreover, he argued that the decisions in *Lawrence* and *Gomez* may produce absurd and grotesque results. He argued that the mental requirements of dishonesty and intention of permanently depriving the owner of property are insufficient to filter out some cases of conduct which should not sensibly be regarded as theft ...

[I]n such cases a prosecution is hardly likely and if mounted, is likely to founder on the basis that the jury will not be persuaded that there was dishonesty in the required sense. And one must retain a sense of perspective ... If the law is restated by adopting a narrower definition of appropriation, the outcome is likely to place beyond the reach of the criminal law dishonest persons who should be found guilty of theft. ...

Counsel for the appellant further pointed out that the law as stated in *Lawrence* and *Gomez* creates a tension between the civil and the criminal law. In other words, conduct which is not wrongful in a civil law sense may constitute the crime of theft. Undoubtedly, this is so. The question whether the civil claim to title by a convicted thief, who committed no civil wrong, may be defeated by the principle that nobody may benefit from his own civil *or criminal* wrong does not arise for decision. Nevertheless, there is a more general point, namely that the interaction between criminal law and civil law can cause problems ... The purposes of the civil law and the criminal law are somewhat different. In theory the two systems should be in perfect harmony. In a practical world there will sometimes be some disharmony between the two systems. In any event, it would be wrong to assume on *a priori* grounds that the criminal law rather than the civil law is defective ... The tension between the civil and the criminal law is therefore not in my view a factor which justifies a departure from the law as stated in *Lawrence* and *Gomez*. Moreover, these decisions of the House have a marked beneficial consequence. While in some contexts of the law of theft a judge cannot avoid explaining civil law concepts to a jury (*e.g.* in respect of section 2(1)(a)), the decisions of the House of Lords eliminate the need for such explanations in respect of appropriation. That is a great advantage in an overly complex corner of the law.

My Lords, if it had been demonstrated that in practice *Lawrence* and *Gomez* were calculated to produce injustice that would have been a compelling reason to revisit the merits of the holdings in those decisions. That is, however, not the case. In practice, the mental requirements of theft are an adequate protection against injustice. In these circumstances I would not be willing to depart from the clear decisions of the House in *Lawrence* and *Gomez*. This brings me back to counsel's principal submission, namely that a person does not appropriate property unless the other (the owner) retains, beyond the instant of the alleged theft, some proprietary interest or the right to resume or recover some proprietary interest. This submission is directly contrary to the holdings in *Lawrence* and *Gomez*. It must be rejected. The alternative submission is that the word 'appropriates' should be interpreted as if the word 'unlawfully' preceded it so that only an act which is unlawful under the general law can be an appropriation. This submission is an invitation to interpolate a word in the carefully crafted language of the 1968 Act. It runs counter to the decisions in *Lawrence* and *Gomez* and must also be rejected. It follows that the certified question must be answered in the affirmative. ...

I would dismiss the appeal to the House."

Lord Hobhouse (dissenting):

"The reasoning of the Court of Appeal therefore depends upon the disturbing acceptance that a criminal conviction and the imposition of custodial sanctions may be based upon conduct which involves no inherent illegality and may only be capable of being criticised on grounds of lack of morality. This approach itself raises fundamental questions. An essential function of the criminal law is to define the boundary between what conduct is criminal and what merely immoral. Both are the subject of the disapprobation of ordinary right-thinking citizens and the distinction is liable to be arbitrary or at least strongly influenced by considerations subjective to the individual members of the tribunal. To treat otherwise lawful conduct as criminal merely because it is open to such disapprobation would be contrary to principle and open to the objection that it fails to achieve the objective and transparent certainty required of the criminal law by the principles basic to human rights ...

If one treats the 'acceptance' of the gift as an appropriation, and this was the approach of the judge and is implicit in the judgment of the Court of Appeal (despite their choice of words), there are immediate difficulties with section 2(1)(a). The defendant did have the right to deprive the donor of the property. The donor did consent to the appropriation; indeed, he intended it. There are also difficulties with section 6 as she was not acting regardless of the donor's rights; the donor has already surrendered his rights. The only way that these conclusions can be displaced is by showing that the gift was not valid. There are even difficulties with section 3 itself. The donee is not 'assuming the rights of an owner': she has them already ...

Section 3 does not use any qualitative expression such as '*mis*appropriates' nor does it repeat the Larceny Act expression 'without the consent of the owner'. It has thus been read by some as if 'appropriates' was a wholly colourless expression. This reading declines to draw any guidance from the context in which the word is used in the definition in section 1(1) and the scheme of sections 2 to 6. It also declines to attach any significance to the use of the word 'assumption'. This led some curious submissions being made to your Lordships.

It was for example suggested that the garage repair mechanic employed to change the oil of a car would have appropriated the car. The reasoning is that only the owner has the right to do this or tell someone to do it therefore to do it is to assume the rights of the owner. This is an absurdity even when one takes into account that some of the absurd results can be avoided by other parts of the definition of theft. The mechanic is not assuming any right; he is merely carrying out the instructions of the owner. The person who accepts a valid gift is simply conforming to the wishes of the owner. The words 'appropriate' (property belonging to another) and 'assume' (the rights of that other) have a useful breadth of meaning but each of them in its natural meaning includes an element of doing something which displaces the rights of that other person. The rights of that other (the owner) include the right to authorise another (the defendant) to do things which would otherwise be an infringement of the rights of the owner. . . .

My Lords, the relevant law is contained in sections 1 to 6 of the Act. They should be construed as a whole and applied in a manner which presents a consistent scheme both internally and with the remainder of the Act. The phrase 'dishonestly appropriates' should be construed as a composite phrase. It does not include acts done in relation to the relevant property which are done in accordance with the actual wishes or actual authority of the person to whom the property belongs. This is because such acts do not involve any assumption of the rights of that person within section 3(1) or because, by necessary implication from section 2(1), they are not to be regarded as dishonest appropriations of property belonging to another.

Actual authority, wishes, consent (or similar words) mean, both as a matter of language and on the authority of the three House of Lords cases, authorisation not obtained by fraud or misrepresentation. The definition of theft therefore embraces cases where the property has come to the defendant by the mistake of the person to whom it belongs and there would be an obligation to restore it—section 5(4)–or property in which the other still has an equitable proprietary interest—section 5(1). This would also embrace property obtained by undue influence or other cases coming within the classes of invalid transfer . . .

In cases of alleged gift, the criteria to be applied are the same. But additional care may need to be taken to see that the transaction is properly explained to the jury. It is unlikely that a charge of theft will be brought where there is not clear evidence of at least some conduct of the defendant which includes an element of fraud or overt dishonesty or some undue influence or knowledge of the deficient capacity of the alleged donor. This was the basis upon which the prosecution of the appellant was originally brought in the present case. On this basis there is no difficulty in explaining to the jury the relevant parts of section 5 and section 2(1) and the effect of the phrase 'assumption of the rights of an owner'. . . .

I would answer the certified question in the negative. But, in any event, I would allow the appeal and quash the conviction because the summing up failed to direct the jury adequately upon the other essential elements of theft, not just appropriation."

Appeal dismissed

Certain conclusions can be drawn from *Gomez* and *Hinks* as to the present meaning of 'appropriation'.

First, an appropriation involves the assumption of *any* of the rights of the owner. There need not be an assumption of *all* of the rights of the owner.

Secondly, where the defendant obtains property by deception there is an appropriation: it is irrelevant that the owner of the property "consents" to the transfer. For example, in *Atakpu*[50] the defendants, using false passports and licences, deceived a car-rental firm in Germany into parting with cars to them. They brought the cars to England with a view to selling them here. It was held that the theft had been committed in Germany and therefore there could be no theft in

---

[50] [1993] 4 All E.R. 215.

England. This means that there is now an almost[51] complete overlap between theft and the offence of obtaining property by deception under section 15 of the Theft Act 1968. In any case where the defendant deceives the victim into parting with property the prosecution has the choice of charging either offence.

Thirdly, because the victim's consent is irrelevant, it is unnecessary for the defendant to do anything involving "adverse interference with or usurpation of" the owner's rights. For example, in *Atakpu* the defendants who rented the cars in Germany did nothing beyond what they were permitted to do but were nevertheless held to have stolen the cars in Germany. The method of receiving the property is irrelevant: it can be pursuant to a valid contract or a gift.

Finally, it is irrelevant that the person receiving the property acquires an indefeasible title to the property. On the facts of *Hinks* itself the woman might only in fact have acquired a voidable title in civil law if there had been undue influence. It was emphasised, however, that the validity of the gift was irrelevant.

The approach adopted by the House of Lords in *Lawrence*, *Gomez* and, particularly, *Hinks* is most unfortunate. First, it is lamentable that leading House of Lords decisions on the meaning of "appropriation" such as *Gomez* and *Hinks* do not even bother to specify the precise actions that constitute the appropriation.[52] This leads to a failure to consider whether *at the time of the appropriation* the property still belongs to another. For instance, it is arguable that if the appropriation in *Gomez* occurred when the goods were physically collected by the rogue, ownership had already passed to him and so there was no appropriation of property belonging to another.[53]

Secondly, the concept of appropriation has become "wholly colourless" (Lord Hobhouse in *Hinks*); it has been emasculated of any practical meaning and has become no more than a minimal triggering condition for theft with the entire emphasis transferred to whether the conduct was dishonest or not. The absurdity of this approach is revealed in the following examples, considered *obiter* in *Gallasso*,[54] a case decided prior to *Hinks*:

"for example, the shopper carelessly knocks an article off the shelf; if he bends down and replaces it on the shelf nobody could regard that as an act of appropriation. Or suppose a lady drops her purse in the street. If a passer-by picks it up and hands it back there is no appropriation even though the passer-by is in temporary control."

As a result of *Hinks*, these actions, along with those of Lord Hobhouse's motor mechanic, all now amount to an appropriation. An appropriation has become a neutral, value-free act with the mental element of the defendant being irrelevant. This purely objective description ignores the definition of appropriation in section 3(1) that it must involve an "*assumption* by a person of the rights of the an owner".

[51] Certain categories of land, wild flowers and wild animals cannot be stolen (s.4(2)–(4)) but can be obtained by deception as these subsections do not apply to s.15 (s.34(1)). Further, Heaton ("Deceiving without Thieving" [2001] Crim.L.R.712) has argued that there will be cases where, as a result of the defendant's deception, ownership passes to the defendant prior to any appropriation so while property has been obtained by deception, there is no theft because the defendant is not appropriating property belonging to another.
[52] Heaton, "Deceiving without Thieving" [2001] Crim.L.R.712.
[53] *ibid.*
[54] (1994) 98 Cr.App.R.284.

As seen above, "assumption" is not a value-free word. It suggests that one is laying claim to rights one does not have over property. There must be an assertion of dominion over the property; it involves a positive decision to treat the property as one's own.[55] It is patently ridiculous to assert that picking up a dropped purse to hand it back to the owner is assuming the rights of the owner.

For similar reasons it is objectionable that persons who have done nothing wrong yet, but have secret dishonest intentions, should be liable for theft. As seen above, the defendant in *Eddy v Niman* took goods from a shelf in a store and, intending not to pay for them, placed them in a trolley. Following *Hinks* this would now be an appropriation and, because of the *mens rea*, theft. Again, it is difficult to accept that this is *assuming* the rights of an owner. One can surely only lay claim, or assert, the rights of an owner if there is an open representation that one is assuming such a right. In the supermarket situation, as long as the goods are in the trolley the defendant is recognising and respecting the rights of the owner by doing exactly what he is expected to do. It is quite different if the defendant slips the goods into his own pocket. He is thereby laying claim to the goods; he is treating them as owner without any recognition of the rights of another. Using Fletcher's test of "manifest criminality" discussed earlier, the reasonable observer would recognise the theftuous criminality of the defendant's actions.[56] However, following *Hinks*, such considerations are irrelevant. This marks an alarming return to 'protectionist criminology' whereby liability is imposed primarily on the basis of the defendant's blameworthy state of mind—even if he has done nothing observably wrong.

A third objection to the ruling in *Hinks* is that persons can be liable for theft despite committing no civil wrong thus creating a conflict between the civil law and the criminal law: "It is surely intolerable that the performance of a perfectly valid contract should be a crime."[57] With regard to valid gifts, the recipient acquires an indefeasible title to property and can sue the donor if she takes the property back. This amounts to the civil law "assisting [the defendant] to enjoy, or to recover, the fruits of his crime".[58] It has been argued, however, that congruence between these two areas of law is not possible: criminal courts are not well placed to determine whether a valid title has been acquired; civil courts are unable to determine liability for theft which depends on the establishment of dishonesty (a question of fact for a jury or magistrate). Nor is harmony necessary because the relevant rules of civil and criminal law are not aimed at the same thing: for example, the civil law has an interest, *inter alia*, in protecting the rights of third parties who subsequently acquire property.[59] The problem with these views is that criminal courts do have to decide questions of civil law[60] and civil courts do have to decide questions of dishonesty.[61]

---

[55] Smith (A.T.H.), *Property Offences* (1994), p. 163.

[56] See also Giles and Uglow, "Appropriation and Manifest Criminality in Theft" (1992) 56 J.Crim.L. 179. Obviously one could not expressly employ a test of manifest criminality as this would involve asking the jury vague questions such as: does this conduct look like theft to you? What is suggested is that in developing a suitable test of appropriation the courts should have been, and hopefully Parliament will be, *guided* by this test.

[57] Smith, [2001] Crim.L.R.163 at 165.

[58] Smith and Hogan, *Criminal Law* (10th ed, 2002), p. 518.

[59] Gardner, "Property and Theft" [1998] Crim.L.R.35.

[60] For example, in relation to "belonging to another" under s.5.

[61] *Twinsectra Ltd v Yardley* [2002] 2 All E.R. 376.

More significantly, this argument misses the central point that the law of theft is there to protect persons' interests in property. These interests can only exist at civil law: "remove dependence on the law of property, and property offences have no rationale".[62] A different argument in favour of the *Hinks* position is that it is legitimate to criminalise conduct that does not breach civil law proprietary rights because such conduct "may nonetheless have a *tendency* to undermine property rights, either directly by attacking the interests that they protect, or indirectly by weakening an established system of property rights and so threatening the public good that that system represents".[63] Of course, it is legitimate to criminalise conduct that threatens security interests—but that is the function of the law of attempt and the other inchoate and endangerment offences. Attepted theft, for example, involves criminalising conduct that threatens the interests protected by the law of theft. The substantive law of theft should, however, be aimed at protecting existing property rights which can only be established by reference to the civil law.

A final objection to the decisions of *Lawrence*, *Gomez* and *Hinks* is that it is quite wrong to have collapsed the distinction between theft and obtaining property by deception.

### P. R. Glazebrook, "Thief or Swindler: Who Cares?" [1991] C.L.J. 389:

"Should it matter tuppence whether a crook snitched his victim's property or tricked him out of it? Parliament evidently thought not [by originally enacting the same penalties for the two offences] ...

In the ensuing 22 years the courts decided accordingly ... [holding] that though property had been, or might have been, obtained by deception the crook could still be convicted of theft for there was nothing in the definition of stealing in section 1 of the 1968 Act that required the courts to make the trivial and morally irrelevant distinction between someone who dishonestly appropriated another's property by stealth, and one who did so by deceit. The crook is as dishonest in the one case as the other, and the gain to him, and the loss to his victim, is exactly the same ... It would certainly be bizarre if a defendant who appropriated property he had received because the transferor had made a mistake to which the defendant had not contributed were guilty of theft (as he is: s.5(4)), but was not guilty if the property had come to him because of a mistake which he had deliberately induced.

What is more, it may be either difficult to decide, or the merest matter of chance, whether the crook had resorted to deception in order to get his sticky mits on to the property he coveted. In *Lawrence* it would have been as difficult as it would have been pointless to set about deciding whether the travel-weary and English-less Signor Occhi had been deceived by taxi-driver Lawrence ... or whether Signor Occhi was just too bemused to know what exactly was happening as Lawrence helped himself to the notes in his wallet ... Can it really be that Her Majesty's judges think that they must indulge the sensitivities of a con-man who feels hurt at being called a common thief? Indeed, the decision (the Court of Appeal judgment in *Gomez*) looks even sillier now that Parliament has decided to reduce the maximum sentence for theft (but not that for obtaining) from 10 years to 7, for it will enable defendants to demand that they should be acquitted of one offence because they are guilty of a more serious one."

---

[62] Beatson and Simester, "Stealing One's Own Property" (1999) 115 L.Q.R. 372 at 374.
[63] Shute, "Appropriation and the Law of Theft" [2002] Crim.L.R.445 at 455.

**Stephen Shute and Jeremy Horder, "Thieving and Deceiving: What is the Difference?" (1993) 56 M.L.R. 548 at 549–553:**

"It has long been recognised that there is some common sense distinction between theft and obtaining property by deception ... The criminal law seeks to find appropriate labels for different kinds of wrongdoers, as part of its 'representative labelling' function. The label 'thief' does not carry the same moral import as the label 'conman' ...

There is in our society a general social practice of uncoerced voluntary transfers ('givings'), even when they are the product of another's advice, influence or persuasion ... [which] serve[s] to enhance the transferor's autonomy ... [T]he nature of the wrongdoing in theft has a separate moral foundation from that of obtaining by deception. The wrongful conduct in obtaining by deception is internal to the practice of voluntary transfer. Its wrongfulness centres on the abuse of what should have been an autonomy enhancing transaction. The fraudster abuses the control that he or she has over the information on which victims make their decisions about an admittedly voluntary transfer: the victim's chances of making an authentic choice are deliberately or recklessly undermined by the fraudster. The wrongful act in theft, however, is external to the legitimate social practice of voluntary transfers of property. Its wrongfulness centres on the fact that the thief bypasses the entire social practice at the victim's expense. Putting it metaphorically, whereas the thief makes war on a social practice from the outside, the deceiver is the traitor within."

These latter views are surely preferable to those of Glazebrook. Offences should be structured, labelled and punished to reflect the extent of wrongdoing and harm involved. Crimes are generally described in terms of their paradigms. The paradigmatic theft involves a surreptitious or forcible taking while deception offences involve a confrontation and a participation by the victim in the loss of the property.[64] With theft, the owner is generally helpless against such a taking. If interrupted there is a risk of violence. With the typical obtaining, the victim has a real opportunity to prevent the commission of the crime. With greater alertness he might not have been deceived. He has agreed to part with the property. In our society where mutual transactions based on trust are valued and encouraged, the wrong of *deceiving* another into parting with property is a distinctive wrong—quite different in quality from the paradigmatic theft. Parliament has now recognised this by providing different penalties for the two offences. It is unacceptable to brush over these important moral distinctions by the creation of broad morally uninformative offences.

*Appropriation and control*

Another problem that has arisen is whether there can be an appropriation by a defendant who is not in a position to exercise power or control over the property. Can a defendant sitting in a pub in Leicester appropriate the Crown Jewels (situated in the Tower of London) by "selling" them to the mythical, ever-gullible foreign tourist?

**R. v Pitham and Hehl (1976) 65 Cr.App.R.45 (Court of Appeal, Criminal Division)**

A man called Millman, knowing that his friend McGregor was in prison, decided to take advantage of his friend's hapless plight and steal furniture from his house. He took the two

---

[64] Clarkson, "Theft and Fair Labelling" (1993) 56 M.L.R. 554.

appellants to the house and sold them some furniture. Millman was convicted of burglary on the basis that he had entered the building as a trespasser and committed theft therein, contrary to section 9(1)(b) of the Theft Act 1968. The two appellants were convicted of handling stolen goods. They argued that their handling was still "in the course of stealing"; the goods were not yet stolen and therefore they were not handling stolen goods.

Lawton L.J.:
"What was the appropriation in this case? The jury found that the two appellants had handled the property *after* Millman had stolen it ... What had Millman done? He had assumed the rights of the owner. He had done that when he took the two appellants to 20 Parry Road, showed them the property and invited them to buy what they wanted. He was then acting as the owner. He was then, in the words of the statute, 'assuming the rights of the owner'. The moment he did that he appropriated McGregor's goods to himself. The appropriation was complete. After this appropriation had been completed there was no question of these two appellants taking part, in the words of the section 22, in dealing with the goods 'in the course of the stealing'."

**Appeal dismissed**

It has been argued that there can be no assumption of a right of an owner in such a case because an owner has no general right that others shall not contract to sell or purport to pass ownership in his property: "He does not need such a right, because other people, generally, can do him no harm by offering to sell his goods, and cannot pass ownership without his authority."[65] Such an argument seems to suggest that "everyone has the right to sell anyone else's property—which seems a trifle bizarre".[66] Further, the fact that the owner suffers no harm because ownership cannot be passed is irrelevant. It is only in rare cases that theft deprives the owner of his ownership (as opposed to possession) of the goods[67] and causing loss of ownership is simply not a prerequisite of the law of theft.

However, while an offer to sell another's property can probably amount to an appropriation,[68] this should only be so where the actor is in a position to threaten the owner's rights. Sitting in a pub offering the sell the Crown Jewels poses no threat whatsoever and therefore does not amount to an assumption of a right of an owner. Indeed, viewed from another perspective, it would not even amount to an attempted theft as the acts would still be preparatory. On the other hand, the rogue Millman in *Pitham* was in a position to threaten his friend's rights. His was an act of adverse interference with the rights of owner and was an assumption of the rights of owner.

*Bank accounts*
Many of the more recent reported cases concern theft and other property offences where the victim is a bank, or a person who has had money wrongfully

---

[65] Smith (A.T.H.), *Property Offences* (1994), p. 160.
[66] Smith and Hogan, *Criminal Law* (10th ed., 2002), p. 524.
[67] *ibid.*
[68] On its particular facts, *Pitham* is probably wrong. As all the parties concerned knew that Millman had no authority to sell the property, Millman was not "assuming the rights of owner"; it was a joint theft (Smith and Hogan, *Criminal Law* (10th ed., 2002), p. 524).

transferred from a bank account. Accordingly, a brief separate word needs to be added concerning appropriation from bank accounts.

The first point to be noted is that when a customer places money in a bank account, the bank owns that money, but owes the customer a debt.

Accordingly, two situations need to be distinguished. First, what is the position if a customer with no funds in her account and no overdraft facility, writes a cheque, backed by a cheque card, on that account? The bank, because of the use of the cheque card, is forced to honour the cheque. Has the customer appropriated property?

### R. v Navvabi [1986] 3 All E.R. 102 (Court of Appeal, Criminal Division)

Lord Lane C.J.:
"[T]he matter ... turns essentially on the construction of s.3(1): was use of the cheque cards to guarantee payment of a cheque delivered to the casino and drawn on an account with inadequate funds an assumption of the rights of the bank and thus appropriation? In our judgment it was not. That use of the cheque card and delivery of the cheque did no more than give the casino a contractual right as against the bank to be paid a specified sum from the bank's funds on presentation of the guaranteed cheque. That was not in itself an assumption of the rights of the bank to that part of the bank's funds to which the sum specified in the cheque corresponded: there was therefore no appropriation by the drawer either on delivery of the cheque to the casino or when the funds were ultimately transferred to the casino."

Secondly, what is the position if a defendant writes a forged cheque, or in some other way gets money transferred from another person's bank account into his own? This is theft of the debt, or part of it, owed by the bank to the other person—and, as we shall see, debts are "property" capable of being stolen. But when would the appropriation occur in such a case? In *Chan Man-sin* the Privy Council held that "one who draws, presents and negotiates a cheque on a particular bank account is assuming the rights of the owner of the credit in the account or (as the case may be) of the pre-negotiated right to draw on the account up to the agreed figure".[69] This was qualified in the following case.

### R. v Governor of Pentonville Prison, ex parte Osman (1990) 90 Cr.App.R.281 (Queen's Bench Divisional Court)

The applicant sought *habeas corpus* pursuant to section 8 of the Fugitive Offenders Act 1967. It was alleged that he, as chairman of X company, had been bribed in Hong Kong to make loans above authorised amounts to the Carrian group of companies. One alleged method was the sending of a telex to a New York bank instructing payment from X's account to the account of one of the Carrian companies. This was theft of the debt owed by the New York bank to X company. The applicant argued that the Hong Kong courts would have no jurisdiction to hear the case as the theft, if committed, took place in New York.

Lloyd L.J.:
"[Counsel for Osman] argued that the theft of the chose in action took place in the United States when BMFL's account was debited, and not before. That was the moment of appropriation. The dealing ticket, confirmation slip and telex were the means whereby the theft was carried out. The theft was not completed until the account was debited ...

---

[69] *Chan Man-sin v Att-Gen of Hong Kong* (1988) 86 Cr.App.R.303 at 306.

In *R. v Morris* ... the House of Lords made it clear that it is not necessary for an appropriation that the defendant assume all rights of an owner. It is enough that he should assume any of the owner's rights ... If so, then one of the plainest rights possessed by the owner of the chose in action in the present case must surely have been the right to draw on the account in question ... So far as the customer is concerned, he has a right as against the bank to have his cheques met. It is that right which the defendant assumes by presenting a cheque, or by sending a telex instruction without authority. The act of sending the telex is therefore the act of theft itself, and not a mere attempt. It is the last act which the defendant has to perform and not a preparatory act. It would not matter if the account were never in fact debited ...

The theft is complete in law, even though it may be said that it is not complete in fact until the account is debited ... [W]e would hold that Hong Kong was the place of appropriation."

In *Hilton*[70] it was held that the appropriation occurred when the defendant instructed the bank to make a transfer of funds and the transfer was made. The decision in *Osman* is clearly to be preferred. Presenting a cheque is undoubtedly as clear an assumption of ownership as swapping price labels. Whether the transfer of money is ever made is as irrelevant as whether the shopkeeper is fooled by the switched price labels. This better view was adopted in *Sui Soi Ngan*[71] where it was held that the drawing and signing of a cheque (in England) were merely preparatory acts and that the appropriation occurred when the cheque was presented to the bank (in Scotland).

When and where does the appropriation occur when access is gained to a bank's computer in order to divert funds?

### R. v Governor of Brixton Prison and Another, ex p. Levin [1997] 1 Cr.App.R.335 (Queen's Bench Divisional Court)

The applicant using a computer in St Petersburg, Russia gained unauthorised access to an American bank in Parsipenny and diverted funds into false accounts. One of the issues in *habeas corpus* proceedings was whether the appropriation had taken place in Russia when the instructions were typed onto a keyboard.

Beldam L.J.:

"We see no reason why the appropriation of the client's right to give instructions should not be regarded as having taken place in the computer [in the U.S.A.] Lloyd L.J. [in *Osman*] did not rule out the possibility of the place where the telex was received also being counted as the place where the appropriation occurred if the courts ever adopted the view that a crime could have a dual location ... [T]he operation of the keyboard by a computer operator produces a virtually instantaneous result on the magnetic disc of the computer even though it may be 10,000 miles away. It seems to us artificial to regard the act as having been done in one rather than the other place. But, in the position of having to choose ... we would opt for Parsipenny. The fact that the applicant was physically in St Petersburg is of far less significance than the fact that he was looking at and operating on magnetic discs located in Parsipenny. The essence of what he was doing was done there. Until the instruction is recorded on the disc, there is in fact no appropriation ...

[70] [1997] 2 Cr.App.R.445.
[71] [1998] 1 Cr.App.R.331.

In the case of a virtually instantaneous instruction intended to take effect where the computer is situated it seems to us artificial to regard the insertion of an instruction onto the disc as having been done only at the remote place where the keyboard is situated."

### Bona fide purchasers

Section 3(2) provides a special exemption for the bona fide purchaser for value of stolen goods. If a person bought goods at a reasonable price not knowing they were stolen and then later discovered they were, but decided to keep them, this would (without section 3(2)) come within the latter half of section 3(1), namely, he would have come by the property innocently without stealing it but would be appropriating it when he decided to keep it. The Criminal Law Revision Committee specifically proposed this exception on the ground that while there was a case for the imposition of criminal liability in such cases, "on the whole it seems to us that, whatever view is taken of the buyer's moral duty, the law would be too strict if it made him guilty of theft".[72] Accordingly, in *Wheeler* the defendant innocently purchased some stolen military antiques. He was later informed by the police that the goods were stolen but, nevertheless, sold one of the items. It was held that he could not be guilty of theft if he kept the goods for himself or sold them to another.[73] It is, however, possible that in selling such goods the defendant could be liable for the offence of obtaining property by deception (if he represented that he had good title) or of aiding and abetting the offence of handling stolen goods by the purchaser (if both knew the goods were stolen).[74]

## 3. Property

### Theft Act 1968, section 4

"(1) 'Property' includes money and all other property, real or personal, including things in action and other intangible property.

(2) A person cannot steal land, or things forming part of land and severed from it by him or by his directions, except in the following cases, that is to say—

(a) when he is a trustee or personal representative, or is authorised by power of attorney, or as liquidator of a company, or otherwise, to sell or dispose of land belonging to another, and he appropriates the land or anything forming part of it by dealing with it in breach of the confidence reposed in him; or

(b) when he is not in possession of the land and appropriates anything forming part of the land by severing it or causing it to be severed or after it has been severed; or

(c) when, being in possession of the land under a tenancy, he appropriates the whole or part of any fixture or structure let to be used with the land.

For purposes of this subsection 'land' does not include incorporeal hereditaments; 'tenancy' means a tenancy for years or any less period and includes an agreement for such a tenancy, but a person who after the end of a tenancy remains in possession as statutory tenant or otherwise is to be treated as having possession under the tenancy, and 'let' shall be construed accordingly.

(3) A person who picks mushrooms growing wild on any land, or who picks flowers, fruit or foliage from a plant growing wild on any land does not (although not in possession of the land) steal what he picks, unless he does it for reward or for sale or other commercial purpose.

---

[72] C.L.R.C., 8th Report, *Theft and Related Offences* (1966), Cmnd.2977, para. 37.
[73] (1991) 92 Cr.App.R.279 at 283.
[74] *Bloxham* [1983] 1 A.C. 109 at 114 approved in *Wheeler* (*ibid.*) at 284.

For purposes of this subsection 'mushroom' includes any fungus, and 'plant' includes any shrub or tree.

(4) Wild creatures, tamed or untamed, shall be regarded as property; but a person cannot steal a wild creature not tamed nor ordinarily kept in captivity, or the carcase of any such creature, unless either it has been reduced into possession by or on behalf of another person and possession of it has not since been lost or abandoned, or another person is in course of reducing it into possession."

Theft is an offence against property and inevitably the question arises as to the meaning of "property." Section 4(1) provides an extremely wide definition that property includes:

1. money: This refers only to current coins and bank notes, including foreign ones. It does not cover money placed in a bank account, which then constitutes a debt owed by the bank to the account holder.
2. all real property: *i.e.*, land and things attached to the land such as houses. However, the breadth of this provision is greatly limited by sections 4(2), (3) and (4). Section 4(2) isolates the only circumstances in which land and the things attached to the land may be stolen. Section 4(3) deals with the circumstances in which things growing wild on land may be stolen. Section 4(4) deals similarly with wild animals.[75]
3. all personal property: *i.e.* all property that is not real property. This includes:
4. things in action: a thing in action is non-physical property; one's rights in it can only be enforced by a legal action. The best example of such a "thing in action" is a debt. We saw above that a bank owns the money in an account but owes a debt to the account holder. This debt is a thing in action; it is property and can be stolen.[76] For example, in *Williams*[77] the defendant dishonestly overcharged elderly householders for building work; by cashing their cheques he was causing a diminution of their credit balances and so was appropriating their thing in action, namely part of the debt owed to them.

   Problems have arisen with regard to whether cheques can be stolen in the situation where the defendant induces a victim to draw a cheque in her favour. Following dicta in *Preddy*[78] it has been held in *Graham*[79] and *Clark*[80] that cheques cannot be stolen in such cases. This is because the moment the cheque is written, the thing in action belongs to the defendant. It does not belong to the victim because he cannot sue himself. However, the better view is that the requisite property here is not the thing in action, but the cheque itself which is a valuable security ("any document . . . authorising the payment of money"[81]); it is a piece of paper with special qualities like a key to a safe[82]

---

[75] For detail on these provisions, see Smith, *The Law of Theft* (8th ed., 1997), pp. 57–64; Griew, *The Theft Acts 1968 and 1978* (6th ed., 1990), pp. 13–17.

[76] *Kohn* (1979) 69 Cr.App.R.395; *Hilton* [1997] 2 Cr.App.R.445.

[77] [2001] 1 Cr.App.R.362.

[78] [1996] A.C. 815.

[79] [1997] 1 Cr.App.R.302.

[80] [2002] 1 Cr.App.R.141. This case concerned obtaining property by deception. The same principles, with regard to the meaning of property, apply to theft.

[81] Theft Act 1968, s.20(3).

[82] Smith, "Obtaining Cheques by Deception or Theft" [1997] Crim.L.R.396 at 400. See *below*, p. ?.

and is, therefore, capable of being stolen. Other examples of things in action
are a copyright, a trademark and shares in a company.

5. other intangible property: this is also non-physical property in which one can
   have a legal interest: for example, statute has declared that a patent is
   intangible property but not a thing in action.[83]

Three areas are of particular interest and deserve consideration.


## Electricity

In *Low v Blease*[84] it was held that electricity is not property for the purposes of
theft. Section 13 of the Theft Act creates a special offence of abstracting electricity,
carrying a maximum of five years' imprisonment.


## Trade secrets

In *Oxford v Moss*[85] a university student acquired a proof of one of his
examination papers. He read the questions but did not intend to deprive the
University of the piece of paper on which the questions were printed. He was
charged with theft of intangible property, namely, the confidential information
contained in the examination questions. On appeal it was held that this was not
intangible property within the meaning of section 4. Following this, in *Absolom*[86] it
was held that a person who obtained valuable trade secrets relating to oil
exploration, worth between £50,000 and £100,000, and tried to sell them to a rival
oil company could not be guilty of theft as such information did not amount to
property. While there are several other offences of infringing rights in intellectual
property,[87] counterfeiting registered trade marks,[88] and gaining unauthorised
access to data held on a computer,[89] it is nonetheless "absurd and disgraceful that
we should still be making do without any legislation specifically designed to
discourage this modern form of commercial piracy".[90] The Law Commission has
investigated this issue and provisionally concluded that confidential information is
not "property" and that it "would be a mistake for the criminal law to pretend that
it is".[91] However, because "there is no distinction in principle between the harm
caused by such misuse and the harm caused by theft"[92] the Commission has
proposed a new offence covering the use or disclosure of another's trade secret
where the "owner does not consent to its use or disclosure".[93]

---

[83] Patents Act 1977, s.30.
[84] [1975] Crim.L.R.513.
[85] (1978) 68 Cr.App.R.183.
[86] *The Times*, September 14, 1983.
[87] Copyright, Designs and Patents Act 1988, ss.107, 198.
[88] Trade Marks Act 1994, s.92.
[89] Computer Misuse Act 1990, s.1.
[90] Williams, *Textbook of Criminal Law* (2nd ed., 1983), p. 739.
[91] Law Commission Consultation Paper No. 150, *Legislating the Criminal Code: Misuse of Trade Secrets* (1997), para. 3.26. See Hull, "Stealing Secrets: A Review of the Law Commission's Consultation Paper on the Misuse of Trade Secrets" [1998] Crim.L.R.246.
[92] Para. 3.60.
[93] Para. 1.30.

*The human body and its parts*

Can one steal a human body or any parts thereof? It is often stated that "nobody owns my body, not even me".[94] However, in relation to the criminal law the answer may not be that simple and to answer the question, some distinctions need to be drawn.

First, for most practical purposes it seems unlikely that parts of the human body, while still a part of a live person, can be property for purposes of theft. In one case[95] magistrates did hold that it was theft to cut hair from a girl's head, but the status of this decision is doubtful. When Mrs Bobbit cut off her husband's penis this was an offence of violence which infringed his personal rights rather than his proprietary rights. It makes no sense to think of this as an offence against property and, even if it were, her conduct could hardly be described as dishonest.[96] However, once a limb, organ or sample has been removed from the body and stored in, say, a sperm or blood bank, it possesses all the attributes of personal property and should fall within section 4(1). Indeed, it has been held that blood[97] and urine[98] are property capable of being stolen. In the United States it has been held that a university hospital owned a patient's spleen and other body substances after they had been removed.[99] Such organs and tissue can be extremely valuable and while, for policy reasons, it might be appropriate to ban the purchase or sale of, say, organs for transplantation,[1] that should not alter the basic proposition that such organs, once removed, can be property capable of being stolen.

Secondly, in relation to corpses there was a commonly accepted view that a corpse was not property and nobody could have a proprietary right or interest in it. For the purposes of the criminal law this is clearly outmoded. Take, for instance, a cadaver "owned" by a University Medical Faculty. If the University does not "own" the cadaver under property law, it does have a bailment of the corpse,[2] or, at least, "possession or control" over it. However, although there might be a "proprietary right or interest" or "possession or control" over a corpse as required by section 5, that does not conclusively establish that the corpse is "property" under section 4. The traditional rule that a corpse, or part of a corpse, is not property was confirmed in *Kelly and Lindsay*[3] but it was added that parts of a corpse can become property for the purpose of section 4 if they have "acquired different attributes by virtue of the application of skill, such as dissection or preservation techniques, for exhibition or teaching purposes". In this case the defendant was held liable for the theft of some 40 body parts (heads, a part of a brain and an assortment of arms, legs and feet) from the Royal College of Surgeons. These parts were used for the training of surgeons. Rose J. did add that in future body parts might be held to be property "even without the acquisition of different

---

[94] Harris, "Who Owns My Body?" (1996) 16 O.J.L.S. 55. See, generally, Smith (A.T.H.), "Stealing the Body and its Parts" [1976] Crim.L.R.622.
[95] *Herbert* (1960) 25 J.Crim.L. 163.
[96] Smith (A.T.H.), *Property Offences* (1994), p. 49.
[97] *Rothery* [1976] R.T.R. 550.
[98] *Welsh* [1974] R.T.R. 478.
[99] *Moore v Regents of the University of California* [1990] 271 Cal.Rptr. 146.
[1] Human Organs Transplants Act 1989.
[2] Brahams, "Bailment and Donation of Parts of the Human Body" (1989) 139 N.L.J. 803.
[3] [1999] Q.B. 621.

attributes, if they have a use or significance beyond their mere existence ... if, for example, they are intended for use in an organ transplant operation".

This decision, while welcome, is somewhat limited and raises problems as to precisely when such body parts can be regarded as property. Legislation is clearly needed to confirm that, at least for the purposes of theft, corpses and organs or parts of the body removed from either a live person or a corpse, can be regarded as property.

### 4. Belonging to Another

Theft is an interference with the proprietary rights of another. One of the central problems here has been identifying who has sufficient "rights" in property to be afforded protection by the criminal law. The owner clearly needs protection, but ownership is only one form of proprietary right and others, particularly those with possession of property, need similar protection. Accordingly, section 5 of the Theft Act 1968 identifies the situations in which property is regarded as "belonging to another". It must be stressed that in some of these situations the property does not *really* (under the civil law) belong to anyone else, but someone else has an interest thought to be worth protecting and, therefore, the property is artificially *deemed* to belong to that person. Section 5 lays down five situations where property "belongs to another". There is substantial overlap between some of these situations but they are "essentially intended to be cumulative in effect".[4] It is convenient to deal with each of them separately.

### (1) Theft Act 1968, section 5(1)

"Property shall be regarded as belonging to any person having possession or control of it, or having in it any proprietary right or interest (not being an equitable interest arising only from an agreement to transfer or grant an interest)."

#### (a) *Possession or control*

"Possession" is a complex legal concept which involves both physical control and an intention to possess. "Control," on the other hand, signifies no more than its literal meaning, namely, physical control—and, therefore, covers many of the cases that could be described as possession, making it unnecessary to draw any distinction between the two concepts. Thus a customer in a shop examining a book has control of the book; a diner in a restaurant has control over the cutlery with which he is eating; a golf club has either possession or control (it does not matter which) over balls lost on its golf course[5]; a person has possession or control over any articles in his house or on his land even if he has forgotten or does not know they are there.[6]

#### *Theft by owner*

The law of theft is designed to protect a variety of interests in property. The result is that theft can be committed by a person with an interest in the property against

---

[4] *Arnold* [1997] 4 All E.R. 1 at 9.
[5] *Hibbert v McKiernan* [1948] 2 K.B. 142.
[6] *Woodman* [1974] Q.B. 754.

another with an interest (even a lesser interest) in the same property. In particular, this means that the real owner may be guilty of stealing his own property from another who has possession or control of that property. For instance, if a defendant pawns his watch as security for a loan and then surreptitiously takes his watch back, he would be appropriating property (the watch) belonging to another (the pawnbroker who, at a minimum, has possession or control over the watch).

### R. v Turner (No. 2) [1971] 1 W.L.R. 901 (Court of Appeal, Criminal Division)

The defendant took his car to a garage to be repaired. The repairs were almost completed and the car parked outside in the road. The defendant, without telling the garage or offering to pay for the repairs, drove his car away. He was convicted of theft and appealed against his conviction.

Lord Parker C.J.:

"[T]he judge directed the jury that they were not concerned in any way with lien and the sole question was whether Mr Brown [the garage proprietor] had possession or control. This court is quite satisfied that there is no ground whatever for qualifying the words 'possession or control' in any way. It is sufficient if it is found that the person from whom the property is taken ... was at the time in fact in possession or control. At the trial there was a long argument whether that possession or control must be lawful, it being said that by reason of the fact that this car was subject to a hire-purchase agreement, Mr Brown could never even as against the appellant obtain lawful possession or control ... As I have said, this court is quite satisfied that the judge was quite correct in telling the jury that they need not bother about lien, and that they need not bother about hire-purchase agreements. The only question was: was Mr Brown in fact in possession or control?"

Appeal dismissed

Glanville Williams described this case as "one of the most extraordinary cases decided under the Theft Act" and stated that "it is hard to believe that the decision represents the law".[7] The gist of his argument is that if one ignores the lien, which the jury were instructed to do, the defendant had a right to repossess his car whenever he liked and one should not be held guilty of theft for doing what one has a right to do. In similar vein, it has been argued that if a defendant takes back his television set from a thief who has stolen it (but who now has possession), there should be no liability because the thief has "no property rights in the television maintainable against D. *Vis-à-vis* D, the television set belongs to no-one else".[8]

It is submitted that this criticism is misplaced. The Theft Act has chosen to protect a wide range of proprietary interests, including possession and control—irrespective of the rights or interests of the defendant. In *Turner (No. 2)* there can be little doubt that the defendant appropriated property belonging to another (Mr Brown, by virtue of his possession or control). In most cases defendants with greater property rights than their victims, such as rights to repossession of their property, will not be acting dishonestly. Generally, the owner who takes back his own property would not be condemned by ordinary community standards as dishonest and would thus not be convicted of theft. The owner retrieving the stolen television set would argue that he believed he had a legal right to take the property and so was not dishonest under section 2(1)(a) of the Theft Act 1968. But the

[7] *Textbook of Criminal Law* (2nd ed., 1983), pp. 749, 750.
[8] Simester and Sullivan, *Criminal Law: Theory and Doctrine* (2000), p. 428.

defendant in *Turner (No. 2)* surreptitiously removed his car without paying for the repairs and without the garage proprietor knowing his name or address so as to be able to send him his bill. In such a case a conviction for theft, based on the ordinary meaning of the words "possession or control", does seem more appropriate than an acquittal based on a technical analysis of the meaning of a "bailment at will", which is what Mr Brown had at civil law if he did not have a lien. The short point is that whatever else he might have had at civil law, Mr Brown clearly had possession or control of the car and the defendant acted dishonestly and satisfied the remaining elements of the offence of theft. A conviction was inevitable.[9]

### (b) *Proprietary Right or Interest*

The most obvious instance of a proprietary right or interest is that of ownership. Ownership is a proprietary right and thus property belongs to an owner. With co-owners of property, each owner has a proprietary right and therefore one co-owner can steal from another.[10]

Particular problems have arisen here with regard to the "passing of property". This phrase is used to signify ownership passing from one person to another. When goods are bought and paid for in a shop "property passes" from the shop to the purchaser. The basic rule at civil law is that property passes when the parties intend it to pass. For example, in a supermarket parties are deemed normally to intend that property should pass only on payment for the goods.

In some cases, however, the transaction might be defective because one of the parties has made a mistake. Such a mistake might prevent property passing. The basic rule here is that if one of the parties has made a *fundamental mistake,* the transaction is rendered *void* and property does not pass pursuant to a void transaction. On the other hand, a lesser or *non-fundamental mistake* can render a contract merely *voidable* and property *does* pass pursuant to a voidable transaction.

The requirement that at the time of the appropriation the property must "belong to another" used to mean that the imposition of criminal liability and punishment could depend entirely on whether property passed pursuant to a transaction. For example, in *Kaur v Chief Constable of Hampshire*[11] the defendant chose a pair of shoes from a rack of shoes marked £6.99 per pair. One shoe was marked at £6.99 and the other at £4.99. The cashier charged her £4.99. On appeal against a conviction for theft it was held that the appropriation occurred when, having paid, she put the shoes in her bag. The issue was whether property had passed to her when she paid for the goods. If the cashier had made a fundamental mistake, the contract would have been void. As ownership would not then have passed she would have been appropriating property belonging to another. It was held, however, that the cashier had made a mere mistake as to quality, rendering the

---

[9] *cf. Meredith* [1973] Crim.L.R.253 where a defendant who had had his car towed away to a police yard took his car back without paying any fee. It was held that a charge of theft was improper as "The police had no right, as against the owner to retain it." This Crown Court decision cannot be accepted. The police had possession or control of the car; it therefore "belonged" to them for the purposes of theft. The only proper route to an acquittal on these facts should have been lack of dishonesty.

[10] *Bonner* [1970] 1 W.L.R. 838.

[11] [1981] 1 W.L.R. 578.

contract, at most, voidable. Accordingly, the ownership had passed to the defendant and she was not liable as she had not appropriated property belonging to another.

Such cases would be decided differently after *Gomez* and *Hinks* because the appropriation would be held to have taken place at the earlier stage when she took the shoes from the rack. At that point they still belonged to the store. The same would be true of the infamous case of *Gilks*[12] where a punter at the races was mistakenly paid out £106 even though his horse came nowhere. It was held that the bookmaker in paying out the money in the mistaken belief that a certain horse had won was making a fundamental mistake. Accordingly, property did not pass and so when the punter decided to keep the money he was appropriating property that did still belong to another. Again, after *Gomez* and *Hinks* the appropriation would be held to occur as the money was handed over and, at that moment (or, at any rate, the split second before) the money would still have belonged to the bookmaker.[13]

There are interests in property less than ownership that also qualify as "proprietary rights or interests". These interests may be either legal or equitable. An example of a legal right can be seen in *Turner (No. 2)* where the garage proprietor had a lien on the car (although, as seen, the case was not decided on that basis). An example of an equitable interest is that the beneficiary of a trust has an equitable interest in the trust property.

With regard to equitable interests it is important to note that there have been significant changes in the civil law relating to constructive trusts since the coming into force of the Theft Act 1968. For example, it is now possible that even though property has passed, the person who made a mistake in delivering the goods retains an equitable interest in them[14] and so the property "belongs" to her by virtue of section 5(1).[15] Whether these developments in the civil law of constructive trusts should be reflected by a corresponding broadening of the law of theft is considered below.

However, section 5(1) specifically excludes "equitable interests arising only from an agreement to transfer or grant an interest". With some contracts, for example, contracts to buy land or shares, the person contracting to purchase acquires an equitable interest, while the other party retains legal ownership. If that legal owner then sells to a third party he does not commit theft as the orginal contracting party only has an "equitable interest arising from an agreement ..." which is not sufficient for the property to be regarded as belonging to him.

It is with regard to this ascertainment of whether a person has a "proprietary right or interest" that we see the sharpest tensions between the criminal law and the civil law because the criminal law, with its traditional emphasis on blame and harm, is having to define part of the harm component in terms of the civil law. We saw in the introduction to this chapter that there is a conflict between two views.

---

[12] [1972] 1 W.L.R. 1371.

[13] In *Goodwin* [1996] Crim.L.R.262 where a defendant inserted foreign money (of less value than the required coin) into a gaming machine, it was held that ownership in any coins paid out would not have passed. Such a ruling was unnecessary. The appropriation would occur as the defendant received each coin. At that moment the property still belonged to the owner of the machine.

[14] *Chase Manhattan Bank v Israel British Bank*[1981] Ch. 105.

[15] For fuller discussion, see Simester and Sullivan, *Criminal Law: Theory and Doctrine*(2000), pp. 438–444.

On the one hand, there is the view that criminal liability should only be imposed on the blameworthy who cause harm and that this determination should be divorced from technical analyses of the civil law. This view tends to maintain that words in the Theft Acts be given their "ordinary meanings" by ordinary people, the jury. This was the view adopted in *Turner (No. 2)* where the judge refused to direct the jury in terms of liens. This approach has been supported by the House of Lords where dissatisfaction was expressed at allowing criminal liability to turn on fine points of civil law.

### R. v Morris, Anderton v Burnside [1984] A.C. 320 (House of Lords)

Lord Roskill:
"I respectfully suggest that it is on any view wrong to introduce into this branch of the criminal law questions whether particular contracts are void or voidable on the ground of mistake or fraud or whether any mistake is sufficiently fundamental to vitiate a contract. These difficult questions should so far as possible be confined to those fields of law to which they are immediately relevant and I do not regard them as relevant questions under the Theft Act 1968."

Reliance on civil law concepts, particularly whether there is a constructive trust or not, can present extremely complicated questions of civil law and generate uncertainty. For example, in *Powell v McRae*[16] the defendant, a turnstile operator at Wembley Stadium, accepted a bribe and allowed a member of the public to enter the ground without a ticket. On a charge of theft the justices ruled that as the money had been received in the course of employment it belonged to the employer. On appeal, this view was rejected: there was no constructive trust and so the employer had no fiduciary interest in the property. However, since this decision, the Privy Council in *Attorney-General of Hong Kong v Reid*[17] has ruled that a person who receives a bribe holds it on a constructive trust for the person injured. Following this, an employer on facts similar to those in *Powell v McRae* would have a proprietary interest in the bribe. It must be questionable whether criminal liability for theft should depend on changes in the law relating to constructive trusts, particularly as the purposes of the law of constructive trusts are very different to those of the criminal law.[18]

Further, holding such persons liable for theft raises the risk of false labelling. The essence of the defendant's wrongdoing in *Powell v McRae* was that he took a bribe and he should be found liable for that[19] rather than for the subsequent theft of the proceeds.

Responding to these concerns, the Court of Appeal in *Attorney-General's Reference (No. 1 of 1985)*[20] doubted whether a secret profit made by an employee would give rise to a trust but indicated that, even if it did, it would not give rise to a proprietary interest for the purposes of section 5(1) because if conduct is "so far from the understanding of ordinary people as to what constitutes stealing, it should not amount to stealing". This approach was not, however, adopted in *Shadrokh-*

---

[16] [1977] Crim.L.R.571.
[17] [1994] 1 A.C. 324.
[18] Smith (A.T.H.), "Constructive Trusts in the Law of Theft" [1977] Crim.L.R.395.
[19] Prevention of Corruption Act 1906, s.1(1). See Simester and Sullivan, p. 443.
[20] (1986) 83 Cr.App.R.70.

*Cigari*[21] where it was held that an equitable interest arising under a constructive trust was a proprietary interest for the purposes of section 5(1).

While one can sympathise with the approach adopted in *Attorney-General's Reference (No. 1 of 1985)*, the fact remains that theft is an offence involving interference with the property rights of another and such property rights can only exist at civil law (whether the law of property, contract or quasi-contract). It is not justifiable to convict a defendant of theft if nobody else has any interest in the property because, as seen, an owner is generally free to use, enjoy and abuse her own property as she sees fit. Equally, while other charges might be more appropriate, it is not justifiable to acquit a defendant of theft on the ground that the property does not belong to another when, by civil law, it plainly does. If the existence of property rights are not to be ascertained by reference to the civil law, then how are they to be ascertained?

Of course, it would be possible for the Theft Act 1968 to be amended so that certain property interests, particularly those arising under a constructive trust, are excluded for the purposes of the law of theft. But unless and until that occurs, it is surely inappropriate for criminal courts to depart from the civil law and proceed on a "if it doesn't look like theft, then it isn't theft" basis.

In *Dobson v General Accident Fire and Life Insurance Corp. plc*[22] it was stressed that the issue whether goods belong to another "is a question to which the criminal law offers no answer and which can only be answered by reference to civil law principles". The necessity for reliance on the civil law is demonstrated by the following case.

### R. v Walker [1984] Crim.L.R.112 (Court of Appeal, Criminal Division)

The appellant sold an unsatisfactory video recorder which was returned to him for repair. After some time the purchaser issued a summons claiming the price of the video as the "return of money paid for defective goods". Two days after the summons was served on him the appellant sold the video to another. The judge directed the jury that it was for them to decide on the evidence whether the property belonged to the original purchaser when it was sold by the appellant to another. The appellant was convicted of theft and appealed.

Held,

"[T]he onus was on the prosecution to prove as a matter of law that the video did not belong to the appellant when he sold it to another. In effect the trial judge had withdrawn the issue of law from the jury. The relevant law, which was contained in the Sale of Goods Act 1979 was complicated but the judge had made no attempt to explain it. For centuries juries had decided civil actions on points arising under the law of sale of goods. There was no reason why this jury should not have had the relevant law explained to them and in the absence of such an explanation it was impossible for them to do justice in the case."

**Appeal allowed**

### J. C. Smith, Commentary to R. v Walker [1984] Crim.L.R.113

"As the present case shows, when a question arises whether property belongs to another, recourse to the civil law is inevitable and it must be the whole of the civil law, including that part which determines whether contracts are void or merely voidable when that is relevant ... to determine whether property belongs to another.

---

[21] [1988] Crim.L.R.465: see below at p. 787.
[22] [1989] 3 All E.R. 929 at 937.

In the present case, it is clear that, after the sale, the video belonged to the purchaser and that it continued to do so when it was returned to the appellant for repair. The purchaser was at that stage a bailee of the recorder. It may well be, however, that the service of the summons claiming the return of the price amounted to a rescission of the contract of sale. In that case, the parties would be restored to the position they were in before the contract. Ownership in the recorder would be re-vested in the appellant. If that were so, since the appellant was already in possession he would hold the entire proprietary interest, the property would no longer belong to the purchaser, and theft would be an impossibility."

## (2) Theft Act 1968, section 5(2)

"Where property is subject to a trust, the persons to whom it belongs shall be regarded as including any person having a right to enforce the trust, and an intention to defeat the trust shall be regarded accordingly as an intention to deprive of the property any person having that right."

With most trusts the beneficiary already has a "proprietary right or interest", making section 5(2) unnecessary.[23] However, with charitable trusts there are no beneficiaries having beneficial interests in the trust property. Such trusts are enforced by the Attorney-General[24] and under section 5(2) the trust property is deemed to belong to the Attorney-General.[25]

## (3) Theft Act 1968, section 5(3)

"Where a person receives property from or on account of another, and is under an obligation to the other to retain and deal with that property or its proceeds in a particular way, the property or proceeds shall be regarded (as against him) as belonging to the other."

If a person receives property and ownership passes to him he is generally free to do as he likes with the property. Sometimes, however, even if the recipient has become the "true owner" of the property,[26] he may be obliged to deal with it in a particular way. For instance, a person collecting with a tin can for charity is obliged to hand over the money to the appropriate charity. When the donor places his coin in the tin can this is the clear understanding between donor and collector. Accordingly, section 5(3) deems that money still to belong to the donor and if the collector makes off with the money he is appropriating money "belonging to" the donor.

In many cases, where section 5(3) could apply, the person to whom the obligation is owed will have a legal or equitable interest in the property and so the property will still belong to that person under section 5(1). Under section 5(3), however, it is not necessary for courts to engage with the intricacies of establishing that a trust has been created and that the person supplying the property retains an equitable interest in it.[27] As said in *Klineberg and Marsden*,[28] section 5(3) "is essentially a deeming provision by which property or its proceeds 'shall be regarded' as belonging to another, even though, on a strict civil law analysis, it does

---

[23] *Arnold* [1997] 4 All E.R. 1 at 9.
[24] Charities Act 1997, s.33(7).
[25] This obvious point was overlooked in *Dyke and Munro* [2002] 1 Cr.App.R.404.
[26] *Arnold* [1997] 4 All E.R. 1.
[27] *Klineberg and Marsden* [1999] 1 Cr.App.R.427; *Floyd v D.P.P.* [2000] Crim.L.R.411.
[28] *ibid.*

not". Nevertheless, for section 5(3) to apply, there are several conditions that need to be satisfied:

(i) *The property must have been received from or on account of another to whom the obligation is owed*

Two alternative situations are covered here. First, as with the charity-collector above, the property is received from the person to whom the obligation is owed. Secondly, it can be received from one person on account of another; in this situation the obligation must be owed to that other person. On this basis the charity-collector could also be said to have received the property on account of the charity. The operation of these two principles can be seen in *Floyd v D.P.P.*[29] where the defendant collected money weekly from work colleagues who had ordered goods from a Home Farm but failed to pay the money to the farm. On these facts it would be possible to invoke either of the above bases. First, she received money from her colleagues; being under an obligation to pay the money to the Home Farm, the money would be regarded as belonging to her colleagues. Secondly, and this was the basis of the actual decision, she received money on account of the Home Farm and owed them an obligation to hand over the money,[30] and so the property was regarded as belonging to the Home Farm.

While establishing receipt of property from another is normally a simple matter,[31] the same is not always true where it is alleged that property has been received on account of another.

### Attorney-General's Reference (No. 1 of 1985) (1986) 83 Cr.App.R.70. (Court of Appeal, Criminal Division)

The defendant, a salaried manager of a tied public house, was only allowed to sell his employer's beer and was under a duty to pay all his takings into his employer's account. However, he sold other beer and kept the profit for himself. He was charged with theft from his employers on the basis that the money he received from his customers belonged to his employers by virtue of section 5(3).

The Lord Chief Justice:

"We are told at the outset of this hearing that this sort of behaviour by managers of 'tied' houses is becoming more prevalent. They do not, it seems, appear to be deterred by the prospect of losing their job or of being compelled by civil action to disgorge their illicit profit. An additional deterrent, it is suggested, in the shape of a conviction for theft would not be inappropriate.

That is not a matter which concerns us. We have to decide whether Parliament intended to bring such behaviour within the ambit of the criminal law ...

[Liability] depends on whether A can properly be said to have received property, (*i.e.* the payment over the counter for the beer he has sold to the customer) 'on account of the employers'. We do not think he can. He received the money on his own account as a result of his private venture. No doubt he is in breach of his contract with the employers; not doubt he

---

[29] [2000] Crim.L.R.411.

[30] As there was no evidence of any contract between the defendant and the Home Farm, it is far from clear that she did in fact owe them any obligation. See Smith, [2000] Crim.L.R.412.

[31] However, where the alleged receipt of the property occurs by way of a bank transfer, then, following *Preddy* [1996] A.C. 815, it has not been "received from" anyone as it is a newly created property that never belonged to anyone else: see Smith, Commentary to *Klineberg and Marsden* [1997] Crim.L.R.417. In this case the court failed to distinguish between money handed over by cash or cheque and that secured by bank transfer.

is under an obligation to account to the employers at least for the profit he has made out of his venture, but that is a different matter."

**Declaration accordingly**

(ii) *There has to be an obligation to deal with that property or its proceeds in a particular way*

Under section 5(3) there has to be an obligation to deal with *the property handed over* or *its proceeds* in a particular way. If I give my decorator £100 in order to buy paint, an obligation to use that money or its proceeds is imposed. If I give him £100 as a down-payment no such obligation results. This simple distinction (in theory) has caused problems in practice, particularly in cases where deposits have been paid.

### R. v Hall [1973] 1 Q.B. 496 (Court of Appeal, Criminal Division)

The defendant was a travel agent who accepted deposits for air trips to the United States. The flights never materialised and the money was not refunded. The appellant paid all the monies into the firm's general trading account. He was convicted of theft and appealed on the ground that the monies paid to him became his and therefore did not "belong to another".

Edmund-Davies L.J.:
"Counsel for the appellant ... concedes that [by receiving the monies] the travel agent undertakes a contractual obligation in relation to arranging flights ... But what counsel for the appellant resists is that in such circumstances the travel agent 'is under an obligation' to the client 'to retain and deal with ... in a particular way' sums paid to him in such circumstances.
What cannot of itself be decisive of the matter is the fact that the appellant paid the money into the firm's general trading account ...
Nevertheless, when a client goes to a firm carrying on the business of travel agents and pays them money, he expects that in return he will, in due course, receive the tickets and other documents necessary for him to accomplish the trip for which he is paying, and the firm are 'under an obligation' to perform their part to fulfil his expectation and are liable to pay him damages if they do not. But, in our judgment, what was not here established was that these clients expected them 'to retain and deal with that property or its proceeds in a particular way', and that an 'obligation' to do so was undertaken by the appellant. We must make clear, however, that each case turns on its own facts. Cases could, we suppose, conceivably arise where by some special arrangement (preferably evidenced by documents), the client could impose on the travel agent an 'obligation' falling within section 5(3). But no such special arrangement was made in any of the seven cases here being considered. It follows from this that, despite what on any view must be condemned as scandalous conduct by the appellant, in our judgment on this ground alone this appeal must be allowed and the convictions quashed."

**Appeal allowed**

### R. v Klineberg and Marsden [1999] 1 Cr.App.R.427 (Court of Appeal, Criminal Division)

The appellants sold timeshare apartments in Lanzarote. The purchasers paid money, to be held by a trust company until the apartments were ready to be occupied. Almost none of the money was in fact transmitted to the trust company. The appellants were convicted of theft and appealed.

Kay J.:

"The intending purchasers in each case, and prior to the handing over of any money, were made aware by documents and in at least some cases by oral representations that, if they were to enter into an agreement, they would have the security of knowing that any money they handed over would be held in independent trusteeship until the apartment in question was ready for occupation. . . . One of the pivotal features of the whole scheme was that their money would be safeguarded by trusteeship pending completion. In such circumstances there must have been, at the very least, an implied obligation in favour of each intending purchaser to transfer his money into the appropriate trusteeship without undue delay."

**Appeal allowed in part on other grounds**

Similarly, in *Re Kumar*[32] a travel agent was held to be under an obligation to use money paid to secure flight tickets because there was an agreed trustee relationship for such money to be transferred into specific bank accounts. In *McHugh*[33] it was stressed that both the defendant and the client must "clearly understand" that the client's money is to be kept separate from the defendant's business money. In other cases, whether one is under an obligation to keep a separate fund in existence depends entirely on the facts of each case.

### Davidge v Bunnett [1984] Crim.L.R.297 (Queen's Bench Divisional Court)

The defendant shared a flat with three other women. When the gas bill arrived the others all gave the defendant their shares in cheques made payable to the defendant's employer. They expected her to pay the bill, either by cashing the cheques with her employer and adding her own share, or, alternatively, that her employer, on receipt of all the monies, would write out a cheque for the Gas Board. Instead, the defendant spent most of the money on her Christmas shopping; the gas bill went unpaid. She was convicted of theft and appealed.

Held,

"D was under an obligation to use the cheques or their proceeds in whatever way she saw fit so long as they were applied *pro tanto* to the discharge of the gas bill. This could have been achieved by one cheque from her employer, or a banker's draft, or her own cheque . . . Hence the magistrates' finding that she was not obliged to use the actual banknotes. Using the proceeds of the cheque on presents amounted to a very negation of her obligation to discharge the bill. She was under an obligation to deal with the proceeds in a particular way. As against D, the proceeds of the cheques were properly belonging to another within section 5(3) of the Act."

**Appeal dismissed**

In *Lewis v Lethbridge*[34] the defendant collected sponsorship money for a colleague who had entered the London Marathon. He never handed this money over to the charity. In the Divisional Court it was held that the defendant was not under an obligation to keep a separate fund in existence equivalent to the amount of money he had received. The money thus did not "belong to another" under section 5(3). The defendant was "a civil debtor and a naughty one without question, but not a thief".[35] This decision has now been disapproved.

---

[32] [2000] Crim.L.R.504.
[33] (1993) 97 Cr.App.R.335.
[34] [1987] Crim.L.R.59.
[35] Cited in *Wain* [1995] 2 Cr.App.R.660 at 664.

## R. v Wain [1995] 2 Cr.App.R.660 (Court of Appeal, Criminal Division)

The appellant raised money for a "Telethon" held for charity by Yorkshire Television. He paid the money raised first into a separate bank account and then, with Yorkshire Television's permission, into his own bank account and then spent it. He was convicted of theft and appealed.

McCowan L.J.:
"[Referring to *Lewis v Lethbridge*] the learned judge was forgetting that section 5(3) of the Theft Act 1968 referred not merely to dealing with that property but also its proceeds ...
Professor Smith ... in his *Law of Theft* (6th ed.) at p. 39 [states]
'... In *Lewis v Lethbridge* ... no consideration was given to the question whether any obligation was imposed by the sponsors. Sponsors surely do not give the collector (whether he has a box or not) the money to do as he likes with. Is there not an overwhelming inference ... that the sponsors intend to give the money to the charity, imposing an obligation in the nature of a trust on the collector?'
It seems to us that the approach of the court in the *Lethbridge* case was a very narrow one based, apparently, on the finding by the justices that there was no requirement of the charity that the appellant hand over the same notes and coins. Neither was there in the present case. But what the Divisional Court does not appear to have considered in that case was the trust aspect ... In our judgment, the criticisms of that case by Professor Smith are fully justified ... [His Lordship approved *Davidge v Bunnett*.]
[I]t seems to us that by virtue of section 5(3), the appellant was plainly under an obligation to retain, if not the actual notes and coins, at least their proceeds, that is to say the money credited in the bank account which he opened for the trust with the actual property. When he took the money credited to that account and moved it over to his own bank account, it was still the proceeds of the notes and coins donated which he proceeded to use for his own purposes, thereby appropriating them."

**Appeal dismissed**

## D.P.P. v Huskinson [1988] Crim.L.R.620 (Queen's Bench Divisional Court)

The defendant fell into arrears with his rent. He applied for housing benefit and was sent a cheque for £479 to pay off some of the arrears which then amounted to £800. He gave his landlord £200 and spent the remainder on himself. He was acquitted of theft and the prosecutor appealed by way of case stated.

Held,
"The decision turned on section 5(3) ... and whether the respondent was under an obligation to the Housing Services Department to deal with the cheque or its proceeds in a particular way ... [The obligation had to be a legal one.] Any such obligation would have to be found in the statutory provisions which gave rise to the payment of housing benefit. The court had examined the relevant statute and regulations, (*i.e.* the Social Security and Housing Benefit Act 1982, s.28 and regulations made thereunder which had since been replaced by the Social Security Act, s.26 ... ) It was quite clear that the regulations did not impose an express obligation on the tenant to pay the sum received directly to the landlord and it was impossible to imply any such obligation. Housing benefit provided a fund from which the tenant was expected to pay his rent. He had a legal obligation to the landlord to pay the rent. However there was no obligation to apply the cheque or proceeds directly in satisfaction of any rent. For example, if the tenant obtained the money from some other source before he received the housing benefit he would be quite entitled to use the cheque or its proceeds for his own purposes. The justices had been right to dismiss the charges."

**Appeal dismissed**

## J. C. Smith, Commentary on D.P.P. v Huskinson [1988] Crim.L.R.621:

"Housing benefit, it appears, is the tenant's money to do as he likes with. There is no reason in law why he should not take it to a betting shop and put it straight on a horse. That, perhaps, is a matter which those responsible for the administration of housing benefit may wish to reconsider. No doubt there is a number of considerations which must be taken into account; but the fact that the money is paid to meet a specific need suggests that there ought to be an obligation to apply it for that purpose ...

The court points out that, if the tenant finds the money for his rent from some other source and pays it before he receives the housing benefit from the local authority, he can do as he likes with it. This is obviously so, but it does not follow that, where he has not paid his rent, he is not under an obligation to the local authority to do so and to retain the money paid, until he pays the rent, either with that or other money. Any obligation to retain and deal with money is extinguished when the purpose for which the obligation to retain and deal was imposed is satisfied."

### (iii) *The defendant must have direct knowledge of the obligation*

### R. v Wills (1991) 92 Cr.App.R.297 (Court of Appeal, Criminal Division)

The appellant and two assistants operated a business as financial consultants advising clients on investments and loans. The assistants each received money from different clients with instructions to invest the money with an insurance company. Those monies were used for the general purposes of the business and not invested in accordance with the clients' instructions. The appellant was not present when either transaction took place and there was no evidence that he personally knew of the obligation. The appellant was convicted of theft (as were the assistants) and appealed.

Farquharson L.J.:

"[T]here can be no doubt in this case that such an obligation had been attached to the monies by the two customers ...

Whether a person is under an obligation to deal with property in a particular way can only be established by proving that he had knowledge of that obligation. Proof that property was not dealt with in conformity with the obligation is not sufficient in itself ... [I]t was submitted that where there was knowledge by the agent of the extent of the obligation imposed on the disposal of the property such knowledge was to be imputed to the principal, in this case the appellant ... [F]or purposes of the criminal law it is necessary for the prosecution to prove that the principal had knowledge of the nature and extent of the obligation to deal with property in a particular way before section 5(3) of the 1968 Act can apply."

**Appeal allowed**

In *Wain* it was stated that whether the defendant "is a trustee is to be judged on an objective basis. It is an obligation on him by law. It is not essential that he should have realised that he was a trustee, but of course the question remains as to whether he was acting honestly or dishonestly".[36] Thus the defendant must have knowledge of the facts giving rise to the obligation but need not know that he is under a civil legal obligation.[37] However, if a defendant genuinely believes he is legally justified in doing what he does with the money, it will be difficult to establish the requisite dishonesty.

[36] [1995] 2 Cr.App.R.660 at 666.
[37] See also *Dubar* [1995] 1 Cr.App.R.280 at 287.

(iv) *The obligation must be a legal one*

It is not enough that the defendant is under a social or moral obligation to deal with the property in a particular way. He must be under a legal obligation. This means that the party imposing the obligation must be able to commence legal proceedings against the defendant at civil law for a failure to perform his obligation. One must be careful here to distinguish a legal obligation to do something (for example, pay one's rent as in *Huskinson*) from a legal obligation to use particular property or its proceeds in the performance of that obligation (for example, using the housing benefit to pay one's rent). It is only when there is a legal obligation of the latter kind that property is deemed to belong to another for the purposes of the law of theft.

Whether the obligation for the purposes of section 5(3) had to be a "legal" one or not used to be controversial. One school of thought was that "obligation" was an ordinary word—like many of the other "ordinary words" used in the Theft Act. Whether there was an obligation or not was simply a matter of fact to be left to the jury. As the jury know no law, this means that they can only decide on the basis of whether they think the defendant ought to be under an obligation, *i.e.* whether a moral obligation exists.[38]

However, it was the opposing school of thought that won the day here in the continuing see-saw battle between "ordinary meaning" and "civil law meaning". In *Mainwaring*[39] it was held that there must be a legal obligation at civil law for the purposes of section 5(3). This was confirmed in *Dubar* where it was stated that it is "the trial judge's function to direct the jury as to matters of law, including the existence of an obligation within section 5(3) if, but only if, he fully and fairly leaves it to the jury to decide the facts which give rise to such an obligation".[40] While this means, yet again, that criminal liability can depend on highly complex points of civil law,[41] nevertheless such an approach can be supported on the basis that: "Parliament is not in the habit of legislating about moral obligations as such; and that Parliament should do so without making its meaning plain is inconceivable."[42]

*Section 5(3) and fair labelling*

A large proportion of reported cases involving section 5(3) involve dishonest business operations by travel agents, estate agents, investment companies and so on.

### L. H. Leigh (with assistance of Susannah Brown), "Crimes in Bankruptcy" in L. H. Leigh (ed.), Economic Crime in Europe (1980), pp. 194–195:

"We appear, indeed, to be witnessing a transition from the employment, in corporate matters, of criminal sanctions, to the employment of administrative disabilities. The emphasis is less upon fraud than upon the fitness of individuals to conduct enterprises.

---

[38] *Hayes* (1977) 64 Cr.App.R.82. There are also dicta in *Hall* [1973] 1 Q.B. 496 to this effect.

[39] (1982) 74 Cr.App.R.99.

[40] [1995] 1 Cr.App.R. 280 at 287. Approved in *Arnold* [1997] 4 All E.R. 1 at 10 and *Breaks and Huggan* [1998] Crim.L.R.349.

[41] See, for example, *Williams and Lamb* [1995] Crim.L.R.77. In *Hallam and Blackburn* [1995] Crim.L.R.323 the Court of Appeal was highly critical of the civil law technicalities that have been grafted on to s.5.

[42] Williams, *Textbook of Criminal Law* (2nd ed., 1983), p. 752.

Whether loss is caused to investors and the public by ineptitude or by fraud is no doubt an important distinction, but it is not all-important ... [R]ecent legislation provides for the disqualification from acting as directors ... [Such measures are] intended to prevent incompetents from managing companies; it also can be used to strike at persons who loot companies, or who arrange insolvencies as part of a scheme of fraud ...

In effect, governments necessarily become more flexible in their search for measures to combat forms of economic criminality; less imbued with the desirability of employing the criminal model purely; and more respectful, perhaps, of some of the traditional limitations attaching to the use of the criminal law. Problems posed by difficulties of proof do not stand alone, of course: there is also the problem of defining standards in such a way as to leave scope for what are thought to be desirable entrepreneurial practices while protecting the public from imposition or worse. Thus, it becomes difficult to define offences."

Since this was written in 1980 there has been a marked increase in the intervention of the criminal law into a wide variety of conduct not previously criminalised. Whether this is an appropriate use of the criminal law was discussed in chapter 1. However, assuming criminalisation is justified in such cases, the question becomes: is section 5(3) so defined as to criminalise behaviour that ought to be subject to criminal sanctions and, if so, is theft the correct label to describe such wrongdoing?

In *Hall* the defendant was dishonest (the jury at first instance convicted him) and Edmund-Davies L.J. described his conduct as scandalous. Yet he escaped liability. Is it justifiable to draw a moral line between his conduct and that of the applicant in *Re Kumar* purely because there was an agreed trustee relationship in the latter case? Part of the problem is that section 5(3) is embracing conduct too far removed from the paradigm of theft. This explains the comments in some of the above cases such as *Lewis v Lethbridge* that the defendant was a "civil debtor and a naughty one without question, but not a thief" and *Attorney-General's Reference (No. 1 of 1985)* that the defendant's conduct was "so far from the understanding of ordinary people as to what constitutes stealing, it should not amount to stealing." In *Klineberg and Marsden* the essence of the prosecution case was that the appellants "were involved in a timeshare fraud". Indeed, in many of the above cases the real wrongdoing constituted fraud and not theft. As shall be seen, the Law Commission[43] has proposed a radical reform of the law of fraud with the introduction of a broadly-based single fraud offence which would catch many of the above defendants. If this new offence were to be created, consideration should be given to the repeal of, or substantial revision to, section 5(3).

*Criminalising breach of contract*

In many of the above cases, the defendant was in breach of contract. In some of these cases (for example, *Re Kumar*) there was liability; in others (for example, *Attorney-General's Reference (No. 1 of 1985)*) there was no liability. Whether a dishonest breach of contract should be criminalised has also arisen in cases not turning on section 5(3). For example, in *Clowes (No. 2)*[44] a central point on appeal

---

[43] See p. 834.
[44] [1994] 2 All E.R. 316.

was whether signed agreements were contracts or trust documents. Criminal liability could only be imposed in the latter situation as only then would the property "belong to another".

Quite apart from the above point concerning the appropriateness of "theft" as the offence label, this raises the broader question whether *all* dishonest breaches of contract should be criminalised. A breach of contract can have as disastrous an impact upon the innocent party as stealing from her. If accompanied by dishonesty, why should it not be criminalised?

It could be asserted that there is the entire structure of the civil law to provide remedies for breach of contract. Criminalisation is unnecessary. This argument, however, collapses when one recalls that there are similar civil remedies provided for those who "lose" their property wrongfully. The existence of civil remedies is no argument for the decriminalisation of theft. So the question remains: why is theft a crime but *dishonest* breach of contract not a crime?

Apart from historical explanations relating to the evolution of the law of larceny and its metamorphosis into theft, an explanation of principle is not easy. It is perhaps best to focus on the paradigmatic instances of theft and breach of contract. A typical theft involves a surreptitious or forceful taking. The victim is helpless against such a taking. If the thief is interrupted there is a risk of violence. Because of his anonymity there is extra difficulty in identifying and apprehending the thief. With the typical breach of contract, however, one is dealing with two parties, both "free" and "equal" who have both chosen to enter into a contractual nexus. The risk of one party breaching his contract was always there and, in a free market economy, a factor to be assessed at the time of entering into the contract—taking account of the civil remedies available. Bearing in mind the basic proposition that conduct should not be made criminal merely because it is immoral, but that, additionally, criminalisation should be "necessary" and "profitable"[45] one should only expand the reaches of the criminal law with the utmost caution. Certain instances of dishonest breach of contract have already been made criminal, particularly where the contract is breached by deception, or the defendant is attempting unilaterally to avoid his liability in circumstances where it would be difficult to trace him.[46] Beyond such cases the criminal law should not go. Section 5(3) does extend the tentacles of the law of theft beyond the paradigmatic instances. Great caution must be exercised to keep some rein over the subsection so that it does not stray too far from ordinary understanding of criminality.

Further, returning to the earlier point, in those cases where criminalisation of dishonest breach of contract is thought to be "necessary", it should be brought under the umbrella of a new fraud offence rather than being falsely labelled "theft".

## (4) Theft Act 1968, section 5(4)

"Where a person gets property by another's mistake, and is under an obligation to make restoration (in whole or in part) of the property or its proceeds or of the value thereof, then to the extent of that obligation the property or proceeds shall be regarded (as against him) as belonging to the person entitled to restoration, and an intention not to make restoration shall be regarded accordingly as an intention to deprive that person of the property or proceeds."

[45] *Above*, p. 18.
[46] *Below*, pp. 830, 835.

This subsection was specifically enacted to combat the mischief revealed in the case of *Moynes v Cooper*[47] where an employee was given a pay packet which, owing to a mistake, contained too much money. When he opened the packet and saw the excess he dishonestly kept the whole. He was acquitted of larceny. If these facts were to reoccur, the case could be brought within section 5(4) and, therefore, even though property in the excess money might have passed to the employee when his wages were handed over, he could be liable: on discovering and keeping the excess money there was an appropriation of property (the money) which was deemed to belong to the employer by virtue of section 5(4) because he had got the money by mistake and was under an obligation to make restoration of the excess—or its proceeds or value.

Section 5(4) is in fact of limited use. Where a person receives property by another's mistake, the mistake may be fundamental, in which case property does not pass at all and the property will still belong to the other by virtue of section 5(1) (proprietary right or interest). Section 5(4) is not needed in such cases. On the other hand, where the mistake is not so fundamental as to prevent property passing,[48] the receiver of the property will not necessarily be under an obligation to make restoration of the property. Whether there is an obligation to make restoration is a complex matter governed by the law of restitution.

Accordingly, the following points can be made about section 5(4):

1. The obligation must be a legal one—*i.e.* under the civil law of restitution.[49]
2. The obligation must be to return *the* property or *its* proceeds or the *value* thereof. (Under section 5(3) only the property or its proceeds is specified.)
3. The subsection says "is" under an obligation. The use of the present tense is significant here. If in a supermarket a cashier makes a mistake as a result of which the contract is *voidable*, property does pass, but the recipient of the property *is* not *there and then* under an obligation to make restitution. The obligation to make restitution only comes into existence when the person who made the mistake "avoids" the contract. At that point the recipient will become under an obligation to make restitution and only then does the present tense "is" become applicable. However, as Heaton[50] points out, upon rescission ownership in the property will revert to the person who made the mistake and any subsequent "keeping or dealing with it as owner" will be an appropriation of property that belongs to another by virtue of section 5(1).

It ought to be pointed out, however, that courts have not been rigorous in their application of these civil law principles and, while insisting with one breath that the obligation be a legal one, they have at the same time tended to adopt a more cavalier approach.

---

[47] [1956] 1 Q.B. 439.
[48] In *Chase Manhattan Bank N.A. v Israel-British Bank London Ltd* [1981] Ch. 105 Goulding J. held that where an action lies to recover money paid under a mistake of fact, the payer retains an equitable interest in that property and therefore it belongs to him by virtue of section 5(1). This was approved in *Shadrokh-Cigari* [1988] Crim.L.R.465. See, however, *Westdeutche v Islington London Borough Council* [1996] 2 All E.R. 961 and discussion in Smith, *Law of Theft* (8th ed., 1997), pp. 53–54.
[49] *Gilks* [1972] 1 W.L.R. 1341.
[50] "Deceiving without Thieving" [2001] Crim.L.R.712 at 723.

## Attorney-General's Reference (No. 1 of 1983) [1985] Q.B. 182 (Court of Appeal, Criminal Division)

The defendant, a policewoman, was overpaid her wages. The money was paid by direct debit straight into her bank account. When she realised the mistake she decided to keep the excess. The judge directed an acquittal and the Attorney-General referred a question on a point of law for the court's opinion under section 36 of the Criminal Justice Act 1972.

Lord Lane C.J.:
"In order to determine the effect of that subsection upon this case one has to take it piece by piece to see what the result is read against the circumstances of this particular prosecution. First of all: 'Did the respondent get property?' The word 'get' is about as wide a word as could possibly have been adopted by the draftsman of the Act. The answer is 'Yes', the respondent in this case did get her chose in action, that is, her right to sue the bank for the debt which they owed her—money which they held in their hands to which she was entitled by virtue of the contract between bank and customer.

Secondly: 'Did she get it by another's mistake?' The answer to that is plainly 'Yes'. The Receiver of the Metropolitan Police made the mistake of thinking she was entitled to £74.74 when she was not entitled to that at all.

'Was she under an obligation to make restoration of either the property or its proceeds or its value?' We take each of those in turn. 'Was she under an obligation to make restoration of the property?'—the chose in action. The answer to that is 'No'. It was something which could not be restored in the ordinary meaning of the word. 'Was she under an obligation to make restoration of its proceeds?' The answer to that is 'No'. There were no proceeds of the chose in action to restore. 'Was she under an obligation to make restoration of the value thereof?'—the value of the chose in action. The answer to that seems to us to be 'Yes'.

I should say here, in parenthesis, that a question was raised during the argument this morning as to whether 'restoration' is the same as 'making restitution'. We think that on the wording of section 5(4) as a whole, the answer to that question is 'Yes'. One therefore turns to see whether, under the general principles of restitution, this respondent was obliged to restore or pay for the benefit which she received. Generally speaking, the respondent, in these circumstances, is obliged to pay for a benefit received when the benefit has been given under a mistake on the part of the giver as to a material fact. The mistake must be as to a fundamental or essential fact and the payment must have been due to that fundamental or essential fact. The mistake here was that this police officer had been working on a day when she had been at home and not working at all. . . .

As a result of the provisions of section 5(4) the debt of £74.74 due from the respondent's bank to the respondent notionally belonged to the Receiver of the Metropolitan Police; therefore the prosecution, up to this point, have succeeded in proving—remarkable though it may seem—that the 'property' in this case belonged to another within the meaning of section 1 in the Theft Act 1968 from the moment when the respondent became aware that this mistake had been made and that her account had been credited with the £74.74 and she consequently became obliged to restore the value. . . .

Before parting with the case we would like to say that it should often be possible to resolve this type of situation without resorting to the criminal law. We do, however, accept that there may be occasions—of which this may have been one—where a prosecution is necessary."

**Opinion accordingly**

The defendant here owed a debt and dishonestly tried to avoid paying that debt. This is yet another instance of the grey area of criminality discussed above: when, if ever, should not paying one's debts or in other ways breaching one's contract be a crime? In one sense the defendant in this case was even more blameless than most debtors because she did not choose to incur the debt. It was thrust upon her by the mistake of another. And again, there were civil remedies available. The money could have been recovered. The court rightly stressed that such cases could usually be dealt with without resort to the criminal law. In *Attorney-General's Reference (No. 1 of 1983)* the amount of the overpayment was some £74. In *Shadrokh-Cigari*[51] a bank account was credited $286,000 instead of $286. English law does not formally take account of the value of property in assessing criminality, or level thereof. Yet this is surely an instance where the sums involved are so huge that perhaps criminal liability is appropriate. Or is it that the value of the property affects our assessment as to dishonesty? We can conceive of perhaps "turning a blind eye" to an extra £74 credited to our bank account, but when the excess amount is some $286,000, an assessment of dishonesty becomes inevitable.

### R. v Davis (1989) 88 Cr.App.R. 347 (Court of Appeal, Criminal Division)

The defendant was entitled to housing benefit from the local authority. By mistake the authority's computer issued duplicate issues of a number of cheques. When he ceased to be eligible for housing benefit only one of the computer entries was deleted and he continued to be sent one cheque. He kept the proceeds of the cheque and appealed against his conviction for theft.

Mustill L.J.:
"[T]he language of the first part of [section 5(4)] was framed to cater for the ordinary tangible article, and to recognise that by the time the defendant comes to commit his dishonest appropriation, the article may be in one of three conditions: it may still exist, so that it can and should be returned; it may have been exchanged for money or goods, in which case the defendant may be under an obligation to account for the fruits of the exchange, at least if they are traceable; and it may have ceased to exist altogether or to have gone out of reach of recovery, in which event the defendant may be obliged to 'restore' the value. In those cases where the defendant is indeed under a duty to 'make restoration' the second part of the subsection will put him in peril of conviction for stealing the article or its proceeds, although not its value, since there is no reference to value in this part of the subsection.
Now, the deceptively plain words of section 5(4) unquestionably give rise to problems. How does one know when the defendant is obliged to 'make restoration'? Again, what happens where the property, which the defendant has received by mistake, is exchanged for something else? ... [W]e do not need to answer [these questions] here. What does seem to us quite plain is that if an article is sold for cash, the sum received represents the 'proceeds' of the article; and there is no reason why this should be any the less so where the transaction involves not simply the piece of paper, but also the rights which it conveys. Accordingly, on the assumption that the defendant was paid cash for the cheque, the offences were made out subject to the proof of dishonesty ...
[In relation to the count concerning the duplicate cheque] there is no true difference between an overpayment effected by an excessive number of coins inserted in the same pay packet and an excessive number of cheques transferred separately. When the 'property' was turned into 'proceeds', in circumstances where those proceeds formed an undifferentiated whole, it is in accordance with the words as well as the spirit of the statute to regard the surplus as the subject matter of the theft, without engaging on the task of ascertaining the exact source of that surplus."

**Appeal allowed in part**

---

[51] [1988] Crim.L.R.465.

## 5. Dishonesty

The *mens rea* of theft is twofold: dishonesty and intention of permanent deprivation. Blameworthiness is generally a pre-requisite to the imposition of criminal liability and *mens rea* is an important indicator of blame. *Mens rea* is normally taken to refer to a state of mind in relation to consequences or circumstances of a defendant's actions—for example, did she intend, foresee or know of something happening? But, apart from the requirement of intending permanent deprivation, this traditional concept of *mens rea* fits ill with property offences where, in essence, a judgment is being made about behaviour and the general state of mind of the defendant in relation to her actions. As was said in one of the leading cases, *Feely*,[52] the taking of property must be one to which "moral obloquy can reasonably" be attached.

The interference with property rights must be such that we can blame the defendant for disregarding the value system inherent in the law of theft. The requirement of "dishonesty" is introduced as a mechanism by which moral judgments can be made and blame attributed.

Dishonesty is only partially defined by the Theft Act 1968. Where defined, the meaning of dishonesty is a question of law. Where undefined, it is a question of fact.

### A. *Question of Law*

#### Theft Act 1968, section 2

"(1) A person's appropriation of property belonging to another is not to be regarded as dishonest—
  (a) if he appropriates the property in the belief that he has in law the right to deprive the other of it, on behalf of himself or of a third person; or
  (b) if he appropriates the property in the belief that he would have the other's consent if the other knew of the appropriation and the circumstances of it; or
  (c) (except where the property came to him as trustee or personal representative) if he appropriates the property in the belief that the person to whom the property belongs cannot be discovered by taking reasonable steps.
(2) A person's appropriation of property belonging to another may be dishonest notwithstanding that he is willing to pay for the property."

#### Theft Act 1968, section 1(2)

"It is immaterial whether the appropriation is made with a view to gain, or is made for the thief's own benefit."

### (a) *Belief in legal right*

Section 2(1)(a) allows a person who genuinely believes he has a legal right to the property to be regarded as honest—irrespective of the reasonableness or otherwise of the belief.[53] There is a well known maxim that "ignorance of the law is no defence". This, however, relates to ignorance of the criminal law, for instance, to a defendant who claims he did not know theft was a crime. Section 2(1)(a) only applies to persons who have made a mistake as to the *civil law*—believing they have legal rights to property when, perhaps, they have no such rights.

---

[52] [1973] 1 Q.B. 530.
[53] *Small* (1988) 86 Cr.App.R.170; *Holden* [1991] Crim.L.R.480.

(b) *Belief in consent*

It will be recalled that under *Gomez* a defendant can appropriate property even though the other has consented to such appropriation. However, if the defendant genuinely believes he has the other's real consent to deal with the property he cannot be condemned as dishonest. Again, the reasonableness of his belief is irrelevant except in evidential terms.

(c) *Belief that property lost*

Lost property continues to belong to the owner therefore the finder of lost property is appropriating property belonging to another. However, if he genuinely (again, a subjective test) believes that the owner "*cannot* be discovered by taking reasonable steps", he is not to be condemned for deciding to keep the property. Obviously, factors such as the type and value of the property and the location where it was found will be important evidence in assessing the defendant's belief.

It should be noted that section 2(1)(c) relates to lost property which does still belong to someone else. It does not concern property which the defendant believes is abandoned. Of course, if property actually is abandoned, it does not belong to another and so the *actus reus* of theft will not be made out. However, what is the position if property is not abandoned but the defendant believes that it has been abandoned? As a matter of strict interpretation, because this situation is not covered by the exclusions in section 2, whether there is dishonesty should be determined as a matter of fact under the rules about to be examined.[54] However, in *Wood*[55] it was held as a *matter of law* that if the defendant genuinely believed that the property was abandoned there would be no dishonesty.

(d) *Willingness to pay*

Section 2(2) makes it clear that a willingness to pay will not necessarily exempt one from a finding of dishonesty. The owner might not wish to sell at whatever price, and it would be unthinkable to allow the unscrupulous to help themselves to other people's property and escape liability simply by being able to pay.

(e) *Not for thief's benefit*

Despite dishonesty being a moral concept, section 1(2) makes it clear that even though the theft is for the good of others, with the thief himself gaining nothing, he can still be found dishonest.[56]

## B. *Question of Fact*

Apart from the above specific instances, the concept of dishonesty was left undefined in the Theft Act 1968 although judges soon began to give the concept a legal meaning.[57] However, in 1973 the Court of Appeal embarked on a new course.

---

[54] Also, there could hardly be an intention permanently to deprive another of the property if the defendant believes it has been abandoned.

[55] [2002] EWCA Crim 832.

[56] The Criminal Law Revision Committee gave two more limited instances that section 1(2) was designed to meet, *viz.*, taking property that is either useless to the taker or which he intends to destroy (8th Report, *Theft and Related Offences* (1966) Cmnd.2977, p. 125).

[57] *Rao* [1972] Crim.L.R.451.

## R. v Feely [1973] 1 Q.B. 530 (Court of Appeal, Criminal Division)

The defendant was employed by a firm of bookmakers as manager of one of their branches. The employer sent round a circular to all managers stating that the practice of borrowing from tills was to stop. The defendant, knowing this, "borrowed" £30. When the deficiency was discovered (but not yet attributed to him) he immediately offered an IOU. He was owed more than twice that sum by his employers. The trial judge directed the jury that this was dishonest, and he was convicted of theft and appealed on the ground that this question should have been left to the jury.

Lawton L.J.:
"The design of the new Act is clear ... Words in everyday use have replaced legal jargon in many parts of the Act ...

In section 1(1) of the Theft Act 1968 the word 'dishonesty' can only relate to the state of mind of the person who does the act which amounts to appropriation. Whether an accused person has a particular state of mind is a question of fact which has to be decided by the jury ... We do not agree that judges should define what 'dishonesty' means.

This word is in common use ... Jurors, when deciding whether an appropriation was dishonest can be reasonably expected to, and should, apply the current standards of ordinary decent people. In their own lives they have to decide what is and what is not dishonest. We can see no reason why, when in a jury box, they should require the help of a judge to tell them what amounts to dishonesty."

**Appeal allowed**

It is for the jury (or magistrates) to determine whether the defendant has acted dishonestly by the standards of ordinary and decent people. To do this they must, of course, try to establish what was in the defendant's mind. For example, in *Price*[58] the defendant issued cheques, which were later dishonoured, claiming that he was the beneficiary of a £100,000 trust fund. The jury first has to decide whether they believe the defendant's story, that is, whether he genuinely believed he was such a beneficiary. Having established the defendant's state of mind, they must decide, applying their own moral standards,[59] whether it is dishonest.[60] In *Price* the jury disbelieved the defendant's story and decided he was dishonest. Thus, using the facts of *Feely*, the jury might find that the defendant did believe he could, and did intend to, repay the money. The jury, now armed with this knowledge, must make a moral assessment as to whether such conduct, in the circumstances, was dishonest.

But what of the defendant whose actions might be regarded as dishonest by the jury applying their standards but who insists (and is believed) that, according to *his* systems of values, he was acting honestly? For example, in *Gilks*[61] the defendant claimed that he thought he was honest in keeping money mistakenly paid to him by a bookmaker because he thought bookmakers were "a race apart" and thus fair game.

---

[58] [1990] Crim.L.R.200.

[59] It is a misdirection to use a witness reaction (for example, of shock) as the yardstick for measuring objective standards of dishonesty (*Green* [1992] Crim.L.R.292).

[60] The courts sometimes fall into error here. For example, in *Buzalek and Schiffer* [1991] Crim.L.R.130 the defendant admitted he had lied about certain payments. The court concluded for itself that he "was confessing to being dishonest". This was, in fact, a legal pronouncement and so inconsistent with *Feely*. Having ascertained he had lied, it should have been for the jury to establish whether he was dishonest. (The defendant claimed these were "white lies" which he believed were justified in the circumstances.)

[61] (1972) 56 Cr.App.R.734.

## R. v Ghosh [1982] Q.B. 1053 (Court of Appeal, Criminal Division)

The defendant was a consultant who acted as a locum at a hospital. He falsely claimed fees in respect of an operation that he had not carried out. He claimed that he thought he was not dishonest by his standards because the same amount of money was legitimately payable to him for consultation fees. The judge directed the jury that they must simply apply their own standards. He was convicted of an offence contrary to section 15 of the Theft Act 1968 (which uses the same concept "dishonesty") and appealed against his conviction.

Lord Lane C.J.:

"The sentence [in *Feely*] requiring the jury to apply current standards leads up to the prohibition on judges from applying *their* standards. That is the context in which the sentence appears. It seems to be reading too much into that sentence to treat it as authority for the view that 'dishonesty can be established independently of the knowledge or belief of the defendant'. If it could, then any reference to the state of mind of the defendant would be beside the point.

This brings us to the heart of the problem. Is 'dishonestly' in section 1 of the Theft Act 1968 intended to characterise a course of conduct? Or is it intended to describe a state of mind? If the former, then we can well understand that it could be established independently of the knowledge or belief of the accused. But if, as we think, it is the latter, then the knowledge and belief of the accused are at the root of the problem.

Take for example a man who comes from a country where public transport is free. On his first day here he travels on a bus. He gets off without paying. He never had any intention of paying. His mind is clearly honest; but his conduct, judged objectively by what he has done, is dishonest. It seems to us that in using the word 'dishonestly' in the Theft Act 1968, Parliament cannot have intended to catch dishonest conduct in that sense, that is to say conduct to which no moral obloquy could possibly attach. This is sufficiently established by the partial definition in section 2 of the Theft Act itself. All the matters covered by section 2(1) relate to the belief of the accused. Section 2(2) relates to his willingness to pay. A man's belief and his willingness to pay are things which can only be established subjectively. It is difficult to see how a partially subjective definition can be made to work in harness with the test which in all other respects is wholly objective.

If we are right that dishonesty is something in the mind of the accused (what Professor Glanville Williams calls 'a special mental state'), then if the mind of the accused is honest, it cannot be deemed dishonest merely because members of the jury would have regarded it as dishonest to embark on that course of conduct.

So we would reject the simple uncomplicated approach that the test is purely objective, however attractive from the practical point of view that solution may be.

There remains the objection that to adopt a subjective test is to abandon all standards but that of the accused himself, and to bring about a state of affairs in which 'Robin Hood would be no robber': *R. v Greenstein* [1975] 1 W.L.R. 1353. This objection misunderstands the nature of the subjective test. It is no defence for a man to say 'I knew that what I was doing is generally regarded as dishonest; but I do not regard it as dishonest myself. Therefore I am not guilty.' What he is however entitled to say is 'I did not know that anybody would regard what I was doing as dishonest.' He may not be believed; just as he may not be believed if he sets up 'a claim of right' under section 2(1) of the Theft Act 1968, or asserts that he believed in the truth of a misrepresentation under section 15 of the Act of 1968. But if he *is* believed, or raises a real doubt about the matter, the jury cannot be sure that he was dishonest.

In determining whether the prosecution has proved that the defendant was acting dishonestly, a jury must first of all decide whether according to the ordinary standards of reasonable and honest people what was done was dishonest. If it was not dishonest by those standards, that is the end of the matter and the prosecution fails.

If it was dishonest by those standards, then the jury must consider whether the defendant himself must have realised that what he was doing was by those standards dishonest. In most cases, where the actions are obviously dishonest by ordinary standards, there will be no doubt about it. It will be obvious that the defendant himself knew that he was acting dishonestly. It is dishonest for a defendant to act in a way which he knows ordinary people consider to be dishonest, even if he asserts or genuinely believes that he is morally justified in acting as he did. For example, Robin Hood or those ardent anti-vivisectionists who remove animals from vivisection laboratories are acting dishonestly, even though they may consider themselves to be morally justified in doing what they do, because they know that ordinary people would consider these actions to be dishonest."

**Appeal dismissed**

The enquiry is thus two-fold:

1. The jury, applying their own standards, must judge the defendant's actions and beliefs and decide whether he was honest or dishonest.
2. If the jury find that according to their standards he was dishonest, they must then establish whether the defendant knew that ordinary people would regard such conduct as dishonest.[62]

In *Roberts*[63] it was held that this second limb of the *Ghosh* direction need only be put to the jury in those cases where the defendant raised the special plea that he did not think he was being dishonest by his own standards.[64] This was confirmed in *Wood*: "the *Ghosh* direction ... is best left only for that kind of case where there is a dispute about whether ordinary people would have different views from a defendant as to whether what he was doing was honest or not."[65]

### Edward Griew, "Dishonesty: The Objections to Feely and Ghosh" [1985] Crim.L.R.341:

"The question tends to increase the number of trials. Whereas a different approach to the dishonesty issue might make it clear that given conduct was dishonest as a matter of law and therefore constituted an offence, the *Feely* question leaves the issue open. It may be worth a defendant's while to take his chance with the jury ... [B]efore *Feely* defendants might have felt constrained to plead guilty.

The question tends to complicate and lengthen contested cases ... [I]t may be in the interests of some defendants to extend and complicate trials in order to obfuscate the issue ...

The *Feely* question carries an unacceptable risk of inconsistency of decision ...

[It] implies the existence of a relevant community norm. In doing so it glosses over differences of age, class and cultural background ... It is simply naive to suppose ... that there is, in respect of the dishonesty question, any such single thing as 'the standards of ordinary decent folk ...'

[It is] unsuitable where the context of the case is a specialised one, involving intricate financial activities or dealings in a specialised market. It is neither reasonable nor rational to expect ordinary people to judge as 'dishonest' or 'not dishonest' conduct of which, for want of relevant experience, they cannot appreciate the contextual flavour ... [O]rdinary people (might) have no standards in relation to the conduct in question ...

A person may defend his attack on another's property by reference to a moral or political conviction so passionately held that he believed (so he claims) that 'ordinary decent'

---

[62] When utilising this two-fold test it must be put to the jury in this order (*Green* [1992] Crim.L.R.292).

[63] (1987) 84 Cr.App.R.117.

[64] It has been suggested (Halpin, "The Test for Dishonesty" [1996] Crim.L.R.283) that *Roberts* allows the second limb of the *Ghosh* direction to be withheld from the jury in cases of "obvious dishonesty" even if the defendant raises the possibility that he believed others would not regard his conduct as dishonest. This view is not reflected in the practice of the courts. See, for example, *Price* [1990] Crim.L.R.200; *Hyam* [1997] Crim.L.R.439; *Clarke* [1996] Crim.L.R.824.

[65] [2002] EWCA Crim 832.

members of society would regard his conduct as proper, even laudable. If the asserted belief is treated as a claim to have been ignorant that the conduct was 'dishonest' by ordinary standards ... and if the jury think (as exceptionally they might) that the belief may have been held, *Ghosh* produces an acquittal. The result is remarkable. Robin Hood must be a thief even if he thinks the whole of the right-thinking world is on his side.

A person reared or moving in an environment in which it is generally regarded as legitimate to take advantage of certain classes of people—perhaps bookmakers or employers—may plausibly claim that he did not realise that his conduct, of which a member of such a class was a victim, was generally regarded as dishonest. It is not acceptable that a claim of that sort should be capable even of being advanced."

## Glanville Williams, Textbook of Criminal Law (2nd ed., 1983), pp. 726–730:

"The practice of leaving the whole matter to the jury might be workable if our society were culturally homogeneous, with known and shared values, as it once very largely was. But the object of the law of theft is to protect property rights; and disrespect for these rights is now widespread. Since the jury are chosen at random, we have no reason to suppose that they will be any more honest and 'decent' in their standards than the average person ...

Evidence of the poor level of self-discipline now prevailing abounds—and this without taking any account of tax defaults. Observers agree upon a very large scale of theft: not merely shoplifting and fare bilking but stealing from employers by employees and an assortment of frauds perpetrated upon customers by employees. Great numbers of employed people of all classes believe, or affect to believe, that systematic dishonesty of various kinds is a 'perk'. It is tolerated by many employers, provided that it does not exceed some ill-defined limit; and some employers even encourage fiddles when they are at the expense of customers, since this is a way of increasing employees' remuneration without cost to the employers. For the employee, illicit remuneration has the advantage of being untaxed. Fiddling also brings non-material rewards: it is a pleasant departure from routine, a game of chance against the risk of detection, all the better since the consequences of detection are now rarely serious. So highly do some workers value the practice that a change in the system of work threatening to interfere with it, or an attempt by employers to prosecute offenders, is met by strikes. Notable examples were the strike at Heathrow Airport when baggage loaders were arrested for pilferage in 1973 ... If ordinary people in steady employment develop these lax notions about the right of property, it seems from the judgment in *Feely* that the law of theft is to be automatically adjusted to suit ...

[Commenting on *Gilks* Professor Williams continues] Subjectivism of this degree gives subjectivism a bad name. The subjective approach to criminal liability, properly understood, looks to the defendant's intention and to the facts as he believed them to be, not to his system of values ...

What must be found is a definition of dishonesty ... I would suggest that the definition should be that dishonesty involves a disregard for rights of property. Professor Smith's suggestion, however, is that a judicial definition of dishonesty might be ... : a person appropriates dishonestly 'where he knows that it will or may be detrimental to the interests of the other in a significant practical way'. ([1982] Crim.L.R. 609) We can at least be certain that almost any definition making the position independent of current social attitudes would be better than the rule in *Ghosh*."[66]

Williams assumes that because large numbers of employees "fiddle" from their employers, for example, that such employees have lost all standards of knowing right from wrong and therefore, being in a moral vacuum, would be unable to

---

[66] Further calls have been made for a comprehensive statutory definition of dishonesty: Glazebrook, "Revising the Theft Act" (1993) 52 C.L.J. 191; Halpin, "The Test for Dishonesty" [1996] Crim.L.R.283.

assess "dishonesty" if sitting in a jury box. But surely a plausible explanation is that most such employees know perfectly well their conduct is dishonest, but have chosen nevertheless to go ahead and do it. Such persons are perfectly capable of sitting on a jury and judging standards of dishonesty. And charges of hypocrisy will not do, otherwise any juror who had ever committed a (relevant) offence would have to be disqualified—an impossible task given the vast unknown figure of unrecorded property crime.

### Law Commission, Report No. 276, Fraud (2002), paras. s.9–s.10.

"5.9 There is some evidence that people's moral standards are surprisingly flexible. A MORI poll for the *Sunday Times* in October 1985 found that only 35% of those questioned thought it morally wrong to accept payment in cash in order to evade liability for tax. On the other hand, it does not follow that the other 65%, if sitting on a jury in a case of tax evasion where dishonesty was in issue, would necessarily have acquitted. Indeed, the proportion of those questioned who thought that such conduct was morally acceptable to most people was only 37%. This may suggest that people do not generally assume that their own moral standards are the norm. Indeed it indicates that a majority of respondents thought that their own moral standards fell below those of most others.
5.10 It seems, therefore, that the first stage of the *Ghosh* test may not necessarily result in the jury simply applying their own standards of honesty. It may, indeed, be quite natural for fact-finders to form a view of what reasonable, honest, people would consider dishonest, as distinct from their decision reflecting their own personal moral view."

The earlier Glanville Williams extract also challenges the view that the defendant's system of values are relevant in an assessment of culpability.

### C. M. V. Clarkson, Understanding Criminal Law (3rd ed., 2001), pp. 227–228:

"The courts were faced with a quandary here. Acceptance of such pleas [*viz.*, that the defendant did not think he was dishonest by his own standards] would undercut the moral imperative laid down by the criminal law. The criminal law largely reflects (and attempts to uphold) community values. The *Feely* test allows these community values to be enunciated by a so-called representative section of the community, namely, the jury. If the values of the jury and the community are to be ignored and replaced by the values of the defendant (who, for example, might endorse the political ideology that 'property is theft'), the result would be a complete absence of any objective standard. The door would be open to the 'Robin Hood defence'. The defendant would effectively become his own judge and jury.
On the other hand, the courts were reluctant to dismiss such pleas totally. The criminal law is based largely on the premise of moral responsibility. We blame those who are morally at fault. If a defendant openly rejects the value system inherent in the law of theft, he can be blamed even if, according to his own values, he thinks his actions are honest. He has knowingly 'declared war' on the values of society and can be blamed for doing this. It can never be an excuse in the criminal law that one does not agree with any given law. But what of the defendant who genuinely thinks he is acting honestly according to his values—*and* who really believes that most other people would agree with him as to the morality of his conduct—and can convince a jury of these beliefs? Such a defendant is not openly defying the law; he believes he is upholding the value system inherent in the law of theft. The case for exempting such a defendant from blame becomes strong.
This latter thinking was endorsed in the leading decision of *Ghosh* ...
The quest throughout the criminal law is for the isolation of the blameworthy. If the jury, reflecting community standards, can attach 'moral obloquy' to the defendant's actions and

are satisfied that the defendant knows he is acting contrary to the moral standards of ordinary people, a judgment of blameworthiness is truly appropriate. The test has tried to combine the need to preserve objective standards within the criminal law with the need to maintain the importance of moral fault."

Such thinking, allowing a context-dependent and individualised assessment of moral blameworthiness, was initially disapproved by the Law Commission.

### Law Commission Consultation Paper No. 155, Fraud and Deception (1999), para. 7.52:

"7.52 [W]e are not aware of any other area of criminal law which recognises an open-ended defence that the conduct in question is morally blameless. The general approach in English law is for elements of the offence to spell out the conduct it is sought to criminalise, and similarly to provide defences by specifying excusable forms of conduct which would otherwise be caught. There is no specific requirement of morally blameworthy conduct in the law of (for example) assaults, sexual offences, corruption or criminal damage ... [O]ffences are defined in such a way that conduct which satisfies their requirements (and does not fall within a recognised general defence) will *normally* be blameworthy; but the element of moral blame is incorporated in the definition of the conduct prohibited, not superimposed upon it. There is always the possibility that blameless conduct may occasionally be caught, but that possibility is dealt with via prosecutorial discretion and sentencing options. It is not clear why theft and deception should be thought unique in this respect."

However, in its subsequent Report, the Law Commission has partially resiled from this position.

### Law Commission, Report No. 276, Fraud (2002), paras. 5.5–5.8:

"5.5 It may be that moral elements such as dishonesty can only be defined with reference to the fact-finder's judgment. Richard Tur argues that 'what may constitute a just excuse is so context-dependent that exhaustive definition must necessarily limit the range of circumstances which might excuse' ("Dishonesty and the Jury" in Griffiths (ed.), *Philosophy and Practice* (1985), p. 75). Therefore, if an exhaustive definition of 'just excuse' or 'dishonesty' were incorporated into the law, there would inevitably be examples of behaviour which were legally dishonest, but which the fact-finders would characterise as morally blameless.

5.16 ... We have also concluded that it would not be possible to define dishonesty exhaustively ...

5.17 ... We have come to agree with the argument put forward by Richard Tur ...

5.18 The fact that *Ghosh* dishonesty leaves open a possibility of variance between cases with essentially similar facts is, in our judgment, a theoretical risk. Many years after its adoption, the *Ghosh* test remains, in practice, unproblematic. We also recognise the fact that the concept of dishonesty is now required in a very large number of criminal cases, so to reject it at this stage would have a far-reaching effect on the criminal justice system."

### 6. Intention of permanent deprivation

### Theft Act 1968, section 6

"(1) A person appropriating property belonging to another without meaning the other permanently to lose the thing itself is nevertheless to be regarded as having the intention of permanently depriving the other of it if his intention is to treat the thing as his own to dispose of regardless of the other's rights; and a borrowing or lending of it may amount to so treating it if, but only if, the borrowing or lending is for a period and in circumstances making it equivalent to an outright taking or disposal.

(2) Without prejudice to the generality of subsection (1) above, where a person, having possession or control (lawfully or not) of property belonging to another, parts with the property under a condition as to its return which he may not be able to perform, this (if done for purposes of his own and without the other's authority) amounts to treating the property as his own to dispose of regardless of the other's rights."

This is not a definition of "intention of permanent deprivation". Rather, it *extends* the natural meaning of the phrase and provides that in certain circumstances even though the defendant did not "mean" the other to lose the thing permanently he is "to be regarded" as having an intention of permanent deprivation. In *Lloyd*[67] it was made clear that section 6 should only be referred to in exceptional cases; for most purposes it would be unnecessary to go beyond section 1(1).[68]

Section 6(1) contains two limbs. The first refers to a defendant whose "intention is to treat the thing as his own to dispose of regardless of the other's rights". The second limb is a specific illustration of this in that certain borrowings "may amount to so treating it" as his own. Section 6(2) provides that the situation covered therein "amounts to treating the property as his own to dispose of regardless of the other's rights". This is thus just another specific illustration of the principle contained in the first limb of section 6(1).[69] Nevertheless, it is useful to look at the three situations separately.

## (a) Section 6(1)

[i] *if his intention is to treat the thing as his own to dispose of regardless of the other's rights:*

### R. v Coffey [1987] Crim.L.R.498 (Court of Appeal, Criminal Division)

The defendant obtained machinery from another with whom he was having a dispute. He decided to exert pressure on the victim by keeping the machinery as "ransom" until the victim gave in, at which point he would return the property. He appealed against conviction on the ground, *inter alia*, that the judge's direction did not accurately state the law as to intention.

Held,
"The culpability of the appellant's act depended upon the quality of the intended detention, considered in all its aspects, including in particular the appellant's own assessment at the time as to the likelihood of the victim coming to terms and of the time for which the machinery would have to be retained. The Court preferred this view.

[67] [1985] Q.B. 829.
[68] *Warner* (1970) 55 Cr.App.R.93; *Cocks* (1976) 63 Cr.App.R.79.
[69] *Fernandez* [1996] 1 Cr.App.R.175 at 188.

This was one of the rare cases where it was right for the judge to bring section 6(1) before the jury. The judge could usefully have illustrated the first part of section 6(1) by the expression 'equivalent to an outright taking or disposal'. If they thought that the appellant might have intended to return the goods even if the victim did not do what he wanted, they would not convict unless they were sure that he intended that the period of detention should be so long as to amount to an outright taking. Even if they did conclude that the appellant had in mind not to return the goods if the victim failed to do what he wanted, they would still have to consider whether the appellant had regarded the likelihood of this happening as being such that his intended conduct could be regarded as equivalent to an outright taking."

**Appeal allowed**

In *Cahill*[70] it was held that the words "to dispose of" mean more than "merely to use the thing as one's own"; they imply that the defendant must intend "to get rid of; to get done with; to ... sell" the goods. This was, however, doubted in *Lavender*[71] where a defendant removed doors from one council property undergoing repairs and used them to replace damaged doors at another council property. It was held that this was a "disposal" under section 6(1) because the defendant "intended to treat the doors as his own, regardless of the council's rights". The problem with this latter interpretation is that it renders section 6 redundant in that an intention to treat property as one's own is already a necessary requirement for an appropriation.

In *Marshall*[72] ticket touts obtained unexpired London Underground tickets and sold them to other potential customers. It was argued that there was no intention of permanent deprivation because the tickets would, in due course, be returned to the possession of London Underground. It was held, however, that the ticket touts had, under section 6(1), an intention to treat the tickets as their own to dispose of regardless of London Underground's rights.

[ii] *Borrowing or lending for a period and in circumstances making it equivalent to an outright taking or disposal:*

This makes it clear that certain borrowings are to be treated the same as outright takings. The classic example here is borrowing another's football season ticket and then returning the piece of paper at the end of the season after watching all the matches. At that stage the ticket has no value and is useless; the "virtue" has gone out of the thing.

### R. v Lloyd [1985] Q.B. 829 (Court of Appeal, Criminal Division)

Films were removed from a cinema for a few hours and "pirate" copies made of them; the originals were then returned. The defendant appealed against his conviction for conspiracy to steal.

[70] [1993] Crim.L.R.141.
[71] [1994] Crim.L.R.297.
[72] [1998] 2 Cr.App.R.282. See Smith, "Stealing Tickets" [1998] Crim.L.R.723. See also *D.P.P. v J* LTL, February 20, 2002, where it was held that an intention to render something useless demonstrated an intention of treating an article as one's own to dispose of.

Lord Lane C.J.:

"[T]he intention of the appellants could more accurately be described as an intention temporarily to deprive the owner of the film and was indeed the opposite of an intention permanently to deprive.

What then was the basis of the prosecution case and the basis of the judge's direction to the jury? It is said that section 6(1) of the Theft Act 1968 brings such actions as the appellants performed here within the provisions of section 1 ... [T]he first part of section 6(1) seems to us to be aimed at the sort of case where a defendant takes things and then offers them back to the owner for the owner to buy if he wishes. If the taker intends to return them to the owner only upon such payment, then, on the wording of section 6(1), that is deemed to amount to the necessary intention permanently to deprive: ...[73]

Borrowing is *ex hypothesi* not something which is done with an intention permanently to deprive. This half of the subsection, we believe, is intended to make it clear that a mere borrowing is never enough to constitute the necessary guilty mind unless the intention is to return the 'thing' in such a changed state that it can truly be said that all its goodness or virtue has gone: for example *R. v Beecham* (1851) 5 Cox C.C. 181, where the defendant stole railway tickets intending that they should be returned to the railway company in the usual way only after the journeys had been completed. He was convicted of larceny....

That being the case, we turn to inquire whether the feature films in this case can fall within that category. Our view is that they cannot. The goodness, the virtue, the practical value of the films to the owners has not gone out of the article. The film could still be projected to paying audiences....

Our view is that those particular films which were the subject of this alleged conspiracy had not themselves diminished in value at all. What had happened was that the borrowed film had been used or was going to be used to perpetrate a copyright swindle on the owners whereby their commercial interests were grossly and adversely affected in the way that we have endeavoured to describe at the outset of this judgment. That borrowing, it seems to us, was not for a period, or in such circumstances, as made it equivalent to an outright taking or disposal. There was still virtue in the film."

**Appeals allowed**

Difficult questions of fact will, of course, remain. In *Lloyd* Lord Lane spoke in terms of "all" the virtue or goodness being gone. This raises the problem of the football season ticket which is returned after it has been used for 19 matches, but is still valid for one final match. The ticket clearly has *some* value or virtue left. Presumably, questions such as these, were they to arise, would be left to the jury as questions of fact.

## (b) Section 6(2)

This is dealing with the situation of a person who takes unacceptable risks with the property of another. For example, he may pawn such property realising he may be unable to redeem it. In *Fernandez* a solicitor dishonestly made an insecure investment of a client's money. It was held that "section 6 may apply to a person in possession or control of another's property who, dishonestly and for his own purpose, deals with that property in such a manner that he knows he is risking its loss".[74] It is uncertain whether the defendant must himself realise that he may be unable to redeem the property or whether it suffices that he "may" objectively be so unable. Griew says: "The former view is doctrinally the purer; the latter is more

---

[73] In *Fernandez* [1996] 1 Cr.App.R. 175 at 188 it was stressed that section 6(1) is not limited in its application to these illustrations.

[74] [1996] 1 Cr.App.R.175 at 188.

readily suggested by the terms of the poorly-drafted section."[75] However, in *Fernandez* it was stated that the defendant must *know* he is risking the loss of the property.[76]

## Dishonest borrowings

Apart from these specific situations where section 6 has deemed dishonest borrowings to be the equivalent of permanent deprivation, the Theft Act 1968 has generally chosen not to punish dishonest borrowings. Why?

### Criminal Law Revision Committee, 8th Report, Theft and Related Offences (1966) Cmnd.2977, para. 56:

"[A]n intention to return the property, even after a long time makes the conduct essentially different from stealing. Apart from this ... [criminalising temporary deprivations] would be a considerable extension of the criminal law, which does not seem to be called for by any existing serious evil. It might moreover have undesirable social consequences. Quarrelling neighbours and families would be able to threaten one another with prosecution. Students and young people sharing accommodation who might be tempted to borrow one another's property in disregard of a prohibition by the owner would be in danger of acquiring a criminal record. Further, it would be difficult for the police to avoid being involved in wasteful and undesirable investigations into alleged offences which had no social importance."

### Glanville Williams, "Temporary Appropriation should be Theft" [1981] Crim.L.R.129, 131–132, 135:

"Suppose that a person removes a small piece of sculpture from a private exhibition, or a valuable book from a University library, and returns it after a year. During that time it has of course been lost to its owner; and both the owner and the police have been put to trouble ... The taker of the article may use it in such a way as to put it at risk, or he may make a profit from it, or he may return it in an impaired condition; and if he is a person of no substance the owner's civil remedy against him will be insufficient penalty ...

If a person has gone off with the property of another, and upon being apprehended and charged with theft swears that he meant to return it, is his statement to be accepted or not? To accept it too readily gives guilty defendants an easy line of escape; to reject it carries the risk of convicting people who are technically innocent, even though they are morally guilty because they have taken the article dishonestly ... Why should not the dishonest taking be sufficient to constitute the offence of theft, thus relieving the prosecution of a very difficult burden of proof? ...

When an article is unlawfully taken, even if only for a temporary purpose and without substantial risk of permanent loss of the article, the owner suffers an immediate loss, namely in respect of the use of it ... Sometimes the economic loss resulting from the loss of use of an article that is essential to an undertaking can be considerable.

One of the principal arguments for changing the law is that the value of articles lies in their use. More and more things are used by way of hiring ... Many articles of use have comparatively short useful 'lives'. In a few years they wear out or become unfashionable or technically obsolete ... Besides, the owner is in a dilemma of either being without the article for that time or putting himself to the expense of buying another—an expense that may turn out to have been unnecessary if the article is returned."

---

[75] *The Theft Acts* (7th ed., 1995), p. 66.
[76] This view is supported by Smith, *The Law of Theft* (8th ed., 1997), p. 82.

This reasoning was largely accepted by the Law Commission whose provisional view was that temporary deprivation of property is wrong in principle and so should be criminal.[77]

There are two well-known exceptions[78] to the intention of permanent deprivation rule (apart from the exceptions within section 6 itself). Section 11 creates the offence of removing articles from places open to the public, for example, removing works of art from museums or galleries albeit intending to return them at some time. Section 12 of the Theft Act 1968 creates the second exceptional offence of taking a motor vehicle or other conveyance without authority. This is designed to prevent "joyriding", where a car is taken and, after being driven around, abandoned. In such cases an intention of permanent deprivation would be difficult to establish.

It is interesting to contrast this last activity of joyriding with the conduct of a person who walks into a bookshop and dishonestly removes a book which he takes home and reads before returning it to the shop. It appears that the only reasons for the criminalisation of the former but not the latter activity are, first, the prevalence of joyriding[79] and secondly, the difficulty of proving the necessary intent with taking cars (with the book example, a finding of intention of permanent deprivation would be almost irresistible and thus a conviction for theft would result in fact).

It is worth pausing at this point for a little futher reflection, as perhaps some insight can here be gleaned into the real harm that is sought to be prevented by the crime of theft. When the book is dishonestly taken from the store, the store clearly suffers a harm. First, there is economic harm. The book is removed from their shelves, meaning it cannot be sold to another. The used book that is returned is not the same thing that was taken, which was a new book. The store sustains an economic loss of the difference in value between the new book and the secondhand book.[80] Secondly, there is all the non-economic harm associated with most thefts. The shop has had its rights of ownership assaulted. It has lost control of its property, lost the power to make choices and decisions about it. The identity of the borrower is probably unknown and, therefore, there can be no certainty as to when and if the property will be returned. For instance, the Criminal Law Revision Committee considered the striking example of someone who "borrowed" Goya's portrait of the Duke of Wellington from the National Gallery for four years.[81]

It is worth stressing at this stage that it is not necessary for a victim to lose his property permanently. What matters is that the defendant, at the time of the appropriation, *intends* that he shall lose it permanently. Thus the result may be the same as with cases of borrowing. In our example, the book is ultimately returned. It is the intention of the taker that distinguishes the cases. Why? Is this approach justifiable?

---

[77] Law Commission Consultation Paper No. 155, *Fraud and Deception* (1999), para. 19. While this proposal was made in relation to deception offences, the reasoning is equally applicable to theft.

[78] For further exceptions, see *e.g.* Post Office Act 1953, s.53, and see Williams, "Temporary Appropriation should be Theft" [1981] Crim.L.R.129 at 130.

[79] C.L.R.C., *above*, n.56. The offence was first created by s.28 of the Road Traffic Act 1930 "to deal with a mischief which had even then become common" (para. 82).

[80] Fletcher, *Rethinking Criminal Law* (1978), p. 48.

[81] *Above*, n.56.

## O. W. Holmes, The Common Law (1882), pp. 70–72:

"[In theft] acts are punished which of themselves would not be sufficient to accomplish the evil which the law seeks to prevent, and which are treated as equally criminal, whether the evil has been accomplished or not ...

In larceny the consequences immediately flowing from the act are generally exhausted with little or no harm to the owner. Goods are removed from his possession by trespass, and that is all, when the crime is complete. But they must be permanently kept from him before the harm is done which the law seeks to prevent. A momentary loss of possession is not what has been guarded against with such severe penalties. What the law means to prevent is the loss of it wholly and forever ...

The reason is plain enough. The law cannot wait until the property has been used up or destroyed in other hands than the owner's, or until the owner has died, in order to make sure that the harm which it seeks to prevent has been done ...

There must be an intent to deprive such owner of his ownership ... But why? ... The true answer is, that the intent is an index to the external event which probably would have happened, and that, if the law is to punish at all, it must, in this case, go on probabilities, not on accomplished facts. The analogy to the manner of dealing with attempts is plain. Theft may be called an attempt to permanently deprive a man of his property, which is punished with the same severity whether successful or not. If theft can rightly be considered in this way, intent must play the same part as in other attempts. An act which does not fully accomplish the prohibited result may be made wrongful by evidence that but for some interference it would have been followed by other acts co-ordinated with it to produce that result. This can only be shown by showing intent. In theft the intent to deprive the owner of his property establishes that the thief would have retained, or would not have taken steps to restore, the stolen goods."

The real harm in theft is, thus, that when a defendant intends permanent deprivation there is a greater risk to the victim that he will lose his property permanently. (In most cases he will, in fact, have already lost the property.) As with the law of attempt, the threat to the property amounts to a "second order harm". This, however, only explains why the actual loss of property need not occur—but still does not explain why there must be an intention of permanent deprivation as opposed to an intention to borrow dishonestly.

What is being punished is disapproved-of behaviour which poses an unacceptable risk to the property of another. It is fairly obvious that where there is an intention of permanent deprivation there is a greater risk of actual permanent deprivation occurring (for much the same reason that there is greater danger when a defendant is intending a consequence than when he is being reckless as to it: he is trying to achieve the objective and must, in general, stand more chance of success than if not so trying). So the question reduces itself to whether permanent deprivation is sufficiently "worse" than temporary deprivation to justify criminalisation of the former but not the latter. Most people would surely agree that, in general, a permanent loss is qualitatively worse than a temporary loss. The owner has been deprived completely and irrevocably of his property. Insurance, if obtainable, will not compensate for such loss of power and control over the property. Whether it is so *much* worse as to justify the criminalisation line being drawn between the two is uncertain. Perhaps, it is best at this stage to conclude that while a temporary loss caused by dishonest conduct is unfortunate and deserves moral condemnation, one should refrain from expanding the role of the criminal law without clear and strong reasons.

*Particular property*

There must be an intention permanently to deprive the other of the *particular* property alleged to be appropriated. It is no defence that similar property was to be returned. This rule is most often applied to coins and banknotes. It is clear law that if one "borrows" money, intending to repay it the next day, one is not intending to return the same notes or coins; one therefore does have an intention of permanently depriving the other of the particular property alleged to be stolen.[82] Of course, actual liability still depends on a finding of dishonesty which, in such cases, may be difficult to establish.

*Cheques*

There is a particular problem with cheques in that if a defendant wrongfully obtains and cashes another's cheque, that cheque will often ultimately be returned to that other and so the defendant could assert he had no intention of permanently depriving the other of that piece of paper.[83] In *Duru*[84] it was held that in such a case the defendant would have an intention of depriving the other permanently of the thing in action represented by the cheque. *Duru* was overruled by *Preddy*[85] on the ground that the thing in action (the defendant's right to sue the other on the cheque) was not property belonging to another and there would be no intention to deprive the drawer of the cheque form which will ultimately be returned to her.[86]

There are two ways of overcoming this problem. First, when the defendant presents the cheque to the bank he is appropriating the other's bank balance—a thing of action. In *Hilton*[87] it was held that the thing in action (the debt from the bank to the other person) in such cases has been wholly or partially destroyed. An intention to destroy the property of another amounts to an intention to permanently deprive the other of it. Secondly, with regard to the cheque itself, it has been argued that, when receiving the cheque, the defendant could be regarded as appropriating a piece of paper with special qualities in that it is effectively the key to the drawer's bank account.[88] When that piece of paper is returned to the other (or his bank) it will simply be a worthless piece of paper with all its virtue gone. The defendant therefore had an intention of permanently depriving the other of the piece of paper with special qualities. The problem with this analysis is that these "special qualities" are simply those that render the cheque a thing in action. As demonstrated by *Preddy*, this thing in action never belonged to another. However, Smith's analysis could be utilised in cases where the property is *deemed* to belong to another as in section 5(3). In such a case an intention that "the document should find its way back to the transferor only after all benefit to the transferor has been lost or removed as a result of its use in breach of such obligation"[89] can amount to an intention to deprive the other permanently of the cheque.

---

[82] *Williams* [1953] 1 Q.B. 660; *Velumyl* [1989] Crim.L.R.299.
[83] A similar argument was advanced in relation to London Underground tickets in *Marshall* [1998] 2 Cr.App.R.282.
[84] (1973) 58 Cr.App.R.151.
[85] [1996] A.C. 815.
[86] This was followed in *Clark* [2001] EWCA Crim. 884.
[87] [1997] 2 Cr.App.R.445, approving *Kohn* (1979) 69 Cr.App.R.395.
[88] Smith, "Obtaining Cheques by Deception or Theft" [1997] Crim.L.R.396.
[89] *Arnold* [1997] 4 All E.R. 1 at 15.

### III. Offences Involving Deception

### A. *The Sociological Background*

The terms "theft", "robbery", and "burglary" evoke immediate understanding in the hearer (even if that understanding is less than perfect); the same is less true of offences involving deception. The behaviour encompassed by this group of offences may, however, be just as devastating to the victim, or just as close to the fringes of criminality. It may be the classic con-man who tricks an elderly lady into parting with her valuable antique for vastly less than it is worth; it may be the individual passing bad cheques or falsely claiming social security; it may be the employee who abuses his position of trust to defraud his employers or it may be a company perpetrating a fraud against the public or the state. An increasing threat is perceived in the rise in the use of computers to commit crime. Large amounts of money may be stolen through "salami" methods, where by rounding up, or down, small amounts are diverted from accounts into the offender's account or, for example, by "trojan horse" methods where secret codes are hidden in somebody else's computer program.[90] Such offending may go on for years without detection and then only come to light through accident. To try to prevent or detect computer crime, companies may be told by security specialists to watch for staff living beyond their means, staff having drug or alcohol problems or staff being unwilling to take holidays, change jobs or be promoted.[91]

Certainly, such advice ties in with classic studies on embezzlement such as that by Cressey. He discovered that much embezzlement occurred in situations where a trusted person found himself with a financial problem which was non-shareable, but was in an occupation where his difficulties could be secretly resolved by violating his position of trust. The offender then felt able to rationalise and justify his behaviour to himself.[92]

The examples given should indicate two other features of offences involving deception: that the amount of money involved, as with theft, may vary from small to huge and it is inevitable that much of the offending will remain hidden and not appear in the official statistics. According to such statistics there is far less offending of this nature than there is of theft. In 2001/02, 51 per cent of recorded property crime was theft, handling stolen goods and "vehicle crime" (the majority of which was theft of or from a vehicle), while fraud and forgery, which includes all the deception offences, amounted to only seven per cent of property offences.[93]

Given the secretive nature of deception offences (the victim may never learn of the loss), reliable estimates about the level of offending are impossible to come by, although it would seem reasonable to conclude that more is left hidden than is the case with other property offences. But work has been done to estimate the financial losses involved in fraud. Levi's major study on fraud gathers together statistics from a variety of sources to conclude that "those data that are available show that in purely financial terms losses from fraud dwarf all other types of property

---

[90] Bequi, *Computer Crime* (1978); Levi, *Regulating Fraud* (1987), pp. 37–41.
[91] Doswell and Simons, *Fraud and Abuse of IT Systems* (1986).
[92] Cressey, *Other People's Money* (1953).
[93] Home Office Statistical Bulletin, *Crime in England and Wales 2001/02* (2002).

crime".[94] For instance, it has been estimated that fraud in the United Kingdom financial community results in losses of up to nearly £14 billion a year with fraud linked to plastic payment cards amounting to £135 million.[95] Benefits fraud amounts to £2 billion a year with Customs and Excise fraud totalling around £7 billion a year.[96]

Whilst more research is obviously necessary in this area, one thing is clear: it is fundamentally flawed to conceive of the "crime problem" in terms of traditional street activities; it does contain within it the stereo-typical working-class villain and his species of fraud, but it also contains the sophisticated frauds by "respectable", powerful members of society.

## B. *The Legal Background*

Whilst the protection of property by means of a law of theft (or larceny) has very early origins in the common law, the emergence of laws protecting those who parted with their property because of fraud or deceit was rather slower. The ruling spirit of "caveat emptor" made it inappropriate to use the criminal law in such instances. "[W]e are not to indict one for making a fool of another",[97] and similarly, "[It is] needless to provide severe laws for such mischiefs, against which common prudence and caution may be a sufficient security."[98]

Just as elsewhere in the law, however, the principle of "caveat emptor" was gradually eroded, so that by the time of the Theft Act 1968 distinct offences existed dependent upon the type of title obtained; if *ownership* passed by means of deception the offence was obtaining by false pretences. If the defendant gained *possession* only, the offence was larceny by a trick. Not only did this cause difficulties in distinguishing the two but there were other separate offences as well, such as larceny by a servant, fraudulent conversion and embezzlement.

All of these were swept away by the reforms of 1968.

### Criminal Law Revision Committee, Theft and Related Offences, Eighth Report (1966) Cmnd.2977, para. 38:

"The sub-committee for a considerable time proposed that the general offence of theft should be made to cover the present offence of obtaining by false pretences under [the Larceny Act] 1916, s.32(1). It might seem appropriate to extend theft in this way in order to make it cover as many ways as possible of getting property dishonestly. But in the end the sub-committee gave up the idea (to the regret of some members), and the full committee agreed. In spite of its attractions, it seemed to the majority of the committee that the scheme would be unsatisfactory. Obtaining by false pretences is ordinarily thought of as different from theft, because in the former the owner in fact consents to part with his ownership; a bogus beggar is regarded as a rogue but not as a thief, and so are his less petty counterparts. To create a new offence of theft to include conduct which ordinary people would find difficult to regard as theft would be a mistake. The unnaturalness of including obtaining by false pretences in theft is emphasised by the difficulty of drafting a satisfactory definition to cover both kinds of conduct."

---

[94] Levi, *Regulating Fraud* (1987), p. 23.
[95] Home Office, *Information on the Criminal Justice System in England and Wales: Digest 4*, (1999).
[96] Home Office Research Bulletin, *Crime in England and Wales: Quarterly Update* (2003).
[97] *Per* Holt C.J. in *Jones* (1703) 91 Eng.Rep. 330.
[98] Hawkins, *Pleas of the Crown* 344 (6th ed. 1788).

Under the Theft Acts 1968 and 1978 there are now eight offences of dishonestly obtaining something by deception:

1. obtaining property[99]
2. obtaining a money transfer[1]
3. obtaining a pecuniary advantage[2]
4. procuring the execution of a valuable security[3]
5. obtaining services[4]
6. securing the remission of liability[5]
7. inducing a creditor to wait for or to forgo payment[6]
8. obtaining an exemption from, or an abatement of, a liability.[7]

From a starting point of not being regarded as warranting criminal status, it now seems that cases involving deception may well be regarded more seriously by the courts than those involving theft (perhaps because of the element of rational execution or betrayal of trust), although not as seriously as robbery or burglary. Section 15, for example, bears a higher maximum penalty than theft, *i.e.* 10 years rather than 7 years.[8] However, in practice, the sentencing patterns for this offence are largely comparable with those for theft. Both are broad offences. Large-scale commercial frauds attract the heaviest custodial sentences while, usually, non-custodial sentences will be imposed for the activities of the "con man", but even for the latter custodial sentences are likely when there has been a deception of the vulnerable, such as the elderly.[9] Generalisations are, however, difficult to draw in this area: the sentencing task is more than ordinarily complicated. The problem has been described as paradoxically having to sentence *offences* of high gravity but *offenders* of low "essential" badness and light prior records.[10]

This problem consists of two main factors, the first of which is the strong positive relationship between the scale of the offence and the status of the offender[11] and, secondly, there is the issue of public attitudes towards "white-collar" offences. Accepted wisdom suggests ignorance of, and indifference to, "white-collar" crime on the part of the public. However, more recent studies suggest that the picture is rather more complex than that. Not only does it depend on the sector of the "public" to which one addresses enquiries (top executives, for example, rating fraud more seriously and police rating it less seriously than the "public") but upon the type and amount of harm caused. For example, in one survey members of the public rated fraud offences involving, respectively, sums of £1,000 and £2,000

---

[99] Theft Act 1968, s.15.
[1] Theft Act 1968, s.16A, inserted by Theft (Amendment) Act 1996.
[2] Theft Act 1968, s.16.
[3] Theft Act 1968, s.20(2).
[4] Theft Act 1978, s.1.
[5] Theft Act 1978, s.2(1)(a).
[6] Theft Act 1978, s.2(1)(b).
[7] Theft Act 1978, s.2(1)(c).
[8] Until 1991 both bore the same maximum of 10 years. It is probably unwise, however, to infer too much from the fact that the maximum for theft was reduced but the maximum for s.15 was not.
[9] See, generally, Wasik, *Emmins on Sentencing* (4th ed., 2001), pp. 337–338.
[10] Levi, p. 234. See also *Barrick* (1985) 7 Cr.App.R.(S.) 142 and *Aspin* (1987) 9 Cr.App.R.(S.) 288 and *Aragon* (1995) 16 Cr.App.R.(S) 930 as examples of this.
[11] Wheeler and Rothman, "The Organisation as Weapon in White-Collar Crime" (1982) 80 Mich.L.R. 1403.

more seriously than a domestic burglary in which £20 was taken. Members of the public also distinguished between, for example, income tax frauds and social security frauds, more people regarding the latter as more morally wrong than the former.[12]

Surveys such as these suggest an intolerance towards commercial fraud at the very least; further, those frauds that result in *physical* harm will be regarded very seriously indeed.[13] Public opinion can, of course, be ignored or heeded as suits the interests of the user, but generally it ought to play a part in the formulation of sentences. To that extent it would appear that sentencing patterns do broadly reflect the views of the public, although it may be that too much credit is given to the previous good character of the defendant for the public's liking.

## C. *The Law*

It is not proposed to deal with all the offences involving deception in great detail. Instead, we shall concentrate on the three elements common to these offences as this should illustrate the principles that have emerged in this area of law.[14] This will be followed by a brief sketch of a few of the main deception offences.

### 1. Common elements

There are certain elements shared by most of these offences:

  (i) There must be a deception.
 (ii) The deception must cause the prohibited result.
(iii) There must be dishonesty on the part of the defendant.

#### (i) *Deception*

#### Theft Act 1968, section 15(4)

"For purposes of this section 'deception' means any deception (whether deliberate or reckless) by words or conduct as to fact or as to law, including a deception as to the present intentions of the person using the deception or any other person."[15]

#### A. T. H. Smith, "The Idea of Criminal Deception" [1982] Crim.L.R.721 at 722–723:

"Deception could have been explained by the legislators in the Theft Act, but it was not. The Act confines itself to the somewhat unhelpful observation that ' "deception" means any deception', the remainder of the section being devoted to reversing certain of the old common law rules surrounding the former 'false pretences'. To some extent this left the courts free to apply their own gloss to the word as the need to do so arose. But 'deception' already had, by the time the Theft Act became law in 1968, acquired a reasonably settled

---

[12] Levi, pp. 57–75 and 136–144.
[13] *cf.* Schrager and Short, "How Serious a Crime?" in Geis and Stotland (eds). *White-Collar Crime* (1980).
[14] For a fuller discussion see the specialist texts: Smith, *The Law of Theft* (8th ed., 1997); Griew, *The Theft Acts 1968 and 1978* (7th ed., 1995) and Smith (A.T.H.), *Property Offences* (1994).
[15] ss.16(3) Theft Act 1968 and 5(1) Theft Act 1978 import the same meaning into the other offences.

meaning, classically that stated by Buckley J. in *Re London and Globe Finance Corporation* ([1903] 1 Ch. 728 at p. 732) 'to deceive is, I apprehend, to induce a man to believe that a thing is true which is false … to deceive is by falsehood to induce a state of mind'. The Criminal Law Revision Committee explained its use of 'deception' by saying:

> 'The substitution of "deception" for "false pretence" is chiefly a matter of language. The word "deception" seems to us (as to the framers of the American Law Institute's Model Penal Code) to have the advantage of directing attention to the effect that the offender deliberately produced on the mind of the person deceived, whereas "false pretence" makes one think of what exactly the offender did in order to deceive. "Deception" seems also more apt in relation to deception by conduct.' (8th Report, Cmnd.2977, para. 187).

This reinforces the suggestion in Buckley J.'s definition that it is essential that the representation must operate on the conscious mind of the victim and cause him to believe that the facts are otherwise than they really are."

The essence of a deception is two-fold: first, the defendant must make an untrue representation, and second, as a result of this, the victim must believe that the untrue representation is true. These are questions of fact for the jury.[16]

Section 15(4) specifies the circumstances and/or conditions in which the untrue representation must be made:

(a) words.

This is generally the most obvious way of practising a deception—for example, telling a victim one is selling a diamond when it is, in fact, glass.

(b) conduct.

Difficulties are raised here in that it is necessary to determine what may be implied by the conduct of the defendant. The following are important instances of such implied representations.[17]

[i] hotels

If one books into a hotel one is taken to be representing that one intends to pay the bill at the end of one's stay.[18]

[ii] restaurants

Ordering and eating a meal in a restaurant is a representation that one intends to pay for that meal. If during or after the meal one decides not to pay, then remaining at the table thereafter is a false representation that one still intends to pay.[19]

[iii] quotations

### R. v Silverman (1988) 86 Cr.App.R.213 (Court of Appeal, Criminal Division)

The appellant charged two elderly sisters grossly excessive prices for work done to the central heating and wiring of their flat. They had trusted him to charge a fair price because of previous work done by him for their family. The appellant placed no pressure on them to accept his quotation and there was nothing wrong with the work done. He was charged and convicted under section 15. He appealed on the grounds, *inter alia*, that an excessively high quotation did not amount to a false representation and that the trial judge had erred in not putting his defence (that the sisters seemed happy with his work) to the jury in express terms.

---

[16] See, *e.g. Adams* [1993] Crim.L.R.525 and commentary thereto.
[17] See further, Smith (A.T.H.), *Property Offences* (1994), pp. 472–480.
[18] *Harris* (1975) 62 Cr.App.R.28.
[19] *D.P.P. v Ray* [1974] A.C. 370.

Watkins L.J.:

"Mr Hopmeier, who appears here for the appellant, has argued, first, that the appellant made no representations to the complainants. He has not shrunk from conceding that the appellant was dishonest. He has submitted that the appellant quoted the sisters for the work to be done but that it was open to them either to accept or reject the quotation upon such advice as they might seek and perhaps in the light of tenders by others, and that the appellant was in much the same position as anyone else who is asked to quote for work to be done. He has argued that it is a dangerous concept to introduce into the criminal law that an excessively high quotation amounts to a false representation under section 15(1) of the Theft Act 1968. In certain circumstances that submission may we think be well founded. But whether a quotation amounts to false representation must depend upon the circumstances.

It seems clear to us that the complainants, far from being worldly wise, were unquestionably gullible. Having left their former home, they relied implicitly upon the word of the appellant about their requirements in their maisonette. In such circumstances of mutual trust, one party depending upon the other for fair and reasonable conduct, the criminal law may apply if one party takes dishonest advantage of the other by representing as a fair charge that which he but not the other knows is dishonestly excessive. ...

There was material for a finding that there had been a false representation although it is true that the appellant had said nothing at the time he made his representations to encourage the sisters to accept the quotations. He applied no pressure upon them, and apart from mentioning the actual prices to be charged was silent as to other matters that may have arisen for question in their minds.

On the matter of representation we have been referred to *D.P.P. v Ray* [1974] A.C. 370, which concerned someone leaving a restaurant without paying for a meal. At p. 379 Lord Reid said: 'So the accused, after he changed his mind, must have done something intended to induce the waiter to believe that he still intended to pay before he left. Deception, to my mind, implies something positive.'

Mr Hopmeier submits that nothing positive was done in this case. Lord Reid continued (*ibid.*): 'It is quite true that a man intending to deceive can build up a situation in which his silence is as eloquent as an express statement.'

Here the situation has been built up over a long period of time. It was a situation of mutual trust and the appellant's silence on any matter other than the sums to be charged were, we think, as eloquent as if he had said: 'What is more, I can say to you that we are going to get no more than a modest profit out of this.'

There is, we think, no foundation for the criticism of the judge in the first ground of appeal nor any substance in this ground in law ...' [However, it was decided that the judge should have included D's defence 'worthless though it might have been in the minds of the jury' in the summing up]."

**Appeal allowed**

The implications of this decision are immense. In a free market economy it is regarded as acceptable to maximise one's profits—in short, to make as big a profit as possible. Those making grossly inflated quotations had, in the past, only to contend with the risk of their quotation being rejected. Now the risk of criminal prosecution is a possibility. Again, we are dealing with dubious business practice being criminalised. Rather than continually extending the reaches of the criminal law, it would surely be better here for the victim to resort to civil remedies.

To prevent any such expansion of the law it is important to stress two features of the above decision that would need to be satisfied in any case before an inflated quotation could give rise to liability. First, there was the rather special circumstance of a relationship of mutual trust that had been built up over a long time. Such special circumstances will seldom exist. Second, for all the deception offences it is necessary to prove dishonesty. It is highly unlikely that any jury would convict in cases of excessive quotations unless there were some very special circumstances as in *Silverman*.

[iv] Cheques

Handing over a signed cheque is an implied representation that when the cheque is presented to the bank it will be honoured.[20]

[v] Cheque cards

The nature of the representation changes when one uses a cheque card to support a cheque. This is because the cheque is bound to be honoured by the bank if certain conditions have been fulfilled and, therefore, the representation made with respect to the cheque is in fact true.

The representation thus is not about the cheque but about the cheque card itself. Issuing a cheque supported by a cheque card is an implied representation by conduct that one has actual authority from the bank to use the card and to contract on behalf of the bank that it will honour the cheque. If this representation is untrue (because, say, the bank has withdrawn its authority) it becomes a deception.[21]

[vi] Credit cards

Acceptance of a credit card gives rise to a contract between the acceptor and the credit card company under which the latter must honour the relevant voucher on presentation. Use of a credit card is thus an implied representation that one has actual authority from the credit card company:

1. to use the card to make contracts on behalf of that company, and
2. to bind the credit card company to honour the relevant voucher on presentation.

If these representations are untrue, then use of the credit card amounts to a deception.

[vii] Silence

What is the law's response where there is no "conduct" at all? What if, for example, the defendant silently acquiesces in the self-deception of another? Here there is nothing to which the intent of the defendant to profit by the misapprehension of another can be attached; he has produced no change of mind in another and there can be no liability.[22]

[viii] Change of circumstances

The rule that silence is no deception is a limited one. If a representation, which was true when made, becomes untrue, the failure to reveal the change of circumstances can amount to a deception. In *D.P.P. v Ray*[23] the defendant ordered a meal in a restaurant with the intention of paying for it. He subsequently formed an intention not to pay. It was held that by remaining at the table, without notifying

[20] *M.P.C. v Charles* [1977] A.C. 177 at 182. In *Hamilton* (1991) 92 Cr.App.R.54 it was held that presenting a signed withdrawal slip at the bank is a representation that the bank is indebted to the person to that amount.
[21] *ibid.*
[22] See further, Smith, *The Law of Theft*, p. 101 and Smith (A.T.H.), "The Idea of Criminal Deception" [1982] Crim.L.R.721 at 729–731.
[23] [1974] A.C. 370.

the waiter of his changed intention, he was practising a deception that he still intended to pay. In *Rai*[24] the defendant applied for a council grant for a bathroom for his elderly mother. Before the work was done, his mother died. It was held that his failure to inform the council of the change of circumstances amounted to a deception.

It is interesting to compare the behaviour in all these cases with that required for theft. We saw earlier that the paradigmatic case of theft involves actions which are objectively inconsistent with the rights of the owner and thus accords with Fletcher's theory of manifest criminality.[25] Deception offences, on the other hand, are more indicative of a theory of subjective liability: the actions of the defendant have to look innocent in order to deceive, but his state of mind renders them criminal.[26] However, as a result of the case of *Gomez* this distinction is all but lost. Cases that have all the hallmarks of deception offences may now be charged as theft under section 1. This overlap raises the question whether the deception offences are redundant. It hardly seems likely to have been Parliament's intention that they should have no role to play, and, indeed, such offences now have a higher maximum penalty than theft. One suggestion is that we should regard obtaining by deception as an aggravated form of theft in much the same way as robbery, the aggravating feature being "a feeling of intellectual vulnerability".[27] If this translates into a fear of being made a fool of or a distrust in one's own judgment, it is hard to see why this particular feature should be singled out. After all, the employer who takes into his employ somebody who subsequently steals from him might feel similarly threatened but may not be able to point to any relevant deception. As stated earlier, it is unfortunate that the House of Lords in *Gomez* has chosen to go down this route.

(c) Deception as to fact or law or present intentions.

Section 15(4) refers to a deception as to fact or law and states that this includes deceptions as to present intentions. This latter inclusion must be right: the implied representation of the restaurant customer that she intends to pay is just as much a fact as the "fact" that she has sufficient money to pay. The Act is, however, silent as to whether statements of opinion are capable of being deceptions although they were not under the pre-1968 law.[28] Given that there are difficulties distinguishing fact from opinion, and given that mere advertising puffs would be excluded by potential victims not being fooled by them, there seems to be some force to the argument that opinions ought to be included. "[D]eliberate mis-statements of opinion would today be generally condemned as dishonest, no less dishonest, indeed, than mis-statements of other facts—for whether an opinion is held or not is a fact."[29] Moreover, such an inclusion would be in line with the subjectivist pattern of liability discernible elsewhere in deception offences.

---

[24] [2000] 1 Cr.App.R.242.
[25] *Above*, p. 752.
[26] Fletcher *Rethinking Criminal Law* (1978), p. 118.
[27] Gardiner, "Appropriation in Theft: The Last Word?" (1993) 109 L.Q.R. 194 at 198.
[28] Larceny Act 1916. See *Bryan* (1857) Deers & B. 265.
[29] Smith, *The Law of Theft* (8th ed., 1997), p. 108.

**(d) Deliberate or reckless.**

Section 15(4) requires the deception to be "deliberate or reckless". A deception will be deliberate where the defendant is aware of the falsity of the statement and knows that the victim will (or may) believe in its truth. Recklessness here bears its subjective *Cunningham* meaning: the defendant must have adverted to the possibility of the representation being false and have gone ahead and taken the risk.[30] The additional requirement of dishonesty dictates such a result; the defendant who does not realise the possibility of his representation being false cannot be described as dishonest.[31]

**Deceiving machines**

The essence of a deception is that the other person must believe the representation is true and act on that belief. A machine has no mind and so cannot be deceived. The scale of this problem in the past was limited to the sort of case where foreign coins were inserted into vending machines. Now, however, with the greatly increased use of internet service providers and automated call centres, this problem has become acute. Under the present law, using credit card details to pay for goods purchased over the internet does not amount to a deception offence (although it could be theft). Efforts to plug this gap will be considered later in this chapter.

**(ii) *The deception must cause the prohibited result***

The deception must be operative, that is, it has to be established that the representation deceived the victim, for example, into providing a meal or a hotel room or accepting a cheque. Logically, therefore the deception must precede the obtaining.[32] If the victim does not rely on the representation for whatever reason (say, for example, he is aware of its falsity),[33] the offence has not been committed. It may, of course, be possible to charge the defendant with attempting to obtain by deception.

### D.P.P. v Ray [1974] A.C. 370 (House of Lords)

The defendant and four other young men went to a Chinese restaurant for a meal, intending at that stage to pay for it. After eating the meal they decided not to pay but only left when the waiter left the room. The defendant's conviction under s.16(2)(a) Theft Act 1968 (now repealed) was quashed by the Divisional Court for lack of deception. The prosecution appealed to the House of Lords.

Lord Morris of Borth-y-Gest:
"In the present case it is found as a fact that when the respondent ordered his meal he believed that he would be able to pay. One of his companions had agreed to lend him money.

---

[30] Smith (A.T.H.), *Property Offences* (1994), pp. 508–509, states that an objective meaning would be "out of accord" with the spirit of the Theft Act, which emphasises the mental state.

[31] See *Large v Mainprize* [1989] Crim.L.R.213; *Goldman* [1997] Crim.L.R.894.

[32] See, *e.g. Coady* [1996] Crim.L.R.518.

[33] See *e.g. Miller* [1992] Crim.L.R.744. In this case the defendant taxi-driver charged his customer 10 times the correct fare for a trip from Heathrow to Gatwick. On the journey the customer realised that the defendant had been lying but felt compelled to pay the extortionate sum. The court looked at the whole of the incident rather than the point at which payment was made to find a causal link between the deception and the payment. In his commentary, Smith is, rightly, doubtful about the validity of this (pp. 745–746).

He therefore intended to pay. So far as the waiter was concerned the original implied representation made to him by the respondent must have been a continuing representation so long as he (the respondent) remained in the restaurant. There was nothing to alter the representation. ... But the moment came when the respondent decided and therefore knew that he was not going to pay: but he also knew that the waiter still thought that he was going to pay ... [C]ontinuing in the same role and behaving just as before he was representing that his previous intention continued. That was a deception because his intention, unknown to the waiter, had become quite otherwise. The dishonest change of intention was not likely to produce the result that the waiter would be told of it. The essence of the deception was that the waiter should not know of it or be given any sort of clue that it (the change of intention) had come about. Had the waiter suspected that by a change of intention a secret exodus was being planned, it is obvious that he would have taken action to prevent its being achieved. ...

The final question which arises is whether, if there was deception and if there was pecuniary advantage, it was by the deception that the respondent obtained the pecuniary advantage. In my view, this must be a question of fact and the magistrates have found that it was by his deception that the respondent dishonestly evaded payment. It would seem to be clear that if the waiter had thought that if he left the restaurant to go to the kitchen the respondent would at once run out, he (the waiter) would not have left the restaurant and would have taken suitable action. The waiter proceeded on the basis that the implied representation made to him (*i.e.* of an honest intention to pay) was effective. The waiter was caused to refrain from taking certain courses of action which but for the representation he would have taken. In my view, the respondent during the whole time that he was in the restaurant made and by his continuing conduct continued to make a representation of his intention to pay before leaving. When in place of his original intention he substituted the dishonest intention of running away as soon as the waiter's back was turned, he was continuing to lead the waiter to believe that he intended to pay. He practised a deception on the waiter and by so doing he obtained for himself the pecuniary advantage of evading his obligation to pay before leaving. That he did so dishonestly was found by the magistrates who, in my opinion, rightly convicted him.

I would allow the appeal."

Appeal allowed[34]

### R. v Laverty [1970] 3 All E.R. 432 (Court of Appeal, Criminal Division)

(The facts appear from the judgment)

Lord Parker C.J.:

"[T]he appellant was convicted of obtaining property by deception, the property being £65 in cash and a cheque for £165, and was sentenced to six months' imprisonment suspended for two years. He now appeals against his conviction.

The facts are in a very short compass. The car bearing number plates DUV 111C, a Hillman Imp, was bought by a Mr Bedborough from the appellant, and a cheque was given as part of the price. In fact that car bearing those number plates was a car originally bearing number plates JPA 945C which had been stolen. According to the appellant when he got the car, and there was no question of his having stolen it, it was in a bad condition, he repaired it and he put on to it the chassis and rear number plates of DUV 111C, those plates having been obtained from another source relating of course to another car.

The charge made in the indictment in count 3 took the form of alleging a false representation which here was by conduct. It was not a false representation that the appellant was the owner and had a good title to sell but the false representation was by purporting that a Hillman Imp motor car which the appellant sold to Roy Clinton Bedborough was the original Hillman Imp motor car, index number DUV 111C.

---

[34] Lord Reid dissented on the basis that dishonest evasion of an obligation to pay was not a deception and that there was no evidence that the waiter had been deceived. See *below*, p. 835 for s.3 of the Theft Act 1978 which would now apply in such situations.

... [I]t was conceded in this court that there was a representation by conduct that the car being sold to Mr Bedborough was the original Hillman Imp to which the chassis plate and rear plate which it bore had been assigned. It is conceded that such a representation was made by conduct; it is clear that that was false, and false to the knowledge of the appellant. The sole question was whether this false representation operated on Mr Bedborough's mind so as to cause him to hand over this cheque.

As sometimes happens, in this case Mr Bedborough did not give the answers which were helpful to the prosecution, and no leading questions could be put. The nearest answer was 'I bought this because I thought the appellant was the owner'. In other words Mr Bedborough was saying: 'What induced me to part with my money was the representation by conduct that the appellant had a title to sell. ...'

The proper way of proving these matters is through the mouth of the person to whom the false representation is conveyed, and further it seems to the court in the present case that no jury could say that the only inference here was that Mr Bedborough parted with his money by reason of this false representation. Mr Bedborough may well have been of the mind as he stated he was, namely that what operated on his mind was the belief that the appellant was the owner. Provided the appellant was the owner it may well be that Mr Bedborough did not mind that the car did not bear its original number plates. At any rate as it seems to the court it cannot be said that the only possible inference here is that it actuated on Mr Bedborough's mind.

In those circumstances, although with some reluctance, this court feels that the proper course here is to allow the appeal and quash the conviction."

**Appeal allowed. Conviction quashed**

### R. v King (1987) 84 Cr.App.R.357 (Court of Appeal, Criminal Division)

The appellants went to the house of a 68-year-old widow, falsely representing themselves as from a firm of tree surgeons, of whom she had heard. They purported to examine the trees in her garden and told her that four trees needed to be removed urgently to prevent damage to a gas main and the house foundations. They offered to do it if paid £470 in cash. Before being paid, the police were informed and the appellants were arrested and charged with attempting to obtain property by deception contrary to section 1(1) of the Criminal Attempts Act 1981. They were convicted and appealed on the ground that their conduct would not have constituted the criminal offence of obtaining property by deception because as a matter of causation, the relevant property would have been obtained by reason of the work carried out (the felling of the trees) rather than by reason of any deception.

Neill L.J.:

"[W]e have come to the conclusion that on the facts of the present case the argument is fallacious.

In our view, the question in each case is: was the deception an operative cause of the obtaining of the property? This question falls to be answered as a question of fact by the jury applying their commonsense. ...

In the present case there was, in our judgment, ample evidence upon which the jury could come to the conclusion that had the attempt succeeded the money would have been paid over by the victim as a result of the lies told to her by the appellants. ...

For the reasons which we have set out, we consider that the appellants were rightly convicted in this case, and the appeals must therefore be dismissed."[35]

**Appeals dismissed**

---

[35] The law of remoteness applies to criminal deception just as is applies in civil law. Here the court decided that the causal connection was not too remote. *Contra, Clucas* [1949] 2 K.B. 226. In this case, decided under the old law of false pretences (similar in relation to remoteness), the defendant induced a book-maker to accept bets on credit by falsely representing that the bets came from a number of persons. When the bet was successful, it was held that the winnings had not been obtained by the false pretences but by the horse winning the race; *cf. Levene v Pearcey* [1976] Crim.L.R.63.

The decision of *Ray* lies somewhere between *Laverty* (where it would have been improper for causal inferences to be drawn) and *King* (where any other inference would have been absurd). Whilst it is true that the waiter in *Ray* would not have left the room had he known of the defendant's change of mind, it does not automatically follow that he left the room *because* of the defendant's continuing representation. Not having the evidence of the crucial witness—the waiter, himself—the majority still felt, however, that there was enough evidence to enable the justices to have inferred the causal link. This rather cavalier approach to the question of causation has been taken much further in other cases.

### R. v Lambie [1982] A.C. 449 (House of Lords)

The defendant purchased goods using a credit card for payment. She had grossly exceeded her credit limit and knew that the bank was trying to recover the card. The shop manager checked her signature, the date on the card and that it was not on the current stop list. She was charged with obtaining a pecuniary advantage by deception, contrary to section 16(1) of the Theft Act 1968, (now repealed) in that she dishonestly obtained for herself the evasion of a debt for which she then made herself liable by deception, namely by false representations that she was authorised to use a credit card to obtain goods. She was convicted, but the Court of Appeal (Criminal Division) allowed her appeal against conviction.

Lord Roskill:
"My Lords, as the appellant says ... the Court of Appeal (Criminal Division) laid too much emphasis upon the undoubted, but to my mind irrelevant, fact that Miss Rounding said she made no assumption about the respondent's credit standing with the bank. They reasoned from the absence of assumption that there was no evidence from which the jury could conclude that she was 'induced by a false representation that the defendant's credit standing at the bank gave her authority to use the card'. But, my Lords, with profound respect to the learned Lord Justice, that is not the relevant question. Following the decision of this House in *R. v Charles* ([1977] A.C. 177) it is in my view clear that the representation arising from the presentation of a credit card has nothing to do with the respondent's credit standing at the bank but is a representation of actual authority to make the contract with, in this case, Mothercare on the bank's behalf that the bank will honour the voucher upon presentation. Upon that view, the existence and terms of the agreement between the bank and Mothercare are irrelevant, as is the fact that Mothercare, because of that agreement, would look to the bank for payment. That being the representation to be implied from the respondent's actions and use of the credit card, the only remaining question is whether Miss Rounding was induced by that representation to complete the transaction and allow the respondent to take away the goods. My Lords, if she had been asked whether, had she known the respondent was acting dishonestly and, in truth, had no authority whatever from the bank to use the credit card in this way, she (Miss Rounding) would have completed the transaction, only one answer is possible—no. Had an affirmative answer been given to this question, Miss Rounding would, of course, have become a participant in furtherance of the respondent's fraud and a conspirator with her to defraud both Mothercare and the bank. Leading counsel for the respondent was ultimately constrained, rightly as I think, to admit that had that question been asked of Miss Rounding and answered, as it must have been, in the negative, this appeal must succeed. But both he and his learned junior strenuously argued that, as my noble and learned friend, Lord Edmund-Davies, pointed out in his speech in *R. v Charles*, the question whether a person is or is not induced to act in a particular way by a dishonest representation is a question of fact, and since what they claimed to be the crucial question had not been asked of Miss Rounding, there was no adequate proof of the requisite inducement. In her deposition, Miss Rounding stated, no doubt with complete truth, that she only remembered this particular transaction with the respondent because some one

subsequently came and asked her about it after it had taken place. My Lords, credit card frauds are all too frequently perpetrated, and if conviction of offenders for offences against sections 15 or 16 of the Act of 1968 can only be obtained if the prosecution are able in each case to call the person upon whom the fraud was immediately perpetrated to say that he or she positively remembered the particular transaction and, had the truth been known, would never have entered into that supposedly well-remembered transaction, the guilty would often escape conviction. In some cases, of course, it may be possible to adduce such evidence if the particular transaction is well remembered. But where as in the present case no one could reasonably be expected to remember a particular transaction in detail, and the inference of inducement may well be in all the circumstances quite irresistible, I see no reason in principle why it should not be left to the jury to decide, upon the evidence in the case as a whole, whether that inference is in truth irresistible as to my mind it is in the present case. In this connection it is to be noted that the respondent did not go into the witness box to give evidence from which that inference might conceivably have been rebutted. . . .

My Lords, I would . . . allow the appeal and restore the conviction of the respondent."

**Appeal allowed**

## R. v Doukas [1978] 1 W.L.R. 372 (Court of Appeal, Criminal Division)

The defendant, a hotel waiter, was found in the hotel with six bottles of wine on him of a kind not stocked by the hotel. He was charged and convicted under section 25 of the Theft Act 1968 with going equipped to cheat having admitted that he intended to sell the wine to the hotel customers for his own profit.

Lane L.J.:
"There must be proof that the obtaining would have been, wholly or partially, by virtue of the deception. The prosecution must prove that nexus between the deception and obtaining. It is this last and final ingredient which, as we see it in the present case, is the only point which raises any difficulty. . . .

We have . . . been referred to the decision in *Rashid* [1977] 1 W.L.R. 298, which was a decision by another division of this court. That case concerned not a waiter in a hotel, but a British Rail waiter who substituted not bottles of wine for the railway wine but his own tomato sandwiches for the railway tomato sandwiches; and it is to be observed that the basis of the decision in that case was that the summing up of the judge to the jury was inadequate. On that basis the appeal was allowed. But the court went on to express its views obiter on the question whether in those circumstances it could be said that the obtaining was by virtue of deception, and it came to the conclusion, as I say obiter, that the answer was probably no.

Of course each case of this type may produce different results according to the circumstances of the case and according, in particular, to the commodity which is being proffered. But, as we see it, the question has to be asked of the hypothetical customer, 'Why did you buy this wine; or, if you had been told the truth, would you or would you not have bought the commodity?' It is, at least in theory, for the jury in the end to decide that question.

Here, as the ground of appeal is simply the judge's action in allowing the case to go to the jury, we are answering that question, so to speak, on behalf of the judge rather than the jury. Was there evidence of the necessary nexus fit to go to the jury? Certainly so far as the wine is concerned, we have no doubt at all that the hypothetical customer, faced with the waiter saying to him: 'This of course is not hotel wine, this is stuff which I imported into the hotel myself and I am going to put the proceeds of the wine, if you pay, into my own pocket,' would certainly answer, so far as we can see, 'I do not want your wine, kindly bring me the hotel carafe wine.' Indeed it would be a strange jury that came to any other conclusion, and a stranger guest who gave any other answer, for several reasons. First of all, the guest would not know what was in the bottle which the waiter was proffering. True, he may not know what was in the carafe which the hotel was proffering, but he would at least be able to have recourse to the hotel if something was wrong with the carafe wine, but he would have no such recourse with the waiter; if he did, it would be worthless.

It seems to us the matter can be answered on a much simpler basis. The hypothetical customer must be reasonably honest as well as being reasonably intelligent and it seems to us incredible that any customer, to whom the true situation was made clear, would willingly make himself a party to what was obviously a fraud by the waiter upon his employers. If that conclusion is contrary to the obiter dicta in *Rashid* then we must respectfully disagree with those dicta.

It is not necessary to examine the question any further as to whether we are differing from *Rashid* or not. But it seems to us beyond argument that the judge was right in the conclusion he reached and was right to allow the matter to go to the jury on the basis which he did."

**Application refused**[36]

In a more recent case, it was indicated, *obiter*, in the Court of Appeal that the court had "the gravest possible doubt" whether the supplier of goods in a credit card transaction was interested in the authority of the card-user: "suppliers of goods were generally concerned to ensure that they would receive payment when a credit card was issued, but there was room to doubt whether they were interested in how the holder got the card, provided that the transaction would be honoured".[37]

The decisions of *Charles*, *Lambie*, *Rashid* and *Doukas* have generated much debate. A. T. H. Smith argues that their combined effect is to extend "the concept of deception beyond what it meant when the Theft Act was framed in 1968, to mean something much more like fraud. ... [W]hereas elsewhere in the criminal law the conduct objected to must be an 'operating and substantial cause' the courts are now saying that a man has been deceived when he has been told an untruth (verbally or by conduct) and where it may be assumed that he would have done otherwise had he known the truth."[38] In other words, causation is reduced to the *sine qua non* level.

### J. C. Smith, Commentary to Lambie [1981] Crim.L.R.716–717:

"Such straining of language and of concepts has been all too common a feature of the law of stealing and related offences for at least 150 years but it has usually been directed to procuring the conviction of a rogue who clearly ought to be guilty of a crime. In the present case it is not so clear. One view is that it is the responsibility of the banks and credit companies to ensure that these cards are given only to creditworthy and responsible people and that they should not look to the criminal law to protect them from dishonest breaches of contract by their clients. They put great temptation in the way of ordinary people, often young and inexperienced, some of whom take too literally the slogan that the card 'takes the waiting out of wanting.' ... The Council of Europe Committee on Crime Problems considered this problem recently: Report on Decriminalisation (1980) Chapter XIII. They found that the law of most member states covered cases where there is a false declaration, forgery or falsification of identity but, they said (p. 201)—'it is not appropriate to criminalise other forms of credit cards abuse (*e.g.* exceeding the credit allowed) since there is a civil law contract freely entered into between the credit institution and its customer for which the guarantee of civil damages seems adequate. It is up to the banks and credit institutions to

---

[36] But see *Cooke* [1986] A.C. 909 where Lord Bridge commented: "Upright citizens as the ordinary run of British Rail passengers may be presumed to be, I am not prepared to assume that they would necessarily refuse to take and pay for refreshments even if they knew perfectly well that the buffet staff were practising the kind of 'fiddle' here involved." See also *Kassim* [1991] 3 All E.R. 713.

[37] *Nabina* [2000] Crim.L.R.481.

[38] "The Idea of Criminal Deception" [1982] Crim.L.R.721.

look to the "morality" of their credit policy by making all necessary checks beforehand on the reliability of their customers and their financial standing, applying the necessary safeguards, moderating their advertising policy, etc.

Criminalisation in this field might have the contrary effect of encouraging banks and credit institutions to be irresponsible and hence increase credit card abuse.'

As for cheques, the committee would decriminalise the use of guaranteed cheques in countries where their use is an offence.

If we followed these recommendations, neither *Charles* nor *Lambie* would be guilty of an offence.

There is a good deal of force in these observations though it may be a bit unrealistic to suggest a civil remedy as a solution in the United Kingdom. The offending party would usually not be worth suing and, if he were, the cost involved would probably be uneconomic. Furthermore, while these modern methods of credit and of trading are certainly of benefit to the banks and to the traders, they are also of benefit to the public, as is apparent from the readiness of the public to take advantage of them. Most people, it is thought, would regard the conduct of *Charles* and of *Lambie* as fraudulent."

As we shall see, the Law Commission has responded to these various concerns by proposing the introduction of a general fraud offence. To avoid the *Lambie*-type problem of holding that a person is deceived when that person really could not care less, and also to overcome one of the gaps in the law that a machine cannot be deceived, the Law Commission proposes replacing the concept of deception for these offences with, *inter alia*, the requirement of a misrepresentation.

### Law Commission, Report No. 276, Fraud (2002), para. 7.16:

"We now believe that [the misuse of credit cards and other payment instruments] would be covered in a more convincing and less artificial way if the concept of deception were replaced by that of misrepresentation. Since the merchant who accepts the card in payment does not care whether the defendant has authority to use it, it is debatable whether the merchant can be said to be *deceived*. It is clear from *Charles* and *Lambie*, however, that by tendering the card the defendant is impliedly and falsely *representing* that he or she has authority to use it for the transaction in question. In our view that should suffice, even if the defendant knows that the representee is indifferent whether the representation is true. We have therefore concluded that this form of the new offence should be defined in terms of misrepresentation rather then deception."

Under this proposal the focus would be on the wrongdoing of the defendant rather than on whether the other person was induced to act in reliance on the misrepresentation. This approach would have the advantage that it would make no difference whether the misrepresentation was directed at a person or a machine. However, under these proposals, as we shall see, even the requirement of a misrepresentation will no longer be an *essential* element of fraud. It will simply become one way (albeit, probably, the most important) in which the proposed offence of fraud can be committed.

Another interesting aspect of the cases of *Charles*, *Lambie* and *Doukas* is that they reveal much about the interests protected by the deception offences. In none of these cases did the so-called victim (the person who was deceived) "lose out" in the sense of suffering detriment as a consequence of the defendant's actions. In *Lambie*, the shop was paid by the bank that issued the credit card. It was described as "irrelevant" that the shop assistant was unconcerned about the creditworthiness of the defendant. In *Rasbid and Doukas*, where the so-called victims were members of the public consuming sandwiches and wine, it was irrelevant that they might have been receiving better value for money. One way of rationalising this approach is that liability should not depend on whether the so-called victims suffer harm to their "net wealth" but on whether their autonomy to direct their assets, without being deceived by another's fraud, has been infringed.[39] The interest the law is seeking to protect is commercial freedom and the defendant is seen as threatening this interest.

The approach, advocated by the Law Commission, shifts the focus away from the "victim" and effectively adopts an inchoate model of liability with the emphasis on the "anti-social" conduct of the defendant.

### Law Commission, Report No. 276, Fraud (2002), paras 7.49–7.54:

"7.49 [T]he law should take a robust and realistic line on this issue. It may be that, where a person's dishonest conduct has genuinely caused no harm whatsoever to anyone else, that conduct is not appropriately described as fraud. However, for every case where this is truly so, there will be many where the loss to others is hard to identify but is none the less real ... [In the] Guinness fraud ... there were many losers, but it would have been very hard to bring evidence of these widely dispersed losses. Similarly, in cases of insider dealing it is clear that market participants suffer as a result of the insiders' actions, but the losses are indirect and diffuse. The fact that the defendant has dishonestly made a gain is not itself the *reason* for criminalising the defendant's conduct. It is, however, the obvious and visible symptom of conduct which, on closer inspection, proves to be anti-social in less obvious ways ...

7.51 For these reasons we believe that it would be unrealistic and artificial to say that the new fraud offence requires proof of loss to others. The dishonest making of a financial gain should suffice ... It should be sufficient that the defendant *either* causes financial loss to another *or* makes a financial gain ...

7.54 Arguably the full offence should not be committed unless the defendant has succeeded in *actually* causing a loss or making a gain: where the defendant has acted with *intent* to cause loss or make a gain, but that intent has been frustrated, a conviction of attempt would adequately reflect the criminality of the defendant's conduct. It may sometimes be debatable, however, whether a loss has actually been caused or a gain made, whilst it is clear beyond doubt that the defendant *intended* to bring about one or both of these outcomes. We think it would be unfortunate if, in such a case, it had to be determined whether there had in fact been gain or loss within the meaning of the Act, when that question had little bearing on the gravity of the defendant's conduct or the appropriate sentence ... [I]t should be sufficient if the defendant acts *with intent* to make a gain or to cause a loss."

### (iii) *Dishonesty*

The partial definition of dishonesty contained in section 2 of the Theft Act 1968 does not apply to the deception offences.[40] However, in other respects, the same meaning is to be given to dishonesty in this context as under section 1.[41]

### Criminal Law Revision Committee, Eighth Report, Theft and Related Offences, 1966, Cmnd.2977, para. 88:

"The provision in (section 15(1)) making a person guilty of criminal deception if he 'dishonestly obtains' the property replaces the provision in [the Larceny Act] 1916, s.32(1),

---

[39] *cf.* Fletcher, *Rethinking Criminal Law* (1978), pp. 51–57.
[40] The Theft Act 1968, s.1(3).
[41] *Melwani* [1989] Crim.L.R.565.

making a person guilty of obtaining by false pretences if he 'with intent to defraud, obtains' the things there mentioned. The change will correspond to the change from 'fraudulently' to 'dishonestly' in the definition of stealing ... 'Dishonestly' seems the right word to use in relation to criminal deception also. Owing to the words 'dishonestly obtains' a person who uses deception in order to obtain property to which he believes himself entitled will not be guilty; for though the deception may be dishonest, the obtaining is not. In this respect also the offence will be in line with theft because a belief in a legal right to deprive an owner of property is for the purpose of theft inconsistent with dishonesty and is specifically made a defence by the partial definition of 'dishonesty' in (section) 2(1)."

In the case of *Woolven*[42] the defendant claimed that whilst ordinary people might have found his behaviour dishonest he did not think it was because he was trying to get the money for his employer (to whom he thought the money belonged). The Court of Appeal concluded that it was unnecessary to direct the jury in terms similar to those in section 2(1)(a) relating to a claim of right: a direction based on *Ghosh* was likely to say everything that was needed. This does not mean, however, that a *Ghosh* direction has to be given in every case. Indeed, in *Price* it was held that it was both unnecessary and potentially misleading in the majority of cases to do so.[43] The direction must be given where the defendant "might have believed that what he is alleged to have done was in accordance with the ordinary person's idea of honesty".[44] It must also be made clear that dishonesty is a separate element to the requirement that the deception be "deliberate or reckless".[45]

With theft, dishonesty performs a *positive* role. As seen, particularly after *Gomez* and *Hinks*, it is an inculpatory requirement. It is what can render otherwise innocent conduct criminal. With the deception offences, however, it has a *negative* or exculpatory role. As there must have been a deception, it is only in very exceptional cases that the conduct would not automatically be regarded as dishonest. Accordingly, the Law Commission in its Consultation Paper[46] recommended abolishing the dishonesty requirement for deception offences and replacing it with specific defences, for example, that the defendant believed she was legally entitled to the property. However, in its final report[47] the Law Commission was persuaded by the view of Tur that "what may constitute a just excuse is so context-dependent that exhaustive definition must necessarily limit the range of circumstances which might exist"[48] and, accordingly, no longer proposes to dispense with dishonesty as a negative requirement for fraud offences.

## 2. The offences

Having examined the central, common elements of deception, obtaining and dishonesty, the specific deception offences can be covered briefly.

---

[42] (1983) 73 Cr.App.R.231.
[43] (1990) 90 Cr.App.R.409 at 411.
[44] *ibid.*
[45] *Feeny* (1992) 94 Cr.App.R.1; *O'Connell* (1992) 94 Cr.App.R.39; *Goldman* [1997] Crim.L.R.894.
[46] Law Commission Consultation Paper No. 155, *Fraud and Deception* (1999), paras 7.39–7.53.
[47] Law Commission, No. 276, *Fraud* (2002).
[48] "Dishonesty and the Jury" in Griffiths (ed.), *Philosophy and Practice* (1985), p. 75.

*(i) Obtaining property by deception*

## Theft Act 1968, section 15(1)

"A person who by any deception dishonestly obtains property belonging to another, with the intention of permanently depriving the other of it, shall on conviction on indictment be liable to imprisonment for a term not exceeding 10 years."

### (a) *Actus reus*

The *actus reus* of this offence is complete if the defendant:
1. by deception
2. obtains
3. property
4. belonging to another.

1. Deception.
This is discussed above.

2. Obtains.

The requirement that the deception must cause the obtaining of the property has been discussed above. There is, however, a specific provision here relating to the meaning of "obtaining".

## Theft Act 1968, section 15(2)

"For purposes of this section a person is to be treated as obtaining property if he obtains ownership, possession or control of it, and 'obtain' includes obtaining for another or enabling another to obtain or to retain."

The defendant must obtain ownership, possession or control for himself or another. It is not sufficient that he is allowed to "retain" property for himself[49] but enabling another to retain the property does suffice.

It would appear that "obtaining" does not necessitate any positive act by the defendant. Once the deception has been practised, no further action is required by the defendant. Accordingly, ownership of property could be transferred to the defendant, pursuant to a deception, even though he was unaware of the fact. Consequently, it has been argued[50] that while it is widely thought that, as a result of *Gomez*,[51] almost all cases of obtaining property by deception will also be theft, in the situation where the defendant obtains ownership of the property prior to there being any appropriation, any subsequent appropriation will provide no basis for theft as, at the time of the appropriation, the property will not belong to another.

3. Property.
Section 34(1) of the 1968 Act makes it clear that the definition of property given in section 4(1) applies here. The only distinction to be drawn is that the limitations

---

[49] The defendant could probably be convicted of theft if, lawfully in possession, he deceives the rightful owner of the property into allowing him to retain it if he has an intention to permanently deprive.
[50] Heaton, "Deceiving without Thieving" [2001] Crim.L.R.712.
[51] [1993] A.C. 442

upon what can be stolen for the purposes of theft found in ss.4(2)–4(4) do not apply to section 15. Land may thus be obtained by deception. For reasons explored earlier[52] and canvassed further in the next section, cheques cannot be obtained (just as they cannot be stolen).[53]

4. Belonging to another.

By virtue of section 34(1), section 5(1) applies to section 15. Thus the artificial definitions of "belonging to another" contained in sections 5(2), (3) and (4) do not apply here.

Until the decision of *Preddy*[54] it was common for prosecutions for mortgage fraud to be brought under section 15.[55] However, in this case the House of Lords held that in cases where a deception results in money being transferred by electronic transfer, CHAPS order[56] or cheque into another's account (whether as part of a mortgage or other fraud), no offence under section 15 has been committed. The basis for this decision was that the defendant could not be said to have obtained property "belonging to another".[57] This is because when the bank account of the defendant is credited, he does not obtain the victim's thing in action (the right to sue on the debt). Instead, the victim's thing in action is either extinguished or reduced in proportion to the sum involved. A new thing in action is created, representing a debt (of the same amount) owed by the bank holding the defendant's account to the defendant. Lord Goff stated:

"In truth the property which the defendant has obtained is the new chose in action constituted by the debt now owed to him by his bank, and represented by the credit entry in his own bank account. This did not come into existence until the debt so created was owed to him by his bank, and *so never belonged to anyone else.*"[58]

This decision exposed a very substantial lacuna in the applicability of section 15 and sent shock-waves through financial institutions. It meant that section 15 was inapt for almost all cases of obtaining a thing in action.[59] Almost immediately, the Law Commission responded by a review of the problems created by *Preddy*.[60] It considered that it would be unsatisfactory to attempt to extend existing offences and as a consequence a new offence of obtaining a money transfer by deception was created.[61]

However, Smith has pointed out that the new offence will not cover all cases. In cases involving payment by cheque, the new offence is only committed when a cheque is honoured and the defendant's account credited. Thus, it is still important to assess whether section 15 may be invoked at an earlier stage. Smith has argued

---

[52] *Above*, p. 768.
[53] *Graham* [1997] 1 Cr.App.R.302; *Clarke* [2002] 1 Cr.App.R.141; *Burke* [2000] Crim.L.R.413.
[54] [1996] A.C. 815.
[55] This charge was relied upon because *Halai* [1983] Crim.L.R.624 had held that a mortgage advance was not a service for the purposes of obtaining services by deception under s.1 of the Theft Act 1978. In *Cooke* [1997] Crim.L.R.436 it was held that *Halai* was wrongly decided. But, *cf. Naviede* [1997] Crim.L.R.662.
[56] Clearing House Automated Payment System.
[57] Overruling *Duru* (1973) 58 Cr.App.R.151.
[58] At 834 (our emphasis).
[59] Except in "the rare case in which what is induced by deception is the transfer or assignment of an existing thing". (Griew, *Archbold News* Issue 7, August 15, 1996, p. 1).
[60] Law Commission No. 243, *Offences of Dishonesty: Money Transfers* (1996).
[61] s.15A of the Theft Act 1968 as inserted by the Theft (Amendment) Act 1996. *Below*, p. 823.

that this is possible if one looks at the nature of the property involved in a different way. If the cheque is perceived not as a thing in action but as a piece of paper with special qualities (rather like a key to a safe) it becomes a valuable security which does *belong to another*—the writer of the cheque—at the time of the deception.[62] The Court of Appeal has found Smith's analysis "highly persuasive" but concluded it was bound by *Preddy* even in relation to cheques.[63] The drawing of a cheque in favour of the defendant creates a new chose in action, which never belonged to anyone else. While the piece of paper on which the cheque is drawn is, of course, property belonging to another, it will ultimately be returned to the drawer via her bank, so there is no intention of permanent deprivation.

In a different context, Smith's view has received some support in *Arnold*[64] where it was stated that "the 'substance' of a cheque lies in the right to present it and obtain the benefit of its proceeds".[65] The logic of this is somewhat difficult to follow. A cheque, before it is made out, is simply a piece of paper. Once made out to the payee, it does indeed become a "key to a safe" or has special "substance", but these are simply euphemisms for the fact that it has become a chose in action and, while the piece of paper might have belonged to the drawer of the cheque, the chose in action never did and, therefore, it was never property belonging to another.[66]

### (b) *Mens rea*

The *mens rea* requirements for section 15 are:
1. dishonestly
2. with intent permanently to deprive
3. deliberately or recklessly makes a false statement.

These requirements have already been discussed. It should be noted that section 15(3) specifically makes section 6 applicable to section 15.

### (c) *Punishment*

Section 15(1) states that a person convicted of obtaining property by deception shall be liable to a term of imprisonment not exceeding 10 years. This offence would appear, therefore, to be regarded more seriously than the other deception offences although it is not immediately clear why obtaining *property* by deception should be so much more serious than obtaining *services* by deception (punishable by a maximum of five years).[67]

---

[62] "Obtaining Cheques by Theft or Deception" [1997] Crim.L.R.396 at 400, 404. Another possibility would be to bring a prosecution for procuring the execution of a valuable security contrary to s.20 of the Theft Act 1968.

[63] *Clarke* [2002] 1 Cr.App.R.151.

[64] [1997] 4 All E.R. 1.

[65] See further, Smith's commentry to *Horseman* [1998] Crim.L.R.128.

[66] The Law Commission was not convinced of the desirability of an amendment to make it clear that obtaining a cheque by deception could be charged under s.15. In its view either s.20(2) or the new 15A were more appropriate charges: Law Commission No. 243 *Offences of Dishonesty: Money Transfers* (1996), pp. 30–31.

[67] The guideline sentence for magistrates is: "is it so serious that only custody is appropriate?" Magistrates' Association, *Sentencing Guidelines* (2001). Penalties are higher when the evidence shows a number of deliberately dishonest transactions over a period of time: Smith (A.T.H.), *Property Offences* (1994), p. 465.

(ii) *Obtaining a money transfer by deception*

### Theft Act 1968, section 15A

"(1) A person is guilty of an offence if by any deception he dishonestly obtains a money transfer for himself or another.
(2) A money transfer occurs when—
(a) a debit is made to one account,
(b) a credit is made to another, and
(c) the credit results from the debit or the debit results from the credit.
(3) References to a credit and to a debit are to a credit of an amount of money and to a debit of an amount of money."

(a) *Actus reus*

This new offence, enacted by the Theft (Amendment) Act 1996, applies to offences committed after December 18, 1996 and remedies the lacuna created by the decision of *Preddy* discussed above. Whilst the mischief primarily aimed at is the electronic transfer of funds and transfers by CHAPS order, the offence also applies to payment by cheque once the cheque has been honoured and the other account credited. This offence is not committed when a cheque is cashed as this would not amount to a money transfer as defined in section 15A(2). The result of the changes is that the prosecution may have a number of possible offences to choose from, depending upon the circumstances of the case. For example, where a mortgage loan is obtained by deception, involving a transfer of funds from one account to another, the prosecution could bring a charge under section 15A or the (amended) section 1 of the 1978 Act. However, in other situations the new offence may be the only possible charge, as, for example, where a defendant obtains an electronic transfer of funds other than a loan by deception.

(b) *Mens rea*

The *mens rea* requirement is that of dishonesty. There is no additional requirement that the defendant intend to retain the credit.

(c) *Punishment*

The offence is punishable to the same extent as section 15, that is, by a maximum of 10 years' imprisonment.

(iii) *Obtaining pecuniary advantage by deception*

### Theft Act 1968, section 16

"(1) A person who by any deception dishonestly obtains for himself or another any pecuniary advantage shall on conviction on indictment be liable to imprisonment for a term not exceeding five years.
(2) The cases in which a pecuniary advantage within the meaning of this section is to be regarded as obtained for a person are cases where—
(a) [Repealed]
(b) he is allowed to borrow by way of overdraft, or to take out any policy of insurance or annuity contract, or obtains an improvement of the terms on which he is allowed to do so; or
(c) he is given the opportunity to earn remuneration or greater remuneration in an office or employment, or to win money by betting.

(3) For purposes of this section 'deception' has the same meaning as in section 15 of this Act."

## (a) *Background*

The history behind this section is a most unhappy one. In its draft Bill the Criminal Law Revision Committee had proposed two offences (obtaining credit by deception and inducing an act by deception with a view to gain), but these foundered in the House of Lords. Instead, section 16 was passed containing within section 16(2)(a) references to the reduction, evasion or deferment of a debt or charge. This quickly proved to be the sort of section likely to keep lawyers in work for the rest of their days. Following intense academic and judicial criticism the Criminal Law Revision Committee was invited to resolve the difficulties; its report became the basis for the 1978 Act and section 16(2)(a) was repealed.[68]

What is left is *one* offence which can be committed in two different ways (subsections (b) and (c)).[69] Fletcher suggests that the language of section 16 indicates some movement towards the protection of economic interests[70] (a movement which would presumably pay more heed to the actual value of the property "lost"), rather than, as suggested above, being more concerned with the protection of commercial autonomy. However, the movement is only linguistic. In neither situation is it necessary for any *actual* advantage to be obtained. For example, under subsection (c) the offence will be made out if the defendant secures the opportunity to earn, even though he may not actually have earned anything. In such situations the defendant is deemed to have obtained a pecuniary advantage.[71] As Fletcher points out, "the basic principle is still the protection of commercial autonomy".[72]

## (b) *Actus reus*

The *actus reus* of section 16 is:

1. deception
2. obtains for himself or another
3. pecuniary advantage.

"Pecuniary advantage" is given a precise definition in sections 16(2)(b) and (c). It covers four situations:

[i] Being allowed to borrow by way of overdraft. The word "allow" here has presented some problems in that *prima facie* it implies a consensual act with the bank agreeing to the overdraft facility. However, in *Charles*[73] the court accepted without question that the defendant had been "allowed" to borrow when his account had become overdrawn without permission. The point was faced more squarely in *Waites*[74]: by issuing a cheque card to the

---

[68] Thirteenth Report, 1977 (Cmnd.6733).
[69] The indictment should, however, specify under which subsection the prosecution is being brought: *Aston and Hadley* [1970] 3 All E.R. 1045.
[70] *Rethinking Criminal Law* (1978), p. 56.
[71] *D.P.P. v Turner* [1974] A.C. 357.
[72] At 57.
[73] [1977] A.C. 177.
[74] [1982] Crim.L.R.369.

defendant (which was then used to borrow by way of overdraft) the bank was giving the card-holder the power to use that card; by binding themselves to honour cheques drawn in excess of the amount in the defendant's account they were in effect "allowing" him to overdraw his account. And in *Bevan*[75] it was held that "the overdraft was consensual, since the appellant impliedly requested it and the bank had, albeit reluctantly, agreed".

[ii] Being allowed to take out an insurance policy or annuity contract or obtain improved terms thereon.

[iii] Being given an opportunity to earn remuneration in an office or employment. This provision is broad enough to cover persons who practice deceptions to gain promotion. It is unnecessary that the remuneration actually be paid. What matters is that the person is given the opportunity to earn it. If the wages or salary are actually received, it is possible[76] that the defendant could be liable under section 15 of the Theft Act 1968 if it were established that the deception was the cause of the obtaining of the salary, as opposed to the money being paid solely for the work done. This provision covers not only employment situations but also independent contractors.[77]

[iv] Being given an opportunity to win money by betting.

### (c) *Mens rea*

The *mens rea* requirements under section 16 are:
1. dishonestly[78]
2. deliberately or recklessly makes a deception.

Must the defendant intend to obtain a pecuniary advantage? For example, a person could practice a deception to be awarded a new position within a company without realising that the new post involves greater remuneration. Smith argues that there must be an intention to obtain the pecuniary advantage.[79] However, section 16 is silent on this point and so it is likely that such a question would be subsumed within the enquiry as to whether there was dishonesty.

### (d) *Punishment*

Section 16(1) lays down the maximum penalty for obtaining a pecuniary advantage by deception as five years' imprisonment upon conviction on indictment.

### (iv) *Procuring the Execution of a Valuable Security*

### Theft Act 1968, section 20

"(2) A person who dishonestly, with a view to gain for himself or another or with intent to cause loss to another, by any deception procures the execution of a valuable security shall on

[75] [1987] Crim.L.R.129.
[76] *King and Stockwell* [1987] Q.B. 547.
[77] *Callender* [1992] 3 W.L.R. 501.
[78] See *Clarke (Victor)* [1996] Crim.L.R.824.
[79] Smith and Hogan, *Criminal Law* (10th ed., 2002) p. 606.

conviction on indictment be liable to imprisonment for a term not exceeding seven years; and this subsection shall apply in relation to the making, acceptance, endorsement, alteration, cancellation or destruction in whole or in part of a valuable security, and in relation to the signing or sealing of any paper or other material in order that it may be made or converted into, or used or dealt with as, a valuable security, as if that were the execution of a valuable security.

(3) [definition of valuable security is provided]"

Detail of this offence cannot be provided in a book of this nature. The following summary encapsulates the essence of the offence.

### Law Commission Consultation Paper No. 155, Fraud and Deception (1999), paras 2.22–2.23:

"2.22 Section 20(2) of the Theft Act 1968 makes it an offence, dishonestly and with a view to gain or with intent to cause loss, by deception to procure the execution of a valuable security. 'Valuable security' is defined in section 20(3) in unmodernised language redolent of the offence's nineteenth century roots, and it is clear that the offence was originally aimed at cheques, bills of exchange and other negotiable instruments. The courts have extended it to include a CHAPS order requiring the electronic transfer of funds from one bank to another, but not to the telegraphic transfer of funds.

2.23 Section 20(2) contains a list of acts which are to count as 'execution'. The House of Lords [*Kassim* [1992] 1 A.C. 9] has held that the term refers to acts done *to* the document (such as signing it) or in connection with it. It does not include *giving effect* to the document by carrying out the instructions in it, such as delivering goods or paying money."

The main importance of this offence is that it covers the situation where a defendant by deception procures another to draw a cheque in favour of herself. The offence is constituted by the drawing and signing of the cheque. The problems, already discussed, of bringing such cheques within the ambit of theft or obtaining property by deception are avoided.

(v) *Obtaining Services by Deception*

### Theft Act 1978, section 1

"(1) A person who by any deception dishonestly obtains services from another shall be guilty of an offence.

(2) It is an obtaining of services where the other is induced to confer a benefit by doing some act, or causing or permitting some act to be done, on the understanding that the benefit has been or will be paid for.

(3) Without prejudice to the generality of subsection (2) above, it is an obtaining of services where the other is induced to make a loan, or to cause or permit a loan to be made, on the understanding that any payment (whether by way of interest or otherwise) will be or has been made in respect of the loan."

This section remedies an obvious defect of section 15, namely, that the latter does not cover the situation where someone is deceived into providing a service rather than parting with property. For example, someone could be induced to mow a lawn or provide a ride in a taxi by being falsely told he will be paid. In other cases, the use of section 15, while theoretically possible, would amount to gross false labelling. For example, if a meal or haircut is provided as a result of a deception, it could be established that the food or shampoo is property that was obtained. However, this does not accurately describe the wrong committed which is obtaining the labour of another by deception. The only surprising thing is that it took so long to recognise the need for a separate offence.[80]

(a) *Actus reus*
The elements of the *actus reus* are that the defendant:
1. by any deception
2. obtains
3. services.

1. By any deception.
Two points need to be added to the earlier discussion of deception. First, the obtaining can be by any deception and not just a deception as to payment.[81] So, for example, if the defendant induces a friend to drive him to work by falsely representing that he is still over the legal limit because of alcohol drunk the previous night, he commits the offence if the friend is to be paid for the acts. The deception must cause the victim to provide the services on the understanding that he will be paid. The Act thus excludes deceptions which induce gratuitous services.

Secondly, the victim need not have suffered economically by the defendant's deception. In the above example the defendant may have paid the victim as agreed. Whilst it may well be that a jury would be reluctant to find the defendant dishonest in such circumstances,[82] this approach is consistent with the view expressed earlier that deception offences are primarily concerned with the protection of commercial autonomy, and not with the protection of economic interests.

2. Obtains.
Causation must be established. It must be proved that the deception causes the services to be obtained.

3. Services.
The term "services" is given a wide definition by subsection (2): "Services" can be regarded as a "joker word, standing only for the notion defined in subsection (2). It is narrower than the usual meaning of 'services' because it does not cover gratuitous services. It is wider because it covers much conduct that would not ordinarily be described as performing a service."[83] In other words, *any* act, so long as it confers a "benefit" and is done on the understanding that it will be paid for, amounts to a service.

This very wide interpretation can be illustrated by *Widdowson*[84] where it was held that obtaining a van on hire-purchase was obtaining services. The effect of this is to create considerable overlap between section 15 of the 1968 Act and section 1 of the 1978 Act. A narrower approach was adopted in *Halai*[85] where it was held

[80] The defendant in such circumstances might have been liable under (the now repealed) s.16(2)(a) of the Theft Act 1968 for obtaining a pecuniary advantage by deception through deferment of the debt.
[81] *Naviede* [1997] Crim.L.R.662.
[82] Smith, *The Law of Theft* (8th ed., 1997), p. 130.
[83] Glanville Williams, *Textbook of Criminal Law* (2nd ed., 1983), p. 798.
[84] (1986) 82 Cr.App.R.314.
[85] [1983] Crim.L.R.624. See further, Smith (A.T.H.), *Property Offences* (1994), pp. 540–546.

that obtaining a mortgage advance by deception was not obtaining a service. This decision was subsequently disapproved.[86] The problem in relation to mortgage frauds has now been resolved by the Theft (Amendment) Act 1996 which inserted subsection (3) above. A mortgage advance is now a service and the broad interpretation of that term is re-established.

It is irrelevant that the service is obtained pursuant to an illegal or otherwise unenforceable contract. So, for example, a man who by deception induces a prostitute to provide sexual services is liable even though the contract is illegal and unenforceable.

What is the position if the services amount to a criminal offence? It has been suggested that if the criminal offence has the object of protecting the defendant there could be no "benefit". For example, if a 17–year-old deceives another into tattooing her, there would be no liability as the offence in question (under the Tattooing of Minors Act 1969) is designed to protect her and so there is no benefit to her.[87] This principle ought surely to be extended to all cases where the "services" amount to a criminal offence. If a gangster induces a "hit-man" to kill another by falsely promising payment it would be absurd to assert that the gangster obtained services by deception—quite apart from the obvious point that the gangster would be guilty of far more serious offences. The purpose of section 1 is to protect persons from wasting their labour which, like property, has intrinsic economic value. It is not the purpose of the law to protect those, like the "hit-man", who devote their labour and time to the commission of criminal offences.

The section only applies to those services induced on the understanding that they will be paid for.[88] Thus the more effective one's lies, the less the chance of liability here. If one's deception is so convincing that a service is provided free, there is no liability. Deceiving someone into the provision of a gratuitous service may, however, fall within section 2(1)(c) of the 1978 Act.

What is meant by "paid for" here? One view is that it extends to recompense in forms other than money.[89] The better view is that the criminal law should not extend its reach into non-commercial, perhaps purely social, transactions, such as where a person induces another into fixing a broken tap by falsely stating that, in return, dinner will be cooked for the tap-mender.

## (b) *Mens rea*

The *mens rea* requirements of section 1 are:
1. dishonesty
2. deliberately or recklessly making the deception.

## (c) *Punishment*

Section 4 lays down the maximum penalties for offences under the 1978 Act. Section 1 is punishable on indictment by up to five years' imprisonment. On

---

[86] *Graham* [1997] Crim.L.R.340 and *Cooke* [1997] Crim.L.R.436 appeared to settle that the case was wrongly decided. However, *Naviede* [1997] Crim.L.R.662 merely distinguished it in a manner which Smith in his commentary describes as deplorable (p. 664).
[87] Smith *The Law of Theft* (8th ed., 1997), p. 133. See also Spencer, "The Theft Act 1978" [1979] Crim.L.R.24 at 27–28. *cf.* Griew, *The Theft Acts 1968 and 1978* (7th ed., 1995), p. 181.
[88] *Shortland* [1995] Crim.L.R.893.
[89] Smith and Hogan, *Criminal Law* (10th ed., 2002), p. 609.

summary conviction the maximum penalty is six months' imprisonment and/or a fine of (currently) a maximum of £5,000.

(vi) *Evasion of liability by deception*

(a) *Introduction*

We saw earlier that the criminal law does not generally punish those who breach their contracts—even those who dishonestly and blatantly refuse to pay their debts. Such matters are more appropriately dealt with by the civil law. The extension of the reaches of the criminal law should always be limited by the criteria of necessity and effectiveness. However, when the breach of contract is secured by deception, in addition to dishonesty, then even though there is no greater harm, the law feels that this added blameworthiness now pushes the case into territory where criminalisation is appropriate. Whether this approach is appropriate is a controversial matter.[90]

(b) *The Law*

### Theft Act 1978, section 2

"(1) Subject to subsection (2) below, where a person by any deception—
(a) dishonestly secures the remission of the whole or part of any existing liability to make a payment, whether his own liability or another's; or
(b) with intent to make permanent default in whole or in part on any existing liability to make a payment, or with intent to let another do so, dishonestly induces the creditor or any person claiming payment on behalf of the creditor to wait for payment (whether or not the due date for payment is deferred) or to forgo payment; or
(c) dishonestly obtains any exemption from or abatement of liability to make a payment;
he shall be guilty of an offence.
(2) For purposes of this section 'liability' means legally enforceable liability; and subsection (1) shall not apply in relation to a liability that has not been accepted or established to pay compensation for a wrongful act or omission.
(3) For purposes of subsection (1)(b) a person induced to take in payment a cheque or other security for money by way of conditional satisfaction of a pre-existing liability is to be treated not as being paid but as being induced to wait for payment.
(4) For purposes of subsection (1)(c) 'obtains' includes obtaining for another or enabling another to obtain."

It would appear that section 2 creates three *separate* offences unlike section 16.[91] This is because there are material differences between the subsections, although it is also the case that there is considerable overlap, all of them dealing in one way or another with the dishonest debtor.

### J. R. Spencer, "The Theft Act 1978" [1979] Crim.L.R.24 at 34–35:

"There seems little practical need for 2(1)(a). Where it applies, D has been fraudulent and dishonest, but his conduct is unlikely to have done P any harm. In theory harm has been caused: P used to own a debt against D; by deceiving P into waiving it, D has deprived him of it. So, it may be said, D ought to be punished just as if he had deprived P of any other item of

---

[90] Spencer, "The Theft Act 1978" [1979] Crim.L.R.24.
[91] Although in *Holt* [1981] 1 W.L.R. 1000, Lawson J. was unsure whether one or three offences had been created, the latter would appear to be the better view.

his property—his car, for example—by deception. But the analogy is false. Where D obtains P's car by deception, P once had a car, and is left with a civil remedy against D which usually is worthless. Where D secures the remission of a debt by deception, P is also left with a probably worthless civil remedy. He can rescind the remission for fraud, and then enforce the debt—but D probably has no assets with which to pay it. However, in this case what did P have *before* D deprived him of it by deception? Merely a debt—a right to sue D for the money. It is possible that D had the money to pay at the time of the deception, and spent it on beer after the debt was remitted; but this is most unlikely. Usually, the reason why D deceived P will be that D had no money but lacked the effrontery to say so. Therefore, as a result of D's deception, P is unlikely to be any the worse off. The only result of fining and imprisoning D if he is caught will be to make P's civil remedy against D worthless in the rare case where D was, before the prosecution, worth powder and shot.

Section 2(1)(b) seems to have little more rhyme or reason to it. It is said to be aimed mainly at those who knowingly write dud cheques in purported settlement of existing liability—conduct which frequently does the creditor good rather than harm [giving the creditor the right to sue on the cheque as well as the debt]. It is harmful in only two ways. First, the payee may unsuspectingly draw against the cheque and so overdraw his own bank account. If this is the mischief aimed at, however, 2(1)(b) is too narrow, because the offence is only committed where D intends never to pay, and P is equally likely to overdraw whatever D's intentions. Secondly, tendering the cheque may enable D to disappear without trace. However, the mischief here is only the same as that involved in 'making off without payment'. Why should running away after telling lies carry a sentence of five years' imprisonment under 2(1)(b), when running away without telling lies—which is more harmful, because D is likely to be harder to trace—only carries a sentence of two years under section 3? Furthermore, as against any dubious benefits to society which 2(1)(b) may provide, there is the uncomfortable fact that because of it, anyone who, however innocently, tenders a cheque which is dishonoured, can be threatened with a prosecution which is likely to get past the committal stage.

The only part of section 2 which seems to strike accurately at an evil worthy of criminal sanction is 2(1)(c), which applies to the evasion of future liability by deception. Although originally intended partly to cover obtaining services cheap or free by deception, and now in that respect redundant [because section 1 is wider in scope than intended by the C.L.R.C.], it still covers conduct which is really harmful to the victim and amounts to no other criminal offence. Take for example the case of the council-house tenant who by deception has his rent halved by way of rent rebate. The council will thereafter fail to collect half his rent as it would otherwise have fallen due. If the fraud is not discovered for several years, the council may lose thousands of pounds. On discovery of the fraud, the council will have in theory a right to sue the tenant for the money, but whereas he could have paid it in instalments over the years, the chance of his ever finding it now—in addition to future rent at the proper rate—is remote. This sort of conduct surely does deserve a prosecution.

A final criticism of section 2 is that it is complicated. Long, expensive hours will be spent in the courts discussing arid procedural questions resulting from a failure to specify what the relationship between the three main clauses is, and whether they are three offences or one. It is an ill wind of legal change which blows no barrister any good."

All these offences deal with a debtor who *is* ((a) and (b)), or *may become* ((c)), liable to a creditor and, in one of the specified ways, seeks to evade this liability. The liability must be legally enforceable (section 2(2)). So these offences would not cover a defendant who dishonestly evades his debts to a prostitute. Also, these offences do not cover liability that has not been accepted to pay compensation for a wrongful act or omission. For example, if the defendant has negligently injured a victim and then, without accepting liability, deceives the victim into thinking he is impecunious and not worth suing, no offence is committed. This limitation is understandable otherwise there could potentially be criminal liability in every tort incident where a defendant lied about the relevant facts. While such lies might be morally reprehensible, the criminal law cannot, and should not, intervene except to protect fairly clearly defined interests.

As seen, section 2 creates three offences:

## (1) Securing the remission of liability

*Remission* of liability means reducing or extinguishing a liability. Section 2(1)(a) covers *existing* liability to make payment. It thus deals with the defendant who has an existing debt and who persuades his creditor to let him off the whole or part of the debt. The creditor must agree to the remission of the liability. An example, given by the Criminal Law Revision Committee,[92] is where the defendant, who has borrowed money from a neighbour, tells a false hard luck story of family tragedy at the time of repayment and is thus let off the loan. This offence would seem to take place whether or not the creditor's promise is binding because it is secured by deception.[93] On the other hand, it would not be appropriate to charge under this subsection where the defendant deceives the creditor into thinking that the debt has already been paid or that it is less than the true figure. In this situation the proper charge is under section 2(1)(b).

## (2) Inducing a creditor to wait for or forgo payment

Two situations are covered by this subsection: inducing a creditor to wait for payment and inducing a creditor to forgo payment. Inducing a creditor to *wait for* payment covers the classic cases of "stalling" payment. Examples would be where a debtor sends his child to the door to tell the rent collector that the parents are out or handing over a dud cheque as payment for an existing debt. However, in most cases of "stalling" the debtor does eventually mean to pay. There is only an offence under section 2(1)(b) if there is an intention of making permanent default as where the family in the above example are moving out of the house the next day and mean to avoid payment permanently. *Forgoing* payment involves inducing the creditor to abandon seeking payment as in *Holt*[94] where the defendant, having dined in a restaurant, told the waiter that another waiter had already taken payment. Again, there must be an intention to make permanent default.

In these cases, unlike section 2(1)(a), the *agreement* of the creditor is not necessary. In the above examples, none of the victims (the rent collector, the recipient of the dud cheque, the waiter) agreed to wait for or forgo payment. The deception must be made to the creditor and not to another party who is not privy to the contract, even though it results in the creditor waiting for or forgoing payment.[95]

This offence is important because it specifically caters for dud cheques.[96] Section 2(3) provides that a person who is induced to take a cheque as payment for a debt is deemed to have been induced to wait for payment.

---

[92] Thirteenth Report, 1977, (Cmnd.6733), para. 13.
[93] But see Smith, *The Law of Theft* (8th ed., 1997), pp. 138–139.
[94] [1981] 1 W.L.R. 1000.
[95] *Gee* [1999] Crim.L.R.397.
[96] The Crown court case of *Andrews* and *Hedges* [1981] Crim.L.R.106 decided that this will only be the case where the creditor is induced to accept a cheque instead of cash. This is criticised by Smith (A.T.H.), *Property Offences* (1994), p. 624.

It has been held that the fact that the offence may be committed either for oneself or another is relevant to the issue of dishonesty and ought to be included in directions to the jury.[97]

### (3) Obtaining exemption from or abatement of liability

Whilst the previous two offences are limited to existing debts by the express wording of the provisions, section 2(1)(c) also covers prospective debts.[98] As with "remission" in section 2(1)(a), it seems that the agreement of the creditor is required.

*Exemption* from liability involves being let off the obligation to pay. An example would be falsely claiming to be a pensioner in order to secure free bus travel. *Abatement* involves a reduction in the amount that must be paid. An example would be falsely claiming to be a pensioner to secure a reduction in the price of a haircut. This offence could have great importance to tax evasion. A person, who, by deception, obtains a lower tax assessment, has obtained an abatement of future liability. In practice, however, this offence is not used for this purpose.

Strictly speaking, an exemption or abatement should be legally effective to eliminate or reduce the obligation to pay. However, this does not appear to be the approach adopted and giving these words their "ordinary meaning"[99] it suffices that the creditor has simply agreed to the exemption from or abatement of liability.

In *Sibartie*[1] the defendant flashed an invalid season ticket to evade paying a train fare. It was held that this could[2] be obtaining an exemption from liability to pay the fare:

> "He was saying, albeit tacitly, by waving the supposed season ticket in the air that he was a holder of a ticket authorising him to be making the journey without further payment and consequently he was not under any liability to pay any more. In the ordinary meaning of words that was dishonestly obtaining an exemption from the liability to pay the excess which, had he been honest, he would have had to pay."

This reasoning is flawed. Because of the deception the inspector would have believed there was no liability to pay because payment would already have been made by the purchase of the season ticket. The inspector was not "exempting" the defendant from any liability to pay. The more appropriate charge would have been under section 2(1)(b).

As the above examples illustrate, many of the factual scenarios falling within section 2(1)(c) will also fall within section 1 (obtaining services by deception) and should be charged as such. The overlap is not total, however; if the defendant induces another to provide her with a free service, section 1 is inapplicable because there is no understanding that the service will be paid for; it would, however, fall within section 2(1)(c).

[97] *Attewell-Hughes* [1991] 1 W.L.R. 955.
[98] *Firth* [1990] Crim.L.R.327.
[99] *Sibartie* [1983] Crim.L.R.470.
[1] *ibid.*
[2] On the facts it was an attempt to commit s.2(1)(c).

## (c) *Punishment*

By virtue of section 4 the offences contained within section 2 are punishable to the same extent as obtaining services by deception under section 1: *i.e.* the maximum penalty for conviction on indictment is five years' imprisonment and six months' imprisonment on summary conviction.

## (d) *Conclusion*

As the discussion of these three offences in section 2 illustrates, there is an enormous overlap between the offences and with other property offences and, as suggested earlier by Spencer, one has to question whether, or to what extent, these offences are really necessary. Perhaps the best way forward is a more radical overhaul of all the deception offences, a matter to which we now turn.

### D. *Rethinking the Structure of Deception Offences*

Three points should have emerged from the above discussion of the eight deception offences. First, there is an enormous overlap between them—quite apart from the overlap, already discussed, with theft. Such blurring of offences is morally confusing in fair labelling terms and makes it difficult for prosecutors to know which charge to select. Secondly, some of the offences are unduly complex: a lawyer's dream or nightmare, depending on one's point of view. Thirdly, many of the offences were drafted in a different technological era. While the existing law has necessarily had to be adapted, both by the courts and Parliament, to cater for the modern reality of a commercial world dominated by credit cards, electronic transfers of money and the provision of goods or services through the internet and call centres, the result is messy and confusing and there are gaps, for example, in relation to deceiving machines. Accordingly, the Law Commission has proposed abolition of all the deception offences and their replacement by a general offence of fraud along with one separate offence of obtaining services dishonestly.

### Law Commission, Report No. 276, Fraud (2002) paras 1.6–1.9:

"1.6 [The issue is] whether the introduction of a general fraud offence would improve the criminal law. We have come to the conclusion that it would ...
  (1) It should make the law more comprehensible to juries, especially in serious fraud trials. The charges which are currently employed in such trials are numerous, and none of them adequately describe or encapsulate the meaning of 'fraud'. The statutory offences are too specific to offer a general description of fraud; while the common law offence of conspiracy to defraud is so wide that it offers little guidance on the difference between fraudulent and lawful conduct ...
  (2) A general offence of fraud would be a useful tool in effective prosecutions. Specific offences are sometimes wrongly charged, in circumstances when another offence would have been more suitable. This can result in unjustified acquittals and costly appeals ...
  (3) Introducing a single crime of fraud would dramatically simplify the law of fraud. Clear, simple law is fairer than complicated, inaccessible law. If a citizen is contemplating activities which could amount to a crime, a clear, simple law gives better guidance on whether the conduct is criminal ...
  (4) A general offence of fraud would be aimed at encompassing fraud in all its forms. It would not focus on particular ways or means of committing frauds. Thus it should be better able to keep pace with developing technology.

1.7 In line with these recommendations, we recommend that the eight offences of deception created by the Theft Acts 1968–96 should be repealed and that the common law offence of conspiracy to defraud should be abolished. In their place we recommend the creation of two new statutory offences—one of fraud, and one of obtaining services dishonestly.

1.8 The offence of fraud would be committed where, with intent to make a gain or to cause loss or to expose another to the risk of loss, a person dishonestly:

(1) makes a false representation,

(2) wrongfully fails to disclose information, or

(3) secretly abuses a position of trust.

1.9 The offence of obtaining services dishonestly would be committed where a person by *any dishonest act* obtains services in respect of which payment is required, with intent to avoid payment. Deception is not an essential element of the offence. It would therefore extend to the obtaining of services by providing false information to computers and machines, which under the present law may not amount to an offence at all."

Of course, more radical options are possible. The Law Commission's proposed offences pre-suppose the existence of the remaining property offences such as theft, handling stolen goods and so on. It could be possible to go further and introduce an even broader offence, such as a general offence of dishonesty. Such proposals will be discussed after some other property offences have been canvassed.

## IV. Making Off Without Payment

### A. *Introduction*

We have already examined the general rule that the criminal law does not punish non-payment of debt even when dishonest, unless there has been a deception. It is the element of deception in securing such non-payment that marks conduct out as deserving of criminal liability.

However, in certain situations where debts have been incurred, such as at restaurants, hotels and petrol stations, it has been felt necessary to criminalise dishonest avoidance of payment even in the absence of a deception. This is because of problems of law enforcement. Normally in contractual situations the identity of the other person is known (or where it is not, as in contracts in shops, a charge of theft will often be possible) and, therefore, it is appropriate to leave remedies to the civil law. However, in restaurants or petrol stations, for example, debts are incurred by anonymous debtors in circumstances where a charge of theft is not possible because property might have passed prior to the appropriation. Accordingly, as civil remedies are useless against the unknown, a special criminal offence has been created to deal with such situations and, to secure its effectiveness, a power of arrest has been given to "any person". Thus, a restaurateur or petrol station attendant has the power to arrest any person who is reasonably suspected of committing the offence.[3]

---

[3] Normally a warrant is required for an offence carrying such a low maximum penalty. See section 24, Police and Criminal Evidence Act 1984.

## B. *The Law*

### Theft Act 1978, section 3

"(1) Subject to subsection (3) below, a person who, knowing that payment on the spot for any goods supplied or service done is required or expected from him, dishonestly makes off without having paid as required or expected and with intent to avoid payment of the amount due shall be guilty of an offence.

(2) For purposes of this section 'payment on the spot' includes payment at the time of collecting goods on which work has been done or in respect of which service has been provided.

(3) Subsection (1) above shall not apply where the supply of the goods or the doing of the service is contrary to law, or where the service done is such that payment is not legally enforceable.

(4) Any person may arrest without warrant anyone who is, or whom he, with reasonable cause, suspects to be, committing or attempting to commit an offence under this section."

Strange though it may seem to start with a list of what does not have to be proved under this section, it is, nevertheless, a useful way of proceeding. Thus, one does not need to determine whether or not property has passed; one does not need to establish deception at any stage of the conduct and, finally, one does not have to show dishonesty any earlier than at the time of making off.

### 1. Actus reus

#### (i) *Makes off*

In the case of *Brooks and Brooks*[4] the court said that making off "may be an exercise accompanied by the sound of trumpets or a silent stealing away after the folding of tents". In more prosaic words, there is no need for the leaving to be done by stealth. All that making off requires is that the defendant leave the place where payment is required for another place. So, if a dissatisfied diner openly storms out of a restaurant without paying, she clearly "makes off". (Criminal liability in such a case would turn on whether her actions were regarded as dishonest.) It would appear to be irrelevant that the defendant has the victim's consent to her leaving, whether it is obtained by deception (for example, inducing the creditor to believe payment has already been made) or not (for example, leaving a name and address). In both cases the defendant "makes off" but, again, criminal liability will depend on other elements of the crime such as dishonesty or, in the case of the name and address being left, whether payment was expected on the spot.

#### (ii) *The spot*

What constitutes the "spot" is a matter of some importance: it will determine whether the defendant can be charged with the full offence or only with an attempt. If the spot is deemed to be the premises, as is likely, for example, in the case of leaving a restaurant without paying, then the offence is only committed when the defendant has left the premises. So in *MacDavitt*[5] where the spot was held to be the restaurant, the defendant, who was apprehended as he made for the door, could only be convicted of attempting to make off without payment.

---

[4] (1983) 76 Cr.App.R.66 at 69.
[5] [1981] Crim.L.R.843. See also *Aziz* [1993] Crim.L.R.708.

(iii) *Goods supplied or service done*

In order to understand the phrase "goods supplied" four situations may be compared. In the first, the defendant drives into a petrol station and fills his tank with petrol. He then decides not to pay and makes off. He has had "goods supplied" to him and will be liable under section 3. In the second situation, the defendant takes goods from a shelf in a supermarket and then leaves without paying. The supermarket, by displaying the goods, can be regarded as having "supplied" them and, accordingly, the defendant can be liable under section 3.[6] In the third situation, the defendant walks into a non-self-service shop and asks for and receives a pack of cigarettes. She then walks off without paying and is again liable under section 3 because she has had "goods supplied" to her. In the fourth situation, the defendant leans over the counter and helps himself to the cigarettes. If he makes off without paying he cannot be liable under section 3 because he has not had "goods supplied" to him.

Neither the term "goods" nor "service" is defined by section 3, but it seems unlikely that this omission will lead to practical difficulties. "Service" may well bear a similar meaning to "services" under section 1 although there are suggestions that it is narrower.[7] Just as the goods must be "supplied", so the service must be "done". Clearest examples of this will be the meal provided in a restaurant or the accommodation provided by a hotel, but it would also seem broad enough to cover the defendant who parks his car in someone's car park, thereby taking up the offer to do so.

(iv) *Without having paid*

In practice, the only area likely to cause difficulties here is in relation to payment by dud cheques. The issue is whether such cheques are to be regarded as payment or not. Various views have been expressed about this. On the one hand, it is argued that such payment is not "as required or expected"[8] and should not, therefore, be regarded as payment. The other view is that such cheques should be regarded as payment because they conditionally discharge the defendant's liability to pay (although this does not apply to forged cheques because they do not amount to such a conditional discharge of liability).[9] If the problem of dud cheques (as opposed to forged cheques) is still to be dealt with under the criminal law, then the best way to proceed in such instances is to use section 2(1)(b) and not section 3 at all. Paradoxically, however, this would have the effect of bringing the defendant within a more serious offence.

(v) *As required or expected*

The only situation likely to cause a problem here is where payment is normally required or expected at a certain time but the creditor, because of a deception, agrees to accept payment at a later time. In *Vincent*[10] the proprietors of hotels agreed to accept postponed payment at a time later than normally required or

---

[6] Smith, *The Law of Theft* (8th ed., 1997), pp. 144–145.
[7] See Smith, *ibid*. p. 145 and Williams, *Textbook of Criminal Law* (2nd ed., 1983), p. 878.
[8] Smith, *ibid*. p. 147.
[9] See Syrota, "Are Cheque Frauds covered by Section 3 of the Theft Act 1978?" [1981] Crim.L.R.412 and *Hammond* [1982] Crim.L.R.611.
[10] [2001] Cr.App.R.150.

expected. It was held to be irrelevant that they had only agreed to this because of the defendant's dishonest deception. Section 3 creates a "simple and straightforward offence". Payment was not required or expected at the usual time. The reasons were irrelevant.

### (vi) *Unenforceable debts*

Making off without payment will not be an offence where the payment is legally unenforceable or the supply of goods or services is contrary to law. The defendant who leaves a prostitute without paying commits no offence under section 3.

### Troughton v The Metropolitan Police [1987] Crim.L.R.138 (Queen's Bench Divisional Court)

"The appellant was convicted before the magistrates of making-off without payment of a taxi-fare contrary to section 3 of the Theft Act 1978. ... A taxi driver agreed to take the appellant to his home somewhere in Highbury. The appellant, having had a great deal to drink, had not told the driver his address. The driver had to stop to obtain directions from the appellant at some point. There was an argument, the appellant accusing the driver of making an unnecessary diversion. The taxi driver, being unable to get an address from the appellant, drove to the nearest police station to see if someone else could help. ... The Crown Court having dismissed the appeal the appellant appealed by case stated to the High Court.

Held,
... The basis for allowing this appeal was that the journey had not been completed and the consequence of that was a breach of contract by the taxi driver. Instead of resolving the argument about further instructions during the journey the driver broke away from the route which would have taken the appellant home in order to go to the police station. The driver being in breach of contract was not lawfully able to demand the fare at any time thereafter. For that reason, among others, the appellant was never in a situation in which he was bound to pay or even tender the money for the journey, and thus it could not be contended that he made off without payment."

**Appeal allowed**

## 2. Mens rea

The *mens rea* required under section 3 is: *knowing* that payment on the spot is required the defendant makes off *dishonestly with intent to avoid payment*.

It is clear that there has to be an intent to make permanent default.[11]

## 3. Punishment

The maximum penalty for an offence under section 3 is two years' imprisonment.[12]

### V. OTHER PROPERTY OFFENCES

There are a large number of other property offences, some serious like blackmail, robbery, burglary and handling stolen goods and some not so serious, like taking a conveyance. Whilst it is beyond the scope of this book to deal with all these offences in detail, the chief provisions of some of these offences will be sketched.

---

[11] *Allen* [1985] A.C. 1029.
[12] The guideline sentence for magistrates is: "is discharge or fine appropriate?" (Magistrates' Association, *Sentencing Guidelines* (2001).

## A. *Sociological Background*

The gravity of the conduct encompassed by these offences varies enormously. Robbery is regarded as the most serious because it is not only a property offence, but also an offence of violence. Robberies, which account for two per cent of recorded crime,[13] range from professional armed robberies on banks and the causing of serious injury to relatively minor street "muggings"[14] where the victim is threatened with a punch if she does not hand over some money or a mobile phone.[15]

England and Wales have a worryingly high robbery rate compared with other countries and the number of recorded robberies has increased sharply in recent years despite the overall recorded crime rate having fallen.[16] While women are more worried about being mugged than men,[17] 76 per cent of victims are male and robberies from males are likely to be more physically intrusive (for example, being physically searched). 70 per cent of robberies from female victims involve property such as handbags and mobile phones being snatched from them. Nearly half of all robbery victims are under 20 years old. Weapons are used or displayed in 33 per cent of personal robberies and 40 per cent of personal robberies result in some form of injury to the victim.[18]

About half of all robberies are reported and, of these, only half are recorded. A mere 18 per cent of recorded robberies are "cleared up" meaning that only about five per cent of robberies "remain in the system".[19]

The other major property offence that is the subject of much media attention is burglary which accounts for 16 per cent of all recorded crime (about half of which is from a dwelling)[20] and eight per cent of all crime according to the British Crime Survey.[21]

The threat of burglary is a particular source of anxiety for both men and women with 15 per cent of adults indicating they had "high levels of worry" about burglary.[22] Indeed, a higher proportion of English and Welsh households have taken security measures (such as burglar alarms) to protect their property against the risk of burglary than in other countries.[23] Perhaps this fear would be even higher if it was commonly known that in 54 per cent of domestic burglaries somebody is in the house.[24] Victims of burglary run a greatly increased risk of repeat victimisation.

---

[13] Home Office Statistical Bulletin, *Crime in England and Wales 2001/02* (2002).

[14] For an account of the importation of this term from the U.S.A. with the consequential "moral panic" generated (where official and media reaction was out of all proportion to the threat posed) see Hall, *Policing the Crisis* (1978).

[15] In 2001/02, some 35 per cent of robberies involved a mobile phone (Home Office Statistical Bulletin, *Crime in England and Wales 2001/02*(2002).).

[16] Smith, *The Nature of Personal Robbery* (H.O.R.S. No. 254, 2003).

[17] Home Office Statistical Bulletin, *Crime in England and Wales 2001/02* (2002).

[18] Smith, *The Nature of Personal Robbery* (H.O.R.S. No. 254, 2003).

[19] Ashworth, "Robbery Re-assessed" [2002] Crim.L.R.851 and references cited therein.

[20] Home Office, *Information on the Criminal Justice System in England and Wales: Digest 4* (1999).

[21] Home Office Statistical Bulletin, *Crime in England and Wales 2001/02* (2002).

[22] Home Office Statistical Bulletin, *Crime in England and Wales: Quarterly Update* (2003).

[23] Mayhew and van Dijk, *Criminal Victimisation in Eleven Industrialised Countries: Key Findings from the International Crime Victims Survey* (1997).

[24] Home Office Statistical Bulletin, *Crime in England and Wales 2001/02: Supplementary Volume* (2003).

The areas most likely to be targeted are socio-economically disadvantaged neighbourhoods that are vulnerable to high crime generally. On the other hand, in 59 per cent of all burglaries no property is in fact stolen[25] and there is no threat or violence in 89 per cent of burglaries.[26] Further, despite its prevalence, the rate of burglaries has in fact declined over recent years.[27] Fear, of course, has to be judged against risk. The B.C.S. reveals that, overall, 3.5 per cent of households in England and Wales interviewed in 2001/02 had experienced at least one domestic burglary in the previous 12 months.[28] However, it goes without saying that fear of crime need not be rationally based. To many, burglary is a particularly distressing crime, not just because of loss of property or risk of violence, but because it amounts to an attack on the bastion of one's privacy: the home. Evidence suggests that victims of domestic burglary are emotionally affected in 81 per cent of incidents.[29]

The reporting and recording rates for burglary are higher than for robbery largely because insurance claims cannot be made without the crime being reported. In 2001/02, just over 60 per cent of all burglaries were reported to the police with 70 per cent of these being recorded. Where there had been property lost in the burglary, the reporting rate rose to 84 per cent with 90 per cent of those being recorded.[30] However, the clear-up rate for domestic burglary is only 19 per cent.[31]

## B. *The Legal Background*

Some of the offences incorporated in the Theft Act of 1968 were already statutory, such as burglary and handling stolen goods under the Larceny Act of 1916; others were common law offences, such as robbery. There can be no doubt, however, that the reforms introduced were timely. Burglary had become a particularly complex offence, with distinctions having to be drawn between "breaking in the night" and "breaking in the day". Fletcher makes the point that the insistence upon the requirement of "breaking" in the development of this offence marks an adherence to a theory of manifest liability, where the actions of the defendant had to be manifestly criminal for an offence to be committed.[32] What has happened since has been a retreat from that position; the new law not only does away with the archaic distinction between breaking by day and night but does away with the requirement of breaking altogether. The replacement, trespass, however, "retains at least a trace of the traditional rule that the entry must be manifestly suspicious".[33]

The severity with which most of these offences are regarded is indicated not only by the maximum sentences available for the offences: robbery and aggravated burglary are punishable by up to life imprisonment and domestic burglary and

---

[25] Home Office Statistical Bulletin, *Crime in England and Wales 2001/02* (2002). This is the B.C.S. estimate. This figure includes attempted burglaries. Where entry is gained to a home, there is theft of property in just under three quarters of cases (Sentencing Advisory Panel, *Annual Report 2001/02* (2002).

[26] *ibid.*

[27] Home Office Research Bulletin, *Crime in England and Wales 2001/02* (2002).

[28] Home Office Statistical Bulletin, *Crime in England and Wales 2001–02* (2002).

[29] *ibid.*

[30] *ibid.*

[31] Home Office, *Criminal Statistics England and Wales 1998* (1998).

[32] Fletcher, *Rethinking Criminal Law* (1978), pp. 124–128.

[33] *ibid.* at p. 128.

handling stolen goods by up to 14 years' imprisonment,[34] but also by the sentences actually handed down by the courts. Of those convicted of robbery in 2000, 69 per cent received custodial sentences with most of the remainder being persons aged between 10 and 17. Professional armed robbers receive sentences in the 18–20 years' imprisonment range while less serious robberies (for example, lesser street "muggings") attract sentences in the 3–5 years' imprisonment range.[35] Robbery with a firearm or imitation firearm is a "serious offence" which involves an automatic sentence of life imprisonment for a second offence unless there are "exceptional circumstances".[36]

Of those sentenced for domestic burglary in 2000 in the Crown Court, 77 per cent were given immediate custodial sentences (average length: 20.9 months), while of those sentences in the magistrates' courts (about 32 per cent of the total) 29 per cent were sentenced to immediate custody (average sentence length: 5.3 months).[37] In the sentencing guideline judgment of *McInerney; Keating*[38] the Court of Appeal largely followed the advice of the Sentencing Advisory Panel but advocated more extensive use of community sentences than advised by the Panel. For a domestic burglary displaying most of the features of a "standard domestic burglary" committed by a first or second time domestic burglar, a community sentence should be imposed to tackle the offender's behaviour. Custodial sentences should only be imposed if the offender has demonstrated by his or her behaviour that a community sentence is not practicable.[39] Where a person convicted of domestic burglary has two or more qualifying previous convictions, there is now a presumptive minimum sentence of three years' custody.[40]

## C. *The Law*

Only the main features of these offences will be highlighted.

### 1. Robbery

#### Theft Act 1968, section 8

"(1) A person is guilty of robbery if he steals, and immediately before or at the time of doing so, and in order to do so, he uses force on any person or puts or seeks to put any person in fear of being then and there subjected to force.

(2) A person guilty of robbery, or of an assault with intent to rob, shall on conviction on indictment be liable to imprisonment for life."

Robbery is theft aggravated by the threat or use of force. The elements of theft must be established if a conviction for robbery is to be obtained. If the defendant

---

[34] Theft Act 1968, ss.8(2), 9(4), 10(2) and 22(2).
[35] Ashworth, "Robbery Re-assessed" [2002] Crim.L.R.851.
[36] Powers of the Criminal Courts (Sentencing) Act 2000, s.109.
[37] Sentencing Advisory Panel, *Annual Report 2001/02* (2002).
[38] [2002] EWCA Crim 3003. See above pp. 77–79 for an extract from this case.
[39] These guidelines, somewhat misrepresented, caused a furore in the national press and prompted Lord Woolf to state that all sentencers would be written to, to clarify the position.
[40] Powers of the Criminal Courts (Sentencing) Act 2000, s.111.

believes he has a legal right to the property he takes (even if not to the way he takes it) then there can be no theft and, therefore, no robbery.[41]

The element additional to theft is that of force and a number of points need to be made about this. First, force is a question of fact to be determined by a jury, although it would seem that very little force is actually required.[42] Wrenching a shopping basket[43] or handbag[44] from the owner can suffice. Secondly, the force must take place immediately before or at the time of the theft.[45] Lastly, the threat of force must be used in order to steal and not for any other purpose such as rape.[46] While the *mens rea* of theft is not spelt out in section 8, it is clear that there must be the *mens rea* of theft, and the force or threatened force must be *in order to steal*; an accidental, negligent or even reckless use of force will not suffice.

Robbery is an extremely broad offence and while some robberies can be extremely serious, others can be relatively minor as where there is no more than a threat of a punch in order to steal a mobile phone. As the threat by itself would amount to no more than an assault (carrying a maximum penalty of six months' imprisonment) and the theft, although carrying a maximum penalty of seven years' imprisonment, would not be severely punished, one is forced to question whether the combination of the two elements justifies such a serious offence carrying a maximum penalty of life imprisonment.

### Andrew Ashworth, "Robbery Re-assessed" [2002] Crim.L.R.851 at 871:

"Violence can be a serious matter, and the law distinguishes serious from less serious degrees. Robbery can also be serious, but the law fails to distinguish very serious from less serious degrees. The result is that the label 'robbery' carries connotations that sometimes grossly misrepresent the seriousness of an offence. A radical approach would be to abolish the offence of robbery, leaving its ingredients to be charged separately. Another approach would be to divide the offence into at least two degrees, using the law of offences against the person as the basis. That would have the procedural benefit of ensuring that lesser offences become triable either way, rather than sending all offenders aged 18 and over to the Crown Court.

One desirable consequence of such a re-assessment would be that sentencing guidance is focused on the amount of the theft and the degree of force used or threatened."

### 2. Burglary and Aggravated Burglary

### Theft Act 1968, sections 9 and 10

"9.—(1) A person is guilty of burglary if—
(a) he enters any building or part of a building as a trespasser and with intent to commit any such offence as is mentioned in subsection (2) below; or
(b) having entered any building or part of a building as a trespasser he steals or attempts to steal anything in the building or that part of it or inflicts or attempts to inflict on any

---

[41] *Robinson* [1977] Crim.L.R.173.
[42] *Dawson and James* (1976) 64 Cr.App.R.170; *Clouden* [1987] Crim.L.R.56.
[43] *Clouden* [1987] Crim.L.R.56.
[44] *Corcoran v Anderton* (1980) 71 Cr.App.R.104.
[45] In *Atakpu* [1994] Q.B. 69 the court was of the view that it should be left to the common sense of the jury to decide at what point the theft finished. This will determine whether the force was used at the time of the theft.
[46] In a situation such as this the defendant may be convicted of theft or possibly attempted rape.

person therein any grievous bodily harm.

(2) The offences referred to in subsection (1)(a) above are offences of stealing anything in the building or part of a building in question, of inflicting on any person therein any grievous bodily harm or raping any person therein, and of doing unlawful damage to the building or anything therein. . . .

(3) A person guilty of burglary shall on conviction on indictment be liable to imprisonment for a term not exceeding—

    (a) where the offence was committed in respect of a building or part of a building which is a dwelling, fourteen years;

    (b) in any other case, ten years.

(4) References in subsections (1) and (2) above to a building, and the reference in subsection (3) above to a building which is a dwelling, shall apply also to an inhabited vehicle or vessel, and shall apply to any such vehicle or vessel at times when the person having a habitation in it is not there as well as at times when he is.

10.—(1) A person is guilty of aggravated burglary if he commits any burglary and at the time has with him any firearm or imitation firearm, any weapon of offence, or any explosive; and for this purpose—

    (a) 'firearm' includes an airgun or air pistol, and 'imitation firearm' means anything which has the appearance of being a firearm, whether capable of being discharged or not; and

    (b) 'weapon of offence' means any article made or adapted for use for causing injury to or incapacitating a person, or intended by the person having it with him for such use; and

    (c) 'explosive' means any article manufactured for the purpose of producing a practical effect by explosion, or intended by the person having it with him for that purpose.

(2) A person guilty of aggravated burglary shall on conviction on indictment be liable to imprisonment for life."

There are now four offences of burglary within section 9. Under section 9(1)(a) there are two offences of entering a building as a trespasser with the intention of stealing, inflicting grievous bodily harm, raping a person or doing unlawful damage—one committed where the building is a "dwelling" and one where it is not. The former offence is known as "domestic burglary".[47] Similarly, under section 9(1)(b) having entered a "dwelling" as a trespasser and then stealing, etc. is distinguished from other buildings or parts thereof. Section 10 creates a more serious offence: burglary aggravated by the presence of weapons.

### R. v Collins [1973] Q.B. 100 (Court of Appeal, Criminal Division)

(The facts appear in the judgment)

Edmund-Davies L.J.:

"Let me relate the facts. Were they put into a novel or portrayed on the stage, they would be regarded as being so improbable as to be unworthy of serious consideration and as verging at times on farce. At about 2 o'clock in the early morning of Saturday, July 24, 1971, a young lady of 18 went to bed at her mother's home in Colchester. She had spent the evening with her boyfriend. She had taken a certain amount of drink, and it may be that this fact affords some explanation of her inability to answer satisfactorily certain crucial questions put to her at the trial.

She has the habit of sleeping without wearing night apparel in a bed which is very near the lattice-type window of her room. At one stage in her evidence she seemed to be saying that the bed was close up against the window which, in accordance with her practice, was wide open. In the photographs which we have before us, however, there appears to be a gap of some sort between the two, but the bed was clearly quite near the window.

---

[47] This is the terminology employed by the Powers of Criminal Courts (Sentencing) Act 2000, s.111.

At about 3.30 or 4 o'clock she awoke and she then saw in the moonlight a vague form crouched in the open window. She was unable to remember, and this is important, whether the form was on the outside of the window sill or on that part of the sill which was inside the room, and for reasons which will later become clear, that seemingly narrow point is of crucial importance.

The young lady then realised several things: first of all that the form in the window was that of a male; secondly, that he was a naked male; and thirdly, that he was a naked male with an erect penis. She also saw in the moonlight that his hair was blond. She thereupon leapt to the conclusion that her boyfriend, with whom for some time she had been on terms of regular and frequent sexual intimacy, was paying her an ardent nocturnal visit. She promptly sat up in bed, and the man descended from the sill and joined her in bed and they had full sexual intercourse. But there was something about him which made her think that things were not at as they usually were between her and her boyfriend. The length of his hair, his voice as they had exchanged what what was described as 'love talk', and other features led her to the conclusion that somehow there was something different. So she turned on the bed-side light, saw that her companion was not her boyfriend and slapped the face of the intruder, who was none other than the defendant. He said to her, 'Give me a good time tonight', and got hold of her arm, but she bit him and told him to go. She then went into the bathroom and he promptly vanished.

The complainant said that she would not have agreed to intercourse if she had known that the person entering her room was not her boyfriend. But there was no suggestion of any force having been used upon her, and the intercourse which took place was undoubtedly effected with no resistance on her part.

The defendant was seen by the police at about 10.30 later that same morning. According to the police, the conversation which took place then elicited these points: He was very lustful the previous night. He had taken a lot of drink. . . . He went on to say that he knew the complainant because he had worked around her house. On this occasion, desiring sexual intercourse—and according to the police evidence he added that he was determined to have a girl, by force if necessary, although that part of the police evidence he challenged—he went on to say that he walked around the house, saw a light in an upstairs bedroom, and he knew that this was the girl's bedroom. He found a step ladder, leaned it against the wall and climbed up and looked into the bedroom. He could see through the wide-open window a girl who was naked and asleep. So he descended the ladder and stripped off all his clothes, with the exception of his socks, because apparently he took the view that if the girl's mother entered the bedroom is would be easier to effect a rapid escape if he had his socks on than if he was in his bare feet. That is a matter about which we are not called upon to express any view, and would in any event find ourselves unable to express one.

Having undressed, he then climbed the ladder and pulled himself up on to the window sill. His version of the matter is that he was pulling himself in when she awoke. She then got up and knelt on the bed, she put her arms around his neck and body, and she seemed to pull him into the bed. He went on: 'I was rather dazed because I didn't think she would want to know me. We kissed and cuddled for about 10 or 15 minutes and then I had it away with her but found it hard because I had had so much to drink.' . . .

Now, one feature of the case which remained at the conclusion of the evidence in great obscurity is where exactly Collins was at the moment when, according to him, the girl manifested that she was welcoming him. Was he kneeling on the sill outside the window or was he already inside the room, having climbed through the window frame, and kneeling upon the inner sill? It was a crucial matter, for there were certainly three ingredients that it was incumbent upon the Crown to establish. Under section 9 of the Theft Act, 1968, which renders a person guilty of burglary if he enters any building or part of a building as a trespasser and with the intention of committing rape, the entry of the accused into the building must first be proved. Well, there is no doubt about that, for it is common ground that he did enter this girl's bedroom. Secondly, it must be proved that he entered as a trespasser. We will develop that point a little later. Thirdly, it must be proven that he entered as a trespasser with intent at the time of entry to commit rape therein.

The second ingredient of the offence—the entry must be as a trespasser—is one which has not, to the best of our knowledge, been previously canvassed in the courts. ...

What does that involve? ...

... In the judgment of this court there cannot be a conviction for entering premises 'as a trespasser' within the meaning of section 9 of the Theft Act unless the person entering does so knowing that he is a trespasser and nevertheless deliberately enters, or, at the very least, is reckless as to whether or not he is entering the premises of another without the other party's consent.

Having so held, the pivotal point of this appeal is whether the Crown established that this defendant at the moment that he entered the bedroom knew perfectly well that he was not welcome there or, being reckless as to whether he was welcome or not, was nevertheless determined to enter. That in turn involves consideration as to where he was at the time that the complainant indicated that she was welcoming him into her bedroom. If, to take an example that was put in the course of argument, her bed had not been near the window but was on the other side of the bedroom, and he (being determined to have her sexually even against her will) climbed through the window and crossed the bedroom to reach her bed, then the offence charged would have been established. But in this case, as we have related, the layout of the room was different, and it became a point of nicety which had to be conclusively established by the Crown as to where he was when the girl made welcoming signs, as she unquestionably at some stage did ...

Unless the jury were entirely satisfied that the defendant made an effective and substantial entry into the bedroom without the complainant doing or saying anything to cause him to believe that she was consenting to his entering it, he ought not to be convicted of the offence charged. The point is a narrow one, as narrow maybe as the window sill which is crucial to this case. ...

We have to say that his appeal must be allowed on the basis that the jury were never invited to consider the vital question whether this young man did enter the premises as a trespasser, that is to say knowing perfectly well that he had no invitation to enter or reckless of whether or not his entry was with permission."

**Appeal allowed**

(i) *Actus reus*

From this case it can be seen that the offence of burglary contrary to section 9(1)(a) involves the following elements.[48]

(a) Enters.

Whether there has been an entry is a question of fact for the jury. In giving them guidance the court in *Collins* held that there had been to be an "effective and substantial" entry. In *Brown*[49] the court qualified this approach requiring only an "effective" entry. Thus it is unnecessary for the entire body of the defendant to be inside the building but minimal intrusions such as a few fingers would be generally insufficient. In *Ryan*[50] it was held that the jury was entitled to consider whether there was an entry in a case where the defendant's head and arm were inside a window when he became trapped. It is difficult to see how this could amount to an "effective" entry.

(b) As a trespasser.

Reference must be made to the civil law in order to understand the term "trespass". Under civil law, trespass is entry without the consent of the lawful

---

[48] The same elements are required under s.9(1)(b) subject to the necessary modifications.
[49] [1985] Crim.L.R.212.
[50] [1996] Crim.L.R.320.

possessor. No conviction for burglary can be obtained without a finding of civil trespass but, as *Collins* makes clear, more than this is required: the defendant must enter "knowing that he is a trespasser ... or, at the very least, is reckless whether or not he is entering the premises of another without the other party's consent". This was the point at issue in *Collins*. Had he entered the building prior to being invited in? If so, he was a trespasser.

Even if there is consent, if the defendant acts in a way that goes beyond what the possessor would have consented to, he may be deemed to enter as a trespasser. Thus in *Jones and Smith*[51] the defendant had left his parents' home but was a frequent, welcome visitor. One night he entered their home and stole two television sets. Despite the father's loyal statement that his son was welcome at *any* time, the court held that an inference could be drawn that he would not have consented to entry for the purposes of theft. The son was thus held to have entered as a trespasser.

(c) Any building or part of a building.

Two issues are raised here. First, what constitutes a "building"? Section 9(4) gives an extended meaning to the term by including within it inhabited vehicles and vessels such as caravans and houseboats. The occupant does not have to be present at the time in order to render it "inhabited" but it would seem that it would have to be lived in.

Little other statutory guidance is given as to the ambit of "building"; generally it would seem appropriate to take a commonsense view of it. It would be too restrictive to think in terms of just houses, flats, offices and the like. Outbuildings such as garages and sheds must also be included. The courts have tended to regard both a degree of permanence and considerable size as appropriate criteria to determine whether something constitutes a "building".[52] As Smith points out, for example, tents and telephone kiosks are, therefore, probably not buildings for the purposes of burglary.[53]

The second issue relates to "part of a building". This does not necessarily mean a separate room. It includes areas such as those behind counters in shops from which the defendant is excluded.[54]

(ii) *Dwelling*

The Criminal Justice Act 1991 created the new offences of domestic burglary in respect of section 9(1)(a) and (b) where the building is a "dwelling". Dwelling is not defined but presumably means a building (or vessel or vehicle) in which someone lives as their home. Smith argues that because this is an aggravating element it should import a requirement of *mens rea*; the defendant should only be guilty if he knows or thinks somebody might be living there.[55]

(iii) *Mens rea*

The *mens rea* requirement for burglary under section 9(1)(a) is:

(i) intention or recklessness as to trespass

---

[51] [1976] 1 W.L.R. 672.
[52] *Stevens v Gorley* (1859) 7 C.B.(N.S.) 99.
[53] Smith, *The Law of Theft* (8th ed., 1997), p. 197.
[54] Either expressly or impliedly: *Walkington* [1979] 1 W.L.R. 1169.
[55] Smith and Hogan, *Criminal Law* (10th ed., 2002), pp. 641–642.

(ii) intention to commit one of the offences in section 9(2).

### (iv) *Aggravated burglary*

If a person "commits any burglary and at the time has with him any firearm or imitation firearm, any weapon of offence, or any explosive", the offence becomes aggravated burglary.[56] For the purposes of this offence it does not matter whether the burglary is of a dwelling or not.

For the purposes of section 9(1)(a) (entry with intent), the defendant must have the article of aggravation with him at the time of entry. For the purposes of section 9(1)(b) (having entered), the relevant time is when the specified offence is committed. So, if a defendant, having entered as a trespasser, picks up a kitchen knife and uses it to force the householder to hand over the property, aggravated burglary is committed. In *Klass*[57] it was held that the weapon must be carried by the person at the time of entering the building. The offence is not committed if another party outside the building is in sole possession of a weapon.

### (v) *Punishment*

A person found guilty of burglary of a dwelling is liable to imprisonment for up to 14 years. In other circumstances the maximum is now 10 years.[58] If the burglary is aggravated the maximum is life imprisonment.

### 3. Handling Stolen Goods

### (i) *Introduction*

The offence of handling stolen goods is closely related to that of theft and there is a considerable overlap between the two offences. Many thieves literally handle the property they have stolen and so, to prevent such persons being liable for both offences, careful demarcation of the two crimes is necessary. Also, many handlers satisfy the test of appropriation and the other elements in the definition of theft. The Criminal Law Revision Committee was fully aware of this overlap, but saw "no reason in principle or convenience" against it, although circumstances and evidentiary requirements may dictate the more natural charge.[59] Handling is a very broad offence covering a wide range of circumstances. The handler could be a professional "fence" or an otherwise law-abiding person buying a stolen video recorder at a car-boot sale. It is thought that without professional handlers of stolen goods, so-called "fences" and "placers", there would be a lot less theft. Handling thus has a higher maximum sentence (of 14 years' imprisonment) than theft to deal with large-scale handling operations. However, the majority of handlers are not such professional criminals[60] and the sentences most frequently

---

[56] Theft Act 1968, s.10.
[57] [1998] 1 Cr.App.R.453.
[58] For sentencing guidelines, see *above*, p. 841.
[59] Criminal Law Revision Committee, Eighth Report (1966), Cmnd.2977, para. 132.
[60] Mode of trial guidelines state that handling cases should be tried summarily unless the handler commissioned the theft, the offence has professional hallmarks or the property was worth over £10,000 (Criminal Justice Consultative Council, *National Mode of Trial Guidelines* (1995), revising *Practice Note (Mode of Trial: Guidelines)* (1990) 92 Cr.App.R.142.

imposed are community sentences, fines and discharges. Only about 20 per cent of persons convicted of this offence receive custodial sentences.[61]

(ii) *The law*

## Theft Act 1968, section 22

"(1) A person handles stolen goods if (otherwise than in the course of the stealing) knowing or believing them to be stolen goods he dishonestly receives the goods, or dishonestly undertakes or assists in their retention, removal, disposal or realisation by or for the benefit of another person, or if he arranges to do so.

(2) A person guilty of handling stolen goods shall on conviction on indictment be liable to imprisonment for a term not exceeding 14 years."

It should be noted that section 22 creates only *one* offence, although there are a large number of ways in which this offence can be committed. In fact, it renders culpable almost any way of dealing with stolen goods as long as there is *mens rea*. So, for example, the person who arranges to handle stolen goods commits the offence under section 22 despite the fact that, but for the provision, he would not even have done enough to be liable for an attempt.

### (a) Actus reus

The elements of the *actus reus* are:
1. the goods must be stolen at the time of handling
2. there must be a handling of the goods.

1. The goods must be stolen at the time of handling.

Section 34(2)(b) defines "goods" as including money and every other description of property, except land. In addition, section 24 defines stolen goods as those obtained by theft under section 1, those obtained by deception under section 15 and those obtained by blackmail under section 21. Importantly, the goods must remain stolen at the time the handling occurs; so, for example, where the goods have been reduced to police custody and used to bait a trap to catch handlers there can be no conviction under section 22.[62]

The handling must be "otherwise than in the course of the stealing". This provision is necessary to prevent thieves being simultaneously guilty of both theft and handling. This raises the problem of when theft ends which depends upon whether an appropriation can be regarded as a continuing act.[63] In *Atakpu*[64] it was held that an appropriation continued as long as the thief was "on the job". Inevitably, such a fluid test raises problems. If a burglar steals valuables from a house and hands them to his "fence" in a car parked outside on the street, is he still "on the job"? The liability of the "fence" for theft or handling will depend upon such a determination.

---

[61] Sentencing Advisory Panel, *Handling Stolen Goods* (2001).
[62] See s.24 and (3) *Attorney-General's Reference (No. 1 of 1974)* [1974] 2 All E.R. 899. The exception will be where it is possible to establish arranging to handle at some earlier time. Alternatively, a charge of attempting to handle stolen goods may be possible.
[63] See *Hale* (1979) 68 Cr.App.R.415; *Lockley* [1995] Crim.L.R.656.
[64] [1994] Q.B. 69.

A further problem arose as a consequence of the House of Lords' decision of *Preddy*.[65] One effect of holding that a section 15 offence was not committed when a money transfer was obtained by CHAPS order, electronic transfer or cheques was that the credit balance created in the recipient's account could not constitute stolen goods for the purposes of handling. The Law Commission took the view that there were difficulties with amending section 22 and instead, a new, analogous offence under section 24A has been created of dishonestly retaining a wrongful credit.[66]

2. There must be a handling of the goods.

Although the preferred view, as indicated above, is that there is only one offence, there are 18 ways in which the property may be handled.[67] The stereo-typical case of handling will involve receiving the goods but it will also encompass disposal (even by way of destruction) and assisting another to deal with the stolen goods. A brief look at the interpretation of this latter form of handling reinforces how very wide this offence is. In *Kanwar*,[68] the Court of Appeal held that "assistance" requires that something be done to aid the retention, removal, disposal or realisation of the goods but that this was not limited to physical acts. On the facts of the case, lying to protect one's husband who had brought stolen goods into the house was held to be sufficient.

### (b) Mens rea

The *mens rea* requirement for handling under section 22 is:
1. the defendant must know or believe the goods to be stolen. There seems to be hardly any difference in the meaning of these words in this context. Belief, if anything, falls only just short of knowledge: where no other reasonable conclusion can be drawn by the defendant but that the goods were stolen.[69] Mere suspicion that the goods could be stolen is, however, not sufficient.
2. there must be dishonesty. Dishonesty here bears the same meaning as for theft. Accordingly, a person could receive stolen goods knowing that they are stolen but intending to return them to the owner. In such a case a finding of dishonesty would be unlikely under the *Ghosh* test.

### (c) Punishment

The maximum penalty for handling stolen goods is 14 years' imprisonment.[70]

---

[65] [1996] A.C. 815.
[66] Theft (Amendment) Act 1996. See further, the Law Commission, No. 243, *Offences of Dishonesty: Money Transfers*, (1996), pp. 36–43 and Smith, *The Law of Theft* (8th ed., 1997), pp. 239–241.
[67] *Nicklin* [1977] 1 W.L.R. 403.
[68] [1982] 1 W.L.R. 845.
[69] In directing the jury, the judge should avoid trying to distinguish the two terms: *Forsyth* [1997] 2 Cr.App.R.299.
[70] The guideline sentence for magistrates is: "is it serious enough for a community penalty?": Magistrates' Association, *Sentencing Guidelines* (2001). The guideline decision is *Wilson* (1980) 2 Cr.App.R.(S.) 196.

## VI. Conclusion

An evaluation of these property offences cannot be undertaken until the underlying elements and rationale of such offences have been exposed. Only then can comment about structure and sentencing levels be made.

### A. *Underlying Rationale*

What do all the different property offences have in common? Clearly, the common denominator in such offences is that they all involve an interference with the property interests of the victim. But what degree of interference is necessary?

We have already seen that the emphasis is *not* on actual loss of property. Indeed, there need not be any loss of property. In theft, for example, there need only be an *intention* of permanent deprivation; there need be no actual deprivation. In burglary, there need only be an entry to a building with one of the specified intents. No property need be taken. This same point emerged strongly when dealing with the non-criminalisation of breach of contract.[71] Losses from theft can be minimal, or non-existent, in comparison with losses from breach of contract and many losses from theft and other property offences can be made good—either by actions for recovery of the goods or by insurance.

It thus seems clear that the emphasis is not on the loss of the property (which could be described as the direct or "first order" harm), but on the quality of the defendant's actions. The focus is on *wrongdoing*. The requirement of dishonesty for most property offences underlines this. The defendant's actions must be such that the community as a whole can reject them as "wrong". The defendant's actions pose a threat to the value system inherent in our whole concept of property. This threat, which raises the risk that there will be actual loss to property, can be seen as the real harm in the property offences. It is not the only harm. Many of the offences have their own special and distinctive harms, but this threat is the harm common to all of them and can be seen as a "second-order" harm analagous to the "second-order" harms encountered in the law of attempt.[72]

### B. *Structure of Property Offences*

Many of the property offences are so similar that perhaps one ought to consider abolishing most of them and introducing a single broad offence of dishonesty or wrongful interference with property rights. The Law Commission[73] has considered this option and rejected it on the grounds that it could extend the reach of the criminal law too far, would place too much reliance on the elusive concept of "dishonesty" and would probably be incompatible with Articles 5 and 7 of the European Convention on Human Rights which has been interpreted to require that offences be formulated with sufficient precision to enable people to regulate their conduct. Such a broad offence would clearly breach the principle of fair labelling whereby different offences should encapsulate different wrongs in a morally informative manner. It would be unthinkable to conflate all the existing property

[71] *Above*, p. 784.
[72] *Above*, p. 465.
[73] Law Commission Consultation Paper No. 155, *Fraud and Deception* (1999).

offences into a single new crime. For example, burglary and robbery involve wrongs quite separate from mere interference with property rights. The same is equally true of other offences such as handling and blackmail.

An alternative solution could be the introduction of a smaller (than at present) number of more broadly drawn offences. For example, the Law Commission has proposed abolishing the existing deception offences and replacing them with a new single offence of fraud, and a new specific offence of obtaining services dishonestly. Other possibilities remain. Given the present overlap between theft and section 15, the latter could be abolished and absorbed into theft or, perhaps, an expanded form of theft. This new offence could be drafted to encompass the present offence of handling stolen goods. In most cases a person who handles stolen goods is "assuming the rights of owner" over property and is thereby appropriating it, becoming guilty of theft. The official Criminal Statistics do not even distinguish between these two offences.

It is submitted, however, that such an approach would be misguided. While there is much to be said for a tidying up of the present deception offences along the lines proposed by the Law Commission, most of the core central property offences should be retained in something like their present form. Criminal offences should describe as accurately as possible the conduct which is prohibited. The moral messages sought to be communicated by the criminal law and by the punishment of offenders become confused if offence categorisations are not clearly understood by the public. There are important moral distinctions between these offences which the public, albeit only intuitively, recognise and which need protecting.

Let us consider two examples, the first of which has already been discussed earlier in this chapter. This was the argument that theft and section 15 should be retained as separate offences and that it is regrettable that *Gomez* has largely collapsed the distinction between them. The typical theft is very different from the typical obtaining by deception: it involves a surreptitious taking against which the owner is helpless; there is a risk of violence if the thief is interrupted; because of the thief's anonymity there are extra difficulties in identifying and apprehending the thief. On the other hand, with the typical obtaining by deception the victim hands over the property "voluntarily": he has an opportunity to resist; he can avoid being deceived (or, at least, more easily than general theft can be avoided); the deceiver has to face the victim openly, thereby increasing the chances of subsequent identification and apprehension. The differences between the paradigmatic instances of the two offences suggest their retention as separate offences.

The second example relates to theft and handling. Apart from the fact that the overlap between these two crimes is not complete with not all cases of handling amounting to theft, there are important differences between these offences in terms of fair labelling. Handling is a very different offence in terms of public perception, (see below) and in terms of the need to be able to impose high deterrent sentences (hence the 14 years maximum). Handlers of stolen goods provide much of the market for theft; their activities are a significant source of the economic motivation behind much theft. If the law could stamp out professional handlers much of the incentive to commit theft would be reduced.

Alternatively, we should consider whether the present offences are too broadly drawn. Should there be some further subdivision? This has already been achieved with burglary. Burglary involves a special harm, namely the violation of the security and sanctity of the home. This can cause special psychological harm: distress, alarm, and the fear of knowing one is not safe even in one's own home.[74] Accordingly, the Criminal Justice Act 1991 drew a distinction between burglaries of dwellings where these harms would be most acutely felt (maximum 14 years' imprisonment) and burglaries of non-dwellings (maximum 10 years' imprisonment).[75] Further, section 10 of the Theft Act 1968 creates the separate offence of aggravated burglary where there is the extra harm of possession of a weapon of offence at the scene of the burglary. This is not only more frightening but increases the risk of violence actually being used, in that the burglar might be "tempted to use it if challenged".[76]

### C. M. V. Clarkson, Understanding Criminal Law (3rd ed., 2001), pp. 238–239:

"[M]ost people today regard handling as a lesser offence in terms of moral stigma; defendants will often plead guilty to handling on condition that all charges of theft are dropped. This attitude has come about because of a growing view that handlers and purchasers of stolen goods are 'only slightly dishonest people' (Spencer, 1985) who are not as blameworthy as those who actually steal or burgle. Buying and selling stolen goods are the most common offences amongst young offenders (Graham and Bowling, 1995). Theft and burglary create an immediate sense of danger in the community; there must often be a risk of violence with such activities; the thief or burglar is the primary cause of harm, directly invading the rights of the owner of property. In contrast, the criminal receiver, the 'fence', is regarded only as a shady, somewhat disreputable character—and the secondary purchaser as simply someone who has succumbed to the 'natural temptation' of buying something very cheap.

The law is accordingly faced with a dilemma. On the one hand, it recognises that the punishment of handlers is crucial if theft and burglary is to be reduced but, on the other hand, it is faced by an apathetic public almost prepared to 'turn a blind eye' to handling. A possible way out of this dilemma could be to divide the offence of handling stolen goods into degrees. The more serious offence could be reserved for the professional 'fence', the lesser offence covering secondary purchasers. Such a division might be a fairer reflection of the moral stigma felt by most to attach to the two categories of handlers and could have the advantage of underwriting the necessity of enforcement against, and harm caused by, the professional handler. The danger with such an approach, however, could be that even less moral stigma would be attached to secondary purchasers than at present and, after all, it is these purchasers who buy stolen goods from fences who are the 'key element in the incentive structure that supports property crime.' "

Another suggestion is that property offences should be subdivided into separate offences based on the value of the property interfered with. In the United States the Model Penal Code states that theft of property worth less than $50 constitutes a petty misdemeanour, theft of property valued at between $50 and $500 constitutes a misdemeanour and theft of property with a value exceeding $500 constitutes a felony of the third degree.[77] Each offence category carries its own range of penalties.

---

[74] The lives of a large majority of victims of burglary are affected for some weeks after a burglary, and over a quarter of such victims suffer serious shock (Maguire, "The Impact of Burglary upon Victims" (1980) 20 Brit. J. Criminol. 261).

[75] Theft Act 1968, s.9(3), as amended by the Criminal Justice Act 1991, s.26(2).

[76] *Stones* [1989] 1 W.L.R. 156.

[77] M.P.C. s.223.1(2).

In England, on the other hand, the same crime of theft is committed whether it is a magazine or a million pounds that is stolen.

## Criminal Law Revision Committee, Eighth Report, Theft and Related Offences, Cmnd.2977 (1966), para. 62:

"We considered whether instead of a general maximum of 10 years there should be different maximum penalties depending on the value of the property stolen. But although there is a case for specially high penalties for stealing large sums, we are not in favour of such a provision. Apart from the difficulty of laying down a satisfactory scale, the value of the property is only one of the possible aggravating features of theft, and it seems to us wrong to single this out. Besides, the property may be far more or far less valuable than the thief imagined."

The value of property is at present taken into account procedurally. For example, criminal damage is only triable summarily if the value of the property does not exceed £5000.[78] Mode of Trial Guidelines suggest that handling offences should be tried summarily if the value of the property is under £10,000.[79] Over the years there have been several proposals to extend this approach to other offences such as theft.[80] The value of property is also an important factor in sentencing.[81] Accordingly, the real debate is not as to *whether* the value of the property should be taken into consideration, but *how* this should be achieved: whether at the mode of trial stage, the substantive level or the sentencing stage.

The present approach of English law is consistent with the underlying rationale of the property offences that the focus is on the wrongdoing of the defendant and not on the direct harm caused. If it is not necessary that *any* direct harm be caused, it follows that the *extent* of that harm is not important and thus the value of the property interfered with should not be taken into account. This is consistent with the widely held view that the causing of resulting harm (and the extent thereof) is irrelevant as it can be "chance" whether a large or small sum is stolen. The criminal law is not a "lottery"[82] with criminal liability being governed by "the invisible hand of Fate".[83] It is also argued that the value of property in abstract terms is irrelevant. What matters is the value of the property relative to the particular victim. Stealing £20 from a pensioner is worse than stealing £20 worth of goods from a large supermarket. Further, it is argued that the value of the property is only one way of assessing the extent of the harm and should not be made decisive. Other factors are equally important: the characteristics of the offender (*e.g.* theft by persons in

---

[78] Magistrates' Court Act 1980, s.22.

[79] *Above*, n.60.

[80] For example, James Report, *The Distribution of Criminal Business between the Crown Court and Magistrates' Courts* (Cmnd.6323, 1975).

[81] The Magistrates' Association specify the value of the property as a factor which will aggravate or mitigate the seriousness of the offence: *Sentencing Guidelines* (2001). In *Barrick* (1985) 7 Cr.App.R.(S.) 142, the sentencing guideline case on theft in breach of trust, the court specifically distinguished between thefts of more and less than £10,000.

[82] Smith, "The Element of Chance in Criminal Liability" [1971] Crim.L.R.63.

[83] Schulhofer, "Harm and Punishment: A Critique of Emphasis on Results of Conduct in the Criminal Law" (1974) 122 U.Penn.L.R. 1497 at 1516.

positions of trust); the characteristics of the victim (*e.g.* theft from the old or disabled); and the circumstances of the offence (*e.g.* pickpocketing, thefts committed jointly with others).

On the other hand, it is interesting to contrast these property offences with offences against the person where the level of harm (physical and psychiatric injury) is crucial in distinguishing offences of different gravity (for example, actual bodily harm as opposed to grievous bodily harm), whereas the other factors, such as characteristics of the victim, are taken into account at the sentencing stage. There is a logic to this. At the substantive stage the law can only deal with *standard* harms.

### Andrew von Hirsch and Nils Jareborg, "Gauging Criminal Harm: A Living-Standard Analysis" (1991) 11 O.J.L.S. 1 at 4–5:

"Why this emphasis on standard harm? Particular criminal acts are too diverse to be rated on an individualised basis. The analysis is aided when one (1) rates the standard case of an offence, and then (2) addresses unusual cases through principles of aggravation and mitigation ... The standard harm in any given type of criminal conduct is, ordinarily, foreseeable. However, when one is talking about atypical harms, foreseeability diminishes. The burglar may be expected to understand the typical consequences of a burglary, but not, ordinarily, Mary Smith's particular situation—*e.g.* the extraordinary value the vase had for her as a gift from a deceased friend. The rules on aggravation/mitigation will thus have to be more complex, because they need to consider not only the special harm involved in unusual cases, but also ... the foreseeability of such special harm ...

The criminal law is a system of rules, not an arena for personalized judgments. If the law can assess crime-seriousness in the standard case, and then make deviations from that assessment for certain types of special circumstances, this is all one can reasonably hope to accomplish."

Following this, it is possible to argue that the most appropriate measure of the standard harm (or threat thereof) in property offences is the value of the property which, like the level of personal injury or success or failure in the law of attempt, is critical in our moral assessments of the defendant's actions. Such an approach might well help to counteract the commonly held view that there is currently one law for wealthy, white-collar criminals (such as those involved in the Guinness frauds) and another for the rest of those who steal. Other factors such as the circumstances of the offence which are simply too diverse to be reduced to substantive rules are best left to the "rules on aggravation/mitigation", *i.e.* to the sentencing stage.

The logic of the argument to this point has been that there could be different levels of property offences based purely on the economic value of the goods interfered with (as suggested by the Model Penal Code). However, an alternative solution could be to subject to separate treatment certain property offences where the economic value of the goods is *generally* small. Shoplifting might be regarded as a prime candidate for this. In Denmark the authorities refuse to prosecute in cases of shoplifting of items of relatively low value.[84] A case can be made for the decriminalisation of some of the activities presently covered by the Theft Acts—particularly in those areas where civil remedies such as breach of contract

---

[84] Fitzmaurice and Pease, *The Psychology of Judicial Sentencing* (1968); *cf.* Murphy, *Customers and Thieves* (1986), p. 239.

seem more appropriate. However, it is highly questionable whether such thinking can or should be applied to shoplifting.

### Daniel J. I. Murphy, Customers and Thieves—an Ethnography of Shoplifting (1986), p. 240:

"[T]here are essentially two methods for controlling shoplifters on the shopfloor: 'law-enforcement' and 'peace-keeping'. It is obvious that the numbers of suspects who are handed to the police differ dramatically according to which model is being pursued. The peace-keeping model is the preferred one of a few retailers who acknowledge the temptation to steal which modern marketing techniques create and they accept the responsibility to convert ordinary shoppers who have succumbed to this temptation. Retailers who pursue the law-enforcement model would criticise the peace-keeping model for being an insufficient deterrent to shoplifters, and the Home Office Standing Committee supports their position: 'A reminder to pay without fear of penalty is no deterrent, and in effect would mean that the thief could not lose.' However, the research clearly demonstrates that all stores on occasions use this method to control shoplifting. ... The point made here is that there are methods of controlling shoplifting which do not involve the criminal justice system and these should be given more public discussion."

The real point is surely that there are indeed ways of dealing with many offences outside the criminal justice system—but that these alternatives presuppose the existence of criminal laws as an ultimate threat or moral backdrop.

Perhaps an easier case can be made for treating shoplifting as a separate and lesser offence.

### Andrew Ashworth, Sentencing and Penal Policy (1983), pp. 186–187:

"[T]here are three major reasons for regarding offences against larger companies, such as Woolworth and Marks and Spencer, as less serious than an offence involving the same amount of property but committed against an individual victim. First, an individual's possessions are more likely to have a personal ('sentimental') value to him which is additional to, and may indeed be more important to him than, the economic value ... Secondly, thefts from individuals are more likely to cause fear and alarm than thefts from companies ... Thirdly, companies would generally be better able than individuals to afford and to off-set any loss through theft."

The case for a separate lesser offence is strengthened when one considers that the value of the property stolen in shops is generally small, such thefts are regarded by the public as the least serious of the various types of theft that can be committed,[85] and even when shoplifters are detected prosecutions are often not brought[86] "in order to avoid 'image' problems, because of the claimed risk of false arrest tort actions by innocent customers, and because of the claimed cost of time away from work when security personnel have to testify".[87]

On the other hand, there is the clear view expressed by Lawton L.J. in *Wood* that "Shoplifting is stealing and stealing is a serious offence."[88] A Home Office Working Party Report on internal shop security was to similar effect:

---

[85] Sparks, Genn and Dodd, *Surveying Victims* (1977).
[86] In 1971 prosecution followed in only 39.9 per cent of cases reported to the police (Home Office, *Shoplifting, and Thefts by Shop Staff* (1973), para. 6.11).
[87] Foote and Levy, *Criminal Law: Cases and Materials* (1981), p. 757.
[88] (1979) 1 Cr.App.R.(S.) 34.

"We also noted the suggestion ... that shoplifting should be made an administrative offence. This would do nothing to reduce the number of shoplifting offences. Indeed, it might increase it. We see no reason why shoplifting should be treated differently from any other type of crime." [89]

A central problem with this approach, as with all attempts to divide offences into narrower subcategories, is that the subdivision has to be rational and must not miss any important moral distinctions. This raises the question: What is so special about shoplifting? Why not make pickpocketing or employee theft a separate offence?

### L. R. Zeitlin, "A Little Larceny can do a Lot for Employee Morale" Psychology Today (June 1974), 22–26, 64:

"Thefts of merchandise alone amount to approximately five per cent of the yearly sales of American retail establishments, and internal losses outweigh external losses by about three to one. That is, the stores' own employees steal three times as much as do shoplifters ... [W]ell over 75 per cent of all employees participate to some extent in merchandise shrinkage ... [I]n retail establishments internal theft averages out to an unevenly distributed five per cent to eight per cent of the typical employee's salary ...

When the average retail employee becomes dissatisfied with his job, if he doesn't quit, he starts stealing from his employer. He gets back at the system. In a sense, the intellectual and physical challenges provided by opportunities to steal represent a significant enrichment of the individual's job. He can take matters into his own hands, assume responsibility, make decisions and face challenges ... He is in business for himself ...

The dishonest worker is enriching his own job in a manner that is very satisfactory (for him) ... [and] management gets a bargain. By permitting a controlled amount of theft, management can avoid reorganising jobs and raising wages ...

[M]anagement may decide that the monetary cost of enforcing honesty is too great ... [M]anagement would have to maintain a figurehead security system. After all, the major benefit of employee theft is the job enrichment provided by the individual's attempt to beat the system. If all need for precaution is eliminated, then the employee gets no satisfaction from theft. All he gets is a slight addition to his income in merchandise instead of cash ...

Uncontrolled theft can be disastrous for any business concern but *controlled* theft can be useful. Employee theft, used as a motivational tool, can be an economic benefit to an organisation, if management finds it too costly to meet its traditional responsibilities to make jobs rewarding and to pay a living wage."

In the United States an examination was made into several substantive offences to ascertain whether subcategorisation was feasible.[90] The bulk of the examination was devoted to the crime of armed robbery with the conclusion that armed robbery be divided into six degrees. Yet these six divisions only take account of two variables: the type of weapon used and the extent of physical violence threatened. No account is taken of the numerous other variables that would normally affect the type and length of sentence imposed. Accordingly, it has been pointed out that:

"if the legislature actually *tried* to anticipate every conceivable offence and offender variation, the result would be a penal law of enormous length and complexity, replete with hair-splitting distinctions. We doubt whether any legislature would be willing or able to spend all its time hammering out a definition of robbery in the 68th degree (and deciding upon the appropriate

---

[89] *Above*, n.86, para. 6.16.
[90] Report of the Twentieth Century Fund Task Force on Criminal Sentencing, *Fair and Certain Punishment* (1976), p. 18.

penalty); but even if it were, it is doubtful whether all offence variations could really be anticipated."[91]

It thus seems clear that little can be gained from subdividing the property offences into smaller separate offences such as shoplifting. No area of law can be adequately, and with sufficient specificity, subcategorised to reflect the nuances of situation, blameworthiness and harm that condition the seriousness of particular criminal acts. Accordingly, perhaps the best way forward is to build on the approach already being adopted by English law. Some reform of the substantive offence definitions and categories clearly needs to be undertaken. Movement in this direction is possible following the Law Commission's proposals to collapse the various deception offences into a broad offence of fraud. At the procedural mode of trial level, more thought should be given to making other offences only triable summarily where the value of the property is low. And, finally, clear sentencing guidelines for the various offences should be developed. Important work has already been done on this by the Sentencing Advisory Panel that has suggested various levels of seriousness for offences with a starting sentence for each level which can be varied by the presence of listed aggravating or mitigating circumstances. Proposals from the Sentencing Advisory Panel have already been made for the offences of robbery, domestic burglary and handling stolen goods and, as has been seen, this advice is increasingly being accepted by the Court of Appeal, for example in relation to domestic burglary.

However, while these developments are to be welcomed, they do not foreclose further consideration of the structure of property offences at the substantive level—for example, whether there should be two categories of robbery and handling stolen goods. But, of course, this whole question of the structure of property offences raises similar issues to those already canvassed with regard to the structure of offences against the person. As suggested there, answers to all such questions depend on the basic philosophy underlying the construction of criminal liability and the criminal justice system.

---

[91] Executive Advisory Committee on Sentencing in New York, *Crime and Punishment in New York* (1979), p. 220.

# INDEX